MW01717400

How to Prepare for the

GMAT®

Graduate Management Admission Test

Tenth Edition

EUGENE D. JAFFE, M.B.A., Ph.D.
Associate Professor, School of Business Administration, Bar-Ilan University, Israel, and formerly Visiting Professor of Marketing and International Business, Baruch College, The City University of New York

STEPHEN HILBERT, Ph.D.
Professor of Mathematics, Ithaca College

BARRON'S

For Liora, Iris and Nurit
and for Susan

All inquiries should be addressed to:
Barron's Educational Series, Inc.
250 Wireless Boulevard
Hauppauge, New York 11788

International Standard Book No. 0-8120-8303-2 (book/disk package)
0-8120-1920-2 (book)

Library of Congress Card Catalog No. 94-9170

Library of Congress Cataloging-in-Publication Data

Jaffe, Eugene D.
How to prepare for the graduate management admission test. GMAT / Eugene D. Jaffe, Stephen Hilbert. — 10th ed.
p. cm.
ISBN 0-8120-1920-2
1. Graduate Management Admission Test. 2. Management—Examinations, questions, etc. 3. Business—Examinations, questions, etc. I. Hilbert, Stephen. II. Title.
HF1118.J33 1994
650'.076—dc20 94-9170
CIP

PRINTED IN THE UNITED STATES OF AMERICA

5 6 7 8 9 0 100 12 11 10 9 8

Contents

Preface

Barron's How to Prepare for the Graduate Management Admission Test (GMAT) is designed to assist students planning to take the official Graduate Management Admission Test administered by the Educational Testing Service of Princeton, New Jersey. Since the results of the GMAT are used by many graduate schools of business as a means for measuring the qualifications of their applicants, it is important that the prospective student do as well as possible on this exam. Admission to business school may well depend on it.

A study guide, although not able to guarantee a perfect score, can provide a good deal of assistance in test preparation by enabling students to become familiar with the material they will encounter on the exam and supplying them with ample opportunity for practice and review. With this in mind, we have developed a study guide that goes further than the simple simulation of the official GMAT in its effort to offer a sound basis of test preparation. Besides containing six practice tests with questions (and answers) similar to those students will encounter on the actual exam, it offers invaluable advice on *how* to prepare for the exam, ranging from a general discussion of the purpose and various formats of the GMAT to a step-by-step program of subject analysis and review designed to help students discover their weak points and take measures to correct them. A tactics section is included that covers every question type. These tactics give students practical instructions and hints on how to analyze and answer each question.

Review sections for each subject area appearing on the exam have been especially developed to meet the specific needs of students who may feel a deficiency in any of these areas. Each review provides both an explanation of the material and exercises for practical work. The six practice exams included in the guide have self-scoring tables to help students evaluate their results and check their progress. All answers to the test questions are fully explained to ensure complete understanding.

The authors would also like to extend their appreciation to Mrs. Susan Hilbert and Ms. Dawn Murcer for their excellent job in typing the manuscript, to Professor Shirley Hockett for several helpful discussions, and to Professor Justin Longenecker for his generous advice.

How to Use This Guide

The step-by-step study program appearing below outlines the recommended study plan you should follow when preparing for the GMAT. By making use of this procedure, you will be able to take full advantage of the material presented in this guide.

1. Familiarize yourself with the purpose and general format of the GMAT (Chapter One).
2. Study the analysis of each type of question on the exam (Chapter Two).
3. Take the GMAT Diagnostic Test (Chapter Three) and use the Self-Scoring Table at the end of the test to evaluate your results.
4. Study the review sections (Chapters Four, Five, Six, Seven, and Eight), spending more time on areas where you scored poorly on the Diagnostic Test.
5. Take the five sample GMAT tests (Chapters Nine, Ten, Eleven, Twelve, and Thirteen) and evaluate your results after completing each one.
6. Review again any areas you discover you are still weak in after you have evaluated your test results.

Acknowledgments

The authors gratefully acknowledge the kindness of all organizations concerned with granting us permission to reprint passages, charts, and graphs. The copyright holders and publishers of quoted passages are listed on this and the following pages.

Sources and permissions for charts and graphs appear on the appropriate pages throughout the book through the courtesy of the following organizations: the New York Times Company; U.S. Department of Labor; Dow Jones & Company, Inc.; U.S. Department of Health, Education, and Welfare; United Nations Economics Bulletin for Europe; Social Security Bulletin, Statistical Abstract of the U.S., U.S. Department of Commerce, Bureau of Economic Analysis; Federal Reserve Bank of New York; European Economic Community; U.S. Department of Commerce, Bureau of the Census; New York State Department of Labor; Federal Power Commission; U.S. Treasury Department; U.S. Bureau of Labor Statistics; Institute of Life Insurance; and the Statistical Abstract of Latin America.

Page 15, Sample Passage: Reprinted with permission of the author, Virgil Thomson.

Page 37, Passage 1: Reprinted from *The Bible on Broadway*. by Arthur T. Buch © Arthur T. Buch 1968, Hamden, CT., Archon Books, with the permission of The Shoe String Press, Inc.

Page 42, Passage 3: Petra Karin Kelly, "Cancer A European Conquest?" *European Community*, April–May, 1976, pp. 23–24. Reprinted from *Europe* Magazine.

Pages 56–58, Section V, 21 Questions (with Explained Answers): Murray Rockowitz et al., *Barron's How to Prepare for the New High School Equivalency Examination (GED)*, © 1979 Barron's Educational Series, Inc., Hauppauge, N.Y.

Page 59, Passage 1: Kenneth R. Seeskin, "Never Speculate, Never Explain: The State of Contemporary Philosophy." Reprinted from *The American Scholar*, Volume 49, No. 1. Winter 1979–80. Copyright © 1979 by the United Chapters of Phi Beta Kappa. By permission of the publishers.

Page 61, Passage 2: By Michael Useem, Professor of Sociology, Boston University, "Government Patronage of Science and Art in America," from *The Production of Culture*, Richard A. Peterson, ed., © 1976 Sage Publications, Inc. Reprinted by permission of the author and the publisher.

Portions of the "Essay Writing Review": George Ehrenhaft, *How to Prepare for SAT II: Writing*, © 1994 Barron's Educational Series, Inc., Hauppaugem N.Y.

Portions of the "Reading Comprehension Review": Eugene J. Farley, *Barron's How to Prepare for the High School Equivalency Examination Reading Interpretation Test*, © 1970 Barron's Educational Series, Inc., Hauppauge, N.Y.

Page 102, Example 2: "Skye, Lonely Scottish Isle," *Newark Sunday News*, June 9, 1968, C 16, Sec. 2.

Page 121, Example 4: David Gunter, "Kibbutz Life Growing Easier," *Newark News*, May 6, 1968, p. 5.

Page 124, Example 2: Reprinted with permission from "Understanding Foreign Policy," by Saul K. Padover, *Public Affairs Pamphlet #280*. Copyright, Public Affairs Committee, Inc.

Page 126, Exercise B: Marina Gazzo and Catherine Browne, "Venice Rising," *Europe*, November–December, 1975, pp. 15–16. © The European Community, 1975. Europe is an independent publication available by subscription.

Page 230, Passage 1: From *Our Dynamic World: A Survey in Modern Geography* by A. Joseph Wraight, © 1966 by the author. Reproduced by permission of the publisher, Chilton Book Company, Radnor, Pennsylvania.

Pages 248–250, Section 5, 21 Questions (with Explained Answers): Samuel C. Brownstein and Mitchel Weiner, *Barron's How to Prepare for College Entrance Examinations (SAT)*, © 1980 Barron's Educational Series, Inc., Hauppauge, N.Y.

Pages 256–258, Section 7, 5 Questions (with Explained Answers): Murray Rockowitz et al., *Barron's How to Prepare for the New High School Equivalency Examination (GED)*, © 1979 Barron's Educational Series, Inc., Hauppauge, N.Y.

Page 292, Passage 1: *Improving Executive Development in the Federal Government*, copyright 1964 by the Committee for Economic Development.

Page 294, Passage 2: G. R. Crone, *Background to Geography*, 1964, by permission of Pitman Publishing Ltd., London.

Page 296, Passage 3: Jean Hollander, "Cops and Writers," Reprinted from *The American Scholar*, Volume 49, No. 2, Spring 1980. Copyright 1980 by the author.

Page 298, Passage 1: "Open Admissions Assessed: The Example of The City University of New York, 1970–1975" by Irwin Polishook, Professor of History, Lehman College, CUNY. "Open Admissions Assessed" originally appeared in *Midstream* (April, 1976), © 1976, The Theodor Herzl Foundation.

Page 301, Passage 2: Robert D. Hershey, Jr., "A Perilous Time for World Trade," *New York Times*, August 1, 1982. © 1982 by The New York Times Company. Reprinted by permission.

Pages 324–326, Section 7, 21 Questions (with Explained Answers): Samuel C. Brownstein and Mitchel Weiner, *Barron's How to Prepare for College Entrance Examinations (SAT)*, © 1980 Barron's Educational Series, Inc., Hauppauge, N.Y.

Pages 324–326, Section 7, 3 Questions (with Explained Answers): Murray Rockowitz et al., *Barron's How to Prepare for the New High School Equivalency Examination (GED)*, © 1979 Barron's Educational Series, Inc., Hauppauge, N.Y.

Page 360, Passage l: *The Hebrew Impact on Western Civilization*, edited by Dagobert Runes. The Philosophical Library.

Page 362, Passage 2: *Budgeting for National Objectives*, copyright 1966 by the Committee on Economic Development.

Page 364, Passage 3: From *The American Guide*, edited by Henry G. Alsberg. Copyright © 1949, by permission of Hastings House, Publishers.

Pages 381–384, Section 5, 17 Questions (with Explained Answers): Murray Rockowitz et al., *Barron's How to Prepare for the New High School Equivalency Examination (GED)*, © 1979 Barron's Educational Series, Inc., Hauppauge, N.Y.

Pages 432–434, Section 1, 14 Questions (with Explained Answers): Sharon Green and Mitchel Weiner, *Barron's How to Prepare for the Test of Standard Written English*, © 1982, Barron's Educational Series, Inc., Hauppauge, N.Y.

Pages 432–434, Section 1, 6 Questions (with Explained Answers): Samuel C. Brownstein and Mitchel Weiner, *Barron's How to Prepare for the College Entrance Examinations (SAT)*, © 1980, Barron's Educational Series, Inc., Hauppauge, N.Y.

Page 439, Passage 1: *Trade Policy Toward Low-Income Countries*, copyright 1967 by the Committee for Economic Development.

Page 442, Passage 2: James Hitchcock, "Postmortem on a Rebirth: The Catholic Intellectual Renaissance." Reprinted from *The American Scholar*, Volume 50, Number 2, Spring 1980. Copyright 1980 by the author.

Page 504, Passage 2: From *The Social Bond*, by Robert A. Nisbet. Copyright © 1970 by Alfred A. Knopf, Inc. Reprinted by permission of the publisher.

Pages 512–515, Section 4, 9 Questions (with Explained Answers): Sharon Green and Mitchel Weiner, *Barron's How to Prepare for the Test of Standard Written English*, © 1982, Barron's Educational Series, Inc., Hauppauge, N.Y.

Pages 512–515, Section 4, 3 Questions (with Explained Answers): Samuel C. Brownstein and Mitchel Weiner, *Barron's How to Prepare for the College Entrance Examinations (SAT)*, © 1980, Barron's Educational Series, Inc., Hauppauge, N.Y.

WHAT YOU NEED TO KNOW ABOUT THE GMAT

1 AN INTRODUCTION TO THE GMAT

The most productive approach to undertaking the actual study and review necessary for any examination is first to determine the answers to some basic questions: What? Where? When? and How? In this case, what is the purpose of the Graduate Management Admission Test (GMAT)? What does it measure? Where and when is the exam given? And most important, how can you prepare to demonstrate aptitude and ability to study business at the graduate level?

The following discussion centers on the purpose behind the Graduate Management Admission Test and answers basic questions about the general format and procedure used on the GMAT.

The Purpose of the GMAT

The purpose of the GMAT is to measure your ability to think systematically and to employ the verbal and mathematical skills that you have acquired throughout your years of schooling. The types of questions that are used to test these abilities are discussed in the next chapter. It should be noted that the test does not aim to measure your knowledge of specific business or academic subjects. No specific business experience is necessary, nor will any specific academic subject area be covered. You are assumed to know basic algebra, geometry, and arithmetic, to know the basic conventions of standard written English, and to be able to write an analytical essay.

In effect, the GMAT provides business school admission officers with an objective measure of academic abilities to supplement subjective criteria used in the selection process, such as interviews, grades, and references. Suppose you are an average student in a college with high grading standards. Your overall grade average may be lower than that of a student from a college with lower grading standards. The GMAT allows you and the other student to be tested under similar conditions using the same grading standard. In this way, a more accurate picture of your all-around ability can be established.

Where to Apply

Information about the exact dates of the exam, fees, testing locations, and a test registration form can be found in the "GMAT Bulletin of Information" for candidates published by ETS. You can obtain a copy by writing:

Graduate Management Admission Test
Educational Testing Service
P.O. Box 6103
Princeton, New Jersey 08541-6103

The GMAT is generally given in October, January, March, and June. Since the majority of business schools send out their acceptances in the spring, it is wise to take the exam as early as possible to ensure that the schools you are applying to receive your scores in time.

The Test Format

The latest GMAT has contained questions of the following types: Reading Comprehension, Problem Solving, Data Sufficiency, Critical Reasoning, and Sentence Correction. Starting in October 1994, the GMAT will include a writing section as well. The writing section will consist of two 30-minute analytical essays. An answer sheet consisting of three lined 8½" × 11" pages will be supplied for each essay. *All versions* of the test with start with these two essays.

There are many different formats for the portion of the test following the written essays, but each version of the test will contain at least one section each of Problem Solving, Reading Comprehension, Sentence Correction, Data Sufficiency, and Critical Reasoning. The remaining two sections will be picked from these five types and will differ from test to test—for example, Problem Solving and Critical Reasoning may appear twice on one version of the test, while on another version of the test Data Sufficiency and Critical Reasoning may appear twice. Usually only six of the seven sections are counted in your score. The other section either contains experimental questions or is used to calibrate different versions of

FORM A

Section	Type of Question	Number of Questions	Time (Min.)
1	Reading Comprehension	23	30
2	Critical Reasoning	16	25
3	Problem Solving	16	25
	(15 minute break)		
4	Sentence Correction	22	25
5	Data Sufficiency	20	25
6	Critical Reasoning	16	25
7	Problem Solving	16	25
Total		129	180

FORM B

Section	Type of Question	Number of Questions	Time (Min.)
1	Reading Comprehension	23	30
2	Problem Solving	16	25
3	Sentence Correction	22	25
	(15 minute break)		
4	Data Sufficiency	20	25
5	Critical Reasoning	16	25
6	Critical Reasoning	16	25
7	Problem Solving	16	25
Total		129	180

the GMAT. However, you will not know which sections are going to count in your score, so you must do your best on every section.

Each section of the GMAT must be completed within the specified time limit. If you finish the section before the allotted time has elapsed, you must spend the remaining time working on that section *only*. You may *not* work on other sections of the test at all.

Specific directions telling you exactly how to answer the questions appear at the beginning of each section of the exam. Keep in mind that although the directions for answering the sample questions in this guide are designed to simulate as closely as possible those on the actual test, the format of the test you take may vary. Therefore, it is important that you read the directions on the actual test very carefully before attempting to answer the questions. You also should be certain of the exact time limit you are allowed.

Your Scores and What They Mean

You will receive four scores on the GMAT exam: a total score, a verbal score, a writing score, and a quantitative score. The total score ranges from 200 to 800; the verbal and quantitative scores range from 0 to 60. You will also be given a percentile ranking for each of the four scores. The percentile ranking gives you the percentage of the test scores in the last three years lower than yours. Thus, a percentile ranking of 75 would mean that 75% of the test scores in the last three years were below your score.

Your total score will be based on your raw score, which is the total number of correct answers minus one fourth of the number of wrong answers. The GMAT subtracts one fourth of the number of wrong answers to compensate for random guessing. The verbal score is based on the answers to the questions in the Reading Comprehension, Critical Reasoning, and Sentence Correction sections. The quantitative score is based on the answers to the questions in the Problem Solving and Data Sufficiency sections. The writing score ranges from 0 to 6 and is based upon the two written essays.

The scores you receive are *scaled scores*. Since there are many different versions of the exam, the use of scaled scores allows test results based on different versions of the exam to be compared. The same *raw score* (total number of correct answers minus one fourth of the number of wrong answers) will be converted into a higher scaled score if you took a more difficult version of the exam. If you take several versions of the exam, your scaled scores should cluster about your "true" scaled score. Thus, your scaled score in some sense represents a range of possibilities. A score of 510 means that your "true" score is probably between 480 and 540.

In general, no particular score can be called good or bad, and no passing or failing grade has been established. Scores above 700 or below 250 are unusual. In recent years, about two thirds of all scores have fallen between 380 and 600, with the average between 480 and 490. In the verbal and quantitative scores, grades above 46 or below 10 are unusual. About two thirds of these scores fall between 20 and 38, with the average about 30. The average verbal score is slightly lower than the average quantitative score.

Importance of the GMAT

Students often ask what is an adequate GMAT score. The answer is that every university and college requiring the GMAT sets its own requirements. Average scores throughout the United States are reported by the Graduate Management Admission Council of the Educational Testing Service. For example, the average GMAT score of all test-takers in the United States during 1991–92 was 502, with a standard deviation of 90 to 110. This means that two thirds of the grades ranged from 412 to 612. Average grades on the GMAT also differed by undergraduate major, with physics majors scoring 561, math majors 548, English majors 541, and political science majors 540. What these results show is that there are not very significant differences between the average scores of liberal arts and science undergraduate majors.

Most college catalogs do not state what the minimum GMAT requirement is, but the annual reports of most MBA programs do note the average GMAT score of the last incoming student body. This is probably a good indication of the necessary ball-park figure for admission. However, obtaining a score somewhat below that figure does not mean that acceptance is not possible. First of all, it is an average figure. Some scored below, but were accepted. The GMAT is only one of a number of criteria for admission. Students who obtain a score below some required average may nevertheless make up for this by their undergraduate grade average or by writing a very good essay as part of the application process. In some cases, doing well in the personal interview with an admissions officer or other university representative may be just as, or even more, important. So, while scoring high on the GMAT is a desired goal and should be pursued with all the means possible, it is not the only requirement for admission to an MBA program. Before applying to a college or university, determine what criteria are considered for admission and how these criteria are ranked by order of importance. Directors of MBA programs, admissions officers, college catalogs, and annual reports should provide this information.

Your score on the GMAT is only one of several factors examined by admissions officers. Your undergraduate record, for example, is at least as important as your GMAT score. Thus, a low score does not mean that no school will accept you, nor does a high GMAT score guarantee acceptance at the school of your choice. However, since your score is one important factor, you should try to do as well as you can on the exam. Using this book should help you to maximize your score.

How to Prepare for the GMAT

You should now be aware of the purpose of the GMAT and have a general idea of the format of the test. With this basic information, you are in a position to begin your study and review. The rest of this guide represents a study plan that will enable you to prepare for the GMAT. If used properly, it will help you diagnose your weak areas and take steps to remedy them.

Begin your preparation by becoming as familiar as possible with the various types of questions that appear on the exam. The analysis of typical GMAT questions in the next chapter is designed for this purpose. Test-taking tactics provide hints on how to approach the different types of questions. When you feel you understand this material completely, take the Diagnostic Test that follows and evaluate your results on the Self-Scoring Table provided at the end of the test. (An explanation of how to use these tables follows.) A low score in any area indicates that you should spend more time reviewing that particular material. Study the review section for that area until you feel you have mastered it and then take one of the sample GMATs at the back of the book. Continue this pattern of study until you are completely satisfied with your performance. For best results, try to simulate exam conditions as closely as possible when taking sample tests: no unscheduled breaks or interruptions, strict adherence to time limits, and no use of outside aids.

The Answer Sheet

You could know the answer to every question on the test and still score lower than you deserve *if* you make mistakes in marking your answer sheet. Under the pressures of time and test-day anxiety, filling in the correct ovals and referring back and forth between an examination booklet and a separate answer sheet is not always as easy as it may sound, especially if it is unfamiliar to you. We strongly encourage you to make use of the sample answer sheets provided in this book for taking the practice tests and recommend that you simulate test-day procedures as much as possible. In self-scoring your practice exams, you may find on occasion that you marked the wrong oval when you did in fact know the right answer. This is a cautionary warning to be careful and pay attention when marking your answer sheet. The sample answer sheets in this book should help familiarize you with their use. You may find you have no problems with this. In that case, continue to be careful. On test day you will get to fill in up to 140 ovals. Each error in this mundane, mechanical process could cost you 1¼ points off your raw score (since not only do you not earn one point for getting the right answer, you are penalized ¼ point for marking the wrong answer). This could represent a loss of 5 points off your total score for each slip in marking your answer sheet. If you have done the work of finding the right answer, it is a shame to lose credit through inattention in the last step. You don't get credit for the right answer unless you fill in the correct oval.

Familiarity with the structure and the instructions for filling out the answer sheet prior to taking the exam can save valuable time and prevent costly mistakes. First, bring several #2 pencils with you to the exam. You will not be able to use a pen. Second, in marking the answer sheet be sure to choose the oval that corresponds to the answer you select. Third, be careful to blacken the entire oval, e.g., 1. Ⓐ Ⓑ ● Ⓓ Ⓔ. Partially blackening a oval may not register. Fourth, if you must erase your selection in order to change your answer, be sure to remove all of your pencil mark. Failure to do so, e.g., 1. Ⓐ Ⓑ Ⓒ Ⓓ ◒ may result in the optic scanner picking up both what you (thought) you erased and your subsequent mark. In this case, it will result in a wrong answer.

The Self-Scoring Tables

The Self-Scoring Tables for each sample test in this guide can be used as a means of evaluating your weaknesses in particular subject areas and should help you plan your study program most effectively.

After completing a sample test, turn to the Answers section which immediately follows each test. First, determine the number of *correct* answers you had for each section. Next, subtract *one-fourth* the number of *wrong* answers for each part from the number of correct answers. This is done to eliminate the benefits of wild guessing. Do *not* subtract for any answers left blank. For example, suppose that in Section 1 you answered 15 out of 25 questions correctly, with 6 incorrect responses and 4 blanks. Subtract ¼ of 6 (1½) from 15 to obtain a final score of 13½. Now turn to the section Evaluating Your Score, which follows the Answers Explained section of each test. Record your scores in the appropriate score boxes in the Self-scoring Table as shown below.

Self-Scoring Table

SECTION	SCORE	RATING
1	13½	FAIR
2		
3		
4		
5		
6		
7		

Use the Rating scale to find your rating for each section. A typical rating scale follows.

***Self-Scoring Scale*—RATING**

SECTION	POOR	FAIR	GOOD	EXCELLENT
1	0 – 12+	13 – 17+	18 – 21+	22 – 25
2	0 – 9+	10 – 13+	14 – 17+	18 – 21
3	0 – 9+	10 – 13+	14 – 17+	18 – 21
4	0 – 8+	9 – 11+	11+ – 14	14 – 17
5	0 – 8+	9 – 11+	11+ – 14	14+ – 17
6	0 – 9+	10 – 13+	14 – 17+	18+ – 21
7	0 – 8+	9 – 11+	11+ – 14	14+ – 17

In the rating scale, numbers such as 12+ mean numbers larger than 12 but less than 13. For example, if your raw score on Section 1 of the exam was 21½, then this translates to GOOD on the Self-Scoring Table.

A rating of FAIR or POOR in any area indicates that you need to spend more time reviewing that material.

Scaled Scores

The rules below will give you a method for converting your raw score on a practice exam into a scaled score. This is not the same procedure that the GMAT uses, but it should give you some idea of what your scaled score would be on the exam. Note that your raw score on an exam is the number of correct answers minus one fourth of the incorrect answers, with no deduction for answers left blank.

Use the following rule to convert your raw score into a scaled score.

SCALED SCORE = 225 + (4.25 × RAW SCORE)

If the rule gives a scaled score greater than 800, then the scaled score is 800.

If the rule gives a scaled score less than 200, then the scaled score is 200.

EXAMPLE

You have a raw score of 117 on a test.

(A) 4.25 × RAW SCORE = 497.25
(B) 497.25 is rounded to 497
(C) So the scaled score is 225 + 497 = 722

To find a scaled quantitative score, take the raw score from the Problem Solving and Data Sufficiency sections. Use the following rule to convert this raw score into a scaled score between 0 and 60.

QUANTSCORE = 9 + (.8 × RAW SCORE)

To find a scaled verbal score, take the raw score from the Critical Reasoning, Reading Comprehension, and Sentence Correction sections. Use the following rule to convert this raw score into a scaled score between 0 and 60.

VERBAL SCORE = 2 + (.65 × RAW SCORE)

If your scaled scores are low on the first practice exams you take, don't get discouraged. Your scaled score should improve on the later practice exams after you have used the various reviews to strengthen your weaknesses. The tests were made hard. That way you can discover your weaknesses and try to correct them. Easy practice tests are not good practice for a difficult exam. Remember that, on the GMAT itself, you shouldn't expect to be able to answer every single question. Don't worry about that. To maximize your score, you want to answer as many questions as you can correctly in the given amount of time.

Guessing

Many students ask the question: Does it pay to guess? If so, under what circumstances? Only a minority of test-takers are able to complete all questions in the allotted time period. Suppose that only a minute remains for completion of a given test section, and you have two or three questions unanswered. Should you guess at the answers?

Two elements should be considered in addressing the question of guessing. First, consider the way your score is determined by the Educational Testing Service, the administrators of the GMAT. If you do not answer, say, three questions on a test section, you do not incur a penalty, but of course you do not earn any points for questions unanswered. If you complete the questions and your answers are incorrect, you are penalized ¼ of a point for each incorrect answer. So, by not answering questions that you are unsure about, or do not have sufficient time to consider, you are not penalized. Two, the probability of selecting the correct answer by random guessing is 1 out of 5, or .20, which is rather low. However, suppose that you have had time to read the question and have been able to eliminate two answer alternatives, but are still unsure of the correct answer. Now, a random guess of the correct answer among the remaining alternatives has a probability of .33. Obviously, if you are able to eliminate three alternatives, you then have a 50–50 chance of guessing the correct answer. Assuming that time has run out, guessing in this situation is a very low risk.

So, there is a difference between random and educated guessing. An educated guess occurs when you have eliminated three alternatives and now have a reasonable chance of selecting the correct answer. Elimination of three alternatives should be possible for most questions. Here are some examples. The first example is a critical reasoning question:

EXAMPLE

The college tenure system provides long-term job security for established professors, but at the same time prevents younger instructors from entering the system. But instructors are familiar with current teaching material and therefore may provide students with a better education. Thus, it is a shame that many students are unable to be taught by instructors who cannot find employment because of the tenure system.

Which of the following is an assumption made in the argument above?

(A) Most tenured professors do not make an effort to provide quality education.
(B) Most instructors are against the tenure system.
(C) University students generally prefer to be taught by instructors.
(D) Instructors have received their graduate degrees more recently than professors.
(E) Tenured professors are not familiar with current teaching material.

In questions of this type, the assumption is usually one of the answer alternatives rather than part of the text. In any case, let us see how several alternatives may be readily eliminated. The fourth alternative (D), is true by definition, but is not even remotely a subject of the text, nor an assumption. Alternative (C) can not be assumed; there is simply no evidence pointing in this direction. Likewise, there is no evidence for alternative (B). By process of elimination, alternatives (A) and (E) remain. Alternative (A), if true, would certainly buttress the claim that it is a shame that students cannot be taught by new instructors, rather than by tenured professors. But this assumes that instructors are better teachers than professors, either because professors do not make an effort to provide quality education (A) or because they are unfamiliar with up-to-date teaching material (E). So, both alternatives are plausible, and if we have to guess, we have a 50–50 chance of answering correctly. However, the claim above is that instructors are "familiar" with teaching material, but that professors are not familiar (E). So, (E) is the assumption made. The argument runs like this:

1. Instructors are familiar with teaching material and can thus provide students with a better education than professors.
2. The college tenure system . . . prevents instructors from entering the system.
(E) 3. Professors are not familiar with current teaching materials.
4. It is a shame for students that they cannot be taught by instructors.

The conclusion, "it is a shame that many students are unable to be taught by instructors" is buttressed by the addition of the premise (3) that professors are not familiar with current teaching materials.

Another example of how two or three alternatives may be quickly eliminated may be demonstrated by taking the reading comprehension passage concerning the "land bridge" on pp. 10–11 and question number 1 on page 11:

1. According to the passage, the major alternative to a U.S. land bridge is the
   (A) Panama Canal
   (B) Suez Canal
   (C) air-freight system
   (D) all land route
   (E) military transport system

Alternative (C) may be quickly eliminated because it is not mentioned. Also (E), military transport system, can be eliminated because it is a user and not an alternative. An all land route (D) is analogous to the U.S. land bridge, and so cannot be an alternative. So, three alternative answers have been quickly eliminated. The choice is between (A) or (B). If we read the passage carefully, we note that the Suez Canal (B) is not mentioned. However, the Panama Canal (A) is noted as the existing alternative to a land bridge.

To summarize, guessing is not advisable unless you can eliminate three incorrect alternative answers. However, if you have succeeded in doing that, you may have sufficient time left for carefully selecting the correct answer rather than guessing at all. If not, an educated guess may be preferable to no answer.

After You Take the Exam

You will usually receive your scores about four weeks after the exam.

You may take the GMAT as many times as you wish. However, if you repeat the test, your scores from that test and the two most recent previous test results will be sent to all institutions you designate as score recipients. Many schools average your scores if you take the test more than once. So unless there is a reason to expect a substantial improvement in your score, it usually is *not* worthwhile to retake the exam.

Currently, you can receive a copy of your answer sheet, a booklet containing all questions that were counted in scoring your exam, an answer key, and the scale used to translate your raw scores into scaled scores. This test disclosure service is available for a fee of $8 for regular forms of the test given on the scheduled Saturday test dates. The service is available for only 90 days after scores are first reported. You should request the test disclosure service if you are considering retaking the exam. You can see if there was any particular section that hurt your score and concentrate on those questions as you study.

You can also cancel your scores if you act *before* receiving them. If you wish to cancel your scores, you must indicate this on your answer sheet, notify the supervisor before you leave the test center, or notify ETS by mail (your request must be received no later than seven days after you take the test). If you cancel your scores, the fact that you took the test will be reported to all the places you designated as score recipients. Thus, it is generally not advantageous to cancel your scores unless there is reason to believe that you have done substantially worse on the test than you would if you took the test again; for example, if you became ill while taking the exam. Once a score is canceled from your record it cannot be put back on your record or reported at a later date.

As a general rule, it is better to retake the exam after looking over your previous results (questions, answers, and so on) than it is to cancel your scores. You can do well on the exam without finishing every section. In addition, each version of the exam contains questions or sections that are experimental and are not counted towards your score, so your score may be better than you expect. Thus, you usually are better off waiting to see your score before deciding whether or not to retake the exam.

2 TYPICAL GMAT QUESTIONS AND HOW TO APPROACH THEM

A logical first step in preparing for the GMAT is to become as familiar as possible with the types of questions that usually appear on this exam. The following analysis of typical GMAT questions explains the purpose behind each type and the best method for answering it. Tactics for handling each of the different types of questions are also given. These tactics provide practical tools and advice to help you prepare for the exam and take it more efficiently. Samples of the questions with a discussion of their answers are also included. More detailed discussions and reviews for each section of the test are presented in the Correct Your Weaknesses part of this book.

Analytical Writing Assessment

The Analytical Writing Assessment section is designed to assess your ability to think critically and to communicate complex ideas. The writing task consists of two sections that require you to examine the composition of an issue, take a position on the basis of the details of the issue, and present a critique of the conclusion derived from a specific way of thinking. The issues are taken from topics of general interest related to business or to other subjects. There is no presumption of any specific knowledge about business or other areas.

Types of Analytical Writing Assessment Tasks

There are two types of Analytical Writing Assessment tasks: *Analysis of an Issue* and *Analysis of an Argument.* Following is an example of each:

EXAMPLE

Analysis of an Issue

Some analysts complain that consumers do not receive enough information to make rational purchase decisions. When the consumer is unable to make rational decisions, the economy suffers. Behavioral scientists contend that emotional and psychological factors play an important role in the satisfaction of consumer wants and that the measurable quantitative information being proposed by others is not as relevant for consumer decision-making as purported to be.

Which do you find more convincing: the complaint of the analysts or the contention of the behavioral scientists? State your position using relevant reasons and examples from your own experience, observation, or reading.

Test-Taking Tactics

1. Identify the issue or argument. For additional practice doing this, read the Critical Reasoning Review on pages 142–150.

In the example, the claim or conclusion is that the economy suffers when consumers cannot make rational decisions. Consumers cannot make rational decisions whenever information is lacking. The counter-view is that consumer decision-making is based more on emotion than on rational reasoning. If that is the case, then information is not so important.

2. Outline your ideas. You are asked to take sides. If you believe that consumers make decisions mainly on a rational basis, you will have to support your view by giving examples based on experience or on the facts that you have acquired from study or reading. You must state why you support this view and not the other. Do you have any facts on the issue? If so, list them along with examples. If you do not have facts, you will need to deal with the issue inferentially—by reasoning inductively. Here, experience and observation will be important to buttress your claims.

Another possibility in this case is that consumer decision-making depends on the sort of product. When it comes to purchasing a house or making a similar capital investment, the decision is mainly rational, and so it depends on a good deal of information. Most consumer purchases, however, are not of this kind; for example, clothing, food, leisure activities—whose motivation is largely emotional. Thus, for most purchases, a lot of information is not necessary, and so the economy does not suffer as is claimed.

EXAMPLE

Analysis of an Argument

The computerized water-irrigation system to be installed by farmers will prevent crops from drying out. The soil moisture is measured by sensors in the ground that send signals back to the irrigation control system. On the basis of this information, the system automatically regulates the amount and time of irrigation.

Discuss how logically persuasive you find this argument. In presenting your point of view, analyze the sort of reasoning used and its supporting evidence. In addition, state what further evidence, if any, would make the argument more sound and convincing or would make you better able to evaluate its conclusion.

Test-Taking Tactics

1. Identify the parts of the argument. For additional practice doing this, read the Critical Reasoning Review on pages 142–150.

2. State how convincing (or unconvincing) you find the argument. The persuasiveness of an argument depends on its logic; that is, on whether the conclusion follows from the evidence presented. You are also asked to discuss what would make the argument more sound and persuasive or would help to evaluate its conclusion. To make an argument more sound, it is necessary to provide more evidence that will buttress the conclusion.

In the example, the conclusion is found in the first sentence: the irrigation system will prevent crops from drying out. What evidence is given that the irrigation system will indeed perform this task? Overall, the argument is sound and convincing, assuming that proper irrigation is all that is needed to keep crops from drying out. What then could strengthen the conclusion? Evidence that systems similar to the one described are already in place and working. This last point is important because we have no evidence about the reliability of the system. Moreover, there may be a question of cost-effectiveness. Will farmers be willing to adopt such a system? If evidence of these factors could be provided, the conclusion would be strengthened.

Reading Comprehension

The Reading Comprehension section tests your ability to analyze written information and includes passages from the humanities, the social sciences, and the physical and biological sciences. The typical Reading Comprehension section consists of three or four passages with a total of 25 questions that must be completed in 30 minutes. You will be allowed to turn back to the passages when answering the questions. However, many of the questions may be based on what is *implied* in the passages, rather than on what is explicitly stated. Your ability to draw inferences from the material is critical to successfully completing this section. You are to select the best answer from five alternatives.

Major Types of Reading Comprehension Questions

Reading comprehension questions usually fall into several general categories. In most questions, you will be asked about one of the following:

Main Idea. In this type of question you may be asked about the main idea or theme of the passage, about a possible title, or about the author's primary objective. Usually the main idea refers to the passage as a whole, not to some segment or part of the passage. The main idea is typically (but not always) found in the first paragraph. It will be a statement that gives the overall theme of the passage. In many cases, it will be in the form of an argument, including a premise and conclusion. (For the identification of the structure of an argument, see the Critical Reasoning Review later in this book.)

A frequent question on Reading Comprehension tests asks you to select the title or theme that best summarizes the passage.

EXAMPLE

Government policy in Frieland has traditionally favored foreign investment. Leaders of all political parties have been virtually unanimous in their belief that foreign investment in Frieland would contribute to speeding that country's economic development, a major priority of both the ruling coalition and opposition parties. Of special interest to the government were those industries that exported a significant share of their total output. Since Frieland had a relatively small population, there was a limit to the amount of goods that could be produced for the local market. Also, the government did not want to encourage foreign investors to compete with local industry, even though new industries might alleviate the already high unemployment rate.

1. The best possible title of the passage is
   (A) Government Policy in Frieland.
   (B) How To Provide Employment.
   (C) Attracting Foreign Investment.
   (D) The Economics of Developing Countries.
   (E) Foreign Investment and Economic Development.

All of the above alternatives can be found in the passage, with the exception of (D)—we don't know if Frieland is a developing country. However, note that the words "foreign investment" are mentioned three times in the passage, and in lines 5–6 it is linked with economic development. Clearly then, the main idea or subject is foreign investment, and the appropriate answer is (E).

Additional questions may ask you to identify the author's purpose in writing the passage.

EXAMPLE

2. It can be concluded that the aim of the author is to
   (A) increase foreign investment.
   (B) protect local industry from foreign competition.
   (C) increase unemployment benefits for workers.
   (D) develop a theory of foreign investment.
   (E) increase the indigenous population of Frieland.

The most appropriate answer to the above question is (A). The author gives some of the reasons and under what conditions foreign investment would be beneficial to Frieland.

Supporting Ideas. In this type of question, you may be asked about the idea expressed in one part of the passage, rather than about the passage as a whole. Questions of this type test your ability to distinguish between the main idea and those themes that support it, some of which may be implicit or implied rather than explicitly stated.

EXAMPLE

Some economists believe that the United States can be utilized as a "land bridge" for the shipment of containerized cargo between Europe and the Far East. Under the land-bridge concept, containerized freight traveling between Europe Line and the Far East would be shipped by ocean carrier to the United States East Coast, unloaded and placed on special railway flatcars, and shipped via railroad to a West Coast port. At this port, the containers would then be loaded on ships bound to a Far East port of entry. This procedure would be reversed for material traveling in the opposite direction. Thus, a land transportation system would be substituted for marine transportation during part of the movement of goods between Europe and the Far East.

If a land-bridge system of shipment were deemed feasible and competitive with alternative methods, t would open a completely new market for both United States steamship lines and railroads. At present, foreign lines carry all Far East-Europe freight. American carriers get none of this trade, and the all-water route excludes the railroads.

The system established by a land bridge could also serve to handle goods now being shipped between the United States West Coast and Europe, or goods shipped between the Far East and the United States Gulf and East Coasts. Currently, there are 20 foreign lines carrying West Coast freight to Europe via the Panama Canal, but not one United States line. Thus, in addition to the land bridge getting this new business for the railroads, it also gives the United States East Coast ships an opportunity to compete for this trade.

While this method of shipment will probably not add to the labor requirements at East and West Coast piers, it does have the potential of absorbing some of the jobs that the containerization of current cargo has eliminated or could eliminate. Thus, the possibility of creating new jobs for longshoremen is not an expected benefit of such a system, but it will most certainly create other labor requirements. The land-bridge concept has the potential of offering new job openings for United States railway workers and seamen. In addition, there would be expansion of labor requirements for people in the shipbuilding and container manufacturing business.

By making United States rail transportation an export service, the land-bridge system would have a favorable effect on our balance of payments. Such a system also has the potential of relieving the United States government of part of the burden it now bears in the form of subsidies to the shipping industry. The federal government subsidizes the construction and operation of scheduled vessels. Some 52 percent of the income from their operation comes from the government in that these ships are used for all our military and other government-related export shipments. The land-bridge requirement for scheduled sailings could effect a shift from the use of these subsidized lines for shipment of government goods to commercial cargo of the land bridge. This would then open some of the lucrative government business to the unscheduled, unsubsidized lines.

The main idea in this passage is that the United States may be utilized as a land bridge for the shipment of containerized cargo between Europe and the Far East. This is evidenced by the first sentence in the passage. Supporting ideas would include any facts or arguments that buttress the main idea. A number of these may be found in the passage:

1. The opening of a *new market.* (paragraph 2)
2. Obtaining *new business.* (paragraph 3)
3. Creating *labor requirements.* (paragraph 4) and
4. Improving U.S. *balance of payments.* (paragraph 5).

EXAMPLE

1. According to the passage, if a land-bridge system were feasible, it would
   (A) create employment in the bridge-building industry
   (B) decrease the amount of air freight
   (C) create a new market for steamship lines and railroads
   (D) make Amerian railroads more efficient
   (E) increase foreign trade

2. The author implies that which of the following would be provided employment by the development of a land bridge?

   I. Longshoremen
   II. U.S. railway workers
   III. U.S. seamen

   (A) I only
   (B) III only
   (C) I and II only
   (D) II and III only
   (E) I, II, and III

The answer to question 1 is alternative (C), which refers to supporting idea (1) listed above and summarized in paragraph 2 of the passage. A land bridge would create a new market for U.S. steamship lines and railroads.

Question 2 is developed from an idea *implied* in the passage. Answer choice (D) is correct, because, in paragraph 4, it is argued that new jobs will be created for U.S. railway workers and seamen, but not for longshoremen.

Drawing Inferences. Questions of this sort ask about ideas that are not explicitly stated in a passage. These questions refer to meanings *implied* by the author based on information given in the passage. Typical questions are:

1. The author feels (believes) that . . .
2. In reference to (event) it may be inferred that . . .

EXAMPLE

Refer to the land bridge passage on page 11.

Which of the following might least benefit from a land bridge?

(A) U.S. railway workers.
(B) U.S. seamen.
(C) U.S. scheduled shipping lines.
(D) U.S. unscheduled shipping lines.
(E) U.S. government.

The author specifically gives reasons why each of the factors mentioned in all alternative answers might benefit from a land bridge. However, the author states in the last paragraph that some one half of the total income of scheduled shipping lines is subsidized by the government. A land bridge would provide increased business for these lines, enabling the government to shift subsidies from scheduled to unscheduled lines. Thus, it may be inferred that the increased traffic will replace subsidized income. Therefore, scheduled shipping lines might *least* benefit from the land bridge, and answer choice (C) is correct.

Specific Details. In this type of question you may be asked about specific facts or details the author has stated explicitly in the passage. This sort of question may take the following forms:

1. Which of the following statements is mentioned by the author?
2. All of the following are given as reasons for ( ) except:
3. The author argues that . . .

EXAMPLE

Refer to the land bridge passage on page 11.

1. According to the passage, the major alternative to a U.S. land bridge is the
   (A) Panama Canal
   (B) Suez Canal
   (C) air-freight system
   (D) all land route
   (E) military transport system

2. The passage states that a land bridge would improve United States
   (A) foreign trade
   (B) balance of payments
   (C) railroad industry
   (D) international relations
   (E) gold reserves

3. A land bridge would *not*
   (A) aid U.S. steamship lines
   (B) handle goods shipped between Europe and the Far East
   (C) create new jobs for longshoremen
   (D) supply new business for U.S. railroads
   (E) create business for unscheduled shipping lines

The answer to specific detail questions may always be found in the passage. These questions do not deal with implications or inferences. The answer to question 1 above is (A); paragraph 3 discusses use of the Panama Canal as a route for freight lines. The answer to question 2 is (B), which is given in paragraph 5. The answer to question 3 is (C); in paragraph 4, it is specifically stated that longshoremen would not benefit from a land bridge.

Applying Information from the Passage to Other Situations. These questions ask you to make an analogy between a situation described in the passage and a similar situation or event listed in the question. Unlike other types of questions, these describe situations *not* given in the passage, but rather those that are analogous to those in the passage. In order to answer a question of this kind, you must be able to draw a parallel between the situation in the question and its counterpart in the passage.

EXAMPLE

The Danes are widely renowned for their business orientation, which is reflected in their export promotion policies. Without any raw materials of their own, except for agricultural produce, the Danes obtain a third of their GNP from their export trade. This magnitude has been achieved only through a thorough exploitation of export potential and the implementation of a wide range of promotional activities. The latter emphasize the practical rather than the theoretical, and actual business encounters rather than such indirect, and previously popular, means as cultural events and Danish weeks.

1. Which of the following countries should succeed in exporting?
   (A) Countries without domestic raw materials.
   (B) Countries with a growing GNP.
   (C) Countries with a practical approach to business.
   (D) Countries with a thoroughly produced and diverse promotional campaign.
   (E) Countries with some export potential based on a wide range of products.

This question asks you to project the Danish experience to similar events in other countries. The analogy, of course, is "what helped the Danes to export will help other countries as well." And what helped the Danes in this case was the "implementation of a wide range of promotional activities." The correct answer is (D). Note that you were not asked to comment on the validity of the analogy, but only to identify the parallel case.

Tone or Attitude of the Passage. These questions concentrate on the author's style, attitude, or mood. In order to determine this attitude, look for key words, such as adjectives that reveal if the author is "pessimistic," "critical," "supportive," or "objective" about an event, idea, or situation in the passage.

Typical questions are:

1. For what audience is the passage intended?

2. The passage indicates that the author expresses a feeling of

   (A) Hope
   (B) Confidence
   (C) Enthusiasm
   (D) Instability
   (E) Pleasure

3. It can be concluded that the author of the passage is

   (A) sympathetic to John Doe's ideas
   (B) uncritical of John Doe's interpretation of history
   (C) politically conservative
   (D) a believer in mysticism
   (E) a political dilettante

Technique Used by the Author in the Passage. A reader can detect certain techniques used by authors, depending on the subject matter of the material.

If the subject matter of the passage is from the *social studies*, authors tend to

- make comparisons ("The ABC company uses a production process that can be likened to. . .")
- describe cause and effect relationships ("The development of the harbor can be attributed to. . .")
- opinionate or reason ("The author belongs to which of the following schools of thought?")

If the subject matter is from the *sciences,* writers deal with

- problem solving ("Serious unemployment leads labor groups to demand . . .")
- cause and effect ("Government investment in industry should result in . . .")
- classification of things and events ("According to the passage, the waves occur most frequently in the area of . . .")

- experimentation ("Given present wave tracking systems, scientists can forecast all of the following except:")

If the subject matter is *literature,* authors tend to

- create moods ("Which of the following best describes the author's tone in the passage?")
- narrate events ("The author's treatment of the topic can be best described as . . .")
- describe settings and characters ("The main character is a person attempting to . . .")

The Logical Structure of the Passage. These types of questions test your understanding of the overall meaning, logic, or organization of a passage. You may be asked how several ideas in a passage are interrelated or how a passage is constructed, classifies, compares, describes events, or situations. You may be asked about the strengths or weaknesses of the argument the author is making, to identify assumptions, or to evaluate counter-arguments.

Typical questions are:

1. John Doe's judgment that he failed was based on an assumption. Which of the following could have served as that assumption?
2. Which of the following, if true, weaken the above argument?
3. If the statement in the passage is true, which of the following must also be true?
4. Which of the following conclusions can be drawn from the passage?

Determining the Meaning of Words from the Context. When a question asks for the meaning of a word, it can usually be deduced from the context of the passage. Remember, you are not required to know the meaning of technical or foreign words.

EXAMPLE

During the 1980 campaign to clean the streets of undesirables and criminal elements, a force of 10,000 special police was used to maintain order. Nevertheless, many of the hunted crime figures fought back with live weapons and the streets looked like a battlefield. Almost as many policemen were injured as criminals. This year's *aktion* will have to be better planned.

1. The planned *aktion* can be described as a

(A) police offensive
(B) political campaign
(C) battle
(D) law and order
(E) none of the above.

The passage tells us that that this year's *aktion* will have to be planned better. From this, we know that it is being compared to something that happened before, which in the passage was during 1980. That was the campaign to clean the streets. Therefore, the best answer choice is (A) and we know that the meaning of *aktion* is the police offensive described in the passage.

Test-Taking Tactics

1. Answer passages with familiar subject matter first. You may encounter a passage that contains familiar material, perhaps subjects you have studied or read. You should be able to do better on these or at least read the passage more quickly. However, even though you have some familiarity with the subject of a passage, do not let your knowledge influence your choice of answer alternatives. You must answer the questions only on what is written or implied in the passage.

2. Read the question first, then the passage. Reading the question first enables you to identify the question *type*. However, do not read the answer alternatives at this time. If you are familiar with the question type, such as identifying a main idea or drawing inferences, you know what to look for in the passage. After you know the question type, carefully read the passage.

Read as quickly as you can, but not in haste. Each Reading Comprehension section contains about 1,500 words, so even if you read at a medium rate of 300 words a minute, you will read the passages in approximately 5 minutes, leaving 25 minutes for answering the questions.

If the question asks you to identify the main idea, remember that often it will be found in the opening sentences or in the summary part of the passage. In order to identify the main idea, first determine the object, person, or thing that is the subject of the passage. Ask yourself: "What is the main point the author is making?"

3. Underline parts of the passage. Underlining or marking key points, such as the main idea and supporting ideas, arguments, and conclusions, may be helpful in answering the questions later on. It will enable you to refer quickly to these points without having to go over all the material again. However, underlining a passage in the test is not the same as simply underlining in a textbook. Since time is limited in the test, you must use a different system. We suggest using marks such as MI for the main idea and SD for specific detail. These marks should be placed near each appropriate part of the passage without extensive underlining or without underlining at all.

4. Read all the answer alternatives. Read *all* the answer choices. Never assume you have found the correct answer until you have considered all the alternatives. Choose the best possible answer on the basis of what is written in the passage and not on your own knowledge from other sources.

5. Learn to identify the major question types. Before taking a Reading Comprehension test, make sure that you are thoroughly familiar with the major question types. This will save you time on the test and increase your effectiveness in choosing the correct answer. Time will be saved because you will know in advance what to look for and how to read the passage. You will be more effective because you will immediately know what reading tactic to apply. To become familiar with the various question types be sure to read the "Major Types of Reading Comprehension Questions" earlier in this chapter.

Sample Passage and Questions

The following passage will give you an idea of the format of the Reading Comprehension section. Read the passage through and then answer the questions, making sure to leave yourself enough time to complete them all.

TIME: 10 minutes

Political theories have, in fact, very little more to do with musical creation than electronics theories have. Both merely determine methods of distribution. The exploitation of these methods is subject to political regulation and is quite rigidly regulated in many countries. The revolutionary parties, both in Russia and elsewhere, have tried to turn composers on to supposedly revolutionary subject-matter. The net result for either art or revolution has not been very important. Neither has official fascist music accomplished much either for music or for Italy or Germany.

Political party-influence on music is just censorship anyway. Performances can be forbidden and composers disciplined for what they write, but the creative stimulus comes from elsewhere. Nothing really "inspires" an author but money or food or love.

That persons or parties subventioning musical uses should wish to retain veto power over the works used is not at all surprising. That our political masters (or our representatives) should exercise a certain negative authority, a censorship, over the exploitation of works whose content they consider dangerous to public welfare is also in no way novel or surprising. But that such political executives should think to turn the musical profession into a college of political theorists or a bunch of hired propagandists is naïve of them. Our musical civilization is older than any political party. We can deal on terms of intellectual equality with acoustical engineers, with architects, with poets, painters, and historians, even with the Roman clergy if necessary. We cannot be expected to take very seriously the inspirational dictates of persons or of groups who think they can pay us to get emotional about ideas. They can pay us to get emotional all right. Anybody can. Nothing is so emotion-producing as money. But emotions are factual; they are not generated by ideas. On the contrary, ideas are generated by emotions; and emotions, in turn, are visceral states produced directly by facts like money and food and sexual intercourse. To have any inspirational quality there must be present facts or immediate anticipations, not pie-in-the-sky.

Now pie-in-the-sky has its virtues as a political ideal, I presume. Certainly most men want to work for an eventual common good. I simply want to make it quite clear that ideals about the common good (not to speak of mere political necessity) are not very stimulating subject-matter for music. They don't produce visceral movements the way facts do. It is notorious that musical descriptions of hell, which is something we can all imagine, are more varied and vigorous than the placid banalities that even the best composers have used to describe heaven; and that all composers do better on really present matters than on either: matters like love and hatred and hunting and war and dancing around and around.

The moral of all this is that the vetoing of objective subject-matter is as far as political stimulation or censorship can go in advance. Style is personal and emotional, not political at all. And form or design, which is impersonal, is not subject to any political differences of opinion.

1. The author is making a statement defending

   I. intellectual freedom
   II. the apolitical stance of most musicians
   III. emotional honesty

   (A) I only
   (B) II only
   (C) I and II only
   (D) I and III only
   (E) I, II, and III

2. The tone of the author in the passage is

   (A) exacting
   (B) pessimistic
   (C) critical
   (D) optimistic
   (E) fatalistic

3. The author's reaction to political influence on music is one of

   (A) surprise
   (B) disbelief
   (C) resignation
   (D) deference
   (E) rancor

4. According to the author, political attempts to control the subject-matter of music
   (A) will be resisted by artists wherever they are made
   (B) may succeed in censoring but not in inspiring musical works
   (C) will succeed only if the eventual goal is the common good
   (D) are less effective than the indirect use of social and economic pressure
   (E) have profoundly influenced the course of modern musical history

5. The author refers to "musical descriptions of hell" (lines 53–54) to make the point that
   (A) musical inspiration depends on the degree to which the composer's imagination is stimulated by his subject
   (B) composers are better at evoking negative emotions and ideas than positive ones
   (C) music is basically unsuited to a role in support of political tyranny
   (D) religious doctrines have inspired numerous musical compositions
   (E) political ideals are a basic motivating force for most contemporary composers

6. The author implies that political doctrines usually fail to generate artistic creativity because they are too
   (A) naïve
   (B) abstract
   (C) rigidly controlled
   (D) concrete
   (E) ambiguous

Answers:

1. **(D)**	3. **(C)**	5. **(A)**
2. **(C)**	4. **(B**	6. **(B)**

Analysis:

1. **(D)** The author is arguing that musicians will not conform to any control over their creativity. Thus, they want to be intellectually free and emotionally honest. It does not mean that they could not be active in politics (apolitical).
2. **(C)** The author is critical of attempts to censor the arts, especially music.
3. **(C)** The author does not find censorship surprising (lines 19–21), nor does he take it seriously (lines 34–37). He is resigned to attempts at censorship, although hc docs not believe it can inspire creativity.
4. **(B)** See paragraph 2.
5. **(A)** See lines 53–57.
6. **(B)** See paragraph 4, in which the author states that "ideals" do not inspire music as "facts" do; and also see lines 16–18 and 43–45.

Now that you have reviewed the answers, let us see how successful you were in marking the passage. Below is the same passage marked with cues to the major question types.

MI Political theories have, in fact, very little more to do with musical creation than electronics theories have. Both merely determine methods of distribution. The exploitation of these methods is subject to political regulation and is quite rigidly regulated in many countries. The revolutionary parties, both in Russia and elsewhere, have tried to turn composers on to supposedly revolutionary subject-matter. The net result for either art or revolution has not been very important. Neither has official fascist music accomplished much either for music or for Italy or Germany.

SI Political party-influence on music is just censorship anyway. Performances can be forbidden and composers disciplined for what they write, but the creative stimulus comes from elsewhere. Nothing ***SD*** really "inspires" an author but money or food or love.

That persons or parties subventioning musical uses should wish to retain veto power over the works used is not at all surprising. That our political masters (or ***SI*** our representatives) should exercise a certain negative authority, a censorship, over the exploitation of works whose content they consider dangerous to public welfare is also in no way novel or surprising. But that such political executives should think to turn the musical profession into a college of ***SI*** political theorists or a bunch of hired propagandists is naïve of them. Our musical civilization is older than any political party. We can deal on terms of intellectual equality with acoustical engineers, with architects, with poets, painters, and historians, even with the Roman clergy if necessary. We cannot be expected to take very seriously the inspirational dictates of persons or of groups who think they can pay us to get emotional about ideas. They can pay us to get emotional all right. Anybody can. Nothing is so emotion-producing as money. But emotions are factual; they are not generated by ideas. On the contrary, ideas are generated by emotions; and emotions, in turn, are visceral states produced directly by facts like money and food and sexual intercourse. To have any inspirational quali- ***SI*** ty there must be present facts or immediate anticipations, not pie-in-the-sky.

Now pie-in-the-sky has its virtues as a political ideal, I presume. Certainly most men want to work for an eventual common good. I simply want to

SI make it quite clear that ideals about the common good (not to speak of mere political necessity) are not very stimulating subject-matter for music. They don't produce visceral movements the way facts do. It is notorious that musical descriptions of *SI* hell, which is something we can all imagine, are more varied and vigorous than the placid banalities that even the best composers have used to describe heaven; and that all composers do better on really present matters than on either: matters like love and hatred and hunting and war and dancing around and around.

The moral of all this is that the vetoing of objective subject-matter is as far as political stimulation or censorship can go in advance. Style is personal and emotional, not political at all. And form or design, which is impersonal, is not subject to any political differences of opinion.

Note the marked passage above. Cue words have been circled, and major question types have been marked in the margins. For example, in the first paragraph the cue words "net result" have been circled. These words refer to the sentences above and to the main idea (MI)—found in the first sentence—that politics and the arts are foreign to each other and that political regulation of music and the arts does nothing for them.

In the second paragraph there are a supporting idea (SI) and a specific detail (SD). The word "that," which appears three times at the beginning of the third paragraph, signals that a statement is to be made. The first two introduce a supporting idea to the effect that it is not surprising to find censorship of artistic works considered to be dangerous to a (totalitarian) state. The "But" before the third "that" signals a different thought: that while censorship may be applied, it will not politicize the musical profession. A second "But" and the phrase "On the contrary" signal that the following ideas or details present a contrasting argument to what was previously presented.

The word "Now" at the beginning of the fourth paragraph clues us to the introduction of another idea, namely, that inspiration, contrary to political ideals, is based on the happenings of everyday life and not on theory.

The cue word "moral" in the last paragraph signals a summing up or a conclusion. The conclusion of the passage is that, while censorship of objective subject matter is possible, the arts cannot be politicized.

Since the main idea is concerned with the politicizing of the arts, the word "political" was underlined every time it appeared. Since musical or artistic creation is also a subject of the passage, the word "emotional" was underlined. As can be seen from the marked passage, underlining was done very sparingly.

Looking now at the passage as a whole, we can see that the first paragraph contains the main idea, the second, third, and fourth paragraphs contain supporting ideas and details buttressing (or, in other passages, sometimes negating) the main idea, while the last paragraph sums up and gives a conclusion. This is a typical structure of a Reading Comprehension passage. You will find that questions will usually follow this order.

After answering the questions and checking answers in practice tests, you should see whether you marked each reading passage properly. Were you able to find the answers by referring to your marks? Or did you miss too many important points? For example, by underlining the word "emotional" in the passage above, we would have easily found the answer to question 1. The answer to question 3 would also have been found since we marked SI (supporting idea) and circled the word "that" each time it occurred at the beginning of paragraph 3. Likewise, signals to the answers of questions 4 and 6 were marked in the sample passage. Continued practice in this manner will improve your score on the Reading Comprehension test.

Sentence Correction

The Sentence Correction part of the exam tests your understanding of the basic rules of English grammar and usage. To succeed in this section, you need a command of sentence structure including tense and mood, subject and verb agreement, proper case, parallel structure, and other basics. No attempt is made to test for punctuation, spelling, or capitalization.

In the Sentence Correction section you will be given sentences in which all or part of the sentence is underlined. You will then be asked to choose the best phrasing of the underlined part from five alternatives. (A) will always be the original phrasing.

Test-Taking Tactics

1. Remember that any error in the sentence must be in the underlined part. Do not look for errors in the rest of the sentence.

2. If you determine that there is an error in the underlined part of the sentence, immediately eliminate answer choice (A), which always repeats the wording of the original sentence. Also eliminate any other answer alternatives that repeat the specific error. Then, concentrate on the remaining answer alternatives to choose your answer.

3. Do not choose as an answer any alternative that changes the meaning of the original sentence.

4. Determine if the parts of the sentence are linked logically. Are the clauses of a sentence equal ("and," "or," etc.) or is one clause subordinate to another ("because," "since," "who," etc.)?

5. Look at the changes made in the answer alternatives. This will tell you what specific error or usage problem is being tested. This can be particularly helpful if you know that there is an error in the original sentence—your ear tells you the sentence is wrong—but you cannot pinpoint the error. Noticing what you have to choose between will help you identify the error and then select what you think is correct.

6. Be aware of the common grammar and usage errors tested on the GMAT. Among the most common errors are errors in verb tense and formation and errors in the use of infinitives and gerunds in verb complements; errors in pronoun case and agreement with subject-object; errors in use of adjectives and adverbs, especially after verbs of sense; errors in comparatives, connectors, parallel construction, and unnecessary modifiers.

There are also commonly confused words—for example, affect and effect, afflict and inflict, prescribe and proscribe. Be sure you know the meaning and spelling of these words and check that they are used correctly in the sentence.

Chapter Six—Sentence Correction Review—reviews those errors in grammar and usage commonly found on the GMAT. Examples of incorrect and correct sentences are given and a list of frequently misused words and prepositional idioms is provided.

Sample Question

Since the advent of cable television, at the beginning of <u>this decade, the video industry took</u> a giant stride forward in this country.

(A) this decade, the video industry took
(B) this decade, the video industry had taken
(C) this decade, the video industry has taken
(D) this decade saw the video industry taking
(E) the decade that let the video industry take

Answer: (C)

Analysis:

The phrase "Since the advent . . ." demands a verb in the present perfect form; thus, *"has taken,"* not *"took,"* is correct. Choice (E) changes the meaning of the original sentence.

Critical Reasoning

The Critical Reasoning section of the GMAT is designed to test your ability to evaluate an assumption, inference, or argument. Each question consists of a short statement followed by a question or assumption about the statement. Each question or assumption has five possible answers. Your task is to evaluate each of the five possible choices and select the one that is the best alternative.

Types of Critical Reasoning Questions

There are a number of different question types.

Inference or Assumption. These questions test your ability to evaluate an assumption, inference, or argument. You will be given a statement, position, argument, or fact and will be asked to identify a conclusion or claim and the premise on which it is based.

EXAMPLE

Four years ago the government introduced the Youth Training Program to guarantee teenagers leaving school an alternative to the dole. Today, over 150,000 16- and 17-year-olds are still signing on for unemployment benefits.

Each of the following, if true, could account for the above except

(A) The program provides uninteresting work.
(B) It is difficult to find work for all the program's graduates.
(C) The number of 16- and 17-year-old youths has increased over the past four years.
(D) Unemployment benefits are known while future salaries are not.
(E) Youths are unaware of the program's benefits.

The correct answer is (C). The fact that the number of 16- and 17-year-old youths has increased does not explain *why* unemployed high school graduates do not opt for the training program. All other answer alternatives do give possible reasons.

Flaws. In this type of question you are asked to choose the best alternative answer that either represents a flaw in the statement position, or if true, would weaken the argument or conclusion.

EXAMPLE

"Many people are murdered by killers whose homicidal tendencies are triggered by an official execution. Since 1977, for each execution there were about four homicides. . . . If each of the 1,788 death row prisoners were to be executed, up to 7,152 additional murders would be one of the results."

Which of the following, if true, would weaken the above argument?

(A) The rate of murders to executions is 1 to 1.66
(B) There is no relation between executions and murders.
(C) Executions result from the higher incidence of violent crime.
(D) The death penalty will be abolished.
(E) Not all death row prisoners will be executed.

The correct answer is (B). The author's assumption is that there is a relation between executions and homicides. As executions increase, so will homicides—at a given rate. Of course, if (D) occurred, presumably the homicide rate, according to the author's argument, will decline. However, (B) is the strongest argument—if true—against the author's premise.

Statements of Fact. With this type of question, you will be asked to find the answer that best agrees with, summarizes, or completes the statement.

EXAMPLE

When Herodotus wrote his history of the ancient world, he mixed the lives of the famous with those of the everyday. He wanted not only to record the events that shaped his world but also to give his readers a taste of life in past times and faraway places.

Which of the following best summarizes the above?

(A) Herodotus performed the tasks of both historian and journalist.
(B) Historians alone cannot reconstruct times and social circles.
(C) Herodotus relied on gossip and hearsay to compile his essays.
(D) Herodotus's history was based on scanty evidence.
(E) Herodotus preferred writing about the elite, rather than the lower classes.

The correct answer is (A). Herodotus wrote about all classes of people, recording not only momentous events but also the mundane. Therefore, he could be classified as an historian and as a journalist.

Test-Taking Tactics

1. First, read the question and then read the passage. If you can identify the question type, you will know what to look for in the passage.

2. Learn to spot major critical reasoning question types. The categories of questions and how to identify them were discussed. If you are able to recognize what a question is asking, you will know what reasoning tactic to apply. For example, if you recognize a question to be the flaw type, you are alerted to the fact that you must identify the argument and conclusion in the passage. If the question is "Which of the following, if true, would weaken the above argument?," your task is to find the author's argument by identifying the premise(s) and conclusion.

In the factual type of question—for example, "Which of the following best summarizes the statement above?" or "If the information in the statement is true, which of the following must also be true?"—you look for the main facts, and what is claimed from the facts. The next step is to determine to what extent the conclusion is substantiated by the facts. In making your judgment as to whether or not the conclusion is substantiated rely only on the facts presented in the passage and not on any outside information. Moreover, assume that the facts are true, without making any value judgment.

3. Look for the conclusion first. Critical reasoning questions are preceded by an argument or statement that has a conclusion or claim. While it may seem logical that a conclusion appears at the end of a passage, it might be given at the beginning or in the middle. Clues to help you find the conclusion are given in the Critical Reasoning Review.

4. Find the premises. Premises are facts or evidence. Determine whether or not the conclusion follows logically from the premises or whether it is merely alleged. A conclusion may not follow, even though premises may be true. You must determine the legitimacy of assumptions and final conclusions. A number of methods for doing this are given in the Review.

A typical question might ask you to attack or find a fact that weakens an argument. You must find the premise (one of the answer alternatives) that defeats the author's assumption.

EXAMPLE

"The United States gives billions of dollars in foreign aid to Balonia. Leaders of Balonia resent foreign aid. The United States should discontinue direct foreign aid to developing countries."

Which of the following statements, if true, would weaken the above argument?

(A) Balonia doesn't need foreign aid.
(B) Balonia isn't a developing country.
(C) Balonia is ruled by a dictator.
(D) Balonia's balance of payments is in surplus.
(E) Balonia's economy is growing.

In the above argument, only one example (that of Balonia) was used as a premise for reaching the conclusion that foreign aid should be discontinued. If it could be shown that Balonia is not a developing country (Choice B), then the premise is false and the conclusion invalid.

5. Do not be opinionated. The statement given in a question may contain a specific point of view. Do not form an opinion about the statement or its claim. Concentrate on the structure of the argument and whether or not the structure and logic is valid. Accept each statement, argument, or trend as fact and proceed accordingly.

6. Do not be overwhelmed by unfamiliar subjects. You are not expected to be familiar with subject matter in a particular field—say, economics or political history. Most scientific and technical words will be explained.

Problem Solving

The Problem Solving section of the GMAT is designed to test your ability to work with numbers. There are a variety of questions in this section dealing with the basic principles of arithmetic, algebra, and geometry. These questions may take the form of word problems or require straight calculation. In addition, questions involving the interpretation of tables and graphs may be included.

Starting in October 1994, the Problem Solving sections will consist of 16 questions that must be answered within a time limit of 25 minutes. These questions range from very easy to quite challenging and are not always arranged in order of difficulty. Make sure you budget your time so that you can try each question.

Test-Taking Tactics

1. Don't waste time. To maximize your score on this section, you must answer as many questions correctly as you can. Don't waste time on a question you can't figure out in a minute or two. Most candidates do not finish every section of the exam. A typical candidate will answer 12 or 13 out of the 16 questions on these sections. So don't worry about questions you can't answer; make sure you answer correctly all the questions you can. Your score will be better if you answer correctly two easy questions than if you answer correctly one difficult question in the same time. Most sections start with a few fairly easy questions but the last part of the section may also have some easy questions—in other words, the questions are not always arranged in order of difficulty. Try to budget your time so that you will have a chance to try to answer each question.

2. Don't perform unnecessary calculations. If you can, answer the question by estimating or doing a rough calculation rather than by figuring it out exactly. The time you save can be used to answer other questions in the section.

EXAMPLE

Find the value of $2x + 2y$ if $x + 2y = 6$ and $x + y = 10$.

(A) –4
(B) 6
(C) 10
(D) 14
(E) 20

You could solve for x and y and then evaluate $2x + 2y$. It is much faster to use the fact that $2(x + y)$ is $2x + 2y$ so the correct answer is 2(10) or 20.

3. Look at the answer choices before you start to work on the problem. For some questions, it may be easier and quicker to check the answers than to solve the problem.

EXAMPLE

Which of the following numbers is the closest to the square root of .0017?

(A) .005
(B) .05
(C) .13
(D) .4
(E) .04

To answer this question, do not try to find the exact square root of .0017 and then see which of the choices is closest to your answer. Instead simply square each answer choice and then determine which is closest to .0017. (E) is the correct answer ($.04 \times .04 = .0016$, which is closer to .0017 than the square of any of the other choices).

4. Answer the question that is asked. Read the question carefully. If your answer matches one of the choices given, your answer is not necessarily correct. Some of the choices given correspond to answers you would obtain by making simple errors, such as adding instead of subtracting or confusing area and perimeter.

EXAMPLE 1

If $x + y = 2$ and $x = 4$, then $x + 2y$ is

(A) −4
(B) −2
(C) 0
(D) 2
(E) 8

Since $x = 4$, then $x + y = 2$ means that y must be −2, and choice (B) is −2. But (B) is not the answer to the question. The question asked for the value of $x + 2y$, not for the value of y. The correct answer is (C), since $x + 2y$ is $4 + 2(-2) = 0$. If you forgot the minus sign and used $y = 2$ in evaluating $x + 2y$, your answer would be 8, which is choice (E).

To give you practice in avoiding these types of mistakes, some of the choices given on the sample tests in this book will be answers you would obtain if you made simple errors. After you have worked through the tests, you will know how to avoid errors of this kind.

EXAMPLE 2

How much will it cost to fence in a field that is 12 feet long and 42 feet wide with fence that costs $10 a yard?

(A) $180
(B) $360
(C) $504
(D) $540
(E) $1,080

If you multiply 12 × 42, you get 504; however, this is the area of the field in square feet. What you need to determine to answer this question is the perimeter of the field. The perimeter of the field is 12 + 12 + 42 + 42 = 108 feet. If you multiply 108 by $10, you get $1,080, or (E). However, this is incorrect. The price is $10 *per yard.* You must change the perimeter to yards before calculating the price. 108 feet ÷ 3 = 36 yards (there are 3 feet in 1 yard). 36 yards multiplied by $10 per yard equals $360, which is answer choice (B).

5. Use intelligent guessing to improve your score. If you have no idea what the correct answer is, you should not guess. However, if you can eliminate even a single choice, you should guess one of the remaining answers. In problem solving, you may be able to eliminate one or two choices by performing a quick estimate. Look at each choice offered. Some choices may obviously be incorrect. This tactic can be very useful for inference questions.

EXAMPLE

If xy is positive, then which of the following conclusions is valid? (x and y are integers.)

I. x must be positive.
II. x is not zero.
III. x must be negative.

(A) Only I
(B) Only II
(C) I and II only
(D) II and III only
(E) I, II, and III

Since 0 times any number is 0 it is easy to see that II is valid. Even if you can't go any further on this problem you know that the correct answer must be a choice that has II as part of the answer. So you know that (A) is incorrect. Guess one of the remaining choices.

EXAMPLE

What is the product of 21.84 × 32.78?

(A) 615.9152
(B) 715.8152
(C) 715.902
(D) 715.9152
(E) 725.9152

Since the product asked for will be greater than 21 × 32, which is 672, you can eliminate choice (A). Also each term has two decimal places, so the answer must have four decimal places; therefore you can eliminate choice (C). If you can't do the calculation, then guess (B), (D), or (E). The correct answer is (D).

6. Mark up diagrams and write in your test booklet. You are allowed to write in the test book so make whatever marks will help you to answer questions. If you are given the dimension of part of a diagram, write it on the diagram. If you are told parts are equal, mark them as equal. Cross out answers you have eliminated as you work on a problem. If a diagram is not supplied, draw a picture whenever possible.

7. If you need to compare non-adjacent entries in tables or graphs, use a pencil or the edge of the answer sheet as a ruler.

8. Check your work if you can. If you can check your work quickly, do so. This will help you avoid silly mistakes. For example if you are asked to solve an equation, check that your answer actually does satisfy the equation. In many questions, you can catch an obvious error by simply asking if your answer makes sense or by looking at an easy case of the problem.

EXAMPLE

What is the solution set to the inequality $2x > 5x - 18$

(A) $x > 6$
(B) $x < 6$
(C) $x > -6$
(D) $x < -6$
(E) $x > \frac{18}{7}$

The correct answer is (B). However, a mistake in algebra could give one of the other choices. For instance if you thought the answer was (C) try x = –5 and see if it works and try x = –7 and see if it doesn't work. Since x = –7 satisfies 2x > 5x – 18 answer (C) must not be correct. If you thought (A) was the answer then check that x = 7 works and x = 5 doesn't work, etc.

9. If a problem involves units, keep track of the units. Make sure your answer has the correct units. If a problem asks for the area of a figure, then your answer should be in square inches or some *square measurement*. Volumes should be in *cubic measurements*. Speed is measured in *miles per hour* or *feet per second*, etc.

EXAMPLE

How much fence will be needed to enclose a rectangular field that is 20 feet long and 100 feet wide?

(A) 120 feet
(B) 140 feet
(C) 200 feet
(D) 240 feet
(E) 2,000 feet

The correct answer is 240 feet, which is the perimeter of the field. If you made a mistake and multiplied length × width (i.e., you found the area of the field), then your answer would be 20 feet × 100 feet = 2,000 *square feet*, which is not the same as choice (E). If you only looked at the number 2,000 you might have made the wrong choice.

10. Use numerical values to find or check answers that involve formulas. Some questions will have answers that use given quantities whose numerical value is not given. For example, a question may ask for the cost of making *y* objects and the answer choices will all involve *y*. In such problems, assigning a value that is easy to compute with can simplify the problem and enable you to check your answer.

EXAMPLE

The first 100 copies of a poster cost x cents each; after the first 100 copies have been made, extra copies cost $\frac{x}{4}$ cents each. How many cents will it cost to make 300 copies of the poster?

(A) $100x$
(B) $150x$
(C) $200x$
(D) $300x$
(E) $400x$

The correct answer is $100x$ plus $200(\frac{x}{4})$ or $150x$ which is (B). Let $x = 8$. (Since the problem has $\frac{x}{4}$, choose a number divisible by 4.) Then the first 100 copies cost 800 cents and extra copies cost $\frac{8}{4} = 2$ cents each. 200 extra copies will cost $200 \times 2 = 400$ cents. The total cost is 800 + 400, or 1200. Letting $x = 8$, the possible answers are 800, 1200, 1600, 2400, and 3200, so (B) is correct.

When assigning variables avoid the values 0 or 1, since 0 times any number is 0 and 1 times a number does not change the number. If there is more than one unknown quantity in the answer, assign different numbers to each quantity.

This technique can sometimes help you eliminate answers to a problem so that you can make an intelligent guess.

In many cases you can eliminate all the incorrect choices by this technique. Start with the easiest formula to compute and work towards the hardest. If the formulas are complicated, this approach may take too much time. So be sure to check the time left and the number of questions left in the section before you use this approach on complicated formulas.

EXAMPLE

Box seats for a ball game cost $\$b$ each and general admission seats cost $\$g$ each. If 10,000 seats are sold, and x of the seats are box seats, which expression gives the fraction of money made on seat sales that came from box seats?

(A) $\dfrac{bx}{bx+(10{,}000-x)g}$

(B) $1 + (10{,}000 - x)g$

(C) $\frac{bx}{10,000}$

(D) $\frac{b}{(b+g)}$

(E) $\frac{x}{10,000}$

Since 10,000 – x general admission tickets are sold, the total from seat sales is $bx + (10,000 - x)g$. Thus the fraction made on box seats sales is $\frac{bx}{bx+(10,000-x)g}$ or (A). If you couldn't solve this problem, assign values to each quantity. For instance, let $b = 20$, $g = 10$ and $x = 2,000$ (note $x = 5,000$ is not a good choice since then the number of box seats and general admission seats will be identical). Then 2,000 box seats were sold and 8,000 general admission seats were sold. The total from box seats is $2,000 \times 20 = 40,000$ and the total from general admission is $8,000 \times 10 = 80,000$. So the total from ticket sales is 120,000, and 40,000 came from box seats; therefore, the answer is $\frac{40,000}{120,000} = \frac{1}{3}$.

The value of answer (C) is $\frac{40,000}{10,000} = 4$, so (C) is wrong; the value of (D) is $\frac{20}{(20+10)} = \frac{2}{3}$, which is wrong; and the value of (E) is $\frac{2,000}{10,000} = \frac{2}{10}$, which is wrong. The value of (B) is $1 + (8,000)(10) = 80,001$, which is incorrect. So the only possible answer is (A). When you substitute the values into choice (A), the result is $\frac{40,000}{[40,000+(8,000)10]} = \frac{40,000}{120,000} = \frac{1}{3}$, which agrees with the correct answer. So the correct answer is (A).

WARNING: If you use this method and one choice gives you the correct answer be sure to check the remaining choices. Different formulas may give the same result for one assignment of quantities.

11. Always remember that x or y could be negative, especially if you need to know whether it is "larger than" or "smaller than." For example, if $x = 3y$, this does not imply that x is greater than y, since if $y = -1$, then x is -3, which is less than -1.

12. Always remember that there are a positive and a negative root to $x^2 = a$. For example, $x^2 = 4$ does not mean that $x = 2$. You only know that $x = 2$ or $x = -2$.

13. Translate the information you are given into numerical or algebraic equations to start working a problem. If there is more than one variable in the problem, keep track of what each variable represents. It is helpful to use variables that suggest what the variable represents. For example, if you have the equation Profit = Revenue – Cost, use the variables P = Profit, R = Revenue, and C = Cost. The equation becomes $P = R - C$, which is much more informative than $x = y - z$.

14. If you skip a question on the test, be sure to skip the question on your answer sheet. It is a good idea to give yourself some indication of a skipped question, possibly by circling the number of that question on the answer sheet. However, be careful, since stray marks near the answers can be interpreted as an answer by the machine that grades the tests.

Long Term Strategy for Problem Solving

1. Practice arithmetic. Most Problem Solving sections contain one or two basic computational questions, such as multiplying two decimals or finding the largest number in a collection of fractions. If you are used to using a calculator to do all your arithmetic, these easy questions may be difficult for you. *You cannot use a calculator on the GMAT,* so practice your arithmetic before you take the exam. You already know how to do basic computation; you just need to practice to improve your speed and accuracy. See the Math Review for computational details and practice.

2. Try to think quantitatively. If you want to be a good reader, you should read a lot. In the same way, if you want to improve your quantitative skills, you should exercise them frequently. When you go grocery shopping, try to figure out whether the giant size is cheaper per ounce than the economy size. When you look at the news, try to make comparisons when figures are given. If you get used to thinking quantitatively, the Problem Solving sections will be much easier for you and you will feel more confident about the entire exam.

Sample Problem Solving Questions

Solve the following sample questions, allowing yourself 12 minutes to complete all of them. As you work try to use the above tactics. Any figure that appears with a problem is drawn as accurately as possible. All numbers used are real numbers.

TIME: 12 minutes

1. A train travels from Albany to Syracuse, a distance of 120 miles, at the average rate of 50 miles per hour. The train then travels back to Albany from Syracuse. The total traveling time of the train is 5 hours and 24 minutes. What was the average rate of speed of the train on the return trip to Albany?

   (A) 60 mph
   (B) 48 mph
   (C) 40 mph
   (D) 50 mph
   (E) 35 mph

2. A parking lot charges a flat rate of X dollars for any amount of time up to two hours, and $\frac{1}{6}X$ for each hour or fraction of an hour after the first two hours. How much does it cost to park for 5 hours and 15 minutes?

   (A) $3X$
   (B) $2X$
   (C) $1\frac{2}{3}X$
   (D) $1\frac{1}{2}X$
   (E) $1\frac{1}{6}X$

3. How many two-digit numbers are divisible by both 5 and 6?

   (A) none
   (B) one
   (C) two
   (D) three
   (E) more than three

4. What is 1 percent of .023?

   (A) .00023
   (B) .0023
   (C) .23
   (D) 2.3
   (E) 23

5. A window has the shape of a semicircle placed on top of a square. If the length of a side of the square is 20 inches, how many square inches is the area of the window?

   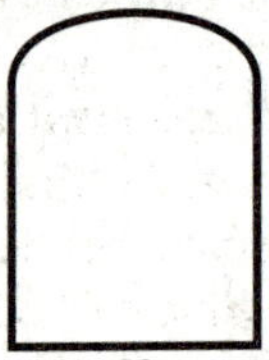

   (A) 400
   (B) 200π
   (C) $50(8 + \pi)$
   (D) $200(2 + \pi)$
   (E) $400(1 + \pi)$

6. Which of the following sets of values for w, x, y, and z, respectively, are possible if ABCD is a parallelogram?

   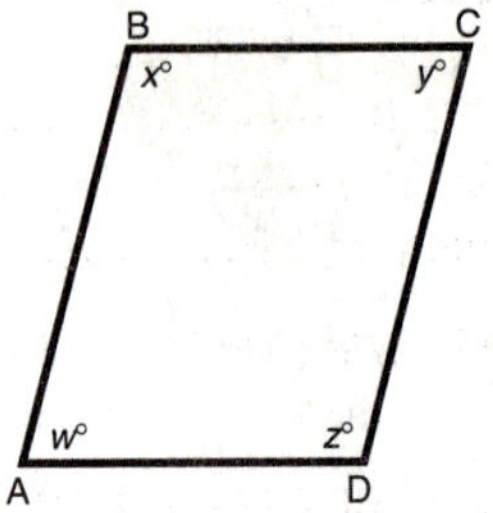

   I. 50, 130, 50, 130
   II. 60, 110, 70, 120
   III. 60, 150, 50, 150

   (A) I only
   (B) II only
   (C) I and II only
   (D) I and III only
   (E) I, II, and III

7. John weighs twice as much as Marcia. Marcia's weight is 60% of Bob's weight. Dave weighs 50% of Lee's weight. Lee weighs 190% of John's weight. Which of these 5 persons weighs the least?

   (A) Bob
   (B) Dave
   (C) John
   (D) Lee
   (E) Marcia

8. There were P people in a room when a meeting started. Q people left the room during the first hour, while R people entered the room during the same time. What expression gives the number of people in the room after the first hour as a percentage of the number of people in the room who have been there since the meeting started?

   (A) $\frac{(P-Q)}{(P-Q+R)}$
   (B) $100\times\frac{(P-Q+R)}{(P-Q)}$
   (C) $\frac{(P+R)}{(P-Q)}$
   (D) $100\times\frac{(P-Q)}{(P-Q+R)}$
   (E) $100\times\frac{(P+R)}{(P-Q)}$

Answers:

1. **(C)**	3. **(D)**	5. **(C)**	7. **(E)**
2. **(C)**	4. **(A)**	6. **(A)**	8. **(B)**

Analysis:

1. **(C)** The train took $\frac{120}{50} = 2\frac{2}{5}$ hours to travel from Albany to Syracuse. Since the total traveling time of the train was $5\frac{2}{3}$ hours, it must have taken the train

3 hours for the trip from Syracuse to Albany. Since the distance traveled is 120 miles, the average rate of speed on the return trip to Albany was $(\frac{1}{3})(120)$ mph = 40 mph.

2. **(C)** It costs X for the first 2 hours. If you park 5 hours and 15 minutes there are 3 hours and 15 minutes left after the first 2 hours. Since this time is charged at the rate of $\frac{X}{6}$ for each hour or fraction thereof, it costs $4\left(\frac{X}{6}\right)$ for the last 3 hours and 15 minutes. Thus the total $X+\frac{4}{6}X=1\frac{2}{3}X$.
3. **(D)** Since 5 and 6 have no common factors any number divisible by both 5 and 6 must be divisible by the product of 5 times 6 or 30. The only two digit numbers divisible by 30 are 30, 60, and 90. So the correct answer is (D).
4. **(A)** Remember that the decimal equivalent of 1 percent is .01. To find 1 percent of .023 you simply multiply .023 by .01. The answer must have five decimal places since .023 has three decimal places and .01 has two decimal places. Therefore, the correct answer is .00023 or choice (A). This is an example of the type of simple calculation that many versions of the GMAT will have in one question in a Problem-Solving section.
5. **(C)** Mark up the diagram by dividing the given figure into a square and a semicircle as shown below. Label all the lengths that you are given. The area of the window is the area of the square plus the area of the semicircle. The area of the square is 20^2 or 400 square inches. The area of the semicircle is $\frac{1}{2}$ of πr^2 where r is the radius of the semicircle. Since the side of the square is a diameter of the semicircle, the radius is $\frac{1}{2}$ of 20, or 10 inches. The area of the semicircle is $\frac{1}{2} \times \pi \times 100 = 50\pi$ square inches. Therefore, the area of the window is $400 + 50\pi = 50(8 + \pi)$ Note that you must be able to change your answer into the correct form to answer this question.

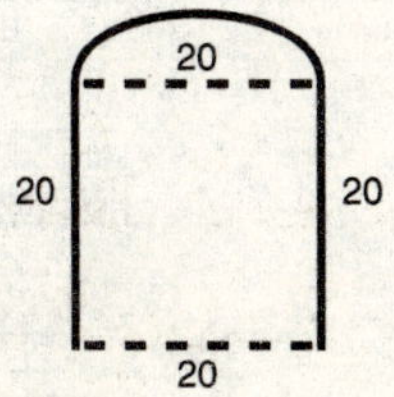

6. **(A)** The sum of the angles of a parallelogram (which is 4-sided) must be $(4 - 2)180° = 360°$. Since the sum of the values in III is 410, III cannot be correct. The sum of the numbers in II is 360, but in a parallelogram opposite angles must be equal so x must equal z and y must equal w. Since 60 is unequal to 70, II cannot be correct. The sum of the values in I is 360 and opposite angles will be equal, so I is correct.
7. **(E)** John weighs twice as much as Marcia, so John cannot weigh the least. Marcia's weight is less than Bob's weight, so Bob's weight is not the least. Dave's weight is $\frac{1}{2}$ of Lee's weight, so Lee can't weigh the least. The only possible answers are Marcia or Dave. So only (B) and (E) are possible; if you can't get any further, you should choose one of the two as your answer, since you have eliminated three choices. Let J, M, B, D, and L stand for the weights of John, Marcia, Bob, Dave, and Lee respectively. Then $D = .5L = .5(1.9)J$. So $D = .95J$. Since $J = 2M$, we know $M = .5J$. Therefore Marcia weighs the least.
8. **(B)** Although this problem looks difficult, it is fairly simple if you approach it in a step-by-step manner. First, express the number of people in the room after the first hour. There were P to begin with and Q left while R entered, so after the first hour there were $P - Q + R$ in the room. Second, express the number of people who have been in the room since the meeting started. R people entered while the meeting was in progress, so $P - Q$ people were in the room the entire hour. Therefore $\frac{(P-Q+R)}{(P-Q)}$ is the desired expression. But the question asks for a percentage. To change a number (fraction) into a percentage, simply multiply the number by 100. The correct answer is (B).

Data Sufficiency

This section of the GMAT is designed to test your reasoning ability. Like the Problem Solving section, it requires a basic knowledge of the principles of arithmetic, algebra, and geometry. Each Data Sufficiency question consists of a mathematical problem and two statements containing information relating to it. You must decide whether the problem can be solved by using information from: (A) the first statement alone, but not the second statement alone; (B) the second statement alone, but not the first statement alone; (C) both statements together, but neither alone; or (D) either of the statements alone. Choose (E) if the problem cannot be solved, even by using both statements together. A typical section will consist of 20 questions to be answered in 25 minutes. As in the Problem Solving section, time is of the utmost importance. Approaching Data Sufficiency problems properly will help you use this time wisely.

Test-Taking Tactics

1. Make sure you understand the directions. Reread the paragraph above. Make sure you know what is being asked. If you have never seen this type of question before, make sure you do the practice problems that follow. At first, these questions may seem difficult, but once you have worked through several examples, you will start to feel comfortable with them.

2. Don't waste time figuring out the exact answer. Always keep in mind that you are never asked to supply an answer for the problem; you are only asked to determine if there is sufficient data available to find the answer. Once you know whether or not it is possible to find the answer from the given information, you are done. If you waste time figuring out the exact answer, you may not be able to finish the entire section.

EXAMPLE

The profits of a company are the revenues the company receives minus the costs that the company pays. How much were the profits of the XYZ company in 1988?

(1) The XYZ company had revenues of $112,234,567 in 1988.
(2) The costs of the XYZ company were $102,479,345 in 1988.

The information given states that to find the profit you need to know both the revenues and the costs. So it is easy to see that both (1) and (2) are needed and that the profit could be determined using (1) and (2). So the answer is (C). Do not compute the profit. If you perform the subtraction needed to compute the profit, you are just wasting time that could be spent on other problems.

3. Draw a picture whenever possible. If a diagram is not supplied, draw one. Remember you can write in the test booklet. Pictures can be especially helpful in any question that involves geometry.

4. Don't make extra assumptions. You are only allowed to use the information given and facts that are always true (such as the number of hours in a day) to answer these questions. Do not make assumptions about things such as prices rising every year. If you are given a diagram don't assume two lines that appear to be perpendicular are perpendicular unless you are given specific information that says the lines are perpendicular. If an angle looks like a 45° angle don't assume it is 45° unless you are given that fact.

5. Use a system to work through the questions. Try to adopt a consistent approach to these types of problems. The system that follows will help you to answer the questions and also let you guess intelligently, if you can't complete the problem. You will have to invest some time to understand the method, but once you have done so, you should be much better prepared for these types of questions.

System for Data Sufficiency Questions

A systematic analysis can improve your score on Data Sufficiency sections. By answering three questions, you will always arrive at the correct choice. In addition, if you can answer any one of the three questions, you can eliminate at least one of the possible choices so that you can make an intelligent guess.

The three questions are:

I. Is the first statement alone sufficient to solve the problem?
II. Is the second statement alone sufficient to solve the problem?
III. Are both statements together sufficient to solve the problem?

As a general rule try to answer the questions in order I, II, III, since in many cases you will not have to answer all three to get the correct choice.

Here is how to use the three questions:

If the answer to I is YES, then the only possible choices are (A) or (D). Now, if the answer to II is YES, the choice must be (D), and if the answer to II is NO, the choice must be (A).

If the answer to I is NO then the only possible choices are (B), (C), or (E). Now, if the answer to II is YES, then the choice must be (B), and if the answer to II is NO, the only possible choices are (C) or (E).

So, finally, if the answer to III is YES, the choice is (C), and if the answer to III is NO, the choice is (E).

A good way to see this is to use a decision tree.

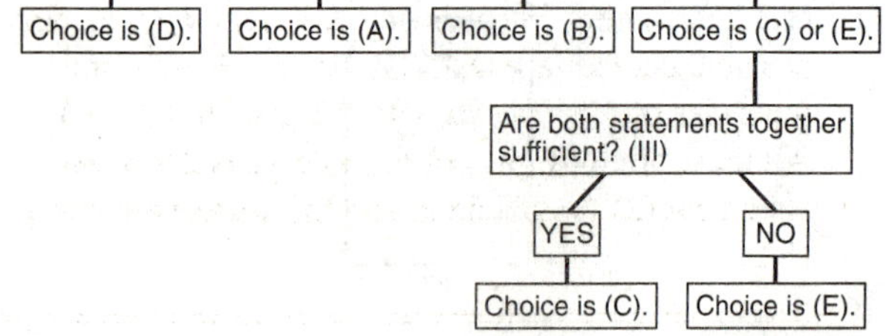

To use the tree simply start at the top and by answering YES or NO move down the tree until you arrive at the correct choice. For example, if the answer to I is YES and the answer to II is NO, then the correct choice is (A). (Notice that in this case you don't need to answer III to find the correct choice.)

The decision tree can also help you make intelligent guesses. If you can only answer one of the three questions, then you can eliminate the choices that follow from the wrong answer to the question.

EXAMPLE 1: You know the answer to I is YES. You can eliminate choices (B), (C), and (E).

EXAMPLE 2: You know the answer to II is NO. You can eliminate choices (D) and (B) since they follow from YES for II.

EXAMPLE 3: You know the answer to III is YES. You can eliminate choice (E) since it follows from NO for III.

EXAMPLE 4: You know the answer to I is NO and the answer to III is YES. You can eliminate (E) since it follows from NO to III. You also can eliminate (A) and (D) since they follow from YES to I.

Since you get one raw score point for each correct choice and lose only one quarter of a point for an incorrect choice, you should guess whenever you can answer one of the three questions.

There is an additional practice section of Data Sufficiency questions following the Math Review on pages 215–216. The analysis of these exercises (on pages 222–224) gives worked-out solutions using this system.

6. In many cases you can use simple values to check quickly whether a statement follows from a given statement. This can be especially useful in deciding that a statement does *not* follow from a given statement.

EXAMPLE

Is k a multiple of 6?

(1) k is a multiple of 3.
(2) k is a multiple of 12.

Write out some simple multiples of 3 ($3 \times 1 = 3$, $3 \times 2 = 6$, etc.). Since 3 is not a multiple of 6, "k is a multiple of 6" does not follow from "k is a multiple of 3." So statement (1) is not sufficient, and the only possible choices are (B), (C), or (E). Write some multiples of 12 (for example, 12, 24, 36, 48, . . .). All these are multiples of 6, since 12 is 2×6. So statement (2) is sufficient, and the correct answer is (B).

7. Remember if there is sufficient information to show that the answer to the question is NO, that means that there is sufficient information to answer the question.

EXAMPLE

Is n an even integer?

(1) $n = 3k$, for some integer k.
(2) $n = 2j + 1$, for some integer j.

The first statement is not sufficient, since 3×2 is 6, which is even, but 3×3 is 9, which is odd. The second statement is sufficient, since it means that n is odd. This means that the answer to the main question is "no," and therefore (B) is the correct choice.

Long Term Strategy for Data Sufficiency Questions

Practice Working Data Sufficiency Questions. Most people have not had much experience with these types of questions. The more examples you work out the better you will perform on this section of the test. By the time you have finished the sample exams, you should feel confident about your ability to answer Data Sufficiency questions.

Sample Questions

Read the following directions carefully and then try the sample Data Sufficiency questions below. Allow yourself 8 minutes total time. All numbers used are real numbers. A figure given for a problem is intended to provide information consistent with that in the question, but not necessarily consistent with the additional information contained in the statements.

TIME: 8 minutes

Directions: Each of the following problems has a question and two statements which are labeled (1) and (2). Use the data given in (1) and (2) together with other available information (such as the number of hours in a day, the definition of *clockwise,* mathematical facts, etc.) to decide whether the statements are *sufficient* to answer the question. Then choose

(A) if you can get the answer from **(1) ALONE** but not from (2) alone
(B) if you can get the answer from **(2) ALONE** but not from (1) alone
(C) if you can get the answer from **BOTH (1) and (2) TOGETHER,** but not from (1) alone or (2) alone
(D) if **EITHER** statement **(1) ALONE OR** statement **(2) ALONE** suffices

(E) if you **CANNOT** get the answer from statements **(1) and (2) TOGETHER,** but need even more data

All numbers used are real numbers. A figure given for a problem is intended to provide information consistent with that in the question, but not necessarily consistent with the additional information contained in the statements.

1. A rectangular field is 40 yards long. Find the area of the field.

   (1) A fence around the entire boundary of the field is 140 yards long.
   (2) The field is more than 20 yards wide.

2. Is X a number greater than zero?

   (1) $X^2 - 1 = 0$
   (2) $X^3 + 1 = 0$

3. An industrial plant produces bottles. In 1991 the number of bottles produced by the plant was twice the number produced in 1990. How many bottles were produced altogether in the years 1990, 1991, and 1992?

   (1) In 1992 the number of bottles produced was 3 times the number produced in 1990.
   (2) In 1993 the number of bottles produced was one half the total produced in the years 1990, 1991, and 1992.

4. A man 6 feet tall is standing near a pole. On the top of the pole is a light. What is the length of the shadow cast by the man?

   (1) The pole is 18 feet high.
   (2) The man is 12 feet from the pole.

5. Find the length of RS if z is 90° and $PS = 6$.

   (1) $PR = 6$
   (2) $x = 45°$

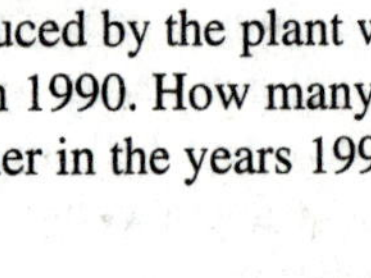

6. Working at a constant rate and by himself, it takes worker U 3 hours to fill up a ditch with sand. How long would it take for worker V to fill up the same ditch working by himself?

   (1) Working together but at the same time U and V can fill in the ditch in 1 hour $52\frac{1}{2}$ minutes.
   (2) In any length of time worker V fills in only 60% as much as worker U does in the same time.

7. Did John go the beach yesterday?

   (1) If John goes to the beach, he will be sunburned the next day.
   (2) John is sunburned today.

Answers:

1. **(A)**	3. **(E)**	5. **(D)**	7. **(E)**
2. **(B)**	4. **(C)**	6. **(D)**	

Analysis:

1. **(A)** The area of a rectangle is the length multiplied by the width. Since you know the length is 40 yards, you must find out the width in order to solve the problem. Since statement (2) simply says the width is greater than 20 yards you cannot find out the exact width using (2). So (2) alone is not sufficient. Statement (1) says the length of a fence around the entire boundary of the field is 140 yards. The length of this fence is the perimeter of the rectangle, the sum of twice the length and twice the width. If we replace the length by 40 in $P = 2L + 2W$ we have $140 = 2(40) + 2W$, which can be solved for W. On the test don't waste time calculating W or the area. At this point you know that (1) alone is sufficient. So the correct choice is (A).
2. **(B)** Statement (1) means $X^2 = 1$, but there are two possible solutions to this equation, $X = 1$, $X = -1$. Thus using (1) alone you cannot deduce whether X is positive or negative. Statement (2) means $X^3 = -1$, but there is only one possible (real) solution to this, $X = -1$. Thus X is not greater than zero, which answers the question. And (2) alone is sufficient.
3. **(E)** T, the total produced in the three years, is the sum of $P_0 + P_1 + P_2$, where P_0 is the number produced in 1990, P_1 the number produced in 1991, and P_2 the number produced in 1992. You are given that $P_1 = 2P_0$. Thus $T = P_0 + P_1 + P_2 = P_0 + 2P_0 + P_2 = 3P_0 + P_2$. So we must find out P_0 and P_2 to answer the question. Statement (1) says $P_2 = 3P_0$; thus by using (1) if we can find the value of P_0 we can find T. But (1) gives us no further information about P_0. Statement (2) says T equals the number produced in 1993, but it does not say what this number is. Since there are no relations given between production in 1993 and production in the individual years 1990, 1991, or 1992 you cannot use (2) to find out what P_0 is. Thus (1) and (2) together are not sufficient.
4. **(C)** Sometimes it may help to draw a picture. By proportions or by similar triangles the height of the

pole, h, is to 6 feet as the length of shadow, s, + the distance to the pole, x, is to s. So $\frac{h}{6}=\frac{(s+x)}{s}$. Thus

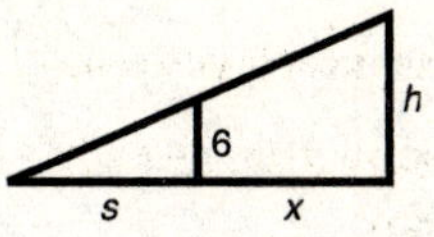

$hs = 6s + 6x$ by cross-multiplication. Solving for s gives $hs - 6s = 6x$, or $s(h - 6) = 6x$, or, finally, we have $s=\frac{6x}{(h-6)}$. Statement (1) says $h = 18$; thus

$s=\frac{6x}{12}=\frac{x}{2}$, **but using (1) alone we cannot deduce the**

value x. Thus (1) alone is not sufficient. Statement (2) says x equals 12; thus, using (1) and (2) together we deduce $s = 6$, but using (2) alone all we can deduce

is that $s=\frac{72}{(h-6)}$, which cannot be solved for s unless

we know h. Thus using (1) and (2) together we can deduce the answer but (1) alone is not sufficient nor is (2) alone.

5. **(D)** Since z is a right angle, $(RS)^2 = (PS)^2 + (PR)^2$, so $(RS)^2 = (6)^2 + (PR)^2$, and RS will be the positive square root of $36 + (PR)^2$. Thus if you can find the length of PR the problem is solved. Statement (1) says $PR = 6$, thus $(RS)^2 = 36 + 36$, so $RS = 6\sqrt{2}$. Thus (1) alone is sufficient. Statement (2) says $x =$ 45° but since the sum of the angles in a triangle is 180° and z is 90° then $y = 45°$. So x and y are equal angles and that means the sides opposite x and opposite y must be equal or $PS = PR$. Thus $PR = 6$ and $RS = 6\sqrt{2}$ so (2) alone is also sufficient.
6. **(D)** (1) says U and V together can fill in the ditch in $1\frac{7}{8}$ hours. Since U can fill in the ditch in 3 hours, in 1 hour he can fill in one-third of the ditch. Hence, in $1\frac{7}{8}$ hours U would fill in $\left(\frac{1}{3}\right)\left(\frac{15}{8}\right)=\frac{5}{8}$ of the ditch. So V fills in $\frac{3}{8}$ of the ditch in $1\frac{7}{8}$ hours. Thus V would take $\left(\frac{8}{3}\right)\left(\frac{15}{8}\right)=5$ hours to fill in the ditch working by himself. Therefore statement (1) alone is sufficient. According to statement (2) since U fills the ditch in 3 hours, V will fill $\frac{3}{5}$ of the ditch in 3 hours. Thus V will take 5 hours to fill in the ditch working by himself.
7. **(E)** Obviously, neither statement alone is sufficient. John *could* have gotten sunburned at the beach, but he might have gotten sunburned somewhere else. Therefore (1) and (2) together are not sufficient. This problem tests your grasp of an elementary rule of logic rather than your mathematical knowledge.

DIAGNOSE YOUR PROBLEM

Answer Sheet
DIAGNOSTIC TEST

Section 1 [Reading Comprehension]

1 (A) (B) (C) (D) (E)	6 (A) (B) (C) (D) (E)	11 (A) (B) (C) (D) (E)	16 (A) (B) (C) (D) (E)	21 (A) (B) (C) (D) (E)
2 (A) (B) (C) (D) (E)	7 (A) (B) (C) (D) (E)	12 (A) (B) (C) (D) (E)	17 (A) (B) (C) (D) (E)	22 (A) (B) (C) (D) (E)
3 (A) (B) (C) (D) (E)	8 (A) (B) (C) (D) (E)	13 (A) (B) (C) (D) (E)	18 (A) (B) (C) (D) (E)	23 (A) (B) (C) (D) (E)
4 (A) (B) (C) (D) (E)	9 (A) (B) (C) (D) (E)	14 (A) (B) (C) (D) (E)	19 (A) (B) (C) (D) (E)	24 (A) (B) (C) (D) (E)
5 (A) (B) (C) (D) (E)	10 (A) (B) (C) (D) (E)	15 (A) (B) (C) (D) (E)	20 (A) (B) (C) (D) (E)	25 (A) (B) (C) (D) (E)

Section 2 [Problem Solving]

1 (A) (B) (C) (D) (E)	6 (A) (B) (C) (D) (E)	11 (A) (B) (C) (D) (E)	16 (A) (B) (C) (D) (E)	21 (A) (B) (C) (D) (E)
2 (A) (B) (C) (D) (E)	7 (A) (B) (C) (D) (E)	12 (A) (B) (C) (D) (E)	17 (A) (B) (C) (D) (E)	22 (A) (B) (C) (D) (E)
3 (A) (B) (C) (D) (E)	8 (A) (B) (C) (D) (E)	13 (A) (B) (C) (D) (E)	18 (A) (B) (C) (D) (E)	23 (A) (B) (C) (D) (E)
4 (A) (B) (C) (D) (E)	9 (A) (B) (C) (D) (E)	14 (A) (B) (C) (D) (E)	19 (A) (B) (C) (D) (E)	24 (A) (B) (C) (D) (E)
5 (A) (B) (C) (D) (E)	10 (A) (B) (C) (D) (E)	15 (A) (B) (C) (D) (E)	20 (A) (B) (C) (D) (E)	25 (A) (B) (C) (D) (E)

Section 3 [Critical Reasoning]

1 (A) (B) (C) (D) (E)	6 (A) (B) (C) (D) (E)	11 (A) (B) (C) (D) (E)	16 (A) (B) (C) (D) (E)	21 (A) (B) (C) (D) (E)
2 (A) (B) (C) (D) (E)	7 (A) (B) (C) (D) (E)	12 (A) (B) (C) (D) (E)	17 (A) (B) (C) (D) (E)	22 (A) (B) (C) (D) (E)
3 (A) (B) (C) (D) (E)	8 (A) (B) (C) (D) (E)	13 (A) (B) (C) (D) (E)	18 (A) (B) (C) (D) (E)	23 (A) (B) (C) (D) (E)
4 (A) (B) (C) (D) (E)	9 (A) (B) (C) (D) (E)	14 (A) (B) (C) (D) (E)	19 (A) (B) (C) (D) (E)	24 (A) (B) (C) (D) (E)
5 (A) (B) (C) (D) (E)	10 (A) (B) (C) (D) (E)	15 (A) (B) (C) (D) (E)	20 (A) (B) (C) (D) (E)	25 (A) (B) (C) (D) (E)

Section 4 [Problem Solving]

1 (A) (B) (C) (D) (E)	6 (A) (B) (C) (D) (E)	11 (A) (B) (C) (D) (E)	16 (A) (B) (C) (D) (E)	21 (A) (B) (C) (D) (E)
2 (A) (B) (C) (D) (E)	7 (A) (B) (C) (D) (E)	12 (A) (B) (C) (D) (E)	17 (A) (B) (C) (D) (E)	22 (A) (B) (C) (D) (E)
3 (A) (B) (C) (D) (E)	8 (A) (B) (C) (D) (E)	13 (A) (B) (C) (D) (E)	18 (A) (B) (C) (D) (E)	23 (A) (B) (C) (D) (E)
4 (A) (B) (C) (D) (E)	9 (A) (B) (C) (D) (E)	14 (A) (B) (C) (D) (E)	19 (A) (B) (C) (D) (E)	24 (A) (B) (C) (D) (E)
5 (A) (B) (C) (D) (E)	10 (A) (B) (C) (D) (E)	15 (A) (B) (C) (D) (E)	20 (A) (B) (C) (D) (E)	25 (A) (B) (C) (D) (E)

Section 5 [Sentence Correction]

1 (A) (B) (C) (D) (E)	6 (A) (B) (C) (D) (E)	11 (A) (B) (C) (D) (E)	16 (A) (B) (C) (D) (E)	21 (A) (B) (C) (D) (E)
2 (A) (B) (C) (D) (E)	7 (A) (B) (C) (D) (E)	12 (A) (B) (C) (D) (E)	17 (A) (B) (C) (D) (E)	22 (A) (B) (C) (D) (E)
3 (A) (B) (C) (D) (E)	8 (A) (B) (C) (D) (E)	13 (A) (B) (C) (D) (E)	18 (A) (B) (C) (D) (E)	23 (A) (B) (C) (D) (E)
4 (A) (B) (C) (D) (E)	9 (A) (B) (C) (D) (E)	14 (A) (B) (C) (D) (E)	19 (A) (B) (C) (D) (E)	24 (A) (B) (C) (D) (E)
5 (A) (B) (C) (D) (E)	10 (A) (B) (C) (D) (E)	15 (A) (B) (C) (D) (E)	20 (A) (B) (C) (D) (E)	25 (A) (B) (C) (D) (E)

Section 6 [Reading Comprehension]

1 (A) (B) (C) (D) (E)	6 (A) (B) (C) (D) (E)	11 (A) (B) (C) (D) (E)	16 (A) (B) (C) (D) (E)	21 (A) (B) (C) (D) (E)
2 (A) (B) (C) (D) (E)	7 (A) (B) (C) (D) (E)	12 (A) (B) (C) (D) (E)	17 (A) (B) (C) (D) (E)	22 (A) (B) (C) (D) (E)
3 (A) (B) (C) (D) (E)	8 (A) (B) (C) (D) (E)	13 (A) (B) (C) (D) (E)	18 (A) (B) (C) (D) (E)	23 (A) (B) (C) (D) (E)
4 (A) (B) (C) (D) (E)	9 (A) (B) (C) (D) (E)	14 (A) (B) (C) (D) (E)	19 (A) (B) (C) (D) (E)	24 (A) (B) (C) (D) (E)
5 (A) (B) (C) (D) (E)	10 (A) (B) (C) (D) (E)	15 (A) (B) (C) (D) (E)	20 (A) (B) (C) (D) (E)	25 (A) (B) (C) (D) (E)

Section 7 [Data Sufficiency]

1 (A) (B) (C) (D) (E)	6 (A) (B) (C) (D) (E)	11 (A) (B) (C) (D) (E)	16 (A) (B) (C) (D) (E)	21 (A) (B) (C) (D) (E)
2 (A) (B) (C) (D) (E)	7 (A) (B) (C) (D) (E)	12 (A) (B) (C) (D) (E)	17 (A) (B) (C) (D) (E)	22 (A) (B) (C) (D) (E)
3 (A) (B) (C) (D) (E)	8 (A) (B) (C) (D) (E)	13 (A) (B) (C) (D) (E)	18 (A) (B) (C) (D) (E)	23 (A) (B) (C) (D) (E)
4 (A) (B) (C) (D) (E)	9 (A) (B) (C) (D) (E)	14 (A) (B) (C) (D) (E)	19 (A) (B) (C) (D) (E)	24 (A) (B) (C) (D) (E)
5 (A) (B) (C) (D) (E)	10 (A) (B) (C) (D) (E)	15 (A) (B) (C) (D) (E)	20 (A) (B) (C) (D) (E)	25 (A) (B) (C) (D) (E)

Cut along dashed line to remove answer sheet

3 DIAGNOSTIC TEST
with Answers and Analysis

Now that you have become familiar with the various types of questions appearing on the GMAT and have had a chance to sample each type, you probably have an idea of what to expect from an actual exam. The next step, then, is to take a sample test to see how you do.

The Diagnostic Test that follows has been designed to resemble the format of the new GMAT. When taking it, try to simulate actual test conditions as closely as possible. For example, time yourself as you work on each section so that you don't go over the allotted time limit for that section. After you have completed the test, check your answers and use the self-scoring chart to evaluate the results. Use these results to determine which review sections you should spend the most time studying before you attempt the 5 sample GMATs at the end of the book. To assist you in your review, all answers to mathematics questions are keyed so that you can easily refer to the section in the Mathematics Review that discusses the material tested by a particular question.

In the following Diagnostic Test, all sections are headed with the name of the test. In the actual GMAT exam, there are no headings that identify the exam, so all of the sample tests in this book follow the actual GMAT structure and do not name the section. After you have finished using this book, you will be so familiar with the structure of each type of test that you will be able to identify it according to the passage or the structure of the first question.

Writing Assessment

Part I: Analysis of an Issue

TIME: 30 minutes

Directions: Write a clear, logical, and well-organized response to the following issue or argument. Your response should be in the form of a short essay, following the conventions of standard written English. Your answer should fit on three pages of lined 8½" × 11" paper. Write legibly. Essays that are illegible or that are written on a topic other than the one outlined in the question will not be scored.

The fear is widespread among environmentalists that free trade increases economic growth and that growth harms the environment. That fear is misplaced. Growth enables governments to tax and to raise resources for a variety of objectives, including the abatement of pollution and the general protection of the environment. Without such revenues, little can be achieved, no matter how pure one's motives may be.

Which do you find more compelling, the fear of free trade or the response to it? Explain the position you take by using appropriate reasons, examples from your experience, reading, and study.

STOP

IF THERE IS STILL TIME REMAINING,
YOU MAY REVIEW THE QUESTIONS IN THIS SECTION ONLY.
YOU MAY NOT TURN TO ANY OTHER SECTION OF THE TEST.

Part II: Analysis of an Argument

TIME: 30 minutes

Directions: Write a clear, logical, and well-organized response to the following issue or argument. Your response should be in the form of a short essay, following the conventions of standard written English. Your answer should fit on three pages of lined 8½" × 11" paper. Write legibly. Essays that are illegible or that are written on a topic other than the one outlined in the question will not be scored.

The installation of electronic, high-speed scanning devices at the entrances and exits of toll roads will obviate the need for toll booths. Automobiles will have scanner sensitive license plates—like the bar codes on consumer packaged products—so that the scanner devices will record the license number of cars entering and exiting the toll road. Car owners will be billed monthly by the highway authorities.

Discuss how logically persuasive you find the above argument. In presenting your point of view, analyze the sort of reasoning used and supporting evidence. In addition, state what further evidence, if any, would make the argument more sound and convincing or would make you better able to evaluate its conclusion.

STOP

IF THERE IS STILL TIME REMAINING,
YOU MAY REVIEW THE QUESTIONS IN THIS SECTION ONLY.
YOU MAY NOT TURN TO ANY OTHER SECTION OF THE TEST.

1 1 1 1 1 1 1 1 1 1 1

Section 1 [Reading Comprehension]

TIME: 30 minutes
25 Questions

Directions: This part contains three reading passages. You are to read each one carefully. When answering the questions, you *will* be able to refer to the passages. The questions are based on what is *stated* or *implied* in each passage.

Passage 1:

Morally and culturally, American society, as reflected in our TV programs, our theatrical fare, our literature and art appears to have hit bottom.

Gen. David Sarnoff felt prompted to issue a statement in defense of the TV industry. He pointed out that there was much good in its programs that was being overlooked while its occasional derelictions were being overly stressed. It struck me that what he was saying about TV applied to other aspects of American culture as well, particularly to the theatrical productions.

Without necessarily resting on his conviction that the good outweighed the bad in American cultural activity, I saw further implications in Gen. Sarnoff's declaration. Audiences needed to be sensitized more and more to the positive qualities of the entertainment and cultural media. In addition, through such increased public sensitivity, producers would be encouraged to provide ever more of the fine, and less of the sordid.

Here is where questions arise. If the exemplary aspects of TV are not being recognized, what is the reason for such a lack of appreciation? Similarly, and further, if the theatre, including in this term the legitimate stage, on and off Broadway as well as the moving pictures, has large measures of goodness, truth and beauty which are unappreciated, how are we to change this situation?

All in all, what should be done to encourage and condone the good, and to discourage and condemn the unsavory in the American cultural pattern?

These are serious and pressing questions—serious for the survival of the American Way of Life, and pressing for immediate and adequate answers. Indeed the simple truth is that the face that America shows the world affects seriously the future of democracy all over the globe.

Since the theatre in its broadest sense is a large aspect of American culture—its expression as well as its creation—I saw the urgent importance of bringing the worthwhile elements in the American Theatre to the fore. Especially was this importance impressed on me when I realized how much Hollywood was involved in exporting American life to the world, and how much Broadway with all its theatres meant to the modern drama.

Then the thought of the Bible came to me in this connection. Was not the Bible the basis of Western civilization as far as morals are concerned? Why not use the Bible as guide and touchstone, as direction and goal in the matter of the cultural achievements of Western society? Thus was born "The Bible on Broadway."

The birth of the idea accomplished, rearing it brought the usual difficulties of raising a child—albeit in this case a "brain" one. There was first the fact that the Bible, although the world's best seller, is not the world's best read book. Second was the current impression that "message-plays" must necessarily be dull and unpopular....

Still, I was drawn to the project of a series of lectures on the Bible and the contemporary theatre. What if the Bible is not well known? Teach it! Plays with a message dull? All plays by reason of their being works of art have been created by their authors' selection and ordering of experience. As such, plays are proponents of ideas—and certainly they are not meant to be uninteresting....

That there are spiritual, even religious ideas, in the contemporary theatre should be no cause for wonderment. It is well known that the drama had its origin in religion. The Greeks, the Romans, as well as the early Hebrews, all had forms of the drama which among the first two developed into our classical plays.

In the Middle Ages, it was the Church in the Western World that produced the morality and mystery plays. With such a long history it is not surprising to find an affinity between the Bible and the Theatre.

GO ON TO THE NEXT PAGE ➤

1. The author is primarily concerned with

   (A) the declining pattern of morality in America
   (B) promoting American theatre
   (C) the role of the Bible in the contemporary theatre
   (D) comparing the theatre with other art forms
   (E) preserving the "American Way of Life"

2. With which of the following statements regarding the theatre would the author most likely agree?

   (A) The theatre does not reflect American culture.
   (B) Critics of American cultural life are biased.
   (C) While the entertainment media can be criticized, they contain much wholesome material.
   (D) The advertising media are largely to blame for criticisms leveled at the theatre.
   (E) The Bible should be used as our primary source of entertainment ideas.

3. Which of the following statements best reflects the author's own ideas?

   (A) American art forms have degenerated to a new low.
   (B) The good outweighs the bad in American cultural activity.
   (C) American culture has positive content, but it is not appreciated by the public.
   (D) Only the Biblical content of American theatre has positive meaning.
   (E) American theatre is currently dull and unpopular.

4. The author implies that he will deal with which of the following questions?

   I. What is the reason for the lack of appreciation of the theatre?
   II. To what extent have Bible themes been used in or influenced American theatrical productions?
   III. What should be done to encourage the good in American culture?

   (A) I only
   (B) II only
   (C) I and II only
   (D) I and III only
   (E) I, II, and III

5. It can be inferred from the passage that the author's background might be in any of the following occupations *except*

   (A) theatrical producer
   (B) thespian
   (C) humorist
   (D) writer
   (E) critic

GO ON TO THE NEXT PAGE ➤

6. The author implies that, if the public is made aware of the positive qualities of American entertainment, it will

   I. demand more high-quality entertainment
   II. demand less low-quality entertainment
   III. attend the theater more often

   (A) I only
   (B) II only
   (C) I and II only
   (D) I and III only
   (E) I, II, and III

7. When the author uses the expression ''the Bible as guide and touchstone" in line 50, he probably means to refer to

   (A) the interrelationship of the Bible and the "American Way of Life"
   (B) an academic approach to researching the theatre and religion
   (C) the relationship of Biblical concepts to basic ideas and values contained in theatrical productions
   (D) the use of the Bible as a guide to everyday life
   (E) the Bible as a source of inspiration for all

8. According to the author, which of the following media have low cultural and moral values?

   I. Movies
   II. TV
   III. Literature

   (A) I only
   (B) II only
   (C) I and II only
   (D) II and III only
   (E) I, II, and III

9. The author believes that high American moral and cultural values are important because they determine

   (A) what is produced in Hollywood
   (B) the future of world democracy
   (C) whether the Bible will be studied
   (D) the basis for Western civilization
   (E) educational trends in the school system

GO ON TO THE NEXT PAGE ➤

Passage 2:

It is easy to accept Freud as an applied scientist, and, indeed he is widely regarded as the twentieth century's master clinician. However, in viewing Marx as an applied social scientist the stance needed is that of a Machiavellian operationalism. The objective is neither to bury nor to praise him. The assumption is simply that he is better understood for being understood as an applied sociologist. This is in part the clear implication of Marx's *Theses on Feurbach*, which culminate in the resounding 11th thesis: "The philosophers have only interpreted the world in different ways; the point, however, is to change it." This would seem to be the tacit creed of applied scientists everywhere.

Marx was no Faustian, concerned solely with understanding society, but a Promethean who sought to understand it well enough to influence and to change it. He was centrally concerned with the social problems of a lay group, the proletariat, and there can be little doubt that his work is motivated by an effort to reduce their suffering, as he saw it. His diagnosis was that their increasing misery and alienation engendered endemic class struggle; his prognosis claimed that this would culminate in revolution; his therapeutic prescription was class consciousness and active struggle.

Here, as in assessing Durkheim or Freud, the issue is not whether this analysis is empirically correct or scientifically adequate. Furthermore, whether or not this formulation seems to eviscerate Marx's revolutionary core, as critics on the left may charge, or whether the formulation provides Marx with a new veneer of academic respectability, as critics on the right may allege, is entirely irrelevant from the present standpoint. Insofar as Marx's or any other social scientist's work conforms to a generalized model of applied social science, insofar as it is professionally oriented to the values and social problems of laymen in his society, he may be treated as an applied social scientist.

Despite Durkheim's intellectualistic proclivities and rationalistic pathos, he was too much the product of European turbulence to turn his back on the travail of his culture. "Why strive for knowledge of reality, if this knowledge cannot aid us in life," he asked. "Social science," he said, "can provide us with rules of action for the future." Durkheim, like Marx, conceived of science as an agency of social action, and like him was professionally oriented to the values and problems of laymen in his society. Unless one sees that Durkheim was in some part an applied social scientist, it is impossible to understand why he concludes his monumental study of *Suicide* with a chapter on "Practical Consequences," and why, in the *Division of Labor*, he proposes a specific remedy for anomie.

Durkheim is today widely regarded as a model of theoretic and methodologic sophistication, and is thus usually seen only in his capacity as a pure social scientist. Surely this is an incomplete view of the man who regarded the *practical* effectiveness of a science as its principal justification. To be more fully understood, Durkheim also needs to be seen as an applied sociologist. His interest in religious beliefs and organization, in crime and penology, in educational methods and organization, in suicide and anomie, are not casually chosen problem areas. Nor did he select them only because they provided occasions for the development of his theoretical orientation. These areas were in his time, as they are today, problems of indigenous interest to applied sociologists in Western society, precisely because of their practical significance.

10. Which of the following best describes the author's conception of an applied social scientist?

    (A) A professional who listens to people's problems
    (B) A professional who seeks social action and change
    (C) A student of society
    (D) A proponent of class struggle
    (E) A philosopher who interprets the world in a unique way

11. According to the author, which of the following did Marx and Durkheim have in common?

    (A) A belief in the importance of class struggle
    (B) A desire to create a system of social organization
    (C) An interest in penology
    (D) Regard for the practical applications of science
    (E) A sense of the political organization of society

GO ON TO THE NEXT PAGE ➤

12. It may be inferred from the passage that the applied social scientist might be interested in all of the following subjects *except*

    (A) the theory of mechanics
    (B) how to make workers more efficient
    (C) rehabilitation of juvenile delinquents
    (D) reduction of social tensions
    (E) industrial safety

13. According to the passage, applied social science can be distinguished from pure social science by its

    (A) practical significance
    (B) universal application
    (C) cultural pluralism
    (D) objectivity
    (E) emphasis on the problems of the poor

14. Which of the following best summarizes the author's main point?

    (A) Marx and Durkheim were similar in their ideas.
    (B) Freud, Marx, and Durkheim were all social scientists.
    (C) Philosophers, among others, who are regarded as theoreticians can also be regarded as empiricists.
    (D) Marx and Durkheim were applied social scientists because they were concerned with the solution of social problems.
    (E) Pure and applied sciences have fundamentally similar objects.

15. All of the following are mentioned as topics of interest to Durkheim *except*

    (A) suicide
    (B) psychiatry
    (C) crime
    (D) education
    (E) religion

16. What action did Marx prescribe for the proletariat?

    I. Class consciousness
    II. Passive resistance
    III. Alienation

    (A) I only
    (B) II only
    (C) I and II only
    (D) II and III only
    (E) I, II, and III

17. Marx sought to

    I. understand society
    II. change the educational system
    III. apply science to philosophy

    (A) I only
    (B) II only
    (C) I and II only
    (D) II and III only
    (E) I, II, and III

GO ON TO THE NEXT PAGE ➤

Passage 3:

In Aachen, Germany, and environs, many children have been found to have an unusually high lead content in their blood and hair. The amount of lead in the children tested has risen above the amount found in workers in heavy-metal industries. The general public is no longer surprised that the lead has been traced to Stolberg near Aachen: Stolberg is surrounded by brass foundries and slag heaps which supply building materials to construct schoolyards and sports halls.

This is but one example....

When Dr. John W. Gofman, professor of medical physics at the University of California and a leading nuclear critic, speaks of "ecocide" in his adversary view of nuclear technology, he means the following: A large nuclear plant like that in Kalkar, the Netherlands, would produce about 200 pounds of plutonium each year. One pound, released into the atmosphere, could cause 9 billion cases of lung cancer. This waste product must be stored for 500,000 years before it is of no further danger to man. In the anticipated reactor economy, it is estimated that there will be 10,000 tons of this material in western Europe, of which one tablespoonful of plutonium-239 represents the official maximum permissible body burden for 200,000 people. Rather than being biodegradable, plutonium destroys biological properties.

In 1972 the U.S. Occupational Safety and Health Administration ruled that the asbestos level in the work place should be lowered to 2 fibers per cubic centimeter of air, but the effective date of the ruling has been delayed until now. The International Federation of Chemical and General Workers' Unions report that the 2-fiber standard was based primarily on one study of 290 men at a British asbestos factory. But when the workers at the British factory had been reexamined by another physician, 40–70 percent had x-ray evidence of lung abnormalities. According to present medical information at the factory in question, out of a total of 29 deaths thus far, seven were caused by lung cancer and three by mesothelioma, a cancer of the lining of the chest-abdomen. An average European or American worker comes into contact with six million fibers a day. And when this man returns home at night, samples of this fireproof product are on his clothes, in his hair, in his lunchpail. "We are now, in fact, finding cancer deaths within the family of the asbestos worker," states Dr. Irving Selikoff, of the Mount Sinai Medical School in New York.

It is now also clear that vinyl chloride, a gas from which the most widely used plastics are made, causes a fatal cancer of the blood-vessel cells of the liver. However, the history of the research on vinyl chloride is, in some ways, more disturbing than the "Watergate cover-up" "There has been evidence of potentially serious disease among polyvinyl chloride workers for 25 years that has been incompletely appreciated and inadequately approached by medical scientists and by regulatory authorities," summed up Dr. Selikoff in the *New Scientist.* At least 17 workers have been killed by vinyl chloride because research over the past 25 years was not followed up. And for over 10 years, workers have been exposed to concentrations of vinyl chloride 10 times the "safe limit" imposed by Dow Chemical Company. In the United Kingdom, a threshold limit value was set after the discovery of the causal link with osteolysis, but the limit was still higher than that set by Dow Chemical. The Germans set a new maximum level in 1970, but also higher than that set by Dow. No other section of U.S. or European industry has followed Dow's lead.

18. Which of the following titles best describes the contents of the passage?

    (A) *The Problems of Nuclear Physics*
    (B) *Advanced Technology and Cancer*
    (C) *Occupational Diseases*
    (D) *Cancer in Germany*
    (E) *The Ecology of Cancer*

19. The author provides information that would answer which of the following questions?

    (A) What sort of legislation is needed to prevent cancer?
    (B) Should nuclear plants be built?
    (C) What are some causes of lung cancer?
    (D) What are the pros and cons of nuclear energy?
    (E) Which country has the lowest incidence of occupational disease?

GO ON TO THE NEXT PAGE ➤

1 1 1 1 1 1 1 1 1 1 1

20. According to the author, all the following are causes of cancer *except*
    (A) plutonium
    (B) asbestos
    (C) vinyl chloride
    (D) osteolysis
    (E) lead

21. The style of the passage is mainly
    (A) argumentative
    (B) emotional
    (C) factual
    (D) clinical
    (E) vitriolic

22. It can be inferred from the passage that the author believes that
    (A) industrialization must be halted to prevent further spread of cancer-producing agents
    (B) only voluntary, industry-wide application of antipollution devices can halt cancer
    (C) workers are partly to blame for the spread of disease because of poor work habits
    (D) more research is needed into the causes of cancer before further progress can be made
    (E) tougher legislation is needed to set lower limits of worker exposure to harmful chemicals and fibers

23. Some workers have been killed by harmful pollutants because
    (A) they failed to take the required precautions and safety measures
    (B) not enough research has been undertaken to find solutions to the pollution problem
    (C) available research was not followed up
    (D) production cannot be halted
    (E) factory owners have failed to provide safety equipment

24. It is mentioned in the passage that the asbestos level
    (A) should be lowered
    (B) causes heart problems
    (C) is linked with osteolysis
    (D) is similar to the level of vinyl chloride
    (E) is not linked with any known disease

25. The passage is based on evidence of pollutants in the following countries *except*
    (A) United Kingdom
    (B) United States
    (C) Sweden
    (D) Germany
    (E) Netherlands

STOP

IF THERE IS STILL TIME REMAINING,
YOU MAY REVIEW THE QUESTIONS IN THIS SECTION ONLY.
YOU MAY NOT TURN TO ANY OTHER SECTION OF THE TEST.

2 2 2 2 2 2 2 2 2 2 2

Section 2 [Problem Solving]

TIME: 25 minutes
17 Questions

Directions: Solve each of the following problems; then indicate the correct answer on the answer sheet.

NOTE: A figure that appears with a problem is drawn as accurately as possible so as to provide information that may help in answering the question. Numbers in this test are real numbers.

1. If the length of a rectangle is increased by 20% and the width is decreased by 20%, then the area

 (A) decreases by 20%
 (B) decreases by 4%
 (C) stays the same
 (D) increases by 10%
 (E) increases by 20%

2. If it is 250 miles from New York to Boston and 120 miles from New York to Hartford, what percentage of the distance from New York to Boston is the distance from New York to Hartford?

 (A) 12
 (B) 24
 (C) 36
 (D) 48
 (E) 52

3. The lead in a mechanical pencil is 5 inches long. After pieces $\frac{1}{8}$ of an inch long, $1\frac{3}{4}$ inches long, and $1\frac{1}{12}$ inches long are broken off, how long is the lead left in the pencil?

 (A) 2 in.
 (B) $2\frac{1}{24}$ in.
 (C) $2\frac{1}{12}$ in.
 (D) $2\frac{1}{4}$ in.
 (E) $2\frac{1}{2}$ in.

GO ON TO THE NEXT PAGE ➤

2 2 2 2 2 2 2 2 2 2 2

4. It costs x dollars each to make the first thousand copies of a compact disk and y dollars to make each subsequent copy. If z is greater than 1,000, how many dollars will it cost to make z copies of the compact disk?

(A) $1{,}000x + yz$
(B) $zx - zy$
(C) $1{,}000\,(z - x) + xy$
(D) $1{,}000\,(z - y) + xz$
(E) $1{,}000\,(x - y) + yz$

5. How many two-digit numbers satisfy the following property: the last digit (units digit) of the square of the two-digit number is 8?

(A) none
(B) 1
(C) 2
(D) 3
(E) more than 3

6. If $x + y = 3$ and $\frac{y}{x} = 2$, then y is equal to

(A) 0
(B) $\frac{1}{2}$
✓(C) 1
(D) $\frac{3}{2}$
(E) 2

7. Ms. Taylor purchased stock for $1,500 and sold $\frac{2}{3}$ of it after its value doubled. She sold the remaining stock at 5 times its purchase price. What was her total profit on the stock?

(A) $1,500
(B) $2,000
(C) $2,500
(D) $3,000
(E) $6,000

8. City B is 8 miles east of City A. City C is 6 miles north of City B. City D is 16 miles east of City C, and City E is 12 miles north of City D. What is the distance from City A to City E?

(A) 10 miles
(B) 20 miles
(C) 24 miles
✓(D) 30 miles
(E) 42 miles

9. A car goes 15 miles on a gallon of gas when it is driven at 50 miles per hour. When the car is driven at 60 miles per hour it only goes 80% as far. How many gallons of gas will it take to travel 120 miles driving at 60 miles per hour?

(A) 2
(B) 6.4
(C) 8
(D) 9.6
(E) 10

GO ON TO THE NEXT PAGE ➤

2 2 2 2 2 2 2 2 2 2 2

10. If $x + y = z$ and x and y are positive, then which of the following statements can be inferred?

    I. $x < y$
    II. $x < z$
    III. $x < 2z$

    (A) I only
    (B) II only
    (C) I and II only
    (D) II and III only
    (E) I, II, and III

11. Mr. Smith drove at an average speed of 50 mph for the first two hours of his trip. For the next three hours, he averaged 20 mph. What was Mr. Smith's average speed for the five-hour trip?

    (A) 30 mph
    (B) 32 mph
    (C) 35 mph
    (D) 38 mph
    (E) 160 mph

12. If in 1967, 1968, and 1969 a worker received 10% more in salary each year than he did the previous year, how much more did he receive in 1969 than in 1967?

    (A) 10%
    (B) 11%
    (C) 20%
    (D) 21%
    (E) 30%

13. If x is a number satisfying $2 < x < 3$ and y is a number satisfying $7 < y < 8$, which of the following expressions will have the largest value?

    (A) x^2y
    (B) xy^2
    (C) $5xy$
    (D) $\frac{4x^2y}{3}$
    (E) $\frac{x^2}{y}$

14. If 50 apprentices can finish a job in 4 hours and 30 journeymen can finish the same job in $4\frac{1}{2}$ hours, how much of the job should be completed by 10 apprentices and 15 journeymen in one hour?

    (A) $\frac{1}{9}$
    (B) $\frac{29}{180}$
    (C) $\frac{26}{143}$
    (D) $\frac{1}{5}$
    (E) $\frac{39}{121}$

GO ON TO THE NEXT PAGE ➤

2 2 2 2 2 2 2 2 2 2 2

15. If the shaded area is one half the area of triangle ABC and angle ABC is a right angle, then the length of line segment AD is

(A) $\frac{1}{2}w$

(B) $\frac{1}{2}(w+x)$

(C) $\sqrt{2x^2+z^2}$

(D) $\sqrt{w^2-3y^2}$

(E) $\sqrt{y^2+z^2}$

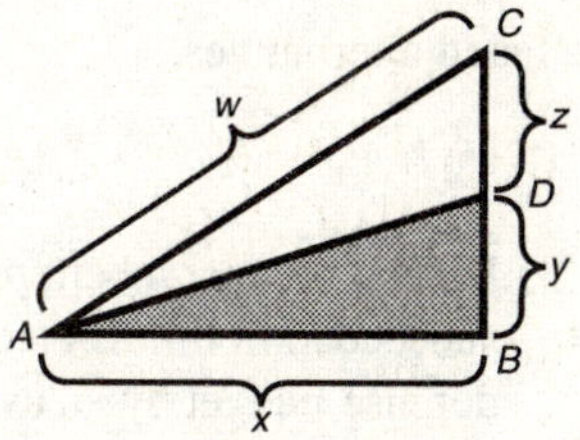

16. There are 4 quarts in a gallon. A gallon of motor oil sells for $12 and a quart of the same oil sells for $5. The owner of a rental agency has 6 machines and each machine needs 5 quarts of oil. What is the minimum amount of money she must spend to purchase enough oil?

(A) $84
✓ (B) $94
(C) $96
(D) $102
(E) $150

17. A store has a parking lot that contains 70 parking spaces. Each row in the parking lot contains the same number of parking spaces. The store has bought additional property in order to build an addition to the store. When the addition is built, 2 parking spaces will be lost from each row; however, 4 more rows will be added to the parking lot. After the addition is built, the parking lot will still have 70 parking spaces, and each row will contain the same number of parking spaces as every other row. How many rows were in the parking lot before the addition was built?

(A) 5
(B) 6
(C) 7
(D) 10
(E) 14

STOP

**IF THERE IS STILL TIME REMAINING,
YOU MAY REVIEW THE QUESTIONS IN THIS SECTION ONLY.
YOU MAY NOT TURN TO ANY OTHER SECTION OF THE TEST.**

Section 3 [Critical Reasoning]

TIME: 25 minutes
17 Questions

Directions: For each question, choose the best answer among the listed alternatives.

1. In winning its bitter, protracted battle to acquire Blue Industries, Inc., Belle Industries has fulfilled its goal to lessen its reliance on tobacco holdings, while the $5.2 billion deal may spur more takeover activity in the insurance industry, analysts said.

   Which of the following can be inferred from the passage?

   (A) Blue Industries is in the tobacco industry.
   (B) Belle Industries is in the insurance business.
   (C) Blue Industries is in the insurance business.
   (D) More divestment takes place in the tobacco industry than in the insurance industry.
   (E) More divestment takes place in the insurance industry than in the tobacco industry.

2. Typically, the entrepreneur is seen as an individual who owns and operates a small business. But, simply to own and operate a small business—or even a big business—does not make someone an entrepreneur. If this person is a true entrepreneur, then new products are being created, new ways of providing services are being implemented.

   Which of the following conclusions can best be drawn from the above passage?

   (A) An owner of a large business may be an entrepreneur.
   (B) Someone who develops an enterprise may be considered an entrepreneur.
   (C) Entrepreneurs do not own and operate small businesses.
   (D) Entrepreneurs are the main actors in economic growth.
   (E) Entrepreneurs are inventors.

3. During the incumbent president's term of office he succeeded in limiting annual increases in the defense budget by an average of 5 percent. His predecessor experienced annual increases of 8 percent. Therefore, the incumbent president should be given credit for the downturn in defense outlays.

   Which of the following statements, if true, would most seriously weaken the above conclusion?

   (A) Some generals have claimed that the country's defenses have weakened in the past year.
   (B) More soldiers were drafted during the former president's term of office.
   (C) The incumbent president advocates peaceful resolution of international disputes.
   (D) The average annual inflation rate during the incumbent president's term was 4 percent, while during his predecessor's term it was 10 percent.
   (E) A disarmament treaty with a major adversary was signed by the incumbent president.

4. Ira is taller than Sam.
   Elliot is taller than Harold.
   Harold is shorter than Gene.
   Sam and Gene are the same height.

   If the above is true, which of the following conditions must also be true?

   (A) Elliot is taller than Gene.
   (B) Elliot is taller than Ira.
   (C) Sam is shorter than Elliot.
   (D) Ira is taller than Harold.
   (E) Sam is shorter than Harold

GO ON TO THE NEXT PAGE ➤

5. Buy Plenty, a supermarket chain, had successfully implemented an in-store promotional campaign based on video messages flashed on a large screen. The purpose of the campaign was to motivate customers to purchase products which they had not planned to buy before they entered the store. The sales manager of Build-It Inc., a chain of do-it-yourself hardware stores, saw the campaign and plans to introduce it in Build-It locations.

   The sales manager's plan assumes that

   (A) supermarket and hardware products are the same.
   (B) products cannot be sold successfully without a video sales campaign.
   (C) supermarket chains do not sell hardware products.
   (D) consumer decision making to buy products does not differ substantially when it comes to both supermarket and hardware products.
   (E) in-store campaigns are more effective than out-of-store advertising and sales promotion.

6. The movement to ownership by unions is the latest step in the progression from management ownership to employee ownership. Employee ownership can save depressed and losing companies.

   All the following statements, if true, provide support for the claim above *except:*

   (A) Employee-owned companies generally have higher productivity.
   (B) Employee participation in management raises morale.
   (C) Employee union ownership drives up salaries and wages.
   (D) Employee union ownership enables workers to share in the profits.
   (E) Employee union ownership makes it easier to layoff redundant workers.

7. The burning of coal, oil and other combustible energy sources produces carbon dioxide, a natural constituent of the atmosphere. Elevated levels of carbon dioxide are thought to be responsible for half the greenhouse effect. Enough carbon dioxide has been sent into the atmosphere already to cause a significant temperature increase. Growth in industrial production must be slowed, or production processes must be changed.

   Which of the following, if true, would tend to weaken the strength of the above conclusion?

   (A) Many areas of the world are cold anyway, so a small rise in temperature would be welcome.
   (B) Carbon dioxide is bad for the health.
   (C) Most carbon dioxide is emitted by automobiles.
   (D) Industry is switching over to synthetic liquid fuel extracted from coal.
   (E) A shift to other energy sources would be too costly.

Questions 8 and 9 are based on the following passage.

Contrary to charges made by opponents of the new trade bill, the bill's provisions for taking action against foreign countries that place barriers against American exports, is justified. Opponents should take note that restrictive trade legislation in the 1930s succeeded in improving the U.S. trade balance even though economists were against it.

8. The author's method of rebutting opponents of the new trade bill is to

   (A) attack the patriotism of its opponents.
   (B) attack the opponents' characters rather than their claims.
   (C) imply an analogy between the new trade bill and previous trade legislation.
   (D) suggest that economists were against both pieces of legislation.
   (E) imply that previous legislation also permitted retaliatory action against foreign countries.

GO ON TO THE NEXT PAGE ➤

9. Opponents of the new legislation could defend themselves against the author's strategy by arguing that:

   (A) the fact that past trade legislation improved the trade balance does not mean that the present bill will do the same.
   (B) economists are not always right.
   (C) the United States had a trade deficit both in the 1930s and at the time of the new bill.
   (D) the new law is not as strong as the 1930s bill.
   (E) America's trading partners have also passed similar legislation.

10. During 1985, advertising expenditures on canned food products increased by 20 percent, while canned food consumption rose by 25 percent.

    Each of the following, if true, could help explain the increase in food consumption *except:*

    (A) Advertising effectiveness increased.
    (B) Canned food prices decreased relative to substitutes.
    (C) Canned food products were available in more stores.
    (D) Can opener production doubled.
    (E) Per-capita consumption of frozen foods declined.

11. Inflation rose by 5.1% over the 2nd quarter, up from 4.1% during the first quarter of the year, and higher than the 3.3 % recorded during the same time last year. However, the higher price index did not seem to alarm Wall Street, as stock prices remained steady.

    Which of the following, if true, could explain the reaction of Wall Street?

    (A) Stock prices were steady because of a fear that inflation would continue.
    (B) The President announced that he was concerned about rising inflation.
    (C) Economists warned that inflation would persist.
    (D) Much of the quarterly increase in the price level was due to a summer drought's effect on food prices.
    (E) Other unfavorable economic news had overshadowed the fact of inflation.

12. "Ever since I arrived at the college last week, I've been shocked by the poor behavior of students, the unfriendly attitude of the townspeople, but the professors are very erudite and genuinely helpful. Still, I wonder if I should have come here in the first place."

    Which of the following, if true, would weaken the above conclusion?

    (A) Professors are not always helpful to students.
    (B) The college numbers over 50,000 students.
    (C) The college is far from the student's home.
    (D) Not all professors have doctorates.
    (E) The narrator was unsure of staying at the college.

13. A local garbage disposal company increased its profitability even though it reduced its prices in order to attract new customers. This was made possible through the use of automated trucks, thereby reducing the number of workers needed per truck. The company also switched from a concentration on household hauling to a concentration on commercial hauling. As a result of its experience, company management planned to replace all their old trucks and increase the overall size of the truck fleet, doubling hauling capacity.

    The company's plan, as outlined above, takes into consideration each of the following *except:*

    (A) Commercial clients have more potential than household customers.
    (B) The demand for garbage removal services is sensitive to price.
    (C) Demand for garbage removal services would increase in the future.
    (D) Doubling of capacity would not necessitate a substantial increase in workforce.
    (E) Doubling of capacity would not cause bottlenecks, leading to a decrease in productivity.

GO ON TO THE THE NEXT PAGE ➤

3 3 3 3 3 3 3 3 3 3 3

14. Every town with a pool hall has its share of unsavory characters. This is because the pool hall attracts gamblers and all gamblers are unsavory.

    Which of the following, if true, cannot be inferred from the above?

    (A) All gamblers are unsavory.
    (B) All pool halls attract gamblers.
    (C) Every town has unsavory characters.
    (D) All gamblers are attracted by pool halls.
    (E) An explanation of what attracts gamblers.

15. In August 1980, according to a *New York Times*/CBS news poll, 36 percent of the voters called themselves Republican or said they were independents leaning towards being Republicans. In November 1984, the Republican figure rose to 47 percent. But in the latest *Times*/CBS survey, the Republicans were down to 38 percent. Therefore, the Democrats are likely to win the next election.

    Which of the following, if true, would most seriously weaken the above conclusion?

    (A) Republicans were a minority in 1984, but a Republican president was elected.
    (B) People tend to switch their votes at the last minute.
    (C) People vote for the best candidate, not for a political party.
    (D) No one can predict how people will vote.
    (E) It has been shown that 85 percent of Republicans vote in an election, compared to 50 percent of the Democrats.

16. Thirty years after African colonies began emerging as nations, modern loyalties still often go first to the tribe. From Angola to Ethiopia, ethnic hatred has forced hundreds of thousands of people to flee their homes, making Africa the continent with the world's largest number of refugees.

    Which of the following statements best summarizes the above?

    (A) Africa is best characterized by ethnic fractionalization.
    (B) Angola and Ethiopia have the worst record of interethnic strife in Africa.
    (C) Continued warfare has made Africa a nation of refugees.
    (D) Africa is best characterized as a federation of many states.
    (E) Africa is best characterized as a continent without loyalties.

17. Average family income is right where it was 20 years ago, even though in most families these days, husbands and wives are working.

    The above statement implies all of the following, *except:*

    (A) Even though nominal family income may have increased, inflation has risen at an equal rate.
    (B) More husbands and wives are working today than 20 years ago.
    (C) It was more prevalent for one spouse to work 20 years ago than today.
    (D) Wives earn more than husbands today.
    (E) The price level was lower 20 years ago.

STOP

IF THERE IS STILL TIME REMAINING,
YOU MAY REVIEW THE QUESTIONS IN THIS SECTION ONLY.
YOU MAY NOT TURN TO ANY OTHER SECTION OF THE TEST.

4 4 4 4 4 4 4 4 4 4 4

Section 4 [Problem Solving]

TIME: 25 minutes
17 Questions

Directions: Solve each of the following problems; then indicate the correct answer on your answer sheet.

NOTE: A figure that appears with a problem is drawn as accurately as possible unless the words "Figure not drawn to scale" appear next to the figure. Numbers in this test are real numbers.

1. .03 times .05 is

(A) 15%
(B) 1.5%
(C) .15%
(D) .015%
(E) .0015%

2. Which of the following are possible values for the angles of a parallelogram?

I. 90°, 90°, 90°, 90°
II. 40°, 70°, 50°, 140°
III. 50°, 130°, 50°, 130°

(A) I only
(B) II only
(C) I and III only
(D) II and III only
(E) I, II, and III

3. For every novel in the school library there are two science books; for each science book there are seven economics books. Express the ratio of economics books to science books to novels in the school library as a triple ratio.

(A) 7 : 2 : 1
(B) 7 : 1 : 2
(C) 14 : 7 : 2
(D) 14 : 2 : 1
(E) 14 : 2 : 7

4. There are 50 employees in the office of ABC company. Of these, 22 have taken an accounting course, 15 have taken a course in finance, and 14 have taken a marketing course. Nine of the employees have taken exactly two of the courses, and one employee has taken all three of the courses. How many of the 50 employees have taken none of the courses?

(A) 0
(B) 9
(C) 10
(D) 11
(E) 26

GO ON TO THE NEXT PAGE ➤

4 4 4 4 4 4 4 4 4 4 4

5. If $x + y = 4$ and $x - y = 3$, then $x + 2y$ is

   (A) $\frac{1}{2}$

   (B) $3\frac{1}{2}$

   (C) 4

   (D) $4\frac{1}{2}$

   (E) $7\frac{1}{2}$

6. How much interest will $2,000 earn at an annual rate of 8% in one year if the interest is compounded every 6 months?

   (A) $160.00
   (B) $163.20
   (C) $249.73
   (D) $332.80
   (E) $2,163.20

7. If BC is parallel to AD and CE is perpendicular to AD, then the area of $ABCD$ is

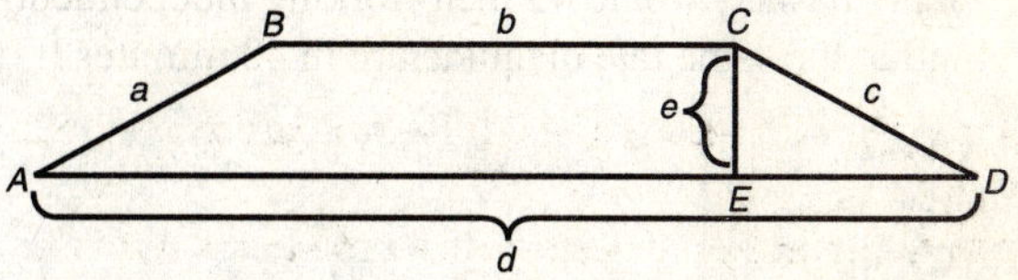

   (A) bd
   (B) $bd + ac$
   (C) ed
   (D) $e(b + d)$
   (E) $.5eb + .5ed$

8. A company makes a profit of 6% on its first $1,000 of sales each day, and 5% on all sales in excess of $1,000 for that day. How many dollars in profit will the company make in a day when sales are $6,000?

   (A) $250
   (B) $300
   (C) $310
   (D) $320
   (E) $360

GO ON TO THE NEXT PAGE ➤

9. If 15 men working independently and at the same rate can manufacture 27 baskets in an hour, how many baskets would 45 men working independently and at the same rate manufacture in 40 minutes?

(A) 27
(B) 35
(C) 40
(D) 54
(E) 81

10. A conveyer belt moves grain at the rate of 2 tons in 5 minutes and a second conveyer belt moves grain at the rate of 3 tons in 7 minutes. How many minutes will it take to move 20 tons of grain using both conveyer belts?

(A) 12
(B) $16\frac{4}{7}$
(C) $18\frac{3}{26}$
(D) 21
(E) $24\frac{4}{29}$

11. A field is rectangular and its width is $\frac{1}{3}$ as long as its length. What is the area of the field if the length of the field is 120 yards?

(A) 480 square yards
(B) 2,400 square yards
(C) 4,800 square yards
(D) 5,000 square yards
(E) 7,200 square yards

12. If the price of steak is currently \$1.00 a pound, and the price triples every 6 months, how long will it be until the price of steak is \$81.00 a pound?

(A) 1 year
(B) 2 years
(C) $2\frac{1}{2}$ years
(D) 13 years
(E) $13\frac{1}{2}$ years

GO ON TO THE NEXT PAGE ➤

4 4 4 4 4 4 4 4 4 4 4

13. If $\frac{x}{y} = \frac{2}{3}$, then $\frac{y^2}{x^2}$ is

(A) $\frac{4}{9}$

(B) $\frac{2}{3}$

(C) $\frac{3}{2}$

(D) $\frac{9}{4}$

(E) $\frac{5}{2}$

14. The entry following a_n in a sequence is determined by the rule $(a_n - 1)^2$. If 1 is an entry in the sequence, the next three entries are

(A) 0, –1, 2
(B) 0, –1, 1
(C) 0, 1, 2
(D) 2, 3, 4
(E) 0, 1, 0

15. An employer pays 3 workers *X*, *Y*, and *Z* a total of $610 a week. *X* is paid 125% of the amount *Y* is paid and 80% of the amount *Z* is paid. How much does *X* make a week?

(A) $150
(B) $175
(C) $180
(D) $195
(E) $200

16. What is the maximum number of points of intersection of two circles which have unequal radii?

(A) none
(B) 1
(C) 2
(D) 3
(E) infinite

17. If the area of a rectangle is equal to the area of a square, then the perimeter of the rectangle must be

(A) $\frac{1}{2}$ the perimeter of the square
(B) equal to the perimeter of the square
(C) equal to twice the perimeter of the square
(D) equal to the square root of the perimeter of the square
(E) none of the above

STOP

**IF THERE IS STILL TIME REMAINING,
YOU MAY REVIEW THE QUESTIONS IN THIS SECTION ONLY.
YOU MAY NOT TURN TO ANY OTHER SECTION OF THE TEST.**

5 5 5 5 5 5 5 5 5 5 5

Section 5 [Sentence Correction]

TIME: 25 minutes
21 Questions

Directions: This test consists of a number of sentences, in each of which some part or the whole is underlined. Each sentence is followed by five alternative versions of the underlined portion. Select the alternative you consider both most correct and most effective according to the requirements of standard written English. Answer A is the same as the original version; if you think the original version is best, select answer A.

In considering the answer choices, be attentive to matters of grammar, diction, and syntax, as well as clarity, precision, and fluency. Do not select an answer which alters the meaning of the original sentence.

1. The principal reason for our failure was quite apparent to those whom we had brought into the venture.
   (A) to those whom we had brought
   (B) to them whom we had brought
   (C) to the ones whom we had brought
   (D) to those who we had brought
   (E) to those who we had brung

2. Although he was the most friendly of all present and different from the others, he hadn't hardly any friends except me.
   (A) different from the others, he hadn't hardly any friends except me
   (B) different than the others, he had hardly any friends except me
   (C) different from the others, he had hardly any friends except me
   (D) different than the others, he hadn't hardly any friends except I
   (E) different from the others, he hardly had any friends except I

3. It was us who had left before he arrived.
   (A) us who had left before he arrived
   (B) we who had left before he arrived
   (C) we who had went before he arrived
   (D) us who had went before he arrived
   (E) we who had left before the time he had arrived

4. He is the sort of person who I feel would be capable of making these kind of statements.
   (A) sort of person who I feel would be capable of making these kind of
   (B) sort of a person who I feel would be capable of making these kind of
   (C) sort of person who I feel would be capable of making these kinds of
   (D) sort of person whom I feel would be capable of making these kinds of
   (E) sort of person whom I feel would be capable of making this kind of

5. Due to the continual rain, a smaller number of spectators witnessed the game than had been expected.
   (A) Due to the continual rain, a smaller number
   (B) Due to the continuous rain, a smaller number
   (C) Due to the continual rain, a lesser number
   (D) Because of the rain that kept falling now and then, a smaller number
   (E) Because of the continual rain, a smaller number

6. Beside me, there were many persons who were altogether aggravated by his manners.
   (A) Beside me, there were many persons who were altogether aggravated
   (B) Beside me, there were many persons who were all together aggravated
   (C) Besides me, there were many persons who were altogether aggravated
   (D) Besides me, there were many persons who were altogether irritated
   (E) Beside me, there were many persons who were all together irritated

GO ON TO THE NEXT PAGE ➤

5 5 5 5 5 5 5 5 5 5 5

7. The owner, who was a kind man, spoke to the boy and he was very rude.
   (A) , who was a kind man, spoke to the boy and he
   (B) was a kind man and he spoke to the boy and he
   (C) spoke to the boy kindly and the boy
   (D) , a kind man, spoke to the boy who
   (E) who was a kind man spoke to the boy and he

8. Because we cooperated together, we divided up the work on the report which had been assigned.
   (A) together, we divided up the work on the report which had been assigned
   (B) together, we divided the work on the report which had been assigned
   (C) , we divided up the work on the report which was assigned
   (D) , we divided the work on the assigned report
   (E) we divided up the work on the assigned report

9. The senator rose up to say that, in his opinion, he thought the bill should be referred back to committee.
   (A) rose up to say that, in his opinion, he thought the bill should be referred back
   (B) rose up to say that he thought the bill should be referred back
   (C) rose up to say that he thought the bill should be referred
   (D) rose up to say that, in his opinion, the bill should be referred
   (E) rose to say that he thought the bill should be referred

10. I don't know as I concur with your decision to try and run for office.
   (A) as I concur with your decision to try and
   (B) that I concur in your decision to try to
   (C) as I concur in your decision to try and
   (D) that I concur with your decision to try to
   (E) as I concur with your decision to try, to

11. Jones, the president of the union and who is also a member of the community group, will be in charge of the negotiations.
   (A) and who is also a member of the community group
   (B) since he is a member of the community group
   (C) a member of the community group
   (D) also being a member of the community group
   (E) in addition, who is a member of the community group

12. The instructor told the student to hold the club lightly, keeping his eye on the ball and drawing the club back quickly, but too much force should not be used on the downward stroke.
   (A) to hold the club lightly, keeping his eye on the ball and drawing the club back quickly, but too much force should not be used
   (B) to hold the club lightly, keep his eye on the ball, and drawing the club back quickly, and too much force should not be used
   (C) to hold the club lightly, keep his eye on the ball, draw the club back quickly, and not use too much force
   (D) to hold the club lightly, keep his eye on the ball, draw the club back quickly and too much force should not be used
   (E) he should hold the club lightly, keeping his eye on the ball, drawing the club back quickly, and not using too much force

13. The horse, ridden by the experienced jockey with the broken leg, had to be destroyed.
   (A) horse, ridden by the experienced jockey with the broken leg, had
   (B) horse ridden by the experienced jockey with the broken leg had
   (C) horse with the broken leg ridden by the experienced, jockey had
   (D) horse with the broken leg ridden by the experienced jockey, had
   (E) horse with the broken leg, ridden by the experienced jockey, had

14. Our guest let us know that he would be arriving next week in his last letter.
   (A) that he would be arriving next week in his last letter
   (B) that he was arriving next week in his last letter
   (C) that he will arrive next week in his last letter
   (D) in his last letter that he would be arriving next week
   (E) in his last letter that he was arriving next week

GO ON TO THE NEXT PAGE ➤

5 5 5 5 5 5 5 5 5 5 5

15. Whoever objects to me going to the convention ought to state his position promptly.
    - (A) Whoever objects to me
    - (B) Whomever objects to me
    - (C) Whomever objects to my
    - (D) Whoever objects to my
    - (E) Whoever has an objection to me

16. The reason that the number of accidents this year is greater than that of last year is because Americans are uninterested in safety techniques.
    - (A) is greater than that of last year is because
    - (B) is greater than last year is because
    - (C) is greater than last year is that
    - (D) is greater than that of last year is that
    - (E) is greater than the number of accidents last year is because

17. Julio found the new job more preferable to the one he had left so he decided to continue on for a while.
    - (A) more preferable to the one he had left so he decided to continue on
    - (B) preferable to the one he had left so he decided to continue on
    - (C) more preferable to the one he had left so he decided to continue
    - (D) preferable to the one he had left so he decided to continue
    - (E) more preferable than the one he had left so he decided to continue

18. Since we are living in New York for five years, we are reluctant to move to another city.
    - (A) Since we are living
    - (B) Being that we are living
    - (C) Being that we have been
    - (D) Since we have been living
    - (E) Since we were living

19. As a child, my parents took me to Chicago to visit my grandfather.
    - (A) As a child, my parents took me to Chicago to visit my grandfather.
    - (B) My parents took me to Chicago to visit my grandfather as a child.
    - (C) My parents took me, as a child, to Chicago to visit my grandfather.
    - (D) A child, my parents took me to Chicago to visit my grandfather.
    - (E) When I was a child, my parents took me to Chicago to visit my grandfather.

20. He said that, if he were elected president and that if funds were available, that he would create a national theater.
    - (A) he were elected president and that if funds were available, that
    - (B) elected president, and funds were available, that
    - (C) he were elected president and funds were available, that
    - (D) he were elected president and funds were available,
    - (E) elected president, and funds were available,

21. Having managed the team for years, he understood the players.
    - (A) Having managed the team for years, he understood the players.
    - (B) After managing the team for years, the players were understood by him.
    - (C) Having managed the team for years, the players were understood by him.
    - (D) For years having managed the team, its players were understood by him.
    - (E) Because he had managed the team for years, its players were understood by him.

STOP

IF THERE IS STILL TIME REMAINING,
YOU MAY REVIEW THE QUESTIONS IN THIS SECTION ONLY.
YOU MAY NOT TURN TO ANY OTHER SECTION OF THE TEST.

6 6 6 6 6 6 6 6 6 6 6

Section 6 [Reading Comprehension]

TIME: 30 minutes
25 Questions

Directions: This part contains three reading passages. You are to read each one carefully. When answering the questions, you *will* be able to refer to the passages. The questions are based on what is *stated* or *implied* in each passage.

Passage 1:

Although the number of journals has never been greater and the flyers announcing new conferences, colloquia, and societies never as ambitious, it is no secret that something is wrong with philosophy in the English-speaking world. The advances made by Russell, Whitehead, Wittgenstein, and Husserl are now studied by historians, and the boldness which characterized their age, roughly from 1900 to 1950, has given way to a spirit of caution, qualification, and retreat. This is not to say that talented people no longer study philosophy, nor that worthwhile contributions have ceased. Promising work is being done, but too often it is overwhelmed by pettifogging or left to die in obscurity.

Those unaware of what is happening in philosophy today may be surprised to learn that few academic philosophers address the sort of problems one studied in college: death, the existence of God, the cardinal virtues, the external world, or the prospects for happiness. Instead, if one walks into a classroom or lecture hall, one is likely to find brief discussions dealing with an odd assortment of issues about such things as time machines, adverbs, pains, possible worlds, sexual perversion. Even the language has changed. In many cases, English prose has been replaced by codes, symbols, and dialects incomprehensible to those outside the profession and not much better known to some of those inside.

It is not altogether surprising that philosophy has fallen on hard times. Throughout much of this century, people believed that philosophical questions were the result of logical or linguistic confusions. The task of philosophy was to eliminate them and thereby do away with itself. . . .

The problem is that philosophy is unique among academic disciplines in that the philosopher is forever plagued by the question of what his discipline is about. . . . A beginning student is usually told that philosophy does not deal with facts but with the analysis of concepts. But this characterization is inadequate because it seems to suggest that the distinction between the factual and the conceptual is absolute and that concepts can be analyzed entirely on their own. The philosopher, in other words, need not bother with what is, has been, or is likely to be the case.

What emerges is a conception of philosophy that retains its purity by making a radical distinction between itself and virtually every other form of knowledge. C. D. Broad once described philosophy at Cambridge as "almost completely out of touch with general history, with political theory and sociology, and with jurisprudence." Few eyebrows would have been raised if he had thrown in a dozen other departments and perhaps three or four additional disciplines as well. As for how it is possible to do, say, ethics in such an environment, Broad and his cohorts had a ready answer: the moral philosopher must be distinguished from the moralist. The latter takes a stand on important ethical questions and can be refuted should his evidence prove insufficient. For him to be ignorant of history, political theory, and jurisprudence is to run the risk of being wrong. The moral philosopher, however, only reflects on the language employed by the moralist. Since the philosopher is not in the business of recommending or criticizing courses of action, he can comfortably ignore the lessons the moralist has to learn.

This conception of philosophy prevailed in the English-speaking world for about forty years until it fell into disrepute during the turmoil of the sixties. Then sticky questions began to be asked: To whom was such analysis addressed and for what purpose? If the moral philosopher had studied the great ethical systems of the past, why should he not bring his knowledge to bear on the controversial issues of the present? Recently a number of articles have sprung up in the philosophical journals dealing with abortion, homosexuality, recombinant DNA research, intelligence testing, and

GO ON TO THE NEXT PAGE ➤

other issues once thought to be beyond the scope of philosophical inquiry. Their presence raises the obvious question: What unique subject or set of problems distinguishes philosophical inquiry from everything else?

One difficulty is that while other disciplines investigate a specific range of phenomena, philosophy, particularly in the hodgepodge conception of it, investigates all of existence. Worse, while the natural sciences seem to get better as they get older, philosophy does not. Without a body of accepted beliefs to build on, philosophers can make interesting points, but not step-by-step progress. A researcher in physics does not have to make a new beginning each time he walks into his lab; he can assume that there is a consensus on a large number of issues and thus can direct his efforts to a few highly restricted problems.

1. Which of the following titles best exemplifies the passage?

   (A) *Declines and Falls*
   (B) *Nationalism and Philosophy*
   (C) *Contemporary American Literature*
   (D) *The State of Contemporary Philosophy*
   (E) *The Study of Philosophy*

2. According to the passage, philosophers are concerned today with the subject of

   (A) political theory
   (B) philosophical inquiry
   (C) outdated works
   (D) abstract versions of social theory
   (E) public affairs

3. The author states that the philosopher is constantly

   (A) out of touch with general history
   (B) defining his discipline
   (C) determining objectives
   (D) investigating specific phenomena
   (E) providing radical alternatives

4. The moral philosopher does not have to

   (A) be in touch with general history
   (B) recommend a course of action
   (C) account to his colleagues
   (D) study linguistics
   (E) be in touch with reality

5. Many philosophers feel that the study of philosophy should become more

   (A) technical
   (B) popular
   (C) cautious
   (D) moralistic
   (E) dialectic

6. Which of the following subjects *is not* generally studied by academic philosophers?

   (A) Time machines
   (B) Possible worlds
   (C) External worlds
   (D) Linguistics
   (E) Moral issues

7. Recently, the field of philosophy has included

   I. intelligence testing
   II. language training
   III. pure research

   (A) I only
   (B) II only
   (C) I and II only
   (D) II and III only
   (E) I, II, and III

8. Which of the following statements best exemplifies the author's feelings?

   (A) Philosophy is in moral decay.
   (B) Talented people no longer study philosophy.
   (C) Historians have replaced philosophers.
   (D) Few academic philosophers are left.
   (E) Philosophers are too cautious.

9. A criticism of philosophy is its lack of

   (A) models and constructs
   (B) concepts
   (C) scientific logic
   (D) purity
   (E) thematic perception

GO ON TO THE NEXT PAGE ➤

6 6 6 6 6 6 6 6 6 6 6

Passage 2:

One of the most rapidly expanding sectors in American life since World War II has been the government. Local, state, and national government expenditures for goods and services rose from 13% of the gross national product in 1950 to 23% in 1970, reflecting a sixfold absolute increase in government spending. The expansion was not limited to traditional domains, such as defense and welfare. New target areas of government spending include the physical sciences, social sciences, and the arts. Federal outlays for research in the physical sciences rose from $0.6 billion in fiscal 1956 to $2.9 billion in 1963 and $3.8 billion in 1973. Federal support of social science research, which stood at $30 million in 1956, reached $412 million in 1973 (National Science Foundation, 1970: 243; 1974a: 149). Expenditures by the National Endowment for the Arts (1973: 111–112) evidenced a similar trend: initially appropriated $3 million during its first year of operation in 1966, the National Endowment's budget reached $15 million in 1971 and $61 million by 1974.

The institutions engaged in artistic or scientific activity are centrally concerned with the maintenance and extension of cultural systems (Parsons, 1961; Peterson, 1976). The growth of government patronage for these areas suggests that the facilitation and production of culture has become a major state activity in the United States. The objectives underlying this state intervention are not well understood. The central purpose of this paper is to evaluate the relative strengths of several alternative explanations for the government's involvement in the production of culture. A second purpose is to suggest the likely impact of government patronage on the physical sciences, social sciences, and arts in America.

Four distinct models for explaining the state's growing interest in the production of culture can be identified. One model emphasizes the value of patronage for the maintenance of the cultural institutions in question. A second model stresses the utility of the investment for capital accumulation. A third model points toward the value of supporting science and art for the administration of government programs. The fourth model identifies the ideological potential of science and art as a primary reason for government patronage.

Science and art for their own sake. The first model of government patronage is predicated on the structural-functionalist assumption that the government is a relatively neutral instrument for the articulation and pursuit of collective goals in a society with relatively autonomous subsystems (Parsons, 1969). Pure science and art are vital societal subsystems, and the government moves to protect and develop these areas to ensure the continued production of culture for the benefit of all members of society. Thus, the government intervenes directly as the final patron of public goods that would otherwise be unavailable. Increasingly, the paradigms (Kuhn, 1970: 175) in science and art dictate expenditures that increasingly outstrip the resources of the institutions themselves. Equipment, staff, and data-processing costs of physical science research far exceed the commercial potential of most scientific projects; the cost of conducting systematic and reliable social scientific investigations can no longer be met through product marketing or private foundations; what is more, artistic organizations are increasingly incapable of underwriting all production costs through income and contributions. Under these conditions, government patronage is introduced to ensure the flow of cultural goods to society.

Two important corollaries follow from this formulation, which make it empirically testable. First, the timing of government intervention should primarily be related to economic crises faced by the arts and science themselves, not to crises in the political system, economy, or elsewhere. Second, government intervention should generally take the form of protecting the paradigm of the arts and sciences. Specifically, federal funding should be allocated to the most creative artists and organizations, as defined by the relevant artistic community. Similarly, funding should be preferentially bestowed on scientists whose research is making the greatest contribution to the advance of the scientific discipline, regardless of its relevance for outside problems or crises.*

GO ON TO THE NEXT PAGE ➤

*Reprinted from Michael Useem, "Government Patronage of Science and Art in America," pp. 123–142 in Richard A. Peterson, ed., *The Production of Culture,* © Sage Publications, Inc.

10. According to the passage, the growth in federal support was greatest for

    (A) goods and services
    (B) social science research
    (C) defense and welfare
    (D) endowment for the arts
    (E) physical sciences

11. The major objective of the passage is to

    (A) increase appreciation for the arts
    (B) provide an ideological basis for artistic funding
    (C) explain why government supports cultural activities
    (D) argue for more government support of the arts and sciences
    (E) demonstrate cultural activities in the United States

12. Which of the models discussed in the passage represents the statement: "Funding should be provided to the best artists and scientists"?

    (A) Science and art for their own sake
    (B) Science and art for business application
    (C) Science and art for government programs
    (D) Science and art for ideological control
    (E) All models for government investment

13. A corollary of the science and art for government programs is

    (A) funding should be provided by government only as a last resort
    (B) funding will be geared to projects of value to the government
    (C) funding is to be provided only to nongovernmental employees
    (D) funding by the government is self-defeating
    (E) funding by the government is inflationary

14. A conclusion reached by the author of the passage is that

    (A) the arts and sciences have been funded by the government for different reasons
    (B) government is a neutral observer of the arts and sciences
    (C) government intervention in the arts and sciences is declining
    (D) the arts and sciences are not dependent on government funding
    (E) politics and science go together

15. Government intervention in the arts and sciences should coincide with

    (A) government's ability to pay
    (B) fluctuations in the business cycle
    (C) political needs
    (D) economic needs of the arts and sciences community
    (E) the number of needy scientists

16. The idea that government should support the arts and sciences only when the market does not provide enough funds belongs to which school?

    (A) "Their own sake"
    (B) "Business application"
    (C) "Government programs"
    (D) "Ideological control"
    (E) All of the above

17. The idea that cultural goods can no longer be provided solely by the market system is given by

    (A) the author of the passage
    (B) the first model of government patronage
    (C) the second model of government patronage
    (D) the third model of government patronage
    (E) the fourth model of government patronage

GO ON TO THE NEXT PAGE ➤

6 6 6 6 6 6 6 6 6 6 6

Passage 3:

Unemployment is an important index of economic slack and lost output, but it is much more than that. For the unemployed person, it is often a damaging affront to human dignity and sometimes a catastrophic blow to family life. Nor is this cost distributed in proportion to ability to bear it. It falls most heavily on the young, the semiskilled and unskilled, the black person, the older worker, and the underemployed person in a low income rural area who is denied the option of securing more rewarding urban employment . . . .

The concentrated incidence of unemployment among specific groups in the population means far greater costs to society than can be measured simply in hours of involuntary idleness or dollars of income lost. The extra costs include disruption of the careers of young people, increased juvenile delinquency, and perpetuation of conditions which breed racial discrimination in employment and otherwise deny equality of opportunity.

There is another and more subtle cost. The social and economic strains of prolonged underutilization create strong pressures for cost-increasing solutions.... On the side of labor, prolonged high unemployment leads to "share-the-work" pressures for shorter hours, intensifies resistance to technological change and to rationalization of work rules, and, in general, increases incentives for restrictive and inefficient measures to protect existing jobs. On the side of business, the weakness of markets leads to attempts to raise prices to cover high average overhead costs and to pressures for protection against foreign and domestic competition. On the side of agriculture, higher prices are necessary to achieve income objectives when urban and industrial demand for foods and fibers is depressed and lack of opportunities for jobs and higher incomes in industry keep people on the farm. In all these cases, the problems are real and the claims understandable. But the solutions suggested raise costs and promote inefficiency. By no means the least of the advantages of full utilization will be a diminution of these pressures. They will be weaker, and they can be more firmly resisted in good conscience, when markets are generally strong and job opportunities are plentiful.

The demand for labor is derived from the demand for the goods and services which labor participates in producing. Thus, unemployment will be reduced to 4 percent of the labor force only when the demand for the myriad of goods and services—automobiles, clothing, food, haircuts, electric generators, highways, and so on—is sufficiently great in total to require the productive efforts of 96 percent of the civilian labor force.

Although many goods are initially produced as materials or components to meet demands related to the further production of other goods, all goods (and services) are ultimately destined to satisfy demands that can, for convenience, be classified into four categories: consumer demand, business demand for new plants and machinery and for additions to inventories, net export demand of foreign buyers, and demand of government units, Federal, state, and local. Thus gross national product (GNP), our total output, is the sum of four major components of expenditure; personal consumption expenditures, gross private domestic investment, net exports, and government purchases of goods and services.

The primary line of attack on the problem of unemployment must be through measures which will expand one or more of these components of demand. Once a satisfactory level of employment has been achieved in a growing economy, economic stability requires the maintenance of a continuing balance between growing productive capacity and growing demand. Action to expand demand is called for not only when demand actually declines and recession appears but even when the rate of growth of demand falls short of the rate of growth of capacity.

18. According to the passage, unemployment is an index of
    - (A) overutilization of capacity
    - (B) economic slack and lost output
    - (C) diminished resources
    - (D) the employment rate
    - (E) undercapacity

GO ON TO THE NEXT PAGE ➤

19. While unemployment is damaging to many, it falls most heavily upon all except the

(A) black
(B) semiskilled
(C) unskilled
(D) underemployed
(E) white middle class

20. The cost to society of unemployment can be measured by all except

(A) lost incomes
(B) idleness
(C) juvenile delinquency
(D) disruption of careers
(E) the death rate

21. Serious unemployment leads labor groups to demand

(A) more jobs by having everyone work shorter hours
(B) higher wages to those employed
(C) "no fire" policies
(D) cost-cutting solutions
(E) higher social security payments

22. According to the passage, a typical business reaction to a recession is to press for

(A) higher unemployment insurance
(B) protection against imports
(C) government action
(D) restrictive business practices
(E) restraint against union activity

23. The demand for labor is

(A) a derived demand
(B) declining
(C) about 4 percent of the total work force
(D) underutilized
(E) dependent upon technology

24. Gross national product (GNP) is a measure of

(A) personal consumption
(B) net exports
(C) domestic investment
(D) government purchases of goods and services
(E) our total output

25. According to the passage, a satisfactory level of unemployment is

(A) 85 percent of the civilian work force
(B) 90 percent of the civilian work force
(C) 4 percent unemployment
(D) 2 percent unemployment
(E) no unemployment

STOP

IF THERE IS STILL TIME REMAINING,
YOU MAY REVIEW THE QUESTIONS IN THIS SECTION ONLY.
YOU MAY NOT TURN TO ANY OTHER SECTION OF THE TEST.

7 7 7 7 7 7 7 7 7 7 7

Section 7 [Data Sufficiency]

TIME: 25 minutes
21 Questions

Directions: Each of the following problems has a question and two statements which are labeled (1) and (2). Use the data given in (1) and (2) together with other available information (such as the number of hours in a day, the definition of *clockwise*, mathematical facts, etc.) to decide whether the statements are *sufficient* to answer the question. Then fill in space

(A) if you can get the answer from **(1) ALONE** but not from (2) alone
(B) if you can get the answer from **(2) ALONE** but not from (1) alone
(C) if you can get the answer from **BOTH (1) and (2) TOGETHER,** but not from (1) alone or (2) alone
(D) if **EITHER** statement **(1) ALONE OR** statement **(2) ALONE** suffices
(E) if you **CANNOT** get the answer from statements (1) and (2) **TOGETHER,** but need even more data

All numbers used in this section are real numbers. A figure given for a problem is intended to provide information consistent with that in the question, but not necessarily with the additional information contained in the statements.

1. A piece of wood 5 feet long is cut into three smaller pieces. How long is the longest of the three pieces?
   (1) One piece is 2 feet 7 inches long.
   (2) One piece is 7 inches longer than another piece and the remaining piece is 5 inches long.

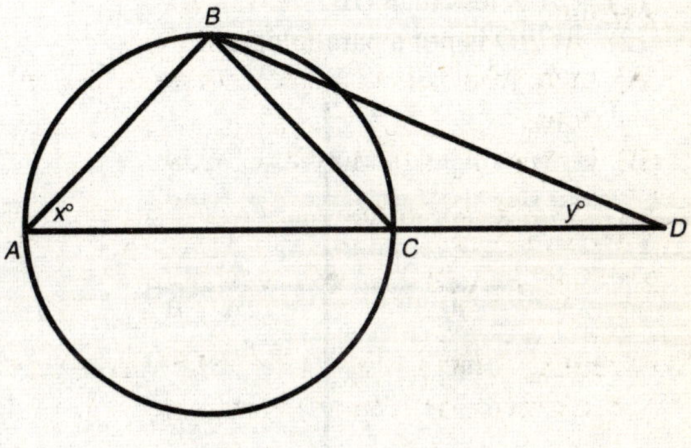

2. *AC* is a diameter of the circle. *ACD* is a straight line. What is the value of *x*?
   (1) $AB = BC$
   (2) $x = 2y$

3. What is the value of *y*?
   (1) $x + 2y = 6$
   (2) $y^2 - 2y + 1 = 0$

GO ON TO THE NEXT PAGE ➤

7 7 7 7 7 7 7 7 7 7 7

(A) if you can get the answer from **(1) ALONE** but not from (2) alone
(B) if you can get the answer from **(2) ALONE** but not from (1) alone
(C) if you can get the answer from **BOTH (1) and (2) TOGETHER,** but not from (1) alone or (2) alone
(D) if **EITHER** statement **(1) ALONE OR** statement **(2) ALONE** suffices
(E) if you **CANNOT** get the answer from statements (1) and (2) **TOGETHER,** but need even more data

4. Two pipes, *A* and *B*, empty into a reservoir. Pipe *A* can fill the reservoir in 30 minutes by itself. How long will it take for pipe *A* and pipe *B* together to fill up the reservoir?

   (1) By itself, pipe *B* can fill the reservoir in 20 minutes.
   (2) Pipe *B* has a larger cross-sectional area than pipe *A*.

5. *AB* is perpendicular to *CO*. Is *A* or *B* closer to *C*?

   (1) *OA* is less than *OB*.
   (2) *ACBD* is not a parallelogram.

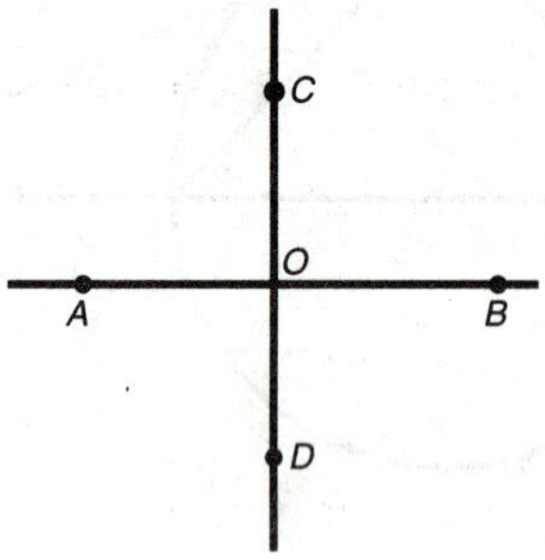

6. Is xy greater than 1? x and y are both positive.

   (1) x is less than 1.
   (2) y is greater than 1.

7. Does $x = y$?

   (1) $z = u$
   (2) *ABCD* is a parallelogram.

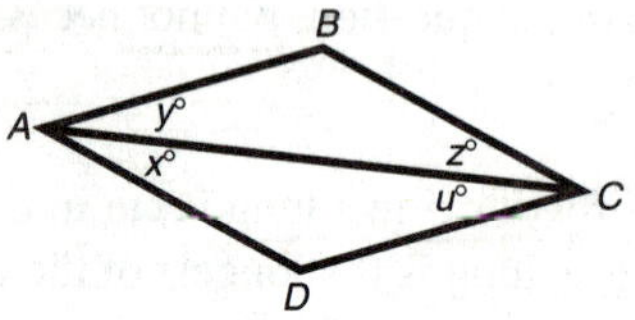

8. Train *T* leaves town *A* for town *B* and travels at a constant rate of speed. At the same time, train *S* leaves town *B* for town *A* and also travels at a constant rate of speed. Town *C* is between *A* and *B*. Which train is traveling faster? Towns *A*, *C*, *B* lie on a straight line.

   (1) Train *S* arrives at town *C* before train *T*.
   (2) *C* is closer to *A* than to *B*.

GO ON TO THE NEXT PAGE ➤

7 7 7 7 7 7 7 7 7 7 7

(A) if you can get the answer from **(1) ALONE** but not from (2) alone
(B) if you can get the answer from **(2) ALONE** but not from (1) alone
(C) if you can get the answer from **BOTH (1) and (2) TOGETHER,** but not from (1) alone or (2) alone
(D) if **EITHER** statement **(1) ALONE OR** statement **(2) ALONE** suffices
(E) if you **CANNOT** get the answer from statements (1) and (2) **TOGETHER,** but need even more data

9. Does $x = y$?

   (1) BD is perpendicular to AC.
   (2) AB is equal to BC.

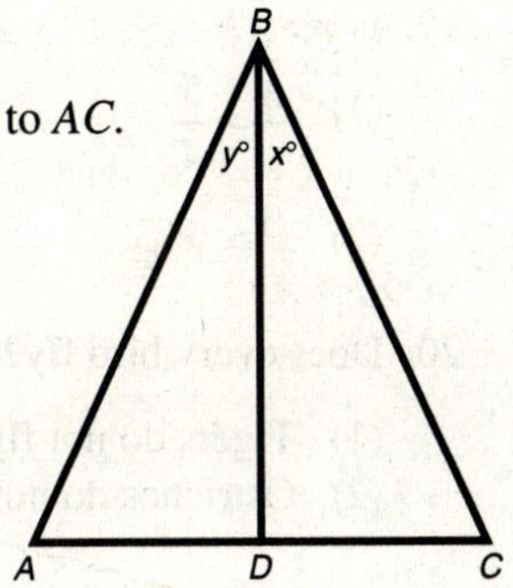

10. What is the value of $x + y$?

    (1) $x - y = 4$
    (2) $3x + 3y = 4$

11. Did the *XYZ* Corporation have higher sales in 1988 or in 1989? Assume sales are positive.

    (1) In 1988 the sales were twice the average (arithmetic mean) of the sales in 1988, 1989, and 1990.
    (2) In 1990, the sales were three times those in 1989.

12. Is *ABDC* a square?

    (1) BC is perpendicular to AD.
    (2) $BE = EC$.

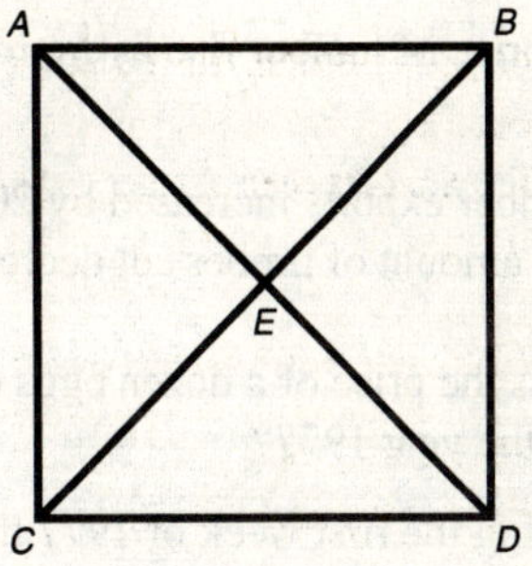

13. k is an integer. Is k divisible by 12?

    (1) k is divisible by 4.
    (2) k is divisible by 3.

14. How far is it from A to B?

    (1) It is 15 miles from A to C.
    (2) It is 25 miles from C to B.

GO ON TO THE NEXT PAGE ➤

(A) if you can get the answer from **(1) ALONE** but not from (2) alone
(B) if you can get the answer from **(2) ALONE** but not from (1) alone
(C) if you can get the answer from **BOTH (1) and (2) TOGETHER,** but not from (1) alone or (2) alone
(D) if **EITHER** statement **(1) ALONE OR** statement **(2) ALONE** suffices
(E) if you **CANNOT** get the answer from statements (1) and (2) **TOGETHER,** but need even more data

15. Is x an even integer? Assume n and p are integers.
    (1) $x = (n + p)^2$
    (2) $x = 2n + 10p$

16. Did the price of lumber rise by more than 10% last year?
    (1) Lumber exports increased by 20%
    (2) The amount of timber cut decreased by 10%.

17. What was the price of a dozen eggs during the 15th week of the year 1977?
    (1) During the first week of 1977 the price of a dozen eggs was 75¢.
    (2) The price of a dozen eggs rose 1¢ a week every week during the first four months of 1977.

18. Is DE parallel to BC? $DB = AD$:
    (1) $AE = EC$
    (2) $DB = EC$

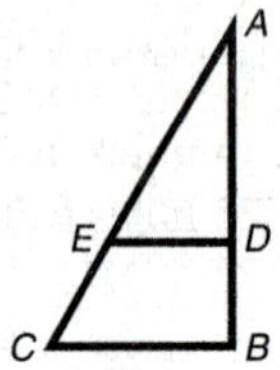

19. Is $x > y$?
    (1) $\frac{x}{y} = \frac{5}{4}$
    (2) $x^2 > y^2$

20. Does every bird fly?
    (1) Tigers do not fly.
    (2) Ostriches do not fly.

21. Find $x + 2y$.
    (1) $x - y = 12$
    (2) $3x - 3y = 36$

STOP

IF THERE IS STILL TIME REMAINING,
YOU MAY REVIEW THE QUESTIONS IN THIS SECTION ONLY.
YOU MAY NOT TURN TO ANY OTHER SECTION OF THE TEST.

Answers
DIAGNOSTIC TEST

Section 1 [Reading Comprehension]

1	C	6	C	11	D	16	A	21	C
2	C	7	C	12	A	17	A	22	E
3	C	8	E	13	A	18	B	23	C
4	B	9	B	14	D	19	C	24	A
5	C	10	B	15	B	20	D	25	C

Section 2 [Problem Solving]

1	B	6	E	11	B	16	B	21	
2	D	7	D	12	D	17	D	22	
3	B	8	D	13	B	18		23	
4	E	9	E	14	B	19		24	
5	A	10	D	15	D	20		25	

Section 3 [Critical Reasoning]

1	C	6	C	11	D	16	A	21	
2	B	7	C	12	B	17	D	22	
3	D	8	C	13	E	18		23	
4	D	9	A	14	C	19		24	
5	D	10	D	15	E	20		25	

Section 4 [Problem Solving]

1	C	6	B	11	C	16	C	21	
2	C	7	E	12	B	17	E	22	
3	D	8	C	13	D	18		23	
4	C	9	D	14	E	19		24	
5	D	10	E	15	E	20		25	

Section 5 [Sentence Correction]

1	A	6	D	11	C	16	D	21	A
2	C	7	D	12	C	17	D	22	
3	B	8	D	13	E	18	D	23	
4	C	9	E	14	D	19	E	24	
5	E	10	B	15	D	20	D	25	

Section 6 [Reading Comprehension]

1	D	6	C	11	C	16	A	21	A
2	B	7	A	12	A	17	B	22	B
3	B	8	E	13	B	18	B	23	A
4	B	9	A	14	A	19	E	24	E
5	A	10	D	15	D	20	E	25	C

Section 7 [Data Sufficiency]

1	D	6	E	11	A	16	E	21	E
2	A	7	C	12	E	17	C	22	
3	B	8	C	13	C	18	A	23	
4	A	9	C	14	E	19	E	24	
5	A	10	B	15	B	20	B	25	

Self-Scoring Guide—Analytical Writing

Evaluate your writing tests (or have a friend or teacher evaluate them for you) on the following basis. Read each essay completely, paying special attention to its logical organization and use of examples and facts to buttress its claims or position. Assign a holistic score between 0 and 6, using the scale below. Your writing score will be the average of the scores of the two essays.

6	**Outstanding**	Cogent, well-articulated analysis of the issue or critique of the argument. Develops a position with insightful reasons and persuasive examples. Well organized. Superior command of language and variety of syntax. Only minor flaws in grammar, usage, and mechanics.
5	**Strong**	Well-developed analysis or critique. Develops a position with well-chosen examples or reasons. Generally well organized. Clear control of language and variety of syntax. Minor flaws in grammar, usage, and mechanics.
4	**Adequate**	Competent analysis or critique. Develops a position with relevant reasons or examples. Adequately organized. Adequate control of language, but may lack syntactic variety. May have some flaws in grammar, usage, and mechanics.
3	**Limited**	Competent but clearly flawed analysis or critique. Vague or limited in developing a position. Poorly organized. Weak in using relevant examples or reasons. Language used imprecisely or lacking in sentence variety. Contains major errors or frequent minor errors in grammar, usage, and mechanics.
2	**Seriously Flawed**	Serious weaknesses in analysis and organization. Unclear or seriously limited in presenting or developing a position. Disorganized. Few relevant examples or reasons. Frequent serious problems in language and sentence structure. Numerous errors in grammar, usage, or mechanics that interfere with meaning.
1	**Fundamentally Deficient**	Little evidence of ability to organize and develop a coherent response to issue or argument. Severe and persistent errors in language and sentence structure. Pervasive pattern of errors in grammar, usage, and mechanics that severely interfere with meaning.
0	**Unscorable**	Illegible or not written on the assigned topic.

Analysis

Section 1
Reading Comprehension

(The passage for questions 1–9 appears on page 37.)

1. The author is primarily concerned with

(A) the declining pattern of morality in America
(B) promoting American theatre
(C) the role of the Bible in the contemporary theatre
(D) comparing the theatre with other art forms
(E) preserving the "American Way of Life"

(C) While the author is concerned with the moral and cultural aspects of American society (lines 1, 32–38), his major concern is to show how the Bible has been used as a guide for some theatrical productions. See especially lines 47–53, and 69ff.

2. With which of the following statements regarding the theatre would the author most likely agree?

(A) The theatre does not reflect American culture.
(B) Critics of American cultural life are biased.
(C) While the entertainment media can be criticized, they contain much wholesome material.
(D) The advertising media are largely to blame for criticisms leveled at the theatre.
(E) The Bible should be used as our primary source of entertainment ideas.

(C) This central theme of the author's concern is contained in lines 4–20.

3. Which of the following statements best reflects the author's own ideas?

(A) American art forms have degenerated to a new low.
(B) The good outweighs the bad in American cultural activity.
(C) American culture has positive content, but it is not appreciated by the public.
(D) Only the Biblical content of American theatre has positive meaning.
(E) American theatre is currently dull and unpopular.

(C) Statements (A) and (B) were not originally voiced by the author, but rather by Gen. Sarnoff. See lines 1–3, 12–15. Statements (D) and (E) are taken out of context. See lines 49–60. Statement (C) reflects the author's own ideas. See lines 21–28.

4. The author implies that he will deal with which of the following questions?

I. What is the reason for the lack of appreciation of the theatre?
II. To what extent have Bible themes been used in or influenced American theatrical productions?
III. What should be done to encourage the good in American culture?

(A) I only
(B) II only
(C) I and II only
(D) I and III only
(E) I, II, and III

(B) Question I is found in lines 21–28, question III in lines 29–31. However, the author does not present evidence that he intends to answer them. Only answers to question II are implied throughout.

5. It can be inferred from the passage that the author's background might be in any of the following occupations *except*

(A) theatrical producer
(B) thespian
(C) humorist
(D) writer
(E) critic

(C) The author does not state his background or profession, but it might be any of the choices except (C), since there are no traces of humor in this passage.

6. The author implies that, if the public is made aware of the positive qualities of American entertainment, it will

I. demand more high-quality entertainment
II. demand less low-quality entertainment
III. attend the theatre more often

(A) I only
(B) II only
(C) I and II only
(D) I and III only
(E) I, II, and III

(C) Both these ideas are implied in lines 15–20.

7. When the author uses the expression "the Bible as guide and touchstone" in line 50, he probably means to refer to

(A) the interrelationship of the Bible and the "American Way of Life"
(B) an academic approach to researching the theatre and religion
(C) the relationship of Biblical concepts to basic ideas and values contained in theatrical productions
(D) the use of the Bible as a guide to everyday life
(E) the Bible as a source of inspiration for all

(C) Examined in context, (C) is the most probable answer. See lines 49–53.

8. According to the author, which of the following media have low cultural and moral values?

I. Movies
II. TV
III. Literature

(A) I only
(B) II only
(C) I and II only
(D) II and III only
(E) I, II, and III

(E) The answer includes all three items. Movies are included in the answer because they are considered part of "theatrical fare." See lines 1–3 and 23–27 of the passage.

9. The author believes that high American moral and cultural values are important because they determine

(A) what is produced in Hollywood
(B) the future of world democracy
(C) whether the Bible will be studied
(D) the basis for Western civilization
(E) educational trends in the school system

(B) The author believes that the "face that America shows the world"—i.e., its moral and cultural values—"affects seriously the future of democracy all over the globe." See lines 32–37.

(The passage for questions 10–17 appears on page 40.)

10. Which of the following best describes the author's conception of an applied social scientist?

(A) A professional who listens to people's problems
(B) A professional who seeks social action and change
(C) A student of society
(D) A proponent of class struggle
(E) A philosopher who interprets the world in a unique way

(B) Lines 11–13 quote Marx as saying that philosophers only want to interpret the world, when what should be done is to change it. Change, the author states on line 14, is the "creed of applied scientists everywhere."

11. According to the author, which of the following did Marx and Durkheim have in common?

(A) A belief in the importance of class struggle
(B) A desire to create a system of social organization
(C) An interest in penology
(D) Regard for the practical applications of science
(E) A sense of the political organization of society

(D) Durkheim also valued the application of science rather than theoretical constructs alone. See lines 58–65.

12. It may be inferred from the passage that the applied social scientist might be interested in all of the following subjects *except*

(A) the theory of mechanics
(B) how to make workers more efficient
(C) rehabilitation of juvenile delinquents
(D) reduction of social tensions
(E) industrial safety

(A) Items (B) through (E) deal with *applied* problems, which are the main concern of the social scientist, according to the passage.

13. According to the passage, applied social science can be distinguished from pure social science by its

(A) practical significance
(B) universal application
(C) cultural pluralism
(D) objectivity
(E) emphasis on the problems of the poor

(A) See lines 61–65.

14. Which of the following best summarizes the author's main point?

(A) Marx and Durkheim were similar in their ideas.
(B) Freud, Marx, and Durkheim were all social scientists.
(C) Philosophers, among others, who are regarded as theoreticians can also be regarded as empiricists.
(D) Marx and Durkheim were applied social scientists because they were concerned with the solution of social problems.
(E) Pure and applied sciences have fundamentally similar objects.

(D) This point is stressed in lines 7–8, 18–19, 27ff, 48–52, 61–63, and 71ff.

15. All of the following are mentioned as topics of interest to Durkheim *except*

(A) suicide
(B) psychiatry
(C) crime
(D) education
(E) religion

(B) All but choice (B) are mentioned in the last paragraph.

16. What action did Marx prescribe for the proletariat?

I. Class consciousness
II. Passive resistance
III. Alienation

(A) I only
(B) II only
(C) I and II only
(D) II and III only
(E) I, II, and III

(A) Marx prescribed (lines 25 and 26) class consciousness and active struggle. This rules out alternative II. Alternative III was thought to be a causal factor.

17. Marx sought to

I. understand society
II. change the educational system
III. apply science to philosophy

(A) I only
(B) II only
(C) I and II only
(D) II and III only
(E) I, II, and III

(A) Marx sought to understand *and* change society (lines 17 and 18).

(The passage for questions 18–25 appears on page 42.)

18. Which of the following titles best describes the contents of the passage?

(A) *The Problems of Nuclear Physics*
(B) *Advanced Technology and Cancer*
(C) *Occupational Diseases*
(D) *Cancer in Germany*
(E) *The Ecology of Cancer*

(B) The passage deals with the harmful effects of certain production processes on workers and others.

19. The author provides information that would answer which of the following questions?

(A) What sort of legislation is needed to prevent cancer?
(B) Should nuclear plants be built?
(C) What are some causes of lung cancer?
(D) What are the pros and cons of nuclear energy?
(E) Which country has the lowest incidence of occupational disease?

(C) This answer is clear from lines 29–52 of the passage.

20. According to the author, all the following are causes of cancer *except*

(A) plutonium
(B) asbestos
(C) vinyl chloride
(D) osteolysis
(E) lead

(D) Osteolysis is not mentioned as a cause. (A) can be found in lines 16–20; (B) in lines 29ff.; (C) in lines 53–56; and (E) in lines 3ff.

21. The style of the passage is mainly

(A) argumentative
(B) emotional
(C) factual
(D) clinical
(E) vitriolic

(C) The author does not argue for remedial action in the passage, but merely presents the facts concerning cancer-producing occupational hazards.

22. It can be inferred from the passage that the author believes that

(A) industrialization must be halted to prevent further spread of cancer-producing agents
(B) only voluntary, industry-wide application of antipollution devices can halt cancer
(C) workers are partly to blame for the spread of disease because of poor work habits
(D) more research is needed into the causes of cancer before further progress can be made
(E) tougher legislation is needed to set lower limits of worker exposure to harmful chemicals and fibers

(E) This is implied in lines 56ff. Existing legislated-maximum levels of vinyl chloride exposure are higher than that set by Dow Chemical and apparently higher than a medically permissible safe limit.

23. Some workers have been killed by harmful pollutants because

(A) they failed to take the required precautions and safety measures
(B) not enough research has been undertaken to find solutions to the pollution problem
(C) available research was not followed up
(D) production cannot be halted
(E) factory owners have failed to provide safety equipment

(C) The passage relates that at least 17 workers were killed because of the failure by authorities to follow up on available research. See lines 64–66.

24. It is mentioned in the passage that the asbestos level

(A) should be lowered
(B) causes heart problems
(C) is linked with osteolysis
(D) is similar to the level of vinyl chloride
(E) is not linked with any known disease

(A) According to the U.S. Occupational Safety and Health Administration, the asbestos level should be lowered. See lines 30–32.

25. The passage is based on evidence of pollutants in the following countries *except*

(A) United Kingdom
(B) United States
(C) Sweden
(D) Germany
(E) Netherlands

(C) The United Kingdom is mentioned in line 69, the United States in line 29, Germany in the first paragraph, and the Netherlands in line 17. Sweden is not mentioned.

Section 2
Problem Solving

(Numbers in parentheses at the end of each explanation indicate the section in the Mathematics Review where material addressed in the question is discussed.)

1. If the length of a rectangle is increased by 20% and the width is decreased by 20%, then the area

(A) decreases by 20%
(B) decreases by 4%
(C) stays the same
(D) increases by 10%
(E) increases by 20%

(B) Let L be the original length and W the original width. The new length is 120% of L which is $(1.2)L$; the new width is 80% of W which is $(.8)W$. The area of a rectangle is length times width, so the original area is LW and the new area is $(1.2)(L)(.8)W$ or $(.96)LW$. Since the new area is 96% of the original area, the area has decreased by 4%. (I-4)

2. If it is 250 miles from New York to Boston and 120 miles from New York to Hartford, what percentage of the distance from New York to Boston is the distance from New York to Hartford?

(A) 12
(B) 24
(C) 36
(D) 48
(E) 52

(D) The distance from New York to Hartford divided by the distance from New York to Boston is $\frac{120}{250}$ or .48, and .48 = 48%. (I-4)

3. The lead in a mechanical pencil is 5 inches long. After pieces $\frac{1}{8}$ of an inch long, $1\frac{3}{4}$ inches long, and $1\frac{1}{12}$ inches long are broken off, how long is the lead left in the pencil?

(A) 2 in.

(B) $2\frac{1}{24}$ in.

(C) $2\frac{1}{12}$ in.

(D) $2\frac{1}{4}$ in.

(E) $2\frac{1}{2}$ in.

(B) The amount broken off is $\frac{1}{8} + 1\frac{3}{4} + 1\frac{1}{12}$ inches.

Since $\frac{1}{8} + 1\frac{3}{4} + 1\frac{1}{12} = \frac{3}{24} + \frac{42}{24} + \frac{26}{24} = \frac{71}{24}$ and

the lead was 5 inches long to begin with, the amount left

$= 5 - \frac{71}{24} = \frac{120}{24} - \frac{71}{24} = \frac{49}{24} = 2\frac{1}{24}$ inches. (I-2).

4. It costs x dollars each to make the first thousand copies of a compact disk and y dollars to make each subsequent copy. If z is greater than 1,000, how many dollars will it cost to make z copies of the compact disk?

(A) $1{,}000x + yz$
(B) $zx - zy$
(C) $1{,}000 (z - x) + xy$
(D) $1{,}000 (z - y) + xz$
(E) $1{,}000 (x - y) + yz$

(E) The first 1,000 copies cost x dollars each, so altogether they will cost $1{,}000x$ dollars. Since z is greater than 1,000, there are $(z - 1{,}000)$ copies left, which each cost y dollars. Their cost is $(z - 1{,}000)y$. Thus the total cost is $1{,}000x + (z - 1{,}000)y$. However, this is not one of the answer choices. But $(z - 1{,}000)y = zy - 1{,}000y$, so the total cost is $1{,}000x - 1{,}000y + yz$ or $1{,}000(x - y) + yz$, which is choice (E). If you want to check your work let $x = 5$, $y = 2$, and $z = 3{,}000$. (II-3)

5. How many two-digit numbers satisfy the following property: the last digit (units digit) of the square of the two-digit number is 8?

(A) none
(B) 1
(C) 2
(D) 3
(E) more than 3

(A) When two numbers are multiplied, the units digit of the product will be the last digit of the product of the last digit of each of the numbers. For example, the product of 22×18 is 396. The last digit of 396 is 6. 6 is also the last digit of 16 which is the product of 2 (the last digit of 22) times 8 (the last digit of 18). When a number is squared, the last digit of the square will be the last digit of the square of the last digit. Squaring an odd number gives an odd number and odd numbers cannot end in 8. Squaring a number that ends in 0 gives a number that ends in 0. Squaring a number that ends in 2 or 8 gives a number that ends in 4. Squaring a number that ends in 4 or 6 results in a number that ends in 6. So no number squared will end in 8. Therefore, the correct choice is (A). (I-1)

6. If $x + y = 3$ and $\frac{y}{x} = 2$, then y is equal to

(A) 0

(B) $\frac{1}{2}$

(C) 1

(D) $\frac{3}{2}$

(E) 2

(E) Since $\frac{y}{x} = 2$, $y = 2x$. Therefore, $x + y = x + 2x = 3x$ which equals 3. So $3x = 3$, which means $x = 1$. Thus, $y = 2$ because $y = 2x$. (II-2).

7. Ms. Taylor purchased stock for $1,500 and sold $\frac{2}{3}$ of it after its value doubled. She sold the remaining stock at 5 times its purchase price. What was her total profit on the stock?

(A) $1,500
(B) $2,000
(C) $2,500
(D) $3,000
(E) $6,000

(D) $\frac{2}{3}$ of the stock cost $\frac{2}{3}$ of $1,500, or $1,000. So, when its value doubled, it was worth $2,000. The profit on this part of the stock is $2,000 – $1,000 = $1,000. The remaining stock cost $1,500 – $1,000 = $500. 5 times the purchase price for this part of the stock is 5 × $500 = $2,500. The profit on this part is $2,500 – $500 = $2,000. So the total profit is $1,000 + $2,000 = $3,000, which is choice (D). (II-3)

8. City B is 8 miles east of City A. City C is 6 miles north of City B. City D is 16 miles east of City C, and City E is 12 miles north of City D. What is the distance from City A to City E?

(A) 10 miles
(B) 20 miles
(C) 24 miles
(D) 30 miles
(E) 42 miles

(D) Drawing a picture makes this problem easy. One way to solve the problem is to use coordinate geometry. Let A have coordinates (0,0), then the coordinates for B, C, D, and E are (8,0), (8,6), (24,6), and (24,18), respectively. So the distance from A to E is the square root of $24^2 + 18^2 = \sqrt{576+324} = \sqrt{900}$, which is 30. (III-9)

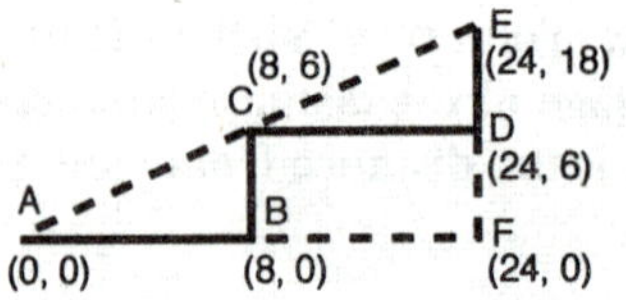

9. A car goes 15 miles on a gallon of gas when it is driven at 50 miles per hour. When the car is driven at 60 miles per hour it only goes 80% as far. How many gallons of gas will it take to travel 120 miles driving at 60 miles per hour?

(A) 2
(B) 6.4
(C) 8
(D) 9.6
(E) 10

(E) Let x be the number of miles the car travels on a gallon of gas when driven at 60 miles an hour. Then 80% of 15 is x; so $\frac{4}{5} \cdot 15 = x$ and $x = 12$. So it will take $\frac{120}{12} = 10$ gallons of gas to travel 120 miles at 60 miles per hour.

Notice that many of the other choices correspond to misconceptions. If you divided $\frac{120}{15}$ you get 8 which is choice (C), but this is how many gallons to travel 120 miles at 50 mph. If you take 80% of 8 gallons you get choice (B), and if you take 120% of 8 you get choice (D). So the fact that your answer matches one of the given choices does not mean it is correct. (II-3)

10. If $x + y = z$ and x and y are positive, then which of the following statements can be inferred?

I. $x < y$
II. $x < z$
III. $x < 2z$

(A) I only
(B) II only
(C) I and II only
(D) II and III only
(E) I, II, and III

(D) STATEMENT I cannot be inferred since if $x = 2$ and $y = 1$, then x and y are positive but x is not less than y.

STATEMENT II is true since $x + y = z$ and y is positive so $x < z$.

STATEMENT III is true. z is positive since it is the sum of two positive numbers and so $z < 2z$. Since we know $x < z$ and $z < 2z$, then $x < 2z$.

Therefore, only STATEMENTS II and III can be inferred. (II-7)

11. Mr. Smith drove at an average speed of 50 mph for the first two hours of his trip. For the next three hours, he averaged 20 mph. What was Mr. Smith's average speed for the five-hour trip?

(A) 30 mph
(B) 32 mph
(C) 35 mph
(D) 38 mph
(E) 160 mph

(B) To find the average speed for the five hour period first you need to know how far the car traveled in the five hour period. In the first two hours the car traveled 50 mph × 2 hours or 100 miles. In the next three hours the car traveled 20 mph × 3 hours or 60 miles. So the total distance traveled was 100 + 60 = 160 miles. Therefore,

the average speed was $\frac{160 \text{ miles}}{15 \text{ hours}} = 32$ miles per hour.

Note that the total distance was 160 miles and that 160 miles per hour was a possible choice. You must be sure to answer the question that is asked. Find the average speed, not the total distance. Keeping track of the units in your answer would avoid this mistake. (II-3)

12. If in 1967, 1968, and 1969 a worker received 10% more in salary each year than he did the previous year, how much more did he receive in 1969 than in 1967?

(A) 10%
(B) 11%
(C) 20%
(D) 21%
(E) 30%

(D) Let S denote the worker's salary in 1967. In 1968 he received 110% of S which is $(1.1)S$, and in 1969 he received 110% of $(1.1)S$ which is $(1.1)(1.1)S$ or $1.21\ S$. Therefore, he received 21% more in 1969 than he did in 1967. (I-4)

13. If x is a number satisfying $2 < x < 3$ and y is a number satisfying $7 < y < 8$, which of the following expressions will have the largest value?

(A) x^2y
(B) xy^2
(C) $5xy$
(D) $\frac{4x^2y}{3}$
(E) $\frac{x^2}{y}$

(B) From the information given you know that x and y are both positive and that $x < y$. So, we know that xy is positive. Since $xy = xy$ and $x < y$, we have that $x(xy) < y(xy)$ so (A) < (B). Since $5 < 7 < y$, we know that $5(xy) < y(xy)$ so (C) < (B). Since $x < 3$, we know $\left(\frac{4}{3}\right)x < 4$ so $\left(\frac{4}{3}\right)x(xy) < 4xy$ so (D) < (B). Since $y > 7$ and $x < 3$, (E) is obviously less than (B). Therefore, (B) has the greatest value and is the correct choice. (II-7)

14. If 50 apprentices can finish a job in 4 hours and 30 journeymen can finish the same job in $4\frac{1}{2}$ hours, how much of the job should be completed by 10 apprentices and 15 journeymen in one hour?

(A) $\frac{1}{9}$

(B) $\frac{29}{180}$

(C) $\frac{26}{143}$

(D) $\frac{1}{5}$

(E) $\frac{39}{121}$

(B) Since 10 is $\frac{1}{5}$ of 50, the 10 apprentices should do $\frac{1}{5}$ as much work as 50 apprentices. 50 apprentices did the job in 4 hours, so in 1 hour 50 apprentices will do $\frac{1}{4}$ of the job. Therefore, 10 apprentices should do $\frac{1}{5}$ of $\frac{1}{4} = \frac{1}{20}$ of the job in an hour.

Since 15 is $\frac{1}{2}$ of 30, 15 journeymen will do half as much work as 30 journeymen. The 30 journeymen finished the job in $4\frac{1}{2}$ hours, so in 1 hour they will do $\frac{2}{9}$ of the job. Therefore, 15 journeymen will do $\frac{1}{2}$ of $\frac{2}{9} = \frac{1}{9}$ of the job in an hour. So both groups will do $\frac{1}{20} + \frac{1}{9} = \frac{9}{180} + \frac{20}{180} = \frac{29}{180}$ of the job in an hour. (II-3)

15. If the shaded area is one half the area of triangle *ABC* and angle *ABC* is a right angle, then the length of line segment *AD* is

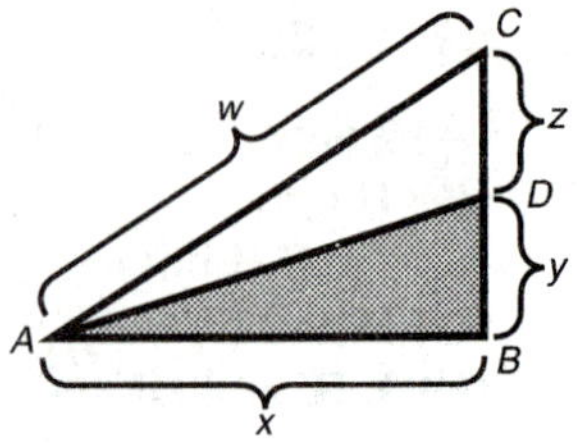

(A) $\frac{1}{2}w$

(B) $\frac{1}{2}(w+x)$

(C) $\sqrt{2x^2+2^2}$

(D) $\sqrt{w^2-3y^2}$

(E) $\sqrt{y^2+z^2}$

(D) Since angle *ABC* is a right angle, we know the length of *AD* squared is equal to the sum of y^2 and x^2. However, none of the answers given is $\sqrt{x^2+y^2}$. The area of triangle *ABC* is $\frac{1}{2}x(y+z)$, and the area of triangle *ABD*, which is $\frac{1}{2}xy$, must be one half of $\frac{1}{2}x(y+z)$. So $\frac{1}{4}xy+\frac{1}{4}xz=\frac{1}{2}xy$, which can be solved to give $y = z$. Since angle *ABC* is a right angle, $w^2 = (y + z)^2 + x^2 = (2y)^2 + x^2$. So $w^2 = 4y^2 + x^2$. Since we want $x^2 + y^2$, we subtract $3y^2$ from each side to get $w^2 - 3y^2 = y^2 + x^2$. Therefore, the length of *AD* squared is $w^2 - 3y^2$. (III-4, III-7)

16. There are 4 quarts in a gallon. A gallon of motor oil sells for \$12 and a quart of the same oil sells for \$5. The owner of a rental agency has 6 machines and each machine needs 5 quarts of oil. What is the minimum amount of money she must spend to purchase enough oil?

(A) \$84
(B) \$94
(C) \$96
(D) \$102
(E) \$150

(B) The total amount of oil needed is $6 \times 5 = 30$ quarts, or 7 gallons and 2 quarts. Since the cost of oil per quart is cheaper when you purchase by the gallon, the owner should buy at least 7 gallons of oil. However, in order to get the remaining 2 gallons, it is cheaper to buy 2 quarts individually rather than another gallon. So the minimum amount is 7 × \$12 + 2 × \$5 = \$84 + \$10 = \$94. The correct answer is (B). (II-3)

17. A store has a parking lot that contains 70 parking spaces. Each row in the parking lot contains the same number of parking spaces. The store has bought additional property in order to build an addition to the store. When the addition is built, 2 parking spaces will be lost from each row; however, 4 more rows will be added to the parking lot. After the addition is built, the parking lot will still have 70 parking spaces, and each row will contain the same number of parking spaces as every other row. How many rows were in the parking lot before the addition was built?

(A) 5
(B) 6
(C) 7
(D) 10
(E) 14

(D) Call s the number of spaces in each row and r the number of rows in the parking lot before the addition is built. The parking lot had 70 parking spaces, so $sr = 70$. Since after the addition is built there are 4 more rows, 2 less spaces in each row, and a total of 70 spaces, we know that $(s - 2)(r + 4) = 70$. You could solve these two equations by algebra, but there is a faster method. Since the number of rows and the number of spaces must be positive integers, you are looking for a way to write 70 as the product of two factors s and r with the additional property that $s - 2$ and $r + 4$ also have 70 as their product. Writing 70 as a product of primes, we get $70 = 2 \times 35 = 2 \times 5 \times 7$. Therefore, the only possibilities for s and r are listed here:

s	r	s	r
1	70	10	7
2	35	14	5
5	14	35	2
7	10	70	1

Now just check whether any pair of solutions (s, r) has the property that $s - 2$ and $r + 4$ is a solution. For example, if $s = 5$ and $r = 14$, then $s - 2 = 3$ and $r + 4 = 18$, which are not solutions. But if $s = 7$ and $r = 10$, then $s - 2 = 5$ and $r + 4 = 14$, which is also a solution. It is easy to see this is the only solution that works. So before the addition was built, there were 10 rows each with 7 spaces. (I-1)

Section 3
Critical Reasoning

1. In winning its bitter, protracted battle to acquire Blue Industries, Inc., Belle Industries has fulfilled its goal to lessen its reliance on tobacco holdings, while the $5.2 billion deal may spur more takeover activity in the insurance industry, analysts said.

Which of the following can be inferred from the passage?

(A) Blue Industries is in the tobacco industry.
(B) Belle Industries is in the insurance business.
(C) Blue Industries is in the insurance business.
(D) More divestment takes place in the tobacco industry than in the insurance industry.
(E) More divestment takes place in the insurance industry than in the tobacco industry.

(C) The passage states that Belle Industries has lessened its reliance on tobacco holdings by virtue of acquiring Blue Industries. Hence, Belle Industries is in the tobacco industry and Blue Industries is not. This rules out answers (A) and (B). The part of the passage that says that the deal may spur more takeover activity in the insurance industry indicates that Blue Industries is in the insurance industry. Thus, answer (C) is correct. Answers (D) and (E) are incorrect because the passage does not state or imply that divestment has taken place, but merely implies that takeover activity in the insurance industry may increase. And, even if one could infer a reference to divestment, the passage makes no assumption about relative magnitude between the two industries.

2. Typically, the entrepreneur is seen as an individual who owns and operates a small business. But, simply to own and operate a small business—or even a big business—does not make someone an entrepreneur. If this person is a true entrepreneur, then new products are being created, new ways of providing services are being implemented.

Which of the following conclusions can best be drawn from the above passage?

(A) An owner of a large business may be an entrepreneur.
(B) Someone who develops an enterprise may be considered an entrepreneur.
(C) Entrepreneurs do not own and operate small businesses.
(D) Entrepreneurs are the main actors in economic growth.
(E) Entrepreneurs are inventors.

(B) Answer (B) is the best choice. Note the cue word "then" before "new products" and "new ways." An entrepreneur is one who creates or implements change, not necessarily an inventor, as in answer (E). Answer (A) is true (the owner of a large business may be an entrepreneur), but it is not the best conclusion that can be drawn from the passage. It is a necessary but insufficient condition. Note that the text states that to own a small or large business does not make someone an entrepreneur. Answer (C) is not supported by the passage, and not enough information is given to conclude answer (D).

3. During the incumbent president's term of office he succeeded in limiting annual increases in the defense budget by an average of 5 percent. His predecessor experienced annual increases of 8 percent. Therefore, the incumbent president should be given credit for the downturn in defense outlays.

Which of the following statements, if true, would most seriously weaken the above conclusion?

(A) Some generals have claimed that the country's defenses have weakened in the past year.
(B) More soldiers were drafted during the former president's term of office.
(C) The incumbent president advocates peaceful resolution of international disputes.
(D) The average annual inflation rate during the incumbent president's term was 4 percent, while during his predecessor's term it was 10 percent.
(E) A disarmament treaty with a major adversary was signed by the incumbent president.

(D) If inflation averaged 4 percent and spending increased by 5 percent, the *real* value of defense outlays actually increased by 25 percent. During the former president's term, outlays actually declined faster than inflation, indicating a real decrease of 25 percent. The passage and conclusions concern defense outlays only; the strength of the defenses (A), number of draftees (B), presidential views (C), or international treaties (E) are not mentioned in the passage and no direct inferences can be made; therefore all other alternatives are not relevant. The argument may be summarized as follows:

1. Annual increases of incumbent were 5 percent.
2. Annual increases of predecessor were 8 percent.

These two premises lead to a conclusion:

5 percent < 8 percent

However, converting the nominal to real increases as we showed above weakens this conclusion.

4. Ira is taller than Sam.
Elliot is taller than Harold.
Harold is shorter than Gene.
Sam and Gene are the same height.

If the above is true, which of the following conditions must also be true?

(A) Elliot is taller than Gene.
(B) Elliot is taller than Ira.
(C) Sam is shorter than Elliot.
(D) Ira is taller than Harold.
(E) Sam is shorter than Harold.

(D) As Harold is shorter than Gene, and as Gene is the same height as Sam, Harold also is shorter than Sam. As Ira is taller than Sam, Ira must also be taller than Harold. Therefore, (D) is the best answer. Choices (A), (B), and (C) might be inferred if one knew more about Elliot's height in relation to the height of the others. Choice (E) cannot be inferred from the information given. The following diagram helps make the situation clear:
$I > S = G > E > H$

5. Buy Plenty, a supermarket chain, had successfully implemented an in-store promotional campaign based on video messages flashed on a large screen. The purpose of the campaign was to motivate customers to purchase products which they had not planned to buy before they entered the store. The sales manager of Build-It Inc., a chain of do-it-yourself hardware stores, saw the campaign and plans to introduce it in Build-It locations.

The sales manager's plan assumes that

(A) supermarket and hardware products are the same.
(B) products cannot be sold successfully without a video sales campaign.
(C) supermarket chains do not sell hardware products.
(D) consumer decision making to buy products does not differ substantially when it comes to both supermarket and hardware products.
(E) in-store campaigns are more effective than out-of-store advertising and sales promotion.

(D) Build-It's sales manager assumes via analogy that consumers behave the same way when it comes to buying do-it-yourself hardware products as they behave in a supermarket even though no evidence for this is given in the passage. Answer choice (A) cannot be inferred, and there is no evidence to support choices (B), (C), or (E).

6. The movement to ownership by unions is the latest step in the progression from management ownership to employee ownership. Employee ownership can save depressed and losing companies.

All the following statements, if true, provide support for the claim above *except:*

(A) Employee-owned companies generally have higher productivity.
(B) Employee participation in management raises morale.
(C) Employee union ownership drives up salaries and wages.
(D) Employee union ownership enables workers to share in the profits.
(E) Employee union ownership makes it easier to layoff redundant workers.

(C) Statement (C) is the best choice because increased salaries and wages will make the company less profitable and thus not help save a losing company. All other statements, if true, would lend credence to the claim.

7. The burning of coal, oil and other combustible energy sources produces carbon dioxide, a natural constituent of the atmosphere. Elevated levels of carbon dioxide are thought to be responsible for half the greenhouse effect. Enough carbon dioxide has been sent into the atmosphere already to cause a significant temperature increase. Growth in industrial production must be slowed, or production processes must be changed.

Which of the following, if true, would tend to weaken the strength of the above conclusion?

(A) Many areas of the world are cold anyway, so a small rise in temperature would be welcome.
(B) Carbon dioxide is bad for the health.
(C) Most carbon dioxide is emitted by automobiles.
(D) Industry is switching over to synthetic liquid fuel extracted from coal.
(E) A shift to other energy sources would be too costly.

(C) Choice (C) would weaken the conclusion the most. If most carbon dioxide is emitted by automobiles, then cutting industrial production or changing production processes would only solve a small part of the problem. Alternative (A) weakens the conclusion, but not as much. It does not attack the basic premise of the passage—namely, that industrial production is responsible for elevated carbon dioxide levels. It also disregards the effect of a temperature increase even in cold areas. Alternative (B) adds to the conclusion. Alternative (D) would not change the conclusion because liquid fuel may also produce carbon dioxide (in actuality, it produces quite a bit). Alternative (E) does not weaken the conclusion because even if a shift to other energy sources were too costly, this does not mean that a slowing of or changes in production would be too costly.

8. Contrary to charges made by opponents of the new trade bill, the bill's provisions for taking action against foreign countries that place barriers against American exports, is justified. Opponents should take note that restrictive trade legislation in the 1930s succeeded in improving the U.S. trade balance even though economists were against it.

The author's method of rebutting opponents of the new trade bill is to

(A) attack the patriotism of its opponents.
(B) attack the opponents' characters rather than their claims.
(C) imply an analogy between the new trade bill and previous trade legislation.
(D) suggest that economists were against both pieces of legislation.
(E) imply that previous legislation also permitted retaliatory action against foreign countries.

(C) The author refers to 1930s trade legislation to justify the new bill. Therefore, choice (C) is the best answer. There is no information to conclude (A) or (B); the author does not attack the character of the opposition, nor their patriotism. In choice (D), it is assumed that the opposition infers that economists were against both pieces of legislation, but there is no evidence of this in the passage. Choice (E) is wrong because the passage does not stipulate what sort of action was permitted by the earlier legislation.

9. Opponents of the new legislation could defend themselves against the author's strategy by arguing that:

(A) the fact that past trade legislation improved the trade balance does not mean that the present bill will do the same.
(B) economists are not always right.
(C) the United States had a trade deficit both in the 1930s and at the time of the new bill.
(D) the new law is not as strong as the 1930s bill.
(E) America's trading partners have also passed similar legislation.

(A) The opponents could argue that two similar pieces of legislation passed and implemented at different times may not have the same effect because they face a different set of circumstances. Even though both bills may have similar provisions, they may be applied under different sets of economic and political conditions. Therefore, (A) is the best answer. Alternatives (C) and (E) strengthen the author's argument rather than the opponent's rebuttal. Alternative (B) may be so, but it does not necessarily apply in this case. There is not enough information to conclude (D).

10. During 1985, advertising expenditures on canned food products increased by 20 percent, while canned food consumption rose by 25 percent.

Each of the following, if true, could help explain the increase in food consumption *except:*

(A) Advertising effectiveness increased.
(B) Canned food prices decreased relative to substitutes.
(C) Canned food products were available in more stores.
(D) Can opener production doubled.
(E) Per-capita consumption of frozen foods declined.

(D) The problem in this example is finding cause and effect. However, some plausible relationships exist. Assuming a positive relationship between advertising outlay and consumption, if advertising is more effective, a smaller increase in expenditure should lead to an increase in consumption, the conclusion in (A), even though we do not have information about the absolute, base amounts of either advertising or consumption expenditures. If people buy more of a substitute product when its price is lower, then alternative (B) will occur. If canned food is made more available, consumption should increase (C). If consumption of substitute products decrease (E), canned products should increase. However, an increase in can opener production may be a result of increased canned food consumption (D), and not the other way around.

11. Inflation rose by 5.1% over the 2nd quarter, up from 4.1% during the first quarter of the year, and higher than the 3.3 % recorded during the same time last year. However, the higher price index did not seem to alarm Wall Street, as stock prices remained steady.

Which of the following, if true, could explain the reaction of Wall Street?

(A) Stock prices were steady because of a fear that inflation would continue.
(B) The President announced that he was concerned about rising inflation.
(C) Economists warned that inflation would persist.
(D) Much of the quarterly increase in the price level was due to a summer drought's effect on food prices.
(E) Other unfavorable economic news had overshadowed the fact of inflation.

(D) Answer (D) is most appropriate. If most of the quarterly inflation was due to a rise in food prices caused by a drought, then other prices rose less or no more than in the last quarter. Since the drought is probably a temporary phenomenon, it may be expected that the price level will decline next quarter. A fear that inflation would continue (A), an announcement by the president that he was concerned about inflation (B), economists' warnings about inflation (C), and other unfavorable economic news (E) would all tend to cause stock prices to decline and cause alarm on Wall Street.

12. "Ever since I arrived at the college last week, I've been shocked by the poor behavior of students, the unfriendly attitude of the townspeople, but the professors are very erudite and genuinely helpful. Still, I wonder if I should have come here in the first place."

Which of the following, if true, would weaken the above conclusion?

(A) Professors are not always helpful to students.
(B) The college numbers over 50,000 students.
(C) The college is far from the student's home.
(D) Not all professors have doctorates.
(E) The narrator was unsure of staying at the college.

(B) If, as the passage states, the narrator spent only a week at a college that has over 50,000 students, how could he or she possibly draw a conclusion about the entire group. This is an example of an overgeneralization, so choice (B) is correct. Choice (A) would support the conclusion. Choices (C), (D), and (E) are irrelevant to the issue.

13. A local garbage disposal company increased its profitability even though it reduced its prices in order to attract new customers. This was made possible through the use of automated trucks, thereby reducing the number of workers needed per truck. The company also switched from a concentration on household hauling to a concentration on commercial hauling. As a result of its experience, company management planned to replace all their old trucks and increase the overall size of the truck fleet, doubling hauling capacity.

The company's plan, as outlined above, takes into consideration each of the following *except:*

(A) Commercial clients have more potential than household customers.
(B) The demand for garbage removal services is sensitive to price.
(C) Demand for garbage removal services would increase in the future.
(D) Doubling of capacity would not necessitate a substantial increase in workforce.
(E) Doubling of capacity would not cause bottlenecks, leading to a decrease in productivity.

(E) There is no evidence that the doubling of capacity is linked to productivity. All other answer choices can be inferred. Choice (A) is inferred from the fact that the company switched from household to commercial customers. Choice (B) is inferred from the company's decision to lower charges which will result in greater demand for its services. Choices (C) and (D) are inferred from the decision to switch to labor-saving trucks.

14. Every town with a pool hall has its share of unsavory characters. This is because the pool hall attracts gamblers and all gamblers are unsavory.

Which of the following, if true, cannot be inferred from the above?

(A) All gamblers are unsavory.
(B) All pool halls attract gamblers.
(C) Every town has unsavory characters.
(D) All gamblers are attracted by pool halls.
(E) An explanation of what attracts gamblers.

(C) The statement's conclusion is that all towns have unsavory characters. This conclusion is false. According to the passage, only towns with pool halls have unsavory characters; and since we cannot infer that all towns have pool halls, conclusion (C) is wrong. Alternatives (A) and (B) are stated in the passage, while alternatives (D) and (E) can be deduced. A diagram will help:

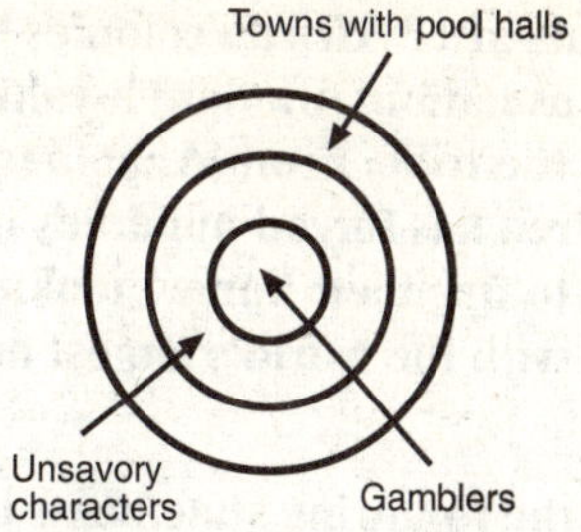

The argument may be summarized as follows:

1. Pool halls attract gamblers.
2. Gamblers are unsavory.
3. *Therefore*, towns with pool halls have unsavory characters.

Check this argument and the diagram with alternative statements in the question.

15. In August 1980, according to a *New York Times*/CBS news poll, 36 percent of the voters called themselves Republican or said they were independents leaning towards being Republicans. In November 1984, the Republican figure rose to 47 percent. But in the latest *Times*/CBS survey, the Republicans were down to 38 percent. Therefore, the Democrats are likely to win the next election.

Which of the following, if true, would most seriously weaken the above conclusion?

(A) Republicans were a minority in 1984, but a Republican president was elected.
(B) People tend to switch their votes at the last minute.
(C) People vote for the best candidate, not for a political party.
(D) No one can predict how people will vote.
(E) It has been shown that 85 percent of Republicans vote in an election, compared to 50 percent of the Democrats.

(E) 85 percent of 38 percent is 32 percent, while 50 percent of 62 percent is 31 percent; therefore, it can be expected that more Republicans will vote. Alternative (A) shows that even though 47 percent of the voters called themselves Republicans, the Republican Party won the election. In the latest poll, the proportion of Republicans declined to 38 percent. (A) weakens the conclusion but not as strongly as (E). Alternatives (B) and (C) hold equally for both Republicans and Democrats. Alternative (D) weakens the conclusion but not as much as (E); the fact that no one can predict how people will vote does not imply that results cannot be forecast with a high probability.

16. Thirty years after African colonies began emerging as nations, modern loyalties still often go first to the tribe. From Angola to Ethiopia, ethnic hatred has forced hundreds of thousands of people to flee their homes, making Africa the continent with the world's largest number of refugees.

Which of the following statements best summarizes the above?

(A) Africa is best characterized by ethnic fractionalization.
(B) Angola and Ethiopia have the worst record of interethnic strife in Africa.
(C) Continued warfare has made Africa a nation of refugees.
(D) Africa is best characterized as a federation of many states.
(E) Africa is best characterized as a continent without loyalties.

(A) Ethnofractionalization is characteristic of a continent with many tribes that are ethnically different. Statement (B) is flawed; Angola and Ethiopia are not given as worst-case examples. Alternatives (D) and (E) are not true. Alternative (C) is the second best summarization, even though warfare is at most inferred.

17. Average family income is right where it was 20 years ago, even though in most families these days, husbands and wives are working.

The above statement implies all of the following, *except:*

(A) Even though nominal family income may have increased, inflation has risen at an equal rate.
(B) More husbands and wives are working today than 20 years ago.
(C) It was more prevalent for one spouse to work 20 years ago than today.
(D) Wives earn more than husbands today.
(E) The price level was lower 20 years ago.

(D) Alternative (D) cannot be implied from the statement. There is no information in the statement that implies that wives earn more than husbands. Alternative (A) may be implied because as wives contributed to the household nominal income, if prices increased at the same rate as the income, real income would stay the same. Alternatives (B) and (C) are implicit in the statement. If the added income contribution of wives leaves average family income at the level of 20 years ago, then the reason must be that price level was lower 20 years ago, so (E) is implied.

Section 4
Problem Solving

(Numbers in parentheses at the end of each explanation indicate the section in the Mathematics Review where material addressed in the questions is discussed.)

1. .03 times .05 is

(A) 15%
(B) 1.5%
(C) .15%
(D) .015%
(E) .0015%

(C) Remember that the decimal point of the product of two decimals is placed so that the number of decimal places in the product is equal to the total of the number of decimal places in all of the numbers multiplied. Since .03 and .05 each have 2 decimal places, their product must have 4 (2 + 2) decimal places. Because 3 times 5 is 15, you need to add 2 zeros to get the correct number of decimal places, so the product of .03 and .05 is .0015. To change a decimal to a percentage you multiply by 100 (just move the decimal point 2 places to the right), so .0015 is .15%. (I-3, I-4)

2. Which of the following are possible values for the angles of a parallelogram?

I. 90°, 90°, 90°, 90°
II. 40°, 70°, 50°, 140°
III. 50°, 130°, 50°, 130°

(A) I only
(B) II only
(C) I and III only
(D) II and III only
(E) I, II, and III

(C) Since a parallelogram is a 4-sided polygon, the sum of the angles of a parallelogram must be (4 – 2)180° = 360°. (A diagonal divides a parallelogram into 2 triangles and the sum of each triangle's angles is 180°.) Since the sum of the angles in II is not 360°, II is not possible. But I and III both consist of angles whose sum is 360°. Also, since in both I and III opposite angles are equal, C is the correct choice. Note that a rectangle is also a parallelogram, so I does give possible values for the angles of a parallelogram. (III-3, III-5)

3. For every novel in the school library there are two science books; for each science book there are seven economics books. Express the ratio of economics books to science books to novels in the school library as a triple ratio.

(A) 7 : 2 : 1
(B) 7 : 1 : 2
(C) 14 : 7 : 2
(D) 14 : 2 : 1
(E) 14 : 2 : 7

(D) If you know two ratios A : B and B : C, you can combine them into a triple ratio if B is the same number and represents the same quantity in both ratios. We know that the ratio of economics books to science books is 7 : 1 and that the ratio of novels to science books is 1 : 2. However, we can't combine this into the triple ratio 7 : 1 : 2 since 1 in the first ratio represents science books and 1 in the second ratio represents novels. We need science books as the middle term in the triple ratio, so express the second ratio as: the ratio of science books to novels is 2 : 1. Now, the ratio of economics books to science books is 7 : 1 and the ratio of science books to novels is 2 : 1. Since a ratio is unchanged if both sides are multiplied by the same positive number, we can also express the ratio of economics books to science books as 14 : 2. Finally, we can combine these into the triple ratio 14 : 2 : 1 of economics books to science books to novels. (II-5.3)

4. There are 50 employees in the office of ABC company. Of these, 22 have taken an accounting course, 15 have taken a course in finance, and 14 have taken a marketing course. Nine of the employees have taken exactly two of the courses, and one employee has taken all three of the courses. How many of the 50 employees have taken none of the courses?

(A) 0
(B) 9
(C) 10
(D) 11
(E) 26

(C) A picture helps.

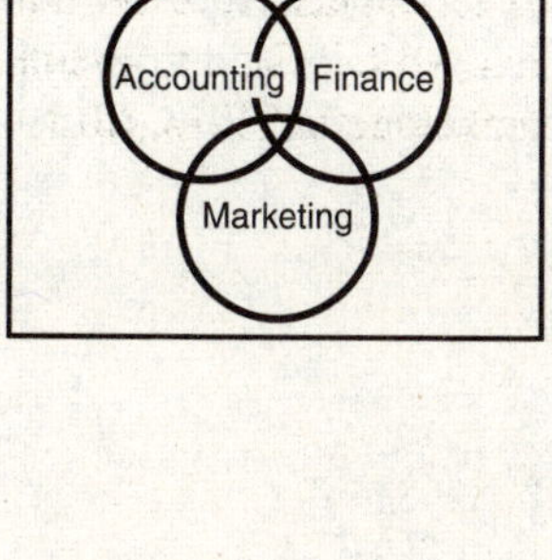

We want to know how many people are not in any of the sets.

The easy way to do this is find the number in at least one of the sets and subtract this number from 50. To find the number of employees in at least one set, *do not count the same employee more than once*. If you add 22, 15, and 14, an employee who took exactly two of the courses will be counted twice and employees who took all three courses will be counted three times. So the number who took at least one course = the number in Accounting + the number in Finance + the number in Marketing – number who took exactly two courses – 2 times the number who took all three courses = 22 + 15 + 14 – 9 – (2 times 1) = 51 – 9 – 2 = 40. Since 40 of the employees took at least one course, 50 – 40 = 10 took none of the courses. (II-4)

5. If $x + y = 4$ and $x - y = 3$, then $x + 2y$ is

(A) $\frac{1}{2}$

(B) $3\frac{1}{2}$

(C) 4

(D) $4\frac{1}{2}$

(E) $7\frac{1}{2}$

(D) Add $x + y = 4$ to $x - y = 3$ to obtain $2x = 7$. Therefore, $x = 3\frac{1}{2}$. Since $x + y = 4$, y must be $4 - 3\frac{1}{2} = \frac{1}{2}$. So $x + 2y = 3\frac{1}{2} + 2\left(\frac{1}{2}\right) = 4\frac{1}{2}$. (II-2)

6. How much interest will $2,000 earn at an annual rate of 8% in one year if the interest is compounded every 6 months?

(A) $160.00
(B) $163.20
(C) $249.73
(D) $332.80
(E) $2,163.20

(B) The interest is compounded every 6 months. At the end of the first 6 months the interest earned is

$\$2{,}000(.08)\left(\frac{1}{2}\right) = \$80$. (Don't forget to change 6 months into $\frac{1}{2}$ year since 8% is the annual—yearly—rate.) Since the interest is compounded, \$2,080 is the amount earning interest for the final 6 months of the year. So the interest earned during the final 6 months of the year is $\$2{,}080(.08)\left(\frac{1}{2}\right) = \$83.20$. Therefore, the total interest earned is \$80 + \$83.20 = \$163.20. (I-4)

7. If *BC* is parallel to *AD* and *CE* is perpendicular to *AD*, then the area of *ABCD* is

(A) *bd*
(B) *bd* + *ac*
(C) *ed*
(D) *e*(*b* + *d*)
(E) .5*eb* + .5*ed*

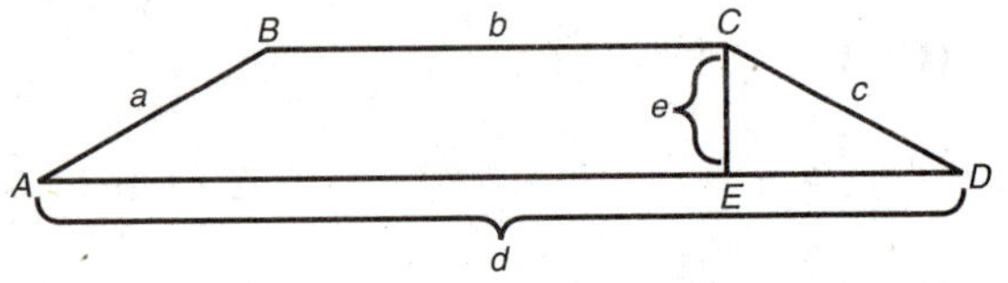

(E) Since *BC* is parallel to *AD*, the figure *ABCD* is a trapezoid. The area of a trapezoid is the average of the parallel sides times an altitude. Since *CE* is perpendicular to *AD*, *e* is an altitude. So the area is $e\left(\frac{1}{2}\right)(b + d) = \left(\frac{1}{2}\right)eb + \left(\frac{1}{2}\right)ed$. Since $\frac{1}{2} = .5$, (E) is the correct answer. (III-7)

8. A company makes a profit of 6% on its first \$1,000 of sales each day, and 5% on all sales in excess of \$1,000 for that day. How many dollars in profit will the company make in a day when sales are \$6,000?

(A) \$250
(B) \$300
(C) \$310
(D) \$320
(E) \$360

(C) The profit is 6% of \$1,000 plus 5% of (\$6,000 – \$1,000) which is (.06)(\$1,000) + (.05)(\$5,000). Therefore, the profit equals \$60 + \$250, which is \$310. (I-4)

9. If 15 men working independently and at the same rate can manufacture 27 baskets in an hour, how many baskets would 45 men working independently and at the same rate manufacture in 40 minutes?

(A) 27
(B) 35
(C) 40
(D) 54
(E) 81

(D) Since the number of baskets manufactured in an hour is proportional to the number of workers, $\frac{15}{45} = \frac{27}{x}$, where x is the number of baskets manufactured by 45 men in an hour. Therefore, x is 81. Since 40 minutes is $\frac{2}{3}$ of an hour, 45 men will make $\frac{2}{3}$ of 81 or 54 baskets in 40 minutes. (II-5)

10. A conveyer belt moves grain at the rate of 2 tons in 5 minutes and a second conveyer belt moves grain at the rate of 3 tons in 7 minutes. How many minutes will it take to move 20 tons of grain using both conveyer belts?

(A) 12
(B) $16\frac{4}{7}$
(C) $18\frac{3}{26}$
(D) 21
(E) $24\frac{4}{29}$

(E) The first belt lifts $\frac{2}{5}$ of a ton per minute and the second belt lifts $\frac{3}{7}$ of a ton per minute, so both belts together will lift $\frac{2}{5} + \frac{3}{7} = \frac{29}{35}$ of a ton per minute.

Therefore, using both belts it will take $\frac{20}{\frac{29}{35}} = \frac{35}{29} \times$

$20 = \frac{700}{29}$ or $24\frac{4}{29}$ minutes to lift 20 tons. (II-3)

11. A field is rectangular and its width is $\frac{1}{3}$ as long as its length. What is the area of the field if the length of the field is 120 yards?

(A) 480 square yards
(B) 2,400 square yards
(C) 4,800 square yards
(D) 5,000 square yards
(E) 7,200 square yards

(C) Since the width is $\frac{1}{3}$ of the length and the length is 120 yards, the width of the field is 40 yards. The area of a rectangle is length times width, so the area of the field is 120 yards time 40 yards, which is 4,800 square yards. (III-7)

12. If the price of steak is currently $1.00 a pound, and the price triples every 6 months, how long will it be until the price of steak is $81.00 a pound?

(A) 1 year

(B) 2 years

(C) $2\frac{1}{2}$ years

(D) 13 years

(E) $13\frac{1}{2}$ years

(B) The price will be $3.00 a pound 6 months from now and $9.00 a pound a year from now. The price is a geometric progression of the form $$3^j$ where j is the number of 6-month periods which have passed. Since $3^4 = 81$, after 4 six-month periods, the price will be $81.00 a pound. Therefore, the answer is two years, since 24 months is 2 years. (II-6, I-8)

13. If $\frac{x}{y} = \frac{2}{3}$, then $\frac{y^2}{x^2}$ is

(A) $\frac{4}{9}$

(B) $\frac{2}{3}$

(C) $\frac{3}{2}$

(D) $\frac{9}{4}$

(E) $\frac{5}{2}$

(D) Since $\frac{x}{y} = \frac{2}{3}$, $\frac{y}{x}$, which is the reciprocal of $\frac{x}{y}$, must be equal to $\frac{3}{2}$. Also, $\frac{y^2}{x^2}$ is equal to $\left(\frac{y}{x}\right)^2$, so $\frac{y^2}{x^2}$ is equal to $\frac{9}{4}$. (I-2, I-8)

14. The entry following a_n in a sequence is determined by the rule $(a_n - 1)^2$, If 1 is an entry in the sequence, the next three entries are

(A) 0, –1, 2
(B) 0, –1, 1
(C) 0, 1, 2
(D) 2, 3, 4
(E) 0, 1, 0

(E) Starting with $a_n = 1$ the rule $(a_n - 1)^2 = (1 - 1)^2 = 0^2 = 0$ so the next entry is 0. Using 0 as a_n gives $(0 - 1)^2 = (-1)^2 = 1$ so the second entry is 1. Since using 1 as a_n gives 0 as the next entry, the entries after 1 should be 0, 1, 0. (II-6, II-1)

15. An employer pays 3 workers *X, Y,* and *Z* a total of $610 a week. *X* is paid 125% of the amount *Y* is paid and 80% of the amount *Z* is paid. How much does *X* make a week?

(A) $150
(B) $175
(C) $180
(D) $195
(E) $200

(E) X is paid 125%, or $\frac{5}{4}$ of Y's salary, so Y makes $\frac{4}{5}$ of what X makes. X makes 80% or $\frac{4}{5}$ of Z's salary, so Z makes $\frac{5}{4}$ of what X makes. Thus, the total salary of X, Y, and Z is the total of X's salary, $\frac{4}{5}$ of X's salary and $\frac{5}{4}$ X's salary. Therefore, the total is $\frac{61}{20}$ of X's salary. Since the total of the salaries is $610, X makes $\frac{20}{61}$ of $610, or $200. (II-3)

16. What is the maximum number of points of intersection of two circles which have unequal radii?

(A) none
(B) 1
(C) 2
(D) 3
(E) infinite

(C) Since the radii are unequal, the circles cannot be identical, thus (E) is incorrect. If two circles intersect in 3 points they must be identical, so (D) is also incorrect. Two different circles can intersect in 2 points without being identical, so (C) is the correct answer. (III–6)

17. If the area of a rectangle is equal to the area of a square, then the perimeter of the rectangle must be

(A) $\frac{1}{2}$ the perimeter of the square
(B) equal to the perimeter of the square
(C) equal to twice the perimeter of the square
(D) equal to the square root of the perimeter of the square
(E) none of the above

(E) Let L be the length and W be the width of the rectangle, and let S be the length of a side of the square. It is given that $LW = S^2$. A relation must be found between $2L + 2W$ and $4S$. It is possible to construct squares and rectangles so that (A), (B), (C), or (D) is false, so (E) is correct. For example, if the rectangle is a square, then the two figures are identical and (A), (C) and (D) are false. If the rectangle is not equal to a square, then the perimeter of the rectangle is larger than the perimeter of the square, so (B) is also false. (III-7)

Section 5
Sentence Correction

1. The principal reason for our failure was quite apparent to those whom we had brought into the venture.

(A) to those whom we had brought
(B) to them whom we had brought
(C) to the ones whom we had brought
(D) to those who we had brought
(E) to those who we had brung

(A) No error.

2. Although he was the most friendly of all present and different from the others, he hadn't hardly any friends except me.

(A) different from the others, he hadn't hardly any friends except me
(B) different than the others, he had hardly any friends except me
(C) different from the others, he had hardly any friends except me
(D) different than the others, he hadn't hardly any friends except I
(E) different from the others, he hardly had any friends except I

(C) This corrects the double negative (*hadn't hardly*). *Different from* is the correct idiom. *Me* is the correct form of the pronoun after the preposition *except*.

3. It was us who had left before he arrived.

(A) us who had left before he arrived
(B) we who had left before he arrived
(C) we who had went before he arrived
(D) us who had went before he arrived
(E) we who had left before the time he had arrived

(B) *We* is correct; a predicate pronoun is in the nominative case. *Had went* is an incorrect verb form (either *went* or *had gone*). (E) is not only wordy but the tense sequence is wrong (the *leaving* occurred before the *arriving*).

4. He is the sort of person who I feel would be capable of making these kind of statements.

(A) sort of person who I feel would be capable of making these kind of
(B) sort of a person who I feel would be capable of making these kind of
(C) sort of person who I feel would be capable of making these kinds of
(D) sort of person whom I feel would be capable of making these kinds of
(E) sort of person whom I feel would be capable of making this kind of

(C) An adjective should agree in number with the noun it modifies (*these kinds*). Although in choice (E) *this kind* is also correct, *whom* is not, since *who* is needed as the subject of *would be*. *The sort of a* is not correct idiom.

5. Due to the continual rain, a smaller number of spectators witnessed the game than had been expected.

(A) Due to the continual rain, a smaller number
(B) Due to the continuous rain, a smaller number
(C) Due to the continual rain, a lesser number
(D) Because of the rain that kept falling now and then, a smaller number
(E) Because of the continual rain, a smaller number

(E) *Because of* is used in an adverbial modifier. Although (D) does use *because of*, it is a wordier sentence. (C) is incorrect also because *lesser* is used to refer only to noncountable nouns.

6. Beside me, there were many persons who were altogether aggravated by his manners.

(A) Beside me, there were many persons who were altogether aggravated
(B) Beside me, there were many persons who were all together aggravated
(C) Besides me, there were many persons who were altogether aggravated
(D) Besides me, there were many persons who were altogether irritated
(E) Beside me, there were many persons who were all together irritated

(D) *Besides* means *in addition to*. *Irritated* is correct. A person is irritated; a situation or condition is aggravated.

7. The owner, who was a kind man, spoke to the boy and he was very rude.

(A) , who was a kind man, spoke to the boy and he
(B) was a kind man and he spoke to the boy and he
(C) spoke to the boy kindly and the boy
(D) , a kind man, spoke to the boy who
(E) who was a kind man spoke to the boy and he

(D) The appositive, *a kind man*, can easily replace the clause *who was a kind man*. The words *and he*, where the antecedent of *he* is vague, should be replaced by *who*, which refers specifically to *boy*.

8. Because we cooperated together, we divided up the work on the report which had been assigned.

(A) together, we divided up the work on the report which had been assigned
(B) together, we divided the work on the report which had been assigned
(C) , we divided up the work on the report which was assigned
(D) , we divided the work on the assigned report
(E) we divided up the work on the assigned report

(D) *Together* and *up* are included in the meaning of other words in the sentence. The adjective *assigned* is preferable stylistically to the adjective clause *which was assigned*.

9. The senator rose up to say that, in his opinion, he thought the bill should be referred back to committee.

(A) rose up to say that, in his opinion, he thought the bill should be referred back
(B) rose up to say that he thought the bill should be referred back
(C) rose up to say that he thought the bill should be referred
(D) rose up to say that, in his opinion, the bill should be referred
(E) rose to say that he thought the bill should be referred

(E) The words *up*, *in his opinion*, and *back* are unnecessary.

10. I don't know as I concur with your decision to try and run for office.

(A) as I concur with your decision to try and
(B) that I concur in your decision to try to
(C) as I concur in your decision to try and
(D) that I concur with your decision to try to
(E) as I concur with your decision to try, to

(B) *As* is an incorrect vulgarism after the verb *know*. One concurs *in* a decision. The infinitive *try* should be followed by *to*.

11. Jones, the president of the union and who is also a member of the community group, will be in charge of the negotiations.

(A) and who is also a member of the community group
(B) since he is a member of the community group
(C) a member of the community group
(D) also being a member of the community group
(E), in addition, who is a member of the community group

(C) Nouns in apposition must be parallel to one another: "Jones, the *president* ... and a *member*..."

12. The instructor told the student to hold the club lightly, keeping his eye on the ball and drawing the club back quickly, but too much force should not be used on the downward stroke.

(A) to hold the club lightly, keeping his eye on the ball and drawing the club back quickly, but too much force should not be used
(B) to hold the club lightly, keep his eye on the ball, and drawing the club back quickly, and too much force should not be used
(C) to hold the club lightly, keep his eye on the ball, draw the club back quickly, and not use too much force
(D) to hold the club lightly, keep his eye on the ball, draw the club back quickly and too much force should not be used
(E) he should hold the club lightly, keeping his eye on the ball, drawing the club back quickly, and not using too much force

(C) Four infinitives are in parallel form and much clearer than the mixture of an infinitive (*to hold*), two verbals (*keeping* and *drawing*), and a clause (*too much force should not be used*).

13. The horse, ridden by the experienced jockey with the broken leg, had to be destroyed.

(A) horse, ridden by the experienced jockey with the broken leg, had
(B) horse ridden by the experienced jockey with the broken leg had
(C) horse with the broken leg ridden by the experienced, jockey had
(D) horse with the broken leg ridden by the experienced jockey, had
(E) horse with the broken leg, ridden by the experienced jockey, had

(E) *With the broken leg* is a misplaced modifier. Commas are needed to set off the nonrestrictive clause *ridden by the experienced jockey*.

14. Our guest let us know that he would be arriving next week in his last letter.

(A) that he would be arriving next week in his last letter
(B) that he was arriving next week in his last letter
(C) that he will arrive next week in his last letter
(D) in his last letter that he would be arriving next week
(E) in his last letter that he was arriving next week

(D) The misplaced modifier, *in his last letter*, gives the mistaken impression that the guest would be arriving *in* the letter. The phrase should be near *know*, which it modifies. In choice (E) the tense is incorrect.

15. Whoever objects to me going to the convention ought to state his position promptly.

(A) Whoever objects to me
(B) Whomever objects to me
(C) Whomever objects to my
(D) Whoever objects to my
(E) Whoever has an objection to me

(D) The possessive form of *me* (*my*) is used before a verb form ending in *ing* and used as a noun (*going*). *Whoever* is correct as the subject.

16. The reason that the number of accidents this year is greater than that of last year is because Americans are uninterested in safety techniques.

(A) is greater than that of last year is because
(B) is greater than last year is because
(C) is greater than last year is that
(D) is greater than that of last year is that
(E) is greater than the number of accidents last year is because

(D) Don't use the expression *the reason is because*; both *reason* and *because* have similar meanings. Choice (C) is incorrect because it compares *number of accidents* with *last year*.

17. Julio found the new job more preferable to the one he had left so he decided to continue on for a while.

(A) more preferable to the one he had left so he decided to continue on
(B) preferable to the one he had left so he decided to continue on
(C) more preferable to the one he had left so he decided to continue
(D) preferable to the one he had left so he decided to continue
(E) more preferable than the one he had left so he decided to continue

(D) The words *more* and *on* are unnecessary.

18. Since we are living in New York for five years, we are reluctant to move to another city.

(A) Since we are living
(B) Being that we are living
(C) Being that we have been
(D) Since we have been living
(E) Since we were living

(D) The present perfect tense is required for action begun in the past and continuing into the present. *Being that* is an incorrect idiom.

19. As a child, my parents took me to Chicago to visit my grandfather.

(A) As a child, my parents took me to Chicago to visit my grandfather.
(B) My parents took me to Chicago to visit my grandfather as a child.
(C) My parents took me, as a child, to Chicago to visit my grandfather.
(D) A child, my parents took me to Chicago to visit my grandfather.
(E) When I was a child, my parents took me to Chicago to visit my grandfather.

(E) This corrects the modifier *as a child*, which is incorrectly referring to *my parents*.

20. He said that, if he were elected president and that if funds were available, that he would create a national theater.

(A) he were elected president and that if funds were available, that
(B) elected president, and funds were available, that
(C) he were elected president and funds were available, that
(D) he were elected president and funds were available,
(E) elected president, and funds were available,

(D) Two *that*'s can be dispensed with, as well as one *if*.

21. Having managed the team for years, he understood the players.

(A) Having managed the team for years, he understood the players.
(B) After managing the team for years, the players were understood by him.
(C) Having managed the team for years, the players were understood by him.
(D) For years having managed the team, its players were understood by him.
(E) Because he had managed the team for years, its players were understood by him.

(A) No error. The use of the passive voice in choice (C) is less preferable.

Section 6 Reading Comprehension

(The passage for questions 1–9 appears on page 59.)

1. Which of the following titles best exemplifies the passage?

(A) ***Declines and Falls***
(B) ***Nationalism and Philosophy***
(C) ***Contemporary American Literature***
(D) ***The State of Contemporary Philosophy***
(E) ***The Study of Philosophy***

(D) Alternatives (A) and (E) are too general. The passage does not deal with nationalism (B) nor American literature (C). The passage considers the present state or condition of philosophy.

2. According to the passage, philosophers are concerned today with the subject of

(A) political theory
(B) philosophical inquiry
(C) outdated works
(D) abstract versions of social theory
(E) public affairs

(B) While philosophers may be concerned with subjects such as (A) and (E), the passage poses a philosophical inquiry in paragraph 6.

3. The author states that the philosopher is constantly

(A) out of touch with general history
(B) defining his discipline
(C) determining objectives
(D) investigating specific phenomena
(E) providing radical alternatives

(B) In lines 36–39, the author states that "the philosopher is forever plagued by the question of what his discipline is about," i.e., defining his discipline.

4. The moral philosopher does not have to

(A) be in touch with general history
(B) recommend a course of action
(C) account to his colleagues
(D) study linguistics
(E) be in touch with reality

(B) The difference between a moral philosopher and a moralist is that the latter must present solutions, or courses of action. The moral philosopher, on the other hand, only considers moral questions without taking a position on them. See paragraph 5.

5. Many philosophers feel that the study of philosophy should become more

(A) technical
(B) popular
(C) cautious
(D) moralistic
(E) dialectic

(A) The author states in the second paragraph that the study of philosophy has, in many cases, embraced the use of codes, symbols, and dialects instead of prose. In short, studies have become more technical (hence the use of symbols).

6. Which of the following subjects *is not* generally studied by academic philosophers?

(A) Time machines
(B) Possible worlds
(C) External worlds
(D) Linguistics
(E) Moral issues

(C) Few academic philosophers study the subject of the external world. See paragraph 2.

7. Recently, the field of philosophy has included

I. intelligence testing
II. language training
III. pure research

(A) I only
(B) II only
(C) I and II only
(D) II and III only
(E) I, II, and III

(A) Of the three alternatives, only I (intelligence testing) is mentioned. See the next to last paragraph.

8. Which of the following statements best exemplifies the author's feelings?

(A) Philosophy is in moral decay.
(B) Talented people no longer study philosophy.
(C) Historians have replaced philosophers.
(D) Few academic philosophers are left.
(E) Philosophers are too cautious.

(E) An examination of the alternatives can be made by reading paragraph 1. Alternatives (A) and (B) are ruled out. (C) is not true; or, rather, some of the subjects studied by philosophers are now studied by historians. (D) is not mentioned anywhere in the passage.

9. A criticism of philosophy is its lack of

(A) models and constructs
(B) concepts
(C) scientific logic
(D) purity
(E) thematic perception

(A) The author claims that philosophy does not have "a body of accepted beliefs to build on" (last paragraph)—i.e., frameworks, or models and constructs.

(The passage for questions 10–17 appears on page 61.)

10. According to the passage, the growth in federal support was greatest for

(A) goods and services
(B) social science research
(C) defense and welfare
(D) endowment for the arts
(E) physical sciences

(D) Federal expenditure on goods and services increased sixfold (from 1950 to 1970): for social science research, federal support increased 13 times; for defense and welfare no figures were given; for endowment for the arts expenditures increased 20 times (between 1966 and 1974); and for the physical sciences the increase was 6 times. (See paragraph 1.)

11. The major objective of the passage is to

(A) increase appreciation for the arts
(B) provide an ideological basis for artistic funding
(C) explain why government supports cultural activities
(D) argue for more government support of the arts and sciences
(E) demonstrate cultural activities in the United States

(C) The author's objective is to provide "alternative explanations for the government's involvement in the production of culture" (paragraph 2).

12. Which of the models discussed in the passage represents the statement: "Funding should be provided to the best artists and scientists"?

(A) Science and art for their own sake
(B) Science and art for business application
(C) Science and art for government programs
(D) Science and art for ideological control
(E) All models for government investment

(A) See lines 85–92: ". . . federal funding should be allocated to the most creative artists . . . ."

13. A corollary of the science and art for government programs is

(A) funding should be provided by government only as a last resort
(B) funding will be geared to projects of value to the government
(C) funding is to be provided only to non-governmental employees
(D) funding by the government is self-defeating
(E) funding by the government is inflationary

(B) Alternative (A) belongs to the first model; alternatives (C) through (E) are not given in the passage.

14. A conclusion reached by the author of the passage is that

(A) the arts and sciences have been funded by the government for different reasons
(B) government is a neutral observer of the arts and sciences
(C) government intervention in the arts and sciences is declining
(D) the arts and sciences are not dependent on government funding
(E) politics and science go together

(A) The author is trying to show empirically how the government funds the arts and sciences, but for different reasons, i.e., as a consumer, as an influencer, and as a subsidizer.

15. Government intervention in the arts and sciences should coincide with

(A) government's ability to pay
(B) fluctuations in the business cycle
(C) political needs
(D) economic needs of the arts and sciences community
(E) the number of needy scientists

(D) See the second sentence of the last paragraph.

16. The idea that government should support the arts and sciences only when the market does not provide enough funds belongs to which school?

(A) "Their own sake"
(B) "Business application"
(C) "Government programs"
(D) "Ideological control"
(E) All of the above

(A) The idea expressed in the question is suggested by the "science and art for their own sake" model, in the sentence: ". . . the government intervenes directly as the final patron of public goods that would otherwise be unavailable," i.e., not purchased or supported by non-governmental or market forces.

17. The idea that cultural goods can no longer be provided solely by the market system is given by

(A) the author of the passage
(B) the first model of government patronage
(C) the second model of government patronage
(D) the third model of government patronage
(E) the fourth model of government patronage

(B) The idea expressed in the question can be found in the section "Science and art for their own sake," especially in the first paragraph of the section.

(The passage for questions 18–25 appears on page 63.)

18. According to the passage, unemployment is an index of

(A) overutilization of capacity
(B) economic slack and lost output
(C) diminished resources
(D) the employment rate
(E) undercapacity

(B) See paragraph 1, line 1: "Unemployment is an important index of economic slack and lost output . . . ."

19. While unemployment is damaging to many, it falls most heavily upon all except the

(A) black
(B) semiskilled
(C) unskilled
(D) underemployed
(E) white middle class

(E) See paragraph 1: "It falls most heavily on the young, the semiskilled [B] and unskilled [C], the black person [A], the older worker, and the underemployed person [D]."

20. The cost to society of unemployment can be measured by all except

(A) lost incomes
(B) idleness
(C) juvenile delinquency
(D) disruption of careers
(E) the death rate

(E) See paragraph 2: In the first line are included the costs of involuntary idleness (B) and income lost (A), followed by (C) and (D) in the next sentence.

21. Serious unemployment leads labor groups to demand

(A) more jobs by having everyone work shorter hours
(B) higher wages to those employed
(C) "no fire" policies
(D) cost-cutting solutions
(E) higher social security payments

(A) See paragraph 3: "On the side of labor, prolonged high unemployment leads to 'share-the-work' pressures for shorter hours . . ."; i.e., if workers are employed fewer hours, there will be "more jobs."

22. According to the passage, a typical business reaction to a recession is to press for

(A) higher unemployment insurance
(B) protection against imports
(C) government action
(D) restrictive business practices
(E) restraint against union activity

(B) In paragraph 3: "On the side of business, the weakness of markets [i.e., a recession] leads to . . . pressures for protection against foreign . . . competition"—i.e., protection against imports. (A) was not mentioned, (C) is too vague, and (D) was implied by "protection against . . . domestic competition" but is also vague.

23. The demand for labor is

(A) a derived demand
(B) declining
(C) about 4 percent of the total work force
(D) underutilized
(E) dependent upon technology

(A) See paragraph 4: "The demand for labor is derived from the demand for the goods and services which labor participates in producing."

24. Gross national product (GNP) is a measure of

(A) personal consumption
(B) net exports
(C) domestic investment
(D) government purchases of goods and services
(E) our total output

(E) See paragraph 5: GNP is a measure of the total goods and services produced, "our total output." It consists of the components in (A), (B), (C), and (D).

25. According to the passage, a satisfactory level of unemployment is

(A) 85 percent of the civilian work force
(B) 90 percent of the civilian work force
(C) 4 percent unemployment
(D) 2 percent unemployment
(E) no unemployment

(C) Mention was made in paragraph 4 of reducing unemployment to a level of 4 percent (employment of 96 percent of the civilian work force), and it can be inferred that this figure constitutes a ''satisfactory level'' of unemployment.

Section 7
Data Sufficiency

1. A piece of wood 5 feet long is cut into three smaller pieces. How long is the longest of the three pieces?

(1) One piece is 2 feet 7 inches long.
(2) One piece is 7 inches longer than another piece and the remaining piece is 5 inches long.

(D) STATEMENT (1) alone is sufficient. 2 feet 7 inches is more than half of 5 feet, so the piece which is 2 feet 7 inches long must be longer than the other two pieces put together.

STATEMENT (2) alone is sufficient. Since one piece is 5 inches long, the sum of the lengths of the remaining two pieces is 4 feet, 7 inches. Since one piece is 7 inches longer than the other, $L + (L + 7 \text{ in.}) = 4 \text{ ft. } 7 \text{ in.}$, where L is the length of the smaller of the two remaining pieces. Solving the equations yields $L + 7$ in. as the length of the longest piece.

2. AC is a diameter of the circle. ACD is a straight line. What is the value of x?

(1) $AB = BC$
(2) $x = 2y$

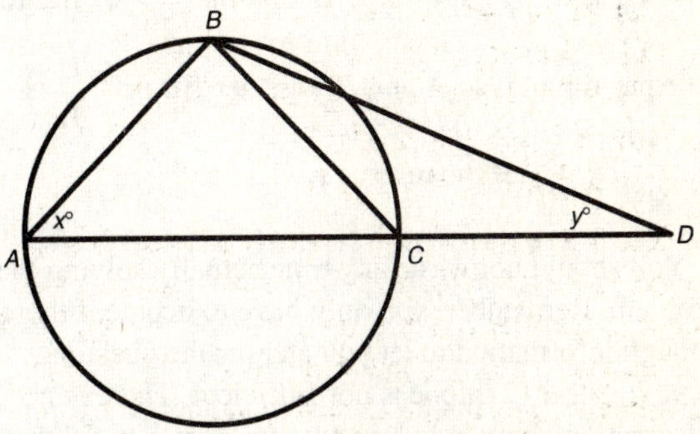

(A) Since AC is a diameter, angle ABC is inscribed in a semicircle and is therefore a right angle.

STATEMENT (1) alone is sufficient since it implies the two other angles in the triangle must be equal. Since the sum of the angles of a triangle is 180°, we can deduce that $x = 45$.

STATEMENT (2) alone is not sufficient. There is no information about the angle ABD; so STATEMENT (2) cannot be used to find the angles of triangle ABD.

3. What is the value of y?

(1) $x + 2y = 6$
(2) $y^2 - 2y + 1 = 0$

(B) STATEMENT (2) alone is sufficient, $y^2 - 2y + 1$ equals $(y - 1)^2$, and the only solution of $(y - 1)^2 = 0$ is $y = 1$.

STATEMENT (1) alone is not sufficient. $x + 2y = 6$ implies $y = 3 - \frac{x}{2}$, but there are no data given about the value of x.

4. Two pipes, A and B, empty into a reservoir. Pipe A can fill the reservoir in 30 minutes by itself. How long will it take for pipe A and pipe B together to fill up the reservoir?

(1) By itself, pipe B can fill the reservoir in 20 minutes.
(2) Pipe B has a larger cross-sectional area than pipe A.

(A) STATEMENT (1) alone is sufficient. Pipe A fills up $\frac{1}{30}$ of the reservoir per minute.

STATEMENT (1) says pipe B fills up $\frac{1}{20}$ of the reservoir per minute, so A and B together fill up $\frac{1}{20} + \frac{1}{30}$ or $\frac{5}{60}$ or $\frac{1}{12}$ of the reservoir.

You should not waste any time actually solving the problem. Remember, you only have to decide if there is enough information to let you answer the question.

STATEMENT (2) alone is not sufficient. There is no information about how long it takes pipe B to fill the reservoir.

5. *AB* is perpendicular to *CO*. Is *A* or *B* closer to *C*?

(1) *OA* is less than *OB*.
(2) *ACBD* is not a parallelogram.

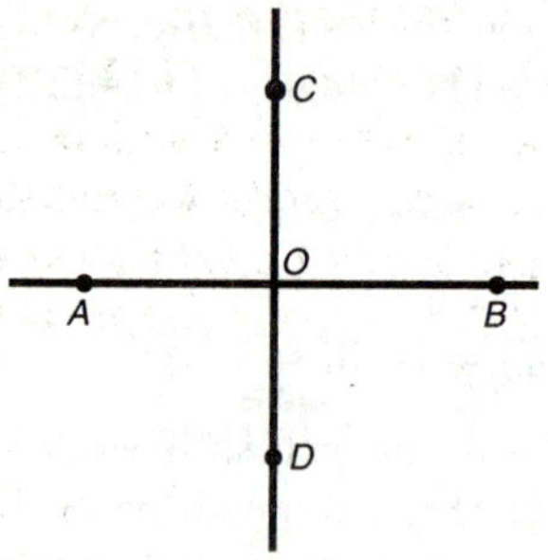

(A) STATEMENT (1) alone is sufficient . Draw the lines AC and BC; then AOC and BOC are right triangles, since AB is perpendicular to CO. By the Pythagorean theorem, $(AC)^2 = (AO)^2 + (CO)^2$ and $(BC)^2 = (OB)^2 + (CO)^2$; so if AO is less than OB, then AC is less than BC.

STATEMENT (2) alone is not sufficient. There is no restriction on where the point D is.

6. Is *xy* greater than 1? *x* and *y* are both positive.

(1) *x* is less than 1.
(2) *y* is greater than 1.

(E) STATEMENTS (1) and (2) together are not sufficient. If $x = \frac{1}{2}$ and $y = 3$, then xy is greater than 1, but if $x = \frac{1}{2}$ and $y = \frac{3}{2}$, then xy is less than 1. This is a good example of the use of specific values for x and y to decide whether the given statements are sufficient to deduce the desired conclusion.

7. Does $x = y$?

(1) $z = u$
(2) *ABCD* is a parallelogram.

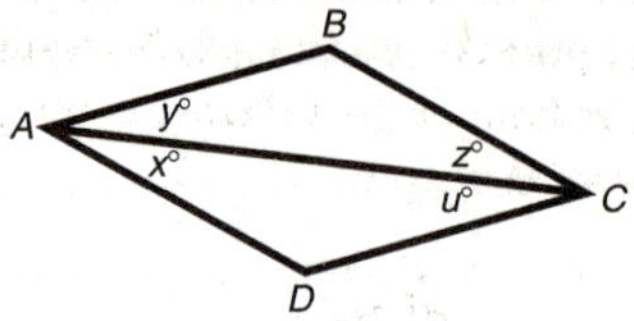

(C) STATEMENT (1) alone is not sufficient. By moving the point B along the original side BC, we can have either $x = y$ or $x \neq y$ and still have $z = u$.

STATEMENT (2) alone is not sufficient. It implies that $x = z$ and $y = u$, but gives no information to compare x and y. STATEMENTS (1) and (2) together, however, yield $x = y$.

8. Train *T* leaves town *A* for town *B* and travels at a constant rate of speed. At the same time, train *S* leaves town *B* for town *A* and also travels at a constant rate of speed. Town *C* is between *A* and *B*. Which train is traveling faster? Towns A, C, B lie on a straight line.

(1) Train *S* arrives at town *C* before train *T*.
(2) *C* is closer to *A* than to *B*.

(C) STATEMENT (1) alone is not sufficient. If town C were closer to B, even if S were going slower than T, S could arrive at C first. But if you also use STATEMENT (2), then train S must be traveling faster than train T, since it is further than B to C than it is from A to C.

So STATEMENTS (1) and (2) together are sufficient.

STATEMENT (2) alone is insufficient since it gives no information about the trains.

9. Does $x = y$?

(1) *BD* is perpendicular to *AC*.
(2) *AB* is equal to *BC*.

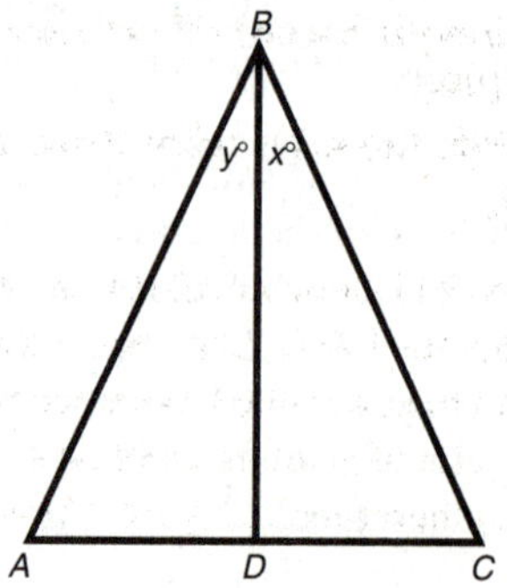

(C) STATEMENT (2) alone is not sufficient, since D can be any point on the line AC if we assume only STATEMENT (2).

STATEMENT (1) alone is not sufficient. Depending on the position of point C, x and y can be equal or unequal. For example, in both of the following triangles BD is perpendicular to AC.

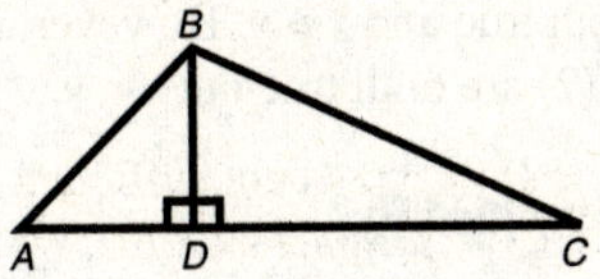

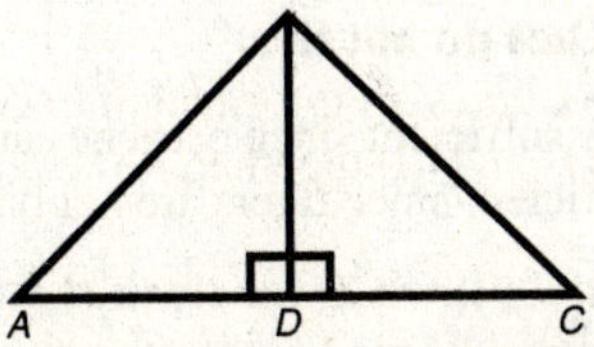

If STATEMENTS (1) and (2) are both true, then $x = y$. The triangles ABD and BDC are both right triangles with two pairs of corresponding sides equal; the triangles are therefore congruent and $x = y$.

10. What is the value of $x + y$?

(1) $x - y = 4$
(2) $3x + 3y = 4$

(B) STATEMENT (2) alone is sufficient, since $3x + 3y$ is $3(x + y)$. (Therefore, if $3x + 3y = 4$, then $x + y = \frac{4}{3}$.)

STATEMENT (1) alone is not sufficient, since you need another equation besides $x - y = 4$ to find the values of x and y.

11. Did the *XYZ* Corporation have higher sales in 1988 or in 1989? Assume sales are positive.

(1) In 1988 the sales were twice the average (arithmetic mean) of the sales in 1988, 1989, and 1990.
(2) In 1990, the sales were three times those in 1989.

(A) STATEMENT (1) alone is sufficient. We know that the total of sales for 1988, 1989, and 1990 is three times the average and that sales in 1988 were twice the average. Then the total of sales in 1989 and 1990 was equal to the average. Therefore, sales were less in 1989 than in 1968.

STATEMENT (2) alone is insufficient, since it does not relate sales in 1989 to sales in 1988.

12. Is *ABDC* a square?

(1) *BC* is perpendicular to *AD*.
(2) *BE* = *EC*.

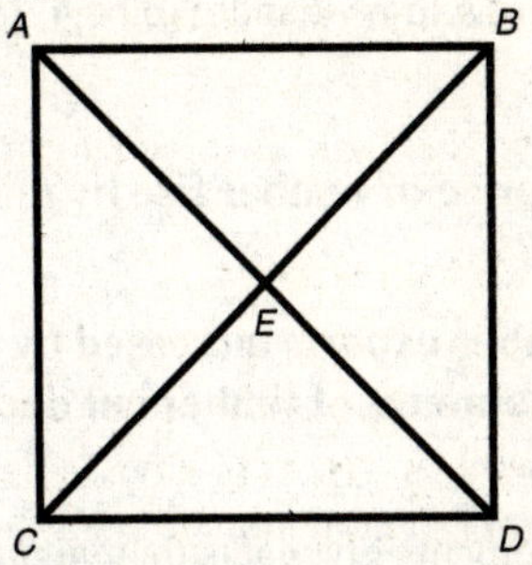

(E) STATEMENTS (1) and (2) together are not sufficient, since the points A and D can be moved and STATEMENTS (1) and (2) will still be satisfied.

13. k is an integer. Is k divisible by 12?

(1) k is divisible by 4.
(2) k is divisible by 3.

(C) List the first few numbers that are divisible by 4, such as 4, 8, 12, 16, 20, 24, . . . and list the first few numbers that are divisible by 3, such as 3, 6, 9, 12, 15, 18, 21, 24, ... Notice that the integers that appear in both lists are divisible by 12. STATEMENT (1) alone is not sufficient, since 24 and 16 are both divisible by 4 but only 24 is divisible by 12.

STATEMENT (2) alone is not sufficient, since 24 and 15 are divisible by 3 but 15 is not divisible by 12.

STATEMENT (1) implies that $k = 4m$ for some integer m. If you assume STATEMENT (2), then since k is divisible by 3, either 4 or m is divisible by 3. Since 4 is not divisible by 3, m must be. Therefore, $m = 3j$, where j is some integer and $k = 4 \times 3j$ or $12j$. So k is divisible by 12. Therefore, STATEMENTS (1) and (2) together are sufficient.

14. How far is it from *A* to *B*?

(1) It is 15 miles from *A* to *C*.
(2) It is 25 miles from *C* to *B*.

(E) STATEMENTS (1) and (2) together are not sufficient, because there is no information about the location of C relative to the locations of A and B.

15. Is x an even integer? Assume n and p are integers.

(1) $x = (n + p)^2$
(2) $x = 2n + 10p$

(B) An even integer is an integer divisible by 2. Since $2n + 10p$ is 2 times $(n + 5p)$ using (2) lets you deduce that x is even. (1) by itself is not sufficient. If n were 2 and p were 3, $(n + p)^2$ would be 25 which is not even, but by choosing n to be 2 and p to be 4, $(n + p)^2$ is 36 which is even.

16. Did the price of lumber rise by more than 10% last year?

(1) Lumber exports increased by 20%
(2) The amount of timber cut decreased by 10%.

(E) Both statements give facts that *might* explain why the price of lumber rose. However, even using both statements you can't deduce what happened to the price of lumber.

17. What was the price of a dozen eggs during the 15th week of the year 1977?

(1) During the first week of 1977 the price of a dozen eggs was 75¢.
(2) The price of a dozen eggs rose 1¢ a week every week during the first four months of 1977.

(C) You need (1) to know what the price was at the beginning of 1977. Using (2) you could then compute the price during the fifteenth week. Either statement alone is insufficient. You should not actually compute the price since it would only waste time.

18. Is DE parallel to BC? $DB = AD$:

(1) $AE = EC$
(2) $DB = EC$

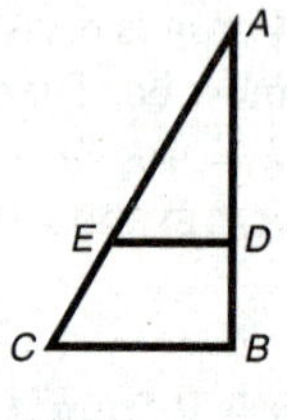

(A) (1) alone is sufficient since the line connecting the midpoints of 2 sides of a triangle is parallel to the third side. (2) alone is insufficient. In an isosceles triangle statement (2) would imply that ED is parallel to BC, but in a non-isosceles triangle, (2) would imply that ED and BC are not parallel.

19. Is $x > y$?

(1) $\frac{x}{y} = \frac{5}{4}$

(2) $x^2 > y^2$

(E) If you answered incorrectly you probably assumed that x and y were positive. If $x = 5$ and $y = 4$, then (1) and (2) are both true and $x > y$. However, if $x = -5$ and $y = -4$, (1) and (2) are both true but $x < y$.

20. Does every bird fly?

(1) Tigers do not fly.
(2) Ostriches do not fly.

(B) (2) alone is sufficient since ostriches are birds. (1) alone is not sufficient since tigers are not birds.

21. Find $x + 2y$.

(1) $x - y = 12$
(2) $3x - 3y = 36$

(E) Since the equation in (2) has exactly the same solutions as the equation in (1), $3(x - y) = 3x - 3y$ and $3(12) = 36$, you can't determine x and y even by using both (1) and (2). If $x = 12$ and $y = 0$, then (1) and (2) are true and $x + 2y = 12$, but if $x = 6$ and $y = -6$, (1) and (2) are again true but $x + 2y = -6$.

Evaluating Your Score

Tabulate your score for each section of the Diagnostic Test according to the directions on pages 6–7 and record the results in the Self-Scoring Table below. Then find your rating for each score on the Self-Scoring Scale and record it in the appropriate blank.

Self-Scoring Table

SECTION	SCORE	RATING
1		
2		
3		
4		
5		
6		
7		

***Self-Scoring Scale*—RATING**

SECTION	POOR	FAIR	GOOD	EXCELLENT
1	0 – 12+	13 – 17+	18 – 21+	22 – 25
2	0 – 8+	9 – 11	11+ – 14	14+ – 17
3	0 – 8+	9 – 11	11+ – 14	14+ – 17
4	0 – 8+	9 – 11	11+ – 14	14+ – 17
5	0 – 9+	10 – 13+	14 – 17+	18 – 21
6	0 – 12+	13 – 17+	18 – 21+	22 – 25
7	0 – 9+	10 – 13+	14 – 17+	18 – 21

The following Review sections cover material for each type of question on the GMAT. Spend more time studying those sections for which you had a rating of FAIR or POOR on the Diagnostic Test.

To obtain an approximation of your actual GMAT score, see page 6.

4 ESSAY WRITING REVIEW

The GMAT Analytical Writing Assessment

The addition of a one-hour "analytical writing assessment" to the GMAT exam, beginning in October of 1994, is the most significant change in the test since it was first administered. The Analytical Writing Assessment (AWA) consists of two essay questions, each of which is allotted 30 minutes.

In general, the addition of the essay questions (and the reduction of the number of multiple-choice questions) will probably favor persons accustomed to expressing their thoughts in concise and well-organized written English. The Analytical Writing Assessment will be the first portion of the test administered, so be prepared to start when you are fresh.

Each essay will be scored by two graders, who are college and university instructors from various schools and departments experienced in teaching and evaluating writing. Each essay will be scored "holistically," which means that it will be assigned one score (between 0 and 6, with 0 being the lowest and 6 the highest) by each reader, based on its overall quality. The two scores for each essay are averaged, and then the two average scores (one for each essay) are averaged again to produce the writing score, which is reported on a scale of 0 to 6, rounded off to the nearest half point.

Each essay must be written in a number 2 pencil in the answer booklet provided at the test center. Three pages are allotted for each essay. You must fit your essay in the space provided and write as legibly as you can. Essays that cannot be read will receive a score of 0.

Writing an Essay

Many students dread the thought of writing an essay on an assigned topic, but it need not be that difficult. Writing an essay that will receive a holistic score of 4, 5, or even 6 requires no more than some common sense, a little on-the-spot planning, familiarity with the standards of written English, and a healthy amount of practice. Indeed, the best way to improve your writing ability is through practice. The more you write, the more comfortable and confident you become with the process, and this will show in the essays you produce.

This chapter cannot substitute for a writing course or for a lifetime of practice, but it will outline some helpful points and strategies for improving your writing and scoring higher on the GMAT Analytical Writing Assessment.

Types of Questions

The essay questions on the GMAT fall into two types: the analysis of an issue and the analysis of an argument. Both types of questions expect you to explore some complexities of the topic, to take a position, and to demonstrate critical reasoning abilities. The questions will not require you to have any pre-existing knowledge of the subject or any specific business training or experience. Some topics may relate to business, but others will be about areas of general interest or current events and issues.

General Strategy

The most important thing your essay must do is take a position. Even if you are not entirely sure that you would always agree with that position, *take a position.* You are not deciding on an irrevocable course in life—you are writing an essay to be assessed on the basis of how well it is written. Support your position with examples organized in a logical order; restate your position in a conclusion. Remember that there are no right or wrong answers to these questions, just well-written or poorly written ones. Don't try to guess what the graders' feelings about the issue might be so you can agree. Take a position upon which you can develop examples and supportive arguments. Make it a specific position; don't try to be too broad: it is much easier to put together ideas about banning automatic assault rifles than it is to discuss the use or misuse of firearms in general.

The second most important thing your essay needs is good organization. Stop and plan before you begin writing. Place your arguments or examples in the most logical order and provide reasonable transitions between them. Usually, three examples are enough.

Finally, you need to concentrate on writing a good beginning and a good conclusion. Your opening sets the stage and draws the reader in; your conclusion clinches your point and leaves your argument fresh in the graders' minds when they assign a score.

Overall Strategy

1. Narrow the topic.
2. Take a position.
3. Use three examples or points and connect them logically.
4. Write a good, interesting opening and a strong, memorable conclusion.

How to Write an Essay in 30 Minutes

Don't be misled by the title of this section. It promises more than it can deliver. For one thing, writing an essay in 30 minutes may be a contradiction in terms. An essay is essentially the product of a writer's thinking about a topic. It expresses a point of view arrived at after reflection, analysis, or interpretation of a subject or issue. When you are given an assignment only 30 minutes before the essay is due, you can't expect to pore over the topic for long. If you think too deeply, before you know it you'll have thought the allotted time away.

A second reason to distrust the title is that no one learns to write well by reading a "how-to" book on the subject. You learn essay writing by taking a pen in hand, by messing around with ideas and words, and by experimenting, practicing, and doing. Many of the in-class essays you've had to produce for social science or humanities courses have probably been good training for the kind of instant essay required by the GMAT Analytical Writing Assessment. In your classes, though, success was often determined by how closely your essay resembled what the teacher had in mind. That's not true on the GMAT, which won't give you a topic with a predetermined answer. You can't study for this essay writing test the way you can study calculus or Spanish. What you need to know is already lodged inside you. The task you face on test day is to organize your ideas and put them into readable form on a piece of paper, which takes practice, practice, practice. Just as athletic skills improve with repetition, so do essay writing skills. All you need each time you schedule a writing session is 30 minutes.

The next several pages will take you inside essay writing. By entering the territory, you won't become a world-class author of essays, but you'll see what most good writers do as they write essays. You'll be shown what works and what to watch out for. The rest is up to you.

A Dozen Principles of Good Writing

Success in essay writing depends in large measure on how completely you can master these 12 guidelines:

1. Study the topic closely.
2. Narrow the topic.
3. Decide what point(s) to make about the topic.
4. Collect ideas and put them in order.
5. Start with an appealing and informative introduction.
6. Develop your ideas with specific examples and details.
7. Guide readers with transitions.
8. Use plain, precise, lively, and fresh words.
9. Omit needless words.
10. Vary your sentences.
11. End your essay unforgettably.
12. Follow the conventions of standard English.

Refer to these guidelines often. If your writing usually demonstrates mastery of these 12 principles, you're undoubtedly a terrific writer. To be a still better one, though, you must know that occasionally one or more of the principles ought to be set aside. When a principle leads you to say something barbaric, ignore it for the time being. Let your intuition and good judgment guide you instead. The principles, after all, merely describe what most good writers do; they are not commandments.

Through experience, accomplished and experienced essayists have absorbed good writing habits into their craft. Professionals needn't be reminded, for example, to cut needless words from their writing or to prefer the plain word to the pompous one.

The Process of Writing an Essay

To start, plan what to do during each stage of the process. The first stage, *prewriting*, consists of all you do before you actually begin writing the text of your essay. During the second stage, *composing*, you are choosing the words and forming the sentences that contain your thoughts. And finally, during the *revising and proofreading* stage, you polish and refine the text of your essay word by word, making it true, clear, and graceful. Actually, the lines between the stages are not at all distinct. Sometimes it helps to put words on paper during the prewriting stage. Writers compose, revise, and proofread simultaneously. New ideas may sprout at any time. No stage really ends until the final period of the last sentence is securely in place—or until time is up and test booklets are closed.

In spite of the blurry boundaries between the stages of the writing process, it pays to keep the functions of each stage in mind as you study in detail how the dozen principles of good writing contribute to the growth of a successful essay.

1. Study the Topic Closely

Obviously, your work on the GMAT essay question should start with a meticulous reading of the topic. Read it more than once, underscoring key ideas and words until you know it intimately. If in doubt, read it again.

Here is a typical essay topic for your scrutiny.

EXAMPLE

Concerned about the survival of democracy, the president of the University of Chicago, Robert Maynard Hutchings, once wrote, "The death of democracy is not likely to be an assassination from ambush. It will be a slow extinction from apathy, indifference, and undernourishment."

While democracy may still be alive and well, situations often arise that do not coincide with the democratic principles on which America was founded. Using examples based on your studies, on reading, or on personal experience, write an essay that illustrates your view on the current health of democracy.

Before reading the explanation, briefly write your understanding of what the topic asks you to do:

Explanation: The basic task is clearly spelled out in the last clause: *write an essay that illustrates your view on the current health of democracy.* The prompt and everything else merely creates a context for the task and provides some general clues to the meaning of "health of democracy." Other essential information is that the essay must use examples drawn from your studies—that is, course work or independent study; your reading, which includes fiction and nonfiction read for school or on your own; or relevant personal experiences.

All told, the topic gives students considerable leeway for interpretation. In fact, lengthy and complicated topics like this one often encourage students to blaze their own trails. Shorter topics, on the other hand, often tighten the reins on creativity.

Although writing about one's experience has a lot of merit, not every GMAT question allows students to write a personal response. But when possible, it's an option that may be too good to refuse, especially when the topic leaves you cold. Students are leading authorities on their own life and times. With a little finesse, almost any topic on the GMAT can be shaped into an interesting and readable personal essay.

2. Narrow the Topic Unmercifully

Because a GMAT topic must suit a multiethnic, multicultural, and multitalented student audience, it is bound to be very broad. Your first job is to reduce it to a size snug enough to fit your answer sheet. In fact, the quality of the essay you write could depend on how narrowly you define the topic. Think small. A cosmic approach won't work, and you are not likely to err by narrowing the topic too much. If you were to run out of things to say about a narrowed topic, the simple solution would be to expand the main idea in midstream, a far easier task than hacking away at an overweight topic after you've already filled most of a page.

It would be beyond the hope and talent of most students to compose a substantive 300 or 400 word essay on such topics as *democracy*, *psychology*, or *jazz*—subjects so vast you could probably fill a barn with books about them. The same holds true for any general subject, from *alcoholism* to *zoology*. Therefore, to keep your essay from being stuck in a mess of generalities, narrow the topic ruthlessly.

Try building a ladder of abstraction. Start at the top with the most general word. As you descend the ladder, make each rung increasingly specific. When you reach the bottom, you may have a topic sufficient for a short essay. Here are some examples:

SUBJECT: *Democracy*

Democracy	*Highest level of abstraction*
Democracy in conflict with totalitarianism	*Too broad for a short essay*
People's rights vs. government control	*Still too broad*
Freedom of press vs. government restrictions	*Still too broad*
The right to print opinions vs. censorship	*Still broad, but getting there*
The right to print a scandalous story in a school newspaper	*Possible topic for a short essay*
What happened to Pete when *The Globe* published a story about incompetent teachers	*Distinct possibility for an essay*

SUBJECT: *Alcoholism*

Alcoholism	*Highest level of abstraction*
The effects of alcoholism on society	*Extremely broad for a short essay*
Family problems resulting from alcoholism	*Still too broad*
Alcoholism as a cause of broken families	*Very broad, but getting closer*
The effects of alcoholism on children from broken homes	*Good only for a lengthy research paper*
The experience of Betsy G., the daughter of an alcoholic	*A definite topic for a short essay*

SUBJECT: *Zoology*

Zoology	*Highest level of abstraction*
The study of mammals	*Too broad*
The study of primates	*Still very broad*
Researching the behavior of chimpanzees	*Still too broad*
Teaching of chimps	*Still rather broad*
Training chimps to distinguish colors	*A reasonable topic*
My job in the primate lab working on the color recognition project	*A fine topic for a short paper*

Each subject has been pared down to a scale appropriate for a GMAT essay. Topics on the bottom rungs offer students a chance to write a thorough essay that will fit comfortably on the answer sheet. Focusing on a single idea may deny them the chance to demonstrate the scope of their knowledge. The GMAT, however, is not a place to show off breadth, but rather to display depth. Business school applications show breadth. For the present, it's depth that counts.

Practice in Narrowing Topics

Reduce several of the following subjects to a level of specificity concise enough to be used for a GMAT essay. Try constructing a ladder of abstraction for each one. Put the broadest topic on the top. Don't stop descending until you have a topic suitable for a short essay.

Youth and Age	Calamities
Procrastination	Probability
Jealousy	Truth
Taking Risks	Style
Change vs. Permanence	Wonder

3. Decide What Point(s) to Make About the Topic

An essay needs a point. Nothing will disappoint a reader more than arriving at the end only to discover that the essay lacks a point. Essays may be written with beautiful words, contain profound thoughts, and make readers laugh or weep. But without a point, sometimes called a *main idea* or a *thesis*, an essay remains just words in search of a meaning. After they've finished, readers may scratch their heads, say "Huh?" and resent having wasted their time. Don't confuse the topic of an essay with its point, for even a pointless essay is likely to be about something. But a topic isn't enough. An essay must also say something about its topic. It can be basically factual, but it should express a point of view about an issue.

Finding a Point for Your GMAT Essay

TOPIC: The topic will be given to you in the instructions for writing the essay.

Purpose: The purpose of the essay will be explained by the wording of the topic. Look for such words as *describe, compare, contrast, persuade, explain, report, analyze,* and *interpret.* Each requires a slightly different response. Or the purpose of the essay may be left up to you.

Point: The point is the essay's main idea or thesis, or what the essay demonstrates, proves, or argues.

Even if you have no particular opinion on an issue or topic, the hard fact is that you must still try to create the illusion that you care deeply about the issue. Doing so may rub your conscience the wrong way, but rather than raise a stink, which won't get you anywhere, make the best of it. This time go along to get along. Don't regard it as a cop-out. Rather, consider it a survival tactic, a challenge to your resilience and creativity, qualities that schools and businesses seek and admire.

Faced with the prospect of writing an essay about a topic that leaves you cold, you have some choices to make: Fake it, fight it, drop it, or psych yourself to do the best you can.

1. *Fake it.* Writing to say something even when you have nothing to say inevitably leads to words on a page that sound forced, like a conversation you might have with an aging aunt at Thanksgiving. Not a good choice.
2. *Fight it.* Some resentful students turn on the test or the test makers by attacking the admissions testing system in America. They write statements declaring their refusal to participate in a dehumanizing charade that fails to take into account each student as a unique individual. After the test, such students may feel relieved for having spoken their minds, but their position also will have irreparably damaged their chances of being admitted to the school of their choice. While admissions officials generally approve of individual initiative and an independent spirit, they won't bother with students who respond defiantly to a GMAT essay question. Not a good choice.
3. *Drop it.* Although this is the only foolproof way to keep yourself from writing a pointless essay, it's not a viable option when you're striving for good grades and high test scores. Not a good choice.
4. *Psych yourself.* This is the most promising solution. Begin by asking yourself ten or a dozen questions about the topic. Start with easy questions and work toward the harder ones.

Here, for example, are questions on the general topic

Dangerous Pursuits:
What are some dangerous pursuits?
Why do some people go bungee jumping?
Why don't I go bungee jumping?
Why does my cousin Henry go?

After a while, the questions and answers become more provocative:

When is it okay to gamble with your life?
Does the state have the right to forbid you from risking your life?
At what point in lawmaking does the government overstep its bounds?

Obviously, at the beginning of a 30-minute essay test, you won't have time to ask and answer dozens of questions, but the more thoughts you can generate, the richer your writing will be.

If self-psyching fails to work, try this alternative: As rapidly as possible write a list of anything, literally anything, that might qualify as a response to the topic. Like pulling a stopper, making a list often starts the flow of ideas. Your mind makes connections as one idea calls up memories of another, and then another. Don't be particular. After a short time, review the list and choose the idea that holds promise for your essay. Even if the list doesn't thrill you, pick the least objectionable item and begin to write on it. Who knows, you may have accidentally stumbled upon a rich lode of ideas. Writers often discover what they really want to say only after they've written for a while, even as long as 10 minutes. After that, time and space won't permit a complete rewrite, but a few crucial sentences could change the emphasis of what they've written, and they can quickly relocate ideas and restructure their essays with neatly drawn arrows.

Sometimes a better thesis suddenly swims into view halfway through the test. Should you change course or stick with what you have? It takes courage to return to "Go" and to start over. Because of time and space restraints on the GMAT, a switch could be fatal. In general, the new idea ought to be out of this world to justify trashing what you've written.

If you find yourself in such a predicament, don't switch unless you'll never again be able to look yourself in the eye. Grit your teeth and finish what you began. Resist the temptation to shift from your original idea even if you don't believe in it anymore. You won't be penalized for hypocrisy, but you will surely damage your essay with a confusing or ambivalent presentation.

Normally, the wording of a GMAT essay question forces you to take a position on the issue or topic. It might say to you directly, "State your opinion," or ask "Do you agree or disagree?" Your view then becomes the point, or thesis, of your essay. In the essay itself the thesis is usually stated outright in a simple declarative sentence, as in these examples:

TOPIC:	Democracy	Thesis: Democracy is a far more cumbersome form of government than dictatorship.
TOPIC:	Psychology	Thesis: When disciplining children, instilling a fear of punishment is more effective than promising a reward.
TOPIC:	War	Thesis: War is hell.

On the other hand, the thesis of an essay may be so strongly implied by the cumulative weight of evidence that stating the thesis is unnecessary. Whichever way you decide to inform the reader of your essay's thesis—by announcing it directly or by weaving it subtly into the fabric of the text—be sure to lock onto it as you write. Let it guide you from the opening lines to your conclusion. Omit material that causes the essay to wander from its point. Readers will appreciate an essay that rarely deviates from a well-defined path.

4. Collect Ideas and Arrange Them in Order

Unless you are blessed with a lightning-quick mind that instantly analyzes issues and draws conclusions in a logical sequence, you'll have to gather and organize ideas for your essay the way ordinary mortals do. You'll search your knowledge and experience for ideas and examples to support your thesis. You'll keep them in mind as you write, note them on paper as you think of them, or prepare a sketchy outline. Jotting down a brief list of ideas that occur to you, or possibly preparing a sketchy outline, is all it takes.

While you reflect on your jottings, a better thesis may come to mind, or you may run into new ideas that bolster your first one. Before you write a word on your answer sheet, though, you probably should devote at least a few minutes to collecting your thoughts. Obviously, on the GMAT, you'll have to think rapidly, but better in haste than not at all.

The Formula

Most essays are variations and adaptations of the formula. Using the formula will not make your prose immortal, but it could help turn a muddle of words into a model of clear thinking. The formula is simply an all-purpose plan for putting ideas into a clear, easy-to-follow order. It uses a beginning, a middle, and an end. It's not sensational, but it works for virtually any essay. Its greatest virtue is simplicity. Each part has its place and purpose:

THE FORMULA

Introduction

Body { Point 1, Point 2, Point 3 }

Conclusion

The formula prescribes a three-stage structure for an essay. It also requires a body consisting of three points. Why three? Mainly because three is a number that works. If you can make three different statements about a topic, you probably know what you're talking about. One is too simple, two is better but is still shallow. Three, however, is thoughtful. It suggests depth. Although every short essay needn't include three points to support its thesis, three carries a voice of authority. If you can't think of three, stick with two, and don't make up a third that is simply a rehash of one of the first two disguised as something new. Psychologically, three also creates a sense of wholeness for the reader, like the beginning, middle, and end of a story. It's no accident that the number three recurs in all literature, from *The Three Little Pigs* to *The Bible*.

The order of ideas is important too. What comes first? Second? Third? The best order is the clearest order, the arrangement that readers can follow with the least effort. No plan is superior to another provided you have a valid reason for using it. The plan least likely to succeed is the aimless one, the one in which you state and develop ideas in the random order they happened to come to mind. It's better to rank your ideas in the order of importance. Decide which provides the strongest support of your thesis. Although your best argument may be listed first in your notes, save it for last on the essay. Giving it away at the start is self-defeating, because everything that follows will be anticlimactic. In other words, work toward your best point, not away from it. An excellent way to plot three good ideas is to lead with your second best, save your best for the end, and sandwich your least powerful idea between the others. This structure recognizes that the end and the beginning of an essay are its critical parts. A good opening draws the reader in and creates an all-important first impression, but a memorable ending, coming last, is what readers have fresh in their minds when they assign you a grade.

5. Start With an Appealing and Informative Introduction

The opening lines of an essay tell readers what to expect. If the opening is dull or confusing, readers will brace themselves for a less than thrilling reading experience. Some essays become clear and engaging by the second paragraph, but an essay with an unimaginative start begins with a handicap, and the writer will have to work that much harder to overcome the reader's first impressions.

It pays, therefore, to write an opening that stops readers in their tracks. Begin with something to lure the reader into the piece. Use a hook—a phrase, sentence, or idea to grab your readers so firmly that they'll desperately want to read on. Hooks must be very crisp, very clean. They must surprise, inform, or tickle the reader in an instant, and say "Read on; you'll be glad you did." A dull hook just won't do. In a short essay, a hook can't take up more than a couple of lines. Anything longer will erode the heart of the essay.

A concise one-sentence opening is probably harder to write than a longer one. In other words, you can't fool around when space is tight. It's not unheard of for students, smitten with an inventive idea, to write half a page before they start to deal directly with the topic. Some students need that much space to put their thoughts in order. Either way, on the GMAT, beware of an introduction that drags on.

Beware also of openings that are too cute or too precious, as in

> *Little did George Washington know as he sat sipping a brew on the veranda at Mount Vernon with his little woman Martha beside him, that . . .*

Be thoughtful and clever, yes, but not obnoxious. Above all, steer clear of an all-inclusive opening that grandiloquently reviews the history of mankind in fifteen words or less, as in

> *Throughout recorded time, man has struggled to keep the flame of freedom alive, . . .*

Be intelligent and perceptive, yes, but not pompous.

Techniques for pulling readers into the body of an essay are unlimited. Yet many successful openings are merely unique variations of one of these popular formats:

1. Begin with a brief incident or anecdote that relates to the point of your essay.

   When Joan S. entered Springdale College early last September, she didn't know that she had left her constitutional rights at the campus gate.

2. State a provocative idea in an ordinary way or an ordinary idea in a provocative way. Either will arrest the reader's interest.

   That a person is supposed to be innocent until proven guilty is an alien concept in my university.

3. Use a quote from the test question, Bruce Springsteen, or any other source—maybe even your grandmother. But be sure the quote relates to the topic of your essay and says it better than you can.

   "All animals are equal, but some animals are more equal than others." George Orwell said that.

4. Knock down a commonly held assumption or define a word in a new and startling way.

   When Ulov, a Russian immigrant, arrived in Shaftsbury, Vermont, he learned that freedom does not mean cutting down a neighbor's maple tree.

5. Ask an interesting question or two, which you will answer in your essay.

   Is true democracy possible? Or is it just an ideal to work for?

6. Make an unexpected connection between your topic and a bit of culture. By offering readers a second layer of meaning, your writing is enriched.

   We'll get by with a little help from our friends. That, at least, was the hope of Hurricane Andrew's victims after the winds died down.

7. Create suspense by waiting until the end of your opening passage to reveal your topic.

   Michael Jackson takes his everywhere, while Julia Roberts takes hers to bed. Rob Lowe keeps one in each Porsche, and Jennifer Jason Leigh has one made of gold. Happiness, for all these stars, depends on having a telephone at their fingertips.

If none of these techniques works for you, or if you don't have time on the GMAT to devise a good hook, rely on the direct approach. Just declare your thesis right up front. But don't phrase it like an announcement, as in "In this essay, I am going to prove that democracy is not dead." State your point, as in "Democracy is far from dead," and take it from there.

If at first you can't find a suitable opening, don't put off writing the rest of your essay. Just skip a few lines and begin with the body of your essay. As you write, a pleasing opening idea might strike you. Add it later. Whatever you do, though, be sure that your opening fits your writing style and personality. Work hard to get it right, but not so hard that it will seem forced or too cute or too long. Ideally, it should introduce your topic so naturally and unobtrusively that readers will not even realize that they are being enticed into reading past the first sentence.

6. Develop Your Ideas Fully With Examples and Details

Precise, well-documented information is far more convincing than general and unsubstantiated opinion. In an essay, the information used to give credence to the writer's main point is commonly called *development*. Because development indicates how deeply a student can think—a matter of great concern to business schools—it counts heavily in grading GMAT essays. Development does not mean number of words. An essay of a thousand words can still be underdeveloped. Some students, unaware of the difference between development and throwing the bull, fill their essays with verbal waste. They write even when they have nothing to say. Perhaps you've done it yourself on occasion. Be assured that essays short on development but long on refuse will be found wanting by GMAT readers, who know bull when they see it.

Nor is development simply the range of evidence summoned to uphold a thesis. Not every good essay needs, say, three or five or a dozen supporting ideas. The fact is that superior development skills can be demonstrated on the GMAT with a single vivid example. It's depth that counts.

Each paragraph in your essay should contribute to the development of the main idea. It should contain facts, data, arguments, examples—testimony of all kinds to corroborate the thesis. If you are unsure how a particular paragraph lends support to the thesis, cross it out or revise it. If you're perplexed, just imagine how your readers will feel. Be merciless with your writing. Even though you may admire a paragraph, give it the boot if it doesn't help to make your case.

A paragraph indentation ordinarily signals readers to get ready for a change in thought or idea. Yet not every new paragraph signals a drastic change in direction. It may simply move the essay ahead one small step at a time. Paragraphs also permit readers to skim your writing. Readers in a hurry focus on opening and closing sentences and skip what lies between, but you can force readers to slow down by varying the location of the most important idea in each paragraph, usually called the *topic sentence*.

While topic sentences come in assorted guises, they share a common trait. They are helpful in keeping both writers and readers on the track. When you write, assume that readers have a poor sense of direction. Given half a chance, they'll lose their way. Therefore, remind them often of where they are. Lead them with topic sentences, but be sure that whatever you say in the rest of the paragraph supports what the topic sentence says.

7. Guide Readers With Transitions

Readers need to be guided through an essay. Consider them visitors in a strange place. As the writer you must show them around by setting up verbal guideposts. Tell them where they are going, show them their progress, and remind them often of the destination. If you've done your job, they should be ready for what they find at the end. By repeatedly alluding to the main idea, you'll not only compel readers to focus on your point, but you'll keep readers at your side from start to finish.

Help readers along, too, by choosing words that establish relationships between one thought and the next. This can be done with words such as *this*, which happens to tie the sentence you are reading to the one before. (The word *too* in the first sentence of this paragraph serves the same function; it serves as a link between this and the earlier paragraph.) The English language is rich with words and phrases that serve to tie sentences and ideas together. Here is a brief thesaurus of common transitions grouped according to their customary use. With a bit of thought, you probably can think of others.

When you **ADD** ideas	*in addition, furthermore, moreover, further, besides, too, also, and then, then too, again, next, secondly, equally important*
When you **COMPARE** or **CONTRAST**	*similarly, likewise, in comparison, in like manner, however, in contrast, conversely, on the other hand, but, nevertheless, and yet, even so, still*
When you cite an **EXAMPLE**	*for example, for instance*
When you **REINFORCE** an idea	*indeed, in fact, as a matter of fact, to be sure, of course, in any event, by all means*
When you show **RESULTS**	*as a result, as a consequence, consequently, therefore, thus, hence, accordingly*
When you express a **SEQUENCE** or the passing of **TIME**	*soon after, then, previously, meanwhile, in the meantime, later, at length, after a while, immediately, next*

When you show **PROXIMITY**	*here, nearby, at this spot, near at hand, in this vicinity, on the opposite side, across from, adjacent to, not far from*
When you **CONCLUDE**	*finally, in short, in other words, in a word, to sum up, in conclusion, in the end*

Not every sentence needs to be tied to the previous one with a particular transitional word or phrase. The ideas themselves sometimes create a natural link.

Whenever you use a transition to tie one sentence to another, you do your readers a favor. You guarantee them a smooth trip through your essay. Otherwise, each sentence stands like a disconnected link in a chain, and readers bump along, often losing the point you are trying to make. Although many sentences won't contain transitions, three or four sentences in succession without a link of some sort may leave readers doubting that this trip is worth taking.

8. Choose Plain, Precise, Lively, and Fresh Words

Use Plain Words

That's a principle easy to say but hard to live by when you're hoping to impress readers with your intellect and sophistication. Yet nothing, truly nothing, conveys your erudition better than plain words. However big your vocabulary, never use a complex word on the GMAT essay to show off. You'll get no extra credit for an essay crammed with ornate, multisyllabic words used for no other purpose than to sound ornate and multisyllabic. There's always a risk, in fact, that words that sound profound to you may seem pompous to your readers. Or worse, they could make you appear foolish.

The student who wrote, "I am of the opinion that a prerequisite for parenthood includes disbursement of penal adjudication among siblings with an even, dispassionate hand," needs a basic lesson in plain writing. How much clearer to have written, "I think that good parents should know how to be fair in disciplining their children" or "I think that being equally strict with all their children is a prerequisite of being good parents." Words should be like gifts, carefully chosen to give pleasure to someone you like. High gloss is not a measure of value. You won't gain much by dressing ordinary ideas in fancy robes or from trying to appear more impressive than you already are.

This admonition to use plain words, however, shouldn't be regarded as a license to use current, everyday slang or street talk in your essays. Spoken language, which contains many colorful words and expressions like *chill*, *pig out*, *dissed*, and *freak out*, has its place, but its place is not in a GMAT essay unless you definitely need current lingo to create an effect that you can't get any other way. If you must write slang terms, don't highlight them with quotation marks. Why call attention to the fact that you can't think of standard or more original words?

Use plain words even for profound thoughts—correction, *especially* for profound thoughts. By writing "I think. Therefore, I am," the seventeenth-century philosopher René Descartes reshaped the way humans think about existence. He could have used more exotic words, of course, words more in keeping with the florid writing style of his time, but his statement probably derives its power from its simplicity. A sign of true intelligence is the ability to convey deep meanings with simple words.

Simple doesn't necessarily mean short. It's true that the plain words tend to be the short ones, but not always. The word *fid* is short, but it's not plain, unless you are a sailor, in which case you'd know that a fid supports the mast on your boat or is used to pry open a tight knot in your lines. On the other hand, *spontaneously* is five syllables long. Yet it is a plain and simple word because of its frequent use. It springs, well, spontaneously from the mouth.

For any GMAT essay, a plain, conversational style is appropriate. The language should sound like you. In formal writing, custom requires you to remove yourself from stage center and focus on the subject matter. At some point in your schooling, you may have been warned never to use "I" in an essay. That caveat may apply to some forms of exposition, but not to GMAT essays. In fact, GMAT topics often encourage first-person responses by asking you to state your opinion or preference. How do you do that without using "I"? It can be done, of course, by using pronouns like *one*, as in "When *one* is getting ready for graduate school, *one* sometimes writes funny," or *you*, as in "Sometimes *you* feel like a dope," or by avoiding pronouns altogether. But an essay that expresses the writer's personal opinion will sound a lot more natural when cast in the first-person singular.

GMAT essay readers are old hands at rooting pretense out of student writing. Unless students are exceptionally astute, they usually give themselves away by using elaborate words that fall a mite short of precise diction. Writers who leave no clue that they are posing as bright, witty, clever, articulate people, on the other hand, are probably bright, witty, clever, and articulate enough to write essays in their natural voice, so why pretend?

The point is, don't be phony! Just let your genuine voice ring out, although the way you speak is not necessarily the way you should write. Most speaking is vague, clumsy, confused, and wordy. Consider writing as the casual speech of someone who speaks exceedingly well. It's grammatically correct and is free of pop expressions and clichés. Think of it as the kind of speech expected of you in an interview. Or maybe even the way this paragraph sounds. You could do a lot worse!

Choose Precise Words

Hazy, vague, and abstract words fade as quickly from a reader's memory as last night's dream. They indicate a lack of clear and precise thinking. How much easier it is to say that a book is *good*, *interesting*, or *exciting* than to search for words that will precisely describe the book's appeal. Similarly, it's more convenient to resort to words like *nice*, *fine*, *stupid*, *boring*, and *pretty* than to explain in detail what you mean by each word. But to write something that will stick in a reader's mind, use well-defined, hard-edged words. Exact words help you express exact thoughts. To write precisely is to write with pictures, sounds, and actions that are as vivid in words as in reality. Exact words leave a distinct mark; general ones, only a blurry impression.

Good writers often experience the world more intensely than other people. Like artists, they think visually. They listen hard to the sounds and voices around them and are extra-sensitive to smells, to tastes, and to the feel of things. They keep their senses at full throttle in order, as the writer James Baldwin once said, "to describe things which other people are too busy to describe." They understand that good writing must sometimes appeal to their readers' senses.

To evoke a strong response from your readers, make use of the principle that a picture is worth a thousand words. Actually, whether it's more or less than a thousand is debatable, but the point is clear: words should help readers *see*. Therefore, *show* more than you *tell*! Instead of describing your uncle as "absent-minded," show him stepping into his morning shower with his pajamas on. Rather than saying that your room is a "mess," show the pile of wrinkled clothes in the corner and the books and Snickers wrappers scattered on the floor next to your unmade bed. The same principle applies to smells: "Her breath was foul with a stale whiskey stench"; to sounds: "the hum and throb of big machines in the distance"; to touch: "the feel of cool, linen bedsheets"; and to tastes: "a cold, sweet drink of clear water on a hot day." In short, by writing vividly, you prevent readers from misinterpreting what you have to say.

Essays bogged down in detail no doubt grow tedious both to read and to write. Authors need to choose what readers need to see and know. Excessive analysis is boring, but so is too little. A balance is best. No one can tell you precisely how to achieve the balance. The feel of what seems right takes time and practice. In the end, the content and purpose of an essay will have to determine how detailed it needs to be. Every time you mention a meal, it's not necessary to recite the menu unless there's a good reason for doing so. When you use an abstract word, ask what is more important, to give details to readers or to push on to other matters? The context, as well as your judgment and experience as a writer, will determine what you can expect readers to understand. To get the knack a little more quickly, reread any interesting passage from a book or other publication. Pick out the details and the broad statements. What did the passage show, and what did it tell? Since the passage held your interest, perhaps you will have found a model worth emulating in your own writing.

By no means does this plea for verbal precision suggest that abstract words be eliminated from the langugage. After all, we need them to talk to each other about *beauty*, *love*, *fairness*, *satisfaction*, *power*, *enlightenment*, and thousands of other notions that exist in our hearts and minds. The ability to think abstractly, to invent theories, to express feelings, and to articulate ideals and lofty principles is a gift that separates human beings from all other creatures, and we should delight in it, but remember that most readers are an impatient lot. They will reject essays that don't, at some point, come down to earth.

Use Lively Language

Active and Passive Verbs: Unlike the machine-scored multiple-choice questions, your GMAT essay will be read by people—real people with feelings, moods, likes and dislikes, and the capacity to laugh, grow angry, and be moved. They are usually teachers who know that student writing can be lively, interesting, and clear. Like any readers, they will be put off by writing that is dull.

The most efficient way to inject life into your writing is to pay close attention to your choice of verbs. Verbs, as you've no doubt been taught, show action or state of being. To a writer, the fact that verbs show action is extremely important. Active verbs stimulate interest by waking up the language. They create movement, perform, stir things up, and move around. They excel all other words in their power to restore life to lifeless prose. They add energy and vitality to sentences, and, as a bonus, they help you to write more economically.

While *active* verbs are full of life, *being* verbs are not. They stagnate. They don't do anything but connect one thought to another, especially forms of the verb *to be*: *is*, *are*, *was*, *were*, *am*, *has been*, *had been*, *will be*. When used in sentences, each of these being verbs joins a subject to a predicate, and that's all. In fact, the verb *to be* in all its forms acts much like a verbal equal sign, as in "Seven plus three *is* ten" (7 + 3 = 10) or "Sam *is* a genius" (Sam = genius), or "Your GMAT score *is* going up" (That = good news!). Because being verbs (and equal signs) show little life, use active verbs whenever possible.

Here are some ways to pump life into sluggish sentences:

1. Try to substitute an active verb drawn from another word in the sentence.

BEING VERB: Monica and Phil *were* the highest scorers on the GMAT practice test.

ACTIVE VERB: Monica and Phil *scored* highest on the GMAT practice test.

The verb "*scored*" has been drawn from the noun "*scorers*."

Active verbs may also be extracted from adjectives:

BEING VERB: Achievement *is* the determining factor in GMAT grades.
ACTIVE VERB: Achievement *determines* GMAT grades.

The verb "*determines*" has been drawn from the adjective "*determining*."

2. Sometimes it's preferable to find an altogether new verb:

BEING VERB: It *is* logical that admission to business school is the result of a student's effort and achievement.
ACTIVE VERB: Logic *dictates* that a student's effort and achievement lead to business school admission.

Being verbs are perfectly acceptable in speech and writing. We can hardly get along without them. But use them sparingly in your essays. As a rule of thumb, if more than one in four of your sentences relies on a form of the verb *to be* as its main verb, you may be depending excessively on passive verbs.

When you start to weed *being* verbs out of your writing, you're likely to find that some sentences resist easy change. Some need to be thoroughly recast. Subjects become verbs, verbs turn into nouns, unnecessary phrases are eliminated entirely—alterations that result in sentences that bear little resemblance to the original. At the same time, though, your writing may get an unexpected lift. Verb-swapping tends to eliminate needless words, thereby improving your writing.

Once you get into the habit of clearing dead verbs out of your prose, you may notice that certain nouns limit your options for using active verbs. That is, certain nouns, when used as the subject of a sentence, determine your chances for finding a lively verb. Some abstract nouns, in fact, cut the choices drastically. Take, for example, sentences starting with "The reason," as in "The reason for taking the GMAT is . . ." Verb choices are also severely reduced by subject nouns like *thought*, *idea*, *issue*, *way*, *notion*, *concept*, or any other essentially abstract nouns. The same holds true for sentences that begin with "There," as in "There are 2,400 colleges in America," and often for sentences that begin with "It," as in "It is difficult to choose just one." On the other hand, nouns that name people, places, concrete objects, or events almost cry out for active verbs. When the subject can perform an action, like a person, for instance, you'll never run out of verb choices.

As these examples illustrate, whenever you insert a concrete, easy-to-define noun in place of an abstraction, you are apt to write a tighter, more energetic, and more readable sentence.

ABSTRACT: The *cause* of the strike was the students' demand for freedom.
DEFINITE: The *students* struck for freedom.

ABSTRACT: The *way* to the dean's office is down the next corridor.
DEFINITE: The next *corridor* goes to the dean's office.

ABSTRACT: *There* are students who are good in chemistry but not in physics.
DEFINITE: Some *students* excel in chemistry but not in physics.

Being verbs are not the only verbs that sap the life out of sentences. They share that distinction with several other verbs, such as any form of *to have*, *to come*, *to go*, *to make*, *to move*, and *to get*. They are convenient and versatile, but because of constant use, such verbs pale next to more animated verbs. But, like *being* verbs, they are indispensable. When they show up in your writing, stick with them only if you can swear that no other words will do. Unless they fit perfectly, however, trade them in for better, livelier ones.

DULL: The line to the lunch counter *moved* very slowly.
LIVELY: The line *crept* (crawled, poked, inched) to the lunch counter.

Note that by using a more animated verb, you eliminate the need for "very slowly," which would be redundant.

DULL: The dean *gave* permission to the students to eat in the staff room.
LIVELY: The dean *permitted* the students to eat in the staff room.

Active and Passive Sentences

To write lively prose, also keep in mind the distinction between *active* and *passive* sentences. A passive sentence is one in which the performer of the action is not mentioned until late in the sentence or is left out altogether. Any time you restructure passive sentences, you pep up the prose.

PASSIVE: This book was recommended by my teacher.
ACTIVE: My teacher recommended this book.

PASSIVE: It was bought for me by my mother.
ACTIVE: My mother bought it for me.

Although active sentences usually sound more natural and interesting, sometimes a passive sentence will work better. When it's immaterial who performed an action, for example, or when the actor can't be identified, passive voice makes perfect stylistic sense.

ACTIVE: The exam proctor gave the starting signal at 8:30.
PASSIVE: The starting signal was given at exactly 8:30.

In the passive version the important fact is the starting time. Who gave the signal is secondary.

Use Fresh Language

Here's your chance to do yourself and your readers a favor. Instead of relying on safe, customary language, take a chance now and then and give your readers a verbal surprise. GMAT essay readers, especially after reading hundreds of predictable essays on the same topic, will do cartwheels for something fresh, something new—a word, a phrase, a sentence still wet behind the ears. A pleasant verbal surprise or two will give your readers, as well as your essay, a boost.

A verbal surprise is simply a unique and interesting choice of words. You don't have to turn exotic phrases in order to dazzle your reader. Common words, deftly used, will do the job just as well—better, probably, for they will sound more natural than something forced onto the page just to sound unusual.

ORDINARY: He wrote a magnificent essay on baseball.
SURPRISING: He pitched a magnificent essay on baseball.

Since essays are not normally *pitched*, the unexpected shift from *wrote* to *pitched* is modestly surprising. The verb *pitched* works well only because the topic is baseball. It might be silly in an essay on another topic.

ORDINARY: The shark bit the swimmers.
SURPRISING: The shark dined on the swimmers.

Changing *bit* to *dined* suggests good manners and gentility, qualities that sharks rarely enjoy.

ORDINARY: The gunshot frightened the pigeons, which flew away.
SURPRISING: The gunshot filled the sky with frightened pigeons.

The ordinary sentence states literally what happened: the sound of the gunshot scared the pigeons silly. In the second version, though, the shot becomes a vital force with the power to fill the sky. Both the pigeons and the sentence have sprung to life.

Surprise with Comparisons

Does this sound familiar? You can't find the words to express a feeling that you have inside you. You know what you want to say, but the words won't come. Although our language is filled with wonderful words to describe virtually anything, sometimes emotions and experiences seem almost inexpressible. How, for instance, do you show the look you got from the bus driver when you didn't have the exact fare? How do you describe street sounds at 5 o'clock on a summer morning or the feel of clean bedsheets?

Comparisons are economical. They condense a lot of thought and feeling into a few words. Ernie Pyle, a famous newspaper correspondent in World War II, reported his stories as though they were being told by the average GI lying in a foxhole. He said, "I write from a worm's eye point of view." What a terrific comparison! Who ever thought that worms have eyes, much less a point of view? The idea gives a fresh slant to the old expression "bird's eye view" and cleverly emphasizes Pyle's position on the battlefield.

Similes ("Norma babbles like a brook") and *metaphors* ("Norma is a babbling brook") compare something known (a babbling brook) to something unknown (Norma). Little kids use such figures of speech instinctively. Because their vocabularies are limited, they compare what they know with what they can't yet express. "When my foot is asleep, it feels like seltzer," says a boy to his daddy, or "Today is chocolate sunshine." As people grow up, they lose the knack of making colorful comparisons and have to relearn it. When you actively look for comparisons, they sprout, like weeds in the garden, all around.

Every familiar combination of words, such as "I could care less," or "you've got to be kidding," or "what a bummer," was once new, cool, or poetic. But constant repetition turned them into clichés, and clichés, by definition, have lost their zing and their power to surprise. Still, clichés crowd our conversations, swamp our airwaves, and deluge the media. Like the air we breathe (a cliché), we hardly notice them. In an essay, however, especially one that is supposed to demonstrate your unique cast of mind, you must avoid clichés like the plague. "*Like the plague*," in fact, is one you should avoid, along with other secondhand phrases and expressions like *the bottom line, how does that sit with you, to touch base with, off the top of my head, I'm outta here, a point well taken, two sides of the same coin, getting psyched, go off the deep end, life in the fast lane, for openers, flipped out, get off my back, get a life!, super, so amazing, at the cutting edge of,* and would you believe, *would you believe?* Using such trite phrases and expressions declares that you'd rather borrow what someone else has said than think of something on your own. Spewing one cliché after another is also the sign of a poverty-stricken mind.

Expunge clichés that sneak into your prose *when your back is turned, when your defenses are down*, and *when you least expect them.* Be vigilant, and purge them from your prose. Don't use an expression that you've ever heard or seen before. If you've written a phrase with a familiar ring, drop it, not *like a hot potato*, but just as quickly.

Your GMAT essay won't be penalized for an absence of inventive and scintillating expressions, but it is sure to suffer if infested with clichés. Get into the habit of expelling all trite phrases from your writing vocabulary. *Half the battle*, as they say, is knowing a cliché when you see one. The other half—removing them—is still to be fought and won.

9. Omit Needless Words

In *Hamlet*, the old windbag Polonius knew what he was talking about when he said "Brevity is the soul of wit." What he meant, in brief, is that Brief is Better. Never use two words when one will do. Readers want to be told quickly and directly what you have to say. They value economy and resent reading more words than necessary.

Here's a word to the wise:

> *Work through all the sentences you write by examining each one and crossing out all the words you don't definitely need.*

Actually, that's 21 words to the wise—probably more than are needed.

> *Go through every sentence you write and cross out unnecessary words.*

That's better—11 words of free advice, but still too many. The sentence could be trimmed still further:

> *Cut extra words out of every sentence.*

Aha! This streamlined version contains just 7 words, one third of the original. If you can regularly trim that proportion of words from your writing without changing meaning or intent, you will have gone about as far as you can to make your writing interesting, although a ruthless, sharp-eyed editor might cut even more:

> *Omit unnecessary words.*

The ultimate goal in economical writing is to make every word count, so that omitting a single word will alter or distort the meaning.

Sentences are trimmed by squeezing them through various wringers.

Wringer #1. Look for repetition. Then combine sentences.

FAT: In his last and final year in college, Bill was elected to be the head of the statewide SADD organization. As head of the statewide organization, he learned about the details of laws dealing with DWI convictions and had many experiences talking in public to large groups of people. (49 words)

TRIMMED: Elected head of the statewide SADD organization in his senior year, Bill learned about DWI laws and spoke often to large groups. (21 words)

Wringer #2. Look for telltale words like *which, who, that, thing, all.* They sometimes indicate the presence of fat.

FAT: Football is a sport that millions of fans enjoy. (9 words)

TRIMMED: Millions of fans enjoy football. (5 words)

Wringer #3. Look for phrases that add words but little meaning.

FAT: *By that point in time*, people will be ready for a change. (12 words)

TRIMMED: By then, people will be ready for a change. (9 words)

FAT: Hamlet returned home *as a result of* his father's death. (10 words)

TRIMMED: Hamlet returned home because his father died. (7 words)

Fat phrases	**Trimmed**
what I mean is	I mean
on account of	because
due to the fact that	
in the final analysis	finally
the bottom line is	
few and far between	few
insignificant in number	
each and every one	each
this is a subject that	this subject
ten in number	ten
at the age of six years old	at age six
most unique	unique
true fact	fact
biography of his life	biography
in regard to	about
with regard to	
in relation to	
with reference to	

Wringer #4. Search for redundancies. Countless words are wasted on reiteration of what has already been said, on restating the obvious, on repeating the same ideas, on saying the same darn thing again and again.

FAT: While carefully scrutinizing her patient's medical history, the doctor seemed fully absorbed by what she was reading. (17 words)

Because scrutinize means "to study carefully," the word "carefully" is unnecessary. Also, absorbed by what she was reading repeats what has already been stated.

TRIMMED: While scrutinizing her patient's medical history, the doctor seemed absorbed. (10 words)

After you've pared your sentences to the bone, study the remains. Cut away still more by tracking down little words like the, a, an, up, down, its, and and. Don't remove whatever gives writing its energy and character, but neither should you spare yourself the pain of removing what you worked hard to put in. Throwing away your precious words may feel sometimes as though you are chopping off your hand, but count on it, your writing will gain life and strength without unnecessary words.

10. Vary Your Sentences

In writing, it's easy to fall into a rut by repeatedly using the same sentence pattern. To avoid boring your readers to death, serve them a variety of sentences. Your prose will be invigorated and your readers will be happy. Because English is such a pliant language, sentences can be endlessly revised until you've got a mix that works.

You probably know that most simple declarative sentences start with the subject, followed by the verb:

The peaches (subject) *are* (verb) not yet ripe or ready to eat.

They (subject) *left* (verb) for the airport at dusk.

This policy (subject) *is* (verb) not easy to enforce.

Several sentences in a row with this subject-verb pattern will make writing sound like a chapter from a grade-school primer. Take steps to more mature prose by checking an essay you've recently written. If several of your sentences lead off with the subject, try starting some of them with a preprositional phrase, with an adverb or adjective, or with some other grammatical unit. By varying sentence openings, you make your writing bolder and more readable.

The following pairs of sentences illustrate ways in which a subject can be shifted from its customary position:

BEFORE THE SHIFT: Poison ivy thrives in the woods.
AFTER THE SHIFT: In the woods and meadows, poison ivy thrives.

After a prepositional phrase the subject of the sentence appears.

BEFORE: Poison ivy is apparently one of the most poisonous plants.
AFTER: Apparently, poison ivy is one of the most poisonous plants.

Obviously, the revised sentence begins with an adverb.

BEFORE: Many people still don't know what it looks like.
AFTER: Still, many people don't know what it looks like.

Well, here the sentence subject is snuck in after an opening connective.

BEFORE: People should keep their eyes peeled for an innocent-looking three-leaved plant on a single stem whenever they go out to the country.
AFTER: Whenever people are out in the country, they should keep their eyes peeled for an innocent-looking three-leaved plant on a single stem.

After introducing this sentence with a dependent clause, the writer named the subject and then added the rest of the sentence.

BEFORE: A prudent person should take a shower with plenty of soap and water as soon as possible after brushing up against the plant to guard against infection.
AFTER: To guard against infection after brushing up against the plant, a prudent person should take a shower with plenty of soap and water as soon as possible.

To revise this sentence the writer began with a *verbal,* in this case "to guard," the infinitive form of the verb. Verbals look and feel a lot like verbs (hence, their name), but are not. (The infinitive form of any verb, for example, cannot serve as the main verb of a sentence.) Verbals, though, come from verbs, which explains the resemblance.

BEFORE: Some people walk through patches of poison ivy without worrying, thinking that they are immune.
AFTER: Thinking that they are immune from poison ivy, some people walk through patches of the stuff without worrying.

Hoping to add diversity to sentence openings, the writer began this sentence with another kind of verbal, known as a *participle.* Most of the time the *-ing* ending is a clue that the word is a participle.

BEFORE: Such people, who were unconcerned about becoming infected, may be shocked to discover that their immunity has suddenly disappeared.

AFTER: Unconcerned about becoming infected, such people may be shocked to discover that their immunity has suddenly disappeared.

Determined to try something different, the writer picked an adjective that happens to sound like a verb because of its *-ed* ending.

Another variation to try occasionally is the sentence with a paired construction. Two equal and matched ideas are set against each other, often differing by only one or two words:

It wasn't that David caught poison ivy, it was poison ivy that caught him.

"Ask not what your country can do for you, ask what you can do for your country."
—John F. Kennedy, January 20, 1961

The strength of such a sentence lies in the balance of parallel parts. Each part could stand alone, but together the thought is expressed more vigorously.

No rule of thumb governs the proportion of sentences in an essay that should depart from the usual subject-verb word order. Much depends on the intent and content of the essay.

Don't deliberately scramble up sentence types just to make a sentence potpourri, for you may end up with a mess on your hands. Be guided always by what seems clearest and by what seems varied enough to hold reader interest.

Use of Repetition

Contrary to what this book has stated previously, repetition deserves a place in an essay writing repertoire. Some kinds of repetition are boring, true, but adept use of repetition lets a writer stress important ideas in an unusual way. People naturally repeat words for emphasis, anyway, as in "I love you. I love you very much" and "Knock it off. I said knock it off!"

While effective repetition leaves its mark, accidental repetition can be annoying. Watch out for avoidable repetitions:

At the end of the hall stood a clock. The clock said five o'clock.

Columbus made three voyages. The voyages took him across the Atlantic.

Usually, combining such sentences will keep you from ending one sentence and starting the next one with the same words:

The clock at the end of the hall said five.

Columbus made three voyages across the Atlantic.

Occasionally sentences are plagued by a word or sound that won't let go. One student wrote:

Maybe some people don't have as much freedom as others, but the freedom they do have is given to them for free. Therefore, freedom is proof enough that the best things in life are free.

Another student wrote:

The members of the assembly remembered that November was just around the corner.

These authors weren't listening to the sound of their own words. Had they read their sentences aloud, their ears would probably have noticed that the record seemed to be stuck. In fact, reading your work aloud allows you to step back (Hold it! Those two words—aloud and allows—should not be allowed to stand. They sound sour, don't you agree?) Anyway, when you say your written words out loud, you gain perspective and notice repetitive bumps that need repair. Or better still, let your essay cool for a spell, then recruit a friend to read it to you. That's how to achieve real objectivity.

Short and Long Sentences

Sentences can be written in any length, from one word to thousands. A long sentence demands more from readers because, while stepping from one part of the sentence to the next, they must keep track of more words, modifiers, phrases (not to speak of parenthetical asides), and clauses without losing the writer's main thought, which may be buried amid any number of secondary, or less important, thoughts. Short sentences are easier to grasp. A brief sentence makes its point quickly and often with considerable force, as in this passage about a family trip:

For three days, my parents and I sat in our Toyota and drove from college to college, looking for the perfect place for me to spend the next four years. For 72 hours we lived as one person, sharing thoughts and dreams, stating opinions about each college we visited, taking guided tours, interviewing students and college officials, asking directions a hundred times, eating together in town after town, and even sleeping in the same motel rooms. But mostly, we fought.

The blunt closing sentence, particularly after a windy 46-word sentence, produces a mild jolt. To be sure, it's meant to shock, but placing a tight, terse sentence against a long one intensifies the effect. Like all stylistic techniques, this one mustn't be used too often. Overuse dilutes its impact, but when it works well, it's indelible.

Short and long sentences create the rhythm of writing. Because readers usually pause, subconsciously at least, at every period, short sentences slow the tempo. Long sentences may speed it up, but the pace depends a lot on the placement of clauses, the amount of parenthetical matter, and word choices.

In any case, a string of short, simple sentences can be as tiresome to read as series of long, complex ones strung end to end. A balance is best. A sequence of four or five equally short (or long) sentences should be given the fission-or-fusion treatment. That is, split the big ones and combine the others.

Passages consisting of short sentences can also be made more readable by fusing ideas.

When sentences are combined, words are excised and the writing often becomes livelier. Not only that, but when some ideas are subordinated to others, not every thought receives equal emphasis.

To Vary Your Sentences—A Summary

Start sentences with:

1. A prepositional phrase: *In the beginning*, *From the start*, *In the first place*
2. Adverbs and adverbial phrases: *Originally*, *At first*, *Initially*
3. Dependent clauses: *If you follow my lead*, *When you start with this*
4. Conjunctions: *And*, *But*, *Not only*, *Either*, *So*, *Yet*
5. Verbal infinitives: *To launch*, *To take the first step*, *To get going*
6. Adjectives and adjective phrases: *Fresh from*, *Introduced with*, *Headed by*
7. Participles: *Leading off*, *Starting up*, *Commencing with*
8. Inversions: *Unique is the writer who embarks . . .*

Use a variety of sentence types.
Balance long and short sentences.
Combine series of very short sentences.
Dismember very long sentences.

11. End Your Essay Unforgettably

When you reach the end of your GMAT or any other essay, you can lift your pen off the paper and be done with it, or you can leave your readers a little gift to remember you by. What you leave can be a little piece of insight, wisdom, or humor to make readers glad that they stayed with you to the end. It may be something to tease their brains, tickle their funny bones, or make them feel smart.

Whatever you give, choose it carefully, and let it spring naturally from the text of your essay. A good essay can easily be spoiled by an ill-fitting ending. Also, don't be tempted to use an ending that is too coy, corny, or cute, such as *that's all, folks*; *it was a dream come true*; *a good time was had by all*; *tune in next week—same time, same station*; or *a nice place to visit, but I wouldn't want to live there*. These are outrageously trite endings that leave behind an impression that the writer was either too cheap to leave a better gift or too dull to think of something classier. Readers will appreciate almost any gift you give them, provided you've put some thought into its selection. Don't spoil a fresh essay with a stale conclusion.

Nor must you tack on an ending just for the sake of good form. The best endings grow organically out of the essay's content. Endings are so crucial in works of creative art that specific words have been designated to name them. A piece of music has a *coda*; a story or play, a *denouement*, a musical show, a *grand finale*. When an ending approaches, you sense it at hand and expect soon to be bathed with a feeling of satisfaction. Good endings please both heart and mind.

Choose the gift judiciously. Leave behind a memento of your thinking, your sense of humor, or your vision. Even an ordinary thought, uniquely presented, will shed an agreeable afterglow.

1. Have some fun with your ending. A reader may remember your sense of humor long after forgetting the essay that struck his funny bone.

SUBJECT: Stricter gun control laws
GIFT: On this issue, the legislature has taken a cheap shot at many law-abiding citizens.

2. End with an apt quotation taken from the essay, from the assigned topic or from some other source.

SUBJECT: The nobility of the teaching profession
GIFT: As a wise person once said, "Catch a fish and you feed a man his dinner, but teach a man to fish, and you feed him for life."

SUBJECT: The costs of racial disharmony
GIFT: Now, more than ever, Rodney King's question, "Can we all get along?" has a new meaning.

3. Finish by reviewing the paper's main point, but with new words. Add a short tag line, perhaps.

SUBJECT: The low quality of art supplies used in school, arguing that money should be devoted to support the art program.
GIFT: Colors fade rapidly when exposed to sunlight, a true indication of the paint's poor quality. How frustrating!

SUBJECT: The purported death of democracy
GIFT: Our victory over the forces of the communist menace must mean that democracy has the power to endure and must mean that it is healthy.

4. Project your readers into the future. What will happen in the months or years ahead?

SUBJECT: Being adventurous
GIFT: By late spring I had my fill of studying the river; it was time to get a raft and try the rapids myself.

SUBJECT: The misuse of our environment
GIFT: We must all do our part to save the planet, or there won't be a planet left to save.

A catchy conclusion isn't always needed, but some sort of ending is necessary to make readers feel they've arrived somewhere. They won't be satisfied with an essay that just evaporates. A short one is better than none at all. Stay away from summary endings, particularly when the essay is short, as on the GMAT. It's insulting, in fact, to review for the readers what is evident on the page in front of them. Readers are intelligent people. Trust them to remember what the essay says.

12. Follow the Conventions of Standard English

This book is too lean to house a complete handbook of standard English usage. For a full treatment of English usage, however, see the Sentence Correction Review in Chapter 6 or go to the library and check out one of the hefty books on the subject. Look, for instance, at H. W. Fowler's *Modern English Usage*, the definitive reference work, in which you can find a page-long discussion of such arcane usage questions as the difference between *farther* and *further*, or when to use *that*, as in "Is it my Mazda Miata *that* is parked illegally?" and when to use *which*, as in "Yes, your Mazda Miata, *which* is now being ticketed, is parked illegally." Numerous other books, such as *The New York Times Manual of Style and Usage* and *The Careful Writer* by Theodore M. Bernstein are packed with solutions to literally thousands of usage problems.

Unhappily, there is no particular logic to standard English usage. Like the famous definition of pornography, it's hard to define but easy to spot when you see it. Standard English is merely a badge of an educated person, the level of writing and speech expected of people who are literate and who, to some degree, must depend on their language skills to help them make their way in the world.

Essay Topics for Further Practice

Directions: Write a clear, logical, and well-organized response to the following issue or argument. Your response should be in the form of a short essay, following the conventions of standard written English. Your answer should fit on three pages of lined 8½" × 11" paper. Write legibly. Essays that are illegible or that are written on a topic other than the one outlined in the question will not be scored.

Eighteen topics are suggested for practice, but if you write on the same topic again and again, the number of topics is two, three, or even ten times as many. Since it's virtually impossible to write the same essay twice, you could try the same topic over and over without repeating yourself. Each time you write on the same topic, choose another point of view to defend. They say that one sign of erudition is the ability to argue both sides of an issue equally well. Then compare the results.

1. Adlai Stevenson once commented, "It is often easier to fight for principles than to live up to them."

   Based on your reading, observation, or experience, to what extent to you agree or disagree with Stevenson's words? Please give examples that support your point of view.

2. The former secretary general of the United Nations, Dag Hammarskjöld wrote, "Never look down to test the ground before taking your next step: only he who keeps his eye fixed on the far horizon will find his right road."

   While such a philosophy may be appropriate for the leader of the United Nations, it may not be an acceptable practice for ordinary individuals to follow as they go about their daily lives. What is your opinion? Support your position with illustrations from your observation, study, reading, or personal experience.

3. The German poet Goethe once wrote, "Treat people as if they were what they ought to be and you help them to become what they are capable of being."

   Goethe's statement could probably apply to schools, government, social services, business, even to families—anyplace, really, where people interact with each other. Is Goethe just expressing pretty-sounding, idealistic nonsense, or does his idea have real-life applicability? Based on your experience, observation, or reading, please comment on the usefulness of Goethe's statement as a realistic guide to human relationships.

4. Some cultures view life as a line, extending from point A to point B. Others view life as a circle.

Explain which of these two views coincides with yours. If neither, what shape or form would you propose? Please explain.

5. After rescuing a child from a burning building, Jim Smith, a fireman, commented, "Courage is just a matter of luck—of being in the right place at the right time."

   Do you think that courage is common to most of us, but that most of us never have an opportunity to show it? Or is physical courage like Jim Smith's an unusual quality in most of us?

6. Why are you such an awful procrastinator? Or why doesn't this question apply to you?

   Explain your answer to one of the above questions. Use illustrations from your personal experience to support your views.

7. "Ignorance of the law is no excuse for breaking it."

   Do you agree or disagree with this legal principle? If you do, should exceptions ever be made? Under what circumstances? If you don't, why do you suppose such a principle exists? What would you propose as an alternative?

8. There's an old proverb, "Spare the rod and spoil the child." To put it another way, fear of punishment keeps people in line. Do you agree or disagree with this view of human nature? Is the hope of reward ever a better way to control behavior?

9. There's an old proverb, "There's no great loss without some gain." Another way to put it is, "Every cloud has a silver lining."

   Do you agree or disagree with this observation? Support your position with illustrations from your observation, studies, reading, or personal experience.

10. An old English proverb says, "What you don't know can't hurt you."

    Do you think that this proverb is generally true or generally false, or do you think that its validity lies somewhere in between? Defend your opinion using examples from life, literature, or your studies.

11. Thomas Jefferson said, "When a man assumes a public trust, he should consider himself public property." In other words, public figures, such as a president and other government officials, should not expect to have the same right of privacy as ordinary citizens.

    To what extent do you support or oppose this point of view? Be as specific as you can in explaining your position.

12. On whom should the moral responsibility for battlefield atrocities lie? Does it rest on military leaders, soldiers who carry out orders, the makers of weapons, or on the people as a whole? Or do you think that no person has the right to hold another person morally responsible for anything—in wartime or any other time?

    Where do you stand on this issue? Please explain and defend your position.

13. It has been said that a great man cannot be overly cautious.

    To what extent do you agree or disagree with this statement? Support your point of view using examples from your observation, experience, reading, or study of history.

14. By law, cigarettes and liquor may not be advertised on television. Some people think there should also be an advertising ban on foods that are unhealthy for children, such as candy and heavily sugared cereals. Opponents view such a ban as an infringement of basic freedoms.

    What is your opinion? Explain and defend your viewpoint, using examples from your observation, study, or experience.

15. Two existing government organizations are the National Endowment for the Humanities, which supports art and culture, and the National Academy of the Sciences, which supports endeavors in the sciences. If you had the opportunity to propose the creation of a new organization to support a cause, it would be the National ____________________. Fill in the blank and explain why you would support such a venture.

16. After some sixteen years of schooling you are likely to have had some good teachers. In your view what makes a good teacher?

17. In most colleges, students who fail a certain number of academic courses are ineligible to participate in intercollegiate athletics until their grades have improved. Do you believe it is proper to link participation in athletics to classroom performance? Write an essay in which you defend or criticize this policy.

18. As a visitor from another planet, you have been observing humankind and its behavior on Earth. One of the oddest features you have observed is ____________________. Fill in the blank, and explain why you singled out that particular feature.

5 READING COMPREHENSION REVIEW

A large proportion of the GMAT is designed to test your ability to comprehend material contained in reading passages. The Reading Comprehension review is preparation for not only the Reading Comprehension section of the test but also the Critical Reasoning section. The Reading Comprehension sections of the GMAT do allow you to turn back to the passages when answering the questions. However, many of the questions may be based on what is *implied* in the passages, rather than on what is explicitly stated. Your ability to draw inferences from the material is critical to successfully completing this section. It is also critical to your success in the Critical Reasoning section which tests your ability to evaluate assumptions, inferences, and arguments.

In each case, success depends on the extent of your reading comprehension skills. The following discussion is designed to help you formulate an approach to reading passages that will enable you to better understand the material you will be asked to read on the GMAT. Practice exercises at the end of this review will give you an opportunity to try out this approach.

Basic Reading Skills

A primary skill necessary for good reading comprehension and recall is the understanding of the meanings of individual words. Knowledge of a wide and diversified vocabulary enables you to detect subtle differences in sentence meaning that may hold the key to the meaning of an entire paragraph or passage. For this reason, it is important that you familiarize yourself with as many words as possible.

A second reading skill to be developed is the ability to discover the central theme of a passage. By making yourself aware of what the entire passage is about, you are in a position to relate what you read to this central theme, logically picking out the main points and significant details as you go along. Although the manner in which the central theme is stated may vary from passage to passage, it can usually be found in the title (if one is presented), in the "topic sentence" of a paragraph in shorter passages, or, in longer passages, by reading several paragraphs.

A third essential skill is the capacity to organize mentally how the passage is put together and determine how each part is related to the whole. This is the skill you will have to use to the greatest degree on the GMAT, where you must pick out significant and insignificant factors, remember main details, and relate information you have read to the central theme.

In general, a mastery of these three basic skills will provide you with a solid basis for better reading comprehension wherein you will be able to read carefully to draw a conclusion from the material, decide the meanings of words and ideas presented and how they in turn affect the meaning of the passage, and recognize opinions and views that are expressed.

Applying Basic Reading Skills

The only way to become adept at the three basic reading skills outlined above is to practice using the techniques involved as much as possible. Studying the meanings of new words you encounter in all your reading material will soon help you establish a working knowledge of many words. In the same manner, making an effort to locate topic sentences, general themes, and specific details in material you read will enable you to improve your skills in these areas. The following drills will help. After you have read through them and answered the questions satisfactorily, you can try the longer practice exercises at the end.

Finding the Topic Sentence

The term "topic sentence" is used to describe the sentence that gives the key to an entire paragraph. Usually the topic sentence is found in the beginning of a paragraph. However, there is no absolute rule. A writer may build his paragraph to a conclusion, putting the key sentence at the end. Here is an example in which the topic sentence is located at the beginning:

EXAMPLE 1

The world faces a serious problem of overpopulation. Right now many people starve from lack of adequate food. Efforts are being made to increase the rate of food production, but the number of people to be fed increases at a faster rate.

The idea is stated directly in the opening sentence. You know that the passage will be about "a serious problem of overpopulation." Like a heading or caption, the topic sentence sets the stage or gets your mind ready for what follows in that paragraph.

Before you try to locate the topic sentence in a paragraph you must remember that this technique depends upon reading and judgment. Read the whole passage first. Then try to decide which sentence comes closest to expressing the main point of the paragraph. Do not worry about the position of the topic sentence in the paragraph; look for the most important statement. Find the idea to which all the other sentences relate.

Try to identify the topic sentence in this passage:

EXAMPLE 2

During the later years of the American Revolution, the Articles of Confederation government was formed. This government suffered severely from a lack of power. Each state distrusted the others and gave little authority to the central or federal government. The Articles of Confederation produced a government which could not raise money from taxes, prevent Indian raids, or force the British out of the United States.

What is the topic sentence? Certainly the paragraph is about the Articles of Confederation. However, is the key idea in the first sentence or in the second sentence? In this instance, the *second* sentence does a better job of giving you the key to this paragraph—the lack of centralized power that characterized the Articles of Confederation. The sentences that complete the paragraph relate more to the idea of "lack of power" than to the time when the government was formed. Don't assume that the topic sentence is always the first sentence of a paragraph. Try this:

EXAMPLE 3

There is a strong relation between limited education and low income. Statistics show that unemployment rates are highest among those adults who attended school the fewest years. Most jobs in a modern industrial society require technical or advanced training. The best pay goes with jobs that demand thinking and decisions based on knowledge. A few people manage to overcome their limited education by personality or a "lucky break." However, studies of lifetime earnings show that the average high school graduate earns more than the average high school dropout, who in turns earns more than the average adult who has not finished eighth grade.

Here, the first sentence contains the main idea of the whole paragraph. One more example should be helpful:

EXAMPLE 4

They had fewer men available as soldiers. Less than one third of the railroads and only a small proportion of the nation's industrial production was theirs. For most of the war their coastline was blockaded by Northern ships. It is a tribute to Southern leadership and the courage of the people that they were not defeated for four years.

In this case you will note that the passage builds up to its main point. The topic sentence is the last one. Practice picking out the topic sentences in other material you read until it becomes an easy task.

Finding the General Theme

A more advanced skill is the ability to read several paragraphs and relate them to one general theme or main idea. The procedure involves careful reading of the entire passage and deciding which idea is the central or main one. You can tell you have the right idea when it is most frequent or most important, or when every sentence relates to it. As you read the next passage, note the *underlined* parts.

EXAMPLE 1

True democracy means direct rule by the people. A good example can be found in a modern town meeting in many small New England towns. All citizens aged twenty-one or over may vote. They not only vote for officials, but they also get together to vote on local laws (or ordinances). The small size of the town and the limited number of voters make this possible.

In the cities, voters cast ballots for officials who get together to make the laws. Because the voters do not make the laws directly, this system is called indirect democracy or representative government. There is no problem of distance to travel, but it is difficult to run a meeting with hundreds of thousands of citizens.

Representation of voters and a direct voice in making laws are more of a problem in state or national governments. The numbers of citizens and the distances to travel make representative government the most practical way to make laws.

Think about the passage in general and the underlined parts in particular. Several examples discuss voting for officials and making laws. In the first paragraph both of these are done by the voters. The second paragraph describes representative government in which voters elect officials who make laws. The last paragraph emphasizes the problem of size and numbers and says that representative government is more practical. In the following question, put all these ideas together.

The main theme of this passage is that

(A) the United States is not democratic
(B) citizens cannot vote for lawmakers
(C) representative government does not make laws
(D) every citizen makes laws directly
(E) increasing populations lead to less direct democracy

The answer is choice (E). Choices (B), (C), and (D) can be eliminated because they are not true of the passage. Choice (A) may have made you hesitate a little. The passage makes comments about *less direct* democracy, but it never says that representative government is *not democratic.*

The next three passages offer further practice in finding the main theme. Answer the question following each example and check the analysis to make sure you understand.

EXAMPLE 2

Skye, 13 miles off the northwest coast of Scotland, is the largest and most famous of the Hebrides. Yet fame has neither marred its natural beauty nor brought affectation to its inhabitants. The scene and the people are almost as they were generations ago.

The first sight that impresses the visitor to Skye is its stark beauty. This is not beauty of the usual sort, for the island is not a lush green "paradise." It is, on the other hand, almost devoid of shrubbery. Mountains, moorlands, sky, and sea combine to create an overpowering landscape. Endless stretches of rocky hills dominate the horizon. Miles of treeless plains meet the eye. Yet this scene has a beauty all its own.

And then cutting into the stark landscape are the fantastic airborne peaks of the Cuillins, rising into the clear skies above. The Cuillins are the most beloved mountains in Scotland and are frequently climbed. Their rugged, naked grandeur, frost-sculptured ridges and acute peaks even attracted Sir Edmund Hillary.

The main idea of this passage is

(A) the sky over Skye
(B) the lack of trees on Skye
(C) the natural beauty of Skye
(D) the lack of affectation on Skye
(E) the Cuillins in the skies of Skye

All of the answers have some truth to them. The problem is to find the *best* answer. Four of the choices are mentioned in the passage only by a small comment. But choice (C) is discussed throughout every part of the passage. The clue to the correct answer was how often the same theme was covered.

EXAMPLE 3

Trade exists for many reasons. No doubt it started from a desire to have something different. Men also realized that different men could make different products. Trade encouraged specialization, which led to improvement in quality.

Trade started from person to person, but grew to involve different towns and different lands. Some found work in transporting the goods or selling them. Merchants grew rich as the demand for products increased. Craftsmen were able to sell more products at home and abroad. People in general had a greater variety of things to choose.

The knowledge of new products led to an interest in the lands which produced them. More daring persons went to see other lands. Others stayed at home, but asked many questions of the travelers. As people learned about the products and the conditions in other countries, they compared them with their own. This often led to a desire for better conditions or a hope for a better life. Trade was mainly an economic force, but it also had other effects.

The general theme of the passage is how

(A) trade makes everyone rich
(B) trade divides the world
(C) products are made
(D) trade changes people's lives
(E) people find new jobs

This is not easy, as you may feel that all the choices are good. Most of them were mentioned in some part of the passage. However, you must select the *best* choice. If you had trouble, let us analyze the passage.

Paragraph one emphasizes a "desire" for "something different" and "improvement." The second paragraph mentions "found work," "merchants grew rich," "craftsmen . . . sell more," and "greater variety of things to choose." The third paragraph covers "interest in the lands," "compared them with their own," "desire for better conditions," and "better life." All these are evidence of the same general theme of how trade brings changes in the lives of people. Choice (D) is the best answer.

Choice (A) is tempting because of the comment on merchants getting rich. However, this idea is not found all through the passage. Choice (B) may catch the careless thinker. Trade does not divide the world, even though the passage talks about dividing jobs. Choice (C) is weak. Some comment is made about making products, but not in all parts of the passage. Choice (E) is weak for the same reason as choice (C).

EXAMPLE 4

The enormous problems of turning swamps and desert into fields and orchards, together with the ideal of share-and-share-alike, gave birth to the kibbutz.

In those days, the kibbutz member had to plow the fields with a rifle slung over his shoulder.

Today security is still a factor in the kibbutz. Shelters are furrowed into the ground along every walk among the shade trees, near the children's house, where all the young children of the kibbutz live, and near the communal dining room.

But the swamps have been conquered, and the desert is gradually becoming green. And while kibbutz members once faced deprivation and a monotonous diet, today they reap the harvest of hard work and success.

One such kibbutz is Dorot, at the gateway to the Negev desert and typical of the average size Israeli communal settlement.

Life on the kibbutz has become more complex through growth and prosperity. While once the land barely yielded enough for a living, Dorot, like many other kibbutzim, now exports some of its crops. It also has become industrialized, another trend among these settlements. Dorot has a factory which exports faucets to a dozen countries, including the United States.

The main theme of this article is

(A) the manufacture of faucets is a sign of growth and prosperity in the kibbutz
(B) with the solving of agricultural problems the kibbutz has become a more complex society
(C) since security is a problem for the kibbutz, it has become industrialized
(D) Dorot is the prosperous gateway to the Negev desert
(E) kibbutzim are good places to live, although they are located in swamps and deserts

Choice (A) receives brief mention at the end of the passage. It is an idea in the passage, but certainly not the general idea of the passage. Choice (D) is the same kind of answer as choice (A)—it is too specific a fact. Choice (E) is unrelated to the passage. We now have choices (B) and (C) as possible answers. Choice (C) seems reasonable until you analyze it. Did the need for security *cause* the industrialization? Or are there better examples of how life has become more complex now that agricultural problems have been solved? The evidence leans more to choice (B).

In summary, in order to find the general theme:

1. Read at your normal speed.
2. Locate the topic sentence in each paragraph.
3. Note ideas that are frequent or emphasized.
4. Find the idea to which most of the passage is related.

Finding Logical Relationships

In order to understand fully the meaning of a passage, you must first look for the general theme and then relate the ideas and opinions found in the passage to this general theme. In this way, you can determine not only what is important but also how the ideas interrelate to form the whole. From this understanding, you will be better able to answer questions that refer to the passage.

As you read the following passages, look for general theme and supporting facts, words or phrases that signal emphasis or shift in thought, and the relation of one idea to another.

EXAMPLE 1

The candidate who wants to be elected pays close attention to statements and actions that will make the voters see him favorably. In ancient Rome candidates wore pure white togas (the Latin word *candidatus* means "clothed in white") to indicate that they were pure, clean, and above any "dirty work." However, it is interesting to note that such a toga was not worn after election.

In more modern history, candidates have allied themselves with political parties. Once a voter knows and favors the views of a certain political party, he may vote for anyone with that party's label. Nevertheless, divisions of opinion develop, so that today there is a wide range of candidate views in any major party.

1. The best conclusion to be drawn from the first paragraph is that after an election

   (A) all candidates are dishonest
   (B) candidates are less concerned with symbols of integrity
   (C) candidates do not change their ideas
   (D) officials are always honest
   (E) policies always change

You noted the ideas about a candidate in Rome. You saw the word "however" signal a shift in ideas or thinking. Now the third step rests with your judgment. You cannot jump to a conclusion; you must see which conclusion is reasonable or fair. Choices (A), (D), and (E) should make you wary. They say "all" or "always" which means without exception. The last sentence is not that strong or positive. Choices (B) and (C) must be considered. There is nothing in the paragraph that supports the fact that candidates do not change their ideas. This forces you into choice (B) as the only statement logically related to what the paragraph said.

2. A fair statement is that most candidates from the same political party today are likely to

   (A) have the same views
   (B) be different in every view
   (C) agree on almost all points
   (D) agree on some points and disagree on others
   (E) agree only by accident

Here again, the burden rests on your judgment after following ideas and word clues. The paragraph makes the point that there is a wide range of views. That eliminates choice (A). Choice (B) is not logical because the candidates would not likely be in the same party if they disagree on every view. The remaining choices are different degrees of agreement. Choice (E) is weak because candidates are too interested to arrive at agreement only by accident. The wide range mentioned seems to oppose choice (C) and favor choice (D) as a little more likely. You may say that choice (C) sounds pretty good. Again we stress that you *are picking the very best choice*, not just a good choice. That is what we mean by reflecting carefully on all possibilities and selecting the best available choice.

EXAMPLE 2

In 1812 Napoleon had to withdraw his forces from Russia. The armies had invaded successfully and reached the city of Moscow. There was no question of French army disloyalty or unwillingness to fight. As winter came, the Russian army moved out of the way, leaving a wasted land and burned buildings. Other conquered European nations seized upon Napoleon's problems in Russia as their chance to rearm and to break loose from French control.

According to the passage, it may be inferred that the main reason for Napoleon's withdrawal from Russia was the

(A) disloyalty of the French troops
(B) Russian winter
(C) burned buildings
(D) revolts in other countries
(E) Russian army

In this passage, only choice (A) is totally incorrect. Choice (E) is very weak because the Russian army was not able to stop the invasion. The choices narrow to which is the best of (B), (C), and (D). It seems that all three answers are supported by the passage. There needs to be some thought and judgment by you. Which of these could be overcome easily and which could be the strongest reason for Napoleon leaving Russia? The burned buildings could be overcome by the troops making other shelters. The Russian winter was severe and the army did not want to face it. However, marching out of Russia in the winter was also a great problem. Napoleon probably would have stayed in Moscow except for a more serious problem—the loss of the control he had established over most of Europe. Thus, answer (D) is best.

EXAMPLE 3

By 1915 events of World War I were already involving the United States and threatening its neutrality. The sinking of the British liner *Lusitania* in that year by a German submarine caused great resentment among Americans. Over a hundred United States citizens were killed in the incident. President Wilson had frequently deplored the use of submarines by Germany against the United States. Since the United States was neutral, it was not liable to acts of war by another nation.

However, Wilson resolved to represent the strong feeling in the country (notably in the Midwest) and in the Democratic Party that United

States neutrality should be maintained. He felt that the United States should have "peace with honor," if possible.

There were also people, mostly in the East, that wanted to wage a preventive war against Germany. Such men as Theodore Roosevelt bitterly attacked Wilson as one who talked a great deal but did nothing.

By 1917 Germany again used unrestricted submarine warfare and Wilson broke off relations with Germany. In February British agents uncovered the Zimmerman Telegram. This was an attempt by the German ambassador to Mexico to involve that nation in a war against the United States. And in March several American merchant ships were sunk by German submarines. His patience at an end, Wilson at last took the position of a growing majority of Americans and asked Congress to declare war on Germany. Thus, the United States entered World War I.

1. This passage tries to explain that
   (A) Wilson wanted the United States to go to war against Germany
   (B) Wilson tried to avoid war with Germany
   (C) Germany wanted the United States to enter the war
   (D) other nations were pressuring the United States to enter the war
   (E) Mexico was our main enemy

2. We can conclude from the passage that most citizens of the United States in 1917 were
   (A) totally opposed to war with Germany
   (B) in favor of war before Wilson was
   (C) willing to accept war after Wilson persuaded them
   (D) neutral
   (E) trying to avoid war

3. The last event in the series of happenings that led to a declaration of war against Germany was
   (A) the Zimmerman Telegram
   (B) attacks on U.S. merchant ships
   (C) Wilson's war message to Congress
   (D) a change in public opinion
   (E) the sinking of the *Lusitania*

In question 1, the key is to note Wilson's actions discussed in paragraph two. Near the end of the passage there is a phrase about "his patience at an end." This describes a man who was trying to avoid a conflict, as in answer choice (B).

Question 2 rests on two ideas. There was a change in the feeling of the American people about war. The other idea is that Wilson responded after he felt that they had changed. The phrase "took the position of a growing majority of Americans" tells us that Wilson followed the change in opinion, as in answer choice (B).

In question 3, you need to check the sequence of events. The declaration of war followed the president's request.

Making Inferences

An inference is not stated. It is assumed by the reader from something said by the writer. An inference is the likely or probable conclusion rather than the direct, logical one. It usually involves an opinion or viewpoint that the writer wants the reader to follow or assume. In another kind of inference, the reader figures out the author's opinion even though it is not stated. The clues are generally found in the manner in which facts are presented and in the choice of words and phrases. Opinion is revealed by the one-sided nature of a passage in which no opposing facts are given. It is shown further by "loaded" words that reveal the author's feelings.

It is well worth noting that opinionated writing is often more interesting than straight factual accounts. Some writers are very colorful, forceful, or amusing in presenting their views. You should understand that there is nothing wrong with reading opinion. You should read varied opinions, but know that they are opinions. Then make up your own mind.

Not every writer will insert his opinion obviously. However, you can get clues from how often the same idea is said (frequency), whether arguments are balanced on both sides (fairness), and the choice of wording (emotional or loaded words). Look for the clues in this next passage.

Example 1

Slowly but surely the great passenger trains of the United States have been fading from the rails. Short-run commuter trains still rattle in and out of the cities. Between major cities you can still find a train, but the schedules are becoming less frequent. The Twentieth Century Limited, The Broadway Limited, and other luxury trains that sang along the rails at 60 to 80 miles an hour are no longer running. Passengers on other long runs complain of poor service, old equipment, and costs in time and money. The long-distance traveler today accepts the noise of jets, the congestion at airports, and the traffic between airport and city. A more elegant and graceful way is becoming only a memory.

1. With respect to the reduction of long-run passenger trains, this writer expresses

(A) regret
(B) pleasure
(C) grief
(D) elation
(E) anger

Before you choose the answer, you must deduce what the writer's feeling is. He does not actually state his feeling, but clues are available so that you may infer what it is. Choices (B) and (D) are impossible, because he gives no word that shows he is pleased by the change. Choice (C) is too strong, as is choice (E). Choice (A) is the most reasonable inference to make. He is sorry to see the change. He is expressing regret.

2. The author seems to feel that air travel is

(A) costly
(B) slow
(C) streamlined
(D) elegant
(E) uncomfortable

Here we must be careful because he says very little about air travel. However, his one sentence about it presents three negative or annoying points. The choice now becomes fairly clear. Answer (E) is correct.

EXAMPLE 2

When the United States was founded at the end of the eighteenth century, it was a small and weak country, made up mostly of poor farmers. Foreign policy, reflecting this domestic condition, stressed "no entangling alliances." The State Department then had a staff of less than half a dozen persons, whose total salary was $6,600 (of which $3,500 went to the Secretary of State), and a diplomatic service budget (July, 1790) of $40,000. Militarily, too, the country was insignificant. The first United States army, soon after the American Revolution, was made up of one captain (John Doughty) and 80 men. Clearly, the United States did not consider itself a real power and was not taken seriously by the rest of the world.

It was not until immense changes took place *inside* the United States that the country began to play an important role in foreign affairs. By the beginning of the twentieth century, the United States had ceased to be a predominantly agricultural nation and had become an industrial one. Its population had grown to more than 30 times its original number. George Washington was president of 3,000,000 Americans; Theodore Roosevelt, of 100,000,000.

1. A country today cannot expect to play an important part in world affairs unless it

I. has wealth
II. has a large population
III. is strong internally

(A) I only
(B) III only
(C) I and II only
(D) II and III only
(E) I, II, and III

This is a slightly different style of question. You must look at each of the answer choices in I, II, and III. As you consider the passage and what it suggests, you note that each of the answer choices in I, II, and III make good sense. Therefore, answer choice (E) is the best answer because it includes all of the correct statements. Again, this is not designed to trick you. The purpose of such a question is to be sure that you have read all the choices.

2. The writer seems to think that a major factor in making the United States a world power was

(A) industrialization
(B) the passing of time
(C) a change in government policies
(D) the presidency of Theodore Roosevelt
(E) the avoidance of entangling alliances

The passage does not answer the question directly. You must infer what is meant by the author. However, there is a clue in the author's comment that changes inside a country make a big difference in its foreign policy. The big internal changes noted are the growth of America's population and industrial power. By correctly interpreting the passage, you will be led to choice (A) for this question.

In Example 3 you will find three short statements by three different writers. The questions will require that you make inferences about each writer and then make comparisons of one against the other two.

EXAMPLE 3

Writer I

No nation should tolerate the slacker who will not defend his country in time of war. The so-called conscientious objector is a coward who accepts the benefits of his country but will not accept the responsibility. By shirking his fair share, he forces another person to assume an unfair burden.

Writer II

A democratic nation should have room for freedom of conscience. Religious training and belief may make a man conscientiously opposed to participation in war. The conscientious objector should be permitted to give labor service or some form of non-combat military duty. His beliefs should be respected.

Writer III

The rights of the conscientious objector should be decided by each individual. No government should dictate to any person or require him to endanger his life if the person, in conscience, objects. There need be no religious basis. It is enough for a free individual to think as he pleases and to reject laws or rules to which he conscientiously objects.

1. A balanced opinion on this subject is presented by

   (A) Writer I
   (B) Writer II
   (C) Writer III
   (D) all of the writers
   (E) none of the writers

2. We can conclude that the writer most likely to support a person who refuses any military service is

   (A) Writer I
   (B) Writer II
   (C) Writer III
   (D) all of the writers
   (E) none of the writers

3. An authoritarian person is most likely to agree with

   (A) Writer I
   (B) Writer II
   (C) Writer III
   (D) all of the writers
   (E) none of the writers

Look for clues in the language or choice of words that are loaded with feeling such as "slacker," "so-called," and "shirking" by Writer I and "dictate," "endanger," and "as he pleases" by Writer III. Compare them with the language used by Writer II. Then see if you can connect what these writers say with views you have heard or read. We are not asking you to accept any of these opinions. You are using your skill in reading what the writers think and adding it to your own knowledge. Then you make logical inferences. The correct answers are 1 (B), 2 (C), and 3 (A).

Now that you have spent time reviewing the three basic skills you should master for better reading comprehension ability, try the two practice exercises that follow. Answers to these exercises appear after Exercise B. You should also try to spend time using this reading approach as you read other material not related to the GMAT.

Practice Exercises

The following two reading passages are similar to the Reading Comprehension passages found on the GMAT. You should read each one and then answer the questions that follow according to the directions. Remember that in Reading Comprehension sections you are permitted to refer to the passage while answering the questions.

Exercise A

TIME: 9 minutes

Directions: This part contains a reading passage. You are to read it carefully. When answering the questions, you *will* be able to refer to the passages. The questions are based on what is stated or *implied* in the passage. You have nine minutes to complete this part.

Above all, colonialism was hated for its explicit assumption that the civilizations of colonized peoples were inferior. Using slogans like *The White Man's Burden* and *La Mission Civilicatrice*, Europeans asserted their moral obligation to impose their way of life on those endowed with inferior cultures. This orientation was particularly blatant among the French. In the colonies, business was conducted in French. Schools used that language and employed curricula designed for children in France. One scholar suggests that Muslim children probably learned no more about the Maghreb than they did about Australia. In the Metropole, intellectuals discoursed on the weakness of Araboislamic culture. A noted historian accused Islam of being hostile to science. An academician wrote that Arabic—the holy language of religion, art and the Muslim sciences—is ''more of an encumbrance than an aid to the mind. It is absolutely devoid of precision.'' There was of course an element of truth in the criticisms. After all, Arab reformists had been engaging in self-criticism for decades. Also, at least some Frenchmen honestly believed they were helping the colonized. A Resident General in Tunisia, for example, told an assemblage of Muslims with sincerity, "We shall distribute to you all that we have of learning; we shall make you a party to everything that makes for the strength of our intelligence." But none of this could change or justify the cultural racism in colonial ideologies. To the French, North Africans were only partly civilized and could be saved only by becoming Frenchmen. The reaction of the colonized was of course to defend his identity and to label colonial policy, in the words of Algerian writer Malek Hadad, "cultural asphyxia." Throughout North Africa, nationalists made the defense of Arabo-Islamic civilization a major objective, a value in whose name they demanded independence. Yet the crisis of identity, provoked by colonial experiences, has not been readily assured and lingers into the post-colonial period. A French scholar describes the devasting impact of colonialism by likening it to "the role played for us (in Europe) by the doctrine of original sin." Frantz Fanon, especially in his *Studies in a Dying Colonialism*, well expresses the North African perspective.

Factors producing militant and romantic cultural nationalism are anchored in time. Memories of colonialism are already beginning to fade and, when the Maghreb has had a few decades in which to grow, dislocations associated with social change can also be expected to be fewer. Whether this means that the cultural nationalism characteristic of the Maghreb today will disappear in the future cannot be known. But a preoccupation with identity and culture and an affirmation of Arabism and Islam have characterized the Maghreb since independence and these still remain today important elements in North African life.

A second great preoccupation in independent North Africa is the promotion of a modernist social revolution. The countries of the Maghreb do not pursue development in the same way and there have been variations in policies within each country. But all three spend heavily on development. In Tunisia, for example, the government devotes 20–25% of its annual budget to education, and literacy has climbed from 15% in 1956 to about 50% today. A problem, however, is that such advances are not always compatible with objectives flowing from North African nationalism. In Morocco, for instance, when the government decided to give children an "Arab" education, it was forced to limit enrollments because, among other things, most Moroccans had been educated in French and the country consequently had few teachers qualified to teach in Arabic. Two years later, with literacy rates declining, this part of the Arabization program was postponed. The director of Arabization declared, "We are not fanatics; we want to enter the modern world."

1. Which of the following titles best describes the content of the passage?

   (A) *Education in the Levant*
   (B) *Nationalism in North Africa*
   (C) *Civilization in the Middle East*
   (D) *Muslim Science*
   (E) *Culture and Language*

2. Which of the following is not used by the author in the presentation of his arguments?

   (A) Colonialism demoralized the local inhabitants.
   (B) Colonialism produced an identity crisis.
   (C) Cultural nationalism will soon disappear.
   (D) Decolonization does not always run smoothly.
   (E) Colonialists assumed that local cultures were inferior.

3. The author's attitude toward colonialism is best described as one of

   (A) sympathy
   (B) bewilderment
   (C) support
   (D) hostility
   (E) ambivalence

4. Which of the following does the author mention as evidence of cultural colonialism?

   (A) Native children in North Africa learned little about local culture.
   (B) Science was not taught in the Arabic language.
   (C) Colonial policy was determined in France.
   (D) Colonialists spent little on development.
   (E) Native teachers were not employed in public schools.

5. The author provides information that would answer which of the following questions?

   (A) What was the difference between French and German attitudes toward their colonies?
   (B) Why did Europeans impose their way of life on their colonies?
   (C) Why was colonialism bad?
   (D) Why was colonialism disliked?
   (E) When did colonialism end in North Africa?

Exercise B

TIME: 9 minutes

Directions: This part contains a reading passage. You are to read it carefully. When answering the questions, you will be able to refer to the passages. The questions are based on what is stated or implied in the passage. You have nine minutes to complete this part.

Man and nature were the culprits as Venice sank hopelessly—or so it seemed—into the 177 canals on which the city is built. While nature's work took ages, man's work was much quicker and more brutal. But now man is using his ingenuity to save what he had almost destroyed. The sinking has been arrested and Venice should start rising again, like an oceanic phoenix from the canals.

The saving of Venice is the problem of the Italian Government, of course, but Venice is also a concern for Europe. And it happened that in the second half of 1975 Italy was in the chair of the European Council of Ministers. But the EC as such has no program for the salvation of Venice. "The Community is not a cultural community," explained one Commission official. "There are some areas where it just does not have competence, the preservation of historical landmarks being one of them." So the efforts to save Venice have taken on a worldwide, rather than a Community-wide dimension.

Industrialization of the Porto Marghera area brought economic benefits to Venice, but it also raped the city as growing air and water pollution began to take their toll on the priceless works of art and architecture. The danger of the imminent disappearance of Venice's cultural heritage was first brought to public attention in November 1966 when tides rose over six feet to flood Venice's canals and squares. Since then, various national and international organizations have sought ways and means to halt the destruction of the "queen of the Adriatic," though no one program has proved wholly satisfactory.

The US "Save Venice" group and the British "Venice in Peril" committee were formed to raise money for the restoration of priceless works of art and monuments. In 1967 the United Nations Educational, Scientific and Cultural Organization (UNESCO) took on the task of helping to save Venice by setting up a joint international advisory committee with the Italian Government. Such distant lands as Pakistan, no stranger to aid programs itself, joined in the effort, giving UNESCO a gift of 10,000 postage stamps for "Venice in Peril." Even a group of famous cartoonists felt moved to draw attention to the fact that "Venice must be saved" and organized an exhibit in 1973, with the Council of Europe in Strasbourg, France, and this year a ballet festival drew people and funds to Venice.

Though Venice, the city of bridge-linked islands, was built in the fifth century, the land on which it was built has been sinking "naturally" for a billion years. Movements of the earth's crust have caused the very slow and gradual descent of the Po Valley. And nature's forces aren't easily countered. Each year, Venice has been sinking about one millimeter into the lagoon which holds this Adriatic jewel. To add to Venice's peril, the slow melting of the polar cap causes the level of the sea to rise another millimeter. If nothing is done to reverse nature's work, Venice is doomed to be another Atlantis, lost for ever beneath the murky sea.

Man's part in the sink-Venice movement has been for reasons mainly economic. For the last 400 years, the population of Venice has been drifting toward the mainland to escape the isolation and inconvenience of living on a series of islets. Between 1951 and 1971, Venice lost 63,000 inhabitants. To curtail this migration, new, artificial land areas, on the Dutch model, were added to the old Venice. Venice's original builders had not been far-sighted enough and set the ground level at only a few inches above what they expected to be the maximum tides. The combination of reclaimed land and Porto Marghera industrialization have "squeezed" the lagoon until its waters have no place to go but . . . up.

As Porto Marghera grows as an industrial port, and more and deeper channels are added for larger ships, currents become faster and dikes make the ravaging tides even more violent. The "acqua alta" has always been a problem for Venice, but with increased industrialization, flooding has become more frequent, sometimes occurring 50 times a year. Added to the violent "scirocco" that blows up to 60 miles an hour, Venice is rendered all the more vulnerable.

Yet Venice is not crumbling. Despite the visible decay caused by repeated floods and despite pollution that peels the stucco off the palazzi and eats away at their bottom-most steps, the structures are solid. The Rialto Bridge still stands safely on its ancient foundations supported by 6000 piles.

And something has been done to stop the damage done by water. Indeed, one simple measure has proved to work miracles; The ban on pumping from the thousands of artesian wells in and around the city—an easy source of water, but also a folly that caused a further descent of 5 millimeters a year—has been so effective that Venice should rise an inch in the next twenty years.

1. According to the passage, between 1951 and 1971, Venice lost approximately how many residents annually?

   (A) 475
   (B) 3,150
   (C) 6,300
   (D) 15,500
   (E) 63,000

2. The author's point of view is that Venice

   (A) cannot be saved from destruction
   (B) is in danger of imminent disappearance
   (C) is doomed to become another "Atlantis"
   (D) can be saved, but much work is necessary
   (E) must become a member of the EC

3. Which of the following conditions has *not* contributed to Venice's peril?

   (A) Movement of the earth's crust
   (B) Natural causes
   (C) Melting of the polar cap
   (D) Industrialization
   (E) Shipping on the canals

4. According to the passage, which of the following figures indicates the approximate year when Venice first began sinking?

   (A) 400 B.C.
   (B) A.D. 1400
   (C) A.D. 1966
   (D) A.D. 1970
   (E) None of the above

5. The author feels that Venice is an example of

   (A) a doomed city like Atlantis
   (B) uncontrolled conditions
   (C) a combination of natural and human destruction
   (D) international neglect
   (E) benign concern by international agencies

Answers and Analysis

Exercise A

1. **(B)** Clearly, the main subject of the passage is nationalism. This is given in the statement on line 1, "Above all, colonialism was hated . . ." and in lines 36ff, and 49ff.
2. **(C)** Choice (E) is given in lines 1–3, (D) in lines 71–73, (B) in lines 40–42, and (A) is implied throughout; while the opposite of (C) is found in lines 54–57.
3. **(D)** See, for instance, the reference to "cultural racism" in line 30, as well as the general tone of paragraph 1.
4. **(A)** This is mentioned in lines 9–11. The fact that children were taught very little about their own culture and history was due to cultural colonialism.
5. **(D)** This theme begins on line 1 and continues throughout much of the passage.

Exercise B

1. **(B)** 63,000 people were lost over a twenty-year period (1951–1971), or approximately 3,150 annually.
2. **(D)** Venice can be saved, but much work is necessary. See lines 5–8.
3. **(E)** Answer (A) appears in line 55, (B) in 54, (C) in 60–61, and (D) in lines 80–83. Choice (E) is not mentioned.
4. **(E)** In lines 53-55 it is stated that the land on which Venice is situated has been sinking for a billion years.
5. **(C)** The theme is given in the first line and repeated in lines 54, 60, 65, 76, 77, and 87.

6 SENTENCE CORRECTION REVIEW

The Sentence Correction section of the GMAT tests your understanding of the basic rules of English grammar and usage. This chapter reviews those errors in grammar and usage that appear most frequently on the GMAT.

In the GMAT Sentence Correction section you will be given sentences in which all or part of the sentence is underlined. You will then be asked to choose the best phrasing of the underlined part from five alternatives. (A) will always be the original phrasing.

EXAMPLE

Not having heard clearly, the speaker was asked to repeat his statement.

(A) the speaker was asked to repeat his statement.
(B) she asked the speaker to repeat again his statement.
(C) the speaker was asked to repeat his statement again.
(D) she asked the speaker to repeat his statement.
(E) she then asked the speaker again to repeat his statement.

Answer

(D) is the best choice.

Review of Errors Commonly Found in the Sentence Correction Section

Since you need only *recognize* errors in grammar and usage for this part of the exam, this section of the book will review those errors most commonly presented in the GMAT and teach you *what to look for*. We will not review the *basic* rules of grammar, such as the formation and use of the different tenses and the passive voice, the subjective and objective cases of pronouns, the position of adjectives and adverbs, and the like. We assume that a candidate for the GMAT is familiar with basic grammar, and we will concentrate on error recognition based on that knowledge.

Verb Errors

1. Errors in Verb Tense. Check if the correct verb *tense* has been used in the sentence.

INCORRECT: When I came home, the children still didn't finish dinner.
CORRECT: When I came home, the children still hadn't finished dinner.

INCORRECT: As we ate dinner, the phone rang.
CORRECT: As we were eating dinner, the phone rang.

In REPORTED SPEECH, check that the rule of *sequence of tenses* has been observed.

INCORRECT: She promised she will come.
CORRECT: She promised she would come.

INCORRECT: She said she doesn't know his phone number.
CORRECT: She said she didn't know his phone number.

INCORRECT: She claimed she has never been there.
CORRECT: She claimed she had never been there.

2. Errors in Tense Formation. Check if the tense has been formed correctly. *Know* the past participle of irregular verbs!

INCORRECT: He throwed it out the window.
CORRECT: He threw it out the window.

INCORRECT: Having just drank some water, I wasn't thirsty.
CORRECT: Having just drunk some water, I wasn't thirsty.

3. Errors in Subject-Verb Agreement. Check if the subject of the verb is singular or plural. Does the verb agree in number?

Multiple subjects will be connected by the word AND:

Ted, John, and I are going.

If a singular subject is separated by a comma from an accompanying phrase, *it remains singular*:

The bride, together with the groom and her parents, is receiving at the door.

INCORRECT: There is many reasons why I can't help you.
CORRECT: There are many reasons why I can't help you.

INCORRECT: Sir Lloyd, accompanied by his wife, were at the party.
CORRECT: Sir Lloyd, accompanied by his wife, was at the party.

INCORRECT: His mastery of several languages and the social graces make him a sought-after dinner guest.
CORRECT: His mastery of several languages and the social graces makes him a sought-after dinner guest.

4. Errors in Conditional Sentences. In conditional sentences, the word *if* will NEVER be followed by the words *will* or *would*.

Here are the correct conditional forms:

FUTURE: If I have time, I will do it tomorrow.
PRESENT: If I had time, I would do it now.
PAST: If I had had time, I would have done it yesterday.

Sentences using the words *when*, *as soon as*, *the moment*, etc., are formed like future conditionals:

I will tell him if I see him.

I will tell him when I see him.

The verb *to be* will ALWAYS appear as *were* in the present conditional:

If I were you, I wouldn't do that.

She wouldn't say so if she weren't sure.

NOTE: Not all sentences containing *if* are conditionals. When *if* appears in the meaning of *whether*, it may take the future:

I don't know if he will be there. (I don't know whether he will be there.)

INCORRECT: If I would have known, I wouldn't have gone.
CORRECT: If I had known, I wouldn't have gone.

INCORRECT: You wouldn't be so tired if you weren't going to bed so late.
CORRECT: You wouldn't be so tired if you didn't go to bed so late.

INCORRECT: Call me the moment you will get home.
CORRECT: Call me the moment you get home.

INCORRECT: We could go to the beach if it wasn't so hot.
CORRECT: We could go to the beach if it weren't so hot.

5. Errors in Expressions of Desire. Unfulfilled desires are expressed by the form "_____ had hoped that _____ would (or *could*, or *might*) do _____."

I had hoped that I would pass the exam.

Expressions with *wish* are formed as follows:

PRESENT: I wish I knew him.
FUTURE: I wish you could (would) come.
PAST: I wish he had come. (or could have come, would have come, might have come)

NOTE: As in conditionals, the verb *to be* will ALWAYS appear as *were* in the present: I wish she were here.

INCORRECT: I wish I heard that story about him before I met him.
CORRECT: I wish I had heard (or could have heard or would have heard) that story about him before I met him.

INCORRECT: She wishes you will be on time.
CORRECT: She wishes you could (or would) be on time.

6. Errors in Verbs Followed by VERB WORDS. The following list consists of words and expressions that are followed by a VERB WORD (the infinitive without the *to*):

ask	prefer	requirement
demand	recommend	suggest
desire	recommendation	suggestion
insist	require	urge

It is essential/imperative/important/necessary that…

INCORRECT: She ignored the doctor's recommendation that she stops smoking.
CORRECT: She ignored the doctor's recommendation that she stop smoking.

INCORRECT: It is essential that you are on time.
CORRECT: It is essential that you be on time.

INCORRECT: He suggested that we should meet at the train.
CORRECT: He suggested that we meet at the train.

7. Errors in Negative Imperatives. Note the two forms for negative imperatives:

A. Please don't do that.
B. Would you please not do that.

INCORRECT: Would you please don't smoke here.
CORRECT: Please don't smoke here.
OR
Would you please not smoke here.

8. Errors in Affirmative and Negative Agreement of Verbs. Note the two correct forms for *affirmative* agreement:

A. I am an American and so is she.
B. I am an American and she is too.

A. Mary likes Bach and so does John.
B. Mary likes Bach and John does too.

A. My father will be there and so will my mother.
B. My father will be there and my mother will too.

INCORRECT: I have seen the film and she also has.
CORRECT: I have seen the film and so has she.
OR
I have seen the film and she has too.

Note the two correct forms for *negative* agreement:

A. I'm not American and he isn't either.
B. I'm not American and neither is he.

A. Mary doesn't like Bach and John doesn't either.
B. Mary doesn't like Bach and neither does John.

A. My father won't be there and my mother won't either.
B. My father won't be there and neither will my mother.

INCORRECT: I haven't seen the film and she hasn't neither.
CORRECT: I haven't seen the film and she hasn't either.
OR
I haven't seen the film and neither has she.

9. Errors of Infinitives or Gerunds in the Complement of Verbs. Some verbs may be followed by either an infinitive or a gerund:

I love swimming at night.
I love to swim at night.

Other verbs, however, may require either one *or* the other for idiomatic reasons. Following is a list of the more commonly used verbs in this category:

Verbs requiring an INFINITIVE:

agree	fail	intend	promise
decide	hope	learn	refuse
expect	want	plan	

Verbs requiring a GERUND:

admit	deny	quit
appreciate	enjoy	regret
avoid	finish	risk
consider	practice	stop

Phrases requiring a GERUND:

approve of	do not mind	keep on
be better off	forget about	look forward to
can't help	insist on	think about
count on	get through	think of

INCORRECT: I intend learning French next semester.
CORRECT: I intend to learn French next semester.

INCORRECT: I have stopped to smoke.
CORRECT: I have stopped smoking.

INCORRECT: We are looking forward to see you.
CORRECT: We are looking forward to seeing you.

10. Errors in Verbs Requiring HOW in the Complement. The verbs KNOW, TEACH, LEARN, and SHOW require the word *HOW* before an infinitive in the complement.

INCORRECT: She knows to drive.
CORRECT: She knows how to drive.

INCORRECT: I will teach you to sew.
CORRECT: I will teach you how to sew.

11. Errors in Tag Endings. Check for *three* things in tag endings:

A. Does the ending use the *same person* as the sentence verb?
B. Does the ending use the *same tense* as the sentence verb?
C. If the sentence verb is positive, is the ending negative; if the sentence verb is negative, is the ending positive?

It's nice here, isn't it?
It isn't nice here, is it?

She speaks French, doesn't she?
She doesn't speak French, does she?

They'll be here tomorrow, won't they?
They won't be here tomorrow, will they?

EXCEPTIONS:

I'm right, aren't I?

We ought to go, shouldn't we?

Let's see, shall we?

NOTE: If there is a contraction in the sentence verb, make sure you know what the contraction stands for:

INCORRECT: She's been there before, isn't she?
CORRECT: She's been there before, hasn't she?

INCORRECT: You'd rather go yourself, hadn't you?
CORRECT: You'd rather go yourself, wouldn't you?

12. Errors in Idiomatic Verb Expressions. Following are a few commonly used idiomatic verb expressions. Notice whether they are followed by a verb word, a participle, an infinitive, or a gerund. Memorize a sample of each to check yourself when choosing an answer:

A. *must have* (*done*)—meaning "it is a logical conclusion"

They're late. They must have missed the bus.

There's no answer. They must have gone out.

B. *had better* (*do*)—meaning "it is advisable"

It's getting cold. You had better take your coat.

He still has fever. He had better not go out yet.

C. *used to* (*do*)—meaning "was in the habit of doing in the past"

I used to smoke a pack of cigarettes a day, but I stopped.

When I worked on a farm, I used to get up at 4:30 in the morning.

D. *to be used to*—meaning "to be accustomed to"

to get used to
to become used to } —meaning "to become accustomed to"

The noise doesn't bother me; I'm used to studying with the radio on.

In America you'll get used to hearing only English all day long.

E. *make* someone *do*—meaning "force someone to do"
have someone *do*—meaning "cause someone to do"
let someone *do*—meaning "allow someone to do"

My mother made me take my little sister with me to the movies.

The teacher had us write an essay instead of taking an exam.

The usher didn't let us come in until the intermission.

F. *would rather*—meaning "would prefer"

I would rather speak to her myself.

I would rather not speak to her myself.

But if the preference is for someone *other than the subject* to do the action, use the PAST:

I would rather you spoke to her.

I would rather you didn't speak to her.

Pronoun Errors

1. Errors in Pronoun Subject-Object. Check if a pronoun is the SUBJECT or the OBJECT of a verb or preposition.

INCORRECT: All of us—Fred, Jane, Alice, and me—were late.
CORRECT: All of us—Fred, Jane, Alice, and I—were late.

INCORRECT: How could she blame you and he for the accident?
CORRECT: How could she blame you and him for the accident?

2. Errors with WHO and WHOM. When in doubt about the correctness of WHO/WHOM, try substituting the subject/object of a simpler pronoun to clarify the meaning:

I don't know who/whom Sarah meant.

Try substituting *he/him*; then rearrange the clause in its proper order:

he/him Sarah meant / Sarah meant him

Now it is clear that the pronoun is the *object* of the verb *meant*, so *whom* is called for.

CORRECT: I don't know whom Sarah meant.

ANOTHER EXAMPLE:

There was a discussion as to who/whom was better suited.

Try substituting *she/her*:

she was better suited / her was better suited

Here the pronoun is the *subject* of the verb *suited*:

CORRECT: There was a discussion as to who was better suited.

3. Errors of Pronoun Subject-Verb Agreement. Check if the pronoun and its verb agree in number. Remember that the following are *singular:*

anyone	either	neither	what
anything	everyone	no one	whatever
each	everything	nothing	whoever

These are *plural:*

both	many	several	others
few			

INCORRECT: John is absent, but a few of the class is here.
CORRECT: John is absent but a few of the class are here.

INCORRECT: Everyone on the project have to come to the meeting.
CORRECT: Everyone on the project has to come to the meeting.

INCORRECT: Either of those dresses are suitable for the party.
CORRECT: Either of those dresses is suitable for the party.

INCORRECT: Neither of them are experts on the subject.
CORRECT: Neither of them is an expert on the subject.

NOTE: The forms "either...or" and "neither...nor" are singular and take a singular verb. For reasons of diction, however, if the noun immediately preceding the verb is plural, use a plural verb. An English speaker finds it difficult to pronounce a singular verb after a plural subject, as in "...they is coming," even though "they" is preceded by "Neither he nor..."

Either his parents or he is bringing it.
Either he or his parents are bringing it.
Neither his parents nor he was there.
Neither he nor his parents were there.

4. Errors of Possessive Pronoun Agreement. Check if possessive pronouns agree in *person* and *number*.

INCORRECT: If anyone calls, take their name.
CORRECT: If anyone calls, take his name.

INCORRECT: Those of us who care should write to their congressman.
CORRECT: Those of us who care should write to our congressman.

INCORRECT: Some of you will have to come in their own cars.
CORRECT: Some of you will have to come in your own cars.

5. Errors in Pronouns after the Verb TO BE. TO BE is an intransitive verb and will always be followed by a subject pronoun.

INCORRECT: It must have been her at the door.
CORRECT: It must have been she at the door.

INCORRECT: I wish I were him!
CORRECT: I wish I were he!

INCORRECT: He didn't know that it was me who did it.
CORRECT: He didn't know that it was I who did it.

6. Errors in Position of Relative Pronouns. A relative pronoun refers to the word preceding it. If the meaning is unclear, the pronoun is in the wrong position.

INCORRECT: He could park right in front of the door, which was very convenient.

Since it was not the door which was convenient, the "which" is illogical in this position. In order to correct the sentence, it is necessary to rewrite it completely:

CORRECT: His being allowed to park right in front of the door was very convenient.

INCORRECT: The traffic was very heavy, which made me late.

CORRECT: I was late because of the heavy traffic.

OR

The heavy traffic made me late.

7. Errors in Parallelism of Impersonal Pronouns. In forms using impersonal pronouns, use *either* "one...one's/his or her" *or* "you...your."

INCORRECT: One should take your duties seriously.

CORRECT: One should take one's/ his or her duties seriously.

OR

You should take your duties seriously.

INCORRECT: One should have their blood pressure checked regularly.

CORRECT: One should have one's/ his or her blood pressure checked regularly.

OR

You should have your blood pressure checked regularly.

Adjective and Adverb Errors

1. Errors in the Use of Adjectives and Adverbs. Check if a word modifier is an ADJECTIVE or an ADVERB. Make sure the correct form has been used.

An ADJECTIVE describes a noun and answers the question, *What kind*?

She is a good cook. (What kind of cook?)

An ADVERB describes either a verb or an adjective and answers the question, *How*?

She cooks well. (She cooks how?)

This exercise is relatively easy. (How easy?)

Most adverbs are formed by adding *-ly* to the adjective.

EXCEPTIONS:

Adjective	*Adverb*
early	early
fast	fast
good	well
hard	hard (*hardly* means *almost not*)
late	late (*lately* means *recently*)

INCORRECT: I sure wish I were rich!

CORRECT: I surely wish I were rich!

INCORRECT: The young man writes bad.

CORRECT: The young man writes badly.

INCORRECT: He's a real good teacher.

CORRECT: He's a really good teacher.

2. Errors of Adjectives with Verbs of Sense. The following verbs of sense are intransitive and are described by ADJECTIVES:

be	look	smell	taste
feel	seem	sound	

INCORRECT: She looked very well.

CORRECT: She looked very good.

NOTE: "He is well" is also correct in the meaning of "He is healthy" or in describing a person's well-being.

INCORRECT: The food tastes deliciously.

CORRECT: The food tastes delicious.

NOTE: When the above verbs are used as transitive verbs, modify with an adverb, as usual: She tasted the soup quickly.

3. Errors in Comparatives

A. Similar comparison

ADJECTIVE: She is as pretty as her sister.

ADVERB: He works as hard as his father.

B. Comparative (of two things)

ADJECTIVE: She is prettier than her sister.
She is more beautiful than her sister.
She is less successful than her sister.

ADVERB: He works harder than his father.
He reads more quickly than I.
He drives less carelessly than he used to.

NOTE 1: A pronoun following *than* in a comparison will be the *subject pronoun*:

You are prettier than she (is).

You drive better than he (does).

NOTE 2: In using comparisons, adjectives of one syllable, or of two syllables ending in *-y*, add *-er*: smart, smarter; pretty, prettier. Other words of more than one syllable use *more*: interesting, more interesting. Adverbs of one syllable add *-er*; longer adverbs use *more*: fast, faster; quickly, more quickly.

NOTE 3: The word *different* is followed by *from*:

You are different from me.

C. Superlative (comparison of more than two things)

ADJECTIVE: She is the prettiest girl in her class.
He is the most successful of his brothers.
This one is the least interesting of the three.

ADVERB: He plays the best of all.
He speaks the most interestingly.
He spoke to them the least patronizingly.

EXCEPTIONAL FORMS:

good	better	best
bad	worse	worst
much/many	more	most
little	less	least

INCORRECT: This exercise is harder then the last one.
CORRECT: This exercise is harder than the last one.

INCORRECT: He works faster than her.
CORRECT: He works faster than she.

INCORRECT: She is the more responsible person of the three.
CORRECT: She is the most responsible person of the three.

INCORRECT: She was much different than I expected.
CORRECT: She was much different from what I expected.

INCORRECT: This year I'll have littler free time.
CORRECT: This year I'll have less free time.

4. Errors in Parallel Comparisons. In parallel comparisons, check if the correct form has been used.

INCORRECT: The more you practice, you will get better.
CORRECT: The more you practice, the better you will get.

INCORRECT: The earlier we leave, we will get there earlier.
CORRECT: The earlier we leave, the earlier we will get there.

INCORRECT: The busier you become, lesser time you have for reading.
CORRECT: The busier you become, the less time you have for reading.

5. Errors of Illogical Comparatives. Check comparisons to make sure they *make sense*.

INCORRECT: Texas is bigger than any state in the United States.
CORRECT: Texas is bigger than any other state in the United States. (If Texas were bigger than *any state*, it would be bigger than itself!)

INCORRECT: That is the most important of any other reason.
CORRECT: That is the most important reason.

INCORRECT: Of the two books, this one is best.
CORRECT: Of the two books, this one is better.

6. Errors of Identical Comparisons. Something can be *the same as* OR *like* something else. Do not mix up the two forms.

INCORRECT: Your dress is the same like mine.
CORRECT: Your dress is like mine.
OR
Your dress is the same as mine.

7. Errors in Idioms Using Comparative Structures. Some idiomatic terms are formed like comparatives, although they are not true comparisons:

as high as	as much as	as few as
as little as	as many as	

INCORRECT: You may have to spend so much as two hours waiting.
CORRECT: You may have to spend as much as two hours waiting.

INCORRECT: It cost twice more than I thought it would.
CORRECT: It cost twice as much as I thought it would.

8. Errors in Noun-Adjectives. When a NOUN is used as an ADJECTIVE, treat it as an adjective. Do not pluralize or add *'s*.

INCORRECT: You're talking like a two-years-old child!
CORRECT: You're talking like a two-year-old child!

9. Errors in Ordinal and Cardinal Numbers. Ordinal numbers (first, second, third, etc.) are preceded by *the*. Cardinal numbers (one, two, three, etc.) are not.

We missed the first act.

We missed Act One.

NOTE: Ordinarily, either form is correct. There are two exceptions:

A. In *dates* use only *ordinal* numbers:
May first (*not* May one)
the first of May

B. In terms dealing with *travel*, use only *cardinal* numbers, as "Gate Three" may not actually be the third gate. It is Gate Number Three.

INCORRECT:	We leave from the second pier.
CORRECT:	We leave from Pier Two.
INCORRECT:	His birthday is on February twenty-two.
CORRECT:	His birthday is on February twenty-second.

10. Errors in Modifying Countable and Noncountable Nouns. If a noun can be preceded by a number, it is a countable noun and will be modified by these words:

a few	many, more	some
few, fewer	number of	

If it cannot be preceded by a number, it is noncountable and will be modified by these words:

amount of	little, less	some
a little	much, more	

INCORRECT:	I was surprised by the large amount of people who came.
CORRECT:	I was surprised by the large number of people who came.
INCORRECT:	You need only a little eggs in this recipe.
CORRECT:	You need only a few eggs in this recipe.

Errors in Usage

1. Errors in Connectors. There are several ways of connecting ideas. Do not mix the different forms:

and	also	not only...but also
too	as well as	both...and

INCORRECT: She speaks not only Spanish but French as well.

CORRECT: She speaks Spanish and French.

She speaks Spanish. She also speaks French.

She speaks Spanish and French too.

She speaks not only Spanish but also French.

She speaks both Spanish and French.

She speaks Spanish as well as French.

2. Errors in Question Word Connectors. When a question word such as *when* or *what* is used as a connector, the clause that follows is *not* a question. Do not use the interrogative form.

INCORRECT:	Do you know when does the movie start?
CORRECT:	Do you know when the movie starts?
INCORRECT:	I don't know what is his name.
CORRECT:	I don't know what his name is.
INCORRECT:	Did he tell you why hasn't he come yet?
CORRECT:	Did he tell you why he hasn't come yet?

3. Errors in Purpose Connectors. The word *so* by itself means *therefore.*

It was too hot to study, so we went to the beach.

So that means *in order to* or *in order that.*

INCORRECT:	We took a cab so we would be on time.
CORRECT:	We took a cab so that we would be on time.

4. Errors with BECAUSE. It is incorrect to say: *The reason is because . . .* Use: *The reason is that . . .*

INCORRECT: The reason he was rejected was because he was too young.

CORRECT: The reason he was rejected was that he was too young.

OR

He was rejected because of his young age.

OR

He was rejected because he was too young.

5. Errors of Dangling Modifiers. An introductory verbal modifier should be directly followed by the noun or pronoun that it modifies. Such a modifier will start with a gerund or participial phrase and be followed by a comma. Look for the modified noun or pronoun *immediately* after the comma.

INCORRECT:	Seeing that the hour was late, it was decided to postpone the committee vote.
CORRECT:	Seeing that the hour was late, the committee decided to postpone the vote.
INCORRECT:	Unaccustomed to getting up early, it was difficult for him to get to work on time.
CORRECT:	Unaccustomed to getting up early, he found it difficult to get to work on time.

INCORRECT: Wanting to get feedback, a questionnaire was handed out to the audience.

CORRECT: Since the speaker wanted to get feedback, he handed out a questionnaire to the audience.

6. Errors in Parallel Construction. In sentences containing a series of two or more items, check if the same form has been used for all the items in the series. Do *not* mix infinitives with gerunds, adjectives with participial phrases, or verbs with nouns.

INCORRECT: The film was interesting, exciting, and it was made well.

CORRECT: The film was interesting, exciting, and well made.

INCORRECT: The purpose of the meeting is to introduce new members and raising money.

CORRECT: The purpose of the meeting is to introduce new members and to raise money.

OR

The purpose of the meeting is introducing new members and raising money.

INCORRECT: He died unloved, unknown, and without any money.

CORRECT: He died unloved, unknown, and penniless.

INCORRECT: He was popular because of his sense of humor, his intelligence, and he could get along with people.

CORRECT: He was popular because of his sense of humor, his intelligence, and his ability to get along with people.

OR

He was popular because he had a sense of humor, was intelligent, and could get along with people.

7. Errors of Unnecessary Modifiers. In general, the more simply an idea is stated, the better it is. An adverb or adjective can often eliminate extraneous words.

INCORRECT: He drove in a careful way.

CORRECT: He drove carefully.

INCORRECT: The problem was difficult and delicate in nature.

CORRECT: It was a difficult, delicate problem.

Beware of words with the same meaning in the same sentence.

INCORRECT: The new innovations were startling.

CORRECT: The innovations were startling.

INCORRECT: Would you please repeat again what you said?

CORRECT: Would you please repeat what you said?

INCORRECT: He left more richer than when he came.

CORRECT: He left richer than when he came.

Beware of general wordiness.

INCORRECT: That depends on the state of the general condition of the situation.

CORRECT: That depends on the situation.

8. Errors of Commonly Confused Words. Following are some of the more commonly misused words in English:

to lie	lied	lied	lying	to tell an untruth
to lie	lay	lain	lying	to recline
to lay	laid	laid	laying	to put down

(*Idiomatic* usage: LAY THE TABLE, put dishes, etc., on the table; CHICKENS LAY EGGS; LAY A BET, make a bet)

to rise	rose	risen	rising	to go up; to get up
to arise	arose	arisen	arising	to wake up; to get up

(*Idiomatic* usage: A PROBLEM HAS ARISEN, a problem has come up)

to raise	raised	raised	raising	to lift; bring up

(*Idiomatic* usage: TO RAISE CHILDREN, to bring up children; TO RAISE VEGETABLES, to grow vegetables; TO RAISE MONEY, to collect funds for a cause)

to set	set	set	setting	to put down

(*Idiomatic* usage: SET A DATE, arrange a date; SET THE TABLE, put dishes, etc., on the table; THE SUN SET, the sun went down for the night; TO SET THE CLOCK, to adjust the timing mechanism of a clock)

to sit	sat	sat	sitting	to be in or get into a sitting position
to let	let	let	letting	to allow; to rent
to leave	left	left	leaving	to go away

formerly—previously
formally—in a formal way

to affect—to influence (verb)
effect—result (noun)

INCORRECT: He was laying in bed all day yesterday.
CORRECT: He was lying in bed all day yesterday.

INCORRECT: It had laid in the closet for a week before we found it.
CORRECT: It had lain in the closet for a week before we found it.

INCORRECT: The price of gas has raised three times last year.
CORRECT: The price of gas rose three times last year.
OR
The price of gas was raised three times last year.

INCORRECT: He raised slowly from his chair.
CORRECT: He arose slowly from his chair.

INCORRECT: We just set around the house all day.
CORRECT: We just sat around the house all day.

INCORRECT: His mother wouldn't leave him go with us.
CORRECT: His mother wouldn't let him go with us.

INCORRECT: All the men were dressed formerly.
CORRECT: All the men were dressed formally.

INCORRECT: My words had no affect on him.
CORRECT: My words had no effect on him.

9. Errors of Misused Words and Prepositional Idioms.

A. **in spite of; despite**

The two expressions are synonymous; use *either* one *or* the other.

INCORRECT: They came despite of the rain.
CORRECT: They came in spite of the rain.
OR
They came despite the rain.

B. **scarcely; barely; hardly**

All three words mean *almost not at all*; do NOT use a negative with them.

INCORRECT: I hardly never see him.
CORRECT: I hardly ever see him.

INCORRECT: He has scarcely no money.
CORRECT: He has scarcely any money.

C. Note and memorize the prepositions in these common idioms:

agree/disagree with
approve/disapprove of
be afraid of
be ashamed of
be bored with
be conscious of
be equal to
be interested in
capable/incapable of
compare to (point out similarities between things of a different order)
compare with (point out differences between things of the same order)
dependent on
except for
in the habit of
independent of
next to
related to
similar to

D. Confusion of words that *sound alike*:

adapt—to change, to adjust
adept—skilled

advice—counsel (n.)
advise—to give advice (v.)

affect—to influence (v.)
effect—result (n.)

afflicted—stricken
inflicted—caused or imposed something negative

affront—to insult
confront—to face

alteration—a change
altercation—argument

allude—to refer to indirectly
elude—to evade

allusion—a reference to
illusion—unreal image
delusion—false belief

apprise—to let know
appraise—to estimate the value of

beside—near
besides—in addition

capital—money; punishable by death; large form of letter
Capitol—the U.S. house of legislature

caret—a mark used in proofreading
carat—unit of gem weight
carrot—an orange vegetable

censor—one who screens objectionable material
censure—condemnation

cite—to quote
sight—vision
site—location

coherent—intelligible
inherent—a naturally included quality

collaborate—to work together
corroborate—to confirm

command—to order
commend—to praise

compile—to collect
comply—to consent

complement—to make complete
compliment—to praise

continual—happening often
continuous—happening uninterruptedly

conscientious—diligent
conscious—aware; awake

credible—believable
creditable—worthy of credit or praise
credulous—believing anything

depredation—a robbing
deprecation—disapproval

detain—to keep or hold up
retain—to keep in possession; to remember

detracted—taken away from
distracted—diverted

devise—to create
revise—to change; to improve

devolve—to deliver from one possessor to another
evolve—to develop

discouraging—seeming to be with no chance of success
disparaging—belittling

disinterested—having nothing personal to gain; impartial
uninterested—having no interest in

elegant—graceful; refined; with good taste
eloquent—persuasive; fluent (speech or writing)

elicit—to draw out
illicit—unlawful

emigrant—one who leaves a country to settle in another
immigrant—one who comes to a new country to settle

eminent—famous; prominent
imminent—impending
immanent—universal

epaulet—a shoulder decoration (usually on a uniform)
epithet—a descriptive word or phrase

epic—a long poem dealing with heroic deeds
epoch—a period of time marked by noteworthy people or events

flouting—scorning
flaunting—showing off provocatively

foreword—introduction to a book
forward—toward the front

gorilla—an ape
guerrilla—a soldier of the underground

horde—a crowd
hoard—to store up a supply

human—belonging to the race of man
humane—kind

immoral—without a sense of morality
immortal—able to live forever

imply—to hint
infer—to conclude from a known fact

in—within
inn—a pub or hostel

incandescent—glowing
clandestine—secret

incite—to urge to action
insight—quality of perceptiveness

incorporate—to include; to merge
incarcerate—to imprison

incredible—unbelievable
incredulous—doubting

ingenious—clever
ingenuous—frank

irrelevant—having no bearing on a matter
irreverent—lacking respect

loath—reluctant
loathe—to hate

luxuriant—growing thickly; highly ornamented
luxurious—rich; having an aura of wealth

perpetuate—to cause to continue
perpetrate—to do (something evil)

persecute—to affflict constantly in order to injure
prosecute—to institute legal proceedings against

personal—private
personnel—employees

perspective—appearance as determined by distance and position
prospective—likely

precede—to come before
proceed—to continue

prescribe—to order; to advise (as medicine)
proscribe—to outlaw

principal—the amount of a debt; the head of a school
principle—a fundamental law

profuse—excessive
profess—to declare

prophecy—prediction (n.)
prophesy—to predict (v.)

relay—to convey; a race between teams
relate—to tell; to connect

repel—to reject
repeal—to cancel

respectful—showing regard for
respective—particular

rightly—with good reason
rightfully—having a lawful claim
righteously—acting in a virtuous way

ruminating—meditating
fulminating—shouting
culminating—ending

sensual—of the body
sensuous—appealing to the senses

staple—basic commodity; a pin holding papers together
stable—firm; a shed for horses

stationary—immobile
stationery—writing materials

supplement—to add to something
supplant—to forcefully replace

temerity—boldness
timidity—shyness

their—belonging to them
there—in that place
they're—they are

troop—a group of people
troupe—a company of singers, dancers, or actors

weigh—to measure the weight of
way—road
whey—a part of milk that is separated from the curds in cheese making

weather—atmospheric conditions
whether—if

wholesome—healthful
fulsome—disgusting because of excessiveness

Strategy for Sentence Correction Questions

The first step in the Sentence Correction part of the exam is to read the sentence carefully in order to spot an error of grammar or usage. Once you have found an error, eliminate choice (A) and ALL OTHER ALTERNATIVES CONTAINING THAT ERROR. Concentrate on the remaining alternatives to choose your answer. Do not select an alternative that has changed the *meaning* of the original sentence.

EXAMPLE 1

If I knew him better, I would have insisted that he change the hour of the lecture.

(A) I would have insisted that he change
(B) I would have insisted that he changed
(C) I would insist that he change
(D) I would insist for him to change
(E) I would have insisted him to change

Since we must assume the unmarked part of the sentence to be correct, this is a PRESENT CONDITIONAL sentence; therefore, the second verb in the sentence should read *I would insist.* Glancing through the alternatives, you can eliminate (A), (B), and (E). You are left with (C) and (D). Remember that the word *insist* takes a *verb word* after it. (C) is the only correct answer.

If you do not find any grammatical error in the underlined part, read the alternatives to see if one of them does not use a clearer or more concise style to express the same thing. Do not choose an alternative that changes the meaning of the original sentence.

EXAMPLE 2

The couple, who had been married recently, booked their honeymoon passage through an agent who lived near them.

(A) The couple, who had been married recently, booked their honeymoon passage through an agent who lived near them.
(B) The couple, who had been recently married, booked their honeymoon passage through an agent who lived not far from them.
(C) The newlyweds booked their honeymoon passage through a local agent.
(D) The newlyweds booked their passage through an agent that lived not far from them.
(E) The couple lived not far from the agent who through him they booked their passage.

Although (A), the original, has no real errors, (C) expresses the same thing more concisely, without distorting the original meaning of the sentence.

Remember: If you find no errors, and if you find that none of the alternatives improve the original, choose (A).

Practice Exercise

Directions: This exercise consists of a number of sentences, in each of which some part or the whole is underlined. Each sentence is followed by five alternative versions of the underlined portion. Select the alternative you consider both most correct and most effective according to the requirements of standard written English. Answer (A) is the same as the original version; if you think the original version is best, select answer (A).

In considering the answer choices, be attentive to matters of grammar, diction, and syntax, as well as clarity, precision, and fluency. Do not select an answer that alters the meaning of the original sentence.

1. A good doctor inquires not only about his patients' physical health, but about their mental health too.

   (A) but about their mental health too
   (B) but their mental health also
   (C) but also he inquires about their mental health
   (D) but also about their mental health
   (E) but too about their mental health

2. Knowing that the area was prone to earthquakes, all the buildings were reinforced with additional steel and concrete.

   (A) Knowing that the area was prone to earthquakes,
   (B) Having known that the area was prone to earthquakes,
   (C) Since the area was known to be prone to earthquakes,
   (D) Since they knew that the area was prone to earthquakes,
   (E) Being prone to earthquakes,

3. John would never have taken the job if he had known what great demands it would make on his time.

   (A) if he had known
   (B) if he knew
   (C) if he had been knowing
   (D) if he knows
   (E) if he was knowing

4. Anyone wishing to enroll in the program should send in their applications before the fifteenth of the month.

   (A) send in their applications
   (B) send their applications in
   (C) send in their application
   (D) send their application in
   (E) send in his application

5. Start the actual writing only after having thoroughly researched your subject, organized your notes, and you have planned an outline.

   (A) you have planned an outline
   (B) planned an outline
   (C) you having planned an outline
   (D) an outline has been planned
   (E) an outline was planned

Answers and Analysis

1. **(D)** The connective *not only* MUST be accompanied by *but also*. Eliminate (A), (B), and (E). (C) repeats *he inquires* unnecessarily. (D) is correct.
2. **(C)** *All the buildings* couldn't have known that the area was prone to earthquakes. Since the unmarked part of the sentence must be assumed to be correct, eliminate all alternatives beginning with a dangling modifier: (A), (B), and (E). In (D) the word *they* is unclear. Where there is no definite subject, the passive is preferable. (C) is correct.
3. **(A)** This is a past conditional sentence. (A) is correct.
4. **(E)** *Anyone* is singular. At one glance eliminate every choice but (E).
5. **(B)** Here is a series of three verbs: having *researched*, *organized*, and *planned*. (B) is correct.

7 CRITICAL REASONING REVIEW

The principal object of the critical reasoning questions in the GMAT is to test skills in constructing and evaluating arguments. An argument is a sequence of two or more phrases, clauses, sentences or statements, one of which is a claim or conclusion, which follows the premises. For example:

> "The ground was wet, so it must have been raining."

The first part of the sentence, "The ground was wet....," is called a *premise*. The *conclusion* of the sentence, "it must have been raining," is based on the premise. Taken together, the premise and the conclusion form an *argument*. The method of reasoning in this example can be termed an *inference*. It is the inference that links the conclusion to the premises. Whether or not the argument and conclusion are valid is another question. In this case, the conclusion is not valid. The ground could have been wet for a variety of reasons, not necessarily connected with the weather.

Identifying the Premise and Conclusion

In evaluating an argument and its strength and validity, the first step is to identify the components—the premises and conclusion. There are several things to keep in mind when doing this.

Cue Words. Very often you will be helped in identifying the parts of an argument by the presence of cue words. Words such as "if," "given that," "since," "because," "for," " suppose," and "in view of" signal the presentation of evidence and reasons in support of a fact or claim. These cues identify premises. Conclusions, on the other hand, may often be preceded by words such as "thus," "hence," "so," and "therefore."

Without cue words, identifying and analyzing an argument become more difficult. For example, in conversation one might say:

> "The roads were empty yesterday. It was Sunday."

This example seems to contain two simple assertions that do not necessarily constitute an argument. However, the juxtaposition of the two facts may indicate that one statement was intended to be a conclusion based on the fact stated in the other statement. In the example given, one is really saying:

> "In view of the fact that it was Sunday, the roads were empty yesterday."

Fortunately, examples with no cue words at all are not common.

Position of Conclusion. Conclusions do not have to be at the end of an argument, as in the first example about wet streets and rain. Conclusions and premises may be reversed while the same meaning is conveyed. For example:

> "David was talking during the lesson, so he didn't understand the teacher's instructions."
> "David did not understand the teacher's instructions because he was talking during the lesson."

In both statements, the conclusion is "David did not understand the teacher's instructions."

Connecting Events to Draw Conclusions. Arguments frequently contain a number of premises and possibly more than one conclusion. Therefore, it is necessary to classify and connect things and events in order to analyze the arguments. To aid this analysis, think of events in terms of time sequence or causal relationships. For example:

> "Sarah overslept, which caused her to be late leaving for school; therefore, she ran all the way, causing her to be out of breath."

Sometimes we predict future events, basing our prediction on regular sequences we have previously experienced. An example of such a sequence:

"The sun rose this morning. The sun rose yesterday. Therefore, it will rise tomorrow."

Note that we are not using our previous experience to prove anything, but rather applying our knowledge about what has happened before as a basis for our conclusion about what will happen in the future.

Determining What the Writer Is Trying to Prove. At first glance the analysis of some arguments looks difficult because of the absence of cue words. In these cases, ask yourself, "What is the writer trying to prove?" Once you have identified the main point of the argument, define it. Ask "How great a claim (or 'How limited a claim') is the author making?" "What precisely is the author talking about?" "What was the author's purpose in making the claim?"

To answer the first of these questions, look again for signal words—for instance "all," "none," "never," "always," "some," and "sometimes." There is a big difference, for example, between "all cars are red" and "some cars are red." The first statement is false. The second is most definitely true. Similarly, note the difference between "I have never seen him before" and "I have not seen him today."

Often the use of different verbs and adverbs can change the meaning of similar claims. Consider the first example used in this chapter: "The ground was wet, so it must have been raining." We can limit the claim by changing "must" to "probably." "The ground was wet. So it probably has been raining." The first statement stands more chance of being proven false. Anything else that can be shown to have made the ground wet limits the chance that it must have been the rain that caused the wetness. However, it could still have been raining, and there is always the probability, no matter how small, that it may have been.

Descriptive words, both nouns and adjectives, in a passage are also used to limit or expand claims made by another. Take the example:

"Teachers in New York deserve extra pay for the dangers they face in the classroom."

Here the claim is made about teachers; it cannot be extended (without further information) to members of any other occupation or to teachers from any other place, except New York.

Another example:

"Prisoners in San Quentin rioted today because they were angry about their conditions."

The author's choice of the word "Prisoners" indicates merely that more than one prisoner rioted. Maybe all or maybe only some prisoners rioted. Note also that the author claims to know the reason for the riot—namely, that the prisoners were angry about their conditions and for no other reason. However, you cannot assume that just because an author states a reason for a claim, he or she is correct in that assumption. And if an author makes a claim about the cause of some event, he or she may either endorse or condemn it. Endorsement of a claim without any supporting evidence is not a substitute for proof.

The use of assumptions is vital in evaluating an argument. We have seen earlier that the conclusion of one argument can act as the premise for a further argument. In practice, we do not extend arguments indefinitely, but we stop at the conclusion we set out to prove, having begun from what seems to be a convenient and secure starting point. The strength of the argument depends on the legitimacy of its assumptions.

Deductive and Inductive Arguments

An argument may be deductive or inductive, depending on how the conclusion follows or is inferred from the premises.

An argument may be defined as deductive if it is *impossible* for the conclusion to be false if all the premises are true. In other words, in a deductive argument, the premises necessitate the conclusion. An example of a deductive argument is:

All men are mortals.
Brian is a man.
Therefore, Brian is a mortal.

If both premises are true, then the conclusion follows automatically.

An argument is inductive if it is *improbable* that the conclusion is false if all premises are true. The premises do not necessitate but do make probable the conclusion. The conclusion may be false even if all the premises are true.

Determining if the conclusion in an argument has been arrived at through deductive reasoning or through inductive reasoning can often be discerned from the wording of the statement or sentence. Words such as "usually," "sometimes," and "generally," are usually signals of induction.

An example of an inductive argument is:

(1) Freshmen usually find Economics I difficult.
(2) Jones is a freshman.
(3) Therefore, Jones finds Economics I difficult.

In the above statement, both premises are true. If the premises are true, does the conclusion automatically follow? No, because not all freshmen find Economics I difficult, and Jones may be one of the minority of freshmen who do not.

The distinction between deduction and induction should not be taken as a distinction between a good or superior way of arguing or reasoning and an inferior way. An inductive argument is not necessarily a bad argument. The two methods of argument serve different and complementary purposes. The distinction is in the manner by which a conclusion follows its premise(s).

Types of Inductive Arguments

Inductive arguments may be based on examples, generalizations, analogy, causal connection or other grounds for belief. We shall discuss a few types of inductive arguments.

Argument by Example

Arguing by example means inferring conclusions from specific cases or examples. The number of cases or examples used may vary from one to several. Example:

> The U.S. gives billions of dollars in foreign aid to Balonia. Leaders of Balonia resent foreign aid. The U.S. should discontinue direct foreign aid to developing countries.

In the above argument, only one example—that of Balonia—was used as a premise for reaching the conclusion that foreign aid should be discontinued. If it could be shown that Balonia is not a developing country, then one premise is false, and the argument and conclusion are invalid.

Assume for the moment that both premises are true. Is the conclusion then valid? Remember: only one example was given. One might argue that most developing countries welcome foreign aid and, therefore, that the single example given is irrelevant or atypical.

A typical critical reasoning question on the GMAT may ask you to select an answer that weakens an argument. In other words, you will be asked to select an answer that falsifies a premise or casts doubt on a generalization. One way to do this is to show that the specific example(s) given is (are) not typical or relevant and therefore cannot be the basis of a valid inductive argument in which examples are used to build a generalization.

Argument by Analogy

Arguing or reasoning by analogy consists of making a comparison between two similar cases, and inferring that what is true in one case is true in the other. A model for argument by analogy is as follows:

> Two things A and B are alike in respect to $C1, \ldots Cn$.
> A has characteristic $Cn + 1$.
> Therefore, B will have characteristic $Cn + 1$.

This model may be illustrated by the following example:

(1) The Conservative and Labor parties support a viable economy, including economic growth, industrialization, a fair wage policy, and unrestricted immigration.
(2) The Conservative party endorsed free trade.
(3) Therefore, the Labor party will endorse free trade.

In premise (1), both parties (A and B) have the same characteristics ($C1, \ldots Cn$). In premise (2), the Conservative Party (A) takes on an additional characteristic—that of endorsing free trade ($Cn + 1$). In the conclusion (3), it is claimed by analogy that the Labor Party (B) will also take on the characteristic ($Cn + 1$). This is an invalid argument by analogy—even though the arguer has shown that the two parties are similar in some ways. Because the Conservative and Labor parties are alike in some ways does not necessarily mean that they are alike in other ways.

In some arguments there is a lack of similar shared characteristics. For example:

(1) France and England have nearly the same population size.
(2) France has fluoridated drinking water.
(3) England will have fluoridated drinking water.

The problem in the above example is that there are not enough points of similarity between France and England to lead to the conclusion. Critical differences might involve income, drinking habits, attitudes toward medicine, and many other things.

Causal Arguing

In causal arguing, one infers that an act or factor (cause) produces a result (effect). This may be illustrated as:

Cause (Known)

↓

Effect (Inferred)

An X may be said to be a cause of Y if the occurrence of X is sufficient for the occurrence of Y. Whenever X occurs, Y follows, so that X determines Y. (Note here that factors other than X may also determine Y and that this does not alter the validity of the stated argument.)

Determining the Logical Sequence of an Argument

Having discussed types of arguments, we will now demonstrate in more detail how an argument can be identified and analyzed. You must be able to determine what the writer is trying to establish.

In order to identify an argument:

1. Find the conclusion first. This may be done by locating the cue that introduces the conclusion.
2. Find the premise(s). Again, locate the cue words (if present) that signal premises.
3. Determine if the premise(s) are true.
4. Determine the logical form of the argument.

A good way to check whether or not a conclusion follows from the premise(s) is to draw a Venn diagram, a device named after the British logician John Venn (1834–1923). A simplified form of the Venn diagram may consist of circles, one for each term of an argument. Take a simple argument:

"All weeds are plants; all daisies are weeds. Therefore, all daisies are plants."

We can now classify the various things (terms) in this argument and enclose each in a circle. Thus:

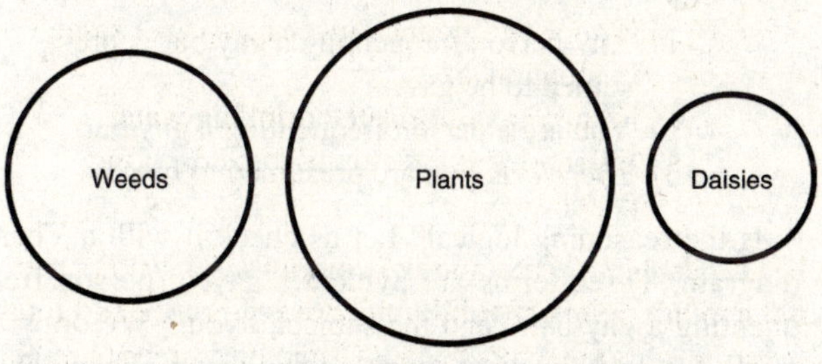

This deductive argument can be arranged to show the premises and conclusion, by showing that "daisies" are totally included in "weeds" and "weeds" are totally included in "plants."

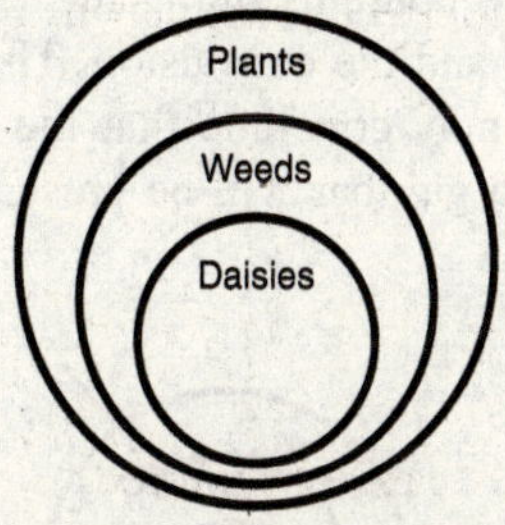

Since "daisies" are totally included in "plants," the conclusion of the argument is valid.

Venn diagrams can also be used to show if arguments are invalid. For example, take the argument:

"Because all dollars are money and all yen are money, then all dollars must be yen."

By placing dollars, money, and yen in circles and arranging them appropriately, we arrive at:

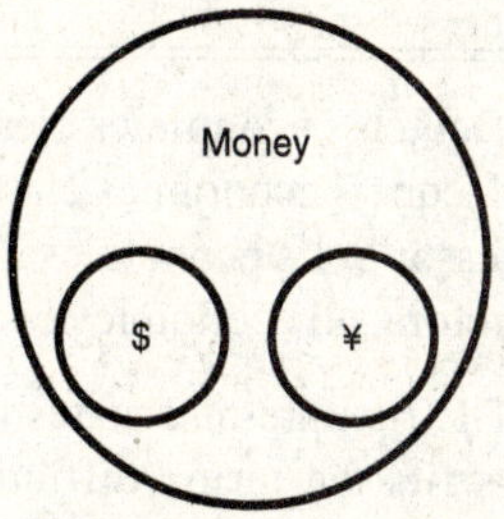

We can see that the conclusion—all dollars are yen—does not stand under scrutiny, since dollars and yen are not in the same small circle. All we can conclude is that both dollars and yen are money.

Using Venn Diagrams

Using examples, we shall now discuss the steps involved in using Venn diagrams to analyze the structure and logical sequence of an argument.

Study the following example.

(1) All men are mortal.
(2) Brian is a man.
(3) Brian is a mortal.

Step One. The first premise states that all men belong to a term which is called mortality. Therefore, we need one circle to represent the term and another circle for "men."

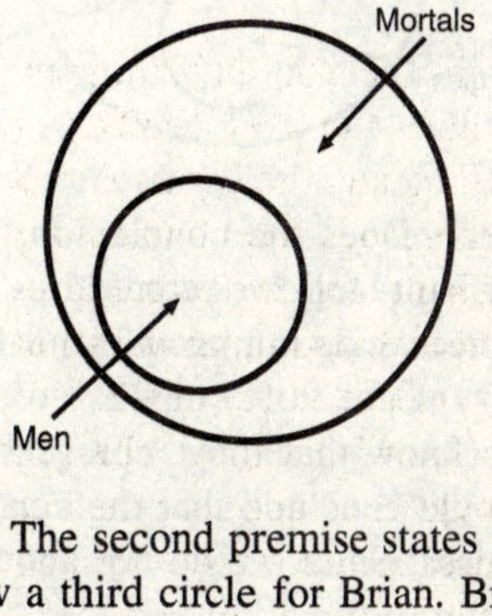

Step Two. The second premise states that Brian is a man. We draw a third circle for Brian. Brian's circle is within the circle of men.

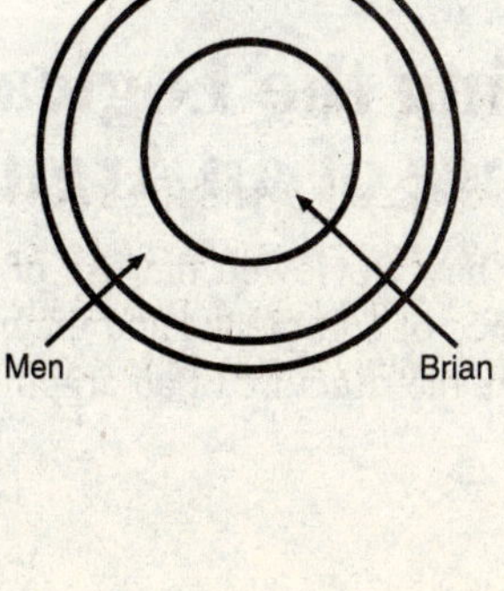

Step Three. Is the argument valid? Certainly, because we see that the conclusion—Brian is mortal—follows from the premises. Brian is in the "mortal" space, so he is mortal as well.

EXAMPLE

(1) Dr. Deutch's economics class is difficult.
(2) Dr. Jacque's economics class is difficult.
(3) Professor Sol's economics class is difficult.
(4) Therefore, all economic classes are difficult.

Step One. The first premise states that Dr. Deutch's economics class fits the term "difficult." This can be represented by two circles, one for the term "difficult," one for Dr. Deutch's class.

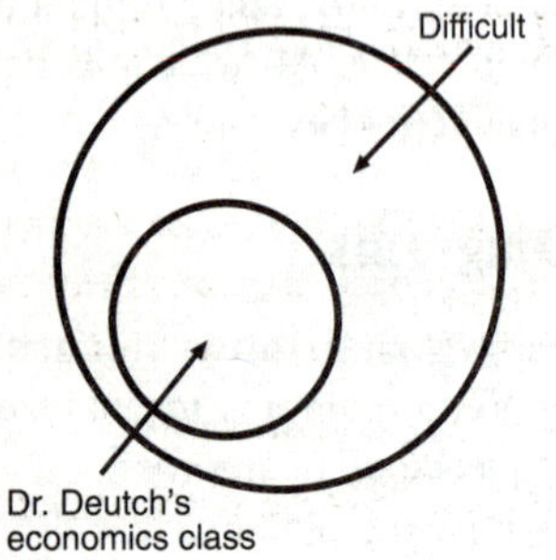

Step Two. Following step one, we are given two similar premises. We will add one circle for each.

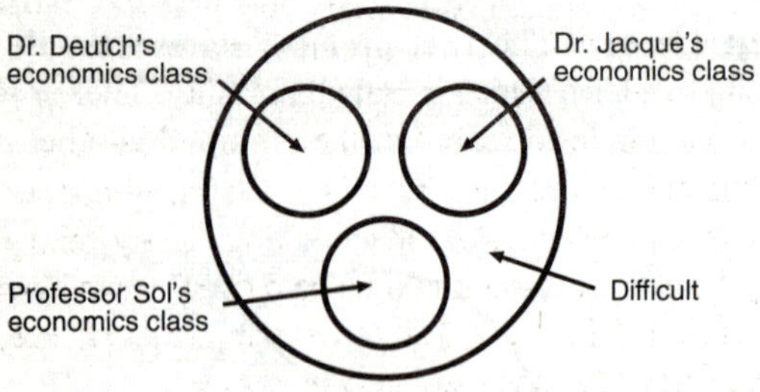

Step Three. Does the conclusion "all economics classes are difficult" follow the premises? The argument is inductive since we do not know if the three economics classes represent all, 90%, or 20% of all economics classes. If we know that they represent all economics classes, we could conclude that the conclusion follows from its premises. Since we do not know this, the conclusion is invalid.

Analyzing the Logical Sequence of an Argument

Now that we have reviewed the use of cue words, the logical sequence of arguments, and the use of Venn diagrams to check the structure of an argument, let us apply these concepts to some examples. The following letter was written to the columnist Ann Landers:

> Dear Ann Landers: I am a 21-year-old guy who is perfectly straight. I like to go to a gay bar in our neighborhood because the music is good and the people are very friendly.
> My dad sat me down last night and asked me if I was a switch-hitter. I told him absolutely not. He said he was very relieved because he had heard I was a steady at this place. When I explained I liked the ambiance, he advised me to find my fun someplace else because everyone assumes that a guy who goes to a gay bar is gay. I think he is wrong....*

What is the reasoning shown in the letter? Clearly, the young man's father believes that his son is guilty by association. The father claims that anyone frequenting a gay bar will be associated with the company he (or she) keeps. What evidence is given for the claim? Searching for key words shows that "because" appears three times. First, in line 2 "because" explains why the son goes to a gay bar. Second, in line 4 "because" signals evidence that the son is a steady patron of the gay bar. Third, in line 5, "because" signals the important assumption that people frequenting a gay bar are presumed to be gay. The father's reasoning may be summarized as follows:

(1) Any person frequenting a gay bar is presumed to be gay.
(2) You are a person frequenting a gay bar.
(3) *Therefore*, you are presumed to be gay.

Is the reasoning logical? Let us check it with a Venn diagram. Three terms are evident: "gay," "person frequenting a gay bar," and the subject, "you." We draw a circle for each of these terms as explained above. The rule for putting the circles together is that the outermost circle contains the term that appears in a premise and the conclusion. That term is "gay." Next, the middle circle contains the term that appears in both premises. That term is "person frequenting a gay bar." Finally, the innermost circle contains the term that appears in the middle premise and the conclusion. That term is "you." Therefore, we may conclude that the son (the "you") who frequents a gay bar will be presumed to belong to the term "gay."

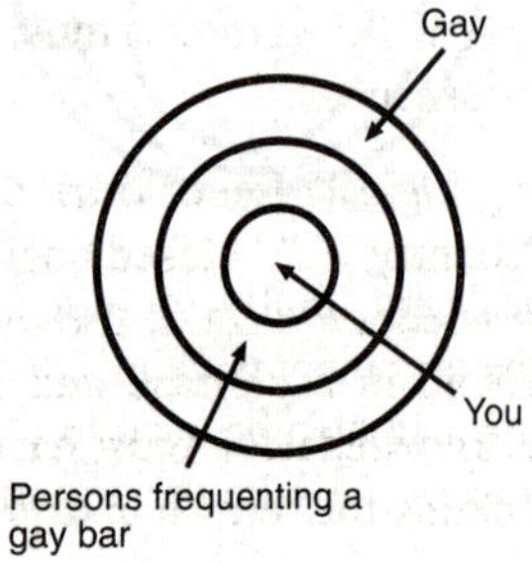

Now let us take another example, from a question that appeared on a recent exam.

EXAMPLE

A weapons-smuggling incident recently took place in country Y. We all know that Y is a closed society. So Y's government must have known about the weapons.

Which of the following is an assumption that would make the conclusion above logically correct?

(A) If a government knows about a particular weapons-smuggling incident, it must have intended to use the weapons for its own purposes.
(B) If a government claims that it knew nothing about a particular weapons-smuggling incident, it must have known everything about it.
(C) If a government does not permit weapons to enter a country, it is a closed society.
(D) If a country is a closed society, its government has a large contingent of armed guards patrolling its borders.
(E) If a country is a closed society, its government has knowledge about everything that occurs in the country.

The only cue word in the above passage is "so," which signals a conclusion: Y's government must have known about the weapons. What evidence is available to buttress this conclusion? The first premise is that "Y is a closed society." Now the question is, How can we link the premise with its conclusion? We need a second premise, but we do not have it in the passage. Surely, a "weapons-smuggling incident" is not the linkage. Therefore, we have what is called a "hidden" premise, one that is not given but must be assumed. However, in passages of this sort, the "hidden" premise is usually one of the answer alternatives. In fact, the question stem asks us to find the alternative that would make the conclusion logically correct. That alternative is (E). The complete argument is:

(1) If a country is a closed society, its government has knowledge.
(2) Y is a closed society.
(3) *Therefore*, Y's government must have known about the weapons.

Is the reasoning logical? Let us draw a Venn diagram. The terms are "country Y," "closed society," and "government has knowledge." Again, the outer circle contains the term found in a premise and the conclusion: "government has knowledge" ("must have known"). The middle circle contains the term found in both premises: "closed society." Finally, the innermost circle contains the term found in the middle premise and the conclusion: "country Y." The Venn diagram shows that the reasoning is logical.

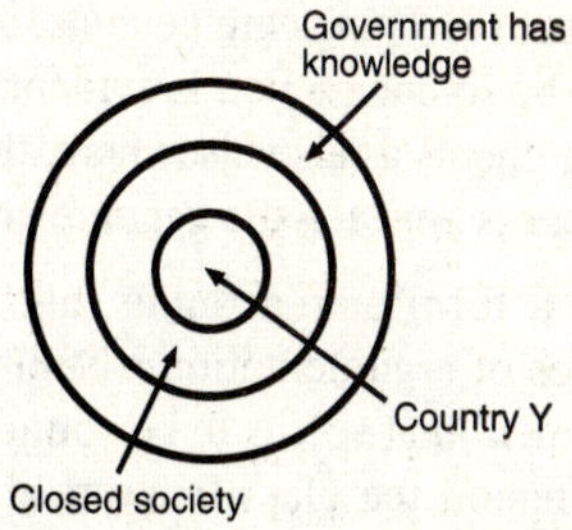

Attacking the Assumptions of an Argument

In the GMAT test, one often has to attack or find a fact that weakens an argument. The most effective way of doing this is to defeat the assumptions. Consider the following argument:

(1) "Cooking classes take place on Tuesdays"
(2) "Today is Tuesday"
(3) "Therefore, cooking classes take place today."

We may be able to defeat this argument by analyzing the first premise. If we assume that cooking classes usually take place on a Tuesday, then there is a probability that if today is Tuesday it will be one of those Tuesdays when cooking classes are held, but this is obviously not certain. Premise (1) does not state that cooking classes take place every Tuesday; classes could be held every other Tuesday or every third Tuesday. Therefore, the third sentence, the conclusion of the argument *may* be false.

Often, the attack on the argument will not be so obvious because the assumptions on which the argument is built are hidden or concealed. Someone who is making a totally honest and correct argument will not explicitly acknowledge all of the assumptions he or she makes. These hidden assumptions may be open to attack. Bear this in mind, particularly if you are presented with an argument that seems logical and correct but which reaches a factually impossible or absurd result. This could indicate the existence of hidden assumptions that make the argument invalid.

Fallacies

As mentioned earlier, the thought process that links the premise of an argument to its conclusion is called an inference. Errors may occur in any part of the argumentation process. These errors in reasoning are called *fallacies* or *flaws*.

Logicians have been studying flaws since Aristotle considered them in his *On Sophistical Refutations*. He wrote:

> That some reasonings are genuine, while others seem to be so but are not, is evident. This happens with arguments as also elsewhere, through a certain likeness between the genuine and the sham.

A fallacy is a form of reasoning that is illogical or violates the rules of argumentation. A fallacy is, in other words, an argument that seems to be sound but is not.

Scholars differ on the classification of fallacies. We shall discuss the most common types of fallacies and those that appear most often on the GMAT.

Guilt by Association

One type of fallacy is guilt by association. Suppose that one proves that educator John Doe is a dues-paying member of the Association for Fairy Teeth (A.F.T.), a fact not denied by Doe. Suppose that three members of the association have been found to be subversives. An argument may be:

> (1) John Doe is a member of the A.F.T.
> (2) X, Y, and Z are members of the A.F.T. and are subversives.
> Therefore, (3) John Doe is a subversive

This argument involves an invalid induction from premise (2) to a (missing) premise: all members of the A.F.T. are subversives. This has not been proven in the argument. It is left for the reader to draw his or her own—in this case, fallacious—conclusion, namely, that John Doe is a subversive.

A Venn diagram may be helpful. The largest circle represents all members of the A.F.T. A small circle within the larger one represents the three A.F.T. members that are known subversives. We are told in the statements that X, Y, and Z are known subversives, but we are not told that it is known that they are the *only* subversives in the A.F.T. membership. Therefore, we have no way of knowing whether or not John Doe is a subversive. In terms of a Venn diagram, we have no way of knowing whether or not the circle representing subversives should represent more than three members or whether or not the John Doe circle should overlap a larger circle representing all subversives.

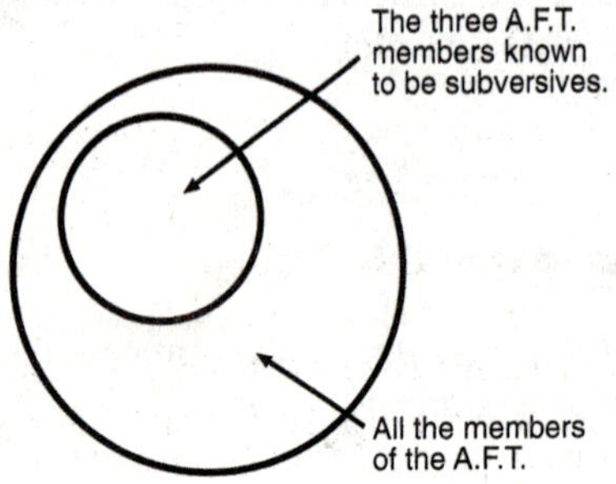

Faulty Analogy

Another type of fallacy is that of faulty analogy. A faulty analogy assumes that things that are similar in one respect must be similar in other respects. In general, analogies may be a useful form of communication. They enable a speaker to convey concepts in terms already familiar to the audience. A statement such as "our civilization is flowering" may be helpful in making a point, but the generalization is faulty. May we conclude that civilizations are in need of fertilizer?

Suppose that an economist argues that a "tariff on textiles will help our textile industry, a tariff on steel will help the steel industry, a tariff on every imported product will benefit the economy."

The above analogy may be stated as:

> (1) Tariffs on textiles benefit the textile industry.
> (2) Tariffs on steel benefit the steel industry.
> Therefore (3), a tariff on every imported product benefits the economy.

A Venn diagram of the above argument is:

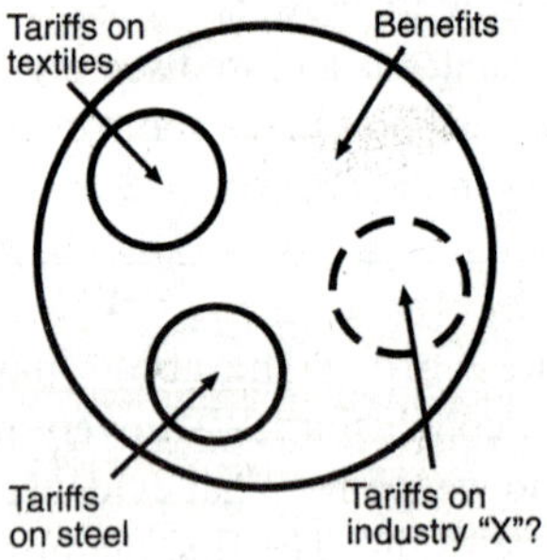

The analogy here assumes that because two industries benefit from tariffs, all others will also benefit. However, no proof for this argument is given.

Causal Fallacies

Some of the common causal fallacies are treating an insignificant relationship as a causal factor and assuming that a sequential relationship implies a causal relationship. That two events occur in sequence is not evidence of a causal relationship. For example, Herbert Hoover was elected President of the United States in 1928, an act followed by a recession in 1929. Did Hoover's policies cause the recession or were there other intervening factors? (There were).

The following is an example of a causal fallacy.

> Roni develops a rash whenever exposed to cactus weed. On his way home from a hike, he breaks out in a rash. Upon applying some ointment, he exclaims, "I must have brushed by cactus weed."

Roni's argument may be expanded as:

(1) Rashes are caused by cactus weed.
(2) I have a rash.
Therefore (3), I must have touched cactus weed.

Roni may be correct. However, other phenomena may have caused his rash: an allergy to certain food, contact with other plants, or many other things. Unless these can be ruled out, Roni's argument is fallacious.

Post Hoc Ergo Hoc ("After this, on account of this"). One type of fallacy of causality is a fallacy termed *post hoc ergo hoc*. This is the proposition that because events follow one another, one causes the other.

Consider the following scenario. In one of a company's five sales districts, the advertising budget was increased 20 percent, while in the other four districts, advertising expenditure was unchanged. Sales increased in the first district by nearly 20 percent, while sales remained unchanged in the other four districts. Did the increased advertising cause the sales increase?

This argument is in the form:

(1) Event Y followed event X
(2) So X is the cause of Y

The inference is weak. Y may be effected by a third factor Z. For example, in the sales district with the increase, a major competitor may have withdrawn from the market.

Fallacies of Relevance

Fallacies of relevance involve arguments wherein one or more of the premises are irrelevant to the conclusion. Some examples are as follows.

Ad Hominem (Personal attacks). One type of fallacy of relevance is the *ad hominem* fallacy. In this type of fallacy, the person is attacked, not his or her argument. Attacking an opponent may well be easier than rebutting the merit of the argument. The role of the demagogue is to assasinate the character of his or her opponent, thereby casting doubt on his/her argument.

For example, an economics professor exclaims to her class: "Even a freshman knows that good economists don't necessarily have to be good mathematicians." Or, "Congressman Goodboy has argued eloquently in favor of increasing public spending in his district. Isn't he the same congressman who was accused of wasting taxpayers' money on new autobuses whose air conditioning systems didn't work?"

The fallacy in these examples is that arguments are not treated on their merit. The arguments follow the form:

(1) Z asserts B.
(2) Z would benefit if we accept B.
(3) Z's assertion of B is insufficient to accept B as true.

This sort of argument attempts to show that B is not a reliable source because of some self-interest.

Another form of *ad hominem* argument is an appeal to the special position or vested interest of the person being argued with. Such arguments may include phrases such as "You, as members of the armed forces, can be counted on . . ." or "As a lover of the arts, you will be the first to agree that we need to raise taxes to support them."

Suppose that the listener does not agree to increased taxes. The argument then takes on the form:

(1) You believe X (that taxes shouldn't be raised).
(2) It is in your interest to reject X (your belief).
(3) You should reject X.

The conclusion does not show that personal gain is evidence enough to reject the belief against increased taxes.

Tu Quoque (You Too). This fallacy of relevance occurs when an argument is weakened by the assertion that its proponent is guilty by commission. A typical argument of this sort is, "You implore me not to drink, but you drink. Therefore, I can ignore your advice and do as I please." Here, the proponent's case is turned against him. This argument takes the form:

(1) You assert not to do X.
(2) But you do X.
(3) I can ignore your advice not to do X.

The above argument is invalid because (2) is not relevant to the advice given. The behavior of the person giving the advice has nothing to do with the validity of the claim or advice.

Fallacies of Language (Ambiguity)

Ambiguity occurs when there are two or more meanings for a word, phrase, statement, or expression, especially when the meanings are easily confused. Another problem occurs when it is not clear in what context the meaning is being used. Words and expressions such as "democracy," "teamwork," "the American way," and "payoff" have different meanings to different people and may be used in different contexts. For example, is the United States government a democracy in the same sense as the Indian government? Does teamwork mean the same thing to Japanese and American workers? The only way to avoid ambiguity is to carefully define the meaning of words in context.

Let us look at some cases where ambiguity is used with intent to deceive or confuse.

Equivocation (Double Meaning). The fallacy of equivocation occurs when words or phrases that have more than one meaning are used. An arguer using this fallacy relies on the fact that the audience fails to realize that some word or expression occurring more than once is used in different ways. The ambiguity may occur in both premises or in a premise and the conclusion. In the following for example, the structure of the argument is valid but an equivocation occurs.

(1) Happiness is the end of life. (X is Y)
(2) The end of life is death. (Y is Z)
(3) So happiness is death. (X is Z)

The fallacy is that the expression "end of life" has a different meaning in each premise. What has been asserted with one sense of the expression is then wrongly regarded as having been proved with respect to the other expression. An equivocation has been committed on the expression.

Amphiboly (Double Talk). This fallacy results whenever there is ambiguity in sentence structure. For example:

"Can you spell backwards?"
"I have filled out the claim form for my damaged car which I enclose."

Most logic textbooks quote a story in Herodotus about Croesus and the oracle. Croesus asked the oracle what would be the outcome if he attacked Cyrus the Great of Persia. The oracle's reply was that, "He would destroy a great empire." Of course, the empire that was destroyed was his own. In both possible outcomes, the oracle would have been correct. Fallacies of these sorts can usually be corrected by changing the syntax or punctuation, as in the first example above: "Can you spell 'backwards'?"

Accent. The meaning of statements can change depending on which words are stressed. Placing stress on certain words can change the meaning from the original unaccented statement. See the following example:

"Throw away your food."
to:
"Throw away your *food*." (instead of something else).
"*Throw away* your food." (instead of eating it?).
"Throw away *your* food." (instead of someone else's?).

Some Final Hints

Sherlock Holmes once said, "When you have eliminated the impossible, whatever remains, *however improbable,* must be the truth." Can this statement be a true guide to critical reasoning problems? When taking the test, be sure to relate the possible answers to the actual statements, without drawing on prior conceptions or possible misconceptions. Each of us perceives a thing in his or her own way, but critical reasoning problems can only have one solution.

Some final tactics to consider:

1. Never rule out the blatantly obvious; it may just be the only solution possible.
2. Never rule out the blatantly ridiculous; it could also be the only reasonable conclusion to be drawn from a specific set of criteria.
3. Always treat each conclusion in isolation, since only one answer can be correct.

8 MATHEMATICS REVIEW

For Problem Solving and Data Sufficiency Sections

The Problem Solving and Data Sufficiency areas of the GMAT require a working knowledge of mathematical principles, including an understanding of the fundamentals of algebra, geometry, and arithmetic, and the ability to interpret graphs. The following review covers these areas thoroughly and if used properly, will prove helpful in preparing for the mathematical parts of the GMAT.

Read through the review carefully. You will notice that each topic is keyed for easy reference. Use the key number next to each answer given in the Sample Tests to refer to those sections in the review that cover material you may have missed and therefore will need to spend more time on.

I. ARITHMETIC

I–1. Integers

➤I–1.1

The numbers 1, 2, 3, . . . are called the positive integers. –1, –2, –3, . . . are called the negative integers. An integer is a positive or negative integer or the number 0.

➤I–1.2

If the integer k divides m evenly, then we say *m is divisible by k* or *k is a factor of m*. For example, 12 is divisible by 4, but 12 is not divisible by 5. The factors of 12 are 1, 2, 3, 4, 6, and 12.

If k is a factor of m, then there is another integer n such that $m = k \times n$; in this case, m is called a *multiple of k*.

Since $12 = 4 \times 3$, 12 is a multiple of 4 and also 12 is a multiple of 3. For example, 5, 10, 15, and 20 are all multiples of 5, but 15 and 5 are not multiples of 10.

Any integer is a multiple of each of its factors.

➤I–1.3

Any whole number is divisible by itself and by 1. If p is a whole number greater than 1, which has *only* p and 1 as factors, then p is called a *prime number*. 2, 3, 5, 7, 11, 13, 17, 19, and 23 are all primes. 14 is not a prime since it is divisible by 2 and by 7.

A whole number which is divisible by 2 is called an *even* number; if a whole number is not even, then it is an *odd* number. 2, 4, 6, 8, and 10 are even numbers, and 1, 3, 5, 7, and 9 are odd numbers.

A collection of numbers is *consecutive* if each number is the successor of the number which precedes it. For example, 7, 8, 9, and 10 are consecutive, but 7, 8, 10, 13 are not. 4, 6, 8, 10 are consecutive even numbers. 7, 11, 13, 17 are consecutive primes. 7, 13, 19, 23 are not consecutive primes since 11 is a prime between 7 and 13.

➤I–1.4

Any integer greater than 1 is a prime or can be written as a product of primes.

To write a number as a *product of prime factors:*

- **A** Divide the number by 2 if possible; continue to divide by 2 until the factor you get is not divisible by 2.
- **B** Divide the result from (A) by 3 if possible; continue to divide by 3 until the factor you get is not divisible by 3.
- **C** Divide the result from (B) by 5 if possible; continue to divide by 5 until the factor you get is not divisible by 5.
- **D** Continue the procedure with 7, 11, and so on, until all the factors are primes.

EXAMPLE 1

Express 24 as a product of prime factors.

Ⓐ $24 = 2 \times 12$, $12 = 2 \times 6$, $6 = 2 \times 3$ so $24 = 2 \times 2 \times 2 \times 3$. Since each factor (2 and 3) is prime, $24 = 2 \times 2 \times 2 \times 3$.

EXAMPLE 2

Express 252 as a product of primes.

Ⓐ $252 = 2 \times 126$, $126 = 2 \times 63$ and 63 is not divisible by 2, so $252 = 2 \times 2 \times 63$.
Ⓑ $63 = 3 \times 21$, $21 = 3 \times 7$ and 7 is not divisible by 3. Since 7 is a prime, then $252 = 2 \times 2 \times 3 \times 3 \times 7$ and all the factors are primes.

EXAMPLE 3

A class of 45 students will sit in rows with the same number of students in each row. Each row must contain at least 2 students and there must be at least 2 rows. A row is parallel to the front of the room. How many different arrangements are possible?

Since 45 = (the number of rows)(the number of students per row), the question can be answered by finding how many different ways to write 45 as a product of two positive integers each of which is larger than 1. (The integers must be larger than 1 since there must be at least 2 rows and at least 2 students per row.) So write 45 as a product of primes $45 = 3 \times 15 = 3 \times 3 \times 5$. Therefore 3×15, 5×9, 9×5, and 15×3 are the only possibilities. So the correct answer is 4. The fact that a row is parallel to the front of the room means that 3×15 and 15×3 are different arrangements.

➤I–1.5

A number m is a *common multiple* of two other numbers k and j if it is a multiple of each of them. For example, 12 is a common multiple of 4 and 6, since $3 \times 4 = 12$ and $2 \times 6 = 12$. 15 is not a common multiple of 3 and 6, because 15 is not a multiple of 6.

A number k is a *common factor* of two other numbers m and n if k is a factor of m and k is a factor of n.

The *least common multiple* (L.C.M.) of two numbers is the smallest number that is a common multiple of both numbers. To find the least common multiple of two numbers k and j:

Ⓐ Write k as a product of primes and j as a product of primes.
Ⓑ If there are any common factors *delete* them in *one* of the products.
Ⓒ Multiply the remaining factors; the result is the least common multiple.

EXAMPLE 1

Find the L.C.M. of 12 and 11.

Ⓐ $12 = 2 \times 2 \times 3$, $11 = 11 \times 1$.
Ⓑ There are no common factors.
Ⓒ The L.C.M. is $12 \times 11 = 132$.

EXAMPLE 2

Find the L.C.M. of 27 and 63.

Ⓐ $27 = 3 \times 3 \times 3$, $63 = 3 \times 3 \times 7$.
Ⓑ $3 \times 3 = 9$ is a common factor so delete it once.
Ⓒ The L.C.M. is $3 \times 3 \times 3 \times 7 = 189$.

You can find the L.C.M. of a collection of numbers in the same way except that if in step (B) the common factors are factors of more than two of the numbers, then delete the common factor in *all but one* of the products.

EXAMPLE 3

Find the L.C.M. of 27, 63 and 72.

Ⓐ $27 = 3 \times 3 \times 3$, $63 = 3 \times 3 \times 7$, $72 = 2 \times 2 \times 2 \times 3 \times 3$.
Ⓑ Delete 3×3 from two of the products.
Ⓒ The L.C.M. is $3 \times 7 \times 2 \times 2 \times 2 \times 3 \times 3 = 21 \times 72 = 1,512$.

EXAMPLE 4

It takes Eric 20 minutes to inspect a car. John only needs 15 minutes to inspect a car. If they both start inspecting cars at 9:00 A.M., what is the first time they will finish inspecting a car at the same time?

Since Eric will finish k cars after $k \times 20$ minutes and John will finish j cars after $j \times 15$ minutes, they will both finish inspecting a car at the same time when $k \times 20 = j \times 15$. Since k and j must be integers (they represent the number of cars finished), this question is asking you to find a common multiple of 20 and 15. The question asks for the first time they will finish at the same time, so you must find the least common multiple.

Ⓐ $20 = 4 \times 5 = 2 \times 2 \times 5$, $15 = 3 \times 5$
Ⓑ Delete 5 from one of the products
Ⓒ So the L.C.M. is $2 \times 2 \times 5 \times 3 = 60$.

So Eric and John will finish inspecting a car at the same time 60 minutes after they start, or at 10:00 A.M. (By that time, Eric will have inspected 3 cars and John will have inspected 4 cars.)

➤I–1.6

The numbers 0, 1, 2, 3, 4, 5, 6, 7, 8, and 9 are called *digits*. The number 132 is a three-digit number. In the number 132, 1 is the first or hundreds digit, 3 is the second or tens digit, and 2 is the last or units digit.

EXAMPLE

Find x if x is a two-digit number whose last digit is 2. The difference of the digits of x is 5.

The two digit numbers whose last digits are 2 are 12, 22, 32, 42, 52, 62, 72, 82, and 92. The difference of the digits of 12 is either 1 or −1 so 12 is not x. Since 7 − 2 is 5, x is 72.

I–2. Fractions

➤I–2.1

A FRACTION is a number that represents a ratio or division of two numbers. A fraction is written in the form $\frac{a}{b}$.

The number on the top, a, is called the numerator; the number on the bottom, b, is called the denominator. The denominator tells how many equal parts there are (for example, parts of a pie); the numerator tells how many of these equal parts are taken. For example, $\frac{5}{8}$ is a fraction whose numerator is 5 and whose denominator is 8; it represents taking 5 of 8 equal parts, or dividing 8 into 5.

> *A fraction cannot have 0 as a denominator since division by 0 is not defined.*

A fraction with 1 as the denominator is the same as the whole number which is its numerator. For example, $\frac{12}{1}$ is 12, $\frac{0}{1}$ is 0.

If the numerator and denominator of a fraction are identical, the fraction represents 1. For example, $\frac{3}{3} = \frac{9}{9} = \frac{13}{13} = 1$. Any whole number, k, is represented by a fraction with a numerator equal to k times the denominator. For example, $\frac{18}{6} = 3$, and $\frac{30}{5} = 6$.

➤I–2.2

Mixed Numbers. A mixed number consists of a whole number and a fraction. For example, $7\frac{1}{4}$ is a mixed number; it means $7 + \frac{1}{4}$ and $\frac{1}{4}$ is called the fractional part of the mixed number $7\frac{1}{4}$. Any mixed number can be changed into a fraction:

Ⓐ Multiply the whole number by the denominator of the fractional part.
Ⓑ Add the numerator of the fraction to the result of step A.
Ⓒ Use the result of step B as the numerator and use the denominator of the fractional part of the mixed number as the denominator. This fraction is equal to the mixed number.

EXAMPLE 1

Write $7\frac{1}{4}$ as a fraction.

Ⓐ $4 \times 7 = 28$
Ⓑ $28 + 1 = 29$
Ⓒ so $7\frac{1}{4} = \frac{29}{4}$.

A fraction whose numerator is larger than its denominator can be changed into a mixed number.

Ⓐ Divide the denominator into the numerator; the result is the whole number of the mixed number.
Ⓑ Put the remainder from step A over the denominator; this is the fractional part of the mixed number.

EXAMPLE 2

If a pizza pie has 8 pieces, how many pizzas pies have been eaten at a party where 35 pieces were eaten?

Since there are 8 pieces in a pie, $\frac{35}{8}$ pies were eaten. To find the number of pies, we need to change $\frac{35}{8}$ into a mixed number.

Ⓐ Divide 8 into 35; the result is 4 with a remainder of 3.
Ⓑ $\frac{3}{8}$ is the fractional part of the mixed number.
Ⓒ So $\frac{35}{8} = 4\frac{3}{8}$.

We can regard any whole number as a mixed number with 0 as the fractional part. For example, $\frac{18}{6} = 3$.

> In calculations with mixed numbers, change the mixed numbers into fractions.

➤I–2.3

Multiplying Fractions. To multiply two fractions, multiply their numerators and divide this result by the product of their denominators.

EXAMPLE

John saves $\frac{1}{3}$ of \$240. How much does he save?

$\frac{1}{3} \times \frac{240}{1} = \frac{240}{3}$ = \$80, the amount John saves.

➤I–2.4

Dividing Fractions. To divide one fraction (the dividend) by another fraction (the divisor), invert the divisor and multiply. To invert a fraction, turn it upside down; for example, if you invert $\frac{3}{4}$, the result is $\frac{4}{3}$.

EXAMPLE 1

$$\frac{5}{6} \div \frac{3}{4} = \frac{5}{6} \times \frac{4}{3} = \frac{20}{18}$$

EXAMPLE 2

A worker makes a basket in $\frac{2}{3}$ of an hour. If the worker works for $7\frac{1}{2}$ hours, how many baskets will he make?

We want to divide $\frac{2}{3}$ into $7\frac{1}{2}$, and $7\frac{1}{2} = \frac{15}{2}$, so we want to divide $\frac{15}{2}$ by $\frac{2}{3}$.

Thus $\frac{15}{2} \div \frac{2}{3} = \frac{15}{2} \bullet \frac{3}{2} = \frac{45}{4} = 11\frac{1}{4}$ baskets.

➤I–2.5

Dividing and Multiplying by the Same Number. *If you multiply the numerator and denominator of a fraction by the same nonzero number the fraction remains the same.*

If you divide the numerator and denominator of any fraction by the same nonzero number, the fraction remains the same.

Consider the fraction $\frac{3}{4}$. If we multiply 3 by 10 and 4 by 10, then $\frac{30}{40}$ must equal $\frac{3}{4}$.

When we multiply fractions, if any of the numerators and denominators have a common factor (see Section I–1.2 for factors) we can divide each of them by the common factor and the fraction remains the same. This process is called *cancelling* and can be a great time-saver.

EXAMPLE

Multiply $\frac{4}{9} \times \frac{75}{8}$.

Since 4 is a common factor of 4 and 8, divide 4 and 8 by 4, getting $\frac{4}{9} \times \frac{75}{8} = \frac{1}{9} \times \frac{75}{2}$. Since 3 is a common factor of 9 and 75, divide 9 and 75 by 3 to get $\frac{1}{9} \times \frac{75}{2} = \frac{1}{3} \times \frac{25}{2}$. So $\frac{4}{9} \times \frac{75}{8} = \frac{1}{3} \times \frac{25}{2} = \frac{25}{6}$.

This is denoted by striking or crossing out the appropriate numbers. For instance, the example would be written as $\frac{\overset{1}{\cancel{4}}}{\underset{3}{\cancel{9}}} \times \frac{\overset{25}{\cancel{75}}}{\underset{2}{\cancel{8}}} = \frac{1}{3} \times \frac{25}{2} = \frac{25}{6}$.

Since you want to work as fast as possible on the GMAT exam, cancel whenever you can.

➤I–2.6

Equivalent Fractions. Two fractions are equivalent or equal if they represent the same ratio or number. In the last section, you saw that if you multiply or divide the numerator and denominator of a fraction by the same nonzero number the result is equivalent to the original fraction. For example, $\frac{7}{8} = \frac{70}{80}$ since $70 = 10 \times 7$ and $80 = 10 \times 8$.

> *In the test there will only be five choices, so your answer to a problem may not be the same as any of the given choices.* You may have to express a fraction as an equivalent fraction.

To find a fraction with a known denominator equal to a given fraction:

A divide the denominator of the given fraction into the known denominator;

B multiply the result of (A) by the numerator of the given fraction; this is the numerator of the required equivalent fraction.

EXAMPLE

Find a fraction with a denominator of 30 which is equal to $\frac{2}{5}$:

A 5 into 30 is 6;

B $6 \bullet 2 = 12$ so $\frac{12}{30} = \frac{2}{5}$.

➤I-2.7

Reducing a Fraction to Lowest Terms. A fraction has been reduced to lowest terms when the numerator and denominator have no common factors.

For example, $\frac{3}{4}$ is reduced to lowest terms, but $\frac{3}{6}$ is not because 3 is a common factor of 3 and 6.

> To reduce a fraction to lowest terms, cancel all the common factors of the numerator and denominator. (Cancelling common factors will not change the value of the fraction.)

For example, $\frac{\overset{2}{\cancel{\overset{10}{\cancel{100}}}}}{\underset{3}{\cancel{\underset{15}{\cancel{150}}}}} = \frac{2}{3}$. Since 2 and 3 have no common factors, $\frac{2}{3}$ is $\frac{100}{150}$ reduced to lowest terms.

A fraction is equivalent to the fraction reduced to lowest terms.

If you aren't sure if there are any common factors, write the numerator and denominator as products of primes. Then it will be easy to cancel any common factors.

$$\frac{63}{81} = \frac{3 \bullet 3 \bullet 7}{3 \bullet 3 \bullet 3 \bullet 3} = \frac{7}{9}$$

➤I-2.8

Adding Fractions. If the fractions have the same denominator, then the denominator is called a *common denominator*. Add the numerators, and use this sum as the new numerator with the common denominator as the denominator of the sum.

EXAMPLE 1

$$\frac{5}{12} + \frac{3}{12} = \frac{5+3}{12} = \frac{8}{12} = \frac{2}{3}$$

EXAMPLE 2

A box of light bulbs contains 24 bulbs. A worker replaces 17 bulbs in the shipping department and 13 bulbs in the accounting department. How many boxes of bulbs did the worker use?

The worker used $\frac{17}{24}$ of a box in the shipping department and $\frac{13}{24}$ of a box in the accounting department. So the total used was $\frac{17}{24} + \frac{13}{24} = \frac{30}{24} = 1\frac{1}{4}$ boxes.

If the fractions don't have the same denominator, you must first find a common denominator. One way to get a common denominator is to multiply all the denominators.

For example, to find $\frac{1}{2} + \frac{2}{3} + \frac{7}{4}$, note that $2 \bullet 3 \bullet 4 = 24$ is a common denominator.

There are many common denominators; the smallest one is called the *least common denominator*. For the previous example, 12 is the least common denominator.

Once you have found a common denominator, express each fraction as an equivalent fraction with the common denominator, and add as you did for the case when the fractions had the same denominator.

EXAMPLE

$\frac{1}{2}+\frac{2}{3}+\frac{7}{4}=?$

Ⓐ 24 is a common denominator.

Ⓑ $\frac{1}{2}=\frac{12}{24}, \frac{2}{3}=\frac{16}{24}, \frac{7}{4}=\frac{42}{24}.$

Ⓒ $\frac{1}{2}+\frac{2}{3}+\frac{7}{4}=\frac{12}{24}+\frac{16}{24}+\frac{42}{24}=\frac{12+16+42}{24}=$

$\frac{70}{24}=\frac{35}{12}.$

➤I–2.9

Subtracting Fractions. When the fractions have the same denominator, subtract the numerators and place the result over the denominator.

EXAMPLE

There are 5 tacos in a lunch box. Jim eats two of the tacos. What fraction of the original tacos are left in the lunch box?

Jim took $\frac{2}{5}$ of the original tacos, so $1-\frac{2}{5}$ are left.

Write 1 as $\frac{5}{5}$; then $\frac{5}{5}-\frac{2}{5}=\frac{(5-2)}{5}=\frac{3}{5}$. So $\frac{3}{5}$ are left in the lunch box.

When the fractions have different denominators:

Ⓐ Find a common denominator.
Ⓑ Express the fractions as equivalent fractions with the same denominator.
Ⓒ Subtract.

EXAMPLE

$\frac{3}{5}-\frac{2}{7}=?$

Ⓐ A common denominator is 5 • 7 = 35.

Ⓑ $\frac{3}{5}=\frac{21}{35}, \frac{2}{7}=\frac{10}{35}.$

Ⓒ $\frac{3}{5}-\frac{2}{7}=\frac{21}{35}-\frac{10}{35}=\frac{21-10}{35}=\frac{11}{35}.$

➤I–2.10

Complex Fractions. A fraction whose numerator and denominator are themselves fractions is called a *complex fraction*. For example $\frac{\frac{2}{3}}{\frac{4}{5}}$ is a complex fraction. A complex fraction can always be simplified by dividing the fraction.

EXAMPLE 1

$\frac{2}{3}\div\frac{4}{5}=\frac{\cancel{2}^{1}}{3}\bullet\frac{5}{\cancel{4}_{2}}=\frac{1}{3}\bullet\frac{5}{2}=\frac{5}{6}$

EXAMPLE 2

It takes $2\frac{1}{2}$ hours to get from Buffalo to Cleveland traveling at a constant rate of speed. What part of the distance is traveled in $\frac{3}{4}$ of an hour?

$\frac{\frac{3}{4}}{2\frac{1}{2}}=\frac{\frac{3}{4}}{\frac{5}{2}}=\frac{3}{4}\bullet\frac{2}{5}=\frac{3}{2}\bullet\frac{1}{5}=\frac{3}{10}$ of the distance.

I–3. Decimals

➤I–3.1

A collection of digits (the digits are 0, 1, 2, . . . 9) after a period (called the decimal point) is called a *decimal fraction*. For example, .503, .5602, .32, and .4 are all decimal fractions. A zero to the left of the decimal point is optional in a decimal fraction. So, 0.503 and .503 are equal.

Every decimal fraction represents a fraction. To find the fraction that a decimal fraction represents:

Ⓐ The denominator is 10 × 10 × 10 × . . . × 10. The number of copies of 10 is equal to the number of digits to the right of the decimal point.
Ⓑ The numerator is the number represented by the digits to the right of the decimal point.

EXAMPLE 1

What fraction does 0.503 represent?

A There are 3 digits to the right of the decimal point, so the denominator is $10 \times 10 \times 10 =$ 1,000.

B The numerator is 503, so the fraction is $\frac{503}{1000}$.

EXAMPLE 2

Find the fraction that .05732 represents.

A There are five digits to the right of the decimal point, so the denominator is $10 \times 10 \times 10 \times 10 \times 10 = 100{,}000$.

B The numerator is 5,732, so the fraction is $\frac{5{,}732}{100{,}000}$.

> *You can add any number of zeros to the right of a decimal fraction without changing its value.*

EXAMPLE

$.3 = \frac{3}{10} = \frac{30}{100} = .30 = .30000 = \frac{30{,}000}{100{,}000} =$

.300000000 . . .

➤I–3.2

We call the first position to the right of the decimal point the tenths place, since the digit in that position tells you how many tenths you should take. (It is the numerator of a fraction whose denominator is 10.) In the same way, we call the second position to the right the hundredths place, the third position to the right the thousandths, and so on. This is similar to the way whole numbers are expressed, since 568 means $5 \times 100 + 6 \times 10 + 8 \times 1$. The various digits represent different numbers depending on their position: the first place to the left of the decimal point represents units, the second place to the left represents tens, and so on.

The following diagram may be helpful:

THOUSANDS	HUNDREDS	TENS	UNITS	•	TENTHS	HUNDREDTHS	THOUSANDTHS

Thus, 5,342.061 means 5 thousands + 3 hundreds + 4 tens + 2 + 0 tenths + 6 hundredths + 1 thousandth.

➤I–3.3

A DECIMAL is a whole number plus a decimal fraction; the decimal point separates the whole number from the decimal fraction. For example, 4,307.206 is a decimal which represents 4,307 added to the decimal fraction .206. A decimal fraction is a decimal with zero as the whole number.

➤I–3.4

A fraction whose denominator is a power of 10 is equivalent to a decimal. The denominator tells you the last place that is filled to the right of the decimal point. Place the decimal point in the numerator so that the last place to the right of the decimal point corresponds to the denominator. If the numerator does not have enough digits, add the appropriate number of zeros *before* the numerator.

EXAMPLE 1

Find the decimal equivalent of $\frac{5{,}732}{100}$.

Since the denominator is 100, you need two places to the right of the decimal point so $\frac{5{,}732}{100} = 57.32$.

EXAMPLE 2

What is the decimal equivalent of $\frac{57}{10{,}000}$?

The denominator is 10,000, so you need 4 decimal places to the right of the decimal point. Since 57 only has two places, we add two zeros in front of 57; thus, $\frac{57}{10{,}000} = .0057$.

Do not make the error of adding the zeros to the right of 57 instead of the left. .5700 is $\frac{5,700}{10,000}$, not $\frac{57}{10,000}$.

➤I–3.5

Adding Decimals. Decimals are much easier to add than fractions. To add a collection of decimals:

Ⓐ Write the decimals in a column with the decimal points vertically aligned.
Ⓑ Add enough zeros to the right of the decimal point so that every number has an entry in each column to the right of the decimal point.
Ⓒ Add the numbers in the same way as whole numbers.
Ⓓ Place a decimal point in the sum so that it is directly beneath the decimal points in the decimals added.

EXAMPLE 1

How much is 5 + 3.43 + 16.021 + 3.1?

Ⓐ
```
      5
      3.43
     16.021
   +  3.1
```
Ⓑ
```
      5.000
      3.430
     16.021
   +  3.100
```
Ⓒ
```
      5.000
      3.430
     16.021
   +  3.100
```
Ⓓ 27.551 The answer is 27.551.

EXAMPLE 2

If Mary has $.50, $3.25, and $6.05, how much does she have?

```
   $ .50
     3.25
   + 6.05
   $9.80
```
So Mary has $9.80.

➤I–3.6

Subtracting Decimals. To subtract one decimal from another:

Ⓐ Put the decimals in a column so that the decimal points are vertically aligned.
Ⓑ Add zeros so that every decimal has an entry in each column to the right of the decimal point.
Ⓒ Subtract the numbers as you would whole numbers.
Ⓓ Place the decimal point in the result so that it is directly beneath the decimal points of the numbers you subtracted.

EXAMPLE 1

Solve 5.053 – 2.09.

Ⓐ
```
    5.053
  – 2.09
```
Ⓑ
```
    5.053
  – 2.090
```
Ⓒ
```
    5.053
  – 2.090
```
Ⓓ 2.963 The answer is 2.963.

EXAMPLE 2

If Joe has $12 and he loses $8.40, how much money does he have left?

Since $12.00 – $8.40 = $3.60, he has $3.60 left.

➤I–3.7

Multiplying Decimals. Decimals are multiplied like whole numbers. *The decimal point of the product is placed so that the number of decimal places in the product is equal to the total of the number of decimal places in all of the numbers multiplied.*

EXAMPLE 1

What is (5.02)(.6)?

(502)(6) = 3012. There were 2 decimal places in 5.02 and 1 decimal place in .6, so the product must have 2 + 1 = 3 decimal places. Therefore, (5.02)(.6) = 3.012.

EXAMPLE 2

If eggs cost $.06 each, how much should a dozen eggs cost?

Since (12)(.06) = .72, a dozen eggs should cost $.72.

Computing Tip: To multiply a decimal by 10, just move the decimal point to the right one place; to multiply by 100 or move the decimal point two places to the right and so on.

EXAMPLE

$9{,}983.456 \times 100 = 998{,}345.6$

➤I–3.8

Dividing Decimals. To divide one decimal (the dividend) by another decimal (the divisor):

- **A** Move the decimal point in the divisor to the right until there is no decimal fraction in the divisor (this is the same as multiplying the divisor by a multiple of 10).
- **B** Move the decimal point in the dividend the same number of places to the right as you moved the decimal point in step (A).
- **C** Divide the result of (B) by the result of (A) as if they were whole numbers.
- **D** The number of decimal places in the result (quotient) should be equal to the number of decimal places in the result of step (B).
- **E** You may obtain as many decimal places as you wish in the quotient by adding zeros to the right in the dividend and then repeating step (C). For each zero you add to the dividend, you need one more decimal place in the quotient.

EXAMPLE 1

Divide .05 into 25.155.

- **A** Move the decimal point two places to the right in .05; the result is 5.
- **B** Move the decimal point two places to the right in 25.155; the result is 2515.5.
- **C** Divide 5 into 25155; the result is 5031.
- **D** Since there was one decimal place in the result of (B), the answer is 503.1.
- **E** There is no need to continue the division.

The work for this example might look like this:

$$.05\overline{)25.155}\quad = 503.1$$

You can always check division by multiplying.

$(503.1)(.05) = 25.155$ so our answer checks.

If you write division as a fraction, example 1 would be expressed as $\frac{25.155}{.05}$.

You can multiply both the numerator and denominator by 100 without changing the value of the fraction, so

$$\frac{25.155}{.05} = \frac{25.155 \times 100}{.05 \times 100} = \frac{2515.5}{5.}.$$

So steps (A) and (B) always change the division of a decimal by a decimal into the division of a decimal by a whole number.

To divide a decimal by a whole number, divide them as if they were whole numbers. Then place the decimal point in the quotient so that the quotient has as many decimal places as the dividend.

EXAMPLE 2

$\frac{100.11}{.8} = ?$

- **A** Move the decimal point one place to the right in .8; the result is 8.
- **B** Move the decimal point one place to the right in 100.11; the result is 1001.1.
- **C** Divide 8 into 10011; the result is 1251, with a remainder of 3. Since the division is not exact, we use step (D).
- **D** Add 3 zeros to the right of 1001.1 and repeat (C). So we divide 8 into 10011000; the result is 1251375.
- **E** The result must have four decimal places (1 from step (B) and 3 from step (D)), so the answer is 125.1375.

The work for this example might look like this:

$$.8\overline{)100.11000}\quad = 125.1375$$

CHECK: $(.8)(125.1375) = 100.11000 = 100.11$ so this is correct.

EXAMPLE 3

If oranges cost 42¢ each, how many oranges can you buy for \$2.52? Make sure the units are compatible, so 42¢ is \$0.42. Therefore, the number of oranges is

$$\frac{2.52}{.42} = \frac{252}{42} = 6.$$

Computing Tip. To divide a decimal by 10, move the decimal point *to the left* one place; to divide by 100, move the decimal point two places to the left, and so on.

EXAMPLE

Divide 5,637.6471 by 1,000.

The answer is 5.6376471, since to divide by 1,000 you move the decimal point 3 places to the left.

➤I–3.9

Converting a Fraction into a Decimal. To convert a fraction into a decimal, divide the denominator into the numerator. For example, $\frac{3}{4} = \frac{3.00}{4} = .75$. Some fractions give a repeating decimal when you divide the denominator into the numerator, for example, $\frac{1}{3} = .333\ldots$ where the three dots mean you keep on getting 3 with each step of division. .333 . . . is a *repeating decimal.*

You should know the following decimal equivalents of fractions:

$\frac{1}{100} = .01$	$\frac{1}{10} = .1$	$\frac{2}{5} = .4$
$\frac{1}{50} = .02$	$\frac{1}{9} = .111\ldots$	$\frac{1}{2} = .5$
$\frac{1}{40} = .025$	$\frac{1}{8} = .125$	$\frac{5}{8} = .625$
$\frac{1}{25} = .04$	$\frac{1}{6} = .1666\ldots$	$\frac{2}{3} = .666\ldots$
$\frac{1}{20} = .05$	$\frac{1}{5} = .2$	$\frac{3}{4} = .75$
$\frac{1}{16} = .0625$	$\frac{1}{4} = .25$	$\frac{7}{8} = .875$
$\frac{1}{15} = .0666\ldots$	$\frac{1}{3} = .333\ldots$	$\frac{3}{2} = 1.5$
$\frac{1}{12} = .0833\ldots$	$\frac{3}{8} = .375$	

Any decimal with . . . is a repeating decimal.

If a fraction has a repeating decimal, use the fraction in any computation.

EXAMPLE 1

What is $\frac{2}{9}$ of $3,690.90?

Since the decimal for $\frac{2}{9}$ is .2222 . . . use the fraction $\frac{2}{9}$.

$\frac{2}{9} \times \$3,690.90 = 2 \times \$410.10 = \$820.20.$

I–4. Percentage

➤I–4.1

PERCENTAGE is another method of expressing fractions or parts of an object. Percentages are expressed in terms of hundredths, so 100% means 100 hundredths or 1, and 50% would be 50 hundredths or $\frac{1}{2}$.

A decimal is converted to a percentage by multiplying the decimal by 100. Since multiplying a decimal by 100 is accomplished by moving the decimal point two places to the right, *you convert a decimal into a percentage by moving the decimal point two places to the right.* For example, .134 = 13.4%.

If you wish to convert a percentage into a decimal, you divide the percentage by 100. There is a shortcut for this also. To divide by 100 you move the decimal point two places to the left.

Therefore, *to convert a percentage into a decimal, move the decimal point two places to the left.* For example, 24% = .24.

A fraction is converted into a percentage by changing the fraction to a decimal and then changing the decimal to a percentage. A percentage is changed into a fraction by first converting the percentage into a decimal and then changing the decimal to a fraction. *You should know the following fractional equivalents of percentages:*

$1\% = \frac{1}{100}$	$25\% = \frac{1}{4}$	$80\% = \frac{4}{5}$
$2\% = \frac{1}{50}$	$33\frac{1}{3}\% = \frac{1}{3}$	$83\frac{1}{3}\% = \frac{5}{6}$
$4\% = \frac{1}{25}$	$37\frac{1}{2}\% = \frac{3}{8}$	$87\frac{1}{2}\% = \frac{7}{8}$
$5\% = \frac{1}{20}$	$40\% = \frac{2}{5}$	$100\% = 1$
$8\frac{1}{3}\% = \frac{1}{12}$	$50\% = \frac{1}{2}$	$120\% = \frac{6}{5}$
$10\% = \frac{1}{10}$	$60\% = \frac{3}{5}$	$125\% = \frac{5}{4}$
$12\frac{1}{2}\% = \frac{1}{8}$	$62\frac{1}{2}\% = \frac{5}{8}$	$133\frac{1}{3}\% = \frac{4}{3}$
$16\frac{2}{3}\% = \frac{1}{6}$	$66\frac{2}{3}\% = \frac{2}{3}$	$150\% = \frac{3}{2}$
$20\% = \frac{1}{5}$	$75\% = \frac{3}{4}$	

Note, for example, that $133\frac{1}{3}\% = 1.33\frac{1}{3} = 1\frac{1}{3} = \frac{4}{3}$.

When you compute with percentages, it is usually easier to change the percentages to decimals or fractions.

EXAMPLE 1

A company has 6,435 bars of soap. If the company sells 20% of its bars of soap, how many bars of soap did it sell?

Change 20% into .2. Thus, the company sold (.2)(6,435) = 1287.0 = 1,287 bars of soap. An alternative method would be to convert 20% to $\frac{1}{5}$.

Then, $\frac{1}{5} \times 6{,}435 = 1{,}287$.

EXAMPLE 2

In a class of 60 students, 18 students received a grade of B. What percentage of the class received a grade of B?

$\frac{18}{60}$ of the class received a grade of B. $\frac{18}{60} = \frac{3}{10} =$ .3 = 30%, so 30% of the class received a grade of B.

EXAMPLE 3

If the population of Dryden was 10,000 in 1960 and the population of Dryden increased by 15% between 1960 and 1970, what was the population of Dryden in 1970?

The population increased by 15% between 1960 and 1970, so the increase was (.15)(10,000) which is 1,500. The population in 1970 was 10,000 + 1,500 = 11,500.

A quicker method: The population increased 15%, so the population in 1970 is 115% of the population in 1960. Therefore, the population in 1970 is 115% of 10,000 which is (1.15)(10,000) = 11,500.

➤I–4.2

Interest and Discount. Two of the most common uses of percentages are in interest and discount problems.

The rate of interest is usually given as a percentage. The basic formula for interest problems is:

INTEREST = AMOUNT × TIME × RATE

You can assume the rate of interest is the annual rate of interest unless the problem states otherwise; so you should express the time in years.

EXAMPLE 1

How much interest will $10,000 earn in 9 months at an annual rate of 6%?

9 months is $\frac{3}{4}$ of a year and $6\% = \frac{3}{50}$, so using the formula, the interest is $\$10{,}000 \times \frac{3}{4} \times \frac{3}{50} = \$50 \times 9 = \$450$.

EXAMPLE 2

What annual rate of interest was paid if $5,000 earned $300 in interest in 2 years?

Since the interest was earned in 2 years, $150 is the interest earned in one year. $\frac{150}{5,000} = .03 = 3\%$, so the annual rate of interest was 3%.

The type of interest described above is called *simple interest.*

There is another method of computing interest called *compound interest.* In computing compound interest, the interest is periodically added to the amount (or principal) which is earning interest.

EXAMPLE 3

What will $1,000 be worth after three years if it earns interest at the rate of 5% compounded annually?

Compounded annually means that the interest earned during one year is added to the amount (or principal) at the end of each year. The interest on $1,000 at 5% for one year is $(1,000)(.05) = $50. So you must compute the interest on $1,050 (not $1,000) for the second year. The interest is $(1,050)(.05) = $52.50. Therefore, during the third year interest will be computed for $1,102.50. During the third year the interest is $(1,102.50)(.05) = $55.125 = $55.13. Therefore, after 3 years the original $1,000 will be worth $1,157.63.

If you calculated simple interest on $1,000 at 5% for three years, the answer would be $(1,000)(.05)(3) = $150. Therefore, using simple interest, $1,000 is worth $1,150 after 3 years. You earn more interest with compound interest.

You can assume that interest means simple interest unless a problem states otherwise.

The basic formula for discount problems is:

DISCOUNT = COST × RATE OF DISCOUNT

EXAMPLE 1

What is the discount if a car which cost $3,000 is discounted 7%? The discount is $3,000 × .07 = $210 since 7% = .07.

If we know the cost of an item and its discounted price, we can find the rate of discount by using the formula

$$\text{rate of discount} = \frac{\text{cost} - \text{price}}{\text{cost}}$$

EXAMPLE 2

What was the rate of discount if a boat which cost $5,000 was sold for $4,800?

Using this formula, we find that the rate of discount equals

$$\frac{5,000 - 4,800}{5,000} = \frac{200}{5,000} = \frac{1}{25} = .04 = 4\%.$$

After an item has been discounted once, it may be discounted again. This procedure is called *successive* discounting.

EXAMPLE 3

A bicycle originally cost $100 and was discounted 10%. After three months it was sold after being discounted 15%. How much was the bicycle sold for?

After the 10% discount the bicycle was selling for $100(.90) = $90. An item which costs $90 and is discounted 15% will sell for $90(.85) = $76.50, so the bicycle was sold for $76.50.

Notice that if you added the two discounts of 10% and 15% and treated the successive discounts as a single discount of 25%, your answer would be that the bicycle sold for $75, which is incorrect. Successive discounts are *not* identical to a single discount of the sum of the discounts. The previous example shows that successive discounts of 10% and 15% are not identical to a single discount of 25%.

I–5. Rounding Off Numbers

➤I–5.1

Many times an approximate answer can be found more quickly and may be more useful than the exact answer. For example, if a company had sales of $998,875.63 during a year, it is easier to remember that the sales were about $1 million.

Rounding off a number to a decimal place means finding the multiple of the representative of that decimal place which is closest to the original number. Thus, rounding off a number to the nearest hundred means finding the multiple of 100 which is closest to the original number. Rounding off to the nearest tenth means finding the multiple of $\frac{1}{10}$ which is closest to the original number. After a number has been rounded off to a particular decimal place, all the digits to the right of that particular decimal place will be zero.

To round off a number to the *r*th decimal place:

A Look at the digit in the place to the right of the *r*th place;

B *If the digit is 4 or less, change all the digits in places to the right of the rth place to 0* to round off the number.

C *If the digit is 5 or more, add 1 to the digit in the rth place and change all the digits in places to the right of the rth place to 0* to round off the number.

For example, the multiple of 100 which is closest to 5,342.1 is 5,300.

EXAMPLE 1

Round off 3.445 to the nearest tenth.

The digit to the right of the tenths place is 4, so 3.445 is 3.4 to the nearest tenth.

Most problems dealing with money are rounded off to the nearest hundredth or cent if the answer contains a fractional part of a cent. This is common business practice.

EXAMPLE 2

If 16 cookies cost $1.00, how much should three cookies cost?

Three cookies should cost $\frac{3}{16}$ of $1.00. Since $\frac{3}{16} \times 1 = .1875$, the cost would be $.1875. In practice, you would round it up to $.19 or 19¢.

Rounding off numbers can help you get quick, approximate answers. Since many questions require only rough answers, you can save time on the test by rounding off numbers.

EXAMPLE 3

If 5,301 of the 499,863 workers employed at the XYZ factory don't show up for work on Monday, about what percentage of the workers don't show up?

(A) 1
(B) 2
(C) 3
(D) 4
(E) 5

You can quickly see that the answer is (A) by rounding off both numbers to the nearest thousand before you divide, because $\frac{5{,}000}{500{,}000} = \frac{1}{100} = .01 =$ 1%. The exact answer is $\frac{5{,}301}{499{,}863} = .010604$, but it would take much longer to get an exact answer.

EXAMPLE 4

Round off 43.796 to the nearest tenth.

The place to the right of tenths is hundredths, so look in the hundredths place. Since 9 is bigger than 5, add 1 to the tenths place. Therefore, 43.796 is 43.8 rounded off to the nearest tenth.

If the digit in the *r*th place is 9 and you need to add 1 to the digit to round off the number to the *r*th decimal place, put a zero in the *r*th place and add 1 to the digit in the position to the left of the *r*th place. For example, 298 rounded off to the nearest 10 is 300; 99,752 to the nearest thousand is 100,000.

I–6. Signed Numbers

➤I–6.1

A number preceded by either a plus or a minus sign is called a SIGNED NUMBER. For example, + 5, –6, –4.2, and $+\frac{3}{4}$ are all signed numbers. If no sign is given with a number, a plus sign is assumed; thus, 5 is interpreted as +5.

Signed numbers can often be used to distinguish different concepts. For example, a profit of $10 can be denoted by +$10 and a loss of $10 by –$10. A temperature of 20 degrees below zero can be denoted –20°.

➤I–6.2

Signed numbers are also called DIRECTED NUMBERS. You can think of numbers arranged on a line, called a number line, in the following manner:

Take a line which extends indefinitely in both directions, pick a point on the line and call it 0, pick another point on the line to the right of 0 and call it 1. The point to the right of 1 which is exactly as far from 1 as 1 is from 0 is called 2, the point to the right of 2 just as far from 2 as 1 is from 0 is called 3, and so on. The point halfway between 0 and 1 is called $\frac{1}{2}$, the point halfway between $\frac{1}{2}$ and 1 is called $\frac{3}{4}$. In this way, you can identify any whole number or any fraction with a point on the line.

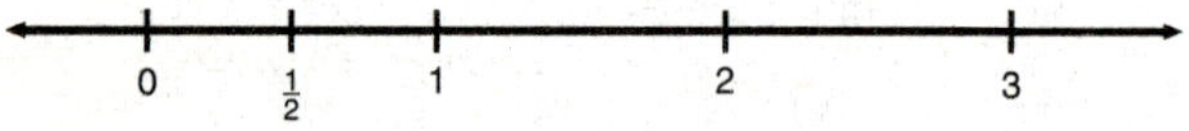

All the numbers which correspond to points to the right of 0 are called *positive numbers*. The sign of a positive number is +.

If you go to the left of zero the same distance as you did from 0 to 1, the point is called –1; in the same way as before, you can find –2, –3, $-\frac{1}{2}$, $-\frac{3}{2}$ and so on.

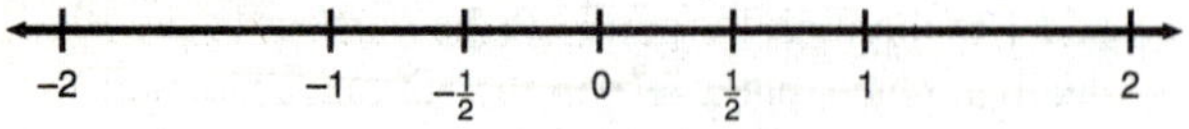

All the numbers which correspond to points to the left of zero are called *negative numbers*. Negative numbers are signed numbers whose sign is –. For example, –3, –5.15, –.003 are all negative numbers.

> *0 is neither positive nor negative; any nonzero number is positive or negative but not both.*

➤I–6.3

Absolute Value. The absolute value of a signed number is the distance of the number from 0. The absolute value of any nonzero number is *positive*. For example, the absolute value of 2 is 2; the absolute value of –2 is 2. The absolute value of a number a is denoted by $|a|$, so $|-2| = 2$. The absolute value of any number can be found by dropping its sign, $|-12| = 12$, $|4| = 4$. *Thus* $|-a| = |a|$ *for any number a*. The only number whose absolute value is zero is zero.

➤I–6.4

Adding Signed Numbers.

Case I. Adding numbers with the <u>*same sign*</u>:

A The sign of the sum is the same as the sign of the numbers being added.
B Add the absolute values.
C Put the sign from step (A) in front of the number you obtained in step (B).

EXAMPLE 1

What is –2 + (–3.1) + (–.02)?

A The sign of the sum will be –.
B $|-2| = 2$, $|-3.1| = 3.1$, $|-.02| = .02$, and 2 + 3.1 + .02 = 5.12.
C The answer is –5.12.

Case II. Adding *two* numbers with *different signs*:

A The sign of the sum is the sign of the number which is largest in absolute value.
B Subtract the absolute value of the number with the smaller absolute value from the absolute value of the number with the larger absolute value.
C The answer is the number you obtained in step (B) preceded by the sign from part (A).

EXAMPLE 2

How much is –5.1 + 3?

A The absolute value of – 5.1 is 5.1 and the absolute value of 3 is 3, so the sign of the sum will be –.
B 5.1 is larger than 3, and 5.1 – 3 = 2.1.
C The sum is –2.1.

Case III. Adding *more than two* numbers with *different signs*:

A Add all the positive numbers; the result is positive (this is Case I).
B Add all the negative numbers; the result is negative (this is Case I).
C Add the result of step (A) to the result of step (B), by using Case II.

EXAMPLE 3

Find the value of 5 + 52 + (–3) + 7 + (–5.1).

A 5 + 52 + 7 = 64.
B –3 + (–5.1) = –8.1.
C 64 + (–8.1) = 55.9, so the answer is 55.9.

Example 4

If a store made a profit of \$23.50 on Monday, lost \$2.05 on Tuesday, lost \$5.03 on Wednesday, made a profit of \$30.10 on Thursday, and made a profit of \$41.25 on Friday, what was its total profit (or loss) for the week? Use + for profit and – for loss.

The total is 23.50 + (–2.05) + (–5.03) + 30.10 + 41.25 which is 94.85 + (–7.08) = 87.77. So the store made a profit of \$87.77.

➤I–6.5

Subtracting Signed Numbers. When subtracting signed numbers:

Ⓐ Change the sign of the number you are subtracting (the subtrahend).

Ⓑ Add the result of step (A) to the number being subtracted from (the minuend) using the rules of the preceding section.

Example 1

Subtract 4.1 from 6.5.

Ⓐ 4.1 becomes –4.1.

Ⓑ 6.5 + (–4.1) = 2.4.

Example 2

What is 7.8 – (–10.1)?

Ⓐ –10.1 becomes 10.1.

Ⓑ 7.8 + 10.1 = 17.9.

So we subtract a negative number by adding a positive number with the same absolute value, and we subtract a positive number by adding a negative number of the same absolute value.

➤I–6.6

Multiplying Signed Numbers.

Case I. Multiplying two numbers:

Ⓐ Multiply the absolute values of the numbers.

Ⓑ If both numbers have the same sign, the result of step (A) is the answer—i.e. the product is positive. If the numbers have different signs, then the answer is the result of step (A) with a minus sign.

Example 1

(–5)(–12) = ?

Ⓐ $5 \times 12 = 60$

Ⓑ Both signs are the same, so the answer is 60.

Example 2

(4)(–3) = ?

Ⓐ $4 \times 3 = 12$

Ⓑ The signs are different, so the answer is –12.

You can remember the sign of the product in the following way:

$$(-)(-) = +$$
$$(+)(+) = +$$
$$(-)(+) = -$$
$$(+)(-) = -$$

Case II. Multiplying more than two numbers:

Ⓐ Multiply the first two factors using Case I.

Ⓑ Multiply the result of (A) by the third factor.

Ⓒ Multiply the result of (B) by the fourth factor.

Ⓓ Continue until you have used each factor.

Example 3

$(-5)(4)(2)(-\frac{1}{2})(\frac{3}{4}) = ?$

Ⓐ (–5)(4) = –20

Ⓑ (–20)(2) = –40

Ⓒ $(-40)(-\frac{1}{2}) = 20$

Ⓓ $(20)(\frac{3}{4}) = 15$, so the answer is 15.

➤I–6.7

Dividing Signed Numbers. Divide the absolute values of the numbers; the sign of the quotient is determined by the same rules as you used to determine the sign of a product. Thus,

$$+ \div + = +$$
$$- \div - = +$$
$$+ \div - = -$$
$$- \div + = -$$

Example 1

Divide 53.2 by –4.

53.2 divided by 4 is 13.3. Since one of the numbers is positive and the other negative, the answer is –13.3.

Example 2

$$\frac{-5}{-2} = \frac{5}{2} = 2.5$$

> *The sign of the product or quotient is + if there are no negative factors or an even number of negative factors. The sign of the product or quotient is – if there are an odd number of negative factors.*

I–7. Averages and Medians

➤I–7.1

Mean. The *average* or *arithmetic mean* of N numbers is the sum of the N numbers divided by N.

EXAMPLE 1

The scores of 9 students on a test were 72, 78, 81, 64, 85, 92, 95, 60, and 55. What was the average score of the students?

Since there are 9 students, the average is the total of all the scores divided by 9.

So the average is $\frac{1}{9}$ of (72 + 78 + 81 + 64 + 85 + 92 + 95 + 60 + 55), which is $\frac{1}{9}$ of 682 or $75\frac{7}{9}$.

EXAMPLE 2

The temperature at noon in Coldtown, U.S.A. was 5° on Monday, 10° on Tuesday, 2° below zero on Wednesday, 5° below zero on Thursday, 0° on Friday, 4° on Saturday, and 1° below zero on Sunday. What was the average temperature at noon for the week?

Use negative numbers for the temperatures below zero. The average temperature is the average of 5, 10, –2, –5, 0, 4, and –1, which is $\frac{5+10+(-2)+(-5)+0+4+(-1)}{7}=\frac{11}{7}=1\frac{4}{7}$.

Therefore, the average temperature at noon for the week is $1\frac{4}{7}^{\circ}$.

EXAMPLE 3

If the average annual income of 10 workers is \$15,665 and two of the workers each made \$20,000 for the year, what is the average annual income of the remaining 8 workers?

The total income of all 10 workers is 10 times the average income which is \$156,650. The two workers made a total of \$40,000, so the total income of the remaining 8 workers was \$156,650 – \$40,000 = \$116,650. Therefore, the average annual income of the 8 remaining workers is $\frac{\$116,650}{8}$ = \$14,581.25.

➤I–7.2

The Median. If we arrange N numbers in order, the *median* is the middle number if N is odd and the average of the two middle numbers if N is even. In example 1 above, the median score was 78, and in example 2, the median temperature for the week was 0. Notice that the medians were different from the averages. In example 3, we don't have enough data to find the median although we know the average.

> *In general the median and the average of a collection of numbers are different.*

I–8. Powers, Exponents, and Roots

➤I–8.1

If b is any number and n is a positive integer, b^n means the product of n factors each of which is equal to b. Thus,

$b^n = b \times b \times b \times \cdots \times b$ where there are n copies of b.

If $n = 1$, there is only one copy of b so $b^1 = b$. Here are some examples:

$2^5 = 2 \times 2 \times 2 \times 2 \times 2 = 32$, $(-4)^3 = (-4) \times (-4) \times (-4) = -64$, $\frac{3^2}{4}=\frac{3\times 3}{4}=\frac{9}{4}$,

$$1^n = 1 \text{ for any } n,\ 0^n = 0 \text{ for any } n.$$

b^n is read as "b raised to the nth power." b^2 is read "b squared." b^2 is always greater than 0 (positive) if b is not zero, since the product of two negative numbers is positive. b^3 is read "b cubed." b^3 can be negative or positive.

You should know the following squares and cubes:

$1^2 = 1$	$9^2 = 81$	$1^3 = 1$
$2^2 = 4$	$10^2 = 100$	$2^3 = 8$
$3^2 = 9$	$11^2 = 121$	$3^3 = 27$
$4^2 = 16$	$12^2 = 144$	$4^3 = 64$
$5^2 = 25$	$13^2 = 169$	$5^3 = 125$
$6^2 = 36$	$14^2 = 196$	
$7^2 = 49$	$15^2 = 225$	
$8^2 = 64$		

If you raise a fraction, $\frac{p}{q}$, to a power, then $\left(\frac{p}{q}\right)^n = \frac{p^n}{q^n}$. For example,

$$\left(\frac{5}{4}\right)^3 = \frac{5^3}{4^3} = \frac{125}{64}.$$

EXAMPLE

If the value of an investment triples each year, what percent of its value today will the investment be worth in 4 years?

The value increases by a factor of 3 each year. Since the time is 4 years, there will be four factors of 3. So the investment will be worth $3 \times 3 \times 3 \times 3 = 3^4$ as much as it is today. $3^4 = 81$, so the investment will be worth 8,100% of its value today in four years.

➤I–8.2

Exponents. In the expression b^n, b is called the *base* and n is called the *exponent*. In the expression 2^5, 2 is the base and 5 is the exponent. The exponent tells how many factors there are.

The three basic formulas for problems involving exponents are:

A $b^n \times b^m = b^{n+m}$

B $a^n \times b^n = (a \bullet b)^n$

C *If $a^x = a^y$, then $x = y$, provided a is not 1.*

(A) and (B) are called *laws of exponents.*

EXAMPLE 1

What is 6^3?

Since $6 = 3 \times 2$, $6^3 = 3^3 \times 2^3 = 27 \times 8 = 216$.

or

$6^3 = 6 \times 6 \times 6 = 216$.

EXAMPLE 2

Find the value of $2^3 \times 2^2$.

Using (A), $2^3 \times 2^2 = 2^{2+3} = 2^5$ which is 32. You can check this, since $2^3 = 8$ and $2^2 = 4$; $2^3 \times 2^2 = 8 \times 4 = 32$.

➤I–8.3

Negative Exponents. *$b^0 = 1$ for any nonzero number b.* If we want (A) to hold, then $b^n \times b^0$ should be b^{n+0} which is b^n. So b^0 must be 1. For example, $3^0 = 1$. (NOTE: 0^0 is not defined.)

Using the law of exponents once more, you can define b^{-n} where n is a positive number. If (A) holds, $b^{-n} \times b^n = b^{-n+n} = b^0 = 1$, so $b^{-n} = \frac{1}{b^n}$. *Multiplying by b^{-n} is the same as dividing by b^n.*

EXAMPLE 1

$$2^{-3} = \frac{1}{2^3} = \frac{1}{8}$$

EXAMPLE 2

$$\left(\frac{1}{2}\right)^{-1} = \frac{1}{\frac{1}{2}} = 2$$

EXAMPLE 3

Find the value of $\frac{6^4}{3^3}$.

$$\frac{6^4}{3^3} = \frac{(3\bullet2)^4}{3^3} = \frac{3^4\bullet2^4}{3^3} = 3^4\times2^4\times3^{-3}$$

$$= 3^4 \times 3^{-3} \times 2^4 = 3^1 \times 2^4 = 48.$$

➤I–8.4

Roots. If you raise a number d to the nth power and the result is b, then d is called the nth root of b, which is usually written $\sqrt[n]{b} = d$. Since $2^5 = 32$, then $\sqrt[5]{32} = 2$. The second root is called the square root and is written $\sqrt{\ }$; the third root is called the cube root. If you read the columns of the table in Section I–8.1 from right to left, you have a table of square roots and cube roots. For example, $\sqrt{225} = 15$; $\sqrt{81} = 9$; $\sqrt[3]{64} = 4$.

There are two possibilities for the square root of a positive number; the positive one is called the square root. Thus we say $\sqrt{9} = 3$ although $(-3) \times (-3) = 9$.

Since the square of any nonzero number is positive, *the square root of a negative number is not defined as a real number*. Thus $\sqrt{-2}$ is not a real number. There are cube roots of negative numbers. $\sqrt[3]{-8} = -2$, because $(-2) \times (-2) \times (-2) = -8$.

You can also write roots as exponents; for example, $\sqrt[n]{b} = b^{\frac{1}{n}}$; so $\sqrt{b} = b^{\frac{1}{2}}$, $\sqrt[3]{b} = b^{\frac{1}{3}}$.

Since you can write roots as exponents, formula (B) under Section I–8.2 is especially useful.

> $a^{\frac{1}{n}} \times b^{\frac{1}{n}} = (a \bullet b)^{\frac{1}{n}}$ or $\sqrt[n]{a \times b} = \sqrt[n]{a} \times \sqrt[n]{b}$ This formula is the basic formula for simplifying square roots, cube roots and so on. *On the test you must state your answer in a form that matches one of the choices given.*

EXAMPLE 1

$\sqrt{54} = ?$

Since $54 = 9 \times 6$, $\sqrt{54} = \sqrt{9 \times 6} = \sqrt{9} \times \sqrt{6}$. Since $\sqrt{9} = 3$, $\sqrt{54} = 3\sqrt{6}$.

You cannot simplify by adding square roots unless you are taking square roots of the same number. For example,

$\sqrt{3} + 2\sqrt{3} - 4\sqrt{3} = -\sqrt{3}$, but $\sqrt{3} + \sqrt{2}$ is not equal to $\sqrt{5}$.

EXAMPLE 2

Simplify $6\sqrt{12} + 2\sqrt{75} - 3\sqrt{98}$.

Since $12 = 4 \times 3$, $\sqrt{12} = \sqrt{4 \times 3} = \sqrt{4} \times \sqrt{3} = 2\sqrt{3}$;

$75 = 25 \times 3$, so $\sqrt{75} = \sqrt{25} \times \sqrt{3} = 5\sqrt{3}$;

and $98 = 49 \times 2$, so $\sqrt{98} = \sqrt{49} \times \sqrt{2} = 7\sqrt{2}$.

Therefore, $6\sqrt{12} + 2\sqrt{75} - 3\sqrt{98}$
$= 6 \times 2\sqrt{3} + 2 \times 5\sqrt{3} - 3 \times 7\sqrt{2}$
$= 12\sqrt{3} + 10\sqrt{3} - 21\sqrt{2} = 22\sqrt{3} - 21\sqrt{2}$.

EXAMPLE 3

Simplify $27^{\frac{1}{3}} \times 8^{\frac{1}{3}}$.

$27^{\frac{1}{3}} = \sqrt[3]{27} = 3$ and $8^{\frac{1}{3}} = 2$, so $27^{\frac{1}{3}} \times 8^{\frac{1}{3}} = 3 \times 2 = 6$. Notice that 6 is $\sqrt[3]{216}$ and $27^{\frac{1}{3}} \times 8^{\frac{1}{3}} = (27 \times 8)^{\frac{1}{3}} = 216^{\frac{1}{3}}$.

II. Algebra

II–1. Algebraic Expressions

➤II–1.1

Often it is necessary to deal with quantities that have a numerical value that is unknown. For example, we may know that Tom's salary is twice as much as Joe's salary. If we let the value of Tom's salary be called T and the value of Joe's salary be J, then T and J are numbers which are unknown. However, we do know that the value of T must be twice the value of J, or $T = 2J$.

T and $2J$ are examples of algebraic expressions. An algebraic expression may involve letters in addition to numbers and symbols; however, *in an algebraic expression a letter always stands for a number*. Therefore, you can multiply, divide, add, subtract and perform other mathematical operations on a letter. Thus, x^2 would mean x times x. Some examples of algebraic expressions are: $2x + y$, $y^3 + 9y$, $z^3 - 5ab$, $c + d + 4$, $5x + 2y(6x - 4y + z)$. When letters or numbers are written together without any sign or symbol between them, multiplication is assumed. Thus $6xy$ means 6 times x times y. $6xy$ is called a term; terms are separated by + or – signs. The expression $5z + 2 + 4x^2$ has three terms, $5z$, 2, and $4x^2$. Terms are often called monomials (mono = one). If an expression has more than one term, it is called a *polynomial* (poly = many). The letters in an algebraic expression are called *variables* or *unknowns*. When a variable is multiplied by a number, the number is called the *coefficient* of the variable. So in the expression $5x^2 + 2yz$, the coefficient of x^2 is 5, and the coefficient of yz is 2.

➤II–1.2

Simplifying Algebraic Expressions. *Since there are only five choices of an answer given for the test questions, you must be able to recognize algebraic expressions which are equal.* It will also save time when you are working problems if you can change a complicated expression into a simpler one.

Case I. Simplifying expressions which don't contain parentheses:

A Perform any multiplications or divisions before performing additions or subtractions. Thus, the expression $6x + y \div x$ means add $6x$ to the quotient of y divided by x. Another way of writing the expression would be $6x + \frac{y}{x}$. This is not the same as $\frac{6x+y}{x}$.

B The order in which you multiply numbers and letters in a term does not matter. So $6xy$ is the same as $6yx$.

C The order in which you add terms does not matter; for instance, $6x + 2y - x = 6x - x + 2y$.

D If there are roots or powers in any terms, you may be able to simplify the term by using the laws of exponents. For example, $5xy \bullet 3x^2y = 15x^3y^2$.

E Combine like terms. *Like terms* (or similar terms) are terms which have exactly the same letters raised to the same powers. So x, $-2x$, $\frac{1}{3}x$ are like terms.

For example, $6x - 2x + x + y$ is equal to $5x + y$. In combining like terms, you simply add or subtract the coefficients of the like terms, and the result is the coefficient of that term in the simplified expression. In the example given, the coefficients of x were $+6$, -2, and $+1$; since $6 - 2 + 1 = 5$ the coefficient of x in the simplified expression is 5.

F Algebraic expressions which involve divisions or factors can be simplified by using the techniques for handling fractions and the laws of exponents. Remember dividing by b^n is the same as multiplying by b^{-n}.

EXAMPLE 1

$3x^2 - 4\sqrt{x} + \sqrt{4x} + xy + 7x^2 = ?$

D $\sqrt{4x} = \sqrt{4}\,\sqrt{x} = 2\sqrt{x}$.

E $3x^2 + 7x^2 = 10x^2$, $-4\sqrt{x} + 2\sqrt{x} = -2\sqrt{x}$.

The original expression equals $3x^2 + 7x^2 - 4\sqrt{x} + 2\sqrt{x} + xy$. Therefore, the simplified expression is $10x^2 - 2\sqrt{x} + xy$.

EXAMPLE 2

Simplify $\frac{21x^4y^2}{3x^6y}$.

F $\frac{21}{3}x^4y^2x^{-6}y^{-1}$.

B $7x^4x^{-6}y^2y^{-1}$.

D $7x^{-2}y$, so the simplified term is $\frac{7y}{x^2}$.

EXAMPLE 3

Write $\frac{2x}{y} - \frac{4}{x}$ as a single fraction.

F A common denominator is xy so

$$\frac{2x}{y} = \frac{2x \bullet x}{y \bullet x} = \frac{2x^2}{xy}, \text{ and } \frac{4}{x} = \frac{4y}{xy}.$$

Therefore, $\frac{2x}{y} - \frac{4}{x} = \frac{2x^2}{xy} - \frac{4y}{xy} = \frac{2x^2 - 4y}{xy}$

Case II. Simplifying expressions which have parentheses:

The first rule is to perform the operations inside parentheses first. So $(6x + y) \div x$ means divide the sum of $6x$ and y by x. Notice that $(6x + y) \div x$ is different from $6x + y \div x$.

The main rule for getting rid of parentheses is the distributive law, which is expressed as $a(b + c) = ab + ac$. In other words, if any monomial is followed by an expression contained in a parenthesis, then *each* term of the expression is multiplied by the monomial. Once we have gotten rid of the parentheses, we proceed as we did in Case I.

EXAMPLE 4

$2x(6x - 4y + 2) = (2x)(6x) + (2x)(-4y) + (2x)(2) = 12x^2 - 8xy + 4x$.

If an expression has more than one set of parentheses, get rid of the *inner parentheses first* and then *work out* through the rest of the parentheses.

EXAMPLE 5

$2x - (x + 6(x - 3y) + 4y) = ?$

To remove the inner parentheses we multiply $6(x - 3y)$ getting $6x - 18y$. Now we have $2x - (x + 6x - 18y + 4y)$ which equals $2x - (7x - 14y)$. Distribute the minus sign (multiply by -1), getting $2x - 7x - (-14y) = -5x + 14y$. Sometimes brackets are used instead of parentheses.

EXAMPLE 6

Simplify $-3x\left[\frac{1}{2}(3x-2y)-2(x(3+y)+4y)\right]$

$$= -3x\left[\frac{1}{2}(3x-2y)-2(3x+xy+4y)\right]$$

$$= -3x\left[\frac{3}{2}x-y-6x-2xy-8y\right]$$

$$= -3x\left[-\frac{9}{2}x-2xy-9y\right]$$

$$= \frac{27}{2}x^2 + 6x^2y + 27xy.$$

➤II–1.3

Adding and Subtracting Algebraic Expressions. Since algebraic expressions are numbers, they can be added and subtracted.

> *The only algebraic terms which can be combined are like terms.*

EXAMPLE 1

$(3x + 4y - xy^2) + (3x + 2x(x - y)) = ?$

The expression $= (3x + 4y - xy^2) + (3x + 2x^2 - 2xy)$, removing the inner parentheses;

$= 6x + 4y + 2x^2 - xy^2 - 2xy$, combining like terms.

EXAMPLE 2

$(2a + 3a^2 - 4) - 2(4a^2 - 2(a + 4)) = ?$

It equals $(2a + 3a^2 - 4) - 2(4a^2 - 2a - 8)$, removing inner parentheses;

$= 2a + 3a^2 - 4 - 8a^2 + 4a + 16$, removing outer parentheses;

$= -5a^2 + 6a + 12$, combining like terms.

➤II–1.4

Multiplying Algebraic Expressions. When you multiply two expressions, you multiply *each term of the first by each term of the second.*

EXAMPLE 1

$(b - 4)(b + a) = b(b + a) - 4(b + a) = ?$

$= b^2 + ab - 4b - 4a.$

EXAMPLE 2

$(2h - 4)(h + 2h^2 + h^3) = ?$

$= 2h(h + 2h^2 + h^3) - 4(h + 2h^2 + h^3)$

$= 2h^2 + 4h^3 + 2h^4 - 4h - 8h^2 - 4h^3$

$= -4h - 6h^2 + 2h^4$, which is the product.

If you need to multiply more than two expressions, multiply the first two expressions, then multiply the result by the third expression, and so on until you have used each factor. Since algebraic expressions can be multiplied, they can be squared, cubed, or raised to other powers.

EXAMPLE 3

$(x - 2y)^3 = (x - 2y)(x - 2y)(x - 2y).$

Since $(x - 2y)(x - 2y)$
$= x^2 - 2yx - 2yx + 4y^2$
$= x^2 - 4xy + 4y^2,$
$(x - 2y)^3 = (x^2 - 4xy + 4y^2)(x - 2y)$
$= x(x^2 - 4xy + 4y^2) - 2y(x^2 - 4xy + 4y^2)$
$= x^3 - 4x^2y + 4xy^2 - 2x^2y + 8xy^2 - 8y^3$
$= x^3 - 6x^2y + 12xy^2 - 8y^3.$

The order in which you multiply algebraic expressions does not matter. Thus $(2a + b)(x^2 + 2x) = (x^2 + 2x)(2a + b)$.

EXAMPLE 4

If a and b are two-digit numbers, and the last digit of a is 7 and the last digit of b is 8, what is the last digit of a times b?

The key to problems such as this is to think of a number in terms of its digits. So a must be written as $x7$, where x is a digit. This means $a = 10x + 7$. In the same way $b = 10y + 8$ for some digit y. So a times b is $(10x + 7)(10y + 8)$, which is $100xy + 80x + 70y + 56$. The digits x and y all are multiplied by 10 or 100 so they will not affect the units place. The only term that will affect the units place is 56. So the unit digit or last digit of a times b is 6. This pattern works all the time and can be expressed by the following rule: the last digit of the product of two numbers is the last digit of the product of the last digits of the two numbers. For example, the last digit of 136 times 157 is 2 because the last digit of 6 times 7 is 2.

➤II–1.5

Factoring Algebraic Expressions. If an algebraic expression is the product of other algebraic expressions, then the expressions are called factors of the original expression. For instance, we claim that $(2h - 4)$ and $(h + 2h^2 + h^3)$ are factors of $-4h - 6h^2 + 2h^4$. We can always check to see if we have the correct factors by multiplying; so by example 2 above we see that our claim is correct. We need to be able to factor algebraic expressions in order to solve quadratic equations. It also can be helpful in dividing algebraic expressions.

First remove any monomial factor that appears in every term of the expression.

Some examples:

$3x + 3y = 3(x + y)$: 3 is a monomial factor.

$15a^2b + 10ab = 5ab(3a + 2)$: $5ab$ is a monomial factor.

$$\frac{1}{2}hy - 3h^3 + 4hy = h\left(\frac{1}{2}y - 3h^2 + 4y\right),$$

$$= h\left(\frac{9}{2}y - 3h^2\right)$$: h is a monomial factor.

You may also need to factor expressions that contain squares or higher powers into factors that only contain linear terms. (Linear terms are terms in which variables are raised only to the first power.) The first rule to remember is that since $(a + b)(a - b) = a^2 + ba - ba - b^2 = a^2 - b^2$, the difference of two squares can always be factored.

EXAMPLE 1

Factor $(9m^2 - 16)$.

$9m^2 = (3m)^2$ and $16 = 4^2$, so the factors are $(3m - 4)(3m + 4)$.

Since $(3m - 4)(3m + 4) = 9m^2 - 16$, these factors are correct.

EXAMPLE 2

Factor $x^4y^4 - 4x^2$.

$x^4y^4 = (x^2y^2)^2$ and $4x^2 = (2x)^2$, so the factors are $x^2y^2 + 2x$ and $x^2y^2 - 2x$.

You also may need to factor expressions that contain squared terms and linear terms, such as $x^2 + 4x + 3$. The factors will be of the form $(x + a)$ and $(x + b)$. Since $(x + a)(x + b) = x^2 + (a + b)x + ab$, you must look for a pair of numbers a and b such that $a \bullet b$ is the numerical term in the expression and $a + b$ is the coefficient of the linear term (the term with exponent 1).

EXAMPLE 3

Factor $x^2 + 4x + 3$.

You want numbers whose product is 3 and whose sum is 4. Look at the possible factors of 3 and check whether they add up to 4. Since $3 = 3 \times 1$ and $3 + 1$ is 4, the factors are $(x + 3)$ and $(x + 1)$. Remember to check by multiplying.

EXAMPLE 4

Factor $y^2 + y - 6$.

Since -6 is negative, the two numbers a and b must be of opposite sign. Possible pairs of factors for -6 are -6 and $+1$, 6 and -1, 3 and -2, and -3 and 2. Since $-2 + 3 = 1$, the factors are $(y + 3)$ and $(y - 2)$. So $(y + 3)(y - 2) = y^2 + y - 6$.

EXAMPLE 5

Factor $a^3 + 4a^2 + 4a$.

Factor out a, so $a^3 + 4a^2 + 4a = a(a^2 + 4a + 4)$. Consider $a^2 + 4a + 4$; since $2 + 2 = 4$ and $2 \times 2 = 4$, the factors are $(a + 2)$ and $(a + 2)$. Therefore, $a^3 + 4a^2 + 4a = a(a + 2)^2$.

If the term with the highest exponent has a coefficient unequal to 1, divide the entire expression by that coefficient. For example, to factor $3a^3 + 12a^2 + 12a$, factor out a 3 from each term, and the result is $a^3 + 4a^2 + 4a$ which is $a(a + 2)^2$. Thus, $3a^3 + 12a^2 + 12a = 3a(a + 2)^2$.

There are some expressions that cannot be factored, for example, $x^2 + 4x + 6$. In general, if you can't factor something by using the methods given above, don't waste a lot of time on the question. Sometimes you may be able to check the answers given to find out what the correct factors are.

➤II–1.6

Division of Algebraic Expressions. The main things to remember in division are:

❶ When you divide a sum, you can get the same result by dividing each term and adding quotients. For example, $\frac{9x+4xy+y^2}{x} = \frac{9x}{x}+\frac{4xy}{x}+\frac{y^2}{x} = 9+4y+\frac{y^2}{x}$.

❷ You can cancel common factors, so the results on factoring will be helpful. For example, $\frac{x^2-2x}{x-2} = \frac{x(x-2)}{x-2} = x$.

EXAMPLE 1

$$\frac{2x+2y+x^2-y^2}{x+y} = ?$$

$$\begin{aligned}\frac{2x+2y+x^2-y^2}{x+y} &= \frac{2x+2y}{x+y}+\frac{x^2-y^2}{x+y}\\ &= \frac{2(x+y)}{x+y}+\frac{(x-y)(x+y)}{x+y}\\ &= 2+x-y\end{aligned}$$

You can also divide one algebraic expression by another using long division.

EXAMPLE 2

$(15x^2 + 2x - 4) \div 3x - 1 = ?$

$$\begin{array}{r} 5x+2 \\ 3x-1\overline{)15x^2+2x-4} \\ \underline{15x^2-5x} \\ 7x-4 \\ \underline{6x-2} \\ x-2 \end{array}$$

So the answer is $5x + 2$ with a remainder of $x - 2$. You can check by multiplying,
$(5x + 2)(3x - 1) = 15x^2 + 6x - 5x - 2$
$= 15x^2 + x - 2$; now add the remainder $x - 2$ and the result is $15x^2 + x - 2 + x - 2$
$= 15x^2 + 2x - 4$.

Division problems where you need to use (1) and (2) are more likely than problems involving long division.

II–2. Equations

➤II–2.1

An EQUATION is a statement that says two algebraic expressions are equal. $x + 2 = 3$, $4 + 2 = 6$, $3x^2 + 2x - 6 = 0$, $x^2 + y^2 = z^2$, $\frac{y}{x} = 2 + z$, and $A = LW$ are all examples of equations. We will refer to the algebraic expressions on each side of the equals sign as the left side and the right side of the equation. Thus, in the equation $2x + 4 = 6y + x$, $2x + 4$ is the left side and $6y + x$ is the right side.

➤II–2.2

If we assign specific numbers to each variable or unknown in an algebraic expression, then the algebraic expression will be equal to a number. This is called *evaluating* the expression. For example, if you evaluate $2x + 4y^2 + 3$ for $x = -1$ and $y = 2$, the expression is equal to $2(-1) + 4 \bullet 2^2 + 3 = -2 + 4 \bullet 4 + 3 = 17$.

If we evaluate each side of an equation and the number obtained is the same for each side of the equation, then the specific values assigned to the unknowns are called a *solution of the equation.* Another way of saying this is that the choices for the unknowns satisfy the equation.

EXAMPLE 1

Consider the equation $2x + 3 = 9$.

If $x = 3$, then the left side of the equation becomes $2 \bullet 3 + 3 = 6 + 3 = 9$, so both sides equal 9, and $x = 3$ is a solution of $2x + 3 = 9$. If $x = 4$, then the left side is $2 \bullet 4 + 3 = 11$. Since 11 is not equal to 9, $x = 4$ is *not* a solution of $2x + 3 = 9$.

EXAMPLE 2

Consider the equation $x^2 + y^2 = 5x$.

If $x = 1$ and $y = 2$, then the left side is $1^2 + 2^2$ which equals $1 + 4 = 5$. The right side is $5 \bullet 1 = 5$; since both sides are equal to 5, $x = 1$ and $y = 2$ is a solution.

If $x = 5$ and $y = 0$, then the left side is $5^2 + 0^2 = 25$ and the right side is $5 \bullet 5 = 25$, so $x = 5$ and $y = 0$ is also a solution.

If $x = 1$ and $y = 1$, then the left side is $1^2 + 1^2 = 2$ and the right side is $5 \bullet 1 = 5$. Therefore, since $2 \neq 5$, $x = 1$ and $y = 1$ is not a solution.

There are some equations that *do not have any solutions that are real numbers.* Since the square of any real number is positive or zero, the equation $x^2 = -4$ does not have any solutions that are real numbers.

➤II–2.3

Equivalence. One equation is *equivalent* to another equation, if they have exactly the same solutions. The basic idea in solving equations is to transform a given equation into an equivalent equation whose solutions are obvious.

> The two main tools for solving equations are:
>
> **A** If you add or subtract the same algebraic expression to or from *each side* of an equation, the resulting equation is equivalent to the original equation.
>
> **B** If you multiply or divide both sides of an equation by the same *nonzero* algebraic expression, the resulting equation is equivalent to the original equation.

The most common type of equation is the linear equation with only one unknown. $6z = 4z - 3$, $3 + a = 2a - 4$, $3b + 2b = b - 4b$, are all examples of linear equations with only one unknown.

Using (A) and (B), you can solve a linear equation in one unknown in the following way:

1. Group all the terms that involve the unknown on one side of the equation and all the terms that are purely numerical on the other side of the equation. This is called *isolating the unknown.*
2. Combine the terms on each side.
3. Divide each side by the coefficient of the unknown.

EXAMPLE 1

Solve $6x + 2 = 3$ for x.

1. Using (A) subtract 2 from each side of the equation. Then $6x + 2 - 2 = 3 - 2$ or $6x = 3 - 2$.
2. $6x = 1$.
3. Divide each side by 6. Therefore, $x = \frac{1}{6}$.

You should always check your answer in the original equation.

CHECK: Since $6\left(\frac{1}{6}\right) + 2 = 1 + 2 = 3$, $x = \frac{1}{6}$ is the solution.

EXAMPLE 2

Solve $3x + 15 = 3 - 4x$ for x.

1. Add $4x$ to each side and subtract 15 from each side; $3x + 15 - 15 + 4x = 3 - 15 - 4x + 4x$.
2. $7x = -12$.
3. Divide each side by 7, so $x = \frac{-12}{7}$ is the solution.

CHECK: $3\left(\frac{-12}{7}\right) + 15 = \frac{-36}{7} + 15 = \frac{69}{7}$ and

$3 - 4\left(\frac{-12}{7}\right) = 3 + \frac{48}{7} = \frac{69}{7}$.

If you do the same thing to each side of an equation, the result is still an equation but it may not be equivalent to the original equation. Be especially careful if you square each side of an equation. For example, $x = -4$ is an equation; square both sides and you get $x^2 = 16$ which has both $x = 4$ and $x = -4$ as solutions. *Always check your answer in the original equation.*

If the equation you want to solve involves square roots, get rid of the square roots by squaring each side of the equation. Remember to check your answer since squaring each side does not always give an equivalent equation.

EXAMPLE 3

Solve $\sqrt{4x+3} = 5$.

Square both sides: $\left(\sqrt{4x+3}\right)^2 = 4x + 3$ and $5^2 = 25$, so the new equation is $4x + 3 = 25$. Subtract 3 from each side to get $4x = 22$ and now divide each side by 4. The solution is $x = \frac{22}{4} = 5.5$. Since $4(5.5) + 3 = 25$ and $\sqrt{25} = 5$, $x = 5.5$ is a solution to the equation $\sqrt{4x+3} = 5$.

If an equation involves fractions, multiply through by a common denominator and then solve. Check your answer to make sure you did not multiply or divide by zero.

EXAMPLE 4

Solve $\frac{3}{a} = 9$ for a.

Multiply each side by a: the result is $3 = 9a$. Divide each side by 9, and you obtain $\frac{3}{9} = a$ or $a = \frac{1}{3}$. Since $\frac{3}{\frac{1}{3}} = 3 \bullet 3 = 9$, $a = \frac{1}{3}$ is a solution.

➤II-2.4

Solving Two Equations in Two Unknowns. You may be asked to solve two equations in two unknowns. Use one equation to solve for one unknown in terms of the other; now change the second equation into an equation in only one unknown which can be solved by the methods of the preceding section.

EXAMPLE 1

Solve for x and y: $\begin{cases} \dfrac{x}{y} = 3 \\ 2x + 4y = 20. \end{cases}$

The first equation gives $x = 3y$. Using $x = 3y$, the second equation is $2(3y) + 4y = 6y + 4y$ or $10y = 20$, so $y = \frac{20}{10} = 2$. Since $x = 3y$, $x = 6$.

CHECK: $\frac{6}{2} = 3$, and $2 \bullet 6 + 4 \bullet 2 = 20$, so $x = 6$ and $y = 2$ is a solution.

EXAMPLE 2

If $2x + y = 5$ and $x + y = 4$, find x and y.

Since $x + y = 4$, $y = 4 - x$, so $2x + y = 2x + 4 - x = x + 4 = 5$ and $x = 1$. If $x = 1$, then $y = 4 - 1 = 3$. So $x = 1$ and $y = 3$ is the solution.

CHECK: $2 \bullet 1 + 3 = 5$ and $1 + 3 = 4$.

Sometimes we can solve two equations by adding them or by subtracting one from the other. If we subtract $x + y = 4$ from $2x + y = 5$ in example 2, we have $x = 1$. However, the previous method will work in cases when the addition method does not work.

➤II–2.5

Solving Quadratic Equations. If the terms of an equation contain squares of the unknown as well as linear terms, the equation is called *quadratic*. Some examples of quadratic equations are $x^2 + 4x = 3$, $2z^2 - 1 = 3z^2 - 2z$, and $a + 6 = a^2 + 6$.

To solve a quadratic equation:

Ⓐ Group all the terms on one side of the equation so that the other side is *zero*.
Ⓑ Combine the terms on the nonzero side.
Ⓒ Factor the expression into linear expressions.
Ⓓ Set the linear factors equal to zero and solve.

The method depends on the fact that if a product of expressions is zero then at least one of the expressions must be zero.

EXAMPLE 1

Solve $x^2 + 4x = -3$.

Ⓐ $x^2 + 4x + 3 = 0$
Ⓒ $x^2 + 4x + 3 = (x + 3)(x + 1) = 0$
Ⓓ So $x + 3 = 0$ or $x + 1 = 0$. Therefore, the solutions are $x = -3$ and $x = -1$.

CHECK: $(-3)^2 + 4(-3) = 9 - 12 = -3$

$(-1)^2 + 4(-1) = 1 - 4 = -3$, so $x = -3$ and $x = -1$ are solutions.

A quadratic equation will usually have 2 different solutions, but it is possible for a quadratic to have only one solution or even no real solution.

EXAMPLE 2

If $2z^2 - 1 = 3z^2 - 2z$, what is z?

Ⓐ $0 = 3z^2 - 2z^2 - 2z + 1$
Ⓑ $z^2 - 2z + 1 = 0$
Ⓒ $z^2 - 2z + 1 = (z - 1)^2 = 0$
Ⓓ $z - 1 = 0$ or $z = 1$

CHECK: $2 \bullet 1^2 - 1 = 2 - 1 = 1$ and $3 \bullet 1^2 - 2 \bullet 1 = 3 - 2 = 1$, so $z = 1$ is a solution.

Equations that may not look like quadratics may be changed into quadratics.

EXAMPLE 3

Find a if $a - 3 = \frac{10}{a}$.

Multiply each side of the equation by a to obtain $a^2 - 3a = 10$, which is quadratic.

Ⓐ $a^2 - 3a - 10 = 0$
Ⓒ $a^2 - 3a - 10 = (a - 5)(a + 2)$
Ⓓ So $a - 5 = 0$ or $a + 2 = 0$

Therefore, $a = 5$ and $a = -2$ are the solutions.

CHECK: $5 - 3 = 2 = \frac{10}{5}$ so $a = 5$ is a solution.

$-2 - 3 = -5 = \frac{10}{-2}$ so $a = -2$ is a solution.

You can also solve quadratic equations by using the *quadratic formula*. The quadratic formula states that the solutions of the quadratic equation

$ax^2 + bx + c = 0$ are $x = \frac{1}{2a}\left[-b + \sqrt{b^2 - 4ac}\right]$

and

$$x = \frac{1}{2a}\left[-b - \sqrt{b^2 - 4ac}\right]$$

This is usually written $x = \frac{1}{2a}\left[-b \pm \sqrt{b^2 - 4ac}\right]$

Use of the quadratic formula would replace steps (C) and (D).

EXAMPLE 4

Find x if $x^2 + 5x = 12 - x^2$.

(A) $x^2 + 5x + x^2 - 12 = 0$
(B) $2x^2 + 5x - 12 = 0$

So $a = 2$, $b = 5$ and $c = -12$. Therefore, using the quadratic formula, the solutions are

$x = \frac{1}{4}\left[-5 \pm \sqrt{25 - 4 \bullet 2 \bullet (-12)}\right]$

$= \frac{1}{4}\left[-5 \pm \sqrt{25 + 96}\right] = \frac{1}{4}\left[-5 \pm \sqrt{121}\right]$. So we have

$x = \frac{1}{4}[-5 \pm 11]$. The solutions are $x = \frac{3}{2}$ and $x = -4$.

CHECK:

$\left(\frac{3}{2}\right)^2 + 5 \bullet \frac{3}{2} = \frac{9}{4} + \frac{15}{2} = \frac{39}{4} = 12 - \frac{9}{4} = 12 - \left(\frac{3}{2}\right)^2$

$(-4)^2 + 5(-4) = 16 - 20 = -4 = 12 - 16 = 12 - (-4)^2$

NOTE: If $b^2 - 4ac$ is negative, then the quadratic equation $ax^2 + bx + c = 0$ has no real solutions because negative numbers do not have real square roots.

The quadratic formula will always give you the solutions to a quadratic equation. If you can factor the equation, factoring will usually give you the solution in less time. Remember, you want to answer as many questions as you can in the time given. So factor if you can. If you don't see the factors immediately, then use the formula.

II-3. Word Problems

➤II–3.1

The general method for solving word problems is to translate them into algebraic problems. The quantities you are seeking are the unknowns, which are usually represented by letters. The information you are given in the problem is then turned into equations. Words such as "is," "was," "are," and "were" mean equals, and words like "of" and "as much as" mean multiplication.

EXAMPLE 1

A coat was sold for \$75. The coat was sold for 150% of the cost of the coat. How much did the coat cost?

You want to find the cost of the coat. Let \$$C$ be the cost of the coat. You know that the coat was sold for \$75 and that \$75 was 150% of the cost. So \$75 = 150% of \$$C$ or $75 = 1.5C$. Solving for C you get $C = \frac{75}{1.5} = 50$, so the coat cost \$50.

CHECK: (1.5)\$50 = \$75.

EXAMPLE 2

Tom's salary is 125% of Joe's salary; Mary's salary is 80% of Joe's salary. The total of all three salaries is \$61,000. What is Mary's salary?

Let M = Mary's salary, J = Joe's salary and T = Tom's salary. The first sentence says T = 125% of J or $T = \frac{5}{4}J$, and M = 80% of J or $M = \frac{4}{5}J$. The second sentence says that $T + M + J = \$61,000$. Using the information from the first sentence, $T + M + J = \frac{5}{4}J + \frac{4}{5}J + J = \frac{25}{20}J + \frac{16}{20}J + J = \frac{61}{20}J$. So $\frac{61}{20}J = 61{,}000$; solving for J you have $J = \frac{20}{61} \times 61{,}000 = 20{,}000$. Therefore, $T = \frac{5}{4} \times \$20{,}000 = \$25{,}000$ and $M = \frac{4}{5} \times \$20{,}000 = \$16{,}000$.

CHECK: \$25,000 + \$16,000 + \$20,000 = \$61,000.

So Mary's salary is \$16,000.

EXAMPLE 3

Steve weighs 25 pounds more than Jim. The combined weight of Jim and Steve is 325 pounds. How much does Jim weigh?

Let S = Steve's weight in pounds and J = Jim's weight in pounds. The first sentence says $S = J + 25$, and the second sentence becomes $S + J = 325$. Since $S = J + 25$, $S + J = 325$ becomes $(J + 25) + J = 2J + 25 = 325$. So $2J = 300$ and $J = 150$. Therefore, Jim weighs 150 pounds.

CHECK: If Jim weighs 150 pounds, then Steve weighs 175 pounds and $150 + 175 = 325$.

EXAMPLE 4

A carpenter is designing a closet. The floor will be in the shape of a rectangle whose length is 2 feet more than its width. How long should the closet be if the carpenter wants the area of the floor to be 15 square feet?

The area of a rectangle is length times width, usually written $A = LW$, where A is the area, L is the length, and W is the width. We know $A = 15$ and $L = 2 + W$. Therefore, $LW = (2 + W)W = W^2 + 2W$; this must equal 15. So we need to solve $W^2 + 2W = 15$ or $W^2 + 2W - 15 = 0$. Since $W^2 + 2W - 15$ factors into $(W + 5)(W - 3)$, the only possible solutions are $W = -5$ and $W = 3$. Since W represents a width, -5 cannot be the answer; therefore the width is 3 feet. The length is the width plus two feet, so the length is 5 feet. Since $5 \times 3 = 15$, the answer checks.

➤II–3.2

Distance Problems. A common type of word problem is a distance or velocity problem. The basic formula is:

DISTANCE TRAVELED = RATE X TIME

The formula is abbreviated $d = rt$.

EXAMPLE 1

A train travels at an average speed of 50 miles per hour for $2\frac{1}{2}$ hours and then travels at a speed of 70 miles per hour for $1\frac{1}{2}$ hours. How far did the train travel in the entire 4 hours?

The train traveled for $2\frac{1}{2}$ hours at an average speed of 50 miles per hour, so it traveled $50 \times \frac{5}{2} =$ 125 miles in the first $2\frac{1}{2}$ hours. Traveling at a speed of 70 miles per hour for $1\frac{1}{2}$ hours, the distance traveled will be equal to $r \times t$ where $r = 70$ m.p.h. and $t = 1\frac{1}{2}$, so the distance is $70 \times \frac{3}{2} = 105$ miles. Therefore, the total distance traveled is $125 + 105 =$ 230 miles.

EXAMPLE 2

The distance from Cleveland to Buffalo is 200 miles. A train takes $3\frac{1}{2}$ hours to go from Buffalo to Cleveland and $4\frac{1}{2}$ hours to go back from Cleveland to Buffalo. What was the average speed of the train for the round trip from Buffalo to Cleveland and back?

The train took $3\frac{1}{2} + 4\frac{1}{2} = 8$ hours for the trip. The distance of a round trip is $2(200) = 400$ miles. Since $d = rt$ then 400 miles $= r \times 8$ hours. Solve for r and you have $r = \frac{400 \text{ miles}}{8 \text{ hours}} = 50$ miles per hour.

Therefore the average speed is 50 miles per hour.

The speed in the formula is the average speed. If you know that there are different speeds for different lengths of time, then you must use the formula more than once, as we did in example 1.

➤II–3.3

Work Problems. In this type of problem you can always assume all workers in the same category work at the same rate. The main idea is: If it takes k workers 1 hour to do a job then *each worker does* $\frac{1}{k}$ *of the job in an hour* or he works at the rate of $\frac{1}{k}$ of the job per hour. If it takes m workers h hours to finish a job then each worker does $\frac{1}{m}$ of the job in h hours so he does $\frac{1}{h}$ of $\frac{1}{m}$ in an hour. Therefore, each worker *works at the rate of* $\frac{1}{mh}$ *of the job per hour.*

EXAMPLE 1

If 5 men take an hour to dig a ditch, how long should it take 12 men to dig a ditch of the same type?

Since 5 workers took an hour, each worker does $\frac{1}{5}$ of the job in an hour. So 12 workers will work at the rate of $\frac{12}{5}$ of the job per hour. Thus if T is the time it takes for 12 workers to do the job, $\frac{12}{5} \times T = 1$ job and $T = \frac{5}{12} \times 1$, so

$$T = \frac{5}{12} \text{ hours or 25 minutes.}$$

EXAMPLE 2

Worker A takes 8 hours to do a job. Worker B takes 10 hours to do the same job. How long should it take worker A and worker B working together, but independently, to do the same job?

Worker A works at a rate of $\frac{1}{8}$ of the job per hour, since he takes 8 hours to finish the job. Worker B finished the job in 10 hours, so he works at a rate of $\frac{1}{10}$ of the job per hour. Therefore, if they work together they should complete $\frac{1}{8} + \frac{1}{10} = \frac{18}{80} = \frac{9}{40}$, so they work at a rate of $\frac{9}{40}$ of the job per hour together. So if T is the time it takes them to finish the job, $\frac{9}{40}$ of the job per hour $\times$ T hours must equal 1 job. Therefore,

$$\frac{9}{40} \times T = 1 \text{ and } T = \frac{40}{9} = 4\frac{4}{9} \text{ hours.}$$

EXAMPLE 3

There are two taps, tap 1 and tap 2, in a keg. If both taps are opened, the keg is drained in 20 minutes. If tap 1 is closed and tap 2 is open, the keg will be drained in 30 minutes. If tap 2 is closed and tap 1 is open, how long will it take to drain the keg?

Tap 1 and tap 2 together take 20 minutes to drain the keg, so together they drain the keg at a rate of $\frac{1}{20}$ of the keg per minute. Tap 2 takes 30 minutes to drain the keg by itself, so it drains the keg at the rate of $\frac{1}{30}$ of the keg per minute. Let r be the rate at which tap 1 will drain the keg by itself. Then $\left(r + \frac{1}{30}\right)$ of the keg per minute is the rate at which both taps together will drain the keg, so $r + \frac{1}{30} = \frac{1}{20}$. Therefore, $r = \frac{1}{20} - \frac{1}{30} = \frac{1}{60}$, and tap 1 drains the keg at the rate of $\frac{1}{60}$ of the keg per minute, so it will take 60 minutes or 1 hour for tap 1 to drain the keg if tap 2 is closed.

II–4. Counting Problems

➤II–4.1

An example of one type of counting problem is: 50 students signed up for both English and Math. 90 students signed up for either English or Math. If 25 students are taking English but not taking Math, how many students are taking Math but not taking English?

In these problems, "either . . . or . . ." means you can take both, so the people taking both are counted among the people taking either Math or English.

You must avoid counting the same people twice in these problems. The formula is:

> the number taking English or Math = the number taking English + the number taking Math – the number taking both.

You have to subtract the number taking both subjects since they are counted once with those taking English and counted again with those taking Math.

A person taking English is either taking Math or not taking Math, so there are 50 + 25 = 75 people taking English, 50 taking English and Math and 25 taking English but not taking Math. Since 75 are taking English, 90 = 75 + number taking Math – 50; so there are 90 – 25 = 65 people taking Math. 50 of the people taking Math are taking English so 65 – 50 or 15 are taking Math but not English.

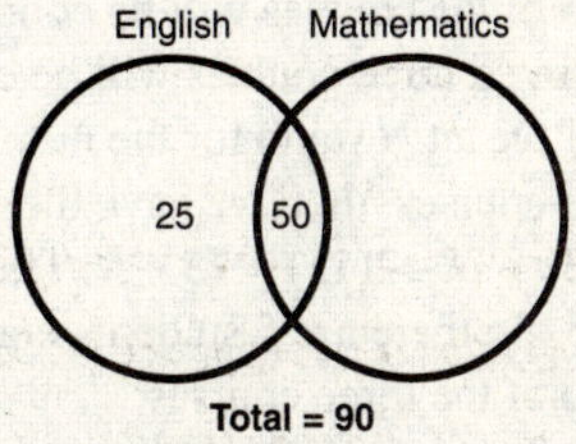

The figure shows what is given. Since 90 students signed up for English or Mathematics, 15 must be taking Mathematics but not English.

EXAMPLE 1

In a survey, 60% of those surveyed owned a car and 80% of those surveyed owned a TV. If 55% owned both a car and a TV, what percent of those surveyed owned a car or a TV or both?

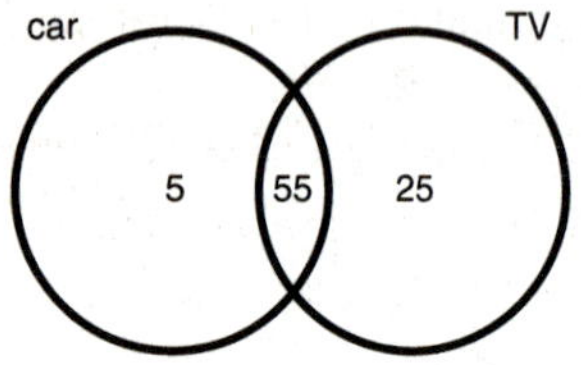

The basic formula is:

people who own a car or a TV = people who own a car + people who own a TV – people who own both a car and a TV.

So the people who own a car or a TV = 60% + 80% – 55% = 85%. Therefore, 85% of the people surveyed own either a car or a TV.

If we just add 60% and 80% the result is 140% which is impossible. This is because the 55% who own both are counted twice.

This type of problem can involve three or more groups. The basic principle remains to avoid counting the same person more than once.

EXAMPLE 2

70 students are enrolled in Math, English, or German. 40 students are in Math, 35 are in English, and 30 are in German. 15 students are enrolled in all three of the courses. How many of the students are enrolled in exactly two of the courses: Math, English, and German?

If we add 40, 35, and 30, the people enrolled in exactly two of the courses will be counted twice and the people in all three courses will be counted three times. So if we let N stand for the number enrolled in exactly two courses, then we have the equation $70 = 40 + 35 + 30 - N - 2(15) = 75 - N$. Therefore, N is $75 - 70 = 5$. So there are 5 students enrolled in exactly two of the three courses.

➤II–4.2

> If an event can happen in m different ways, and each of the m ways is followed by a second event which can occur in k different ways, then the first event can be followed by the second event in $m \bullet k$ different ways. This is called the *fundamental principle of counting.*

EXAMPLE 1

If there are 3 different roads from Syracuse to Binghamton and 4 different roads from Binghamton to Scranton, how many different routes are there from Syracuse to Scranton that go through Binghamton?

There are 3 different ways to go from Syracuse to Binghamton. Once you are in Binghamton, there are 4 different ways to get to Scranton. So using the fundamental principle of counting, there are $3 \times 4 = 12$ different ways to get from Syracuse to Scranton going through Binghamton.

EXAMPLE 2

A club has 20 members. They are electing a president and a vice-president. How many different outcomes of the election are possible? (Assume the president and vice-president must be different members of the club.)

There are 20 members, so there are 20 choices for president. Once a president is chosen, there are 19 members left who can be vice-president. So there are $20 \bullet 19 = 380$ different possible outcomes of the election.

II–5. Ratio and Proportion

➤II–5.1

Ratio. A ratio is a comparison of two numbers by division. The ratio of a to b is written as $a : b = \frac{a}{b} = a \div b$. We can handle ratios as fractions, since a ratio is a fraction. In the ratio $a : b$, a and b are called the *terms* of the ratio.

Since a : b *is a fraction,* b *can never be zero.* The fraction $\frac{a}{b}$ is usually different from the fraction $\frac{b}{a}\left(\text{for example, } \frac{3}{2} \text{ is not the same as } \frac{2}{3}\right)$ so *the order of the terms in a ratio is important.*

EXAMPLE 1

If an orange costs 20¢ and an apple costs 12¢, what is the ratio of the cost of an orange to the cost of an apple?

The ratio is $\frac{20¢}{12¢} = \frac{5}{3}$ or 5 : 3. Notice that the ratio of the cost of an apple to the cost of an orange is $\frac{12¢}{20¢} = \frac{3}{5}$ or 3 : 5. So the order of the terms is important.

A ratio is a number, so if you want to find the ratio of two quantities they must be expressed in the same units.

EXAMPLE 2

What is the ratio of 8 inches to 6 feet?

Change 6 feet into inches. Since there are 12 inches in a foot, 6 feet = 6 × 12 inches = 72 inches. So the ratio is $\frac{8 \text{ inches}}{72 \text{ inches}} = \frac{1}{9}$ or 1 : 9.

If you regard ratios as fractions, the units must cancel out. In example 2, if you did not change units the ratio would be $\frac{8 \text{ inches}}{6 \text{ feet}} = \frac{4 \text{ inches}}{3 \text{ feet}}$, which is not a number.

If two numbers measure different quantities, their quotient is usually called a rate. For example, $\frac{50 \text{ miles}}{2 \text{ hours}}$, which equals 25 miles per hour, is a rate of speed.

➤II–5.2

Proportion. A proportion is a statement that two ratios are equal. For example, $\frac{3}{12} = \frac{1}{4}$ is a proportion; it could also be expressed as 3 : 12 = 1 : 4 or 3 : 12 :: 1 : 4.

In the proportion $a : b = c : d$, the terms on the outside (a and d) are called the *extremes*, and the terms on the inside (b and c) are called the *means*. Since $a : b$ and $c : d$ are ratios, b and d are both different from zero, so $bd \neq 0$. Multiply each side of $\frac{a}{b} = \frac{c}{d}$ by bd; you get $(bd)\left(\frac{a}{b}\right) = ad$ and $(bd)\left(\frac{c}{d}\right) = bc$. Since $bd \neq 0$, the proportion $\frac{a}{b} = \frac{c}{d}$ is equivalent to the equation $ad = bc$. This is usually expressed in the following way:

In a proportion the product of the extremes is equal to the product of the means.

EXAMPLE 1

Find x if $\frac{4}{5} = \frac{10}{x}$.

In the proportion $\frac{4}{5} = \frac{10}{x}$, 4 and x are the extremes and 5 and 10 are the means, so $4x = 5 \bullet 10 = 50$. Solve for x and we get $x = \frac{50}{4} = 12.5$.

Finding the products ad and bc is also called *cross multiplying the proportion*: $\frac{a}{b} \times \frac{c}{d}$. So cross multiplying a proportion gives two equal numbers. The proportion $\frac{a}{b} = \frac{c}{d}$ is read "a is to b as c is to d."

EXAMPLE 2

Two numbers are in the ratio 5 : 4 and their difference is 10. What is the larger number?

Let m and n be the two numbers. Then $\frac{m}{n} = \frac{5}{4}$ and $m - n = 10$. Cross multiply the proportion and you get $5n = 4m$ or $n = \frac{4}{5}m$. So $m - n = m - \frac{4}{5}m = \frac{1}{5}m = 10$ and $m = 50$, which means $n = \frac{4}{5} \bullet 50 = 40$.

Therefore, the larger number is 50.

CHECK: $\frac{50}{40} = \frac{5}{4}$ and $50 - 40 = 10$.

Two variables, a and b, are *directly proportional* if they satisfy a relationship of the form $a = kb$, where k is a number. The distance a car travels in two hours and its average speed for the two hours are directly proportional, since $d = 2s$ where d is the distance and s is the average speed expressed in miles per hour. Here $k = 2$. Sometimes the word *directly* is omitted, so a and b are proportional means $a = kb$.

EXAMPLE 3

If m is proportional to n and $m = 5$ when $n = 4$, what is the value of m when $n = 18$?

There are two different ways to work the problem.

I. Since m and n are directly proportional, $m = kn$; and $m = 5$ when $n = 4$, so $5 = k \bullet 4$ which means $k = \frac{5}{4}$. Therefore, $m = \frac{5}{4}n$. So when $n = 18$, $m = \frac{5}{4} \bullet 18 = \frac{90}{4} = 22.5$.

II. Since m and n are directly proportional, $m = kn$. If n' is some value of n, then the value of m corresponding to n' we will call m', and $m' = kn'$. So $\frac{m}{n} = k$ and $\frac{m'}{n'} = k$; therefore, $\frac{m}{n} = \frac{m'}{n'}$, is a proportion. Since $m = 5$ when $n = 4$, $\frac{m}{n} = \frac{5}{4} = \frac{m'}{18}$. Cross multiply and we have $4m' = 90$ or $m' = \frac{90}{4} = 22.5$.

If two quantities are proportional, you can always set up a proportion in this manner.

EXAMPLE 4

If a machine makes 3 yards of cloth in 2 minutes, how many yards of cloth will the machine make in 50 minutes?

The amount of cloth is proportional to the time the machine operates. Let y be the number of yards of cloth the machine makes in 50 minutes; then $\frac{2 \text{ minutes}}{50 \text{ minutes}} = \frac{3 \text{ yards}}{y \text{ yards}}$, so $\frac{2}{50} = \frac{3}{y}$. Cross multiply and you have $2y = 150$, so $y = 75$. Therefore, the machine makes 75 yards of cloth in 50 minutes.

Since a ratio is a number, the units must cancel; so put the numbers that measure the same quantity in the same ratio.

> *Any two units of measurement of the same quantity are directly proportional.*

EXAMPLE 5

How many ounces are there in $4\frac{3}{4}$ pounds?

Let x be the number of ounces in $4\frac{3}{4}$ pounds.

Since there are 16 ounces in a pound,

$\frac{x \text{ ounces}}{16 \text{ ounces}} = \frac{4\frac{3}{4} \text{ pounds}}{1 \text{ pound}}$. Cross multiply to get $x = 16 \bullet 4\frac{3}{4} = 16 \bullet \frac{19}{4} = 76$; so $4\frac{3}{4}$ pounds = 76 ounces.

You can always change units by using a proportion. You should know the following measurements:

LENGTH:	1 foot = 12 inches
	1 yard = 3 feet
AREA:	1 square foot = 144 square inches
	1 square yard = 9 square feet
TIME:	1 minute = 60 seconds
	1 hour = 60 minutes
	1 day = 24 hours
	1 week = 7 days
	1 year = 52 weeks
VOLUME:	1 quart = 2 pints
	1 gallon = 4 quarts
WEIGHT:	1 ounce = 16 drams
	1 pound = 16 ounces
	1 ton = 2000 pounds

EXAMPLE 6

On a map, it is $2\frac{1}{2}$ inches from Harrisburg to Gary. The actual distance from Harrisburg to Gary is 750 miles. What is the actual distance from town A to town B if they are 4 inches apart on the map?

Let d miles be the distance from A to B; then $\frac{2\frac{1}{2} \text{ inches}}{4 \text{ inches}} = \frac{750 \text{ miles}}{d \text{ miles}}$. Cross multiply and we have $\left(2\frac{1}{2}\right) d = 4 \times 750 = 3{,}000$, so $d = \frac{2}{5} \times 3{,}000 =$ 1,200. Therefore, the distance from A to B is 1,200 miles. Problems like this one are often called scale problems.

Two variables, a and b, are *indirectly proportional* or *inversely proportional* if they satisfy a relationship of the form $k = ab$, where k is a number. So the average speed of a car and the time it takes the car to travel 300 miles are indirectly proportional, since $st = 300$ where s is the speed and t is the time.

EXAMPLE 7

m is indirectly proportional to n and $m = 5$ when $n = 4$. What is the value of m when $n = 18$?

Since m and n are indirectly proportional, $m \bullet n = k$, and $k = 5 \bullet 4 = 20$ because $m = 5$ when $n = 4$. Therefore, $18m = k = 20$, so $m = \frac{20}{18} = \frac{10}{9}$ when $n = 18$.

Other examples of indirect proportion are work problems (see Section II–3.3).

> If two quantities are directly proportional, then when one increases, the other increases. If two quantities are indirectly proportional, when one quantity increases, the other decreases.

➤II–5.3

It is also possible to compare three or more numbers by a ratio. The numbers A, B, and C are in the ratio 2 : 4 : 3 means $A : B = 2 : 4$, $A : C = 2 : 3$, and $B : C = 4 : 3$. The order of the terms is important: $A : B : C$ is read A is to B is to C.

EXAMPLE 1

What is the ratio of Tom's salary to Martha's salary to Anne's salary if Tom makes $15,000, Martha makes $12,000 and Anne makes $10,000?

The ratio is 15,000 : 12,000 : 10,000 which is the same as 15 : 12 : 10. You can cancel a factor that appears in *every* term.

EXAMPLE 2

The angles of a triangle are in the ratio 5 : 4 : 3; how many degrees are there in the largest angle?

The sum of the angles in a triangle is 180°. If the angles are $a°$, $b°$, and $c°$, then $a + b + c = 180$, and $a : b : c = 5 : 4 : 3$. You could find b in terms of a, since $\frac{a}{b} = \frac{5}{4}$, and c in terms of a, since $\frac{a}{c} = \frac{5}{3}$, and then solve the equation for a.

A quicker method for this type of problem is:

❶ Add all the numbers, so $5 + 4 + 3 = 12$.
❷ Use each number as the numerator of a fraction whose denominator is the result of step (1), getting $\frac{5}{12}, \frac{4}{12}, \frac{3}{12}$.
❸ Each quantity is the corresponding fraction (from step 2) of the total.

Thus

$a = \frac{5}{12}$ of 180 or 75, $b = \frac{4}{12}$ of 180 or 60, and $c = \frac{3}{12}$ of 180 or 45.

So the largest angle is 75°.
CHECK: $75 : 60 : 45 = 5 : 4 : 3$ and $75 + 60 + 45 = 180$.

II-6. Sequences and Progressions

➤II–6.1

A SEQUENCE is an ordered collection of numbers. For example, 2, 4, 6, 8, 10, . . . is a sequence. 2, 4, 6, 8, 10 are called the *terms* of the sequence. We identify the terms by their position in the sequence; so 2 is the first term, 8 is the 4th term and so on. The dots mean the sequence continues; you should be able to figure out the succeeding terms. In the example, the sequence is the sequence of even integers, and the next term after 10 would be 12.

EXAMPLE 1

What is the eighth term of the sequence 1, 4, 9, 16, 25, . . . ?

Since $1^2 = 1$, $2^2 = 4$, $3^2 = 9$, the sequence is the sequence of squares of integers, so the eighth term is $8^2 = 64$.

Sequences are sometimes given by a rule that defines an entry (usually called the n-th entry) in terms of previous entries of the sequence.

EXAMPLE 2

If a sequence is defined by the rule $a_n = (a_{n-1} - 3)^2$, what is a_4 (the fourth term of the sequence) if a_1 is 1?

Since a_1 is 1, a_2 is $(1 - 3)^2 = (-2)^2 = 4$. So a_3 is $(4 - 3)^2 = (1)^2 = 1$. Therefore, a_4 is $(1 - 3)^2 = 4$.

➤II–6.2

An *arithmetic progression* is a sequence of numbers with the property that the *difference* of any two consecutive numbers is always the same. The numbers 2, 6, 10, 14, 18, 22, . . . constitute an arithmetic progression, since each term is 4 more than the term before it. 4 is called the common difference of the progression.

If d is the common difference and a is the first term of the progression, then the nth term will be $a + (n - 1)d$. So a progression with common difference 4 and initial term 5 will have $5 + 6(4) = 29$ as its 7th term. You can check your answer. The sequence would be 5, 9, 13, 17, 21, 25, 29, . . . so 29 is the seventh term.

A sequence of numbers is called a *geometric progression* if the *ratio* of consecutive terms is always the same. So 3, 6, 12, 24, 48, . . . is a geometric progression since $\frac{6}{3} = 2 = \frac{12}{6} = \frac{24}{12} = \frac{48}{24}$, ... *The nth term of a geometric progression is* ar^{n-1} where a is the first term and r is the common ratio. If a geometric progression started with 2 and the common ratio was 3, then the fifth term should be $2 \bullet 3^4 = 2 \bullet 81 = 162$. The sequence would be 2, 6, 18, 54, 162, . . . so 162 is indeed the fifth term of the progression.

We can quickly add up the first n terms of a geometric progression that starts with a and has common ratio r. *The formula for the sum of the first n terms* is $\frac{ar^n - a}{r - 1}$ when $r \neq 1$. (If $r = 1$ all the terms are the same so the sum is na.)

EXAMPLE

Find the sum of the first 7 terms of the sequence 5, 10, 20, 40, ... Since $\frac{10}{5} = \frac{20}{10} = \frac{40}{20} = 2$, the sequence is a geometric sequence with common ratio 2. The first term is 5, so $a = 5$ and the common ratio is 2. The sum of the first seven terms means $n = 7$, thus the sum is

$$\frac{5 \bullet 2^7 - 5}{2 - 1} = 5(2^7 - 1) = 5(128 - 1) = 5 \bullet 127 = 635.$$

CHECK: The first seven terms are 5, 10, 20, 40, 80, 160, 320, and 5 + 10 + 20 + 40 + 80 + 160 + 320 = 635.

II–7. Inequalities

➤II–7.1

A number is positive if it is greater than 0, so 1, $\frac{1}{1000}$, and 53.4 are all positive numbers. Positive numbers are signed numbers whose sign is +. If you think of numbers as points on a number line (see Section I–6.1), positive numbers correspond to points to the right of 0.

A number is negative if it is less than 0. $-\frac{4}{5}$, –50, and –.0001 are all negative numbers. Negative numbers are signed numbers whose sign is –. Negative numbers correspond to points to the left of 0 on a number line.

0 is the only number which is neither positive nor negative.

$a > b$ means the number a is greater than the number b; that is, $a = b + x$ where x is a positive number. If we look at a number line, $a > b$ means a is to the right of b. $a > b$ can also be read as b is less than a, which is also written $b < a$. For example, $-5 > -7.5$ because $-5 = -7.5 + 2.5$ and 2.5 is positive.

The notation $a \leq b$ means a is less than or equal to b, or b is greater than or equal to a. For example, $5 \geq 4$; also $4 \geq 4$. $a \neq b$ means a is not equal to b.

> If you need to know whether one fraction is greater than another fraction, put the fractions over a common denominator and compare the numerators.

EXAMPLE

Which is larger, $\frac{13}{16}$ or $\frac{31}{40}$?

A common denominator is 80. $\frac{13}{16} = \frac{65}{80}$, and $\frac{31}{40} = \frac{62}{80}$; since $65 > 62$, $\frac{65}{80} > \frac{62}{80}$, so $\frac{13}{16} > \frac{31}{40}$.

➤II–7.2

Inequalities have certain properties that are similar to equations. We can talk about the left side and the right side of an inequality, and we can use algebraic expressions for the sides of an inequality. For example, $6x < 5x + 4$. A value for an unknown *satisfies an inequality*, if when you evaluate each side of the inequality the numbers satisfy the inequality. So if $x = 2$, then $6x = 12$ and $5x + 4 = 14$ and since $12 < 14$, $x = 2$ satisfies $6x < 5x + 4$. Two inequalities are equivalent if the same collection of numbers satisfies both inequalities.

The following basic principles are used in work with inequalities:

- **A** Adding the same expression to *each* side of an inequality gives an equivalent inequality (written $a < b \leftrightarrow a + c < b + c$ where $\leftrightarrow$ means equivalent).
- **B** Subtracting the same expression from *each* side of an inequality gives an equivalent inequality ($a < b \leftrightarrow a - c < b - c$).
- **C** Multiplying or dividing *each* side of an inequality by the same *positive* expression gives an equivalent inequality ($a < b \leftrightarrow ca < cb$ for $c > 0$).
- **D** Multiplying or dividing each side of an inequality by the same *negative* expression *reverses* the inequality ($a < b \leftrightarrow ca > cb$ for $c < 0$).
- **E** If both sides of an inequality have the same sign, inverting both sides of the inequality *reverses* the inequality.

$$0 < a < b \leftrightarrow 0 < \frac{1}{b} < \frac{1}{a}$$

$$a < b < 0 \leftrightarrow \frac{1}{b} < \frac{1}{a} < 0$$

- **F** If two inequalities are of the same type (both greater or both less), adding the respective sides gives the same type of inequality.

$$(a < b \text{ and } c < d, \text{ then } a + c < b + d)$$

Note that the inequalities are *not* equivalent.

- **G** If $a < b$ and $b < c$ then $a < c$.

EXAMPLE 1

Find the values of x for which $5x - 4 < 7x + 2$.

Using principle (B) subtract $5x + 2$ from each side, so $(5x - 4 < 7x + 2) \leftrightarrow -6 < 2x$. Now use principle (C) and divide each side by 2, so $-6 < 2x \leftrightarrow -3 < x$.

So any x greater than -3 satisfies the inequality. It is a good idea to make a spot check. -1 is > -3; let $x = -1$ then $5x - 4 = -9$ and $7x + 2 = -5$. Since $-9 < -5$, the answer is correct for at least the particular value $x = -1$.

Some inequalities are not satisfied by *any* real number. For example, since $x^2 \geq 0$ for all x, there is no real number x such that $x^2 < -9$.

You may be given an inequality and asked whether other inequalities follow from the original inequality. You should be able to answer such questions by using principles (A) through (G).

If there is any property of inequalities you can't remember, try out some specific numbers. If $x < y$, then what is the relation between $-x$ and $-y$? Since $4 < 5$ but $-5 < -4$, the relation is probably $-x > -y$, which is true by (D).

Probably the most common mistake is forgetting to reverse the inequalities if you multiply or divide by a negative number.

EXAMPLE 2

Find the values of a which satisfy $a^2 + 1 > 2a + 4$.

We will solve this using an alternate method:

- **A** Group all terms on one side, so that the other side will be 0. The result is $a^2 - 2a + 1 - 4 = a^2 - 2a - 3 > 0$.
- **B** Find all values of the variable which make the expression equal 0.

Since $a^2 - 2a - 3 = (a - 3)(a + 1)$, the result is $a = 3$ and $a = -1$. So the only possible solutions are: $a > 3$, $-1 < a < 3$, and $a < -1$.

- **C** Choose points other than those found in (B), and check whether the points are solutions. If $a = 0$, then $a^2 - 2a - 3 = -3$, which is less than 0, so $-1 < a < 3$ is not a solution. If $a = 4$, then $a^2 - 2a - 3 = 5$, which is greater than 0, so $a > 3$ is a solution. Use $a = -2$ to see that $a < -1$ is also a solution. So the solutions are $a > 3$ and $a < -1$.

This method is quicker for solving inequalities that are not linear.

III. Geometry

III–1. Angles

➤III–1.1

If two straight lines meet at a point they form an *angle*. The point is called the *vertex* of the angle and the lines are called the *sides* or *rays* of the angle. The sign for angle is ∠ and an angle can be denoted in the following ways:

A ∠ABC where B is the vertex, A is a point on one side, and C a point on the other side.

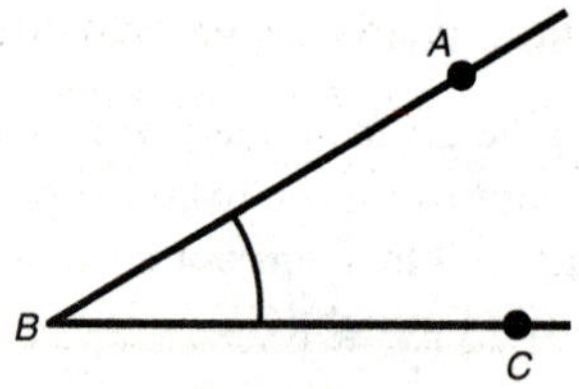

B ∠B where B is the vertex.

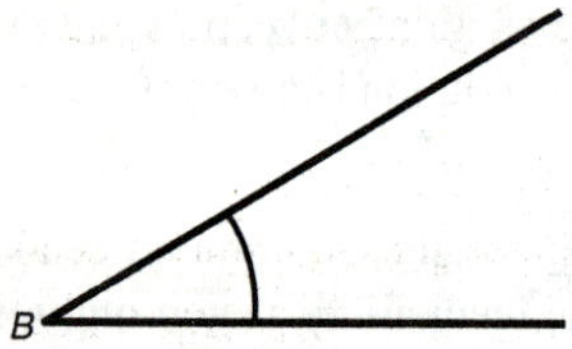

C ∠1 or ∠x where x or 1 is written inside the angle.

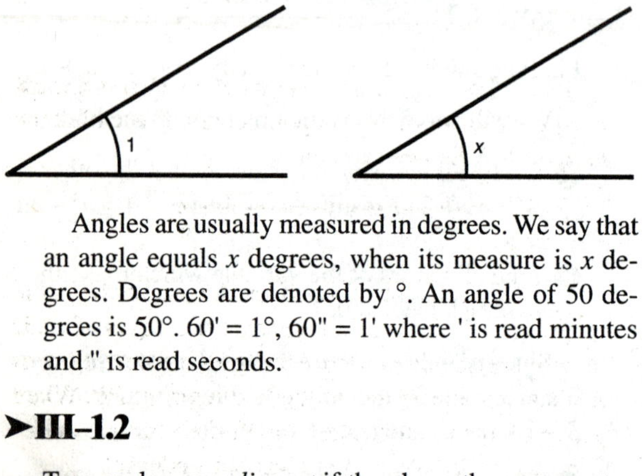

Angles are usually measured in degrees. We say that an angle equals x degrees, when its measure is x degrees. Degrees are denoted by °. An angle of 50 degrees is 50°. 60' = 1°, 60" = 1' where ' is read minutes and " is read seconds.

➤III–1.2

Two angles are *adjacent* if they have the same vertex and a common side and one angle is not inside the other.

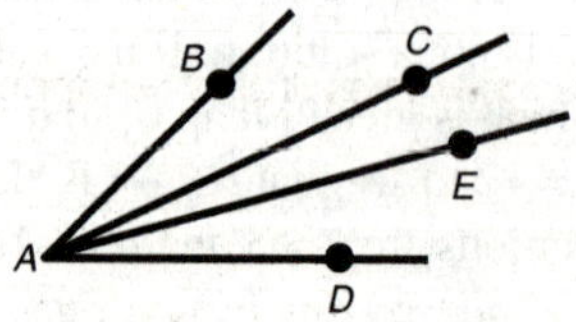

∠BAC and ∠CAD are adjacent, but ∠CAD and ∠EAD are not adjacent.

Where two lines intersect at a point, they form 4 angles. The angles opposite each other are called vertical angles. ∠1 and ∠3 are vertical angles. ∠2 and ∠4 are vertical angles.

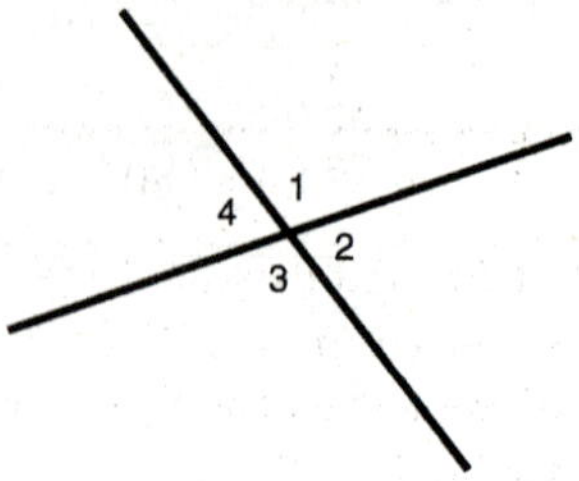

Vertical angles are equal,

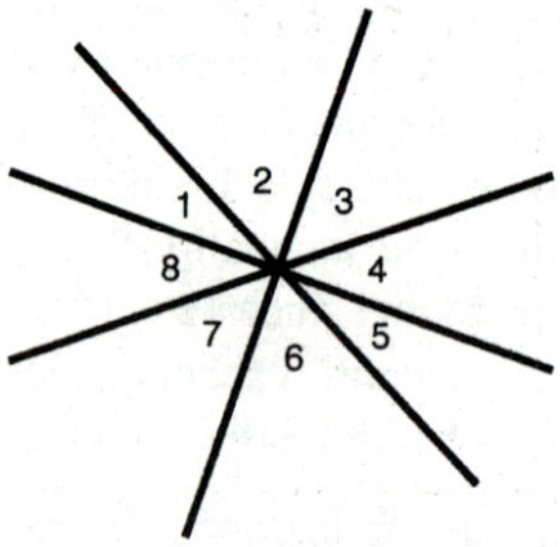

so ∠1 = ∠5, ∠2 = ∠6, ∠3 = ∠7, ∠4 = ∠8.

➤III–1.3

A straight angle is an angle whose sides lie on a straight line. *A straight angle equals 180°.*

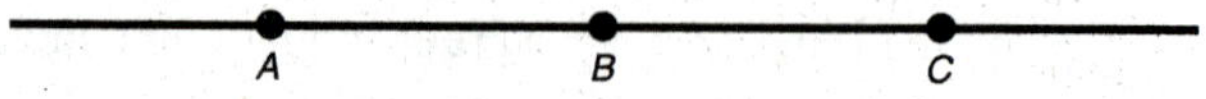

∠ABC is a straight angle.

If the sum of two adjacent angles is a straight angle, then the angles are *supplementary* and each angle is the supplement of the other.

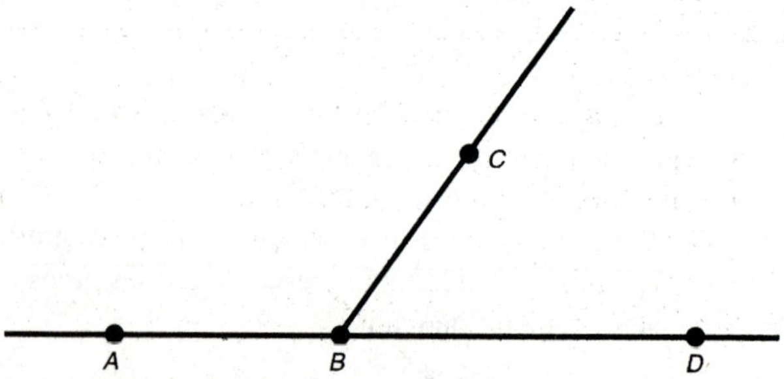

∠ABC and ∠CBD are supplementary.

If an angle of $x°$ and an angle of $y°$ are supplements, then $x + y = 180$.

If two supplementary angles are equal, they are both *right angles*. A right angle is half of a straight angle. A right angle = 90°.

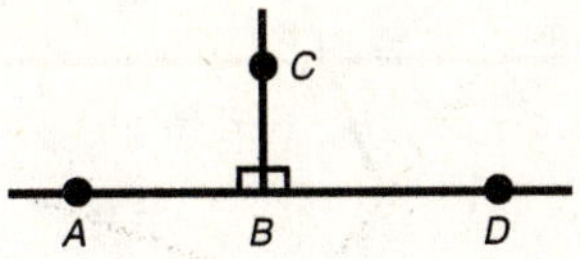

$\angle ABC = \angle CBD$ and they are both right angles. A right angle is denoted by ⊾. When 2 lines intersect and all four of the angles are equal, then each of the angles is a right angle.

If the sum of two adjacent angles is a right angle, then the angles are *complementary* and each angle is the complement of the other.

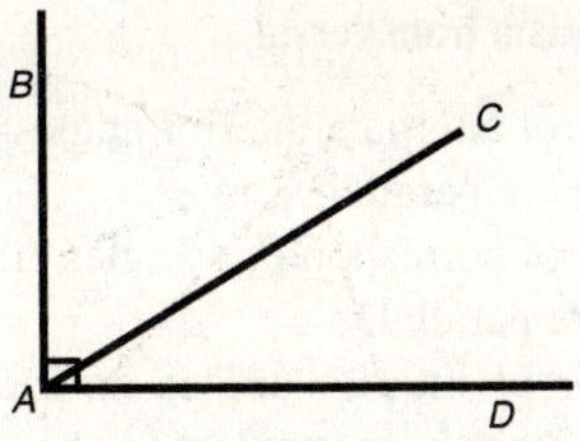

$\angle BAC$ and $\angle CAD$ are complementary.

If an angle of $x°$ and an angle of $y°$ are complementary, then $x + y = 90$.

EXAMPLE

If the supplement of angle x is three times as much as the complement of angle x, how many degrees is angle x?

Let d be the number of degrees in angle x; then the supplement of x is $(180 - d)°$, and the complement of x is $(90 - d)°$. Since the supplement is 3 times the complement, $180 - d = 3(90 - d) = 270 - 3d$ which gives $2d = 90$, so $d = 45$.

Therefore, angle x is 45°.

If an angle is divided into two equal angles by a straight line, then the angle has been *bisected* and the line is called the *bisector* of the angle.

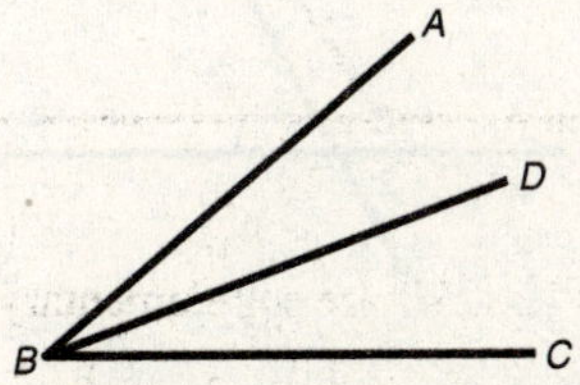

BD bisects $\angle ABC$; so $\angle ABD = \angle DBC$.

An *acute angle* is an angle less than a right angle. An *obtuse* angle is an angle greater than a right angle, but less than a straight angle.

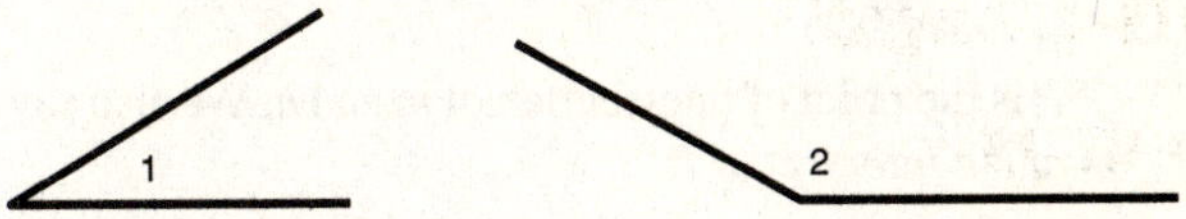

$\angle 1$ is an acute angle, and $\angle 2$ is an obtuse angle.

III–2. Lines

➤III–2.1

A line is understood to be a straight line. A line is assumed to extend indefinitely in both directions. *There is one and only one line between two distinct points.* There are two ways to denote a line:

1. by a single letter: l is a line;

2. by two points on the line:

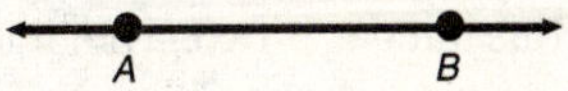

AB is a line.

A *line segment* is the part of a line between two points called *endpoints*. A line segment is denoted by its endpoints.

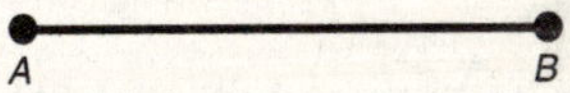

AB is a line segment. If a point P on a line segment is equidistant from the endpoints, then P is called the *midpoint* of the line segment.

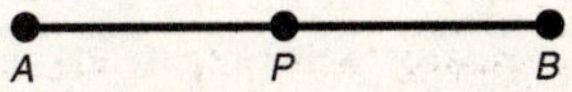

P is the midpoint of AB if the length of AP = the length of PB. Two line segments are equal if their lengths are equal; so $AP = PB$ means the line segment AP has the same length as the line segment PB. When a line segment is extended indefinitely in one direction, it is called a *ray*. A ray has one endpoint.

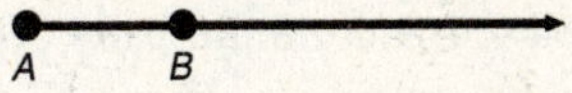

AB is a ray which has A as its endpoint.

➤III–2.2

P is a *point of intersection* of two lines if P is a point which is on both of the lines. *Two different lines cannot have more than one point of intersection*, because there is only one line between two points.

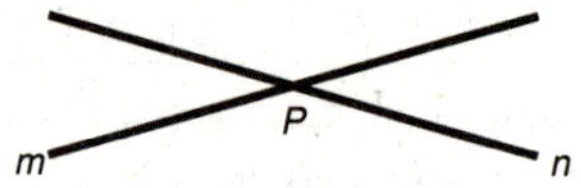

P is the point of intersection of *m* and *n*. We also say *m and n intersect at P*.

Two lines are parallel if they do not intersect no matter how far they are extended.

m and *n* are parallel, but *k* and *l* are not parallel since if *k* and *l* are extended they will intersect. Parallel lines are denoted by the symbol ||; so *m* || *n* means *m* is parallel to *n*.

If two lines are parallel to a third line, then they are parallel to each other.

If a third line intersects two given lines, it is called a *transversal*. A transversal and the two given lines form eight angles. The four inside angles are called *interior* angles. The four outside angles are called *exterior* angles. If two angles are on opposite sides of the transversal they are called *alternate* angles.

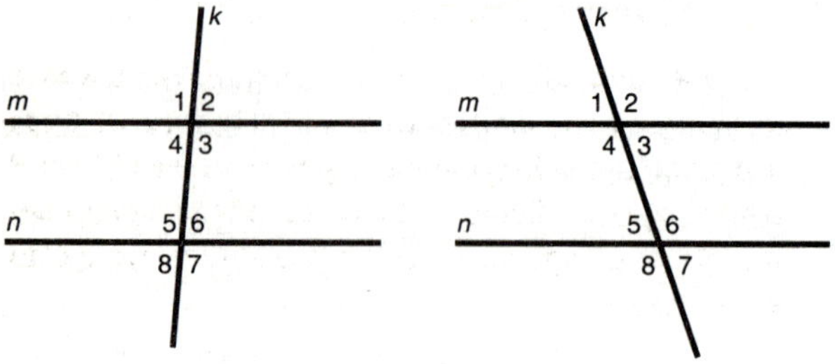

k is a transversal of the lines *m* and *n*. Angles 1, 2, 7, and 8 are the exterior angles, and angles 3, 4, 5, and 6 are the interior angles. ∠4 and ∠6 are an example of a pair of alternate angles. ∠1 and ∠5, ∠2 and ∠6, ∠3 and ∠7, and ∠4 and ∠8 are pairs of *corresponding* angles.

If two parallel lines are intersected by a transversal then:

❶ Alternate interior angles are equal.
❷ Corresponding angles are equal.
❸ Interior angles on the same side of the transversal are supplementary.

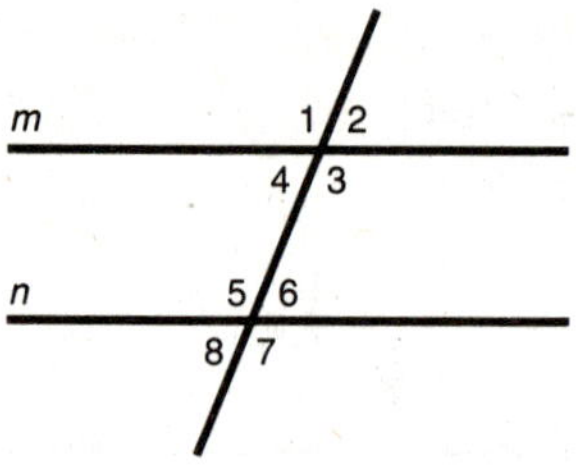

If we use the fact that vertical angles are equal, we can replace "interior" by "exterior" in (1) and (3).

m is parallel to *n* implies:

❶ ∠4 = ∠6 and ∠3 = ∠5
❷ ∠1 = ∠5, ∠2 = ∠6, ∠3 = ∠7 and ∠7 and ∠4 = ∠8
❸ ∠3 + ∠6 = 180° and ∠4 + ∠5 = 180°

The reverse is also true. Let *m* and *n* be two lines that have *k* as a transversal.

❶ If a pair of alternate interior angles are equal, then *m* and *n* are parallel.
❷ If a pair of corresponding angles are equal, then *m* and *n* are parallel.
❸ If a pair of interior angles on the same side of the transversal are supplementary, then *m* is parallel to *n*.

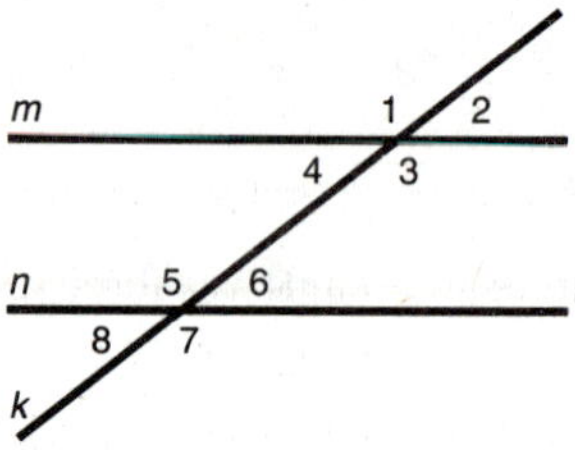

If ∠3 = ∠5, then *m* || *n*. If ∠4 = ∠6 then *m* || *n*. If ∠2 = ∠6 then *m* || *n*. If ∠3 + ∠6 = 180°, then *m* || *n*.

EXAMPLE

If *m* and *n* are two parallel lines and angle 1 is 60°, how many degrees is angle 2?

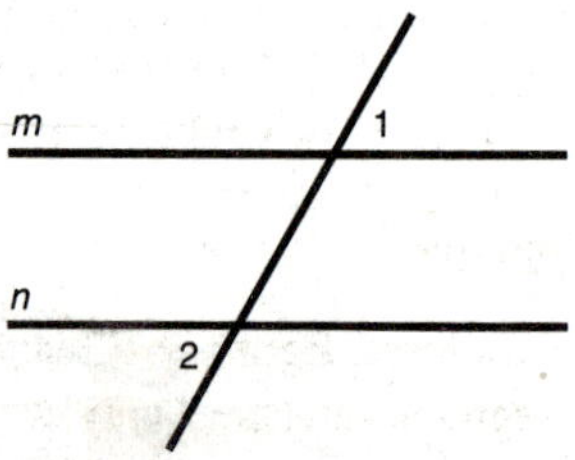

Let ∠3 be the vertical angle equal to angle 2.

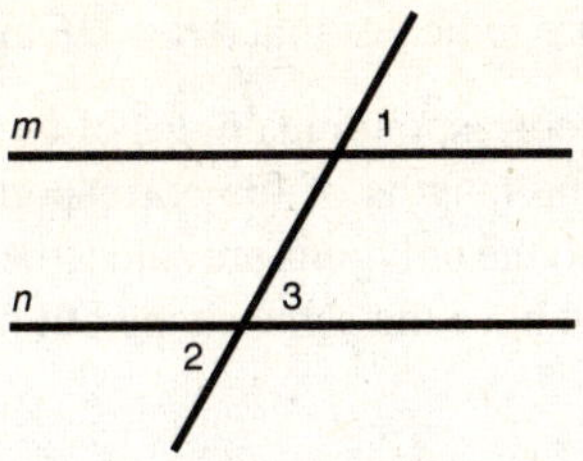

$\angle 3 = \angle 2$. Since *m* and *n* are parallel, corresponding angles are equal. Since $\angle 1$ and $\angle 3$ are corresponding angles, $\angle 1 = \angle 3$. Therefore, $\angle 1 = \angle 2$, and $\angle 2$ equals 60° since $\angle 1 = 60°$.

➤III–2.3

When two lines intersect and all four of the angles formed are equal, the lines are said to be *perpendicular*. If two lines are perpendicular, they are the sides of right angles whose vertex is the point of intersection.

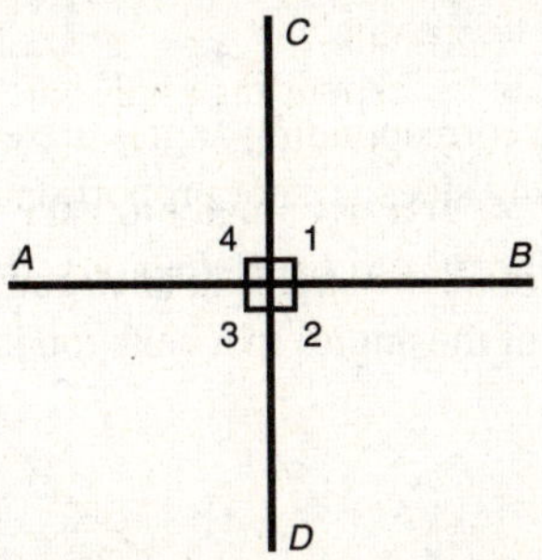

AB is perpendicular to *CD*, and angles 1, 2, 3, and 4 are all right angles. ⊥ is the symbol for perpendicular; so $AB \perp CD$.

If two lines in a plane are perpendicular to the same line, then the two lines are parallel.

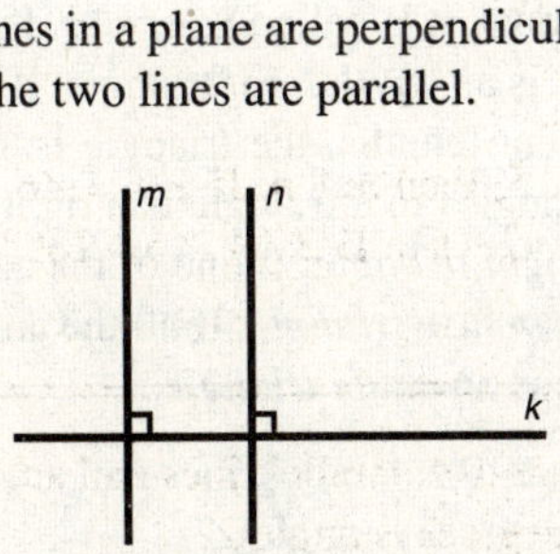

$m \perp k$ and $n \perp k$ imply that $m \parallel n$.

If *any one* of the angles formed when two lines intersect is a right angle, then the lines are perpendicular.

➤III–3. Polygons

A POLYGON is a closed figure in a plane that is composed of line segments that meet only at their endpoints. The line segments are called *sides* of the polygon, and a point where two sides meet is called a *vertex* (plural *vertices*) of the polygon.

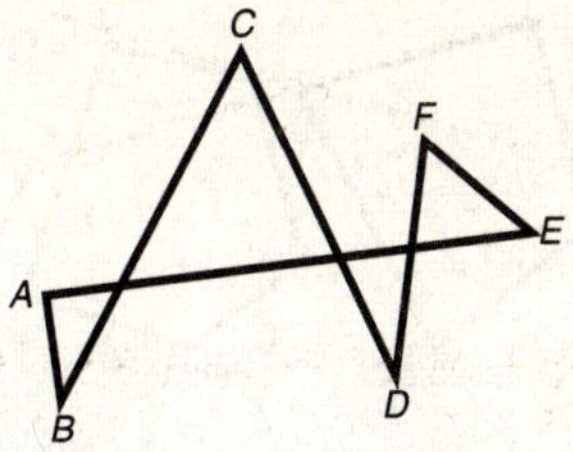

ABCDEF is not a polygon since the line segments intersect at points that are not endpoints.

Some examples of polygons are:

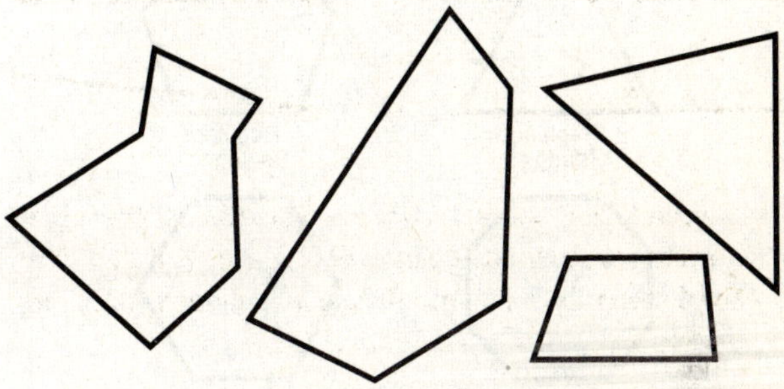

A polygon is usually denoted by the vertices given in order.

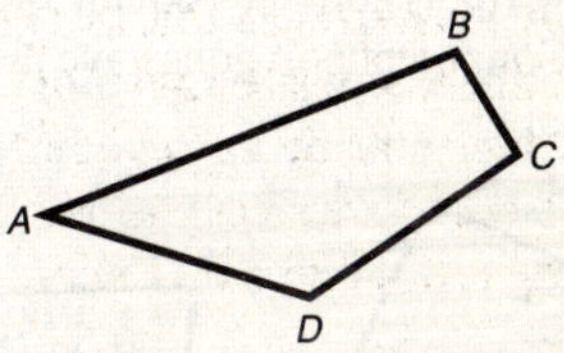

ABCD is a polygon.

A *diagonal* of a polygon is a line segment whose endpoints are nonadjacent vertices. The *altitude* from a vertex *P* to a side is the line segment with endpoint *P* which is perpendicular to the side. In the diagram below, *AC* is a diagonal, and *CE* is the altitude from *C* to *AD*.

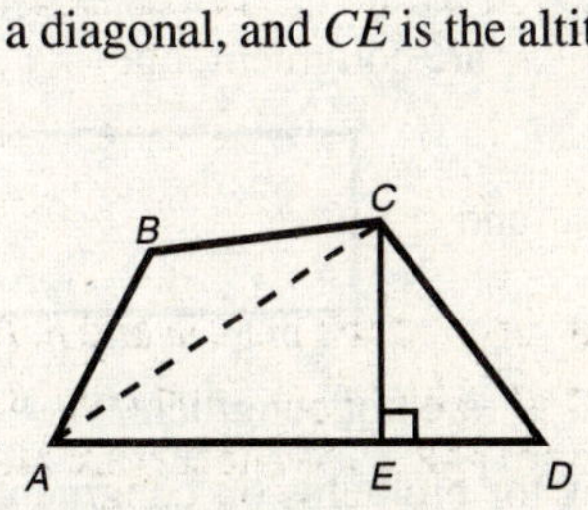

Polygons are classified by the number of angles or sides they have. A polygon with three angles is called a *triangle*; a four-sided polygon is a *quadrilateral*; a polygon with five angles is a *pentagon*; a polygon with six angles is a *hexagon*; an eight-sided polygon is an *octagon*. The number of angles is always equal to the number of sides in a polygon, so a six-sided polygon is a hexagon. The term *n*-gon refers to a polygon with *n* sides.

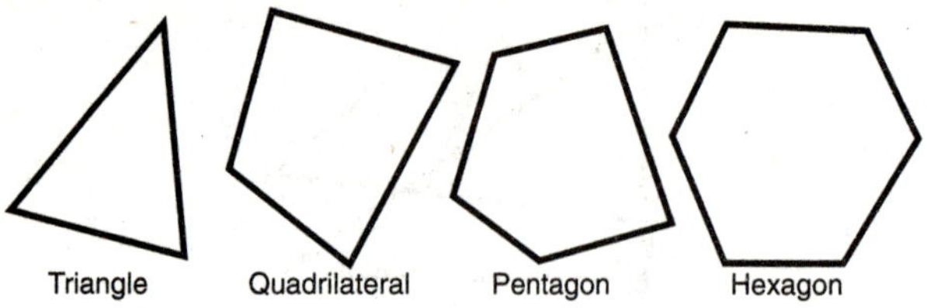

If the sides of a polygon are all equal in length and if all the angles of a polygon are equal, the polygon is called a *regular* polygon.

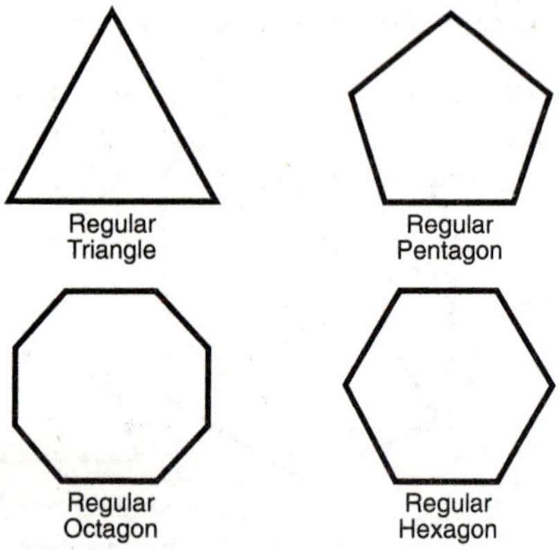

If the corresponding sides and the corresponding angles of two polygons are equal, the polygons are *congruent*. Congruent polygons have the same size and the same shape:

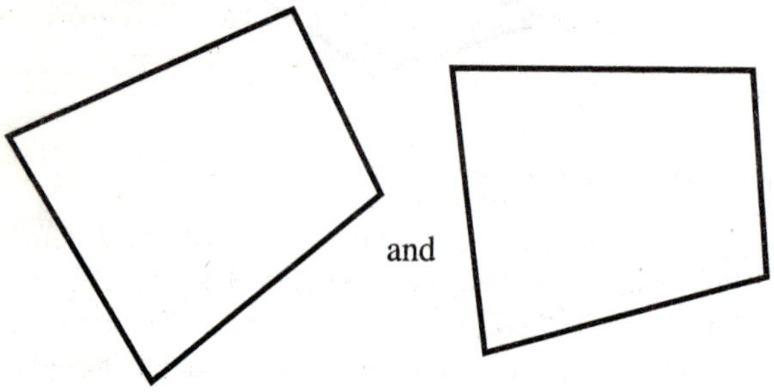

are congruent, but

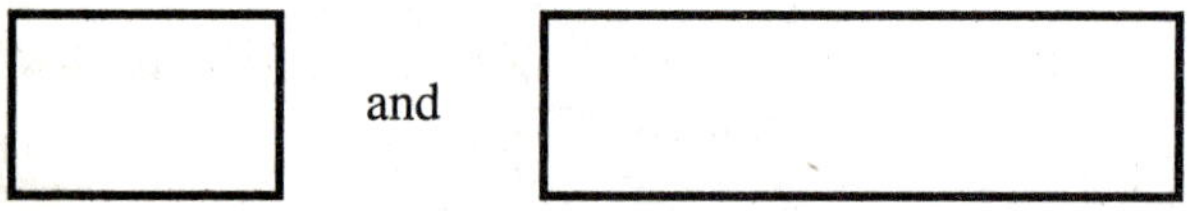

are not congruent

In figures for problems on congruence, sides with the same number of strokes through them are equal.

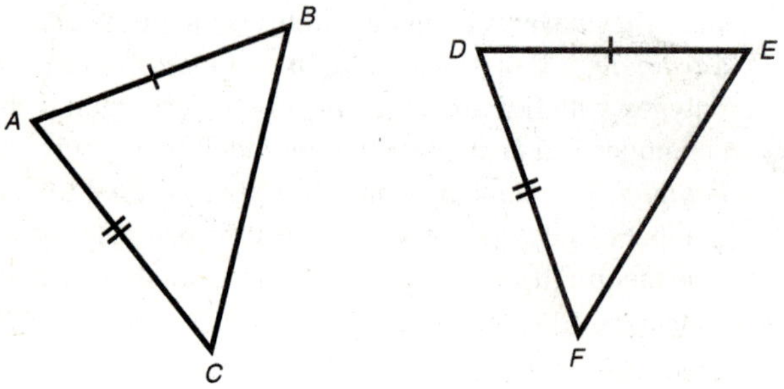

This figure indicates that $AB = DE$ and $AC = DF$.

If all the corresponding angles of two polygons are equal and the lengths of the corresponding sides are proportional, the polygons are said to be *similar*. Similar polygons have the same shape but need not be the same size.

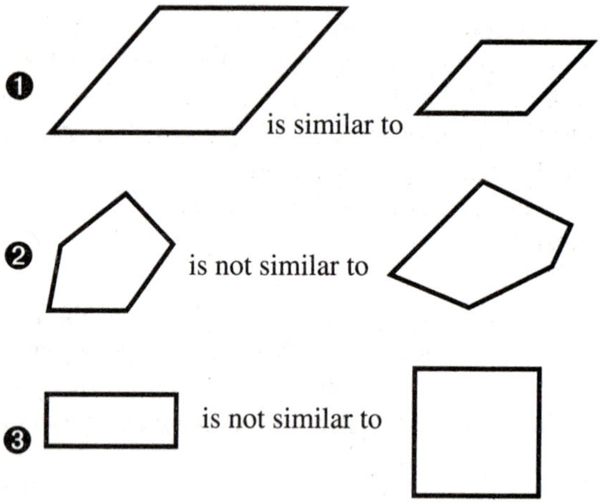

In (3) the corresponding angles are equal, but the corresponding sides are not proportional.

The sum of all the angles of an n-gon is $(n - 2)180°$. So the sum of the angles in a hexagon is $(6 - 2)180° = 720°$.

III–4. Triangles

➤III–4.1

A TRIANGLE is a 3-sided polygon. If two sides of a triangle are equal, it is called *isosceles*. If all three sides are equal, it is an *equilateral* triangle. If all of the sides have different lengths, the triangle is *scalene*. When one of the angles in a triangle is a right angle, the triangle is a *right triangle*. If one of the angles is obtuse we have an *obtuse triangle*. If all the angles are acute, the triangle is an *acute triangle*.

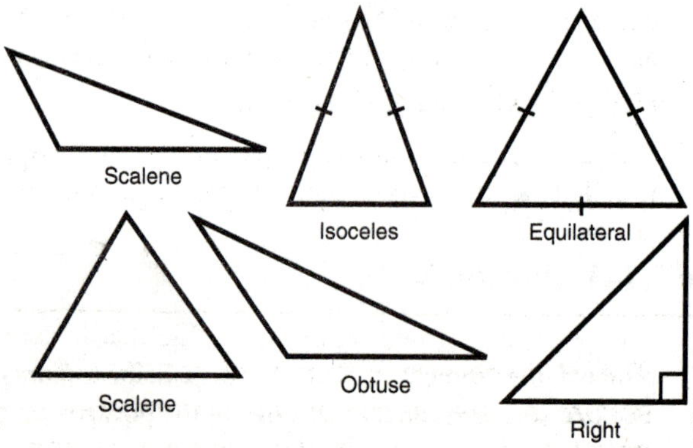

The symbol for a triangle is Δ; so ΔABC means a triangle whose vertices are A, B, and C.

The sum of the angles in a triangle is 180°.

The sum of the lengths of any two sides of a triangle must be longer than the remaining side.

If two angles in a triangle are equal, then the lengths of the sides opposite the equal angles are equal. If two sides of a triangle are equal, then the angles opposite the two equal sides are equal. In an equilateral triangle all the angles are equal and each angle = 60°. If each of the angles in a triangle is 60°, then the triangle is equilateral.

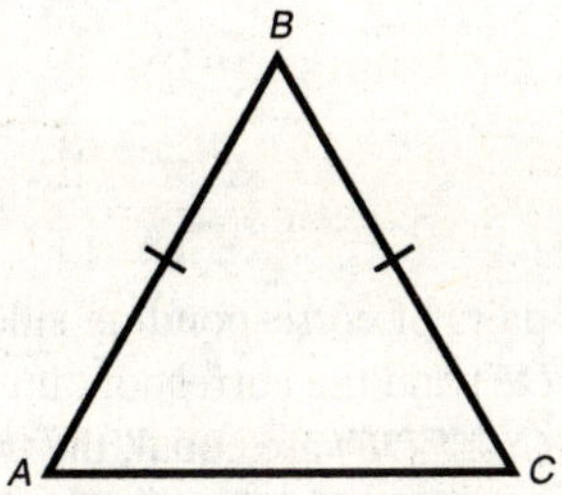

If $AB = BC$, then $\angle BAC = \angle BCA$.

If one angle in a triangle is larger than another angle, the side opposite the larger angle is longer than the side opposite the smaller angle. If one side is longer than another side, then the angle opposite the longer side is larger than the angle opposite the shorter side.

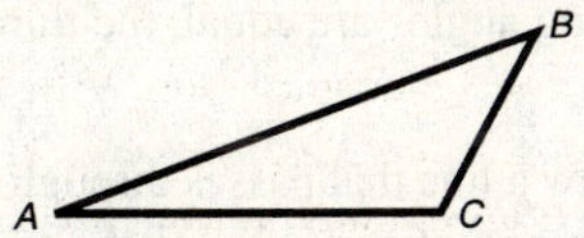

$AB > AC$ implies $\angle BCA > \angle ABC$.

If the side of a triangle is extended, then the resulting exterior angle is greater than either of the opposite and interior angles. So in the triangle above, if we had extended the side *AC* beyond *C* to a point *D*, then the angle *BCD* would be greater than the angle *BAC* and greater than the angle *ABC*.

In a right triangle, the side opposite the right angle is called the *hypotenuse*, and the remaining two sides are called *legs*.

The Pythagorean Theorem states that the square of the length of the hypotenuse is equal to the sum of the squares of the lengths of the legs.

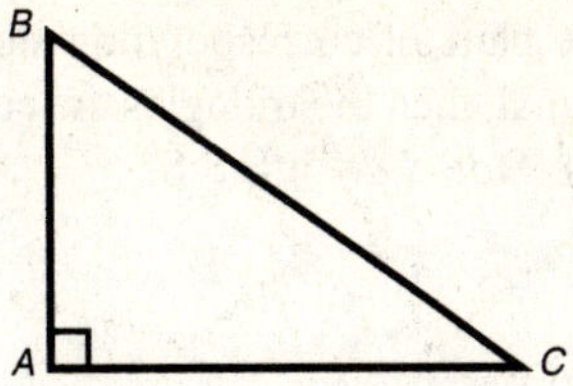

$(BC)^2 = (AB)^2 + (AC)^2$

If $AB = 4$ and $AC = 3$ then $(BC)^2 = 4^2 + 3^2 = 25$ so $BC = 5$. If $BC = 13$ and $AC = 5$, then $13^2 = 169 = (AB)^2 + 5^2$. So $(AB)^2 = 169 - 25 = 144$ and $AB = 12$.

If the lengths of the three sides of a triangle are a, b, and c and $a^2 = b^2 + c^2$, then the triangle is a right triangle where a is the length of the hypotenuse.

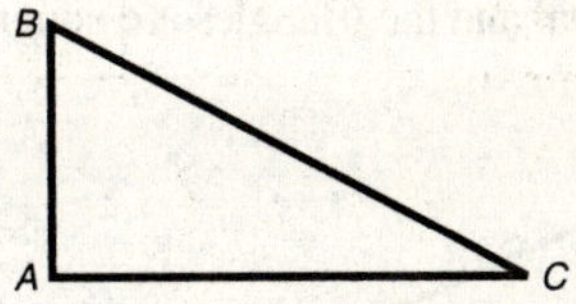

If $AB = 8$, $AC = 15$, and $BC = 17$, then since $17^2 = 8^2 + 15^2$, $\angle BAC$ is a right angle.

➤III–4.2

Congruence. Two triangles are congruent if two pairs of corresponding sides and the corresponding *included* angles are equal. This is called *Side-Angle-Side* and is denoted by S.A.S.

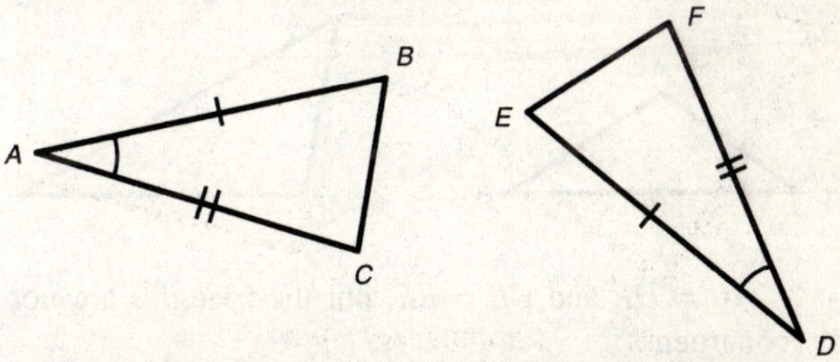

$AB = DE$, $AC = DF$ and $\angle BAC = \angle EDF$ imply that $\Delta ABC \cong \Delta DEF$. $\cong$ means congruent.

Two triangles are congruent if two pairs of corresponding angles and the corresponding *included* sides are equal. This is called *Angle-Side-Angle* or A.S.A.

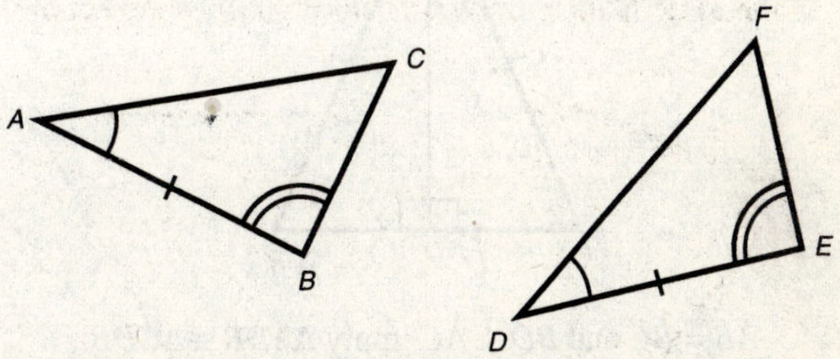

If $AB = DE$, $\angle BAC = \angle EDF$, and $\angle CBA = \angle FED$ then $\Delta ABC \cong \Delta DEF$.

If all three pairs of corresponding sides of two triangles are equal, then the triangles are congruent. This is called *Side-Side-Side* or S.S.S.

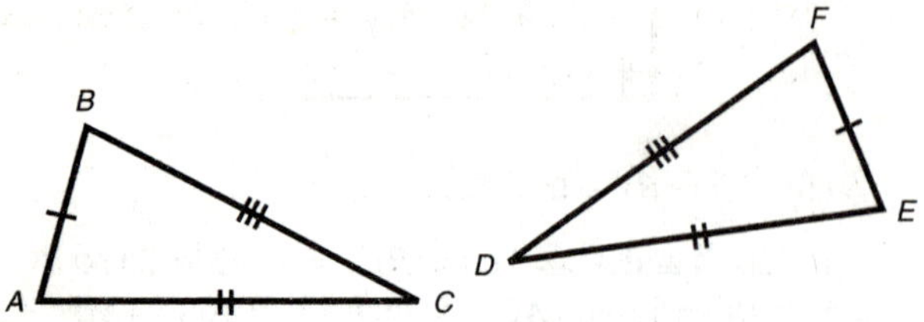

$AB = EF$, $AC = ED$, and $BC = FD$ imply that $\Delta ABC \cong \Delta EFD$.

Because of the Pythagorean Theorem, if any two corresponding sides of two right triangles are equal, the third sides are equal and the triangles are congruent.

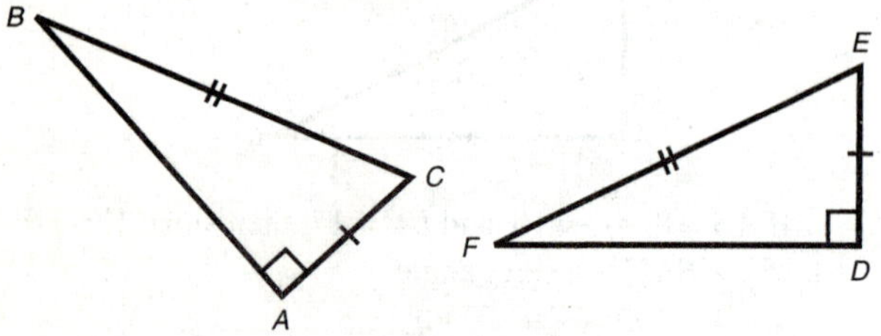

$AC = DE$ and $BC = EF$ imply $\Delta ABC \cong \Delta DFE$.

In general, if two corresponding sides of two triangles are equal, we cannot infer that the triangles are congruent.

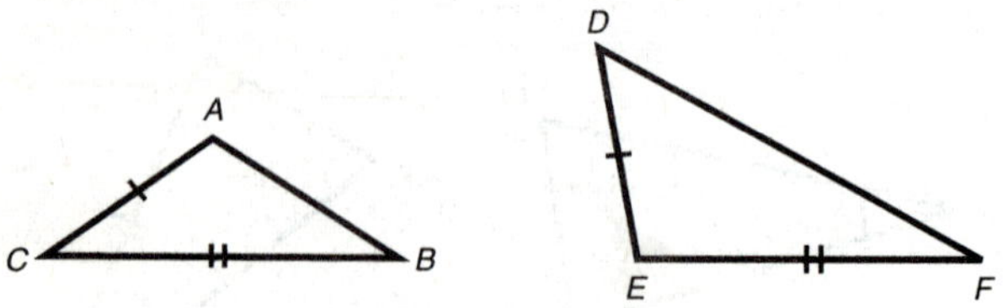

$AC = DE$ and $CB = EF$, but the triangles are not congruent.

If two sides of a triangle are equal, then the altitude to the third side divides the triangle into two congruent triangles.

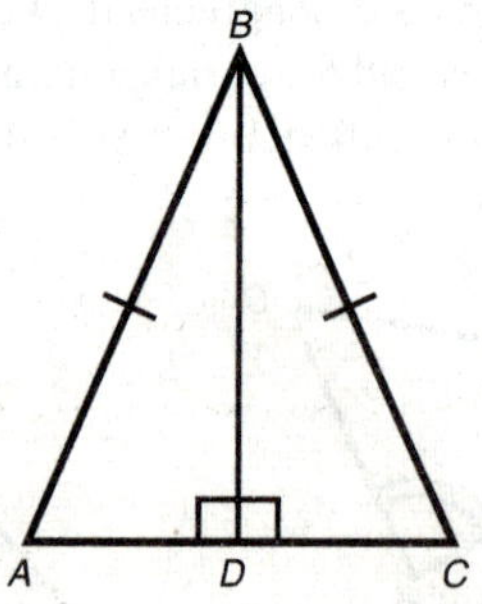

$AB = BC$ and $BD \perp AC$ imply $\Delta ADB \cong \Delta CDB$.

Therefore, $\angle ABD = \angle CBD$, so BD bisects $\angle ABC$. Since $AD = DC$, D is the midpoint of AC so BD is the median from B to AC. A *median* is the segment from a vertex to the midpoint of the side opposite the vertex.

EXAMPLE

If $AB = 4$, $AC = 4.5$ and $BC = 6$, $\angle BAC = \angle EDF$, $DE = 4$, and $DF = 4.5$, what is EF?

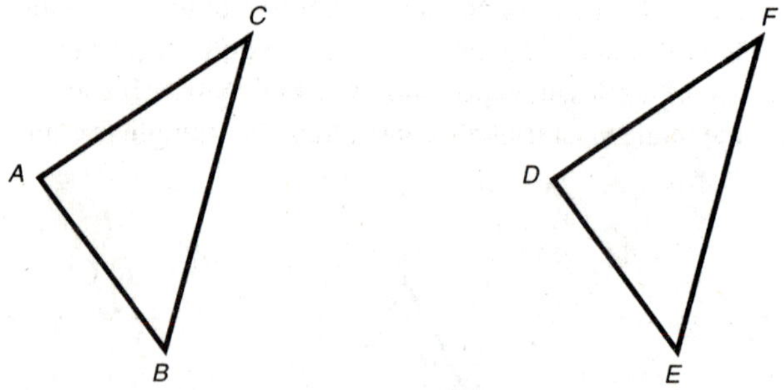

Since two pairs of corresponding sides (AB and DE, AC and DF) and the corresponding included angles ($\angle BAC$, $\angle EDF$) are equal, the triangles ABC and DEF are congruent by S.A.S. Therefore, $EF = BC = 6$.

➤III–4.3

Similarity. *Two triangles are similar if all three pairs of corresponding angles are equal.* Since the sum of the angles in a triangle is 180°, it follows that if two corresponding angles are equal, the third angles must be equal.

If you draw a line that passes through a triangle and is parallel to one of the sides of the triangle, the triangle formed is similar to the original triangle.

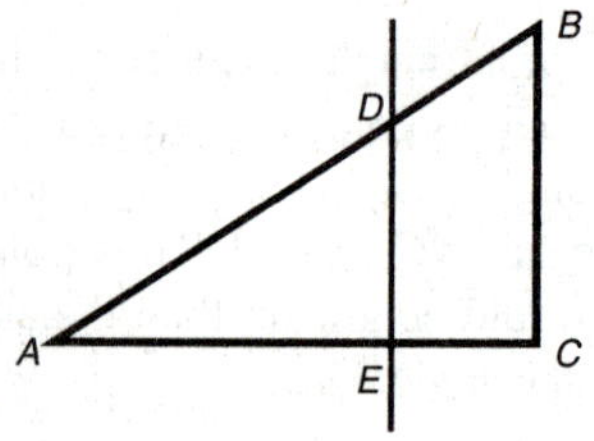

If $DE \parallel BC$ then $\Delta ADE \sim \Delta ABC$. The symbol ~ means similar.

EXAMPLE

A man 6 feet tall casts a shadow 4 feet long; at the same time a flagpole casts a shadow which is 50 feet long. How tall is the flagpole?

The man with his shadow and the flagpole with its shadow can be regarded as the pairs of corresponding sides of two similar triangles.

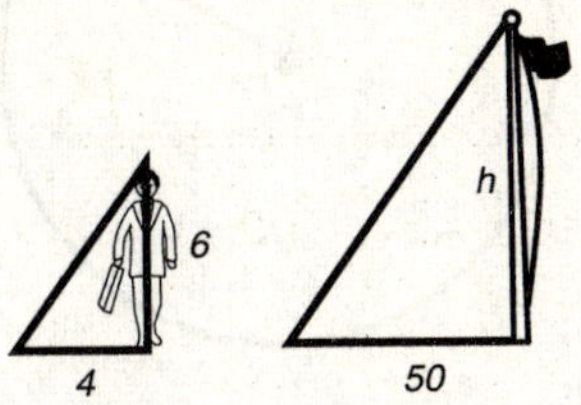

Let h be the height of the flagpole. Since corresponding sides of similar triangles are proportional, $\frac{4}{50} = \frac{6}{h}$. Cross multiply, getting $4h = 6 \bullet 50 = 300$; so $h = 75$. Therefore, the flagpole is 75 feet high.

III–5. Quadrilaterals

A QUADRILATERAL is a polygon with four sides. The sum of the angles in a quadrilateral is 360°. If both sets of opposite sides of a quadrilateral are parallel, the figure is a *parallelogram.*

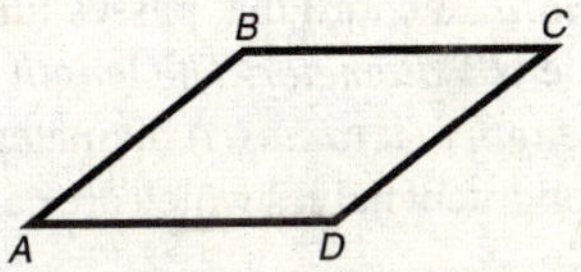

ABCD is a parallelogram.

In a parallelogram:

❶ The opposite sides are equal.
❷ The opposite angles are equal.
❸ Any diagonal divides the parallelogram into two congruent triangles.
❹ The diagonals bisect each other. (A line *bisects* a line segment if it intersects the segment at the midpoint of the segment.)

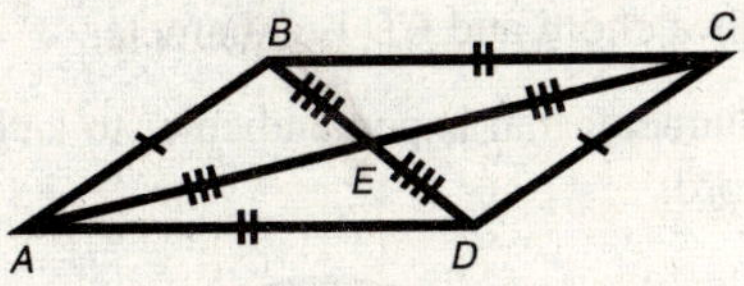

ABCD is a parallelogram.

❶ $AB = DC$, $BC = AD$.
❷ $\angle BCD = \angle BAD$, $\angle ABC = \angle ADC$.
❸ $\Delta ABC \cong \Delta ADC$, $\Delta ABD \cong \Delta CDB$.
❹ $AE = EC$ and $BE = ED$.

If *any* of the statements (1), (2), (3) and (4) are true for a quadrilateral, then the quadrilateral is a parallelogram.

If all of the sides of a parallelogram are equal, the figure is called a *rhombus.*

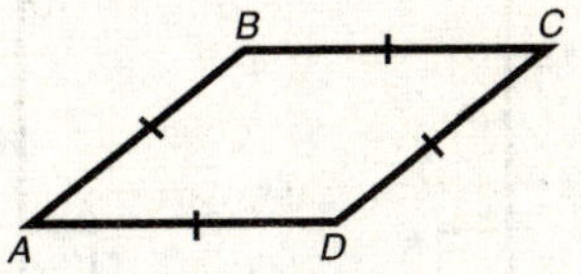

ABCD is a rhombus.

The diagonals of a rhombus are perpendicular.

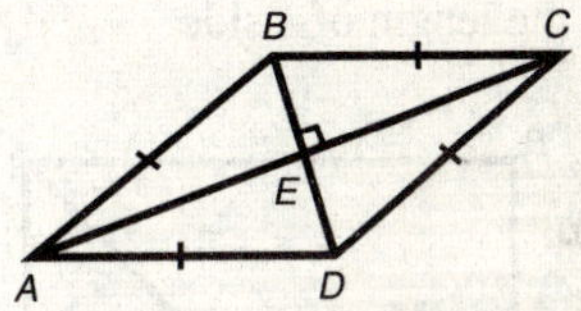

$BD \perp AC$; $\angle BEC = \angle CED = \angle AED = \angle AEB = 90°$.

If all the angles of a parallelogram are right angles, the figure is a *rectangle.*

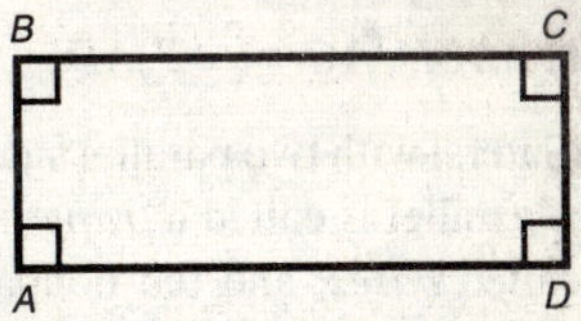

ABCD is a rectangle.

Since the sum of the angles in a quadrilateral is 360°, if *all* the angles of a quadrilateral are equal then the figure is a rectangle. The diagonals of a rectangle are equal. The length of a diagonal can be found by using the Pythagorean Theorem.

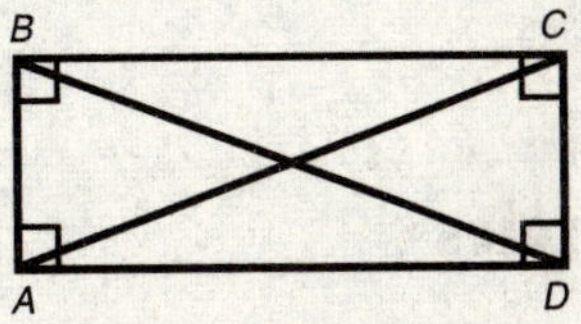

If *ABCD* is a rectangle, $AC = BD$ and $(AC)^2 = (AD)^2 + (DC)^2$.

If all the sides of a rectangle are equal, the figure is a *square*.

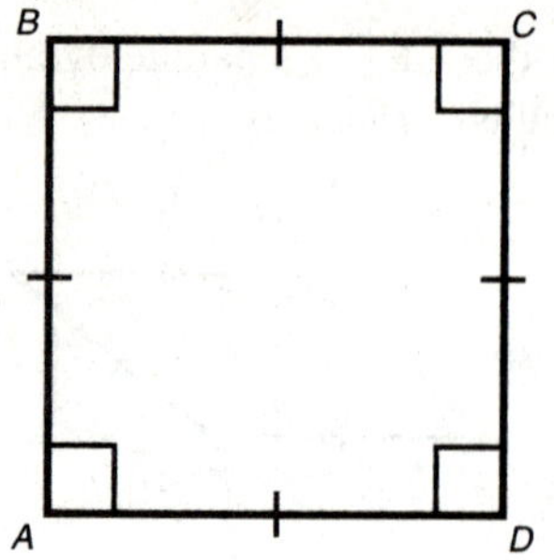

ABCD is a square.

If all the angles of a rhombus are equal, the figure is a square. The length of the diagonal of a square is $\sqrt{2}\,s$ where *s* is the length of a side.

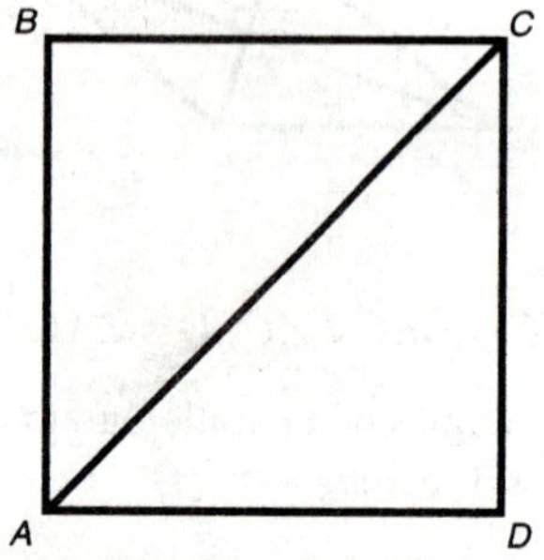

In square *ABCD*, $AC = (\sqrt{2})AD$.

A quadrilateral with two parallel sides and two sides that are not parallel is called a *trapezoid*. The parallel sides are called *bases*, and the nonparallel sides are called *legs*.

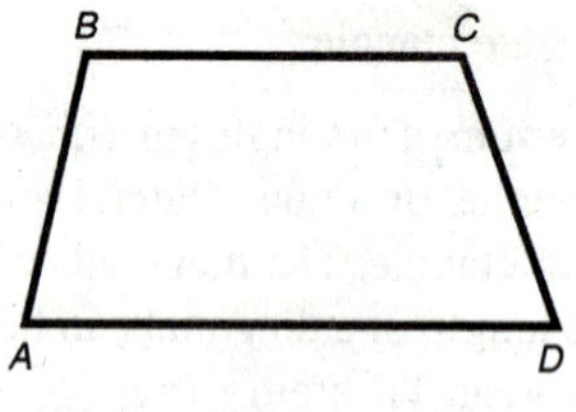

If $BC \parallel AD$ then *ABCD* is a trapezoid; *BC* and *AD* are the bases.

III–6. Circles

A CIRCLE is a figure in a plane consisting of all the points that are the same distance from a fixed point called the *center* of the circle. A line segment from any point on the circle to the center of the circle is called a *radius* (plural: *radii*) of the circle. All radii of the same circle have the same length.

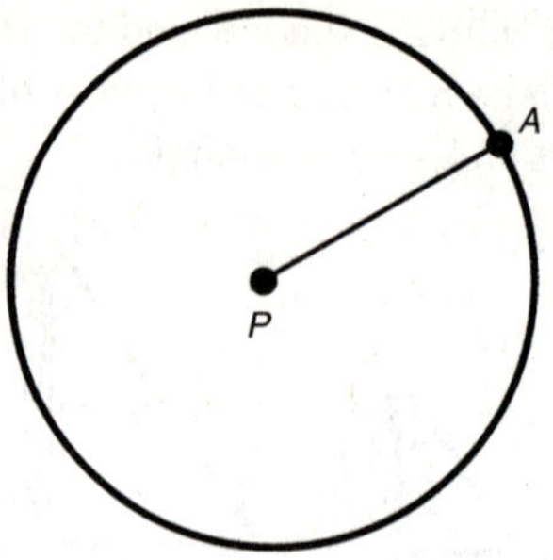

This circle has center *P* and radius *AP*.

A circle is denoted by a single letter, usually its center. Two circles with the same center are *concentric*.

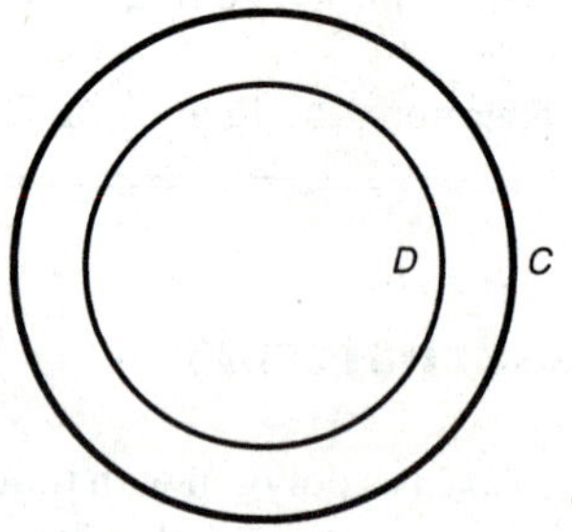

C and *D* are concentric circles.

A line segment whose endpoints are on a circle is called a *chord*. A chord that passes through the center of the circle is a *diameter*. *The length of a diameter is twice the length of a radius.* A diameter divides a circle into two congruent halves which are called *semicircles*.

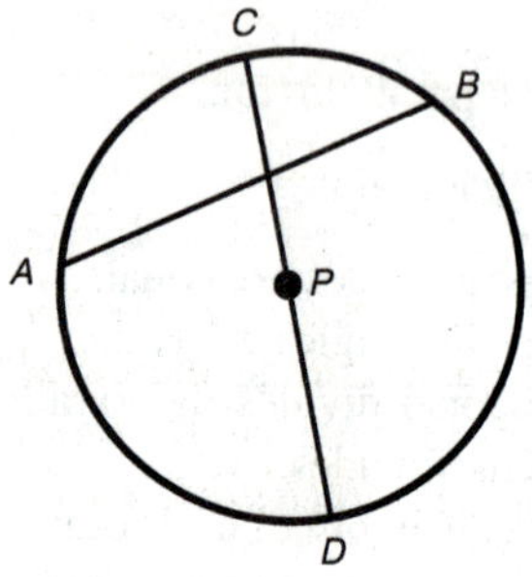

P is the center of the circle.

AB is a chord and *CD* is a diameter.

A diameter that is perpendicular to a chord bisects the chord.

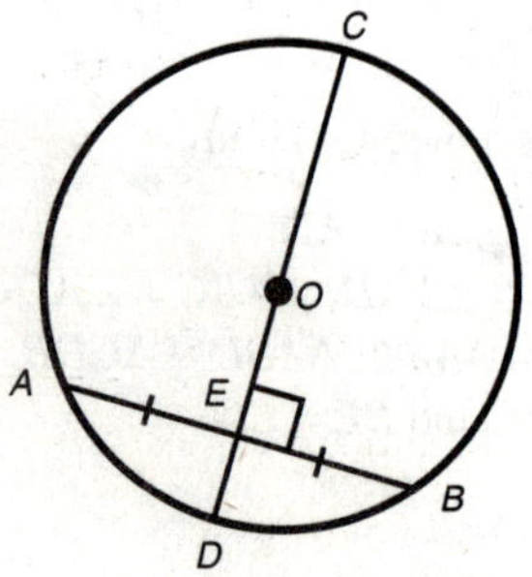

O is the center of this circle and $AB \perp CD$; then $AE = EB$.

If a line intersects a circle at one and only one point, the line is said to be a *tangent* to the circle. The point common to a circle and a tangent to the circle is called the *point of tangency*. The radius from the center to the point of tangency is perpendicular to the tangent.

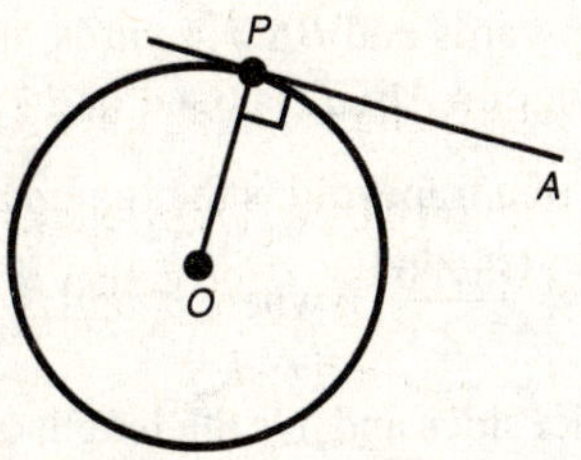

AP is tangent to the circle with center O. P is the point of tangency and $OP \perp PA$.

A polygon is *inscribed* in a circle if all of its vertices are points on the circle.

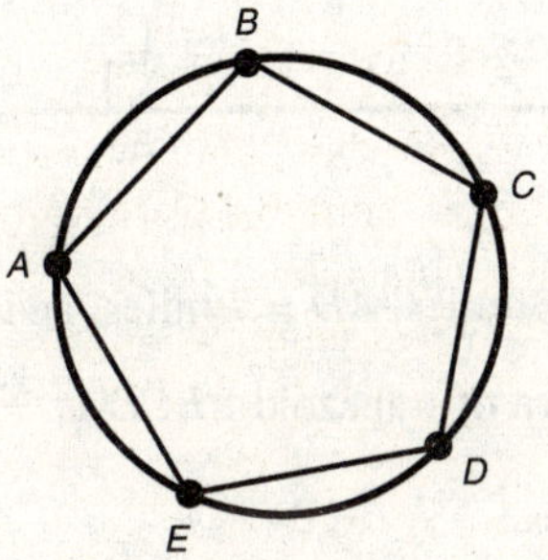

$ABCDE$ is an inscribed pentagon.

An angle whose vertex is a point on a circle and whose sides are chords of the circle is called an *inscribed angle*. An angle whose vertex is the center of a circle and whose sides are radii of the circle is called a *central angle*.

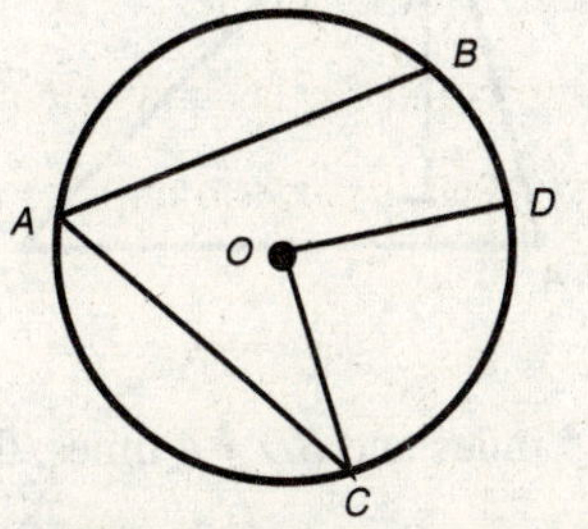

$\angle BAC$ is an inscribed angle.

$\angle DOC$ is a central angle.

An *arc* is a part of a circle.

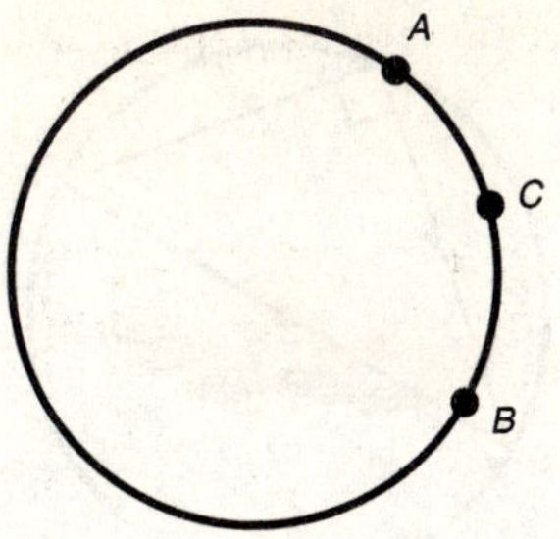

ACB is an *arc*. Arc ACB is written $\overset{\frown}{ACB}$.

If two letters are used to denote an arc, they represent the smaller of the two possible arcs. So $\overset{\frown}{AB} = \overset{\frown}{ACB}$.

An arc can be measured in degrees. The entire circle is 360°; thus an arc of 120° would be $\frac{1}{3}$ of a circle.

A central angle is equal in measure to the arc it intercepts.

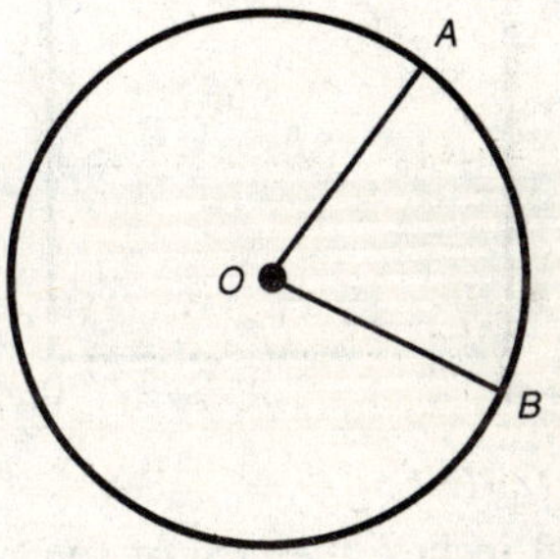

$\angle AOB = \overset{\frown}{AB}$

An inscribed angle is equal in measure to $\frac{1}{2}$ *the arc it intercepts.*

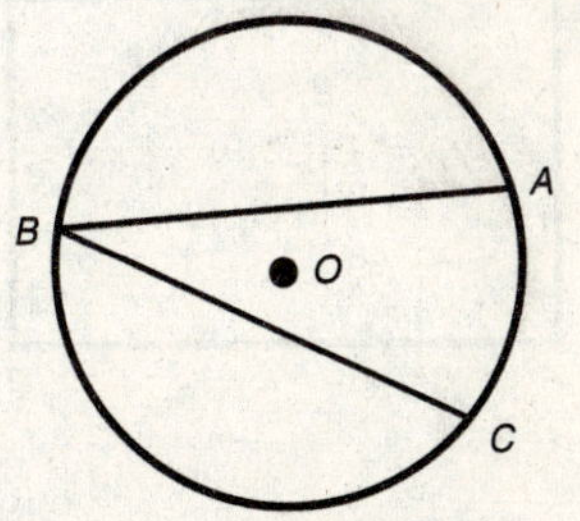

$\angle ABC = \frac{1}{2}\overset{\frown}{AC}$

An angle inscribed in a semicircle is a *right angle*.

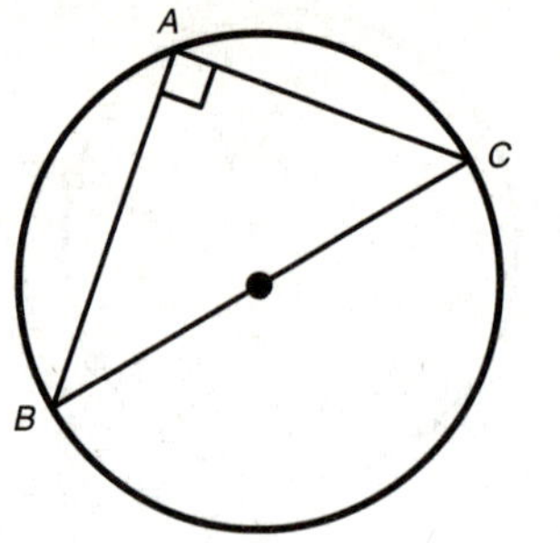

If BC is a diameter, then $\angle BAC$ is inscribed in a semicircle; so $\angle BAC = 90°$.

III–7. Area and Perimeter

➤III–7.1

The area A of a square equals s^2, where s is the length of a side of the square. Thus, $A = s^2$.

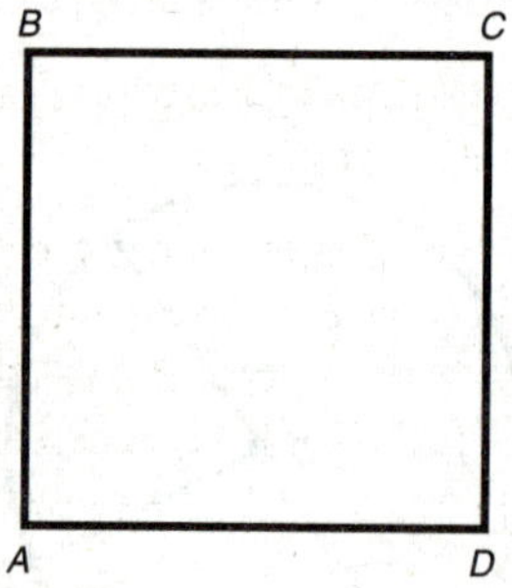

If $AD = 5$ inches, the area of square $ABCD$ is 25 square inches.

The area of a rectangle equals length times width; if L is the length of one side and W is the length of a perpendicular side, then the area $A = LW$.

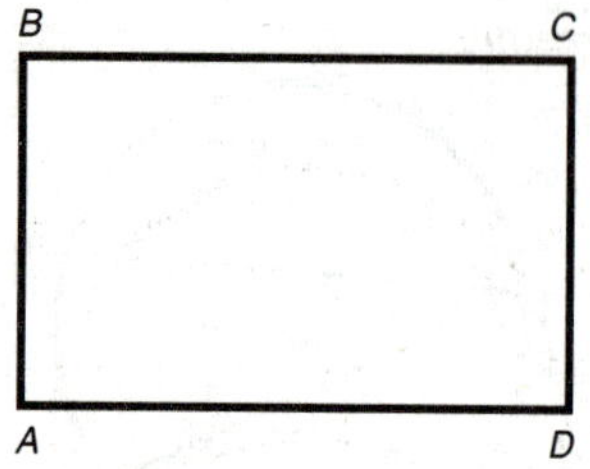

If $AB = 5$ feet and $AD = 8$ feet, then the area of rectangle $ABCD$ is 40 square feet.

The area of a parallelogram is base × height; $A = bh$, where b is the length of a side and h is the length of an altitude to that side.

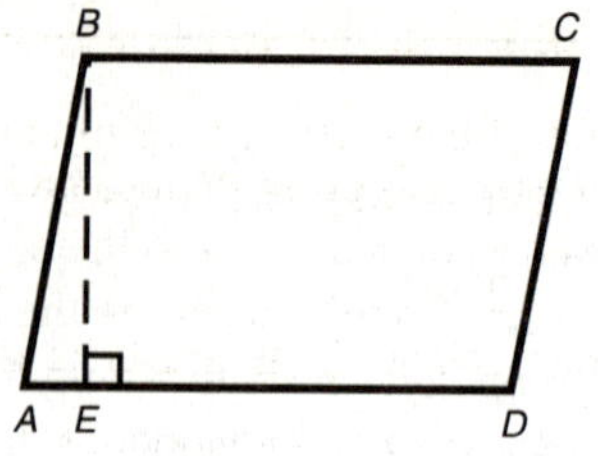

If $AD = 6$ yards and $BE = 4$ yards, then the area of the parallelogram $ABCD$ is $6 \bullet 4$ or 24 square yards.

The area of a trapezoid is the (average of the bases) × height. $A = \frac{(b_1+b_2)}{2}h$ where b_1 and b_2 are the lengths of the parallel sides and h is the length of an altitude to one of the bases.

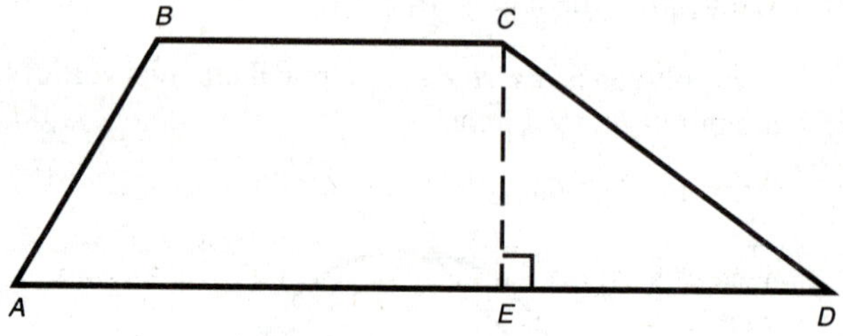

If $BC = 3$ miles, $AD = 7$ miles, and $CE = 2$ miles, then the area of trapezoid $ABCD$ is $\frac{(3+7)}{2} \bullet 2 = 10$ square miles.

The area of a triangle is $\frac{1}{2}$ (base × height); $A = \frac{1}{2}bh$, where b is the length of a side and h is the length of the altitude to that side.

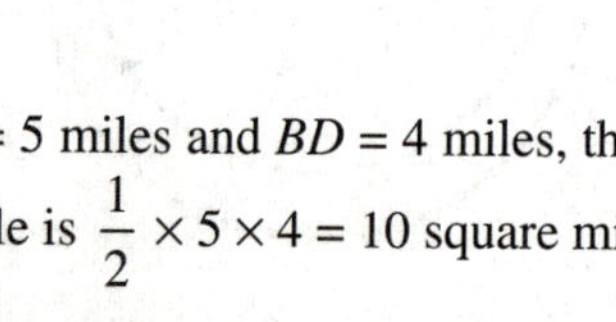

If $AC = 5$ miles and $BD = 4$ miles, then the area of the triangle is $\frac{1}{2} \times 5 \times 4 = 10$ square miles.

Since the legs of a right triangle are perpendicular to each other, the area of a right triangle is one-half the product of the lengths of the legs.

EXAMPLE

If the lengths of the sides of a triangle are 5 feet, 12 feet, and 13 feet, what is the area of the triangle?

Since $5^2 + 12^2 = 25 + 144 = 169 = 13^2$, the triangle is a right triangle and the legs are the sides with lengths 5 feet and 12 feet. Therefore, the area is $\frac{1}{2} \times 5 \times 12 = 30$ square feet.

If we want to find the area of a polygon that is not of a type already mentioned, we break the polygon up into smaller figures such as triangles or rectangles, find the area of each piece, and add these to get the area of the given polygon.

The area of a circle is πr^2 where r is the length of a radius. Since $d = 2r$ where d is the length of a diameter, $A = \pi\left(\frac{d}{2}\right)^2 = \pi\frac{d^2}{4}$. π is a number which is approximately $\frac{22}{7}$ or 3.14; however, there is *no fraction which is exactly equal to* π. π is called an *irrational number.*

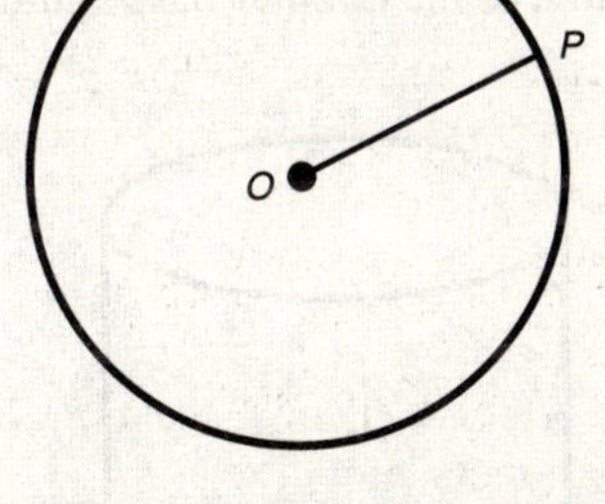

If $OP = 2$ inches, then the area of the circle with center O is $\pi 2^2$ or 4π square inches. The portion of the plane bounded by a circle and a central angle is called a *sector* of the circle.

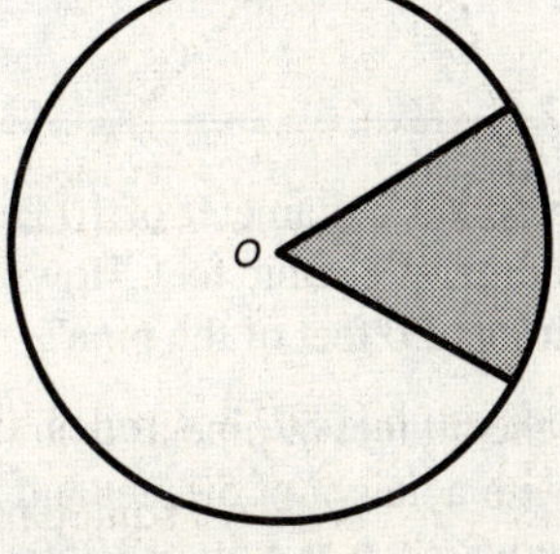

The shaded region is a sector of the circle with center O. The area of a sector with central angle $n°$ in a circle of radius r is $\frac{n}{360}\pi r^2$.

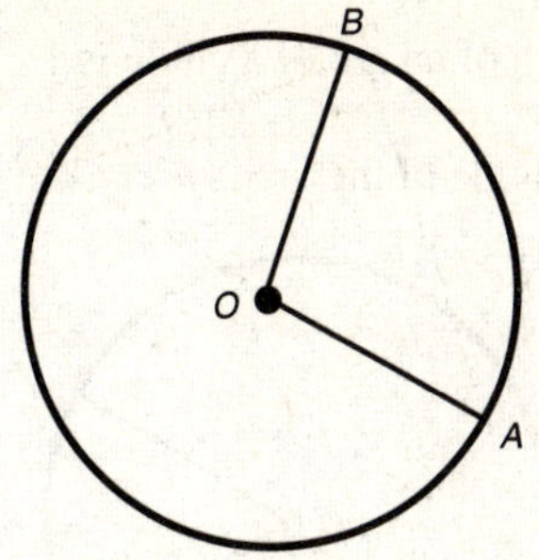

If $OB = 4$ inches and $\angle BOA = 100°$, then the area of the sector is $\frac{100}{360}\pi \bullet 4^2 = \frac{5}{18} \bullet 16\pi = \frac{40}{9}\pi$ square inches.

➤III–7.2

The *perimeter* of a polygon is the sum of the lengths of the sides.

EXAMPLE 1

What is the perimeter of a regular pentagon whose sides are 6 inches long?

A pentagon has 5 sides. Since the pentagon is regular, all sides have the same length which is 6 inches. Therefore, the perimeter of the pentagon is 5×6 which equals 30 inches or 2.5 feet.

The *perimeter of a rectangle is 2(L + W)* where L is the length and W is the width.

The *perimeter of a square is 4s* where s is the length of a side of the square.

The *perimeter of a circle* is called the *circumference* of the circle. The *circumference of a circle is* πd *or* $2\pi r$, where d is the length of a diameter and r is the length of a radius.

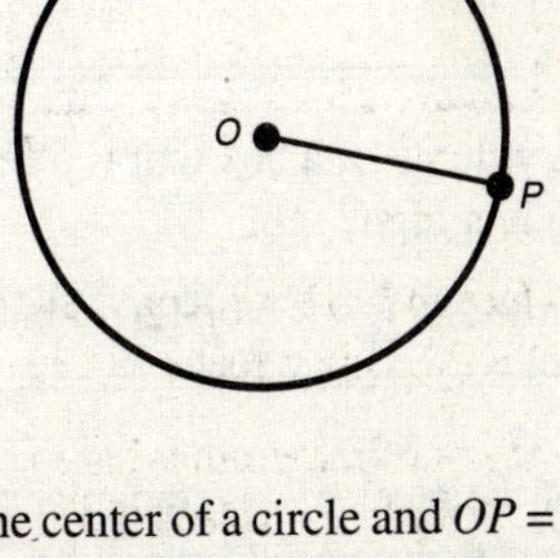

If O is the center of a circle and $OP = 5$ feet, then the circumference of the circle is $2 \times 5\pi$ or 10π feet.

The length of an arc of a circle is $\left(\frac{n}{360}\right)\pi d$ where the central angle of the arc is $n°$.

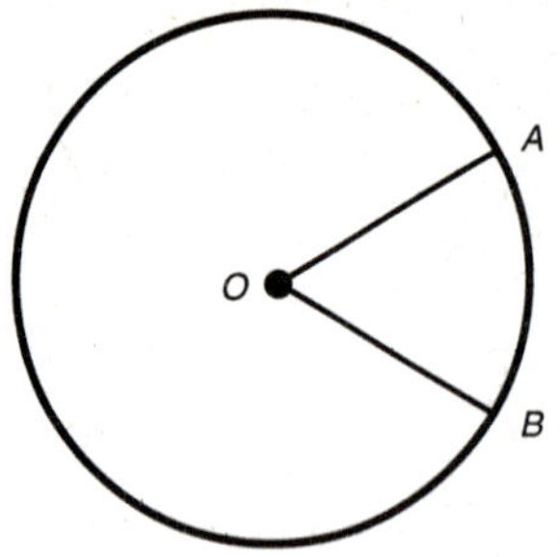

If O is the center of a circle where $OA = 5$ yards and $\angle AOB = 60°$, then the length of arc AB is $\frac{60}{360}\pi \times 10 = \frac{10}{6}\pi = \frac{5}{3}\pi$ yards.

EXAMPLE 2

How far will a wheel of radius 2 feet travel in 500 revolutions? (Assume the wheel does not slip.)

The diameter of the wheel is 4 feet; so the circumference is 4π feet. Therefore, the wheel will travel $500 \times 4\pi$ or $2{,}000\pi$ feet in 500 revolutions.

III–8. Volume and Surface Area

➤III–8.1

The volume of a rectangular prism or box is length times width times height.

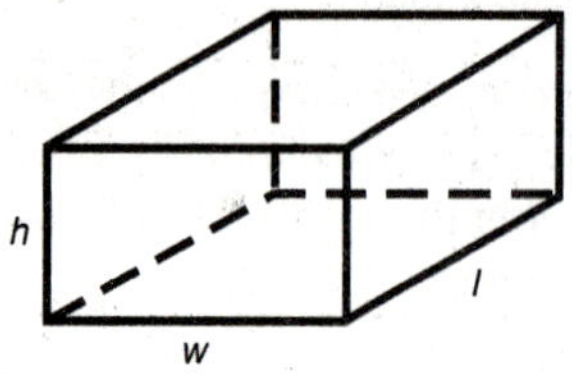

$V = lwh$

EXAMPLE 1

What is the volume of a box that is 5 feet long, 4 feet wide, and 6 feet high?

The volume is $5 \times 4 \times 6$ or 120 cubic feet.

If each of the faces of a rectangular prism is a congruent square, then the solid is a *cube*. The volume of a cube is the length of a side (or edge) cubed.

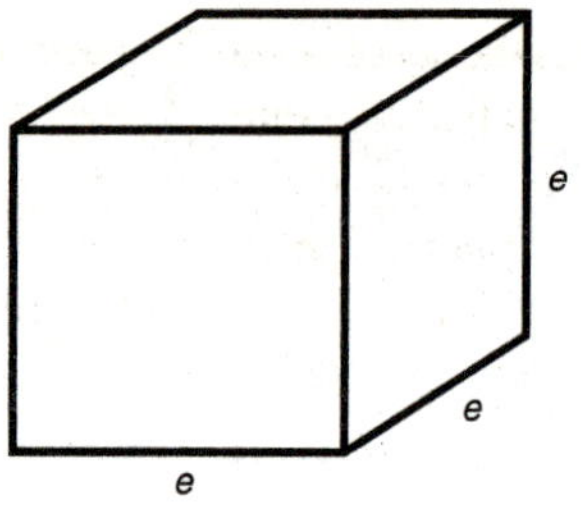

$V = e^3$

If the side of a cube is 4 feet long, then the volume of the cube is 4^3 or 64 cubic feet.

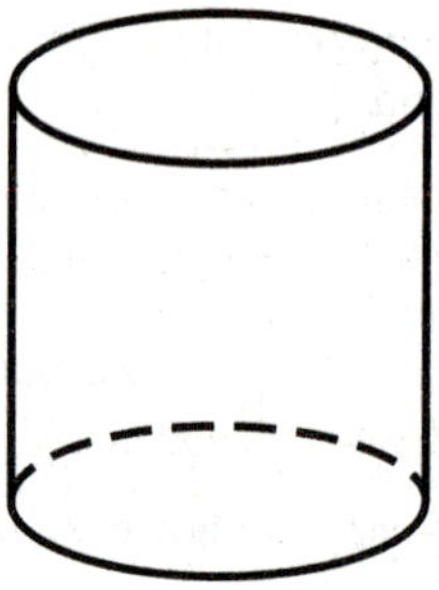

This solid is a circular cylinder. The top and the bottom are congruent circles. Most tin cans are circular cylinders. The volume of a circular cylinder is the product of the area of the circular base and the height.

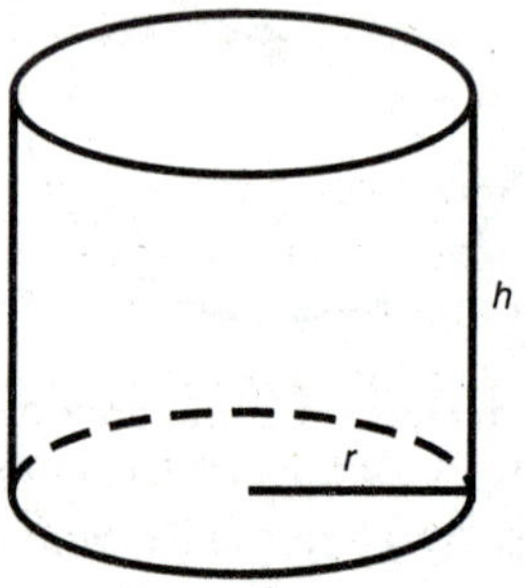

$V = \pi r^2 h$

EXAMPLE 2

A circular pipe has a diameter of 10 feet. A gallon of oil has a volume of 2 cubic feet. How many gallons of oil can fit into 50 feet of the pipe?

Think of the 50 feet of pipe as a circular cylinder on its side with a height of 50 feet and a radius of 5 feet. Its volume is $\pi \bullet 5^2 \bullet 50$ or $1{,}250\pi$ cubic feet. Since a gallon of oil has a volume of 2 cubic feet, 50 feet of pipe will hold $\frac{1250\pi}{2}$ or 625π gallons of oil.

A *sphere* is the set of points in space equidistant from a fixed point called the center. The length of a segment from any point on the sphere to the center is called the radius of the sphere. *The volume of a sphere of radius r is $\frac{4}{3}\pi r^3$.*

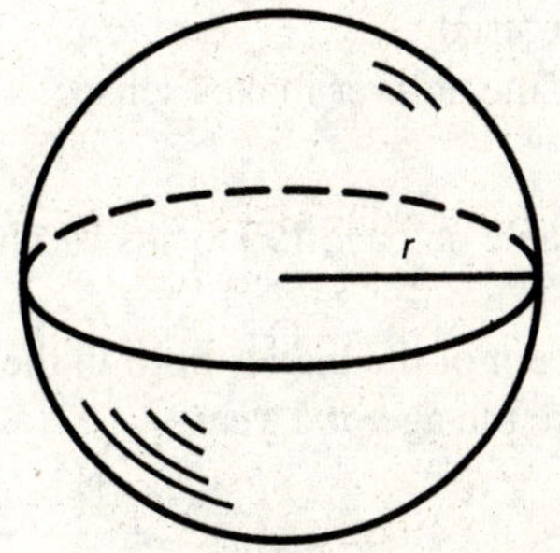

$$V = \frac{4}{3}\pi r^3$$

The volume of a sphere with radius 3 feet is $\frac{4}{3}\pi 3^3 = 36\pi$ cubic feet.

➤III–8.2

The surface area of a rectangular prism is $2LW + 2LH + 2WH$ where L is the length, W is the width, and H is the height.

EXAMPLE 1

If a roll of wallpaper covers 30 square feet, how many rolls are needed to cover the walls of a rectangular room 10 feet long by 8 feet wide by 9 feet high? There are no windows in the room.

We have to cover the surface area of the walls which equals $2(10 \times 9 + 8 \times 9)$ or $2(90 + 72)$ or 324 square feet. (Note that the product omits the area of the floor or the ceiling.) Since a roll covers 30 square feet, we need $\frac{324}{30} = 10\frac{4}{5}$ rolls.

The surface area of a cube is $6e^2$ where e is the length of an edge.

The area of the circular part of a cylinder is called the lateral area. The lateral area of a cylinder is $2\pi rh$, since if we unroll the circular part, we get a rectangle whose dimensions are the circumference of the circle and the height of the cylinder. The total surface area is the lateral surface area plus the areas of the circles on top and bottom, so the total surface area is $2\pi rh + 2\pi r^2$.

EXAMPLE 2

How much tin is needed to make a tin can in the shape of a circular cylinder whose radius is 3 inches and whose height is 5 inches?

The area of both the bottom and top is $\pi \cdot 3^2$ or 9π square inches. The lateral area is $2\pi \cdot 3 \cdot 5$ or 30π square inches. Therefore, we need $9\pi + 9\pi + 30\pi$ or 48π square inches of tin.

III–9. Coordinate Geometry

In coordinate geometry, every point in the plane is associated with an ordered pair of numbers called *coordinates*. Two perpendicular lines are drawn; the horizontal line is called the x-axis and the vertical line is called the y-axis. The point where the two axes intersect is called the *origin*. Both of the axes are number lines with the origin corresponding to zero (see I–6). Positive numbers on the x-axis are to the right of the origin, negative numbers to the left. Positive numbers on the y-axis are above the origin, negative numbers below the origin. The coordinates of a point P are (x, y) if P is located by moving x units along the x-axis from the origin and then moving y units up or down. *The distance along the x-axis is always given first.*

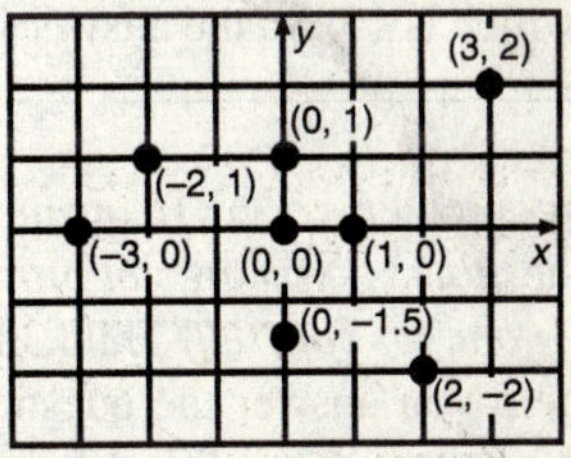

The numbers in parentheses are the coordinates of the point. Thus "$P = (3, 2)$" means that the coordinates of P are (3, 2). *The distance between the point with coordinates (r, s) and the point with coordinates (a, b) is* $\sqrt{(r-a)^2 + (s-b)^2}$. You should be able to answer most questions by using the distance formula.

$$d = \sqrt{(r-a)^2 + (s-b)^2}$$

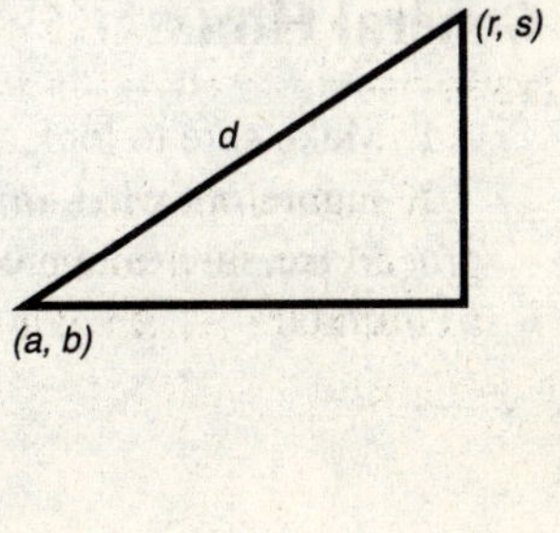

EXAMPLE

Is $ABCD$ a parallelogram?

$A = (3, 2)$, $B = (1, -2)$, $C = (-2, 1)$, $D = (1, 5)$. The length of AB is $\sqrt{(3-1)^2 + (2-(-2))^2} = \sqrt{2^2 + 4^2}$ $= \sqrt{20}$. The length of CD is $\sqrt{(-2-1)^2 + (1-5)^2} =$ $\sqrt{(-3)^2 + (-4)^2} = \sqrt{25}$. Therefore, $AB \neq CD$, so $ABCD$ cannot be a parallelogram, since in a parallelogram the lengths of opposite sides are equal.

You can often use coordinate geometry to solve problems that do not appear to involve coordinates.

EXAMPLE

City A is 5 miles north of City B and City C is 12 miles west of City B. How far is it between City A and City C?

Set up a coordinate axis with City B at the origin, east-west as the x axis, and north-south as the y axis, as in the diagram.

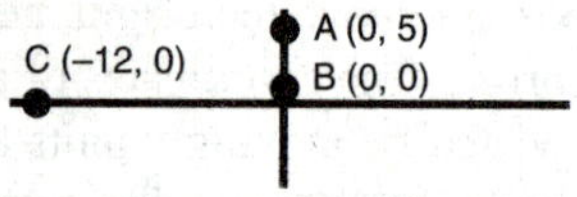

Then City A has coordinates (0, 5) and City C has coordinates (–12, 0). So the distance from A to C is the square root of $(-12-0)^2 + (5-0)^2$ or $\sqrt{144+25}$ $= \sqrt{169}$, which is 13. So the answer is 13 miles.

Geometry problems occur frequently in the data sufficiency questions. *If you are not provided with a diagram, draw one for yourself.* Think of any conditions that will help you answer the question; perhaps you can see how to answer a different question that will lead to an answer to the original question. It may help to draw in some diagonals, altitudes, or other auxiliary lines in your diagram.

IV. TABLES AND GRAPHS

IV–1. Tables

General Hints

1. Make sure to look at the *entire* table or graph.
2. Figure out what *units* the table or graph is using. Make sure to express your answer in the correct units.
3. Look at the possible answers before calculating. Since many questions only call for an approximate answer, it may be possible to round off (see I–5), saving time and effort.
4. Don't confuse decimals and percentages. If the units are percentages, then an entry of .2 means .2% which is equal to .002.
5. In inference questions, only the information given can be used.
6. See if the answer makes sense.

(Refer to the table on page 199 to answer these questions.)

1. What percent of the babies born in the U.S. in 1947 died before the age of 1 year?

   (A) 3.22
   (B) 4.7
   (C) 26.7
   (D) 32.2
   (E) 47

To find a percentage, use the information given in the rate columns. The rate is given *per thousand.* In 1947 the rate was 32.2 per thousand which is $\frac{32.2}{1000} =$ .0322 or 3.22%. So the correct answer is (A). If you assumed incorrectly that the rate was per hundred, you would get the incorrect answer (D); if you looked in the wrong column you might get (B) or (E) as your answer.

2. Which state had the most infant deaths in 1940?

   (A) California
   (B) New Mexico
   (C) New York
   (D) Pennsylvania
   (E) Texas

Look in the numbers column under 1940. Only Texas had more than 8,000 in 1940, so the correct answer is (E). New Mexico had a higher rate, but the question asked for the *highest amount. Make sure you answer the question that is asked.*

3. Which of the following statements can be inferred from the table?

   I. In 1950 less than $\frac{1}{20}$ of the babies born in the U.S. died before the age of 1 year.
   II. The number of infant deaths in the U.S. decreased from 1945 to 1950.
   III. More than 5% of the infant deaths in the U.S. in 1950 occurred in California.
   IV. The number of infant deaths in North America in 1950 was less than 150,000.

INFANT DEATHS (UNDER 1 YEAR OF AGE) AND RATES PER 1,000 LIVE BIRTHS, BY STATES: 1940 TO 1950

State	Number of Infant Deaths					Rate per 1,000 Live Births				
	1940	1947	1948	1949	1950	1940	1947	1948	1949	1950
United States	110,984	119,173	113,169	111,531	103,825	47.0	32.2	32.0	31.3	29.2
Alabama	3,870	3,301	3,228	3,345	3,044	61.5	37.5	37.8	39.6	36.8
Arizona	983	973	1,083	1,034	953	85.5	50.8	56.4	51.0	45.8
Arkansas	1,810	1,445	1,363	1,539	1,209	47.0	29.5	28.4	33.7	26.5
California	4,403	7,233	6,885	6,574	6,115	39.2	29.4	28.6	26.8	25.0
Colorado	1,270	1,234	1,267	1,153	1,167	60.4	37.5	38.4	35.1	34.4
Connecticut	868	1,150	1,026	943	886	34.0	25.2	24.3	23.1	21.8
Delaware	217	239	214	224	235	47.7	31.0	29.5	30.4	30.7
District of Columbia	554	691	531	576	603	49.3	31.9	25.5	29.1	30.4
Florida	1,818	2,285	2,103	2,088	2,078	53.8	38.2	35.3	33.8	32.1
Georgia	3,744	3,251	3,169	3,101	3,064	57.8	34.2	34.2	33.3	33.5
Idaho	506	478	481	431	434	42.9	29.4	29.8	27.0	27.1
Illinois	4,398	5,672	5,123	5,195	4,868	35.3	28.9	27.7	27.4	25.6
Indiana	2,595	2,949	2,760	2,746	2,520	42.1	30.6	29.8	29.1	27.0
Iowa	1,636	1,817	1,610	1,591	1,555	36.5	28.5	26.6	25.7	24.8
Kansas	1,106	1,251	1,151	1,136	1,130	38.3	28.1	26.9	25.9	25.7
Kentucky	3,387	2,971	3,073	3,139	2,616	53.1	37.1	39.8	41.2	34.9
Louisiana	3,268	2,773	2,779	2,810	2,639	64.3	37.2	37.9	37.2	34.6
Maine	810	853	706	713	650	53.2	35.7	32.0	32.5	30.9
Maryland	1,590	1,794	1,537	1,636	1,465	49.1	31.6	28.8	30.5	27.0
Massachusetts	2,458	3,027	2,613	2,347	2,240	37.5	28.1	26.8	24.5	23.3
Michigan	4,032	5,080	4,639	4,545	4,230	40.7	31.5	30.0	28.9	26.3
Minnesota	1,758	2,165	1,959	1,893	1,889	33.2	28.6	26.9	25.6	25.1
Mississippi	2,869	2,448	2,474	2,631	2,385	54.4	36.8	37.9	39.6	36.7
Missouri	2,885	2,929	2,585	2,563	2,510	46.9	32.5	30.3	30.0	29.2
Montana	537	484	461	457	441	46.5	32.1	30.7	29.7	28.2
Nebraska	792	894	835	761	796	36.0	27.8	26.8	24.1	25.0
Nevada	109	134	147	118	139	51.7	33.2	39.8	32.1	37.9
New Hampshire	341	399	361	333	282	40.9	30.1	29.1	27.9	24.5
New Jersey	2,121	2,965	2,585	2,534	2,467	35.5	27.9	26.5	26.0	25.2
New Mexico	1,488	1,379	1,438	1,408	1,211	100.6	67.9	70.1	65.1	54.8
New York	7,297	9,123	8,258	7,878	7,429	37.2	28.2	27.3	26.1	24.7
North Carolina	4,631	3,938	3,858	4,113	3,674	57.6	34.9	35.3	38.1	34.5
North Dakota	593	523	487	517	453	45.1	30.6	29.4	30.7	26.6
Ohio	4,744	5,817	5,693	5,315	4,990	41.4	29.5	30.5	28.1	26.8
Oklahoma	2,238	1,733	1,731	1,531	1,514	49.9	32.3	34.4	30.8	30.2
Oregon	585	895	897	869	812	33.2	24.7	25.5	24.6	22.5
Pennsylvania	7,404	7,741	6,442	6,567	6,126	44.7	31.1	28.4	29.2	27.6
Rhode Island	410	522	444	395	450	37.9	28.2	26.3	24.0	27.8
South Carolina	3,042	2,352	2,331	2,283	2,220	68.2	39.5	40.4	39.0	38.6
South Dakota	466	511	525	448	473	38.7	30.9	32.0	26.0	26.6
Tennessee	2,954	3,144	3,098	3,331	2,961	53.5	36.3	37.7	40.2	36.4
Texas	8,675	8,161	9,131	8,628	7,630	68.3	41.1	46.2	42.7	37.4
Utah	539	545	568	535	503	40.4	25.1	27.4	25.3	23.7
Vermont	309	303	271	301	221	44.5	31.2	28.9	32.4	24.5
Virginia	3,335	3,142	3,163	3,162	2,836	58.5	36.6	38.5	38.1	34.6
Washington	992	1,643	1,537	1,530	1,522	35.2	28.1	27.5	27.1	27.3
West Virginia	2,269	2,091	2,108	2,082	1,822	53.7	38.0	40.2	39.6	36.1
Wisconsin	2,046	2,476	2,148	2,202	2,121	37.3	29.5	26.3	26.5	25.7
Wyoming	232	249	293	280	247	44.7	34.0	39.5	37.4	32.5

SOURCE: Department of Health, Education, and Welfare, Public Health Service, National Office of Vital Statistics; annual report *Vital Statistics of the United States.*

(A) I only
(B) II only
(C) I and III only
(D) I, III, IV only
(E) I, II, III, IV

Analysis:

Statement I can be inferred since $\frac{1}{20}$ of 1,000 = 50 which exceeds the rate per thousand of 29.2 in 1950.

Statement II can't be inferred since the table has no information about 1945. Infant deaths decreased between 1940 and 1950, but that doesn't mean they decreased between 1945 and 1950.

Statement III can be inferred from the table. The total number of infant deaths in 1950 was 103,825, and 6,115 occurred in California. A calculation of $\frac{6{,}115}{103{,}825}$ could be made, but it is much quicker to find 5% of 103,825 which is 5,191. Since 6,115 is greater than 5,191, more than 5% of the infant deaths in the U.S. occurred in California.

Statement IV can't be inferred, because the table only gives information about the U.S. and there are other countries in North America.

So the correct answer is (C).

IV–2. Circle Graphs

CIRCLE GRAPHS are used to show how various sectors share in the whole. Circle graphs are sometimes called pie charts. Circle graphs usually give the percentage that each sector receives.

(Refer to the graph that follows to answer these questions.)

1. The amount spent on materials in 1960 was 120% of the amount spent on

(A) research in 1960
(B) compensation in 1960
(C) advertising in 1970
(D) materials in 1970
(E) legal affairs in 1960

When using circle graphs to find ratios of various sectors, don't find the amounts each sector received and then the ratio of the amounts. Find the *ratio of the percentages*, which is much quicker. In 1960, 18% of the expenditures were for materials. We want x where 120% of x = 18%; so x = 15%. Any category which received 15% of 1960 expenditures gives the correct answer, but only one of the five choices is correct. Here, the answer is (A) since research received 15% of the expenditure in 1960. Check the 1960 answers first since you need look only at the percentages, which can be done quickly. Notice that (C) is incorrect, since 15% of the expenditures for 1970 is different from 15% of the expenditures for 1960.

EXPENDITURES OF GENERAL INDUSTRIES
(by major categories)

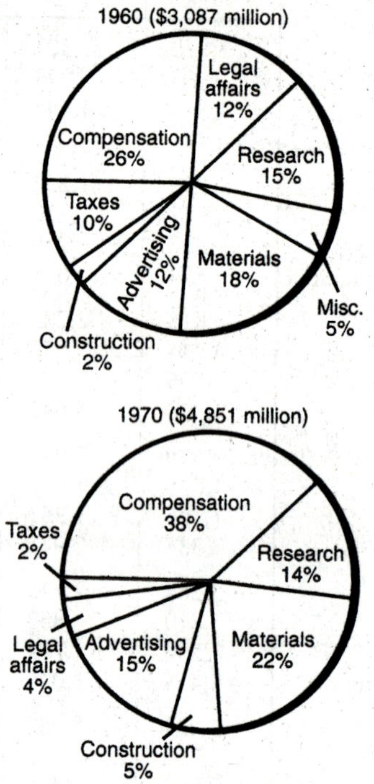

2. The fraction of the total expenditures for 1960 and 1970 spent on compensation was about

(A) $\frac{1}{5}$

(B) $\frac{1}{4}$

(C) $\frac{1}{3}$

(D) $\frac{3}{7}$

(E) $\frac{1}{2}$

In 1960, 26% of $3,087 million was spent on compensation and in 1970 compensation received 38% of $4,851 million. The total expenditures for 1960 and 1970 are $(3,087 + 4,851) million. So the exact answer is $\frac{[(.26)(3,087)+(.38)(4,851)]}{(3,087+4,851)}$. Actually calculating the answer, you will waste a lot of time. Look at the answers and think for a second.

We are taking a weighted average of 26% and 38%. To find a weighted average, we multiply each value by a weight and divide by the total of all the weights. Here 26% is given a weight of 3,087 and 38% a weight of

4,851. The following general rule is often useful in average problems: The average or weighted average of a collection of values can *never* be:

1. less than the smallest value in the collection, or
2. greater than the largest value in the collection.

Therefore, the answer to the question must be greater than or equal to 26% and less than or equal to 38%.

Since $\frac{1}{5} = 20\%$ and $\frac{1}{4} = 25\%$, which are both less than 26%, neither (A) nor (B) can be the correct answer. Since $\frac{3}{7} = 42\frac{6}{7}\%$ and $\frac{1}{2} = 50\%$, which are both greater than 38%, neither (D) nor (E) can be correct. Therefore, by elimination (C) is the correct answer.

3. The amount spent in 1960 for materials, advertising, and taxes was about the same as

   (A) $\frac{5}{4}$ of the amount spent for compensation in 1960
   (B) the amount spent for compensation in 1970
   (C) the amount spent on materials in 1970
   (D) $\frac{5}{3}$ of the amount spent on advertising in 1970
   (E) the amount spent on research and construction in 1970

First calculate the combined percentage for materials, advertising, and taxes in 1960. Since 18% + 12% + 10% = 40%, these three categories accounted for 40% of the expenditures in 1960. You can check the one answer that involves 1960 now. Since $\frac{5}{4}$ of 26% = 32.5%, (A) is incorrect. To check the answers that involve 1970, you must know the amount spent on the three categories above in 1960. 40% of 3,087 is 1,234.8; so the amount spent on the three categories in 1960 was $1,234.8 million. You could calculate the amount spent in each of the possible answers, but there is a quicker way. Find the *approximate* percentage that 1,234.8 is of 4,851, and check this against the percentages of the answers. Since $\frac{12}{48} = \frac{1}{4}$, the amount for the 3 categories in 1960 is about 25% of the 1970 expenditures. Compensation received 38% of 1970 expenditures, so (B) is incorrect. Materials received 22% and research and construction together received 19%; since advertising received 15%, $\frac{5}{3}$ of the amount for advertising yields 25%. So (D) is probably correct. You can check by calculating 22% of 4,851 which is 1,067.22, while 25% of 4,851 = 1,212.75. Therefore, (D) is correct.

In inference questions involving circle graphs, *do not compare different percentages*. Note in question 3 that the percentage of expenditures in 1960 for the three categories (40%) is *not equal* to 40% of the expenditures in 1970.

IV–3. Line Graphs

LINE GRAPHS are used to show how a quantity changes continuously. Very often the quantity is measured as time changes. If the line goes up, the quantity is increasing; if the line goes down, the quantity is decreasing; if the line is horizontal, the quantity is not changing. To measure the height of a point on the graph, use your pencil or a piece of paper (for example, the admission card to the exam) as a straight edge.

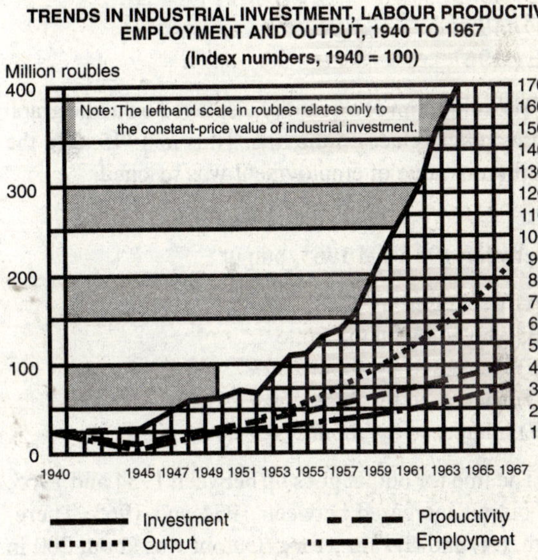

SOURCE: United Nations Economics Bulletin for Europe

(Refer to the graph above to answer these questions.)

1. The ratio of productivity in 1967 to productivity in 1940 was about

   (A) 1 : 4
   (B) 1 : 3
   (C) 3 : 1
   (D) 4 : 1
   (E) 9 : 1

In 1967 productivity had an index number of 400, and the index numbers are based on 1940 = 100. So the ratio is 400 : 100 = 4 : 1. Therefore, the answer is (D). [If you used (incorrectly) output or employment (instead of productivity) you would get the wrong answer (E) or (C); if you confused the order of the ratio you would have incorrectly answered (A).]

2. If 1 rouble = $3, then the constant-price value of industrial investment in 1959 was about

   (A) $1.9 million
   (B) $200 million
   (C) $420.000,000
   (D) $570,000,000
   (E) $570,000 million

In 1959, the value was about 190 million roubles. (It was a little below 200 million.) The answers are all in dollars, so multiply 190 by 3 to get $570 million or $570,000,000 (D). If you are not careful about units, you may answer (B) or (E), which are incorrect.

3. Employment was at its minimum during the years shown in

   (A) 1940
   (B) 1943
   (C) 1945
   (D) 1953
   (E) 1967

The minimum of a quantity displayed on a line graph is the lowest place on the line. Thus in 1945, (C), the minimum value of employment was reached.

4. Between 1954 and 1965, output

   (A) decreased by about 10%
   (B) stayed about the same
   (C) increased by about 200%
   (D) increased by about 250%
   (E) increased by about 500%

The line for output goes up between 1954 and 1965, so output increased between 1954 and 1965. Therefore, (A) and (B) are wrong. Output was about 200 in 1954 and about 700 in 1965, so the increase was 500. Since $\frac{500}{200} = 2.5 = 250\%$, the correct answer is (D).

IV–4. Bar Graphs

Quantities can be compared by the height or length of a bar in a bar graph. A bar graph can have either vertical or horizontal bars. You can compare different quantities or the same quantity at different times. Use your pencil or a piece of paper to compare bars that are not adjacent to each other.

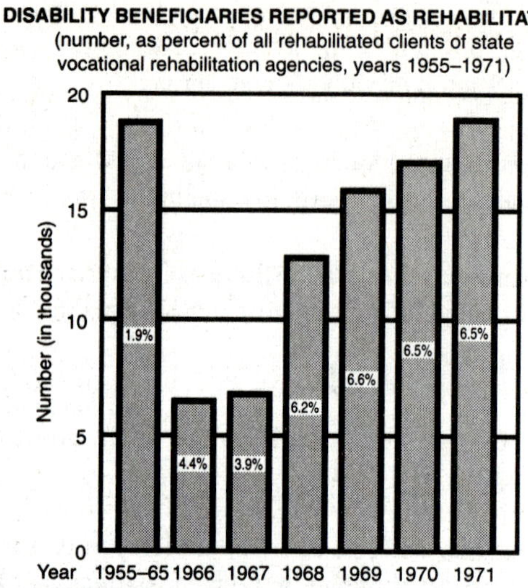

SOURCE: Social Security Bulletin

(Refer to the graph above to answer these questions.)

1. Between 1967 and 1971, the largest number of disability beneficiaries were reported as rehabilitated in the year

   (A) 1967
   (B) 1968
   (C) 1969
   (D) 1970
   (E) 1971

The answer is (E) since the highest bar is the bar for 1971. The percentage of disability beneficiaries out of all rehabilitated clients was higher in 1969, but the *number* was lower.

2. Between 1955 and 1965, about how many clients were rehabilitated by state vocational rehabilitation agencies?

   (A) 90,000
   (B) 400,000
   (C) 1,000,000
   (D) 1,900,000
   (E) 10,000,000

1.9% of those rehabilitated were disability beneficiaries, and there were about 19,000 disability beneficiaries rehabilitated. So if T is the total number rehabilitated, then 1.9% of T = 19,000 or $.019T = 19,000$. Thus $T = \frac{19,000}{.019} = 1,000,000$ and the answer is (C).

IV-5. Cumulative Graphs

You can compare several categories by a graph of the cumulative type. These are usually bar or line graphs where the height of the bar or line is divided up proportionately among different quantities.

FEDERAL PRISONERS RECEIVED FROM THE COURTS, BY MAJOR OFFENSE GROUPS: YEARS 1944–1952

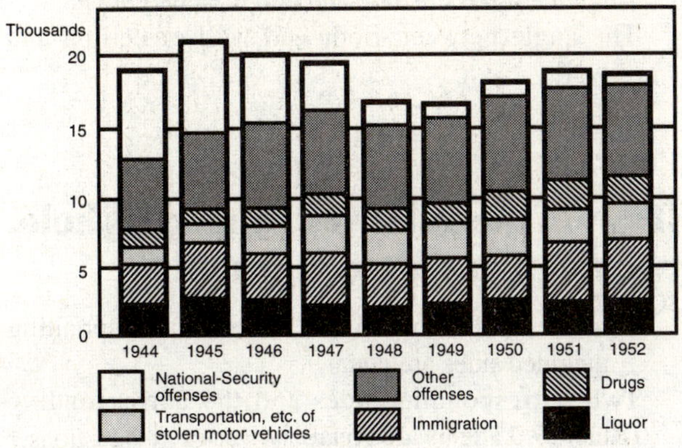

SOURCE: Statistical Abstract of the U.S. 1953

Refer to the graph above to answer these questions.

1. In 1946, roughly what percent of the federal prisoners received from the courts were national-security offenders?

   (A) 10
   (B) 15
   (C) 25
   (D) 30
   (E) 35

The total number of prisoners in 1946 was about 20,000, and national-security offenders accounted for the part of the graph from just above 15,000 to just above 20,000. Therefore, there were about 20,000 – 15,000 = 5,000 prisoners convicted of national-security offenses. Since $\frac{5,000}{20,000} = \frac{1}{4} = 25\%$, the correct answer is (C).

2. Of the combined total for the four years 1947 through 1950, the largest number of offenders were in the category

   (A) national-security offenses
   (B) other offenses
   (C) drugs
   (D) immigration
   (E) liquor

The correct answer is (B). Since other offenses had the most offenders in each year, that category must have the largest total number of offenders. [If you answered this question for the years 1944–1946, then (A) would be correct.]

3. Which of the following statements can be inferred from the graph?

   I. The number of federal prisoners received from the courts decreased each year from 1946 to 1948.
   II. More than 40% of the prisoners between 1944 and 1952 came from the other offenses category.
   III. 2% of the federal prisoners received in 1952 were convicted on heroin charges.

   (A) I only
   (B) III only
   (C) I and II only
   (D) I and III only
   (E) I, II, and III

Statement I is true, since the height of the bar for each year was lower than the height of the bar for the previous year in 1946, 1947, and 1948.

Statement II is not true. For most of the years, other offenses accounted for about 25–30%, and it never was more than 40% in any year. Therefore, it could not account for more than 40% of the total.

Statement III cannot be inferred. There is a category of drug offenders, but there is no information about specific drugs.

So, the correct answer is (A).

REVIEW OF FORMULAS

(Numbers next to the formulas refer to the section of the Math Review where the formula is discussed.)

Interest = Amount × Time × Rate	I–4
Discount = Cost × Rate of Discount	I–4
Price = Cost × (100% – Rate of Discount)	I–4
$x^2 - y^2 = (x + y)(x - y)$	II–1
$x = \frac{1}{2a}[-b \pm \sqrt{b^2 - 4ac}]$ (quadratic formula)	II–2

Distance = Rate × Time II–3
$a^2 + b^2 = c^2$ when a and b are the legs and c is the hypotenuse of a right triangle (Pythagorean Theorem) III–4
Diameter of a circle = 2 × Radius III–6
Area of a square = s^2 III–7
Area of a rectangle = LW III–7
Area of a triangle = $\frac{1}{2}bh$ III–7
Area of a circle = πr^2 III–7
Area of a parallelogram = bh III–7
Area of a trapezoid = $\frac{1}{2}(b_1 + b_2)h$ III–7
Circumference of a circle = πd III–7
Perimeter of a square = $4s$ III–7
Perimeter of a rectangle = $2(L + W)$ III–7
Volume of a box = lwh III–8
Volume of a cube = e^3 III–8
Volume of a cylinder = $\pi r^2 h$ III–8
Volume of a sphere = $\frac{4}{3}\pi r^3$ III–8
Surface area of a box = $2LW + 2LH + 2WH$ III–8
Surface area of a cube = $6e^2$ III–8
Surface area of a cylinder = $2\pi rh + 2\pi r^2$ III–8
Distance between points (x,y) and (a,b) is $\sqrt{(x-a)^2 + (y-b)^2}$ III–9

The following are always equal:

Any two radii of the same circle.
The two sides opposite equal angles of a triangle.
The two angles opposite equal sides of a triangle.
Opposite angles formed by intersecting lines.
Alternate angles formed by parallel lines.
The four sides of a square.
The three sides of an equilateral triangle.
Opposite sides (and angles) of a parallelogram.
The sides (and angles) of any regular polygon.
Corresponding angles of similar polygons.
All right angles.
The square of the hypotenuse and the sum of the squares of two remaining sides of a right triangle.
The difference of two squares and the product of the sum and difference of their square roots.

The following are always right angles:

Any angle whose measure is 90 degrees.
Angles formed by perpendicular lines.
Any of four equal angles formed by intersection of two lines.
Any angle that is equal to its supplement.
All angles of a square, rectangle, or cube.
Any angle inscribed in a semi-circle.
The angle formed by a circle's radius and tangent.
The angle opposite the longest side of a right triangle.
The angles between north, south, east, and west.
Angle between the base and height of a triangle.
Angle between the base and height of a cylinder.
The angle between floor and wall or ceiling and wall.

If any of the following properties hold, two triangles are congruent:

Two corresponding angles and the corresponding included sides are equal.
Two corresponding sides and the corresponding included angles are equal.
All three corresponding sides are equal.
Two right triangles that have any two corresponding sides equal.

Hints for Answering Mathematics Questions

1. Make sure you answer the question you are asked to answer.
2. Look at the answers before you start to work out a problem; you can save a lot of time.
3. Don't waste time on superfluous computations.
4. *Estimate* whenever you can to save time.
5. Budget your time so you can try all the questions. (Bring a watch.)
6. You probably won't be able to answer all the questions; don't waste time worrying about it.
7. Do all the problems you know how to work *before* you start to think about those that you can't answer in a minute or two.
8. If you skip a question, make sure you skip that number on the answer sheet.
9. Don't make extra assumptions on inference questions.
10. Work efficiently; don't waste time worrying during the test.
11. Make sure you express your answer in the units asked for.
12. On data sufficiency questions, don't do any more work than is necessary. (Don't solve the problem; you only have to know that the problem can be solved.)

PRACTICE EXERCISES

The four exercises that follow will give you an indication of your ability to handle both mathematics and data sufficiency questions. The time for each practice mathematics exercise is 30 minutes. Scoring for each of the mathematics exercises may be interpreted as follows:

22 – 25	EXCELLENT
18 – 21+	GOOD
13 – 17+	FAIR
0 – 12+	POOR

Your score should be determined by counting the number of correct answers minus ¼ the number of incorrect answers.

Mathematics Exercise A

<u>Directions:</u> Solve each of the following problems.

NOTE: A figure that appears with a problem is drawn as accurately as possible unless the words "Figure not drawn to scale" appear next to the figure. Numbers in this test are real numbers.

1. In 1955, it cost \$12 to purchase one hundred pounds of potatoes. In 1975, it cost \$34 to purchase one hundred pounds of potatoes. The price of one hundred pounds of potatoes increased X dollars between 1955 and 1975 with X equal to:

   (A) 1.20
   (B) 2.20
   (C) 3.40
   (D) 22
   (E) 34

2. A house cost Ms. Jones C dollars in 1965. Three years later she sold the house for 25% more than she paid for it. She has to pay a tax of 50% of the gain. (The gain is the selling price minus the cost.) How much tax must Ms. Jones pay?

   (A) $\frac{1}{24}C$
   (B) $\frac{C}{8}$
   (C) $\frac{1}{4}C$
   (D) $\frac{C}{2}$
   (E) $.6C$

3. If the length of a rectangle is increased by 20%, and the width of the same rectangle is decreased by 20%, then the area of the rectangle

   (A) decreases by 20%
   (B) decreases by 4%
   (C) is unchanged
   (D) increases by 20%
   (E) increases by 40%

Use the following graph for questions 4–7.

WORLDWIDE MILITARY EXPENDITURES

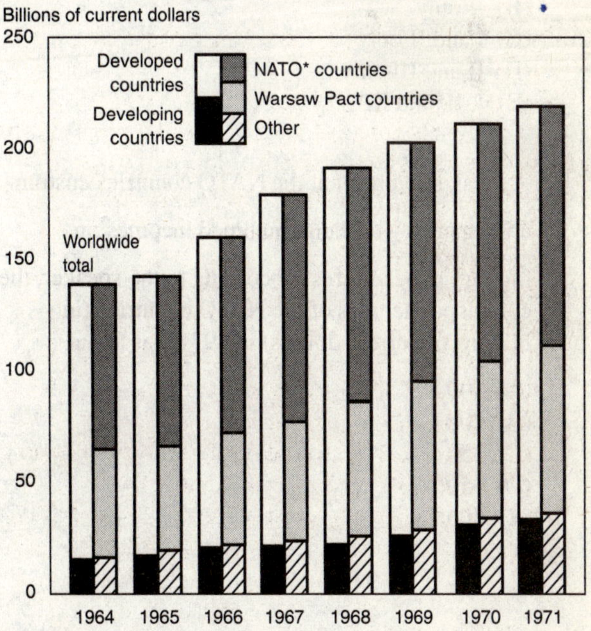

*North Atlantic Treaty Organization

SOURCE: Pocket Data Book U.S.A. 1973.

4. Between 1964 and 1969, worldwide military expenditures

(A) increased by about 50%
(B) roughly doubled
(C) increased by about 150%
(D) almost tripled
(E) increased by 10%

5. The average yearly military expenditure by the developing countries between 1964 and 1971 was approximately how many billions of current dollars?

(A) 20
(B) 50
(C) 100
(D) 140
(E) 175

6. Which of the following statements can be inferred from the graph?

I. The NATO countries have higher incomes than the Warsaw Pact countries.
II. Worldwide military expenditures have increased each year between 1964 and 1971.
III. In 1972 worldwide military expenditures were more than 230 billion current dollars.

(A) I only
(B) II only
(C) I and II only
(D) II and III only
(E) I, II, and III

7. A speaker claims that the NATO countries customarily spend $\frac{1}{3}$ of their combined incomes on military expenditures. According to the speaker, the combined incomes of the NATO countries (in billions of current dollars) in 1971 was about

(A) 100
(B) 200
(C) 250
(D) 350
(E) 500

8. 8% of the people eligible to vote are between 18 and 21. In an election 85% of those eligible to vote who were between 18 and 21 actually voted. In that election, people between 18 and 21 who actually voted were what percent of those people eligible to vote?

(A) 4.2
(B) 6.4
(C) 6.8
(D) 8
(E) 68

9. If n and p are both odd numbers, which of the following numbers *must* be an even number?

(A) $n + p$
(B) np
(C) $np + 2$
(D) $n + p + 1$
(E) $2n + p$

10. It costs g cents a mile for gasoline and m cents a mile for all other costs to run a car. How many *dollars* will it cost to run the car for 100 miles?

(A) $\frac{g+m}{100}$
(B) $100g + 100m$
(C) $g + m$
(D) $g + .1m$
(E) g

11. What is the length of the line segment that connects A to B?

(A) $\sqrt{3}$
(B) 2
(C) $2\sqrt{2}$
(D) 4
(E) 8

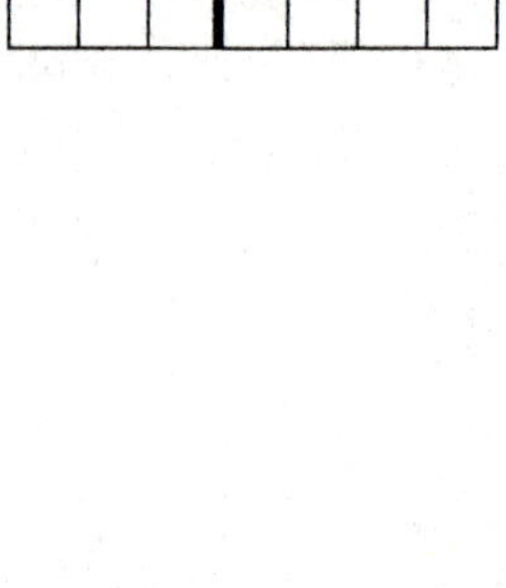

12. A cabdriver's income consists of his salary and tips. His salary is $50 a week. During one week his tips were $\frac{5}{4}$ of his salary. What fraction of his income for the week came from tips?

(A) $\frac{4}{9}$
(B) $\frac{1}{2}$
(C) $\frac{5}{9}$
(D) $\frac{5}{8}$
(E) $\frac{5}{4}$

Use the following table for questions 13–17.

INCOME (IN DOLLARS)	TAX (IN DOLLARS)
0 – 4,000	1% of income
4,000 – 6,000	40 + 2% of income over 4,000
6,000 – 8,000	80 + 3% of income over 6,000
8,000 – 10,000	140 + 4% of income over 8,000
10,000 – 15,000	220 + 5% of income over 10,000
15,000 – 25,000	470 + 6% of income over 15,000
25,000 – 50,000	1,070 + 7% of income over 25,000

13. How much tax is due on an income of $7,500?

(A) $75
(B) $80
(C) $125
(D) $150
(E) $225

14. Your income for a year is $26,000. You receive a raise so that next year your income will be $29,000. How much more will you pay in taxes next year if the tax rate remains the same?

(A) $70
(B) $180
(C) $200
(D) $210
(E) $700

15. Joan paid $100 tax. If X was her income, which of the following statements is true?

(A) $0 < X < 4{,}000$
(B) $4{,}000 < X < 6{,}000$
(C) $6{,}000 < X < 8{,}000$
(D) $8{,}000 < X < 10{,}000$
(E) $10{,}000 < X < 15{,}000$

16. The town of Zenith has a population of 50,000. The average income of a person who lives in Zenith is $3,700 per year. What is the total amount paid in taxes by the people of Zenith? Assume each person pays tax on $3,700.

(A) $37
(B) $3,700
(C) $50,000
(D) $185,000
(E) $1,850,000

17. A person who has an income of $10,000 pays what percent (to the nearest percent) of his or her income in taxes?

(A) 1
(B) 2
(C) 3
(D) 4
(E) 5

18. Given that x and y are real numbers, let $S(x, y) = x^2 - y^2$. Then $S(3, S(3, 4)) =$

(A) –40
(B) –7
(C) 40
(D) 49
(E) 56

19. Eggs cost 90¢ a dozen. Peppers cost 20¢ each. An omelet consists of 3 eggs and $\frac{1}{4}$ of a pepper. How much will the ingredients for 8 omelets cost?

(A) $.90
(B) $1.30
(C) $1.80
(D) $2.20
(E) $2.70

20. It is 185 miles from Binghamton to New York City. If a bus takes 2 hours to travel the first 85 miles, how long must the bus take to travel the final 100 miles in order to average 50 miles an hour for the entire trip?

(A) 60 min.
(B) 75 min.
(C) 94 min.
(D) 102 min.
(E) 112 min.

21. What is the area of this figure? *ABDC* is a rectangle and *BDE* is an isosceles right triangle.

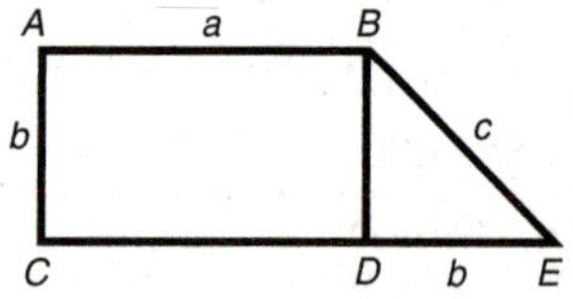

(A) ab
(B) ab^2
(C) $b\left(a+\frac{b}{2}\right)$
(D) cab
(E) $\frac{1}{2}bc$

22. If $2x + y = 5$ then $4x + 2y$ is equal to

(A) 5
(B) 8
(C) 9
(D) 10
(E) none of these

23. In 1967, a new sedan cost $2,500; in 1975, the same type of sedan cost $4,800. The cost of that type of sedan has increased by what percent between 1967 and 1975?

(A) 48
(B) 52
(C) 92
(D) 152
(E) 192

24. What is the area of the square *ABCD*?

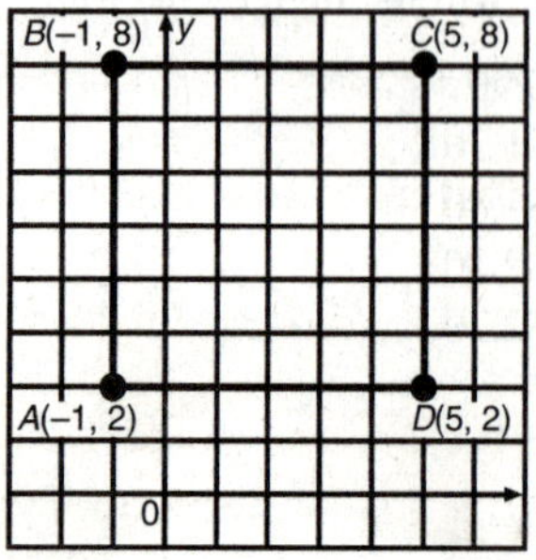

(A) 10
(B) 18
(C) 24
(D) 36
(E) 48

25. If $x + y = 6$ and $3x - y = 4$, then $x - y$ is equal to

(A) –1
(B) 0
(C) 2
(D) 4
(E) 6

Mathematics Exercise B

Directions: Solve each of the following problems.

NOTE: A figure that appears with a problem is drawn as accurately as possible so as to provide information that may help in answering the question. Numbers in this test are real numbers.

Use the graphs below for questions 1–5.

WOMEN IN THE LABOR FORCE

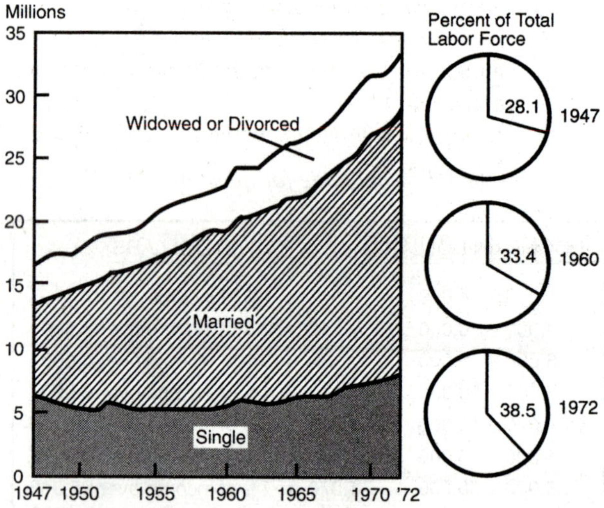

SOURCE: Pocket Data Book U.S.A. 1973. Bureau of the Census.

1. The total labor force in 1960 was about *y* million with *y* equal to about

(A) 22
(B) 65
(C) 75
(D) 80
(E) 85

2. In 1947, the percentage of women in the labor force who were married was about

(A) 28
(B) 33
(C) 38
(D) 50
(E) 65

3. What was the first year when more than 20 million women were in the labor force?

(A) 1950
(B) 1953
(C) 1956
(D) 1958
(E) 1964

4. Between 1947 and 1972, the number of women in the labor force

(A) increased by about 50%
(B) increased by about 100%
(C) increased by about 150%
(D) increased by about 200%
(E) increased by about 250%

5. Which of the following statements about the labor force can be inferred from the graphs?

I. Between 1947 and 1957, there were no years when more than 5 million widowed or divorced women were in the labor force.
II. In every year between 1947 and 1972, the number of single women in the labor force has increased.
III. In 1965, women made up more than $\frac{1}{3}$ of the total labor force.

(A) I only
(B) II only
(C) I and II only
(D) I and III only
(E) I, II, and III

6. If $\frac{x}{y} = \frac{2}{3}$ then $\frac{y^2}{x^2}$ is equal to

(A) $\frac{4}{9}$
(B) $\frac{2}{3}$
(C) $\frac{3}{2}$
(D) $\frac{9}{4}$
(E) $\frac{5}{2}$

7. In the figure, *BD* is perpendicular to *AC*. *BA* and *BC* have length *a*. What is the area of the triangle *ABC*?

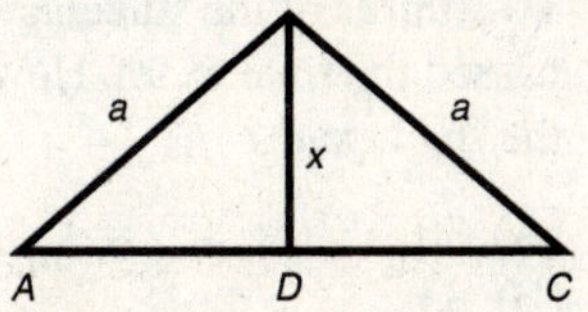

(A) $2x\sqrt{a^2 - x^2}$
(B) $x\sqrt{a^2 - x^2}$
(C) $a\sqrt{a^2 - x^2}$
(D) $2a\sqrt{x^2 - a^2}$
(E) $x\sqrt{x^2 - a^2}$

8. If two places are one inch apart on a map, then they are actually 160 miles apart. (The scale on the map is one inch equals 160 miles.) If Seaton is $2\frac{7}{8}$ inches from Monroe on the map, how many miles is it from Seaton to Monroe?

(A) 3
(B) 27
(C) 300
(D) 360
(E) 460

9. In the accompanying diagram *ABCD* is a rectangle. The area of isosceles right triangle *ABE* = 7, and *EC* = 3(*BE*). The area of *ABCD* is

(A) 21
(B) 28
(C) 42
(D) 56
(E) 84

10. An automobile tire has two punctures. The first puncture by itself would make the tire flat in 9 minutes. The second puncture by itself would make the tire flat in 6 minutes. How long will it take for both punctures together to make the tire flat? (Assume the air leaks out at a constant rate.)

(A) $3\frac{3}{5}$ minutes
(B) 4 minutes
(C) $5\frac{1}{4}$ minutes
(D) $7\frac{1}{2}$ minutes
(E) 15 minutes

11. If n^3 is odd, which of the following statements are true?

I. n is odd.
II. n^2 is odd.
III. n^2 is even.

(A) I only
(B) II only
(C) III only
(D) I and II only
(E) I and III only

Use the table below for questions 12–15.

PARTICIPATION IN NATIONAL ELECTIONS

Persons in millions. Civilian noninstitutional population as of Nov. 1. Based on post-election surveys of persons reporting whether or not they voted.

	1964		1968		1972	
Characteristic	**Persons of voting age**	**Percent voted**	**Persons of voting age**	**Percent voted**	**Persons of voting age**	**Percent voted**
Total	111	69	117	68	136	63
Male	52	72	54	70	64	64
Female	58	67	62	66	72	62
White	99	71	105	69	121	64
Negro and other	11	57	12	56	15	51
Negro	10	58	11	58	13	52
Region:						
North and West	78	75	82	71	94	66
South	32	57	35	60	43	55
Age:						
18–24 years	10	51	12	50	25	50
25–44 years	45	69	46	67	49	63
45–64 years	38	76	40	75	42	71
65 years and over	17	66	18	66	40	63

SOURCE: U.S. Bureau of the Census.

12. Which of the following groups had the highest percentage of voters in 1968?

(A) 18–24 years
(B) Female
(C) South
(D) 25–44 years
(E) Male

13. In 1972, what percent (to the nearest percent) of persons of voting age were female?

(A) 52
(B) 53
(C) 62
(D) 64
(E) 72

14. In 1968, how many males of voting age voted?

(A) 37,440,000
(B) 37,800,000
(C) 42,160,000
(D) 62,000,000
(E) 374,400,000

15. Let X be the number (in millions) of persons of voting age in the range 25–44 years who lived in the North and West in 1964. Which of the following includes all possible values and only possible values of X?

(A) $0 \leqq X \leqq 45$
(B) $13 \leqq X \leqq 45$
(C) $13 \leqq X \leqq 78$
(D) $45 \leqq X \leqq 78$
(E) $75 \leqq X \leqq 78$

16. There are 50 students enrolled in Business 100. Of the enrolled students, 90% took the final exam. Two-thirds of the students who took the final exam passed the final exam. How many students passed the final exam?

(A) 30
(B) 33
(C) 34
(D) 35
(E) 45

17. If a is less than b, which of the following numbers is greater than a and less than b?

(A) $\frac{(a+b)}{2}$
(B) $\frac{(ab)}{2}$
(C) $b^2 - a^2$
(D) ab
(E) $b - a$

18. In the figure, OR and PR are radii of circles. The length of OP is 4. If $OR = 2$, what is PR? PR is tangent to the circle with center O.

(A) 2
(B) $\frac{5}{2}$
(C) 3
(D) $2\sqrt{3}$
(E) $3\sqrt{2}$

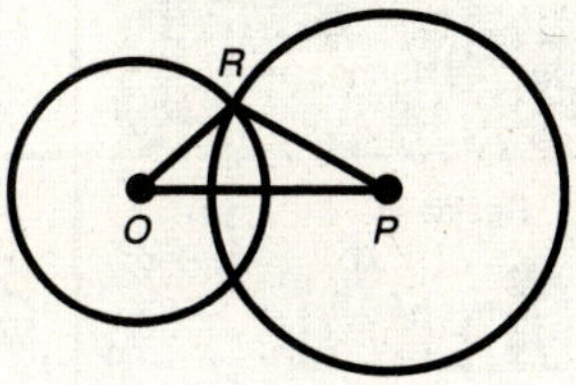

19. A bus uses one gallon of gasoline to travel 15 miles. After a tune-up, the bus travels 15% farther on one gallon. How many gallons of gasoline (to the nearest tenth) will it take for the bus to travel 150 miles after a tune-up?

(A) 8.5
(B) 8.7
(C) 8.9
(D) 9.0
(E) 10.0

20. If $x + 2y = 4$ and $\frac{x}{y} = 2$, then x is equal to

(A) 0
(B) $\frac{1}{2}$
(C) 1
(D) $\frac{3}{2}$
(E) 2

Use the following table for questions 21–23.

SPEED OF A TRAIN OVER A 3-HOUR PERIOD								
TIMED PERIOD *(in minutes)*	0	30	45	60	90	120	150	180
SPEED AT TIME *(in m.p.h.)*	40	45	47.5	50	55	60	65	70

21. How fast was the train traveling $2\frac{1}{2}$ hours after the beginning of the timed period?

(A) 50 m.p.h.
(B) 55 m.p.h.
(C) 60 m.p.h.
(D) 65 m.p.h.
(E) 70 m.p.h.

22. During the three hours shown on the table the speed of the train

(A) increased by 25%
(B) increased by 50%
(C) increased by 75%
(D) increased by 100%
(E) increased by 125%

23. At time t measured in minutes after the beginning of the timed period, which of the following gives the speed of the train in accordance with the table?

(A) $\frac{1}{6}t$
(B) $10t$
(C) $40 + t$
(D) $40 + \frac{1}{6}t$
(E) $40 + 10t$

24. It costs $1,000 to make the first thousand copies of a book and x dollars to make each subsequent copy. If it costs a total of $7,230 to make the first 8,000 copies of a book, what is x?

(A) .89
(B) .90375
(C) 1.00
(D) 89
(E) 90.375

25. If 16 workers can finish a job in three hours, how long should it take 5 workers to finish the same job?

(A) $3\frac{1}{2}$ hours
(B) 4 hours
(C) 5 hours
(D) $7\frac{1}{16}$ hours
(E) $9\frac{3}{5}$ hours

Mathematics Exercise C

Directions: Solve each of the following problems.

NOTE: A figure that appears with a problem is drawn as accurately as possible so as to provide information that may help in answering the question. Numbers in this test are real numbers.

1. A box contains 12 poles and 7 pieces of net. Each piece of net weighs .2 pounds; each pole weighs 1.1 pounds. The box and its contents together weigh 16.25 pounds. How much does the empty box weigh?

(A) 1.2 pounds
(B) 1.65 pounds
(C) 2.75 pounds
(D) 6.15 pounds
(E) 16 pounds

2. If $a + b + c + d$ is a positive number, a minimum of x of the numbers a, b, c, and d must be positive where x is equal to

(A) 0
(B) 1
(C) 2
(D) 3
(E) 4

3. Consider the accompanying diagram. Which of the following statements is true?

(A) $KM < KL$
(B) $KM < LM$
(C) $KL + LM < KM$
(D) $KL < LM$
(E) $LM < KL$

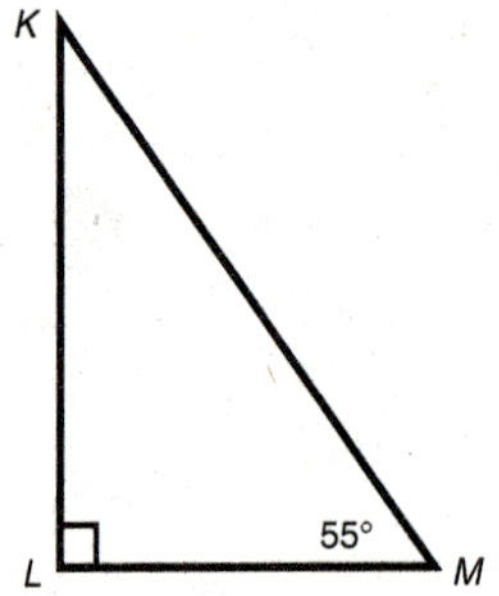

Use the graphs below for questions 4–6.

POPULATION CHARACTERISTICS

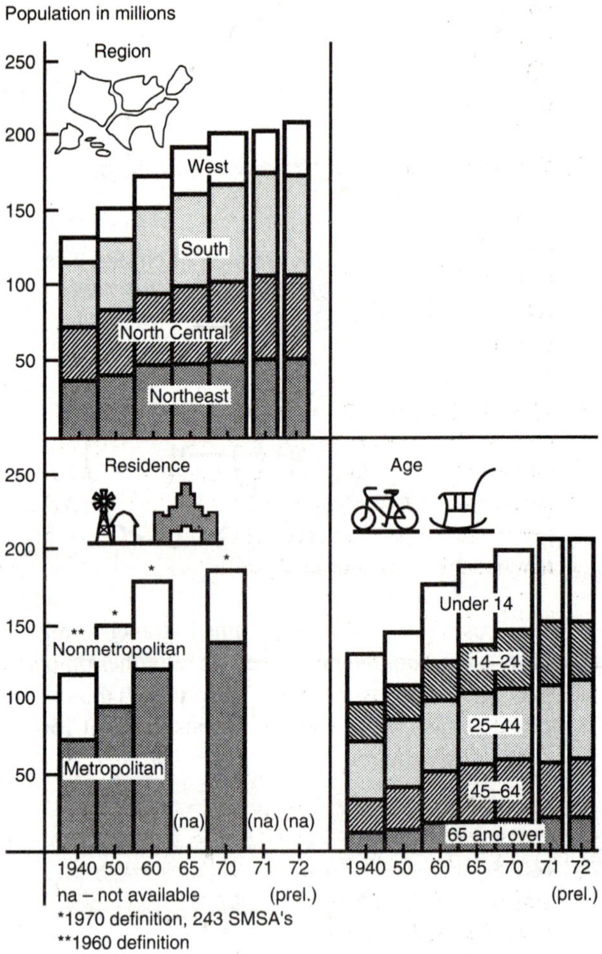

SOURCE: Pocket Data Book U.S.A. 1973. Bureau of the Census.

4. In 1970, the ratio of the population living in metropolitan areas to the population living in nonmetropolitan areas was approximately

(A) 1 to 2
(B) 2 to 3
(C) 7 to 5
(D) 2 to 1
(E) 3 to 1

5. In 1950, the age group that had the fewest people was

(A) under 14
(B) 14–24
(C) 25–44
(D) 45–64
(E) 65 and over

6. How many of the regions shown had a population increase of less than 5% between 1940 and 1972?

(A) 0
(B) 1
(C) 2
(D) 3
(E) 4

7. Which of the following numbers is the largest?

(A) $(2+2+2)^2$
(B) $[(2+2)^2]^2$
(C) $(2\times 2\times 2)^2$
(D) $2+2^2+(2^2)^2$
(E) 4^3

8. In a survey of the town of Waso, it was found that 65% of the people surveyed watched the news on television, 40% read a newspaper, and 25% read a newspaper and watched the news on television. What percent of the people surveyed neither watched the news on television nor read a newspaper?

(A) 0%
(B) 5%
(C) 10%
(D) 15%
(E) 20%

9. A worker is paid d dollars an hour for the first 8 hours she works in a day. For every hour after the first 8 hours, she is paid c dollars an hour. If she works 12 hours in one day, what is her average hourly wage for that day?

(A) $\frac{(2d+c)}{3}$
(B) $8d+4c$
(C) $\frac{(8d+12c)}{12}$
(D) $\frac{(4d+8c)}{12}$
(E) $d+\left(\frac{1}{3}\right)c$

10. A screwdriver and a hammer currently have the same price. If the price of a screwdriver rises by 5% and the price of a hammer goes up by 3%, how much more will it cost to buy 3 screwdrivers and 3 hammers?

(A) 3%
(B) 4%
(C) 5%
(D) 8%
(E) 24%

11. If the radius of a circle is increased by 6%, then the area of the circle is increased by

(A) .36%
(B) 3.6%
(C) 6%
(D) 12.36%
(E) 36%

12. Given that a and b are real numbers, let $f(a, b) = ab$ and let $g(a) = a^2 + 2$. Then $f[3, g(3)] =$

(A) $3a^2+2$
(B) $3a^2+6$
(C) 27
(D) 29
(E) 33

13. A share of stock in Ace Enterprises cost D dollars on Jan. 1, 1975. One year later, a share increased to Q dollars. The fraction by which the cost of a share of stock has increased in the year is

(A) $\frac{(Q-D)}{D}$
(B) $\frac{(D-Q)}{Q}$
(C) $\frac{D}{Q}$
(D) $\frac{Q}{D}$
(E) $\frac{(Q-D)}{Q}$

14. *ABCD* is a square, *EFGH* is a rectangle. $AB = 3$, $EF = 4$, $FG = 6$. The area of the region outside of *ABCD* and inside *EFGH* is

(A) 6
(B) 9
(C) 12
(D) 15
(E) 24

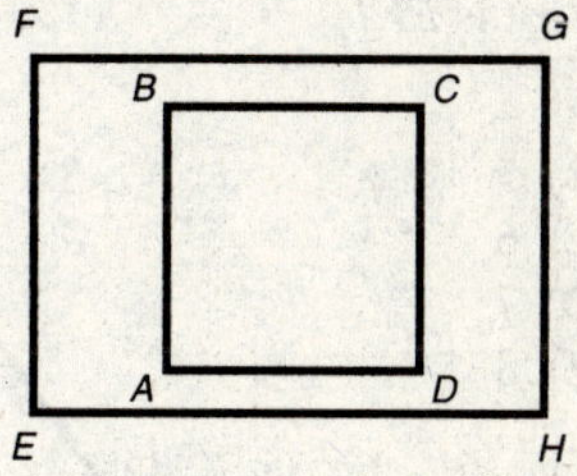

Use the table below for questions 15–17.

	% OF PROTEIN	% OF CARBOHYDRATES	% OF FAT	COST PER 100 GRAMS
FOOD A	10	20	30	$1.80
FOOD B	20	15	10	$3.00
FOOD C	20	10	40	$2.75

15. If you purchase x grams of Food A, y grams of Food B, and z grams of Food C, the cost will be

(A) $\left(\frac{9}{5}x+3y+\frac{11}{4}z\right)$¢

(B) $\$\left(\frac{9}{5}x+3y+\frac{11}{4}z\right)$

(C) $\$(1.8x + 3z + 2.75y)$

(D) $(3x + 1.8y + 2.75z)$¢

(E) $\$(x + y + z)$

16. Which of the following diets would supply the most grams of protein?

(A) 500 grams of A
(B) 250 grams of B
(C) 350 grams of C
(D) 150 grams of A and 200 grams of B
(E) 200 grams of B and 200 grams of C

17. All of the following diets would supply at least 75 grams of fat. Which of the diets costs the least?

(A) 200 grams of A, 150 grams of B
(B) 500 grams of B, 100 grams of A
(C) 200 grams of C
(D) 150 grams of A, 100 grams of C
(E) 300 grams of A

18. CD is parallel to EF. $AD = DF$, $CD = 4$, and $DF = 3$. What is EF?

(A) 4
(B) 5
(C) 6
(D) 7
(E) 8

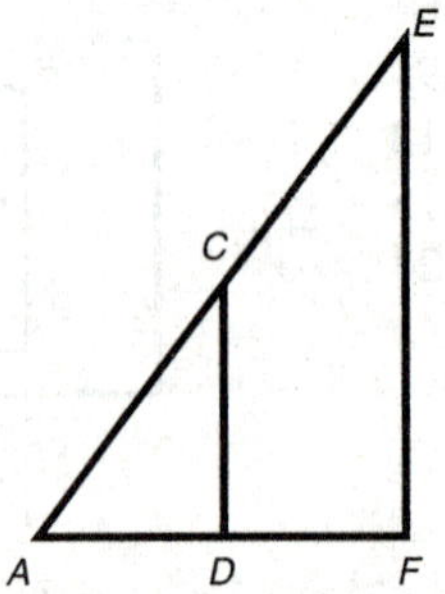

19. Which of the following fractions is the largest?

(A) $\frac{5}{6}$

(B) $\frac{11}{14}$

(C) $\frac{12}{15}$

(D) $\frac{17}{21}$

(E) $\frac{29}{35}$

20. How much simple interest will $2,000 earn in 18 months at an annual rate of 6%?

(A) $120
(B) $180
(C) $216
(D) $1,800
(E) $2,160

21. If $x + y > 5$ and $x - y > 3$, then which of the following gives all possible values of x and only possible values of x?

(A) $x > 3$
(B) $x > 4$
(C) $x > 5$
(D) $x < 5$
(E) $x < 3$

22. If the average (or arithmetic mean) of 6 numbers is 4.5, what is the sum of the numbers?

(A) 4.5
(B) 24
(C) 27
(D) 30
(E) cannot be determined

23. A silo is filled to capacity with W pounds of wheat. Rats eat r pounds a day. After 25 days, what percentage of the silo's capacity have the rats eaten?

(A) $\frac{25r}{W}$

(B) $\frac{25r}{100W}$

(C) $2{,}500\left(\frac{r}{w}\right)$

(D) $\frac{r}{W}$

(E) $\frac{r}{25W}$

24. If $x^2 + 2x - 8 = 0$, then x is either –4 or
    - (A) –2
    - (B) –1
    - (C) 0
    - (D) 2
    - (E) 8

25. The interest charged on a loan is p dollars per \$1,000 for the first month and q dollars per \$1,000 for each month after the first month. How much interest will be charged during the first three months on a loan of \$10,000?
    - (A) $30p$
    - (B) $30q$
    - (C) $p + 2q$
    - (D) $20p + 10q$
    - (E) $10p + 20q$

Data Sufficiency Exercise

We have included one data sufficiency exercise to give you practice in answering this type of problem. The time allotted for this practice exercise is 18 minutes. Scoring may be interpreted as follows:

13 – 15	EXCELLENT
10 – 12+	GOOD
7 – 9+	FAIR
0 – 6+	POOR

Determine your score by counting the number of correct answers minus 1/4 the number of incorrect answers. Before starting this practice exercise, refer to the system for answering data sufficiency questions as outlined on pages 26–27 of this book.

Directions: Each of the following problems has a question and two statements which are labeled (1) and (2). Use the data given in (1) and (2) together with other available information (such as the number of hours in a day, the definition of *clockwise*, mathematical facts, etc.) to decide whether the statements are *sufficient* to answer the question. Then fill in space

(A) if you can get the answer from **(1) ALONE** but not from (2) alone
(B) if you can get the answer from **(2) ALONE** but not from (1) alone
(C) if you can get the answer from **BOTH (1) and (2) TOGETHER,** but not from (1) alone or (2) alone
(D) if **EITHER** statement **(1) ALONE OR** statement **(2) ALONE** suffices
(E) if you **CANNOT** get the answer from statements (1) and (2) **TOGETHER,** but need even more data

All numbers used in this section are real numbers. A figure given for a problem is intended to provide information consistent with that in the question, but not necessarily with the additional information contained in the statements.

1. Find the value of the expression $x^3y - \left(\frac{x^3}{y}\right)$.
   (1) $x = 2$
   (2) $y = 1$

2. If x is a two-digit number (so $x = ba$ with b and a digits), what is the last digit a of x?
   (1) The number $3x$ is a three-digit number whose last digit is a.
   (2) The digit a is less than 7.

3. Is the number $\frac{N}{3}$ an odd integer? (You may assume that $\frac{N}{3}$ is an integer.)
   (1) $N = 3K$ where K is an integer.
   (2) $N = 6J + 3$ where J is an integer.

4. How many families in Jaytown own exactly two phones?
   (1) 150 families in Jaytown own at least one telephone.
   (2) 45 families in Jaytown own at least three telephones.

5. Is the line PQ parallel to the line SR?
   (1) $w = q$
   (2) $y = z$

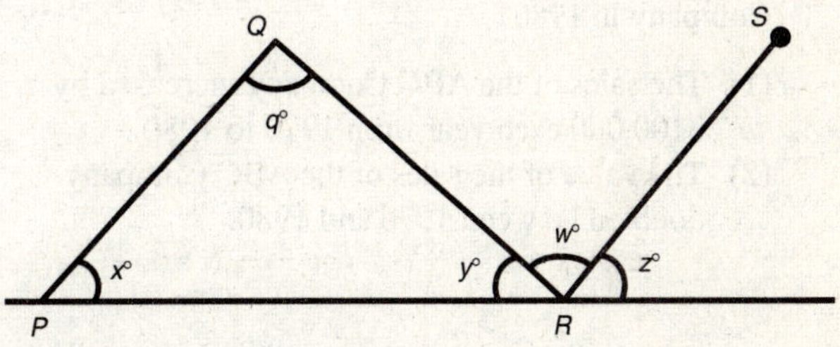

6. What is the value of $x^3 - y^3$?
   (1) $x^6 - y^6 = 0$
   (2) $y = 0$

7. How much does John weigh? Tim weighs 200 pounds.

   (1) Tim's weight plus Moe's weight is equal to John's weight.
   (2) John's weight plus Moe's weight is equal to twice Tim's weight.

8. Which triangle, *ADE* or *AEC*, has the larger area? *ABCD* is a rectangle.

   (1) *DE* is longer than *EC*.
   (2) *AC* is longer than *AE*.

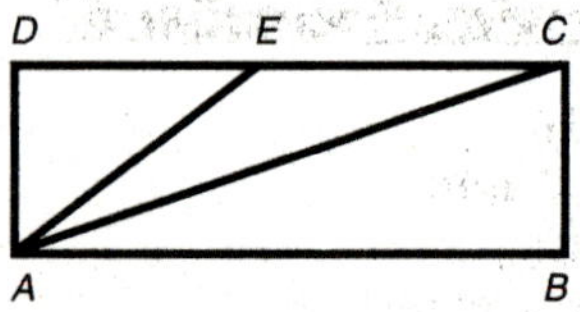

9. *ABCDEFGH* is a cube. What is the length of the line segment *AG*?

   (1) The length of the line segment *AB* is 4 inches.
   (2) The area of the square *BCGH* is 16 square inches.

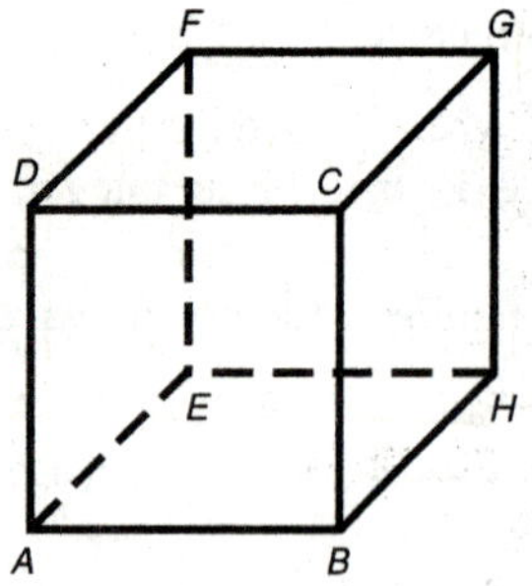

10. Is the integer *K* an odd integer?

    (1) $K = 3M$ where *M* is an integer.
    (2) $K = 6J$ where *J* is an integer.

11. What was the value of the sales of the ABC Company in 1980?

    (1) The sales of the ABC Company increased by $100,000 each year from 1970 to 1980.
    (2) The value of the sales of the ABC Company doubled between 1970 and 1980.

12. Is *x* greater than 2? (You may assume *y* is not equal to zero.)

    (1) $\left(\frac{x}{y}\right)$ is greater than 2.
    (2) $\left(\frac{1}{y}\right)$ is less than 1.

13. How many gallons of a chemical can be stored in a cylindrical tank if the radius of the tank is 15 feet? One gallon is equal to 231 cubic inches.

    (1) The height of the tank is 20 feet.
    (2) The temperature is 60 degrees Fahrenheit.

14. Is the area of the circle with center *O* larger than the area of the region outside the circle and inside the square *ABCD*? The straight line *OEF* is parallel to *AB*.

    (1) $OE < \left(\frac{1}{4}\right)AB$
    (2) $EF < \left(\frac{1}{4}\right)AB$

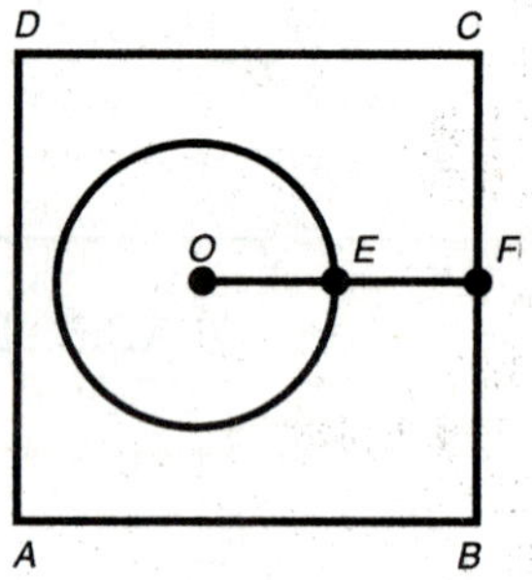

15. If $x^6 - y^6 = 0$, what is the value of $x^3 - y^3$?

    (1) *x* is positive.
    (2) *y* is greater than 1.

Answers

The letter following each question number is the correct answer. The numbers in parentheses refer to the sections of this chapter that explain the necessary mathematics principles. A more detailed explanation of all answers follows.

Mathematics Exercise A

1. **D** (I-1)
2. **B** (I-4)
3. **B** (III-7, I-4)
4. **A** (IV-4, IV-5, I-4)
5. **A** (IV-4, I-7)
6. **B** (IV-4)
7. **D** (IV-4, I-2)
8. **C** (I-4)
9. **A** (I-1)
10. **C** (II-1)
11. **C** (III-9, I-8)
12. **C** (I-2)
13. **C** (I-4)
14. **D** (I-4)
15. **C** (I-4)
16. **E** (I-7, I-4)
17. **B** (I-4, I-5)
18. **A** (II-1)
19. **D** (I-2)
20. **D** (II-3)
21. **C** (III-7, II-1, I-8)
22. **D** (II-2)
23. **C** (I-4)
24. **D** (III-9, III-7)
25. **A** (II-2)

Mathematics Exercise B

1. **B** (IV-2, IV-3)
2. **D** (IV-3)
3. **C** (IV-3)
4. **B** (IV-3)
5. **A** (IV-3)
6. **D** (I-8)
7. **B** (III-4, III-7)
8. **E** (II-5)
9. **D** (III-7)
10. **A** (II-3)
11. **D** (I-1)
12. **E** (IV-1)
13. **B** (IV-1)
14. **B** (IV-1)
15. **B** (IV-1, II-7)
16. **A** (I-4, I-2)
17. **A** (II-7)
18. **D** (III-6, III-4)
19. **B** (I-4)
20. **E** (II-2)
21. **D** (IV-1)
22. **C** (IV-1)
23. **D** (II-1)
24. **A** (II-2)
25. **E** (II-3)

Mathematics Exercise C

1. **B** (I-3)
2. **B** (II-7, I-6)
3. **E** (III-4)
4. **E** (IV-5, II-5)
5. **E** (IV-5)
6. **A** (IV-5)
7. **B** (I-8)
8. **E** (II-4)
9. **A** (I-7, II-I)
10. **B** (I-4)
11. **D** (III-7)
12. **E** (II-1)
13. **A** (I-2)
14. **D** (III-7)
15. **A** (II-1)
16. **E** (I-4)
17. **E** (IV-1)
18. **E** (III-4)
19. **A** (I-1, I-2, III-7)
20. **B** (I-4)
21. **B** (II-7)
22. **C** (I-7)
23. **C** (I-4)
24. **D** (II-1, II-2)
25. **E** (II-1)

Data Sufficiency Exercise

1. **(B)**
2. **(E)**
3. **(B)**
4. **(E)**
5. **(A)**
6. **(C)**
7. **(C)**
8. **(A)**
9. **(D)**
10. **(B)**
11. **(C)**
12. **(E)**
13. **(A)**
14. **(A)**
15. **(C)**

Explanation of Answers

Mathematics Exercise A

1. **D** The price increased by 34 – 12 = 22 dollars.
2. **B** She sold the house for 125% of C or $\frac{5}{4}C$.

   Thus, the gain is $\frac{5}{4}C - C = \frac{C}{4}$. She must pay a tax of 50% of $\frac{C}{4}$ or $\frac{1}{2}$ of $\frac{C}{4}$. Therefore, the tax is $\frac{C}{8}$. Notice that the three years has nothing to do with the problem. Sometimes a question contains unnecessary information.
3. **B** The area of a rectangle is length times width. Let L and W denote the original length and width. Then the new length is $1.2L$ and the new width is $.8W$. Therefore, the new area is $(1.2L)(.8W) = .96LW$ or 96% of the original area. So the area has decreased by 4%.
4. **A** In 1964 military expenditures were about 140 billion and by 1969 they had increased to about 200 billion. $\frac{60}{140} = \frac{3}{7}$ which is almost 50%. By using a straight edge, you may see that the bar for 1969 is about half again as long as the bar for 1964.
5. **A** Since the developing countries' military expenditures for every year were less than 30 billion, choice A is the only possible answer. Notice that by reading the possible answers first, you save time. You don't need the exact answer.
6. **B** I. cannot be inferred since the graph indicates *only* the dollars spent on military expenditures, not the percent of income and not total income. II. is true since each bar is higher than the previous bar to the left. III. cannot be inferred since the graph gives no information about 1972. So only statement II. can be inferred from the graph.
7. **D** In 1971 the NATO countries spent over 100 billion and less than 150 billion on military expenditures. Since this was $\frac{1}{3}$ of their combined incomes the combined income is between 300 billion and 450 billion. Thus choice D must be the correct answer.
8. **C** Voters between 18 and 21 who voted are 85% of the 8% of eligible voters. Thus, (.08)(.85) = .068, so 6.8% of the eligible voters were voters between 18 and 21 who voted.
9. **A** Odd numbers are of the form $2x + 1$ where x is an integer. Thus if $n = 2x + 1$ and $p = 2k + 1$, then $n + p = 2x + 1 + 2k + 1 = 2x + 2k + 2$ which is even. Using $n = 3$ and $p = 5$, all the other choices give an odd number. In general, if a problem involves odd or even numbers, try using the fact that odd numbers are of the form $2x + 1$ and even numbers of the form $2y$ where x and y are integers.
10. **C** To run a car 100 miles will cost $100(g + m)$ cents. Divide by 100 to convert to dollars. The result is $g + m$.
11. **C** Using the distance formula, the distance from A to B is $\sqrt{(1-(-1))^2+(3-5)^2} = \sqrt{4+4} = \sqrt{8} = \sqrt{4\times 2} = \sqrt{4}\sqrt{2} = 2\sqrt{2}$. You have to be able to simplify $\sqrt{8}$ in order to obtain the correct answer.
12. **C** Tips for the week were $\frac{5}{4} \bullet 50$ so his total income was $50 + \frac{5}{4}(50) = \frac{9}{4}(50)$. Therefore, tips made up $\frac{\frac{5}{4}(50)}{\frac{9}{4}(50)} = \frac{\frac{5}{4}}{\frac{9}{4}} = \frac{5}{9}$ of his income.

    Don't waste time figuring out the total income and the tip income. You can use the time to answer other questions.
13. **C** 7,500 is in the 6,000–8,000 bracket so the tax will be 80 + 3% of the income over 6,000. Since 7,500 – 6,000 = 1,500, the income over 6,000 is 1,500. 3% of 1,500 = (.03)(1,500) = 45, so the tax is 80 + 45 = 125.
14. **D** The tax on 26,000 is 1,070 + 7% of (26,000 – 25,000). Thus, the tax is 1,070 + 70 = 1,140. The tax on 29,000 is 1.070 + 7% of (29,000 – 25,000). Thus, the tax on 29,000 is 1,070 + 280 = 1,350. Therefore, you will pay 1,350 – 1,140 = $210 more in taxes next year. A faster method is to use the fact that the $3,000 raise is income over 25,000, so it will be taxed at 7%. Therefore, the tax on the extra $3,000 will be (.07)(3,000) = 210.
15. **C** If income is less than 6,000, then the tax is less than 80. If income is greater than 8,000, then the tax is greater than 140. Therefore, if the tax is 100, the income must be between 6,000 and 8,000. You *do not* have to calculate her exact income.
16. **E** Each person pays the tax on $3,700 which is 1% of 3,700 or $37. Since there are 50,000 people in Zenith, the total taxes are (37)(50,000) = $1,850,000.

17. **B** The tax on 10,000 is 220, so taxes are $\frac{220}{10,000} = .022 = 2.2\%$ of income. 2.2% is 2% after rounding to the nearest percent.

18. **A** $S(3, 4) = 3^2 - 4^2 = 9 - 16 = -7$. Therefore, $S(3, S(3, 4)) = S(3, -7) = 3^2 - (-7)^2 = 9 - 49 = -40$.

19. **D** 8 omelets will use $8 \bullet 3 = 24$ eggs and $8 \bullet \frac{1}{4} =$ 2 peppers. Since 24 is two dozen, the cost will be (2)(90¢) + (2)(20¢) = 220¢ or $2.20.

20. **D** In order to average 50 m.p.h. for the trip, the bus must make the trip in $\frac{185}{50} = 3\frac{7}{10}$ hours which is 222 minutes. Since 2 hours or 120 minutes were needed for the first 85 miles, the final 100 miles must be completed in 222 – 120 which is 102 minutes.

21. **C** The area of a rectangle is length times width so the area of *ABDC* is *ab*. The area of a triangle is one half of the height times the base. Since *BDE* is an isosceles right triangle, the base and height both are equal to *b*. Thus, the area of *BDE* is $\frac{1}{2}b^2$. Therefore, the area of the figure is $ab + \frac{1}{2}b^2$ which is equal to $b\left(a + \frac{b}{2}\right)$. You have to express your answer as one of the possible answers, so you need to be able to simplify.

22. **D** Since $4x + 2y$ is equal to $2(2x + y)$ and $2x + y = 5$, $4x + 2y$ is equal to 2(5) or 10.

23. **C** The cost has increased by $4,800 minus $2,500, or $2,300, between 1967 and 1975. So the cost has increased by $\frac{2,300}{2,500}$ which is .92 or 92%. Answer (E) is incorrect. The price in 1975 is 192% of the price in 1967, but the *increase* is 92%.

24. **D** The distance from (–1, 2) to (5, 2) is 6. (You can use the distance formula or just count the blocks in this case.) The area of a square is the length of a side squared, so the area is 6^2 or 36.

25. **A** Since $x + y = 6$ and $3x - y = 4$, we may add the two equations to obtain $4x = 10$, or $x = 2.5$. Then, because $x + y = 6$, y must be 3.5. Therefore, $x - y = -1$.

Mathematics Exercise B

1. **B** In 1960 women made up 33.4% or about $\frac{1}{3}$ of the labor force. The line graph shows there were about 22 million women in the labor force in 1960. So the labor force was about 3(22) or 66 million. The closest answer among the choices is 65 million.

2. **D** In 1947, there were about 16 million women in the labor force, and about 14 – 6 or 8 million of them were married. Therefore, the percentage of women in the labor force who were married is $\frac{8}{16}$ or 50%.

3. **C** Look at the possible answers first. You can use your pencil and admission card as straight edges.

4. **B** In 1947, there were about 16 million women in the labor force. By 1972 there were about 32 million. Therefore, the number of women doubled which is an increase of 100%. (Not of 200%.)

5. **A** I. is true since the width of the band for widowed or divorced women was never more than 5 million between 1947 and 1957. II. is false since the number of single women in the labor force decreased from 1947 to 1948. III. cannot be inferred since there is no information about the total labor force or women as a percent of it in 1965. Thus, only I. can be inferred.

6. **D** If $\frac{x}{y}$ is $\frac{2}{3}$, then $\frac{y}{x}$ is $\frac{3}{2}$. Since $\left(\frac{y}{x}\right)^2$ is equal to $\frac{y^2}{x^2}$, $\frac{y^2}{x^2}$ is $\left(\frac{3}{2}\right)^2$ or $\frac{9}{4}$.

7. **B** The area of a triangle is $\frac{1}{2}$ altitude times base. Since *BD* is perpendicular to *AC*, *x* is the altitude. Using the Pythagorean theorem, $x^2 + (AD)^2 = a^2$ and $x^2 + (DC)^2 = a^2$. Thus, $AD = DC$, and $AD = \sqrt{a^2 - x^2}$. So the base is $2\sqrt{a^2 - x^2}$. Therefore, the area is $\frac{1}{2}(x)(2\sqrt{a^2 - x^2})$ which is choice B.

8. **E** $1 : 160 = 2\frac{7}{8} : x$. $x = 2\frac{7}{8}$ (160). $2\frac{7}{8}$ is $\frac{23}{8}$ so the distance from Seton to Monroe is $\frac{23}{8}(160) = 460$ miles.

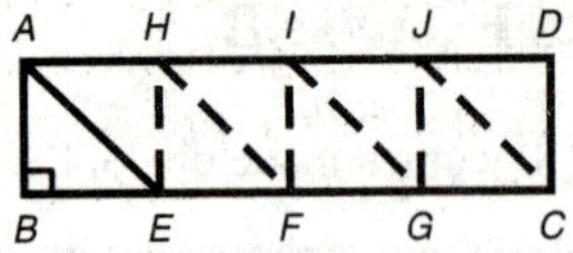

9. **D** Let $EF = FG = GC$. Therefore, $BE = EF = FG = GC$. Draw perpendiculars EH, FI, GJ. Draw diagonals HF, IG, JC. The 8 triangles are equal in area since they each have the same altitude (AB or DC) and equal bases (BE, EF, FG, GC, AH, HI, IJ, JD). Since the area of $ABE = 7$, the area of $ABCD = (8)(7)$ or 56.

10. **A** In each minute the first puncture will leak $\frac{1}{9}$ of the air and the second puncture will leak $\frac{1}{6}$ of the air. Together $\frac{1}{9} + \frac{1}{6} = \frac{5}{18}$. So $\frac{5}{18}$ of the air will leak out in each minute. In $\frac{18}{5}$ or $3\frac{3}{5}$ minutes the tire will be flat.

11. **D** Since an even number times any number is even, and n times n^2 is odd, neither n nor n^2 can be even. Therefore, n and n^2 must both be odd for n^3 to be odd. I and II are true, and III is false.

12. **E** Look in the fourth column.

13. **B** In 1972 there were 72 million females out of 136 million persons of voting age. $\frac{72}{136} =$ .529 which is 53% to the nearest percent.

14. **B** In 1968, 70% of the 54 million males of voting age voted, and $(.7)(54{,}000{,}000) = 37{,}800{,}000$.

15. **B** Since 78 million persons of voting age lived in the North and West in 1964, and there were 65 million persons of voting age not in the 25–44 year range, there must be at least $78 - 65 = 13$ million people in the North and West in the 25–44 year range. X must be greater than or equal to 13. Since there were 45 million people of voting age in the 25–44 year range, X must be less than or equal to 45.

16. **A** 90% of 50 is 45, so 45 students took the final. $\frac{2}{3}$ of 45 is 30. Therefore, 30 students passed the final.

17. **A** The average of two different numbers is always between the two. If $a = 2$ and $b = 3$, then $b^2 - a^2 = 5$, $ab = 6$, and $b - a = 1$ so C, D, and E must be false. If $a = \frac{1}{2}$ and $b = 1$, then $\frac{(ab)}{2} = \frac{1}{4}$, so B is also false.

18. **D** Since the radius to the point of tangency is perpendicular to the tangent OR must be perpendicular to PR. Therefore, ORP is a right triangle, and $(PO) = (OR)^2 + (PR)^2$. Then, $(PR)^2 = (PO)^2 - (OR)^2$. Thus $(PR)^2 = 4^2 - 2^2$, and $PR = \sqrt{16-4} = \sqrt{12} = \sqrt{4}\sqrt{3} = 2\sqrt{3}$.

19. **B** After the tune-up, the bus will travel $(1.15)(15) = 17.25$ miles on a gallon of gas. Therefore, it will take $(150) \div (17.25) = 8.7$ (to the nearest tenth) gallons of gasoline to travel 150 miles.

20. **E** If $\frac{x}{y} = 2$, then $x = 2y$, so $x + 2y = 2y + 2y = 4y$. But $x + 2y = 4$, so $4y = 4$, or $y = 1$. Since $x = 2y$, x must be 2.

21. **D** $2\frac{1}{2}$ hours is 150 minutes.

22. **C** The train's speed increased by $70 - 40$, which is 30 miles per hour. $\frac{30}{40}$ is 75%.

23. **D** When $t = 0$, the speed is 40, so A and B are incorrect. When $t = 180$, the speed is 70, so C and E are incorrect. Choice D gives all the values that appear in the table.

24. **A** The cost of producing the first 8,000 copies is $1{,}000 + 7{,}000x$. $1{,}000 + 7{,}000x = \$7{,}230$. Therefore, $7{,}000x = 6230$ and $x = .89$.

25. **E** Assume all workers work at the same rate unless given different information. Since 16 workers take 3 hours, each worker does $\frac{1}{48}$ of the job an hour. Thus, the 5 workers will finish $\frac{5}{48}$ of the job each hour. $\frac{5}{48}x = \frac{48}{48}$. It will take $\frac{48}{5} = 9\frac{3}{5}$ hours for them to finish the job.

Mathematics Exercise C

1. **B** The 12 poles weigh $(12)(1.1) = 13.2$ pounds and the 7 pieces of net weigh $7(.2) = 1.4$ pounds, so the contents of the box weigh $13.2 + 1.4 = 14.6$ pounds. Therefore, the box by itself must weigh $16.25 - 14.6 = 1.65$ pounds.

2. **B** If all the numbers were not positive, then the sum could not be positive so A is incorrect. If a, b, and c were all -1 and d were 5, then $a + b + c + d$ would be positive so C, D, and E are incorrect.

3. **E** Since the measure of angle M is 55°, the measure of angle K is 35°. Therefore, $LM < KL$ since the larger side is opposite the larger angle.

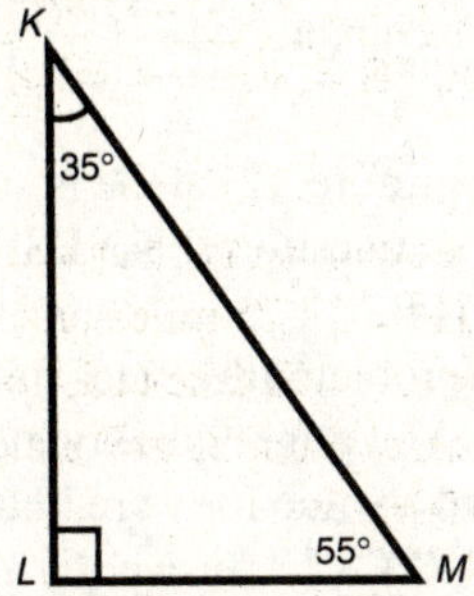

4. **E** The population in metropolitan areas in 1970 was about 140 million, and the population in nonmetropolitan areas was about 190 – 140 or 50 million. Therefore, the ratio was about 140 to 50 and 3 to 1 is the best choice.
5. **E** Compare the segments of the second bar under "age."
6. **A** All regions increased by at least 10%. Compare the segments of the first bar with those of the last bar under "Region."
7. **B** Choice A gives 6^2 or 36. Choice B gives 4^4 or 256. Choice C is 8^2 or 64. Choice D is 2 + 4 + 16 or 22. Choice E is 4^3 or 64.
8. **E** Since 25% read the newspaper and watched the news on television and 40% read the newspaper, 40% – 25% or 15% read the newspaper but did not watch the news on television. Thus 65% + 15% or 80% read the newspaper or watched the news on television, so 100% – 80% or 20% neither read the newspaper nor watched the news on television.
9. **A** For the first 8 hours, she is paid a total of $8d$. For the final 4 hours (12 – 8), she is paid $4c$. Therefore, her total pay is $8d + 4c$. To find the average hourly pay, divide by 12. To find the correct answer among the choices, you have to reduce the fraction. Divide the numerator by four and the denominator by four.
10. **B** If the price of one screwdriver increases by 5%, then the price of three screwdrivers increases by 5% (not 15%). The percentage change is the same regardless of the number sold. Since a screwdriver and a hammer currently cost the same, the screwdrivers and the hammers each cost one half of the total price. So one half of the total is increased by 5%. The other half is increased by 3%. Therefore, the total price is increased by $\frac{1}{2}(5\%) + \frac{1}{2}(3\%) = 4\%$.
11. **D** After the radius is increased by 6%, the radius will be 1.06 times the original radius. Since the area of a circle is πr^2, the new area will be $\pi(1.06r)^2 = \pi(1.1236r^2)$ or $1.12361\pi r^2$. Thus, the area has been increased by .1236 or by 12.36%.
12. **E** Since $g(a) = a^2 + 2$, $g(3)$ is $3^2 + 2$ or 11. So $f[3, g(3)]$ is $f(3, 11) = 3 \times 11$ or 33.
13. **A** The difference in the price is $Q - D$. So the fraction by which it has increased is $\frac{(Q-D)}{D}$. Note that the denominator is the *original* price.
14. **D** Since $ABCD$ is a square, the area of $ABCD$ is 3^2 or 9. The area of the rectangle $EFGH$ is *length* times *width* or $4 \times 6 = 24$. Thus, the area outside the square and inside the rectangle is 24 – 9 or 15.
15. **A** The cost of food A is \$1.80 per hundred grams or 1.8¢ a gram, so x grams cost $(1.8x)$¢ or $\left(\frac{9}{5}\right)x$¢. Each gram of food B costs 3¢ so y grams of food B will cost $3y$¢. Each gram of food C costs 2.75¢ or $\left(\frac{11}{4}\right)$¢; thus, z grams of food C will cost $\left(\frac{11}{4}\right)z$¢. Therefore, the total cost is $[\left(\frac{9}{5}\right)x + 3y + \left(\frac{11}{4}\right)z]$¢.
16. **E** Since food A is 10% protein, 500 grams of food A will supply 50 grams of protein. Food B is 20% protein so 250 grams of food B will supply 50 grams of protein. 350 grams of food C will supply 70 grams of protein. 150 grams of food A and 200 grams of food B will supply 15 + 40 = 55 grams of protein. 200 grams of food B and 200 grams of food C will supply 40 + 40 or 80 grams of protein. Choice E supplies the most protein.
17. **E** The diet of choice A will cost 2(\$1.80) + $\left(\frac{3}{2}\right)$(\$3) = \$3.60 + \$4.50 = \$8.10. Choice B will cost 5(\$3) + \$1.80 = \$16.80. Choice C costs 2(\$2.75) = \$5.50. Choice D costs $\left(\frac{3}{2}\right)$(\$1.80) + \$2.75 = \$2.70 + \$2.75 = \$5.45. The diet of Choice E costs 3(\$1.80) or \$5.40, so Choice E costs the least.

18. **E** Since CD is parallel to EF, the triangles ACD and AEF are similar. Therefore, corresponding sides are proportional. So CD is to EF as AD is to AF. Since $AD = DF$, $\frac{AD}{AF}$ is $\frac{1}{2}$. Therefore, EF is twice CD or 8.

19. **A** You need to find a common denominator for the fractions. One method is to multiply all the denominators. A quicker method is to find the least common multiple of the denominators. Since $6 = 3 \times 2$, $14 = 2 \times 7$, $15 = 3 \times 5$, $21 = 3 \times 7$, and $35 = 5 \times 7$, the least common multiple is $2 \times 3 \times 5 \times 7 = 210$. $\frac{5}{6}$ is $\frac{175}{210}$, $\frac{11}{14}$ is $\frac{165}{210}$, $\frac{12}{15}$ is $\frac{168}{210}$, $\frac{17}{21}$ is $\frac{170}{210}$, and $\frac{29}{35}$ is $\frac{174}{210}$. So $\frac{5}{6}$ is the largest.

20. **B** 18 months is $\frac{3}{2}$ of a year. Interest = Amount × Time × Rate. $(\$2{,}000)\left(\frac{3}{2}\right)(.06) = \$180$.

21. **B** If $x + y > 5$ and $x - y > 3$, then, since both inequalities are of the same type, the corresponding sides can be added to obtain $2x > 8$ or $x > 4$.

22. **C** The average of 6 numbers is the sum of the numbers divided by 6. Thus, the sum of the numbers is the average multiplied by 6 or 4.5×6 which is 27.

23. **C** After 25 days the rats have eaten $25r$ pounds of wheat. So $\frac{(25r)}{W}$ is the fraction of the capacity eaten by the rats. To change this to percent, multiply by 100. $\frac{(25r)}{W} \times 100 = 2500\left(\frac{r}{W}\right)$.

24. **D** Factor $x^2 + 2x - 8$ into $(x + 4)(x - 2)$. If x is either -4 or 2, $x^2 + 2x - 8 = 0$, and D is the correct answer.

25. **E** The interest on the $10,000 for the first month will be $10p$. For the next 2 months the interest will be $20q$. The total interest is $10p + 20q$.

Data Sufficiency Exercise

(Refer to pages 26–27 for an explanation of the system used in solving the following problems.)

1. **B** If STATEMENT (1) is true, then $x^3y - \left(\frac{x^3}{y}\right)$ is equal to $8y - \left(\frac{8}{y}\right)$, but the value of y is needed to find the value of the expression. Therefore, (1) alone is not sufficient. So the answer to question I is NO, and the only possible choices are B, C, or E.

   If STATEMENT (2) alone is true, then $x^3y - \left(\frac{x^3}{y}\right)$ is equal to $x^3 1 - \left(\frac{x^3}{1}\right)$, which is equal to 0. Therefore, (2) alone is sufficient, and the answer to question II is YES. So the correct choice is B.

   This problem illustrates the need to be careful. You might quickly infer that a value for x and a value for y are both needed and INCORRECTLY answer C. To understand the problem, you need to simplify the expression by factoring out an x^3 from each term. So $x^3y - \left(\frac{x^3}{y}\right)$ is equal to $x^3(y - \left(\frac{1}{y}\right))$, which is equal to 0 if $x = 0$ or if $y - \left(\frac{1}{y}\right) = 0$. Thus, the expression's value is determined if $x = 0$ or if $y = 1$; otherwise, you need both a value for x and a value for y.

2. **E** If STATEMENT (1) is true, then since $x = ba$, $3x = 3(10b + a) = 30b + 3a$. Now, because b is multiplied by 10 in the expression for $3x$, the final digit of $3x$ must be the final digit of $3a$. Since a is a digit, $0 \le a \le 9$, which implies $0 \le 3a \le 27$. So for the last digit of $3a$ to be equal to a, $3a$ must equal a or $10 + a$ or $20 + a$. If $a = 3a$, then $a = 0$. If $10 + a = 3a$, then $10 = 2a$ or $a = 5$. If $20 + a = 3a$, then $20 = 2a$ or $a = 10$, but since 10 is not a digit this is not possible. So if (1) is true, then a is 0 or 5, and (1) alone is not sufficient. Thus the answer to question I is NO, and the only possible choices are B, C, or E.

   Now since 26 and 25 are both two-digit numbers whose last digits are less than 7, STATEMENT (2) alone is not sufficient. So the answer to question II is NO, and the only possible choices are C or E. Also, since (2) does not allow us to choose between 0 and 5, STATEMENTS (1) and (2) together are not sufficient, so the correct choice is E.

   Many people would be able to see that STATEMENT (2) alone would be insufficient but might not be able to decide whether (1) is sufficient. You can use the strategy to make an intelligent guess. Since (2) alone is not sufficient, the answer to question II on the decision tree is NO. Since choices B and D need an answer of YES to II, the only possible choices are A, C, or E. Since you can eliminate two choices, it is worthwhile to guess.

3. **B** STATEMENT (1) alone is not sufficient since then $\frac{N}{3} = \frac{(3K)}{3} = K$. Now if $K = 1$, then $\frac{N}{3} = 1$, which is odd, but if $K = 2$, then $\frac{N}{3} = 2$, which is even. So the answer to question I is NO, and the only possible choices are B, C, or E.

STATEMENT (2) alone is sufficient since then $\frac{N}{3} = \frac{(6J+3)}{3} = 2J + 1$, which is always odd since J is an integer. So the answer to question II is YES, and the correct choice is B.

4. **E** If you use STATEMENTS (1) and (2) together, you can deduce that $150 - 45 = 105$ families own at least one telephone and less than three telephones. However, since this is the total of families with one phone and families with two phones, we cannot find the number of families with exactly two phones. So (1) and (2) together are not sufficient. Thus, the answer to question III is NO, and the correct choice is E.

5. **A** Since w and q are alternate interior angles, if STATEMENT (1) is true then PQ is parallel to SR. So (1) alone is sufficient. Thus, the answer to question I is YES and the only possible choices are A and D.

STATEMENT (2) alone is not sufficient since the line RS can be moved so that y is still equal to z but PQ and RS are not parallel. (See the diagram below.)

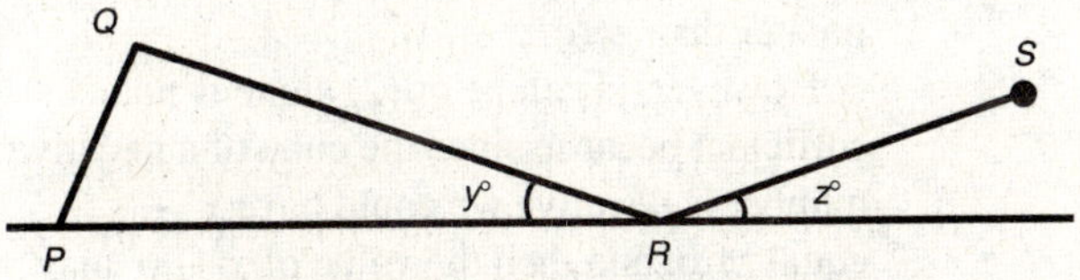

Therefore, the answer to question II is NO, and the correct choice is A.

6. **C** If STATEMENT (1) alone is true, then since $x^6 - y^6$ can be factored into $(x^3 + y^3)(x^3 - y^3)$, either $x^3 + y^3 = 0$ or $x^3 - y^3 = 0$. So (1) alone is not sufficient, and the answer to question I is NO. Thus, the only possible choices are B, C, or E.

STATEMENT (2) alone is insuffficient since if $y = 0$, then $x^3 - y^3 = x^3$, and we have no value for x. So the answer to question II is NO, and the only possible choices are C or E.

If (1) and (2) are both true, then we can deduce that x and y must both be equal to zero, which is sufficient. Thus, the answer to question III is YES, and the correct choice must be C.

7. **C** Let J, M, and T stand for the weights of John, Moe, and Tim respectively. We need to find J and we know $T = 200$. STATEMENT (1) gives the equation $200 + M = J$, but since we don't know M, (1) alone is not sufficient.

STATEMENT (2) alone gives the equation $J + M = 2T = 400$, and since we don't know M, (2) alone is insufficient.

However, if we use STATEMENTS (1) and (2) together, then we have two linear equations in two unknowns, which we know can be solved to find J and M.

NOTE: Don't waste time actually solving the equations. You only have to decide if there is enough information to answer the question; you don't have to compute the actual answer.

8. **A** Since the area of a triangle is $\left(\frac{1}{2}\right)$ (altitude) (base) and since both triangles have DA as an altitude, if the base (DE) of triangle ADE is larger than the base (EC) of triangle AEC, then the area of ADE is larger than the area of AEC. So STATEMENT (1) alone is sufficient, and the answer to question I is YES.

STATEMENT (2) alone is not sufficient since for any point E between D and C (2) will be true, but, depending on whether E is closer to D or C, a different triangle will have the larger area. So the answer to question II is NO, and the correct choice is A.

9. **D** By using the distance formula (Pythagorean theorem) you could find the length of AG if you knew the lengths of AH and GH (or if you knew the lengths of AC and CG or many other combinations). If you knew the lengths of AB and BH, then you could find the length of AH. Thus, it is sufficient to know the lengths of AB, BH, and GH. Since $ABCDEFGH$ is a cube, AB, BH, and GH all have the same length since they are all edges of the cube. So it is sufficient to know the length of an edge of the cube. Now STATEMENTS (1) and (2) are equivalent since the area of a square face of the cube is 16 if and only if the length of an edge is 4. Therefore, (1) alone and (2) alone are sufficient, and the correct choice is D.

Notice that, if you knew that (1) and (2) are equivalent, then the only possible choices are D or E, so you *can* make an intelligent guess.

10. **B** STATEMENT (2) alone is sufficient since if (2) is true, then $K = 2(3J)$, which means that K is even. Note this is sufficient to answer the question even though the answer is NO.

STATEMENT (1) alone is not sufficient since if M is even, then K is even, but if M is odd, then K is odd.

11. **C** STATEMENT (1) alone is insufficient since we don't know the sales for any year. Thus, the answer to question I is NO. Therefore, the only possible choices are B, C, or E.

STATEMENT (2) alone is not sufficient since we don't know the value of the sales in 1970. So the answer to question III is NO, and the only possible choices are C and E.

Using (1), we can calculate the change in sales from 1970 to 1980, and then by using (2), we can find the value of the sales in 1980. Therefore, the answer to question III is YES, and the correct choice is C.

12. **E** Since $x = 3$, $y = 1$, and $x = 1$, $y = \left(\frac{1}{3}\right)$ both make STATEMENT (1) true, (1) alone is not sufficient. So the answer to question I is NO, and the only possible choices are B, C, or E.

STATEMENT (2) alone is obviously not sufficient since it gives no information about x. Thus, the answer to question II is NO, and the only possible choices are C or E. (NOTE: Even if you can't answer question I for this problem, you should be able to answer question II, and you would be able to guess either A, C, or E.)

Now if y were positive, we could use STATEMENT (2) to deduce that $y > 1$ and then (1) would imply that $x > 2$. However, negative values of y can also satisfy (2) (for example, $y = -1$) and then (1) would have solutions with $x < 2$. So (1) and (2) together are not sufficient, and the answer to question III is NO. Thus the correct choice is E.

13. **A** STATEMENT (1) alone is sufficient since it will allow you to compute the volume of the tank in cubic feet. To actually find the answer, you would then change cubic feet into gallons using the fact that 231 cubic inches is one gallon. However, do not perform the calculation since it will only waste time.

Since using STATEMENT (2) alone will not allow you to find the volume of the tank, the correct answer is A.

14. **A** The area of the circle plus the area of the region outside the circle and inside the square is equal to the area of the square, which is $(AB)^2$. Thus if you can determine whether one area is larger (or smaller) than $\left(\frac{1}{2}\right)AB^2$, that is sufficient.

STATEMENT (1) alone is sufficient since the area of the circle is $\pi(OE)^2$, and if (1) holds, then $\pi(OE)^2 < \pi\left(\left(\frac{1}{4}\right)AB\right)^2 = \left(\frac{1}{16}\right)AB^2$. But since $\frac{\pi}{16}$ is less than $\left(\frac{1}{2}\right)$, we can answer the question. So the answer to question I is YES, and the only possible choices are A or D.

STATEMENT (2) alone is not sufficient since (2) does not give any information about the radius of the circle. Note you might think that $OE + EF = \left(\frac{1}{2}\right)AB$; however, that requires the additional information that O is also the center of the square, which is NOT given. So the answer to question II is NO, and the correct choice is A.

15. **C** The key to solving this problem is to relate $x^3 - y^3$ to the information $x^6 - y^6 = 0$. If you think of $x^6 - y^6$ as $(x^3)^2 - (y^3)^2$, then you can factor the equation into $(x^3 - y^3)(x^3 + y^3) = 0$. So if $x^3 + y^3$ is not zero, then $x^3 - y^3$ must be zero. Thus STATEMENTS (1) and (2) together are sufficient because they imply that $x^3 + y^3$ is greater than zero.

However, (1) alone or (2) alone is not sufficient because since the cube of a negative number is negative we could have $x^3 + y^3$ equal zero, and then the value of $x^3 - y^3$ may not be determined. For example, $x = 1$, $y = 1$ and $x = 1$, $y = -1$ show (1) alone is not sufficient, and $x = 2$, $y = 2$ and $x = -2$, $y = 2$ show (2) alone is not sufficient.

TEST YOURSELF

Answer Sheet
SAMPLE TEST 1

Section 1

1 Ⓐ Ⓑ Ⓒ Ⓓ Ⓔ	6 Ⓐ Ⓑ Ⓒ Ⓓ Ⓔ	11 Ⓐ Ⓑ Ⓒ Ⓓ Ⓔ	16 Ⓐ Ⓑ Ⓒ Ⓓ Ⓔ	21 Ⓐ Ⓑ Ⓒ Ⓓ Ⓔ
2 Ⓐ Ⓑ Ⓒ Ⓓ Ⓔ	7 Ⓐ Ⓑ Ⓒ Ⓓ Ⓔ	12 Ⓐ Ⓑ Ⓒ Ⓓ Ⓔ	17 Ⓐ Ⓑ Ⓒ Ⓓ Ⓔ	22 Ⓐ Ⓑ Ⓒ Ⓓ Ⓔ
3 Ⓐ Ⓑ Ⓒ Ⓓ Ⓔ	8 Ⓐ Ⓑ Ⓒ Ⓓ Ⓔ	13 Ⓐ Ⓑ Ⓒ Ⓓ Ⓔ	18 Ⓐ Ⓑ Ⓒ Ⓓ Ⓔ	23 Ⓐ Ⓑ Ⓒ Ⓓ Ⓔ
4 Ⓐ Ⓑ Ⓒ Ⓓ Ⓔ	9 Ⓐ Ⓑ Ⓒ Ⓓ Ⓔ	14 Ⓐ Ⓑ Ⓒ Ⓓ Ⓔ	19 Ⓐ Ⓑ Ⓒ Ⓓ Ⓔ	24 Ⓐ Ⓑ Ⓒ Ⓓ Ⓔ
5 Ⓐ Ⓑ Ⓒ Ⓓ Ⓔ	10 Ⓐ Ⓑ Ⓒ Ⓓ Ⓔ	15 Ⓐ Ⓑ Ⓒ Ⓓ Ⓔ	20 Ⓐ Ⓑ Ⓒ Ⓓ Ⓔ	25 Ⓐ Ⓑ Ⓒ Ⓓ Ⓔ

Section 2

1 Ⓐ Ⓑ Ⓒ Ⓓ Ⓔ	6 Ⓐ Ⓑ Ⓒ Ⓓ Ⓔ	11 Ⓐ Ⓑ Ⓒ Ⓓ Ⓔ	16 Ⓐ Ⓑ Ⓒ Ⓓ Ⓔ	21 Ⓐ Ⓑ Ⓒ Ⓓ Ⓔ
2 Ⓐ Ⓑ Ⓒ Ⓓ Ⓔ	7 Ⓐ Ⓑ Ⓒ Ⓓ Ⓔ	12 Ⓐ Ⓑ Ⓒ Ⓓ Ⓔ	17 Ⓐ Ⓑ Ⓒ Ⓓ Ⓔ	22 Ⓐ Ⓑ Ⓒ Ⓓ Ⓔ
3 Ⓐ Ⓑ Ⓒ Ⓓ Ⓔ	8 Ⓐ Ⓑ Ⓒ Ⓓ Ⓔ	13 Ⓐ Ⓑ Ⓒ Ⓓ Ⓔ	18 Ⓐ Ⓑ Ⓒ Ⓓ Ⓔ	23 Ⓐ Ⓑ Ⓒ Ⓓ Ⓔ
4 Ⓐ Ⓑ Ⓒ Ⓓ Ⓔ	9 Ⓐ Ⓑ Ⓒ Ⓓ Ⓔ	14 Ⓐ Ⓑ Ⓒ Ⓓ Ⓔ	19 Ⓐ Ⓑ Ⓒ Ⓓ Ⓔ	24 Ⓐ Ⓑ Ⓒ Ⓓ Ⓔ
5 Ⓐ Ⓑ Ⓒ Ⓓ Ⓔ	10 Ⓐ Ⓑ Ⓒ Ⓓ Ⓔ	15 Ⓐ Ⓑ Ⓒ Ⓓ Ⓔ	20 Ⓐ Ⓑ Ⓒ Ⓓ Ⓔ	25 Ⓐ Ⓑ Ⓒ Ⓓ Ⓔ

Section 3

1 Ⓐ Ⓑ Ⓒ Ⓓ Ⓔ	6 Ⓐ Ⓑ Ⓒ Ⓓ Ⓔ	11 Ⓐ Ⓑ Ⓒ Ⓓ Ⓔ	16 Ⓐ Ⓑ Ⓒ Ⓓ Ⓔ	21 Ⓐ Ⓑ Ⓒ Ⓓ Ⓔ
2 Ⓐ Ⓑ Ⓒ Ⓓ Ⓔ	7 Ⓐ Ⓑ Ⓒ Ⓓ Ⓔ	12 Ⓐ Ⓑ Ⓒ Ⓓ Ⓔ	17 Ⓐ Ⓑ Ⓒ Ⓓ Ⓔ	22 Ⓐ Ⓑ Ⓒ Ⓓ Ⓔ
3 Ⓐ Ⓑ Ⓒ Ⓓ Ⓔ	8 Ⓐ Ⓑ Ⓒ Ⓓ Ⓔ	13 Ⓐ Ⓑ Ⓒ Ⓓ Ⓔ	18 Ⓐ Ⓑ Ⓒ Ⓓ Ⓔ	23 Ⓐ Ⓑ Ⓒ Ⓓ Ⓔ
4 Ⓐ Ⓑ Ⓒ Ⓓ Ⓔ	9 Ⓐ Ⓑ Ⓒ Ⓓ Ⓔ	14 Ⓐ Ⓑ Ⓒ Ⓓ Ⓔ	19 Ⓐ Ⓑ Ⓒ Ⓓ Ⓔ	24 Ⓐ Ⓑ Ⓒ Ⓓ Ⓔ
5 Ⓐ Ⓑ Ⓒ Ⓓ Ⓔ	10 Ⓐ Ⓑ Ⓒ Ⓓ Ⓔ	15 Ⓐ Ⓑ Ⓒ Ⓓ Ⓔ	20 Ⓐ Ⓑ Ⓒ Ⓓ Ⓔ	25 Ⓐ Ⓑ Ⓒ Ⓓ Ⓔ

Section 4

1 Ⓐ Ⓑ Ⓒ Ⓓ Ⓔ	6 Ⓐ Ⓑ Ⓒ Ⓓ Ⓔ	11 Ⓐ Ⓑ Ⓒ Ⓓ Ⓔ	16 Ⓐ Ⓑ Ⓒ Ⓓ Ⓔ	21 Ⓐ Ⓑ Ⓒ Ⓓ Ⓔ
2 Ⓐ Ⓑ Ⓒ Ⓓ Ⓔ	7 Ⓐ Ⓑ Ⓒ Ⓓ Ⓔ	12 Ⓐ Ⓑ Ⓒ Ⓓ Ⓔ	17 Ⓐ Ⓑ Ⓒ Ⓓ Ⓔ	22 Ⓐ Ⓑ Ⓒ Ⓓ Ⓔ
3 Ⓐ Ⓑ Ⓒ Ⓓ Ⓔ	8 Ⓐ Ⓑ Ⓒ Ⓓ Ⓔ	13 Ⓐ Ⓑ Ⓒ Ⓓ Ⓔ	18 Ⓐ Ⓑ Ⓒ Ⓓ Ⓔ	23 Ⓐ Ⓑ Ⓒ Ⓓ Ⓔ
4 Ⓐ Ⓑ Ⓒ Ⓓ Ⓔ	9 Ⓐ Ⓑ Ⓒ Ⓓ Ⓔ	14 Ⓐ Ⓑ Ⓒ Ⓓ Ⓔ	19 Ⓐ Ⓑ Ⓒ Ⓓ Ⓔ	24 Ⓐ Ⓑ Ⓒ Ⓓ Ⓔ
5 Ⓐ Ⓑ Ⓒ Ⓓ Ⓔ	10 Ⓐ Ⓑ Ⓒ Ⓓ Ⓔ	15 Ⓐ Ⓑ Ⓒ Ⓓ Ⓔ	20 Ⓐ Ⓑ Ⓒ Ⓓ Ⓔ	25 Ⓐ Ⓑ Ⓒ Ⓓ Ⓔ

Section 5

1 Ⓐ Ⓑ Ⓒ Ⓓ Ⓔ	6 Ⓐ Ⓑ Ⓒ Ⓓ Ⓔ	11 Ⓐ Ⓑ Ⓒ Ⓓ Ⓔ	16 Ⓐ Ⓑ Ⓒ Ⓓ Ⓔ	21 Ⓐ Ⓑ Ⓒ Ⓓ Ⓔ
2 Ⓐ Ⓑ Ⓒ Ⓓ Ⓔ	7 Ⓐ Ⓑ Ⓒ Ⓓ Ⓔ	12 Ⓐ Ⓑ Ⓒ Ⓓ Ⓔ	17 Ⓐ Ⓑ Ⓒ Ⓓ Ⓔ	22 Ⓐ Ⓑ Ⓒ Ⓓ Ⓔ
3 Ⓐ Ⓑ Ⓒ Ⓓ Ⓔ	8 Ⓐ Ⓑ Ⓒ Ⓓ Ⓔ	13 Ⓐ Ⓑ Ⓒ Ⓓ Ⓔ	18 Ⓐ Ⓑ Ⓒ Ⓓ Ⓔ	23 Ⓐ Ⓑ Ⓒ Ⓓ Ⓔ
4 Ⓐ Ⓑ Ⓒ Ⓓ Ⓔ	9 Ⓐ Ⓑ Ⓒ Ⓓ Ⓔ	14 Ⓐ Ⓑ Ⓒ Ⓓ Ⓔ	19 Ⓐ Ⓑ Ⓒ Ⓓ Ⓔ	24 Ⓐ Ⓑ Ⓒ Ⓓ Ⓔ
5 Ⓐ Ⓑ Ⓒ Ⓓ Ⓔ	10 Ⓐ Ⓑ Ⓒ Ⓓ Ⓔ	15 Ⓐ Ⓑ Ⓒ Ⓓ Ⓔ	20 Ⓐ Ⓑ Ⓒ Ⓓ Ⓔ	25 Ⓐ Ⓑ Ⓒ Ⓓ Ⓔ

Section 6

1 Ⓐ Ⓑ Ⓒ Ⓓ Ⓔ	6 Ⓐ Ⓑ Ⓒ Ⓓ Ⓔ	11 Ⓐ Ⓑ Ⓒ Ⓓ Ⓔ	16 Ⓐ Ⓑ Ⓒ Ⓓ Ⓔ	21 Ⓐ Ⓑ Ⓒ Ⓓ Ⓔ
2 Ⓐ Ⓑ Ⓒ Ⓓ Ⓔ	7 Ⓐ Ⓑ Ⓒ Ⓓ Ⓔ	12 Ⓐ Ⓑ Ⓒ Ⓓ Ⓔ	17 Ⓐ Ⓑ Ⓒ Ⓓ Ⓔ	22 Ⓐ Ⓑ Ⓒ Ⓓ Ⓔ
3 Ⓐ Ⓑ Ⓒ Ⓓ Ⓔ	8 Ⓐ Ⓑ Ⓒ Ⓓ Ⓔ	13 Ⓐ Ⓑ Ⓒ Ⓓ Ⓔ	18 Ⓐ Ⓑ Ⓒ Ⓓ Ⓔ	23 Ⓐ Ⓑ Ⓒ Ⓓ Ⓔ
4 Ⓐ Ⓑ Ⓒ Ⓓ Ⓔ	9 Ⓐ Ⓑ Ⓒ Ⓓ Ⓔ	14 Ⓐ Ⓑ Ⓒ Ⓓ Ⓔ	19 Ⓐ Ⓑ Ⓒ Ⓓ Ⓔ	24 Ⓐ Ⓑ Ⓒ Ⓓ Ⓔ
5 Ⓐ Ⓑ Ⓒ Ⓓ Ⓔ	10 Ⓐ Ⓑ Ⓒ Ⓓ Ⓔ	15 Ⓐ Ⓑ Ⓒ Ⓓ Ⓔ	20 Ⓐ Ⓑ Ⓒ Ⓓ Ⓔ	25 Ⓐ Ⓑ Ⓒ Ⓓ Ⓔ

Section 7

1 Ⓐ Ⓑ Ⓒ Ⓓ Ⓔ	6 Ⓐ Ⓑ Ⓒ Ⓓ Ⓔ	11 Ⓐ Ⓑ Ⓒ Ⓓ Ⓔ	16 Ⓐ Ⓑ Ⓒ Ⓓ Ⓔ	21 Ⓐ Ⓑ Ⓒ Ⓓ Ⓔ
2 Ⓐ Ⓑ Ⓒ Ⓓ Ⓔ	7 Ⓐ Ⓑ Ⓒ Ⓓ Ⓔ	12 Ⓐ Ⓑ Ⓒ Ⓓ Ⓔ	17 Ⓐ Ⓑ Ⓒ Ⓓ Ⓔ	22 Ⓐ Ⓑ Ⓒ Ⓓ Ⓔ
3 Ⓐ Ⓑ Ⓒ Ⓓ Ⓔ	8 Ⓐ Ⓑ Ⓒ Ⓓ Ⓔ	13 Ⓐ Ⓑ Ⓒ Ⓓ Ⓔ	18 Ⓐ Ⓑ Ⓒ Ⓓ Ⓔ	23 Ⓐ Ⓑ Ⓒ Ⓓ Ⓔ
4 Ⓐ Ⓑ Ⓒ Ⓓ Ⓔ	9 Ⓐ Ⓑ Ⓒ Ⓓ Ⓔ	14 Ⓐ Ⓑ Ⓒ Ⓓ Ⓔ	19 Ⓐ Ⓑ Ⓒ Ⓓ Ⓔ	24 Ⓐ Ⓑ Ⓒ Ⓓ Ⓔ
5 Ⓐ Ⓑ Ⓒ Ⓓ Ⓔ	10 Ⓐ Ⓑ Ⓒ Ⓓ Ⓔ	15 Ⓐ Ⓑ Ⓒ Ⓓ Ⓔ	20 Ⓐ Ⓑ Ⓒ Ⓓ Ⓔ	25 Ⓐ Ⓑ Ⓒ Ⓓ Ⓔ

✂ Cut along dashed line to remove answer sheet.

9 SAMPLE TEST 1
with Answers and Analysis

Writing Assessment

Part I

TIME: 30 minutes

Directions: Write a clear, logical, and well-organized response to the following issue or argument. Your response should be in the form of a short essay, following the conventions of standard written English. Your answer should fit on three pages of lined $8\frac{1}{2}" \times 11"$ paper. Write legibly. Essays that are illegible or that are written on a topic other than the one outlined in the question will not be scored.

The Japanese always have to consult a companion or call a conference to solve even the most trivial things. In India, there are definite rules for family members (and this is also true for other social groups), so that when one wants to do something, one knows whether it is all right by following those rules. Because of the rule system, things get done more quickly in India.

Discuss how logically persuasive you find the above argument. In presenting your point of view, analyze the sort of reasoning used and its supporting evidence. In addition, state what further evidence, if any, would make the argument more sound and convincing or would make you better able to evaluate its conclusion.

Part II

TIME: 30 minutes

Directions: Write a clear, logical, and well-organized response to the following issue or argument. Your response should be in the form of a short essay, following the conventions of standard written English. Your answer should fit on three pages of lined $8\frac{1}{2}" \times 11"$ paper. Write legibly. Essays that are illegible or that are written on a topic other than the one outlined in the question will not be scored.

The economic penetration by multinational corporations shapes and distorts cultural patterns in developing countries. The Westernization, particularly the Americanization, of culture presents a formidable threat to the cultural integrity of the non-Western world. Nevertheless, the know-how of these corporations is necessary to fuel the economic development of developing countries.

Which of the attributes of the multinational corporation do you agree with: a contributor to growth or a threat to culture? Support your point of view with specific reasons or examples that you have observed or read about.

STOP

IF THERE IS STILL TIME REMAINING,
YOU MAY REVIEW THE QUESTIONS IN THIS SECTION ONLY.
YOU MAY NOT TURN TO ANY OTHER SECTION OF THE TEST.

1 1 1 1 1 1 1 1 1 1 1

Section 1

TIME: 30 minutes
25 Questions

Directions: This part contains three reading passages. You are to read each one carefully. When answering the questions you *will* be allowed to refer back to the passages. The questions are based on what is *stated* or *implied* in each passage.

Passage 1:

These huge waves wreak terrific damage when they crash on the shores of distant lands or continents. Under a perfectly sunny sky and from an apparently calm sea, a wall of water may break twenty or thirty feet high over beaches and waterfronts, crushing houses and drowning unsuspecting residents and bathers in its path.

How are these waves formed? When a submarine earthquake occurs, it is likely to set up a tremendous amount of shock, disturbing the quiet waters of the deep ocean. This disturbance travels to the surface and forms a huge swell in the ocean many miles across. It rolls outward in all directions, and the water lowers in the center as another swell looms up. Thus, a series of concentric swells are formed similar to those made when a coin or small pebble is dropped into a basin of water. The big difference is in the size. Each of the concentric rings of basin water traveling out toward the edge is only about an inch across and less than a quarter of an inch high. The swells in the ocean are sometimes nearly a mile wide and rise to several multiples of ten feet in height.

Many of us have heard about these waves, often referred to by their Japanese name of "tsunami." For ages they have been dreaded in the Pacific, as no shore has been free from them. An underwater earthquake in the Aleutian Islands could start a swell that would break along the shores and cause severe damage in the southern part of Chile in South America. These waves travel hundreds of miles an hour, and one can understand how they would crash as violent breakers when caused to drag in the shallow waters of a coast.

Nothing was done about tsunamis until after World War II. In 1947 a particularly bad submarine earthquake took place south of the Aleutian Islands. A few hours later, people bathing in the sun along the quiet shores of Hawaii were dashed to death and shore-line property became a mass of shambles because a series of monstrous, breaking swells crashed along the shore and drove far inland. Hundreds of lives were lost in this catastrophe, and millions upon millions of dollars' worth of damage was done.

Hawaii (at that time a territory) and other Pacific areas then asked the U.S. Coast and Geodetic Survey to attempt to forecast these killer waves. With the blessing of the government, the Coast and Geodetic Survey initiated a program in 1948 known as the Seismic Seawave Warning System, using the earthquake-monitoring facilities of the agency, together with the world seismological data center, to locate submarine earthquakes as soon as they might occur. With this information they could then tell how severe a submarine earthquake was and could set up a tracking chart, with the center over the area of the earthquake, which would show by concentric time belts the rate of travel of the resulting wave. This system would indicate when and where, along the shores of the Pacific, the swells caused by the submarine earthquakes would strike.

1. One surprising aspect of the waves discussed in the passage is the fact that they
   (A) are formed in concentric patterns
   (B) often strike during clear weather
   (C) arise under conditions of cold temperature
   (D) are produced by deep swells
   (E) may be forecast scientifically

GO ON TO THE NEXT PAGE ➤

1 1 1 1 1 1 1 1 1 1 1

2. The waves discussed in the passage often strike

(A) along the coasts of the Aleutian Islands
(B) in regions outside the area monitored by the Coast and Geodetic Survey
(C) at great distances from their place of origin
(D) at the same time as the occurrence of earthquakes
(E) in areas outside the Pacific region

3. It is believed that the waves are caused by

(A) seismic changes
(B) concentric time belts
(C) atmospheric conditions
(D) underwater earthquakes
(E) storms

4. The normal maximum width of the waves is approximately

(A) five feet
(B) ten feet
(C) one mile
(D) five miles
(E) thirty miles

5. The U.S. Coast and Geodetic Survey set up a program to

I. Prevent submarine earthquakes
II. Locate submarine earthquakes
III. Determine the severity of submarine earthquakes

(A) I only
(B) III only
(C) I and II only
(D) II and III only
(E) I, II, and III

6. Nothing was done about the waves until

(A) insurance could not cover damages
(B) the outbreak of World War II
(C) a solution was found
(D) millions of dollars worth of damage was incurred in Hawaii
(E) large areas in Chile were devastated

7. The movement of the waves has been measured at a speed of

(A) 30 miles an hour
(B) 40 miles an hour
(C) 50 miles an hour
(D) 100 miles an hour
(E) more than a hundred miles an hour

8. According to the passage, the waves occur most frequently in the area of

(A) the Eastern U.S. seaboard
(B) the Pacific
(C) Argentina
(D) Western Europe
(E) Asia

9. Given present wave-tracking systems, scientists can forecast all of the following *except*

(A) the severity of underwater earthquakes
(B) the wave's rate of travel
(C) when a wave will strike
(D) where a wave will strike
(E) the height of the wave

GO ON TO THE NEXT PAGE ➤

Passage 2:

This passage was written in 1972.

The United States economy made progress in reducing unemployment and moderating inflation. On the international side, this year was much calmer than last. Nevertheless, continuing imbalances in the pattern of world trade contributed to intermittent strains in the foreign exchange markets. These strains intensified to crisis proportions, precipitating a further devaluation of the dollar.

The domestic economy expanded in a remarkably vigorous and steady fashion.... The resurgence in consumer confidence was reflected in the higher proportion of incomes spent for goods and services and the marked increase in consumer willingness to take on installment debt. A parallel strengthening in business psychology was manifested in a stepped-up rate of plant and equipment spending and a gradual pickup in outlays for inventory. Confidence in the economy was also reflected in the strength of the stock market and in the stability of the bond market.... For the year as a whole, consumer and business sentiment benefited from rising public expectations that a resolution of the conflict in Vietnam was in prospect and that East-West tensions were easing.

The underpinnings of the business expansion were to be found in part in the stimulative monetary and fiscal policies that had been pursued. Moreover, the restoration of sounder liquidity positions and tighter management control of production efficiency had also helped lay the groundwork for a strong expansion. In addition, the economic policy moves made by the President had served to renew optimism on the business outlook while boosting hopes that inflation would be brought under more effective control. Finally, of course, the economy was able to grow as vigorously as it did because sufficient leeway existed in terms of idle men and machines.

The United States balance of payments deficit declined sharply. Nevertheless, by any other test, the deficit remained very large, and there was actually a substantial deterioration in our trade account to a sizable deficit, almost two thirds of which was with Japan.... While the overall trade performance proved disappointing, there are still good reasons for expecting the delayed impact of devaluation to produce in time a significant strengthening in our trade picture. Given the size of the Japanese component of our trade deficit, however, the outcome will depend importantly on the extent of the corrective measures undertaken by Japan. Also important will be our own efforts in the United States to fashion internal policies consistent with an improvement in our external balance.

The underlying task of public policy for the year ahead—and indeed for the longer run—remained a familiar one: to strike the right balance between encouraging healthy economic growth and avoiding inflationary pressures. With the economy showing sustained and vigorous growth, and with the currency crisis highlighting the need to improve our competitive posture internationally, the emphasis seemed to be shifting to the problem of inflation. The Phase Three program of wage and price restraint can contribute to dampening inflation. Unless productivity growth is unexpectedly large, however, the expansion of real output must eventually begin to slow down to the economy's larger run growth potential if generalized demand pressures on prices are to be avoided. Indeed, while the unemployment rates of a bit over five percent were still too high, it seems doubtful whether the much lower rates of four percent and below often cited as appropriate definitions of full employment do in fact represent feasible goals for the United States economy—unless there are improvements in the structure of labor and product markets and public policies influencing their operation. There is little doubt that overall unemployment rates can be brought down to four percent or less, for a time at least, by sufficient stimulation of aggregate demand. However, the resultant inflationary pressures have in the past proved exceedingly difficult to contain.

10. The passage was most likely published in a

(A) popular magazine
(B) general newspaper
(C) science journal
(D) financial journal
(E) textbook

GO ON TO THE NEXT PAGE ➤

1 1 1 1 1 1 1 1 1 1 1

11. Confidence in the economy was expressed by all of the following except

(A) a strong stock market
(B) a stable bond market
(C) increased installment debt
(D) increased plant and equipment expenditures
(E) rising interest rates

12. During the year in question, public confidence in the economy resulted in part from which of the following occurrences?

I. Possible peace in Vietnam
II. Reduction in East-West tensions
III. An entente with China

(A) I only
(B) III only
(C) I and II only
(D) II and III only
(E) I, II, and III

13. According to the author, business expansion for the period under review was caused largely by

(A) stimulative monetary and fiscal policies
(B) rising interest rates
(C) increased foreign trade
(D) price and wage controls
(E) implementation of the Phase Three program

14. Most of the trade deficit in the balance of payments was attributed to trade with which country?

(A) United Kingdom
(B) Japan
(C) Germany
(D) France
(E) Saudi Arabia

15. Part of the public policy task, as outlined in the passage, is to

(A) cut consumer spending
(B) prevent balance of payments deficits
(C) devalue the dollar
(D) avoid inflationary pressures
(E) increase the balance of trade

16. The Phase Three program contained

(A) higher income taxes
(B) reduced government spending
(C) devaluation of the dollar
(D) productivity measures
(E) wage and price controls

17. The passage states that the unemployment rate at the time the article was written was

(A) 6 percent
(B) a little over 5 percent
(C) 5 percent
(D) a little over 4 percent
(E) 4 percent

GO ON TO THE NEXT PAGE ➤

Passage 3:

Literature is at once the most intimate and the most articulate of the arts. It cannot impart its effect through the senses or the nerves as the other arts can; it is beautiful only through the intelligence; it is the mind speaking to the mind; until it has been put into absolute terms, of an invariable significance, it does not exist at all. It cannot awaken this emotion in one, and that in another; if it fails to express precisely the meaning of the author, if it does not say *him*, it says nothing, and is nothing. So that when a poet has put his heart, much or little, into a poem, and sold it to a magazine, the scandal is greater than when a painter has sold a picture to a patron, or a sculptor has modelled a statue to order. These are artists less articulate and less intimate than the poet; they are more exterior to their work; they are less personally in it; they part with less of themselves in the dicker. It does not change the nature of the case to say that Tennyson and Longfellow and Emerson sold the poems in which they couched the most mystical messages their genius was charged to bear mankind. They submitted to the conditions which none can escape; but that does not justify the conditions, which are none the less the conditions of hucksters because they are imposed upon poets. If it will serve to make my meaning a little clearer, we will suppose that a poet has been crossed in love, or has suffered some real sorrow, like the loss of a wife or child. He pours out his broken heart in verse that shall bring tears of sacred sympathy from his readers, and an editor pays him a hundred dollars for the right of bringing his verse to their notice. It is perfectly true that the poem was not written for these dollars, but it is perfectly true that it was sold for them. The poet must use his emotions to pay his provision bills; he has no other means; society does not propose to pay his bills for him. Yet, and at the end of the ends, the unsophisticated witness finds the transaction ridiculous, finds it repulsive, finds it shabby. Somehow he knows that if our huckstering civilization did not at every moment violate the eternal fitness of things, the poet's song would have been given to the world, and the poet would have been cared for by the whole human brotherhood, as any man should be who does the duty that every man owes it.

The instinctive sense of the dishonor which money-purchase does to art is so strong that sometimes a man of letters who can pay his way otherwise refuses pay for his work, as Lord Byron did, for a while, from a noble pride, and as Count Tolstoy has tried to do, from a noble conscience. But Byron's publisher profited by a generosity which did not reach his readers; and the Countess Tolstoy collects the copyright which her husband foregoes; so that these two eminent instances of protest against business in literature may be said not to have shaken its money basis. I know of no others; but there may be many that I am culpably ignorant of. Still, I doubt if there are enough to affect the fact that Literature is Business as well as Art, and almost as soon. At present business is the only human solidarity; we are all bound together with that chain, whatever interests and tastes and principles separate us.

18. The author implies that writers are

(A) incompetent businessmen
(B) not sufficiently paid for their work
(C) greedy
(D) hucksters
(E) profiting against their will

19. A possible title that best expresses the meaning of the passage would be

(A) *The Man of Letters as a Man of Business*
(B) *Literature and the Arts*
(C) *Progress in Literature*
(D) *Poets and Writers*
(E) *The State of the Arts*

20. The author laments the fact that Tennyson, Longfellow, and Emerson

(A) wrote mystical poems
(B) had to sell their poetry
(C) were not appreciated in their time
(D) were prolific poets
(E) wrote emotional poetry

GO ON TO THE NEXT PAGE ➤

1 1 1 1 1 1 1 1 1 1 1

21. The passage states that authors such as Tennyson "submitted to the conditions which none can escape." What conditions is the author of the passage referring to?

    (A) An unappreciative audience
    (B) A materialistic society
    (C) The fact that writers had to sell their work to survive
    (D) Authors wrote for an esoteric audience
    (E) Authors wrote what the public wanted

22. According to the author, Lord Byron

    (A) refused payment for his work
    (B) combined business with literature
    (C) did not copyright his work
    (D) was well known in the business community
    (E) founded a school for aspiring writers

23. The author of the passage implies that

    (A) society should subsidize artists and writers
    (B) writers should rebel against the business system
    (C) more writers should follow the example set by Lord Byron
    (D) writers should only accept remuneration that will provide them with a basic standard of living
    (E) writers should not attempt to change society

24. The author of the passage proposes that writers and artists

    (A) make the best out of a bad situation
    (B) attempt to induce society to change its values
    (C) withhold their work until they gain recognition
    (D) adopt the principles of commercialism
    (E) adopt the value system of society

25. By accepting payment for works of literature or art, its creators are

    I. writing and painting solely for monetary gain
    II. justifying the practice of art
    III. exchanging their work for remuneration

    (A) I only
    (B) III only
    (C) I and II only
    (D) II and III only
    (E) I, II, and III

STOP

**IF THERE IS STILL TIME REMAINING,
YOU MAY REVIEW THE QUESTIONS IN THIS SECTION ONLY.
YOU MAY NOT TURN TO ANY OTHER SECTION OF THE TEST.**

Section 2

TIME: 25 minutes
17 Questions

Directions: Solve each of the following problems; then indicate the correct answer on the answer sheet.

NOTE: A figure that appears with a problem is drawn as accurately as possible so as to provide information that may help in answering the question. Numbers in this test are real numbers.

1. A trip takes 6 hours to complete. After traveling $\frac{1}{4}$ of an hour, $1\frac{3}{8}$ hours, and $2\frac{1}{3}$ hours, how much time does one need to complete the trip?

   (A) $2\frac{1}{12}$ hours
   (B) 2 hours, $2\frac{1}{2}$ minutes
   (C) 2 hours, 5 minutes
   (D) $2\frac{1}{8}$ hours
   (E) 2 hours, $7\frac{1}{2}$ minutes

2. It takes 30 days to fill a laboratory dish with bacteria. If the size of the bacteria doubles each day, how long did it take for the bacteria to fill one half of the dish?

   (A) 10 days
   (B) 15 days
   (C) 24 days
   (D) 29 days
   (E) 29.5 days

3. A car wash can wash 8 cars in 18 minutes. At this rate, how many cars can the car wash wash in 3 hours?

   (A) 13
   (B) 40.5
   (C) 80
   (D) 125
   (E) 405

GO ON TO THE NEXT PAGE ➤

2 2 2 2 2 2 2 2 2 2 2

4. If the ratio of the areas of 2 squares is 2 : 1, then the ratio of the perimeters of the squares is

(A) 1 : 2
(B) 1: $\sqrt{2}$
(C) $\sqrt{2}$: 1
(D) 2 : 1
(E) 4 : 1

5. There are three types of tickets available for a concert: orchestra, which cost $12 each; balcony, which cost $9 each; and box, which cost $25 each. There were *P* orchestra tickets, *B* balcony tickets, and *R* box tickets sold for the concert. Which of the following expressions gives the percentage of ticket proceeds due to the sale of orchestra tickets?

(A) $100\times\frac{P}{(P+B+R)}$
(B) $100\times\frac{12P}{(12P+9B+25R)}$
(C) $\frac{12P}{(12P+9B+25R)}$
(D) $100\times\frac{(9B+25R)}{(12P+9B+25R)}$
(E) $100\times\frac{(12P+9B+25R)}{(12P)}$

6. City *B* is 5 miles east of City *A*. City *C* is 10 miles southeast of City *B*. Which of the following is the closest to the distance from City *A* to City *C*?

(A) 11 miles
(B) 12 miles
(C) 13 miles
(D) 14 miles
(E) 15 miles

7. If $3x - 2y = 8$, then $4y - 6x$ is:

(A) –16
(B) –8
(C) 8
(D) 16
(E) cannot be determined

8. It costs 10¢ a kilometer to fly and 12¢ a kilometer to drive. If you travel 200 kilometers, flying *x* kilometers of the distance and driving the rest, then the cost of the trip in dollars is

(A) 20
(B) 24
(C) $24 - 2x$
(D) $24 - .02x$
(E) $2{,}400 - 2x$

GO ON TO THE NEXT PAGE ➤

9. If two identical rectangles R_1 and R_2 form a square when placed next to each other, and the length of R_1 is x times the width of R_1, then x is

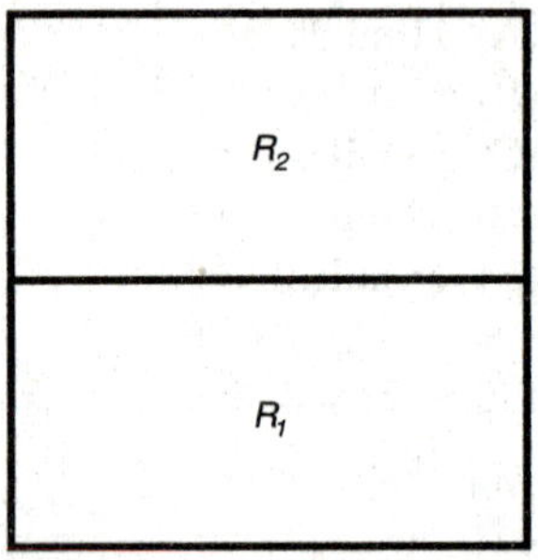

(A) 1
(B) $\frac{3}{2}$
(C) $\frac{5}{4}$
(D) 2
(E) 3

10. If the area of a square increases by 69%, then the side of the square increases by

(A) 13%
(B) 30%
(C) 39%
(D) 69%
(E) 130%

11. There are 30 socks in a drawer. 60% of the socks are red and the rest are blue. What is the minimum number of socks that must be taken from the drawer without looking in order to be certain that at least two blue socks have been chosen?

(A) 2
(B) 3
(C) 14
(D) 16
(E) 20

Use the following table for questions 12–14.

Distribution of Work Hours in a Factory

Number of Workers		*Number of Hours Worked*
20		45–50
15		40–44
25		35–39
16		30–34
4		0–29
80	TOTAL	3,100

12. What percentage of workers worked 40 or more hours?

(A) 18.75
(B) 25
(C) $33\frac{1}{3}$
(D) 40
(E) 43.75

13. The number of workers who worked from 40 to 44 hours is x times the number who worked up to 29 hours, where x is

(A) $\frac{15}{16}$
(B) $3\frac{3}{4}$
(C) 4
(D) 5
(E) $6\frac{1}{4}$

GO ON TO THE NEXT PAGE ➤

2 2 2 2 2 2 2 2 2 2 2

14. Which of the following statements can be inferred from the table?

    I. The average number of hours worked per worker is less than 40.
    II. At least 3 worked more than 48 hours.
    III. More than half of all the workers worked more than 40 hours.

    (A) I only
    (B) II only
    (C) I and II only
    (D) I and III only
    (E) I, II, and III

15. When a truck travels at 60 miles per hour, it uses 30% more gasoline to travel any distance than it does when it travels at 50 miles per hour. The truck can travel 20 miles on a gallon of gas if it is traveling at 50 miles per hour. The truck has only 10 gallons of gas and is 160 miles from its destination. It takes 20 minutes for the truck to stop for gas. How long will it take the truck to reach its final destination if the truck is driven at 60 miles per hour?

    (A) 160 minutes
    (B) 180 minutes
    (C) 190 minutes
    (D) 192 minutes
    (E) 195 minutes

16. Company *A* owns 40% of the stock in the *XYZ* corporation. Company *B* owns 15,000 shares. Company *C* owns all the shares not owned by companies *A* or *B*. How many shares of stock does company *A* own if company *C* has 25% more shares than company *A*?

    (A) 45,000
    (B) 50,000
    (C) 60,000
    (D) 75,000
    (E) 90,000

17. How many squares with sides $\frac{1}{2}$ inch long are needed to cover a rectangle that is 4 feet long and 6 feet wide?

    (A) 24
    (B) 96
    (C) 3,456
    (D) 13,824
    (E) 14,266

STOP

IF THERE IS STILL TIME REMAINING,
YOU MAY REVIEW THE QUESTIONS IN THIS SECTION ONLY.
YOU MAY NOT TURN TO ANY OTHER SECTION OF THE TEST.

Section 3

TIME: 25 minutes
17 Questions

Directions: For each question, choose the best answer among the listed alternatives.

1. Monopoly is characterized by an absence of or decline in competition. The ABC Company realizes that its operations are in competitive industries.

   Which of the following conclusions may be inferred from the above?

   (A) ABC's market is not monopolistic.
   (B) Monopoly is defined as one seller in a market.
   (C) The ABC Company has no domestic competitors.
   (D) The ABC Company is publicly owned.
   (E) The ABC Company is in a service industry.

2. Farmers in the North have observed that heavy frost is usually preceded by a full moon. They are convinced that the full moon somehow generates the frost.

   Which of the following, if true, would weaken the farmers' conviction?

   (A) The temperature must fall below 10 degrees Celsius (50 degrees Fahrenheit) for frost to occur.
   (B) Absence of a cloud cover cools the ground which causes frost.
   (C) Farmers are superstitious.
   (D) No one has proven that the moon causes frost.
   (E) Farmers are not experts in meteorology.

3. Professor Tembel told his class that the method of student evaluation of teachers is not a valid measure of teaching quality. Students should fill out questionnaires at the end of the semester when courses have been completed.

   Which of the following, if true, provides support for Professor Tembel's proposal?

   (A) Professor Tembel received low ratings from his students.
   (B) Students filled out questionnaires after the midterm exam.
   (C) Students are interested in teacher evaluation.
   (D) Teachers are not obligated to use the survey results.
   (E) Student evaluation of teachers is voluntary.

4. The President lobbied for passage of his new trade bill which would liberalize trade with industrialized countries such as Japan, members of the European Community, and Canada.

   Each of the following, if true, could account for the above, except:

   (A) The President is up for re-election and needs to show results.
   (B) Labor unions have petitioned the President to provide more local jobs.
   (C) The trade agreement could bring a *quid pro quo* on pending negotiations.
   (D) Economists claimed that the passage of the bill would increase the country's trade deficit.
   (E) It was politically desirable for a trade bill at the present time.

5. If we are doomed to have local drug rehabilitation centers—and society has determined that we are—then society ought to pay for them.

   Which of the following, if true, would weaken the above argument?

   (A) Drug rehabilitation centers are too expensive to be locally funded.
   (B) Many neighborhood groups oppose rehabilitation centers.
   (C) Drug rehabilitation centers are expensive to maintain.
   (D) Drug addicts may be unwilling to receive treatment.
   (E) A government committee has convinced many groups that local rehabilitation centers are ineffective.

GO ON TO THE NEXT PAGE ➤

6. Surviving this crisis is going to take everything we've got. In addition to ... massive retraining, we may also need subsidies—direct or channeled through the private sector—for a radically expanding service sector. Not merely things like environmental clean-up, but basic human services. (Alvin Toffler, *Previews and Premises* (New York: Bantam Books, 1985), p. 57.)

   Which of the following statements is inconsistent with the above?

   (A) Subsidies are needed to overcome the crisis.
   (B) Environmental controls will be loosened.
   (C) The service sector is going to expand to such an extent that many more workers will be needed.
   (D) The private sector will play a role in retraining workers.
   (E) Before the crisis can end, an environmental clean-up will have to take place.

7. Per-capita income last year was $12,290. Per-capita income is calculated by dividing total aggregate cash income by the total population. Real median income for families headed by a female, with no husband present, was $14,620. Therefore, women wage-earners earned more than the national average.

   Which of the following would, if true, weaken the above conclusion?

   (A) Per-capita income is calculated in real terms.
   (B) In 99 percent of the cases, families headed by a female included no other wage-earner.
   (C) Average income is not significantly different from median income.
   (D) The overall average and per-capita income were the same.
   (E) Only a small proportion of the total wage earners are women family heads.

8. An economist was quoted as saying that the Cost-of-Living index (COL) will go up next month because of a recent increase in the price of fruit and vegetables.

   Which of the following cannot be inferred from the statement?

   (A) The cost of fruits and vegetables has risen sharply.
   (B) Consumers have decreased their consumption of fruits and vegetables.
   (C) The cost of fruit and vegetables is a major item in the COL.
   (D) Food cost changes are reflected quickly in the COL.
   (E) Other items that make up the COL have not significantly decreased in price.

9. The director of the customs administration suggested that customs taxes on automobiles not be reduced as planned by the government because of the high incidence of traffic accidents last year.

   Which of the above statements weakens the argument above?

   I. Although the traffic accident rate last year was high, it was not appreciably higher than previous years and anyway, compulsory insurance covered most physical damage to automobiles and property.
   II. A Commerce Department report showed that the demand for automobiles was highly inelastic. That is, as dealers lowered their prices, sales did not increase appreciably.
   III. A study by the Economics Department at Classics University found that most traffic accidents had been caused by human error although it also concluded that an inadequate road network contributed to at least forty percent of passenger injuries.

   (A) I, but not II and not III.
   (B) II, but not I and not III.
   (C) I and III, but not II.
   (D) II and III, but not I.
   (E) I, II and III.

10. Significant beneficial effects of smoking occur primarily in the area of mental health, and the habit originates in a search for contentment. The life expectancy of our people has increased greatly in recent years; it is possible that the relaxation and contentment and enjoyment produced by smoking has lengthened many lives. Smoking is beneficial.
    Which of the following, if true, weaken the above conclusion?

    (A) That cigarettes are a major health hazard cannot be traced to the willfull act of any human or organization.
    (B) The government earns millions of dollars from the tobacco tax and tens of thousands of civilians are employed in the tobacco industry.
    (C) The evidence cited in the statement covers only one example of the effects of cigarette smoking.
    (D) No mention is made of possible harmful side-effects of smoking.
    (E) No statistical evidence has proven a link between smoking and longevity.

GO ON TO THE NEXT PAGE ➤

11. Many of the convenience foods on the market today, like dry cereals, have less nutrients than natural foods, which were dominant a decade or two ago. Many nutritionists claim that dry cereal gives less nourishment than natural foods like eggs or bacon. Opponents of the nutritionists' views state that examination of grade-school students show less nutritional deficiency than in their parents' time.

    Which of the following, if true, would tend to strengthen the opponents' view?

    (A) Grade school children reported eating no breakfast at all.
    (B) Fewer convenience foods were available to the parents.
    (C) Adults claim to eat convenience foods as well as natural foods.
    (D) Convenience foods can be digested just as quickly as natural foods.
    (E) Consumers are not likely to sacrifice convenience for nutrition.

12. In a world of many trading countries, the trade between two countries need not be balanced for the trade of each to be in global balance. Differing demands and productive capabilities among countries will cause a specific country to have trade deficits with some countries and surpluses with other countries.

    Which of the following conclusions best summarizes the passage above?

    (A) A country's trade will always be in balance even though it runs a deficit with a single country.
    (B) A country's trade deficits and surpluses with other countries always balance out.
    (C) A country's global trade balance is a sign of strength or weakness.
    (D) Countries should not be concerned if they have trade deficits because they will balance out in the long run.
    (E) A country's global trade balance is determined by relative demand and productive capabilities.

13. Foreign investment is composed of direct investment transactions (investment in plant, equipment and land) and securities investment transactions. Throughout the post-World War II period, net increases in U.S. direct investment in Europe (funds outflows) exceeded net new European direct investment in the U.S.

    Each of the following, if true, could help to account for this trend except:

    (A) Land values in Europe were increasing at a faster rate than in the United States.
    (B) Duties on imported goods in Europe were higher than those imposed by the United States.
    (C) The cost of labor (wages) was consistently lower in Europe than in the United States.
    (D) Labor mobility was much higher in the United States than in Europe.
    (E) Corporate liquidity was lower in Europe than in the United States.

14. Most large retail stores hold sales in the month of January. The original idea of price reduction campaigns in January became popular when it was realized that sales of products would generally slow down following the Christmas rush, were it not for some incentive. The lack of demand could be solved by the simple solution of reducing prices.

    There is now an increasing tendency among major department stores in large urban centers to have their "January sales" begin before Christmas, some time before the end of the calendar year. The idea behind this trend is to endeavor to sell the maximum amount of stock at a profit, even if that may not be at the maximum profit.

    Which of the following conclusions cannot be drawn from the above?

    (A) The incidence of "early" January sales results in the lower holdings of stocks with the corollary of lower stock holding costs.
    (B) Demand is a function of price; as you lower price, demand increases.
    (C) Major stores seem to think it makes sense to have the January sales campaigns pre-Christmas.
    (D) It is becoming less popular to start the January sales in the New Year.
    (E) The major department stores do not worry as much about profit maximization as they do about sales maximization.

GO ON TO THE NEXT PAGE ➤

3 3 3 3 3 3 3 3 3 3 3

15. Of the world's largest external-debt countries in 1989, three had the same share of world external-debt as they had in 1980. These three countries may serve as examples of countries that succeeded in holding steady their share of world external-debt.

    Which of the following, if true, would most seriously undermine the idea that these countries serve as examples as described above?

    (A) Of the three countries, two had a much larger share of world external-debt in 1985 than in 1989.
    (B) Some countries strive to reduce their share of world external-debt, not keep it steady.
    (C) The three countries have different rates of economic growth.
    (D) The absolute value of debt of the three countries is different.
    (E) Some countries are more concerned with internal budgets than with external debt.

16. In a famous experiment by Pavlov, when a dog smelled food, it salivated. Subsequently, a bell was rung whenever food was placed near the dog. After a number of trials, only the bell was rung, whereupon the dog would salivate even though no food was present.

    Which of the following conclusions may be drawn from the above experiment?

    (A) Dogs are easily fooled.
    (B) Dogs are motivated only by the sound of a bell.
    (C) The ringing of a bell was associated with food.
    (D) A conclusion cannot be reached on the basis of one experiment.
    (E) Two stimuli are stronger than one.

17. At a political rally at Jefferson Stadium, candidate Smith exclaimed: "Nearly everyone at the rally is behind me. It looks like I am going to be elected."

    Which of the following statements, if true, best supports the above conclusion?

    (A) Smith's opponent also appeared at the rally.
    (B) The rally was attended by almost all the residents of Smith's constituency.
    (C) Smith was never defeated in an election.
    (D) Smith was supported by the local mayor.
    (E) People always vote their emotions.

STOP

IF THERE IS STILL TIME REMAINING,
YOU MAY REVIEW THE QUESTIONS IN THIS SECTION ONLY.
YOU MAY NOT TURN TO ANY OTHER SECTION OF THE TEST.

4 4 4 4 4 4 4 4 4 4 4

Section 4

TIME: 25 minutes
21 Questions

Directions: Each of the following problems has a question and two statements which are labeled (1) and (2). Use the data given in (1) and (2) together with other available information (such as the number of hours in a day, the definition of *clockwise*, mathematical facts, etc.) to decide whether the statements are *sufficient* to answer the question. Then fill in the space.

(A) if you can get the answer from **(1) ALONE** but not from (2) alone
(B) if you can get the answer from **(2) ALONE** but not from (1) alone
(C) if you can get the answer from **BOTH (1) and (2) TOGETHER,** but not from (1) alone or (2) alone
(D) if **EITHER** statement **(1) ALONE OR** statement **(2) ALONE** suffices
(E) if you **CANNOT** get the answer from statements (1) and (2) **TOGETHER,** but need even more data

All numbers used in this section are real numbers. A figure given for a problem is intended to provide information consistent with that in the question, but not necessarily with the additional information contained in the statements.

1. Are two triangles congruent?
   (1) Both triangles are right triangles.
   (2) Both triangles have the same perimeter.

2. Is x greater than zero?
   (1) $x^4 - 16 = 0$
   (2) $x^3 - 8 = 0$

3. If both conveyer belt A and conveyer belt B are used, they can fill a hopper with coal in one hour. How long will it take for conveyer belt A to fill the hopper without conveyer belt B?
   (1) Conveyer belt A moves twice as much coal as conveyer belt B.
   (2) Conveyer belt B would take 3 hours to fill the hopper without belt A.

GO ON TO THE NEXT PAGE ➤

(A) if you can get the answer from **(1) ALONE** but not from (2) alone
(B) if you can get the answer from **(2) ALONE** but not from (1) alone
(C) if you can get the answer from **BOTH (1) and (2) TOGETHER,** but not from (1) alone or (2) alone
(D) if **EITHER** statement **(1) ALONE OR** statement **(2) ALONE** suffices
(E) if you **CANNOT** get the answer from statements (1) and (2) **TOGETHER,** but need even more data

4. A fly crawls around the outside of a circle once. A second fly crawls around the outside of a square once. Which fly travels further?

   (1) The diagonal of the square is equal to the diameter of the circle.
   (2) The fly crawling around the circle took more time to complete his journey than the fly crawling around the square.

5. Is y larger than 1?

   (1) y is larger than 0.
   (2) $y^2 - 4 > 0$.

6. A worker is hired for 6 days. He is paid $2 more for each day of work than he was paid for the preceding day of work. How much was he paid for the first day of work?

   (1) His total wages for the 6 days were $150.
   (2) He was paid 150% of his first day's pay for the sixth day.

7. A car originally sold for $3,000. After a month, the car was discounted x%, and a month later the car's price was discounted y%. Is the car's price after the discounts less than $2,600?

   (1) $y = 10$
   (2) $x = 15$

8. In triangle ABC, find z if $AB = 5$ and $y = 40$.

   (1) $BC = 5$
   (2) The bisector of angle B is perpendicular to AC.

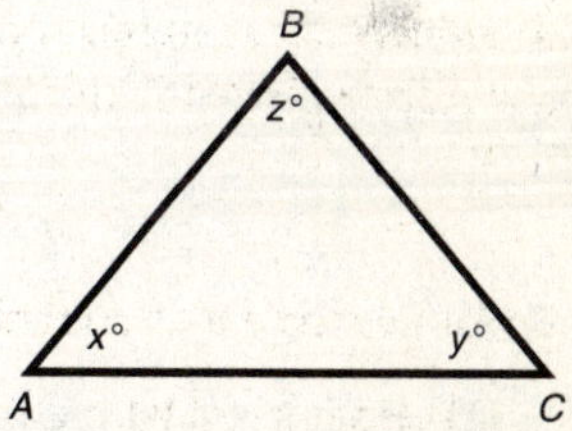

9. How much cardboard will it take to make an open cubical box with no top?

   (1) The area of the bottom of the box is 4 square feet.
   (2) The volume of the box is 8 cubic feet.

GO ON TO THE NEXT PAGE ➤

4 4 4 4 4 4 4 4 4 4 4

(A) if you can get the answer from **(1) ALONE** but not from (2) alone
(B) if you can get the answer from **(2) ALONE** but not from (1) alone
(C) if you can get the answer from **BOTH (1) and (2) TOGETHER,** but not from (1) alone or (2) alone
(D) if **EITHER** statement **(1) ALONE OR** statement **(2) ALONE** suffices
(E) if you **CANNOT** get the answer from statements (1) and (2) **TOGETHER,** but need even more data

10. Is the integer x divisible by 3?

    (1) The last digit in x is 3.
    (2) $x + 5$ is divisible by 6.

11. Is the figure $ABCD$ a rectangle?

    (1) $x = 90$
    (2) $AB = CD$

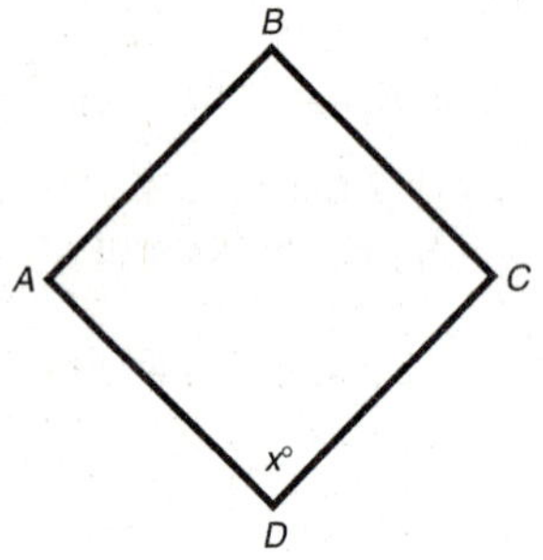

12. A sequence of numbers is given by the rule $a_n = (a_{n-1})^2$. What is a_5?

    (1) $a_1 = -1$
    (2) $a_3 = 1$

13. How much is John's weekly salary?

    (1) John's weekly salary is twice as much as Fred's weekly salary.
    (2) Fred's weekly salary is 40% of the total of Chuck's weekly salary and John's weekly salary.

14. Find $x + 2y$.

    (1) $x + y = 4$
    (2) $2x + 4y = 12$

15. Is angle BAC a right angle?

    (1) $x = 2y$
    (2) $y = 1.5z$

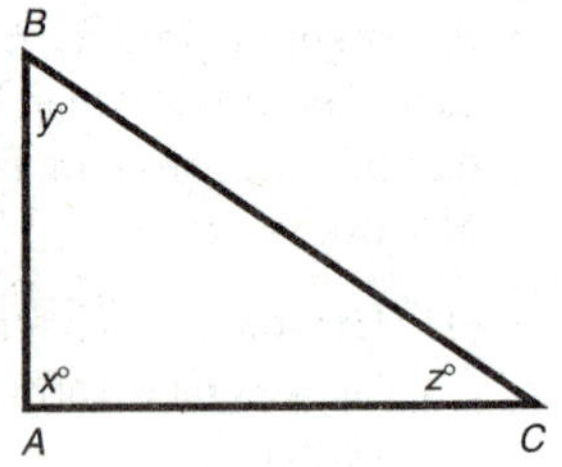

16. If a, b, and c are digits, is $a + b + c$ a multiple of 9? A digit is one of the integers 0, 1, 2, 3, 4, 5, 6, 7, 8, 9.

    (1) The three digit number abc is a multiple of 9.
    (2) $(a \times b) + c$ is a multiple of 9.

GO ON TO THE NEXT PAGE ➤

4 4 4 4 4 4 4 4 4 4 4

(A) if you can get the answer from **(1) ALONE** but not from (2) alone
(B) if you can get the answer from **(2) ALONE** but not from (1) alone
(C) if you can get the answer from **BOTH (1) and (2) TOGETHER,** but not from (1) alone or (2) alone
(D) if **EITHER** statement **(1) ALONE OR** statement **(2) ALONE** suffices
(E) if you **CANNOT** get the answer from statements (1) and (2) **TOGETHER,** but need even more data

17. 50% of the people in Teetown have blue eyes and blond hair. What percent of the people in Teetown have blue eyes but do not have blond hair?

(1) 70% of the people in Teetown have blond hair.
(2) 60% of the people in Teetown have blue eyes.

18. The pentagon *ABCDE* is inscribed in the circle with center *O*. How many degrees is angle *ABC*?

(1) The pentagon *ABCDE* is a regular pentagon.
(2) The radius of the circle is 5 inches.

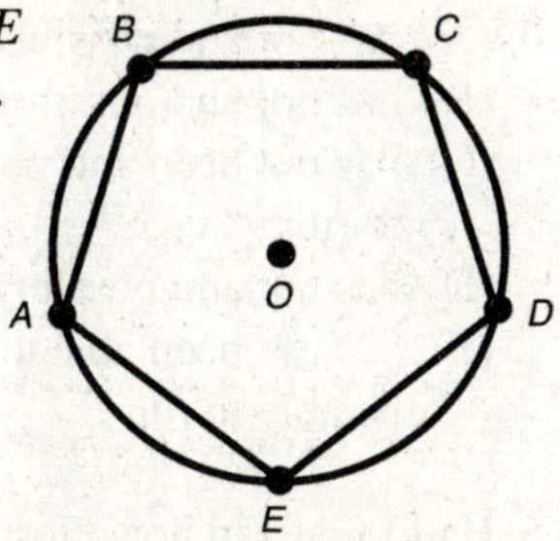

19. What is the area of the circle with center *O*?(*AB* and *DE* are straight lines)

(1) $DE = 5$ inches
(2) $AB = 7$ inches

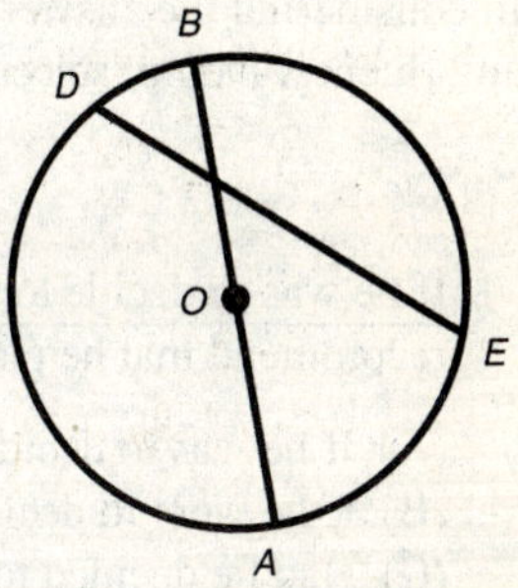

20. Is $k^2 + k - 2 > 0$?

(1) $k < 1$
(2) $k > -1$

21. If a group of 5 craftsmen take 3 hours to finish a job, how long will it take a group of 4 apprentices to do the same job?

(1) An apprentice works at $\frac{2}{3}$ the rate of a craftsman.

(2) The 5 craftsmen and the 4 apprentices working together will take $1\frac{22}{23}$ hours to finish the job.

STOP

IF THERE IS STILL TIME REMAINING,
YOU MAY REVIEW THE QUESTIONS IN THIS SECTION ONLY.
YOU MAY NOT TURN TO ANY OTHER SECTION OF THE TEST.

5 5 5 5 5 5 5 5 5 5 5

Section 5

TIME: 25 minutes
21 Questions

Directions: This test consists of a number of sentences, in each of which some part or the whole is underlined. Each sentence is followed by five alternative versions of the underlined portion. Select an alternative you consider both most correct and most effective according to the requirements of standard written English. Answer A is the same as the original version; if you think the original version is best, select answer A.

In considering the answer choices, be attentive to matters of grammar, diction, and syntax, as well as clarity, precision, and fluency. Do not select an answer that alters the meaning of the original sentence.

1. If he was to decide to go to college, I, for one, would recommend that he plan to go to Yale.
   (A) If he was to decide to go to college,
   (B) If he were to decide to go to college,
   (C) Had he decided to go to college,
   (D) In the event that he decides to go to college,
   (E) Supposing he was to decide to go to college,

2. Except for you and I, everyone brought a present to the party.
   (A) Except for you and I, everyone brought
   (B) With exception of you and I, everyone brought
   (C) Except for you and I, everyone had brought
   (D) Except for you and me, everyone brought
   (E) Except for you and me, everyone had brought

3. When one reads the poetry of the seventeenth century, you find a striking contrast between the philosophy of the Cavalier poets such as Suckling and the attitude of the Metaphysical poets such as Donne.
   (A) When one reads the poetry of the seventeenth century, you find
   (B) When you read the poetry of the seventeenth century, one finds
   (C) When one reads the poetry of the seventeenth century, he finds
   (D) If one reads the poetry of the 17th century, you find
   (E) As you read the poetry of the 17th century, one finds

4. Because of his broken hip, John Jones has not and possibly never will be able to run the mile again.
   (A) has not and possibly never will be able to run
   (B) has not and possibly will never be able to run
   (C) has not been and possibly never would be able to run
   (D) has not and possibly never would be able to run
   (E) has not been able to run and possibly never will be able to run

5. Had I realized how close I was to failing, I would not have gone to the party.
   (A) Had I realized how close
   (B) If I would have realized
   (C) Had I had realized how close
   (D) When I realized how close
   (E) If I realized how close

6. The football team's winning it's first game of the season excited the student body.
   (A) The football team's winning it's first game of the season
   (B) The football team having won it's first game of the season
   (C) The football team's having won it's first game of the season
   (D) The football team's winning its first game of the season
   (E) The football team winning it's first game of the season

GO ON TO THE NEXT PAGE ➤

5 5 5 5 5 5 5 5 5 5 5

7. Anyone interested in the use of computers can learn much <u>if you have access</u> to a state-of-the-art microcomputer.

   (A) if you have access to
   (B) if he has access to
   (C) if access is available to
   (D) by access to
   (E) from access to

8. <u>No student had ought to be put into a situation where</u> he has to choose between his loyalty to his friends and his duty to the class.

   (A) No student had ought to be put into a situation where
   (B) No student had ought to be put into a situation in which
   (C) No student should be put into a situation where
   (D) No student ought to be put into a situation in which
   (E) No student ought to be put into a situation where

9. <u>Being a realist,</u> I could not accept his statement that supernatural beings had caused the disturbance.

   (A) Being a realist,
   (B) Since I am a realist,
   (C) Being that I am a realist,
   (D) Being as I am a realist,
   (E) Realist that I am,

10. The reason <u>I came late to class today is because</u> the bus broke down.

    (A) I came late to class today is because
    (B) why I came late to class today is because
    (C) I was late to school today is because
    (D) that I was late to school today is because
    (E) I came late to class today is that

11. The grocer <u>hadn't hardly any of those kind</u> of canned goods.

    (A) hadn't hardly any of those kind
    (B) hadn't hardly any of those kinds
    (C) had hardly any of those kind
    (D) had hardly any of those kinds
    (E) had scarcely any of those kind

12. <u>Having stole the money, the police searched the thief.</u>

    (A) Having stole the money, the police searched the thief.
    (B) Having stolen the money, the thief was searched by the police.
    (C) Having stolen the money, the police searched the thief.
    (D) Having stole the money, the thief was searched by the police.
    (E) Being that he stole the money, the police searched the thief.

13. The child is <u>neither encouraged to be critical or to examine</u> all the evidence for his opinion.

    (A) neither encouraged to be critical or to examine
    (B) neither encouraged to be critical nor to examine
    (C) either encouraged to be critical or to examine
    (D) encouraged either to be critical nor to examine
    (E) not encouraged either to be critical or to examine

14. The process by which the community <u>influence the actions of its members</u> is known as social control.

    (A) influence the actions of its members
    (B) influences the actions of its members
    (C) had influenced the actions of its members
    (D) influences the actions of their members
    (E) will influence the actions of its members

15. To be sure, there would be scarcely no time left over for other things if school children <u>would have been expected to have considered</u> all sides of every matter on which they hold opinions.

    (A) would have been expected to have considered
    (B) should have been expected to have considered
    (C) were expected to consider
    (D) will be expected to have been considered
    (E) were expected to be considered

GO ON TO THE NEXT PAGE ➤

5 5 5 5 5 5 5 5 5 5 5

16. Depending on skillful suggestion, argument is seldom used in advertising.

(A) Depending on skillful suggestion, argument is seldom used in advertising.
(B) Argument is seldom used by advertisers, who depend instead on skillful suggestion.
(C) Skillfull suggestion is depended on by advertisers instead of argument.
(D) Suggestion, which is more skillful, is used in place of argument by advertisers.
(E) Instead of suggestion, depending on argument is used by skillful advertisers.

17. When this war is over, no nation will either be isolated in war or peace.

(A) either be isolated in war or peace
(B) be either isolated in war or peace
(C) be isolated in neither war nor peace
(D) be isolated either in war or in peace
(E) be isolated neither in war or peace

18. Each will be within trading distance of all the others and will be able to strike them.

(A) within trading distance of all the others and will be able to strike them
(B) near enough to trade with and strike all the others
(C) trading and striking the others
(D) within trading and striking distance of all the others
(E) able to strike and trade with all the others

19. However many mistakes have been made in our past, the tradition of America, not only the champion of freedom but also fair play, still lives among millions who can see light and hope scarcely anywhere else.

(A) not only the champion of freedom but also fair play,
(B) the champion of not only freedom but also of fair play,
(C) the champion not only of freedom but also of fair play,
(D) not only the champion but also freedom and fair play,
(E) not the champion of freedom only, but also fair play,

20. In giving expression to the play instincts of the human race, new vigor and effectiveness are afforded by recreation to the body and to the mind.

(A) new vigor and effectiveness are afforded by recreation to the body and to the mind
(B) recreation affords new vigor and effectiveness to the body and to the mind
(C) there are afforded new vigor and effectiveness to the body and to the mind
(D) by recreation the body and mind are afforded new vigor and effectiveness
(E) the body and the mind afford new vigor and effectiveness to themselves by recreation

21. Play being recognized as an important factor in improving mental and physical health and thereby reducing human misery and poverty.

(A) Play being recognized as
(B) By recognizing play as
(C) Their recognizing play as
(D) Recognition of it being
(E) Play is recognized as

STOP

IF THERE IS STILL TIME REMAINING,
YOU MAY REVIEW THE QUESTIONS IN THIS SECTION ONLY.
YOU MAY NOT TURN TO ANY OTHER SECTION OF THE TEST.

6 6 6 6 6 6 6 6 6 6 6

Section 6

TIME: 25 minutes
17 Questions

Directions: Solve each of the following problems; then indicate the correct answer on the answer sheet.

NOTE: A figure that appears with a problem is drawn as accurately as possible so as to provide information that may help in answering the question. Numbers in this test are real numbers.

Use the following graphs for questions 1–3.

AVERAGE ANNUAL RECEIPTS AND OUTLAYS OF U.S. GOVERNMENT 1967–1970 IN PERCENTAGE

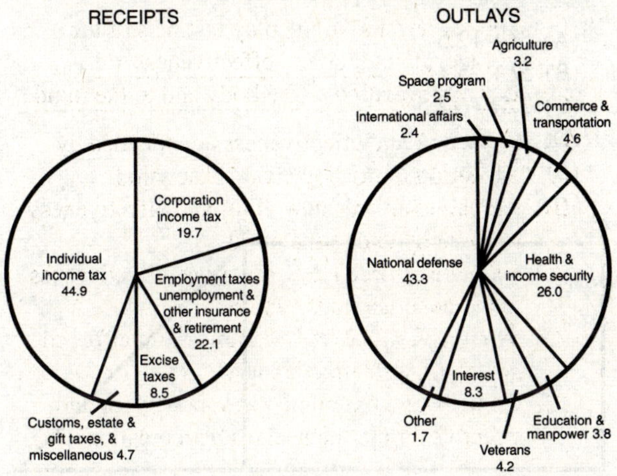

1. If the annual average receipts from the corporation income tax during the years 1967–1970 equal x, then the average annual receipts during this period were about

(A) $\frac{x}{4}$
(B) x^2
(C) $3x$
(D) $5x$
(E) x^5

GO ON TO THE NEXT PAGE ➤

6 6 6 6 6 6 6 6 6 6 6

2. The average annual combined outlay for veterans, education and manpower, and health and income security was roughly what fraction of the average annual outlays?

(A) $\frac{1}{4}$

(B) $\frac{1}{3}$

(C) $\frac{2}{5}$

(D) $\frac{1}{2}$

(E) $\frac{2}{3}$

3. If $\frac{5}{8}$ of the average annual outlays for agriculture was spent in the western U.S., what percentage of average annual outlays was spent on agriculture in the western U.S.?

(A) $\frac{5}{8}$

(B) 1

(C) $1\frac{1}{4}$

(D) 2

(E) 3.2

4. In a group of people solicited by a charity, 30% contributed \$40 each, 45% contributed \$20 each, and the rest contributed \$12 each. What percentage of the total contributed came from people who gave \$40?

(A) 25%
(B) 30%
(C) 40%
(D) 45%
(E) 50%

5. A trapezoid *ABCD* is formed by adding the isosceles right triangle *BCE* with base 5 inches to the rectangle *ABED* where *DE* is *t* inches. What is the area of the trapezoid in square inches?

(A) $5t + 12.5$
(B) $5t + 25$
(C) $2.5t + 12.5$
(D) $(t + 5)^2$
(E) $t^2 + 25$

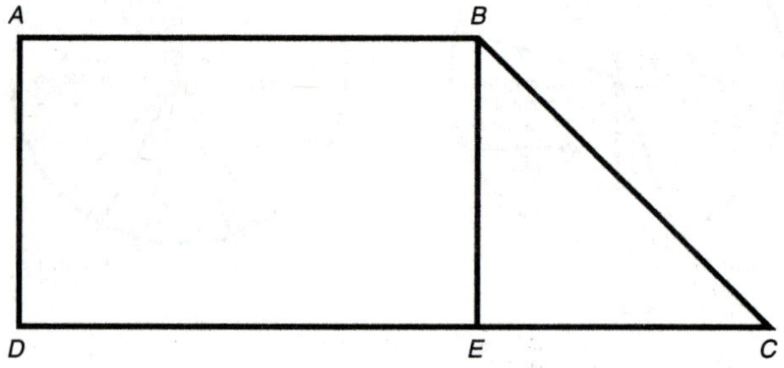

GO ON TO THE NEXT PAGE ➤

6 6 6 6 6 6 6 6 6 6 6

6. A manufacturer of jam wants to make a profit of \$75 when he sells 300 jars of jam. It costs 65¢ each to make the first 100 jars of jam and 55¢ each to make each jar after the first 100. What price should he charge for the 300 jars of jam?

(A) \$75
(B) \$175
(C) \$225
(D) \$240
(E) \$250

7. A car traveled 75% of the way from town *A* to town *B* by traveling for *T* hours at an average speed of *V* mph. The car travels at an average speed of *S* mph for the remaining part of the trip. Which of the following expressions represents the time the car traveled at *S* mph?

(A) $\frac{VT}{S}$
(B) $\frac{VS}{4T}$
(C) $\frac{4VT}{3S}$
(D) $\frac{3S}{VT}$
(E) $\frac{VT}{3S}$

8. A company makes a profit of 7% selling goods which cost \$2,000; it also makes a profit of 6% selling a machine that cost the company \$5,000. How much total profit did the company make on both transactions?

(A) \$300
(B) \$400
(C) \$420
(D) \$440
(E) \$490

9. If $\frac{x}{y} = \frac{3}{z}$, then $9y^2$ equals

(A) $\frac{x^2}{9}$
(B) x^3z
(C) x^2z^2
(D) $3x^2$
(E) $\left(\frac{1}{9}\right)x^2z^2$

10. The operation * applied to a number gives as its result 10 subtracted from twice the number. What is *(*9)?

(A) −11
(B) 6
(C) 8
(D) 9
(E) 36

GO ON TO THE NEXT PAGE ➤

6 6 6 6 6 6 6 6 6 6 6

11. *ABCD* is a rectangle. The length of *BE* is 4 and the length of *EC* is 6. The area of triangle *BEA* plus the area of triangle *DCE* minus the area of triangle *AED* is

(A) 0
(B) .4 of the area of triangle *AEB*
(C) .5 of the area of triangle *AED*
(D) .5 of the area of *ABCD*
(E) cannot be determined

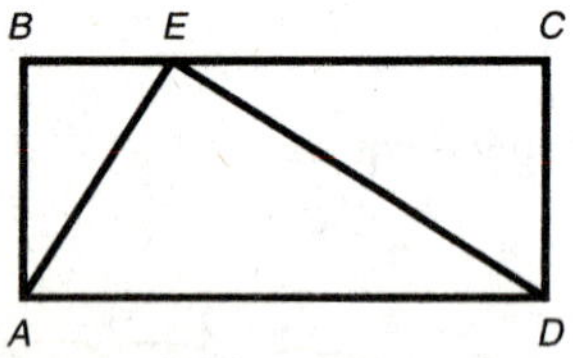

12. 36 identical chairs must be arranged in rows with the same number of chairs in each row. Each row must contain at least three chairs and there must be at least three rows. A row is parallel to the front of the room. How many different arrangements are possible?

(A) 2
(B) 4
(C) 5
(D) 6
(E) 10

13. Which of the following solids has the largest volume? (*Figures are not drawn to scale.*)

I. A cylinder of radius 5 mm and height 11 mm (volume of a cylinder is $\pi r^2 h$)

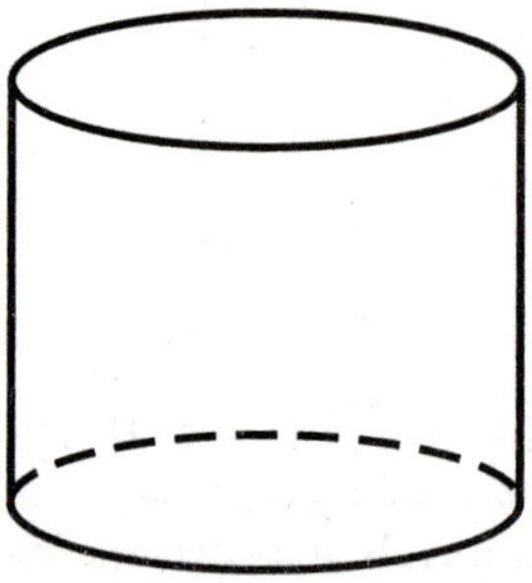

II. A sphere of radius 6mm (volume of a sphere is $\frac{4}{3}\pi r^3$)

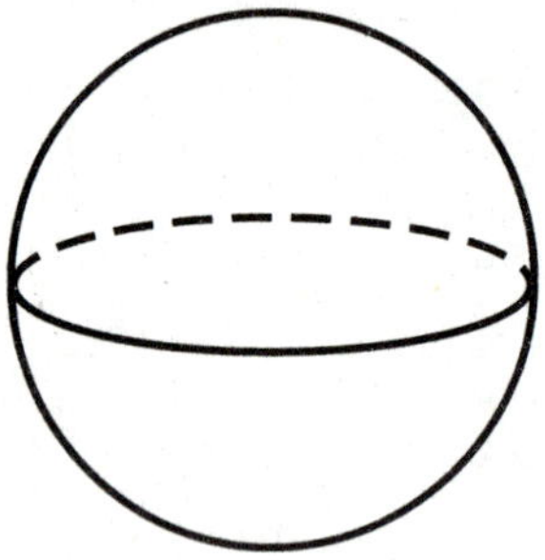

GO ON TO THE NEXT PAGE ➤

6 6 6 6 6 6 6 6 6 6 6

III. A cube with edge of 9mm (volume of a cube is e^3)

(A) I
(B) II
(C) III
(D) I and II
(E) II and III

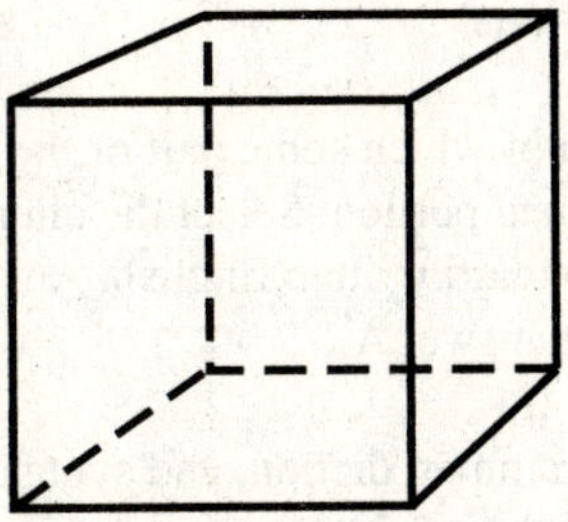

14. A pension fund has a total of $1 million invested in stock of the ABC Company and bonds of the DEF Corporation. The ABC stock yields 12% in cash each year, and the DEF bonds pay 10% in cash each year. The pension fund received a total of $115,000 in cash from ABC stock and DEF bonds last year. How much money was invested in ABC stock?

(A) $750,000.00
(B) $600,000.00
(C) $500,000.00
(D) $333,333.33
(E) $250,000.00

15. The ratio of chickens to pigs to horses on a farm can be expressed as the triple ratio 20 : 4 : 6. If there are 120 chickens on the farm, then the number of horses on the farm is

(A) 4
(B) 6
(C) 24
(D) 36
(E) 60

16. If $x^2 - y^2 = 15$ and $x + y = 3$, then $x - y$ is

(A) –3
(B) 0
(C) 3
(D) 5
(E) cannot be determined

17. What is the area of the shaded region? The radius of the outer circle is a and the radius of each of the circles inside the large circle is $\frac{a}{3}$.

(A) 0
(B) $\left(\frac{1}{3}\right)\pi a^2$
(C) $\left(\frac{2}{3}\right)\pi a^2$
(D) $\left(\frac{7}{9}\right)\pi a^2$
(E) $\left(\frac{8}{9}\right)\pi a^2$

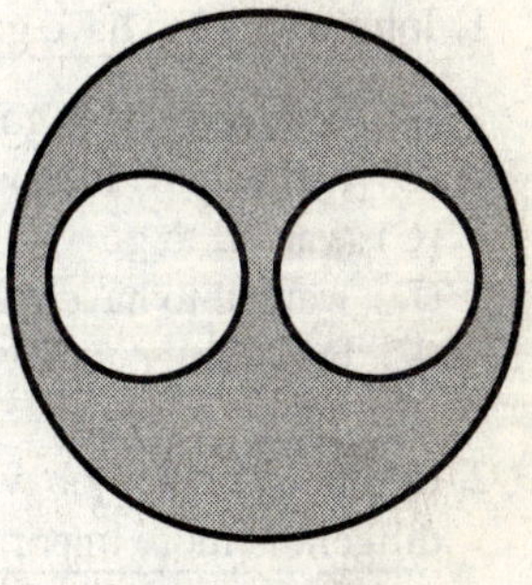

STOP

IF THERE IS STILL TIME REMAINING, YOU MAY REVIEW THE QUESTIONS IN THIS SECTION ONLY. YOU MAY NOT TURN TO ANY OTHER SECTION OF THE TEST.

7 7 7 7 7 7 7 7 7 7 7

Section 7

TIME: 25 minutes
21 Questions

Directions: This test consists of a number of sentences, in each of which some part or the whole is underlined. Each sentence is followed by five alternative versions of the underlined portion. Select the alternative you consider both most correct and most effective according to the requirements of standard written English. Answer A is the same as the original version; if you think the original version is best, select answer A.

In considering the answer choices, be attentive to matters of grammar, diction, and syntax, as well as clarity, precision, and fluency. Do not select an answer that alters the meaning of the original sentence.

1. John wanted to have gone to the movies.
   (A) wanted to have gone
   (B) had wanted to have gone
   (C) wanted to go
   (D) wanted to have went
   (E) had wanted to have went

2. In this particular job we have discovered that to be diligent is more important than being bright.
   (A) to be diligent is more important than being bright
   (B) for one to be diligent is more important than being bright
   (C) diligence is more important than brightness
   (D) being diligent is more important than to be bright
   (E) by being diligent is more important than being bright

3. On their return, they not only witnessed the sinking ship but the amazing escape of the passengers.
   (A) not only witnessed the sinking ship but the
   (B) not only witnessed the sinking ship, but the
   (C) not only witnessed the sinking ship, but also the
   (D) witnessed not only the sinking ship but also the
   (E) witnessed the sinking ship and also the

4. No one but him could have told them that the thief was I.
   (A) him could have told them that the thief was I
   (B) he could have told them that the thief was I
   (C) he could have told them that the thief was me
   (D) him could have told them that the thief was me
   (E) he could have told them the thief was me

5. Either you transfer the data which was demanded or file a report explaining why you did not submit the overall annual figures.
   (A) Either you transfer the data which was demanded
   (B) You either transfer the data, which was demanded,
   (C) You either transfer the data which were demanded
   (D) Either you transfer the data, which was demanded,
   (E) Either you transfer the data, which were demanded,

6. On entering the stadium, cheers greeted them as a sign of universal approval of their great achievement.
   (A) On entering the stadium, cheers greeted them
   (B) On entering the stadium, they were greeted by cheers
   (C) While entering the stadium, cheers greeted them
   (D) On entering the stadium cheers greeted them
   (E) On entering the stadium: cheers greeted them

7. The set of propositions which was discussed by the panel have been published in the society journal.
   (A) which was discussed by the panel have
   (B) which were discussed by the panel have
   (C) that was discussed by the panel has
   (D) which were discussed by the panel has
   (E) which was discussed, by the panel, has

GO ON TO THE NEXT PAGE ➤

7 7 7 7 7 7 7 7 7 7 7

8. They decided to honor Mr. Wilson, who will be president of the club for ten years next Tuesday.

(A) will be president of the club for ten years next Tuesday
(B) shall have been president of the club for ten years next Tuesday
(C) next Tuesday will have been president of the club for ten years
(D) next Tuesday has been president of the club for ten years
(E) had been president of the club for ten years next Tuesday

9. After a careful evaluation of the circumstances surrounding the incident, we decided that we neither have the authority nor the means to cope with the problem.

(A) neither have the authority nor
(B) neither have authority or
(C) have neither the authority nor
(D) have neither the authority or
(E) have not either the authority nor

10. Everyone of us have understood that without him helping us we would not have succeeded in our program over the past six months.

(A) Everyone of us have understood that without him helping us
(B) Everyone of us has understood that without his helping us
(C) Everyone of us have understood that without his help
(D) Everyone of us has understood that without him helping us
(E) Every single one of us have understood that without him helping us

11. On the African continent, the incidence of vitamin deficiencies correlates positively with the level of solar radiation

(A) deficiencies correlates positively with
(B) deficiencies correlate positively with
(C) deficiencies, correlate positively with,
(D) deficiencies correlate positively to
(E) deficiencies correlates positively to

12. A thoroughly frightened child was seen by her cowering in the corner of the room.

(A) A thoroughly frightened child was seen by her cowering in the corner of the room.
(B) Cowering in the corner of the room a thoroughly frightened child was seen by her.
(C) She saw, cowering in the corner of the room, a thoroughly frightened child.
(D) A thoroughly frightened child, cowering in the corner of the room, was seen by her.
(E) She saw a thoroughly frightened child who was cowering in the corner of the room.

13. If they would have taken greater care in the disposal of the nuclear waste, the disaster would not have occurred.

(A) If they would have taken greater care
(B) Unless they took greater care
(C) Had they not taken greater care
(D) If they had taken greater care
(E) If they took greater care

14. Neither the judge nor I am ready to announce who the winner is.

(A) Neither the judge nor I am ready to announce who the winner is.
(B) Neither the judge nor I are ready to announce who the winner is.
(C) Neither the judge nor I are ready to announce who is the winner.
(D) Neither the judge nor I am ready to announce who is the winner.
(E) Neither I or the judge are ready to announce who is the winner.

15. After adequate deliberation, the council can see scarcely any valid reason for its reviewing the request.

(A) can see scarcely any valid reason for its
(B) can not see scarcely any valid reason for its
(C) can see any valid reason scarcely for its
(D) can see scarcely any valid reason for it's
(E) can scarcely see any valid reason for it's

GO ON TO THE NEXT PAGE ➤

7 7 7 7 7 7 7 7 7 7 7

16. If she were I, she would have accepted the prize if she had won it.

    (A) were I, she would have accepted the prize if she had
    (B) was I, she would have accepted the prize if she would have
    (C) was I, she would have accepted the prize if she had
    (D) were I, she would have accepted the prize if she would have
    (E) were me, she would have accepted the prize if she had

17. We expect help in providing adequate facilities and ample funds from everybody in order to advance this vital program.

    (A) in providing adequate facilities and ample funds from everybody
    (B) in the provision of adequate facilities and ample funds from everybody
    (C) in providing adequate facilities and funds from everyone
    (D) with facilities and funds from everyone
    (E) from everybody in providing adequate facilities and ample funds

18. From the moment he took public office, his actions have been loaded with significance and filled with worth.

    (A) been loaded with significance and filled with worth
    (B) been significant and worthwhile
    (C) become loaded with significance and worth
    (D) to be loaded with significance and filled with worth
    (E) been actions of significance and worth

19. After several days' tour, we became convinced that the climate of this deserted island was like Florida in winter.

    (A) the climate of this deserted island was like Florida in winter
    (B) the climate of this deserted island was like that of Florida in winter
    (C) the climate of this desert Island was like Florida in winter
    (D) the climate of this deserted island in winter was like Florida
    (E) the climate of this desert island was as Florida in winter

20. The students have always had a most sincere interest and admiration for the important work of Professor Jakobsen.

    (A) a most sincere interest and admiration for
    (B) a most sincere interest in and admiration for
    (C) mostly a sincere interest and admiration for
    (D) a most sincere interest, and admiration for
    (E) a most sincere interest and an admiration for

21. I might have provided a happier ending if I was the author of that novel.

    (A) ending if I was the author of that novel
    (B) ending, if I were the author of that novel
    (C) ending. If I were the author of that novel
    (D) ending if I had been the author of that novel
    (E) ending, if I had to be the author of that novel

STOP

IF THERE IS STILL TIME REMAINING,
YOU MAY REVIEW THE QUESTIONS IN THIS SECTION ONLY.
YOU MAY NOT TURN TO ANY OTHER SECTION OF THE TEST.

Answers
SAMPLE TEST 1

Section 1 [Reading Comprehension]

1	B	6	D	11	E	16	E	21	C
2	C	7	E	12	C	17	B	22	A
3	D	8	B	13	A	18	E	23	A
4	C	9	E	14	B	19	A	24	A
5	D	10	D	15	D	20	B	25	B

Section 2 [Problem Solving]

1	B	6	D	11	E	16	C	21	
2	D	7	A	12	E	17	D	22	
3	C	8	D	13	B	18		23	
4	C	9	D	14	A	19		24	
5	B	10	B	15	B	20		25	

Section 3 [Critical Reasoning]

1	A	6	B	11	B	16	C	21	
2	B	7	E	12	E	17	B	22	
3	B	8	B	13	D	18		23	
4	D	9	B	14	A	19		24	
5	E	10	E	15	A	20		25	

Section 4 [Data Sufficiency]

1	E	6	D	11	E	16	A	21	D
2	B	7	B	12	D	17	B	22	
3	D	8	D	13	E	18	A	23	
4	A	9	D	14	B	19	B	24	
5	C	10	B	15	C	20	C	25	

Section 5 [Sentence Correction]

1	B	6	D	11	D	16	B	21	E
2	D	7	B	12	B	17	D	22	
3	C	8	D	13	E	18	D	23	
4	E	9	A	14	B	19	C	24	
5	A	10	E	15	C	20	B	25	

Section 6 [Problem Solving]

1	D	6	E	11	A	16	D	21	
2	B	7	E	12	C	17	D	22	
3	D	8	D	13	B	18		23	
4	E	9	C	14	A	19		24	
5	A	10	B	15	D	20		25	

Section 7 [Sentence Correction]

1	C	6	B	11	A	16	A	21	D
2	C	7	D	12	C	17	E	22	
3	D	8	C	13	D	18	B	23	
4	A	9	C	14	A	19	B	24	
5	C	10	B	15	A	20	B	25	

Self-Scoring Guide—Analytical Writing

Evaluate your writing tests (or have a friend or teacher evaluate them for you) on the following basis. Read each essay completely, paying special attention to its logical organization and use of examples and facts to buttress its claims or position. Assign a holistic score between 0 and 6, using the scale below. Your writing score will be the average of the scores of the two essays.

6	**Outstanding**	Cogent, well-articulated analysis of the issue or critique of the argument. Develops a position with insightful reasons and persuasive examples. Well organized. Superior command of language and variety of syntax. Only minor flaws in grammar, usage, and mechanics.
5	**Strong**	Well-developed analysis or critique. Develops a position with well-chosen examples or reasons. Generally well organized. Clear control of language and variety of syntax. Minor flaws in grammar, usage, and mechanics.
4	**Adequate**	Competent analysis or critique. Develops a position with relevant reasons or examples. Adequately organized. Adequate control of language, but may lack syntactic variety. May have some flaws in grammar, usage, and mechanics.
3	**Limited**	Competent but clearly flawed analysis or critique. Vague or limited in developing a position. Poorly organized. Weak in using relevant examples or reasons. Language used imprecisely or lacking in sentence variety. Contains major errors or frequent minor errors in grammar, usage, and mechanics.
2	**Seriously Flawed**	Serious weaknesses in analysis and organization. Unclear or seriously limited in presenting or developing a position. Disorganized. Few relevant examples or reasons. Frequent serious problems in language and sentence structure. Numerous errors in grammar, usage, or mechanics that interfere with meaning.
1	**Fundamentally Deficient**	Little evidence of ability to organize and develop a coherent response to issue or argument. Severe and persistent errors in language and sentence structure. Pervasive pattern of errors in grammar, usage, and mechanics that severely interfere with meaning.
0	**Unscorable**	Illegible or not written on the assigned topic.

Analysis

Section 1
Reading Comprehension

The passage for questions 1–9 appears on page 230.

1. One surprising aspect of the waves discussed in the passage is the fact that they

(A) are formed in concentric patterns
(B) often strike during clear weather
(C) arise under conditions of cold temperature
(D) are produced by deep swells
(E) may be forecast scientifically

(B) See paragraph 1: "Under a perfectly sunny sky and from an apparently calm sea . . ." None of the other answer choices is particularly surprising.

2. The waves discussed in the passage often strike

(A) along the coasts of the Aleutian Islands
(B) in regions outside the area monitored by the Coast and Geodetic Survey
(C) at great distances from their place of origin
(D) at the same time as the occurrence of earthquakes
(E) in areas outside the Pacific region

(C) See the first sentence of the passage: ". . . distant lands or continents."

3. It is believed that the waves are caused by

(A) seismic changes
(B) concentric time belts
(C) atmospheric conditions
(D) underwater earthquakes
(E) storms

(D) See paragraph 2, line 1: "How are these waves formed? When a submarine earthquake occurs . . ."

4. The normal maximum width of the waves is approximately

(A) five feet
(B) ten feet
(C) one mile
(D) five miles
(E) thirty miles

(C) See paragraph 2: "The swells in the ocean are sometimes nearly a mile wide . . ."

5. The U.S. Coast and Geodetic Survey set up a program to

I. Prevent submarine earthquakes
II. Locate submarine earthquakes
III. Determine the severity of submarine earthquakes

(A) I only
(B) III only
(C) I and II only
(D) II and III only
(E) I, II, and III

(D) See paragraph 5: ". . . the Coast and Geodetic Survey initiated a program . . . to locate submarine earthquakes [and] tell how severe a submarine earthquake was . . ."

6. Nothing was done about the waves until

(A) insurance could not cover damages
(B) the outbreak of World War II
(C) a solution was found
(D) millions of dollars worth of damage was incurred in Hawaii
(E) large areas in Chile were devastated

(D) See paragraph 4.

7. The movement of the waves has been measured at a speed of

(A) 30 miles an hour
(B) 40 miles an hour
(C) 50 miles an hour
(D) 100 miles an hour
(E) more than a hundred miles an hour

(E) See paragraph 3: "These waves travel hundreds of miles an hour . . ."

8. According to the passage, the waves occur most frequently in the area of

(A) the Eastern U.S. seaboard
(B) the Pacific
(C) Argentina
(D) Western Europe
(E) Asia

(B) See paragraph 3.

9. Given present wave-tracking systems, scientists can forecast all of the following *except*

(A) the severity of underwater earthquakes
(B) the wave's rate of travel
(C) when a wave will strike
(D) where a wave will strike
(E) the height of the wave

(E) All are mentioned in paragraph 5, except for the height of the wave.

The passage for questions 10–17 appears on page 232.

10. The passage was most likely published in a

(A) popular magazine
(B) general newspaper
(C) science journal
(D) financial journal
(E) textbook

(D) This is clearly a passage dealing with the economy and economic policy. Note that (E) is too vague; an *economic policy* textbook might have been a correct answer.

11. Confidence in the economy was expressed by all of the following except

(A) a strong stock market
(B) a stable bond market
(C) increased installment debt
(D) increased plant and equipment expenditures
(E) rising interest rates

(E) All of the others are given in paragraph 2.

12. During the year in question, public confidence in the economy resulted in part from which of the following occurrences?

I. Possible peace in Vietnam
II. Reduction in East-West tensions
III. An entente with China

(A) I only
(B) III only
(C) I and II only
(D) II and III only
(E) I, II, and III

(C) See paragraph 2: "... consumer and business sentiment benefited from rising public expectations that a resolution of the conflict in Vietnam was in prospect and that East-West tensions were easing."

13. According to the author, business expansion for the period under review was caused largely by

(A) stimulative monetary and fiscal policies
(B) rising interest rates
(C) increased foreign trade
(D) price and wage controls
(E) implementation of the Phase Three program

(A) See paragraph 3, line 1: "The underpinnings of the business expansion were to be found in part in the stimulative monetary and fiscal policies that had been pursued."

14. Most of the trade deficit in the balance of payments was attributed to trade with which country?

(A) United Kingdom
(B) Japan
(C) Germany
(D) France
(E) Saudi Arabia

(B) See paragraph 4: "... there was actually a substantial deterioration in our trade account to a sizable deficit, almost two thirds of which was with Japan."

15. Part of the public policy task, as outlined in the passage, is to

(A) cut consumer spending
(B) prevent balance of payments deficits
(C) devalue the dollar
(D) avoid inflationary pressures
(E) increase the balance of trade

(D) See paragraph 5, lines 59–60: Only (D) was mentioned.

16. The Phase Three program contained

(A) higher income taxes
(B) reduced government spending
(C) devaluation of the dollar
(D) productivity measures
(E) wage and price controls

(E) See paragraph 5, sentence 3: "The Phase Three program of wage and price restraint can contribute to dampening inflation."

17. The passage states that the unemployment rate at the time the article was written was

(A) 6 percent
(B) a little over 5 percent
(C) 5 percent
(D) a little over 4 percent
(E) 4 percent

(B) See paragraph 5: "... the unemployment rates of a bit over 5 percent ..."

The passage for questions 18–25 appears on page 234.

18. The author implies that writers are

(A) incompetent businessmen
(B) not sufficiently paid for their work
(C) greedy
(D) hucksters
(E) profiting against their will

(E) This expression is found throughout the passage, e.g.: in paragraph 1: "... when a poet has put his heart ... into a poem, and sold it to a magazine, the scandal is greater ..."

19. A possible title that best expresses the meaning of the passage would be

(A) *The Man of Letters as a Man of Business*
(B) *Literature and the Arts*
(C) *Progress in Literature*
(D) *Poets and Writers*
(E) *The State of the Arts*

(A) The passage treats the problem of the poet or writer who must "sell" his works to survive; therefore he acts like a businessman.

20. The author laments the fact that Tennyson, Longfellow, and Emerson

(A) wrote mystical poems
(B) had to sell their poetry
(C) were not appreciated in their time
(D) were prolific poets
(E) wrote emotional poetry

(B) See paragraph 1: They sold their poetry, i.e., "... submitted to the conditions which none can escape."

21. The passage states that authors such as Tennyson "submitted to the conditions which none can escape." What conditions is the author of the passage referring to?

(A) An unappreciative audience
(B) A materialistic society
(C) The fact that writers had to sell their work to survive
(D) Authors wrote for an esoteric audience
(E) Authors wrote what the public wanted

(C) See paragraph 1: "... the poem was not written for these dollars, but it is perfectly true that it was sold for them."

22. According to the author, Lord Byron

(A) refused payment for his work
(B) combined business with literature
(C) did not copyright his work
(D) was well known in the business community
(E) founded a school for aspiring writers

(A) See paragraph 2: Lord Byron refused payment for his work (although others gained monetarily from it).

23. The author of the passage implies that

(A) society should subsidize artists and writers
(B) writers should rebel against the business system
(C) more writers should follow the example set by Lord Byron
(D) writers should only accept remuneration that will provide them with a basic standard of living
(E) writers should not attempt to change society

(A) This is implied in paragraph 1: "... the poet would have been cared for by the whole human brotherhood, as any man should be who does the duty that every man owes it."

24. The author of the passage proposes that writers and artists

(A) make the best out of a bad situation
(B) attempt to induce society to change its values
(C) withhold their work until they gain recognition
(D) adopt the principles of commercialism
(E) adopt the value system of society

(A) The author proposes that until society changes its value system (which he does not foresee) the artist and writer must compromise as best they can with the existing system without, however, debasing their work.

25. By accepting payment for works of literature or art, its creators are

I. writing and painting solely for monetary gain
II. justifying the practice of art
III. exchanging their work for remuneration

(A) I only
(B) III only
(C) I and II only
(D) II and III only
(E) I, II, and III

(B) See paragraph 1: Exchanging their work for money does not mean that it was "written for these dollars," even though it was "sold for them." Moreover, the act of selling for gain "does not justify the conditions" or reality of the situation.

Section 2
Problem Solving

(Numbers in parentheses at the end of each explanation indicate the section in the Mathematics Review where material addressed in the question is discussed.)

1. A trip takes 6 hours to complete. After traveling $\frac{1}{4}$ of an hour, $1\frac{3}{8}$ hours, and $2\frac{1}{3}$ hours, how much time does one need to complete the trip?

(A) $2\frac{1}{12}$ hours

(B) 2 hours, $2\frac{1}{2}$ minutes

(C) 2 hours, 5 minutes

(D) $2\frac{1}{8}$ hours

(E) 2 hours, $7\frac{1}{2}$ minutes

(B) The time needed to complete the trip is $\left(6-\frac{1}{4}-1\frac{3}{8}-2\frac{1}{3}\right)$ hours. This equals 6 – (1 + 2) – $\left(\frac{1}{4}+\frac{3}{8}+\frac{1}{3}\right) = 3 - \frac{6+9+8}{24} = 3 - \frac{23}{24} = 2\frac{1}{24}$ = 2 hours $2\frac{1}{2}$ minutes. (I-2)

2. It takes 30 days to fill a laboratory dish with bacteria. If the size of the bacteria doubles each day, how long did it take for the bacteria to fill one half of the dish?

(A) 10 days
(B) 15 days
(C) 24 days
(D) 29 days
(E) 29.5 days

(D) Since the size of the bacteria doubles each day, the dish must be half full one day before it is full. So the correct answer is 29 days, or choice (D). A common mistake is to choose (B), but that gives half the time it takes to fill the dish, not the time when the dish is half-full. If the question asked when the dish was one-quarter full, the correct answer would have been 28 days. (I-6)

3. A car wash can wash 8 cars in 18 minutes. At this rate, how many cars can the car wash wash in 3 hours?

(A) 13
(B) 40.5
(C) 80
(D) 125
(E) 405

(C) Since there are 180 minutes in 3 hours, then $\frac{x}{8} = \frac{180}{18}$, where x is the number of cars washed in 3 hours. Therefore, $x = 8 \times 10 = 80$. (II-5)

4. If the ratio of the areas of 2 squares is 2 : 1, then the ratio of the perimeters of the squares is

(A) 1 : 2
(B) 1: $\sqrt{2}$
(C) $\sqrt{2}$: 1
(D) 2 : 1
(E) 4 : 1

(C) If s and t denote the sides of the two squares, then $s^2 : t^2 = 2 : 1$ or $\frac{s^2}{t^2} = \frac{2}{1}$. Thus $\left(\frac{s}{t}\right)^2 = \frac{2}{1}$ and $\frac{s}{t} = \frac{\sqrt{2}}{1}$.

Since the ratio of the perimeters is $4s : 4t = s : t$, (C) is the correct answer. (II-5, III-7)

5. There are three types of tickets available for a concert: orchestra, which cost $12 each; balcony, which cost $9 each; and box, which cost $25 each. There were *P* orchestra tickets, *B* balcony tickets, and *R* box tickets sold for the concert. Which of the following expressions gives the percentage of ticket proceeds due to the sale of orchestra tickets?

(A) $100 \times \frac{P}{(P+B+R)}$

(B) $100 \times \frac{12P}{(12P+9B+25R)}$

(C) $\frac{12P}{(12P+9B+25R)}$

(D) $100 \times \frac{(9B+25R)}{(12P+9B+25R)}$

(E) $100 \times \frac{12P+9B+25R}{(12P)}$

(B) First find an expression for the proceeds from orchestra tickets, which is $12P$. Next, find an expression for the total proceeds, which is $12P + 9B + 25R$. So $\frac{12P}{(12P+9B+25R)}$ gives the part of the total proceeds due to the sale of orchestra tickets. However, this is not a percentage. You need to multiply this expression by 100 to get a percentage. So the correct choice is (B). (II-3)

6. City B is 5 miles east of City A. City C is 10 miles southeast of City B. Which of the following is the closest to the distance from City A to City C?

(A) 11 miles
(B) 12 miles
(C) 13 miles
(D) 14 miles
(E) 15 miles

(D) Set up a coordinate system with A at (0, 0). Then B is at (5, 0). Since C is southeast of B, then BCD is an

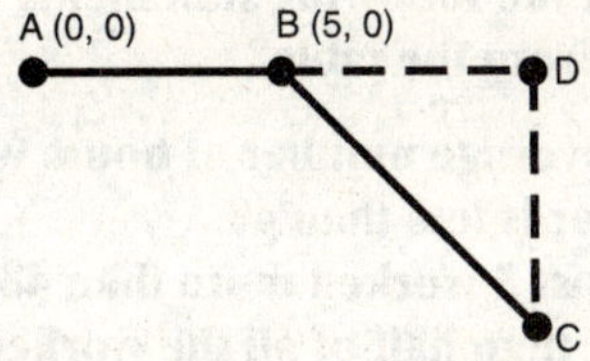

isosceles right triangle whose hypotenuse is 10 miles. So $BD^2 + CD^2 = 10^2 = 100$ and $BD = CD$, so $BD^2 = 50$. Therefore, $BD = \sqrt{50} = \sqrt{25}\sqrt{2} = 5\sqrt{2}$. So the coordinates of C are $(5 + 5\sqrt{2}, -5\sqrt{2})$. Remember, the distance between two points whose coordinates are (x, y) and (a, b) is $\sqrt{(x-a)^2 + (y-b)^2}$. So the distance from A to C is the square root of $(5 + 5\sqrt{2})^2 + (-5\sqrt{2})^2$. You can work with these numbers but it will be messy. It is much faster to use the fact that $\sqrt{2}$ is about 1.4. Remember, the question only asks for an approximate answer. So $5\sqrt{2}$ is about 7, thus the distance is the square root of $(5 + 7)^2 + (-7)^2$. This is equal to the square root of 144 + 49 or 193. *Do not try to find the square root of this number if you don't know it.* Simply square each answer and see which is closest to 193. Since $14^2 = 196$, the correct choice is 14 miles or (D). (III-9)

7. If $3x - 2y = 8$, then $4y - 6x$ is:

(A) –16
(B) –8
(C) 8
(D) 16
(E) cannot be determined

(A) $4y - 6x = -2(3x - 2y) = -2(8) = -16$. (II-2)

8. It costs 10¢ a kilometer to fly and 12¢ a kilometer to drive. If you travel 200 kilometers, flying x kilometers of the distance and driving the rest, then the cost of the trip in dollars is

(A) 20
(B) 24
(C) $24 - 2x$
(D) $24 - .02x$
(E) $2{,}400 - 2x$

(D) Since the total distance is 200 kilometers, of which you fly x kilometers, you drive $(200 - x)$ kilometers. Therefore, the cost is $10x + (200 - x)12$, which is $10x - 12x + 2400$ or $2400 - 2x$ cents. The answer in dollars is obtained by dividing by 100, which is $(24 - .02x)$ dollars. (II-1)

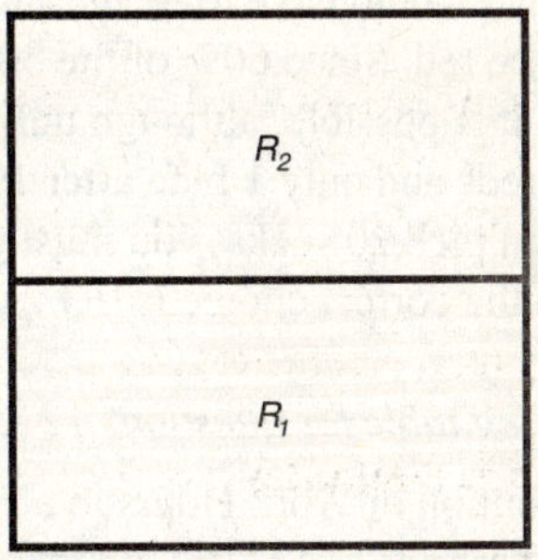

9. If two identical rectangles R_1 and R_2 form a square when placed next to each other, and the length of R_1 is x times the width of R_1, then x is

(A) 1
(B) $\frac{3}{2}$
(C) $\frac{5}{4}$
(D) 2
(E) 3

(D) Since the sides of the square equal the length of the rectangles, which is twice the width, the length of R_1 is 2 times its width. (III-5)

10. If the area of a square increases by 69%, then the side of the square increases by

(A) 13%
(B) 30%
(C) 39%
(D) 69%
(E) 130%

(B) If A_1 denotes the increased area and A the original area, then $A_1 = 1.69A$, since A_1 is A increased by 69%. Thus, $s_1^2 = A_1 = 1.69A = 1.69s^2$, where s_1 is the increased side and s the original side. Since the square root of 1.69 is 1.3, we have $s_1 = 1.3s$ so s is increased by .3 or 30%.

11. There are 30 socks in a drawer. 60% of the socks are red and the rest are blue. What is the minimum number of socks that must be taken from the drawer without looking in order to be certain that at least two blue socks have been chosen?

(A) 2
(B) 3
(C) 14
(D) 16
(E) 20

(E) The key word in this problem is *certain.* If you picked only two socks, you might get a pair of blue socks, but you are not certain. If the question asked for a pair of socks the same color, then after only 3 socks were picked, two would have to be the same color—but the two might be red. Since 60% of the 30 socks, or 18 socks, are red, it is possible, although unlikely, that you could pick 18 reds and only 1 blue after 19 picks. However, if you pick 20 socks, you must get at least 2 blue socks. So the correct choice is (E).

Use the following table for questions 12–14.

Distribution of Work Hours in a Factory

Number of Workers		*Number of Hours Worked*
20		45–50
15		40–44
25		35–39
16		30–34
4		0–29
80	TOTAL	3,100

12. What percentage of workers worked 40 or more hours?

(A) 18.75
(B) 25
(C) $33\frac{1}{3}$
(D) 40
(E) 43.75

(E) The total number of workers is 80, and 35 of them work 40 or more hours. Therefore, $\frac{35}{80} = .4375 =$ 43.75%.

13. The number of workers who worked from 40 to 44 hours is x times the number who worked up to 29 hours, where x is

(A) $\frac{15}{16}$
(B) $3\frac{3}{4}$
(C) 4
(D) 5
(E) $6\frac{1}{4}$

(B) 15 people worked 40 to 44 hours, and 4 worked up to 29 hours. So $4x = 15$, which means $x = \frac{15}{4} = 3\frac{3}{4}$.

14. Which of the following statements can be inferred from the table?

I. The average number of hours worked per worker is less than 40.
II. At least 3 worked more than 48 hours.
III. More than half of all the workers worked more than 40 hours.

(A) I only
(B) II only
(C) I and II only
(D) I and III only
(E) I, II, and III

(A) STATEMENT I can be inferred, since the average number of hours worked is $\frac{3100}{80} = 38\frac{3}{4}$ which is less than 40.

15. When a truck travels at 60 miles per hour, it uses 30% more gasoline to travel any distance than it does when it travels at 50 miles per hour. The truck can travel 20 miles on a gallon of gas if it is traveling at 50 miles per hour. The truck has only 10 gallons of gas and is 160 miles from its destination. It takes 20 minutes for the truck to stop for gas. How long will it take the truck to reach its final destination if the truck is driven at 60 miles per hour?

(A) 160 minutes
(B) 180 minutes
(C) 190 minutes
(D) 192 minutes
(E) 195 minutes

(B) To calculate the driving time, simply divide 160 miles by 60 miles per hour to obtain $2\frac{2}{3}$ hours, or 160 minutes. However, you need to decide whether or not the truck must stop for gasoline. At a speed of 60 mph, the truck will use 30% more fuel, so it will need 1.3 gallons to travel 20 miles. Thus x (the amount of fuel needed to travel 160 miles) must satisfy the proportion $\frac{160}{20} = \frac{x}{1.3}$ or $x = 8\ (1.3) = 10.4$ gallons. So, if the truck is driven at 60 mph, it will have to stop for gas since it has only 10 gallons. Therefore, the total time needed is $160 + 20 = 180$ minutes.

16. Company *A* owns 40% of the stock in the *XYZ* corporation. Company *B* owns 15,000 shares. Company *C* owns all the shares not owned by companies *A* or *B*. How many shares of stock does company *A* own if company *C* has 25% more shares than company *A*?

(A) 45,000
(B) 50,000
(C) 60,000
(D) 75,000
(E) 90,000

(C) If company *C* owns 25% more than company *A*, and *A* owns 40% of *XYZ*, then company *C* must own $1.25 \times .4 = .5$, or 50% of *XYZ*. Since *B* owns all that *A* and *C* do not own, then *B* must own $100\% - 40\% - 50\% = 10\%$.

If 10% of the shares is 15,000 shares, then there must be 150,000 shares in company *XYZ*. Since company *A* owns 40%, it owns $150{,}000 \times 0.40 = 60{,}000$ shares. So (C) is the correct answer. Remember: always answer the question asked. If you picked (D), you found only how many shares company *C* owns.

17. How many squares with sides $\frac{1}{2}$ inch long are needed to cover a rectangle that is 4 feet long and 6 feet wide?

(A) 24
(B) 96
(C) 3,456
(D) 13,824
(E) 14,266

(D) The area of the rectangle is $4 \times 6 = 24$ square feet. Since 1 square foot is 144 square inches, the area of the rectangle is 3,456 square inches. Each square has an area of $\left(\frac{1}{2}\right)^2$ or $\frac{1}{4}$ square inches. Therefore, the number of squares needed $= 3{,}456 \div \frac{1}{4} = 3{,}456 \times 4 = 13{,}824$.

Section 3
Critical Reasoning

1. Monopoly is characterized by an absence of or decline in competition. The ABC Company realizes that its operations are in competitive industries.

Which of the following conclusions may be inferred from the above?

(A) ABC's market is not monopolistic.
(B) Monopoly is defined as one seller in a market.
(C) The ABC Company has no domestic competitors.
(D) The ABC Company is publicly owned.
(E) The ABC Company is in a service industry.

(A) The argument is: (1) in a monopoly situation, there is either no competition or competition is declining. (2) Competition exists in ABC's markets. (3) There is an absence of monopoly in ABC's markets. Therefore, alternative (A) is the correct answer. Alternative (B) is another way of stating premise (1). Alternative (C) cannot be inferred; we are told that competition exists but we have no way of knowing if the competition is domestic and/or foreign. Answer alternatives (D) and (E) are not relevant to the argument.

2. Farmers in the North have observed that heavy frost is usually preceded by a full moon. They are convinced that the full moon somehow generates the frost.

Which of the following, if true, would weaken the farmers' conviction?

(A) The temperature must fall below 10 degrees Celsius (50 degrees Fahrenheit) for frost to occur.
(B) Absence of a cloud cover cools the ground which causes frost.
(C) Farmers are superstitious.
(D) No one has proven that the moon causes frost.
(E) Farmers are not experts in meteorology.

(B) The argument represents a fallacy in causality. Absence of cloud cover enables the moon to be seen. And, it is the absence of cloud cover—not a full moon—that causes the ground to cool and produce frost. Answer choice (A) may be a necessary but insufficient condition for frost to occur; that is, there may be an absence of frost even below 10 degrees Celsius. Farmers may be superstitious, but there is nothing in the statement that links superstition with the farmers' conviction (alternative C). Alternative (D) is inappropriate because, even if true, it could not change the farmers' convictions. Farmers do not have to be experts in meteorology (E) to hold a conviction.

3. Professor Tembel told his class that the method of student evaluation of teachers is not a valid measure of teaching quality. Students should fill out questionnaires at the end of the semester when courses have been completed.

Which of the following, if true, provides support for Professor Tembel's proposal?

(A) Professor Tembel received low ratings from his students.
(B) Students filled out questionnaires after the midterm exam.
(C) Students are interested in teacher evaluation.
(D) Teachers are not obligated to use the survey results.
(E) Student evaluation of teachers is voluntary.

(B) The question concerns Professor Tembel's proposal to improve the validity of the method used to measure teacher quality. Alternative (B) supports the proposal. Students relate only partial experience with a teacher if the questionnaires are completed at midterm. Alternative (A) suggests that Professor Tembel's motive for questioning the present evaluation method stems from his low ratings. It is questionable whether handing out questionnaires at the end of the semester would improve his ratings. Alternatives (C), (D), and (E) are not related to the validity of the evaluation method.

4. The President lobbied for passage of his new trade bill which would liberalize trade with industrialized countries such as Japan, members of the European Community, and Canada.

Each of the following, if true, could account for the above, except:

(A) The President is up for re-election and needs to show results.
(B) Labor unions have petitioned the President to provide more local jobs.
(C) The trade agreement could bring a *quid pro quo* on pending negotiations.
(D) Economists claimed that the passage of the bill would increase the country's trade deficit.
(E) It was politically desirable for a trade bill at the present time.

(D) All of the facts except (D) would be consonant with the President's actions. Fact (D) would be against passage of such a bill.

5. If we are doomed to have local drug rehabilitation centers—and society has determined that we are—then society ought to pay for them.

Which of the following, if true, would weaken the above argument?

(A) Drug rehabilitation centers are too expensive to be locally funded.
(B) Many neighborhood groups oppose rehabilitation centers.
(C) Drug rehabilitation centers are expensive to maintain.
(D) Drug addicts may be unwilling to receive treatment.
(E) A government committee has convinced many groups that local rehabilitation centers are ineffective.

(E) The argument is in the form of a conditional syllogism: (1) *If* we must have drug rehabilitation centers, *then* society ought to pay for them. (2) We must have drug rehabilitation centers. (3) Society ought to pay for them. Alternative (E) falsifies the minor premise 2. Whether or not neighborhood groups oppose the centers (B) or drug addicts will go to them to receive treatment (D) are not relevant to the argument concerning who will pay for them. The level of government funding (A) or the amount of expense (C) are not mentioned in the passage and are not relevant to the argument. However, a government statement that local rehabilitation centers are ineffective would seriously weaken the premise upon which the argument rests.

6. Surviving this crisis is going to take everything we've got. In addition to ... massive retraining, we may also need subsidies—direct or channeled through the private sector—for a radically expanding service sector. Not merely things like environmental clean-up, but basic human services. (Alvin Toffler, *Previews and Premises* (New York: Bantam Books, 1985), p. 57.)

Which of the following statements is inconsistent with the above?

(A) Subsidies are needed to overcome the crisis.
(B) Environmental controls will be loosened.
(C) The service sector is going to expand to such an extent that many more workers will be needed.
(D) The private sector will play a role in retraining workers.
(E) Before the crisis can end, an environmental clean-up will have to take place.

(B) The "crisis" which is alluded to in the statement refers to a need for environmental clean-up and basic human services (the latter mentioned in alternative (E)).

In order to provide these services more workers will be needed (C), many of whom will have to be retrained. This retraining will have to be financed by subsidies (A), which may be provided by the private sector (D). Alternative (B) is inconsistent with the statement which calls for more environmental controls (clean-up), not less.

7. Per-capita income last year was $12,290. Per-capita income is calculated by dividing total aggregate cash income by the total population. Real median income for families headed by a female, with no husband present, was $14,620. Therefore, women wage-earners earned more than the national average.

Which of the following would, if true, weaken the above conclusion?

(A) Per-capita income is calculated in real terms.
(B) In 99 percent of the cases, families headed by a female included no other wage-earner.
(C) Average income is not significantly different from median income.
(D) The overall average and per-capita income were the same.
(E) Only a small proportion of the total wage earners are women family heads.

(E) Total per-capita income includes salaries and wages earned by women. In order to determine if women wage-earners earned more than the overall average, the salaries of all women—not just women heading families with no husband present—would have to be calculated separately. Alternative (E) states that women family heads are not representative of all women wage earners. Thus, the conclusion in the statement is a fallacy of relevance or representativeness. All other alternatives would buttress the conclusion.

8. An economist was quoted as saying that the Cost-of-Living index (COL) will go up next month because of a recent increase in the price of fruit and vegetables.

Which of the following cannot be inferred from the statement?

(A) The cost of fruits and vegetables has risen sharply.
(B) Consumers have decreased their consumption of fruits and vegetables.
(C) The cost of fruit and vegetables is a major item in the COL.
(D) Food cost changes are reflected quickly in the COL.
(E) Other items that make up the COL have not significantly decreased in price.

(B) The claim in the statement is that the COL will go up. The reasoning behind the claim is based on the premise that the cost of fruit and vegetables has risen sharply (A). Since these commodities are major items in the COL (C) and because food cost changes are reflected quickly in the index (D), the index will go up. A premise that could weaken the claim might be (E) *if* other items included in the index and weighted at least as much decreased in price, thus offsetting the cost increases for fruits and vegetables. However, alternative (E) gives evidence to the contrary. Alternative (B) may not be inferred. If consumers reduced consumption of fruits and vegetables, the prices of these items would be expected to drop. In any case, the rate of consumption cannot be inferred.

9. The director of the customs administration suggested that customs taxes on automobiles not be reduced as planned by the government because of the high incidence of traffic accidents last year.

Which of the above statements weakens the argument above?

I. Although the traffic accident rate last year was high, it was not appreciably higher than previous years and anyway, compulsory insurance covered most physical damage to automobiles and property.
II. A Commerce Department report showed that the demand for automobiles was highly inelastic. That is, as dealers lowered their prices, sales did not increase appreciably.
III. A study by the Economics Department at Classics University found that most traffic accidents had been caused by human error although it also concluded that an inadequate road network contributed to at least forty percent of passenger injuries.

(A) I, but not II and not III.
(B) II, but not I and not III.
(C) I and III, but not II.
(D) II and III, but not I.
(E) I, II and III.

(B) The argument claims that fewer cars on the road will lead to fewer accidents. In order to hold down the existing number of cars, it is suggested that custom taxes not be reduced so as not to lower the price to the consumer. Statement I does not weaken the claim because it does not refute the fact of a high incidence of traffic accidents. Statement III strengthens the claim. A higher volume of cars on an inadequate road network should lead to more accidents. Statement II weakens the argument because it provides evidence that even if car prices were reduced it would not lead to increased purchases, which, of course, is the argument in the passage.

10. Significant beneficial effects of smoking occur primarily in the area of mental health, and the habit originates in a search for contentment. The life expectancy of our people has increased greatly in recent years; it is possible that the relaxation and contentment and enjoyment produced by smoking has lengthened many lives. Smoking is beneficial.

Which of the following, if true, weaken the above conclusion?

(A) That cigarettes are a major health hazard cannot be traced to the willfull act of any human or organization.
(B) The government earns millions of dollars from the tobacco tax and tens of thousands of civilians are employed in the tobacco industry.
(C) The evidence cited in the statement covers only one example of the effects of cigarette smoking.
(D) No mention is made of possible harmful side-effects of smoking.
(E) No statistical evidence has proven a link between smoking and longevity.

(E) Statements (A) and (B) do not address themselves to the premise or conclusion. The conclusion in the statement is that smoking is beneficial. Why? Because it leads to longevity through greater relaxation as a result of smoking. Statement (C) is true, but it does not attack the premise. Statement (D) does attack the premise of the beneficiality of smoking, but it does not give evidence of harm. Statement (E) throws doubt on the major premise, and thus on the conclusion.

11. Many of the convenience foods on the market today, like dry cereals, have less nutrients than natural foods, which were dominant a decade or two ago. Many nutritionists claim that dry cereal gives less nourishment than natural foods like eggs or bacon. Opponents of the nutritionists' views state that examination of grade-school students show less nutritional deficiency than in their parents' time.

Which of the following, if true, would tend to strengthen the opponents' view?

(A) Grade school children reported eating no breakfast at all.
(B) Fewer convenience foods were available to the parents.
(C) Adults claim to eat convenience foods as well as natural foods.
(D) Convenience foods can be digested just as quickly as natural foods.
(E) Consumers are not likely to sacrifice convenience for nutrition.

(B) Even if most grade students eat no breakfast (A), they still have ample opportunity to consume convenience foods during other meals (and between them!). That adults today eat both convenience and natural foods (C) does not explain the nutritional discrepancy between the generations. (D) and (E) are not evidence that can support or refute the opposing view. Since during the parents' generation fewer convenience foods were available, we would expect the parents to show better nutrition. Since grade school students show less nutritional deficiency than their parents, apparently convenience foods are not having a negative effect.

12. In a world of many trading countries, the trade between two countries need not be balanced for the trade of each to be in global balance. Differing demands and productive capabilities among countries will cause a specific country to have trade deficits with some countries and surpluses with other countries.

Which of the following conclusions best summarizes the passage above?

(A) A country's trade will always be in balance even though it runs a deficit with a single country.
(B) A country's trade deficits and surpluses with other countries always balance out.
(C) A country's global trade balance is a sign of strength or weakness.
(D) Countries should not be concerned if they have trade deficits because they will balance out in the long run.
(E) A country's global trade balance is determined by relative demand and productive capabilities.

(E) The passage argues that even if any one country has a surplus or deficit with another country, their surpluses or deficits may balance out. Thus, when bilateral trade becomes multilateral, different demand and productive capabilities between the countries will cause any one country to be simultaneously in deficit with some and in surplus with others. Thus, conceivably, a country might be in deficit with one country, but in balance overall. Alternatives (A) and (B) are incorrect because of the word "always." The passage does not claim that all countries' trade be in balance. Nor does the passage equate a trade balance with strength or weakness (C), nor imply that a short-term imbalance is cause for concern. Choice (E) best summarizes the passage: It is relative (compared to other countries) demand and productive abilities that determine a country's global trade balance.

13. Foreign investment is composed of direct investment transactions (investment in plant, equipment and land) and securities investment transactions. Throughout the post-World War II period, net increases in U.S. direct investment in Europe (funds outflows) exceeded net new European direct investment in the U.S.

Each of the following, if true, could help to account for this trend except:

(A) Land values in Europe were increasing at a faster rate than in the United States.
(B) Duties on imported goods in Europe were higher than those imposed by the United States.
(C) The cost of labor (wages) was consistently lower in Europe than in the United States.
(D) Labor mobility was much higher in the United States than in Europe.
(E) Corporate liquidity was lower in Europe than in the United States.

(D) Land values were higher in Europe, attracting U.S. capital (A); higher duties on U.S. exports to Europe (B) brought a substitution of foreign production for U.S. exports; lower labor costs in Europe (C) meant it was cheaper to produce there. Higher liquidity (E) in the U.S. provided the capital for foreign investment. Only D is irrelevant as an explanation of direct investment.

14. Most large retail stores hold sales in the month of January. The original idea of price reduction campaigns in January became popular when it was realized that sales of products would generally slow down following the Christmas rush, were it not for some incentive. The lack of demand could be solved by the simple solution of reducing prices.

There is now an increasing tendency among major department stores in large urban centers to have their "January sales" begin before Christmas, some time before the end of the calendar year. The idea behind this trend is to endeavor to sell the maximum amount of stock at a profit, even if that may not be at the maximum profit.

Which of the following conclusions cannot be drawn from the above?

(A) The incidence of "early" January sales results in the lower holdings of stocks with the corollary of lower stock holding costs.
(B) Demand is a function of price; as you lower price, demand increases.
(C) Major stores seem to think it makes sense to have the January sales campaigns pre-Christmas.
(D) It is becoming less popular to start the January sales in the New Year.
(E) The major department stores do not worry as much about profit maximization as they do about sales maximization.

(A) A number of points are made in the paragraph, and a number of conclusions can be drawn. One is (B), the simple law of economics—that demand varies with price. Also, since it is stated that there is now an increasing tendency to have the January sales in December, it must be becoming less popular to start the sales in January itself. Therefore, the conclusions in (C) and (D) can be drawn, and so choices (C) and (D) are not appropriate. Further, the hypothesis in (C) and also in (E) can be inferred from what is stated in the paragraph about the stores' policies on end-of-year sales. Answer choice (A) introduces a new idea that may be correct and valid, but which cannot be inferred or concluded from what is stated in the paragraph; (A), therefore is the correct answer.

15. Of the world's largest external-debt countries in 1989, three had the same share of world external-debt as they had in 1980. These three countries may serve as examples of countries that succeeded in holding steady their share of world external-debt.

Which of the following, if true, would most seriously undermine the idea that these countries serve as examples as described above?

(A) Of the three countries, two had a much larger share of world external-debt in 1985 than in 1989.
(B) Some countries strive to reduce their share of world external-debt, not keep it steady.
(C) The three countries have different rates of economic growth.
(D) The absolute value of debt of the three countries is different.
(E) Some countries are more concerned with internal budgets than with external debt.

(A) Two of the three countries actually experienced shifts in their share of world external-debt from 1980 to 1989, hardly an example of stability. Answer choice (B) may be true for some countries, but it does not weaken the statement. Answer choices (C) and (D) skirt the issues: rates of economic growth and absolute debt are not related to external debt in the statement. Answer choice (E) may be so, but the example in the statement deals with external, not internal, debt.

16. In a famous experiment by Pavlov, when a dog smelled food, it salivated. Subsequently, a bell was rung whenever food was placed near the dog. After a number of trials, only the bell was rung, whereupon the dog would salivate even though no food was present.

Which of the following conclusions may be drawn from the above experiment?

(A) Dogs are easily fooled.
(B) Dogs are motivated only by the sound of a bell.
(C) The ringing of a bell was associated with food.
(D) A conclusion cannot be reached on the basis of one experiment.
(E) Two stimuli are stronger than one.

(C) In this experiment, the dog was conditioned to associate the ringing of a bell with food. Therefore, when the dog heard the bell, it expected to be fed, even though it could not smell food. Alternative (A) cannot be inferred. Alternative (B) and (D) are incorrect, and there is no proof for (E).

17. At a political rally at Jefferson Stadium, candidate Smith exclaimed: "Nearly everyone at the rally is behind me. It looks like I am going to be elected."

Which of the following statements, if true, best supports the above conclusion?

(A) Smith's opponent also appeared at the rally.
(B) The rally was attended by almost all the residents of Smith's constituency.
(C) Smith was never defeated in an election.
(D) Smith was supported by the local mayor.
(E) People always vote their emotions.

(B) If the behavior at the rally is indicative of how people will vote *and* the rally attendance was representative of the voters, then the conclusion is valid. The argument is thus: (1) The rally is representative of all voters. (2) Most at the rally are for me. (3) Most rally attendees will vote for me. Alternative (A) might also support the conclusion since even with the appearance of the opponent, Smith says "Nearly everyone at the rally is behind me," but this support depends on whether or not the people at the rally are voters in the election, so this is not the best answer. Smith's previous election results (C) or support from the mayor (D) are not relevant to the conclusion. Alternative (E) is also irrelevant; support at a rally does not imply only emotional support.

Section 4
Data Sufficiency

1. Are two triangles congruent?

(1) Both triangles are right triangles.
(2) Both triangles have the same perimeter.

(E) A triangle with sides of lengths 3, 4, and 5 is a right triangle since $3^2 + 4^2 = 5^2$, and its perimeter is 12. A triangle with sides of lengths 2, $4\frac{4}{5}$, and $5\frac{1}{5}$ also has a perimeter of 12. And since $2^2 + \left(4\frac{4}{5}\right)^2 = \left(5\frac{1}{5}\right)^2$, it too is a right triangle. Therefore, two triangles can satisfy STATEMENTS (1) and (2) yet not be congruent. On the other hand, any pair of congruent right triangles satisfy STATEMENTS (1) and (2). Thus, STATEMENTS (1) and (2) together are not sufficient to answer the question.

2. Is x greater than zero?

(1) $x^4 - 16 = 0$
(2) $x^3 - 8 = 0$

(B) $x^3 - 8 = 0$ has only $x = 2$ as a real solution. And 2 is greater than 0, so STATEMENT (2) alone is sufficient.

Since $x = 2$ and $x = -2$ are both solutions of $x^4 - 16 = 0$, STATEMENT (1) alone is not sufficient.

3. If both conveyer belt *A* and conveyer belt *B* are used, they can fill a hopper with coal in one hour. How long will it take for conveyer belt *A* to fill the hopper without conveyer belt *B*?

(1) Conveyer belt *A* moves twice as much coal as conveyer belt *B*.
(2) Conveyer belt *B* would take 3 hours to fill the hopper without belt *A*.

(D) STATEMENT (1) is sufficient since it implies that conveyer belt *A* loads $\frac{2}{3}$ of the hopper while conveyer belt *B* loads only $\frac{1}{3}$ with both working. Since conveyer belt *A* loads $\frac{2}{3}$ of the hopper in a hour, it will take $1 \div \frac{2}{3}$ or $1\frac{1}{2}$ hours to fill the hopper by itself.

STATEMENT (2) is also sufficient since it implies that conveyer belt B fills $\frac{1}{3}$ of the hopper in 1 hour. Thus, conveyer belt A loads $\frac{2}{3}$ in one hour, and that means conveyer belt A will take $1\frac{1}{2}$ hours by itself.

4. A fly crawls around the outside of a circle once. A second fly crawls around the outside of a square once. Which fly travels further?

(1) The diagonal of the square is equal to the diameter of the circle.
(2) The fly crawling around the circle took more time to complete his journey than the fly crawling around the square.

(A) The first fly will travel a distance equal to the circumference of the circle which is π times the diameter. The second fly will travel $4s$ where s is the length of a side. Since the diagonal of a square has length $\sqrt{2}\,s$, the second fly will travel $\frac{4}{\sqrt{2}}$ times the diagonal of the square. Therefore, (1) alone is sufficient, since $\frac{4}{\sqrt{2}} = \frac{4\sqrt{2}}{2} = 2\sqrt{2}$ which is less than π. (2) alone is not sufficient, since one fly might have crawled faster than the other.

5. Is y larger than 1?

(1) y is larger than 0.
(2) $y^2 - 4 > 0$.

(C) (2) alone is not sufficient since both $y = 3$ and $y = -3$ satisfy $y^2 - 4 > 0$. (1) alone is not sufficient, since $\frac{1}{2}$ is larger than 0 but less than 1 while 3 is larger than 0 and larger than 1. If $y^2 - 4 > 0$, then either y is > 2 or $y < -2$. If (1) and (2) both hold, then y must be > 2, which is > 1.

6. A worker is hired for 6 days. He is paid \$2 more for each day of work than he was paid for the preceding day of work. How much was he paid for the first day of work?

(1) His total wages for the 6 days were \$150.
(2) He was paid 150% of his first day's pay for the sixth day.

(D) Let \$$x$ be the amount he was paid the first day. Then he was paid $x + 2$, $x + 4$, $x + 6$, $x + 8$, and $x + 10$ dollars for the succeeding days. (1) alone is sufficient, since the total he was paid is $(6x + 30)$ dollars, and we can solve $6x + 30 = 150$ (to find that he was paid \$20 for the first day). (2) alone is also sufficient. He was paid \$$(x + 10)$ on the sixth day, so (2) means that $(1.5)x = x + 10$ (which is the same as $x = 20$).

7. A car originally sold for \$3,000. After a month, the car was discounted x%, and a month later the car's price was discounted y%. Is the car's price after the discounts less than \$2,600?

(1) $y = 10$
(2) $x = 15$

(B) Since 85% of \$3,000 is \$2,550, (2) alone is sufficient. (1) alone is not sufficient, since if x were 5% (1) would tell us the price of the car is less than \$2,600. But if x were 1%, (1) would imply that the price of the car is greater than \$2,600.

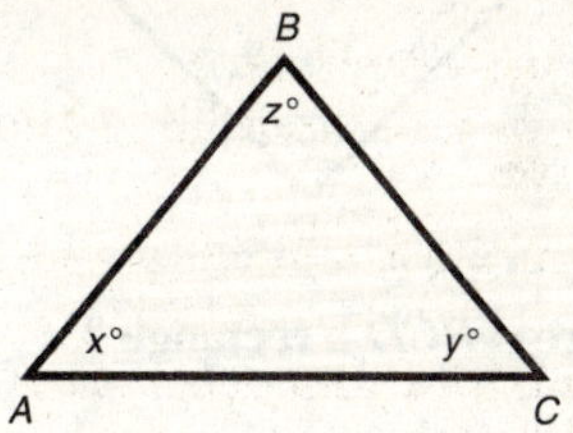

8. In triangle ABC, find z if $AB = 5$ and $y = 40$.

(1) $BC = 5$
(2) The bisector of angle B is perpendicular to AC.

(D) (1) alone is sufficient since $BC = AB$ implies $x = y = 40$. Since the sum of the angles in a triangle is 180°, z must equal 100. (2) alone is sufficient. Let D be the point where the bisector of angle B meets AC. Then according to (2), triangle BDC is a right triangle. Since angle y is 40°, the remaining angle in triangle BDC is 50° and equals $\frac{1}{2}z$, so $z = 100$.

9. How much cardboard will it take to make an open cubical box with no top?

(1) The area of the bottom of the box is 4 square feet.
(2) The volume of the box is 8 cubic feet.

(D) Since there are a bottom and 4 sides, each a congruent square, the amount of cardboard needed will be $5e^2$ where e is the length of an edge of the box. So we need to find e. (1) alone is sufficient.

Since the area of the bottom is e^2, (1) means $e^2 = 4$ with $e = 2$ feet. (2) alone is also sufficient. Since the volume of the box is e^3, (2) means $e^3 = 8$ and $e = 2$ feet.

10. Is the integer x divisible by 3?

(1) The last digit in x is 3.
(2) $x + 5$ is divisible by 6.

(B) STATEMENT (1) is not sufficient. If x is 33, then (1) is true, and x is divisible by 3, but if x is 23, then (1) is true, but x is not divisible by 3.

STATEMENT (2) is sufficient. According to (2) there must be an integer k such that $x + 5 = 6k$, so x is $6k - 5$. But this means that x divided by 3 will be $2k + \frac{5}{3}$, so x is not divisible by 3. So (B) is the correct choice.

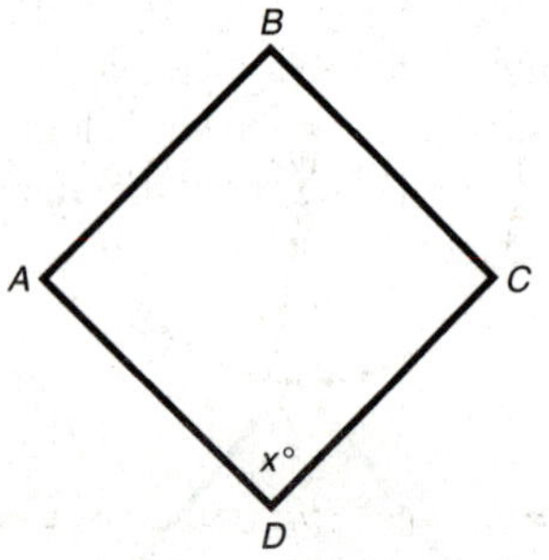

11. Is the figure $ABCD$ a rectangle?

(1) $x = 90$
(2) $AB = CD$

(E) If $ABCD$ has the pairs of opposite sides equal and each angle is 90°, then it is a rectangle. But there are many quadrilaterals that have two opposite sides equal with one angle a right angle. For example, the figure below has $AB = DC$ and $x = 90$, but it is not a rectangle. Therefore, (1) and (2) together are insufficient.

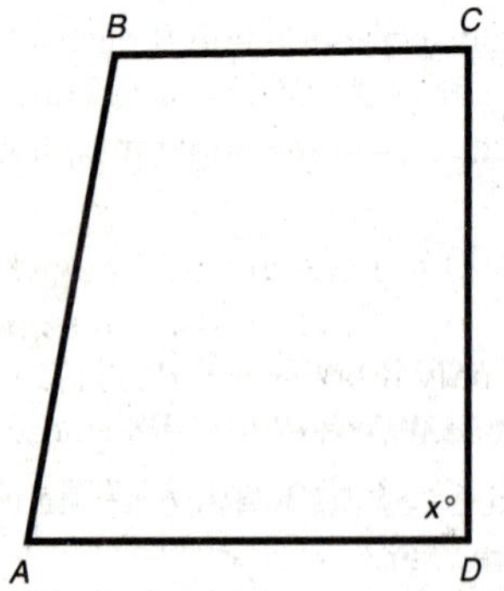

12. A sequence of numbers is given by the rule $a_n = (a_{n-1})^2$. What is a_5?

(1) $a_1 = -1$
(2) $a_3 = 1$

(D) (2) alone is sufficient, since if $a_3 = 1$ then $a_4 = (a_3)^2 = 1^2 = 1$; then $a_5 = (a_4)^2 = 1^2 = 1$. (1) alone is also sufficient. If $a_1 = -1$ then $a_2 = (a_1)^2 = 1$, and $a_3 = (a_2)^2 = 1$, but $a_3 = 1$ is given by (2) which we know is sufficient.

13. How much is John's weekly salary?

(1) John's weekly salary is twice as much as Fred's weekly salary.
(2) Fred's weekly salary is 40% of the total of Chuck's weekly salary and John's weekly salary.

(E) Let J, F, and C stand for the weekly salaries of John, Fred, and Chuck. (1) says $J = 2F$ and (2) says $F = .4(C + J)$. Since there is no information given about the values of C or F, we cannot deduce the value of J. Therefore, (1) and (2) together are insufficient.

14. Find $x + 2y$.

(1) $x + y = 4$
(2) $2x + 4y = 12$

(B) STATEMENT (2) alone is sufficient. $2x + 4y = 2(x + 2y)$, so if $2x + 4y = 12$ then $2(x + 2y) = 12$ and $x + 2y = 6$.

STATEMENT (1) alone is insufficient. If you only use STATEMENT (1) then you can get $x + 2y = x + y + y = 4 + y$ but there is no information on the value of y.

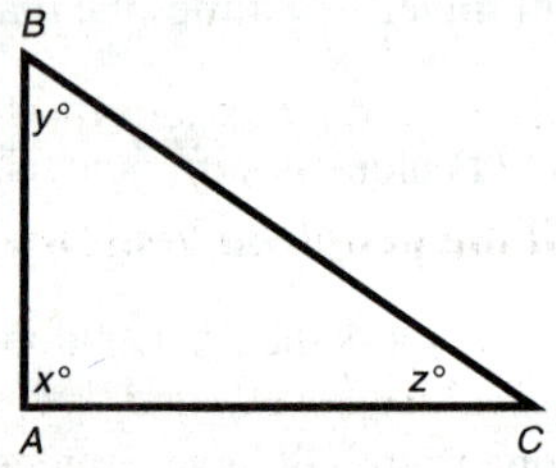

15. Is angle BAC a right angle?

(1) $x = 2y$
(2) $y = 1.5z$

(C) Since the sum of the angles in a triangle is 180°, $x + y + z = 180$. Using STATEMENT (1) alone we have $2y + y + z = 3y + z = 180$, which is insufficient to determine y or z.

Using STATEMENT (2) alone we have $x + 1.5z + z = x + 2.5z = 180$, which is not sufficient to determine x or z.

However, if we use both STATEMENTS (1) and (2) we obtain $3y + z = 4.5z + z = 5.5z = 180$, so $z = \frac{2}{11}$ of 180.

Now $y = \frac{3}{2}$ of z, so $y = \frac{3}{11}$ of 180, and $x = \frac{6}{11}$ of 180.

Therefore, angle BAC is not a right angle and STATEMENTS (1) and (2) are sufficient.

16. If a, b, and c are digits, is $a + b + c$ a multiple of 9? A digit is one of the integers 0, 1, 2, 3, 4, 5, 6, 7, 8, 9.

(1) The three digit number abc is a multiple of 9.
(2) $(a \times b) + c$ is a multiple of 9.

(A) The three digit number *abc* is $(100 \times a) + (10 \times b) + c$. If *abc* is a multiple of 9, then there is an integer *k* such that $k9 = (100 \times a) + (10 \times b) + c$. Divide this equation by 9 and you have

$$k = \left(\frac{100}{9} \times a\right) + \left(\frac{10}{9} \times b\right) + \frac{c}{9}$$

$$= \left(11a + \frac{a}{9}\right) + \left(b + \frac{b}{9}\right) + \frac{c}{9}$$

$$= 11a + b + \left(\frac{a}{9} + \frac{b}{9} + \frac{c}{9}\right)$$

$$= 11a + b + \left(\frac{a+b+c}{9}\right)$$

So (1) alone is sufficient. (2) is not sufficient since choosing $a = 0 = b$ and $c = 9$ makes (2) valid and $a + b + c$ is 9 but choosing $a = 4 = b$ and $c = 2$ also makes (2) valid with $a + b + c$ equal to 10.

17. 50% of the people in Teetown have blue eyes and blond hair. What percent of the people in Teetown have blue eyes but do not have blond hair?

(1) 70% of the people in Teetown have blond hair.
(2) 60% of the people in Teetown have blue eyes.

(B) STATEMENT (2) alone is sufficient. 60% of the people have blue eyes and 50% of the people have blue eyes and blond hair, so 60% – 50% = 10% of the people have blue eyes but do not have blond hair.

STATEMENT (1) alone is not sufficient. Using STATEMENT (1) alone we can only find out how many people have blond hair and do not have blue eyes, in addition to what is given.

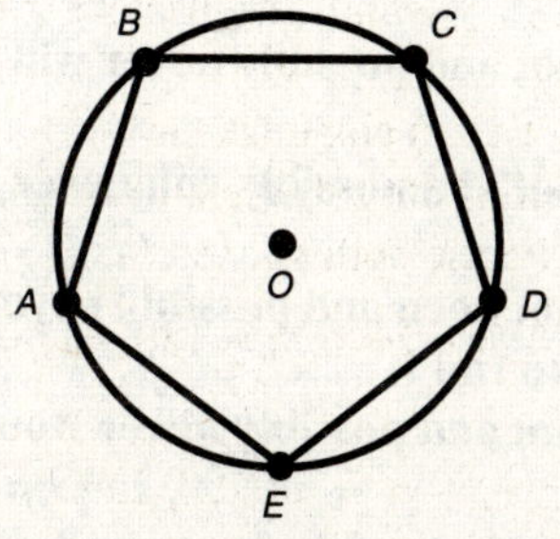

18. The pentagon *ABCDE* is inscribed in the circle with center *O*. How many degrees is angle *ABC*?

(1) The pentagon *ABCDE* is a regular pentagon.
(2) The radius of the circle is 5 inches.

(A) The sum of the angles of the pentagon is 540°. (The sum of the angles of a polygon with *n* sides which is inscribed in a circle is $(n - 2)180°$.)

STATEMENT (1) alone is sufficient. If the polygon is regular, all angles are equal and so angle *ABC* is $\frac{1}{5}$ of 540° or 108°.

STATEMENT (2) alone is insufficient because the radius of the circle does not give any information about the angles of the pentagon.

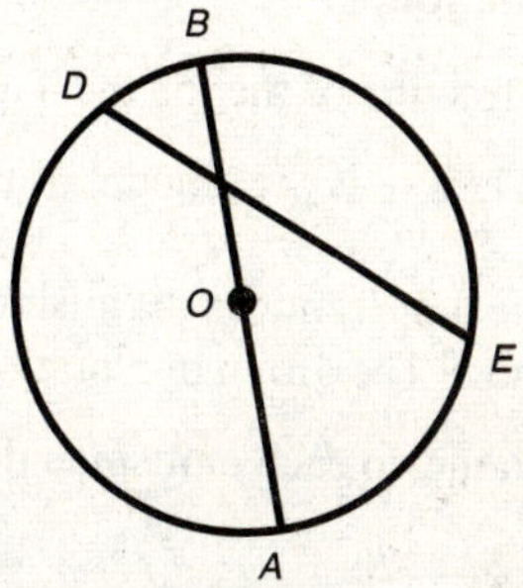

19. What is the area of the circle with center *O*?(*AB* and *DE* are straight lines)

(1) *DE* = 5 inches
(2) *AB* =7 inches

(B) The area of a circle is πr^2, where *r* is the radius of the circle. Since *O* is a point on the line *AB*, *AB* is a diameter of the circle. Therefore, since a radius is one half of a diameter, the radius of the circle is 3.5 inches. Thus, STATEMENT (2) alone is sufficient.

STATEMENT (1) alone is insufficient since there is no relation between *DE* and the radius.

20. Is $k^2 + k - 2 > 0$?

(1) $k < 1$
(2) $k > -1$

(C) The key to this problem is to factor $k^2 + k - 2$ into $(k + 2)(k - 1)$. The product of the two expressions is positive if and only if both expressions have the same sign. When (1) holds, then $k - 1$ is negative, but $k + 2$ can be positive or negative, so (1) alone is not sufficient. When (2) holds, then $k + 2$ is positive, but $k - 1$ can be positive or negative, so (2) alone is not sufficient. However, if both (1) and (2) are true, then *k* is between –1 and 1 and so $k + 2$ is positive and $k - 1$ is negative, which means $(k + 2)(k - 1)$ is negative. This is sufficient to answer the question.

21. If a group of 5 craftsmen take 3 hours to finish a job, how long will it take a group of 4 apprentices to do the same job?

(1) An apprentice works at $\frac{2}{3}$ the rate of a craftsman.

(2) The 5 craftsmen and the 4 apprentices working together will take $1\frac{22}{23}$ hours to finish the job.

(D) Let r be the fraction of the job the 4 apprentices finish in 1 hour. Then $\frac{1}{r}$ is the amount of time in hours that it will take the 4 apprentices to finish the job. So it is sufficient to find r. The group of 5 craftsmen finishes $\frac{1}{3}$ of the job per hour, so each craftsman does $\frac{1}{15}$ of the job per hour.

STATEMENT (1) alone is sufficient. An apprentice will do $\frac{2}{3}$ of $\frac{1}{15} = \frac{2}{45}$ of the job per hour, so $r = \frac{8}{45}$.

STATEMENT (2) alone is sufficient. The craftsmen and the apprentices together will finish $\frac{1}{3} + r$ of the job per hour. Since it takes them $1\frac{22}{23}$ hours to finish the job, $(\frac{1}{3} + r)\left(\frac{45}{23}\right) = 1$ which can be solved for r.

Section 5
Sentence Correction

1. If he was to decide to go to college, I, for one, would recommend that he plan to go to Yale.

(A) If he was to decide to go to college,
(B) If he were to decide to go to college,
(C) Had he decided to go to college,
(D) In the event that he decides to go to college,
(E) Supposing he was to decide to go to college,

(B) This corrects the misuse of the subjunctive.

2. Except for you and I, everyone brought a present to the party.

(A) Except for you and I, everyone brought
(B) With exception of you and I, everyone brought
(C) Except for you and I, everyone had brought
(D) Except for you and me, everyone brought
(E) Except for you and me, everyone had brought

(D) This corrects the error in the case of the pronoun. Choice E corrects the error in case but introduces an error in tense.

3. When one reads the poetry of the seventeenth century, you find a striking contrast between the philosophy of the Cavalier poets such as Suckling and the attitude of the Metaphysical poets such as Donne.

(A) When one reads the poetry of the seventeenth century, you find
(B) When you read the poetry of the seventeenth century, one finds
(C) When one reads the poetry of the seventeenth century, he finds
(D) If one reads the poetry of the 17th century, you find
(E) As you read the poetry of the 17th century, one finds

(C) The improper use of the pronouns *one* and *you* is corrected in Choice C.

4. Because of his broken hip, John Jones has not and possibly never will be able to run the mile again.

(A) has not and possibly never will be able to run
(B) has not and possibly will never be able to run
(C) has not been and possibly never would be able to run
(D) has not and possibly never would be able to run
(E) has not been able to run and possibly never will be able to run

(E) The omission of the past participle *been* is corrected in Choice E.

5. **Had I realized how close I was to failing, I would not have gone to the party.**

   (A) Had I realized how close
   (B) If I would have realized
   (C) Had I had realized how close
   (D) When I realized how close
   (E) If I realized how close

(A) No error.

6. **The football team's winning it's first game of the season excited the student body.**

   (A) The football team's winning it's first game of the season
   (B) The football team having won it's first game of the season
   (C) The football team's having won it's first game of the season
   (D) The football team's winning its first game of the season
   (E) The football team winning it's first game of the season

(D) Misuse of word. The pronoun is *its*.

7. **Anyone interested in the use of computers can learn much if you have access to a state-of-the-art microcomputer.**

   (A) if you have access to
   (B) if he has access to
   (C) if access is available to
   (D) by access to
   (E) from access to

(B) This corrects the unnecessary switch in the pronouns, *anyone—you*.

8. **No student had ought to be put into a situation where he has to choose between his loyalty to his friends and his duty to the class.**

   (A) No student had ought to be put into a situation where
   (B) No student had ought to be put into a situation in which
   (C) No student should be put into a situation where
   (D) No student ought to be put into a situation in which
   (E) No student ought to be put into a situation where

(D) This corrects the error in tense and in the use of adjective or adverbial clauses.

9. **Being a realist, I could not accept his statement that supernatural beings had caused the disturbance.**

   (A) Being a realist,
   (B) Since I am a realist,
   (C) Being that I am a realist,
   (D) Being as I am a realist,
   (E) Realist that I am,

(A) No error.

10. **The reason I came late to class today is because the bus broke down.**

    (A) I came late to class today is because
    (B) why I came late to class today is because
    (C) I was late to school today is because
    (D) that I was late to school today is because
    (E) I came late to class today is that

(E) *The reason is that* is preferable to *The reason is because.*

11. **The grocer hadn't hardly any of those kind of canned goods.**

    (A) hadn't hardly any of those kind
    (B) hadn't hardly any of those kinds
    (C) had hardly any of those kind
    (D) had hardly any of those kinds
    (E) had scarcely any of those kind

(D) This corrects the double negative (*hadn't hardly*) and the misuse of *those* with *kind*.

12. **Having stole the money, the police searched the thief.**

    (A) Having stole the money, the police searched the thief.
    (B) Having stolen the money, the thief was searched by the police.
    (C) Having stolen the money, the police searched the thief.
    (D) Having stole the money, the thief was searched by the police.
    (E) Being that he stole the money, the police searched the thief.

(B) This corrects the dangling participle and the misuse of *stole* for *stolen*.

13. The child is neither encouraged to be critical or to examine all the evidence for his opinion.

(A) neither encouraged to be critical or to examine
(B) neither encouraged to be critical nor to examine
(C) either encouraged to be critical or to examine
(D) encouraged either to be critical nor to examine
(E) not encouraged either to be critical or to examine

(E) This question involves two aspects of correct English. *Neither* should be followed by *nor*; *either* by *or*. Choices A and D are, therefore, incorrect. The words *neither . . . nor* and *either . . . or* should be placed before the two items being discussed—*to be critical* and *to criticize*. Choice E meets both requirements.

14. The process by which the community influence the actions of its members is known as social control.

(A) influence the actions of its members
(B) influences the actions of its members
(C) had influenced the actions of its members
(D) influences the actions of their members
(E) will influence the actions of its members

(B) This question tests agreement. Agreement between subject and verb and pronoun and antecedent are both involved. *Community* (singular) needs a singular verb, *influences*. Also, the pronoun which refers to *community* should be singular (*its*). Choice B is best.

15. To be sure, there would be scarcely no time left over for other things if school children would have been expected to have considered all sides of every matter on which they hold opinions.

(A) would have been expected to have considered
(B) should have been expected to have considered
(C) were expected to consider
(D) will be expected to have been considered
(E) were expected to be considered

(C) *Would have been expected* is incorrect as a verb in a clause introduced by the conjunction *if. Had been expected* or *were expected* is preferable. *To have considered* does not follow correct sequence of tense and should be changed to *to consider.* Choice E changes the thought of the sentence and is illogical. Choice C is best.

16. Depending on skillful suggestion, argument is seldom used in advertising.

(A) Depending on skillful suggestion, argument is seldom used in advertising.
(B) Argument is seldom used by advertisers, who depend instead on skillful suggestion.
(C) Skillfull suggestion is depended on by advertisers instead of argument.
(D) Suggestion, which is more skillful, is used in place of argument by advertisers.
(E) Instead of suggestion, depending on argument is used by skillful advertisers.

(B) As presented, the sentence contains a dangling participle, *depending*. Choice B corrects this error. The other choices change the emphasis presented by the author.

17. When this war is over, no nation will either be isolated in war or peace.

(A) either be isolated in war or peace
(B) be either isolated in war or peace
(C) be isolated in neither war nor peace
(D) be isolated either in war or in peace
(E) be isolated neither in war or peace

(D) This question is similar to question 13. *Either. . . or* should precede the two choices offered (*in war* and *in peace*).

18. Each will be within trading distance of all the others and will be able to strike them.

(A) within trading distance of all the others and will be able to strike them
(B) near enough to trade with and strike all the others
(C) trading and striking the others
(D) within trading and striking distance of all the others
(E) able to strike and trade with all the others

(D) This phrase expresses the thought more compactly than the other four choices.

19. However many mistakes have been made in our past, the tradition of America, not only the champion of freedom but also fair play, still lives among millions who can see light and hope scarcely anywhere else.

(A) not only the champion of freedom but also fair play,
(B) the champion of not only freedom but also of fair play,
(C) the champion not only of freedom but also of fair play,
(D) not only the champion but also freedom and fair play,
(E) not the champion of freedom only, but also fair play,

(C) Parallel structure requires that *not only . . . but also* immediately precede the words they limit.

20. In giving expression to the play instincts of the human race, new vigor and effectiveness are afforded by recreation to the body and to the mind.

(A) new vigor and effectiveness are afforded by recreation to the body and to the mind
(B) recreation affords new vigor and effectiveness to the body and to the mind
(C) there are afforded new vigor and effectiveness to the body and to the mind
(D) by recreation the body and mind are afforded new vigor and effectiveness
(E) the body and the mind afford new vigor and effectiveness to themselves by recreation

(B) Given a choice, most authorities recommend the use of the active voice whenever possible. Thus, *affords* in Choice B is stronger than *are afforded* in Choices A, C, and D. The meaning of the sentence is changed in Choice E.

21. Play being recognized as an important factor in improving mental and physical health and thereby reducing human misery and poverty.

(A) Play being recognized as
(B) By recognizing play as
(C) Their recognizing play as
(D) Recognition of it being
(E) Play is recognized as

(E) This is an incomplete sentence or fragment. The sentence needs a verb to establish a principal clause. Choice E provides the verb (is *recognized*) and presents the only complete sentence in the group.

Section 6
Problem Solving

(Numbers in parentheses at the end of each explanation indicate the section in the Mathematics Review where material addressed in the question is discussed.)

AVERAGE ANNUAL RECEIPTS AND OUTLAYS OF U.S. GOVERNMENT 1967–1970 IN PERCENTAGE

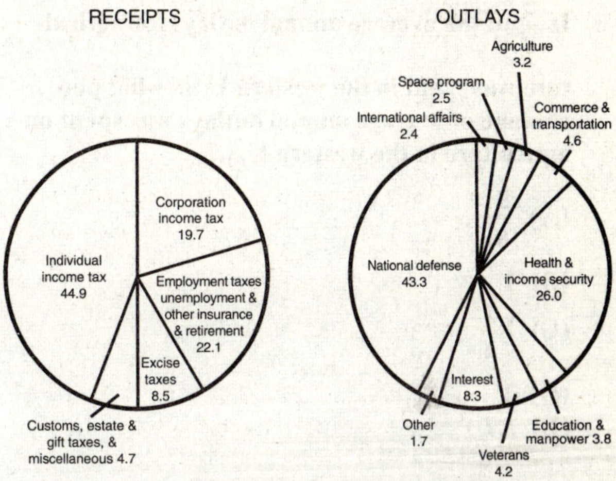

1. If the annual average receipts from the corporation income tax during the years 1967–1970 equal x, then the average annual receipts during this period were about

(A) $\frac{x}{4}$
(B) x^2
(C) $3x$
(D) $5x$
(E) x^5

(D) The corporation income tax accounted for 19.7% of all average annual receipts for the years 1967–1970. Since 19.7% is about 20% or $\frac{1}{5}$, the average annual receipts were about 5 times the average annual receipts from the corporation income tax. Therefore, the answer is $5x$. (IV-2)

2. The average annual combined outlay for veterans, education and manpower, and health and income security was roughly what fraction of the average annual outlays?

(A) $\frac{1}{4}$
(B) $\frac{1}{3}$
(C) $\frac{2}{5}$
(D) $\frac{1}{2}$
(E) $\frac{2}{3}$

(B) Veterans received 4.2%, education and manpower 3.8%, and health and income security 26% of the average annual outlays; so together the three categories received 4.2% + 3.8% + 26% or 34%. Since $\frac{1}{3}$ is $33\frac{1}{3}$%, 34% is roughly $\frac{1}{3}$. (IV-2)

3. If $\frac{5}{8}$ of the average annual outlays for agriculture was spent in the western U.S., what percentage of average annual outlays was spent on agriculture in the western U.S.?

(A) $\frac{5}{8}$
(B) 1
(C) $1\frac{1}{4}$
(D) 2
(E) 3.2

(D) Since $\frac{5}{8}$ of 3.2% = 5 × .4% = 2.0%, the correct answer is (D). (IV-2)

4. In a group of people solicited by a charity, 30% contributed \$40 each, 45% contributed \$20 each, and the rest contributed \$12 each. What percentage of the total contributed came from people who gave \$40?

(A) 25%
(B) 30%
(C) 40%
(D) 45%
(E) 50%

(E) Those who gave \$12 were 25% (100% – 30% – 45% = 25%) of the group. Let *x*, *y*, and *z* stand for the number of people who contributed \$40, \$20, and \$12 respectively. Then, the total number of people (*n*) who contributed is $x + y + z = n$. The total amount (*T*) contributed is

$$\$40x + \$20y + \$12z = T$$

Since 30% contributed \$40., we know that $x = .3n$; in the same way, we know that $y = .45n$ and $z = .25n$. Therefore, the total contributed was

$$\begin{aligned} T &= \$40(.3n) + \$20(.45n) + \$12(.25n) \\ &= 12n + 9n + 3n \\ &= 24n \end{aligned}$$

The amount contributed by those who gave \$40 was, therefore,

$$\$40\,(.3n) = 12n$$

So the percentage contributed by the \$40 donors is

$$100 \times \frac{12n}{24n} \text{ or } 50\%. \text{ (II-2)}$$

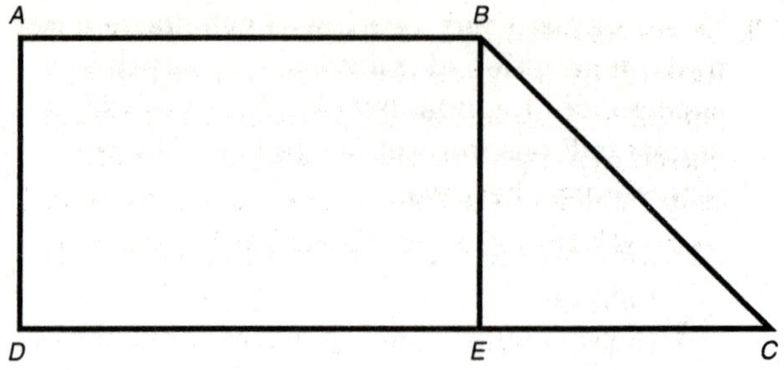

5. A trapezoid *ABCD* is formed by adding the isosceles right triangle *BCE* with base 5 inches to the rectangle *ABED* where *DE* is *t* inches. What is the area of the trapezoid in square inches?

(A) $5t + 12.5$
(B) $5t + 25$
(C) $2.5t + 12.5$
(D) $(t + 5)^2$
(E) $t^2 + 25$

(A) The area of trapezoid *ABCD* equals the area of rectangle *ABED*, which is $t \times 5$ (since $BE = EC = 5$), plus the area of triangle *BEC*, which is $\frac{(5\times5)}{2}$. The answer is thus $5t + 12.5$. (III-7)

6. A manufacturer of jam wants to make a profit of \$75 when he sells 300 jars of jam. It costs 65¢ each to make the first 100 jars of jam and 55¢ each to make each jar after the first 100. What price should he charge for the 300 jars of jam?

(A) \$75
(B) \$175
(C) \$225
(D) \$240
(E) \$250

(E) The selling price of the jars should equal cost + \$75. The cost of making 300 jars = (100)65¢ + (200)55¢ = \$65 + \$110 = \$175. So the selling price should be \$175 + \$75 or \$250. (II-3)

7. A car traveled 75% of the way from town A to town B by traveling for T hours at an average speed of V mph. The car travels at an average speed of S mph for the remaining part of the trip. Which of the following expressions represents the time the car traveled at S mph?

(A) $\frac{VT}{S}$

(B) $\frac{VS}{4T}$

(C) $\frac{4VT}{3S}$

(D) $\frac{3S}{VT}$

(E) $\frac{VT}{3S}$

(E) You need to find the total distance traveled in order to find the total time. Since the car traveled $V \times T$ miles when it averaged V mph, then VT is 75% of the total distance. Therefore, the total distance traveled is

$$\frac{VT}{.75} = \frac{4VT}{3}$$

The distance that was traveled at S mph is the total distance minus the distance at V mph, which is

$$\frac{4}{3}VT - VT = \frac{VT}{3}$$

So the time spent traveling at S mph was

$$\frac{\frac{VT}{3}}{S} = \frac{VT}{3S}$$

(II-3)

8. A company makes a profit of 7% selling goods which cost \$2,000; it also makes a profit of 6% selling a machine that cost the company \$5,000. How much total profit did the company make on both transactions?

(A) \$300
(B) \$400
(C) \$420
(D) \$440
(E) \$490

(D) The company's profit = (2,000)(.07) + (5,000)(.06) = \$140 + \$300 = \$440. (I-4)

9. If $\frac{x}{y} = \frac{3}{z}$, then $9y^2$ equals

(A) $\frac{x^2}{9}$

(B) x^3z

(C) x^2z^2

(D) $3x^2$

(E) $\left(\frac{1}{9}\right)x^2z^2$

(C) Since $\frac{x}{y} = \frac{3}{z}$, $xz = 3y$ and $9y^2 = (3y)^2$; so $9y^2 = (xz)^2 = x^2z^2$. (II-5, I-8)

10. The operation * applied to a number gives as its result 10 subtracted from twice the number. What is *(*9)?

(A) –11
(B) 6
(C) 8
(D) 9
(E) 36

(B) *9 is 10 subtracted from twice 9, or 2(9) – 10. So *9 is 18 – 10 = 8. Thus *(*9) will be *8. *8 is 10 subtracted from twice 8, or 16 – 10 = 6. Therefore 6 is the correct answer. (III-1, III-3)

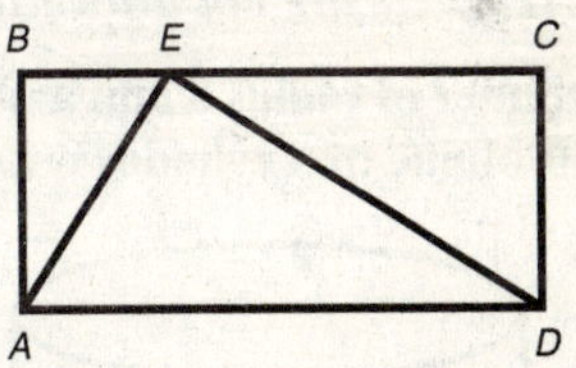

11. $ABCD$ is a rectangle. The length of BE is 4 and the length of EC is 6. The area of triangle BEA plus the area of triangle DCE minus the area of triangle AED is

(A) 0
(B) .4 of the area of triangle AEB
(C) .5 of the area of triangle AED
(D) .5 of the area of $ABCD$
(E) cannot be determined

(A) The area of a triangle is $\frac{1}{2}$ the base times the altitude. Since $ABCD$ is a rectangle, the triangles AED, BEA, and CDE all have the same altitude (AB). The base of AED is AD, which is equal to the base of ABE (BE) plus the base of CDE (EC). So the area af ABE plus the area of CDE is equal to the area of AED. Therefore, subtracting the area of ADE from the sum of the areas of ABE and CDE gives a result of 0. (III-7)

12. 36 identical chairs must be arranged in rows with the same number of chairs in each row. Each row must contain at least three chairs and there must be at least three rows. A row is parallel to the front of the room. How many different arrangements are possible?

(A) 2
(B) 4
(C) 5
(D) 6
(E) 10

(C) Let c be the number of chairs in a row and r be the number of rows. Since each row must have the same number of chairs, c times r must equal 36. We need to know how many ways we can write 36 as a product of two integers each greater than or equal to three, since each way to write 36 corresponds to an acceptable arrangement of the room. (c must be greater than or equal to 3 since each row must contain at least 3 chairs. In the same way, r must be greater than or equal to 3 because there must be at least 3 rows.) Writing 36 as a product of primes, we obtain $36 = 2 \times 18 = 2 \times 2 \times 9 = 2 \times 2 \times 3 \times 3$. So 36 can be written as 1×36, 2×18, 3×12, 4×9, 6×6, 9×4, 12×3, 18×2, and 36×1. Of these possibilities, 5 (3×12, 4×9, 6×6, 9×4, and 12×3) satisfy the requirements. Therefore, there are 5 arrangements. (I-1)

13. Which of the following solids has the largest volume? (*Figures are not drawn to scale.*)

I. A cylinder of radius 5 mm and height 11 mm (volume of a cylinder is $\pi r^2 h$)

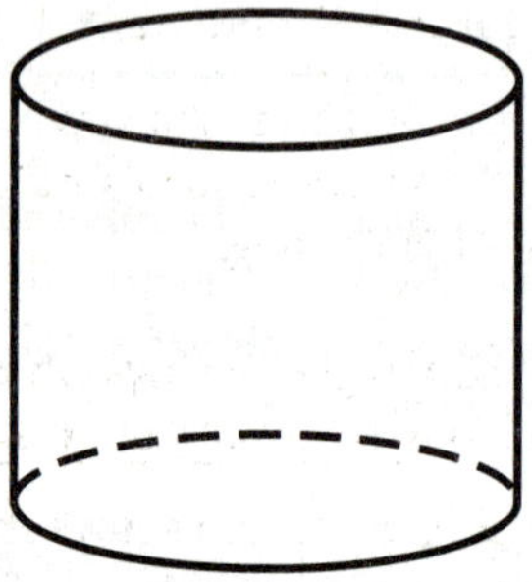

II. A sphere of radius 6mm (volume of a sphere is $\frac{4}{3}\pi r^3$)

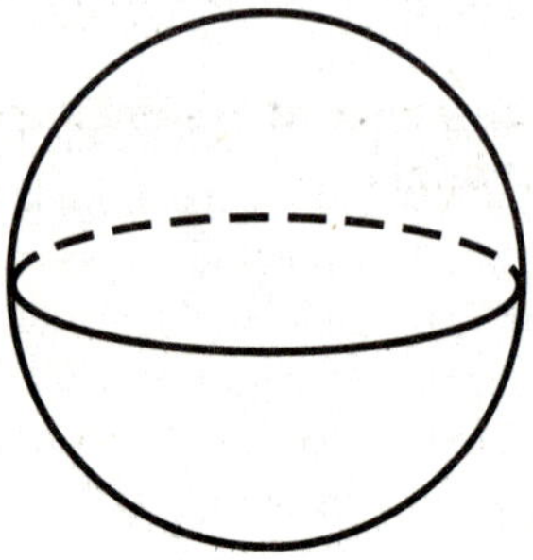

III. A cube with edge of 9mm (volume of a cube is e^3)

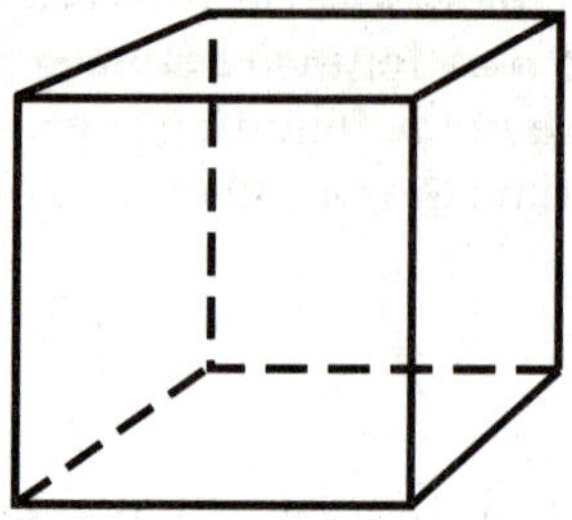

(A) I
(B) II
(C) III
(D) I and II
(E) II and III

(B) Volume of the cube is $9 \times 9 \times 9 = 729$ cubic mm. The sphere has volume $\frac{4}{3}\pi 6 \times 6 \times 6 = 288\pi$. Since π is greater than 3, 288π is greater than 729. The volume of the cylinder is $5 \times 5 \times 11\pi = 275\pi$. So the sphere has the largest volume.

You can save a lot of time in this problem if you do not change π to a decimal and then multiply the answers out. (III-8)

14. A pension fund has a total of $1 million invested in stock of the ABC Company and bonds of the DEF Corporation. The ABC stock yields 12% in cash each year, and the DEF bonds pay 10% in cash each year. The pension fund received a total of $115,000 in cash from ABC stock and DEF bonds last year. How much money was invested in ABC stock?

(A) $750,000.00
(B) $600,000.00
(C) $500,000.00
(D) $333,333.33
(E) $250,000.00

(A) Let s be the amount invested in ABC stock and b be the amount invested in DEF bonds. Then $s + b = 1{,}000{,}000$ and $.12s + .10b = 115{,}000$. Solve $s + b = 1{,}000{,}000$ for b and you get $b = 1{,}000{,}000 - s$. Now substitute this into the second equation. The result is $.12s + .10(1{,}000{,}000 - s) = .12s - .10s + 100{,}000 = 115{,}000$. So $.02s = 15{,}000$, which gives $s = \frac{15{,}000}{.02}$.

Therefore, $s = \$750{,}000$. (II-2)

15. The ratio of chickens to pigs to horses on a farm can be expressed as the triple ratio 20 : 4 : 6. If there are 120 chickens on the farm, then the number of horses on the farm is

(A) 4
(B) 6
(C) 24
(D) 36
(E) 60

(D) A triple ratio is a compact way of expressing three ratios. So the ratio of chickens to pigs to horses, 20 : 4 : 6, means that the ratio of chickens to pigs is 20 : 4 and the ratio of pigs to horses is 4 : 6 and the ratio of chickens to horses is 20 : 6. Thus for every 20 chickens there are 6 horses. So if there are 120 chickens, there are x horses where x satisfies the proportion $\frac{120}{20} = \frac{x}{6}$. Cross multiplying gives $20x = 720$ or $x = 36$. You can check the answer by seeing that the ratio of chickens to horses is 120 : 36, which is the same ratio as 20 : 6. (II-5)

16. If $x^2 - y^2 = 15$ and $x + y = 3$, then $x-y$ is

(A) –3
(B) 0
(C) 3
(D) 5
(E) cannot be determined

(D) $x^2 - y^2$ be factored into $(x + y)(x - y)$. So if $x + y$ is equal to 3, then $x^2 - y^2 = 15$ is equivalent to $3(x - y) = 15$. Dividing each side of the equation by 3, we obtain $x - y = \frac{15}{3} = 5$. (II-1, II-2)

17. What is the area of the shaded region? The radius of the outer circle is a and the radius of each of the circles inside the large circle is $\frac{a}{3}$.

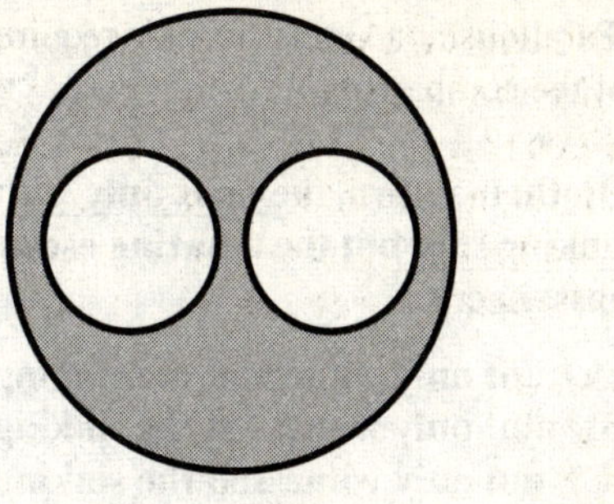

(A) 0
(B) $\left(\frac{1}{3}\right)\pi a^2$
(C) $\left(\frac{2}{3}\right)\pi a^2$
(D) $\left(\frac{7}{9}\right)\pi a^2$
(E) $\left(\frac{8}{9}\right)\pi a^2$

(D) The area of a circle is π times the square of the radius of the circle. So the area of the large circle is πa^2, and the area of each of the interior circles is $\pi\left(\frac{a}{3}\right)^2 = \left(\frac{1}{9}\right)\pi a^2$. Since there are two interior circles the shaded region has area equal to $\pi a^2 - 2\left(\left(\frac{1}{9}\right)\pi a^2\right) = \left(1 - \frac{2}{9}\right)\pi a^2 = \left(\frac{7}{9}\right)\pi a^2$. (III-7)

Section 7 Sentence Correction

1. John wanted to have gone to the movies.

(A) wanted to have gone
(B) had wanted to have gone
(C) wanted to go
(D) wanted to have went
(E) had wanted to have went

(C) The sequence of tenses is incorrect. According to the meaning of the sentence, John's wanting comes *before*, not *after*, John's going.

2. In this particular job we have discovered that to be diligent is more important than being bright.

(A) to be diligent is more important than being bright
(B) for one to be diligent is more important than being bright
(C) diligence is more important than brightness
(D) being diligent is more important than to be bright
(E) by being diligent is more important than being bright

(C) Parallelism: a similar form is required on either side of the comparison.

3. On their return, they not only witnessed the sinking ship but the amazing escape of the passengers.

(A) not only witnessed the sinking ship but the
(B) not only witnessed the sinking ship, but the
(C) not only witnessed the sinking ship, but also the
(D) witnessed not only the sinking ship but also the
(E) witnessed the sinking ship and also the

(D) They did witness two things, *not only the sinking ship* but also the *escape*.

4. No one but him could have told them that the thief was I.

(A) him could have told them that the thief was I
(B) he could have told them that the thief was I
(C) he could have told them that the thief was me
(D) him could have told them that the thief was me
(E) he could have told them the thief was me

(A) *But* meaning *except* is always followed by the objective pronoun, and the copula *was* takes the subjective *I*.

5. Either you transfer the data which was demanded or file a report explaining why you did not submit the overall annual figures.

(A) Either you transfer the data which was demanded
(B) You either transfer the data, which was demanded,
(C) You either transfer the data which were demanded
(D) Either you transfer the data, which was demanded,
(E) Either you transfer the data, which were demanded,

(C) *Either . . . or* connect *transfer* and *file*. *Data* here is plural and requires the verb *were*.

6. On entering the stadium, cheers greeted them as a sign of universal approval of their great achievement.

(A) On entering the stadium, cheers greeted them
(B) On entering the stadium, they were greeted by cheers
(C) While entering the stadium, cheers greeted them
(D) On entering the stadium cheers greeted them
(E) On entering the stadium: cheers greeted them

(B) A participial phrase at the beginning of a sentence must be followed by the word it modifies.

7. The set of propositions which was discussed by the panel have been published in the society journal.

(A) which was discussed by the panel have
(B) which were discussed by the panel have
(C) that was discussed by the panel has
(D) which were discussed by the panel has
(E) which was discussed, by the panel, has

(D) The *set has been* published, while the *propositions* (individually) *were* discussed.

8. They decided to honor Mr. Wilson, who will be president of the club for ten years next Tuesday.

(A) will be president of the club for ten years next Tuesday
(B) shall have been president of the club for ten years next Tuesday
(C) next Tuesday will have been president of the club for ten years
(D) next Tuesday has been president of the club for ten years
(E) had been president of the club for ten years next Tuesday

(C) The future perfect tense is required here, since the action continues from the past into the future (*next Tuesday*).

9. After a careful evaluation of the circumstances surrounding the incident, we decided that we neither have the authority nor the means to cope with the problem.

(A) neither have the authority nor
(B) neither have authority or
(C) have neither the authority nor
(D) have neither the authority or
(E) have not either the authority nor

(C) *Neither . . . nor* apply to *authority* and *means* and must precede them directly.

10. Everyone of us have understood that without him helping us we would not have succeeded in our program over the past six months.

(A) Everyone of us have understood that without him helping us
(B) Everyone of us has understood that without his helping us
(C) Everyone of us have understood that without his help
(D) Everyone of us has understood that without him helping us
(E) Every single one of us have understood that without him helping us

(B) *Everyone* is singular and requires the singular *has.* The preposition *without* requires the gerund *helping* preceded by the possessive *his.*

11. On the African continent, the incidence of vitamin deficiencies correlates positively with the level of solar radiation

(A) deficiencies correlates positively with
(B) deficiencies correlate positively with
(C) deficiencies, correlate positively with,
(D) deficiencies correlate positively to
(E) deficiencies correlates positively to

(A) The *incidence* (singular) *correlates.* The preposition *with* is correct.

12. A thoroughly frightened child was seen by her cowering in the corner of the room.

(A) A thoroughly frightened child was seen by her cowering in the corner of the room.
(B) Cowering in the corner of the room a thoroughly frightened child was seen by her.
(C) She saw, cowering in the corner of the room, a thoroughly frightened child.
(D) A thoroughly frightened child, cowering in the corner of the room, was seen by her.
(E) She saw a thoroughly frightened child who was cowering in the corner of the room.

(C) This is a suspenseful sentence since what *She saw* is held off to the very last word in the sentence. Also, an active verb, *saw,* is preferable to the passive *was seen.*

13. If they would have taken greater care in the disposal of the nuclear waste, the disaster would not have occurred.

(A) If they would have taken greater care
(B) Unless they took greater care
(C) Had they not taken greater care
(D) If they had taken greater care
(E) If they took greater care

(D) The correct form of the past conditional requires the past perfect in the conditional clause: *had taken.*

14. Neither the judge nor I am ready to announce who the winner is.

(A) Neither the judge nor I am ready to announce who the winner is.
(B) Neither the judge nor I are ready to announce who the winner is.
(C) Neither the judge nor I are ready to announce who is the winner.
(D) Neither the judge nor I am ready to announce who is the winner.
(E) Neither I or the judge are ready to announce who is the winner.

(A) In *neither . . . nor* constructions, the verb is matched to the noun or pronoun that immediately precedes it. The sentence is not a question, and thus does not become inverted.

15. After adequate deliberation, the council can see scarcely any valid reason for its reviewing the request.

(A) can see scarcely any valid reason for its
(B) can not see scarcely any valid reason for its
(C) can see any valid reason scarcely for its
(D) can see scarcely any valid reason for it's
(E) can scarcely see any valid reason for it's

(A) *Scarcely* applies to the *valid reason* and thus must precede it directly. *Scarcely,* having a negative connotation, does not require a negation of the verb.

16. If she were I, she would have accepted the prize if she had won it.

(A) were I, she would have accepted the prize if she had
(B) was I, she would have accepted the prize if she would have
(C) was I, she would have accepted the prize if she had
(D) were I, she would have accepted the prize if she would have
(E) were me, she would have accepted the prize if she had

(A) No error. The sequence of tenses requires that the past perfect tense be used in the conditional clause *if she had won it*. Also, *I* is required after a form of the verb *to be*.

17. We expect help in providing adequate facilities and ample funds from everybody in order to advance this vital program.

(A) in providing adequate facilities and ample funds from everybody
(B) in the provision of adequate facilities and ample funds from everybody
(C) in providing adequate facilities and funds from everyone
(D) with facilities and funds from everyone
(E) from everybody in providing adequate facilities and ample funds

(E) *Everybody* is expected to help. The sense demands that *from everybody* be placed in the general position. *In the provision of* makes the sentence unnecessarily bulky.

18. From the moment he took public office, his actions have been loaded with significance and filled with worth.

(A) been loaded with significance and filled with worth
(B) been significant and worthwhile
(C) become loaded with significance and worth
(D) to be loaded with significance and filled with worth
(E) been actions of significance and worth

(B) The original sentence is too wordy.

19. After several days' tour, we became convinced that the climate of this deserted island was like Florida in winter.

(A) the climate of this deserted island was like Florida in winter
(B) the climate of this deserted island was like that of Florida in winter
(C) the climate of this desert Island was like Florida in winter
(D) the climate of this deserted island in winter was like Florida
(E) the climate of this desert island was as Florida in winter

(B) The *climate* can only be compared to another climate.

20. The students have always had a most sincere interest and admiration for the important work of Professor Jakobsen.

(A) a most sincere interest and admiration for
(B) a most sincere interest in and admiration for
(C) mostly a sincere interest and admiration for
(D) a most sincere interest, and admiration for
(E) a most sincere interest and an admiration for

(B) *Interest in* a subject and *admiration for* it: the prepositions must remain.

21. I might have provided a happier ending if I was the author of that novel.

(A) ending if I was the author of that novel
(B) ending, if I were the author of that novel
(C) ending. If I were the author of that novel
(D) ending if I had been the author of that novel
(E) ending, if I had to be the author of that novel

(D) This is a past conditional and requires the past perfect in the conditional clause. There is no punctuation before the *if*.

Evaluating Your Score

Tabulate your score for each section of Sample Test 1 according to the directions on pages 6–7 and record the results in the Self-Scoring Table below. Then find your rating for each score on the Self-Scoring Scale and record it in the appropriate blank.

Self-Scoring Table

SECTION	SCORE	RATING
1		
2		
3		
4		
5		
6		
7		

***Self-Scoring Scale*—RATING**

SECTION	POOR	FAIR	GOOD	EXCELLENT
1	0 – 12+	13 – 17+	18 – 21+	22 – 25
2	0 – 8+	9 – 11	11+ – 14	14+ – 17
3	0 – 8+	9 – 11	11+ – 14	14+ – 17
4	0 – 9+	10 – 13+	14 – 17+	18 – 21
5	0 – 9+	10 – 13+	14 – 17+	18 – 21
6	0 – 8+	9 – 11	11+ – 14	14+ – 17
7	0 – 9+	10 – 13+	14 – 17+	18 – 21

Study again the Review sections covering material in Sample Test 1 for which you had a rating of FAIR or POOR. Then go on to Sample Test 2.

To obtain an approximation of your GMAT score, see page 6.

Answer Sheet
SAMPLE TEST 2

Section 1

1 Ⓐ Ⓑ Ⓒ Ⓓ Ⓔ	6 Ⓐ Ⓑ Ⓒ Ⓓ Ⓔ	11 Ⓐ Ⓑ Ⓒ Ⓓ Ⓔ	16 Ⓐ Ⓑ Ⓒ Ⓓ Ⓔ	21 Ⓐ Ⓑ Ⓒ Ⓓ Ⓔ
2 Ⓐ Ⓑ Ⓒ Ⓓ Ⓔ	7 Ⓐ Ⓑ Ⓒ Ⓓ Ⓔ	12 Ⓐ Ⓑ Ⓒ Ⓓ Ⓔ	17 Ⓐ Ⓑ Ⓒ Ⓓ Ⓔ	22 Ⓐ Ⓑ Ⓒ Ⓓ Ⓔ
3 Ⓐ Ⓑ Ⓒ Ⓓ Ⓔ	8 Ⓐ Ⓑ Ⓒ Ⓓ Ⓔ	13 Ⓐ Ⓑ Ⓒ Ⓓ Ⓔ	18 Ⓐ Ⓑ Ⓒ Ⓓ Ⓔ	23 Ⓐ Ⓑ Ⓒ Ⓓ Ⓔ
4 Ⓐ Ⓑ Ⓒ Ⓓ Ⓔ	9 Ⓐ Ⓑ Ⓒ Ⓓ Ⓔ	14 Ⓐ Ⓑ Ⓒ Ⓓ Ⓔ	19 Ⓐ Ⓑ Ⓒ Ⓓ Ⓔ	24 Ⓐ Ⓑ Ⓒ Ⓓ Ⓔ
5 Ⓐ Ⓑ Ⓒ Ⓓ Ⓔ	10 Ⓐ Ⓑ Ⓒ Ⓓ Ⓔ	15 Ⓐ Ⓑ Ⓒ Ⓓ Ⓔ	20 Ⓐ Ⓑ Ⓒ Ⓓ Ⓔ	25 Ⓐ Ⓑ Ⓒ Ⓓ Ⓔ

Section 2

1 Ⓐ Ⓑ Ⓒ Ⓓ Ⓔ	6 Ⓐ Ⓑ Ⓒ Ⓓ Ⓔ	11 Ⓐ Ⓑ Ⓒ Ⓓ Ⓔ	16 Ⓐ Ⓑ Ⓒ Ⓓ Ⓔ	21 Ⓐ Ⓑ Ⓒ Ⓓ Ⓔ
2 Ⓐ Ⓑ Ⓒ Ⓓ Ⓔ	7 Ⓐ Ⓑ Ⓒ Ⓓ Ⓔ	12 Ⓐ Ⓑ Ⓒ Ⓓ Ⓔ	17 Ⓐ Ⓑ Ⓒ Ⓓ Ⓔ	22 Ⓐ Ⓑ Ⓒ Ⓓ Ⓔ
3 Ⓐ Ⓑ Ⓒ Ⓓ Ⓔ	8 Ⓐ Ⓑ Ⓒ Ⓓ Ⓔ	13 Ⓐ Ⓑ Ⓒ Ⓓ Ⓔ	18 Ⓐ Ⓑ Ⓒ Ⓓ Ⓔ	23 Ⓐ Ⓑ Ⓒ Ⓓ Ⓔ
4 Ⓐ Ⓑ Ⓒ Ⓓ Ⓔ	9 Ⓐ Ⓑ Ⓒ Ⓓ Ⓔ	14 Ⓐ Ⓑ Ⓒ Ⓓ Ⓔ	19 Ⓐ Ⓑ Ⓒ Ⓓ Ⓔ	24 Ⓐ Ⓑ Ⓒ Ⓓ Ⓔ
5 Ⓐ Ⓑ Ⓒ Ⓓ Ⓔ	10 Ⓐ Ⓑ Ⓒ Ⓓ Ⓔ	15 Ⓐ Ⓑ Ⓒ Ⓓ Ⓔ	20 Ⓐ Ⓑ Ⓒ Ⓓ Ⓔ	25 Ⓐ Ⓑ Ⓒ Ⓓ Ⓔ

Section 3

1 Ⓐ Ⓑ Ⓒ Ⓓ Ⓔ	6 Ⓐ Ⓑ Ⓒ Ⓓ Ⓔ	11 Ⓐ Ⓑ Ⓒ Ⓓ Ⓔ	16 Ⓐ Ⓑ Ⓒ Ⓓ Ⓔ	21 Ⓐ Ⓑ Ⓒ Ⓓ Ⓔ
2 Ⓐ Ⓑ Ⓒ Ⓓ Ⓔ	7 Ⓐ Ⓑ Ⓒ Ⓓ Ⓔ	12 Ⓐ Ⓑ Ⓒ Ⓓ Ⓔ	17 Ⓐ Ⓑ Ⓒ Ⓓ Ⓔ	22 Ⓐ Ⓑ Ⓒ Ⓓ Ⓔ
3 Ⓐ Ⓑ Ⓒ Ⓓ Ⓔ	8 Ⓐ Ⓑ Ⓒ Ⓓ Ⓔ	13 Ⓐ Ⓑ Ⓒ Ⓓ Ⓔ	18 Ⓐ Ⓑ Ⓒ Ⓓ Ⓔ	23 Ⓐ Ⓑ Ⓒ Ⓓ Ⓔ
4 Ⓐ Ⓑ Ⓒ Ⓓ Ⓔ	9 Ⓐ Ⓑ Ⓒ Ⓓ Ⓔ	14 Ⓐ Ⓑ Ⓒ Ⓓ Ⓔ	19 Ⓐ Ⓑ Ⓒ Ⓓ Ⓔ	24 Ⓐ Ⓑ Ⓒ Ⓓ Ⓔ
5 Ⓐ Ⓑ Ⓒ Ⓓ Ⓔ	10 Ⓐ Ⓑ Ⓒ Ⓓ Ⓔ	15 Ⓐ Ⓑ Ⓒ Ⓓ Ⓔ	20 Ⓐ Ⓑ Ⓒ Ⓓ Ⓔ	25 Ⓐ Ⓑ Ⓒ Ⓓ Ⓔ

Section 4

1 Ⓐ Ⓑ Ⓒ Ⓓ Ⓔ	6 Ⓐ Ⓑ Ⓒ Ⓓ Ⓔ	11 Ⓐ Ⓑ Ⓒ Ⓓ Ⓔ	16 Ⓐ Ⓑ Ⓒ Ⓓ Ⓔ	21 Ⓐ Ⓑ Ⓒ Ⓓ Ⓔ
2 Ⓐ Ⓑ Ⓒ Ⓓ Ⓔ	7 Ⓐ Ⓑ Ⓒ Ⓓ Ⓔ	12 Ⓐ Ⓑ Ⓒ Ⓓ Ⓔ	17 Ⓐ Ⓑ Ⓒ Ⓓ Ⓔ	22 Ⓐ Ⓑ Ⓒ Ⓓ Ⓔ
3 Ⓐ Ⓑ Ⓒ Ⓓ Ⓔ	8 Ⓐ Ⓑ Ⓒ Ⓓ Ⓔ	13 Ⓐ Ⓑ Ⓒ Ⓓ Ⓔ	18 Ⓐ Ⓑ Ⓒ Ⓓ Ⓔ	23 Ⓐ Ⓑ Ⓒ Ⓓ Ⓔ
4 Ⓐ Ⓑ Ⓒ Ⓓ Ⓔ	9 Ⓐ Ⓑ Ⓒ Ⓓ Ⓔ	14 Ⓐ Ⓑ Ⓒ Ⓓ Ⓔ	19 Ⓐ Ⓑ Ⓒ Ⓓ Ⓔ	24 Ⓐ Ⓑ Ⓒ Ⓓ Ⓔ
5 Ⓐ Ⓑ Ⓒ Ⓓ Ⓔ	10 Ⓐ Ⓑ Ⓒ Ⓓ Ⓔ	15 Ⓐ Ⓑ Ⓒ Ⓓ Ⓔ	20 Ⓐ Ⓑ Ⓒ Ⓓ Ⓔ	25 Ⓐ Ⓑ Ⓒ Ⓓ Ⓔ

Section 5

1 Ⓐ Ⓑ Ⓒ Ⓓ Ⓔ	6 Ⓐ Ⓑ Ⓒ Ⓓ Ⓔ	11 Ⓐ Ⓑ Ⓒ Ⓓ Ⓔ	16 Ⓐ Ⓑ Ⓒ Ⓓ Ⓔ	21 Ⓐ Ⓑ Ⓒ Ⓓ Ⓔ
2 Ⓐ Ⓑ Ⓒ Ⓓ Ⓔ	7 Ⓐ Ⓑ Ⓒ Ⓓ Ⓔ	12 Ⓐ Ⓑ Ⓒ Ⓓ Ⓔ	17 Ⓐ Ⓑ Ⓒ Ⓓ Ⓔ	22 Ⓐ Ⓑ Ⓒ Ⓓ Ⓔ
3 Ⓐ Ⓑ Ⓒ Ⓓ Ⓔ	8 Ⓐ Ⓑ Ⓒ Ⓓ Ⓔ	13 Ⓐ Ⓑ Ⓒ Ⓓ Ⓔ	18 Ⓐ Ⓑ Ⓒ Ⓓ Ⓔ	23 Ⓐ Ⓑ Ⓒ Ⓓ Ⓔ
4 Ⓐ Ⓑ Ⓒ Ⓓ Ⓔ	9 Ⓐ Ⓑ Ⓒ Ⓓ Ⓔ	14 Ⓐ Ⓑ Ⓒ Ⓓ Ⓔ	19 Ⓐ Ⓑ Ⓒ Ⓓ Ⓔ	24 Ⓐ Ⓑ Ⓒ Ⓓ Ⓔ
5 Ⓐ Ⓑ Ⓒ Ⓓ Ⓔ	10 Ⓐ Ⓑ Ⓒ Ⓓ Ⓔ	15 Ⓐ Ⓑ Ⓒ Ⓓ Ⓔ	20 Ⓐ Ⓑ Ⓒ Ⓓ Ⓔ	25 Ⓐ Ⓑ Ⓒ Ⓓ Ⓔ

Section 6

1 Ⓐ Ⓑ Ⓒ Ⓓ Ⓔ	6 Ⓐ Ⓑ Ⓒ Ⓓ Ⓔ	11 Ⓐ Ⓑ Ⓒ Ⓓ Ⓔ	16 Ⓐ Ⓑ Ⓒ Ⓓ Ⓔ	21 Ⓐ Ⓑ Ⓒ Ⓓ Ⓔ
2 Ⓐ Ⓑ Ⓒ Ⓓ Ⓔ	7 Ⓐ Ⓑ Ⓒ Ⓓ Ⓔ	12 Ⓐ Ⓑ Ⓒ Ⓓ Ⓔ	17 Ⓐ Ⓑ Ⓒ Ⓓ Ⓔ	22 Ⓐ Ⓑ Ⓒ Ⓓ Ⓔ
3 Ⓐ Ⓑ Ⓒ Ⓓ Ⓔ	8 Ⓐ Ⓑ Ⓒ Ⓓ Ⓔ	13 Ⓐ Ⓑ Ⓒ Ⓓ Ⓔ	18 Ⓐ Ⓑ Ⓒ Ⓓ Ⓔ	23 Ⓐ Ⓑ Ⓒ Ⓓ Ⓔ
4 Ⓐ Ⓑ Ⓒ Ⓓ Ⓔ	9 Ⓐ Ⓑ Ⓒ Ⓓ Ⓔ	14 Ⓐ Ⓑ Ⓒ Ⓓ Ⓔ	19 Ⓐ Ⓑ Ⓒ Ⓓ Ⓔ	24 Ⓐ Ⓑ Ⓒ Ⓓ Ⓔ
5 Ⓐ Ⓑ Ⓒ Ⓓ Ⓔ	10 Ⓐ Ⓑ Ⓒ Ⓓ Ⓔ	15 Ⓐ Ⓑ Ⓒ Ⓓ Ⓔ	20 Ⓐ Ⓑ Ⓒ Ⓓ Ⓔ	25 Ⓐ Ⓑ Ⓒ Ⓓ Ⓔ

Section 7

1 Ⓐ Ⓑ Ⓒ Ⓓ Ⓔ	6 Ⓐ Ⓑ Ⓒ Ⓓ Ⓔ	11 Ⓐ Ⓑ Ⓒ Ⓓ Ⓔ	16 Ⓐ Ⓑ Ⓒ Ⓓ Ⓔ	21 Ⓐ Ⓑ Ⓒ Ⓓ Ⓔ
2 Ⓐ Ⓑ Ⓒ Ⓓ Ⓔ	7 Ⓐ Ⓑ Ⓒ Ⓓ Ⓔ	12 Ⓐ Ⓑ Ⓒ Ⓓ Ⓔ	17 Ⓐ Ⓑ Ⓒ Ⓓ Ⓔ	22 Ⓐ Ⓑ Ⓒ Ⓓ Ⓔ
3 Ⓐ Ⓑ Ⓒ Ⓓ Ⓔ	8 Ⓐ Ⓑ Ⓒ Ⓓ Ⓔ	13 Ⓐ Ⓑ Ⓒ Ⓓ Ⓔ	18 Ⓐ Ⓑ Ⓒ Ⓓ Ⓔ	23 Ⓐ Ⓑ Ⓒ Ⓓ Ⓔ
4 Ⓐ Ⓑ Ⓒ Ⓓ Ⓔ	9 Ⓐ Ⓑ Ⓒ Ⓓ Ⓔ	14 Ⓐ Ⓑ Ⓒ Ⓓ Ⓔ	19 Ⓐ Ⓑ Ⓒ Ⓓ Ⓔ	24 Ⓐ Ⓑ Ⓒ Ⓓ Ⓔ
5 Ⓐ Ⓑ Ⓒ Ⓓ Ⓔ	10 Ⓐ Ⓑ Ⓒ Ⓓ Ⓔ	15 Ⓐ Ⓑ Ⓒ Ⓓ Ⓔ	20 Ⓐ Ⓑ Ⓒ Ⓓ Ⓔ	25 Ⓐ Ⓑ Ⓒ Ⓓ Ⓔ

✂ Cut along dashed line to remove answer sheet.

10 SAMPLE TEST 2
with Answers and Analysis

Writing Assessment

Part I

TIME: 30 minutes

Directions: Write a clear, logical, and well-organized response to the following issue or argument. Your response should be in the form of a short essay, following the conventions of standard written English. Your answer should fit on three pages of lined 8½" × 11" paper. Write legibly. Essays that are illegible or that are written on a topic other than the one outlined in the question will not be scored.

Forced obsolescence is a strategy that manufacturers use to limit the useful life of some consumer products in order to increase sales. Some commentators complain that this practice results in a waste of resources. What they do not understand is that by shortening the life cycle of products, manufacturers are able to both improve them and lower the cost to the consumer.

Which statement do you find more convincing, that forced obsolescence wastes resources or that it benefits consumers? State your position using relevant reasons from your own experience, observation, or reading.

Part II

TIME: 30 minutes

Directions: Write a clear, logical, and well-organized response to the following issue or argument. Your response should be in the form of a short essay, following the conventions of standard written English. Your answer should fit on three pages of lined 8½" × 11" paper. Write legibly. Essays that are illegible or that are written on a topic other than the one outlined in the question will not be scored.

Women are more fashion conscious than men. Women's clothing styles change every year, forcing them to update their wardrobes so as not to appear behind the times.

Discuss how logically persuasive you find the above argument. In presenting your point of view, analyze the sort of reasoning used and its supporting evidence. In addition, state what further evidence, if any, would make the argument more sound and convincing or would make you better able to evaluate its conclusion.

STOP

**IF THERE IS STILL TIME REMAINING,
YOU MAY REVIEW THE QUESTIONS IN THIS SECTION ONLY.
YOU MAY NOT TURN TO ANY OTHER SECTION OF THE TEST.**

Section 1

TIME: 30 minutes
25 Questions

Directions: This part contains three reading passages. You are to read each one carefully. When answering the questions, you *will* be allowed to refer back to the passages. The questions are based on what is *stated* or *implied* in each passage.

Passage 1:

The following passage was written in 1964.

The main burden of assuring that the resources of the federal government are well managed falls on relatively few of the five million men and women whom it employs. Under the department and agency heads there are 8,600 political, career, military, and foreign service executives—the top managers and professionals—who exert major influence on the manner in which the rest are directed and utilized. Below their level there are other thousands with assignments of some managerial significance, but we believe that the line of demarcation selected is the best available for our purposes in this attainment.

In addition to Presidential appointees in responsible posts, the 8,600 include the three highest grades under the Classification Act; the three highest grades in the postal field service; comparable grades in the foreign service; general officers in the military service; and similar classes in other special services and in agencies or positions excepted from the Classification Act.

There is no complete inventory of positions or people in federal service at this level. The lack may be explained by separate agency statutes and personnel systems, diffusion among so many special services, and absence of any central point (short of the President himself) with jurisdiction over all upper-level personnel of the government.

This Committee considers establishment and maintenance of a central inventory of these key people and positions to be an elementary necessity, a first step in improved management throughout the Executive Branch.

Top Presidential appointees, about 500 of them, bear the brunt of translating the philosophy and aims of the current administration into practical programs. This group includes the secretaries and assistant secretaries of cabinet departments, agency heads and their deputies, heads and members of boards and commissions with fixed terms, and chiefs and directors of major bureaus, divisions, and services. Appointments to many of these politically sensitive positions are made on recommendation by department or agency heads, but all are presumably responsible to Presidential leadership.

One qualification for office at this level is that there be no basic disagreement with Presidential political philosophy, at least so far as administrative judgments and actions are concerned. Apart from the bi-partisan boards and commissions, these men are normally identified with the political party of the President, or are sympathetic to it, although there are exceptions.

There are four distinguishable kinds of top Presidential appointees, including:

—Those whom the President selects at the outset to establish immediate and effective control over the government (e.g., Cabinet secretaries, agency heads, his own White House staff and Executive Office Personnel).

—Those selected by department and agency heads in order to establish control within their respective organizations (e.g.—assistant secretaries, deputies, assistants to, and major line posts in some bureaus and divisions).

—High-level appointees who—though often requiring clearance through political or interest group channels, or both—must have known scientific or technical competence (e.g.—the Surgeon General, the Commissioner of Education).

GO ON TO THE NEXT PAGE ➤

—Those named to residual positions traditionally filled on a partisan patronage basis.

These appointees are primarily regarded as policy makers and overseers of policy execution. In practice, however, they usually have substantial responsibilities in line management, often requiring a thorough knowledge of substantive agency programs.

1. According to the passage, about how many top managerial professionals work for the federal government?

   (A) five million
   (B) two million
   (C) twenty thousand
   (D) nine thousand
   (E) five hundred

2. No complete inventory exists of positions in the three highest levels of government service because

   (A) no one has bothered to count them
   (B) computers cannot handle all the data
   (C) separate agency personnel systems are used
   (D) the President has never requested such information
   (E) the Classification Act prohibits such a census

3. Top Presidential appointees have as their central responsibility the

   (A) prevention of politically motivated interference with the actions of their agencies
   (B) monitoring of government actions on behalf of the President's own political party
   (C) translation of the aims of the administration into practical programs
   (D) investigation of charges of corruption within the government
   (E) maintenance of adequate controls over the rate of government spending

4. One exception to the general rule that top Presidential appointees must be in agreement with the President's political philosophy may be found in

   (A) most cabinet-level officers
   (B) members of the White House staff
   (C) bi-partisan boards and commissions
   (D) those offices filled on a patronage basis
   (E) offices requiring scientific or technical expertise

5. Applicants for Presidential appointments are usually identified with or are members of

   (A) large corporations
   (B) the foreign service
   (C) government bureaus
   (D) academic circles
   (E) the President's political party

6. Appointees that are selected directly by the President include

   (A) U.S. marshals and attorneys
   (B) military officers
   (C) agency heads
   (D) assistant secretaries
   (E) congressional committee members

7. Appointees usually have to possess expertise in

   (A) line management
   (B) military affairs
   (C) foreign affairs
   (D) strategic planning
   (E) constitutional law

8. According to the passage, Presidential appointees are regarded primarily as

   (A) political spokesmen
   (B) policy makers
   (C) staff managers
   (D) scientific or technical experts
   (E) business executives

9. Appointees selected by department and agency heads include

   (A) military men
   (B) cabinet secretaries
   (C) deputy secretaries
   (D) diplomats
   (E) residual position holders

GO ON TO THE NEXT PAGE ➤

Passage 2:

The first and decisive step in the expansion of Europe overseas was the conquest of the Atlantic Ocean. That the nation to achieve this should be Portugal was the logical outcome of her geographical position and her history. Placed on the extreme margin of the old, classical Mediterranean world and facing the untraversed ocean, Portugal could adapt and develop the knowledge and experience of the past to meet the challenge of the unknown. Some centuries of navigating the coastal waters of Western Europe and Northern Africa had prepared Portuguese seamen to appreciate the problems which the Ocean presented and to apply and develop the methods necessary to overcome them. From the seamen of the Mediterranean, particularly those of Genoa and Venice, they had learned the organization and conduct of a mercantile marine, and from Jewish astronomers and Catalan mapmakers the rudiments of navigation. Largely excluded from a share in Mediterranean commerce at a time when her increasing and vigorous population was making heavy demands on her resources, Portugal turned southwards and westwards for opportunities of trade and commerce. At this moment of national destiny it was fortunate for her that in men of the calibre of Prince Henry, known as the Navigator, and King John II she found resolute and dedicated leaders.

The problems to be faced were new and complex. The conditions for navigation and commerce in the Mediterranean were relatively simple, compared with those in the western seas. The landlocked Mediterranean, tideless and with a climatic regime of regular and well-defined seasons, presented few obstacles to sailors who were the heirs of a great body of sea lore garnered from the experiences of many centuries. What hazards there were, in the form of sudden storms or dangerous coasts, were known and could be usually anticipated. Similarly the Mediterranean coasts, though they might be for long periods in the hands of dangerous rivals, were described in sailing directions or laid down on the portolan charts drawn by Venetian, Genoese and Catalan cartographers. Problems of determining positions at sea, which confronted the Portuguese, did not arise. Though the Mediterranean seamen by no means restricted themselves to coastal sailing, the latitudinal extent of the Mediterranean was not great, and voyages could be conducted from point to point on compass bearings; the ships were never so far from land as to make it necessary to fix their positions in latitude by astronomical observations. Having made a landfall on a bearing, they could determine their precise position from prominent landmarks, soundings or the nature of the sea bed, after reference to the sailing directions or charts.

By contrast, the pioneers of ocean navigation faced much greater difficulties. The western ocean which extended, according to the speculations of the cosmographers, through many degrees of latitude and longitude, was an unknown quantity, but certainly subjected to wide variations of weather and without known bounds. Those who first ventured out over its waters did so without benefit of sailing directions or traditional lore. As the Portuguese sailed southwards, they left behind them the familiar constellations in the heavens by which they could determine direction and the hours of the night, and particularly the pole-star from which by a simple operation they could determine their latitude. Along the unknown coasts they were threatened by shallows, hidden banks, rocks and contrary winds and currents, with no knowledge of convenient shelter to ride out storms or of very necessary watering places. It is little wonder that these pioneers dreaded the thought of being forced on to a lee shore or of having to choose between these inshore dangers and the unrecorded perils of the open sea.

10. Before the expansion of Europe overseas could take place

(A) vast sums of money had to be raised
(B) an army had to be recruited
(C) the Atlantic Ocean had to be conquered
(D) ships had to be built
(E) seamen had to be trained

GO ON TO THE NEXT PAGE ➤

11. One of Portugal's leaders, known as the Navigator, was in reality
    (A) Christopher Columbus
    (B) King John II
    (C) a Venetian
    (D) Prince Henry
    (E) Prince Paul

12. Portugal was adept at exploring unknown waters because she possessed all of the following except
    (A) a navy
    (B) past experience
    (C) experienced navigators
    (D) experienced mapmakers
    (E) extensive trade routes

13. In addition to possessing the necessary resources for exploration, Portugal was the logical country for this task because of her
    (A) wealth
    (B) navigational experience
    (C) geographical position
    (D) prominence
    (E) ability

14. The Portuguese learned navigational methods and procedures from all of the following except
    (A) Jews
    (B) Catalans
    (C) Genoese
    (D) Venetians
    (E) Aegeans

15. Mediterranean seamen generally kept close to shore because
    (A) they were afraid of pirates
    (B) they feared being forced to a lee shore
    (C) they lacked navigational ability
    (D) they feared running into storms
    (E) the latitudinal extent of the Mediterranean was not great

16. Hazards such as sudden storms and dangerous coasts were
    (A) predictable risks
    (B) unknown risks
    (C) unknown to the area
    (D) a major threat to exploration
    (E) no threat to navigation

17. Sailing close to the coast enabled seamen to
    (A) reach their destination faster
    (B) navigate without sailing directions
    (C) determine their positions from landmarks
    (D) determine their longitude and latitude
    (E) avoid dangerous shoals

GO ON TO THE NEXT PAGE ➤

Passage 3:

I decided to begin the term's work with the short story since that form would be the easiest for [the police officers], not only because most of their reading up to then had probably been in that genre, but also because a study of the reaction of people to various situations was something they relied on in their daily work. For instance, they had to be able to predict how others would react to their directives and interventions before deciding on their own form of action; they had to be able to take in the details of a situation quickly and correctly before intervening. No matter how factual and sparse police reports may seem to us, they must make use of a selection of vital detail, similar to that which a writer of a short story has to make.

This was taught to me by one of my students, a captain, at the end of the term. I had begun the study of the short story by stressing the differences between a factual report, such as a scientist's or a policeman's report, and the presentation of a creative writer. While a selection of necessary details is involved in both, the officer must remain neutral and clearly try to present a picture of the facts, while the artist usually begins with a preconceived message or attitude which is then transmitted through the use of carefully selected details of action described in words intended to provoke associations and emotional reactions in the reader. Only at the end of the term did the captain point out to me that he and his men also try to evaluate the events they describe and that their description of a sequence of events must of necessity be structured and colored by their understanding of what has taken place.

The policemen's reactions to events and characters in the stories were surprisingly unprejudiced .... They did not object to writers whose stories had to do with their protagonist's rebellion against society's accepted values. Nor did stories in which the strong father becomes the villain and in which our usual ideals of manhood are turned around offend them. The many hunters among my students readily granted the message in those hunting tales in which sensitivity triumphs over male aggressiveness, stories that show the boy becoming a man because he *fails* to shoot the deer, goose, or catbird. The only characters they did object to were those they thought unrealistic. As the previous class had done, this one also excelled in interpreting the ways in which characters reveal themselves, subtly manipulate and influence each other; they, too, understood how the story usually saves its insight, its revelation, for the end.

This almost instinctive grasp of the writing of fiction was revealed when the policemen volunteered to write their own short stories. . . . They not only took great pains with plot and character, but with style and language. The stories were surprisingly well written, revealing an understanding of what a solid short story must contain: the revelation of character, the use of background description and language to create atmosphere and mood, the need to sustain suspense and yet make each event as it occurs seem natural, the insight achieved either by the characters in the story or the reader or both. They tended to favor surprise endings. Some stories were sheer fantasies, or derived from previous reading, films, or television shows. Most wrote stories, obviously based on their own experiences, that revealed the amazing distance they must put between their personal lives and their work, which is part of the training for being a good cop. These stories, as well as their discussions of them, showed how coolly they judged their own weaknesses as well as the humor with which they accepted some of the difficulties or injustices of existence. Despite their authors' unmistakable sense of irony and awareness of corruption, these stories demonstrated how clearly, almost naively, these policemen wanted to continue to believe in some of the so-called American virtues—that courage is worth the effort and will be admired; that hard work will be rewarded; that life is somehow good; and that, despite the weariness, boredom, and occasional ugliness and danger, despite all their dislike of most of their routine and despite their own occasional grousing and complaints, they somehow did like being cops; that life, even in a chaotic and violent world, is worth it after all.

GO ON TO THE NEXT PAGE ➤

1 1 1 1 1 1 1 1 1 1 1

18. Compared to the artist, the policeman is

(A) a man of action, not words
(B) factual and not fanciful
(C) neutral and not prejudiced
(D) stoic and not emotional
(E) aggressive and not passive

19. Policemen reacted to story events and characters

(A) like most other people
(B) according to a policeman's stereotyped image
(C) like dilettantes
(D) unrealistically
(E) without emotion

20. To which sort of characters did policemen object?

I. Unrealistic
II. Emotional
III. Sordid

(A) I only
(B) II only
(C) I and II only
(D) II and III only
(E) I, II, and III

21. According to the passage, a short story should contain

(A) elegant prose
(B) suspense
(C) objectivity
(D) real-life experiences
(E) irony

22. The instructor chose the short story because

I. it was easy for the students
II. students had experience with it
III. students would enjoy it

(A) I only
(B) II only
(C) I and II only
(D) II and III only
(E) I, II, and III

23. Like writers, policemen must

(A) analyze situations
(B) behave coolly
(C) have an artistic bent
(D) intervene quickly
(E) attend college

24. According to the passage, most policemen wrote stories about

(A) films
(B) previous reading
(C) American history
(D) their work
(E) politics

25. According to the author, policemen view their profession as

(A) full of corruption
(B) worth the effort
(C) full of routine
(D) poorly paid
(E) dangerous but adventuresome

STOP

**IF THERE IS STILL TIME REMAINING,
YOU MAY REVIEW THE QUESTIONS IN THIS SECTION ONLY.
YOU MAY NOT TURN TO ANY OTHER SECTION OF THE TEST.**

2 2 2 2 2 2 2 2 2 2 2

Section 2

TIME: 30 minutes
25 Questions

Directions: This part contains three reading passages. You are to be read each one carefully. When answering the questions, you *will* be able to refer to the passages. The questions are based on what is *stated* or *implied* in each passage.

Passage 1:

In the past, American colleges and universities were created to serve a dual purpose—to advance learning and to offer a chance to become familiar with bodies of knowledge already discovered to those who wished it. To create and to impart, these were the hallmarks of American higher education prior to the most recent, tumultuous decades of the twentieth century. The successful institution of higher learning had never been one whose mission could be defined in terms of providing vocational skills or as a strategy for resolving societal problems. In a subtle way Americans believed postsecondary education to be useful, but not necessarily of immediate use. What the student obtained in college became beneficial in later life—residually, without direct application in the period after graduation.

Another purpose has now been assigned to the mission of American colleges and universities. Institutions of higher learning—public or private—commonly face the challenge of defining their programs in such a way as to contribute to the service of the community.

This service role has various applications. Most common are programs to meet the demands of regional employment markets, to provide opportunities for upward social and economic mobility, to achieve racial, ethnic, or social integration, or more generally to produce "productive" as compared to "educated" graduates. Regardless of its precise definition, the idea of a service-university has won acceptance within the academic community.

One need only be reminded of the change in language describing the two-year college to appreciate the new value currently being attached to the concept of a service-related university. The traditional two-year college has shed its pejorative "junior" college label and is generally called a "community" college, a clearly value-laden expression representing the latest commitment in higher education. Even the doctoral degree, long recognized as a required "union card" in the academic world, has come under severe criticism as the pursuit of learning for its own sake and the accumulation of knowledge without immediate application to a professor's classroom duties. The idea of a college or university that performs a triple function—communicating knowledge to students, expanding the content of various disciplines, and interacting in a direct relationship with society—has been the most important change in higher education in recent years.

This novel development is often overlooked. Educators have always been familiar with those parts of the two-year college curriculum that have a "service" or vocational orientation. Knowing this, otherwise perceptive commentaries on American postsecondary education underplay the impact of the attempt of colleges and universities to relate to, if not resolve, the problems of society. Whether the subject under review is student unrest, faculty tenure, the nature of the curriculum, the onset of collective bargaining, or the growth of collegiate bureaucracies, in each instance the thrust of these discussions obscures the larger meaning of the emergence of the service-university in American higher education. Even the highly regarded critique of Clark Kerr, currently head of the Carnegie Foundation, which set the parameters of academic debate around the evolution of the so-called "multiversity," failed to take account of this phenomenon and the manner in which its fulfillment changed the scope of higher education. To the extent that the idea of "multiversity" centered on matters of scale—how big is too big? how complex is too complex?—it obscured the fundamental question posed by the service-university: what is higher education supposed to do? Unless the commitment to what Samuel Gould has properly

GO ON TO THE NEXT PAGE ➤

called the "communiversity" is clearly articulated, the success of any college or university in achieving its service-education functions will be effectively impaired. . . .

The most reliable report about the progress of Open Admissions became available at the end of August, 1974. What the document showed was that the dropout rate for all freshmen admitted in September, 1970, after seven semesters, was about 48 percent, a figure that corresponds closely to national averages at similar colleges and universities. The discrepancy between the performance of "regular" students (those who would have been admitted into the four-year colleges with 80% high school averages and into the two-year units with 75%) and Open Admissions freshmen provides a better indication of how the program worked. Taken together the attrition rate (from known and unknown causes) was 48 percent, but the figure for regular students was 36 percent while for Open Admissions categories it was 56 percent. Surprisingly, the statistics indicated that the four-year colleges retained or graduated more of the Open Admissions students than the two-year colleges, a finding that did not reflect experience elsewhere. Not surprisingly, perhaps, the figures indicated a close relationship between academic success defined as retention or graduation and high school averages. Similarly, it took longer for the Open Admissions students to generate college credits and graduate than regular students, a pattern similar to national averages. The most important statistics, however, relate to the findings regarding Open Admissions students, and these indicated as a projection that perhaps as many as 70 percent would not graduate from a unit of the City University.

1. The dropout rate among regular students in Open Admissions was approximately

(A) 35%
(B) 45%
(C) 55%
(D) 65%
(E) 75%

2. According to the passage, in the past it was *not* the purpose of American higher education to

(A) advance learning
(B) solve societal problems
(C) impart knowledge
(D) train workers
(E) prepare future managers

3. One of the recent, important changes in higher education relates to

(A) student representation on college boards
(B) faculty tenure requirements
(C) curriculum updates
(D) service-education concepts
(E) cost constraints

4. It was estimated that what percentage of Open Admissions students would fail to graduate from City University?

(A) 40%
(B) 50%
(C) 60%
(D) 70%
(E) 80%

GO ON TO THE NEXT PAGE ➤

2 2 2 2 2 2 2 2 2 2 2

5. According to the passage, the two-year college may be described as

   I. a junior college
   II. service-oriented
   III. a community college

   (A) I only
   (B) II only
   (C) I and II only
   (D) II and III only
   (E) I, II, and III

6. The service role of colleges aims to

   (A) improve services
   (B) gain acceptance among educators
   (C) serve the community
   (D) provide skills for future use
   (E) make graduates employable

7. The attrition rate for Open Admissions students was greater than the rate for regular students by what percent?

   (A) 10%
   (B) 20%
   (C) 36%
   (D) 40%
   (E) 46%

8. Clark Kerr failed to take account of

   (A) the "communiversity"
   (B) collegiate bureaucracies
   (C) faculty tenure
   (D) the service-university
   (E) Open Admissions

9. The *average* attrition rate for regular and Open Admissions students was

   (A) 36%
   (B) 46%
   (C) 56%
   (D) 75%
   (E) 92%

GO ON TO THE NEXT PAGE ➤

2 2 2 2 2 2 2 2 2 2 2

Passage 2:

"The United States seems totally indifferent to our problems," charges French Foreign Minister Claude Cheysson, defending his Government's decision to defy President Reagan and proceed with construction of the Soviet gas pipeline. West German Chancellor Helmut Schmidt endorsed the French action and sounded a similar note. Washington's handling of the pipeline, he said, has "cast a shadow over relations" between Europe and the United States, "damaging confidence as regards future agreements."

But it's not just the pipeline that has made a mockery of Versailles. Charges of unfair trade practices and threats of retaliation in a half-dozen industries are flying back and forth over the Atlantic—and the Pacific, too—in a worrisome crescendo. Businessmen, dismayed by the long siege of sluggish economic growth that has left some 30 million people in the West unemployed, are doing what comes naturally: pressuring politicians to restrain imports, subsidize exports, or both. Steelmakers in Bonn and Pittsburgh want help; so do auto makers in London and Detroit, textile, apparel and shoe manufacturers throughout the West and farmers virtually everywhere.

Democratic governments, the targets of such pressure, are worried about their own political fortunes and embarrassed by their failure to generate strong growth and lower unemployment. The temptation is strong to take the path of least resistance and tighten up on trade—even for a Government as devoted to the free market as Ronald Reagan's. In the past 18 months, Washington, beset by domestic producers, has raised new barriers against imports in autos, textiles and sugar. Steel is likely to be next. Nor is the United States alone. European countries, to varying degrees, have also sought to defend domestic markets or to promote exports through generous subsidies. . . .

The upcoming meeting, to consider trade policy for the 1980's, is surely well timed. "It has been suggested often that world trade policy is 'at a crossroads'—but such a characterization of the early 1980's may be reasonably accurate," says C. Fred Bergsten, a former Treasury official in the Carter Administration, now director of a new Washington think tank, the Institute for International Economics.

The most urgent question before the leaders of the industrial world is whether they can change the fractious atmosphere of this summer before stronger protective measures are actually put in place. So far, Mr. Bergsten says, words have outweighed deeds. The trade picture is dismal. World trade reached some $2 trillion a year in 1980 and hasn't budged since. In the first half of this year, Mr. Bergsten suspects that trade probably fell as the world economy stayed flat. But, according to his studies, increased protectionism is not the culprit for the slowdown in trade—at least not yet. The culprit instead is slow growth and recession, and the resulting slump in demand for imports. . . .

But there are fresh problems today that could be severely damaging. Though tariffs and outright quotas are low after three rounds of intense international trade negotiations in the past two decades—new trade restraints, often bound up in voluntary agreements between countries to limit particular imports, have sprouted in recent years like mushrooms in a wet wood. Though the new protectionism is more subtle than the old-fashioned variety, it is no less damaging to economic efficiency and, ultimately, to prospects for world economic growth.

A striking feature is that the new protectionism has focused on the same limited sectors in most of the major industrial countries—textiles, steel, electronics, footwear, shipbuilding and autos. Similarly, it has concentrated on supply from Japan and the newly industrialized countries.

When several countries try to protect the same industries, the dealings become difficult. Take steel. Since 1977, the European Economic Community has been following a plan to eliminate excess steel capacity, using bilateral import quotas along the way to soften the blow to the steelworkers. The United States, responding to similar pressure at home and to the same problem of a world oversupplied with steel, introduced a "voluntary" quota system in 1969, and, after a brief period of no restraint, developed a complex trigger price mechanism in 1978.

GO ON TO THE NEXT PAGE ➤

2 2 2 2 2 2 2 2 2 2 2

10. According to the passage, a "new protectionism" is evidenced by
    - (A) bilateral import quotas
    - (B) political suasion
    - (C) lower than market prices
    - (D) abrogating agreements
    - (E) increased product standards

11. Increased protectionism has been caused by
    - (A) the "cold war"
    - (B) United States economic policy
    - (C) increased unemployment
    - (D) a breakdown in international law
    - (E) a growth in cartels

12. A slowdown in world trade has been caused by
    - (A) protectionism
    - (B) slower population growth
    - (C) less trade with Communist countries
    - (D) economic recession
    - (E) increased oil prices

13. The U.S. Government has increased barriers to the import of
    - (A) autos, textiles, and sugar
    - (B) autos, textiles, and steel
    - (C) autos, electronics, and steel
    - (D) shoes, textiles, and sugar
    - (E) shoes, textiles, and steel

14. The best possible theme for the passage would be
    - (A) "Reagan Administration's Economic Policies"
    - (B) "International Trade Agreements in the 1960's"
    - (C) "Tokyo Round of Trade Negotiations"
    - (D) "A Perilous Time for World Trade"
    - (E) "Problems and Prospects for World Exports"

15. In recent years, trade between nations has been constrained by
    - (A) voluntary agreements limiting imports
    - (B) rhetoric expressed by labor leaders
    - (C) misalignment among world currencies
    - (D) the free international exchange of goods
    - (E) restrictive monetary and fiscal policies

16. While imports are restrained by barriers, exports are encouraged through
    - (A) bargaining
    - (B) lowering prices
    - (C) subsidies
    - (D) advertising
    - (E) dealing

17. A means to decrease steel capacity in the European Economic Community has been the use of
    - (A) voluntary quotas
    - (B) bilateral quotas
    - (C) voluntary and bilateral quotas
    - (D) trigger prices
    - (E) restraints

GO ON TO THE NEXT PAGE ➤

Passage 3:

It is indisputable that in order to fulfill its many functions, water should be clean and biologically valuable. The costs connected with the provision of biologically valuable water for food production with the maintenance of sufficiently clean water, therefore, are primarily production costs. Purely "environmental" costs seem to be in this respect only costs connected with the safeguarding of cultural, recreational and sports functions which the water courses and reservoirs fulfill both in nature and in human settlements.

The pollution problems of the atmosphere resemble those of the water only partly. So far, the supply of air has not been deficient as was the case with water, and the dimensions of the air-shed are so vast that a number of people still hold the opinion that air need not be economized. However, scientific forecasts have shown that the time may be already approaching when clear and biologically valuable air will become problem No. 1.

Air being ubiquitous, people are particularly sensitive about any reduction in the quality of the atmosphere, the increased contents of dust and gaseous exhalations, and particularly about the presence of odors. The demand for purity of atmosphere, therefore, emanates much more from the population itself than from the specific sectors of the national economy affected by a polluted or even biologically aggressive atmosphere.

The households' share in atmospheric pollution is far bigger than that of industry which, in turn, further complicates the economic problems of atmospheric purity. Some countries have already collected positive experience with the reconstruction of whole urban sectors on the basis of new heating appliances based on the combustion of solid fossil fuels; estimates of the economic consequences of such measures have also been put forward.

In contrast to water, where the maintenance of purity would seem primarily to be related to the costs of production and transport, a far higher proportion of the costs of maintaining the purity of the atmosphere derives from environmental considerations. Industrial sources of gaseous and dust emissions are well known and classified; their location can be accurately identified, which makes them controllable. With the exception, perhaps, of the elimination of sulphur dioxide, technical means and technological processes exist which can be used for the elimination of all excessive impurities of the air from the various emissions.

Atmospheric pollution caused by the private property of individuals (their dwellings, automobiles, etc.) is difficult to control. Some sources such as motor vehicles are very mobile, and they are thus capable of polluting vast territories. In this particular case, the cost of anti-pollution measures will have to be borne, to a considerable extent, by individuals, whether in the form of direct costs or indirectly in the form of taxes, dues, surcharges, etc.

The problem of noise is a typical example of an environmental problem which cannot be solved only passively, i.e., merely by protective measures, but will require the adoption of active measures, i.e., direct interventions at the source. The costs of a complete protection against noise are so prohibitive as to make it unthinkable even in the economically most developed countries. At the same time it would not seem feasible, either economically or politically, to force the population to carry the costs of individual protection against noise, for example, by reinforcing the sound insulation of their homes. A solution of this problem probably cannot be found in the near future.

18. According to the passage, the population at large

(A) is unconcerned about air pollution controls
(B) is especially aware of problems concerning air quality and purity
(C) regards water pollution as more serious than air pollution
(D) has failed to recognize the economic consequences of pollution
(E) is unwilling to make the sacrifices needed to ensure clean air

GO ON TO THE NEXT PAGE ➤

2 2 2 2 2 2 2 2 2 2 2

19. Scientific forecasts have shown that clear and biologically valuable air

    (A) is likely to remain abundant for some time
    (B) creates fewer economic difficulties than does water pollution
    (C) may soon be dangerously lacking
    (D) may be beyond the capacity of our technology to protect
    (E) has already become difficult to obtain

20. According to the passage, which of the following contributes *most* to atmospheric pollution?

    (A) industry
    (B) production
    (C) households
    (D) mining
    (E) waste disposal

21. The costs involved in the maintenance of pure water are determined primarily by

    I. production costs
    II. transport costs
    III. research costs

    (A) I only
    (B) III only
    (C) I and II only
    (D) II and III only
    (E) I, II, and III

22. According to the passage, atmospheric pollution caused by private property is

    (A) easy to control
    (B) impossible to control
    (C) difficult to control
    (D) decreasing
    (E) negligible

23. According to the passage, the problem of noise can be solved through

    I. Active measures
    II. Passive measures
    III. Tax levies

    (A) I only
    (B) III only
    (C) I and II only
    (D) II and III only
    (E) I, II, and III

24. According to the passage, the costs of some anti-pollution measures will have to be borne by individuals because

    (A) individuals contribute to the creation of pollution
    (B) governments do not have adequate resources
    (C) industry is not willing to bear its share
    (D) individuals are more easily taxed than producers
    (E) individuals demand production, which causes pollution

25. Complete protection against noise

    (A) may be forthcoming in the near future
    (B) is impossible to achieve
    (C) may have prohibitive costs
    (D) is possible only in developed countries
    (E) has been achieved in some countries

STOP

IF THERE IS STILL TIME REMAINING, YOU MAY REVIEW THE QUESTIONS IN THIS SECTION ONLY. YOU MAY NOT TURN TO ANY OTHER SECTION OF THE TEST.

Section 3

TIME: 25 minutes
17 Questions

Directions: Solve each of the following problems; then indicate the correct answer on the answer sheet.

NOTE: A figure that appears with a problem is drawn as accurately as possible so as to provide information that may help in answering the question. Numbers in this test are real numbers.

1. Water has been poured into an empty rectangular tank at the rate of 5 cubic feet per minute for 6 minutes. The length of the tank is 4 feet and the width is one half of the length. How deep is the water in the tank?

   (A) 7.5 inches
   (B) 3 ft. 7.5 inches
   (C) 3 ft. 9 inches
   (D) 7 ft. 6 inches
   (E) 30 ft.

2. If $2x - y = 4$, then $6x - 3y$ is

   (A) 4
   (B) 6
   (C) 8
   (D) 10
   (E) 12

3. If x, y, z are chosen from the three numbers -3, $\frac{1}{2}$, and 2, what is the largest possible value of the expression $\left(\frac{x}{y}\right)z^2$?

   (A) $-\frac{3}{8}$
   (B) 16
   (C) 24
   (D) 36
   (E) 54

GO ON TO THE NEXT PAGE ➤

4. A survey of n people found that 60 percent preferred brand A. An additional x people were surveyed who all preferred brand A. Seventy percent of all the people surveyed preferred brand A. Find x in terms of n.

(A) $\frac{n}{6}$

(B) $\frac{n}{3}$

(C) $\frac{n}{2}$

(D) n

(E) $3n$

5. The hexagon *ABCDEF* is regular. That means all its sides are the same length and all its interior angles are the same size. Each side of the hexagon is 2 feet. What is the area of the rectangle *BCEF*?

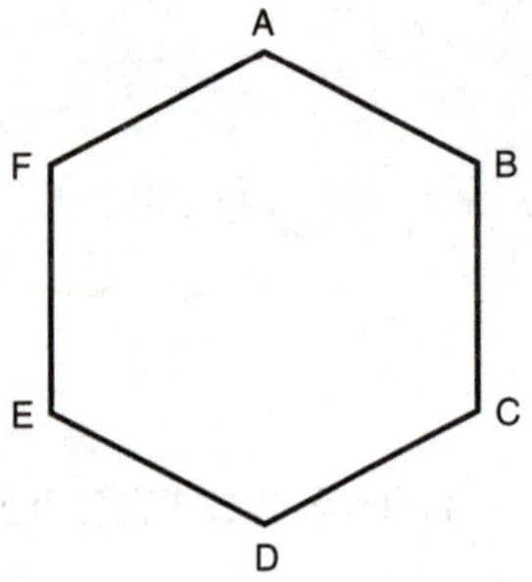

(A) 4 square feet

(B) $4\sqrt{3}$ square feet

(C) 8 square feet

(D) $4 + 4\sqrt{3}$ square feet

(E) 12 square feet

6. A warehouse has 20 packers. Each packer can load $\frac{1}{8}$ of a box in 9 minutes. How many boxes can be loaded in $1\frac{1}{2}$ hours by all 20 packers?

(A) $1\frac{1}{4}$

(B) $10\frac{1}{4}$

(C) $12\frac{1}{2}$

(D) 20

(E) 25

7. In Motor City 90% of the population own a car, 15% own a motorcycle, and everybody owns one or the other or both. What is the percentage of motorcycle owners who own cars?

(A) 5%

(B) 15%

(C) $33\frac{1}{3}\%$

(D) 50%

(E) 90%

GO ON TO THE NEXT PAGE ➤

3 3 3 3 3 3 3 3 3 3 3

8. Jim's weight is 140% of Marcia's weight. Bob's weight is 90% of Lee's weight. Lee weighs twice as much as Marcia. What percentage of Jim's weight is Bob's weight?

(A) $64\frac{2}{7}$

(B) $77\frac{7}{9}$

(C) 90

(D) $128\frac{4}{7}$

(E) $155\frac{5}{9}$

9. Towns A and C are connected by a straight highway which is 60 miles long. The straight-line distance between town A and town B is 50 miles, and the straight-line distance from town B to town C is 50 miles. How many miles is it from town B to the point on the highway connecting towns A and C which is closest to town B?

(A) 30
(B) 40
(C) $30\sqrt{2}$
(D) 50
(E) 60

10. A chair originally cost $50.00. The chair was offered for sale at 108% of its cost. After a week the price was discounted 10% and the chair was sold. The chair was sold for

(A) $45.00
(B) $48.60
(C) $49.00
(D) $49.50
(E) $54.00

11. A worker is paid x dollars for the first 8 hours he works each day. He is paid y dollars per hour for each hour he works in excess of 8 hours. During one week he works 8 hours on Monday, 11 hours on Tuesday, 9 hours on Wednesday, 10 hours on Thursday, and 9 hours on Friday. What is his average daily wage in dollars for the five-day week?

(A) $x + \frac{7}{5}y$

(B) $2x + y$

(C) $\frac{5x + 8y}{5}$

(D) $8x + \left(\frac{7}{5}\right)y$

(E) $5x + 7y$

12. A club has 8 male and 8 female members. The club is choosing a committee of 6 members. The committee must have 3 male and 3 female members. How many different committees can be chosen?

(A) 112,896
(B) 3,136
(C) 720
(D) 112
(E) 9

GO ON TO THE NEXT PAGE ➤

3 3 3 3 3 3 3 3 3 3 3

13. A motorcycle costs \$2,500 when it is brand new. At the end of each year it is worth $\frac{4}{5}$ of what it was at the beginning of the year. What is the motorcycle worth when it is 3 years old?

(A) \$1,000
(B) \$1,200
(C) \$1,280
(D) \$1,340
(E) \$1,430

14. Which of the following inequalities is the solution to the inequality $7x - 5 < 12x + 18$?

(A) $x < -\frac{13}{5}$

(B) $x > -\frac{23}{5}$

(C) $x < -\frac{23}{5}$

(D) $x > \frac{23}{5}$

(E) $x < \frac{23}{5}$

15. If $x + 2y = 2x + y$, then $x - y$ is equal to

(A) 0
(B) 2
(C) 4
(D) 5
(E) cannot be determined

16. Mary, John, and Karen ate lunch together. Karen's meal cost 50% more than John's meal and Mary's meal cost $\frac{5}{6}$ as much as Karen's meal. If Mary paid \$2 more than John, how much was the total that the three of them paid?

(A) \$28.33
(B) \$30.00
(C) \$35.00
(D) \$37.50
(E) \$40.00

17. If the angles of a triangle are in the ratio 1 : 2 : 2, then the triangle

(A) is isosceles
(B) is obtuse
(C) is a right triangle
(D) is equilateral
(E) has one angle greater than 80°

STOP

**IF THERE IS STILL TIME REMAINING,
YOU MAY REVIEW THE QUESTIONS IN THIS SECTION ONLY.
YOU MAY NOT TURN TO ANY OTHER SECTION OF THE TEST.**

4 4 4 4 4 4 4 4 4 4 4

Section 4

TIME: 25 minutes
17 Questions

Directions: For each question, choose the best answer among the listed alternatives.

1. Richard is a terrible driver. He has had at least five traffic violations in the past year.

   Which of the following can be said about the above claim?

   (A) This is an example of an argument that is directed against the source of the claim rather than the claim itself.
   (B) The statement is fallacious because it contains an illegitimate appeal to authority.
   (C) The above argument obtains its strength from a similarity of two compared situations.
   (D) The argument is built upon an assumption that is not stated but rather is concealed.
   (E) In the above statements, there is a shifting in the meaning of terms, causing a fallacy of ambiguity.

2. The exchange rate is the ruling official rate of exchange of dollars for other currencies. It determines the value of American goods in relation to foreign goods. If the dollar is devalued in terms of other currencies, American exports (which are paid for in dollars) become cheaper to foreigners and American imports (paid for by purchasing foreign currency) become more expensive to holders of dollars.

   What conclusion can be drawn from the above?

   (A) There are certain disadvantages for the United States economy attached to devaluation.
   (B) The prospect of devaluation results in a speculative outflow of funds.
   (C) By encouraging exports and discouraging imports, devaluation can improve the American balance of payments.
   (D) The difference between imports and exports is called the Trade Gap.
   (E) It is possible that inflation neutralizes the beneficial effects of devaluation.

3. You have three boxes, each containing two balls, one containing a black pair; one, a white pair; and the third, one white ball and one black ball. On each box are pictures of two balls—either two black ones, two white ones, or one white and one black. You are told that the markings on the boxes are all wrong. You are asked to ascertain the colors of the balls contained in each box.

   Which of the following statements can be inferred from the above?

   (A) You can take out one ball from the box marked with two black balls and, without looking at the second ball, know what each box actually contains.
   (B) You can take out one ball from the box marked with two white balls and, without looking at the second ball, know what each box actually contains.
   (C) You can take out one ball from the box marked with one white ball and one black ball and, without looking at the second ball, know what each box contains.
   (D) You cannot know which balls are contained in which box until you take a ball out of more than one box.
   (E) You cannot know which boxes contain which color balls until you take a ball out of all three boxes.

GO ON TO THE NEXT PAGE ➤

4 4 4 4 4 4 4 4 4 4 4

4. In the human body, platelets promote blood clotting by clumping together. Aspirin has been found to prevent clotting by making platelets less sticky. Research has now shown that heart attacks and strokes caused by blood clots could be avoided by taking one aspirin a day. Statistics show that the incidence of second heart attacks has been reduced by 21% and overall mortality rates by 15% as a result of taking aspirin.

   Unfortunately, the drug has several unpleasant side effects, including nausea, gastric bleeding, and, in severe cases, shock. In children, it has been linked to Reye's Syndrome, a rare, but occasionally fatal, childhood illness.

   On balance, however, for men aged 40 and over, an aspirin a day may present an excellent prophylactic measure for a disease that affects 1.5 million Americans yearly and claims the lives of about 540,000.

   Which of the following conclusions can most properly be drawn from the information above?

   (A) All people should take an aspirin a day to prevent heart attacks.
   (B) Painkillers prevent heart attacks.
   (C) Smokers can safely continue smoking, provided that they take at least one aspirin a day.
   (D) The majority of people suffering second subsequent cardiac arrests could have been saved by taking an aspirin a day.
   (E) Aspirin can be used to reduce mortality rates in patients who have already suffered heart attacks.

5. In the past, to run for one's country in the Olympics was the ultimate achievement of any athlete. Nowadays, an athlete's motives are more and more influenced by financial gain, and consequently we do not see our best athletes in the Olympics, which is still only for amateurs.

   Which of the following will most weaken the above conclusion?

   (A) The publicity and fame that can be achieved by competing in the Olympics makes athletes more "marketable" by agents and potential sponsors, while allowing the athletes to retain their amateur status.
   (B) The winning of a race is not as important as participating.
   (C) There is a widely held belief that our best Olympic athletes already receive enough in terms of promotion and sponsorship.
   (D) It has been suggested that professional athletes should be allowed to compete in the games.
   (E) Athletics as an entertainment is like any other entertainment job and deserves a financial reward.

GO ON TO THE NEXT PAGE ➤

6. The function of a food technologist in a large marketing chain of food stores is to ensure that all foodstuffs which are offered for sale in the various retail outlets meet certain standard criteria for nonperishability, freshness, and fitness for human consumption.

   It is the technologist's job to visit the premises of suppliers and food producers (factory or farm), inspect the facilities and report thereon. His responsibility also includes receiving new products from local and foreign suppliers and performing exhaustive quality control testing on them. Finally, he should carry out surprise spot-checks on goods held in the marketing chain's own warehouses and stores.

   What conclusion can best be drawn from the preceding paragraph?

   (A) A university degree in food technology is a necessary and sufficient condition for becoming a food technologist.
   (B) Imported products, as well as home-produced goods, must be rigorously tested.
   (C) The food technologist stands between the unhygienic producer and the unsuspecting consumer.
   (D) Home-produced foodstuffs are safer to eat than goods imported from abroad because they are subject to more regular and closer inspection procedures.
   (E) Random checking of the quality of goods stored on the shelves in a foodstore is the best way of ensuring that foodstuffs of an inferior quality are not purchased by the general public.

7. The daily journey from his home to his office takes John Bond on average an hour and thirty-five minutes by car. A friend has told him of a different route that is longer in mileage, but will only take an hour and a quarter on average, because it contains stretches of roads where it is possible to drive at higher speeds.

   John Bond's only consideration apart from the time factor is the cost, and he calculates that his car will consume 10% less gasoline if he takes the suggested new route. John decides to take the new route for the next two weeks as an experiment.

   If the above were the only other considerations, which one of the following may have an effect on the decision John has made?

   (A) Major road work is begun on the shorter (in distance) route, which holds up traffic for an extra ten minutes. The project will take six months, but after it, the improvements will allow the journey to be made in half an hour less than at present.
   (B) There is to be a strike at local gas stations and the amount of gasoline drivers may purchase may be rationed.
   (C) John finds a third route which is slightly longer then his old route, but shorter than the suggested route.
   (D) The old route passes the door of a work colleague, who without a ride, would have to go to work by bus.
   (E) None of the above.

GO ON TO THE NEXT PAGE ➤

4 4 4 4 4 4 4 4 4 4 4

8. All elephants are grey.
And all mice are grey.
Therefore, I conclude that all elephants are mice.
The argument above is invalid because

(A) the writer bases his argument on another argument that contains circular reasoning.
(B) the writer has illogically classified two disparate groups together when there is no relationship between them, except that they both have the same attribute.
(C) the writer has made a mistaken analogy between two dissimilar qualities.
(D) the writer has used a fallacy which involves the ambiguous description of animals by their color.
(E) the writer has failed to express his reasoning fully.

9. There are three main factors that control the risks of becoming dependent on drugs. These factors are the type of drug, the personality of the individual, and the circumstances in which the drug is taken. Indeed, it could be said that the majority of the adult population have taken alcohol, yet few have become dependent on it. Also, many strong drugs that have been used for medical purposes have not caused the patient to become addicted.

However, it can be demonstrated that people who have taken drugs for fun are more likely to become dependent on the drug. The dependence is not always physiological but may remain psychological, although the effects are still essentially the same. Those at greatest risk appear to be personalities that are psychopathic, immature, or otherwise unstable.

Psychological dependence is very strong with heroin, morphine, cocaine, and amphetamines. Physiological dependence is great with heroin and morphine, but less with amphetamines, barbiturates, and alcohol.

Which of the following conclusions can be drawn from the text?

(A) One cannot become addicted to certain drugs if one has a strong personality.
(B) Taking drugs for "kicks" increases the possibility of becoming dependent on drugs.
(C) Psychological dependence is greatest with heroin.
(D) Alcohol is a safe drug since very few people become dependent on it.
(E) Long-term use of certain drugs for medical purposes does not cause addiction.

10. Sally overslept. Therefore, she did not eat breakfast. She realized that she was late for school, so she ran as fast as she could and did not see a hole in the ground which was in her path. She tripped and broke her ankle. She was then taken to the hospital and while lying in bed was visited by her friend, who wanted to know why she had got up so late.

Which of the following conclusions can be made from the above passage?

(A) Because Sally did not eat her breakfast, she broke her ankle.
(B) Sally's friend visited her in the hospital because she wanted to know why she was late for school.
(C) Sally did not notice the hole because she overslept.
(D) Sally broke her ankle because she went to bed late the previous night.
(E) Sally's broken ankle meant she did not go to school that day.

11. The owners of a local supermarket have decided to make use of three now-redundant checkout counters. They believe that they will attract those customers who lately have been put off by the long checkout lines during the mid-morning and evening rush hours. The owners have concluded that in order to be successful, the increased revenue from existing and added counters will have to be more than the increase in maintenance costs for the added counters.

The underlying goal of the owners can be summarized thus:

(A) To improve services to all customers.
(B) To attract people who have never been to the store.
(C) To make use of the redundant counters.
(D) To keep maintenance costs on the added counters as low as possible.
(E) To increase monthly profits.

GO ON TO THE NEXT PAGE ➤

4 4 4 4 4 4 4 4 4 4 4

12. The cost of housing in many parts of the United States has become so excessive that many young couples, with above-average salaries, can only afford small apartments. Mortgage commitments are so huge that they cannot consider the possibility of starting a family. A new baby would probably mean either the mother or father giving up a well-paid position. The lack of or great cost of child-care facilities precludes the return of both parents to work.

    Which of the following adjustments could practically be made to the situation described above which would allow young couples to improve their housing prospects?

    (A) Encourage couples to remain childless.
    (B) Encourage couples to have one child only.
    (C) Encourage couples to postpone starting their families until a later age than previously acceptable to society.
    (D) Encourage young couples to move to cheaper areas of the United States.
    (E) Encourage fathers to remain at home while mothers return to work.

13. Unless new reserves are found soon, the world's supply of coal is being depleted in such a way that with demand continuing to grow at present rates, reserves will be exhausted by the year 2050.

    Which of the following, if true, will most weaken the above argument?

    (A) There has been a slowdown in the rate of increase in world demand for coal over the last 5 years from 10% to 5%.
    (B) It has been known for many years that there are vast stocks of coal under Antarctica which have yet to be economically exploited.
    (C) Oil is being used increasingly in place of coal for many industrial and domestic uses.
    (D) As coal resources are depleted more and more marginal supplies, which are more costly to produce and less efficient in use are being mined.
    (E) None of the above.

14. In accordance with their powers, many state authorities are introducing fluoridation of drinking water. This follows the conclusion of 10 years of research that the process ensures that children and adults receive the required intake of fluoride that will strengthen teeth. The maximum level has been set at one part per million. However, there are many who object, claiming that fluoridation removes freedom of choice.

    Which of the following will weaken the claim of the proponents of fluoridation?

    (A) Fluoridation over a certain prescribed level has been shown to lead to a general weakening of teeth.
    (B) There is no record of the long-term effects of drinking fluoridated water.
    (C) The people to be affected by fluoridation claim that they have not had sufficient opportunity to voice their views.
    (D) Fluoridation is only one part of general dental health.
    (E) Water already contains natural fluoride.

15. Mr. and Mrs. Smith and their son John want to cross the Dart River. The only way across is with Mr. Jones in his rowboat. Mr. Jones will not allow anyone to row his boat and will take only one passenger at a time. John is only a little boy so he cannot be left alone on the river bank.

    Which of the following conditions are not part of the successful passage of the Smiths across the river?

    (A) Mr. Smith crosses the river first.
    (B) Mr. Smith crosses the river last.
    (C) Mr. and Mrs. Smith do not cross together.
    (D) John crosses the river first.
    (E) John crosses the river second.

GO ON TO THE NEXT PAGE ➤

16. In 1980, global service exports totaled about $370 billion, approximately 20 percent of world trade. Still, no coherent system of rules, principles, and procedures exists to govern trade in services.

    Which of the following best summarizes the argument?

    (A) Regulatory systems lag behind reality.
    (B) A regulatory system ought to reflect the importance of service exports.
    (C) World trade totaled $1850 billion in 1980.
    (D) Service trade legislation is a veritable wasteland.
    (E) While trade legislation exists, it is uncoordinated.

17. Perhaps the most significant and constructive change in national politics would be the abolition of the Vice Presidency.

    Each of the following, if true, would strengthen the above argument, except:

    (A) There are few, if any, specific duties or responsibilities assigned to the Vice Presidency.
    (B) A historian claimed that the post was "superfluous."
    (C) People of Presidential caliber refused the Vice Presidential nomination.
    (D) The office can waste a good politician for four or eight years.
    (E) The office puts people in line for the Presidency who were not chosen to be President.

STOP

**IF THERE IS STILL TIME REMAINING,
YOU MAY REVIEW THE QUESTIONS IN THIS SECTION ONLY.
YOU MAY NOT TURN TO ANY OTHER SECTION OF THE TEST.**

5 5 5 5 5 5 5 5 5 5 5

Section 5

TIME: 25 minutes
21 Questions

Directions: Each of the following problems has a question and two statements which are labeled (1) and (2). Use the data given in (1) and (2) together with other available information (such as the number of hours in a day, the definition of *clockwise*, mathematical facts, etc.) to decide whether the statements are *sufficient* to answer the question. Then fill in space

(A) if you can get the answer from **(1) ALONE** but not from (2) alone
(B) if you can get the answer from **(2) ALONE** but not from (1) alone
(C) if you can get the answer from **BOTH (1) and (2) TOGETHER,** but not from (1) alone or (2) alone
(D) if **EITHER** statement **(1) ALONE OR** statement **(2) ALONE** suffices
(E) if you **CANNOT** get the answer from statements (1) and (2) **TOGETHER**, but need even more data

All numbers used in this section are real numbers. A figure given for a problem is intended to provide information consistent with that in the question, but not necessarily with the additional information contained in the statements.

1. Is x greater than y?

   (1) $3x = 2k$
   (2) $k = y^2$

2. Is *ABCD* a parallelogram?

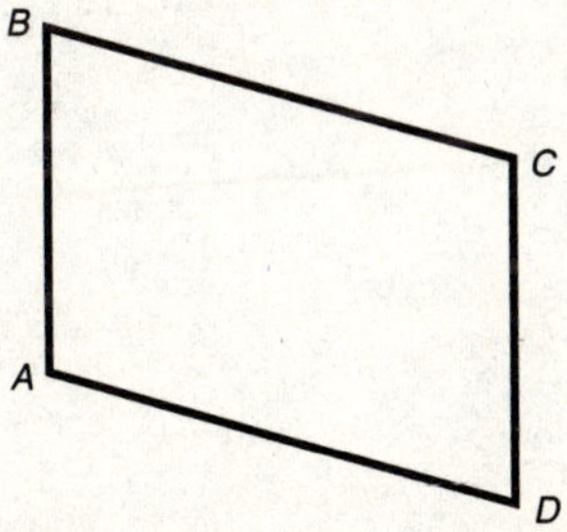

   (1) $AB = CD$
   (2) *AB* is parallel to *CD*

3. What was Mr. Smith's combined income for the years 1965–1970? In 1965 he made $10,000.

   (1) His average yearly income for the years 1965–1970 was $12,000.
   (2) In 1970, his income was $20,000.

4. What is the two digit number whose first digit is a and whose second digit is b? The number is greater than 9.

   (1) $2a + 3b = 11a + 2b$
   (2) The two digit number is a multiple of 19.

GO ON TO THE NEXT PAGE ➤

5 5 5 5 5 5 5 5 5 5 5

(A) if you can get the answer from **(1) ALONE** but not from (2) alone
(B) if you can get the answer from **(2) ALONE** but not from (1) alone
(C) if you can get the answer from **BOTH (1) and (2) TOGETHER,** but not from (1) alone or (2) alone
(D) if **EITHER** statement **(1) ALONE OR** statement **(2) ALONE** suffices
(E) if you **CANNOT** get the answer from statements (1) and (2) **TOGETHER**, but need even more data

5. k is a positive integer. Is k a prime number?

(1) No integer between 2 and $\sqrt{k}$ inclusive divides k evenly.

(2) No integer between 2 and $\frac{k}{2}$ inclusive divides k evenly, and k is greater than 5.

6. The towns *A*, *B*, and *C* lie on a straight line. *C* is between *A* and *B*. The distance from *A* to *B* is 100 miles. How far is it from *A* to *C*?

(1) The distance from *A* to *B* is 25% more than the distance from C to *B*.

(2) The distance from *A* to *C* is $\frac{1}{4}$ of the distance from *C* to *B*.

7. Is *AB* perpendicular to *CD*?

(1) $AC = BD$
(2) $x = y$

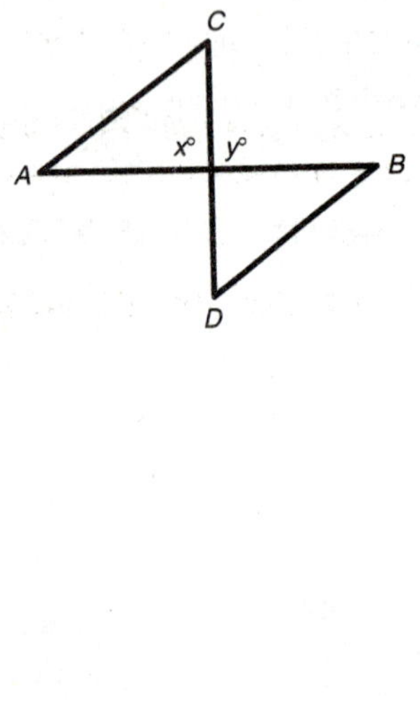

8. What is the value of $x - y$?

(1) $x + 2y = 6$
(2) $x = y$

9. The number of eligible voters is 100,000. How many eligible voters voted?

(1) 63% of the eligible men voted.
(2) 67% of the eligible women voted.

10. How much was the original cost of a car which sold for $2,300?

(1) The car was sold for a discount of 10% from its original cost.
(2) The sales tax was $150.

GO ON TO THE NEXT PAGE ➤

5 5 5 5 5 5 5 5 5 5 5

(A) if you can get the answer from **(1) ALONE** but not from (2) alone
(B) if you can get the answer from **(2) ALONE** but not from (1) alone
(C) if you can get the answer from **BOTH (1) and (2) TOGETHER,** but not from (1) alone or (2) alone
(D) if **EITHER** statement **(1) ALONE OR** statement **(2) ALONE** suffices
(E) if you **CANNOT** get the answer from statements (1) and (2) **TOGETHER**, but need even more data

11. The hexagon *ABCDEF* is inscribed in the circle with center *O*. What is the length of *AB*?

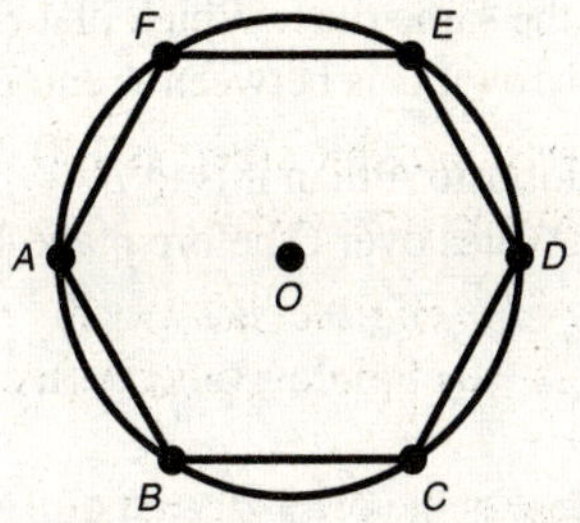

(1) The radius of the circle is 4 inches.
(2) The hexagon is a regular hexagon.

12. What was the percentage of defective items produced at a factory?

(1) The total number of defective items produced was 1,234.
(2) The ratio of defective items to nondefective items was 32 to 5,678.

13. Is *ABC* a right triangle? $AB = 5$; $AC = 4$.

(1) $BC = 3$
(2) $AC = CD$

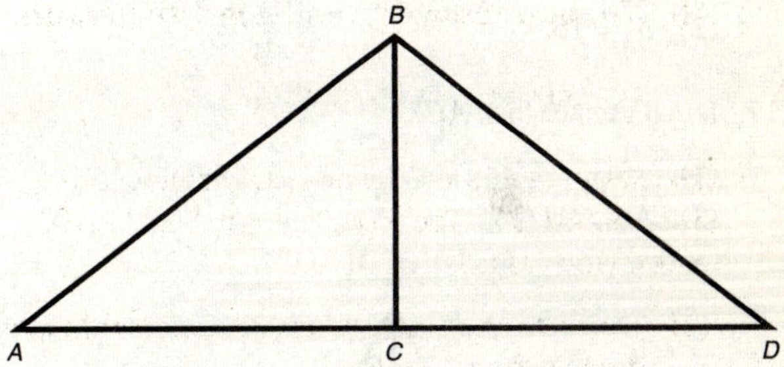

14. Did the price of energy rise last year?

(1) If the price of energy rose last year, then the price of food would rise this year.
(2) The price of food rose this year.

15. How much was a certain Rembrandt painting worth in January 1971?

(1) In January 1977 the painting was worth \$2,000,000.
(2) Over the ten years 1968–1977 the painting increased in value by 10% each year.

GO ON TO THE NEXT PAGE ➤

5 5 5 5 5 5 5 5 5 5 5

(A) if you can get the answer from **(1) ALONE** but not from (2) alone
(B) if you can get the answer from **(2) ALONE** but not from (1) alone
(C) if you can get the answer from **BOTH (1) and (2) TOGETHER,** but not from (1) alone or (2) alone
(D) if **EITHER** statement **(1) ALONE OR** statement **(2) ALONE** suffices
(E) if you **CANNOT** get the answer from statements (1) and (2) **TOGETHER**, but need even more data

16. A sequence of numbers $a_1, a_2, a_3, \ldots$ is given by the rule $a_n^2 = a_{n+1}$. Does 3 appear in the sequence?

 (1) $a_1 = 2$
 (2) $a_3 = 16$

17. Is AB greater than AC?

 (1) $z > x$
 (2) $AC > AD$

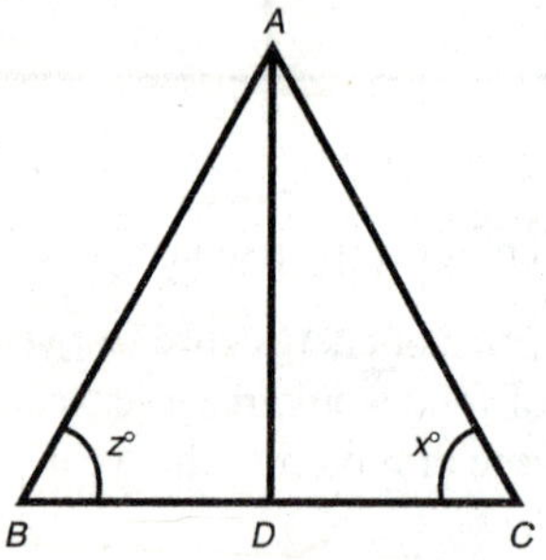

18. Is $\frac{1}{x}$ greater than $\frac{1}{y}$?

 (1) x is greater than 1.
 (2) x is less than y.

19. Plane X flies at r miles per hour from A to B. Plane Y flies at S miles per hour from B to A. Both planes take off at the same time. Which plane flies at a faster rate? Town C is between A and B.

 (1) C is closer to A than it is to B.
 (2) Plane X flies over C before plane Y.

20. Is $\frac{x}{12} > \frac{y}{40}$?

 (1) $10x > 3y$
 (2) $12x < 4y$

21. What is the area of the circular section AOB? A and B are points on the circle which has O as its center.

 (1) Angle $AOB = 36°$
 (2) $OB = OA$

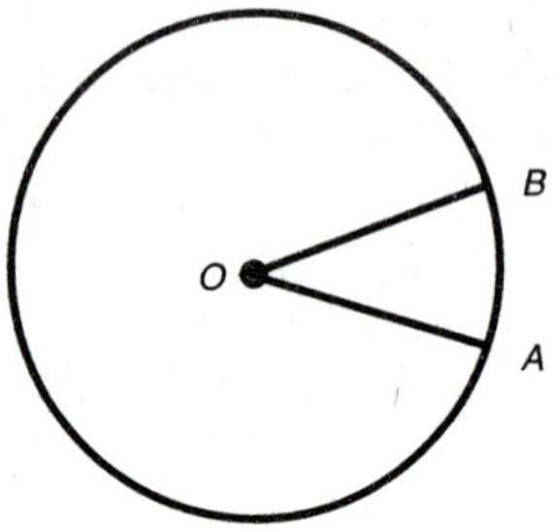

STOP

IF THERE IS STILL TIME REMAINING,
YOU MAY REVIEW THE QUESTIONS IN THIS SECTION ONLY.
YOU MAY NOT TURN TO ANY OTHER SECTION OF THE TEST.

6 6 6 6 6 6 6 6 6 6 6

Section 6

TIME: 25 minutes
17 Questions

Directions: Solve each of the following problems; then indicate the correct answer on the answer sheet.

NOTE: A figure that appears with a problem is drawn as accurately as possible so as to provide information that may help in answering the question. Numbers in this test are real numbers.

1. In a group of people solicited by a charity, 30% contributed $40, 45% contributed $20, and the rest contributed $2. If the charity received a total of $300 from the people who contributed $2, how much was contributed by the entire group?

   (A) $1,200
   (B) $2,400
   (C) $12,600
   (D) $12,900
   (E) $25,800

2. A car currently travels 15 miles on a gallon of gas but after a tune-up the car will use only $\frac{3}{4}$ as much gas as it does now. How many miles will the car travel on a gallon of gas after the tune-up?

   (A) 15
   (B) $16\frac{1}{2}$
   (C) $17\frac{1}{2}$
   (D) $18\frac{3}{4}$
   (E) 20

3. Successive discounts of 20% and 15% are equal to a single discount of

   (A) 30%
   (B) 32%
   (C) 34%
   (D) 35%
   (E) 36%

4. A wall with no windows is 11 feet high and 20 feet long. A large roll of wallpaper costs $25 and will cover 60 square feet of wall. A small roll of wallpaper costs $6 and will cover 10 square feet of wall. What is the least cost for enough wallpaper to cover the wall?

   (A) $75
   (B) $99
   (C) $100
   (D) $120
   (E) $132

GO ON TO THE NEXT PAGE ➤

6 6 6 6 6 6 6 6 6 6 6

5. Mary, John and Karen ate lunch together. Karen's meal cost 50% more than John's meal and Mary's meal cost $\frac{5}{6}$ as much as Karen's meal. If John paid $10 for his meal, what was the total that the three of them paid for lunch?

(A) $28.33
(B) $30.00
(C) $35.00
(D) $37.50
(E) $40.00

Use the following graphs for questions 6–7.

PER CAPITA PERSONAL HEALTH CARE EXPENDITURES

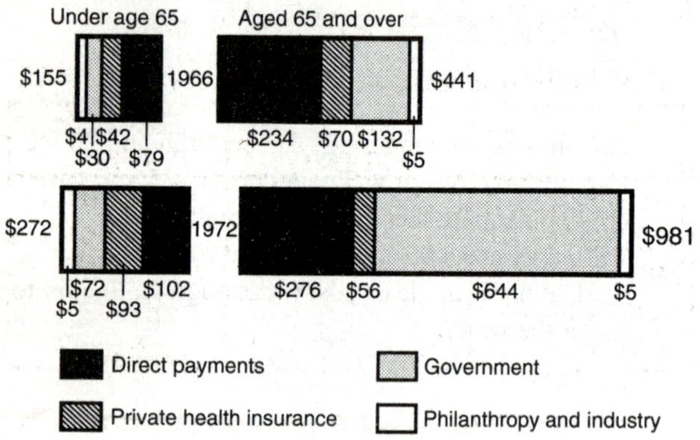

SOURCE: Social Security Bulletin

6. Between 1966 and 1972, the per capita amount spent by the government on personal health care for those under age 65 increased by x% where x is

(A) 100
(B) 120
(C) 140
(D) 220
(E) 240

7. Which of the following statements about expenditures for personal health care between 1966 and 1972 can be inferred from the graphs?

I. The total amount spent for those aged 65 and over in 1972 was more than 3 times as much as the total amount spent on those under 65.
II. Between 1966 and 1972, the amount spent per capita by those aged 65 and over increased in each of the four categories (direct payments, government, private health insurance, philanthropy).
III. The government paid more than $\frac{1}{2}$ the amount of expenditures for those aged 65 and over in 1972.

(A) I only
(B) II only
(C) III only
(D) I and III only
(E) II and III only

GO ON TO THE NEXT PAGE ➤

6 6 6 6 6 6 6 6 6 6 6

8. A car traveled 75% of the way from town A to town B at an average speed of 50 mph. The car travels at an average speed of S mph for the remaining part of the trip. The average speed for the entire trip was 40 mph. What is S?

(A) 10
(B) 20
(C) 25
(D) 30
(E) 37.5

9. If hose A can fill up a tank in 20 minutes, and hose B can fill up the same tank in 15 minutes, how long will it take for the hoses together to fill up the tank?

(A) 5 minutes
(B) $7\frac{1}{2}$ minutes
(C) $8\frac{4}{7}$ minutes
(D) $9\frac{2}{7}$ minutes
(E) 12 minutes

10. It takes Eric 20 minutes to inspect a car. John only needs 18 minutes to inspect a car. If they both start inspecting cars at 8:00 A.M., what is the first time they will finish inspecting a car at the same time?

(A) 9:30 A.M.
(B) 9:42 A.M.
(C) 10:00 A.M.
(D) 11:00 A.M.
(E) 2:00 P.M.

11. In the figure angles A, B, C, D, E, F, G, H are all 90 degrees and $AB = AH = EF = DE$. Also, $BC = CD = HG$ and the Cartesian coordinates of A, C, and E are (1, 2), (2, 5), and (5, 4) respectively. What is the area of the figure $ABCDEFGH$?

(A) 6
(B) 7
(C) 8
(D) 10
(E) 12

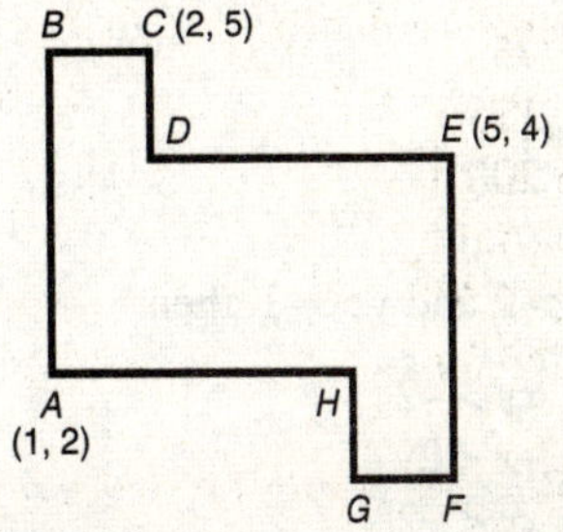

Use the following table for question 12.

Car Production at Plant T for One Week in 1960

	Number of cars produced	Total daily wages
MONDAY	900	\$30,000
TUESDAY	1200	\$40,000
WEDNESDAY	1500	\$52,000
THURSDAY	1400	\$50,000
FRIDAY	1000	\$32,000

12. What was the average cost in wages per car produced for the week?

(A) \$25
(B) \$26
(C) \$29
(D) \$32
(E) \$34

GO ON TO THE NEXT PAGE ➤

6 6 6 6 6 6 6 6 6 6 6

13. If $\frac{x}{y} = 4$ and y is not 0, what percentage (to the nearest percent) of x is $2x - y$?

    (A) 25
    (B) 57
    (C) 75
    (D) 175
    (E) 200

14. If $x > 2$ and $y > -1$, then

    (A) $xy > -2$
    (B) $-x < 2y$
    (C) $xy < -2$
    (D) $-x > 2y$
    (E) $x < 2y$

15. What is the area of the rectangle $ABCD$, if the length of AC is 5 and the length of AD is 4?

    (A) 3
    (B) 6
    (C) 12
    (D) 15
    (E) 20

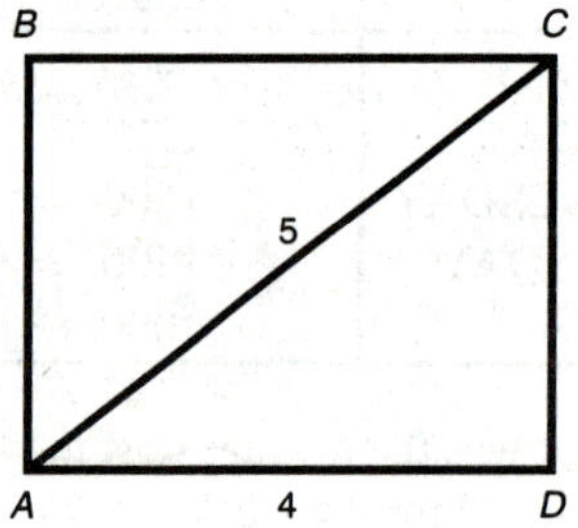

16. If electricity costs k¢ an hour, heat \$$d$ an hour, and water w¢ an hour, how much will all three cost for 12 hours?

    (A) $12(k + d + w)$¢
    (B) $\$(12k + 12d + 12w)$
    (C) $\$(k + 100d + w)$
    (D) $\$\left(12k + \frac{12d}{100} + 12w\right)$
    (E) $\$(.12k + 12d + .12w)$

17. If $x = y = 2z$ and $x \bullet y \bullet z = 256$, then x equals

    (A) 2
    (B) $2\sqrt[3]{2}$
    (C) 4
    (D) $4\sqrt[3]{2}$
    (E) 8

STOP

IF THERE IS STILL TIME REMAINING,
YOU MAY REVIEW THE QUESTIONS IN THIS SECTION ONLY.
YOU MAY NOT TURN TO ANY OTHER SECTION OF THE TEST.

7 7 7 7 7 7 7 7 7 7 7

Section 7

TIME: 25 minutes
21 Questions

Directions: This test consists of a number of sentences, in each of which some part or the whole is underlined. Each sentence is followed by five alternative versions of the underlined portion. Select the alternative you consider both most correct and most effective according to the requirements of standard written English. Answer A is the same as the original version; if you think the original version is best, select answer A.

In considering the answer choices, be attentive to matters of grammar, diction, and syntax as well as clarity, precision, and fluency. Do not select an answer that alters the meaning of the original sentence.

1. Although I calculate that he will be here any minute, I cannot wait much longer for him to arrive.

   (A) Although I calculate that he will be here
   (B) Although I reckon that he will be here
   (C) Because I calculate that he will be here
   (D) Although I think that he will be here
   (E) Because I am confident that he will be here

2. The fourteen-hour day not only has been reduced to one of ten hours but also, in some lines of work, to one of eight or even six.

   (A) The fourteen-hour day not only has been reduced
   (B) Not only the fourteen-hour day has been reduced
   (C) Not the fourteen-hour day only has been reduced
   (D) The fourteen-hour day has not only been reduced
   (E) The fourteen-hour day has been reduced not only

3. The trend toward a decrease is further evidenced in the longer weekend already given to employees in many business establishments.

   (A) already
   (B) all ready
   (C) allready
   (D) ready
   (E) all in all

4. Using it wisely, leisure promotes health, efficiency, and happiness.

   (A) Using it wisely,
   (B) If used wisely,
   (C) Having used it wisely,
   (D) Because it is used wisely,
   (E) Because of usefulness,

5. We want the teacher to be him who has the best rapport with the students.

   (A) We want the teacher to be him
   (B) We want the teacher to be he
   (C) We want him to be the teacher
   (D) We desire that the teacher be him
   (E) We anticipate that the teacher will be him

6. If he were to win the medal, I for one would be disturbed.

   (A) If he were to win the medal,
   (B) If he was to win the medal,
   (C) If he wins the medal,
   (D) If he is the winner of the medal,
   (E) In the event that he wins the medal,

GO ON TO THE NEXT PAGE ➤

7 7 7 7 7 7 7 7 7 7 7

7. The scouts were told to take an overnight hike, pitch camp, prepare dinner, and that they should be in bed by 9 P.M.

    (A) to take an overnight hike, pitch camp, prepare dinner, and that they should be in bed by 9 P.M.
    (B) to take an overnight hike, to pitch camp, to prepare dinner, and that they should be in bed by 9 P.M.
    (C) to take an overnight hike, pitch camp, prepare dinner, and be in bed by 9 P.M.
    (D) to take an overnight hike, pitching camp, preparing dinner and going to bed by 9 P.M.
    (E) to engage in an overnight hike, pitch camp, prepare dinner, and that they should be in bed by 9 P.M.

8. The government's failing to keep it's pledges will earn the distrust of all the other nations in the alliance.

    (A) government's failing to keep it's pledges
    (B) government failing to keep it's pledges
    (C) government's failing to keep its pledges
    (D) government failing to keep its pledges
    (E) governments failing to keep their pledges

9. Her brother along with her parents insist that she remain in school.

    (A) insist
    (B) insists
    (C) are insisting
    (D) were insisting
    (E) have insisted

10. Most students like to read these kind of books during their spare time.

    (A) these kind of books
    (B) these kind of book
    (C) this kind of book
    (D) this kinds of books
    (E) those kind of books

11. She not only was competent but also friendly in nature.

    (A) She not only was competent but also friendly
    (B) Not only was she competent but friendly also
    (C) She not only was competent but friendly also
    (D) She was not only competent but also friendly
    (E) She was not only competent but friendly also

12. In the normal course of events, John will graduate high school and enter college in two years.

    (A) John will graduate high school and enter
    (B) John will graduate from high school and enter
    (C) John will be graduated from high school and enter
    (D) John will be graduated from high school and enter into
    (E) John will have graduated high school and enter

13. With the exception of Frank and I, everyone in the class finished the assignment before the bell rang.

    (A) Frank and I, everyone in the class finished
    (B) Frank and me, everyone in the class finished
    (C) Frank and me, everyone in the class had finished
    (D) Frank and I, everyone in the class had finished
    (E) Frank and me everyone in the class finished

14. Many middle-class individuals find that they cannot obtain good medical attention, despite they need it badly.

    (A) despite they need it badly
    (B) despite they badly need it
    (C) in spite of they need it badly
    (D) however much they need it
    (E) therefore, they need it badly

15. When one eats in this restaurant, you often find that the prices are high and that the food is poorly prepared.

    (A) When one eats in this restaurant, you often find
    (B) When you eat in this restaurant, one often finds
    (C) As you eat in this restaurant, you often find
    (D) If you eat in this restaurant, you often find
    (E) When one ate in this restaurant, he often found

GO ON TO THE NEXT PAGE ➤

7 7 7 7 7 7 7 7 7 7 7

16. Ever since the bombing of Cambodia, there has been much opposition from they who maintain that it was an unauthorized war.
    - (A) from they who maintain that it was an unauthorized war
    - (B) from they who maintain that it had been an unauthorized war
    - (C) from those who maintain that it was an unauthorized war
    - (D) from they maintaining that it was unauthorized
    - (E) from they maintaining that it had been unauthorized

17. I am not to eager to go to this play because it did not get good reviews.
    - (A) I am not to eager to go to this play because it did not get good reviews.
    - (B) Because of its poor reviews, I am not to eager to go to this play.
    - (C) Because of its poor revues, I am not to eager to go to this play.
    - (D) I am not to eager to go to this play because the critics did not give it good reviews.
    - (E) I am not too eager to go to this play because of its poor reviews.

18. It was decided by us that the emphasis would be placed on the results that might be attained.
    - (A) It was decided by us that the emphasis would be placed on the results that might be attained.
    - (B) We decided that the emphasis would be placed on the results that might be attained.
    - (C) We decided to emphasize the results that might be attained.
    - (D) We decided to emphasize the results we might attain.
    - (E) It was decided that we would place emphasis on the results that might be attained.

19. May I venture to say that I think this performance is the most superior I have ever heard.
    - (A) May I venture to say that I think this performance is the most superior
    - (B) May I venture to say that this performance is the most superior
    - (C) May I say that this performance is the most superior
    - (D) I think this performance is superior to any
    - (E) This performance is the most superior of any

20. Completing the physical examination, the tonsils were found to be diseased.
    - (A) Completing the physical examination, the tonsils were found to be diseased.
    - (B) Having completed the physical examination, the tonsils were found to be diseased.
    - (C) When the physical examination was completed, the tonsils were found to be diseased.
    - (D) The physical examination completed, the tonsils were found to be diseased.
    - (E) The physical examination found that the tonsils were diseased.

21. Today this is a totally different world than we have seen in the last decade.
    - (A) than we have seen
    - (B) from what we have seen
    - (C) from what we seen
    - (D) than what we seen
    - (E) then we have seen

STOP

IF THERE IS STILL TIME REMAINING,
YOU MAY REVIEW THE QUESTIONS IN THIS SECTION ONLY.
YOU MAY NOT TURN TO ANY OTHER SECTION OF THE TEST.

Answers
SAMPLE TEST 2

Section 1 [Reading Comprehension]

1	D	6	C	11	D	16	A	21	B
2	C	7	A	12	E	17	C	22	C
3	C	8	B	13	C	18	C	23	A
4	C	9	C	14	E	19	A	24	D
5	E	10	C	15	E	20	A	25	B

Section 2 [Reading Comprehension]

1	A	6	E	11	C	16	C	21	C
2	B	7	B	12	D	17	B	22	C
3	D	8	D	13	A	18	B	23	C
4	D	9	B	14	D	19	C	24	A
5	D	10	A	15	A	20	C	25	C

Section 3 [Problem Solving]

1	C	6	E	11	A	16	B	21	
2	E	7	C	12	B	17	A	22	
3	D	8	D	13	C	18		23	
4	B	9	B	14	B	19		24	
5	B	10	B	15	A	20		25	

Section 4 [Critical Reasoning]

1	D	6	C	11	E	16	B	21	
2	C	7	C	12	C	17	B	22	
3	C	8	B	13	E	18		23	
4	E	9	B	14	B	19		24	
5	A	10	C	15	D	20		25	

Section 5 [Data Sufficiency]

1	E	6	D	11	C	16	D	21	E
2	C	7	B	12	B	17	A	22	
3	A	8	B	13	A	18	C	23	
4	A	9	E	14	E	19	E	24	
5	D	10	A	15	C	20	A	25	

Section 6 [Problem Solving]

1	D	6	C	11	D	16	E	21	
2	E	7	C	12	E	17	E	22	
3	B	8	C	13	D	18		23	
4	B	9	C	14	B	19		24	
5	D	10	D	15	C	20		25	

Section 7 [Sentence Correction]

1	D	6	A	11	D	16	C	21	B
2	E	7	C	12	B	17	E	22	
3	A	8	C	13	C	18	C	23	
4	B	9	B	14	D	19	D	24	
5	B	10	C	15	C	20	E	25	

Self-Scoring Guide—Analytical Writing

Evaluate your writing tests (or have a friend or teacher evaluate them for you) on the following basis. Read each essay completely, paying special attention to its logical organization and use of examples and facts to buttress its claims or position. Assign a holistic score between 0 and 6, using the scale below. Your writing score will be the average of the scores of the two essays.

6	**Outstanding**	Cogent, well-articulated analysis of the issue or critique of the argument. Develops a position with insightful reasons and persuasive examples. Well organized. Superior command of language and variety of syntax. Only minor flaws in grammar, usage, and mechanics.
5	**Strong**	Well-developed analysis or critique. Develops a position with well-chosen examples or reasons. Generally well organized. Clear control of language and variety of syntax. Minor flaws in grammar, usage, and mechanics.
4	**Adequate**	Competent analysis or critique. Develops a position with relevant reasons or examples. Adequately organized. Adequate control of language, but may lack syntactic variety. May have some flaws in grammar, usage, and mechanics.
3	**Limited**	Competent but clearly flawed analysis or critique. Vague or limited in developing a position. Poorly organized. Weak in using relevant examples or reasons. Language used imprecisely or lacking in sentence variety. Contains major errors or frequent minor errors in grammar, usage, and mechanics.
2	**Seriously Flawed**	Serious weaknesses in analysis and organization. Unclear or seriously limited in presenting or developing a position. Disorganized. Few relevant examples or reasons. Frequent serious problems in language and sentence structure. Numerous errors in grammar, usage, or mechanics that interfere with meaning.
1	**Fundamentally Deficient**	Little evidence of ability to organize and develop a coherent response to issue or argument. Severe and persistent errors in language and sentence structure. Pervasive pattern of errors in grammar, usage, and mechanics that severely interfere with meaning.
0	**Unscorable**	Illegible or not written on the assigned topic.

Analysis

Section 1
Reading Comprehension

The passage for questions 1–9 appears on page 292.

1. According to the passage, about how many top managerial professionals work for the federal government?

(A) five million
(B) two million
(C) twenty thousand
(D) nine thousand
(E) five hundred

(D) Note that the question asks "about how many," which requires an approximate figure. Of all the alternative answers, (D) comes closest to the 8,600 employees given in paragraph 1.

2. No complete inventory exists of positions in the three highest levels of government service because

(A) no one has bothered to count them
(B) computers cannot handle all the data
(C) separate agency personnel systems are used
(D) the President has never requested such information
(E) the Classification Act prohibits such a census

(C) See paragraph 3, lines 1 and 2.

3. Top Presidential appointees have as their central responsibility the

(A) prevention of politically motivated interference with the actions of their agencies
(B) monitoring of government actions on behalf of the President's own political party
(C) translation of the aims of the administration into practical programs
(D) investigation of charges of corruption within the government
(E) maintenance of adequate controls over the rate of government spending

(C) See paragraph 5, line 1: "Top Presidential appointees, . . . bear the brunt of translating the philosophy and aims of the current administration into practical programs."

4. One exception to the general rule that top Presidential appointees must be in agreement with the President's political philosophy may be found in

(A) most cabinet-level officers
(B) members of the White House staff
(C) bi-partisan boards and commissions
(D) those offices filled on a patronage basis
(E) offices requiring scientific or technical expertise

(C) See paragraph 6, sentence 2.

5. Applicants for Presidential appointments are usually identified with or are members of

(A) large corporations
(B) the foreign service
(C) government bureaus
(D) academic circles
(E) the President's political party

(E) See paragraph 6, last line.

6. Appointees that are selected directly by the President include

(A) U.S. marshals and attorneys
(B) military officers
(C) agency heads
(D) assistant secretaries
(E) congressional committee members

(C) See paragraph 7: "Those whom the president selects . . ." and following.

7. Appointees usually have to possess expertise in

(A) line management
(B) military affairs
(C) foreign affairs
(D) strategic planning
(E) constitutional law

(A) See paragraph 8: ". . . they usually have substantial responsibilities in line management. . . ."

8. According to the passage, Presidential appointees are regarded primarily as

(A) political spokesmen
(B) policy makers
(C) staff managers
(D) scientific or technical experts
(E) business executives

(B) Paragraph 8, line 1: "These appointees are primarily regarded as policy makers. . . ."

9. Appointees selected by department and agency heads include

(A) military men
(B) cabinet secretaries
(C) deputy secretaries
(D) diplomats
(E) residual position holders

(C) See paragraph 7: "Those selected by department and agency heads . . ." and following.

The passage for questions 10–17 appears on page 294.

10. Before the expansion of Europe overseas could take place

(A) vast sums of money had to be raised
(B) an army had to be recruited
(C) the Atlantic Ocean had to be conquered
(D) ships had to be built
(E) seamen had to be trained

(C) See paragraph 1, line 1: "The first and decisive step in the expansion of Europe overseas was the conquest of the Atlantic Ocean."

11. One of Portugal's leaders, known as the Navigator, was in reality

(A) Christopher Columbus
(B) King John II
(C) a Venetian
(D) Prince Henry
(E) Prince Paul

(D) See paragraph 1, line 26: ". . . in men of the calibre of Prince Henry, known as the Navigator. . . ."

12. Portugal was adept at exploring unknown waters because she possessed all of the following except

(A) a navy
(B) past experience
(C) experienced navigators
(D) experienced mapmakers
(E) extensive trade routes

(E) In paragraph 1, the sentence containing the statement "Portugal could adapt and develop the knowledge and experience of the past to meet the challenge of the unknown . . . ," meets answer (B); also in this paragraph there is mention of experienced Portuguese seamen and a mercantile marine (A), rudiments of navigation (C), and mapmakers (D). Since extensive trade routes are never mentioned, the correct answer is (E).

13. In addition to possessing the necessary resources for exploration, Portugal was the logical country for this task because of her

(A) wealth
(B) navigational experience
(C) geographical position
(D) prominence
(E) ability

(C) Portugal was the logical nation for this task because of her "geographical position and her history." Wealth (A) and navigational experience (B) are resources in context with the question, while (D) and (E) are vague.

14. The Portuguese learned navigational methods and procedures from all of the following except

(A) Jews
(B) Catalans
(C) Genoese
(D) Venetians
(E) Aegeans

(E) See paragraph 1.

15. Mediterranean seamen generally kept close to shore because

(A) they were afraid of pirates
(B) they feared being forced to a lee shore
(C) they lacked navigational ability
(D) they feared running into storms
(E) the latitudinal extent of the Mediterranean was not great

(E) See paragraph 2, line 49: Seamen kept close to shore because ". . . the latitudinal extent of the Mediterranean was not great, and voyages could be conducted from point to point on compass bearings," not because of the other reasons given in the question.

16. Hazards such as sudden storms and dangerous coasts were

(A) predictable risks
(B) unknown risks
(C) unknown to the area
(D) a major threat to exploration
(E) no threat to navigation

(A) See paragraph 2, line 38: ". . . hazards . . . in the form of sudden storms or dangerous coasts, were known and could be usually anticipated."

17. Sailing close to the coast enabled seamen to

(A) reach their destination faster
(B) navigate without sailing directions
(C) determine their positions from landmarks
(D) determine their longitude and latitude
(E) avoid dangerous shoals

(C) See paragraph 2, line 54: "Having made a landfall on a bearing, they could determine their precise position from prominent landmarks. . . ."

The passage for questions 18–25 appears on page 296.

18. Compared to the artist, the policeman is

(A) a man of action, not words
(B) factual and not fanciful
(C) neutral and not prejudiced
(D) stoic and not emotional
(E) aggressive and not passive

(C) The correct answer is given in paragraph 2. The policeman must be neutral and present the facts, while the "artist usually begins with a preconceived message or attitude . . . ," i.e., prejudiced. While artists are "emotional," no mention is made that policemen are stoic (D).

19. Policemen reacted to story events and characters

(A) like most other people
(B) according to a policeman's stereotyped image
(C) like dilettantes
(D) unrealistically
(E) without emotion

(A) The writer explains that the policemen's reactions were "surprisingly unprejudiced." The rest of paragraph 3 explains that policemen reacted to story events and characters according to alternative (A).

20. To which sort of characters did policemen object?

I. Unrealistic
II. Emotional
III. Sordid

(A) I only
(B) II only
(C) I and II only
(D) II and III only
(E) I, II, and III

(A) The only characters that policemen objected to were unrealistic. See paragraph 3.

21. According to the passage, a short story should contain

(A) elegant prose
(B) suspense
(C) objectivity
(D) real-life experiences
(E) irony

(B) Only "suspense" was given in the passage (in paragraph 4).

22. The instructor chose the short story because

I. it was easy for the students
II. students had experience with it
III. students would enjoy it

(A) I only
(B) II only
(C) I and II only
(D) II and III only
(E) I, II, and III

(C) Alternatives I and II may be found in the first paragraph.

23. Like writers, policemen must

(A) analyze situations
(B) behave coolly
(C) have an artistic bent
(D) intervene quickly
(E) attend college

(A) Policemen must "also try to evaluate the events they describe. . . ." The "also" refers to artists and writers. See paragraph 2, and also paragraph 1: ". . . they had to be able to take in the details of a situation quickly. . . ."

24. According to the passage, most policemen wrote stories about

(A) films
(B) previous reading
(C) American history
(D) their work
(E) politics

(D) Policemen wrote about their work. See paragraph 4.

25. According to the author, policemen view their profession as

(A) full of corruption
(B) worth the effort
(C) full of routine
(D) poorly paid
(E) dangerous but adventuresome

(B) Alternative (B) sums up their feeling. Corruption and routine were mentioned as minor annoyances. The issues of pay and adventure were not mentioned. See paragraph 4.

Section 2 Reading Comprehension

The passage for questions 1–9 appears on page 298.

1. The dropout rate among regular students in Open Admissions was approximately

(A) 35%
(B) 45%
(C) 55%
(D) 65%
(E) 75%

(A) The dropout rate on average for all Open Admissions students was 48%; for regular students, 36%; and for Open Admissions categories, 56% (lines 95–98).

2. According to the passage, in the past it was *not* the purpose of American higher education to

(A) advance learning
(B) solve societal problems
(C) impart knowledge
(D) train workers
(E) prepare future managers

(B) See paragraph 1: "The successful institution of higher learning had never been one whose mission could be defined in terms of providing vocational skills or . . . resolving societal problems." This is the sort of question that must be read carefully; it asks for an answer that is *not* among the alternatives given in the passage.

3. One of the recent, important changes in higher education relates to

(A) student representation on college boards
(B) faculty tenure requirements
(C) curriculum updates
(D) service-education concepts
(E) cost constraints

(D) The idea that a university must relate to the problems of society is given in paragraphs 2, 3, and 5.

4. It was estimated that what percentage of Open Admissions students would fail to graduate from City University?

(A) 40%
(B) 50%
(C) 60%
(D) 70%
(E) 80%

(D) See the last sentence.

5. According to the passage, the two-year college may be described as

I. a junior college
II. service-oriented
III. a community college

(A) I only
(B) II only
(C) I and II only
(D) II and III only
(E) I, II, and III

(D) The two-year college is described in paragraph 4 as a "service-related" and "community" college. It is no longer called a "junior" college.

6. The service role of colleges aims to

(A) improve services
(B) gain acceptance among educators
(C) serve the community
(D) provide skills for future use
(E) make graduates employable

(E) The idea of the service-oriented college is to produce "productive" students and, as stated in the third paragraph, to provide programs "to meet the demands of regional employment markets, . . ." i.e., to make graduates employable.

7. The attrition rate for Open Admissions students was greater than the rate for regular students by what percent?

(A) 10%
(B) 20%
(C) 36%
(D) 40%
(E) 46%

(B) The attrition rate for Open Admissions students was 56 percent, and that for regular students 36 percent, a difference of 20 percent. See lines 97–98.

8. Clark Kerr failed to take account of

(A) the "communiversity"
(B) collegiate bureaucracies
(C) faculty tenure
(D) the service-university
(E) Open Admissions

(D) The phrase "this phenomenon" in line 70 refers to the preceding discussion of the service-university, and not just to the "multiversity."

9. The *average* attrition rate for regular and Open Admissions students was

(A) 36%
(B) 46%
(C) 56%
(D) 75%
(E) 92%

(B) The attrition rate for Open Admissions students was 56 percent and for regular students, 36 percent. The average of 56 percent and 36 percent is 48 percent. See lines 97–98.

The passage for questions 10–17 appears on page 301.

10. According to the passage, a "new protectionism" is evidenced by

(A) bilateral import quotas
(B) political suasion
(C) lower than market prices
(D) abrogating agreements
(E) increased product standards

(A) See the example of steel in the last two paragraphs.

11. Increased protectionism has been caused by

(A) the "cold war"
(B) United States economic policy
(C) increased unemployment
(D) a breakdown in international law
(E) a growth in cartels

(C) Increased barriers to trade—protectionism—have been caused by recession and unemployment. See paragraph 2.

12. A slowdown in world trade has been caused by

(A) protectionism
(B) slower population growth
(C) less trade with Communist countries
(D) economic recession
(E) increased oil prices

(D) See line 57: ". . . trade probably fell as the world economy stayed flat."

13. The U.S. Government has increased barriers to the import of

(A) autos, textiles, and sugar
(B) autos, textiles, and steel
(C) autos, electronics, and steel
(D) shoes, textiles, and sugar
(E) shoes, textiles, and steel

(A) See lines 33–35: ". . . Washington . . . has raised new barriers against imports in autos, textiles and sugar."

14. The best possible theme for the passage would be

(A) "Reagan Administration's Economic Policies"
(B) "International Trade Agreements in the 1960's"
(C) "Tokyo Round of Trade Negotiations"
(D) "A Perilous Time for World Trade"
(E) "Problems and Prospects for World Exports"

(D) Alternatives (B) and (E) can be eliminated since the subject of the passage is not trade agreements or world exports (trade, of course, includes imports as well). Alternative (A) is not plausible, because the passage does not emphasize "domestic" but rather international economic policy. The "Tokyo Round," (C), was not mentioned in the passage. Alternative (D) certainly reflects the passage, which is pessimistic about the future of world trade.

15. In recent years, trade between nations has been constrained by

(A) voluntary agreements limiting imports
(B) rhetoric expressed by labor leaders
(C) misalignment among world currencies
(D) the free international exchange of goods
(E) restrictive monetary and fiscal policies

(A) See lines 67–69: ". . . new trade restraints, often bound up in voluntary agreements . . . to limit particular imports . . ."

16. While imports are restrained by barriers, exports are encouraged through

(A) bargaining
(B) lowering prices
(C) subsidies
(D) advertising
(E) dealing

(C) Exports are promoted through subsidies. See lines 37–39.

17. A means to decrease steel capacity in the European Economic Community has been the use of

(A) voluntary quotas
(B) bilateral quotas
(C) voluntary and bilateral quotas
(D) trigger prices
(E) restraints

(B) Bilateral quotas were used by the European Economic Community. See the last paragraph.

The passage for questions 18–25 appears on page 303.

18. According to the passage, the population at large

(A) is unconcerned about air pollution controls
(B) is especially aware of problems concerning air quality and purity
(C) regards water pollution as more serious than air pollution
(D) has failed to recognize the economic consequences of pollution
(E) is unwilling to make the sacrifices needed to ensure clean air

(B) See paragraph 3, sentence 1: ". . . people are particularly sensitive about any reduction in the quality of the atmosphere. . . ."

19. Scientific forecasts have shown that clear and biologically valuable air

(A) is likely to remain abundant for some time
(B) creates fewer economic difficulties than does water pollution
(C) may soon be dangerously lacking
(D) may be beyond the capacity of our technology to protect
(E) has already become difficult to obtain

(C) This is implied in paragraph 2.

20. According to the passage, which of the following contributes *most* to atmospheric pollution?

(A) industry
(B) production
(C) households
(D) mining
(E) waste disposal

(C) See paragraph 4: "The households' share in atmospheric pollution is far bigger than that of industry. . . ." The key word in the question is "most."

21. The costs involved in the maintenance of pure water are determined primarily by

I. production costs
II. transport costs
III. research costs

(A) I only
(B) III only
(C) I and II only
(D) II and III only
(E) I, II, and III

(C) Both production *and* transportation costs are important. Although paragraph 1 states that the costs of maintaining clean water are "primarily" production costs, paragraph 5 states that this problem is "related to the costs of production and transport . . ."

22. According to the passage, atmospheric pollution caused by private property is

(A) easy to control
(B) impossible to control
(C) difficult to control
(D) decreasing
(E) negligible

(C) See paragraph 6, line 54: "Atmospheric pollution caused by the private property of individuals . . . is difficult to control."

23. According to the passage, the problem of noise can be solved through

I. Active measures
II. Passive measures
III. Tax levies

(A) I only
(B) III only
(C) I and II only
(D) II and III only
(E) I, II, and III

(C) See paragraph 7: both active and passive resources. No mention is made of levying taxes.

24. According to the passage, the costs of some anti-pollution measures will have to be borne by individuals because

(A) individuals contribute to the creation of pollution
(B) governments do not have adequate resources
(C) industry is not willing to bear its share
(D) individuals are more easily taxed than producers
(E) individuals demand production, which causes pollution

(A) See paragraph 6: "*In this particular case*, the cost of anti-pollution measures will have to be borne, to a considerable extent, by individuals. . . ." "In this particular case" refers to the situation also described in the paragraph where pollution is caused by the private property of individuals.

25. Complete protection against noise

(A) may be forthcoming in the near future
(B) is impossible to achieve
(C) may have prohibitive costs
(D) is possible only in developed countries
(E) has been achieved in some countries

(C) See paragraph 7: While noise abatement is not impossible to achieve, the "costs of a complete protection against noise are so prohibitive. . . ."

Section 3 Problem Solving

(Numbers in parentheses at the end of each explanation indicate the section in the Mathematics Review where material addressed in the question is discussed.)

1. Water has been poured into an empty rectangular tank at the rate of 5 cubic feet per minute for 6 minutes. The length of the tank is 4 feet and the width is one half of the length. How deep is the water in the tank?

(A) 7.5 inches
(B) 3 ft. 7.5 inches
(C) 3 ft. 9 inches
(D) 7 ft. 6 inches
(E) 30 ft.

(C) The volume of water that has been poured into the tank is 5 cubic feet per minute for 6 minutes, or 30 cubic feet. The tank is rectangular, so its volume is length × width × height, with the answer in cubic units. The width is $\frac{1}{2}$ the length, or $\frac{1}{2}$ of 4 feet, or 2 feet. The volume, which we already know is 30 cubic feet, is, therefore, 4 feet × 2 feet × the height. The height (depth of the water in the tank) is, therefore, $\frac{30}{8} = 3\frac{3}{4}$ feet = 3 feet 9 inches. (III-3)

2. If $2x - y = 4$, then $6x - 3y$ is

(A) 4
(B) 6
(C) 8
(D) 10
(E) 12

(E) $6x - 3y$ is $3(2x - y)$. Since $2x - y = 4$, $6x - 3y = 3 \bullet 4$ or 12. (II-2)

3. If x, y, z are chosen from the three numbers -3, $\frac{1}{2}$, and 2, what is the largest possible value of the expression $\left(\frac{x}{y}\right)z^2$?

(A) $-\frac{3}{8}$
(B) 16
(C) 24
(D) 36
(E) 54

(D) Since -3 has the largest absolute value of the three given numbers, using z as -3 will make z^2 as large as possible. Since $\frac{x}{y}$ is a quotient, to make it as large as possible use the smallest positive number for y and the largest positive number for x. So if you use $x = 2$ and $y = \frac{1}{2}$ then $\frac{x}{y}$ is as large as possible. Therefore, the largest value of the expression is $\left(\frac{2}{\left(\frac{1}{2}\right)}\right)(-3)^2 = 4(9) = 36$. (I-2)

4. A survey of n people found that 60 percent preferred brand A. An additional x people were surveyed who all preferred brand A. Seventy percent of all the people surveyed preferred brand A. Find x in terms of n.

(A) $\frac{n}{6}$

(B) $\frac{n}{3}$

(C) $\frac{n}{2}$

(D) n

(E) $3n$

(B) The total number of people surveyed was $n + x$. Since 70% of the total preferred brand A that means $.7(n + x)$ preferred brand A. However, 60% of the n people and all of the x people preferred brand A. So $.6n + x$ preferred brand A. Therefore, $.7(n + x)$ must equal $.6n + x$. So we have $.7n + .7x = .6n + x$. Solving for x gives $.1n = .3x$ or $x = \frac{n}{3}$. (I-4)

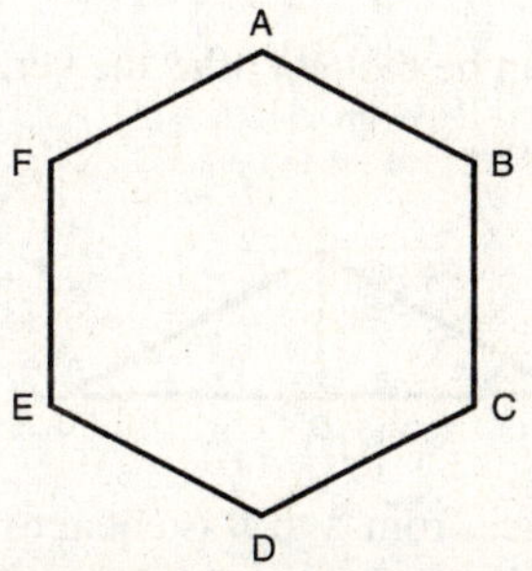

5. The hexagon *ABCDEF* is regular. That means all its sides are the same length and all its interior angles are the same size. Each side of the hexagon is 2 feet. What is the area of the rectangle *BCEF*?

(A) 4 square feet

(B) $4\sqrt{3}$ square feet

(C) 8 square feet

(D) $4 + 4\sqrt{3}$ square feet

(E) 12 square feet

B) A picture always helps. You are given that *BC* and *F* are each 2 feet. Since the area of a rectangle is length imes width, you must find the length (*CE* or *BF*). Look at he triangle *ABF*. It has two equal sides ($AB = AF$), so the

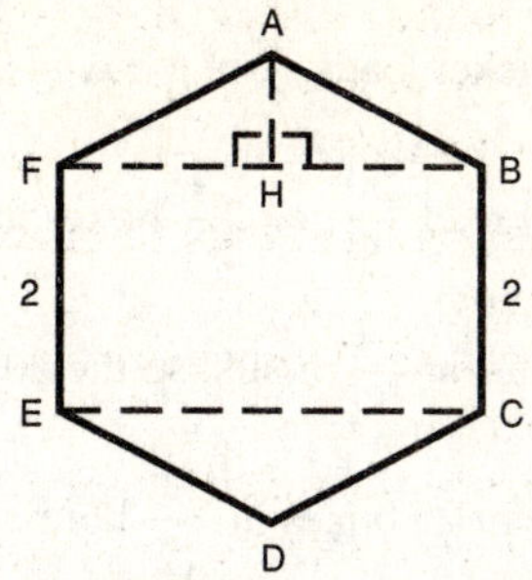

perpendicular from *A* to the line *BF* will divide *ABF* into two congruent right triangles, *AHF* and *AHB*, each with hypotenuse 2. The angle *FAB* is 120°, since the total of all the angles of the hexagon is 720°. So each of the two triangles is a 30° – 60° – 90° triangle with hypotenuse 2.

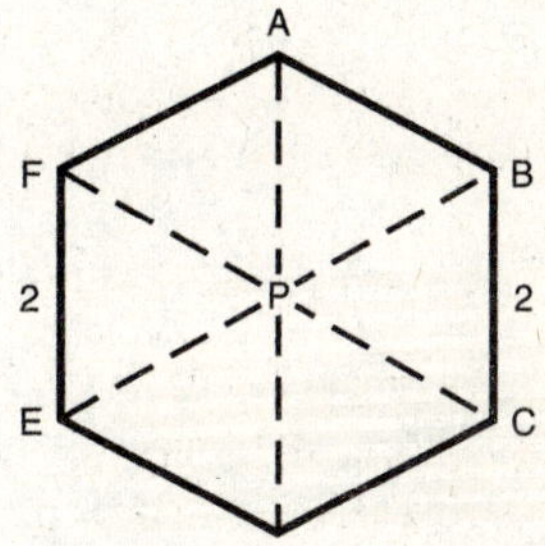

So $AH = 1$ and *FH* and *HB* must equal $\sqrt{3}$. Therefore, *BF* is $2\sqrt{3}$ and the area is $2 \times 2\sqrt{3} = 4\sqrt{3}$ square feet. (You can find the sum of the angles of any convex polygon by connecting all vertices to a fixed interior point, *P*. In the case of the hexagon this will give 6 triangles. The total of all the triangles' angles is $6 \times 180° = 1{,}080°$. Since the angles at the fixed point, which are not part of the hexagon angles, will add up to 360°, the sum of the hexagon's angles is $1{,}080° – 360° = 720°$.) (III-3, III-4)

6. A warehouse has 20 packers. Each packer can load $\frac{1}{8}$ of a box in 9 minutes. How many boxes can be loaded in $1\frac{1}{2}$ hours by all 20 packers?

(A) $1\frac{1}{4}$

(B) $10\frac{1}{4}$

(C) $12\frac{1}{2}$

(D) 20

(E) 25

(E) Since each packer loads $\frac{1}{8}$ of a box in 9 minutes, the 20 packers will load $\frac{20}{8}$, or $2\frac{1}{2}$ boxes in 9 minutes. There are 90 minutes in $1\frac{1}{2}$ hours; so the 20 packers will load $10 \times 2\frac{1}{2}$ or 25 boxes in $1\frac{1}{2}$ hours. (II-5)

7. In Motor City 90% of the population own a car, 15% own a motorcycle, and everybody owns one or the other or both. What is the percentage of motorcycle owners who own cars?

(A) 5%

(B) 15%

(C) $33\frac{1}{3}$%

(D) 50%

(E) 90%

(C) You want the ratio of the percentage who own both a car and a motorcycle to the percentage who own a motorcycle. You know that 15% own a motorcycle so you need to find the percentage who own both a car and a motorcycle. Let A stand for the percentage who own both a car and a motorcycle. Then (the percentage who own a car) + (the percentage who own a motorcycle) – A must equal the percentage who own one or the other or both. Since 100% own one or the other or both, we obtain 90% + 15% – A = 105% – A = 100%. So A = 5%. Since 15% own motorcycles, the percentage of motorcycle owners who own cars is $\frac{5\%}{15\%} = \frac{1}{3} = 33\frac{1}{3}\%$. (II-4)

8. Jim's weight is 140% of Marcia's weight. Bob's weight is 90% of Lee's weight. Lee weighs twice as much as Marcia. What percentage of Jim's weight is Bob's weight?

(A) $64\frac{2}{7}$

(B) $77\frac{7}{9}$

(C) 90

(D) $128\frac{4}{7}$

(E) $155\frac{5}{9}$

(D) To do computations, change percentages to decimals. Let $J, M, B,$ and L stand for Jim's, Marcia's, Bob's, and Lee's respective weights. Then we know $J = 1.4M$, $B = .9L$, and $L = 2M$. We need to know B as a percentage of J. Since $B = .9L$ and $L = 2M$, we have $B = .9(2M) = 1.8M$. $J = 1.4M$ is equivalent to $M = \left(\frac{1}{(1.4)}\right)J$. So $B = 1.8M = 1.8\left(\frac{1}{(1.4)}\right)J = \left(1\frac{2}{7}\right)J$. Converting $1\frac{2}{7}$ to a percentage, we have $1\frac{2}{7} = 1.28\frac{4}{7} = 128\frac{4}{7}\%$, so (D) is the correct answer. (II-2, I-4)

9. Towns A and C are connected by a straight highway which is 60 miles long. The straight-line distance between town A and town B is 50 miles, and the straight-line distance from town B to town C is 50 miles. How many miles is it from town B to the point on the highway connecting towns A and C which is closest to town B?

(A) 30
(B) 40
(C) $30\sqrt{2}$
(D) 50
(E) 60

(B) The towns can be thought of as the vertices of a triangle.

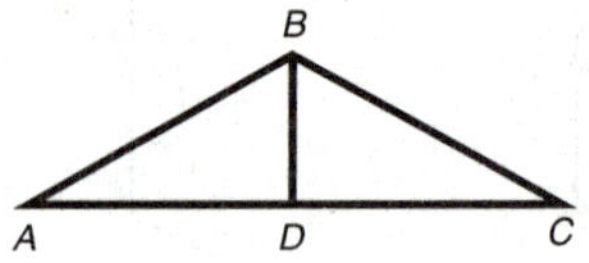

Since the distance from A to B is equal to the distance from B to C, the triangle is isosceles. The point D on AC which is closest to B is the point on AC such that BD is perpendicular to AC. (If BD were not perpendicular to AC, then there would be a point on AC closer to B than D; in the picture, E is closer to B than D is.)

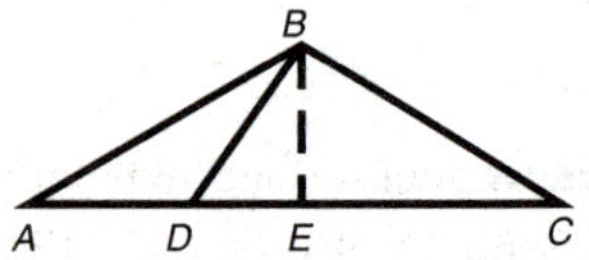

So the triangles ABD and CBD are right triangles with two corresponding sides equal. Therefore ABD is congruent to CBD. Thus $AD = DC$, and since AC is 60, AD must be 30. Since ABD is a right triangle with hypotenuse 50 and another side = 30, the remaining side (BD) must be 40. (III-4)

10. A chair originally cost $50.00. The chair was offered for sale at 108% of its cost. After a week the price was discounted 10% and the chair was sold. The chair was sold for

(A) $45.00
(B) $48.60
(C) $49.00
(D) $49.50
(E) $54.00

(B) Since 108% of $50 = (1.08)(50) = $54, the chair was offered for sale at $54.00. It was sold for 90% of $54 since there was a 10% discount. Therefore, the chair was sold for (.9)($54) or $48.60. (I-4)

11. A worker is paid *x* dollars for the first 8 hours he works each day. He is paid *y* dollars per hour for each hour he works in excess of 8 hours. During one week he works 8 hours on Monday, 11 hours on Tuesday, 9 hours on Wednesday, 10 hours on Thursday, and 9 hours on Friday. What is his average daily wage in dollars for the five-day week?

(A) $x + \frac{7}{5}y$

(B) $2x + y$

(C) $\frac{5x + 8y}{5}$

(D) $8x + \left(\frac{7}{5}\right)y$

(E) $5x + 7y$

(A) Here's a table of the hours worked:

	Mon.	Tues.	Wed.	Thurs.	Fri.	Wages for week
	8	8	8	8	8	$5x$
excess over 8 hrs	0	3	1	2	1	$(0+3+1+2+1)y = 7y.$

The average daily wage equals $\frac{(5x + 7y)}{5}$, or $x + \frac{7}{5}y$.

(II-3)

12. A club has 8 male and 8 female members. The club is choosing a committee of 6 members. The committee must have 3 male and 3 female members. How many different committees can be chosen?

(A) 112,896
(B) 3,136
(C) 720
(D) 112
(E) 9

(B) There are 8 choices for the first female, then 7 choices for the second female, and 6 choices for the third female on the committee. So there are $8 \times 7 \times 6$ different ways to pick the three females in order. However, if member A is chosen first, then member B, then member C, the same three females are chosen as when C is followed by A and B is chosen last. In fact, the same three members can be chosen in $3 \times 2 \times 1$ different orders. So to find the number of different groups of 3 females, DIVIDE $8 \times 7 \times 6$ by $3 \times 2 \times 1$ to obtain 56.

In the same way, there are $8 \times 7 \times 6 = 336$ ways to choose the three males in order, but any group of three males can be put in order $3 \times 2 \times 1 = 6$ different ways. So there are $\frac{336}{6} = 56$ different groups of three males. Therefore, there are $56 \times 56 = 3{,}136$ different committees of 3 males and 3 females. (II-4)

13. A motorcycle costs $2,500 when it is brand new. At the end of each year it is worth $\frac{4}{5}$ of what it was at the beginning of the year. What is the motorcycle worth when it is 3 years old?

(A) $1,000
(B) $1,200
(C) $1,280
(D) $1,340
(E) $1,430

(C) Let x_n be what the motorcycle is worth after *n* years. Then we know $x_0 = \$2{,}500$ and $x_{n+1} = \frac{4}{5} \times x_n$.

So $x_1 = \frac{4}{5} \times 2{,}500$, which is $2,000. x_2 is $\frac{4}{5} \times 2{,}000$, which is 1,600, and finally x_3 is $\frac{4}{5} \times 1{,}600$, which is 1,280. Therefore, the motorcycle is worth $1,280 at the end of three years.

OR

$$x_3 = \frac{4}{5}x_2 = \frac{4}{5}\left(\frac{4}{5}x_1\right) = \left(\frac{4}{5}\right)\left(\frac{4}{5}\right)\left(\frac{4}{5}x_0\right) = \frac{64}{125}x_0.$$

$\left(\frac{64}{125}\right)2500 = 1280.$ (II-6)

14. Which of the following inequalities is the solution to the inequality $7x - 5 < 12x + 18$?

(A) $x < -\frac{13}{5}$

(B) $x > -\frac{23}{5}$

(C) $x < -\frac{23}{5}$

(D) $x > \frac{23}{5}$

(E) $x < \frac{23}{5}$

(B) Simply use the properties of inequalities to solve the given inequality. Subtract $12x$ from each side to get $-5x - 5 < 18$. Next add 5 to each side to obtain $-5x < 23$. Finally, divide each side by -5 to get $x > -\frac{23}{5}$. Remember that if you divide each side of an inequality by a negative number the inequality is reversed. You can make a quick check of your answer by using $x = -5$ which is not $> -\frac{23}{5}$ and $x = -4$, which is $> -\frac{23}{5}$ in the original inequality. Since $x = -5$ does not satisfy the original inequality (-40 is not < -42) and $x = -4$ does satisfy the inequality (-33 is < -30), the answer is correct. You could use the method of checking values to find the correct answer, but it would take longer. (II-7)

15. If $x + 2y = 2x + y$, then $x - y$ is equal to

(A) 0
(B) 2
(C) 4
(D) 5
(E) cannot be determined

(A) Since $x + 2y = 2x + y$, we can subtract $x + 2y$ from each side of the equation and the result is $0 = x - y$. (II-2)

16. Mary, John, and Karen ate lunch together. Karen's meal cost 50% more than John's meal and Mary's meal cost $\frac{5}{6}$ as much as Karen's meal. If Mary paid \$2 more than John, how much was the total that the three of them paid?

(A) \$28.33
(B) \$30.00
(C) \$35.00
(D) \$37.50
(E) \$40.00

(B) Let M, J, and K be the amounts paid by Mary, John, and Karen respectively. Then $K = 1.5J$, $M = \frac{5}{6}K$, and $M = J + 2$. So M, which is $\frac{5}{6}K$ must $= \left(\frac{5}{6}\right)(1.5)J = \left(\frac{5}{6}\right)\left(\frac{3}{2}\right)J = \left(\frac{5}{4}\right)J$. Therefore, we have $\left(\frac{5}{4}\right)J = J + 2$ or $\left(\frac{1}{4}\right)J = 2$, which means $J = 8$. So $K = 1.5J$, or 12 and $M = J + 2$, or 10. So the total is $8 + 12 + 10 = \$30$. (II-2)

17. If the angles of a triangle are in the ratio 1 : 2 : 2, then the triangle

(A) is isosceles
(B) is obtuse
(C) is a right triangle
(D) is equilateral
(E) has one angle greater than 80°

(A) The angles are in the ratio of 1 : 2 : 2, so 2 angles are equal to each other, and both are twice as large as the third angle of the triangle. Since a triangle with two equal angles must have the sides opposite equal, the triangle is isosceles. (Using the fact that the sum of the angles of a triangle is 180°, you can see that the angles of the triangle are 72°, 72° and 36°, so only (A) is true.) (III-4)

Section 4
Critical Reasoning

1. Richard is a terrible driver. He has had at least five traffic violations in the past year.

Which of the following can be said about the above claim?

(A) This is an example of an argument that is directed against the source of the claim rather than the claim itself.
(B) The statement is fallacious because it contains an illegitimate appeal to authority.
(C) The above argument obtains its strength from a similarity of two compared situations.
(D) The argument is built upon an assumption that is not stated but rather is concealed.
(E) In the above statements, there is a shifting in the meaning of terms, causing a fallacy of ambiguity.

(D) Analysis of the two sentences indicates the presence of an assumption that anyone who has had at least five traffic violations in a year is a terrible driver. This assumption is understood but is not stated. Rather, it is a hidden assumption, making (D) the appropriate answer. Alternative (A) is incorrect because there is no attack on the source of the claim. (B) is wrong because there is no appeal to authority—illegitimate or not. (C) is not the correct answer because there is no comparison of two similar situations in the statement. (E) is incorrect because there is no term with a confusing or double meaning.

2. The exchange rate is the ruling official rate of exchange of dollars for other currencies. It determines the value of American goods in relation to foreign goods. If the dollar is devalued in terms of other currencies, American exports (which are paid for in dollars) become cheaper to foreigners and American imports (paid for by purchasing foreign currency) become more expensive to holders of dollars.

What conclusion can be drawn from the above?

(A) There are certain disadvantages for the United States economy attached to devaluation.
(B) The prospect of devaluation results in a speculative outflow of funds.
(C) By encouraging exports and discouraging imports, devaluation can improve the American balance of payments.
(D) The difference between imports and exports is called the Trade Gap.
(E) It is possible that inflation neutralizes the beneficial effects of devaluation.

(C) The best conclusion that can be drawn from the statement is one that sums up the facts that are given in one sentence; thus, (C) is the best answer. Although the given paragraph states that if there is devaluation of the dollar, American imports will become more expensive, this will not necessarily be a disadvantage for the U.S. economy. Hence, (A) is not appropriate. Alternative (B) is also inappropriate, because it highlights a disadvantage that may arise from the expectation of devaluation, but which is not dealt with in the paragraph. Alternatives (D) and (E) are both helpful pieces of information, but they cannot be concluded from the given text.

3. You have three boxes, each containing two balls, one containing a black pair; one, a white pair; and the third, one white ball and one black ball. On each box are pictures of two balls—either two black ones, two white ones, or one white and one black. You are told that the markings on the boxes are all wrong. You are asked to ascertain the colors of the balls contained in each box.

Which of the following statements can be inferred from the above?

(A) You can take out one ball from the box marked with two black balls and, without looking at the second ball, know what each box actually contains.
(B) You can take out one ball from the box marked with two white balls and, without looking at the second ball, know what each box actually contains.
(C) You can take out one ball from the box marked with one white ball and one black ball and, without looking at the second ball, know what each box contains.
(D) You cannot know which balls are contained in which box until you take a ball out of more than one box.
(E) You cannot know which boxes contain which color balls until you take a ball out of all three boxes.

(C) By removing one ball from the box marked with two black balls or removing one ball from the box marked with two white balls, you cannot ascertain the color of the ball left in the box, let alone the color of the balls in the third box. Therefore, answer alternatives (A) and (B) are inappropriate. (D) and (E) are also inappropriate because it is possible by taking out just one ball from the box marked with one white ball and one black ball and ascertain the colors of all the balls contained in each box. The appropriate answer is (C). If you take one ball from the box wrongly marked with one white ball and one black ball, and if the ball is white, it must be one of the white pair. The mixed pair would then have to be in the box marked with two black balls and the remaining box must therefore contain the black pair.

4. In the human body, platelets promote blood clotting by clumping together. Aspirin has been found to prevent clotting by making platelets less sticky. Research has now shown that heart attacks and strokes caused by blood clots could be avoided by taking one aspirin a day. Statistics show that the incidence of second heart attacks has been reduced by 21% and overall mortality rates by 15% as a result of taking aspirin.

Unfortunately, the drug has several unpleasant side effects, including nausea, gastric bleeding, and, in severe cases, shock. In children, it has been linked to Reye's Syndrome, a rare, but occasionally fatal, childhood illness.

On balance, however, for men aged 40 and over, an aspirin a day may present an excellent prophylactic measure for a disease that affects 1.5 million Americans yearly and claims the lives of about 540,000.

Which of the following conclusions can most properly be drawn from the information above?

(A) All people should take an aspirin a day to prevent heart attacks.
(B) Painkillers prevent heart attacks.
(C) Smokers can safely continue smoking, provided that they take at least one aspirin a day.
(D) The majority of people suffering second subsequent cardiac arrests could have been saved by taking an aspirin a day.
(E) Aspirin can be used to reduce mortality rates in patients who have already suffered heart attacks.

(E) According to the passage, all people cannot take aspirin without undesirable side effects, and in some cases, the danger caused by aspirin itself outweighs its benefits. The passage, by saying "On balance, however, for men aged 40 and over, an aspirin a day may present. . . ." also implies that not all, but only some people (men over 40) should take an aspirin a day. Alternative answer (A) clearly cannot be concluded from the passage. Answer alternative (B) is also inappropriate. No painkiller other than aspirin is mentioned in the passage, and it cannot be inferred that all painkillers reduce the "stickiness" of platelets. (C) is incorrect. Smoking is not mentioned in the passage and since studies of the effects of smoking and aspirin have not been reported, no conclusions can be drawn. (D) is wrong because the statistics given in the passage say that 15% of second heart attack victims were saved from death by taking aspirin, and 15% does not constitute a majority. (E) is the correct choice since it simply states that mortality rates can be reduced in patients who have already suffered a heart attack (as stated in the passage), without giving any specific statistics.

5. In the past, to run for one's country in the Olympics was the ultimate achievement of any athlete. Nowadays, an athlete's motives are more and more influenced by financial gain, and consequently we do not see our best athletes in the Olympics, which is still only for amateurs.

Which of the following will most weaken the above conclusion?

(A) The publicity and fame that can be achieved by competing in the Olympics makes athletes more "marketable" by agents and potential sponsors, while allowing the athletes to retain their amateur status.
(B) The winning of a race is not as important as participating.
(C) There is a widely held belief that our best Olympic athletes already receive enough in terms of promotion and sponsorship.
(D) It has been suggested that professional athletes should be allowed to compete in the games.
(E) Athletics as an entertainment is like any other entertainment job and deserves a financial reward.

(A) It is fact that athletes can attract sponsorship and make money and that participation in the Olympics can aid this process. On the basis that it is true that athletes are more and more attracted by the profit motive, the conclusion that the best athletes do not compete in the Olympics is weakened. Therefore, A is the appropriate answer. Alternative (B) is an oft-stated maxim, but in this case, it is not relevant to the argument. The fact that people believe that amateur athletes are receiving adequate alternative remuneration does not bear on the argument for allowing genuine professional athletes into the games. So, (C) is inappropriate. Choice (D) comes close to weakening the argument, because if professional (as well as amateur) athletes were allowed to compete, presuming the participants were selected on merit, then the best athletes would be seen. However, it has only been a suggestion, perhaps in the past, (in which case it was not adopted) or in the future (in which case its adoption is not certain). Choice (E) represents an opinion that might or might not be held by the writer, but, whether or not the author agrees, it does not weaken the argument; therefore (E) is inappropriate.

6. The function of a food technologist in a large marketing chain of food stores is to ensure that all foodstuffs which are offered for sale in the various retail outlets meet certain standard criteria for nonperishability, freshness, and fitness for human consumption.

It is the technologist's job to visit the premises of suppliers and food producers (factory or farm), inspect the facilities and report thereon. His responsibility also includes receiving new products from local and foreign suppliers and performing exhaustive quality control testing on them. Finally, he should carry out surprise spot-checks on goods held in the marketing chain's own warehouses and stores.

What conclusion can best be drawn from the preceding paragraph?

(A) A university degree in food technology is a necessary and sufficient condition for becoming a food technologist.
(B) Imported products, as well as home-produced goods, must be rigorously tested.
(C) The food technologist stands between the unhygienic producer and the unsuspecting consumer.
(D) Home-produced foodstuffs are safer to eat than goods imported from abroad because they are subject to more regular and closer inspection procedures.
(E) Random checking of the quality of goods stored on the shelves in a foodstore is the best way of ensuring that foodstuffs of an inferior quality are not purchased by the general public.

(C) The paragraph demonstrates from beginning to end that the function of the food technologist is to prevent unfit foodstuffs from being marketed by the stores and passed on to the consumer, who relies on the store's control procedures. (C), therefore, is the most appropriate answer. Answer alternative (A) is inappropriate because it cannot be inferred from the text (even if it were true). Answer (B) and possibly answer (D) are factually correct, but these conclusions cannot be drawn from the text itself. (E) is not a correct interpretation of the facts; random checking is not the best way, since below-standard goods are caught in the net only by chance.

7. The daily journey from his home to his office takes John Bond on average an hour and thirty-five minutes by car. A friend has told him of a different route that is longer in mileage, but will only take an hour and a quarter on average, because it contains stretches of roads where it is possible to drive at higher speeds.

John Bond's only consideration apart from the time factor is the cost, and he calculates that his car will consume 10% less gasoline if he takes the suggested new route. John decides to take the new route for the next two weeks as an experiment.

If the above were the only other considerations, which one of the following may have an effect on the decision John has made?

(A) Major road work is begun on the shorter (in distance) route, which holds up traffic for an extra ten minutes. The project will take six months, but after it, the improvements will allow the journey to be made in half an hour less than at present.
(B) There is to be a strike at local gas stations and the amount of gasoline drivers may purchase may be rationed.
(C) John finds a third route which is slightly longer then his old route, but shorter than the suggested route.
(D) The old route passes the door of a work colleague, who without a ride, would have to go to work by bus.
(E) None of the above.

(C) John's decision is to experiment with the new longer (in mileage) route for two weeks, and it is this decision that we have to consider. Choice (C), by offering a third alternative, gives John another possibility and, therefore, another outcome. It may affect his decision, and therefore, is the appropriate answer. Alternatives (A), (B), and (D) alter factors within the calculation affecting the decision, but taken individually and not making any other changes, will definitely not result in a different decision being made. These three are, therefore, not appropriate answers. The existence of a definite answer—in this case, (C)—means that alternative (E) is not appropriate.

8. All elephants are grey.
And all mice are grey.
Therefore, I conclude that all elephants are mice.

The argument above is invalid because

(A) the writer bases his argument on another argument that contains circular reasoning.
(B) the writer has illogically classified two disparate groups together when there is no relationship between them, except that they both have the same attribute.
(C) the writer has made a mistaken analogy between two dissimilar qualities.
(D) the writer has used a fallacy which involves the ambiguous description of animals by their color.
(E) the writer has failed to express his reasoning fully.

(B) There is only one argument in the passage based on two separate premises upon which the writer has based his conclusion. Choice (A) is inappropriate because there is no other argument. Choice (C) is incorrect because the qualities are the same (grey). (D) is inappropriate because the description is not ambiguous, and (E) is wrong because the writer has stated an argument—albeit invalid.

9. There are three main factors that control the risks of becoming dependent on drugs. These factors are the type of drug, the personality of the individual, and the circumstances in which the drug is taken. Indeed, it could be said that the majority of the adult population have taken alcohol, yet few have become dependent on it. Also, many strong drugs that have been used for medical purposes have not caused the patient to become addicted.

However, it can be demonstrated that people who have taken drugs for fun are more likely to become dependent on the drug. The dependence is not always physiological but may remain psychological, although the effects are still essentially the same. Those at greatest risk appear to be personalities that are psychopathic, immature, or otherwise unstable.

Psychological dependence is very strong with heroin, morphine, cocaine, and amphetamines. Physiological dependence is great with heroin and morphine, but less with amphetamines, barbiturates, and alcohol.

Which of the following conclusions can be drawn from the text?

(A) One cannot become addicted to certain drugs if one has a strong personality.
(B) Taking drugs for "kicks" increases the possibility of becoming dependent on drugs.
(C) Psychological dependence is greatest with heroin.
(D) Alcohol is a safe drug since very few people become dependent on it.
(E) Long-term use of certain drugs for medical purposes does not cause addiction.

(B) Although a strong personality might have some resistance to the psychological dependence factors of drug use, it cannot be stated with any certainty that a strong personality can prevent physiological dependence. In this way, (A) is not a reasonable conclusion.

Psychological dependence on heroin is greater than that of drugs such as alcohol and marijuana, but it is not stated to be the greatest since psychological dependence is also great with cocaine and amphetamines. There is no conclusive evidence in the text to support this view, (C) is not, therefore, a reasonable conclusion.

A safe drug implies no danger of addiction, and since it cannot be shown that there is no danger of addiction to alcohol, statement (D) is also not valid.

Although short-term use of certain drugs for medical purposes rarely produces dependence, long-term use of certain drugs often causes physiological dependence; in this respect (E) is not a valid assumption.

(B) is the only conclusion that can probably be true. Statistics show that many hard-drug addicts and regular users started their habit by taking drugs for "kicks." Also the search for drugs to be used for "kicks" almost inevitably causes exposure to localities where harder and more addictive drugs are available, thus increasing the chances of attempting more addictive drugs for "kicks." The passage states that the circumstances in which the drug is taken is one factor controlling the risk of becoming dependent and also that it can be demonstrated that people who have taken drugs for fun are more likely to become dependent on the drug.

10. Sally overslept. Therefore, she did not eat breakfast. She realized that she was late for school, so she ran as fast as she could and did not see a hole in the ground which was in her path. She tripped and broke her ankle. She was then taken to the hospital and while lying in bed was visited by her friend, who wanted to know why she had got up so late.

Which of the following conclusions can be made from the above passage?

(A) Because Sally did not eat her breakfast, she broke her ankle.
(B) Sally's friend visited her in the hospital because she wanted to know why she was late for school.
(C) Sally did not notice the hole because she overslept.
(D) Sally broke her ankle because she went to bed late the previous night.
(E) Sally's broken ankle meant she did not go to school that day.

(C) Here we have a chain of events where the conclusion of one argument becomes the premise for another. Only (C) can be concluded from the facts given in the passage—that is, because Sally overslept she ran toward school, and because she ran, she did not notice the hole. Choice (A) is inappropriate because the chain of events is not linked by the fact that Sally did not eat her breakfast. The passage does not include a consequence emanating from that fact. Choice (B) is not appropriate because there is no way to link Sally's friend to the events in the passage. Similarly, facts not included preclude (D) from being the appropriate answer. Finally, (E) cannot be inferred, as we do not know what Sally did later that day; she may have been released from the hospital and gone to school.

11. The owners of a local supermarket have decided to make use of three now-redundant checkout counters. They believe that they will attract those customers who lately have been put off by the long checkout lines during the mid-morning and evening rush hours. The owners have concluded that in order to be successful, the increased revenue from existing and added counters will have to be more than the increase in maintenance costs for the added counters.

The underlying goal of the owners can be summarized thus:

(A) To improve services to all customers.
(B) To attract people who have never been to the store.
(C) To make use of the redundant counters.
(D) To keep maintenance costs on the added counters as low as possible.
(E) To increase monthly profits.

(E) Services will be improved, it is hoped, for a certain segment of customers—those that shop during the rush hours—but not for all customers. This fact makes choice (A) inappropriate. To attract new customers is not stated in the passage as an objective, so (B) is inappropriate. The utilization of excess capacity, as in (C) is a useful byproduct of the new system, but it is not the main goal. If maintenance costs are kept low, it will probably make the achievement of the main goal that much easier, but this is not the major objective so choice (D) is not appropriate. The principal purpose of the owners is to make more money from the change, by increasing income more than the added costs. Therefore, (E) is the appropriate answer.

12. The cost of housing in many parts of the United States has become so excessive that many young couples, with above-average salaries, can only afford small apartments. Mortgage commitments are so huge that they cannot consider the possibility of starting a family. A new baby would probably mean either the mother or father giving up a well-paid position. The lack of or great cost of child-care facilities precludes the return of both parents to work.

Which of the following adjustments could practically be made to the situation described above which would allow young couples to improve their housing prospects?

(A) Encourage couples to remain childless.
(B) Encourage couples to have one child only.
(C) Encourage couples to postpone starting their families until a later age than previously acceptable to society.
(D) Encourage young couples to move to cheaper areas of the United States.
(E) Encourage fathers to remain at home while mothers return to work.

(C) Encouraging couples to remain childless would have a negative social effect and would not be practical, so answer alternative (A) is not a reasonable suggestion. The income loss involved in having one child is not much more than that involved in having two or more children (assuming the loss of the income of one parent or the expense of child care), so suggestion (B) is also invalid. If couples move to cheaper areas in the country, as suggested in (D), the chances are that work would be less available or possibly that the couple would have a less positive economic future, so the change may not necessarily be financially advantageous. If fathers stayed at home rather than mothers, there would be no improvement in financial status, so suggestion (E) is invalid. Suggestion (C) is the only sensible solution, since financial stability is likely to increase with the length of time in employment.

13. Unless new reserves are found soon, the world's supply of coal is being depleted in such a way that with demand continuing to grow at present rates, reserves will be exhausted by the year 2050.

Which of the following, if true, will most weaken the above argument?

(A) There has been a slowdown in the rate of increase in world demand for coal over the last 5 years from 10% to 5%.
(B) It has been known for many years that there are vast stocks of coal under Antarctica which have yet to be economically exploited.
(C) Oil is being used increasingly in place of coal for many industrial and domestic uses.
(D) As coal resources are depleted more and more marginal supplies, which are more costly to produce and less efficient in use are being mined.
(E) None of the above.

(E) Even if the rate of increase in demand has slowed from 10% per annum to 5% per annum over the last five years, that means that demand is still increasing at 5% per annum. If, as the passage states, demand continues to grow at the present rate—that is, by 5% per annum—the world's resources will be used up by the year 2050. Therefore, the argument is not weakened by the statement in answer alternative (A). Choice (B) introduces the matter of supply, but apparently the reserves in Antarctica have been known for some time, and this, therefore, does not affect the argument that stocks will be depleted unless new reserves are found. Choice (C) informs us that there is an alternative to coal which is being used increasingly. However, the questions of the supply of and the rate of growth of demand for oil do not affect the argument in the paragraph. Choice (D) states an economic fact of life that will have to be faced if the statements in the paragraph are true. It may lead to a search for alternative fuels and consequent decrease in demand for coal, but this is uncertain and cannot be inferred. So, neither (A), (B), (C), or (D) are appropriate. Choice (E) is, therefore, the correct answer.

14. In accordance with their powers, many state authorities are introducing fluoridation of drinking water. This follows the conclusion of 10 years of research that the process ensures that children and adults receive the required intake of fluoride that will strengthen teeth. The maximum level has been set at one part per million. However, there are many who object, claiming that fluoridation removes freedom of choice.

Which of the following will weaken the claim of the proponents of fluoridation?

(A) Fluoridation over a certain prescribed level has been shown to lead to a general weakening of teeth.
(B) There is no record of the long-term effects of drinking fluoridated water.
(C) The people to be affected by fluoridation claim that they have not had sufficient opportunity to voice their views.
(D) Fluoridation is only one part of general dental health.
(E) Water already contains natural fluoride.

(B) Choice (A) contains an important point which would have been considered in setting the maximum treatment level. So it does not weaken the argument of the authorities and is inappropriate. Choice (C) is incorrect as the passage states that the authorities are carrying out this policy in accordance with their powers. Choice (D) is a fact that would be acknowledged by both sides and weakens neither's case, while choice (E) is also a well-known fact, which like the fact in (A), would have been taken into consideration by the researchers, so it is also not appropriate. The fact that the authorities have no record of the long-term good or damage of fluoridation is a significant weakness in their case, and therefore, (B) is the appropriate answer.

15. Mr. and Mrs. Smith and their son John want to cross the Dart River. The only way across is with Mr. Jones in his rowboat. Mr. Jones will not allow anyone to row his boat and will take only one passenger at a time. John is only a little boy so he cannot be left alone on the river bank.

Which of the following conditions are not part of the successful passage of the Smiths across the river?

(A) Mr. Smith crosses the river first.
(B) Mr. Smith crosses the river last.
(C) Mr. and Mrs. Smith do not cross together.
(D) John crosses the river first.
(E) John crosses the river second.

(D) Since John cannot be allowed to remain alone, Mr. Smith must cross the river with Mr. Jones and he must be first or last across the river in order to be with John when Mrs. Smith is crossing. Therefore, both (A) and (B) are possibilities that would lead to the Smiths' successful crossing of the river. Since John cannot be left alone and since Mr. Jones will not allow anyone else to row his boat and neither will he take two passengers together, as (C) states, Mr. and Mrs. Smith cannot cross together. (C) is, therefore, a necessary condition and is therefore not an appropriate answer. (E) is a possible condition, since either Mr. or Mrs. Smith will be on the opposite bank waiting for John so he will not be alone. This too is not an appropriate answer. John however, cannot be the first to cross the river or else he would be left alone on the opposite river bank. (D) is, therefore, the appropriate answer.

16. In 1980, global service exports totaled about $370 billion, approximately 20 percent of world trade. Still, no coherent system of rules, principles, and procedures exists to govern trade in services.

Which of the following best summarizes the argument?

(A) Regulatory systems lag behind reality.
(B) A regulatory system ought to reflect the importance of service exports.
(C) World trade totaled $1850 billion in 1980.
(D) Service trade legislation is a veritable wasteland.
(E) While trade legislation exists, it is uncoordinated.

(B) Choice (A) is vague, while (D) equates service trade with legislation. Choice (C) is irrelevant to the argument. (E) comes close to summarizing the argument, but it is incomplete; uncoordinated is not an antonym for coherent.

17. Perhaps the most significant and constructive change in national politics would be the abolition of the Vice Presidency.

Each of the following, if true, would strengthen the above argument, except:

(A) There are few, if any, specific duties or responsibilities assigned to the Vice Presidency.
(B) A historian claimed that the post was "superfluous."
(C) People of Presidential caliber refused the Vice Presidential nomination.
(D) The office can waste a good politician for four or eight years.
(E) The office puts people in line for the Presidency who were not chosen to be President.

(B) Choice (B) is an example of an illegitimate appeal to authority. If the historian were known and his definition of "superfluous" understood, we might rely on his statement. All other statements, if true, would strengthen the argument.

Section 5
Data Sufficiency

1. Is x greater than y?

(1) $3x = 2k$
(2) $k = y^2$

(E) Since STATEMENT (1) describes only x and STATEMENT (2) describes only y, both are needed to get an answer. Using STATEMENT (2), STATEMENT (1) becomes $3x = 2k = 2y^2$, so $x = \frac{2y^2}{3}$. However, this is not sufficient, since if $y = -1$ then $x = \frac{2}{3}$ and x is greater than y, but if $y = 1$ then again $x = \frac{2}{3}$ but now x is less than y.

Therefore, STATEMENTS (1) and (2) together are not sufficient.

2. Is $ABCD$ a parallelogram?

(1) $AB = CD$
(2) AB is parallel to CD

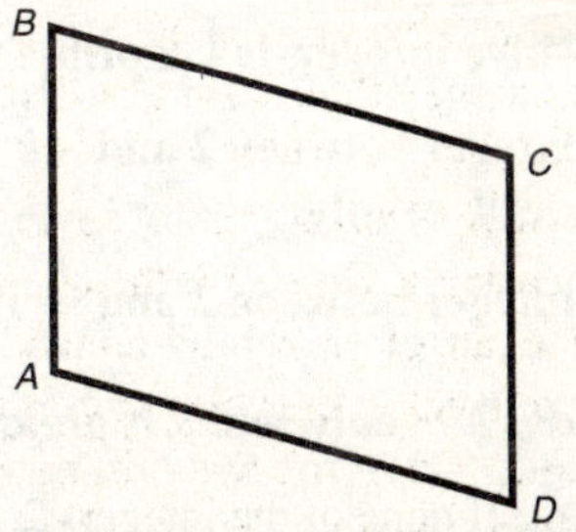

(C) $ABCD$ is a parallelogram if AB is parallel to CD and BC is parallel to AD. STATEMENT (2) tells you that AB is parallel to CD, but this is not sufficient since a trapezoid has only one pair of opposite sides parallel. Thus, STATEMENT (2) alone is not sufficient.

STATEMENT (1) alone is not sufficient since a trapezoid can have the two nonparallel sides equal.

However, using STATEMENTS (1) and (2) together we can deduce that BC is parallel to AD, since the distance from BC to AD is equal along two different parallel lines.

3. What was Mr. Smith's combined income for the years 1965–1970? In 1965 he made $10,000.

(1) His average yearly income for the years 1965–1970 was $12,000.
(2) In 1970, his income was $20,000.

(A) STATEMENT (1) alone is sufficient. The average is the combined income for 1965–1970 divided by 6 (the number of years). Therefore, the combined income is 6 times the average yearly income.

STATEMENT (2) alone is not sufficient since there is no information about his income for the years 1966–1969.

4. What is the two digit number whose first digit is *a* and whose second digit is *b*? The number is greater than 9.

(1) $2a + 3b = 11a + 2b$
(2) The two digit number is a multiple of 19.

(A) Two digit numbers are the integers from 10 to 99. Since you are told that the number is greater than 9, the only possible choices are integers 10, 11, . . . 99.

STATEMENT (1) alone is sufficient since (1) is equivalent to $9a = b$. In this case if a is greater than 1, then $9a$ is not a digit and if a is 0, then the number is not greater than 9. Thus there is only one possible choice, $a = 1$, which yields the number 19, that satisfies (1).

STATEMENT (2) alone is not sufficient since 19, 38, 57, 76, and 95 satisfy (2) and are two digit numbers greater than 9.

So (A) is the correct choice.

5. *k* is a positive integer. Is *k* a prime number?

(1) No integer between 2 and $\sqrt{k}$ inclusive divides *k* evenly.
(2) No integer between 2 and $\frac{k}{2}$ inclusive divides *k* evenly, and *k* is greater than 5.

(D) k is a prime if none of the integers 2, 3, 4, . . . up to $k - 1$ divide k evenly. STATEMENT (1) alone is sufficient since if k is not a prime then $k = (m)(n)$ where m and n must be integers less than k. But this means either m or n must be less than or equal to $\sqrt{k}$, since if m and n are both larger than $\sqrt{k}$, $(m)(n)$ is larger than $(\sqrt{k})(\sqrt{k})$ or k. So STATEMENT (1) implies k is a prime.

STATEMENT (2) alone is also sufficient, since if $k = (m)(n)$ and m and n are both larger than $\frac{k}{2}$, then $(m)(n)$ is greater than $\frac{k^2}{4}$; but $\frac{k^2}{4}$ is greater than k when k is larger than 5. Therefore, if no integer between 2 and $\frac{k}{2}$ inclusive divides k evenly, then k is a prime.

6. The towns *A*, *B*, and *C* lie on a straight line. *C* is between *A* and *B*. The distance from *A* to *B* is 100 miles. How far is it from *A* to *C*?

(1) The distance from *A* to *B* is 25% more than the distance from C to *B*.
(2) The distance from *A* to *C* is $\frac{1}{4}$ of the distance from *C* to *B*.

(D) Since we are given the fact that 100 miles is the distance from A to B, it is sufficient to find the distance from C to B. This is so, because 100 minus the distance from C to B is the distance from A to C. STATEMENT (1) says that 125% of the distance from C to B is 100 miles. Thus, we can find the distance from C to B, which is sufficient. Since the distance from A to C plus the distance from C to B is the distance from A to B, we can use STATEMENT (2) to set up the equation 5 times the distance from A to C equals 100 miles.

Therefore, STATEMENTS (1) and (2) are each sufficient.

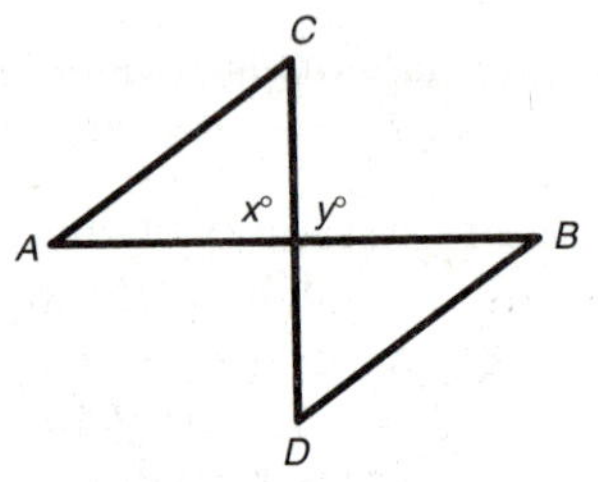

7. Is *AB* perpendicular to *CD*?

(1) $AC = BD$
(2) $x = y$

(B) STATEMENT (1) alone is not sufficient. If the segment AC is moved further away from the segment BD, then the angles x and y will change. So STATEMENT (1) does not ensure that CD and AB are perpendicular.

STATEMENT (2) alone is sufficient. Since AB is a straight line, $x + y$ equals 180. Thus, if $x = y$, x and y both equal 90 and AB is perpendicular to CD. So the correct answer is (B).

8. What is the value of $x - y$?

(1) $x + 2y = 6$
(2) $x = y$

(B) STATEMENT (2) alone is sufficient, since $x = y$ implies $x - y = 0$.

STATEMENT (1) alone is not sufficient. An infinite number of pairs satisfy STATEMENT (1), for example, $x = 2$, $y = 2$, for which $x - y = 0$, or $x = 4$, $y = 1$, for which $x - y = 3$.

9. The number of eligible voters is 100,000. How many eligible voters voted?

(1) 63% of the eligible men voted.
(2) 67% of the eligible women voted.

(E) Since there is no information on how many of the eligible voters are men or how many are women, STATEMENTS (1) and (2) together are not sufficient.

10. How much was the original cost of a car which sold for $2,300?

(1) The car was sold for a discount of 10% from its original cost.
(2) The sales tax was $150.

(A) STATEMENT (1) is sufficient since it means 90% of the original cost is $2,300. Thus, we can solve the equation for the original cost.

STATEMENT (2) alone is insufficient, since it gives no information about the cost.

11. The hexagon *ABCDEF* is inscribed in the circle with center *O*. What is the length of *AB*?

(1) The radius of the circle is 4 inches.
(2) The hexagon is a regular hexagon.

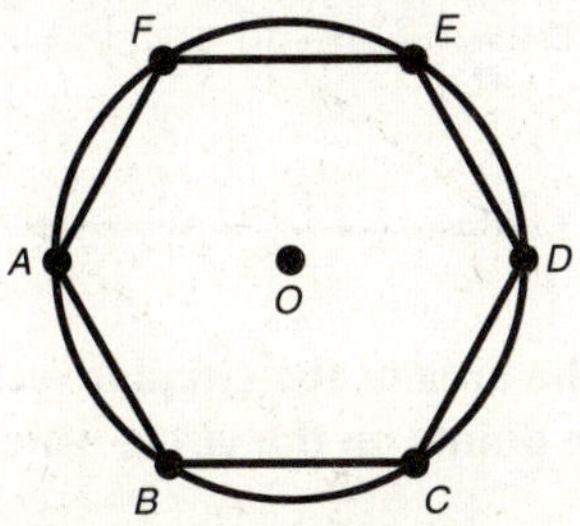

(C) Draw the radii from *O* to each of the vertices. These lines divide the hexagon into six triangles. STATEMENT (2) says that all the triangles are congruent since each of their pairs of corresponding sides is equal. Since there are 360° in a circle, the central angle of each triangle is 60°. And, since all radii are equal, each angle of the triangle equals 60°. Therefore, the triangles are equilateral, and *AB* is equal to the radius of the circle. Thus, if we assume STATEMENT (1), we know the length of *AB*. Without STATEMENT (1), we can't find the length of *AB*.

Also STATEMENT (1) alone is not sufficient, since *AB* need not equal the radius unless the hexagon is regular.

12. What was the percentage of defective items produced at a factory?

(1) The total number of defective items produced was 1,234.
(2) The ratio of defective items to nondefective items was 32 to 5,678.

(B) STATEMENT (2) alone is sufficient. If (2) holds, then $\frac{32}{(32+5,678)}$ represents the ratio of defective items to total items produced. Since any fraction can be changed into a percentage by multiplying by 100, STATEMENT (2) alone is sufficient.

STATEMENT (1) alone is not sufficient since the total number of items produced is also needed to find the percentage of defective items.

Therefore (B) is the correct choice.

13. Is *ABC* a right triangle? *AB* = 5; *AC* = 4.

(1) *BC* = 3
(2) *AC* = *CD*

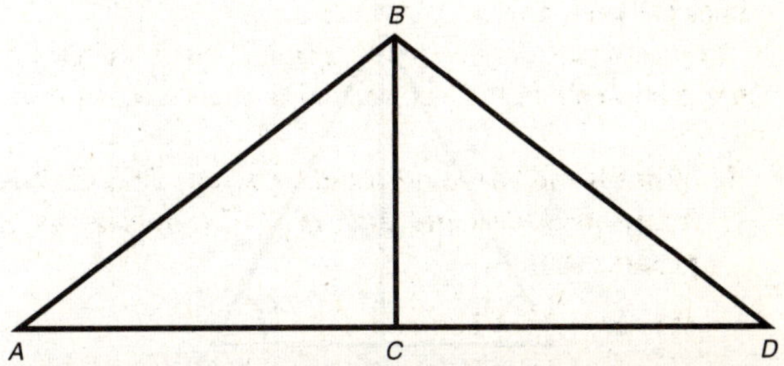

(A) STATEMENT (1) alone is sufficient. Since $3^2 + 4^2 = 5^2$, *ABC* is a right triangle by the Pythagorean theorem.

STATEMENT (2) alone is not sufficient since you can choose a point *D* so that *AC* = *CD* for *any* triangle *ABC*.

14. Did the price of energy rise last year?

(1) If the price of energy rose last year, then the price of food would rise this year.
(2) The price of food rose this year.

(E) (1) and (2) are not sufficient. The price of food could rise for other reasons besides the price of energy rising.

15. How much was a certain Rembrandt painting worth in January 1971?

(1) In January 1977 the painting was worth $2,000,000.
(2) Over the ten years 1968–1977 the painting increased in value by 10% each year.

(C) (1) alone is obviously insufficient. To use (2) you need to know what the painting was worth at some time between 1968 and 1977. So (2) alone is insufficient, but by using (1) and (2) together you can figure out the worth of the painting in January 1971.

16. A sequence of numbers $a_1, a_2, a_3, \ldots$ is given by the rule $a_n^2 = a_{n+1}$. Does 3 appear in the sequence?

(1) $a_1 = 2$
(2) $a_3 = 16$

(D) (1) alone is sufficient since the rule enables you to compute all successive values once you know a_1. Also the rule and (1) tell you that the numbers in the sequence will always increase. Thus, since $a_2 = 4$, 3 will never appear. In the same way, by using (2) and the rule for the sequence you can determine that $a_2 = 4$ and a_1 is 2 or –2, so the reasoning used above shows that 3 will never appear.

17. Is *AB* greater than *AC*?

(1) $z > x$
(2) $AC > AD$

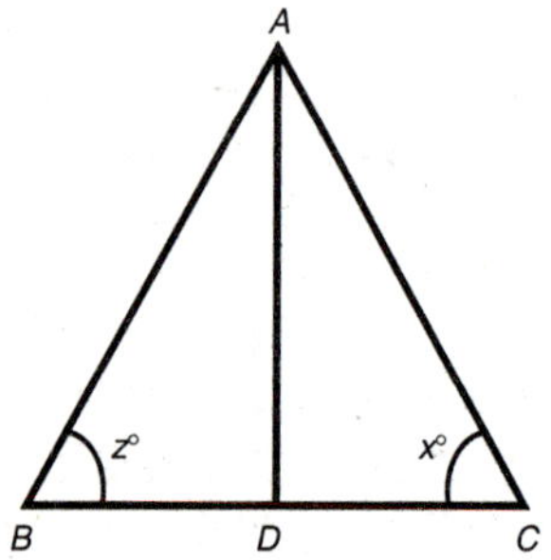

(A) (1) alone is sufficient. If $z > x$ then the side opposite angle *ABC* is larger than the side opposite angle *ACB*. (2) alone is insufficient since *D* can be anywhere between *B* and C, so you can't decide whether *AD* is larger or smaller than *AB*.

18. Is $\frac{1}{x}$ greater than $\frac{1}{y}$?

(1) *x* is greater than 1.
(2) *x* is less than *y*.

(C) STATEMENT (2) alone is not sufficient. –1 is less than 2 and $\frac{1}{-1}$ is less than $\frac{1}{2}$ but 1 is less than 2 and $\frac{1}{1}$ is greater than $\frac{1}{2}$.

STATEMENT (1) alone is insufficient since there is no information about *y*.

STATEMENT (1) and (2) together imply that *x* and *y* are both greater than 1 and for two positive numbers *x* and *y*, if *x* is less than *y* then $\frac{1}{x}$ is greater than $\frac{1}{y}$.

19. Plane *X* flies at *r* miles per hour from *A* to *B*. Plane *Y* flies at *S* miles per hour from *B* to *A*. Both planes take off at the same time. Which plane flies at a faster rate? Town *C* is between *A* and *B*.

(1) *C* is closer to *A* than it is to *B*.
(2) Plane *X* flies over *C* before plane *Y*.

(E) Since *C* is closer to *A*, if plane *X* is flying faster than plane *Y* it will certainly fly over *C* before plane *Y*. However, if plane *X* flies slower than plane *Y*, and *C* is very close to *A*, plane *X* would still fly over *C* before plane *Y* does. Thus, STATEMENTS (1) and (2) together are not sufficient.

20. Is $\frac{x}{12} > \frac{y}{40}$?

(1) $10x > 3y$
(2) $12x < 4y$

(A) To compare two fractions, the fractions must have the same denominator. The least common denominator for both fractions is 120. Using this fact, $\frac{x}{12} = \frac{10x}{120}$ and $\frac{y}{40} = \frac{3y}{120}$. So the relation between the fractions is the same as the relation between $10x$ and $3y$. Therefore, STATEMENT (1) alone is sufficient. STATEMENT (2) alone is not sufficient. Using $y = 13$ and $x = 4$, STATEMENT (2) is true and $\frac{x}{12}$ is greater than $\frac{y}{40}$. However, using $y = 10$ and $x = 2$, STATEMENT (2) is still true, but now $\frac{x}{12}$ is less than $\frac{y}{40}$.

21. What is the area of the circular section *AOB*? *A* and *B* are points on the circle which has *O* as its center.

(1) Angle $AOB = 36°$
(2) $OB = OA$

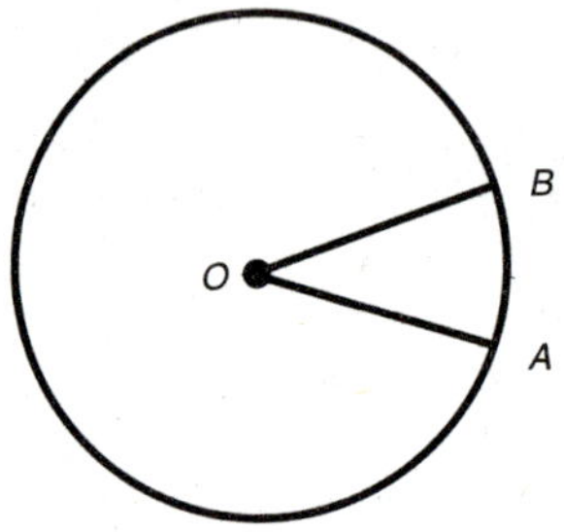

(E) Since the area of a circle is πr^2, the area of the circular section *AOB* is the fraction $\frac{x}{360}$ times πr^2, where angle $AOB = x°$. (There are 360° in the entire circle.) Using STATEMENT (1), we know $x = 36$ so $\left(\frac{x}{360}\right)\pi r^2 = \frac{1}{10}\pi r^2$. However, STATEMENT (1) gives no information about the value of *r*, so STATEMENT (1) alone is insufficient.

STATEMENT (2) gives no information about the value of *r*, so STATEMENTS (1) and (2) together are insufficient.

Section 6
Problem Solving

(Numbers in parentheses at the end of each explanation indicate the section in the Mathematics Review where material addressed in the question is discussed.)

1. In a group of people solicited by a charity, 30% contributed \$40, 45% contributed \$20, and the rest contributed \$2. If the charity received a total of \$300 from the people who contributed \$2, how much was contributed by the entire group?

(A) \$1,200
(B) \$2,400
(C) \$12,600
(D) \$12,900
(E) \$25,800

(D) $\frac{300}{2} = 150$, so there were 150 people who contributed \$2. Since this group was 100% − 30% − 45% = 25% of the total group, there were $\frac{150}{.25} = 600$ people in the total group. So the amount contributed by those who gave \$40 was $.30 \times 600 \times \$40 = \$7{,}200$. The amount contributed by those who gave \$20 was $.45 \times 600 \times \$20 = \$5{,}400$. Therefore the total was \$7,200 + \$5,400 + \$300 = \$12,900. (I-4)

2. A car currently travels 15 miles on a gallon of gas but after a tune-up the car will use only $\frac{3}{4}$ as much gas as it does now. How many miles will the car travel on a gallon of gas after the tune-up?

(A) 15
(B) $16\frac{1}{2}$
(C) $17\frac{1}{2}$
(D) $18\frac{3}{4}$
(E) 20

(E) After the tune-up, the car will travel 15 miles on $\frac{3}{4}$ of a gallon of gas. So it will travel $\frac{15}{\frac{3}{4}}$ or $\frac{4}{3} \times 15$ or 20 miles on one gallon of gas. (I-2)

3. Successive discounts of 20% and 15% are equal to a single discount of

(A) 30%
(B) 32%
(C) 34%
(D) 35%
(E) 36%

(B) The price after a discount of 20% is 80% of P, the original price. After another 15% discount, the price is 85% of 80% of P or $(.85)(.80)P$, which equals $.68P$. Therefore, after the successive discounts, the price is 68% of what it was originally, which is the same as a single discount of 32%. (I-4)

4. A wall with no windows is 11 feet high and 20 feet long. A large roll of wallpaper costs \$25 and will cover 60 square feet of wall. A small roll of wallpaper costs \$6 and will cover 10 square feet of wall. What is the least cost for enough wallpaper to cover the wall?

(A) \$75
(B) \$99
(C) \$100
(D) \$120
(E) \$132

(B) The area of the wall is 11 feet × 20 feet = 220 square feet. Since a large roll of wallpaper gives more square feet per dollar, you should try to use large rolls. $\frac{220}{60} = 3$ with a remainder of 40. So, if you buy 3 large rolls, which cost $3 \times \$25 = \$75$, you will have enough to cover the entire wall, except for 40 square feet. You can cover 40 square feet by either buying 1 large roll or 4 small rolls. A large roll costs \$25 but 4 small rolls cost only \$24. So the minimum cost is \$75 + \$24 = \$99. (II-3)

5. Mary, John and Karen ate lunch together. Karen's meal cost 50% more than John's meal and Mary's meal cost $\frac{5}{6}$ as much as Karen's meal. If John paid \$10 for his meal, what was the total that the three of them paid for lunch?

(A) \$28.33
(B) \$30.00
(C) \$35.00
(D) \$37.50
(E) \$40.00

(D) If John paid \$10, then Karen paid 150% of \$10, or \$15. So Mary paid $\frac{5}{6} \times \$15 = \$12.50$. The total is \$10 + \$15 + \$12.50 = \$37.50. (II-2)

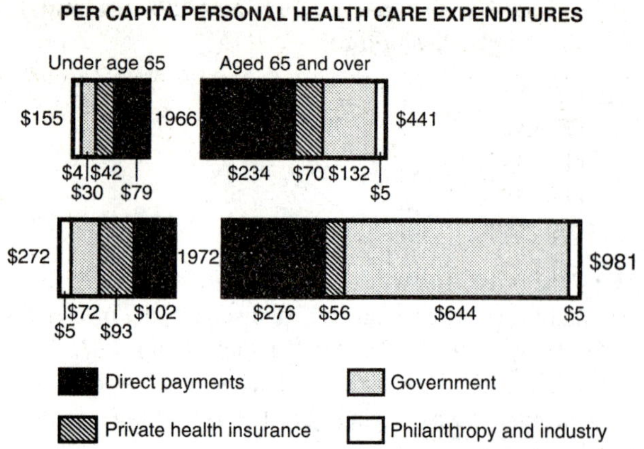

6. Between 1966 and 1972, the per capita amount spent by the government on personal health care for those under age 65 increased by x% where x is

(A) 100
(B) 120
(C) 140
(D) 220
(E) 240

(C) In 1966, the government spent $30 per capita on people under 65; by 1972 the per capita amount for those under 65 was $72. Therefore, the increase was $42. Since $\frac{42}{30} = 1.4 = 140\%$, the correct answer is (C). (IV-5)

7. Which of the following statements about expenditures for personal health care between 1966 and 1972 can be inferred from the graphs?

I. The total amount spent for those aged 65 and over in 1972 was more than 3 times as much as the total amount spent on those under 65.

II. Between 1966 and 1972, the amount spent per capita by those aged 65 and over increased in each of the four categories (direct payments, government, private health insurance, philanthropy).

III. The government paid more than $\frac{1}{2}$ the amount of expenditures for those aged 65 and over in 1972.

(A) I only
(B) II only
(C) III only
(D) I and III only
(E) II and III only

(C) STATEMENT I cannot be inferred since the graph gives only per capita amounts. The total amount will also depend on the number of people in each group.

STATEMENT II is false since private health insurance decreased from $70 to $56 per capita.

STATEMENT III is true since $644 is more than $\frac{1}{2}$ of $981.

Therefore, only STATEMENT III can be inferred from the graphs. (IV-5)

8. A car traveled 75% of the way from town A to town B at an average speed of 50 mph. The car travels at an average speed of S mph for the remaining part of the trip. The average speed for the entire trip was 40 mph. What is S?

(A) 10
(B) 20
(C) 25
(D) 30
(E) 37.5

(C) This problem can be worked out by some complicated algebra if you let D be the distance between the towns and T be the total time of the trip. However, it is much easier to work it out if you simply choose a convenient number for the distance. So let the distance between town A and town B be 1000 miles. Then 75% of the distance is 750 miles, so the car traveled for $\frac{750}{50} =$ 15 hours at 50 mph. If the car averaged 40 mph for the entire trip, then the entire trip took $\frac{1000}{40} = 25$ hours. So the car must have taken 25 – 15 = 10 hours for the part of the trip it traveled at S mph. It traveled 1000 – 750 = 250 miles at S mph, so S is $\frac{250}{10} = 25$. A common mistake is to solve the equation $.75(50) + .25S = 40$ for S. This approach would be correct if the car traveled 75% of the TIME at 50 mph and 25% of the TIME at S mph. However, you are given that the car traveled 75% of the DISTANCE at 50 mph and since the speed changes the time it takes to travel, 75% of the distance will not be 75% of the time. (II-3)

9. If hose A can fill up a tank in 20 minutes, and hose B can fill up the same tank in 15 minutes, how long will it take for the hoses together to fill up the tank?

(A) 5 minutes
(B) $7\frac{1}{2}$ minutes
(C) $8\frac{4}{7}$ minutes
(D) $9\frac{2}{7}$ minutes
(E) 12 minutes

(C) Since hose A takes 20 minutes to fill the tank, it fills up $\frac{1}{20}$ of the tank each minute. Since hose B fills up the tank in 15 minutes, it fills up $\frac{1}{15}$ of the tank each minute. Therefore, hose A and hose B together will fill up $\frac{1}{20} + \frac{1}{15}$ or $\frac{3+4}{60}$ or $\frac{7}{60}$ of the tank each minute. Thus, it will take $\frac{60}{7}$ or $8\frac{4}{7}$ minutes to fill the tank.

(II-3)

10. It takes Eric 20 minutes to inspect a car. John only needs 18 minutes to inspect a car. If they both start inspecting cars at 8:00 A.M., what is the first time they will finish inspecting a car at the same time?

(A) 9:30 A.M.
(B) 9:42 A.M.
(C) 10:00 A.M.
(D) 11:00 A.M.
(E) 2:00 P.M.

(D) Since Eric will finish k cars after $k \times 20$ minutes and John will finish j cars after $j \times 18$ minutes, they both will finish inspecting cars at the same time when $k \times 20 = j \times 18$. Since k and j must be integers (they represent the number of cars finished) this question is asking you to find a common multiple of 20 and 18. The question asks for the first time they will finish a car simultaneously, so you must find the least common multiple. The following 3 steps will find the Least Common Multiple

(A) $20 = 4 \times 5 = 2 \times 2 \times 5$
$18 = 2 \times 3 \times 3$
(B) Delete 2 from one of the products
(C) So the L.C.M. is $2 \times 2 \times 5 \times 3 \times 3 = 180$

So Eric and John will finish inspecting a car at the same time 180 minutes after they start, or at 11:00 A.M. (I-1)

11. In the figure angles A, B, C, D, E, F, G, H are all 90 degrees and $AB = AH = EF = DE$. Also, $BC = CD = HG$ and the Cartesian coordinates of A, C, and E are (1, 2), (2, 5), and (5, 4) respectively. What is the area of the figure *ABCDEFGH*?

(A) 6
(B) 7
(C) 8
(D) 10
(E) 12

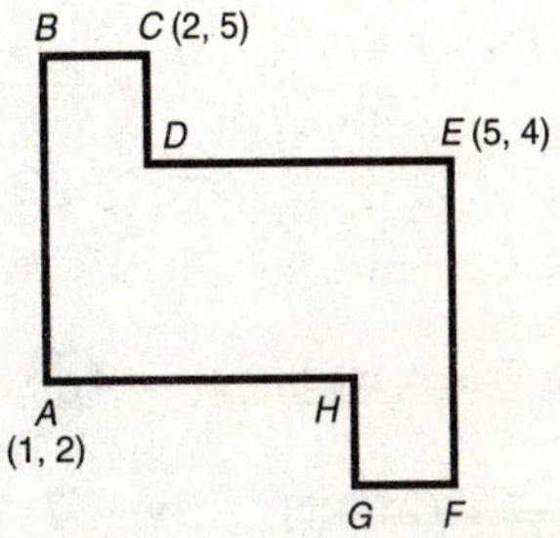

(D) Since the angle B is 90 degrees, the coordinates of B are (1, 5) so $AB = 3$ and $BC = 1$. To find the area, break the figure into three smaller figures by extending the line CD until it meets AH at point J and extending line GH until it meets DE at point K. Then the area sought is the sum of the areas of *ABCJ*, *JDKH*, and *KEFG*. All three figures are rectangles because all their angles are 90 degrees.

The area of *ABCJ* is 3×1 since AB is 3 and BC is 1. The area of *JDKH* is $JD \times JH$. Since the coordinates of D, J, and K are (2, 4), (2, 2) and (4, 4) respectively, the area of *JDKH* is $2 \times 2 = 4$. Finally since $EF = AB = 3$ and $KE = 1$, the area of *EFGH* is $3 \times 1 = 3$. Therefore, the area of the figure is $3 + 4 + 3 = 10$. (III-9)

Car Production at Plant T for One Week in 1960

	Number of cars produced	Total daily wages
MONDAY	900	\$30,000
TUESDAY	1200	\$40,000
WEDNESDAY	1500	\$52,000
THURSDAY	1400	\$50,000
FRIDAY	1000	\$32,000

12. What was the average cost in wages per car produced for the week?

(A) \$25
(B) \$26
(C) \$29
(D) \$32
(E) \$34

(E) There were 6,000 cars produced and the total wages paid for the week was (\$30,000 + \$40,000 + \$52,000 + \$50,000 + \$32,000) or \$204,000. Therefore,

the average cost in wages per car = $\frac{\$204,000}{6,000} = \$34$.

(IV-1, I-7)

13. If $\frac{x}{y} = 4$ and y is not 0, what percentage (to the nearest percent) of x is $2x - y$?

(A) 25
(B) 57
(C) 75
(D) 175
(E) 200

(D) Since $\frac{x}{y} = 4$, we know $x = 4y$. So $2x - y = 2(4y) - y = 7y$. Therefore $\frac{(2x - y)}{x}$ is $\frac{7y}{4y} = \frac{7}{4}$, or 175%. (II-2)

14. If $x > 2$ and $y > -1$, then

(A) $xy > -2$
(B) $-x < 2y$
(C) $xy < -2$
(D) $-x > 2y$
(E) $x < 2y$

(B) Since $x > 2$, then $-x < -2$; but $y > -1$ implies $2y > -2$. Therefore, $-x < -2 < 2y$ so $-x < 2y$. None of the other statements is always true. (A) is false if x is 5 and $y = -\frac{1}{2}$; (C) is false if $x = 3$ and $y = -\frac{1}{2}$; (D) is false if $x = 3$ and $y = 3$, and (E) is false if $x = 3$ and $y = -\frac{1}{2}$. (II-7)

15. What is the area of the rectangle *ABCD*, if the length of *AC* is 5 and the length of *AD* is 4?

(A) 3
(B) 6
(C) 12
(D) 15
(E) 20

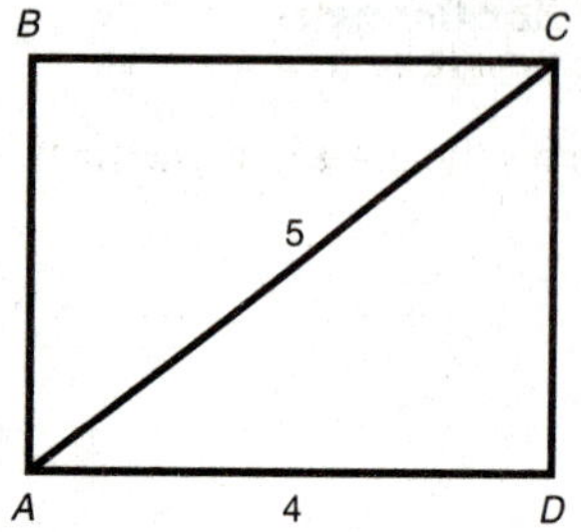

(C) Since *ABCD* is a rectangle, all its angles are right angles. The area of a rectangle is length times width; and the length of *AD* is 4. Using the Pythagorean theorem we have $4^2 + (\text{width})^2 = 5^2$, so the $(\text{width})^2$ is $25 - 16 = 9$. Therefore, the width is 3, and the area is $4 \times 3 = 12$. (III-4, III-7)

16. If electricity costs k¢ an hour, heat \$$d$ an hour, and water w¢ an hour, how much will all three cost for 12 hours?

(A) $12(k + d + w)$¢
(B) \$$(12k + 12d + 12w)$
(C) \$$(k + 100d + w)$
(D) \$$\left(12k + \frac{12d}{100} + 12w\right)$
(E) \$$(.12k + 12d + .12w)$

(E) The electricity costs $12k$¢ for 12 hours, the heat costs \$$12d$ for 12 hours, and the water costs $12w$¢ for 12 hours. So the total is $12k$¢ + \$$12d$ + $12w$¢ or \$$.12k$ + \$$12d$ + \$$.12w$ which is \$$(.12k + 12d + .12w)$. (II-3)

17. If $x = y = 2z$ and $x \bullet y \bullet z = 256$, then x equals

(A) 2
(B) $2\sqrt[3]{2}$
(C) 4
(D) $4\sqrt[3]{2}$
(E) 8

(E) Since $x = 2z$ and $y = 2z$, $x \bullet y \bullet z = (2z)(2z)(z) = 4z^3$; but $x \bullet y \bullet z = 256$ so $4z^3 = 256$. Therefore, $z^3 = 64$ and z is 4; so $x = 8$. (II-2, I-8)

Section 7
Sentence Correction

1. <u>Although I calculate that he will be here</u> any minute, I cannot wait much longer for him to arrive.

(A) Although I calculate that he will be here
(B) Although I reckon that he will be here
(C) Because I calculate that he will be here
(D) Although I think that he will be here
(E) Because I am confident that he will be here

(D) Do not use *calculate* or *reckon* when you mean *think*.

2. The fourteen-hour day not only has been reduced to one of ten hours but also, in some lines of work, to one of eight or even six.

(A) The fourteen-hour day not only has been reduced
(B) Not only the fourteen-hour day has been reduced
(C) Not the fourteen-hour day only has been reduced
(D) The fourteen-hour day has not only been reduced
(E) The fourteen-hour day has been reduced not only

(E) Since the words *but also* precede a phrase, to *one of eight or even six,* the words *not only* should precede a phrase, *to one of ten hours.* This error in parallel structure is corrected in choice E.

3. The trend toward a decrease is further evidenced in the longer weekend already given to employees in many business establishments.

(A) already
(B) all ready
(C) allready
(D) ready
(E) all in all

(A) *Already* is an adverb; *all ready* is an adjectival construction. *Allready* is a misspelling. Choices D and E do not convey the thought of the sentence.

4. Using it wisely, leisure promotes health, efficiency, and happiness.

(A) Using it wisely,
(B) If used wisely,
(C) Having used it wisely,
(D) Because it is used wisely,
(E) Because of usefulness,

(B) One way of correcting a dangling participle is to change the participial phrase to a clause. Choices B and D substitute clauses for the phrase. However, choice D changes the meaning of the sentence.

5. We want the teacher to be him who has the best rapport with the students.

(A) We want the teacher to be him
(B) We want the teacher to be he
(C) We want him to be the teacher
(D) We desire that the teacher be him
(E) We anticipate that the teacher will be him

(B) "He" is the subject of the sentence which takes who as the relative pronoun.

6. If he were to win the medal, I for one would be disturbed.

(A) If he were to win the medal,
(B) If he was to win the medal,
(C) If he wins the medal,
(D) If he is the winner of the medal,
(E) In the event that he wins the medal,

(A) No error.

7. The scouts were told to take an overnight hike, pitch camp, prepare dinner, and that they should be in bed by 9 P.M.

(A) to take an overnight hike, pitch camp, prepare dinner, and that they should be in bed by 9 P.M.
(B) to take an overnight hike, to pitch camp, to prepare dinner, and that they should be in bed by 9 P.M.
(C) to take an overnight hike, pitch camp, prepare dinner, and be in bed by 9 P.M.
(D) to take an overnight hike, pitching camp, preparing dinner and going to bed by 9 P.M.
(E) to engage in an overnight hike, pitch camp, prepare dinner, and that they should be in bed by 9 P.M.

(C) This choice does not violate parallel structure.

8. The government's failing to keep it's pledges will earn the distrust of all the other nations in the alliance.

(A) government's failing to keep it's pledges
(B) government failing to keep it's pledges
(C) government's failing to keep its pledges
(D) government failing to keep its pledges
(E) governments failing to keep their pledges

(C) Choice C corrects errors in the possessive form of *government* (needed before a verbal noun) and *it*.

9. Her brother along with her parents insist that she remain in school.

(A) insist
(B) insists
(C) are insisting
(D) were insisting
(E) have insisted

(B) This corrects the error in agreement: *Her brother . . . insists.*

10. Most students like to read these kind of books during their spare time.

(A) these kind of books
(B) these kind of book
(C) this kind of book
(D) this kinds of books
(E) those kind of books

(C) This is also an error in agreement: *Kind* is singular and requires a singular modifier (*this*).

11. She not only was competent but also friendly in nature.

(A) She not only was competent but also friendly
(B) Not only was she competent but friendly also
(C) She not only was competent but friendly also
(D) She was not only competent but also friendly
(E) She was not only competent but friendly also

(D) This choice eliminates the error in parallel structure.

12. In the normal course of events, John will graduate high school and enter college in two years.

(A) John will graduate high school and enter
(B) John will graduate from high school and enter
(C) John will be graduated from high school and enter
(D) John will be graduated from high school and enter into
(E) John will have graduated high school and enter

(B) The correct idiom is *graduate from.* The active case is preferred to the passive used in choice C. Choice D adds an unnecessary word, *into.*

13. With the exception of Frank and I, everyone in the class finished the assignment before the bell rang.

(A) Frank and I, everyone in the class finished
(B) Frank and me, everyone in the class finished
(C) Frank and me, everyone in the class had finished
(D) Frank and I, everyone in the class had finished
(E) Frank and me everyone in the class finished

(C) This corrects the two errors in this sentence—the error in case (*me* for *I*) and the error in tense (*had finished* for *finished*).

14. Many middle-class individuals find that they cannot obtain good medical attention, despite they need it badly.

(A) despite they need it badly
(B) despite they badly need it
(C) in spite of they need it badly
(D) however much they need it
(E) therefore, they need it badly

(D) *Despite* should be used as a preposition, not as a word joining clauses.

15. When one eats in this restaurant, you often find that the prices are high and that the food is poorly prepared.

(A) When one eats in this restaurant, you often find
(B) When you eat in this restaurant, one often finds
(C) As you eat in this restaurant, you often find
(D) If you eat in this restaurant, you often find
(E) When one ate in this restaurant, he often found

(C) This was an unnecessary shift of pronoun. Do not shift from *you* to *one.* Choice D changes the meaning unnecessarily.

16. Ever since the bombing of Cambodia, there has been much opposition from they who maintain that it was an unauthorized war.

(A) from they who maintain that it was an unauthorized war
(B) from they who maintain that it had been an unauthorized war
(C) from those who maintain that it was an unauthorized war
(D) from they maintaining that it was unauthorized
(E) from they maintaining that it had been unauthorized

(C) The demonstrative pronoun *those* is needed here—*from those* (persons).

17. I am not to eager to go to this play because it did not get good reviews.

- **(A) I am not to eager to go to this play because it did not get good reviews.**
- **(B) Because of its poor reviews, I am not to eager to go to this play.**
- **(C) Because of its poor revues, I am not to eager to go to this play.**
- **(D) I am not to eager to go to this play because the critics did not give it good reviews.**
- **(E) I am not too eager to go to this play because of its poor reviews.**

(E) Choice E corrects the misuse of the word *too*.

18. It was decided by us that the emphasis would be placed on the results that might be attained.

- **(A) It was decided by us that the emphasis would be placed on the results that might be attained.**
- **(B) We decided that the emphasis would be placed on the results that might be attained.**
- **(C) We decided to emphasize the results that might be attained.**
- **(D) We decided to emphasize the results we might attain.**
- **(E) It was decided that we would place emphasis on the results that might be attained.**

(C) Active verbs are preferred to passive verbs.

19. May I venture to say that I think this performance is the most superior I have ever heard.

- **(A) May I venture to say that I think this performance is the most superior**
- **(B) May I venture to say that this performance is the most superior**
- **(C) May I say that this performance is the most superior**
- **(D) I think this performance is superior to any**
- **(E) This performance is the most superior of any**

(D) The phrase *May I venture to say that* is unnecessary, as is *most* before *superior.*

20. Completing the physical examination, the tonsils were found to be diseased.

- **(A) Completing the physical examination, the tonsils were found to be diseased.**
- **(B) Having completed the physical examination, the tonsils were found to be diseased.**
- **(C) When the physical examination was completed, the tonsils were found to be diseased.**
- **(D) The physical examination completed, the tonsils were found to be diseased.**
- **(E) The physical examination found that the tonsils were diseased.**

(E) This answer eliminates the misplaced modifier, *completing*, and the passive verb, *were found*.

21. Today this is a totally different world than we have seen in the last decade.

- **(A) than we have seen**
- **(B) from what we have seen**
- **(C) from what we seen**
- **(D) than what we seen**
- **(E) then we have seen**

(B) The correct idiom is *different from*.

Evaluating Your Score

Tabulate your score for each section of Sample Test 2 according to the directions on pages 6–7 and record the results in the Self-Scoring Table below. Then find your rating for each score on the Self-Scoring Scale and record it in the appropriate blank.

Self-Scoring Table

SECTION	SCORE	RATING
1		
2		
3		
4		
5		
6		
7		

***Self-Scoring Scale*—RATING**

SECTION	POOR	FAIR	GOOD	EXCELLENT
1	0 – 12+	13 – 17+	18 – 21+	22 – 25
2	0 – 12+	13 – 17+	18 – 21+	22 – 25
3	0 – 8+	9 – 11	11+ – 14	14+ – 17
4	0 – 8+	9 – 11	11+ – 14	14+ – 17
5	0 – 9+	10 – 13+	14 – 17+	18 – 21
6	0 – 8+	9 – 11	11 – 14	14+ – 17
7	0 – 9+	10 – 13+	14 – 17+	18 – 21

Study again the Review sections covering material in Sample Test 2 for which you had a rating of FAIR or POOR. Then go on to Sample Test 3.

To obtain an approximation of your actual GMAT score, see page 6.

Answer Sheet
SAMPLE TEST 3

Section 1

1 Ⓐ Ⓑ Ⓒ Ⓓ Ⓔ	6 Ⓐ Ⓑ Ⓒ Ⓓ Ⓔ	11 Ⓐ Ⓑ Ⓒ Ⓓ Ⓔ	16 Ⓐ Ⓑ Ⓒ Ⓓ Ⓔ	21 Ⓐ Ⓑ Ⓒ Ⓓ Ⓔ
2 Ⓐ Ⓑ Ⓒ Ⓓ Ⓔ	7 Ⓐ Ⓑ Ⓒ Ⓓ Ⓔ	12 Ⓐ Ⓑ Ⓒ Ⓓ Ⓔ	17 Ⓐ Ⓑ Ⓒ Ⓓ Ⓔ	22 Ⓐ Ⓑ Ⓒ Ⓓ Ⓔ
3 Ⓐ Ⓑ Ⓒ Ⓓ Ⓔ	8 Ⓐ Ⓑ Ⓒ Ⓓ Ⓔ	13 Ⓐ Ⓑ Ⓒ Ⓓ Ⓔ	18 Ⓐ Ⓑ Ⓒ Ⓓ Ⓔ	23 Ⓐ Ⓑ Ⓒ Ⓓ Ⓔ
4 Ⓐ Ⓑ Ⓒ Ⓓ Ⓔ	9 Ⓐ Ⓑ Ⓒ Ⓓ Ⓔ	14 Ⓐ Ⓑ Ⓒ Ⓓ Ⓔ	19 Ⓐ Ⓑ Ⓒ Ⓓ Ⓔ	24 Ⓐ Ⓑ Ⓒ Ⓓ Ⓔ
5 Ⓐ Ⓑ Ⓒ Ⓓ Ⓔ	10 Ⓐ Ⓑ Ⓒ Ⓓ Ⓔ	15 Ⓐ Ⓑ Ⓒ Ⓓ Ⓔ	20 Ⓐ Ⓑ Ⓒ Ⓓ Ⓔ	25 Ⓐ Ⓑ Ⓒ Ⓓ Ⓔ

Section 2

1 Ⓐ Ⓑ Ⓒ Ⓓ Ⓔ	6 Ⓐ Ⓑ Ⓒ Ⓓ Ⓔ	11 Ⓐ Ⓑ Ⓒ Ⓓ Ⓔ	16 Ⓐ Ⓑ Ⓒ Ⓓ Ⓔ	21 Ⓐ Ⓑ Ⓒ Ⓓ Ⓔ
2 Ⓐ Ⓑ Ⓒ Ⓓ Ⓔ	7 Ⓐ Ⓑ Ⓒ Ⓓ Ⓔ	12 Ⓐ Ⓑ Ⓒ Ⓓ Ⓔ	17 Ⓐ Ⓑ Ⓒ Ⓓ Ⓔ	22 Ⓐ Ⓑ Ⓒ Ⓓ Ⓔ
3 Ⓐ Ⓑ Ⓒ Ⓓ Ⓔ	8 Ⓐ Ⓑ Ⓒ Ⓓ Ⓔ	13 Ⓐ Ⓑ Ⓒ Ⓓ Ⓔ	18 Ⓐ Ⓑ Ⓒ Ⓓ Ⓔ	23 Ⓐ Ⓑ Ⓒ Ⓓ Ⓔ
4 Ⓐ Ⓑ Ⓒ Ⓓ Ⓔ	9 Ⓐ Ⓑ Ⓒ Ⓓ Ⓔ	14 Ⓐ Ⓑ Ⓒ Ⓓ Ⓔ	19 Ⓐ Ⓑ Ⓒ Ⓓ Ⓔ	24 Ⓐ Ⓑ Ⓒ Ⓓ Ⓔ
5 Ⓐ Ⓑ Ⓒ Ⓓ Ⓔ	10 Ⓐ Ⓑ Ⓒ Ⓓ Ⓔ	15 Ⓐ Ⓑ Ⓒ Ⓓ Ⓔ	20 Ⓐ Ⓑ Ⓒ Ⓓ Ⓔ	25 Ⓐ Ⓑ Ⓒ Ⓓ Ⓔ

Section 3

1 Ⓐ Ⓑ Ⓒ Ⓓ Ⓔ	6 Ⓐ Ⓑ Ⓒ Ⓓ Ⓔ	11 Ⓐ Ⓑ Ⓒ Ⓓ Ⓔ	16 Ⓐ Ⓑ Ⓒ Ⓓ Ⓔ	21 Ⓐ Ⓑ Ⓒ Ⓓ Ⓔ
2 Ⓐ Ⓑ Ⓒ Ⓓ Ⓔ	7 Ⓐ Ⓑ Ⓒ Ⓓ Ⓔ	12 Ⓐ Ⓑ Ⓒ Ⓓ Ⓔ	17 Ⓐ Ⓑ Ⓒ Ⓓ Ⓔ	22 Ⓐ Ⓑ Ⓒ Ⓓ Ⓔ
3 Ⓐ Ⓑ Ⓒ Ⓓ Ⓔ	8 Ⓐ Ⓑ Ⓒ Ⓓ Ⓔ	13 Ⓐ Ⓑ Ⓒ Ⓓ Ⓔ	18 Ⓐ Ⓑ Ⓒ Ⓓ Ⓔ	23 Ⓐ Ⓑ Ⓒ Ⓓ Ⓔ
4 Ⓐ Ⓑ Ⓒ Ⓓ Ⓔ	9 Ⓐ Ⓑ Ⓒ Ⓓ Ⓔ	14 Ⓐ Ⓑ Ⓒ Ⓓ Ⓔ	19 Ⓐ Ⓑ Ⓒ Ⓓ Ⓔ	24 Ⓐ Ⓑ Ⓒ Ⓓ Ⓔ
5 Ⓐ Ⓑ Ⓒ Ⓓ Ⓔ	10 Ⓐ Ⓑ Ⓒ Ⓓ Ⓔ	15 Ⓐ Ⓑ Ⓒ Ⓓ Ⓔ	20 Ⓐ Ⓑ Ⓒ Ⓓ Ⓔ	25 Ⓐ Ⓑ Ⓒ Ⓓ Ⓔ

Section 4

1 Ⓐ Ⓑ Ⓒ Ⓓ Ⓔ	6 Ⓐ Ⓑ Ⓒ Ⓓ Ⓔ	11 Ⓐ Ⓑ Ⓒ Ⓓ Ⓔ	16 Ⓐ Ⓑ Ⓒ Ⓓ Ⓔ	21 Ⓐ Ⓑ Ⓒ Ⓓ Ⓔ
2 Ⓐ Ⓑ Ⓒ Ⓓ Ⓔ	7 Ⓐ Ⓑ Ⓒ Ⓓ Ⓔ	12 Ⓐ Ⓑ Ⓒ Ⓓ Ⓔ	17 Ⓐ Ⓑ Ⓒ Ⓓ Ⓔ	22 Ⓐ Ⓑ Ⓒ Ⓓ Ⓔ
3 Ⓐ Ⓑ Ⓒ Ⓓ Ⓔ	8 Ⓐ Ⓑ Ⓒ Ⓓ Ⓔ	13 Ⓐ Ⓑ Ⓒ Ⓓ Ⓔ	18 Ⓐ Ⓑ Ⓒ Ⓓ Ⓔ	23 Ⓐ Ⓑ Ⓒ Ⓓ Ⓔ
4 Ⓐ Ⓑ Ⓒ Ⓓ Ⓔ	9 Ⓐ Ⓑ Ⓒ Ⓓ Ⓔ	14 Ⓐ Ⓑ Ⓒ Ⓓ Ⓔ	19 Ⓐ Ⓑ Ⓒ Ⓓ Ⓔ	24 Ⓐ Ⓑ Ⓒ Ⓓ Ⓔ
5 Ⓐ Ⓑ Ⓒ Ⓓ Ⓔ	10 Ⓐ Ⓑ Ⓒ Ⓓ Ⓔ	15 Ⓐ Ⓑ Ⓒ Ⓓ Ⓔ	20 Ⓐ Ⓑ Ⓒ Ⓓ Ⓔ	25 Ⓐ Ⓑ Ⓒ Ⓓ Ⓔ

Section 5

1 Ⓐ Ⓑ Ⓒ Ⓓ Ⓔ	6 Ⓐ Ⓑ Ⓒ Ⓓ Ⓔ	11 Ⓐ Ⓑ Ⓒ Ⓓ Ⓔ	16 Ⓐ Ⓑ Ⓒ Ⓓ Ⓔ	21 Ⓐ Ⓑ Ⓒ Ⓓ Ⓔ
2 Ⓐ Ⓑ Ⓒ Ⓓ Ⓔ	7 Ⓐ Ⓑ Ⓒ Ⓓ Ⓔ	12 Ⓐ Ⓑ Ⓒ Ⓓ Ⓔ	17 Ⓐ Ⓑ Ⓒ Ⓓ Ⓔ	22 Ⓐ Ⓑ Ⓒ Ⓓ Ⓔ
3 Ⓐ Ⓑ Ⓒ Ⓓ Ⓔ	8 Ⓐ Ⓑ Ⓒ Ⓓ Ⓔ	13 Ⓐ Ⓑ Ⓒ Ⓓ Ⓔ	18 Ⓐ Ⓑ Ⓒ Ⓓ Ⓔ	23 Ⓐ Ⓑ Ⓒ Ⓓ Ⓔ
4 Ⓐ Ⓑ Ⓒ Ⓓ Ⓔ	9 Ⓐ Ⓑ Ⓒ Ⓓ Ⓔ	14 Ⓐ Ⓑ Ⓒ Ⓓ Ⓔ	19 Ⓐ Ⓑ Ⓒ Ⓓ Ⓔ	24 Ⓐ Ⓑ Ⓒ Ⓓ Ⓔ
5 Ⓐ Ⓑ Ⓒ Ⓓ Ⓔ	10 Ⓐ Ⓑ Ⓒ Ⓓ Ⓔ	15 Ⓐ Ⓑ Ⓒ Ⓓ Ⓔ	20 Ⓐ Ⓑ Ⓒ Ⓓ Ⓔ	25 Ⓐ Ⓑ Ⓒ Ⓓ Ⓔ

Section 6

1 Ⓐ Ⓑ Ⓒ Ⓓ Ⓔ	6 Ⓐ Ⓑ Ⓒ Ⓓ Ⓔ	11 Ⓐ Ⓑ Ⓒ Ⓓ Ⓔ	16 Ⓐ Ⓑ Ⓒ Ⓓ Ⓔ	21 Ⓐ Ⓑ Ⓒ Ⓓ Ⓔ
2 Ⓐ Ⓑ Ⓒ Ⓓ Ⓔ	7 Ⓐ Ⓑ Ⓒ Ⓓ Ⓔ	12 Ⓐ Ⓑ Ⓒ Ⓓ Ⓔ	17 Ⓐ Ⓑ Ⓒ Ⓓ Ⓔ	22 Ⓐ Ⓑ Ⓒ Ⓓ Ⓔ
3 Ⓐ Ⓑ Ⓒ Ⓓ Ⓔ	8 Ⓐ Ⓑ Ⓒ Ⓓ Ⓔ	13 Ⓐ Ⓑ Ⓒ Ⓓ Ⓔ	18 Ⓐ Ⓑ Ⓒ Ⓓ Ⓔ	23 Ⓐ Ⓑ Ⓒ Ⓓ Ⓔ
4 Ⓐ Ⓑ Ⓒ Ⓓ Ⓔ	9 Ⓐ Ⓑ Ⓒ Ⓓ Ⓔ	14 Ⓐ Ⓑ Ⓒ Ⓓ Ⓔ	19 Ⓐ Ⓑ Ⓒ Ⓓ Ⓔ	24 Ⓐ Ⓑ Ⓒ Ⓓ Ⓔ
5 Ⓐ Ⓑ Ⓒ Ⓓ Ⓔ	10 Ⓐ Ⓑ Ⓒ Ⓓ Ⓔ	15 Ⓐ Ⓑ Ⓒ Ⓓ Ⓔ	20 Ⓐ Ⓑ Ⓒ Ⓓ Ⓔ	25 Ⓐ Ⓑ Ⓒ Ⓓ Ⓔ

Section 7

1 Ⓐ Ⓑ Ⓒ Ⓓ Ⓔ	6 Ⓐ Ⓑ Ⓒ Ⓓ Ⓔ	11 Ⓐ Ⓑ Ⓒ Ⓓ Ⓔ	16 Ⓐ Ⓑ Ⓒ Ⓓ Ⓔ	21 Ⓐ Ⓑ Ⓒ Ⓓ Ⓔ
2 Ⓐ Ⓑ Ⓒ Ⓓ Ⓔ	7 Ⓐ Ⓑ Ⓒ Ⓓ Ⓔ	12 Ⓐ Ⓑ Ⓒ Ⓓ Ⓔ	17 Ⓐ Ⓑ Ⓒ Ⓓ Ⓔ	22 Ⓐ Ⓑ Ⓒ Ⓓ Ⓔ
3 Ⓐ Ⓑ Ⓒ Ⓓ Ⓔ	8 Ⓐ Ⓑ Ⓒ Ⓓ Ⓔ	13 Ⓐ Ⓑ Ⓒ Ⓓ Ⓔ	18 Ⓐ Ⓑ Ⓒ Ⓓ Ⓔ	23 Ⓐ Ⓑ Ⓒ Ⓓ Ⓔ
4 Ⓐ Ⓑ Ⓒ Ⓓ Ⓔ	9 Ⓐ Ⓑ Ⓒ Ⓓ Ⓔ	14 Ⓐ Ⓑ Ⓒ Ⓓ Ⓔ	19 Ⓐ Ⓑ Ⓒ Ⓓ Ⓔ	24 Ⓐ Ⓑ Ⓒ Ⓓ Ⓔ
5 Ⓐ Ⓑ Ⓒ Ⓓ Ⓔ	10 Ⓐ Ⓑ Ⓒ Ⓓ Ⓔ	15 Ⓐ Ⓑ Ⓒ Ⓓ Ⓔ	20 Ⓐ Ⓑ Ⓒ Ⓓ Ⓔ	25 Ⓐ Ⓑ Ⓒ Ⓓ Ⓔ

✂ Cut along dashed line to remove answer sheet

11 SAMPLE TEST 3
with Answers and Analysis

Writing Assessment

Part I

TIME: 30 minutes

Directions: Write a clear, logical, and well-organized response to the following issue or argument. Your response should be in the form of a short essay, following the conventions of standard written English. Your answer should fit on three pages of lined $8\frac{1}{2}" \times 11"$ paper. Write legibly. Essays that are illegible or that are written on a topic other than the one outlined in the question will not be scored.

It appears that the easiest kind of occupation is that of the forecaster. If a dismal future is forecast and remedial action is taken, the forecaster can claim disaster was avoided because he or she was listened to. However, if the pessimism was well founded, the forecaster can take credit for the ability to predict future events.

Discuss how logically persuasive you find the above argument. In presenting your point of view, analyze the sort of reasoning used and its supporting evidence. In addition, state what further evidence, if any, would make the argument more sound and convincing or would make you better able to evaluate its conclusion.

Part II

TIME: 30 minutes

Directions: Write a clear, logical, and well-organized response to the following issue or argument. Your response should be in the form of a short essay, following the conventions of standard written English. Your answer should fit on three pages of lined $8\frac{1}{2}" \times 11"$ paper. Write legibly. Essays that are illegible or that are written on a topic other than the one outlined in the question will not be scored.

Many workers believe that "whistle-blowers" are company traitors who reveal secrets for their own glorification. They feel that if controversial practices are good for the company, they should be ignored. Others feel, however, that whistle-blowing results in reduction of waste, improved worker morale, and more ethical behavior.

Which do you find more convincing: the argument that whistle-blowing is motivated by selfish reasons or by the good of the company as a whole? State your position using relevant reasons and examples from your own experience, observation, or reading.

STOP

IF THERE IS STILL TIME REMAINING,
YOU MAY REVIEW THE QUESTIONS IN THIS SECTION ONLY.
YOU MAY NOT TURN TO ANY OTHER SECTION OF THE TEST.

Section 1

TIME: 30 minutes
25 Questions

Directions: This part contains three reading passages. You are to read each one carefully. When answering the questions, you *will* be allowed to refer back to the passages. The questions are based on what is *stated* or *implied* in each passage.

Passage 1:

With Friedrich Engels, Karl Marx in 1848 published the *Communist Manifesto*, calling upon the masses to rise and throw off their economic chains. His maturer theories of society were later elaborated in his large and abstruse work *Das Capital.* Starting as a non-violent revolutionist, he ended life as a major social theorist more or less sympathetic with violent revolution, if such became necessary in order to change the social system which he believed to be frankly predatory upon the masses.

On the theoretical side, Marx set up the doctrine of surplus value as the chief element in capitalistic exploitation. According to this theory, the ruling classes no longer employed military force primarily as a means to plundering the people. Instead, they used their control over employment and working conditions under the bourgeois capitalistic system for this purpose, paying only a bare subsistence wage to the worker while they appropriated all surplus values in the productive process. He further taught that the strategic disadvantage of the worker in industry prevented him from obtaining a fairer share of the earnings by bargaining methods and drove him to revolutionary procedures as a means to establishing his economic and social rights. This revolution might be peacefully consummated by parliamentary procedures if the people prepared themselves for political action by mastering the materialistic interpretation of history and by organizing politically for the final event. It was his belief that the aggressions of the capitalist class would eventually destroy the middle class and take over all their sources of income by a process of capitalistic absorption of industry—a process which has failed to occur in most countries.

With minor exceptions, Marx's social philosophy is now generally accepted by leftwing labor movements in many countries, but rejected by centrist labor groups, especially those in the United States. In Russia and other Eastern European countries, however, Socialist leaders adopted the methods of violent revolution because of the opposition of the ruling classes. Yet, many now hold that the present Communist regime in Russia and her satellite countries is no longer a proletarian movement based on Marxist social and political theory, but a camouflaged imperialistic effort to dominate the world in the interest of a new ruling class.

It is important, however, that those who wish to approach Marx as a teacher should not be "buffaloed" by his philosophic approach. They are very likely to in these days, because those most interested in propagating the ideas of Marx, the Russian Bolsheviks, have swallowed down his Hegelian philosophy along with his science of revolutionary engineering, and they look upon us irreverent peoples who presume to meditate social and even revolutionary problems without making our obeisance to the mysteries of Dialectic Materialism, as a species of unredeemed and well-nigh unredeemable barbarians. They are right in scorning our ignorance of the scientific ideas of Karl Marx and our indifference to them. They are wrong in scorning our distaste for having practical programs presented in the form of systems of philosophy. In that we simply represent a more progressive intellectual culture than that in which Marx received his education—a culture farther emerged from the dominance of religious attitudes.

1. According to the passage, the chief element in Marx's analysis of capitalist exploitation was the doctrine of

(A) just wages
(B) the price system
(C) surplus value
(D) predatory production
(E) subsistence work

GO ON TO THE NEXT PAGE ➤

2. *Das Capital* differs from the *Communist Manifesto* in that it

(A) was written with the help of Friedrich Engels
(B) retreated from Marx's earlier revolutionary stance
(C) expressed a more fully developed form of Marxist theory
(D) denounced the predatory nature of the capitalist system
(E) expressed sympathy for the plight of the middle class

3. According to the passage, Marx ended his life

I. a believer in non-violent revolution
II. accepting violent revolution
III. a major social theorist

(A) I only
(B) III only
(C) I and III only
(D) II and III only
(E) Neither I, II, nor III

4. The author suggests that the Communist regime in Russia may best be categorized as a(n)

(A) proletarian movement
(B) social government
(C) imperialistic state
(D) revolutionary government
(E) social democracy

5. Marx's social philosophy is now generally accepted by

(A) centrist labor groups
(B) most labor unions
(C) left-wing labor unions
(D) only those in Communist countries
(E) only those in Russia

6. It can be concluded that the author of the passage is

(A) sympathetic to Marx's ideas
(B) unsympathetic to Marx's ideas
(C) uncritical of Marx's interpretation of history
(D) a believer in Hegelian philosophy
(E) a Leninist-Marxist

7. Which of the following classes did Marx believe should control the economy?

(A) The working class
(B) The upper class
(C) The middle class
(D) The lower class
(E) The capitalist class

8. According to Marx, a social and economic revolution could take place through

I. parliamentary procedures
II. political action
III. violent revolution

(A) I only
(B) III only
(C) I or II only
(D) II or III only
(E) I, II, or III

GO ON TO THE NEXT PAGE ➤

Passage 2:

The basic character of our governmental and political institutions conditions the federal budgetary system. The working relationships between branches, and between the elements within each branch, are intricate, subtle, and in continuous change—affected by partisan politics, personalities, social forces, and public opinion. A few landmark stages in the evolution of the present system provide perspective.

In 1789 Alexander Hamilton, as the first Secretary of the Treasury, affirmed and successfully established a position of strong executive leadership in matters of public finance. His proposals on revenues, banking, and the assumption of prior debts of both national and state governments were based on his philosophy that federal fiscal policies should be designed to encourage economic growth. However, Hamilton's successors, and the Presidents under whom they served, did not follow his concept of executive responsibility for "plans of finance."

Partly through default, Congress took charge of all phases of fiscal policy. At the outset, each chamber was so small that coherent initiative was possible. (The first House had some 60 members—about the number of its present Appropriations Committee.) Spending estimates, considered in Committee of the Whole in 1789, were later referred to the Committee on Ways and Means. In 1865 expenditures were assigned to a new Appropriations Committee while revenues remained with the Ways and Means Committee. In 1885 most spending proposals were subdivided among the legislative committees so that appropriation bills came to be handled by numerous committees (14 in the House and 15 in the Senate), each dealing directly with the departments. The presidential role was minimal.

By the turn of the century there was a clear need for reform in financial management. At all levels of government, officials spent money on activities "as authorized by law" and in line with "appropriations" made by legislative bodies—usually after committee consideration. Other officials collected taxes and fees under various unrelated statutes. Such a system—or lack-of-system—worked within reason as long as governments had little to do. But as government activities grew, becoming more technical and closely interrelated, this lack-of-system bogged down.

Several factors played a part in the eventual breakthrough. In the first decade of the twentieth century, an "executive budget" came into successful use by some cities and states. President Taft's Commission on Efficiency and Economy prepared an illustrative federal budget which—while rejected by Congress—commanded broad public support. The more advanced methods developed by European governments came to American attention. World War I precipitated accounting chaos, with an aftermath of scandal. The need for new and better methods was established beyond dispute.

The Budget and Accounting Act of 1921 placed direct responsibility for preparation and execution of the federal budget upon the President, making a unified federal budget possible for the first time. The Act set up two new organizational units, the General Accounting Office (GAO) and the Bureau of the Budget. GAO is headed by the Comptroller General, appointed by the President *with* Senate approval for a 15-year term, and is regarded as primarily a congressional rather than an executive resource. The Bureau, under a Director appointed by the President *without* Senate confirmation and serving at his pleasure, has from its inception been the President's chief reliance in budgetary and related matters.

9. Alexander Hamilton's philosophy was that federal fiscal policies should

(A) be expansionary
(B) encourage economic growth
(C) be determined by Congress
(D) encourage a balanced budget
(E) be determined by the President

10. Hamilton's successors

I. followed his economic philosophy of "plans of finance"
II. followed his social philosophy
III. did not follow his philosophy of strong executive leadership

(A) I only
(B) III only
(C) I and II only
(D) II and III only
(E) I, II, and III

GO ON TO THE NEXT PAGE ➤

1 1 1 1 1 1 1 1 1 1 1

11. In the history of U.S. fiscal management, spending estimates were *first* considered by the
    (A) Committee of the Whole
    (B) Appropriations Committee
    (C) Ways and Means Committee
    (D) Commission on Efficiency and Economy
    (E) General Accounting Office

12. At the end of the nineteenth century, there was a need for
    (A) more restrained executive leadership
    (B) a new finance commission
    (C) more Congressional interest in finance
    (D) overall reform of financial management
    (E) creation of a new Appropriations committee

13. The "executive budget" was first used
    (A) by Alexander Hamilton
    (B) in the 19th century
    (C) in the first decade of the 20th century
    (D) by President Eisenhower
    (E) by President Truman

14. President Taft's federal budget was
    (A) based on procedures used by some European governments
    (B) enthusiastically accepted by Congress
    (C) a partial cause of accounting chaos during World War I
    (D) rejected by Congress
    (E) vilified by the public

15. In 1921, the responsibility for preparation and execution of the federal budget fell upon the
    (A) President
    (B) Congress
    (C) Bureau of the Budget
    (D) House of Representatives
    (E) Senate

16. All of the following are true about the Bureau of the Budget except
    (A) its Director is appointed by the President
    (B) it assists the President in budgetary matters
    (C) its Director need not be approved by the Senate
    (D) it was established in 1921
    (E) its Director serves for a 15-year term

GO ON TO THE NEXT PAGE ➤

Passage 3:

In describing the Indians of the various sections of the United States at different stages in their history, some of the factors which account for their similarity amid difference can be readily accounted for, others are difficult to discern.

The basic physical similarity of the Indians from Alaska to Patagonia is explained by the fact that they all came originally from Asia by way of the Bering Strait and the Aleutian Islands into Alaska and then southward. They came in different waves, the earliest around 25,000 years ago, the latest probably not long before America was discovered by Europeans. Because these people all came from Asia and were therefore drawn from the same pool of Asiatic people, they tended to look alike. But since the various waves of migration crossed into Alaska at widely separated times, there were differences among them in their physical characteristics.

There were also differences in cultural equipment. The earliest arrivals are known to science only through their simple tools of chipped stone and bone. Despite their limited technical equipment, some of the New Mexico Indians were very successful big game hunters. Twenty-five thousand years ago they were hunting the wooly mammoth, the giant bison, the ground sloth and the camel, all characteristic animals of the closing phases of the last ice age.

After their arrival from Asia in various waves across the Bering Strait, the early peoples in the Americas slowly spread southward into the vast empty spaces of the two continents. A group of people moving slowly down the Mackenzie River valley east of the Rockies into the general region of Southern Alberta, then eastward across the northern prairies reaching the wooded country around the upper Mississippi and the Western Great Lakes, then in a southeastward movement following the Mississippi valley until some final settlement was reached in the Gulf states, would encounter a wide variety of physical environments. At various stages of such wanderings they would have to evolve methods of coping with the cold, barren, tundra country of northern Canada; the prairies, cold, treeless but well stocked with large game; then later the completely different flora and fauna of the Minnesota-Wisconsin-Illinois area, thickly forested and well watered and providing an abundance of small game and wild vegetable foods; then the semi-tropical character of the lower Mississippi country as they neared the Gulf of Mexico. Since such a migration would be spread over many centuries, the modification of whatever basic culture they had on their arrival from Asia would be very slow. Yet the end result would be completely different from their original culture. It would also be different from the final culture of a closely allied group who became separated from them early in their wanderings and whose movements led them into different types of country. In its final form, the culture of this second group would have little in common with that of the first except perhaps a continuing resemblance in language and in physical type.

17. According to the passage, Indians who migrated to what is now the United States originated in

(A) Asia
(B) Africa
(C) South America
(D) Alaska
(E) Patagonia

18. Physical differences among Indians who migrated to Alaska can be accounted for by the fact that they came

(A) from different places
(B) from different tribes
(C) at different times
(D) from different races
(E) to different places

19. It is estimated that Indians first came to what is now the United States about

(A) 5,000 years ago
(B) 10,000 years ago
(C) 15,000 years ago
(D) 25,000 years ago
(E) 50,000 years ago

GO ON TO THE NEXT PAGE ➤

20. The author is most interested in discussing the Indians'

(A) cultural background
(B) eating habits
(C) technical abilities
(D) migration patterns
(E) physical characteristics

21. According to the passage, the southernmost area reached by the earliest Indians was the

(A) northern prairies
(B) upper Mississippi
(C) Great Lakes
(D) Mackenzie River valley
(E) Gulf States

22. Particularly noted for their hunting prowess were the Indians of

(A) Mississippi
(B) Southern Alberta
(C) the Mackenzie River valley
(D) New Mexico
(E) the American prairies

23. What characteristics of Indian culture remained fairly stable despite the Indian migrations?

I. Language
II. Physical type
III. Technical abilities

(A) I only
(B) III only
(C) I and II only
(D) II and III only
(E) I, II, and III

24. Which animals were hunted by the Indians when they first migrated to the Americas?

I. Bison
II. Wooly mammoth
III. Camel

(A) I only
(B) III only
(C) I and II only
(D) II and III only
(E) I, II, and III

25. The passage most likely was written by a(n)

(A) economist
(B) historian
(C) educator
(D) social scientist
(E) anthropologist

STOP

**IF THERE IS STILL TIME REMAINING,
YOU MAY REVIEW THE QUESTIONS IN THIS SECTION ONLY.
YOU MAY NOT TURN TO ANY OTHER SECTION OF THE TEST.**

2 2 2 2 2 2 2 2 2 2 2

Section 2

TIME: 25 minutes
17 Questions

Directions: Solve each of the following problems; then indicate the correct answer on the answer sheet.

NOTE: A figure that appears with a problem is drawn as accurately as possible so as to provide information that may help in answering the question. Numbers in this test are real numbers.

1. A college has raised 75% of the amount it needs for a new building by receiving an average donation of \$60 from the people already solicited. The people already solicited represent 60% of the people the college will ask for donations. If the college is to raise exactly the amount needed for the new building, how much must the remaining people donate per person?

    (A) \$25
    (B) \$30
    (C) \$40
    (D) \$50
    (E) \$60

2. If a worker can pack $\frac{1}{6}$ of a carton of canned food in 15 minutes and there are 40 workers in a factory, how many cartons should be packed in the factory in $1\frac{2}{3}$ hours?

    (A) 16
    (B) $40\frac{2}{9}$
    (C) $43\frac{4}{9}$
    (D) $44\frac{4}{9}$
    (E) $45\frac{2}{3}$

GO ON TO THE NEXT PAGE ➤

3. Which of the following inequalities is the solution to the inequality $7x - 5 < 2x + 18$?

(A) $x < \frac{13}{5}$

(B) $x > \frac{23}{9}$

(C) $x < \frac{23}{9}$

(D) $x > \frac{23}{5}$

(E) $x < \frac{23}{5}$

4. A truck driver must complete a 180-mile trip in 4 hours. If he averages 50 miles an hour for the first three hours of his trip, how fast must he travel in the final hour?

(A) 30 mph
(B) 35 mph
(C) 40 mph
(D) 45 mph
(E) 50 mph

5. If a triangle has base B and the altitude of the triangle is twice the base, then the area of the triangle is

(A) $\frac{1}{2}AB$

(B) AB

(C) $\frac{1}{2}B^2$

(D) B^2
(E) $2B^2$

6. If the product of two numbers is 10 and the sum of the two numbers is 7, then the larger of the two numbers is

(A) −2
(B) 2
(C) 3
(D) $4\frac{1}{4}$

(E) 5

7. If the lengths of the two sides of a right triangle adjacent to the right angle are 8 and 15 respectively, then the length of the side opposite the right angle is

(A) $\sqrt{258}$
(B) 15.8
(C) 16
(D) 17
(E) 17.9

GO ON TO THE NEXT PAGE ➤

2 2 2 2 2 2 2 2 2 2 2

8. It costs x¢ each to print the first 600 copies of a newspaper. It costs $\left(x - \frac{y}{10}\right)$¢ for every copy after the first 600. How much does it cost to print 1,500 copies of the newspaper?

(A) $1500x$¢
(B) $150y$¢
(C) $(1500x - 90y)$¢
(D) \$$(150x - 9y)$
(E) \$$15x$

9. Which of the following sets of values for w, x, y, and z respectively are possible if $ABCD$ is a parallelogram?

I. 50, 130, 50, 130
II. 60, 110, 70, 120
III. 60, 150, 50, 150

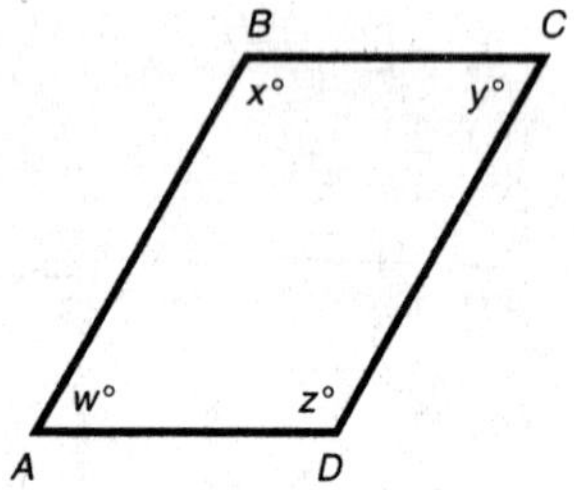

(A) I only
(B) II only
(C) I and II only
(D) I and III only
(E) I, II, and III

10. John weighs twice as much as Marcia. Marcia's weight is 60% of Bob's weight. Dave weighs 50% of Lee's weight. Lee weighs 190% of John's weight. Which of these 5 persons weighs the least?

(A) Bob
(B) Dave
(C) John
(D) Lee
(E) Marcia

11. The sum of 5 consecutive integers is 35. How many of the five consecutive integers are prime numbers?

(A) 0
(B) 1
(C) 2
(D) 3
(E) 4

12. The assessed value of a house is \$72,000. The assessed value is 60% of the market value of the house. If taxes are \$3 for every \$1,000 of the market value of the house, how much are the taxes on the house?

(A) \$216
(B) \$360
(C) \$1,386
(D) \$2,160
(E) \$3,600

13. If the operation * is defined by $*a = a^2 - 2$, then $*(*5)$ is

(A) 23
(B) 527
(C) 529
(D) 621
(E) 623

GO ON TO THE NEXT PAGE ➤

2 2 2 2 2 2 2 2 2 2 2

14. If $\frac{y}{x} = \frac{1}{3}$ and $x + 2y = 10$, then x is

(A) 2
(B) 3
(C) 4
(D) 5
(E) 6

15. What is the area of the parallelogram *ABCD*? The coordinates of the points are: $A = (1, -1)$, $B = (2, 2)$, $C = (5, 2)$ and $D = (4, -1)$.

(A) 3

(B) 4

(C) $4\frac{1}{2}$

(D) 9

(E) 10

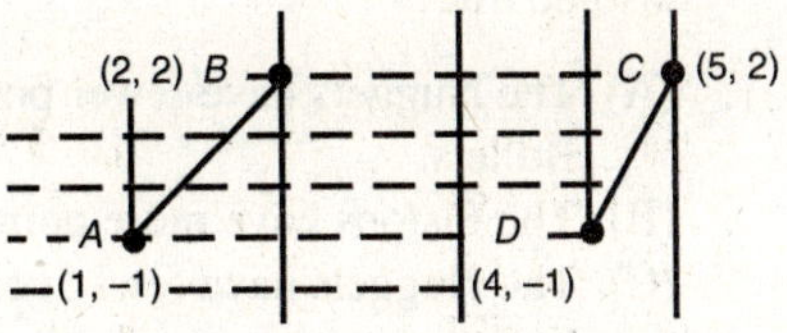

16. The area of a rectangular field is 1,000 square yards. If the length of the field is *y* yards, then how many yards is the perimeter of the field?

(A) $y + \frac{1,000}{y}$

(B) $2y + 1,000$

(C) 1,000

(D) $2y + \frac{1,000}{y}$

(E) $2y + \frac{2,000}{y}$

17. The figure *ABCDEFGH* is a cube. $AB = 10$. What is the length of the line segment *AF*?

(A) 10
(B) $10\sqrt{2}$
(C) $10\sqrt{3}$
(D) 20
(E) $10\sqrt{5}$

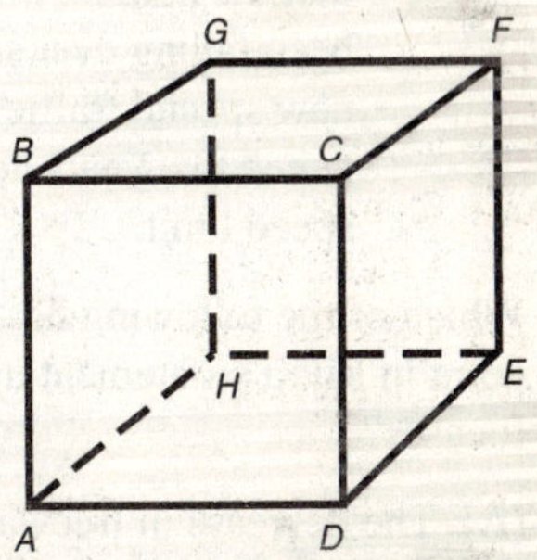

STOP

IF THERE IS STILL TIME REMAINING,
YOU MAY REVIEW THE QUESTIONS IN THIS SECTION ONLY.
YOU MAY NOT TURN TO ANY OTHER SECTION OF THE TEST.

3 3 3 3 3 3 3 3 3 3 3

Section 3

TIME: 25 minutes
17 Questions

Directions: For each question, choose the best answer among the listed alternatives.

1. Myra: The number of freeway accidents this year in the state of North Carolina, where the speed limit on freeways was lowered to fifty miles an hour two years ago, is clear evidence that speed restrictions rigorously enforced, make drivers more aware of the dangers of going too fast.

Lewis: Wrong. A close look at the records shows that the number of freeway accidents has been falling ever since the formation of a new special traffic division, which happened two years before the lowering of the speed limit.

Which of the following best describes the weak point in Myra's statement upon which Lewis focuses?

(A) The decrease in freeway accidents may be a temporary phenomenon.
(B) The evidence Myra cites comes only from one source—the state of North Carolina.
(C) Myra's claim leaves open the possibility that the cause she cites came after the effect she attributes to it.
(D) No exact statistics for freeway accidents are given by Myra.
(E) No mention is made of deaths caused on roads other than freeways.

2. The Pistons have more points than the Nuggets. The Bullets have less points than the Lakers. The Nuggets and the Suns have the same number of points. The Suns have more points than the Bullets.

If the above is true, which of the following must also be true?

(A) The Nuggets have fewer points than the Bullets.
(B) The Pistons have more points than the Bullets.
(C) The Nuggets have fewer points than the Lakers.
(D) The Lakers have more points than the Pistons.
(E) The Lakers have more points than the Suns.

3. The states of New York, Ohio, Pennsylvania, and California provide extensive free higher education to their residents. These states are representative of different geographic areas of the United States. There is little reason why most states cannot provide the same service to their residents.

Which of the following, if true, would weaken the above argument?

(A) Free education is not guaranteed by the constitution.
(B) New York, Ohio, Pennsylvania and California have more qualified high school graduates than other states.
(C) Most other states do not have the tax base that New York, Ohio, Pennsylvania and California have.
(D) Other states do not have as many high school graduates.
(E) Quality education cannot be free; it must be paid for

GO ON TO THE NEXT PAGE ➤

3 3 3 3 3 3 3 3 3 3 3

4. Professor Archibald had the task of giving grades (ranging from A–D in descending value) to his 100 students, based upon the marks they received in three examinations in which the passing mark was 50%. He is instructed to follow the following criteria:

   I. All students that scored between 90 and 100% in any two examinations could receive an A grade.
   II. Students that came in the top decile overall were to be awarded an A.
   III. Notwithstanding I and II, if any student failed an exam, the highest he or she could get was a B.
   IV. The top 20 students in the whole year, when the overall exam percentages were averaged, could receive an A.

   Given the above criteria, which of the following, in the absence of further information, would definitely not be permissible?

   (A) A. Brown, who got 95% in Chemistry and 92% in Biology, received a B grade.
   (B) B. White, who was first in Physics and got 96% in History, received a B grade.
   (C) C. Green failed English, but because he ranked ninth overall out of the 100 students, he was awarded an A grade.
   (D) D. Black was given an A after he came twentieth out of the 100 students and failed to get above 90% in any of the three examinations.
   (E) E. Gray failed his Math exam, but came top in his other two tests and was awarded a B.

5. A company, Marson Ltd., included in its annual financial statements the following note on its policy of accounting for fixed assets and depreciation:

   Fixed Assets

   Fixed assets are stated in the consolidated balance sheet at cost less accumulated depreciation and amortization. Depreciation is provided on all fixed assets, except land, to write off their cost in equal annual installments over the estimated economic useful lives of the assets. The cost of leasehold improvements is amortized over the term of the remaining number of years of the lease in equal annual installments.

   Which of the following statements is relevant to, but not consistent with, the above accounting policy?

   (A) The economic useful life of land and buildings is assumed to be 50 years, and Marson Ltd., therefore, employs a depreciation rate of 2% per annum.
   (B) Marson Ltd. include in their plant inventory equipment that cost $100,000, even though this equipment is more than 10 years old and the depreciation rate on plant and machinery has been 15% for many years.
   (C) Marson Ltd. spent $30,000 on improving a building, which is leased. The period of the lease was seven years, but the lease must be renewed in two years time. Marson Ltd. provided for amortization at 50% for this year.
   (D) Inventories and negotiable securities are not included in fixed assets.
   (E) Amortization of other assets, e.g. goodwill, is provided separately in the financial statements.

GO ON TO THE NEXT PAGE ➤

6. "The last five Wimbledon men's single champions have all changed to Gallenger's new tennis rackets—the only racket that uses genuine X-lon strengthened frames. In that case, isn't now the time to add power to your tennis strokes and to trade in your old racket for a Gallenger?"

Which of the following claims is not made and cannot be inferred from the above ad?

(A) Frames strengthened by X-lon are used only in Gallenger's new rackets.
(B) X-lon strengthened frames make tennis rackets stronger and allow the player to make more powerful strokes.
(C) Former Wimbledon champions know a great deal about tennis and their equipment.
(D) Gallenger tennis rackets helped the last five Wimbledon mens' singles champions achieve their status.
(E) You will improve your tennis play with a Gallenger.

7. The fact that more and more married women are working has placed stress on marriages. The census published data showing the divorce rate for married women earning over $75,000 annually is twice the national average and four times the national average for women in the $150,000 bracket.

Which of the following, if true, would weaken the statement?

(A) Fifteen percent of married women earn over $75,000 per year.
(B) Married couples are more stressed because of their careers.
(C) Married couples where both spouses work have less time to spend together.
(D) Sixty percent of married women earn over $75,000 per year.
(E) The average divorce rate for unemployed women is 40 percent.

8. Prompted by a proposal to convert a shipyard into a complex of condominiums with a full-service marina and boat repair center and by concern about the proposal from local residents, baymen, and environmentalists, the town is considering a one-year building moratorium for the waterfront area.

Which of the following, if true, would most seriously weaken opposition to the complex?

(A) Condominiums would sell for $350,000 each.
(B) There is a large demand for boat repair services.
(C) A growing population results in the closure of shellfish.
(D) There are already 1200 moorings on the waterfront.
(E) The shipyard may be sold for another commercial use.

9. The local education authorities in England have recently issued a "prescribed" list of books that are approved for reading in schools by children aged between 5 and 11.

A furor has arisen among many parents because an authoress by the name of Enid Blyton, very popular with children, has been omitted from the said list. When asked to comment on the omission, the head of the committee that was responsible for preparing the list of books said that the books of Mrs. Blyton have been omitted because "we thought they are of an inferior quality and do not sufficiently stimulate the children's intellectual ability and not because they contain characters which are stereotypes or may show racial prejudice."

Which one of the following statements can be inferred from the above paragraph?

(A) Children are very angry that they will not be reading Enid Blyton in school once this decision is implemented.
(B) The parents' view is that Mrs. Blyton's books might have been left off the list because some of her characters were racist.
(C) If the parents had been consulted, Enid Blyton's books would have been omitted.
(D) The head of the deciding committee implied that Mrs. Blyton was not the only author whose books were banned.
(E) Mrs. Blyton was popular with children and parents because she included stereotype characters in her books.

GO ON TO THE NEXT PAGE ➤

10. Pioneers of the motor-car industry realized that if they were going to meet the growing demand for their product, they had to adapt the labor force used in the productive process. Instead of many men working to complete all the stages of one car at a time, they assigned defined tasks to each man which they would repeat on every car.

    Which of the following can be concluded from the passage?

    (A) Early motor car manufacturers intended to increase productivity by applying the principle of division of labor.
    (B) The car workers became disgruntled because they were assigned monotonous, repetitive tasks on the assembly line.
    (C) Economies of scale enabled early motor companies to expand.
    (D) A bad worker would perform the same task badly on each car, leading to many more rejects.
    (E) The new production process enabled certain car workers to become specialists in the part of the process to which they were assigned.

11. In 1989 Japanese economic growth is expected to increase 50 times more than that of the United States.

    Japanese economic policy ensures that faster growth is caused by greater investment in modern industrial plants. The initial investment leads to lower production costs, increased competitiveness, higher living standards, and low inflation.

    The United States, on the other hand, is more concerned with curbing inflation and is pursuing a policy of slow growth, thus preventing investment in the modernization of American industry.

    Which of the following conclusions can be drawn from the above?

    (A) Slow growth prevents inflation.
    (B) Slow-growth policies reduce inflation, but also decrease the efficiency and competitiveness of industry.
    (C) Investment in industry causes inflation.
    (D) Inflation can be reduced by increasing productivity.
    (E) The U.S. must cure inflation before it can modernize and streamline its industry.

12. A pill that can induce abortions in pregnant women has become available in France. The drug, RU486, has proved more than 95% effective in tests conducted by a scientific team in Paris. The drug is an antihormone which disrupts pregnancy by blocking the implantation of a fertilized egg in the wall of the uterus. In France, the pill will be available to women who are 49 days late in their menstrual cycle. The company that manufactures the pill, Roussel Uclaf, states, however, that the pill is not a "morning after" pill for use as a contraceptive.

    Which of the following statements can be correctly deduced from the text above?

    (A) The drug RU486 is a new type of contraceptive.
    (B) The drug RU486 blocks egg production.
    (C) The drug RU486 can be used to terminate pregnancy.
    (D) The drug RU486 will replace conventional abortion techniques.
    (E) The drug RU486 will only be available in France.

13. Jane and Bella are both successful women who are also members of a minority group. Jane believes in positive discrimination. She believes that if positions of power and honor are offered principally to minority groups, then these groups will begin to play a more significant role in society today.

    Bella, on the other hand, feels that she has succeeded in her chosen field of work on her own merits. She thinks that positive discrimination will lower standards and decrease competition between similarly qualified personnel who will expect to achieve positions because of their minority status rather than their suitability for the particular position.

    Which of the following best sums up Jane's argument?

    (A) Positive discrimination will encourage more people to apply for jobs, previously unavailable to them.
    (B) Positive discrimination will give extra opportunities to minority groups.
    (C) Quality and professionalism will improve because of the greater number of positions held by members of minority groups.
    (D) Positive discrimination will ensure that each position is filled by the most suitably qualified candidate.
    (E) Positive discrimination will eradicate prejudice from the work arena.

GO ON TO THE NEXT PAGE ➤

14. Many countries are facing a potential crisis in 20 to 30 years time. The ratio of pensioners to workers will be changing drastically with a declining birth rate, with more lengthy education of the young, and with a reduced working life. In general, the number of people paying into pension schemes is decreasing all the time. Meanwhile, with increased health care and living standards, more people are living long enough to draw their pension funds.

    A controversial solution to this problem has been proposed in Germany—changing the age of retirement, for both men and women, from the current qualifying age of 63 for men and 60 for women.

    A radical, but socially acceptable, solution to this problem must be found. If this is not done, it is predicted that by the year 2050, one person in three will be 65 or over and the projected work force will be unable to support pensions.

    Assuming the following were all socially acceptable, which one would not improve the situation in the future?

    (A) Lower the retirement age.
    (B) Decrease the school-leaving age.
    (C) Impose larger contributions on employees and employers.
    (D) Cut pensions in half.
    (E) Only give state pensions to retired persons whose income is below a certain level.

15. Before the arrival of Joe, a new partner, sales output in Bill's company Midas In Reverse Ltd. had been rising by 10% per year on average. Innovations by Joe included computerization of technical processes and reductions in the work force, but annual sales output has only risen by 5% per year. It appears that Joe's innovations have caused the reduction in the annual growth rate.

    Which of the following, if true, would most seriously weaken the conclusion above?

    (A) The investment in new machinery entails a provision for depreciation of the cost of the fixed assets, which causes a reduction in profit.
    (B) Midas In Reverse Ltd. does not base increases in the selling price of its products with costs.
    (C) Joe's innovations were intended as long-term investment and not made for short-term profit growth.
    (D) General demand for the product manufactured by the company has declined.
    (E) Workers laid off by Midas In Reverse Ltd. have been hired by a competitor, who is taking an increasing share of the market.

GO ON TO THE NEXT PAGE ➤

3 3 3 3 3 3 3 3 3 3 3

16. Complete the following paragraph with the most suitable sentence.

    In order to boost sales of toys at times other than the peak sale time—Christmas—manufacturers use many techniques. Character toys from movies or TV series are promoted, and all sets are "collectible" by their young purchasers. Collections, however, never appear to be complete, because as soon as all the characters are acquired, the child then requires the "car," the "home," the "mobile home," and even the "airplane" to ensure a happy environment for the toys. Ultimately, the elusive final piece of the series is attained just as the manufacturer and promoter release the next series of "collectibles."

    The prime aim of the manufacturer and promoter is to ensure that . . .

    (A) all children should be happy and no child can be happy without a complete series of toys.
    (B) as soon as one set is complete or almost complete, then the next one arrives on the scene.
    (C) children should be encouraged to complete their collections of toys.
    (D) Christmas must be the peak selling period for toys.
    (E) sales need to be bolstered throughout the year.

17. John Wyndham Lewis, the famous sociologist, postulated that if murder is a worse crime than blackmail and blackmail is a worse crime than theft, how much more so is murder a worse crime than theft.

    Which is a correct analysis of the above argument?

    (A) A case operating in one situation will also be operative in another situation, if both situations are characterized in identical terms.
    (B) A case that operates under certain conditions will surely be operative in other situations in which the same conditions are present in a more acute form.
    (C) A case that clearly expresses the purpose it was meant to serve will also apply in other situations in which the identical purpose may be served.
    (D) A case that begins with a generalization as to its intended application, then continues until the specification of particular cases, and then concludes with a restatement of the generalization, can be applied only to the particular cases specified.
    (E) None of the above.

STOP

IF THERE IS STILL TIME REMAINING,
YOU MAY REVIEW THE QUESTIONS IN THIS SECTION ONLY.
YOU MAY NOT TURN TO ANY OTHER SECTION OF THE TEST.

4 4 4 4 4 4 4 4 4 4 4

Section 4

TIME: 25 minutes
21 Questions

Directions: Each of the following problems has a question and two statements which are labeled (1) and (2). Use the data given in (1) and (2) together with other available information (such as the number of hours in a day, the definition of *clockwise*, mathematical facts, etc.) to decide whether the statements are *sufficient* to answer the question. Then fill in space

(A) if you can get the answer from **(1) ALONE** but not from (2) alone
(B) if you can get the answer from **(2) ALONE** but not from (1) alone
(C) if you can get the answer from **BOTH (1) and (2) TOGETHER**, but not from (1) alone or (2) alone
(D) if **EITHER** statement **(1) ALONE OR** statement **(2) ALONE** suffices
(E) if you **CANNOT** get the answer from statements (1) and (2) **TOGETHER**, but need even more data

All numbers used in this section are real numbers. A figure given for a problem is intended to provide information consistent with that in the question, but not necessarily with the additional information contained in the statements.

1. How many degrees Celsius is 100° Fahrenheit?

 (1) degrees Celsius = $\frac{5}{9}$ (degrees Fahrenheit – 32)

 (2) degrees Fahrenheit = $\frac{9}{5}$ (degrees Celsius) + 32

2. What is the area of the shaded part of the circle? *O* is the center of the circle.

 (1) The radius of the circle is 4.
 (2) *x* is 60.

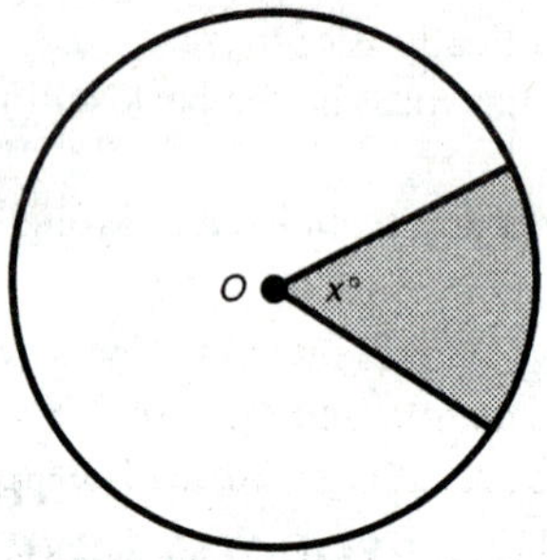

GO ON TO THE NEXT PAGE ➤

4 4 4 4 4 4 4 4 4 4 4

(A) if you can get the answer from **(1) ALONE** but not from (2) alone
(B) if you can get the answer from **(2) ALONE** but not from (1) alone
(C) if you can get the answer from **BOTH (1) and (2) TOGETHER**, but not from (1) alone or (2) alone
(D) if **EITHER** statement **(1) ALONE OR** statement **(2) ALONE** suffices
(E) if you **CANNOT** get the answer from statements (1) and (2) **TOGETHER**, but need even more data

3. What was Mr. Kliman's income in 1990?
   (1) His total income for 1988, 1989, and 1990 was $141,000.
   (2) He made 20% more in 1989 than he did in 1988.

4. If l and l' are straight lines, find y.
   (1) $x = 100$
   (2) $z = 80$

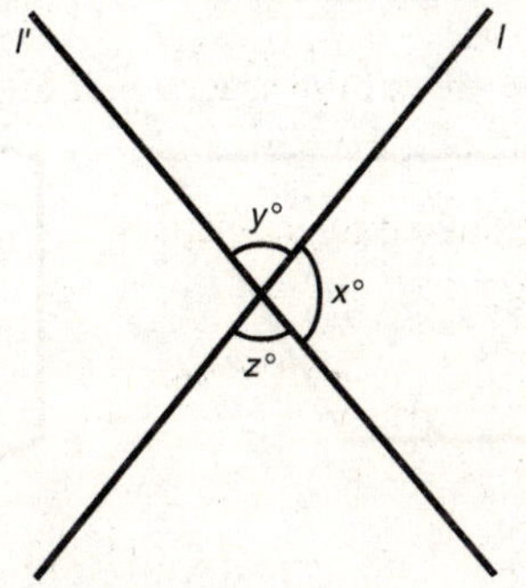

5. Fifty students have signed up for at least one of the courses German I and English I. How many of the 50 students are taking German I but not English I?
   (1) 16 students are taking German I and English I.
   (2) The number of students taking English I but not German I is the same as the number taking German I but not English I.

6. Is $ABCD$ a square?

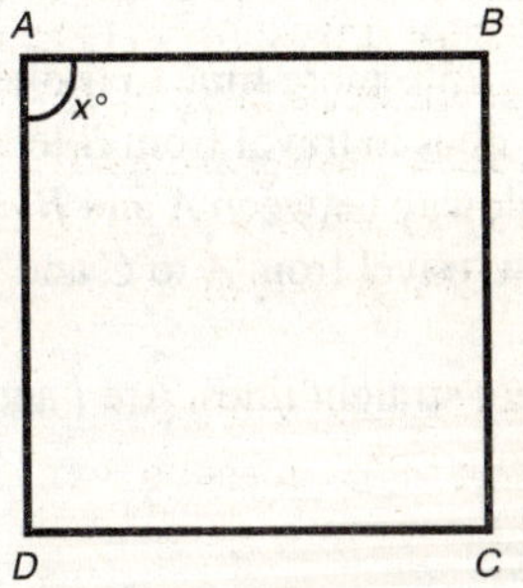

   (1) $AD = AB$
   (2) $x = 90$

7. The XYZ Corporation has 7,000 employees. What is the average yearly wage of an employee of the XYZ Corporation?
   (1) 4,000 of the employees are executives.
   (2) The total amount the company pays in wages each year is $77,000,000.

8. Is $x > y$?
   (1) $(x + y)^2 > 0$
   (2) x is positive

GO ON TO THE NEXT PAGE ➤

4 4 4 4 4 4 4 4 4 4 4

(A) if you can get the answer from **(1) ALONE** but not from (2) alone
(B) if you can get the answer from **(2) ALONE** but not from (1) alone
(C) if you can get the answer from **BOTH (1) and (2) TOGETHER**, but not from (1) alone or (2) alone
(D) if **EITHER** statement **(1) ALONE OR** statement **(2) ALONE** suffices
(E) if you **CANNOT** get the answer from statements (1) and (2) **TOGETHER**, but need even more data

9. How long will it take to travel from *A* to *B*? It takes 4 hours to travel from *A* to *B* and back to *A*.
   (1) It takes 25% more time to travel from *A* to *B* than it does to travel from *B* to *A*.
   (2) *C* is midway between *A* and *B*, and it takes 2 hours to travel from *A* to *C* and back to *A*.

10. *l*, *l'*, and *k* are straight lines. Are *l* and *l'* parallel?
   (1) $x = y$
   (2) $y = z$

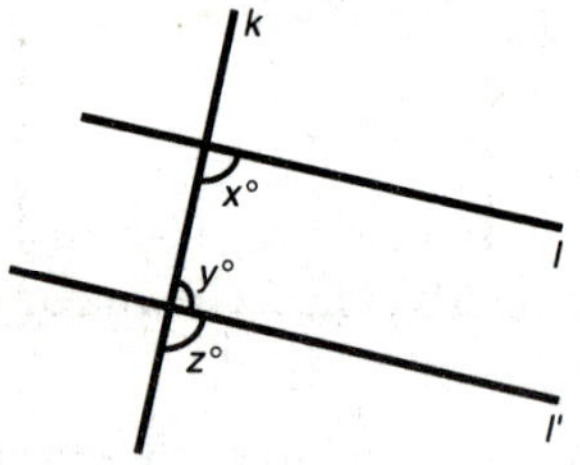

11. What is $x + y + z$?
   (1) $x + y = 3$
   (2) $x + z = 2$

12. If *a*, *b*, and *c* are digits, is $a + b + c$ a multiple of 8? A digit is one of the integers 0, 1, 2, 3, 4, 5, 6, 7, 8, 9.
   (1) The three digit number *abc* is a multiple of 8.
   (2) $a \times b \times c$ is a multiple of 8.

13. Which of the two figures, *ABCD* or *EFGH*, has the largest area?
   (1) The perimeter of *ABCD* is longer than the perimeter of *EFGH*.
   (2) *AC* is longer than *EG*.

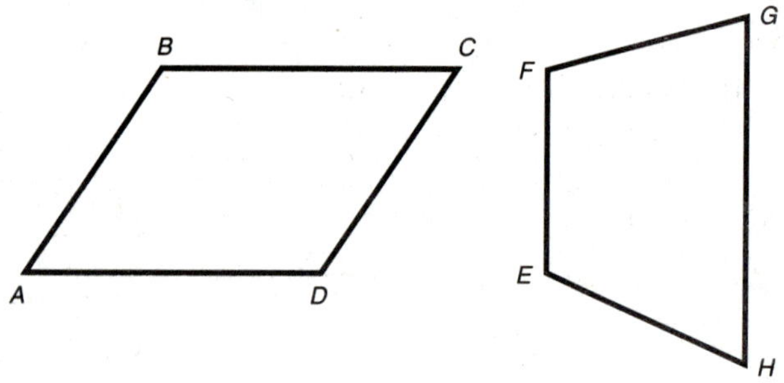

14. Is a number divisible by 9?
   (1) The number is divisible by 3.
   (2) The number is divisible by 27.

GO ON TO THE NEXT PAGE ➤

4 4 4 4 4 4 4 4 4 4 4

(A) if you can get the answer from **(1) ALONE** but not from (2) alone
(B) if you can get the answer from **(2) ALONE** but not from (1) alone
(C) if you can get the answer from **BOTH (1) and (2) TOGETHER**, but not from (1) alone or (2) alone
(D) if **EITHER** statement **(1) ALONE OR** statement **(2) ALONE** suffices
(E) if you **CANNOT** get the answer from statements (1) and (2) **TOGETHER**, but need even more data

15. *ABCD* is a rectangle. Which region, *ABEF* or *CDFE*, has a larger area?

 (1) *BE* is longer than *FD*.
 (2) *BE* is longer than *CD*.

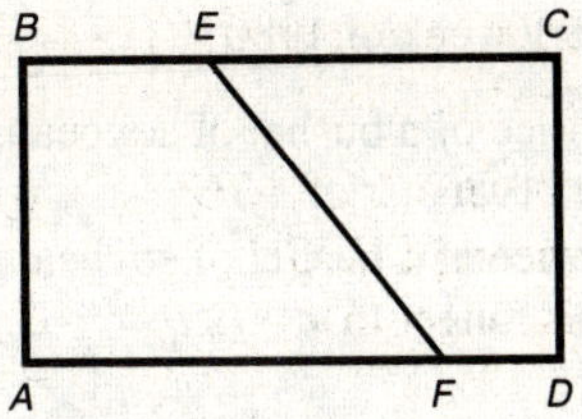

16. Is the integer k odd or even?

 (1) k^2 is odd.
 (2) $2k$ is even.

17. Is x positive?

 (1) $x^2 + 3x - 4 = 0$
 (2) $x > -2$

18. *ABCD* is a square.

 BCO is a semicircle.

 What is the area of *ABOCD*?

 (1) The length of *AC* is $4\sqrt{2}$.
 (2) The radius of the semicircle *BOC* is 2.

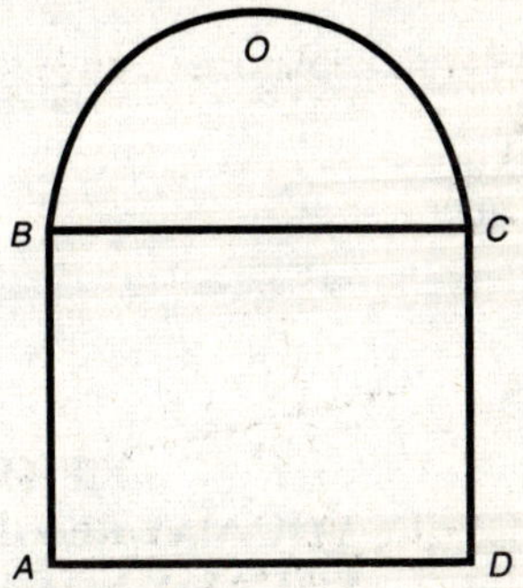

GO ON TO THE NEXT PAGE ➤

4 4 4 4 4 4 4 4 4 4 4

(A) if you can get the answer from **(1) ALONE** but not from (2) alone
(B) if you can get the answer from **(2) ALONE** but not from (1) alone
(C) if you can get the answer from **BOTH (1) and (2) TOGETHER**, but not from (1) alone or (2) alone
(D) if **EITHER** statement **(1) ALONE OR** statement **(2) ALONE** suffices
(E) if you **CANNOT** get the answer from statements (1) and (2) **TOGETHER**, but need even more data

19. Do the points P and Q lie on the same circle with center (0, 0)?

    (1) The coordinates of point P are (2, 3).
    (2) The coordinates of point Q are (4, 1).

20. Is 2^n divisible by 8?

    (1) n is an odd integer.
    (2) n is an integer greater than 5.

21. Did the price of a bushel of soybeans increase during every week of 1980?

    (1) The price of a bushel of soybeans was $2 on Jan. 1, 1980.
    (2) The price of a bushel of soybeans was $4 on Jan. 1, 1981.

STOP

IF THERE IS STILL TIME REMAINING,
YOU MAY REVIEW THE QUESTIONS IN THIS SECTION ONLY.
YOU MAY NOT TURN TO ANY OTHER SECTION OF THE TEST.

5 5 5 5 5 5 5 5 5 5 5

Section 5

TIME: 25 minutes
21 Questions

Directions: This test consists of a number of sentences, in each of which some part or the whole is underlined. Each sentence is followed by five alternative versions of the underlined portion. Select the alternative you consider both most correct and most effective according to the requirements of standard written English. Answer A is the same as the original version; if you think the original version is best, select answer A.

In considering the answer choices, be attentive to matters of grammar, diction, and syntax, as well as clarity, precision, and fluency. Do not select an answer which alters the meaning of the original sentence.

1. If we cooperate together by dividing up the work, we shall be able to finish it quickly.
   (A) If we cooperate together by dividing up the work
   (B) If we cooperate by dividing up the work
   (C) If we cooperate together by dividing the work
   (D) If we cooperate by dividing up the work together
   (E) If we cooperate by dividing the work

2. The vacationers enjoyed swimming in the pool, bathing in the ocean, and, particularly, to snorkel near the reef.
   (A) enjoyed swimming in the pool, bathing in the ocean, and, particularly, to snorkel
   (B) enjoyed swimming in the pool, to bathe in the ocean, and, particularly, to snorkel
   (C) enjoyed swimming in the pool, to bathe in the ocean, and, particularly snorkeling
   (D) enjoyed swimming in the pool, bathing in the ocean, and, particularly, snorkeling
   (E) enjoyed to swim in the pool, to bathe in the ocean, and, particularly, to snorkel

3. Crossing the street, a car almost struck us.
   (A) Crossing the street, a car almost struck us.
   (B) A car almost struck us, crossing the street.
   (C) As we crossed the street, a car almost struck us.
   (D) A car, crossing the street, almost struck us.
   (E) Having crossed the street, a car almost struck us.

4. The theme of this novel is how money doesn't make you happy.
   (A) The theme of this novel is how money doesn't make you happy.
   (B) The theme of this novel is that money doesn't make you happy.
   (C) In this novel, its theme is how money doesn't make you happy.
   (D) In this novel, that money doesn't make you happy is the theme.
   (E) In this novel, you are not made happy by money is the theme.

5. If some Americans look at where they are going, it can be seen that our goal is money.
   (A) look at where they are going, it can be seen that our goal
   (B) look back at where they are going, they see that their goal
   (C) look ahead to where they are going, it can be seen that their goal
   (D) look at where they are going, they can see our goal
   (E) look ahead to where they are going, they can see their goal

GO ON TO THE NEXT PAGE ➤

5 5 5 5 5 5 5 5 5 5 5

6. Mary, a girl with little talent for cooking, enjoys preparing pizza.

   (A) Mary, a girl with little talent for cooking, enjoys preparing
   (B) Mary is a girl who has little talent for cooking who enjoys to prepare
   (C) Mary is a girl with little talent for cooking and who enjoys preparing
   (D) Mary, who has little talent for cooking, enjoys to prepare
   (E) With little talent for cooking, Mary is a girl who enjoys to prepare

7. My grandmother is the most remarkable person of all the persons I have ever met.

   (A) My grandmother is the most remarkable person of all the persons I have ever met.
   (B) Of all the persons I have ever met, my grandmother is the most remarkable person.
   (C) Of all the persons I have ever met, the most remarkable person is my grandmother.
   (D) Of all the persons I have ever met, the most remarkable is my grandmother.
   (E) My grandmother, of all the persons I have ever met, is the most remarkable.

8. Start the motor, and then you should remove the blocks.

   (A) Start the motor, and then you should remove the blocks.
   (B) Start the motor and then remove the blocks.
   (C) Start the motor, then removing the blocks.
   (D) Start the motor, and then the blocks should be removed.
   (E) Starting the motor, the blocks should then be removed.

9. He is a genius, although he is eccentric and wants recognition.

   (A) He is a genius, although he is eccentric and wants recognition.
   (B) Although he is eccentric, he is a genius and wants recognition.
   (C) Although he is eccentric, he is a genius although he wants recognition.
   (D) His is a genius although he is eccentric and although he wants recognition.
   (E) Although he is eccentric and wants recognition, he is a genius.

10. The smaller firms sold either on a price or quality-of-workmanship basis.

    (A) The smaller firms sold either on a price or quality-of-workmanship basis.
    (B) The smaller firms either sold on a price or quality-of-workmanship basis.
    (C) The smaller firms sold on either a price or a quality-of-workmanship basis.
    (D) The smaller firms sold on either a price or on a quality-of-workmanship basis.
    (E) Either the smaller firms sold on a price or on a quality-of-workmanship basis.

11. The matter was referred back to committee since the solution to the problem was different from the one proposed earlier which was not practicable.

    (A) referred back to committee since the solution to the problem was different from the one proposed earlier which was not practicable
    (B) referred to committee since the solution to the problem was different from the one proposed earlier which was not practicable
    (C) referred back to committee since the solution to the problem was different than the one proposed earlier which was not practical
    (D) referred to committee since the solution to the problem was different than the one proposed earlier which was not practicable
    (E) referred back to committee since the solution to the problem was different from the one proposed earlier which was not practical

12. Irregardless of the consequences, the police officer was forbidden from making any pinches.

    (A) Irregardless of the consequences, the police officer was forbidden from making any pinches.
    (B) Irregardless of the consequences, the police officer was forbidden from making any arrests.
    (C) Regardless of the consequences, the police officer was forbidden from making any arrests.
    (D) Irregardless of the consequences, the police officer was forbidden to make any pinches.
    (E) Regardless of the consequences, the police officer was forbidden to make any arrests.

GO ON TO THE NEXT PAGE ➤

5 5 5 5 5 5 5 5 5 5 5

13. The book having been read carefully and extensive notes having been taken, Tom felt confident about the test.

    (A) The book having been read carefully and extensive notes having been taken, Tom
    (B) Tom, who read the book carefully and having taken extensive notes
    (C) Reading the book carefully and taking extensive notes, Tom
    (D) Having read the book carefully and extensive notes having been taken, Tom
    (E) Because he had read the book carefully and had taken extensive notes, Tom

14. He has not only violated the law, but also he has escaped punishment.

    (A) not only violated the law, but also he has escaped punishment
    (B) violated not only the law, but also he has escaped punishment
    (C) violated not only the law, but he has escaped punishment also
    (D) not only violated the law, but also escaped punishment
    (E) not only violated the law, but has escaped punishment

15. Ideally, the fan should be placed in a different room than the one you want to cool.

    (A) the fan should be placed in a different room than
    (B) the fan had ought to be placed in a different room from
    (C) the fan should be placed in a different room from
    (D) the fan had ought to be placed in a different room than
    (E) you should place the fan in a different room than

16. After viewing both movies, John agreed that the first one was the best of the two.

    (A) John agreed that the first one was the best of the two
    (B) John agreed that the first was the best of the two
    (C) John agreed that the first one was the better of the two
    (D) John agreed that of the two the better one was the first
    (E) John agreed that the best of the two was the first

17. Poor product quality angers Bob, who wonders if it is part of a strategy by manufacturers.

    (A) who wonders if it is part of a strategy by manufacturers
    (B) who wonders if manufacturers are part of the strategy
    (C) that wonders if it is part of a strategy by manufacturers
    (D) wondering if this is part of a strategy by manufacturers
    (E) who wonders if they are part of a strategy by manufacturers

18. He noted the dog's soft hair, strong legs, and keen sense of smell.

    (A) the dog's soft hair, strong legs, and keen sense of smell
    (B) the dog's soft hair, strong legs, and that his sense of smell was keen
    (C) the dog's soft hair, and that his legs were strong and sense of smell was keen
    (D) the dog's soft hair, and that his legs were strong and smell was keen
    (E) the dog's soft hair, keen smell and that his legs were strong

19. Having bowed our heads, the minister led us in prayer.

    (A) Having bowed our heads, the minister led
    (B) After we bowed our heads, the minister led
    (C) After we bowed our heads, the minister leads
    (D) After we had bowed our heads, the minister led
    (E) Having bowed our heads, the minister leads

GO ON TO THE NEXT PAGE ➤

20. She seldom ever wants to try and face the true facts.

    (A) seldom ever wants to try and face the true facts
    (B) seldom ever wants to try and face the facts
    (C) seldom ever wants to try to face the facts
    (D) seldom wants to try and face the facts
    (E) seldom wants to try to face the facts

21. The president's talk was directed toward whomever was present.

    (A) was directed toward whomever was present
    (B) was directed toward whoever was present
    (C) was directed at who was present
    (D) was directed at whomever was present
    (E) was directed towards whomever was present

STOP

IF THERE IS STILL TIME REMAINING,
YOU MAY REVIEW THE QUESTIONS IN THIS SECTION ONLY.
YOU MAY NOT TURN TO ANY OTHER SECTION OF THE TEST.

6 6 6 6 6 6 6 6 6 6 6

Section 6

TIME: 25 minutes
17 Questions

Directions: Solve each of the following problems; then indicate the correct answer on the answer sheet.

NOTE: A figure that appears with a problem is drawn as accurately as possible so as to provide information that may help in answering the question. Numbers in this test are real numbers.

1. If the side of a square increases by 40%, then the area of the square increases by

   (A) 16%
   (B) 40%
   (C) 96%
   (D) 116%
   (E) 140%

2. If 28 cartons of soda cost $21.00, then 7 cartons of soda should cost

   (A) $5.25
   (B) $5.50
   (C) $6.40
   (D) $7.00
   (E) $10.50

3. Plane P takes off at 2 A.M. and flies at a constant speed of x mph. Plane Q takes off at 3:30 A.M. and flies the same route as P but travels at a constant speed of y mph. Assuming that y is greater than x, how many hours after 3:30 A.M. will plane Q overtake plane P?

   (A) $\frac{3}{2}x$ hrs.
   (B) $\frac{3}{2}$ hrs.
   (C) $\frac{3}{2y}$ hrs.
   (D) $\frac{3}{2(y-x)}$ hrs.
   (E) $\frac{3x}{2(y-x)}$ hrs.

GO ON TO THE NEXT PAGE ➤

6 6 6 6 6 6 6 6 6 6 6

Use the following table for questions 4–5.

DISTRIBUTION OF TEST SCORES IN A CLASS

Number of Students	*Number of Correct Answers*
10	36 to 40
16	32 to 35
12	28 to 31
14	26 to 27
8	0 to 25

4. What percent of the class answered 32 or more questions correctly?

(A) $16\frac{2}{3}$

(B) 20

(C) $26\frac{2}{3}$

(D) $43\frac{1}{3}$

(E) 52

5. The number of students who answered 28 to 31 questions correctly is x times the number who answered 25 or fewer correctly, where x is

(A) $\frac{2}{3}$

(B) 1

(C) $\frac{3}{2}$

(D) $\frac{7}{4}$

(E) 2

6. If the product of 3 consecutive integers is 210, then the sum of the two smaller integers is

(A) 5
(B) 11
(C) 12
(D) 13
(E) 18

7. Cereal costs $\frac{1}{3}$ as much as bacon. Bacon costs $\frac{5}{4}$ as much as eggs. Eggs cost what fraction of the cost of cereal?

(A) $\frac{5}{12}$

(B) $\frac{4}{5}$

(C) $\frac{5}{4}$

(D) $\frac{5}{3}$

(E) $\frac{12}{5}$

8. A truck gets 15 miles per gallon of gas when it is unloaded. When the truck is loaded, it travels only 80% as far on a gallon of gas as when unloaded. How many gallons will the loaded truck use to travel 80 miles?

(A) $5\frac{1}{3}$

(B) 6

(C) $6\frac{1}{3}$

(D) $6\frac{2}{3}$

(E) $6\frac{3}{4}$

GO ON TO THE NEXT PAGE ➤

9. Both circles have radius 4 and the area enclosed by both circles is 28π. What is the area of the shaded region?

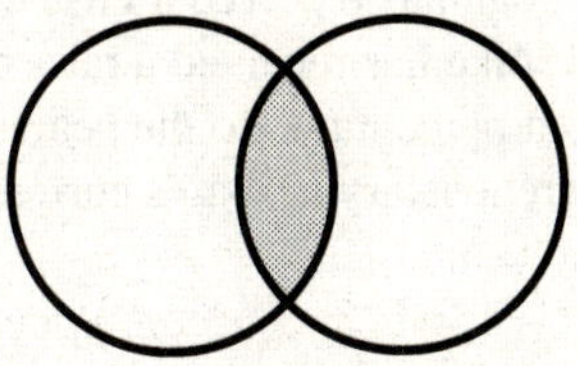

(A) 0
(B) 2π
(C) 4π
(D) $4\pi^2$
(E) 16π

10. For each dollar spent by the sales department, the research department spends 20¢. For every \$4 spent by the research department, the packing department spends \$1.50. The triple ratio of the money spent by the sales department to the money spent by the research department to the money spent by the packing department can be expressed as

(A) 40 : 8 : 3
(B) 20 : 4 : 1
(C) 8 : 4 : 1
(D) 4 : 1 : 5
(E) 2 : 1 : 5

11. *ABCD* has area equal to 28. *BC* is parallel to *AD*. *BA* is perpendicular to *AD*. If *BC* is 6 and *AD* is 8, then what is *CD*?

(A) $2\sqrt{2}$
(B) $2\sqrt{3}$
(C) 4
(D) $2\sqrt{5}$
(E) 6

12. If *X* is an odd integer and *Y* is an even integer, which of the following statements is (are) always true?

I. $X + Y$ is odd.
II. XY is odd.
III. $2X + Y$ is even.

(A) I only
(B) III only
(C) I and III only
(D) II and III only
(E) I, II, and III

GO ON TO THE NEXT PAGE ➤

6 6 6 6 6 6 6 6 6 6 6

13. Find the area of the region inside the circle and outside the square *ABCD*. *A*, *B*, *C*, and *D* are all points on the circle, and the radius of the circle is 4.

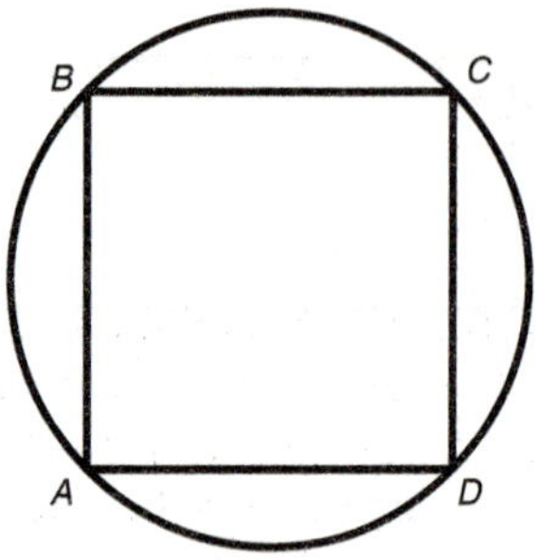

(A) $16\pi - 36$
(B) $16(\pi - 2)$
(C) $16(\pi - 1)$
(D) $16\pi - 4$
(E) 16π

14. $*X$ is defined as the largest integer which is less than X. What is the value of $(*3) + (*4) + (*4.5)$?

(A) 9
(B) 10
(C) 11
(D) 11.5
(E) 12

15. Joan started work 2 years ago. Her starting salary was $\frac{1}{2}$ of Mike's salary at that time. Each year since then Joan has received a raise of 5% in her salary and Mike has received a raise of 10% in his salary. What percentage (to the nearest percent) of Mike's current salary is Joan's current salary?

(A) 45
(B) 46
(C) 48
(D) 50
(E) 220

16. Which of the following integers has the most divisors?

(A) 88
(B) 91
(C) 95
(D) 99
(E) 101

17. The amount of fat in an ounce of food A plus the amount of protein in an ounce of food A is 100 grams. The amount of protein in an ounce of food A minus twice the amount of fat in an ounce of food A is 10 grams. How many grams of protein are there in an ounce of food A?

(A) 30
(B) 45
(C) 50
(D) 55
(E) 70

STOP

**IF THERE IS STILL TIME REMAINING,
YOU MAY REVIEW THE QUESTIONS IN THIS SECTION ONLY.
YOU MAY NOT TURN TO ANY OTHER SECTION OF THE TEST.**

Section 7

TIME: 25 minutes
17 Questions

Directions: For each question, choose the best answer among the listed alternatives.

1. A politician wrote the following: "I realize there are some shortcomings to the questionnaire method. However, since I send a copy of the questionnaire to every home in the district, I believe the results are quite representative . . . I think the numbers received are so large that it is quite accurate even though the survey is not done scientifically."

   The writer of the above statement makes which of the following assumptions:

   (A) Most people who received the questionnaire have replied.
   (B) Most people in the district live in homes.
   (C) The questionnaire method of data collection is unscientific.
   (D) The large number of replies means that a high proportion of those sampled have replied.
   (E) A large, absolute number of replies is synonymous with accuracy.

2. In 1950, Transylvania earned $1 million in tourist revenue. By 1970, tourist revenue doubled and in 1980, it reached the sum of $4 million.

   Each of the following, if true, may explain the trend in tourist revenue except:

   (A) The number of tourists has increased from 1950 to 1980.
   (B) Average expenditure per tourist has increased.
   (C) Average stay per tourist has increased.
   (D) The number of total hotel rooms has increased.
   (E) The average price of tourist services has increased.

3. Donors are almost never offended by being asked for too much (in fact, they are usually flattered). And if you ask for too much, your donor can always suggest a smaller amount. On the other hand, donors are frequently offended by being asked for too little. A common reaction is, "so that's all they think I'm worth."

   The above statement assumes that:

   (A) Donors are usually never asked for enough.
   (B) A good fund raiser will value the worth of the donor.
   (C) It is worth the gamble to ask for large donations.
   (D) Fund raisers often think that donors are incapable of giving much.
   (E) Donors are seldom offended by fund raisers.

4. One major obligation of the social psychologist is to provide his own discipline, the other social sciences, and interested laymen with conceptual tools that will increase the range and the reliability of their understanding of social phenomena. Beyond that, responsible government officials are today turning more frequently to the social scientist for insights into the nature and solution of the problems with which they are confronted.

   The above argument assumes that:

   (A) Social psychologists must have a strong background in other sciences as well as their own.
   (B) A study of social psychology should be a part of the curriculum of government officials.
   (C) The social scientist has an obligation to provide the means by which social phenomena may be understood by others.
   (D) Social phenomena are little understood by those outside the field of social psychology.
   (E) A good social psychologist is obligated principally by the need to solve inter-disciplinary problems.

GO ON TO THE NEXT PAGE ➤

5. New problems require new solutions. And new problems arise with new populations and new technologies. The solutions of these problems require new institutions as well as new political, economic, and social mechanisms. Yet institutions and political and economic arrangements grow slowly and die slowly. Because old institutions die slowly, new institutions should be given every chance of success.

   The writer of the above makes which of the following assumptions:

   (A) New institutions are needed because old institutions are inefficient.
   (B) New institutions are created in order to solve existing problems.
   (C) As old institutions are phased out, new ones take their place.
   (D) If there were no growth, old institutions would die more slowly.
   (E) Socio-technological change requires new forms of institutional arrangements.

6. About 40 percent of American husbands think it is a good idea for wives with school age children to work outside the home. Only one out of ten German household heads approves of mothers working if school age children live at home. Every second American wife, and every third German wife with school age children has a job outside her home.

   If the above is correct, which of the following must be true?

   (A) More German than American wives work outside the home.
   (B) Employment opportunities for American wives are greater than for German wives.
   (C) German husbands have more conservative attitudes than American husbands.
   (D) German husbands would seem to be less satisfied about working wives who have school age children than American husbands.
   (E) German women have fewer children than American women.

7. Building codes required all public buildings constructed after 1980 to have reinforced-steel bomb shelters installed.

   From which of the following can the statement above be inferred?

   (A) Public buildings had to install reinforced-steel bomb shelters after 1980.
   (B) No bomb shelters other than reinforced-steel shelters were installed in public buildings after 1980, but all public buildings constructed after 1980 were required to have bomb shelters.
   (C) Some public buildings constructed before 1980 had installed bomb shelters.
   (D) Bomb shelters were not required in public buildings before 1980, but some were installed voluntarily.
   (E) Before 1980, public buildings had bomb shelters, but not necessarily made of reinforced-steel.

8. In 1950, the average child visited the dentist once a year, by 1970, the number of visits had increased to two. Today, the average child visits the dentist three times a year.

   Each of the following, if true, could explain this trend except:

   (A) Dentist fees have declined over the period.
   (B) Better home care of teeth has reduced the number of cavities.
   (C) Dental care has become less painful.
   (D) Parents are more aware of the importance of dental care.
   (E) Tax benefits for deducting dental expenses have increased.

GO ON TO THE NEXT PAGE ➤

9. Attention is most often focused on net exports (exports less imports) because that figure measures the net effect of a nation's trade in goods and services with the rest of the world. In 1968, net exports were 5.8 percent of GNP (Gross National Product) and in 1975, they were 6.8 percent.

   If the information above is accurate, which of the following must be true?

   (A) If GNP was constant from 1968 to 1975, net exports were greater in 1975 than in 1968.
   (B) Exports were greater than imports in 1975, but not in 1968.
   (C) Exports increased from 1968 to 1975.
   (D) In 1975, the increase in exports was nearly double that in 1968.
   (E) In 1968, net exports were greater than in 1975.

10. Once a company has established an extensive sales network in a foreign market and therefore has achieved substantial sales, it seems that these markets should be treated in a very similar fashion to those in one's own country. It is therefore those countries where only initial sales and representation have been developed where marketing methods will have to differ from domestic activities.

    The above statement assumes that:

    (A) Sales networks can be the same in both foreign and domestic markets.
    (B) Extensive sales networks are preferable to less developed ones.
    (C) Some countries develop economically faster than others.
    (D) Larger markets abroad are more adaptable to domestic marketing methods.
    (E) A study of marketing should consider the adaptability of advertising campaigns in different countries.

11. The principal monetary policy objective is to reduce substantially the import surplus of the coming years while resuming economic growth. Realization of this goal entails a marked structural change of the economy, which can be brought about by freezing the standard of living (per capita private consumption plus public services) and restricting investments that do not further exports.

    The writer of the above policy assumes that:

    (A) Economic growth will result in a structural change of the economy.
    (B) Only if people consume less can the economy grow.
    (C) The import surplus can be reduced if investment is restricted.
    (D) Only a structural change in the economy can substantially increase imports.
    (E) People will have to be persuaded to give up consumption for the national good.

12. The most commonly cited explanation for nationalization of foreign companies is a change in government. Nationalization tends to cover a wide range of industries and is not selective by country of ownership.

    The above statement assumes that:

    (A) Defense-related, government-related, and natural resource industries are most likely to be nationalized.
    (B) The process of nationalization is not limited to any particular industry or country.
    (C) Nationalization of businesses is so widespread as to cause concern.
    (D) Nationalization will not occur in countries with democratic governments.
    (E) Sharing ownership with local nationals will forestall takeovers by foreign governments.

GO ON TO THE NEXT PAGE ➤

13. In 1985 there were 20 deaths from automobile accidents per 1,000 miles traveled. A total of 20,000 miles were traveled via automobiles in 1985. In the same year, 800 people died in airplane crashes and 400 people were killed in train disasters. A statistician concluded from these data alone that it was more dangerous to travel by plane, train, and automobile, in that order.

    Which of the following refutes the statistician's conclusion?

    (A) There is no common denominator by which to compare the number of deaths resulting from each mode of travel.
    (B) One year is insufficient to reach such a conclusion.
    (C) More people travel by car than any other mode of transport, therefore, the probability of a car accident is greater.
    (D) The number of plane flights and train trips is not stated.
    (E) The probability of being killed in a train disaster and as a result of a car crash is the same.

14. From a letter to the commercial editor of a newspaper: Your article of January 9 drew attention to the large deficit in Playland's balance of payments that has worsened over the past three years. Yet, you favor the recent trade treaty signed between Playland and Workland. That treaty results in a lowering of our import duties that will flood us with Workland's goods. This will only exacerbate our balance of trade. How can you be in favor of the treaty?

    Which of the following considerations would weaken the letter writer's argument?

    (A) Import diversion versus import creation.
    (B) Prices paid by importers versus prices paid by consumers.
    (C) Economic goals versus political goals.
    (D) Duties levied increase government revenue.
    (E) Free trade versus protectionism.

15. In 1930, there were, on the average 10 deaths at birth (infant mortality) per 10,000 population. By 1940 there were 8.5, and by 1950, 7.0. Today there are 5.5 deaths at birth per 10,000 population, and it is anticipated that the downward trend will continue.

    Each of the following, if true, would help to account for this trend except:

    (A) Medical care is more widespread and available.
    (B) More effective birth control methods have been implemented.
    (C) Sanitary conditions have improved.
    (D) The number of pediatricians per 10,000 population has increased.
    (E) Midwifery has declined in favor of medical doctors.

16. Product shipments of household appliances are expected to rise to $17 billion next year, an average annual increase of 8.0 percent over the past five years. The real growth rate, after allowing for probable price increases, is expected to be about 4.3 percent each year, resulting in shipments this year of $14 billion in 1987 dollars.

    Each of the following, if true, could help to account for this trend except:

    (A) Increased consumer spending for durable products.
    (B) Household formations have increased.
    (C) Consumer disposable income has increased.
    (D) The consumer price of electricity has decreased.
    (E) Individual tax advantages have decreased.

GO ON TO THE NEXT PAGE ➤

7 7 7 7 7 7 7 7 7 7 7

17. Following is a proposal to amend the constitution of a fraternal club as forwarded to its members for approval:

    When more than one candidate is a nominee for an office, prospective candidates must consent to nomination and, before giving such consent, must be shown the list of all nominees.

    Which of the following statements about the proposal is logical if it cannot be known who the actual candidates are until prospective candidates have consented to be nominated?

    (A) The proposal would guarantee that there would always be more than one candidate.
    (B) If there is more than one prospective candidate, the proposal would preclude any of them from being a nominee.
    (C) The proposal would ensure a wider choice of candidates.
    (D) If there is more than one candidate, a given candidate could withdraw before becoming a nominee.
    (E) The proposal would ensure that each candidate knows the identity of the others

STOP

IF THERE IS STILL TIME REMAINING,
YOU MAY REVIEW THE QUESTIONS IN THIS SECTION ONLY.
YOU MAY NOT TURN TO ANY OTHER SECTION OF THE TEST.

Answers
SAMPLE TEST 3

Section 1 [Reading Comprehension]

1	C	6	B	11	A	16	E	21	E
2	C	7	A	12	D	17	A	22	D
3	D	8	E	13	C	18	C	23	C
4	C	9	B	14	D	19	D	24	E
5	C	10	B	15	A	20	D	25	E

Section 2 [Problem Solving]

1	B	6	E	11	C	16	E	21	
2	D	7	D	12	B	17	C	22	
3	E	8	C	13	B	18		23	
4	A	9	A	14	E	19		24	
5	D	10	E	15	D	20		25	

Section 3 [Critical Reasoning]

1	C	6	D	11	B	16	E	21	
2	B	7	A	12	C	17	B	22	
3	C	8	E	13	B	18		23	
4	C	9	B	14	A	19		24	
5	A	10	A	15	D	20		25	

Section 4 [Data Sufficiency]

1	D	6	E	11	E	16	A	21	E
2	C	7	B	12	E	17	C	22	
3	E	8	E	13	E	18	D	23	
4	D	9	A	14	B	19	C	24	
5	C	10	C	15	A	20	B	25	

Section 5 [Sentence Correction]

1	E	6	A	11	B	16	C	21	B
2	D	7	D	12	E	17	A	22	
3	C	8	B	13	E	18	A	23	
4	B	9	E	14	D	19	D	24	
5	E	10	C	15	C	20	E	25	

Section 6 [Problem Solving]

1	C	6	B	11	D	16	A	21	
2	A	7	E	12	C	17	E	22	
3	E	8	D	13	B	18		23	
4	D	9	C	14	A	19		24	
5	C	10	A	15	B	20		25	

Section 7 [Critical Reasoning]

1	E	6	D	11	E	16	E	21	
2	D	7	B	12	B	17	B	22	
3	C	8	B	13	A	18		23	
4	C	9	A	14	A	19		24	
5	E	10	D	15	B	20		25	

Self-Scoring Guide—Analytical Writing

Evaluate your writing tests (or have a friend or teacher evaluate them for you) on the following basis. Read each essay completely, paying special attention to its logical organization and use of examples and facts to buttress its claims or position. Assign a holistic score between 0 and 6, using the scale below. Your writing score will be the average of the scores of the two essays.

6	**Outstanding**	Cogent, well-articulated analysis of the issue or critique of the argument. Develops a position with insightful reasons and persuasive examples. Well organized. Superior command of language and variety of syntax. Only minor flaws in grammar, usage, and mechanics.
5	**Strong**	Well-developed analysis or critique. Develops a position with well-chosen examples or reasons. Generally well organized. Clear control of language and variety of syntax. Minor flaws in grammar, usage, and mechanics.
4	**Adequate**	Competent analysis or critique. Develops a position with relevant reasons or examples. Adequately organized. Adequate control of language, but may lack syntactic variety. May have some flaws in grammar, usage, and mechanics.
3	**Limited**	Competent but clearly flawed analysis or critique. Vague or limited in developing a position. Poorly organized. Weak in using relevant examples or reasons. Language used imprecisely or lacking in sentence variety. Contains major errors or frequent minor errors in grammar, usage, and mechanics.
2	**Seriously Flawed**	Serious weaknesses in analysis and organization. Unclear or seriously limited in presenting or developing a position. Disorganized. Few relevant examples or reasons. Frequent serious problems in language and sentence structure. Numerous errors in grammar, usage, or mechanics that interfere with meaning.
1	**Fundamentally Deficient**	Little evidence of ability to organize and develop a coherent response to issue or argument. Severe and persistent errors in language and sentence structure. Pervasive pattern of errors in grammar, usage, and mechanics that severely interfere with meaning.
0	**Unscorable**	Illegible or not written on the assigned topic.

Analysis

Section 1
Reading Comprehension

The passage for questions 1–8 appears on page 360.

1. According to the passage, the chief element in Marx's analysis of capitalist exploitation was the doctrine of

(A) just wages
(B) the price system
(C) surplus value
(D) predatory production
(E) subsistence work

(C) See paragraph 2, line 1.

2. *Das Capital* differs from the *Communist Manifesto* in that it

(A) was written with the help of Friedrich Engels
(B) retreated from Marx's earlier revolutionary stance
(C) expressed a more fully developed form of Marxist theory
(D) denounced the predatory nature of the capitalist system
(E) expressed sympathy for the plight of the middle class

(C) See paragraph 1, sentence 2: "His maturer theories of society . . ."

3. According to the passage, Marx ended his life

I. a believer in non-violent revolution
II. accepting violent revolution
III. a major social theorist

(A) I only
(B) III only
(C) I and III only
(D) II and III only
(E) Neither I, II, nor III

(D) See paragraph 1: ". . . he ended life as a major social theorist . . . sympathetic with violent revolution. . . ."

4. The author suggests that the Communist regime in Russia may best be categorized as a(n)

(A) proletarian movement
(B) social government
(C) imperialistic state
(D) revolutionary government
(E) social democracy

(C) See paragraph 3: ". . . Russia . . . is no longer a proletarian movement . . . but a camouflaged imperialistic effort. . . ."

5. Marx's social philosophy is now generally accepted by

(A) centrist labor groups
(B) most labor unions
(C) left-wing labor unions
(D) only those in Communist countries
(E) only those in Russia

(C) See paragraph 3. Of course, it is accepted by some of those in (D) and (E), but also by those in (C).

6. It can be concluded that the author of the passage is

(A) sympathetic to Marx's ideas
(B) unsympathetic to Marx's ideas
(C) uncritical of Marx's interpretation of history
(D) a believer in Hegelian philosophy
(E) a Leninist-Marxist

(B) This can be deduced from the last paragraph.

7. Which of the following classes did Marx believe should control the economy?

(A) The working class
(B) The upper class
(C) The middle class
(D) The lower class
(E) The capitalist class

(A) See paragraph 2.

8. According to Marx, a social and economic revolution could take place through

I. parliamentary procedures
II. political action
III. violent revolution

(A) I only
(B) III only
(C) I or II only
(D) II or III only
(E) I, II, or III

(E) All these are mentioned in paragraph 1.

The passage for questions 9–16 appears on page 362.

9. Alexander Hamilton's philosophy was that federal fiscal policies should

(A) be expansionary
(B) encourage economic growth
(C) be determined by Congress
(D) encourage a balanced budget
(E) be determined by the President

(B) See paragraph 2: ". . . fiscal policies should be designed to encourage economic growth."

10. Hamilton's successors

I. followed his economic philosophy of "plans of finance"
II. followed his social philosophy
III. did not follow his philosophy of strong executive leadership

(A) I only
(B) III only
(C) I and II only
(D) II and III only
(E) I, II, and III

(B) See paragraph 2: they did not.

11. In the history of U.S. fiscal management, spending estimates were *first* considered by the

(A) Committee of the Whole
(B) Appropriations Committee
(C) Ways and Means Committee
(D) Commission on Efficiency and Economy
(E) General Accounting Office

(A) See paragraph 3: the Committee of the Whole.

12. At the end of the nineteenth century, there was a need for

(A) more restrained executive leadership
(B) a new finance commission
(C) more Congressional interest in finance
(D) overall reform of financial management
(E) creation of a new Appropriations committee

(D) See paragraph 4, line 1.

13. The "executive budget" was first used

(A) by Alexander Hamilton
(B) in the 19th century
(C) in the first decade of the 20th century
(D) by President Eisenhower
(E) by President Truman

(C) See paragraph 5: "In the first decade of the twentieth century, an 'executive budget' came into successful use. . . ."

14. President Taft's federal budget was

(A) based on procedures used by some European governments
(B) enthusiastically accepted by Congress
(C) a partial cause of accounting chaos during World War I
(D) rejected by Congress
(E) vilified by the public

(D) See paragraph 5: it was rejected.

15. In 1921, the responsibility for preparation and execution of the federal budget fell upon the

(A) President
(B) Congress
(C) Bureau of the Budget
(D) House of Representatives
(E) Senate

(A) See paragraph 6, line 1: the responsibility was given by the Budget and Accounting Act of 1921.

16. All of the following are true about the Bureau of the Budget except

(A) its Director is appointed by the President
(B) it assists the President in budgetary matters
(C) its Director need not be approved by the Senate
(D) it was established in 1921
(E) its Director serves for a 15-year term

(E) See paragraph 6: the Director of the Bureau of the Budget serves for an indefinite term.

The passage for questions 17–25 appears on page 364.

17. According to the passage, Indians who migrated to what is now the United States originated in

(A) Asia
(B) Africa
(C) South America
(D) Alaska
(E) Patagonia

(A) See paragraph 2.

18. Physical differences among Indians who migrated to Alaska can be accounted for by the fact that they came

(A) from different places
(B) from different tribes
(C) at different times
(D) from different races
(E) to different places

(C) See paragraph 2: they came at different times.

19. It is estimated that Indians first came to what is now the United States about

(A) 5,000 years ago
(B) 10,000 years ago
(C) 15,000 years ago
(D) 25,000 years ago
(E) 50,000 years ago

(D) See paragraph 2.

20. The author is most interested in discussing the Indians'

(A) cultural background
(B) eating habits
(C) technical abilities
(D) migration patterns
(E) physical characteristics

(D) Paragraphs 2 and 4 especially mention the various points of migration which the Indians reached.

21. According to the passage, the southernmost area reached by the earliest Indians was the

(A) northern prairies
(B) upper Mississippi
(C) Great Lakes
(D) Mackenzie River valley
(E) Gulf States

(E) See paragraph 4.

22. Particularly noted for their hunting prowess were the Indians of

(A) Mississippi
(B) Southern Alberta
(C) the Mackenzie River valley
(D) New Mexico
(E) the American prairies

(D) See paragraph 3: ". . . the New Mexico Indians were very successful big game hunters."

23. What characteristics of Indian culture remained fairly stable despite the Indian migrations?

I. Language
II. Physical type
III. Technical abilities

(A) I only
(B) III only
(C) I and II only
(D) II and III only
(E) I, II, and III

(C) See the last line of paragraph 4.

24. Which animals were hunted by the Indians when they first migrated to the Americas?

I. Bison
II. Wooly mammoth
III. Camel

(A) I only
(B) III only
(C) I and II only
(D) II and III only
(E) I, II, and III

(E) All these are given in paragraph 3.

25. The passage most likely was written by a(n)

(A) economist
(B) historian
(C) educator
(D) social scientist
(E) anthropologist

(E) Certainly, alternatives (A) and (C) do not correspond to the contents of the passage, while (B) and (D) are too general. The main point in the passage is the migration of Indians, their cultures, and their acclimation to new surroundings. These subjects are in the domain of the anthropologist.

Section 2
Problem Solving

(Numbers in parentheses at the end of each explanation indicate the section in the Mathematics Review where material addressed in the question is discussed.)

1. A college has raised 75% of the amount it needs for a new building by receiving an average donation of $60 from the people already solicited. The people already solicited represent 60% of the people the college will ask for donations. If the college is to raise exactly the amount needed for the new building, how much must the remaining people donate per person?

(A) $25
(B) $30
(C) $40
(D) $50
(E) $60

(B) Let T be the total amount needed for the building and let L be the total number of people the college will ask for donations. Then there are $.4L$ people left to give donations and they must donate a total of $.25T$. So, if A denotes the amount donated per person by the remaining people, then $(.4L) \times A = .25T$. This equation can be solved for A to yield $A = \frac{(.25T)}{(.4L)} = \left(\frac{5}{8}\right)\left(\frac{T}{L}\right)$. Since 75% of the total was raised by an average donation of $60 each from 60% of the people, we know that $\$60 \times .6L = .75T$. So $\$36L = .75T$, which gives $\frac{T}{L} = \frac{\$36}{.75} = \$48$.

Therefore $A = \left(\frac{5}{8}\right)\$48 = \$30$.

You can avoid the algebra by using a convenient value for the number of donors, such as 100. That means 60 donors have already donated an average of $60 each, for a total of $3,600. Since this is 75% of the total, the total needed is $4,800, which leaves $1,200 to be given by the 40 remaining donors. So the average gift will be $\frac{\$1,200}{40} = \$30$. (II-3)

2. If a worker can pack $\frac{1}{6}$ of a carton of canned food in 15 minutes and there are 40 workers in a factory, how many cartons should be packed in the factory in $1\frac{2}{3}$ hours?

(A) 16

(B) $40\frac{2}{9}$

(C) $43\frac{4}{9}$

(D) $44\frac{4}{9}$

(E) $45\frac{2}{3}$

(D) Since 15 minutes is $\frac{1}{4}$ of an hour, each worker can pack $4 \times \frac{1}{6}$ or $\frac{2}{3}$ of a case an hour. The factory has 40 workers, so they should pack $40 \times \frac{2}{3}$ or $\frac{80}{3}$ cases each hour. Therefore, in $1\frac{2}{3}$ or $\frac{5}{3}$ hours the factory should pack $\left(\frac{5}{3} \times \frac{80}{3}\right)$, which equals $\frac{400}{9}$ or $44\frac{4}{9}$ cases. (II-3)

3. Which of the following inequalities is the solution to the inequality $7x - 5 < 2x + 18$?

(A) $x < \frac{13}{5}$

(B) $x > \frac{23}{9}$

(C) $x < \frac{23}{9}$

(D) $x > \frac{23}{5}$

(E) $x < \frac{23}{5}$

(E) Simply use the properties of inequalities to solve the given inequality. Subtract $2x$ from each side to get $5x - 5 < 18$. Next add 5 to each side to obtain $5x < 23$. Finally divide each side by 5 to get $x < \frac{23}{5}$. (II-9)

4. A truck driver must complete a 180-mile trip in 4 hours. If he averages 50 miles an hour for the first three hours of his trip, how fast must he travel in the final hour?

(A) 30 mph
(B) 35 mph
(C) 40 mph
(D) 45 mph
(E) 50 mph

(A) Since the truck driver averaged 50 miles per hour for the first three hours, he traveled 3×50 or 150 miles during the first three hours. Since he needs to travel 180 – 150 miles in the final hour, he should drive at 30 mph. (II-3)

5. If a triangle has base *B* and the altitude of the triangle is twice the base, then the area of the triangle is

(A) $\frac{1}{2}AB$
(B) AB
(C) $\frac{1}{2}B^2$
(D) B^2
(E) $2B^2$

(D) The area of a triangle is $\frac{1}{2}$ the base times the altitude. The altitude is $2B$, so the area is $\left(\frac{1}{2}\right)(B)(2B)$ or B^2. (III-7)

6. If the product of two numbers is 10 and the sum of the two numbers is 7, then the larger of the two numbers is

(A) –2
(B) 2
(C) 3
(D) $4\frac{1}{4}$
(E) 5

(E) If we denote the two numbers by x and y, then $xy = 10$ and $x + y = 7$. Then x is $7 - y$ and $(7 - y)y = 7y - y^2 = 10$ or $y^2 - 7y + 10 = 0$. But $y^2 - 7y + 10 = (y - 5)(y - 2)$; so the two numbers are 5 and 2. If you can't obtain the quadratic equation or factor the expression, you can still solve the problem. Divide each given answer into 10 and see if the result and the divisor add up to 7. (II-2)

7. If the lengths of the two sides of a right triangle adjacent to the right angle are 8 and 15 respectively, then the length of the side opposite the right angle is

(A) $\sqrt{258}$
(B) 15.8
(C) 16
(D) 17
(E) 17.9

(D) According to the Pythagorean theorem, the length squared equals $8^2 + 15^2$, which is 289. So the length of the side opposite the right angle is 17. If you don't remember that the square root of 289 is 17, see which answer squared gives 289. You can eliminate choice (A) without any calculation. Start with the integer answers, since they are the easiest to calculate. Since $16 \times 16 = 256$, the correct answer must be greater than 16, so you can eliminate choices (B) and (C). Even if you got no further than this, you should guess one of the two remaining choices. (III-4)

8. It costs x¢ each to print the first 600 copies of a newspaper. It costs $\left(x - \frac{y}{10}\right)$¢ for every copy after the first 600. How much does it cost to print 1,500 copies of the newspaper?

(A) $1500x$¢
(B) $150y$¢
(C) $(1500x - 90y)$¢
(D) $\$(150x - 9y)$
(E) $\$15x$

(C) The first 600 copies cost a total of $600x$¢. There are 1,500 – 600 or 900 copies after the first 600, each of which costs $\left(x - \frac{y}{10}\right)$¢; so the 900 copies cost 900 $\left(x - \frac{y}{10}\right)$¢, which equals $(900x - 90y)$¢. Therefore, the total cost is $(1500x - 90y)$¢. (II-3)

9. Which of the following sets of values for $w, x, y,$ and z respectively are possible if $ABCD$ is a parallelogram?

I. 50, 130, 50, 130
II. 60, 110, 70, 120
III. 60, 150, 50, 150

(A) I only
(B) II only
(C) I and II only
(D) I and III only
(E) I, II, and III

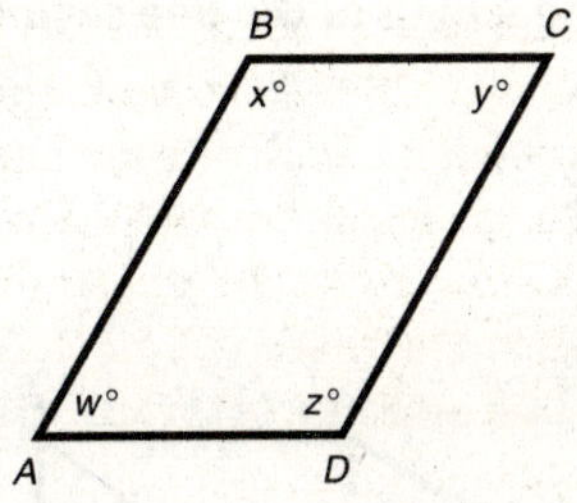

(A) The sum of the angles of a parallelogram (which is 4-sided) must be (4 – 2) 180° = 360°. Since the sum of the values in III is 410, III cannot be correct. The sum of the numbers in II is 360, but in a parallelogram opposite angles must be equal so x must equal z and y must equal w. Since 60 is unequal to 70, II cannot be correct. The sum of the values in I is 360 and opposite angles will be equal, so I is correct. (III-5)

10. John weighs twice as much as Marcia. Marcia's weight is 60% of Bob's weight. Dave weighs 50% of Lee's weight. Lee weighs 190% of John's weight. Which of these 5 persons weighs the least?

(A) Bob
(B) Dave
(C) John
(D) Lee
(E) Marcia

(E) John weighs twice as much as Marcia, so John cannot weigh the least. Marcia's weight is less than Bob's weight, so Bob's weight is not the least. Dave's weight is $\frac{1}{2}$ of Lee's weight, so Lee can't weigh the least. The only possible answers are Marcia or Dave. Let $J, M, B, D,$ and L stand for the weights of John, Marcia, Bob, Dave, and Lee respectively. Then $D = .5L = .5(1.9)J$. So $D = .95J$. Since $J = 2M$, we know $M = .5J$. Therefore Marcia weighs the least. (II-2)

11. The sum of 5 consecutive integers is 35. How many of the five consecutive integers are prime numbers?

(A) 0
(B) 1
(C) 2
(D) 3
(E) 4

(C) Since the sum of the integers is 35, the average is $\frac{35}{5} = 7$. So the "middle" integer should be near 7. Since $5 + 6 + 7 + 8 + 9 = 35$, the five integers are 5, 6, 7, 8, and 9. 6 and 8 are not primes because they are divisible by 2; 9 is not a prime since it is divisible by 3. Only 5 and 7 are primes, so two of the five integers are primes. (I-1)

12. The assessed value of a house is $72,000. The assessed value is 60% of the market value of the house. If taxes are $3 for every $1,000 of the market value of the house, how much are the taxes on the house?

(A) $216
(B) $360
(C) $1,386
(D) $2,160
(E) $3,600

(B) First find the market value of the house. If M is the market value, then 60% of M is $72,000. So $.6M = \$72{,}000$, which means $M = \frac{\$72{,}000}{.6} = \$120{,}000$. The tax rate is $3 for every $1,000 or .003. Therefore thetaxes are $.003 \times \$120{,}000 = \$360$. (I-3, I-4)

13. If the operation * is defined by $*a = a^2 - 2$, then $*(*5)$ is

(A) 23
(B) 527
(C) 529
(D) 621
(E) 623

(B) First evaluate *5. Using the given rule, *5 is $(5 \times 5) - 2 = 25 - 2 = 23$. So *(*5) is *23, which is $(23 \times 23) - 2 = 529 - 2 = 527$. (I-8, II-1)

14. If $\frac{y}{x} = \frac{1}{3}$ and $x + 2y = 10$, then x is

(A) 2
(B) 3
(C) 4
(D) 5
(E) 6

(E) Since $\frac{y}{x} = \frac{1}{3}$, cross multiply to obtain $x = 3y$. Substitute $x = 3y$ into $x + 2y = 10$ to get $3y + 2y = 5y = 10$. Therefore $y = 2$, so $x = 6$. You can check that $\frac{2}{6} = \frac{1}{3}$ and $6 + 2(2) = 10$, so you know your answer is correct. (II-2, II-5)

15. What is the area of the parallelogram *ABCD*? The coordinates of the points are: $A = (1, -1)$, $B = (2, 2)$, $C = (5, 2)$ and $D = (4, -1)$.

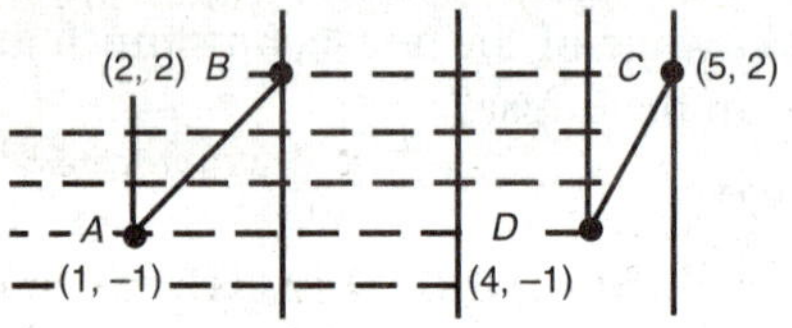

(A) 3
(B) 4
(C) $4\frac{1}{2}$
(D) 9
(E) 10

(D) The area of a parallelogram is the altitude times the base. Since the bottom is part of the line $y = -1$ and the top is part of the line $y = 2$, an altitude is the distance between these two lines. This distance is $|2 - (-1)| = 3$. Since a base is the segment from $(1, -1)$ to $(4, -1)$, the base is $|4 - 1| = 3$. Therefore the area is $3 \times 3 = 9$. (III-7, III-9)

16. The area of a rectangular field is 1,000 square yards. If the length of the field is y yards, then how many yards is the perimeter of the field?

(A) $y + \frac{1{,}000}{y}$
(B) $2y + 1{,}000$
(C) 1,000
(D) $2y + \frac{1{,}000}{y}$
(E) $2y + \frac{2{,}000}{y}$

(E) The perimeter of a rectangle is 2(length) + 2(width). Since we know the length is y, we need to find the width. The area of a rectangle is (length) × (width). So the fact that the area is 1,000 square yards gives the equation y(width) = 1,000. Solving for the width, we get width = $\frac{1{,}000}{y}$. Therefore the perimeter is $2y + 2\left(\frac{1{,}000}{y}\right) = 2y + \frac{2{,}000}{y}$. (III-7)

17. The figure *ABCDEFGH* is a cube. $AB = 10$. What is the length of the line segment *AF*?

(A) 10
(B) $10\sqrt{2}$
(C) $10\sqrt{3}$
(D) 20
(E) $10\sqrt{5}$

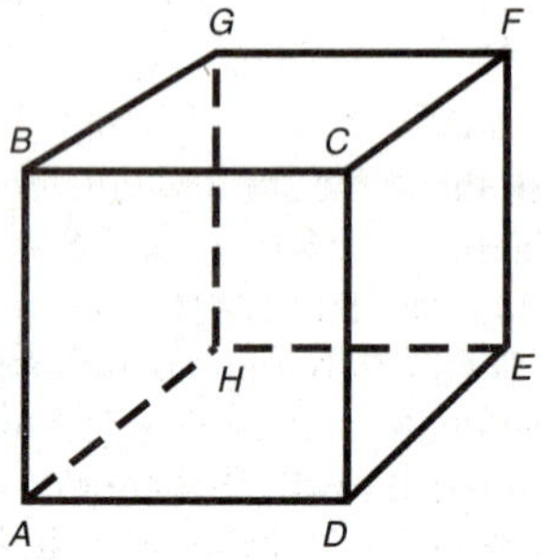

(C) Since the figure is a cube, *ADEH* is a square whose sides have length 10. Therefore *AE*, which is a diagonal of the square, has length $\sqrt{10^2 + 10^2} = \sqrt{200}$. Since *FE* is perpendicular to *AE*, the triangle *AEF* is a right triangle. So *AF* squared is equal to the sum of the square of *AE* and the square of *FE*. Therefore $AF = \sqrt{200 + 10^2} = \sqrt{200 + 100} = \sqrt{300} = \sqrt{3} \times \sqrt{100} = 10\sqrt{3}$. (III-8, III-9)

Section 3
Critical Reasoning

1. Myra: The number of freeway accidents this year in the state of North Carolina, where the speed limit on freeways was lowered to fifty miles an hour two years ago, is clear evidence that speed restrictions rigorously enforced, make drivers more aware of the dangers of going too fast.

Lewis: Wrong. A close look at the records shows that the number of freeway accidents has been falling ever since the formation of a new special traffic division, which happened two years before the lowering of the speed limit.

Which of the following best describes the weak point in Myra's statement upon which Lewis focuses?

(A) The decrease in freeway accidents may be a temporary phenomenon.
(B) The evidence Myra cites comes only from one source—the state of North Carolina.
(C) Myra's claim leaves open the possibility that the cause she cites came after the effect she attributes to it.
(D) No exact statistics for freeway accidents are given by Myra.
(E) No mention is made of deaths caused on roads other than freeways.

(C) It is true that the condition cited by Myra as evidence might be only temporary (A) and also that Myra uses a generalization based on only one source (B), but Lewis does not react to either of these. Lewis' reply also ignores deaths caused on roads other than freeways (E). Further, the fact that no statistics are given (D) has no bearing on Myra's conclusion. So none of these is an appropriate answer. Choice (C) is the correct answer. Myra cites the fact that the number of freeway accidents in North Carolina has decreased with the new speed limit as evidence that this new policy and freeway accidents are causally related. However, Myra fails to establish specifically that the number of freeway accidents was higher under the previous speed limit. Lewis' response centers on this omission.

2. **The Pistons have more points than the Nuggets. The Bullets have less points than the Lakers. The Nuggets and the Suns have the same number of points. The Suns have more points than the Bullets.**

   If the above is true, which of the following must also be true?

   (A) The Nuggets have fewer points than the Bullets.
   (B) The Pistons have more points than the Bullets.
   (C) The Nuggets have fewer points than the Lakers.
   (D) The Lakers have more points than the Pistons.
   (E) The Lakers have more points than the Suns.

(B) Answer alternative (A) can be shown false from the information given—namely, that the Nuggets and the Suns have the same number of points and that the Suns have more points than the Bullets. Choices (C), (D), and (E) might be correct, but it is not possible to confirm these facts from the information given in the paragraph. Details on the number of points the Lakers have in relation to the other teams is not provided. (B) can be demonstrated to be true, since the Bullets have fewer points than the Suns, who have the same number of points as the Nuggets; the Nuggets, therefore, have more points than the Bullets. The Pistons have more points than the Nuggets and, therefore, more than the Bullets.

The information in the passage can best be summarized in the following diagram.

$$B \; {}^{\angle\, L} < S = N < P$$

3. **The states of New York, Ohio, Pennsylvania, and California provide extensive free higher education to their residents. These states are representative of different geographic areas of the United States. There is little reason why most states cannot provide the same service to their residents.**

   Which of the following, if true, would weaken the above argument?

   (A) Free education is not guaranteed by the constitution.
   (B) New York, Ohio, Pennsylvania and California have more qualified high school graduates than other states.
   (C) Most other states do not have the tax base that New York, Ohio, Pennsylvania and California have.
   (D) Other states do not have as many high school graduates.
   (E) Quality education cannot be free; it must be paid for.

(C) It can be argued that New York, Ohio, Pennsylvania, and California have large populations and extensive industry and thus a wide tax base from which to finance higher education. Most other states (there are some exceptions) do not have such an extensive tax base. The argument in the statement is a fallacy of analogy, incorrectly making an analogy between the four states mentioned and most other states. Fewer high school graduates in the other states (B) and (D) could imply reduced costs and thus could possibly strengthen the argument. The fact that free education is not guaranteed (A) does not preclude its being offered and is not relevant to the argument. Alternative (E), a statement of opinion, is also not relevant; the quality of education is not mentioned in the statement.

4. Professor Archibald had the task of giving grades (ranging from A–D in descending value) to his 100 students, based upon the marks they received in three examinations in which the passing mark was 50%. He is instructed to follow the following criteria:

I. All students that scored between 90 and 100% in any two examinations could receive an A grade.
II. Students that came in the top decile overall were to be awarded an A.
III. Notwithstanding I and II, if any student failed an exam, the highest he or she could get was a B.
IV. The top 20 students in the whole year, when the overall exam percentages were averaged, could receive an A.

Given the above criteria, which of the following, in the absence of further information, would definitely not be permissible?

(A) A. Brown, who got 95% in Chemistry and 92% in Biology, received a B grade.
(B) B. White, who was first in Physics and got 96% in History, received a B grade.
(C) C. Green failed English, but because he ranked ninth overall out of the 100 students, he was awarded an A grade.
(D) D. Black was given an A after he came twentieth out of the 100 students and failed to get above 90% in any of the three examinations.
(E) E. Gray failed his Math exam, but came top in his other two tests and was awarded a B.

(C) A. Brown, in choice (A), is eligible for an A grade under condition I, but that condition states that a student could receive an A (not that he must) and anyway, A. Brown may have failed the third examination. So choice (A) is possible and therefore not appropriate. Not enough information is given about B. White to determine his grade, but the data given does not preclude the giving of a B. This makes choice (B) inappropriate. D. Black qualifies for an A on condition IV and E. Gray gets a B by virtue of failing one exam in accordance with condition III, making choices (D) and (E) inappropriate. (C) is not permissible, even though C. Green came in the top decile, because he failed an examination. Therefore, he cannot receive a grade higher than a B.

5. A company, Marson Ltd., included in its annual financial statements the following note on its policy of accounting for fixed assets and depreciation:

Fixed Assets

Fixed assets are stated in the consolidated balance sheet at cost less accumulated depreciation and amortization. Depreciation is provided on all fixed assets, except land, to write off their cost in equal annual installments over the estimated economic useful lives of the assets. The cost of leasehold improvements is amortized over the term of the remaining number of years of the lease in equal annual installments.

Which of the following statements is relevant to, but not consistent with, the above accounting policy?

(A) The economic useful life of land and buildings is assumed to be 50 years, and Marson Ltd., therefore, employs a depreciation rate of 2% per annum.
(B) Marson Ltd. include in their plant inventory equipment that cost $100,000, even though this equipment is more than 10 years old and the depreciation rate on plant and machinery has been 15% for many years.
(C) Marson Ltd. spent $30,000 on improving a building, which is leased. The period of the lease was seven years, but the lease must be renewed in two years time. Marson Ltd. provided for amortization at 50% for this year.
(D) Inventories and negotiable securities are not included in fixed assets.
(E) Amortization of other assets, e.g. goodwill, is provided separately in the financial statements.

(A) The statements given in choices (B) and (C) are relevant to and consistent with the stated policy. (B) is an example of fully written down equipment still being held by the company and is perfectly consistent with the stated accounting policy. (C) is also consistent with the policy as, in accordance with the last sentence on leasehold improvements, the additional costs of leasehold improvements should be written off over the number of years left on the lease. The statements given in choices (D) and (E) are not within the ambit of the policy notes. Inventories and negotiable securities are usually current assets and subject to other accounting policies, and amortization of assets other than fixed assets would be similarly dealt with elsewhere. Therefore, (D) and (E) are neither relevant to nor consistent with the policy stated in the paragraph. The statement in (A) is relevant to but not fully consistent with the accounting policy as by not separating the cost of land from that of land and buildings and depreciating it at a rate of 2%, Marton Ltd. has not acted in accordance with its own policy, which is to provide depreciation on all fixed assets except land. (A) is the correct answer.

6. "The last five Wimbledon men's single champions have all changed to Gallenger's new tennis rackets—the only racket that uses genuine X-lon strengthened frames. In that case, isn't now the time to add power to your tennis strokes and to trade in your old racket for a Gallenger?"

Which of the following claims is not made and cannot be inferred from the above ad?

(A) Frames strengthened by X-lon are used only in Gallenger's new rackets.

(B) X-lon strengthened frames make tennis rackets stronger and allow the player to make more powerful strokes.

(C) Former Wimbledon champions know a great deal about tennis and their equipment.

(D) Gallenger tennis rackets helped the last five Wimbledon mens' singles champions achieve their status.

(E) You will improve your tennis play with a Gallenger.

(D) The ad emphasizes that Gallenger's new rackets are stronger and will add power to your strokes. (B) and (E) are, therefore, inferred. It is intended that the reader of the ad should relate to the judgment of former Wimbledon champions, and, therefore, wish to follow their example; for this reason (C) can be inferred. The claim made in choice (A) is included in the ad. Choices (A), (B), (C), and (E) are all therefore inappropriate. However, the ad does not claim or infer the statement made in (D). In fact, the paragraph states that the five individuals have changed to Gallenger's new rackets, and this implies that they used something else previously. (D) is the appropriate answer.

7. The fact that more and more married women are working has placed stress on marriages. The census published data showing the divorce rate for married women earning over $75,000 annually is twice the national average and four times the national average for women in the $150,000 bracket.

Which of the following, if true, would weaken the statement?

(A) Fifteen percent of married women earn over $75,000 per year.

(B) Married couples are more stressed because of their careers.

(C) Married couples where both spouses work have less time to spend together.

(D) Sixty percent of married women earn over $75,000 per year.

(E) The average divorce rate for unemployed women is 40 percent.

(A) The argument is that married women who work have a higher chance of getting divorced than unemployed married women. However, the statistics do not prove this contention. The census bureau's report of divorce rates is for only married women who earn above $75,000. What about those who earn less? If, as in alternative (A), only 15 percent of married women earn more than $75,000, then what about the other 85 percent? If, among the remaining 85 percent, the divorce rate is equal to or less than that of unemployed married women, then the conclusion is false. Alternatives (B) and (C) buttress the argument. Alternative (D) states evidence that cannot weaken the statement because it does not refer to the divorce rate. Alternative (E) could weaken the statement *if* the divorce rate for employed women was known.

8. Prompted by a proposal to convert a shipyard into a complex of condominiums with a full-service marina and boat repair center and by concern about the proposal from local residents, baymen, and environmentalists, the town is considering a one-year building moratorium for the waterfront area.

Which of the following, if true, would most seriously weaken opposition to the complex?

(A) Condominiums would sell for $350,000 each.

(B) There is a large demand for boat repair services.

(C) A growing population results in the closure of shellfish.

(D) There are already 1200 moorings on the waterfront.

(E) The shipyard may be sold for another commercial use.

(E) If the shipyard is not converted into the proposed complex, it might be sold for another use, which could be more detrimental to the opposition's interests than the current plan. Alternatives (A) and (B) reveal that there are buyers for the proposed complex, but hardly rebut the opposition's argument against the project. The closure of shellfish (C) buttresses the opposition (more population). The number of existing moorings (D) also supports the opposition, i.e. there are sufficient moorings. Alternative (E) implies that another use for the shipyard may be worse than the proposed project.

9. The local education authorities in England have recently issued a "prescribed" list of books that are approved for reading in schools by children aged between 5 and 11.

A furor has arisen among many parents because an authoress by the name of Enid Blyton, very popular with children, has been omitted from the said list. When asked to comment on the omission, the head of the committee that was responsible for preparing the list of books said that the books of Mrs. Blyton have been omitted because "we thought they are of an inferior quality and do not sufficiently stimulate the children's intellectual ability and not because they contain characters which are stereotypes or may show racial prejudice."

Which one of the following statements can be inferred from the above paragraph?

(A) Children are very angry that they will not be reading Enid Blyton in school once this decision is implemented.
(B) The parents' view is that Mrs. Blyton's books might have been left off the list because some of her characters were racist.
(C) If the parents had been consulted, Enid Blyton's books would have been omitted.
(D) The head of the deciding committee implied that Mrs. Blyton was not the only author whose books were banned.
(E) Mrs. Blyton was popular with children and parents because she included stereotype characters in her books.

(B) It may be inferred that the head of the committee is replying to the parents' complaint. As such, the committee head is stating reasons for omitting the books, viz., because they do not stimulate the intellectual ability of children. The mention of stereotypes and racial prejudice may be inferred as a reaction to the parents' comments.

The four remaining answers may have an element of truth in them, but they cannot be inferred from the text.

10. Pioneers of the motor-car industry realized that if they were going to meet the growing demand for their product, they had to adapt the labor force used in the productive process. Instead of many men working to complete all the stages of one car at a time, they assigned defined tasks to each man which they would repeat on every car.

Which of the following can be concluded from the passage?

(A) Early motor car manufacturers intended to increase productivity by applying the principle of division of labor.
(B) The car workers became disgruntled because they were assigned monotonous, repetitive tasks on the assembly line.
(C) Economies of scale enabled early motor companies to expand.
(D) A bad worker would perform the same task badly on each car, leading to many more rejects.
(E) The new production process enabled certain car workers to become specialists in the part of the process to which they were assigned.

(A) Choice (A) sums up the conclusion of the passage and is thus the appropriate answer. It combines the intention of the car manufacturers—to produce more cars—with the chosen method, dividing labor into component tasks. Choice (B) may have been a further outcome of implementing this policy, but the passage does not comment on this; therefore, (B) is not appropriate. Choice (C) mentions another direction in which the car manufacturers may have moved, i.e. opening larger plants, etc. and this process may have been assisted by what is discussed in the passage, but again this cannot be concluded from the passage. So, (C) is also inappropriate.

Choices (D) and (E) are both concomitant with the division of labor process—(D), a disadvantage, and (E), an advantage—but neither of them can be inferred from the passage and therefore are inappropriate.

11. In 1989 Japanese economic growth is expected to increase 50 times more than that of the United States.

Japanese economic policy ensures that faster growth is caused by greater investment in modern industrial plants. The initial investment leads to lower production costs, increased competitiveness, higher living standards, and low inflation.

The United States, on the other hand, is more concerned with curbing inflation and is pursuing a policy of slow growth, thus preventing investment in the modernization of American industry.

Which of the following conclusions can be drawn from the above?

(A) Slow growth prevents inflation.
(B) Slow-growth policies reduce inflation, but also decrease the efficiency and competitiveness of industry.
(C) Investment in industry causes inflation.
(D) Inflation can be reduced by increasing productivity.
(E) The U.S. must cure inflation before it can modernize and streamline its industry.

(B) The statement in choice (A) cannot be inferred or concluded. We may conclude that slow growth may reduce inflation since the United States is pursuing such a policy as part of a concern to curb inflation, but we may not infer or conclude that slow growth can prevent inflation. According to the passage, investment in industry in Japan has been shown to lead to low, not high, inflation; so choice (C) is not appropriate. The statement in choice (D) is partially correct since increased productivity has lowered the rate of inflation in Japan. However, this has been coupled with lowering of production costs. Statement (D) is insufficient by itself, and so is not the correct choice. The statement in (E) is a correct interpretation of U.S. economic policy, but it is not a proven statement, and it cannot be concluded based on the paragraph provided. The text does not state that the United States must cure inflation before improving industry; it merely states that this is current policy and understanding. Choice (B) is the correct choice. Since modernization lowers costs of production, this increases competitiveness and business activity. This has been demonstrated by Japan's high productivity, export record, and low inflation. Slow growth in the United States has had the opposite effect on industry, causing a decrease in efficiency and production. Therefore, (B) is the only conclusion that can be drawn.

12. A pill that can induce abortions in pregnant women has become available in France. The drug, RU486, has proved more than 95% effective in tests conducted by a scientific team in Paris. The drug is an antihormone which disrupts pregnancy by blocking the implantation of a fertilized egg in the wall of the uterus. In France, the pill will be available to women who are 49 days late in their menstrual cycle. The company that manufactures the pill, Roussel Uclaf, states, however, that the pill is not a "morning after" pill for use as a contraceptive.

Which of the following statements can be correctly deduced from the text above?

(A) The drug RU486 is a new type of contraceptive.
(B) The drug RU486 blocks egg production.
(C) The drug RU486 can be used to terminate pregnancy.
(D) The drug RU486 will replace conventional abortion techniques.
(E) The drug RU486 will only be available in France.

(C) Statement (A) cannot be deduced from the text. It is an untrue statement: a contraceptive is something that can prevent conception, and the drug discussed here does not prevent conception. Therefore, (A) is an incorrect choice. Statement (B) is also an untrue statement. The drug is reported to block egg implantation, not egg production. There is nothing in the paragraph concerning the drug's effectiveness, side effects, benefits, or dangers as compared to other abortion techniques, so there is no basis from which the reader can deduce or infer that the new drug will replace conventional abortion techniques. So (D) is not appropriate. Although the drug has been manufactured and tested in France, there is no indication that its use will be limited to that country alone, so statement (E) is not valid. The statement in (C) is the only limited statement that can be deduced from the text—that the drug RU486 can be used to induce abortion, thus terminating pregnancy.

13. Jane and Bella are both successful women who are also members of a minority group. Jane believes in positive discrimination. She believes that if positions of power and honor are offered principally to minority groups, then these groups will begin to play a more significant role in society today.

Bella, on the other hand, feels that she has succeeded in her chosen field of work on her own merits. She thinks that positive discrimination will lower standards and decrease competition between similarly qualified personnel who will expect to achieve positions because of their minority status rather than their suitability for the particular position.

Which of the following best sums up Jane's argument?

(A) Positive discrimination will encourage more people to apply for jobs, previously unavailable to them.
(B) Positive discrimination will give extra opportunities to minority groups.
(C) Quality and professionalism will improve because of the greater number of positions held by members of minority groups.
(D) Positive discrimination will ensure that each position is filled by the most suitably qualified candidate.
(E) Positive discrimination will eradicate prejudice from the work arena.

(B) Improvement in quality and professionalism can only be ensured if the most suitable candidates are chosen. Since positive discrimination does not guarantee this, statement (C) is not valid. Similarly, statement (D) only ensures that the most suitably qualified candidate from a minority group will fill the position and he or she might be less well suited than a candidate from a non-minority group. Therefore, (D) is an incorrect choice. Positive discrimination cannot be shown to be capable of eradicating prejudice, as claimed in (E); this is a totally separate issue and is not covered within the realm of the text. Statement (A) is probably a correct statement of fact, but it is not the basis of Jane's argument. Jane's argument is that, for better or worse, positive discrimination is a tool to be used to enable minority groups to play a more significant role in society. Because applicants from minority groups will receive more favorable consideration with a policy of positive discrimination, it can be assumed that they will receive extra opportunities. These opportunities are Jane's immediate and long-term objectives. Statement (B), which states all the above in one sentence, is, therefore, the best summary of Jane's position and the correct answer.

14. Many countries are facing a potential crisis in 20 to 30 years time. The ratio of pensioners to workers will be changing drastically with a declining birth rate, with more lengthy education of the young, and with a reduced working life. In general, the number of people paying into pension schemes is decreasing all the time. Meanwhile, with increased health care and living standards, more people are living long enough to draw their pension funds.

A controversial solution to this problem has been proposed in Germany—changing the age of retirement, for both men and women, from the current qualifying age of 63 for men and 60 for women.

A radical, but socially acceptable, solution to this problem must be found. If this is not done, it is predicted that by the year 2050, one person in three will be 65 or over and the projected work force will be unable to support pensions.

Assuming the following were all socially acceptable, which one would not improve the situation in the future?

(A) Lower the retirement age.
(B) Decrease the school-leaving age.
(C) Impose larger contributions on employees and employers.
(D) Cut pensions in half.
(E) Only give state pensions to retired persons whose income is below a certain level.

(A) Suggestion (B) would immediately put more people in the job market, and, if they found work, there would be more people contributing to pension funds, thus increasing the amount on hand to pay pensions. Suggestion (C) is also a possible solution to the problem, since again more money would be available for paying those of pensionable age. Thus, both (B) and (C) would improve the situation and are therefore incorrect choices. Suggestions (D) and (E) would reduce the amount of money being paid out. Therefore, they would also help improve the situation and so are incorrect. Choice (A), on the other hand, is a policy that would increase the number of claimants and decrease the number of people providing contributions. This suggestion would not improve the situation, and therefore, (A) is the appropriate answer.

15. Before the arrival of Joe, a new partner, sales output in Bill's company Midas In Reverse Ltd. had been rising by 10% per year on average. Innovations by Joe included computerization of technical processes and reductions in the work force, but annual sales output has only risen by 5% per year. It appears that Joe's innovations have caused the reduction in the annual growth rate.

Which of the following, if true, would most seriously weaken the conclusion above?

(A) The investment in new machinery entails a provision for depreciation of the cost of the fixed assets, which causes a reduction in profit.
(B) Midas In Reverse Ltd. does not base increases in the selling price of its products with costs.
(C) Joe's innovations were intended as long-term investment and not made for short-term profit growth.
(D) General demand for the product manufactured by the company has declined.
(E) Workers laid off by Midas In Reverse Ltd. have been hired by a competitor, who is taking an increasing share of the market.

(D) In order to shift the blame for the reduction in the annual rate of growth of sales output away from Joe's new regime, we must find another reason for the lack of sales. (D) provides us with this alternative, thus weakening the conclusion in the paragraph. (D), therefore, is the appropriate answer. Although a cost is incurred in providing depreciation on the new plan and machinery, as in (A), this does not affect the conclusion drawn. (B) is simply a statement of policy, or rather lack of policy—that is, that there is no strict relationship between sales price and cost of production. (C) is a possible defense of Joe's policy, but it does not weaken the conclusion that implementation of his ideas has been to blame for the reduction in the annual rate of growth in sales output. Finally, the fact that Joe's policy of firing workers has enabled a competitor to recruit the company's ex-employees, as in (E), has no bearing on whether or not implementation of Joe's plans has resulted in the decrease in the growth of sales.

16. Complete the following paragraph with the most suitable sentence.

In order to boost sales of toys at times other than the peak sale time—Christmas—manufacturers use many techniques. Character toys from movies or TV series are promoted, and all sets are "collectible" by their young purchasers. Collections, however, never appear to be complete, because as soon as all the characters are acquired, the child then requires the "car," the "home," the "mobile home," and even the "airplane" to ensure a happy environment for the toys. Ultimately, the elusive final piece of the series is attained just as the manufacturer and promoter release the next series of "collectibles."

The prime aim of the manufacturer and promoter is to ensure that . . .

(A) all children should be happy and no child can be happy without a complete series of toys.
(B) as soon as one set is complete or almost complete, then the next one arrives on the scene.
(C) children should be encouraged to complete their collections of toys.
(D) Christmas must be the peak selling period for toys.
(E) sales need to be bolstered throughout the year.

(E) Sentence (A) is a sublime idea, but it cannot be proven to be the intention of the manufacturer. Similarly, sentence (C) is true, but again, cannot be proven to be the prime motive of the manufacturer. Sentence (B) is a tactical move, not a motive, or aim. Sentence (D) is untrue, and so cannot be the prime aim of the manufacturer. Sentence (E) is the only statement that can be obtained from the paragraph, and thus is the appropriate answer.

17. John Wyndham Lewis, the famous sociologist, postulated that if murder is a worse crime than blackmail and blackmail is a worse crime than theft, how much more so is murder a worse crime than theft.

Which is a correct analysis of the above argument?

(A) A case operating in one situation will also be operative in another situation, if both situations are characterized in identical terms.
(B) A case that operates under certain conditions will surely be operative in other situations in which the same conditions are present in a more acute form.
(C) A case that clearly expresses the purpose it was meant to serve will also apply in other situations in which the identical purpose may be served.
(D) A case that begins with a generalization as to its intended application, then continues until the specification of particular cases, and then concludes with a restatement of the generalization, can be applied only to the particular cases specified.
(E) None of the above.

(B) The statement by Lewis in the extract simply states that if *X* is greater than *Y* and *Y* is greater than *Z*, then *X* is greater than *Z*, i.e. the condition of being greater is more acute. Choice (B), which states this condition, is the appropriate answer. Choice (A) does not describe the argument in the extract; there is a similarity in the terms used, but the extract does not say that murder is as bad as blackmail and the latter is bad as theft, therefore murder is as bad as theft. Therefore (A) is inappropriate. Choice (C) is inapplicable, as the extract does not state a purpose that can be applied to other situations. Similarly, (D) is not appropriate as there is no generalization, followed by specific cases. Since there is one appropriate answer, (E) is not correct.

Section 4
Data Sufficiency

1. How many degrees Celsius is 100° Fahrenheit?

(1) degrees Celsius = $\frac{5}{9}$ (degrees Fahrenheit − 32)

(2) degrees Fahrenheit = $\frac{9}{5}$ (degrees Celsius) + 32

(D) STATEMENT (1) alone is sufficient. Just use 100 for degrees Fahrenheit in the formula. STATEMENT (2) alone is also sufficient, since the formula in STATEMENT (2) can be solved to give the formula of STATEMENT (1) which we know is sufficient.

2. What is the area of the shaded part of the circle? *O* is the center of the circle.

(1) The radius of the circle is 4.
(2) *x* is 60.

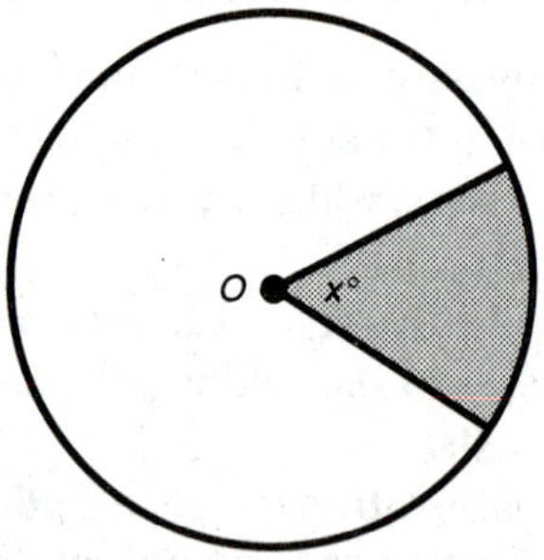

(C) STATEMENT (1) tells us the area of the circle is $\pi 4^2 = 16\pi$. Since there are 360° in the whole circle, (2) tells us that the shaded area is $\frac{60}{360}$ or $\frac{1}{6}$ of the area of the circle. Thus, using both (1) and (2), we can answer the question, but since we need both the radius of the circle and the value of *x*, neither of them alone is sufficient. Therefore, the answer is (C).

3. What was Mr. Kliman's income in 1990?

(1) His total income for 1988, 1989, and 1990 was $141,000.
(2) He made 20% more in 1989 than he did in 1988.

(E) Using STATEMENT (1) we can find the income for 1990 if we know the income for 1988 and 1989, but (1) gives no more information about the income for 1988 and 1989. If we also use (2) we can get the income in 1989 if we know the income for 1988, but we still can't determine the income for 1988. Therefore, both together are not sufficient.

4. If l and l' are straight lines, find y.

(1) $x = 100$
(2) $z = 80$

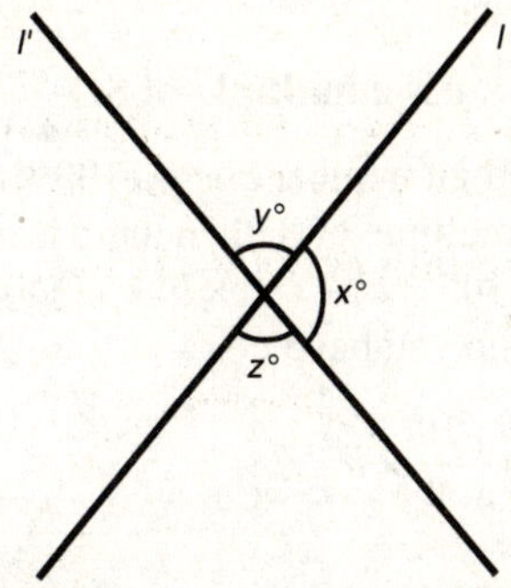

(D) Since a straight line forms an angle of 180° and l' is a straight line, we know $x + y = 180$. If we use STATEMENT (1) we get $y = 80$, so (1) alone is sufficient. When two straight lines intersect, the vertical angles are equal. So $y = z$; thus if we use (2) we get $y = 80$. Therefore, (2) alone is sufficient. Thus, each statement alone is sufficient.

5. Fifty students have signed up for at least one of the courses German I and English I. How many of the 50 students are taking German I but not English I?

(1) 16 students are taking German I and English I.
(2) The number of students taking English I but not German I is the same as the number taking German I but not English I.

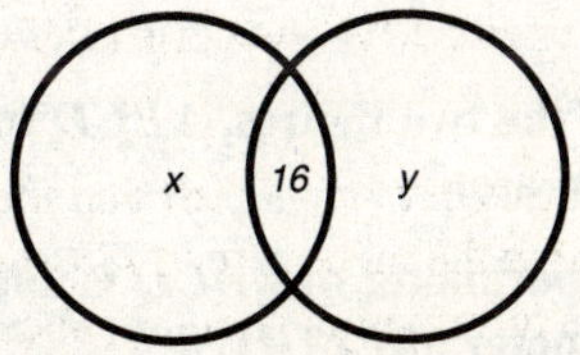

(C) In the figure, x denotes the number taking German I but not English I, and y the number taking English I but not German I. From (1) we know that $x + 16 + y = 50$; from (2), $x = y$. Neither statement alone can be solved for x, but both together are sufficient (and yield $x = 17$).

6. Is $ABCD$ a square?

(1) $AD = AB$
(2) $x = 90$

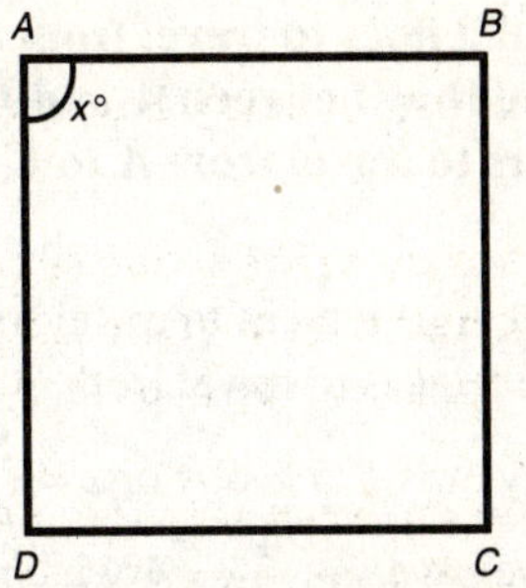

(E) STATEMENT (1) alone is not sufficient because it only says two sides are equal; in a square all four sides are equal. Even if we use (2) we don't know if $ABCD$ is a square since *all* angles have to be right angles in a square. Therefore, both statements together are insufficient.

Another way to solve this problem would be to visualize what happens to the figure $ABCD$ if C is moved while A, B, and D are kept the same. (1) and (2) would still hold even when C is moved, but the figure $ABCD$ could change from a square to a non-square. Thus (1) and (2) together are not sufficient.

7. The *XYZ* Corporation has 7,000 employees. What is the average yearly wage of an employee of the *XYZ* Corporation?

(1) 4,000 of the employees are executives.
(2) The total amount the company pays in wages each year is \$77,000,000.

(B) The average yearly wage per employee is the total amount of wages divided by the number of employees. So STATEMENT (2) alone is sufficient since it gives the total amount of wages and we are given the number of employees. (1) alone is not sufficient, since (1) by itself does not tell us the total wages. Therefore, the answer is (B).

8. Is $x > y$?

(1) $(x + y)^2 > 0$
(2) x is positive

(E) Because $x = 2$, $y = 1$ and $x = 1$, $y = 2$ both satisfy STATEMENTS (1) and (2), the statements together are not sufficient.

9. How long will it take to travel from *A* to *B*? It takes 4 hours to travel from *A* to *B* and back to *A*.

(1) It takes 25% more time to travel from *A* to *B* than it does to travel from *B* to *A*.
(2) *C* is midway between *A* and *B*, and it takes 2 hours to travel from *A* to *C* and back to *A*.

(A) Let x be the time it takes to travel from A to B and let y be the time it takes to travel from B to A. We know $x + y = 4$. (1) says x is 125% of y or $x = \frac{5}{4}y$. So using STATEMENT (1) we have $x + \frac{4}{5}x = 4$ which we can solve for x. Thus, (1) alone is sufficient. (2) alone is not sufficient since we need information about the relation of x to y to solve the problem and (2) says nothing about the relation between x and y. Therefore, (1) alone is sufficient but (2) alone is insufficient.

10. *l*, *l*', and *k* are straight lines. Are *l* and *l*' parallel?

(1) $x = y$
(2) $y = z$

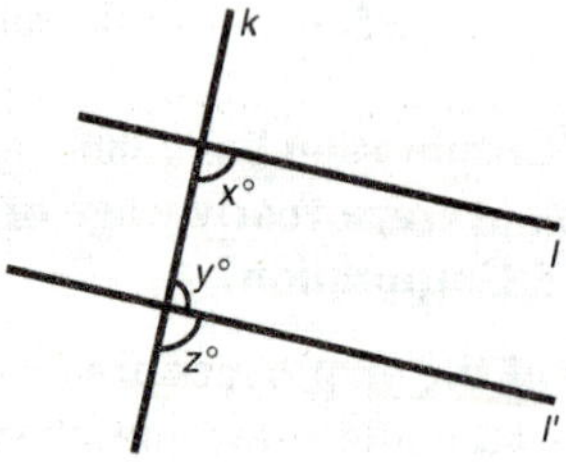

(C) STATEMENT (1) alone is insufficient. If x and y were right angles, (1) would imply that l and l' are parallel, but if x and y are not right angles, (1) would imply that l and l' are not parallel. (2) alone is not sufficient since it gives information only about l' and says nothing about the relation of l and l'. (1) and (2) together give $x = z$ which means that l and l' are parallel. Therefore, (1) and (2) together are sufficient but neither alone is sufficient.

11. What is $x + y + z$?

(1) $x + y = 3$
(2) $x + z = 2$

(E) If we use STATEMENT (1), we have $x + y + z = 3 + z$, but we have no information about z, so (1) alone is insufficient. If we use (2) alone, we have $x + y + z = y + 2$, but since we have no information about y, (2) alone is insufficient. If we use both (1) and (2), we obtain $x + y + z = y + 2 = 3 + z$. We can also add (1) and (2) to obtain $2x + y + z = 5$, but we can't find the value of $x + y + z$ without more information. So the answer is (E).

12. If *a*, *b*, and *c* are digits, is $a + b + c$ a multiple of 8? A digit is one of the integers 0, 1, 2, 3, 4, 5, 6, 7, 8, 9.

(1) The three digit number *abc* is a multiple of 8.
(2) $a \times b \times c$ is a multiple of 8.

(E) The three digit number abc is $(100 \times a) + (100 \times b) + c$. If abc is a multiple of 8, then there is an integer k such that $k8 = (100 \times a) + (10 \times b) + c$. Divide this equation by 8 and you have

$$k = \left(\frac{100}{8} \times a\right) + \left(\frac{10}{8} \times b\right) + \frac{c}{8}$$

$$= \left(12a + \frac{4a}{8}\right) + \left(b + \frac{2b}{8}\right) + \frac{c}{8}$$

$$= 12a + b + \left(\frac{4a}{8} + \frac{2b}{8} + \frac{c}{8}\right)$$

$$= 12a + b + \left(\frac{4a + 2b + c}{8}\right)$$

So STATEMENT (1) alone is not enough since choosing $a = 1 = b$ and $c = 2$ will make abc (112) a multiple of 8 but $a + b + c = 4$, which is not a multiple of 8. However, choosing $a = 8 = b = c$ will make abc (888) a multiple of 8 and $a + b + c = 24$, which is also a multiple of 8. So (1) alone is not sufficient. (1) and (2) together are not sufficient, since the assignment $a = 8 = b = c$ will satisfy both (1) and (2) and $a + b + c = 24$ but the assignment $a = 2$, $b = 4$, and $c = 8$ will satisfy both (1) and (2) and $a + b + c = 14$.

13. Which of the two figures, *ABCD* or *EFGH*, has the largest area?

(1) The perimeter of *ABCD* is longer than the perimeter of *EFGH*.
(2) *AC* is longer than *EG*.

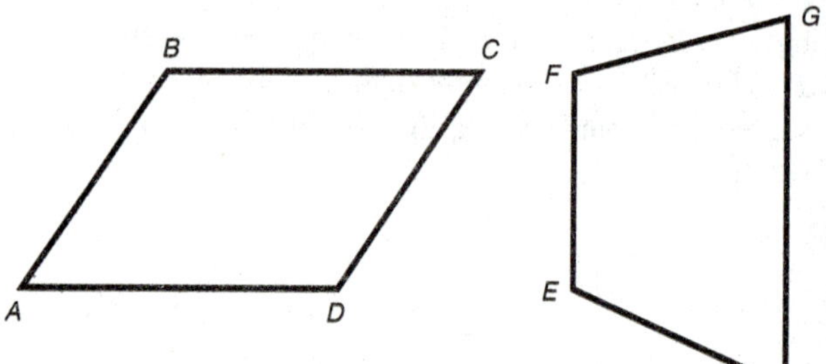

(E) STATEMENT (1) alone is not sufficient. A four-sided figure can have both larger perimeter and smaller area than another four-sided figure, or it could have larger perimeter and larger area. (2) alone is also insufficient since the length of one diagonal does not determine the area of a four-sided figure. (1) and (2) together are also insufficient, as shown by the figure.

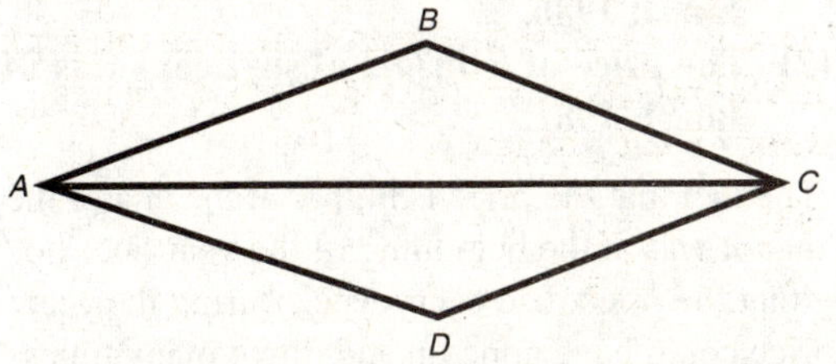

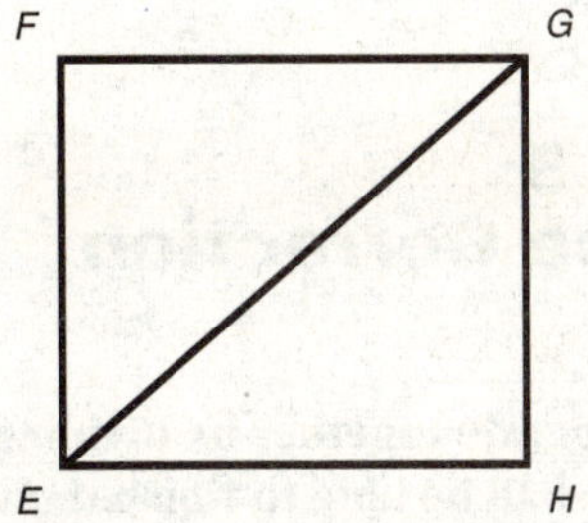

(1) and (2) are both satisfied and the area of *EFGH* is larger than *ABCD*. But (1) and (2) could still be satisfied and the area of *ABCD* be larger than the area of *EFGH*; so the answer is (E).

14. Is a number divisible by 9?

(1) The number is divisible by 3.
(2) The number is divisible by 27.

(B) STATEMENT (1) alone is not sufficient, since 12 is divisible by 3 but 12 is not divisible by 9. STATEMENT (2) alone is sufficient, since if a number is divisible by 27 then, because $27 = 9 \times 3$, the number must be divisible by 9.

15. *ABCD* is a rectangle. Which region, *ABEF* or *CDFE*, has a larger area?

(1) *BE* is longer than *FD*.
(2) *BE* is longer than *CD*.

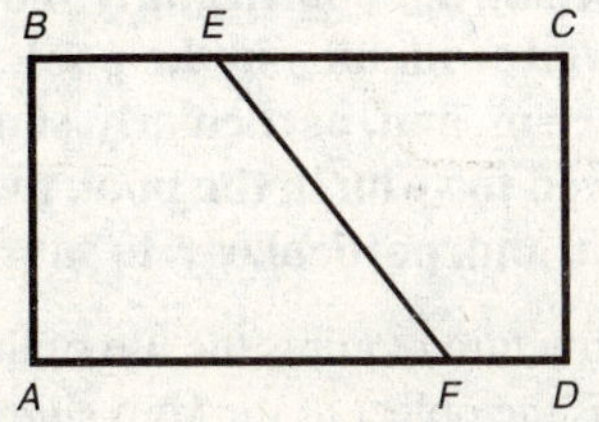

(A) Both regions *ABEF* and *CDFE* are trapezoids, so their area is given by the formula $a\,(\frac{1}{2}[b_1 + b_2])$ where a is an altitude and b_1 and b_2 are the sides perpendicular to the altitude. Because *ABCD* is a rectangle, $AB = CD$, which means the altitudes are the same length for each region. So it is sufficient to know whether $BE + AF$ is larger than $EC + FD$.

STATEMENT (1) alone is sufficient, since, if *BE* is larger than *FD*, then $BC - BE$, which is *EC*, must be smaller than $AD - FD = AF$. ($AD = BC$ since *ABCD* is a rectangle.) So $BE + AF$ is larger than $EC + FD$.

STATEMENT (2) alone is not sufficient, since either region could be larger if *BE* is larger than *CD* (See figures).

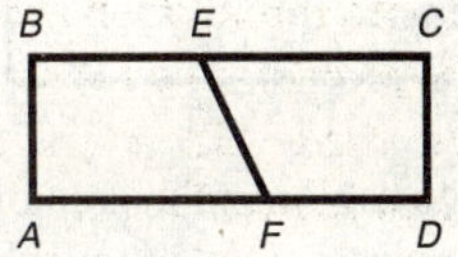

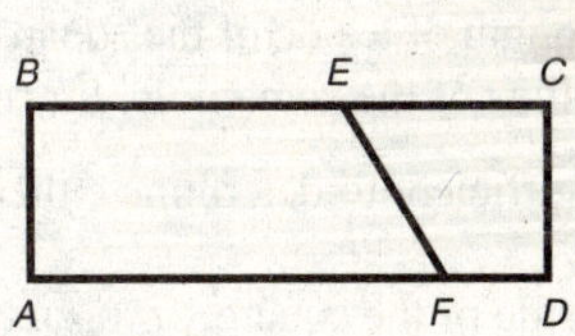

16. Is the integer *k* odd or even?

(1) k^2 is odd.
(2) $2k$ is even.

(A) The square of an even integer is always even. So if k^2 is odd, k can't be even. Therefore, k is odd and (1) alone is sufficient.

STATEMENT (2) alone is not sufficient, since $2k$ is even for every integer k.

17. Is *x* positive?

(1) $x^2 + 3x - 4 = 0$
(2) $x > -2$

(C) STATEMENT (1) alone is not sufficient. Factoring the expression in (1) gives x is equal to -4 or 1.

STATEMENT (2) alone is not sufficient, since there are positive numbers greater than -2 and negative numbers greater than -2.

STATEMENT (1) and (2) together are sufficient, since the only possible value is 1.

18. ***ABCD*** **is a square.**

BCO **is a semicircle.**

What is the area of ***ABOCD*****?**

(1) The length of ***AC*** **is** $4\sqrt{2}$**.**
(2) The radius of the semicircle ***BOC*** **is 2.**

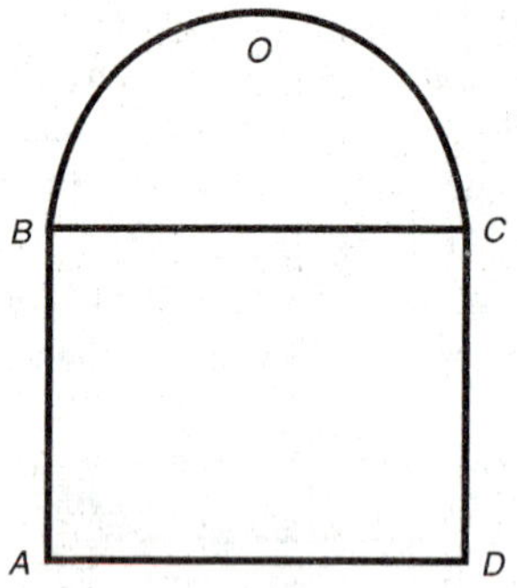

(D) The area of the region is the area of the square plus the area of the semicircle. So you must be able to determine the length of a side of the square and the length of the radius of the semicircle. Since the radius is $\frac{1}{2}$ of *BC*, it is sufficient to determine either the radius or the length of a side of the square. STATEMENT (1) alone is sufficient, since the diagonal of a square is $\sqrt{2}$ times the length of a side. STATEMENT (2) alone is sufficient, since the length of a side of the square is twice the radius.

19. Do the points ***P*** **and** ***Q*** **lie on the same circle with center (0, 0)?**

(1) The coordinates of point ***P*** **are (2, 3).**
(2) The coordinates of point ***Q*** **are (4, 1).**

(C) Using STATEMENTS (1) and (2), you can determine the distance from *P* to (0, 0) and the distance from *Q* to (0, 0). The distances are equal if and only if *P* and *Q* are on the same circle with center (0, 0). Neither statement alone is sufficient, since you need to know both distances.

20. Is 2^n **divisible by 8?**

(1) ***n*** **is an odd integer.**
(2) ***n*** **is an integer greater than 5.**

(B) Since 2^n is *n* "copies" of 2 multiplied together, 2^n is divisible by 8 if and only if *n* is greater than or equal to 3. (This is because $8 = 2 \times 2 \times 2 = 2^3$). Therefore, (2) alone is sufficient.

STATEMENT (1) alone is not sufficient, because there are odd numbers less than 3 (for example, 1) and odd numbers greater than 3.

21. Did the price of a bushel of soybeans increase during every week of 1980?

(1) The price of a bushel of soybeans was $2 on Jan. 1, 1980.
(2) The price of a bushel of soybeans was $4 on Jan. 1, 1981.

(E) The fact that the price is higher at the end of the year than it was at the beginning of the year does not imply that the price rose every week during the year. The price could have gone up and down many times during the year.

Section 5
Sentence Correction

1. If we cooperate together by dividing up the work, we shall be able to finish it quickly.

(A) If we cooperate together by dividing up the work
(B) If we cooperate by dividing up the work
(C) If we cooperate together by dividing the work
(D) If we cooperate by dividing up the work together
(E) If we cooperate by dividing the work

(E) Both *together* and *up* are unnecessary since their meaning is included in the words *cooperate* and *divide.*

2. The vacationers enjoyed swimming in the pool, bathing in the ocean, and, particularly, to snorkel near the reef.

(A) enjoyed swimming in the pool, bathing in the ocean, and, particularly, to snorkel
(B) enjoyed swimming in the pool, to bathe in the ocean, and, particularly, to snorkel
(C) enjoyed swimming in the pool, to bathe in the ocean, and, particularly snorkeling
(D) enjoyed swimming in the pool, bathing in the ocean, and, particularly, snorkeling
(E) enjoyed to swim in the pool, to bathe in the ocean, and, particularly, to snorkel

(D) Parallel structure requires the use of the gerund (verbal noun) as the object of the verb *enjoyed: swimming, bathing, snorkeling. Enjoy* should not be followed by an infinitive construction.

3. **Crossing the street, a car almost struck us.**

   (A) Crossing the street, a car almost struck us.
   (B) A car almost struck us, crossing the street.
   (C) As we crossed the street, a car almost struck us.
   (D) A car, crossing the street, almost struck us.
   (E) Having crossed the street, a car almost struck us.

(C) The other choices all have misplaced modifiers.

4. **The theme of this novel is how money doesn't make you happy.**

   (A) The theme of this novel is how money doesn't make you happy.
   (B) The theme of this novel is that money doesn't make you happy.
   (C) In this novel, its theme is how money doesn't make you happy.
   (D) In this novel, that money doesn't make you happy is the theme.
   (E) In this novel, you are not made happy by money is the theme.

(B) The clause *that money doesn't make you happy* is the predicate nominative of the verb *is*. *How* is inappropriate.

5. **If some Americans look at where they are going, it can be seen that our goal is money.**

   (A) look at where they are going, it can be seen that our goal
   (B) look back at where they are going, they see that their goal
   (C) look ahead to where they are going, it can be seen that their goal
   (D) look at where they are going, they can see our goal
   (E) look ahead to where they are going, they can see their goal

(E) The shift in pronouns from *they* to *our* is incorrect. The active verb *can see* is preferable to the passive verb *can be seen.* Also, one looks *ahead to* where one is going.

6. **Mary, a girl with little talent for cooking, enjoys preparing pizza.**

   (A) Mary, a girl with little talent for cooking, enjoys preparing
   (B) Mary is a girl who has little talent for cooking who enjoys to prepare
   (C) Mary is a girl with little talent for cooking and who enjoys preparing
   (D) Mary, who has little talent for cooking, enjoys to prepare
   (E) With little talent for cooking, Mary is a girl who enjoys to prepare

(A) No error.

7. **My grandmother is the most remarkable person of all the persons I have ever met.**

   (A) My grandmother is the most remarkable person of all the persons I have ever met.
   (B) Of all the persons I have ever met, my grandmother is the most remarkable person.
   (C) Of all the persons I have ever met, the most remarkable person is my grandmother.
   (D) Of all the persons I have ever met, the most remarkable is my grandmother.
   (E) My grandmother, of all the persons I have ever met, is the most remarkable.

(D) Suspense is created by holding *grandmother* to the end of the sentence. The word *person* does not have to be repeated.

8. **Start the motor, and then you should remove the blocks.**

   (A) Start the motor, and then you should remove the blocks.
   (B) Start the motor and then remove the blocks.
   (C) Start the motor, then removing the blocks.
   (D) Start the motor, and then the blocks should be removed.
   (E) Starting the motor, the blocks should then be removed.

(B) The two verbs should be parallel: *start* and *remove.*

9. He is a genius, although he is eccentric and wants recognition.

(A) He is a genius, although he is eccentric and wants recognition.
(B) Although he is eccentric, he is a genius and wants recognition.
(C) Although he is eccentric, he is a genius although he wants recognition.
(D) His is a genius although he is eccentric and although he wants recognition.
(E) Although he is eccentric and wants recognition, he is a genius.

(E) The key idea is that *he is a genius.* To create a suspenseful or periodic sentence, the writer should place *he is a genius* at the end of the sentence.

10. The smaller firms sold either on a price or quality-of-workmanship basis.

(A) The smaller firms sold either on a price or quality-of-workmanship basis.
(B) The smaller firms either sold on a price or quality-of-workmanship basis.
(C) The smaller firms sold on either a price or a quality-of-workmanship basis.
(D) The smaller firms sold on either a price or on a quality-of-workmanship basis.
(E) Either the smaller firms sold on a price or on a quality-of-workmanship basis.

(C) The correlatives *either . . . or* should be placed as near as possible to the words with which they belong: *a price* and *a quality-of-workmanship basis.*

11. The matter was referred back to committee since the solution to the problem was different from the one proposed earlier which was not practicable.

(A) referred back to committee since the solution to the problem was different from the one proposed earlier which was not practicable
(B) referred to committee since the solution to the problem was different from the one proposed earlier which was not practicable
(C) referred back to committee since the solution to the problem was different than the one proposed earlier which was not practical
(D) referred to committee since the solution to the problem was different than the one proposed earlier which was not practicable
(E) referred back to committee since the solution to the problem was different from the one proposed earlier which was not practical

(B) *Referred back* is redundant. The prefix *re* means "back."

12. Irregardless of the consequences, the police officer was forbidden from making any pinches.

(A) Irregardless of the consequences, the police officer was forbidden from making any pinches.
(B) Irregardless of the consequences, the police officer was forbidden from making any arrests.
(C) Regardless of the consequences, the police officer was forbidden from making any arrests.
(D) Irregardless of the consequences, the police officer was forbidden to make any pinches.
(E) Regardless of the consequences, the police officer was forbidden to make any arrests.

(E) *Irregardless* is not a word in current English usage. *Forbidden* requires an infinitive construction (forbidden *to make*). The word *pinch* is slang and should be avoided in writing.

13. The book having been read carefully and extensive notes having been taken, Tom felt confident about the test.

(A) The book having been read carefully and extensive notes having been taken, Tom
(B) Tom, who read the book carefully and having taken extensive notes
(C) Reading the book carefully and taking extensive notes, Tom
(D) Having read the book carefully and extensive notes having been taken, Tom
(E) Because he had read the book carefully and had taken extensive notes, Tom

(E) Active expressions are preferable to passive ones. The two subordinate reasons, reading and note-taking, should be preceded by *because.*

14. He has not only violated the law, but also he has escaped punishment.

(A) not only violated the law, but also he has escaped punishment
(B) violated not only the law, but also he has escaped punishment
(C) violated not only the law, but he has escaped punishment also
(D) not only violated the law, but also escaped punishment
(E) not only violated the law, but has escaped punishment

(D) The correlatives *not only . . . but also* should be placed near to the words with which they belong: *violated* and *escaped.*

15. Ideally, the fan should be placed in a different room than the one you want to cool.

(A) the fan should be placed in a different room than
(B) the fan had ought to be placed in a different room from
(C) the fan should be placed in a different room from
(D) the fan had ought to be placed in a different room than
(E) you should place the fan in a different room than

(C) The correct idiom is *different from. Had ought* is not correct verb form.

16. After viewing both movies, John agreed that the first one was the best of the two.

(A) John agreed that the first one was the best of the two
(B) John agreed that the first was the best of the two
(C) John agreed that the first one was the better of the two
(D) John agreed that of the two the better one was the first
(E) John agreed that the best of the two was the first

(C) In sentences comparing two items, *-er* words are used. When comparing more than two items use *-est* words. Thus the correct form here is *better.* Choice D is more awkward in construction.

17. Poor product quality angers Bob, who wonders if it is part of a strategy by manufacturers.

(A) who wonders if it is part of a strategy by manufacturers
(B) who wonders if manufacturers are part of the strategy
(C) that wonders if it is part of a strategy by manufacturers
(D) wondering if this is part of a strategy by manufacturers
(E) who wonders if they are part of a strategy by manufacturers

(A) No error. *Poor product quality* is singular, so the pronoun must also be singular—*it.* Choice B eliminates the pronoun and changes the meaning. Choice E uses a plural pronoun. Choice C uses an incorrect pronoun, *that,* in place of *who.* Choice D is awkward.

18. He noted the dog's soft hair, strong legs, and keen sense of smell.

(A) the dog's soft hair, strong legs, and keen sense of smell
(B) the dog's soft hair, strong legs, and that his sense of smell was keen
(C) the dog's soft hair, and that his legs were strong and sense of smell was keen
(D) the dog's soft hair, and that his legs were strong and smell was keen
(E) the dog's soft hair, keen smell and that his legs were strong

(A) No error. The phrases are all parallel: soft *hair,* strong *legs,* and keen *sense* of smell.

19. Having bowed our heads, the minister led us in prayer.

(A) Having bowed our heads, the minister led
(B) After we bowed our heads, the minister led
(C) After we bowed our heads, the minister leads
(D) After we had bowed our heads, the minister led
(E) Having bowed our heads, the minister leads

(D) *Having bowed our heads* is a dangling modifier. The act of bowing heads preceded the leading prayer, so the past perfect tense must be used.

20. She seldom ever wants to try and face the true facts.

(A) seldom ever wants to try and face the true facts
(B) seldom ever wants to try and face the facts
(C) seldom ever wants to try to face the facts
(D) seldom wants to try and face the facts
(E) seldom wants to try to face the facts

(E) *Ever* and *true* are unnecessary. The infinitive *to try* is followed by *to,* not *and.*

21. The president's talk was directed toward whomever was present.

(A) was directed toward whomever was present
(B) was directed toward whoever was present
(C) was directed at who was present
(D) was directed at whomever was present
(E) was directed towards whomever was present

(B) The entire clause *whoever was present* is the object of the preposition *toward*; *whoever* is the subject of *was.* Therefore, *whomever,* which is in the objective case, in incorrect.

Section 6
Problem Solving

(Numbers in parentheses at the end of each explanation indicate the section in the Mathematics Review where material addressed in the question is discussed.)

1. If the side of a square increases by 40%, then the area of the square increases by

(A) 16%
(B) 40%
(C) 96%
(D) 116%
(E) 140%

(C) If s is the original side of the square, then s^2 is the area of the original square. The side of the increased square is 140% of s or $(1.4)s$. Therefore, the area of the increased square is $(1.4s)^2$ or $1.96s^2$, which is 196% of the original area. Thus, the area has increased by 96%.

You could also work this problem by letting $s = 10$; then the original area was 100. The increased side is 14 and the increased area is 196, so the area has increased by $\frac{96}{100}$ or 96%. (I-4, III-7)

2. If 28 cartons of soda cost \$21.00, then 7 cartons of soda should cost

(A) \$5.25
(B) \$5.50
(C) \$6.40
(D) \$7.00
(E) \$10.50

(A) If P is the price of 7 cartons, then $\frac{7}{28} = \frac{P}{21}$,

so $P = \frac{1}{4}$ of \$21, which is \$5.25. (II-5)

3. Plane *P* takes off at 2 A.M. and flies at a constant speed of *x* mph. Plane *Q* takes off at 3:30 A.M. and flies the same route as *P* but travels at a constant speed of *y* mph. Assuming that *y* is greater than *x*, how many hours after 3:30 A.M. will plane *Q* overtake plane *P*?

(A) $\frac{3}{2}x$ **hrs.**

(B) $\frac{3}{2}$ **hrs.**

(C) $\frac{3}{2y}$ **hrs.**

(D) $\frac{3}{2(y-x)}$ **hrs.**

(E) $\frac{3x}{2(y-x)}$ **hrs.**

(E) Plane P will travel $\frac{3}{2}$ of an hour before Q takes off, so it will be $\frac{3x}{2}$ miles away at 3:30 A.M. Let t denote the number of hours after 3:30 A.M. it takes Q to overtake P. By then P has flown $tx + \frac{3x}{2}$ miles and Q has flown ty miles. We want the value of t, where $ty = tx + \frac{3x}{2}$, or $t(y - x) = \frac{3x}{2}$. Therefore, $t = \frac{3x}{2(y-x)}$. (II-3)

DISTRIBUTION OF TEST SCORES IN A CLASS

Number of Students	*Number of Correct Answers*
10	36 to 40
16	32 to 35
12	28 to 31
14	26 to 27
8	0 to 25

4. What percent of the class answered 32 or more questions correctly?

(A) $16\frac{2}{3}$

(B) 20

(C) $26\frac{2}{3}$

(D) $43\frac{1}{3}$

(E) 52

(D) There were 26 (16 + 10) students who answered 32 or more questions correctly. The total number of students is 60, and $\frac{26}{60} = .43\frac{1}{3}$. So $43\frac{1}{3}$% of the class answered 32 or more questions correctly. (I-4)

5. The number of students who answered 28 to 31 questions correctly is x times the number who answered 25 or fewer correctly, where x is

(A) $\frac{2}{3}$

(B) 1

(C) $\frac{3}{2}$

(D) $\frac{7}{4}$

(E) 2

(C) 12 students had scores of 28 to 31, and 8 scores of 25 or less; so $8x = 12$ and $x = \frac{12}{8} = \frac{3}{2}$. (II-3)

6. If the product of 3 consecutive integers is 210, then the sum of the two smaller integers is

(A) 5
(B) 11
(C) 12
(D) 13
(E) 18

(B) The product of 3 consecutive integers is of the form $(x-1)(x)(x+1)$ and a good approximation to this is x^3. Since $6^3 = 216$, a good guess for x is 6. 6 is correct since $5 \times 6 \times 7 = 210$. Therefore, the sum of the two smaller integers is 5 + 6 or 11. (I-1)

7. Cereal costs $\frac{1}{3}$ as much as bacon. Bacon costs $\frac{5}{4}$ as much as eggs. Eggs cost what fraction of the cost of cereal?

(A) $\frac{5}{12}$

(B) $\frac{4}{5}$

(C) $\frac{5}{4}$

(D) $\frac{5}{3}$

(E) $\frac{12}{5}$

(E) Let C, B, and E denote the cost of cereal, bacon, and eggs respectively. Then $C = \frac{1B}{3}$ and $B = \frac{5E}{4}$, or $E = \frac{4B}{5}$. Therefore, $E = \frac{4B}{5}$ and $B = 3C$; so we conclude that $E = \left(\frac{4}{5}\right) 3C = \frac{12C}{5}$. (I-2)

8. A truck gets 15 miles per gallon of gas when it is unloaded. When the truck is loaded, it travels only 80% as far on a gallon of gas as when unloaded. How many gallons will the loaded truck use to travel 80 miles?

(A) $5\frac{1}{3}$

(B) 6

(C) $6\frac{1}{3}$

(D) $6\frac{2}{3}$

(E) $6\frac{3}{4}$

(D) Since 80% of 15 is 12, the loaded truck travels 12 miles on a gallon of gas. Therefore, it will use $\frac{80}{12}$ or $6\frac{8}{12}$ or $6\frac{2}{3}$ gallons of gas to travel 80 miles (I-4)

9. Both circles have radius 4 and the area enclosed by both circles is 28π. What is the area of the shaded region?

(A) 0
(B) 2π
(C) 4π
(D) $4\pi^2$
(E) 16π

(C) Think of the area enclosed by both circles as three distinct sections: a, b, and c, as in the illustration below. Then we want to know the value of b. Since each circle has radius 4, the area of each circle is $\pi(4 \times 4) = 16\pi$. So $a + b = 16\pi$ and $b + c = 16\pi$ or $a + 2b + c = 32\pi$. The area enclosed by both circles is $a + b + c$, which must be equal to 28π. Now subtract $a + b + c = 28\pi$ from $a + 2b + c = 32\pi$ to obtain $b = 4\pi$. (II-4, III-7)

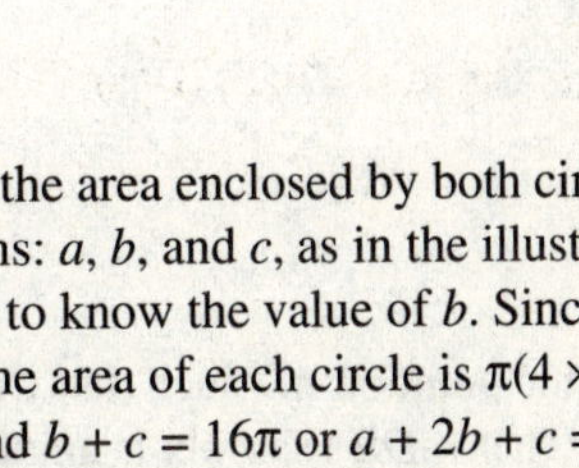

10. For each dollar spent by the sales department, the research department spends 20¢. For every $4 spent by the research department, the packing department spends $1.50. The triple ratio of the money spent by the sales department to the money spent by the research department to the money spent by the packing department can be expressed as

(A) 40 : 8 : 3
(B) 20 : 4 : 1
(C) 8 : 4 : 1
(D) 4 : 1 : 5
(E) 2 : 1 : 5

(A) Let S, R, and P be the respective amounts spent by the sales, research, and packing departments. Then S : R is 1 : .2 and R : P is 4 : 1.5. In order to combine these into a triple ratio for S : R : P, we need to have the same number for R in both the ratios S : R and R : P.

If we multiply each term of the ratio S : R by 20, we obtain 20 : 4. Therefore we can express the triple ratio as 20 : 4 : 1.5. However, this is not one of the given answers. If you multiply every term of a triple ratio by the same nonzero number, the triple ratio remains unchanged. So multiply each term by 2, and the triple ratio becomes 40 : 8 : 3, which is (A). (II-5)

11. *ABCD* has area equal to 28. *BC* is parallel to *AD*. *BA* is perpendicular to *AD*. If *BC* is 6 and *AD* is 8, then what is *CD*?

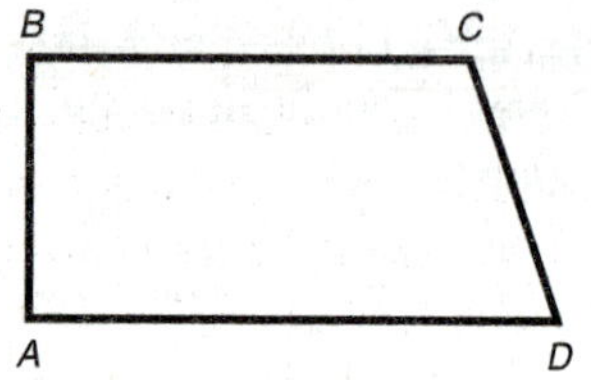

(A) $2\sqrt{2}$
(B) $2\sqrt{3}$
(C) 4
(D) $2\sqrt{5}$
(E) 6

(D) Let *E* be the point on *AD* such that *CE* is perpendicular to *AD*. Then *CDE* is a right triangle, and *CD* can be computed if we know *CE* and *DE*. Since *EC* and *AB* are perpendicular to the same line, *ABCE* is a rectangle. So *AE* is equal to *BC*, which is 6. Therefore *ED* = *AD* – *AE* = 8 – 6 = 2. Since *ABCD* is a trapezoid, its area is the average of *AD* and *BC* multiplied by an altitude. Since the average of *AD* and *BC* is 7, the length of any altitude is $\frac{28}{7}$, which is 4. Since *CE* is perpendicular to *AD*, *CE* is an altitude and so *CE* must equal 4. Finally, using the Pythagorean relation, we have *CD* = $\sqrt{4^2+2^2} = \sqrt{20} = \sqrt{4}\times\sqrt{5} = 2\sqrt{5}$. (III-4, III-7)

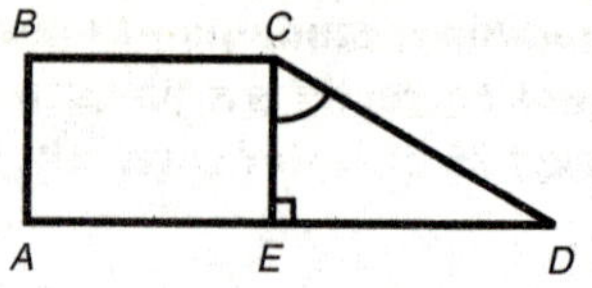

12. If *X* is an odd integer and *Y* is an even integer, which of the following statements is (are) always true?

I. *X* + *Y* is odd.
II. *XY* is odd.
III. 2*X* + *Y* is even.

(A) I only
(B) III only
(C) I and III only
(D) II and III only
(E) I, II, and III

(C) An odd integer can be written as $2j - 1$ for some integer *j*, and an even integer can be written as $2k$ for some integer *k*. So let $x = 2j - 1$ and $y = 2k$. Then $x + y = 2j - 1 + 2k = 2(j + k) - 1$, which is odd. So I is true. Since $xy = (2j - 1)2k = 4jk - 2k = 2(2jk - k)$, *xy* is even and II is false. Finally, $2x + y$ is $2(2j - 1) + 2k = 4j - 2 + 2k = 2(2j - 1 + k)$, which is even. Therefore, III is true. (I-1)

13. Find the area of the region inside the circle and outside the square *ABCD*. *A*, *B*, *C*, and *D* are all points on the circle, and the radius of the circle is 4.

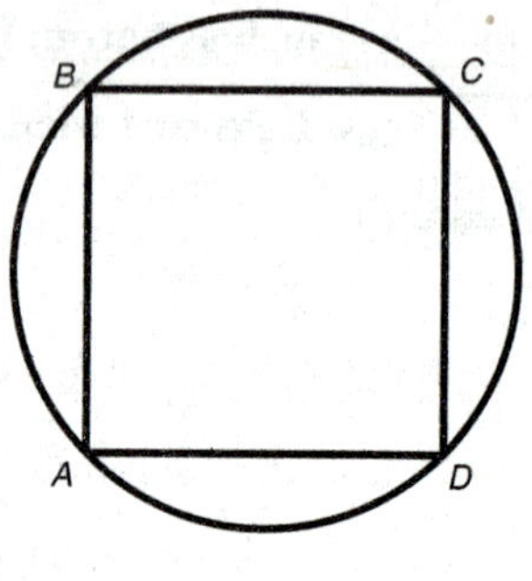

(A) 16π – 36
(B) 16(π – 2)
(C) 16(π – 1)
(D) 16π – 4
(E) 16π

(B) The area of the region is the area of the circle minus the area of the square. Since the radius of the circle is 4, the area of the circle is $\pi(4 \times 4) = 16\pi$. Since *ABCD* is a square, *ABD* is a right triangle with *AB* equal to *AD*. Since *ABD* is a right triangle, *BD* is a diameter of the circle, so *BD* equals 8. Therefore, $s^2 + s^2 = 8^2$ where *s* is the length of a side of the square. So $2s^2 = 64$ or $s^2 = 32$. Since s^2 is the area of the square, 32 is the area of the square. So the area of the region is $16\pi - 32 = 16(\pi - 2)$. (III-7)

14. *X is defined as the largest integer which is less than X. What is the value of (*3) + (*4) + (*4.5)?

(A) 9
(B) 10
(C) 11
(D) 11.5
(E) 12

(A) Since *X is the largest integer which is less than X, *3 is 2 (NOT 3). In the same way *4 is 3 and *4.5 is 4. So (*3) + (*4) + (*4.5) equals 2 + 3 + 4 = 9. (II-1)

15. Joan started work 2 years ago. Her starting salary was $\frac{1}{2}$ of Mike's salary at that time. Each year since then Joan has received a raise of 5% in her salary and Mike has received a raise of 10% in his salary. What percentage (to the nearest percent) of Mike's current salary is Joan's current salary?

(A) 45
(B) 46
(C) 48
(D) 50
(E) 220

(B) Let *JS* and *JC* be Joan's starting and current salaries respectively. Let *MS* and *MC* be Mike's salary when Joan started and his current salary. We know $JS = .5MS$, and we want to find an equation relating *JC* and *MC*. Since Joan received a 5% raise each year, after 1 year her salary was $1.05JS$ and after 2 years her salary is $(1.05)(1.05)JS$. In the same way, we can see that Mike's current salary (*MC*) is $(1.10)(1.10)MS$. So $MC = (1.1)^2MS$. So $JC = (1.05)(1.05)JS = 1.1025JS = .5(1.1025)MS = (.55125)\left(\frac{1}{(1.1)^2}\right)MC = \left(\frac{.55125}{1.21}\right)MC.$

Since we want the answer to the nearest percent, we must divide to three decimal places. So $\frac{.55125}{1.21} = .455 =$ 46% to the nearest percent. (I-8, II-2)

16. Which of the following integers has the most divisors?

(A) 88
(B) 91
(C) 95
(D) 99
(E) 101

(A) Since every integer has 1 and itself as divisors, we shall neglect these. Write each integer as a product of primes to determine its divisors. So $88 = 2 \times 44 = 2 \times 2 \times 22 = 2 \times 2 \times 2 \times 11$. Therefore, the divisors of 88 are 2, 4, 8, 11, 22, and 44, for a total of 6. Since $91 = 7 \times 13$ and $95 = 5 \times 19$, they both have a total of 2 divisors. $99 = 3 \times 33 = 3 \times 3 \times 11$, so the divisors of 99 are 3, 9, 11, and 33, for a total of 4. 101 is a prime, so it has no divisors. (To see that 101 is a prime, you only have to see if primes less than $\sqrt{101}$, which is less than 11, divide 101.) Therefore, 88 has the most divisors. (I-1)

17. The amount of fat in an ounce of food A plus the amount of protein in an ounce of food A is 100 grams. The amount of protein in an ounce of food A minus twice the amount of fat in an ounce of food A is 10 grams. How many grams of protein are there in an ounce of food A?

(A) 30
(B) 45
(C) 50
(D) 55
(E) 70

(E) Let *f* and *p* be the amounts of fat and protein in an ounce of food A. Then we know that $f + p = 100$ and $p - 2f = 10$. So *f* is $100 - p$, and the second equation becomes $p - 2(100 - p) = p - 200 + 2p = 3p - 200 = 10$. So $3p = 210$ or $p = 70$. (II-2)

Section 7
Critical Reasoning

1. A politician wrote the following: "I realize there are some shortcomings to the questionnaire method. However, since I send a copy of the questionnaire to every home in the district, I believe the results are quite representative . . . I think the numbers received are so large that it is quite accurate even though the survey is not done scientifically."

The writer of the above statement makes which of the following assumptions:

(A) Most people who received the questionnaire have replied.
(B) Most people in the district live in homes.
(C) The questionnaire method of data collection is unscientific.
(D) The large number of replies means that a high proportion of those sampled have replied.
(E) A large, absolute number of replies is synonymous with accuracy.

(E) The politician assumes that a large, absolute number of replies means that the survey results are representative of the population (total homes in the district), even though a proportionately small number of replies may have resulted. Alternatives (A), (B), and (D) cannot be assumed from the statement. Alternative (C) is incorrect.

2. In 1950, Transylvania earned $1 million in tourist revenue. By 1970, tourist revenue doubled and in 1980, it reached the sum of $4 million.

Each of the following, if true, may explain the trend in tourist revenue except:

(A) The number of tourists has increased from 1950 to 1980.
(B) Average expenditure per tourist has increased.
(C) Average stay per tourist has increased.
(D) The number of total hotel rooms has increased.
(E) The average price of tourist services has increased.

(D) The number of hotel rooms may be a function of the number of tourists and not vice versa. If average income per tourist did not increase over the time period, an increase in the number of tourists' (doubling every decade) total revenue would double (A). If the number of tourists did not double every decade, but average revenue per tourist doubled (B), total revenue would double. If the average stay per tourist increased, total revenue would increase (assuming that average revenue did not decrease) (C). If the average cost for, say, services, would have doubled during any ten year period, even assuming the same number of tourists and average revenue, total revenue would double. In short, any combination of increases in (A), (B), (C), and (E) could explain the doubling of tourist revenue in any ten year period.

3. Donors are almost never offended by being asked for too much (in fact, they are usually flattered). And if you ask for too much, your donor can always suggest a smaller amount. On the other hand, donors are frequently offended by being asked for too little. A common reaction is, "so that's all they think I'm worth."

The above statement assumes that:

(A) Donors are usually never asked for enough.
(B) A good fund raiser will value the worth of the donor.
(C) It is worth the gamble to ask for large donations.
(D) Fund raisers often think that donors are incapable of giving much.
(E) Donors are seldom offended by fund raisers.

(C) The assumption is that potential donors will be flattered by requests for large donations and frequently offended by requests for smaller amounts. Therefore, it is worth the gamble to start high—at worse the potential donor may decrease his gift. Alternatives (A), (B), and (D) are not assumptions made in the statement. Alternative (E) is partially correct: Donors are seldom offended if they are asked *too much* by fund raisers.

4. One major obligation of the social psychologist is to provide his own discipline, the other social sciences, and interested laymen with conceptual tools that will increase the range and the reliability of their understanding of social phenomena. Beyond that, responsible government officials are today turning more frequently to the social scientist for insights into the nature and solution of the problems with which they are confronted.

The above argument assumes that:

(A) Social psychologists must have a strong background in other sciences as well as their own.
(B) A study of social psychology should be a part of the curriculum of government officials.
(C) The social scientist has an obligation to provide the means by which social phenomena may be understood by others.
(D) Social phenomena are little understood by those outside the field of social psychology.
(E) A good social psychologist is obligated principally by the need to solve inter-disciplinary problems.

(C) The statement refers to the social psychologist's obligation to provide a wide range of people—those in his own discipline, other social scientists, laymen, and government officials—with the tools to understand social phenomena. Alternative (E) might be a correct assumption if it was not linked to inter-disciplinary problems. Alternatives (A), (B), and (D) are incorrect assumptions.

5. New problems require new solutions. And new problems arise with new populations and new technologies. The solutions of these problems require new institutions as well as new political, economic, and social mechanisms. Yet institutions and political and economic arrangements grow slowly and die slowly. Because old institutions die slowly, new institutions should be given every chance of success.

The writer of the above makes which of the following assumptions:

(A) New institutions are needed because old institutions are inefficient.
(B) New institutions are created in order to solve existing problems.
(C) As old institutions are phased out, new ones take their place.
(D) If there were no growth, old institutions would die more slowly.
(E) Socio-technological change requires new forms of institutional arrangements.

(E) New technologies and populations represent socio-technological change problems and require new mechanisms. The other alternatives are incorrect assumptions.

6. About 40 percent of American husbands think it is a good idea for wives with school age children to work outside the home. Only one out of ten German household heads approves of mothers working if school age children live at home. Every second American wife, and every third German wife with school age children has a job outside her home.

If the above is correct, which of the following must be true?

(A) More German than American wives work outside the home.
(B) Employment opportunities for American wives are greater than for German wives.
(C) German husbands have more conservative attitudes than American husbands.
(D) German husbands would seem to be less satisfied about working wives who have school age children than American husbands.
(E) German women have fewer children than American women.

(D) is true. Forty percent of American husbands approve, while 50 percent of American wives work. Ten percent of German husbands approve, while 33 percent of German wives work. Therefore, the gap between German husbands' attitudes towards work and what their wives actually do is much greater than for American husbands and wives.

7. Building codes required all public buildings constructed after 1980 to have reinforced-steel bomb shelters installed.

From which of the following can the statement above be inferred?

(A) Public buildings had to install reinforced-steel bomb shelters after 1980.
(B) No bomb shelters other than reinforced-steel shelters were installed in public buildings after 1980, but all public buildings constructed after 1980 were required to have bomb shelters.
(C) Some public buildings constructed before 1980 had installed bomb shelters.
(D) Bomb shelters were not required in public buildings before 1980, but some were installed voluntarily.
(E) Before 1980, public buildings had bomb shelters, but not necessarily made of reinforced-steel.

(B) Both statements may be inferred; if all public buildings constructed after 1980 were required to have reinforced-steel bomb shelters, then by definition, no bomb shelters other than reinforced-steel ones were installed after 1980. Alternative (A) is incorrect because it refers to *all* public buildings, i.e. those built before 1980. The statement mentions only those constructed *after* 1980.

8. In 1950, the average child visited the dentist once a year, by 1970, the number of visits had increased to two. Today, the average child visits the dentist three times a year.

Each of the following, if true, could explain this trend except:

(A) Dentist fees have declined over the period.
(B) Better home care of teeth has reduced the number of cavities.
(C) Dental care has become less painful.
(D) Parents are more aware of the importance of dental care.
(E) Tax benefits for deducting dental expenses have increased.

(B) (A), (C), (D), and (E) should all encourage more visits to dentists. A decrease in the incidence of cavities should result in a decline of visits to dentists.

9. Attention is most often focused on net exports (exports less imports) because that figure measures the net effect of a nation's trade in goods and services with the rest of the world. In 1968, net exports were 5.8 percent of GNP (Gross National Product) and in 1975, they were 6.8 percent.

If the information above is accurate, which of the following must be true?

(A) If GNP was constant from 1968 to 1975, net exports were greater in 1975 than in 1968.
(B) Exports were greater than imports in 1975, but not in 1968.
(C) Exports increased from 1968 to 1975.
(D) In 1975, the increase in exports was nearly double that in 1968.
(E) In 1968, net exports were greater than in 1975.

(A) The net export figure is measured in absolute terms, while the export and import figures are given as percents of GNP. Therefore, we may compare the trend in percentage terms and relate it to net exports (given in absolute terms) only as a proportion of GNP. If GNP remained constant over the period, we may compare only the percentage terms. Net exports/constant GNP was 5.8 percent in 1968 and 6.8 percent in 1975. Since GNP was constant over the two time periods, net exports were greater in 1975 than in 1968.

10. Once a company has established an extensive sales network in a foreign market and therefore has achieved substantial sales, it seems that these markets should be treated in a very similar fashion to those in one's own country. It is therefore those countries where only initial sales and representation have been developed where marketing methods will have to differ from domestic activities.

The above statement assumes that:

(A) Sales networks can be the same in both foreign and domestic markets.
(B) Extensive sales networks are preferable to less developed ones.
(C) Some countries develop economically faster than others.
(D) Larger markets abroad are more adaptable to domestic marketing methods.
(E) A study of marketing should consider the adaptability of advertising campaigns in different countries.

(D) The assumption is that domestic marketing techniques may be transferable to only those markets that have substantial sales volume. The words "marketing methods" in the last sentence refer to the word "treated" in the first sentence.

11. The principal monetary policy objective is to reduce substantially the import surplus of the coming years while resuming economic growth. Realization of this goal entails a marked structural change of the economy, which can be brought about by freezing the standard of living (per capita private consumption plus public services) and restricting investments that do not further exports.

The writer of the above policy assumes that:

(A) Economic growth will result in a structural change of the economy.
(B) Only if people consume less can the economy grow.
(C) The import surplus can be reduced if investment is restricted.
(D) Only a structural change in the economy can substantially increase imports.
(E) People will have to be persuaded to give up consumption for the national good.

(E) If the principal monetary policy is to be attained—reducing the import surplus while resuming economic growth—per-capita consumption will have to be frozen. Thus, consumers will have to be persuaded to give up consumption to further national economic goals. The assumption is that people will be willing to put a halt to growth in their standard of living.

12. The most commonly cited explanation for nationalization of foreign companies is a change in government. Nationalization tends to cover a wide range of industries and is not selective by country of ownership.

The above statement assumes that:

(A) Defense-related, government-related, and natural resource industries are most likely to be nationalized.
(B) The process of nationalization is not limited to any particular industry or country.
(C) Nationalization of businesses is so widespread as to cause concern.
(D) Nationalization will not occur in countries with democratic governments.
(E) Sharing ownership with local nationals will forestall takeovers by foreign governments.

(B) Even though nationalization is thought to be caused by changes in government, it is not "selective" by country and covers a wide range of industries.

13. In 1985 there were 20 deaths from automobile accidents per 1,000 miles traveled. A total of 20,000 miles were traveled via automobiles in 1985. In the same year, 800 people died in airplane crashes and 400 people were killed in train disasters. A statistician concluded from these data alone that it was more dangerous to travel by plane, train, and automobile, in that order.

Which of the following refutes the statistician's conclusion?

(A) There is no common denominator by which to compare the number of deaths resulting from each mode of travel.
(B) One year is insufficient to reach such a conclusion.
(C) More people travel by car than any other mode of transport, therefore, the probability of a car accident is greater.
(D) The number of plane flights and train trips is not stated.
(E) The probability of being killed in a train disaster and as a result of a car crash is the same.

(A) Note that the casualty figure for automobile deaths is given as the ratio of number of deaths to miles traveled. In order to make a comparison with other modes of transport, the same denominator (miles traveled) would have to be used.

14. From a letter to the commercial editor of a newspaper: Your article of January 9 drew attention to the large deficit in Playland's balance of payments that has worsened over the past three years. Yet, you favor the recent trade treaty signed between Playland and Workland. That treaty results in a lowering of our import duties that will flood us with Workland's goods. This will only exacerbate our balance of trade. How can you be in favor of the treaty?

Which of the following considerations would weaken the letter writer's argument?

(A) Import diversion versus import creation.
(B) Prices paid by importers versus prices paid by consumers.
(C) Economic goals versus political goals.
(D) Duties levied increase government revenue.
(E) Free trade versus protectionism.

(A) If the treaty results in increased Workland exports to Playland at the expense of local producers (import creation), Playland's balance of payments will show a larger deficit. If however, increased Workland exports to Playland merely replace imports from other countries (import diversion), the trade balance will not change. Alternative (C) is a second best consideration, i.e. that political objectives supersede economic goals. The remaining alternatives have no bearing on Playland's balance of trade.

15. In 1930, there were, on the average 10 deaths at birth (infant mortality) per 10,000 population. By 1940 there were 8.5, and by 1950, 7.0. Today there are 5.5 deaths at birth per 10,000 population, and it is anticipated that the downward trend will continue.

Each of the following, if true, would help to account for this trend except:

(A) Medical care is more widespread and available.
(B) More effective birth control methods have been implemented.
(C) Sanitary conditions have improved.
(D) The number of pediatricians per 10,000 population has increased.
(E) Midwifery has declined in favor of medical doctors.

(B) There is no association between birth control and infant mortality. Birth control can prevent pregnancies but not death after birth.

16. Product shipments of household appliances are expected to rise to $17 billion next year, an average annual increase of 8.0 percent over the past five years. The real growth rate, after allowing for probable price increases, is expected to be about 4.3 percent each year, resulting in shipments this year of $14 billion in 1987 dollars.

Each of the following, if true, could help to account for this trend except:

(A) Increased consumer spending for durable products.
(B) Household formations have increased.
(C) Consumer disposable income has increased.
(D) The consumer price of electricity has decreased.
(E) Individual tax advantages have decreased.

(E) If tax advantages (deductions, etc.) decrease, less disposable income is available for spending. All other alternatives explain why total shipments of appliances has increased.

17. Following is a proposal to amend the constitution of a fraternal club as forwarded to its members for approval:

When more than one candidate is a nominee for an office, prospective candidates must consent to nomination and, before giving such consent, must be shown the list of all nominees.

Which of the following statements about the proposal is logical if it cannot be known who the actual candidates are until prospective candidates have consented to be nominated?

(A) The proposal would guarantee that there would always be more than one candidate.
(B) If there is more than one prospective candidate, the proposal would preclude any of them from being a nominee.
(C) The proposal would ensure a wider choice of candidates.
(D) If there is more than one candidate, a given candidate could withdraw before becoming a nominee.
(E) The proposal would ensure that each candidate knows the identity of the others.

(B) A similar question was the final one on a recent GMAT, meaning that it is rather difficult. However, if the order of the argument can be identified, then the correct answer can be found. In shorthand, the argument runs like this:

1. If there is more than one candidate.
2. She or he is told the names of the others.
3. She or he must consent to nomination.

Now, if it cannot be shown who the actual candidate is until prospective candidates have given their consent, then premise (2) and the conclusion (3) are reversed. But this reversal negates the proposal, so (B) is the correct answer.

Evaluating Your Score

Tabulate your score for each section of Sample Test 3 according to the directions on pages 6–7 and record the results in the Self-Scoring Table below. Then find your rating for each score on the Self-Scoring Scale and record it in the appropriate blank.

Self-Scoring Table

SECTION	SCORE	RATING
1		
2		
3		
4		
5		
6		
7		

***Self-Scoring Scale*–RATING**

SECTION	POOR	FAIR	GOOD	EXCELLENT
1	0 – 12+	13 – 17+	18 – 21+	22 – 25
2	0 – 8+	9 – 11	11+ – 14	14+ – 17
3	0 – 8+	9 – 11	11+ – 14	14+ – 17
4	0 – 9+	10 – 13+	14 – 17+	18 – 21
5	0 – 9+	10 – 13+	14 – 17+	18 – 21
6	0 – 8+	9 – 11	11+ – 14	14+ – 17
7	0 – 8+	9 – 11	11+ – 14	14+ – 17

Study again the Review sections covering material in Sample Test 3 for which you had a rating of FAIR or POOR. Then go on the Sample Test 4.

To obtain an approximation of your actual GMAT score, see page 7.

Answer Sheet
SAMPLE TEST 4

Section 1

1 Ⓐ Ⓑ Ⓒ Ⓓ Ⓔ	6 Ⓐ Ⓑ Ⓒ Ⓓ Ⓔ	11 Ⓐ Ⓑ Ⓒ Ⓓ Ⓔ	16 Ⓐ Ⓑ Ⓒ Ⓓ Ⓔ	21 Ⓐ Ⓑ Ⓒ Ⓓ Ⓔ
2 Ⓐ Ⓑ Ⓒ Ⓓ Ⓔ	7 Ⓐ Ⓑ Ⓒ Ⓓ Ⓔ	12 Ⓐ Ⓑ Ⓒ Ⓓ Ⓔ	17 Ⓐ Ⓑ Ⓒ Ⓓ Ⓔ	22 Ⓐ Ⓑ Ⓒ Ⓓ Ⓔ
3 Ⓐ Ⓑ Ⓒ Ⓓ Ⓔ	8 Ⓐ Ⓑ Ⓒ Ⓓ Ⓔ	13 Ⓐ Ⓑ Ⓒ Ⓓ Ⓔ	18 Ⓐ Ⓑ Ⓒ Ⓓ Ⓔ	23 Ⓐ Ⓑ Ⓒ Ⓓ Ⓔ
4 Ⓐ Ⓑ Ⓒ Ⓓ Ⓔ	9 Ⓐ Ⓑ Ⓒ Ⓓ Ⓔ	14 Ⓐ Ⓑ Ⓒ Ⓓ Ⓔ	19 Ⓐ Ⓑ Ⓒ Ⓓ Ⓔ	24 Ⓐ Ⓑ Ⓒ Ⓓ Ⓔ
5 Ⓐ Ⓑ Ⓒ Ⓓ Ⓔ	10 Ⓐ Ⓑ Ⓒ Ⓓ Ⓔ	15 Ⓐ Ⓑ Ⓒ Ⓓ Ⓔ	20 Ⓐ Ⓑ Ⓒ Ⓓ Ⓔ	25 Ⓐ Ⓑ Ⓒ Ⓓ Ⓔ

Section 2

1 Ⓐ Ⓑ Ⓒ Ⓓ Ⓔ	6 Ⓐ Ⓑ Ⓒ Ⓓ Ⓔ	11 Ⓐ Ⓑ Ⓒ Ⓓ Ⓔ	16 Ⓐ Ⓑ Ⓒ Ⓓ Ⓔ	21 Ⓐ Ⓑ Ⓒ Ⓓ Ⓔ
2 Ⓐ Ⓑ Ⓒ Ⓓ Ⓔ	7 Ⓐ Ⓑ Ⓒ Ⓓ Ⓔ	12 Ⓐ Ⓑ Ⓒ Ⓓ Ⓔ	17 Ⓐ Ⓑ Ⓒ Ⓓ Ⓔ	22 Ⓐ Ⓑ Ⓒ Ⓓ Ⓔ
3 Ⓐ Ⓑ Ⓒ Ⓓ Ⓔ	8 Ⓐ Ⓑ Ⓒ Ⓓ Ⓔ	13 Ⓐ Ⓑ Ⓒ Ⓓ Ⓔ	18 Ⓐ Ⓑ Ⓒ Ⓓ Ⓔ	23 Ⓐ Ⓑ Ⓒ Ⓓ Ⓔ
4 Ⓐ Ⓑ Ⓒ Ⓓ Ⓔ	9 Ⓐ Ⓑ Ⓒ Ⓓ Ⓔ	14 Ⓐ Ⓑ Ⓒ Ⓓ Ⓔ	19 Ⓐ Ⓑ Ⓒ Ⓓ Ⓔ	24 Ⓐ Ⓑ Ⓒ Ⓓ Ⓔ
5 Ⓐ Ⓑ Ⓒ Ⓓ Ⓔ	10 Ⓐ Ⓑ Ⓒ Ⓓ Ⓔ	15 Ⓐ Ⓑ Ⓒ Ⓓ Ⓔ	20 Ⓐ Ⓑ Ⓒ Ⓓ Ⓔ	25 Ⓐ Ⓑ Ⓒ Ⓓ Ⓔ

Section 3

1 Ⓐ Ⓑ Ⓒ Ⓓ Ⓔ	6 Ⓐ Ⓑ Ⓒ Ⓓ Ⓔ	11 Ⓐ Ⓑ Ⓒ Ⓓ Ⓔ	16 Ⓐ Ⓑ Ⓒ Ⓓ Ⓔ	21 Ⓐ Ⓑ Ⓒ Ⓓ Ⓔ
2 Ⓐ Ⓑ Ⓒ Ⓓ Ⓔ	7 Ⓐ Ⓑ Ⓒ Ⓓ Ⓔ	12 Ⓐ Ⓑ Ⓒ Ⓓ Ⓔ	17 Ⓐ Ⓑ Ⓒ Ⓓ Ⓔ	22 Ⓐ Ⓑ Ⓒ Ⓓ Ⓔ
3 Ⓐ Ⓑ Ⓒ Ⓓ Ⓔ	8 Ⓐ Ⓑ Ⓒ Ⓓ Ⓔ	13 Ⓐ Ⓑ Ⓒ Ⓓ Ⓔ	18 Ⓐ Ⓑ Ⓒ Ⓓ Ⓔ	23 Ⓐ Ⓑ Ⓒ Ⓓ Ⓔ
4 Ⓐ Ⓑ Ⓒ Ⓓ Ⓔ	9 Ⓐ Ⓑ Ⓒ Ⓓ Ⓔ	14 Ⓐ Ⓑ Ⓒ Ⓓ Ⓔ	19 Ⓐ Ⓑ Ⓒ Ⓓ Ⓔ	24 Ⓐ Ⓑ Ⓒ Ⓓ Ⓔ
5 Ⓐ Ⓑ Ⓒ Ⓓ Ⓔ	10 Ⓐ Ⓑ Ⓒ Ⓓ Ⓔ	15 Ⓐ Ⓑ Ⓒ Ⓓ Ⓔ	20 Ⓐ Ⓑ Ⓒ Ⓓ Ⓔ	25 Ⓐ Ⓑ Ⓒ Ⓓ Ⓔ

Section 4

1 Ⓐ Ⓑ Ⓒ Ⓓ Ⓔ	6 Ⓐ Ⓑ Ⓒ Ⓓ Ⓔ	11 Ⓐ Ⓑ Ⓒ Ⓓ Ⓔ	16 Ⓐ Ⓑ Ⓒ Ⓓ Ⓔ	21 Ⓐ Ⓑ Ⓒ Ⓓ Ⓔ
2 Ⓐ Ⓑ Ⓒ Ⓓ Ⓔ	7 Ⓐ Ⓑ Ⓒ Ⓓ Ⓔ	12 Ⓐ Ⓑ Ⓒ Ⓓ Ⓔ	17 Ⓐ Ⓑ Ⓒ Ⓓ Ⓔ	22 Ⓐ Ⓑ Ⓒ Ⓓ Ⓔ
3 Ⓐ Ⓑ Ⓒ Ⓓ Ⓔ	8 Ⓐ Ⓑ Ⓒ Ⓓ Ⓔ	13 Ⓐ Ⓑ Ⓒ Ⓓ Ⓔ	18 Ⓐ Ⓑ Ⓒ Ⓓ Ⓔ	23 Ⓐ Ⓑ Ⓒ Ⓓ Ⓔ
4 Ⓐ Ⓑ Ⓒ Ⓓ Ⓔ	9 Ⓐ Ⓑ Ⓒ Ⓓ Ⓔ	14 Ⓐ Ⓑ Ⓒ Ⓓ Ⓔ	19 Ⓐ Ⓑ Ⓒ Ⓓ Ⓔ	24 Ⓐ Ⓑ Ⓒ Ⓓ Ⓔ
5 Ⓐ Ⓑ Ⓒ Ⓓ Ⓔ	10 Ⓐ Ⓑ Ⓒ Ⓓ Ⓔ	15 Ⓐ Ⓑ Ⓒ Ⓓ Ⓔ	20 Ⓐ Ⓑ Ⓒ Ⓓ Ⓔ	25 Ⓐ Ⓑ Ⓒ Ⓓ Ⓔ

Section 5

1 Ⓐ Ⓑ Ⓒ Ⓓ Ⓔ	6 Ⓐ Ⓑ Ⓒ Ⓓ Ⓔ	11 Ⓐ Ⓑ Ⓒ Ⓓ Ⓔ	16 Ⓐ Ⓑ Ⓒ Ⓓ Ⓔ	21 Ⓐ Ⓑ Ⓒ Ⓓ Ⓔ
2 Ⓐ Ⓑ Ⓒ Ⓓ Ⓔ	7 Ⓐ Ⓑ Ⓒ Ⓓ Ⓔ	12 Ⓐ Ⓑ Ⓒ Ⓓ Ⓔ	17 Ⓐ Ⓑ Ⓒ Ⓓ Ⓔ	22 Ⓐ Ⓑ Ⓒ Ⓓ Ⓔ
3 Ⓐ Ⓑ Ⓒ Ⓓ Ⓔ	8 Ⓐ Ⓑ Ⓒ Ⓓ Ⓔ	13 Ⓐ Ⓑ Ⓒ Ⓓ Ⓔ	18 Ⓐ Ⓑ Ⓒ Ⓓ Ⓔ	23 Ⓐ Ⓑ Ⓒ Ⓓ Ⓔ
4 Ⓐ Ⓑ Ⓒ Ⓓ Ⓔ	9 Ⓐ Ⓑ Ⓒ Ⓓ Ⓔ	14 Ⓐ Ⓑ Ⓒ Ⓓ Ⓔ	19 Ⓐ Ⓑ Ⓒ Ⓓ Ⓔ	24 Ⓐ Ⓑ Ⓒ Ⓓ Ⓔ
5 Ⓐ Ⓑ Ⓒ Ⓓ Ⓔ	10 Ⓐ Ⓑ Ⓒ Ⓓ Ⓔ	15 Ⓐ Ⓑ Ⓒ Ⓓ Ⓔ	20 Ⓐ Ⓑ Ⓒ Ⓓ Ⓔ	25 Ⓐ Ⓑ Ⓒ Ⓓ Ⓔ

Section 6

1 Ⓐ Ⓑ Ⓒ Ⓓ Ⓔ	6 Ⓐ Ⓑ Ⓒ Ⓓ Ⓔ	11 Ⓐ Ⓑ Ⓒ Ⓓ Ⓔ	16 Ⓐ Ⓑ Ⓒ Ⓓ Ⓔ	21 Ⓐ Ⓑ Ⓒ Ⓓ Ⓔ
2 Ⓐ Ⓑ Ⓒ Ⓓ Ⓔ	7 Ⓐ Ⓑ Ⓒ Ⓓ Ⓔ	12 Ⓐ Ⓑ Ⓒ Ⓓ Ⓔ	17 Ⓐ Ⓑ Ⓒ Ⓓ Ⓔ	22 Ⓐ Ⓑ Ⓒ Ⓓ Ⓔ
3 Ⓐ Ⓑ Ⓒ Ⓓ Ⓔ	8 Ⓐ Ⓑ Ⓒ Ⓓ Ⓔ	13 Ⓐ Ⓑ Ⓒ Ⓓ Ⓔ	18 Ⓐ Ⓑ Ⓒ Ⓓ Ⓔ	23 Ⓐ Ⓑ Ⓒ Ⓓ Ⓔ
4 Ⓐ Ⓑ Ⓒ Ⓓ Ⓔ	9 Ⓐ Ⓑ Ⓒ Ⓓ Ⓔ	14 Ⓐ Ⓑ Ⓒ Ⓓ Ⓔ	19 Ⓐ Ⓑ Ⓒ Ⓓ Ⓔ	24 Ⓐ Ⓑ Ⓒ Ⓓ Ⓔ
5 Ⓐ Ⓑ Ⓒ Ⓓ Ⓔ	10 Ⓐ Ⓑ Ⓒ Ⓓ Ⓔ	15 Ⓐ Ⓑ Ⓒ Ⓓ Ⓔ	20 Ⓐ Ⓑ Ⓒ Ⓓ Ⓔ	25 Ⓐ Ⓑ Ⓒ Ⓓ Ⓔ

Section 7

1 Ⓐ Ⓑ Ⓒ Ⓓ Ⓔ	6 Ⓐ Ⓑ Ⓒ Ⓓ Ⓔ	11 Ⓐ Ⓑ Ⓒ Ⓓ Ⓔ	16 Ⓐ Ⓑ Ⓒ Ⓓ Ⓔ	21 Ⓐ Ⓑ Ⓒ Ⓓ Ⓔ
2 Ⓐ Ⓑ Ⓒ Ⓓ Ⓔ	7 Ⓐ Ⓑ Ⓒ Ⓓ Ⓔ	12 Ⓐ Ⓑ Ⓒ Ⓓ Ⓔ	17 Ⓐ Ⓑ Ⓒ Ⓓ Ⓔ	22 Ⓐ Ⓑ Ⓒ Ⓓ Ⓔ
3 Ⓐ Ⓑ Ⓒ Ⓓ Ⓔ	8 Ⓐ Ⓑ Ⓒ Ⓓ Ⓔ	13 Ⓐ Ⓑ Ⓒ Ⓓ Ⓔ	18 Ⓐ Ⓑ Ⓒ Ⓓ Ⓔ	23 Ⓐ Ⓑ Ⓒ Ⓓ Ⓔ
4 Ⓐ Ⓑ Ⓒ Ⓓ Ⓔ	9 Ⓐ Ⓑ Ⓒ Ⓓ Ⓔ	14 Ⓐ Ⓑ Ⓒ Ⓓ Ⓔ	19 Ⓐ Ⓑ Ⓒ Ⓓ Ⓔ	24 Ⓐ Ⓑ Ⓒ Ⓓ Ⓔ
5 Ⓐ Ⓑ Ⓒ Ⓓ Ⓔ	10 Ⓐ Ⓑ Ⓒ Ⓓ Ⓔ	15 Ⓐ Ⓑ Ⓒ Ⓓ Ⓔ	20 Ⓐ Ⓑ Ⓒ Ⓓ Ⓔ	25 Ⓐ Ⓑ Ⓒ Ⓓ Ⓔ

Cut along dashed line to remove answer sheet.

12 SAMPLE TEST 4
with Answers and Analysis

Writing Assessment

Part I

TIME: 30 minutes

Directions: Write a clear, logical, and well-organized response to the following issue or argument. Your response should be in the form of a short essay, following the conventions of standard written English. Your answer should fit on three pages of lined 8½" × 11" paper. Write legibly. Essays that are illegible or that are written on a topic other than the one outlined in the question will not be scored.

Industrialized nations have now managed to provide their citizens with food, shelter, and clothing. As a result, citizens are becoming aware of other and subtler needs. But a society geared to the production of goods is poorly adapted to providing for psychological needs. The very processes by which we manufacture goods so effectively actually reduce psychological satisfaction.

Which do you find more convincing: the claim that industrialization provides for psychological needs or the opposite view? State your position using relevant reasons and examples from your own experience, observation, or reading.

Part II

TIME: 30 minutes

Directions: Write a clear, logical, and well-organized response to the following issue or argument. Your response should be in the form of a short essay, following the conventions of standard written English. Your answer should fit on three pages of lined 8½" × 11" paper. Write legibly. Essays that are illegible or that are written on a topic other than the one outlined in the question will not be scored.

The Bestvalue Superette chain has nine stores in Mytown, USA. The company's policy is to maintain the same prices for all items at all stores. However, the distribution manager knowingly sends the poorest cuts of meat and the lowest quality produce to the store located in the low-income section of town. He justifies this action based on the fact that this store has the highest overhead because of factors such as employee turnover, theft, and vandalism.

Discuss how logically persuasive you find the above argument. In presenting your point of view, analyze the sort of reasoning used and its supporting evidence. In addition, state what further evidence, if any, would make the argument more sound and convincing or would make you better able to evaluate its conclusion.

STOP

IF THERE IS STILL TIME REMAINING, YOU MAY REVIEW THE QUESTIONS IN THIS SECTION ONLY. YOU MAY NOT TURN TO ANY OTHER SECTION OF THE TEST.

1 1 1 1 1 1 1 1 1 1 1

Section 1

TIME: 25 minutes
21 Questions

Directions: This test consists of a number of sentences, in each of which some part or the whole is underlined. Each sentence is followed by five alternative versions of the underlined portion. Select the alternative you consider both most correct and most effective according to the requirements of standard written English. Answer A is the same as the original version; if you think the original version is best, select answer A.

In considering the answer choices, be attentive to matters of grammar, diction, and syntax, as well as clarity, precision, and fluency. Do not select an answer that alters the meaning of the original sentence.

1. More than any animal, the wolverine exemplifies the unbridled ferocity of "nature red in tooth and claw."

(A) More than any animal
(B) More than any other animal
(C) More than another animal
(D) Unlike any animal
(E) Compared to other animals

2. In 1896, Henri Bequerel found that uranium salts emitted penetrating radiations similar to those which Roentgen produced only a year earlier with a gas discharge tube.

(A) similar to those which Roentgen
(B) like those which Roentgen
(C) similar to those that Roentgen had
(D) similar to them that Roentgen
(E) similar to those Roentgen

3. Unless they reverse present policies immediately, the world may suffer permanent damage from the unregulated use of pesticides.

(A) Unless they reverse present policies
(B) Unless present policies are reversed
(C) Unless present policies will be reversed
(D) If it will not reverse present policies
(E) If present policies will not be reversed

4. He interviewed several candidates who he thought had the experience and qualifications the position required.

(A) who he thought
(B) whom he thought
(C) of whom he thought
(D) he thought who
(E) which he thought

5. The average citizen today is surprisingly knowledgeable about landmark court decisions concerning such questions as racial segregation, legislative appointment, prayer in the public schools, and whether a defendant has a right to counsel in a criminal prosecution.

(A) whether a defendant has a right to counsel
(B) if a defendant has a right to counsel
(C) the right of a defendant to council
(D) the right of a defendant to counsel
(E) is a defendant entitled to counsel

6. The reason we are late is due to the fact that the bus was delayed by heavy traffic.

(A) due to the fact that the bus was delayed by heavy traffic
(B) because the bus was delayed by heavy traffic
(C) that the bus was delayed by heavy traffic
(D) due to the fact that heavy traffic delayed the bus
(E) that the delay of our bus was caused by heavy traffic

7. Before starting a program of diet and exercise, a consultation with your physician is advisable.

(A) a consultation with your physician is advisable
(B) it is advisable to have a consultation with your physician
(C) a physician's consultation is advisable
(D) a consultation with your physician is necessary
(E) you should consult your physician

GO ON TO THE NEXT PAGE ➤

8. The first of a number of receptions and testimonial dinners for the departing school superintendent have been scheduled, with more events still in the planning stage.

   (A) have been scheduled, with more events still
   (B) have been scheduled, and with more events still
   (C) has been scheduled, and with more events still
   (D) has been scheduled, with more events still
   (E) have been scheduled, and there is still more events

9. If the Confederate Army would have carried the day at Gettysburg, the history of America during the past century might have been profoundly altered.

   (A) If the Confederate Army would have carried the day at Gettysburg
   (B) Had the Confederate Army carried the day at Gettysburg
   (C) The Confederate Army having carried the day at Gettysburg
   (D) If the Confederate Army would have won at Gettysburg
   (E) If the Battle of Gettysburg would have been won by the Confederate Army

10. Economic conditions demand that we not only cut wages and prices but also reduce inflation-raised tax rates.

   (A) that we not only cut wages and prices but also
   (B) not only cutting wages and prices but also to
   (C) not only to cut wages and prices but also to
   (D) not only a cut in wages and prices but also to
   (E) not only to cut wages and prices but that we also

11. Legislative effectiveness, in theory, makes good sense; in actuality, however, they are sometimes difficult to enforce.

   (A) they are sometimes difficult to enforce
   (B) it is difficult to enforce them
   (C) laws are sometimes difficult to enforce
   (D) it is sometimes difficult to enforce laws
   (E) this is sometimes difficult for them to enforce

12. Fame as well as fortune were his goals in life.

   (A) Fame as well as fortune were his goals
   (B) Fame as well as fortune was his goals
   (C) Fame as well as fortune were his goal
   (D) Fame and fortune were his goals
   (E) Fame also fortune were his goals

13. Familiar with the terrain from previous visits, the explorer's search for the abandoned mine site was a success.

   (A) the explorer's search for the abandoned mine site was a success
   (B) the success of the explorer's search for the abandoned mine site was assured
   (C) the explorer succeeded in finding the abandoned mine site
   (D) the search by the explorer for the abandoned mine was successful
   (E) the explorer in his search for the abandoned mine site was a success

14. During the first year that he and I were neighbors, our conversations turned frequently on the two cardinal points of poetry: the power of exciting the sympathy of the reader by a faithful adherence to the truth of nature and the power to give the interest of novelty by the modifying colors of imagination.

   (A) power to give
   (B) ability to give
   (C) power to bestow
   (D) ability to bestow
   (E) power of giving

15. Modernization has gone hand in hand and has offered incentives for such things as personal initiative and ambition, hard work, and resourcefulness.

   (A) and has offered incentives for such things as personal initiative and ambition, hard work, and resourcefulness
   (B) with and has offered incentives for such things as personal initiative and ambition, hard work, and resourcefulness
   (C) with and has offered incentives for such things as personal initiative and ambition, hard work, and the ability to be resourceful
   (D) and has offered incentives such as personal initiative and ambition, hard work, and resourcefulness
   (E) and is offering incentives for such things as personal initiative and ambition, hard work, and resourcefulness

GO ON TO THE NEXT PAGE ➤

1 1 1 1 1 1 1 1 1 1 1

16. My objection to him taking part in this dispute is based on my belief that he is not a disinterested party.

(A) My objection to him taking part in this dispute is based on my belief that he is not a disinterested party.
(B) My objection to his taking part in this dispute is based on my belief that he is not a disinterested party.
(C) My objection to him taking part in this dispute is based on my belief that he is not an uninterested party.
(D) My objection to his taking part in this dispute is based on my belief that he is not an uninterested party.
(E) I object to him taking part in this dispute because he is not a disinterested party.

17. Of the two candidates for this government position, Jason Harald is the most qualified because of his experience in the field.

(A) most qualified because of
(B) most qualified due to
(C) more qualified due to
(D) more qualified because of
(E) most qualified as a result of

18. If anyone calls while we are in conference, tell them that I will return their call after the meeting.

(A) them that I will return their call after the meeting
(B) him or her that I will return their call after the meeting
(C) them that I would return their call after the meeting
(D) the person that I will return the call after the meeting
(E) him or her that I would return the call after the meeting is over

19. Neither the earthquake or the subsequent fire was able to destroy the spirit of the city dwellers.

(A) or the subsequent fire was
(B) nor the subsequent fire were
(C) or the subsequent fire were
(D) nor the subsequent fire was
(E) or the fire that occurred subsequently were

20. The Secretary of State reminded his listeners that this country always has and always will try to honor its commitments.

(A) always has and always will try to honor
(B) has always and will always try to honor
(C) always has tried and always will try to honor
(D) always has tried to honor and will always
(E) has always tried to honor and will always

21. Tests show that catfish from Lake Apopka are safe to eat, even though they contain almost twice as much of the pesticide DDT this year than they did in 1982.

(A) than they did
(B) more than they did
(C) as they did
(D) than they had contained
(E) than they contained

STOP

IF THERE IS STILL TIME REMAINING,
YOU MAY REVIEW THE QUESTIONS IN THIS SECTION ONLY.
YOU MAY NOT TURN TO ANY OTHER SECTION OF THE TEST.

Section 2

TIME: 25 minutes
17 Questions

Directions: Solve each of the following problems; then indicate the correct answer on the answer sheet.

NOTE: A figure that appears with a problem is drawn as accurately as possible so as to provide information that may help in answering the question. Numbers in this test are real numbers.

1. If 32 students in a class are female and in the class the ratio of female students to male students is 16 : 9, what percentage of the class is female?

   (A) 32%
   (B) 36%
   (C) 56.25%
   (D) 64%
   (E) 72%

2. If a job takes 12 men 4 hours to complete, how long should it take 15 men to complete the job?

   (A) 2 hrs. 40 min.
   (B) 3 hrs.
   (C) 3 hrs. 12 min.
   (D) 3 hrs. 24 min.
   (E) 3 hrs. 30 min.

3. The schedules of G first-year students were inspected. It was found that M were taking a math course, L were taking a language course, and B were taking both a math course and a language course. Which of the following expressions gives the percentage of the students whose schedules were inspected who were taking neither a math course nor a language course?

   (A) $100 \times \frac{G}{(B+L+M)}$
   (B) $100 \times \frac{(B+L+M)}{G}$
   (C) $100 \times \frac{(G-L-M)}{G}$
   (D) $100 \times \frac{(G-B-L-M)}{G}$
   (E) $100 \times \frac{(G+B-L-M)}{G}$

GO ON TO THE NEXT PAGE ➤

2 2 2 2 2 2 2 2 2 2 2

4. How long must a driver take to drive the final 70 miles of a trip if he wants to average 50 miles an hour for the entire trip and during the first part of the trip he drove 50 miles in $1\frac{1}{2}$ hours?

(A) 54 min.
(B) 1 hr.
(C) 66 min.
(D) 70 min.
(E) 75 min.

5. If $a + 2b = 6$ and $ab = 4$ what is $\frac{2}{a} + \frac{1}{b}$?

(A) $\frac{1}{2}$
(B) 1
(C) $\frac{3}{2}$
(D) 2
(E) $\frac{5}{2}$

6. A is 10 miles west of B. C is 30 miles north of B. D is 20 miles east of C. What is the distance from A to D?

(A) 10 miles
(B) 30 miles
(C) $10\sqrt{10}$ miles
(D) $10\sqrt{13}$ miles
(E) $30\sqrt{2}$ miles

7. What percentage of the numbers from 1 to 50 have squares that end in the digit 1?

(A) 1
(B) 5
(C) 10
(D) 11
(E) 20

8. If a rectangle has length L and the width is one half of the length, then the area of the rectangle is

(A) L
(B) L^2
(C) $\frac{1}{2}L^2$
(D) $\frac{1}{4}L^2$
(E) $2L$

GO ON TO THE NEXT PAGE ➤

2 2 2 2 2 2 2 2 2 2 2

9. If the product of two numbers is 5 and one of the numbers is $\frac{3}{2}$, then the sum of the two numbers is

(A) $4\frac{1}{3}$
(B) $4\frac{2}{3}$
(C) $4\frac{5}{6}$
(D) $5\frac{1}{6}$
(E) $6\frac{1}{2}$

10. Which of the following sets of numbers can be used as the lengths of the sides of a triangle?

I. [5, 7, 12]
II. [2, 4, 10]
III. [5, 7, 9]

(A) I only
(B) III only
(C) I and II only
(D) I and III only
(E) II and III only

11. What is the next number in the arithmetic progression 2, 5, 8 . . . ?

(A) 7
(B) 9
(C) 10
(D) 11
(E) 12

12. The sum of the three digits *a*, *b*, and *c* is 12. What is the largest three digit number that can be formed using each of the digits exactly once?

(A) 921
(B) 930
(C) 999
(D) 1092
(E) 1200

13. Water is poured into an empty cylindrical tank at a constant rate for 5 minutes. After the water has been poured into the tank, the depth of the water is 7 feet. The radius of the tank is 10 feet. Which of the following is the best approximation for the rate at which the water was poured into the tank?

(A) 44 cubic feet/min
(B) 140 cubic feet/min
(C) 440 cubic feet/min
(D) 700 cubic feet/min
(E) 2200 cubic feet/min

GO ON TO THE NEXT PAGE ➤

2 2 2 2 2 2 2 2 2 2 2

14. A car traveled 75% of the way from town A to town B by traveling at T hours at an average speed of V mph. The car travels at an average speed of S mph for the remaining part of the trip. Which of the following expressions represents the average speed for the entire trip?

(A) $.75V + .25S$
(B) $.75T + .25S$
(C) $\dfrac{VT}{(3S)}$
(D) $\dfrac{4VT}{\left(\dfrac{T+S}{3}\right)}$
(E) $\dfrac{4VS}{(3S+V)}$

15. What is the farthest distance between two points on a cylinder of height 8 and radius 8?

(A) $8\sqrt{2}$
(B) $8\sqrt{3}$
(C) 16
(D) $8\sqrt{5}$
(E) $8\,(2\pi + 1)$

16. Rich sold his skis for \$160.00 and his ski boots for \$96.00. He made a profit of 20% on his boots and took a 10% loss on his skis. He ended up with a

(A) loss of \$1.78
(B) loss of \$1.50
(C) gain of \$3.20
(D) gain of \$7.53
(E) gain of \$17.06

17. It costs 10¢ each to print the first 500 copies of a newspaper. It costs $\left(10 - \dfrac{x}{50}\right)$¢ each for every copy after the first 500. What is x if it cost \$75.00 to print 1,000 copies of the newspaper?

(A) 2.5
(B) 100
(C) 25
(D) 250
(E) 300

STOP

IF THERE IS STILL TIME REMAINING,
YOU MAY REVIEW THE QUESTIONS IN THIS SECTION ONLY.
YOU MAY NOT TURN TO ANY OTHER SECTION OF THE TEST.

3 3 3 3 3 3 3 3 3 3 3

Section 3

TIME: 30 minutes
25 Questions

Directions: This part contains three reading passages. You are to read each one carefully. When answering the questions, you will be allowed to refer back to the passages. The questions are based on what is *stated* or *implied* in each passage.

Passage 1:

The economic condition of the low-income regions of the world is one of the great problems of our time. Their progress is important to the high-income countries, not only for humanitarian and political reasons but also because rapid economic growth in the low income countries could make a substantial contribution to the expansion and prosperity of the world economy as a whole.

The governments of most high-income countries have in recent years undertaken important aid programs, both bilaterally and multilaterally, and have thus demonstrated their interest in the development of low-income countries. They have also worked within the General Agreement on Tariffs and Trade (GATT) for greater freedom of trade and, recognizing the special problems of low-income countries, have made special trading arrangements to meet their needs. But a faster expansion of trade with high-income countries is necessary if the low-income countries are to enjoy a satisfactory rate of growth.

This statement is therefore concerned with the policies of high-income countries toward their trade with low-income countries. Our recommendations are based on the conviction that a better distribution of world resources and a more rational utilization of labor are in the general interest. A liberal policy on the part of high-income countries with respect to their trade with low-income countries will not only be helpful to the low-income countries but, when transitional adjustments have taken place, beneficial to the high-income countries as well.

It is necessary to recognize however, that in furthering the development of low-income countries, the high-income countries can play only a supporting role. If development is to be successful, the main effort must necessarily be made by the people of the low-income countries. The high-income countries are, moreover, likely to provide aid and facilitate trade more readily and extensively where the low-income countries are seen to be making sound and determined efforts to help themselves, and thus to be making effective use of their aid and trade opportunities.

It is, then, necessary that the low-income countries take full account of the lessons that have been learned from the experience of recent years, if they wish to achieve successful development and benefit from support from high-income countries. Among the most important of these lessons are the following:

Severe damage has been done by inflation. A sound financial framework evokes higher domestic savings and investment as well as more aid and investment from abroad. Budgetary and monetary discipline and a more efficient financial and fiscal system help greatly to mobilize funds for investment and thereby decisively influence the rate of growth. Foreign aid should also be efficiently applied to this end.

The energies of the people of low-income countries are more likely to be harnessed to the task of economic development where the policies of their governments aim to offer economic opportunity for all and to reduce excessive social inequalities.

GO ON TO THE NEXT PAGE ➤

Development plans have tended to concentrate on industrial investment. The growth of industry depends, however, on concomitant development in agriculture. A steady rise in productivity on the farms, where in almost all low-income countries a majority of the labor force works, is an essential condition of rapid over-all growth. Satisfactory development of agriculture is also necessary to provide an adequate market for an expanding industrial sector and to feed the growing urban population without burdening the balance of payments with heavy food imports. Diminishing surpluses in the high-income countries underline the need for a faster growth of agricultural productivity in low-income countries. Success in this should, moreover, lead to greater trade in agricultural products among the low-income countries themselves as well as to increased exports of some agricultural products to the high-income countries.

There can be no doubt about the urgency of the world food problem. Adequate nourishment and a balanced diet are not only necessary for working adults but are crucial for the mental and physical development of growing children. Yet, in a number of low-income countries where the diet is already insufficient the production of food has fallen behind the increase in population. A continuation of this trend must lead to endemic famine. The situation demands strenuous efforts in the low-income countries to improve the production, preservation, and distribution of food so that these countries are better able to feed themselves.

1. The economic conditions of low-income countries are important to high-income countries because of

    I. economic reasons
    II. political reasons
    III. cultural reasons

    (A) I only
    (B) III only
    (C) I and II only
    (D) II and III only
    (E) I, II, and III

2. According to the passage, governments of most high-income countries have
    (A) not worked for freer trade with low-income countries
    (B) undertaken important aid programs for low-income countries
    (C) injected massive doses of capital into low-income countries
    (D) provided training programs for low-income country entrepreneurs
    (E) helped improve the educational systems of low-income countries

3. The major subject with which the passage is concerned is
    (A) trade policies of high-income countries towards low-income countries
    (B) foreign trade problems of low-income countries
    (C) fiscal and monetary problems of low-income countries
    (D) trade arrangements under the GATT organization
    (E) general economic problems of low-income countries

GO ON TO THE NEXT PAGE ➤

3 3 3 3 3 3 3 3 3 3 3

4. If low-income countries expect aid from high-income countries, they must do all of the following except

   (A) spend the aid wisely
   (B) put their own houses in order first
   (C) learn from the experience of developed countries
   (D) curb inflation
   (E) de-emphasize agricultural development in favor of industrial growth

5. Which of the following is mentioned for its influence upon the rate of economic growth?

   (A) an efficient financial and fiscal system
   (B) a trade surplus
   (C) a democratic government
   (D) little reliance upon foreign aid
   (E) a budgetary surplus

6. Industrial growth depends upon a parallel growth of the

   (A) labor force
   (B) agricultural system
   (C) balance of payments
   (D) urban population
   (E) monetary system

7. The passage states that participation of high-income countries should be limited to

   (A) 10 percent of their GNP
   (B) a supporting role
   (C) regulations stipulated by GATT
   (D) what low-income countries can absorb
   (E) monetary aid only

8. In order to better enlist the support of the population in economic development efforts, low-income countries should

   (A) not accept more foreign aid than they can use
   (B) budget the capital wisely
   (C) reduce excessive social inequalities
   (D) concentrate on commercial development
   (E) establish agricultural communes

9. People will be motivated to work if they are offered

   (A) social equality
   (B) better working conditions
   (C) more money
   (D) shorter hours
   (E) quality jobs

GO ON TO THE NEXT PAGE ➤

Passage 2:

In *Scholasticism and Politics*, written during World War II, Maritain expressed discouragement at the pessimism and lack of self-confidence characteristic of the Western democracies, and in the postwar world he joined enthusiastically in the resurgence of that confidence. While stopping short of asserting that democracy as a political system flowed directly from correct philosophical principles, he nonetheless dismissed Fascism and Communism as inherently irrational. Bourgeois individualism was, however, implicitly immoral and, by breaking down all sense of community and shared moral values, would inevitably end in some form of statism: order imposed from above. In *Integral Humanism* (1936) and later works, he developed a systematic critique of the prevailing modern political ideologies and argued that a workable political order, which might appropriately be democracy, depended on a correct understanding of human nature and of natural moral law.

Maritain became something of an Americanophile, seeking to counter not only what he regarded as European misconceptions about America but also the Americans' own self-deprecation. In *Reflections on America* (1958), he argued that Americans were not really materialistic but were the most idealistic people in the world, although theirs was an idealism often unformed and lacking in philosophical bases. America, he thought, offered perhaps the best contemporary prospect for the emergence of a truly Christian civilization, based not on governmental decree but on the gradual realization of Christian values on the part of a majority of the population. American saints were coming, he predicted.

But his postulation of a possible Christian civilization in America did not in any way temper his optimistic political liberalism—a facet of his thought which caused him to be held in suspicion by some of his fellow Catholics in the 1950s. The Dominican chaplain at Princeton, for example, refused to allow him to address the Catholic students. (One of the exquisite ironies of recent Catholic history was that Maritain in his last books was acerbically critical of secularizing priests, while the Dominican chaplain resigned from the priesthood and ended his days as a real estate salesman in Florida.)

No doubt in part because of Raïssa's background, Maritain had an enduring interest in anti-Semitism, which he analyzed and criticized in two books, and he was one of the principal influences in the effort to establish better Jewish-Catholic relations. Racism he regarded as America's most severe flaw. As early as 1958 he was praising Martin Luther King, Jr., and the Chicago neighborhood organizer Saul Alinsky.

Maritain and, to a lesser extent, Gilson provided the program for a bold kind of Catholic intellectuality—an appropriation of medieval thought for modern use, not so much a medieval revival as a demonstration of the perennial relevance of the medieval philosophical achievement. The modern mind was to be brought back to its Catholic roots, not by the simple disparagement of modernity or by emphasis on the subjective necessity of faith, but by a rigorous and demanding appeal to reason. In the process, Scholastic principles would be applied in new and often daring ways.

In the end the gamble failed. Despite promising signs in the 1940s, secular thinkers did not finally find the Scholastic appeal persuasive. And, as is inevitable when an intellectual community is dominated so thoroughly by a single system of thought, a restiveness was building up in Catholic circles. Although Maritain insisted that Thomism, because of the central importance it gave to the act of existence, was the true existentialism, Catholic intellectuals of the 1950s were attracted to the movement which more usually went by that name; and Gabriel Marcel, a Catholic existentialist of the same generation as Gilson and Maritain, was available to mediate between faith and anguish. Catholic colleges in America were hospitable to existentialist and phenomenological currents at a time when few secular institutions were, and what Catholics sought there was primarily a philosophy which was serious about the metaphysical questions of existence, yet not as rationalistic, rigid, and abstract as Scholasticism often seemed to be.

GO ON TO THE NEXT PAGE ➤

3 3 3 3 3 3 3 3 3 3 3

10. Maritain believed that Americans were

    I. materialistic
    II. idealistic
    III. self-deprecating

    (A) I only
    (B) II only
    (C) I and II only
    (D) II and III only
    (E) I, II, and III

11. Maritain could be characterized as

    (A) anti-Semitic
    (B) materialistic
    (C) a Catholic chaplain
    (D) a historian
    (E) a political liberal

12. Which of the following statements best exemplifies Maritain's belief?

    (A) Democracy was an old-fashioned ideology.
    (B) Democracy and Fascism were both imperfect.
    (C) Democracy flowed from correct philosophical principles.
    (D) Bourgeois individualism would end in statism.
    (E) Fascism and Communism were just as bad.

13. Maritain's program for Catholic intellectuality may be expressed as

    (A) a synthesis of modernity and tradition
    (B) political liberalism
    (C) Dominican Catholicism
    (D) Scholastic reasoning
    (E) medieval Catholic values

14. Scholasticism was not accepted by secular thinkers because it was too

    I. rationalistic
    II. secular
    III. nationalistic

    (A) I only
    (B) II only
    (C) I and II only
    (D) II and III only
    (E) I, II, and III

15. Maritain discussed political ideologies in his publication(s)

    I. *Scholasticism and Politics*
    II. *Integral Humanism*
    III. *Reflections on America*

    (A) I only
    (B) II only
    (C) I and II only
    (D) II and III only
    (E) I, II, and III

16. Catholic intellectuals of the 1950s were attracted to

    (A) eclectic movements
    (B) existentialism
    (C) Scholastic principles
    (D) neo-Scholasticism
    (E) medieval philosophers

17. The most appropriate title for the passage is

    (A) "Catholicism in America"
    (B) "Catholicism and Scholasticism"
    (C) "Christian Civilization and Politics"
    (D) "Catholic Intellectual Renaissance"
    (E) "Catholic Thought on Campus"

GO ON TO THE NEXT PAGE ➤

Passage 3:

Much as an electrical lamp transforms electrical energy into heat and light, the visual "apparatus" of a human being acts as a transformer of light into sight. Light projected from a source or reflected by an object enters the cornea and lens of the eyeball. The energy is transmitted to the retina of the eye whose rods and cones are activated.

The stimuli are transferred by nerve cells to the optic nerve and then to the brain. Man is a binocular animal, and the impressions from his two eyes are translated into sight—a rapid, compound analysis of the shape, form, color, size, position, and motion of the things he sees.

Photometry is the science of measuring light. The illuminating engineer and designer employ photometric data constantly in their work. In all fields of application of light and lighting, they predicate their choice of equipment, lamps, wall finishes, colors of light and backgrounds, and other factors affecting the luminous and environmental pattern to be secured, in great part from data supplied originally by a photometric laboratory. Today, extensive tables and charts of photometric data are used widely, constituting the basis for many details of design.

Although the lighting designer may not be called upon to do the detailed work of making measurements or plotting data in the form of photometric curves and analyzing them, an understanding of the terms used and their derivation form valuable background knowledge.

The perception of color is a complex visual sensation, intimately related to light. The apparent color of an object depends primarily upon four factors: its ability to reflect various colors of light, the nature of the light by which it is seen, the color of its surroundings, and the characteristics and state of adaptation of the eye.

In most discussions of color, a distinction is made between white and colored objects. White is the color name most usually applied to a material that diffusely transmits a high percentage of all the hues of light. Colors that have no hue are termed neutral or achromatic colors. They include white, off-white, all shades of gray, down to black.

All colored objects selectively absorb certain wave-lengths of light and reflect or transmit others in varying degrees. Inorganic materials, chiefly metals such as copper and brass, reflect light from their *surfaces.* Hence we have the term "surface" or "metallic" colors, as contrasted with "body" or "pigment" colors. In the former, the light reflected from the surface is often tinted.

Most paints, on the other hand, have body or pigment colors. In these, light is reflected from the surface without much color change, but the body material absorbs some colors and reflects others; hence, the diffuse reflection from the body of the material is colored but often appears to be overlaid and diluted with a "white" reflection from the glossy surface of the paint film. In paints and enamels, the pigment particles, which are usually opaque, are suspended in a vehicle such as oil or plastic. The particles of a dye, on the other hand, are considerably finer and may be described as coloring matter in solution. The dye particles are more often transparent or translucent.

18. Light projected from a source enters the eyeball through the

    (A) cornea
    (B) retina
    (C) rods
    (D) cones
    (E) brain

19. Photometry is the science of

    (A) studying sight
    (B) color configurations
    (C) light projection
    (D) light and motion
    (E) measuring light

GO ON TO THE NEXT PAGE ➤

3 3 3 3 3 3 3 3 3 3 3

20. According to the passage, lighting engineers need *not*

    (A) plot photometric curves
    (B) understand photometric techniques
    (C) utilize photometric data
    (D) have mathematical expertise
    (E) be college graduates

21. The color black is an example of

    (A) a surface color
    (B) an organic color
    (C) an achromatic color
    (D) a diffuse color
    (E) a pigment color

22. The reflection of light wave-lengths is accomplished by

    (A) all colors
    (B) selective colors
    (C) surface colors
    (D) achromatic colors
    (E) pigment colors

23. Inorganic materials reflect light from their

    (A) hues
    (B) body
    (C) surface
    (D) pigment
    (E) compounds

24. Paint would be an example of a substance containing

    (A) inorganic material
    (B) surface colors
    (C) body colors
    (D) metallic colors
    (E) enamels

25. The perception of color is

    (A) a photometric phenomenon
    (B) activated by the brain
    (C) a complex visual sensation
    (D) light reflected by a source
    (E) energy transmitted from the retina

STOP

**IF THERE IS STILL TIME REMAINING,
YOU MAY REVIEW THE QUESTIONS IN THIS SECTION ONLY.
YOU MAY NOT TURN TO ANY OTHER SECTION OF THE TEST.**

4 4 4 4 4 4 4 4 4 4 4

Section 4

TIME: 25 minutes
17 Questions

Directions: Solve each of the following problems; then indicate the correct answer on your answer sheet.

NOTE: A figure that appears with a problem is drawn as accurately as possible unless the words "figure not drawn to scale" appear next to the figure. Numbers in this test are real numbers.

1. The amount of coal necessary to heat a home cost \$53.00 in 1992 and will increase at the rate of 15% a year. The amount of oil necessary to heat the same home cost \$45.00 in 1992 but will increase at the rate of 20% a year. In 1994 which of the following methods would heat the home for the cheapest price?

(A) Use of only coal
(B) Use of only oil
(C) Use of coal or oil since they cost the same amount
(D) Use of oil for 8 months and coal for 4 months
(E) Use of coal for 8 months and oil for 4 months

2. Train X leaves New York at 1 A.M. and travels east at a constant speed of x mph. If train Z leaves New York at 2 A.M. and travels east, at what constant rate of speed will train Z have to travel in order to catch train X at exactly 5:30 A.M.?

(A) $\frac{5}{6}x$
(B) $\frac{9}{8}x$
(C) $\frac{6}{5}x$
(D) $\frac{9}{7}x$
(E) $\frac{3}{2}x$

Use this graph for question 3.

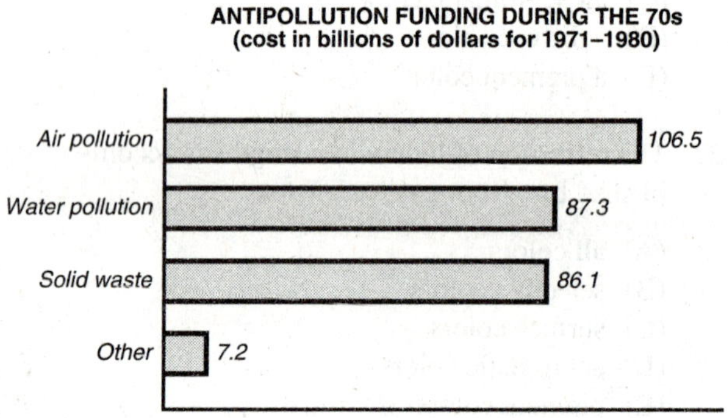

3. The ratio of air pollution funding to water pollution funding is about

(A) 2 to 1
(B) 3 to 2
(C) 6 to 5
(D) 5 to 6
(E) 2 to 3

GO ON TO THE NEXT PAGE ➤

4 4 4 4 4 4 4 4 4 4 4

4. How many of the integers between 110 and 120 are prime numbers?

   (A) 0
   (B) 1
   (C) 2
   (D) 3
   (E) 4

5. A worker is paid r dollars for each hour he works up to 8 hours a day. For any time worked over 8 hours he is paid at the rate of $(1.5)r$ dollars an hour. The total amount of dollars the worker will earn if he works 11 hours in a day is

   (A) $(4.5)r$
   (B) $(5.5)r$
   (C) $(9.25)r$
   (D) $(11)r$
   (E) $(12.5)r$

6. If the product of 3 consecutive integers is 120, then the sum of the integers is

   (A) 9
   (B) 12
   (C) 14
   (D) 15
   (E) 18

7. For which values of x is $x^2 - 5x + 6$ negative?

   (A) $x < 0$
   (B) $0 < x < 2$
   (C) $2 < x < 3$
   (D) $3 < x < 6$
   (E) $x > 6$

8. A plane flying north at 500 mph passes over a city at 12 noon. A plane flying east at the same altitude passes over the same city at 12:30 P.M. The plane is flying east at 400 mph. To the nearest hundred miles, how far apart are the two planes at 2 P.M.?

   (A) 600 miles
   (B) 1000 miles
   (C) 1100 miles
   (D) 1200 miles
   (E) 1300 miles

GO ON TO THE NEXT PAGE ➤

9. Mechanics are paid twice the hourly wage of salesmen. Custodial workers are paid one-third the hourly wage of mechanics. What fraction of the hourly wage of custodial workers are salesmen paid?

(A) $\frac{1}{3}$

(B) $\frac{1}{2}$

(C) $\frac{2}{3}$

(D) $\frac{4}{3}$

(E) $\frac{3}{2}$

10. If $8a = 6b$ and $3a = 0$ then

(A) a and b are equal
(B) $a = 6$
(C) $\frac{b}{a} = \frac{4}{3}$
(D) $a = 6$ and $b = 8$
(E) $\frac{a}{b} = \frac{3}{4}$

11. A horse can travel at the rate of 5 miles per hour for the first two hours of a trip. After the first two hours the horse's speed drops to 3 miles per hour. How many hours will it take the horse to travel 20 miles?

(A) 4
(B) 5
(C) $5\frac{1}{3}$
(D) $5\frac{1}{2}$
(E) $5\frac{2}{3}$

GO ON TO THE NEXT PAGE ➤

4 4 4 4 4 4 4 4 4 4 4

Use the following table for question 12.

THE BUDGET DOLLAR

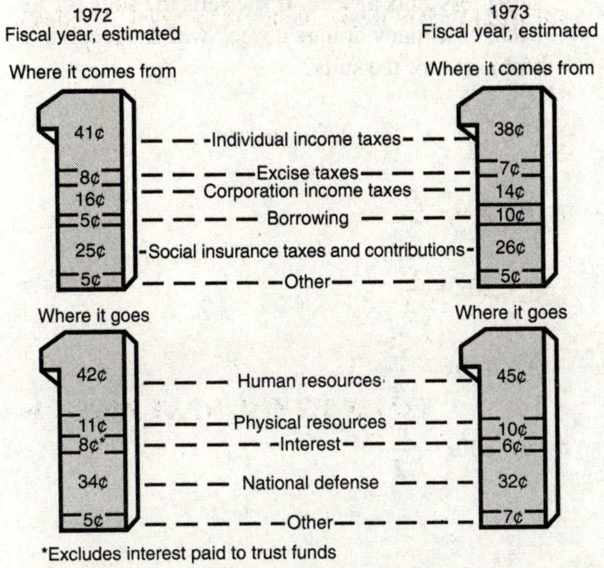

*Excludes interest paid to trust funds

12. Which of the following statements can be inferred from the graph?

    I. The amount of money collected from excise taxes declined from 1972 to 1973.
    II. The government will borrow twice as much money in 1973 as it did in 1972.
    III. Of the total amount of income in 1972 and 1973, 15% came from Corporation Income Taxes.

    (A) None
    (B) III only
    (C) I and II only
    (D) II and III only
    (E) I, II, and III

13. If the ratio of the radii of two circles is 3 to 2, then the ratio of the areas of the two circles is

    (A) 2 to 3
    (B) 3 to 4
    (C) 4 to 9
    (D) 9 to 4
    (E) 3 to 2

14. Ms. Jones has twice as much invested in stocks as bonds. Last year, the stock investments paid 7.5% of their value while the bonds paid 10% of their value. If the total that both investments paid last year was $1,000, how much did Ms. Jones have invested in stocks?

    (A) $3,636
    (B) $4,000
    (C) $7,500
    (D) $8,000
    (E) $10,000

15. If $\frac{1}{x} < \frac{1}{y}$ then

    (A) $x > y$
    (B) x and y are negative
    (C) x and y are positive
    (D) $x < y$
    (E) none of the preceding statements follows

GO ON TO THE NEXT PAGE ➤

4 4 4 4 4 4 4 4 4 4 4

16. A manufacturer of boxes wants to make a profit of x dollars. When she sells 5,000 boxes it costs 5¢ a box to make the first 1,000 boxes and then it costs y¢ a box to make the remaining 4,000 boxes. What price in dollars should she charge for the 5,000 boxes?

    (A) $5{,}000 + 1{,}000y$
    (B) $5{,}000 + 1{,}000y + 100x$
    (C) $50 + 10y + x$
    (D) $5{,}000 + 4{,}000y + x$
    (E) $50 + 40y + x$

17. A clothing manufacturer has determined that she can sell 100 suits a week at a selling price of $200 each. For each rise of $4 in the selling price she will sell 2 less suits a week. If she sells the suits for $$x$ each, how many dollars a week will she receive from sales of the suits?

    (A) $\frac{x^2}{2}$
    (B) $200 - \frac{x}{2}$
    (C) $50x + \frac{x^2}{4}$
    (D) $150x - \frac{x^2}{4}$
    (E) $200x - \frac{x^2}{2}$

STOP

**IF THERE IS STILL TIME REMAINING,
YOU MAY REVIEW THE QUESTIONS IN THIS SECTION ONLY.
YOU MAY NOT TURN TO ANY OTHER SECTION OF THE TEST.**

5 5 5 5 5 5 5 5 5 5 5

Section 5

TIME: 25 minutes
17 Questions

Directions: For each question, choose the best answer among the listed alternatives.

1. 1. All members of Group IV include all members of Group II.
   2. All members of Group III include all members of Group I.
   3. All members of Group IV include all members of Group I.
   4. All members of Group II include all members of Group I.
   5. All members of Group III include all members of Group IV.

   Which of the following statements must be true in order to establish that Group III is the all-embracing group, i.e. includes Groups I, II, & IV?

   (A) Statement 1 is a vital piece of information.
   (B) Statement 2 is a vital piece of information.
   (C) Statement 3 is a vital piece of information.
   (D) Statement 4 is a vital piece of information.
   (E) None of the above statements is a vital piece of information.

2. In Great Britain, the problem of violence among spectators of soccer games last year became more and more serious, with hardly a weekend passing without many arrested and many injured from among those who supposedly came to see a sport.

   Many suggestions have been made to combat this problem, most of them involving the introduction of more restrictions on the freedom of the crowds. Increased police presence at all games, enclosing supporters of opposing teams in pens, preventing the two groups from coming into contact with each other, and the use of membership cards with photographs which must be presented in order to gain access, have all been tried.

   What is needed now is a deterrent factor. Increased fines, Saturday afternoon detention centers, and even jail terms must be introduced speedily and rigorously, if we are going to solve this problem.

   Which of the following if true, would most strengthen the present view of the writer?

   (A) The British Government has just passed legislation outlawing alcoholic drink to be sold at or brought into soccer matches.
   (B) Last week there were 36 arrested and 50 injured in fighting among the top soccer matches. An increase of 25% over the figures for the previous week.
   (C) The soccer clubs should do more to encourage families to attend their games by improving facilities and making special enclosures.
   (D) Violence is on the increase at soccer matches and the authorities must get tougher.
   (E) Closed-circuit television has been set-up to monitor trouble-making elements in the crowd.

GO ON TO THE NEXT PAGE ➤

3. Nursing mothers provide many benefits to their newborn babies. The colostrum produced during the first few days following birth is rich in antibodies and confers on the newborn infant immunity to many diseases. Although milk substitutes are useful in cases where mothers cannot produce their own milk, "natural" milk provides a balanced diet and is ideal for human babies. Indeed substitute milks are derived from cows' milk, intended only for calves. Many large companies that produce milk substitutes operate large sales campaigns in Third World countries arguing that substitute milk is almost the same as mothers' milk.

   Using the facts in the paragraph above, which of the following completes the sentence in an appropriate way?

   Encouraging Third World mothers to adopt the use of milk substitutes instead of nursing is . . .

   (A) praiseworthy because these substitutes are rich in calories, vitamins and minerals.
   (B) unwise because their infants usually are unable to break down lactose.
   (C) unwise because mothers' milk provides immunity against many diseases.
   (D) probably neither really helpful nor harmful to the health of their infants.
   (E) useful because it releases the mothers from their commitment to their infants and allows them to return more rapidly to work.

4. Lavoisier, the 18th-century scientist, became more influential and famous than most of his contemporaries in his field because not only did he discover and isolate many of the chemical elements but he also gave them names which both described the element in terms of its power and function and which came to be accepted by other scientists in subsequent generations.

   Which of the following can be inferred from the above passage?

   (A) Lavoisier strived for fame and influence in the 18th century.
   (B) All elements found in the 18th century were named after Lavoisier.
   (C) Some of the elements that Lavoisier isolated were given names that described their properties.
   (D) Lavoisier was the most influential and famous scientist of his time.
   (E) Lavoisier became famous only because the names that he gave the chemicals became accepted.

5. Contrary to the views of those who oppose recent introduction of the law prohibiting smoking cigarettes, cigars, and pipes in restaurants and other public places, the prohibition is quite justified and long overdue. Those who object would do well to remember that there is much legislation in this country—for example, the law against jaywalking—which is an infringement of civil liberties.

   Which of the following statements about the author's intention is correct?

   (A) He is pointing out that the opponents' rationalization of the argument leads to an unreasonable conclusion.
   (B) He attacks his opponents because they are self-interested smokers.
   (C) He points out that his antagonists' arguments lead to a choice between equally undesirable alternatives.
   (D) He is attempting to draw an analogy between restricting a person's freedom to cross a busy road anywhere one pleases and banning smoking in public places.
   (E) He demonstrates that the law against jaywalking applies in this country, as well as other democracies, in which civil liberties is paramount.

GO ON TO THE NEXT PAGE ➤

5 5 5 5 5 5 5 5 5 5 5

6. The disaster that followed the recent earthquake in Soviet Armenia is tragic and serious, not just because of the fatalities and injuries, but because such widespread and severe damage was avoidable. The earthquake was less than 6 on the open-ended Richter scale, but its effects and aftermath matched the scene of events after much stronger quakes. What caused the casualty figures to reach such horrendous heights was that the buildings in the area were generally of a design that could not be expected to withstand anything more than a minor tremor.

   Which of the following statements can best be inferred from the passage?

   (A) People were not killed and injured by the earthquake, but by the falling masonry.
   (B) Resources should be invested in predicting the location, incidence, and strength of earthquakes.
   (C) Emergency evacuation procedures should be introduced in areas where earthquakes tend to occur frequently.
   (D) It would be better if earthquakes only occurred in areas far away from large centers of population.
   (E) The rescue aid provided by international organizations and other countries after the earthquake will hopefully improve relations.

7. The Greenhouse Effect is causing a general warming of the world. Climatologists are predicting that there will be more droughts and more floods. Soil erosion will also become an increasing problem in semi-arid lands. However, there will be benefits to other areas of the world where agricultural production will increase. An example is Hokkaido, the northern island of Japan, which will experience a temperature rise of 4 degrees Celsius within the next 50 years, and it is predicted that this will increase rice production fourfold. In Iceland and Finland, land fit for pasture could increase by 50% and yields of hay could increase by 60%.

   Based on the above text, which of the following assumptions is correct in planning for future food production?

   (A) The climate of northern parts of the world will be unaffected.
   (B) Pasture land will increase in area.
   (C) The Greenhouse Effect will have a positive effect on certain areas of the world only.
   (D) Desert lands may be flooded.
   (E) Japan will increase its rice production fourfold.

8. Scientists believe they have discovered the wreck of the *USS Harvard*, sunk by Japanese torpedoes during the Second World War. Their conclusions are drawn from underwater searches by mini-submarines of the area about 4 miles west of Midway Island in the Pacific Ocean during what started out as offshore oil platform accident procedures. There are some military historians that are skeptical about the scientists' claim, on the basis that sophisticated sonar equipment has not identified the ship as, indeed, the *Harvard*.

   Which of the following, if true, would weaken the historians' arguments?

   (A) Thorough searching by divers and bathoscopes has not located the wreck.
   (B) Three other ships were sunk in this area during the Second World War.
   (C) The ship's last known position was 20 miles east of Midway.
   (D) The use of sonar only enables the user to identify the shape and dimension of a wreck.
   (E) It is not known whether the *Harvard* suffered much structural damage before being sunk.

GO ON TO THE NEXT PAGE ➤

9. The incidence of stress-related diseases in management workers is increasing at an alarming rate. Between 1982 and 1985 the increase in lost working days in industry for men was up by more than 13% for cardiac disease, 12% for cerebrovascular disease, 16% for psychoses, more than 4% for hypertensive disease, and 3% for neuroses.

   For women workers, comparable figures were a 25% increase for cardiac disease, 73% for cerebrovascular disease, 1% for psychoses, more than 3% for hypertensive disease, 2% for neuroses and 6% for ulcers.

   Prime causes of these increases tend to be corporate merger mania—takeovers, acquisitions, amalgamations, buyouts and coventures.

   Which of the following conclusions *cannot* be deduced from the above?

   (A) More women are suffering from cerebrovascular diseases related to stress than men.
   (B) Crises in industry have a direct effect on the health of management staff.
   (C) Male staff seem to be more sensitive to psychological stress than female staff.
   (D) The rate at which the incidence of cardiac disease for men is increasing in less than the rate for women.
   (E) More and more working days are being lost because of stress-related disease.

10. The United States has the highest rate of poverty in the industrial world. According to data collected, the average family income of the poorest 20% of the population declined by 10.9% from 1979 to 1986. Meanwhile, the average family income of the richest 20% of the country increased by 13.8%.

    Research seems to indicate that this decline has been caused by slow economic growth in the early and mid-1980s while there has been a major redistribution of income from lower-income families toward the most affluent.

    Which of the following conclusions can be deduced from the above text?

    (A) Average income in the United States has declined by 10.9% from 1979 to 1986.
    (B) The gap between rich and poor is widening.
    (C) The income of the poorest families must rise by 20% to retain the differential between rich and poor families.
    (D) Rich families are spreading more.
    (E) An increase in economic growth will equalize the distribution of wealth.

11. Choosing an executive for important positions in top companies can be a chancey business. Many decisions are arbitrary and dependent on personal preferences and prejudices. Appearance, color of clothes, beards, height, can all aid or hinder a candidate's chances for success.

    Additional methods for helping a "head-hunter" to choose the correct candidate can be psychometric testing and handwriting analysis. Although these tests cannot be taken in isolation, they may help to highlight weaknesses and strengths in a candidate's aptitudes. The tests include verbal and numerical critical reasoning tests, detailed personality questionnaires, and often, additional tests to see how candidates organize their time and utilize their resources.

    By also using a personal interview, the company can then find the most suitable person for a job.

    Which of the following statements can be derived from the above?

    (A) Psychometric tests alone should be used to choose candidates.
    (B) Employers choose their executives according to their appearance.
    (C) Psychometric tests are essential in choosing suitable candidates for jobs.
    (D) Psychometric tests show up the weaknesses of candidates.
    (E) Successful candidacy for a top job is dependent only on luck.

12. Which of the statements listed below best completes the passage?

    In department stores the placing of aisles, display stands, and shelves, is designed to direct a customer's movements. Different sorts of products are also situated to ensure that a customer will move through different parts of the store. More expensive items are usually placed on upper floors, while cheaper, impulse items are placed near the entrance and also adjacent to the cashier. This sort of planning is intended to . . . .

    (A) keep traffic flowing in the store as smoothly as possible.
    (B) maximize sales by exposing customers to as many products as possible.
    (C) utilize sales people as efficiently as possible.
    (D) prevent long lines and undue waiting time at cash registers.
    (E) confuse the consumer in order to keep him in the stores as long as possible.

GO ON TO THE NEXT PAGE ➤

5 5 5 5 5 5 5 5 5 5 5

13. Department stores range from two to eight floors in height. If a store has more than three floors, it has an elevator.

    If the statements above are true, which of the following must also be true?

    (A) Second floors do not have elevators.
    (B) Seventh floors have elevators.
    (C) Only floors above the third floor have elevators.
    (D) All floors may be reached by elevators.
    (E) Some two-floor department stores do not have elevators.

14. Bob Boger, along with some other members of his class, took the GMAT exam in July 1989. The average class score was 530 compared to the state average of 524. On learning these results, Bob happily explained that he scored higher than the average state score.

    Which of the following, if true, would weaken the above argument?

    (A) The national average score was 545.
    (B) Bob's class comprised "high achievers."
    (C) The July 1989 exam was especially difficult.
    (D) Bob was not able to complete every question within the allotted time.
    (E) Bob's reported class score was an average: individual scores may have been above or below the state average score.

15. Social security law is an evolving law that tries as far as possible to reflect reality—to adjust to changes in and the needs of society.

    Which of the following statements best summarizes the above?

    (A) Legislation lags behind reality.
    (B) Social security law gradually adapts itself to societal demands.
    (C) A good social security system ought to reflect every change in social values.
    (D) Changes in social conditions and needs imply the necessity for changes in social security legislation.
    (E) We need to study social needs.

16. Starting in 1955, all workers had to wear steel helmets if they were employed in the construction industry.

    From which of the following can the statement above be properly inferred?

    (A) No workers had to wear steel helmets before 1955, but all workers had to wear them after 1955.
    (B) Construction industry workers were the first to be required to wear steel helmets.
    (C) Construction industry workers had to wear steel helmets prior to 1955.
    (D) Some workers may have worn steel helmets before 1955, but all construction workers were required to wear them beginning in 1955.
    (E) Workers may have worn some type of helmet before 1955, but later all had to wear steel-type helmets.

17. Team sports, like baseball, display strong socialist tendencies in their requirement of individual subordination to the authority of coaches and managers.

    Which of the following conclusions may not be inferred from the above information?

    (A) All team sports are authoritarian.
    (B) All team players are subordinate to their coaches.
    (C) Without employee subordination to managerial authority, production for profit would not be possible.
    (D) All team sports have socialist tendencies.
    (E) Individual subordination to authority is an aspect of socialism.

STOP

IF THERE IS STILL TIME REMAINING,
YOU MAY REVIEW THE QUESTIONS IN THIS SECTION ONLY.
YOU MAY NOT TURN TO ANY OTHER SECTION OF THE TEST.

6 6 6 6 6 6 6 6 6 6 6

Section 6

TIME: 25 minutes
21 Questions

Directions: Each of the following problems has a question and two statements which are labeled (1) and (2). Use the data given in (1) and (2) together with other available information (such as the number of hours in a day, the definition of *clockwise*, mathematical facts, etc.) to decide whether the statements are *sufficient* to answer the question. Then fill in space

(A) if you can get the answer from **(1) ALONE** but not from (2) alone
(B) if you can get the answer from **(2) ALONE** but not from (1) alone
(C) if you can get the answer from **BOTH (1) and (2) TOGETHER,** but not from (1) alone or (2) alone
(D) if **EITHER** statement **(1) ALONE OR** statement **(2) ALONE** suffices
(E) if you **CANNOT** get the answer from statements (1) and (2) **TOGETHER**, but need even more data

All numbers used in this section are real numbers. A figure given for a problem is intended to provide information consistent with that in the question, but not necessarily with the additional information contained in the statements.

1. A rectangular field is 40 yards long. Find the area of the field.
   (1) A fence around the outside of the field is 140 yards long.
   (2) The distance from one corner of the field to the opposite corner is 50 yards.

2. Is x greater than 0?
   (1) $x^3 + 1 = 0$
   (2) $x^2 - 1 = 0$

3. There are 450 boxes to load on a truck. *A* and *B* working independently but at the same time take 30 minutes to load the truck. How long should it take *B* working alone to load the truck?
   (1) *A* loads twice as many boxes as *B*.
   (2) *A* would take 45 minutes by himself.

GO ON TO THE NEXT PAGE ➤

6 6 6 6 6 6 6 6 6 6 6

(A) if you can get the answer from **(1) ALONE** but not from (2) alone
(B) if you can get the answer from **(2) ALONE** but not from (1) alone
(C) if you can get the answer from **BOTH (1) and (2) TOGETHER,** but not from (1) alone or (2) alone
(D) if **EITHER** statement **(1) ALONE OR** statement **(2) ALONE** suffices
(E) if you **CANNOT** get the answer from statements (1) and (2) **TOGETHER**, but need even more data

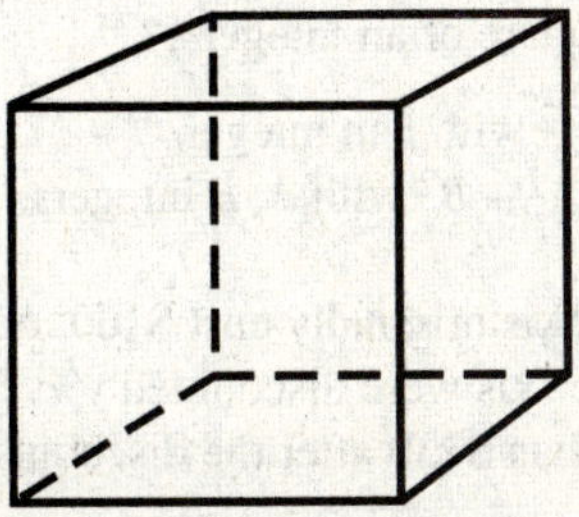

4. Is the above figure a cube?

   (1) The lengths of all edges are equal.
   (2) The angle between any two edges that meet is a right angle.

5. A car drives around a circular track once. A second car drives from point *A* to point *B* in a straight line. Which car travels farther?

   (1) The car driving around the circular track takes a longer time to complete its trip than the car traveling in a straight line.
   (2) The straight line from *A* to *B* is $1\frac{1}{2}$ times as long as the diameter of the circular track.

6. Find $x + y$

   (1) $x - y = 6$
   (2) $2x + 3y = 7$

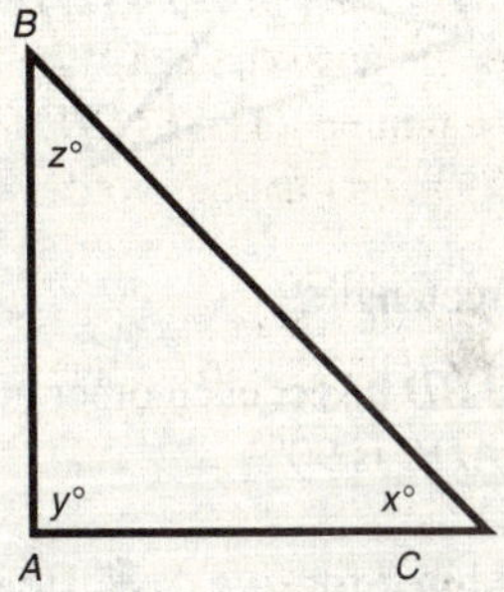

7. Find the length of *AC* if *AB* has length 3 and x is 45.

   (1) $z = 45$
   (2) $y = 90$

8. It costs 50 cents in tolls, 2 dollars in gas, and at least 1 dollar for parking to drive (round trip) from Utopia to Green Acres each day. The train offers a weekly ticket. Which is the cheaper way to travel per week if you work five days per week?

   (1) The weekly train ticket costs 15 dollars.
   (2) Parking costs a total of 6 dollars.

GO ON TO THE NEXT PAGE ➤

6 6 6 6 6 6 6 6 6 6 6

(A) if you can get the answer from **(1) ALONE** but not from (2) alone
(B) if you can get the answer from **(2) ALONE** but not from (1) alone
(C) if you can get the answer from **BOTH (1) and (2) TOGETHER,** but not from (1) alone or (2) alone
(D) if **EITHER** statement **(1) ALONE OR** statement **(2) ALONE** suffices
(E) if you **CANNOT** get the answer from statements (1) and (2) **TOGETHER**, but need even more data

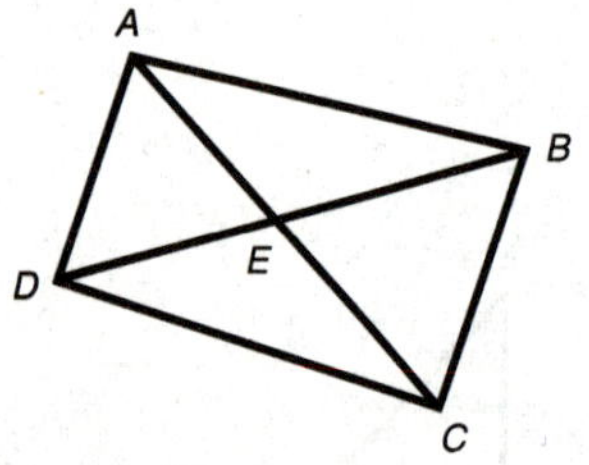

9. Is $ABCD$ a rectangle?

 (1) AC and BD bisect each other at E.
 (2) Angle ADC is 90°

10. A worker is hired for five days. He is paid $5.00 more for each day of work than he was paid for the preceding day of work. What was the total amount he was paid for the five days of work?

 (1) He had made 50% of the total by the end of the third day.
 (2) He was paid twice as much for the last day as he was for the first day.

11. Is y larger than x?

 (1) $x + y = 2$
 (2) $\frac{x}{y} = 2$

12. Is n the square of an integer k?

 (1) $n = 4j^2$ with j an integer.
 (2) $n^2 = A^2 + B^2$ with A, B integers.

13. A pair of skis originally cost $160. After a discount of x%, the skis were discounted y%. Do the skis cost less than $130 after the discounts?

 (1) $x = 20$
 (2) $y = 15$

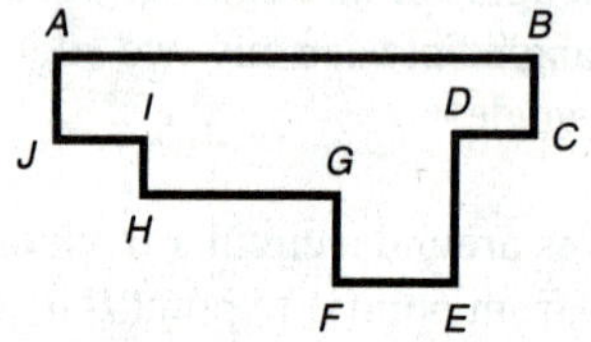

14. What is the length of line segment AB? All lines that meet are perpendicular. AJ, JI, HI, BC, FE, GF and DC are each equal to x. HG and DE are each equal to y.

 (1) $y = 4$
 (2) $x = 2$

GO ON TO THE NEXT PAGE ➤

6 6 6 6 6 6 6 6 6 6 6

(A) if you can get the answer from **(1) ALONE** but not from (2) alone
(B) if you can get the answer from **(2) ALONE** but not from (1) alone
(C) if you can get the answer from **BOTH (1) and (2) TOGETHER,** but not from (1) alone or (2) alone
(D) if **EITHER** statement **(1) ALONE OR** statement **(2) ALONE** suffices
(E) if you **CANNOT** get the answer from statements (1) and (2) **TOGETHER**, but need even more data

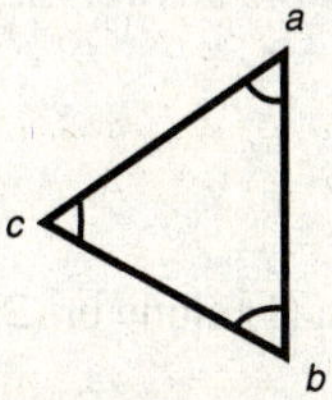

15. Is the angle c larger than 60°?

(1) $a + b$ is greater than c.
(2) a is greater than b which is greater than c.

16. If a and b are both positive numbers, then which is larger, 2^a or 3^b?

(1) a is greater than $2b$.
(2) a is greater than or equal to $b + 3$

17. Will the circle with center O fit inside the square *ABCD*?

(1) The diameter of the circle is less than a side of the square.
(2) The area of the circle is less than the area of the square.

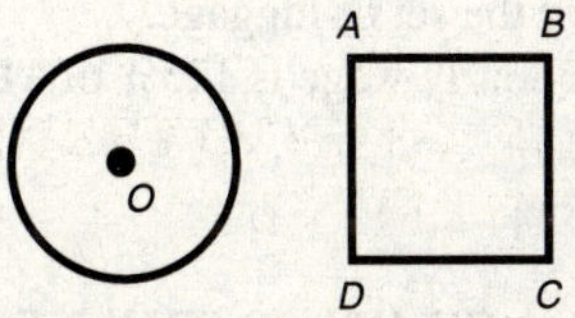

18. Is $xy < 0$?

(1) $\frac{1}{x} < \frac{1}{y}$
(2) $x > 0$

19. A square originally had sides with length s. The length of the side is increased by x%. Did the area of the square increase by more than 10%?

(1) x is greater than 5.
(2) x is less than 10.

20. Is $k^2 + k - 2 > 0$

(1) $k < 1$
(2) $k < -2$

21. How many books are on the bookshelf?

(1) The bookshelf is 12 feet long.
(2) The average weight of each book is 1.2 pounds.

STOP

IF THERE IS STILL TIME REMAINING,
YOU MAY REVIEW THE QUESTIONS IN THIS SECTION ONLY.
YOU MAY NOT TURN TO ANY OTHER SECTION OF THE TEST.

Section 7

TIME: 25 minutes
21 Questions

Directions: Each of the following problems has a question and two statements which are labeled (1) and (2). Use the data given in (1) and (2) together with other available information (such as the number of hours in a day, the definition of *clockwise*, mathematical facts, etc.) to decide whether the statements are *sufficient* to answer the question. Then fill in space

(A) if you can get the answer from **(1) ALONE** but not from (2) alone
(B) if you can get the answer from **(2) ALONE** but not from (1) alone
(C) if you can get the answer from **BOTH (1) and (2) TOGETHER,** but not from (1) alone or (2) alone
(D) if **EITHER** statement **(1) ALONE OR** statement **(2) ALONE** suffices
(E) if you **CANNOT** get the answer from statements (1) and (2) **TOGETHER**, but need even more data

All numbers used in this section are real numbers. A figure given for a problem is intended to provide information consistent with that in the question, but not necessarily with the additional information contained in the statements.

1. How much is the average salary of the 30 assembly workers? The foreman is paid a salary of $12,000.
   (1) The total salary paid to the 30 assembly workers and the foreman is $312,000.
   (2) The foreman's salary is 120% of the average salary of the 30 assembly workers.

2. How far is it from town *A* to town *B*? Town *C* is 12 miles east of town *A*.
   (1) Town *C* is south of town *B*.
   (2) It is 9 miles from town *B* to town *C*.

3. How many vinyl squares with sides 5 inches long will be needed to cover the rectangular floor of a room?
   (1) The floor is 10 feet long.
   (2) The floor is 5 feet wide.

4. Mary must work 15 hours to make in wages the cost of a set of luggage. How many dollars does the set of luggage cost?
   (1) Jim must work 12 hours to make in wages the cost of the set of luggage.
   (2) Jim's hourly wage is 125% of Mary's hourly wage.

GO ON TO THE NEXT PAGE ➤

7 7 7 7 7 7 7 7 7 7 7

(A) if you can get the answer from **(1) ALONE** but not from (2) alone
(B) if you can get the answer from **(2) ALONE** but not from (1) alone
(C) if you can get the answer from **BOTH (1) and (2) TOGETHER,** but not from (1) alone or (2) alone
(D) if **EITHER** statement **(1) ALONE OR** statement **(2) ALONE** suffices
(E) if you **CANNOT** get the answer from statements (1) and (2) **TOGETHER**, but need even more data

5. What is the value of x?

   (1) $\frac{x}{y} = 3$

   (2) $x - y = 9$

6. Is DE parallel to AB?

   (1) $CD = DA$
   (2) $CE = EB$

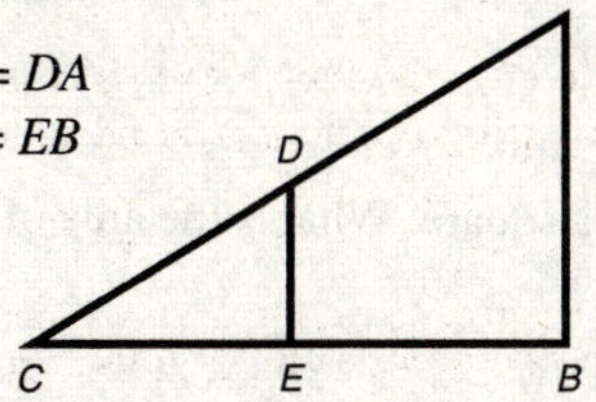

7. How many of the numbers x and y are positive? Both x and y are less than 20.

   (1) x is less than 5.
   (2) $x + y = 24$

8. What is the value of x? $PS = SR$.

   (1) $y = 30$
   (2) $PQ = QR$

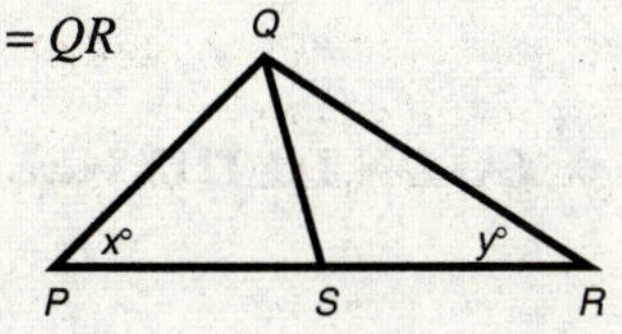

9. How much does the first volume of a 5-volume work weigh?

   (1) The first 3 volumes weigh 4 pounds.
   (2) The second, third and fourth volumes weigh a total of $3\frac{1}{2}$ pounds.

10. A sequence of numbers is given by the rule $a_n = a_{n-1} + 2$. Is a_{10} an even integer?

    (1) a_1 is an even integer.
    (2) a_9 is 24.

11. Is the radius of a circle greater than 3?

    (1) The points with coordinates (2, 4) and (5, 10) are on the circle.
    (2) The points with coordinates (2, 4) and (4, 1) are on the circle.

GO ON TO THE NEXT PAGE ➤

(A) if you can get the answer from **(1) ALONE** but not from (2) alone
(B) if you can get the answer from **(2) ALONE** but not from (1) alone
(C) if you can get the answer from **BOTH (1) and (2) TOGETHER,** but not from (1) alone or (2) alone
(D) if **EITHER** statement **(1) ALONE OR** statement **(2) ALONE** suffices
(E) if you **CANNOT** get the answer from statements (1) and (2) **TOGETHER**, but need even more data

12. If $x = k$, is the expression $x^3 + ax^2 + bx$ equal to zero?

    (1) $a = 0$
    (2) $-b = k^2$

13. A jar is filled with 60 marbles. All the marbles in the jar are either red or green. What is the smallest number of marbles which must be drawn from the jar in order to be certain that a red marble is drawn?

    (1) The ratio of red marbles to green marbles is 2 : 1.
    (2) There are 20 green marbles in the jar.

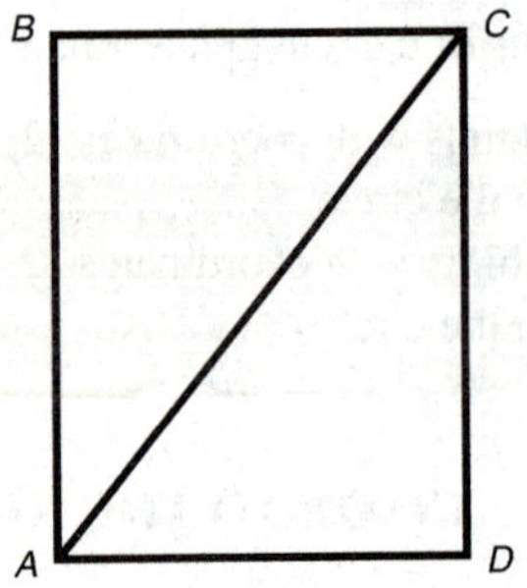

14. What is the area of rectangle $ABCD$?

    (1) $AC = 5$
    (2) $AB = 4$

15. Which is larger, a^b or b^a? $a > 0$ and $b > 0$.

    (1) $a = 1$
    (2) $b > 2$

16. Is x greater than y?

    (1) $xy = 5$
    (2) $\frac{x}{y} = 2$

17. $ABCD$ is a square. What is the area of the triangle ABE?

    (1) $AB = 10$
    (2) $CE = DE$

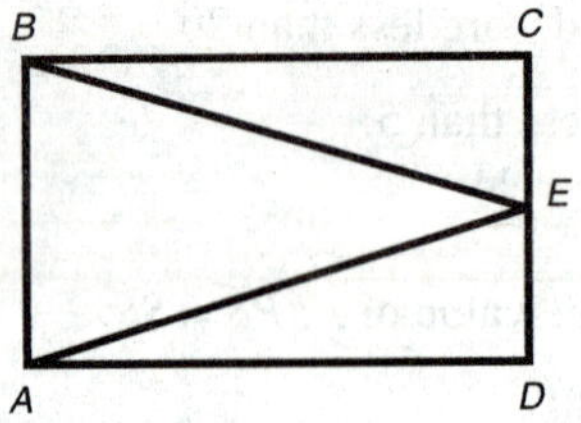

GO ON TO THE NEXT PAGE ➤

7 7 7 7 7 7 7 7 7 7 7

(A) if you can get the answer from **(1) ALONE** but not from (2) alone
(B) if you can get the answer from **(2) ALONE** but not from (1) alone
(C) if you can get the answer from **BOTH (1) and (2) TOGETHER,** but not from (1) alone or (2) alone
(D) if **EITHER** statement **(1) ALONE OR** statement **(2) ALONE** suffices
(E) if you **CANNOT** get the answer from statements (1) and (2) **TOGETHER**, but need even more data

18. Is x greater than y?

    (1) $x = 2y$
    (2) $x = y + 2$

19. A group of 49 consumers were offered a chance to subscribe to 3 magazines: A, B, and C. 38 of the consumers subscribed to at least one of the magazines. How many of the 49 consumers subscribed to exactly two of the magazines?

    (1) Twelve of the 49 consumers subscribed to all three of the magazines.
    (2) Twenty of the 49 consumers subscribed to magazine A.

20. Is k an odd integer?

    (1) k is divisible by 3.
    (2) The square root of k is an integer divisible by 3.

21. Which of the four numbers w, x, y, and z is the largest?

    (1) The average of w, x, y, and z is 25.
    (2) The numbers w, x, and y are each less than 24.

STOP

IF THERE IS STILL TIME REMAINING,
YOU MAY REVIEW THE QUESTIONS IN THIS SECTION ONLY.
YOU MAY NOT TURN TO ANY OTHER SECTION OF THE TEST.

Answers
SAMPLE TEST 4

Section 1 [Sentence Correction]

Q	Ans	Q	Ans	Q	Ans	Q	Ans	Q	Ans
1	B	6	C	11	C	16	B	21	C
2	C	7	E	12	D	17	D	22	
3	B	8	D	13	C	18	D	23	
4	A	9	B	14	E	19	D	24	
5	D	10	A	15	B	20	C	25	

Section 2 [Problem Solving]

Q	Ans	Q	Ans	Q	Ans	Q	Ans	Q	Ans
1	D	6	E	11	D	16	A	21	
2	C	7	E	12	B	17	D	22	
3	E	8	C	13	C	18		23	
4	A	9	C	14	E	19		24	
5	C	10	B	15	D	20		25	

Section 3 [Reading Comprehension]

Q	Ans	Q	Ans	Q	Ans	Q	Ans	Q	Ans
1	C	6	B	11	E	16	B	21	C
2	B	7	B	12	D	17	D	22	A
3	A	8	C	13	E	18	A	23	C
4	E	9	A	14	A	19	E	24	C
5	A	10	D	15	C	20	A	25	C

Section 4 [Problem Solving]

Q	Ans	Q	Ans	Q	Ans	Q	Ans	Q	Ans
1	B	6	D	11	C	16	E	21	
2	D	7	C	12	A	17	E	22	
3	C	8	D	13	D	18		23	
4	B	9	E	14	D	19		24	
5	E	10	A	15	E	20		25	

Section 5 [Critical Reasoning]

Q	Ans	Q	Ans	Q	Ans	Q	Ans	Q	Ans
1	A	6	A	11	E	16	D	21	
2	B	7	C	12	B	17	C	22	
3	C	8	D	13	B	18		23	
4	C	9	A	14	E	19		24	
5	D	10	B	15	B	20		25	

Section 6 [Data Sufficiency]

Q	Ans	Q	Ans	Q	Ans	Q	Ans	Q	Ans
1	D	6	C	11	C	16	A	21	E
2	A	7	D	12	A	17	A	22	
3	D	8	A	13	A	18	C	23	
4	C	9	C	14	D	19	A	24	
5	B	10	D	15	B	20	B	25	

Section 7 [Data Sufficiency]

Q	Ans	Q	Ans	Q	Ans	Q	Ans	Q	Ans
1	D	6	C	11	A	16	E	21	C
2	C	7	B	12	C	17	A	22	
3	C	8	C	13	D	18	B	23	
4	E	9	E	14	C	19	E	24	
5	C	10	D	15	C	20	E	25	

Self-Scoring Guide—Analytical Writing

Evaluate your writing tests (or have a friend or teacher evaluate them for you) on the following basis. Read each essay completely, paying special attention to its logical organization and use of examples and facts to buttress its claims or position. Assign a holistic score between 0 and 6, using the scale below. Your writing score will be the average of the scores of the two essays.

6	**Outstanding**	Cogent, well-articulated analysis of the issue or critique of the argument. Develops a position with insightful reasons and persuasive examples. Well organized. Superior command of language and variety of syntax. Only minor flaws in grammar, usage, and mechanics.
5	**Strong**	Well-developed analysis or critique. Develops a position with well-chosen examples or reasons. Generally well organized. Clear control of language and variety of syntax. Minor flaws in grammar, usage, and mechanics.
4	**Adequate**	Competent analysis or critique. Develops a position with relevant reasons or examples. Adequately organized. Adequate control of language, but may lack syntactic variety. May have some flaws in grammar, usage, and mechanics.
3	**Limited**	Competent but clearly flawed analysis or critique. Vague or limited in developing a position. Poorly organized. Weak in using relevant examples or reasons. Language used imprecisely or lacking in sentence variety. Contains major errors or frequent minor errors in grammar, usage, and mechanics.
2	**Seriously Flawed**	Serious weaknesses in analysis and organization. Unclear or seriously limited in presenting or developing a position. Disorganized. Few relevant examples or reasons. Frequent serious problems in language and sentence structure. Numerous errors in grammar, usage, or mechanics that interfere with meaning.
1	**Fundamentally Deficient**	Little evidence of ability to organize and develop a coherent response to issue or argument. Severe and persistent errors in language and sentence structure. Pervasive pattern of errors in grammar, usage, and mechanics that severely interfere with meaning.
0	**Unscorable**	Illegible or not written on the assigned topic.

Analysis

Section 1
Sentence Correction

1. **More than any animal, the wolverine exemplifies the unbridled ferocity of "nature red in tooth and claw."**

   (A) More than any animal
   (B) More than any other animal
   (C) More than another animal
   (D) Unlike any animal
   (E) Compared to other animals

(B) Choice (B) includes the necessary word *other*, which makes the comparison correct. Choice (D) changes the meaning of the sentence by its implication that the wolverine is *not* an animal.

2. **In 1896, Henri Bequerel found that uranium salts emitted penetrating radiations similar to those which Roentgen produced only a year earlier with a gas discharge tube.**

   (A) similar to those which Roentgen
   (B) like those which Roentgen
   (C) similar to those that Roentgen had
   (D) similar to them that Roentgen
   (E) similar to those Roentgen

(C) The past perfect tense *had produced* is required in this sentence to show that Roentgen's work preceded that of Bequerel.

3. **Unless they reverse present policies immediately, the world may suffer permanent damage from the unregulated use of pesticides.**

   (A) Unless they reverse present policies
   (B) Unless present policies are reversed
   (C) Unless present policies will be reversed
   (D) If it will not reverse present policies
   (E) If present policies will not be reversed

(B) Choice (A) suffers from the use of the ambiguous pronoun *they*. It is not clear whom *they* is supposed to refer to. The use of the future tense in choices (C), (D), and (E) is incorrect.

4. **He interviewed several candidates who he thought had the experience and qualifications the position required.**

   (A) who he thought
   (B) whom he thought
   (C) of whom he thought
   (D) he thought who
   (E) which he thought

(A) Choice (A) is correct because the subject of the verb *had* must be *who*, not *whom*. *Which* in choice (E) should not be used to refer to a person.

5. **The average citizen today is surprisingly knowledgeable about landmark court decisions concerning such questions as racial segregation, legislative appointment, prayer in the public schools, and whether a defendant has a right to counsel in a criminal prosecution.**

   (A) whether a defendant has a right to counsel
   (B) if a defendant has a right to counsel
   (C) the right of a defendant to council
   (D) the right of a defendant to counsel
   (E) is a defendant entitled to counsel

(D) Choices (A), (B), and (E) violate the principle of parallel structure—that parts of a sentence parallel in meaning should be parallel in structure. The nouns *segregation, appointment,* and *prayer* should be followed by the noun *right*, rather than a clause. Choice (C) incorrectly uses *council* (an advisory or legislative body) for *counsel* (a lawyer).

6. **The reason we are late is due to the fact that the bus was delayed by heavy traffic.**

   (A) due to the fact that the bus was delayed by heavy traffic
   (B) because the bus was delayed by heavy traffic
   (C) that the bus was delayed by heavy traffic
   (D) due to the fact that heavy traffic delayed the bus
   (E) that the delay of our bus was caused by heavy traffic

(C) *Due to* in choices (A) and (D) should not be used as a substitute for *because of*. The phrase *the reason is that* (C) is preferable to *the reason is because* (B). Choice (E) is unnecessarily wordy.

7. Before starting a program of diet and exercise, a consultation with your physician is advisable.

(A) a consultation with your physician is advisable
(B) it is advisable to have a consultation with your physician
(C) a physician's consultation is advisable
(D) a consultation with your physician is necessary
(E) you should consult your physician

(E) Choice (E) best indicates the doer of the action in the sentence.

8. The first of a number of receptions and testimonial dinners for the departing school superintendent have been scheduled, with more events still in the planning stage.

(A) have been scheduled, with more events still
(B) have been scheduled, and with more events still
(C) has been scheduled, and with more events still
(D) has been scheduled, with more events still
(E) have been scheduled, and there is still more events

(D) Choices (A), (B), and (E) have an error in agreement: the plural verb *have been scheduled* should be the singular *has been scheduled*, because its subject, *first*, is singular. The word *and* in choices (B) and (C) is unnecessary.

9. If the Confederate Army would have carried the day at Gettysburg, the history of America during the past century might have been profoundly altered.

(A) If the Confederate Army would have carried the day at Gettysburg
(B) Had the Confederate Army carried the day at Gettysburg
(C) The Confederate Army having carried the day at Gettysburg
(D) If the Confederate Army would have won at Gettysburg
(E) If the Battle of Gettysburg would have been won by the Confederate Army

(B) The *if* clause with which the sentence begins expresses a condition contrary to fact and therefore requires the subjunctive mood. Choice (B) provides the necessary subjunctive. Choice (C) changes the meaning of the sentence.

10. Economic conditions demand that we not only cut wages and prices but also reduce inflation-raised tax rates.

(A) that we not only cut wages and prices but also
(B) not only cutting wages and prices but also to
(C) not only to cut wages and prices but also to
(D) not only a cut in wages and prices but also to
(E) not only to cut wages and prices but that we also

(A) Choices (B), (D), and (E) do not maintain parallel structure. The infinitive *to cut* cannot be an object of *demand*, as in choice (C); a noun clause like the one in choice (A) corrects this error.

11. Legislative effectiveness, in theory, makes good sense; in actuality, however, they are sometimes difficult to enforce.

(A) they are sometimes difficult to enforce
(B) it is difficult to enforce them
(C) laws are sometimes difficult to enforce
(D) it is sometimes difficult to enforce laws
(E) this is sometimes difficult for them to enforce

(C) The antecedent of the pronoun *they* should be stated, not merely implied in the sentence, or a noun should be substituted in its place; choice (C) makes clear that *laws*, not *legislative effectiveness*, are what *they* referred to.

12. Fame as well as fortune were his goals in life.

(A) Fame as well as fortune were his goals
(B) Fame as well as fortune was his goals
(C) Fame as well as fortune were his goal
(D) Fame and fortune were his goals
(E) Fame also fortune were his goals

(D) In the original sentence, the subject is *fame*, a singular noun. Therefore, the verb should also be singular. This eliminates choices (A) and (C). In choice (B), *goals* should be *goal*. The word *also* in choice (E) should not be used as a conjunction.

13. Familiar with the terrain from previous visits, the explorer's search for the abandoned mine site was a success.

(A) the explorer's search for the abandoned mine site was a success
(B) the success of the explorer's search for the abandoned mine site was assured
(C) the explorer succeeded in finding the abandoned mine site
(D) the search by the explorer for the abandoned mine was successful
(E) the explorer in his search for the abandoned mine site was a success

(C) In choices (A), (B), and (D), the modifier *familiar* is dangling. The wording in choice (E) suggests that the explorer was a success, whereas the original sentence states that the search was a success—a somewhat different meaning. Choice (C) corrects the error and retains the original meaning of the sentence.

14. During the first year that he and I were neighbors, our conversations turned frequently on the two cardinal points of poetry: the power of exciting the sympathy of the reader by a faithful adherence to the truth of nature and the power to give the interest of novelty by the modifying colors of imagination.

(A) power to give
(B) ability to give
(C) power to bestow
(D) ability to bestow
(E) power of giving

(E) This choice preserves the parallel structure of the sentence.

15. Modernization has gone hand in hand and has offered incentives for such things as personal initiative and ambition, hard work, and resourcefulness.

(A) and has offered incentives for such things as personal initiative and ambition, hard work, and resourcefulness
(B) with and has offered incentives for such things as personal initiative and ambition, hard work, and resourcefulness
(C) with and has offered incentives for such things as personal initiative and ambition, hard work, and the ability to be resourceful
(D) and has offered incentives such as personal initiative and ambition, hard work, and resourcefulness
(E) and is offering incentives for such things as personal initiative and ambition, hard work, and resourcefulness

(B) The preposition *with* is needed to complete the phrase *has gone hand in hand with.* Choice (C) unnecessarily changes the single word *resourcefulness* to *the ability to be resourceful.*

16. My objection to him taking part in this dispute is based on my belief that he is not a disinterested party.

(A) My objection to him taking part in this dispute is based on my belief that he is not a disinterested party.
(B) My objection to his taking part in this dispute is based on my belief that he is not a disinterested party.
(C) My objection to him taking part in this dispute is based on my belief that he is not an uninterested party.
(D) My objection to his taking part in this dispute is based on my belief that he is not an uninterested party.
(E) I object to him taking part in this dispute because he is not a disinterested party.

(B) A pronoun preceding a gerund should be in the possessive case: *his taking part.* Choice (D) incorrectly substitutes *uninterested* (*indifferent*) for *disinterested* (*impartial*).

17. Of the two candidates for this government position, Jason Harald is the most qualified because of his experience in the field.

(A) most qualified because of
(B) most qualified due to
(C) more qualified due to
(D) more qualified because of
(E) most qualified as a result of

(D) The superlative *most* is incorrect here; when two are compared, *more* should be used. Choices (B) and (C) incorrectly substitute *due to* for *because of.* Choice (E) unnecessarily changes the wording.

18. If anyone calls while we are in conference, tell them that I will return their call after the meeting.

(A) them that I will return their call after the meeting
(B) him or her that I will return their call after the meeting
(C) them that I would return their call after the meeting
(D) the person that I will return the call after the meeting
(E) him or her that I would return the call after the meeting is over

(D) There is an error in agreement: The singular pronoun *anyone* requires a singular pronoun or noun. Although choice (B) corrects the first error (changes *them* to *his or her*), *their* should also have been changed. Choice (E) uses the wrong tense and unnecessarily adds words.

19. Neither the earthquake or the subsequent fire was able to destroy the spirit of the city dwellers.

(A) or the subsequent fire was
(B) nor the subsequent fire were
(C) or the subsequent fire were
(D) nor the subsequent fire was
(E) or the fire that occurred subsequently were

(D) The correct correlative conjunctions are *neither . . . nor*. The verb agrees with the noun that follows the correlative *nor: fire was*; therefore (B) is incorrect.

20. The Secretary of State reminded his listeners that this country always has and always will try to honor its commitments.

(A) always has and always will try to honor
(B) has always and will always try to honor
(C) always has tried and always will try to honor
(D) always has tried to honor and will always
(E) has always tried to honor and will always

(C) The original sentence contains an improper ellipsis. The first verb (*has tried*) should not be cut short, because it is not in the same tense as the second one (*will try*).

21. Tests show that catfish from Lake Apopka are safe to eat, even though they contain almost twice as much of the pesticide DDT this year than they did in 1982.

(A) than they did
(B) more than they did
(C) as they did
(D) than they had contained
(E) than they contained

(C) The correct expression is *as much as*.

Section 2
Problem Solving

(Numbers in parentheses at the end of each explanation indicate the section in the Mathematics Review where material addressed in the question is discussed.)

1. If 32 students in a class are female and in the class the ratio of female students to male students is 16 : 9, what percentage of the class is female?

(A) 32%
(B) 36%
(C) 56.25%
(D) 64%
(E) 72%

(D) Since the ratio of female to male is 16 : 9 and there are 32 female students, the number of male students in the class is $\left(\frac{9}{16}\right)32 = 18$. So there are 50 students in the class. Since $\frac{32}{50} = .64$, females make up 64% of the class. You can find the answer faster by using the ratio. Since 16 + 9 = 25, the percentage of female students is $\frac{16}{25}$, which is 64%. (I-4)

2. If a job takes 12 men 4 hours to complete, how long should it take 15 men to complete the job?

(A) 2 hrs. 40 min.
(B) 3 hrs.
(C) 3 hrs. 12 min.
(D) 3 hrs. 24 min.
(E) 3 hrs. 30 min.

(C) Since 15 is $\frac{5}{4}$ of 12, it takes 15 men only $\frac{4}{5}$ as long as 12 men to do the job, $\frac{4}{5}$ of $4 = 3\frac{1}{5}$ hours, or 3 hrs. 12 min. (II-3)

3. The schedules of G first-year students were inspected. It was found that M were taking a math course, L were taking a language course, and B were taking both a math course and a language course. Which of the following expressions gives the percentage of the students whose schedules were inspected who were taking neither a math course nor a language course?

(A) $100 \times \frac{G}{(B+L+M)}$

(B) $100 \times \frac{(B+L+M)}{G}$

(C) $100 \times \frac{(G-L-M)}{G}$

(D) $100 \times \frac{(G-B-L-M)}{G}$

(E) $100 \times \frac{(G+B-L-M)}{G}$

(E) The first step is to find the number taking neither of the courses. A diagram is helpful.

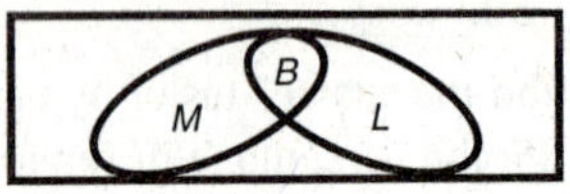

The number taking one or the other or both is $M + L - B$. (Remember: a student taking both courses should only be counted once.) So those taking neither are $G - (M + L - B) = G + B - M - L$. So the percentage taking neither is $100 \times \frac{(G+B-M-L)}{G}$. (II-4)

4. How long must a driver take to drive the final 70 miles of a trip if he wants to average 50 miles an hour for the entire trip and during the first part of the trip he drove 50 miles in $1\frac{1}{2}$ hours?

(A) 54 min.
(B) 1 hr.
(C) 66 min.
(D) 70 min.
(E) 75 min.

(A) The total length of the trip will be 120 miles. Hence to average 50 mph for the trip, he must take 2.4 hrs. total traveling time. Since he has already traveled for 1.5 hrs., he must complete the trip in 2.4 – 1.5 or .9 hrs. or 54 min. (II-3)

5. If $a + 2b = 6$ and $ab = 4$ what is $\frac{2}{a} + \frac{1}{b}$?

(A) $\frac{1}{2}$

(B) 1

(C) $\frac{3}{2}$

(D) 2

(E) $\frac{5}{2}$

(C) Convert $\frac{2}{a} + \frac{1}{b}$ into a single fraction. The fact that you are given the value of ab, which is a common denominator, is a clue. So $\frac{2}{a} + \frac{1}{b} = \frac{2b+a}{ab} = \frac{6}{4} = \frac{3}{2}$. (II-1, II-2).

6. A is 10 miles west of B. C is 30 miles north of B. D is 20 miles east of C. What is the distance from A to D?

(A) 10 miles
(B) 30 miles
(C) $10\sqrt{10}$ miles
(D) $10\sqrt{13}$ miles
(E) $30\sqrt{2}$ miles

(E) Set up a coordinate system with B as the origin. Then A is at (–10, 0), C is at (0, 30), and D is at (20, 30).

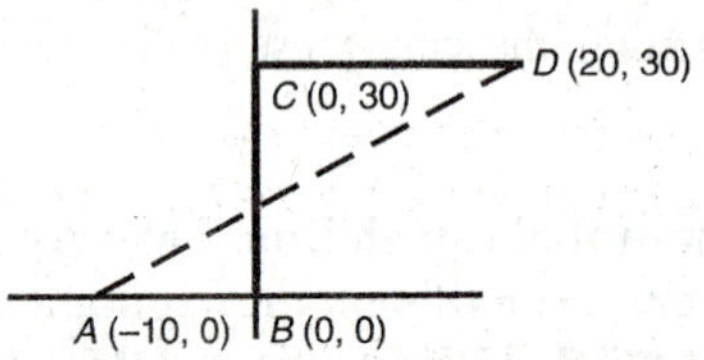

To answer the question you must find the distance between (–10, 0) and (20, 30). Remember the distance between two points whose coordinates are (x, y) and (a, b) is $\sqrt{(x-a)^2 + (y-b)^2}$. So the distance between A and D is the distance between (–10, 0) and (20, 30). The distance is $\sqrt{(-10-20)^2 + (0-30)^2} = \sqrt{30^2 + 30^2} = 30\sqrt{2}$ miles. (III-9)

7. What percentage of the numbers from 1 to 50 have squares that end in the digit 1?

(A) 1
(B) 5
(C) 10
(D) 11
(E) 20

(E) Do not try to square all the numbers from 1 to 50. The last digit of the square of a number is simply the last digit of the square of the last digit of the number. For example, the last digit of the square of 34 is the last digit of 4 squared or 6. Now square each digit from 0 to 9 and you will see that $1^2 = 1$ and $9^2 = 81$, so numbers that end in 1 or 9 will have squares that end in 1. Since 20% of the numbers from 1 to 50 end in 1 or 9, the correct choice is (E). (I-1)

8. If a rectangle has length L and the width is one half of the length, then the area of the rectangle is

(A) L
(B) L^2
(C) $\frac{1}{2}L^2$
(D) $\frac{1}{4}L^2$
(E) $2L$

(C) Area = length times width = $(L)\left(\frac{1}{2}L\right) = \frac{1}{2}L^2$.

(III-7)

9. If the product of two numbers is 5 and one of the numbers is $\frac{3}{2}$, then the sum of the two numbers is

(A) $4\frac{1}{3}$
(B) $4\frac{2}{3}$
(C) $4\frac{5}{6}$
(D) $5\frac{1}{6}$
(E) $6\frac{1}{2}$

(C) Let x be the unknown number. Then $\left(\frac{3}{2}\right)x = 5$; so

$x = (5)\left(\frac{2}{3}\right) = \frac{10}{3}$. The sum of the two numbers is $x +$

$\frac{3}{2} = \frac{10}{3} + \frac{3}{2} = \frac{29}{6} = 4\frac{5}{6}$. (II-2)

10. Which of the following sets of numbers can be used as the lengths of the sides of a triangle?

I. [5, 7, 12]
II. [2, 4, 10]
III. [5, 7, 9]

(A) I only
(B) III only
(C) I and II only
(D) I and III only
(E) II and III only

(B) The length of any side of a triangle must be less than the sum of the lengths of the other two sides. Since 5 + 7 = 12 and 10 is greater than 2 + 4, I and II cannot be the sides of a triangle. 5 + 7 is greater than 9, 5 + 9 is greater than 7, and 7 + 9 is greater than 5. Therefore, there is a triangle whose sides have lengths of 5, 7, and 9. (III-4)

11. What is the next number in the arithmetic progression 2, 5, 8 . . . ?

(A) 7
(B) 9
(C) 10
(D) 11
(E) 12

(D) 2 + 3 = 5 and 5 + 3 = 8, so the next number is 8 +3 or 11. (II-6)

12. The sum of the three digits *a*, *b*, and *c* is 12. What is the largest three digit number that can be formed using each of the digits exactly once?

(A) 921
(B) 930
(C) 999
(D) 1092
(E) 1200

(B) Use 9 for the hundreds position since you want the largest three digit number and 9 is the largest digit. Since the sum is 12, use 12 – 9 = 3 for the tens digit, and 0 for the units. The largest three digit number is (B). Note: (C) uses 9 three times while (D) and (E) are not three digit numbers. (I-3)

13. Water is poured into an empty cylindrical tank at a constant rate for 5 minutes. After the water has been poured into the tank, the depth of the water is 7 feet. The radius of the tank is 10 feet. Which of the following is the best approximation for the rate at which the water was poured into the tank?

(A) 44 cubic feet/min
(B) 140 cubic feet/min
(C) 440 cubic feet/min
(D) 700 cubic feet/min
(E) 2200 cubic feet/min

(C) The amount of water in the tank is 5 × rate, and the volume of a cylinder is $\pi \times (\text{radius})^2 \times \text{height} = \pi \times 10^2 \times 7 = \pi \times 700$ cubic feet. So the rate is $\frac{700\pi}{5} = 140\pi$ cubic feet per minute. Using $\frac{22}{7}$ as an estimate for π, gives $20 \times 22 = 440$ cubic feet/minute as the rate. (III-8)

14. A car traveled 75% of the way from town *A* to town *B* by traveling at *T* hours at an average speed of *V* mph. The car travels at an average speed of *S* mph for the remaining part of the trip. Which of the following expressions represents the average speed for the entire trip?

(A) $.75V + .25S$
(B) $.75T + .25S$
(C) $\frac{VT}{(3S)}$
(D) $\frac{4VT}{\left(\frac{T+S}{3}\right)}$
(E) $\frac{4VS}{(3S+V)}$

(E) You need to find the total distance traveled and the total time. Since the car traveled $V \times T$ when it averaged V mph, then VT is 75% of the total distance. Therefore, the total distance traveled is $\frac{VT}{.75} = \frac{4VT}{3}$. The distance that was traveled at S mph is total distance $- VT = \frac{VT}{3}$.

So the time spent traveling at S mph was

$$\frac{\left(\frac{VT}{3}\right)}{S} = \frac{VT}{(3S)}.$$

Therefore the total time was $T + \frac{VT}{3S}$. So the average speed was

$$\frac{\text{distance}}{\text{time}} = \frac{\left(\frac{4VT}{3}\right)}{T + \frac{VT}{(3S)}}$$

$$= \frac{\left(\frac{4VT}{3}\right)}{\left(\frac{3ST+VT}{(3S)}\right)}$$

$$= \frac{4VTS}{T(3S+V)}$$

$$= \frac{4VS}{(3S+V)} \quad \text{(II-3)}$$

15. What is the farthest distance between two points on a cylinder of height 8 and radius 8?

(A) $8\sqrt{2}$
(B) $8\sqrt{3}$
(C) 16
(D) $8\sqrt{5}$
(E) $8(2\pi + 1)$

(D) Points the farthest apart will be on opposite ends of the cylinder and on opposite sides of the diameter of the circles at the ends. Therefore, the distance between these points will be the hypotenuse of a right triangle with sides equal to the diameter and height of the cylinder. So, since the diameter is 16 and the height is 8, the distance is the square root of $16^2 + 8^2 = 8$ times the square root of $(2^2 + 1^2)$, which is (D). (III-8)

16. Rich sold his skis for $160.00 and his ski boots for $96.00. He made a profit of 20% on his boots and took a 10% loss on his skis. He ended up with a

(A) loss of $1.78
(B) loss of $1.50
(C) gain of $3.20
(D) gain of $7.53
(E) gain of $17.06

(A) Price = (cost)(rate). Let *x* be the original cost of the skis. Then $160 = *x*(.9), so *x* = $177.78. Let *y* be the original cost of the boots; then $96 = *y*(1.2), so *y* = $80. So he made $96 – $80 = $16 on the boots and lost $177.78 – $160 = $17.78 on the skis. Therefore, he lost $1.78.

17. It costs 10¢ each to print the first 500 copies of a newspaper. It costs $\left(10-\frac{x}{50}\right)$¢ each for every copy after the first 500. What is x if it cost $75.00 to print 1,000 copies of the newspaper?

(A) 2.5
(B) 100
(C) 25
(D) 250
(E) 300

(D) The cost in cents of printing 1000 copies equals $500(10) + (1000 - 500)\left(10-\frac{x}{50}\right) = 5000 + 500\left(10-\frac{x}{50}\right)$. Therefore, $7500 = 5000 + 5000 - 10x$, $10x = 2500$, and $x = 250$.

Section 3
Reading Comprehension

The passage for questions 1–9 appears on page 439.

1. The economic conditions of low-income countries are important to high-income countries because of

I. economic reasons
II. political reasons
III. cultural reasons

(A) I only
(B) III only
(C) I and II only
(D) II and III only
(E) I, II, and III

(C) See the second sentence of paragraph 1.

2. According to the passage, governments of most high-income countries have

(A) not worked for freer trade with low-income countries
(B) undertaken important aid programs for low-income countries
(C) injected massive doses of capital into low-income countries
(D) provided training programs for low-income country entrepreneurs
(E) helped improve the educational systems of low-income countries

(B) Paragraph 2: ". . . governments of most high-income countries have in recent years undertaken important aid programs. . . ."

3. The major subject with which the passage is concerned is

(A) trade policies of high-income countries towards low-income countries
(B) foreign trade problems of low-income countries
(C) fiscal and monetary problems of low-income countries
(D) trade arrangements under the GATT organization
(E) general economic problems of low-income countries

(A) See paragraphs 3 and 4 especially.

4. If low-income countries expect aid from high-income countries, they must do all of the following except

(A) spend the aid wisely
(B) put their own houses in order first
(C) learn from the experience of developed countries
(D) curb inflation
(E) de-emphasize agricultural development in favor of industrial growth

(E) Choices (A) through (D) are all mentioned. See paragraphs 4, 6, 7, and 8.

5. Which of the following is mentioned for its influence upon the rate of economic growth?

(A) an efficient financial and fiscal system
(B) a trade surplus
(C) a democratic government
(D) little reliance upon foreign aid
(E) a budgetary surplus

(A) Paragraph 6: ". . . a more efficient financial and fiscal system help[s] greatly to mobilize funds for investment" and following.

6. Industrial growth depends upon a parallel growth of the

(A) labor force
(B) agricultural system
(C) balance of payments
(D) urban population
(E) monetary system

(B) See paragraph 8, the section that states that industrial growth depends upon agricultural productivity.

7. The passage states that participation of high-income countries should be limited to

(A) 10 percent of their GNP
(B) a supporting role
(C) regulations stipulated by GATT
(D) what low-income countries can absorb
(E) monetary aid only

(B) See paragraphs 2 and especially 4: ". . . high-income countries can play only a supporting role."

8. In order to better enlist the support of the population in economic development efforts, low-income countries should

(A) not accept more foreign aid than they can use
(B) budget the capital wisely
(C) reduce excessive social inequalities
(D) concentrate on commercial development
(E) establish agricultural communes

(C) See paragraph 7: "The energies of the people . . . are more likely to be harnessed . . . where . . . governments aim . . . to reduce excessive social inequalities."

9. People will be motivated to work if they are offered

(A) social equality
(B) better working conditions
(C) more money
(D) shorter hours
(E) quality jobs

(A) The answer is implied in paragraph 7.

The passage for questions 10–17 appears on page 442.

10. Maritain believed that Americans were

I. materialistic
II. idealistic
III. self-deprecating

(A) I only
(B) II only
(C) I and II only
(D) II and III only
(E) I, II, and III

(D) Answers were idealistic (II) and self-deprecating (III), but *not* materialistic. See paragraph 2.

11. Maritain could be characterized as

(A) anti-Semitic
(B) materialistic
(C) a Catholic chaplain
(D) a historian
(E) a political liberal

(E) Maritain was a political liberal (paragraph 3), not anti-Semitic (paragraph 4) nor materialistic (the "not really materialistic" reference was to the Americans—paragraph 2). There was no mention of his being a chaplain, nor can it be inferred that he was a historian.

12. Which of the following statements best exemplifies Maritain's belief?

(A) Democracy was an old-fashioned ideology.
(B) Democracy and Fascism were both imperfect.
(C) Democracy flowed from correct philosophical principles.
(D) Bourgeois individualism would end in statism.
(E) Fascism and Communism were just as bad.

(D) Alternatives (A) and (B) were not mentioned. In paragraph 1 the passage states that Maritain "stopped short" of stating that democracy flowed from correct philosophical principles (C). While he believed that both Communism and Fascism were irrational, no statement or inference is made of their morality (E). (D) is mentioned in paragraph 1.

13. Maritain's program for Catholic intellectuality may be expressed as

(A) a synthesis of modernity and tradition
(B) political liberalism
(C) Dominican Catholicism
(D) Scholastic reasoning
(E) medieval Catholic values

(E) Catholic intellectuality was expressed as a "demonstration of the perennial relevance of the medieval philosophical achievement." See paragraph 5.

14. Scholasticism was not accepted by secular thinkers because it was too

I. rationalistic
II. secular
III. nationalistic

(A) I only
(B) II only
(C) I and II only
(D) II and III only
(E) I, II, and III

(A) Only *rationalistic* is given (in the last paragraph) among the reasons why Scholasticism was not accepted by secular thinkers.

15. Maritain discussed political ideologies in his publication(s)

I. *Scholasticism and Politics*
II. *Integral Humanism*
III. *Reflections on America*

(A) I only
(B) II only
(C) I and II only
(D) II and III only
(E) I, II, and III

(C) While the term "political ideologies" is mentioned in paragraph 1 in a discussion of *Integral Humanism,* it is clear that the same topic was examined in *Scholasticism and Politics.*

16. Catholic intellectuals of the 1950s were attracted to

(A) eclectic movements
(B) existentialism
(C) Scholastic principles
(D) neo-Scholasticism
(E) medieval philosophers

(B) See paragraph 6: ". . . Catholic intellectuals . . . were attracted to the movement which more usually went by that name; . . ."—i.e., existentialism.

17. The most appropriate title for the passage is

(A) "Catholicism in America"
(B) "Catholicism and Scholasticism"
(C) "Christian Civilization and Politics"
(D) "Catholic Intellectual Renaissance"
(E) "Catholic Thought on Campus"

(D) While the locus of the passage is America (A), the major theme of the passage focuses on philosophy and is stated in paragraph 5 in the reference to "Catholic intellectuality," not just Catholic thought on campus (E). Alternative (B) is too narrow. The correct answer is (D).

The passage for questions 18–25 appears on page 444.

18. Light projected from a source enters the eyeball through the

(A) cornea
(B) retina
(C) rods
(D) cones
(E) brain

(A) See paragraph 1: "Light projected from a source . . . enters the cornea and lens of the eyeball."

19. Photometry is the science of

(A) studying sight
(B) color configurations
(C) light projection
(D) light and motion
(E) measuring light

(E) See paragraph 3, line 1.

20. According to the passage, lighting engineers need *not*

(A) plot photometric curves
(B) understand photometric techniques
(C) utilize photometric data
(D) have mathematical expertise
(E) be college graduates

(A) See lines 26–29: ". . . lighting designer may not be called upon to do . . . photometric curves . . ."

21. The color black is an example of

(A) a surface color
(B) an organic color
(C) an achromatic color
(D) a diffuse color
(E) a pigment color

(C) See paragraph 6: "Colors that have no hue are termed neutral or achromatic colors. They include . . . black."

22. The reflection of light wave-lengths is accomplished by

(A) all colors
(B) selective colors
(C) surface colors
(D) achromatic colors
(E) pigment colors

(A) See paragraph 7: "All colored objects selectively absorb certain wave-lengths of light and reflect. . . ."

23. Inorganic materials reflect light from their

(A) hues
(B) body
(C) surface
(D) pigment
(E) compounds

(C) See paragraph 7.

24. Paint would be an example of a substance containing

(A) inorganic material
(B) surface colors
(C) body colors
(D) metallic colors
(E) enamels

(C) See line 54: "Most paints . . . have body or pigment colors."

25. The perception of color is

(A) a photometric phenomenon
(B) activated by the brain
(C) a complex visual sensation
(D) light reflected by a source
(E) energy transmitted from the retina

(C) See paragraph 5, line 1.

Section 4
Problem Solving

(Numbers in parentheses at the end of each explanation indicate the section in the Mathematics Review where material addressed in the question is discussed.)

1. The amount of coal necessary to heat a home cost $53.00 in 1992 and will increase at the rate of 15% a year. The amount of oil necessary to heat the same home cost $45.00 in 1992 but will increase at the rate of 20% a year. In 1994 which of the following methods would heat the home for the cheapest price?

(A) Use of only coal
(B) Use of only oil
(C) Use of coal or oil since they cost the same amount
(D) Use of oil for 8 months and coal for 4 months
(E) Use of coal for 8 months and oil for 4 months

(B) The increase in cost between 1992 and 1993 is (cost in 1992) • (rate of increase). The cost in 1993 will be the cost in 1992 (1 + rate of increase). Also, the cost in 1994 will equal (cost in 1993) (1 + rate of increase) or (cost in 1992) (1 + rate of increase)^2. So the cost of coal for 1994 = ($53)$(1.15)^2$ = $(53)(1.32225) = $70.09, and the cost of oil for 1994 = (45)(1.2)^2$ = $(45)(1.44) = $64.80. Since oil is cheaper than coal, (D) and (E) are incorrect because replacing oil by coal for any amount of time raises the cost. (I-4)

2. Train X leaves New York at 1 A.M. and travels east at a constant speed of x mph. If train Z leaves New York at 2 A.M. and travels east, at what constant rate of speed will train Z have to travel in order to catch train X at exactly 5:30 A.M.?

(A) $\frac{5}{6}x$

(B) $\frac{9}{8}x$

(C) $\frac{6}{5}x$

(D) $\frac{9}{7}x$

(E) $\frac{3}{2}x$

(D) By 5:30 A.M. train X will have traveled $\left(4\frac{1}{2}\right)x$ miles. So train Z must travel $\left(4\frac{1}{2}\right)x$ miles in $3\frac{1}{2}$ hours.

The average rate of speed necessary is $\dfrac{4\frac{1}{2}x}{3\frac{1}{2}}$ which equals $\dfrac{\frac{9}{2}x}{\frac{7}{2}}$ or $\frac{9}{7}x$. (II-3)

3. The ratio of air pollution funding to water pollution funding is about

(A) 2 to 1
(B) 3 to 2
(C) 6 to 5
(D) 5 to 6
(E) 2 to 3

ANTIPOLLUTION FUNDING DURING THE 70s
(cost in billions of dollars for 1971–1980)

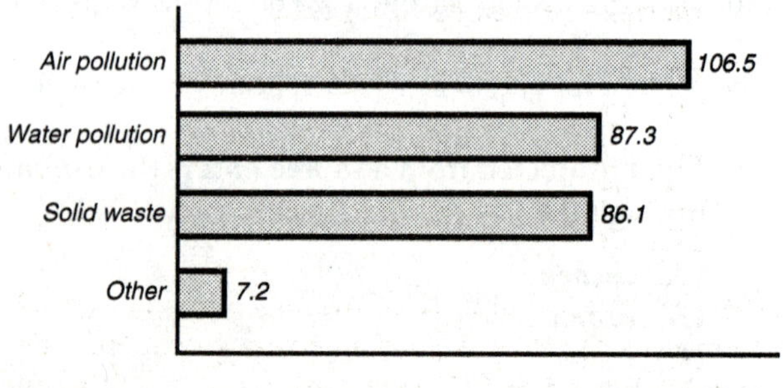

(C) (6)(18) = 108 and (5)(18) = 90. To make quick estimates, check the amount funded for water pollution if air pollution received 100. For example, if the ratio were 3 to 2, water pollution would get only 66.7 billion dollars. You should be able to see that (D) and (E) are incorrect since these choices imply that more money was spent on water pollution than on air pollution. In this case, even if you aren't sure of the correct choice, guess one of the remaining choices—(A), (B), or (C). (IV-3, II-5)

4. How many of the integers between 110 and 120 are prime numbers?

(A) 0
(B) 1
(C) 2
(D) 3
(E) 4

(B) Since any even number is divisible by 2, none of the even integers can be prime. So the only possibilities are 111, 113, 115, 117, and 119. 115 is divisible by 5, so it cannot be prime. You can check the remaining possibilities by seeing if they are divisible by primes less than 11. (If any factor is greater than 11, then there must be divisor less than 11.) So the only divisors you must check are 3, 5, and 7. $3 \times 37 = 111$, so 111 is not prime. 113 is prime. $3 \times 39 = 117$, so 117 is not prime. $7 \times 17 = 119$, so 119 is not prime. Therefore, there is only one prime in the set—113. (I-1)

5. A worker is paid *r* dollars for each hour he works up to 8 hours a day. For any time worked over 8 hours he is paid at the rate of (1.5)*r* dollars an hour. The total amount of dollars the worker will earn if he works 11 hours in a day is

(A) (4.5)*r*
(B) (5.5)*r*
(C) (9.25)*r*
(D) (11)*r*
(E) (12.5)*r*

(E) The amount the worker is paid for working T hours if T is larger than 8 is $8r + (T - 8)(1.5)r$. When $T = 11$, the worker will be paid $8r + 3(1.5)r = (12.5)r$. (II-3)

6. If the product of 3 consecutive integers is 120, then the sum of the integers is

(A) 9
(B) 12
(C) 14
(D) 15
(E) 18

(D) The product of three consecutive integers is of the form $x(x + 1)(x + 2)$. A good approximation to this is $(x + 1)^3$. Since $5^3 = 125$, a good guess is 4, 5, 6. This is correct because $(4)(5)(6) = 120$. The sum of these three numbers is 15. (I-1)

7. For which values of *x* is $x^2 - 5x + 6$ negative?

(A) $x < 0$
(B) $0 < x < 2$
(C) $2 < x < 3$
(D) $3 < x < 6$
(E) $x > 6$

(C) To investigate the sign of an expression, factor it. The given expression factors into $(x - 3)(x - 2)$. If the expression is negative, then the factors must have opposite signs. So if $x - 3$ is positive and $x - 2$ is negative, then the expression would be negative. However, $x - 3$ is positive only when $x > 3$, and $x - 2$ is negative only when $x < 2$. There is no number x which is both greater than 3 and less than 2, so this possibility yields no solutions. But if $x - 3$ is negative and $x - 2$ is positive, then $x > 2$ and $x < 3$. So choice (C) is correct. (II-1, I-6)

8. A plane flying north at 500 mph passes over a city at 12 noon. A plane flying east at the same altitude passes over the same city at 12:30 P.M. The plane is flying east at 400 mph. To the nearest hundred miles, how far apart are the two planes at 2 P.M.?

(A) 600 miles
(B) 1000 miles
(C) 1100 miles
(D) 1200 miles
(E) 1300 miles

(D) Set up a coordinate system with the city at (0, 0). Then the plane going north travels along the y axis, and at 2 o'clock its position will be (0, 1000). The plane flying east travels along the x axis, and it will travel $1.5 \times 400 = 600$ miles east by 2 o'clock. (Remember, it passed over the city at 12:30, so it has only traveled east of the city for 1.5 hours by 2 o'clock.) So the distance between the planes at 2 o'clock is the distance between (0, 1000) and (600, 0), which is $\sqrt{1000^2 + 600^2} = 100\sqrt{10^2 + 6^2} = 100\sqrt{136}$. Since 12 is closer to $\sqrt{136}$ than 11 is (because $12^2 = 144$ and $11^2 = 121$), the correct answer is 100×12 or 1200 miles. (III-9)

9. Mechanics are paid twice the hourly wage of salesmen. Custodial workers are paid one-third the hourly wage of mechanics. What fraction of the hourly wage of custodial workers are salesmen paid?

(A) $\frac{1}{3}$

(B) $\frac{1}{2}$

(C) $\frac{2}{3}$

(D) $\frac{4}{3}$

(E) $\frac{3}{2}$

(E) Let M be the mechanic's hourly wage, C the custodial worker's hourly wage, and S the salesman's hourly wage. Then $M = 2S$, and $C = \frac{1}{3}M$ or $M = 3C$, hence $3C = 2S$, $S = \frac{3}{2}C$. (II-3)

10. If $8a = 6b$ and $3a = 0$ then

(A) a **and** b **are equal**
(B) $a = 6$
(C) $\frac{b}{a} = \frac{4}{3}$
(D) $a = 6$ **and** $b = 8$
(E) $\frac{a}{b} = \frac{3}{4}$

(A) Since $3a = 0$, a must equal 0, which implies that $b = 0$. Note that $\frac{b}{a}$ and $\frac{a}{b}$ are not defined. (I-2, II-2)

11. A horse can travel at the rate of 5 miles per hour for the first two hours of a trip. After the first two hours the horse's speed drops to 3 miles per hour. How many hours will it take the horse to travel 20 miles?

(A) 4
(B) 5
(C) $5\frac{1}{3}$
(D) $5\frac{1}{2}$
(E) $5\frac{2}{3}$

(C) The horse will travel 10 miles in the first two hours. The horse will take $\frac{10}{3}$ or $3\frac{1}{3}$ hours to travel the final 10 miles. So the total time is $5\frac{1}{3}$ hours. (II-3)

12. Which of the following statements can be inferred from the graph?

I. The amount of money collected from excise taxes declined from 1972 to 1973.
II. The government will borrow twice as much money in 1973 as it did in 1972.
III. Of the total amount of income in 1972 and 1973, 15% came from Corporation Income Taxes.

(A) None
(B) III only
(C) I and II only
(D) II and III only
(E) I, II, and III

THE BUDGET DOLLAR

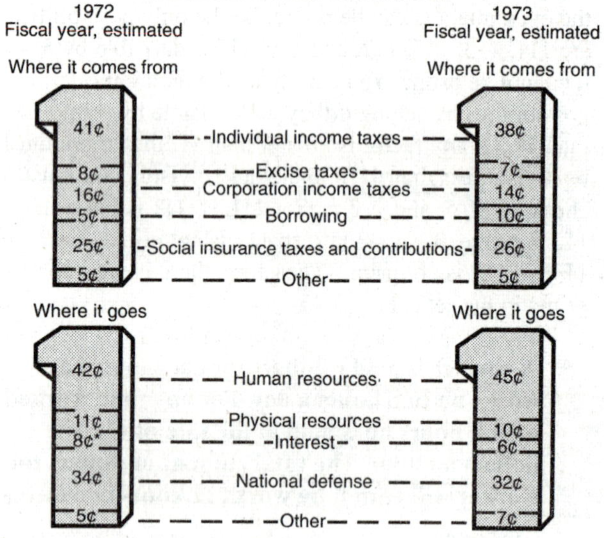

*Excludes interest paid to trust funds

(A) Statement I is false since the graph indicates only that the percentage of the total collected was less. (If the total in 1973 was much larger, the amount collected from excise taxes could have increased.) II is false since, again, the graph gives only percentages not amounts. III is false for the same reason. (IV-2)

13. If the ratio of the radii of two circles is 3 to 2, then the ratio of the areas of the two circles is

(A) 2 to 3
(B) 3 to 4
(C) 4 to 9
(D) 9 to 4
(E) 3 to 2

(D) Let r_1 be the radius of the first circle and r_2 the radius of the second circle. Then $\frac{r_1}{r_2} = \frac{3}{2}$, so $r_1 = \left(\frac{3}{2}\right)r_2$, and $\pi (r_1)^2 = \pi\frac{9}{4}(r_2)^2$. Since the area of a circle is π (radius)^2, then the ratio of the areas is 9 to 4. (III-7, II-5)

14. Ms. Jones has twice as much invested in stocks as bonds. Last year, the stock investments paid 7.5% of their value while the bonds paid 10% of their value. If the total that both investments paid last year was $1,000, how much did Ms. Jones have invested in stocks?

(A) $3,636
(B) $4,000
(C) $7,500
(D) $8,000
(E) $10,000

(D) Let S be the amount invested in stocks and B be the amount invested in bonds. Then $0.75S + .1B = 1{,}000$ and $S = 2B$. So $.075\,(2B) + .1B = .25B = 1000$, which means that $B = \frac{1000}{.25}$ or $B = \$4{,}000$. Finally $S = 2B$, so $S = \$8{,}000$. (II-2)

15. If $\frac{1}{x} < \frac{1}{y}$ then

(A) $x > y$
(B) x and y are negative
(C) x and y are positive
(D) $x < y$
(E) none of the preceding statements follows

(E) Let $x = -3$ and $y = 2$, then $\frac{1}{-3} < \frac{1}{2}$, so (A), (B), and (C) are false. Let $x = 3$ and $y = 2$; then $\frac{1}{3} < \frac{1}{2}$ so (D) is false. (E) is the only correct answer. (II-7)

16. A manufacturer of boxes wants to make a profit of x dollars. When she sells 5,000 boxes it costs 5¢ a box to make the first 1,000 boxes and then it costs y¢ a box to make the remaining 4,000 boxes. What price in dollars should she charge for the 5,000 boxes?

(A) $5{,}000 + 1{,}000y$
(B) $5{,}000 + 1{,}000y + 100x$
(C) $50 + 10y + x$
(D) $5{,}000 + 4{,}000y + x$
(E) $50 + 40y + x$

(E) The selling price of the boxes should equal x plus the cost. The cost in cents of making 5,000 boxes is (1,000)5¢ + (4,000)y which equals $50 + 40y$ in dollars. So the selling price should be $50 + 40y + x$. (I-4, II-3)

17. A clothing manufacturer has determined that she can sell 100 suits a week at a selling price of $200 each. For each rise of $4 in the selling price she will sell 2 less suits a week. If she sells the suits for $x each, how many dollars a week will she receive from sales of the suits?

(A) $\frac{x^2}{2}$

(B) $200 - \frac{x}{2}$

(C) $50x + \frac{x^2}{4}$

(D) $150x - \frac{x^2}{4}$

(E) $200x - \frac{x^2}{2}$

(E) The amount received from suit sales will be equal to the number of suits sold times the price of each suit. Since each suit is sold for $x, we need to know how many suits will be sold. First we must compute the number of $4 price raises. Since $x - 200$ is the increase in price, $\frac{(x-200)}{4}$ is the number of $4 increases. Thus the number of suits sold will decrease by $2\frac{(x-200)}{4}$.

Therefore, the number of suits sold will be 100 – $2\frac{(x-200)}{4} = 100 - \frac{x}{2} + 100 = 200 - \frac{x}{2}$. So the amount received is $x\left(200 - \frac{x}{2}\right) = 200x - \frac{x^2}{2}$. (II-1, II-3)

Section 5
Critical Reasoning

1. 1. All members of Group IV include all members of Group II.
2. All members of Group III include all members of Group I.
3. All members of Group IV include all members of Group I.
4. All members of Group II include all members of Group I.
5. All members of Group III include all members of Group IV.

Which of the following statements must be true in order to establish that Group III is the all-embracing group, i.e. includes Groups I, II, & IV?

(A) Statement 1 is a vital piece of information.
(B) Statement 2 is a vital piece of information.
(C) Statement 3 is a vital piece of information.
(D) Statement 4 is a vital piece of information.
(E) None of the above statements is a vital piece of information.

(A) If you did not have statement 4, you can still know that Group I is in Group III (from statement 2) and Group IV (from statement 3) and that Group II is in Group IV (from statement 1). Because you know Group IV is in Group III (from statement 5), you can still infer that Group III includes all the other groups. Therefore, (D) is inappropriate. Similarly, if you lacked the information in statement 2, or that in statement 3, you could still have sufficient information to conclude what Group II includes. So answer choices (B) and (C) are inappropriate. Statement 1, however is vital, as without it one cannot be certain if Group III includes Group II or vice versa. Therefore, (A) is the appropriate answer. Choice (E) is not appropriate since (A) is vital.

2. In Great Britain, the problem of violence among spectators of soccer games last year became more and more serious, with hardly a weekend passing without many arrested and many injured from among those who supposedly came to see a sport.

Many suggestions have been made to combat this problem, most of them involving the introduction of more restrictions on the freedom of the crowds. Increased police presence at all games, enclosing supporters of opposing teams in pens, preventing the two groups from coming into contact with each other, and the use of membership cards with photographs which must be presented in order to gain access, have all been tried.

What is needed now is a deterrent factor. Increased fines, Saturday afternoon detention centers, and even jail terms must be introduced speedily and rigorously, if we are going to solve this problem.

Which of the following if true, would most strengthen the present view of the writer?

(A) The British Government has just passed legislation outlawing alcoholic drink to be sold at or brought into soccer matches.
(B) Last week there were 36 arrested and 50 injured in fighting among the top soccer matches. An increase of 25% over the figures for the previous week.
(C) The soccer clubs should do more to encourage families to attend their games by improving facilities and making special enclosures.
(D) Violence is on the increase at soccer matches and the authorities must get tougher.
(E) Closed-circuit television has been set-up to monitor trouble-making elements in the crowd.

(B) The question asks which statement would most strengthen the present view of the writer. Answer choice (D) is simply a summation of the author's opinion and is not necessarily likely to strengthen his view. While the writer may agree with the sentiments expressed in (C), it by itself will not reinforce his views. Choices (D) and (C), therefore, cannot be correct. What will harden the author's viewpoint is learning more facts that are not to his liking. Presumably, the developments noted in (A) and (E) will meet with his approval, and are therefore not appropriate. On the other hand, the information conveyed by (B) will serve to increase his anger and resolve and strengthen his present view. (B), therefore, is the appropriate answer.

3. Nursing mothers provide many benefits to their newborn babies. The colostrum produced during the first few days following birth is rich in antibodies and confers on the newborn infant immunity to many diseases. Although milk substitutes are useful in cases where mothers cannot produce their own milk, "natural" milk provides a balanced diet and is ideal for human babies. Indeed substitute milks are derived from cows' milk, intended only for calves. Many large companies that produce milk substitutes operate large sales campaigns in Third World countries arguing that substitute milk is almost the same as mothers' milk.

Using the facts in the paragraph above, which of the following completes the sentence in an appropriate way?

Encouraging Third World mothers to adopt the use of milk substitutes instead of nursing is . . .

(A) praiseworthy because these substitutes are rich in calories, vitamins and minerals.
(B) unwise because their infants usually are unable to break down lactose.
(C) unwise because mothers' milk provides immunity against many diseases.
(D) probably neither really helpful nor harmful to the health of their infants.
(E) useful because it releases the mothers from their commitment to their infants and allows them to return more rapidly to work.

(C) The statement in choice (A) does not express the writer's view presented in the paragraph. The writer clearly points out the value of "natural" milk, especially its antibodies which provide infants with protection from many diseases. Therefore, choice (A) is incorrect. Choice (B) is also incorrect. There is no indication in the paragraph that infants have a problem dealing with lactose (milk sugar) from any source. Choice (D) is also inappropriate, since the writer clearly thinks that nursing provides many benefits to newborns. Choice (E) is not a relevant suggestion since many Third World mothers work while carrying their infants strapped to their bodies, and thus, nursing would present no impediment to their rapid return to work. Only choice (C) is appropriate.

4. Lavoisier, the 18th-century scientist, became more influential and famous than most of his contemporaries in his field because not only did he discover and isolate many of the chemical elements but he also gave them names which both described the element in terms of its power and function and which came to be accepted by other scientists in subsequent generations.

Which of the following can be inferred from the above passage?

(A) Lavoisier strived for fame and influence in the 18th century.
(B) All elements found in the 18th century were named after Lavoisier.
(C) Some of the elements that Lavoisier isolated were given names that described their properties.
(D) Lavoisier was the most influential and famous scientist of his time.
(E) Lavoisier became famous only because the names that he gave the chemicals became accepted.

(C) That Lavoisier strived for fame and influence may be a statement of fact, but not one which may be concluded from the passage. We learn from the passage only that he became famous and influential; therefore, choice (A) is inappropriate. Certainly, some of the elements discovered in the 1700s were named after Lavoisier, as can be learned from the passage, but not all of them. Therefore, choice (B) is also not appropriate. Choice (D) may be ruled out because the presence in the passage of the key words "more influential than most of his contemporaries" and not as choice (D) states "the most influential scientist of his time." There is a comparison between Lavoisier and the other scientists but that is as far as the passage goes. Choice (E) is not appropriate because the passage does not give as fact that the names he allocated to the chemicals he discovered were accepted as the only reason for his subsequent fame. The word "only" rules it out. Choice (C) correctly states the conclusion, which can be drawn from the passage and is, therefore, the appropriate answer.

5. Contrary to the views of those who oppose recent introduction of the law prohibiting smoking cigarettes, cigars, and pipes in restaurants and other public places, the prohibition is quite justified and long overdue. Those who object would do well to remember that there is much legislation in this country—for example, the law against jaywalking—which is an infringement of civil liberties.

Which of the following statements about the author's intention is correct?

(A) He is pointing out that the opponents' rationalization of the argument leads to an unreasonable conclusion.
(B) He attacks his opponents because they are self-interested smokers.
(C) He points out that his antagonists' arguments lead to a choice between equally undesirable alternatives.
(D) He is attempting to draw an analogy between restricting a person's freedom to cross a busy road anywhere one pleases and banning smoking in public places.
(E) He demonstrates that the law against jaywalking applies in this country, as well as other democracies, in which civil liberties is paramount.

(D) The author is claiming that the situation on banning smoking in public places is analogous to that of the law against jaywalking in that in both cases civil rights are interfered with. Therefore, (D) is the correct answer. The answer alternative (A) is inappropriate because the author is not claiming that the opponent's argument is unreasonable; he is claiming that it is wrong. Choice (B) is incorrect because the author is not attacking his opponents for their motives, but rather for their opinion; also the paragraph does not state that the opponents are smokers anyway. The writer's arguments do not lead to the dilemma indicated by (C), and (C) is inappropriate. Statement (E) makes a comparison between the author's country and other countries, thereby adding information that is not given in the paragraph and is not relevant to the question.

6. The disaster that followed the recent earthquake in Soviet Armenia is tragic and serious, not just because of the fatalities and injuries, but because such widespread and severe damage was avoidable. The earthquake was less than 6 on the open-ended Richter scale, but its effects and aftermath matched the scene of events after much stronger quakes. What caused the casualty figures to reach such horrendous heights was that the buildings in the area were generally of a design that could not be expected to withstand anything more than a minor tremor.

Which of the following statements can best be inferred from the passage?

(A) People were not killed and injured by the earthquake, but by the falling masonry.
(B) Resources should be invested in predicting the location, incidence, and strength of earthquakes.
(C) Emergency evacuation procedures should be introduced in areas where earthquakes tend to occur frequently.
(D) It would be better if earthquakes only occurred in areas far away from large centers of population.
(E) The rescue aid provided by international organizations and other countries after the earthquake will hopefully improve relations.

(A) The main inference in the whole paragraph is that an earthquake by itself—that is, a movement of the earth's crust that on the surface is felt as a series of sudden jerks—will not necessarily cause human casualties. It is only when quakes occur in heavily populated areas wherein there are many buildings and the buildings collapse that people are injured and killed by being hit by falling bricks and masonry. (A), therefore, is the appropriate answer. The proposal in choice (B), however laudable, does not emanate from the passage. Choice (C) proposes another alternative measure that cannot be inferred from the passage. (D) presents an opinion with which probably nobody would disagree, but again, this view is not taken from the text. (E) can be ruled out for the same reason: it is not contained in and cannot be inferred from the passage.

7. The Greenhouse Effect is causing a general warming of the world. Climatologists are predicting that there will be more droughts and more floods. Soil erosion will also become an increasing problem in semi-arid lands. However, there will be benefits to other areas of the world where agricultural production will increase. An example is Hokkaido, the northern island of Japan, which will experience a temperature rise of 4 degrees Celsius within the next 50 years, and it is predicted that this will increase rice production fourfold. In Iceland and Finland, land fit for pasture could increase by 50% and yields of hay could increase by 60%.

Based on the above text, which of the following assumptions is correct in planning for future food production?

(A) The climate of northern parts of the world will be unaffected.
(B) Pasture land will increase in area.
(C) The Greenhouse Effect will have a positive effect on certain areas of the world only.
(D) Desert lands may be flooded.
(E) Japan will increase its rice production fourfold.

(C) Statement (A) is incorrect because there will be a general warming of the entire world. Statement (B) says that pasture lands will increase in area, but this is only true for some northern countries, so (B) is not a correct assumption. There is no indication in the paragraph that floods will affect desert lands; in fact, it is more likely that these areas will become even more arid. Thus, choice (D) is invalidated. Although rice production will, it is stated, increase in the northern island of Japan, there is no reason to assume that the rest of Japan will benefit by increased production, so total output could be the same or even less than at present. Therefore, suggestion (E) is not a reasonable assumption. The only valid assumption is that the Greenhouse Effect will only benefit some parts of the earth, while adversely affecting other parts. Assumption (C) is, therefore, correct.

8. Scientists believe they have discovered the wreck of the *USS Harvard*, sunk by Japanese torpedoes during the Second World War. Their conclusions are drawn from underwater searches by mini-submarines of the area about 4 miles west of Midway Island in the Pacific Ocean during what started out as offshore oil platform accident procedures. There are some military historians that are skeptical about the scientists' claim, on the basis that sophisticated sonar equipment has not identified the ship as, indeed, the *Harvard.*

Which of the following, if true, would weaken the historians' arguments?

(A) Thorough searching by divers and bathoscopes has not located the wreck.
(B) Three other ships were sunk in this area during the Second World War.
(C) The ship's last known position was 20 miles east of Midway.
(D) The use of sonar only enables the user to identify the shape and dimension of a wreck.
(E) It is not known whether the *Harvard* suffered much structural damage before being sunk.

(D) The statement in answer choice (A) would strengthen the historian's arguments, so (A) is incorrect. The additional information provided in statement (B) could also be used to strengthen the historian's argument since if there is a wreck of a ship in the location in question, it may not be that of the *Harvard* but rather could be that of any of several ships known to have been sunk in the area during the War. Therefore, (B) is inappropriate. The statement in (E) does not help to determine whether what has been found is or is not a wreck or whether it is or is not the *Harvard*; it is not relevant to the argument, and therefore (E) is incorrect. The fact that the *Harvard's* last known position was not close to the area where the wreck has been found may strengthen the historian's conclusion. It certainly does not weaken his argument. To weaken the historian's argument most effectively, counterevidence that shows that their method of investigation or study produces results that are inconclusive must be brought. Statement (D) does this. It points out shortcomings in the method employed—that is, sonar equipment— thereby making the conclusions reached more tenuous. This is the statement that would most effectively weaken the historian's argument, and thus (D) is the correct answer.

9. The incidence of stress-related diseases in management workers is increasing at an alarming rate. Between 1982 and 1985 the increase in lost working days in industry for men was up by more than 13% for cardiac disease, 12% for cerebrovascular disease, 16% for psychoses, more than 4% for hypertensive disease, and 3% for neuroses.

For women workers, comparable figures were a 25% increase for cardiac disease, 73% for cerebrovascular disease, 1% for psychoses, more than 3% for hypertensive disease, 2% for neuroses and 6% for ulcers.

Prime causes of these increases tend to be corporate merger mania—takeovers, acquisitions, amalgamations, buyouts and coventures.

Which of the following conclusions *cannot* be deduced from the above?

(A) More women are suffering from cerebrovascular diseases related to stress than men.
(B) Crises in industry have a direct effect on the health of management staff.
(C) Male staff seem to be more sensitive to psychological stress than female staff.
(D) The rate at which the incidence of cardiac disease for men is increasing in less than the rate for women.
(E) More and more working days are being lost because of stress-related disease.

(A) Statement (A) is the only conclusion that cannot be deduced from the text. The statistics given only state an increase in the number of days lost due to stress, and this may or may not be due to more women being employed in positions of stress. All the other statements can be inferred from the text, so choices (B), (C), (D), and (E) are incorrect.

10. The United States has the highest rate of poverty in the industrial world. According to data collected, the average family income of the poorest 20% of the population declined by 10.9% from 1979 to 1986. Meanwhile, the average family income of the richest 20% of the country increased by 13.8%.

Research seems to indicate that this decline has been caused by slow economic growth in the early and mid-1980s while there has been a major redistribution of income from lower-income families toward the most affluent.

Which of the following conclusions can be deduced from the above text?

(A) Average income in the United States has declined by 10.9% from 1979 to 1986.
(B) The gap between rich and poor is widening.
(C) The income of the poorest families must rise by 20% to retain the differential between rich and poor families.
(D) Rich families are spreading more.
(E) An increase in economic growth will equalize the distribution of wealth.

(B) The statement in (A) cannot be deduced from the text; it is incorrect. Only the average income of the poorest 20% has declined by 10.9%. Statement (C) is also incorrect. The income of the poor has declined by 10.9% while the income of the rich has increased by 13.8%. Since 13.8% of a higher income is much greater than 10.9% of a smaller income, the total difference cannot be said to be 20%. The statements in (D) and (E) are not indicated in and cannot be deduced from the text. Only statement (B)—a general statement—can be deduced from the text.

11. Choosing an executive for important positions in top companies can be a chancey business. Many decisions are arbitrary and dependent on personal preferences and prejudices. Appearance, color of clothes, beards, height, can all aid or hinder a candidate's chances for success.

Additional methods for helping a "head-hunter" to choose the correct candidate can be psychometric testing and handwriting analysis. Although these tests cannot be taken in isolation, they may help to highlight weaknesses and strengths in a candidate's aptitudes. The tests include verbal and numerical critical reasoning tests, detailed personality questionnaires, and often, additional tests to see how candidates organize their time and utilize their resources.

By also using a personal interview, the company can then find the most suitable person for a job.

Which of the following statements can be derived from the above?

(A) Psychometric tests alone should be used to choose candidates.
(B) Employers choose their executives according to their appearance.
(C) Psychometric tests are essential in choosing suitable candidates for jobs.
(D) Psychometric tests show up the weaknesses of candidates.
(E) Successful candidacy for a top job is dependent only on luck.

(E) Statement (A) cannot be derived since the paragraph indicates that psychometric tests are only an aid in choosing candidates. Although some executives are chosen for their appearance, this is not always true, so statement (B) is not evident from the text. Not all employers are convinced of the validity of psychometric testing. Otherwise, all would use these tests and this is not necessarily true. So statement (C) is not evident from the text. Psychometric tests show up both weaknesses and strengths of candidates, thereby invalidating statement (D). It remains, therefore, that only statement **(E)** can be derived from the test. It may be true that a candidate will perform well in a psychometric test and then fail in the personal interview. His personality might clash with that of the potential employer, so his or her chance of success is not, in fact, governed by any single factor but rather by random selection of several factors.

12. Which of the statements listed below best completes the passage?

In department stores the placing of aisles, display stands, and shelves, is designed to direct a customer's movements. Different sorts of products are also situated to ensure that a customer will move through different parts of the store. More expensive items are usually placed on upper floors, while cheaper, impulse items are placed near the entrance and also adjacent to the cashier. This sort of planning is intended to . . . .

(A) keep traffic flowing in the store as smoothly as possible.
(B) maximize sales by exposing customers to as many products as possible.
(C) utilize sales people as efficiently as possible.
(D) prevent long lines and undue waiting time at cash registers.
(E) confuse the consumer in order to keep him in the stores as long as possible.

(B) A premise in the passage is that customers will spend more effort to search for more expensive products than they will for cheaper products. By placing more expensive products on upper floors, the store exposes the customer to cheaper ones on his or her way up or down, thereby increasing the chance of additional purchases. The conclusion is that sales will be maximized by this type of planning. Nothing in the paragraph refers to smooth traffic flow, use of sales personnel, cashier lines, or a desire to confuse customers, so choices (A), (C), (D) and (E) are all inappropriate.

13. Department stores range from two to eight floors in height. If a store has more than three floors, it has an elevator.

If the statements above are true, which of the following must also be true?

(A) Second floors do not have elevators.
(B) Seventh floors have elevators.
(C) Only floors above the third floor have elevators.
(D) All floors may be reached by elevators.
(E) Some two-floor department stores do not have elevators.

(B) Only choice (B) is buttressed by evidence in the passage. All of the other choices may be true, but they cannot be substantiated from the statements in the passage. Therefore, (A), (C), (D), and (E) are all incorrect.

14. Bob Boger, along with some other members of his class, took the GMAT exam in July 1989. The average class score was 530 compared to the state average of 524. On learning these results, Bob happily explained that he scored higher than the average state score.

Which of the following, if true, would weaken the above argument?

(A) The national average score was 545.
(B) Bob's class comprised "high achievers."
(C) The July 1989 exam was especially difficult.
(D) Bob was not able to complete every question within the allotted time.
(E) Bob's reported class score was an average: individual scores may have been above or below the state average score.

(E) The argument is a fallacy, since the distribution of individual scores around the average class score may be very wide, say more than + or – 10. Thus, Bob could have scored a 520, a score below the average state score. In alternative (A), the national average score is irrelevant. The makeup of Bob's class (B) does not affect Bob's individual score. Whether or not the test was difficult (C) or whether or not Bob completed all the questions (D) are not relevant; only Bob's score is relevant.

15. Social security law is an evolving law that tries as far as possible to reflect reality—to adjust to changes in and the needs of society.

Which of the following statements best summarizes the above?

(A) Legislation lags behind reality.
(B) Social security law gradually adapts itself to societal demands.
(C) A good social security system ought to reflect every change in social values.
(D) Changes in social conditions and needs imply the necessity for changes in social security legislation.
(E) We need to study social needs.

(B) The key phrase in the passage is "tries as far as possible." Social security legislation generally adapts itself to the changing needs of society. The passage says nothing about any other type of legislation, so answer choice (A) is inappropriate. The passage also does not include any statements about social values, the quality of the social security system, or the need to study social needs, so answer alternatives (C) and (E) are not appropriate. While statement (D) is relevant and does relate to the passage, it is not the best summary.

16. Starting in 1955, all workers had to wear steel helmets if they were employed in the construction industry.

From which of the following can the statement above be properly inferred?

(A) No workers had to wear steel helmets before 1955, but all workers had to wear them after 1955.
(B) Construction industry workers were the first to be required to wear steel helmets.
(C) Construction industry workers had to wear steel helmets prior to 1955.
(D) Some workers may have worn steel helmets before 1955, but all construction workers were required to wear them beginning in 1955.
(E) Workers may have worn some type of helmet before 1955, but later all had to wear steel-type helmets.

(D) The passage states that construction workers had to wear steel helmets beginning in 1955; some workers in the construction industry or in other industries may have worn them before 1955. Choice (A) is incorrect because we cannot infer that no workers had to wear helmets before 1955. There is no evidence to assume choices (B) and (C). The first part of the answer choice (E) may be inferred, but the second part ("but later all had to wear steel type helmets") is incorrect; the statement refers only to workers in the construction industry.

17. Team sports, like baseball, display strong socialist tendencies in their requirement of individual subordination to the authority of coaches and managers.

Which of the following conclusions may not be inferred from the above information?

(A) All team sports are authoritarian.
(B) All team players are subordinate to their coaches.
(C) Without employee subordination to managerial authority, production for profit would not be possible.
(D) All team sports have socialist tendencies.
(E) Individual subordination to authority is an aspect of socialism.

(C) The sentence does not contain cue words that could help the reader identify premises and a conclusion. However, two sets of arguments may be identified:

1. all team sports have socialist tendencies.
2. baseball is a team sport.
3. baseball has socialist tendencies.

and

1. individual subordination to authority is a form of socialism.
2. all players in team sports are subordinate to their coaches.

Two diagrams will help:

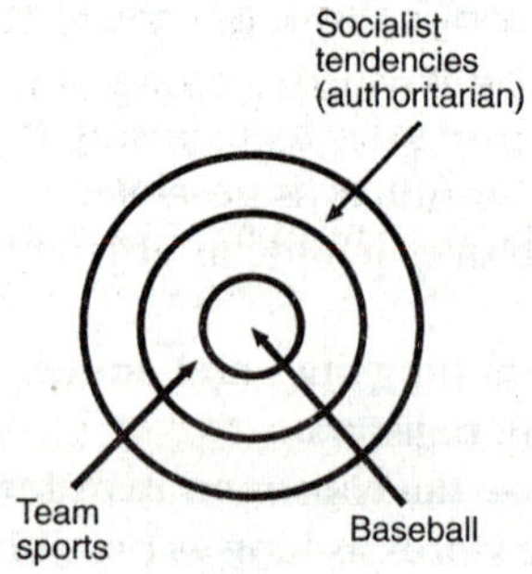

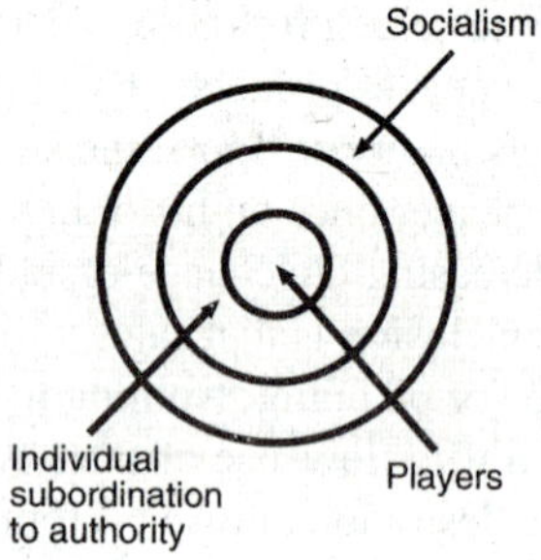

Section 6
Data Sufficiency

1. A rectangular field is 40 yards long. Find the area of the field.

(1) A fence around the outside of the field is 140 yards long.
(2) The distance from one corner of the field to the opposite corner is 50 yards.

(D) Area = (length)(width) = 40(width). So to find the area we must know the width. The perimeter of a rectangle is twice (length + width). STATEMENT (1) tells us the perimeter equals 140 yds. Since the length is 40 yds, the width is 30 yds, so (1) is sufficient. If we connect 2 opposite corners of the field, then it is divided into 2 right triangles where the side opposite the right angle has length 50 and one of the other sides has length 40. Since $(40)^2 + (\text{width})^2 = (50)^2$ the width is 30, and STATEMENT (2) is sufficient by itself.

2. Is x greater than 0?

(1) $x^3 + 1 = 0$
(2) $x^2 - 1 = 0$

(A) STATEMENT (1) is $x^3 + 1 = 0$, which means $x^3 = -1$; the only solution to this equation is -1. So x is not greater than 0. Therefore, (1) alone is sufficient. STATEMENT (2) says $x^2 - 1 = 0$ or $x^2 = 1$. There are two possible solutions to this equation, one positive and the other negative. So (2) by itself is not sufficient.

3. There are 450 boxes to load on a truck. *A* and *B* working independently but at the same time take 30 minutes to load the truck. How long should it take *B* working alone to load the truck?

(1) *A* loads twice as many boxes as *B*.
(2) *A* would take 45 minutes by himself.

(D) STATEMENT (1) is sufficient since it implies that *A* loaded 300 boxes in 30 minutes and *B* loaded 150 boxes. So *B* should take 90 minutes to load the 450 boxes alone. STATEMENT (2) is also sufficient since it implies *A* loads 10 boxes per minute; hence *A* loads 300 boxes in 30 minutes, and by the above argument we can deduce that *B* will take 90 minutes.

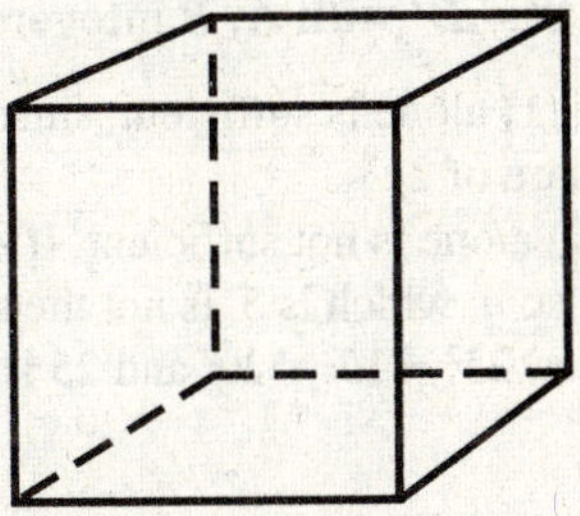

4. Is the above figure a cube?

(1) The lengths of all edges are equal.
(2) The angle between any two edges that meet is a right angle.

(C) A cube is a solid with 6 faces, all of which are congruent squares and any two faces that intersect are perpendicular. STATEMENT (1) is not sufficient since a solid with 2 of the faces as diamonds (rhombus) is not a cube but does satisfy (1) . STATEMENT (2) is not sufficient since a solid with 2 or 4 of the faces as congruent rectangles is not a cube 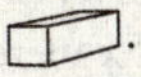. But (1) and (2) together mean that each face is a congruent square.

5. A car drives around a circular track once. A second car drives from point *A* to point *B* in a straight line. Which car travels farther?

(1) The car driving around the circular track takes a longer time to complete its trip than the car traveling in a straight line.
(2) The straight line from *A* to *B* is $1\frac{1}{2}$ times as long as the diameter of the circular track.

(B) The first car will travel a distance equal to the circumference of the circle, which is π times the diameter. Since π is greater than $1\frac{1}{2}$, STATEMENT (2) is sufficient. STATEMENT (1) is not sufficient since one car might have traveled at a faster rate than the other.

6. Find $x + y$

(1) $x - y = 6$
(2) $2x + 3y = 7$

(C) STATEMENT (1) tells us only that $x = 6 + y$, so it is not sufficient. In the same way STATEMENT (2) alone will give only one of the unknowns in terms of the other. However, if we use both (1) and (2), we obtain a system of two equations that can be solved for x and y.

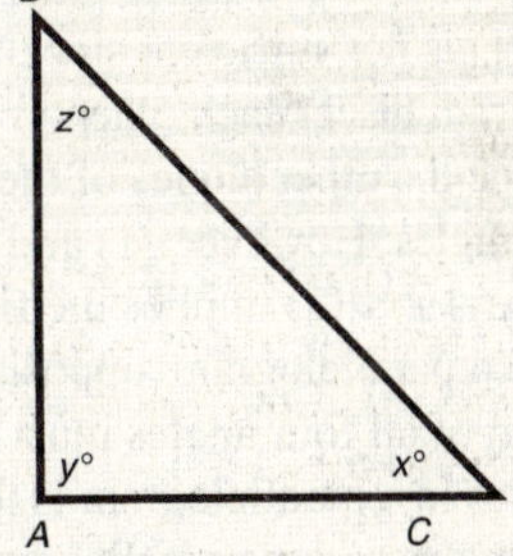

7. Find the length of *AC* if *AB* has length 3 and x is 45.

(1) $z = 45$
(2) $y = 90$

(D) Since we know that the sum of the angles in a triangle is 180° and that $x = 45$, STATEMENT (1) implies STATEMENT (2) and (2) implies (1). Either one is sufficient, since if $z = 45$, then $x = z$ and the sides opposite the equal angles are equal. Hence $AC = AB = 3$.

8. It costs 50 cents in tolls, 2 dollars in gas, and at least 1 dollar for parking to drive (round trip) from Utopia to Green Acres each day. The train offers a weekly ticket. Which is the cheaper way to travel per week if you work five days per week?

(1) The weekly train ticket costs 15 dollars.
(2) Parking costs a total of 6 dollars.

(A) It costs \$10 in gas, \$2.50 in the tolls, and at least \$5 in parking to drive each week. So driving costs at least \$17.50 a week. STATEMENT (1) is sufficient. Without information on the price of the train ticket we cannot compare the two methods, so STATEMENT (2) is not sufficient.

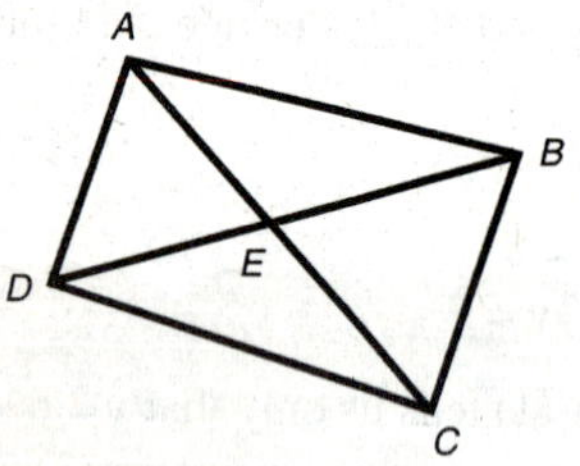

9. Is *ABCD* a rectangle?

(1) *AC* and *BD* bisect each other at *E*.
(2) Angle *ADC* is 90°

(C) STATEMENT (1) is not sufficient since the diagonals of *any* parallelogram bisect each other. STATEMENT (2) is not sufficient since the other angles of the figure do not have to be right angles. However, (1) and (2) together are sufficient. STATEMENT (1) implies the figure is a parallelogram. In a parallelogram, opposite angles are equal and the sum of all four angles must be 360°. Thus, if one of the angles in a parallelogram is 90°, all of the angles are right angles and the parallelogram is a rectangle.

10. A worker is hired for five days. He is paid \$5.00 more for each day of work than he was paid for the preceding day of work. What was the total amount he was paid for the five days of work?

(1) He had made 50% of the total by the end of the third day.
(2) He was paid twice as much for the last day as he was for the first day.

(D) Let x be the amount he was paid on the first day; then he was paid $x + 5$, $x + 10$, $x + 15$, and $x + 20$ for the remaining days of work. The total amount he was paid is $5x + 50$. Thus if we can find x, we can find the total amount he was paid. STATEMENT (1) is sufficient since after 3 days his total pay was $x + x + 5 + x + 10$ or $3x + 15$; this is equal to $\frac{1}{2}(5x + 50)$. So $3x + 15 = 2.5(x) + 25$ which implies $x = 20$. STATEMENT (2)is sufficient since he was paid $x + 20$ on the last day and so $x + 20 = 2x$ which implies $x = 20$.

Remember that to answer the question it is not necessary to actually *solve* the equations given in STATEMENTS 1 and 2. You only have to know that they will give you an equation that can be solved for x. Don't bother to actually solve the problem since you only have a limited amount of time to work all the questions in this section.

11. Is *y* larger than *x*?

(1) $x + y = 2$
(2) $\frac{x}{y} = 2$

(C) STATEMENT (1) alone is not sufficient since $x = 3$, $y = -1$, and $x = -1$, $y = 3$ satisfy $x + y = 2$. STATEMENT (2) alone is not sufficient since $x = 2$, $y = 1$ and $x = -2$, $y = -1$ satisfy (2). However, since (2) says $x = 2y$, using (1) $x + y = 2y + y = 2$ we see that $y = \frac{2}{3}$ and $x = \frac{4}{3}$. So (1) and (2) together are sufficient.

12. Is *n* the square of an integer *k*?

(1) $n = 4j^2$ **with *j* an integer.**
(2) $n^2 = A^2 + B^2$ **with *A*, *B* integers.**

(A) STATEMENT (1) alone is sufficient, since (1) implies that n is the square of $2j$.

STATEMENT (2) alone is not sufficient. If $A = 3$, and $B = 4$, then $n^2 = 25$, so n, which is 5, is not the square of an integer. However, $25^2 = 15^2 + 20^2$ and 25 is the square of an integer.

13. A pair of skis originally cost \$160. After a discount of *x*%, the skis were discounted *y*%. Do the skis cost less than \$130 after the discounts?

(1) $x = 20$
(2) $y = 15$

(A) Since 80% of \$160 = \$128, we know that after the first discount the skis cost less than \$130. Any further discount will only lower the price. So STATEMENT (1) alone is sufficient. STATEMENT (2) alone is not sufficient since if x were 10%, (2) would tell us the price was less than \$130; but if x were 1%, (2) would imply that the price was greater than \$130.

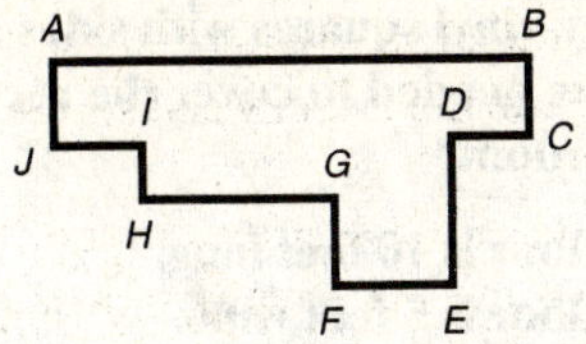

14. What is the length of line segment AB? All lines that meet are perpendicular. AJ, JI, HI, BC, FE, GF and DC are each equal to x. HG and DE are each equal to y.

(1) $y = 4$
(2) $x = 2$

(D) Since $AB = JI + HG + FE + DC$, if we knew the lengths of JI, HG, FE, and DC we could find the length of AB. So we need to know both what x is and what y is. Since $DE = IH + GF$, $y = 2x$. Thus, either STATEMENT (1) alone or (2) alone is sufficient. Marking sides that are equal to each other with either one slash or two slashes will help you to see the relationships.

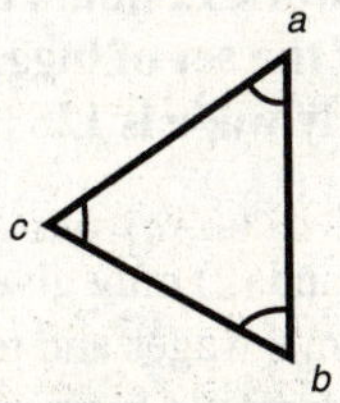

15. Is the angle c larger than 60°?

(1) $a + b$ is greater than c.
(2) a is greater than b which is greater than c.

(B) STATEMENT (1) alone is not sufficient. If $a = 70°$, $b = 25°$ and $c = 85°$, STATEMENT (1) would be true; however, if $a = 90°$, $b = 45°$, and $c = 45°$, STATEMENT (1) would also be true.

STATEMENT (2) alone is sufficient. Since we know that the sum of the angles in a triangle is 180°, the smallest angle is always less than or equal to 60°. Notice that STATEMENT (2) gives enough information to answer the question, but the answer is *no*. Don't confuse answering a question with answering a question affirmatively.

16. If a and b are both positive numbers, then which is larger, 2^a or 3^b?

(1) a is greater than $2b$.
(2) a is greater than or equal to $b + 3$

(A) STATEMENT (1) alone is sufficient. If a is greater than $2b$, then 2^a is greater than $2^{2b} = (2^2)^b = 4^b$, and 4^b is greater than 3^b.

STATEMENT (2) alone is not sufficient. If $b = 1$, then a could be 4 and 2^a would be greater than 3^b; however, if $b = 6$ and $a = 9$ then $2^a = 512$ and this is not greater than $3^b = 729$.

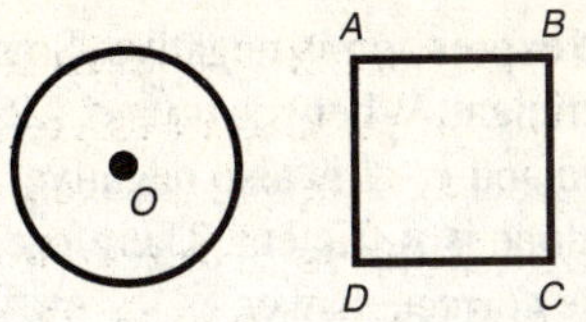

17. Will the circle with center O fit inside the square $ABCD$?

(1) The diameter of the circle is less than a side of the square.
(2) The area of the circle is less than the area of the square.

(A) STATEMENT (1) alone is sufficient. STATEMENT (2) is not sufficient. If the radius of the circle were $\sqrt{\pi}$ then the area of the circle would be $\pi r^2 = \pi^2$, but the diameter of the circle would be $2\sqrt{\pi}$, which is greater than π. So the circle could not fit inside a square with side of length π, although the area of the square would be π^2.

18. Is $xy < 0$?

(1) $\frac{1}{x} < \frac{1}{y}$
(2) $x > 0$

(C) STATEMENT (1) alone is not sufficient. x could be negative or positive with y positive, and (1) would be true.

STATEMENT (2) alone is not sufficient, since it gives no information about y.

STATEMENT (1) and (2) together are sufficient. If $x > 0$ then (1) implies y is > 0, so $xy > 0$.

19. A square originally had sides with length s. The length of the side is increased by x%. Did the area of the square increase by more than 10%?

(1) x is greater than 5.
(2) x is less than 10.

(A) STATEMENT (1) alone is sufficient. If x is greater than 5, then the area must increase by more than 10%, since $(1.05s)^2 = 1.1025(s^2)$.

STATEMENT (2) alone is not sufficient. If x is 1, then the area increases by less than 10%. However, if x is 9, then the area increases by more.

20. Is $k^2 + k - 2 > 0$

(1) $k < 1$
(2) $k < -2$

(B) The key to this problem is to factor $k^2 + k - 2$ into $(k + 2)(k - 1)$. The product of two expressions is positive if and only if both expressions have the same sign. $k = -4$ and $k = 0$ both satisfy STATEMENT (1), but when $k = -4$, the expression $k^2 + k - 2$ is positive, while when $k = 0$, the expression is negative. So STATEMENT (1) alone is not sufficient. When STATEMENT (2) holds, then $k + 2$ is negative and $k - 1$ is also negative. Therefore, STATEMENT (2) alone is sufficient. Therefore, answer choice (B) is the correct answer.

21. How many books are on the bookshelf?

(1) The bookshelf is 12 feet long.
(2) The average weight of each book is 1.2 pounds.

(E) STATEMENT (1) would be sufficient if there were information about the width of each book. Since STATEMENT (2) only gives information about the *weight* of each book, both statements together are not sufficient.

Section 7
Data Sufficiency

1. How much is the average salary of the 30 assembly workers? The foreman is paid a salary of $12,000.

(1) The total salary paid to the 30 assembly workers and the foreman is $312,000.
(2) The foreman's salary is 120% of the average salary of the 30 assembly workers.

(D) STATEMENT (1) is sufficient. Since the foreman's salary is $12,000, the total of the assembly workers' salaries is $300,000. Therefore, the average salary is $300,000 ÷ 30 = $10,000.

STATEMENT (2) is sufficient. If A is the average salary of the assembly workers, then 120% of A is $12,000. Therefore, $A = \$12{,}000 \div \frac{6}{5} = \$10{,}000$.

2. How far is it from town *A* to town *B*? Town *C* is 12 miles east of town *A*.
(1) Town *C* is south of town *B*.
(2) It is 9 miles from town *B* to town *C*.

(C) STATEMENT (2) alone is insufficient since you need to know what direction town *B* is from town *C*.

STATEMENT (1) alone is insufficient, since you need to know how far it is from town *B* to town *C*.

Using both STATEMENTS (1) and (2), *A*, *B* and *C* form a right triangle with legs of 9 miles and 12 miles. The distance from town *A* to town *B* is the hypotenuse of the triangle, so the distance from town *A* to town *B* is $\sqrt{9^2 + 12^2} = 15$ miles.

3. How many vinyl squares with sides 5 inches long will be needed to cover the rectangular floor of a room?

(1) The floor is 10 feet long.
(2) The floor is 5 feet wide.

(C) STATEMENTS (1) and (2) by themselves are insufficient since you need to know the area of the floor, and STATEMENT (1) only gives the length and STATEMENT (2) only gives the width. Using STATEMENTS (1) and (2) together, the area of the floor is $5 \times 10 = 50$ square feet. Since the area of each square is $5^2 = 25$ square inches, each square has area $\frac{25}{144}$ square feet. Therefore, the number of squares is $50 \div \frac{25}{144} = 288$.

4. Mary must work 15 hours to make in wages the cost of a set of luggage. How many dollars does the set of luggage cost?

(1) Jim must work 12 hours to make in wages the cost of the set of luggage.
(2) Jim's hourly wage is 125% of Mary's hourly wage.

(E) STATEMENTS (1) and (2) only give relations between Mary's wages and Jim's wages and tell you the cost of the set of luggage in terms of hours of wages. Since there is no information about the value of the hourly wages in dollars, STATEMENTS (1) and (2) together are not sufficient.

5. What is the value of x?

(1) $\frac{x}{y} = 3$

(2) $x - y = 9$

(C) STATEMENT (1) alone implies $x = 3y$. Since there is no more information about y, STATEMENT (1) alone is insufficient.

STATEMENT 2 alone gives $x = 9 + y$ but there is no information about y, so STATEMENT (2) alone is not sufficient.

STATEMENTS (1) and (2) together are sufficient. If $x = 9 + y$ and $x = 3y$, then $3y = 9 + y$ which gives $y = \frac{9}{2}$, so $x = (3)\left(\frac{9}{2}\right) = \frac{27}{2}$.

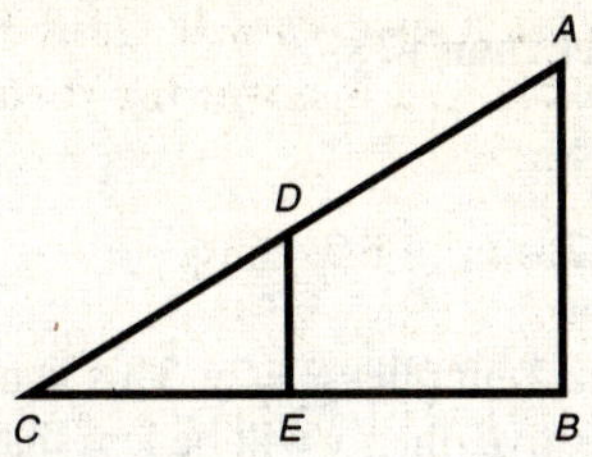

6. Is DE parallel to AB?

(1) $CD = DA$
(2) $CE = EB$

(C) STATEMENT (1) alone is not sufficient since if CD equals DA, E can be any point on the line CB. By the same reasoning, since D could be any point on AC if STATEMENT (2) is true, (2) alone is not sufficient. However, if both (1) and (2) are true, then triangles CDE and CAB are similar, with the corresponding angles CED and CBA equal. Thus the transversal CB has equal corresponding angles with the lines DE and AB, so DE is parallel to AB. Thus (1) and (2) together are sufficient.

7. How many of the numbers x and y are positive? Both x and y are less than 20.

(1) x is less than 5.
(2) $x + y = 24$

(B) If $x + y = 24$ then at least one of the numbers x or y is positive. If x is positive then $y = 24 - x$ and since x is less than 20, $24 - x = y$ is positive. The same argument shows that if y is positive so is x. Therefore, STATEMENT (2) alone is sufficient to show that both numbers are positive.

STATEMENT (1) alone is insufficient, since the fact that x is less than 5 does not tell whether x is positive and no information is given about y.

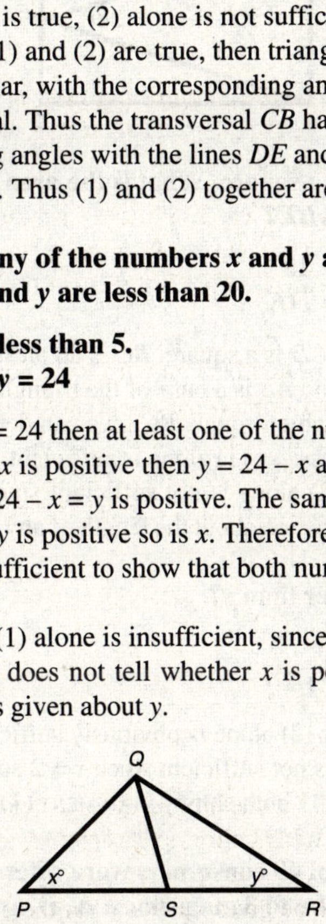

8. What is the value of x? $PS = SR$.

(1) $y = 30$
(2) $PQ = QR$

(C) STATEMENT (2) alone implies $x = y$ since equal sides have equal angles in a triangle. Since there is no information about y, STATEMENT (2) alone is insufficient.

STATEMENT (1) alone is insufficient since there is no relation between x and y without STATEMENT (2).

STATEMENTS (1) and (2) together imply $x = y = 30$, so STATEMENTS (1) and (2) together are sufficient.

9. How much does the first volume of a 5-volume work weigh?

(1) The first 3 volumes weigh 4 pounds.
(2) The second, third and fourth volumes weigh a total of $3\frac{1}{2}$ pounds.

(E) Denote by w_1, the weight of the first volume, by w_2 the weight of the second volume, by w_3 the weight of the third volume and by w_4 the weight of the fourth volume. STATEMENT (1) gives $w_1 + w_2 + w_3 = 4$ and STATEMENT (2) gives $w_2 + w_3 + w_4 = 3\frac{1}{2}$. Using STATEMENTS (1) and (2) you can obtain $w_1 - w_4 = \frac{1}{2}$ so $w_1 = w_4 + \frac{1}{2}$ but no other information is given about w_4. Therefore, STATEMENTS (1) and (2) together are insufficient.

10. A sequence of numbers is given by the rule $a_n = a_{n-1} + 2$. Is a_{10} an even integer?

(1) a_1 is an even integer.
(2) a_9 is 24.

(D) If any value of a_n is an even integer, then all succeeding values are even. (Any even integer + 2 is an even integer.) Since a_{10} appears after a_1 and a_9, both STATEMENT (1) alone and STATEMENT (2) alone are sufficient.

11. Is the radius of a circle greater than 3?

(1) The points with coordinates (2, 4) and (5, 10) are on the circle.
(2) The points with coordinates (2, 4) and (4, 1) are on the circle.

(A) The distance between the points (2, 4) and (5, 10) is the square root of $(2 - 5)^2 + (4 - 10)^2$ which is $\sqrt{45}$. So STATEMENT (1) alone is sufficient since $\sqrt{45}$ is greater than 6. (The distance between any two points is less than or equal to the diameter which is 2 × radius). STATEMENT (2) alone is not sufficient since the distance between (2, 4) and (4, 1) is less than 6. So (A) is the correct choice.

12. If $x = k$, is the expression $x^3 + ax^2 + bx$ equal to zero?

(1) $a = 0$
(2) $-b = k^2$

(C) STATEMENT (1) alone is not sufficient. The expression becomes $x^3 + bx = x(x^2 + b)$, but there is no relationship between the expression and k.

STATEMENT (2) alone is not sufficient, since the roots of the expression will depend on the value of a.

STATEMENTS (1) and (2) together make the expression $x^3 + ax^2 + bx$ into $x^3 - k^2x = x(x^2 - k^2)$, which is equal to zero when $x = k$.

13. A jar is filled with 60 marbles. All the marbles in the jar are either red or green. What is the smallest number of marbles which must be drawn from the jar in order to be certain that a red marble is drawn?

(1) The ratio of red marbles to green marbles is 2 : 1.

(2) There are 20 green marbles in the jar.

(D) If there are x red marbles and y green marbles in the jar, then $y + 1$ marbles must contain at least one red marble. So it is sufficient to know the number of red marbles and the number of green marbles. Since you are given that $x + y = 60$, STATEMENT (2) is obviously sufficient. Also STATEMENT (1) is sufficient since it implies that $x = 2y$, which enables you to find x and y. Therefore, the correct answer choice is (D).

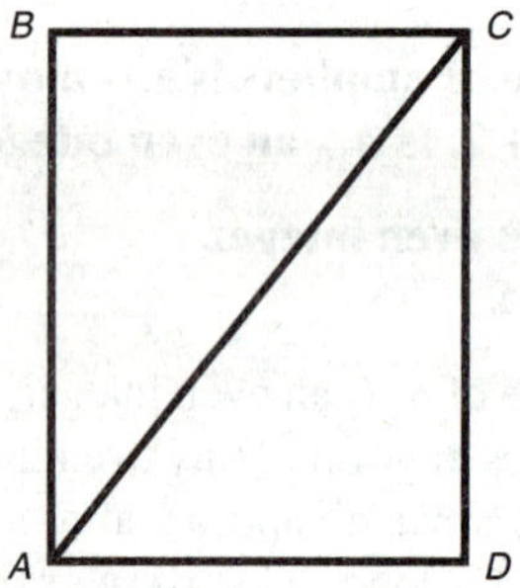

14. What is the area of rectangle *ABCD*?

(1) $AC = 5$

(2) $AB = 4$

(C) Since the figure is a rectangle, ABC is a right triangle. Therefore, using STATEMENTS (1) and (2) you can find BC, which will enable you to compute the area.

STATEMENT (2) alone is not sufficient, since BC could be any value without contradicting STATEMENT (2).

STATEMENT (1) alone is not sufficient. If $AB = 4$ and $BC = 3$, then $AC = 5$, and the area is 12. However, if $AB = 1$ and $BC = \sqrt{24}$, then $AC = 5$, but the area is $\sqrt{24}$ which is not 12.

15. Which is larger, a^b or b^a? $a > 0$ and $b > 0$.

(1) $a = 1$

(2) $b > 2$

(C) STATEMENT (1) reduces a^b to $1^b = 1$, and $b^a = b$.

STATEMENT (2) then allows us to decide, since $b > 2$ implies $b > 1$.

STATEMENT (2) alone is not sufficient. If $a = 1$ and $b = 3$, then $a^b = 1$ is less than $b^a = 3$. However, if $a = 3$ and $b = 4$, then $a^b = 81$, which is greater than $b^a = 64$.

16. Is x greater than y?

(1) $xy = 5$

(2) $\frac{x}{y} = 2$

(E) STATEMENT (2) implies $x = 2y$. This is not sufficient since if x is negative, then x will be less than y, but if x is positive, then x will be greater than y. If we also use STATEMENT (1), we obtain $(2y)y = 2y^2 = 5$, which has two solutions, one positive, the other negative. Thus, both statements together are not sufficient.

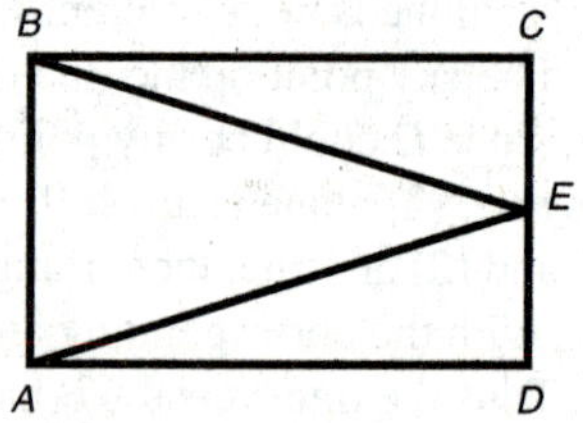

17. *ABCD* is a square. What is the area of the triangle *ABE*?

(1) $AB = 10$

(2) $CE = DE$

(A) Since $ABCD$ is a square, BC is an altitude of the triangle ABE and AB is a base of the triangle ABE. So if we know AB (which equals BC), we can determine the area. Thus STATEMENT (1) alone is sufficient.

STATEMENT (2) alone is not sufficient since it does not give any information about the length of any line segment.

18. Is x greater than y?

(1) $x = 2y$

(2) $x = y + 2$

(B) STATEMENT (2) alone is obviously sufficient. STATEMENT (1) is not sufficient since $x = 2$ and $y = 1$ and $x = -2$ and $y = -1$ both satisfy STATEMENT (1).

19. A group of 49 consumers were offered a chance to subscribe to 3 magazines: A, B, and C. 38 of the consumers subscribed to at least one of the magazines. How many of the 49 consumers subscribed to exactly two of the magazines?

(1) Twelve of the 49 consumers subscribed to all three of the magazines.

(2) Twenty of the 49 consumers subscribed to magazine A.

(E) The number who subscribed to at least one magazine is the sum of the numbers who subscribed to exactly one, two, and three magazines. So $38 = N1 + N2 + N3$, where $N1$, $N2$, and $N3$ are the number who subscribed to 1, 2, and 3 magazines respectively. We need to find $N2$. STATEMENT (1) is not sufficient since it tells the value of $N3$, but $N1$ and $N2$ are still both unknown. Even if we also use STATEMENT (1), we cannot find $N2$ since we have no information about the number of subscribers to magazines B and C.

20. Is k an odd integer?

(1) k is divisible by 3.
(2) The square root of k is an integer divisible by 3.

(E) STATEMENT (1) is insufficient since 9 (which is odd) and 6 (which is even) are both divisible by 3.

STATEMENT (2) is also insufficient since 81 is odd and 36 is even. 81 and 36 are also both divisible by 3, so (1) and (2) together are still insufficient.

21. Which of the four numbers w, x, y, and z is the largest?

(1) The average of w, x, y, and z is 25.
(2) The numbers w, x, and y are each less than 24.

(C) STATEMENT (1) is insufficient since any of the four numbers could be the largest.

STATEMENT (2) alone is insufficient since z could be larger than 24 or it could be smaller than one of the numbers x, y, or w.

STATEMENT (1) and STATEMENT (2) together are sufficient. (1) implies that $w + x + y + z = 100$ or $z = 100 - w - x - y$. Now using (2), we can see that $100 - w - x - y$ is greater than $100 - 24 - 24 - 24 = 28$. So z must be the largest number.

Evaluating Your Score

Tabulate your score for each section of Sample Test 4 according to the directions on pages 6–7 and record the results in the Self-Scoring Table below. Then find your rating for each score on the Self-Scoring Scale and record it in the appropriate blank.

Self-Scoring Table

SECTION	SCORE	RATING
1		
2		
3		
4		
5		
6		
7		

***Self-Scoring Scale*—RATING**

SECTION	POOR	FAIR	GOOD	EXCELLENT
1	0 – 9+	10 – 13+	14 – 17+	18 – 21
2	0 – 8+	9 – 11	11+ – 14	14+ – 17
3	0 – 12+	13 – 17+	18 – 21+	22 – 25
4	0 – 8+	9 – 11	11+ – 14	14+ – 17
5	0 – 8+	9 – 11	11+ – 14	14+ – 17
6	0 – 9+	10 – 13+	14 – 17+	18 – 21
7	0 – 9+	10 – 13+	14 – 17+	18 – 21

Study again the Review sections covering material in Sample Test 4 for which you had a rating of FAIR or POOR. Then go on to Sample Test 5.

To obtain an approximation of your GMAT score, see page 6.

Answer Sheet
SAMPLE TEST 5

Section 1

1 Ⓐ Ⓑ Ⓒ Ⓓ Ⓔ	6 Ⓐ Ⓑ Ⓒ Ⓓ Ⓔ	11 Ⓐ Ⓑ Ⓒ Ⓓ Ⓔ	16 Ⓐ Ⓑ Ⓒ Ⓓ Ⓔ	21 Ⓐ Ⓑ Ⓒ Ⓓ Ⓔ
2 Ⓐ Ⓑ Ⓒ Ⓓ Ⓔ	7 Ⓐ Ⓑ Ⓒ Ⓓ Ⓔ	12 Ⓐ Ⓑ Ⓒ Ⓓ Ⓔ	17 Ⓐ Ⓑ Ⓒ Ⓓ Ⓔ	22 Ⓐ Ⓑ Ⓒ Ⓓ Ⓔ
3 Ⓐ Ⓑ Ⓒ Ⓓ Ⓔ	8 Ⓐ Ⓑ Ⓒ Ⓓ Ⓔ	13 Ⓐ Ⓑ Ⓒ Ⓓ Ⓔ	18 Ⓐ Ⓑ Ⓒ Ⓓ Ⓔ	23 Ⓐ Ⓑ Ⓒ Ⓓ Ⓔ
4 Ⓐ Ⓑ Ⓒ Ⓓ Ⓔ	9 Ⓐ Ⓑ Ⓒ Ⓓ Ⓔ	14 Ⓐ Ⓑ Ⓒ Ⓓ Ⓔ	19 Ⓐ Ⓑ Ⓒ Ⓓ Ⓔ	24 Ⓐ Ⓑ Ⓒ Ⓓ Ⓔ
5 Ⓐ Ⓑ Ⓒ Ⓓ Ⓔ	10 Ⓐ Ⓑ Ⓒ Ⓓ Ⓔ	15 Ⓐ Ⓑ Ⓒ Ⓓ Ⓔ	20 Ⓐ Ⓑ Ⓒ Ⓓ Ⓔ	25 Ⓐ Ⓑ Ⓒ Ⓓ Ⓔ

Section 2

1 Ⓐ Ⓑ Ⓒ Ⓓ Ⓔ	6 Ⓐ Ⓑ Ⓒ Ⓓ Ⓔ	11 Ⓐ Ⓑ Ⓒ Ⓓ Ⓔ	16 Ⓐ Ⓑ Ⓒ Ⓓ Ⓔ	21 Ⓐ Ⓑ Ⓒ Ⓓ Ⓔ
2 Ⓐ Ⓑ Ⓒ Ⓓ Ⓔ	7 Ⓐ Ⓑ Ⓒ Ⓓ Ⓔ	12 Ⓐ Ⓑ Ⓒ Ⓓ Ⓔ	17 Ⓐ Ⓑ Ⓒ Ⓓ Ⓔ	22 Ⓐ Ⓑ Ⓒ Ⓓ Ⓔ
3 Ⓐ Ⓑ Ⓒ Ⓓ Ⓔ	8 Ⓐ Ⓑ Ⓒ Ⓓ Ⓔ	13 Ⓐ Ⓑ Ⓒ Ⓓ Ⓔ	18 Ⓐ Ⓑ Ⓒ Ⓓ Ⓔ	23 Ⓐ Ⓑ Ⓒ Ⓓ Ⓔ
4 Ⓐ Ⓑ Ⓒ Ⓓ Ⓔ	9 Ⓐ Ⓑ Ⓒ Ⓓ Ⓔ	14 Ⓐ Ⓑ Ⓒ Ⓓ Ⓔ	19 Ⓐ Ⓑ Ⓒ Ⓓ Ⓔ	24 Ⓐ Ⓑ Ⓒ Ⓓ Ⓔ
5 Ⓐ Ⓑ Ⓒ Ⓓ Ⓔ	10 Ⓐ Ⓑ Ⓒ Ⓓ Ⓔ	15 Ⓐ Ⓑ Ⓒ Ⓓ Ⓔ	20 Ⓐ Ⓑ Ⓒ Ⓓ Ⓔ	25 Ⓐ Ⓑ Ⓒ Ⓓ Ⓔ

Section 3

1 Ⓐ Ⓑ Ⓒ Ⓓ Ⓔ	6 Ⓐ Ⓑ Ⓒ Ⓓ Ⓔ	11 Ⓐ Ⓑ Ⓒ Ⓓ Ⓔ	16 Ⓐ Ⓑ Ⓒ Ⓓ Ⓔ	21 Ⓐ Ⓑ Ⓒ Ⓓ Ⓔ
2 Ⓐ Ⓑ Ⓒ Ⓓ Ⓔ	7 Ⓐ Ⓑ Ⓒ Ⓓ Ⓔ	12 Ⓐ Ⓑ Ⓒ Ⓓ Ⓔ	17 Ⓐ Ⓑ Ⓒ Ⓓ Ⓔ	22 Ⓐ Ⓑ Ⓒ Ⓓ Ⓔ
3 Ⓐ Ⓑ Ⓒ Ⓓ Ⓔ	8 Ⓐ Ⓑ Ⓒ Ⓓ Ⓔ	13 Ⓐ Ⓑ Ⓒ Ⓓ Ⓔ	18 Ⓐ Ⓑ Ⓒ Ⓓ Ⓔ	23 Ⓐ Ⓑ Ⓒ Ⓓ Ⓔ
4 Ⓐ Ⓑ Ⓒ Ⓓ Ⓔ	9 Ⓐ Ⓑ Ⓒ Ⓓ Ⓔ	14 Ⓐ Ⓑ Ⓒ Ⓓ Ⓔ	19 Ⓐ Ⓑ Ⓒ Ⓓ Ⓔ	24 Ⓐ Ⓑ Ⓒ Ⓓ Ⓔ
5 Ⓐ Ⓑ Ⓒ Ⓓ Ⓔ	10 Ⓐ Ⓑ Ⓒ Ⓓ Ⓔ	15 Ⓐ Ⓑ Ⓒ Ⓓ Ⓔ	20 Ⓐ Ⓑ Ⓒ Ⓓ Ⓔ	25 Ⓐ Ⓑ Ⓒ Ⓓ Ⓔ

Section 4

1 Ⓐ Ⓑ Ⓒ Ⓓ Ⓔ	6 Ⓐ Ⓑ Ⓒ Ⓓ Ⓔ	11 Ⓐ Ⓑ Ⓒ Ⓓ Ⓔ	16 Ⓐ Ⓑ Ⓒ Ⓓ Ⓔ	21 Ⓐ Ⓑ Ⓒ Ⓓ Ⓔ
2 Ⓐ Ⓑ Ⓒ Ⓓ Ⓔ	7 Ⓐ Ⓑ Ⓒ Ⓓ Ⓔ	12 Ⓐ Ⓑ Ⓒ Ⓓ Ⓔ	17 Ⓐ Ⓑ Ⓒ Ⓓ Ⓔ	22 Ⓐ Ⓑ Ⓒ Ⓓ Ⓔ
3 Ⓐ Ⓑ Ⓒ Ⓓ Ⓔ	8 Ⓐ Ⓑ Ⓒ Ⓓ Ⓔ	13 Ⓐ Ⓑ Ⓒ Ⓓ Ⓔ	18 Ⓐ Ⓑ Ⓒ Ⓓ Ⓔ	23 Ⓐ Ⓑ Ⓒ Ⓓ Ⓔ
4 Ⓐ Ⓑ Ⓒ Ⓓ Ⓔ	9 Ⓐ Ⓑ Ⓒ Ⓓ Ⓔ	14 Ⓐ Ⓑ Ⓒ Ⓓ Ⓔ	19 Ⓐ Ⓑ Ⓒ Ⓓ Ⓔ	24 Ⓐ Ⓑ Ⓒ Ⓓ Ⓔ
5 Ⓐ Ⓑ Ⓒ Ⓓ Ⓔ	10 Ⓐ Ⓑ Ⓒ Ⓓ Ⓔ	15 Ⓐ Ⓑ Ⓒ Ⓓ Ⓔ	20 Ⓐ Ⓑ Ⓒ Ⓓ Ⓔ	25 Ⓐ Ⓑ Ⓒ Ⓓ Ⓔ

Section 5

1 Ⓐ Ⓑ Ⓒ Ⓓ Ⓔ	6 Ⓐ Ⓑ Ⓒ Ⓓ Ⓔ	11 Ⓐ Ⓑ Ⓒ Ⓓ Ⓔ	16 Ⓐ Ⓑ Ⓒ Ⓓ Ⓔ	21 Ⓐ Ⓑ Ⓒ Ⓓ Ⓔ
2 Ⓐ Ⓑ Ⓒ Ⓓ Ⓔ	7 Ⓐ Ⓑ Ⓒ Ⓓ Ⓔ	12 Ⓐ Ⓑ Ⓒ Ⓓ Ⓔ	17 Ⓐ Ⓑ Ⓒ Ⓓ Ⓔ	22 Ⓐ Ⓑ Ⓒ Ⓓ Ⓔ
3 Ⓐ Ⓑ Ⓒ Ⓓ Ⓔ	8 Ⓐ Ⓑ Ⓒ Ⓓ Ⓔ	13 Ⓐ Ⓑ Ⓒ Ⓓ Ⓔ	18 Ⓐ Ⓑ Ⓒ Ⓓ Ⓔ	23 Ⓐ Ⓑ Ⓒ Ⓓ Ⓔ
4 Ⓐ Ⓑ Ⓒ Ⓓ Ⓔ	9 Ⓐ Ⓑ Ⓒ Ⓓ Ⓔ	14 Ⓐ Ⓑ Ⓒ Ⓓ Ⓔ	19 Ⓐ Ⓑ Ⓒ Ⓓ Ⓔ	24 Ⓐ Ⓑ Ⓒ Ⓓ Ⓔ
5 Ⓐ Ⓑ Ⓒ Ⓓ Ⓔ	10 Ⓐ Ⓑ Ⓒ Ⓓ Ⓔ	15 Ⓐ Ⓑ Ⓒ Ⓓ Ⓔ	20 Ⓐ Ⓑ Ⓒ Ⓓ Ⓔ	25 Ⓐ Ⓑ Ⓒ Ⓓ Ⓔ

Section 6

1 Ⓐ Ⓑ Ⓒ Ⓓ Ⓔ	6 Ⓐ Ⓑ Ⓒ Ⓓ Ⓔ	11 Ⓐ Ⓑ Ⓒ Ⓓ Ⓔ	16 Ⓐ Ⓑ Ⓒ Ⓓ Ⓔ	21 Ⓐ Ⓑ Ⓒ Ⓓ Ⓔ
2 Ⓐ Ⓑ Ⓒ Ⓓ Ⓔ	7 Ⓐ Ⓑ Ⓒ Ⓓ Ⓔ	12 Ⓐ Ⓑ Ⓒ Ⓓ Ⓔ	17 Ⓐ Ⓑ Ⓒ Ⓓ Ⓔ	22 Ⓐ Ⓑ Ⓒ Ⓓ Ⓔ
3 Ⓐ Ⓑ Ⓒ Ⓓ Ⓔ	8 Ⓐ Ⓑ Ⓒ Ⓓ Ⓔ	13 Ⓐ Ⓑ Ⓒ Ⓓ Ⓔ	18 Ⓐ Ⓑ Ⓒ Ⓓ Ⓔ	23 Ⓐ Ⓑ Ⓒ Ⓓ Ⓔ
4 Ⓐ Ⓑ Ⓒ Ⓓ Ⓔ	9 Ⓐ Ⓑ Ⓒ Ⓓ Ⓔ	14 Ⓐ Ⓑ Ⓒ Ⓓ Ⓔ	19 Ⓐ Ⓑ Ⓒ Ⓓ Ⓔ	24 Ⓐ Ⓑ Ⓒ Ⓓ Ⓔ
5 Ⓐ Ⓑ Ⓒ Ⓓ Ⓔ	10 Ⓐ Ⓑ Ⓒ Ⓓ Ⓔ	15 Ⓐ Ⓑ Ⓒ Ⓓ Ⓔ	20 Ⓐ Ⓑ Ⓒ Ⓓ Ⓔ	25 Ⓐ Ⓑ Ⓒ Ⓓ Ⓔ

Section 7

1 Ⓐ Ⓑ Ⓒ Ⓓ Ⓔ	6 Ⓐ Ⓑ Ⓒ Ⓓ Ⓔ	11 Ⓐ Ⓑ Ⓒ Ⓓ Ⓔ	16 Ⓐ Ⓑ Ⓒ Ⓓ Ⓔ	21 Ⓐ Ⓑ Ⓒ Ⓓ Ⓔ
2 Ⓐ Ⓑ Ⓒ Ⓓ Ⓔ	7 Ⓐ Ⓑ Ⓒ Ⓓ Ⓔ	12 Ⓐ Ⓑ Ⓒ Ⓓ Ⓔ	17 Ⓐ Ⓑ Ⓒ Ⓓ Ⓔ	22 Ⓐ Ⓑ Ⓒ Ⓓ Ⓔ
3 Ⓐ Ⓑ Ⓒ Ⓓ Ⓔ	8 Ⓐ Ⓑ Ⓒ Ⓓ Ⓔ	13 Ⓐ Ⓑ Ⓒ Ⓓ Ⓔ	18 Ⓐ Ⓑ Ⓒ Ⓓ Ⓔ	23 Ⓐ Ⓑ Ⓒ Ⓓ Ⓔ
4 Ⓐ Ⓑ Ⓒ Ⓓ Ⓔ	9 Ⓐ Ⓑ Ⓒ Ⓓ Ⓔ	14 Ⓐ Ⓑ Ⓒ Ⓓ Ⓔ	19 Ⓐ Ⓑ Ⓒ Ⓓ Ⓔ	24 Ⓐ Ⓑ Ⓒ Ⓓ Ⓔ
5 Ⓐ Ⓑ Ⓒ Ⓓ Ⓔ	10 Ⓐ Ⓑ Ⓒ Ⓓ Ⓔ	15 Ⓐ Ⓑ Ⓒ Ⓓ Ⓔ	20 Ⓐ Ⓑ Ⓒ Ⓓ Ⓔ	25 Ⓐ Ⓑ Ⓒ Ⓓ Ⓔ

13 SAMPLE TEST 5
with Answers and Analysis

Writing Assessment

Part I

TIME: 30 minutes

Directions: Write a clear, logical, and well-organized response to the following issue or argument. Your response should be in the form of a short essay, following the conventions of standard written English. Your answer should fit on three pages of lined 8½" × 11" paper. Write legibly. Essays that are illegible or that are written on a topic other than the one outlined in the question will not be scored.

Science may be on the threshold of greatly extending the human life span to 100 years or more. If all causes of biological aging are discovered and cured, man eventually may have an indefinite life span extending for many centuries.

Discuss how logically persuasive you find the above argument. In presenting your point of view, analyze the sort of reasoning used and its supporting evidence. In addition, state what further evidence, if any, would make the argument more sound and convincing or would make you better able to evaluate its conclusion.

Part II

TIME: 30 minutes

Directions: Write a clear, logical, and well-organized response to the following issue or argument. Your response should be in the form of a short essay, following the conventions of standard written English. Your answer should fit on three pages of lined 8½" × 11" paper. Write legibly. Essays that are illegible or that are written on a topic other than the one outlined in the question will not be scored.

Certain schools of thought stress the value to the listener of having some practical experience of music. They suggest that even a rudimentary playing of the piano or some other instrument is better than reading a dozen books about music. There are those, however, who claim that even many concert pianists have only a limited understanding of what music is.

Do you agree with the claim that practical experience is a better teacher of music than learning about it from books? State your position using relevant reasons and examples from your own experience, observation, or reading.

STOP

**IF THERE IS STILL TIME REMAINING,
YOU MAY REVIEW THE QUESTIONS IN THIS SECTION ONLY.
YOU MAY NOT TURN TO ANY OTHER SECTION OF THE TEST.**

Section 1

TIME: 25 minutes
17 Questions

Directions: Solve each of the following problems; then indicate the correct answer on the answer sheet.

NOTE: A figure that appears with a problem is drawn as accurately as possible so as to provide information that may help in answering the questions. Numbers in this test are real numbers.

1. An angle of x degrees has the property that its complement is equal to $\frac{1}{6}$ of its supplement where x is

(A) 30
(B) 45
(C) 60
(D) 63
(E) 72

2. If $y = \frac{3}{(x^2)} + x$ and $x = 3$, then y is

(A) $\frac{2}{3}$
(B) $\frac{10}{3}$
(C) $\frac{12}{3}$
(D) $\frac{18}{3}$
(E) $\frac{36}{6}$

3. Which of the following numbers is the least common multiple of the numbers 2, 3, 4 and 5?

(A) 12
(B) 24
(C) 30
(D) 40
(E) 60

4. In a certain town 40% of the people have brown hair, 25% have brown eyes, and 10% have both brown hair and brown eyes. What percentage of the people in the town have neither brown hair nor brown eyes?

(A) 35
(B) 40
(C) 45
(D) 50
(E) 55

GO ON TO THE NEXT PAGE ➤

5. If the altitude of a triangle increases by 5% and the base of the triangle increases by 7%, by what percent will the area of the triangle increase?

(A) 3.33%
(B) 5%
(C) 6%
(D) 12%
(E) 12.35%

6. A shipping firm charges 2¢ a pound for the first 20 pounds of package weight and 1.5¢ for each pound or fraction of a pound over 20 pounds of package weight. How much will it charge to ship a package which weighs $23\frac{1}{2}$ pounds?

(A) 6¢
(B) 8¢
(C) 45¢
(D) 46¢
(E) 47¢

7. If paper costs 1¢ a sheet, and a buyer gets a 2% discount on all the paper he buys after the first 1,000 sheets, how much will it cost to buy 5,000 sheets of paper?

(A) $49.20
(B) $50.00
(C) $3,920.00
(D) $4,920.00
(E) $5,000.00

8. Tom's salary is 150% of John's salary. John's salary is 80% of Steve's salary. What is the ratio of Steve's salary to Tom's salary?

(A) 1 to 2
(B) 2 to 3
(C) 5 to 6
(D) 6 to 5
(E) 5 to 4

9. A charity solicited *P* persons over the phone who agreed to an average pledge of $*R* each. *Q* of these people who had pledged an average of $*S* each never sent in the pledged amount. Which of the following expressions represents the percentage of pledged money that the charity received?

(A) $100 \times \frac{PR}{QS}$

(B) $100 \times \frac{QS}{PR}$

(C) $100\,PR - 100\,QS$

(D) $100 - \frac{100QS}{PR}$

(E) $100\,PR - \frac{100QS}{PR}$

GO ON TO THE NEXT PAGE ➤

1 1 1 1 1 1 1 1 1 1 1

10. If it takes 50 workers 4 hours to dig a sewer, how long should it take 30 workers to dig the same sewer?

(A) 2 hrs., 24 min.
(B) 5 hrs., 12 min.
(C) 6 hrs., 12 min.
(D) 6 hrs., 20 min.
(E) 6 hrs., 40 min.

11. Three pounds of 05 grass seed contain 5 percent herbicide. A different type of grass seed, 20, which contains 20 percent herbicide, will be mixed with the three pounds of 05 grass seed. How much grass seed of type 20 should be added to the three pounds of 05 so that the resulting mixture contains 15 percent herbicide?

(A) 3 pounds
(B) 3.75 pounds
(C) 4.5 pounds
(D) 6 pounds
(E) 9 pounds

12. A car is traveling on a straight highway. At 10 o'clock, it passes a truck traveling in the same direction. The truck continues on the highway traveling at 50 mph while the car travels at 65 mph. How far apart are the car and the truck at 2 o'clock?

(A) 15 miles
(B) 30 miles
(C) 60 miles
(D) 200 miles
(E) 260 miles

Use the following graph for question 13.

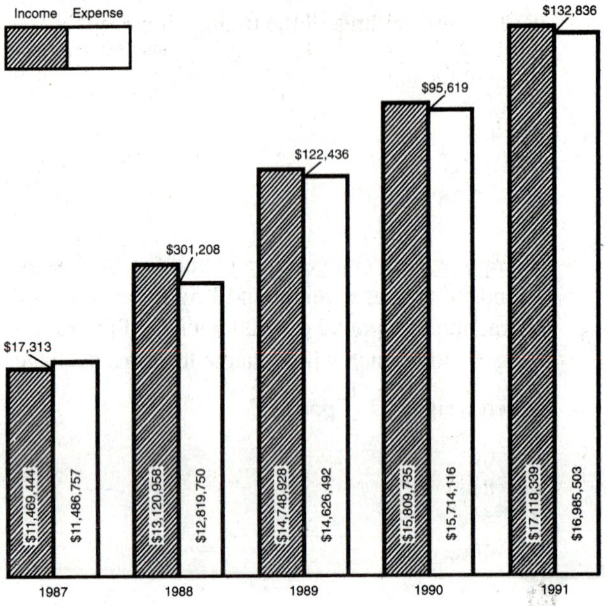

13. Which of the following statements can be inferred from the graph?

I. The company made a profit in all the years shown on the graph.
II. The company's profit increased in every year between 1989 and 1991.
III. The company's expenses increased in each year shown on the graph.

(A) I only
(B) II only
(C) III only
(D) I and III only
(E) I, II, and III

GO ON TO THE NEXT PAGE ➤

1 1 1 1 1 1 1 1 1 1 1

14. Wheat costs \$2.00 a bushel and corn costs \$2.62 a bushel. If the price of wheat rises 10% a month and the price of corn is unchanged, how many months will it take before a bushel of corn costs less than a bushel of wheat?

(A) 2
(B) 3
(C) 4
(D) 5
(E) 6

15. If $\frac{1}{2}+\frac{1}{4}=\frac{x}{15}$, then x is

(A) 10
(B) 11.25
(C) 12
(D) 13.75
(E) 14

16. If $x + y + z + w = 15$, then at least k of the numbers x, y, z, w must be positive where k is

(A) 0
(B) 1
(C) 2
(D) 3
(E) 4

17. Which of the following figures has the largest area?

I. A circle of radius $\sqrt{2}$.
II. An equilateral triangle whose sides each have length 4.
III. A triangle whose sides have lengths 3, 4, and 5.

(A) I
(B) II
(C) III
(D) I and II
(E) II and III

STOP

IF THERE IS STILL TIME REMAINING,
YOU MAY REVIEW THE QUESTIONS IN THIS SECTION ONLY.
YOU MAY NOT TURN TO ANY OTHER SECTION OF THE TEST.

2 2 2 2 2 2 2 2 2 2 2

Section 2

TIME: 30 minutes
25 Questions

Directions: This part contains three reading passages. You are to read each one carefully. When answering the questions, you *will* be allowed to refer back to the passages. The questions are based on what is *stated* or *implied* in each passage. You have thirty minutes to complete this section.

Passage 1:

A newly issued report reveals in facts and figures what should have been known in principle, that quite a lot of business companies are going to go under during the coming decade, as tariff walls are progressively dismantled. Labor and capital valued at $12 billion are to be made idle through the impact of duty-free imports. As a result, 35,000 workers will be displaced. Some will move to other jobs and other departments within the same firm. Around 15,000 will have to leave the firm now employing them and work elsewhere.

The report is measuring exclusively the influence of free trade with Europe. The authors do not take into account the expected expansion of production over the coming years. On the other hand, they are not sure that even the export predictions they make will be achieved. For this presupposes that a suitable business climate lets the pressure to increase productivity materialize.

There are two reasons why this scenario may not happen. The first one is that industry on the whole is not taking the initiatives necessary to adapt fully to the new price situation it will be facing as time goes by.

This is another way of saying that the manufacturers do not realize what lies ahead. The government is to blame for not making the position absolutely clear. It should be saying that in ten years' time tariffs on all industrial goods imported from Europe will be eliminated. There will be no adjustment assistance for manufacturers who cannot adapt to this situation.

The second obstacle to adjustment is not stressed in the same way in the report; it is the attitude of the service sector. Not only are service industries unaware that the Common Market treaty concerns them too, they are artificially insulated from the physical pressures of international competition. The manufacturing sector has been forced to apply its nose to the grindstone for some time now, by the increasingly stringent import-liberalization program.

The ancillary services on which the factories depend show a growing indifference to their work obligations. They seem unaware that overmanned ships, underutilized container equipment in the ports, and repeated work stoppages slow the country's attempts to narrow the trade gap. The remedy is to cut the fees charged by these services so as to reduce their earnings—in exactly the same way that earnings in industrial undertakings are reduced by the tariff reduction program embodied in the treaty with the European Community.

There is no point in dismissing 15,000 industrial workers from their present jobs during the coming ten years if all the gain in productivity is wasted by costly harbor, transport, financial, administrative and other services. The free trade treaty is their concern as well. Surplus staff should be removed, if need be, from all workplaces, not just from the factories. Efficiency is everybody's business.

1. The attitude of the report, as described in the passage, may best be expressed as
   - (A) harshly condemnatory, because industry is not more responsive to the business climate
   - (B) optimistic that government will induce industry to make needed changes
   - (C) critical of labor unions
   - (D) pessimistic that anything can be done to reduce the trade gap
   - (E) objective in assessing the influence of free trade on employment

GO ON TO THE NEXT PAGE ➤

2 2 2 2 2 2 2 2 2 2 2

2. What is the meaning of *free trade* in line 13?

(A) unlimited sale of goods in Europe
(B) trade on a barter basis
(C) the elimination of tariffs
(D) sale of price-discounted goods to European countries
(E) trade with only the so-called "free countries," i.e., Western Europe

3. It can be inferred that the term *adjustment assistance* in line 31 refers mainly to

(A) unemployment compensation
(B) some sort of financial assistance to manufacturers hurt by free trade
(C) help in relocating plants to Europe
(D) aid in reducing work stoppages
(E) subsidy payments to increase exports

4. The author's central recommendation seems to be that

(A) unemployment should be avoided at all costs
(B) redundant labor should be removed in all sectors
(C) government should control the service sector
(D) tariffs should not be lowered
(E) workers should be retrained

5. Which of the following titles best describes the content of the passage?

(A) *The Prospects of Free Trade*
(B) *Government Intervention in World Trade*
(C) *Trade with the Common Market*
(D) *What Lies Ahead?*
(E) *Unemployment and Adjustment Assistance*

6. Which of the following will occur because of duty-free imports?

I. Twelve billion dollars of capital will be idled.
II. Thirty-five thousand workers will be unemployed.
III. Fifteen thousand firms will face bankruptcy.

(A) I only
(B) II only
(C) I and II only
(D) II and III only
(E) I, II, and III

7. According to the passage, the government is responsible for

(A) increasing tariffs
(B) subsidizing exports
(C) not explaining its position
(D) adjustment assistance
(E) overmanned ships

8. Tariffs will be reduced on

(A) all manufactured goods
(B) manufactured and agricultural goods
(C) all goods
(D) industrial goods
(E) industrial and consumer goods

9. Which industries will be affected by tariff reductions?

I. Services
II. Manufacturing
III. Extracting

(A) I only
(B) II only
(C) I and II only
(D) II and III only
(E) I, II, and III

GO ON TO THE NEXT PAGE ➤

Passage 2:

The fundamental objectives of sociology are the same as those of science generally—discovery and explanation. To *discover* the essential data of social behavior and the connections among the data is the first objective of sociology. To *explain* the data and the connections is the second and larger objective. Science makes its advances in terms of both of these objectives. Sometimes it is the discovery of a new element or set of elements that marks a major breakthrough in the history of a scientific discipline. Closely related to such discovery is the discovery of relationships of data that had never been noted before. All of this is, as we know, of immense importance in science. But the drama of discovery, in this sense, can sometimes lead us to overlook the greater importance of explanation of what is revealed by the data. Sometimes decades, even centuries, pass before known connections and relationships are actually explained. Discovery and explanation are the two great interpenetrating, interacting realms of science.

The order of reality that interests the scientists is the *empirical* order, that is, the order of data and phenomena revealed to us through observation or experience. To be precise or explicit about what is, and is not, revealed by observation is not always easy, to be sure. And often it is necessary for our natural powers of observation to be supplemented by the most intricate of mechanical aids for a given object to become "empirical" in the sense just used. That the electron is not as immediately visible as is the mountain range does not mean, obviously, that it is any less empirical. That social behavior does not lend itself to as quick and accurate description as, say, chemical behavior of gases and compounds does not mean that social roles, statuses, and attitudes are any less empirical than molecules and tissues. What is empirical and observable today may have been nonexistent in scientific consciousness a decade ago. Moreover, the empirical is often data *inferred* from direct observation. All of this is clear enough, and we should make no pretense that there are not often shadow areas between the empirical and the nonempirical. Nevertheless, the first point to make about any science, physical or social, is that its world of data is the empirical world. A very large amount of scientific energy goes merely into the work of expanding the frontiers, through discovery, of the known, observable, empirical world.

From observation or discovery we move to *explanation.* The explanation sought by the scientist is, of course, not at all like the explanation sought by the theologian or metaphysician. The scientist is not interested—not, that is, in his role of scientist—in ultimate, transcendental, or divine causes of what he sets himself to explain. He is interested in explanations that are as empirical as the data themselves. If it is the high incidence of crime in a certain part of a large city that requires explanation, the scientist is obliged to offer his explanation in terms of factors which are empirically real as the phenomenon of crime itself. He does not explain the problem, for example, in terms of references to the will of God, demons, or original sin. A satisfactory explanation is not only one that is empirical, however, but one that can be stated in the terms of a *causal proposition.* Description is an indispensable point of beginning, but description is not explanation. It is well to stress this point, for there are all too many scientists, or would-be scientists, who are primarily concerned with data gathering, data counting, and data describing, and who seem to forget that such operations, however useful, are but the first step. Until we have accounted for the problem at hand, explained it causally by referring the data to some principle or generalization already established, or to some new principle or generalization, we have not explained anything.

10. According to the passage, scientists are not interested in theological explanations because

    (A) scientists tend to be atheists
    (B) theology cannot explain change
    (C) theological explanations are not empirical
    (D) theology cannot explain social behavior
    (E) scientists are concerned primarily with data gathering

11. The major objective of the passage is to

    (A) show that explanation is more important than discovery
    (B) prove that sociology is a science
    (C) explain the major objectives of sociology
    (D) discuss scientific method
    (E) describe social behavior

GO ON TO THE NEXT PAGE ➤

2 2 2 2 2 2 2 2 2 2 2

12. Which of the following statements best agrees with the author's position?
    (A) Science is the formulation of unverified hypotheses.
    (B) Explanation is inferred from data.
    (C) Causation is a basis for explanation.
    (D) Generalization is a prerequisite for explanation.
    (E) Empiricism is the science of discovery.

13. Judging from the contents of the passage, the final step in a study of social behavior would be to
    (A) discover the problem
    (B) establish principles
    (C) offer an explanation of the data by determining causation
    (D) collect data
    (E) establish generalizations

14. According to the passage, which of the following activities contribute to the advance of science?
    I. Finding data relationships
    II. Expanding the limits of the empirical
    III. Establishing ultimate causes of phenomena

    (A) I only
    (B) II only
    (C) I and II only
    (D) I and III only
    (E) I, II, and III

15. The author's main point in the first paragraph may best be described by which of the following statements?
    (A) Science and sociology are interdisciplinary.
    (B) The first objective of sociology is discovery.
    (C) Discovery without explanation is meaningless.
    (D) Both discovery and explanation are fundamental to building a science.
    (E) It takes a long time before relationships of data are discovered.

16. According to the author, which of the following explanations would a scientist accept?
    I. Snow falls because angels are having a pillow fight.
    II. Suicide is caused by weak character.
    III. Babies weigh 20% more than the average weight of newborns if their mothers take a 2-hour nap every day during the last 3 months of pregnancy.

    (A) I only
    (B) II only
    (C) III only
    (D) II and III only
    (E) I, II, and III

17. The major objective of the second paragraph is
    (A) to show that electrons are empirical data
    (B) to show that science changes as time passes
    (C) to demonstrate the difference between chemistry and sociology
    (D) to explain how science expands the frontiers of the observable world
    (E) to explain what the term *empirical order* means

GO ON TO THE NEXT PAGE ➤

Passage 3:

A polytheist always has favorites among the gods, determined by his own temperament, age, and condition, as well as his own interest, temporary or permanent. If it is true that everybody loves a lover, then Venus will be a popular deity with all. But from lovers she will elicit special devotion. In ancient Rome, when a young couple went out together to see a procession or other show, they would of course pay great respect to Venus, when her image appeared on the screen. Instead of saying, "Isn't love wonderful?" they would say, "Great art thou, O Venus." In a polytheistic society you could tell a good deal about a person's frame of mind by the gods he favored, so that to tell a girl you were trying to woo that you thought Venus overrated was hardly the way to win her heart. But in any case, a lovesick youth or maiden would be spontaneously supplicating Venus.

The Greeks liked to present their deities in human form; it was natural to them to symbolize the gods as human beings glorified, idealized. But this fact is also capable of misleading us. We might suppose that the ancients were really worshipping only themselves; that they were, like Narcissus, beholding their own image in a pool, so that their worship was *anthropocentric* (man-centered) rather than *theocentric* (god-centered). We are in danger of assuming that they were simply constructing the god in their own image. This is not necessarily so. The gods must always be symbolized in one form or another. To give them a human form is one way of doing this, technically called *anthropomorphism* (from the Greek *anthropos*, a man, and *morphé*, form). People of certain temperaments and within certain types of culture seem to be more inclined to it than are others. It is, however, more noticeable in others than in oneself, and those who affect to despise it are sometimes conspicuous for their addiction to it. A German once said an Englishman's idea of God is an Englishman twelve feet tall. Such disparagement of anthropomorphism occurred in the ancient world, too. The Celts, for instance, despised Greek practice in this matter, preferring to use animals and other such symbols. The Egyptians favored more abstract and stylized symbols, among which a well-known example is the solar disk, a symbol of Rà, the sun-god.

Professor C. S. Lewis tells of an Oxford undergraduate he knew who, priggishly despising the conventional images of God, thought he was overcoming anthropomorphism by thinking of the Deity as infinite vapor or smoke. Of course even the bearded-old-man image can be a better symbol of Deity than ever could be the image, even if this were psychologically possible, of an unlimited smog.

What is really characteristic of all polytheism, however, is not the worship of idols or humanity or forests or stars; it is, rather, the worship of innumerable *powers* that confront and affect us. The powers are held to be valuable in themselves; that is why they are to be worshipped. But the values conflict. The gods do not cooperate, so you have to play them off against each other. Suppose you want rain. You know of two gods, the dry-god who sends drought and the wet-god who sends rain. You do not suppose that you can just pray to the wet-god to get busy, and simply ignore the dry-god. If you do so, the latter may be offended, so that no matter how hard the wet-god tries to oblige you, the dry-god will do his best to wither everything. Because both gods are powerful you must take both into consideration, begging the wet-god to be generous and beseeching the dry-god to stay his hand.

18. It can be inferred from the passage that polytheism means a belief in

(A) Greek gods
(B) more than one god
(C) a god-centered world
(D) powerful deities
(E) infinite numbers of gods

19. The author's statement in lines 13–14 that "you could tell a good deal about a person's frame of mind by the gods he favored" means that

(A) those who believed in gods were superstitious
(B) worship was either anthropocentric or theocentric
(C) gods were chosen to represent a given way of life
(D) the way a person thinks depends on the power of deities
(E) in certain cultures, the gods served as representations of what people thought of themselves

GO ON TO THE NEXT PAGE ➤

2 2 2 2 2 2 2 2 2 2 2

20. It may be inferred from the passage that the author would most likely agree that ancient cultures

    I. symbolized their deities only in human form
    II. symbolized the gods in many forms
    III. were mainly self-worshippers

    (A) I only
    (B) II only
    (C) I and II only
    (D) I and III only
    (E) I, II, and III

21. The main point the author makes about anthropomorphism in lines 34 and 35 is that

    (A) certain cultures are inclined to antropomorphism
    (B) those who demean anthropomorphism may themselves practice it
    (C) the disparagement of anthropomorphism is common to both ancient and modern cultures
    (D) the Germans tend to be more theocentric than the English
    (E) anthropomorphism is a practice common to all cultures

22. It may be inferred from the last paragraph that polytheism entails

    (A) a commonality of interests among the deities
    (B) predictable consequences
    (C) incoherence and conflict among the "powers"
    (D) an orderly universe
    (E) worshipping one god at a time

23. Which people worshipped animals?

    (A) Romans
    (B) Greeks
    (C) Egyptians
    (D) Celts
    (E) Pagans

24. Anthropomorphism may be said to be symbolizing

    (A) a deity in one's own image
    (B) a human form
    (C) any form
    (D) both human and spiritual forms
    (E) an abstract form

25. A polytheist

    I. has favorite gods
    II. simultaneously worships more than one god
    III. lived in Greece

    (A) I only
    (B) II only
    (C) I and II only
    (D) II and III only
    (E) I, II, and III

STOP

IF THERE IS STILL TIME REMAINING,
YOU MAY REVIEW THE QUESTIONS IN THIS SECTION ONLY.
YOU MAY NOT TURN TO ANY OTHER SECTION OF THE TEST.

3 3 3 3 3 3 3 3 3 3 3

Section 3

TIME: 25 minutes
21 Questions

Directions: Each of the following problems has a question and two statements which are labeled (1) and (2). Use the data given in (1) and (2) together with other available information (such as the number of hours in a day, the definition of *clockwise*, mathematical facts, etc.) to decide whether the statements are *sufficient* to answer the question. Then fill in space

(A) if you can get the answer from **(1) ALONE** but not from (2) alone
(B) if you can get the answer from **(2) ALONE** but not from (1) alone
(C) if you can get the answer from **BOTH (1) and (2) TOGETHER**, but not from (1) alone or (2) alone
(D) if **EITHER** statement **(1) ALONE OR** statement **(2) ALONE** suffices
(E) if you **CANNOT** get the answer from statements (1) and (2) **TOGETHER**, but need even more data

All numbers used in this section are real numbers. A figure given for a problem is intended to provide information consistent with that in the question, but not necessarily with the additional information contained in the statements.

1. *ABC* is a triangle inscribed in circle *AOCB*. Is *AC* a diameter of the circle *AOCB*?

   (1) Angle *ABC* is a right angle.

   (2) The length of *AB* is $\frac{3}{4}$ the length of *BC*.

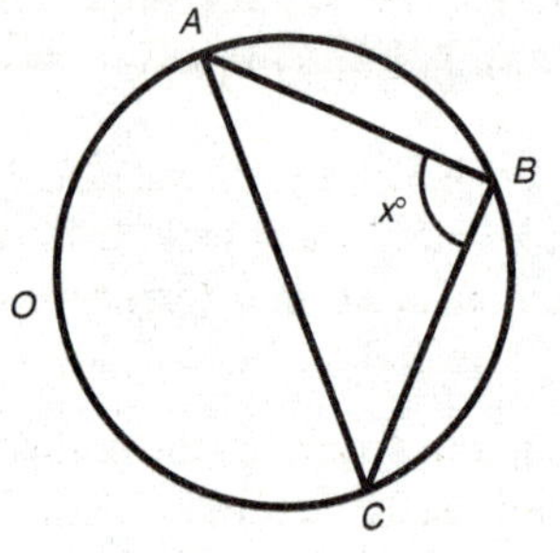

2. How many books are on the bookshelf?

   (1) The average weight of each book is 1.2 pounds.

   (2) The books and the bookshelf together weigh 34 pounds.

GO ON TO THE NEXT PAGE ➤

3 3 3 3 3 3 3 3 3 3 3

(A) if you can get the answer from **(1) ALONE** but not from (2) alone
(B) if you can get the answer from **(2) ALONE** but not from (1) alone
(C) if you can get the answer from **BOTH (1) and (2) TOGETHER**, but not from (1) alone or (2) alone
(D) if **EITHER** statement **(1) ALONE OR** statement **(2) ALONE** suffices
(E) if you **CANNOT** get the answer from statements (1) and (2) **TOGETHER**, but need even more data

3. Is the triangle ABC congruent to the triangle DEF? x is equal to y.

   (1) AB is equal to DE.
   (2) BC is equal to EF.

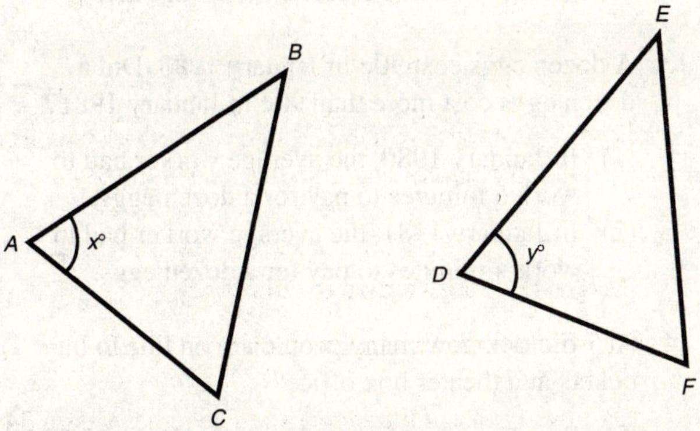

4. Decide whether the square root of the integer x is an integer.

   (1) The last digit of x is 2.
   (2) x is divisible by 3.

5. Do the rectangle $ABCD$ and the square $EFGH$ have the same area?

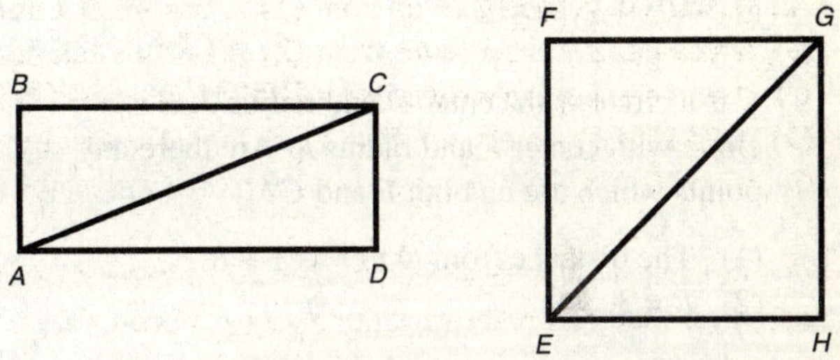

   (1) $AC = EG, AB = \frac{1}{2}\ EH$
   (2) The area of triangle ABC is not equal to the area of triangle EFG.

6. How much does Susan weigh?

   (1) Susan and Joan together weigh 250 pounds.
   (2) Joan weighs twice as much as Susan.

7. Two different holes, hole A and hole B, are put in the bottom of a full water tank. If the water drains out through the holes, how long before the tank is empty?

   (1) If only hole A is put in the bottom, the tank will be empty in 24 minutes.
   (2) If only hole B is put in the bottom, the tank will be empty in 42 minutes.

GO ON TO THE NEXT PAGE ➤

3 3 3 3 3 3 3 3 3 3 3

(A) if you can get the answer from **(1) ALONE** but not from (2) alone
(B) if you can get the answer from **(2) ALONE** but not from (1) alone
(C) if you can get the answer from **BOTH (1) and (2) TOGETHER**, but not from (1) alone or (2) alone
(D) if **EITHER** statement **(1) ALONE OR** statement **(2) ALONE** suffices
(E) if you **CANNOT** get the answer from statements (1) and (2) **TOGETHER**, but need even more data

8. Find $x + y$

   (1) $x - y = 6$
   (2) $-2x + 2y = -12$

9. C is a circle with center D and radius 2. E is a circle with center F and radius R. Are there any points which are on both E and C?

   (1) The distance from D to F is $1 + R$.
   (2) $R = 3$.

10. Mr. Parker made $20,000 in 1967. What is Mr. Parker's average yearly income for the three years 1967 to 1969?

   (1) He made 10% more in each year than he did in the previous year.
   (2) His total combined income for 1968 and 1969 was $46,200.

11. Is the integer n divisible by 9? n is a two digit number.

   (1) When n is divided by 3 the remainder is 2.
   (2) When n is divided by 7 the remainder is 1.

12. John and Paul are standing together on a sunny day. John's shadow is 10 feet long. Paul's shadow is 9 feet long. How tall is Paul?

   (1) John is 6 feet tall.
   (2) John is standing 2 feet away from Paul.

13. A dozen eggs cost 90¢ in January 1980. Did a dozen eggs cost more than 90¢ in January 1981?

   (1) In January 1980, the average worker had to work 5 minutes to pay for a dozen eggs.
   (2) In January 1981, the average worker had to work 4 minutes to pay for a dozen eggs.

14. At 7 o'clock how many people are on line to buy tickets at a theater box office?

   (1) People are getting on the line at the rate of 2 people per minute at 7 o'clock.
   (2) People are buying tickets and leaving the line at the rate of 4 people every 2 minutes at 7 o'clock.

15. What is the value of $\frac{x}{y}$? $x > 0$.

   (1) $x = \frac{1}{4}y$
   (2) $y = 400\%$ of x

GO ON TO THE NEXT PAGE ➤

3 3 3 3 3 3 3 3 3 3 3

(A) if you can get the answer from **(1) ALONE** but not from (2) alone
(B) if you can get the answer from **(2) ALONE** but not from (1) alone
(C) if you can get the answer from **BOTH (1) and (2) TOGETHER**, but not from (1) alone or (2) alone
(D) if **EITHER** statement **(1) ALONE OR** statement **(2) ALONE** suffices
(E) if you **CANNOT** get the answer from statements (1) and (2) **TOGETHER**, but need even more data

16. How many of the numbers x, y, and z are positive? x, y, and z are all less than 30.

 (1) $x + y + z = 61$
 (2) $x + y = 35$

17. How far is it from town A to town B? Town C is 15 miles west of town A.

 (1) It is 10 miles from town B to town C.
 (2) There is a river between town A and town B.

18. Is $2 < x < 4$?

 (1) $x^2 - 5x + 6 < 0$
 (2) $5x^2 - 25x > 0$

19. What percentage of families in the state have annual incomes over $25,000 and own a sailboat?

 (1) 28% of all the families in the state have an annual income over $25,000
 (2) 40% of the families in the state with an annual income over $25,000 own a sailboat.

20. What is the two-digit number whose first digit is a and whose second digit is b? The number is greater than 9.

 (1) The number is a multiple of 51.
 (2) The sum of the digits a and b is 6.

21. What is the radius of the circle with center O?

 (1) The area of the circle is 25π.
 (2) The area of the circle divided by the diameter of the circle is equal to π times $\frac{1}{2}$ of the radius of the circle.

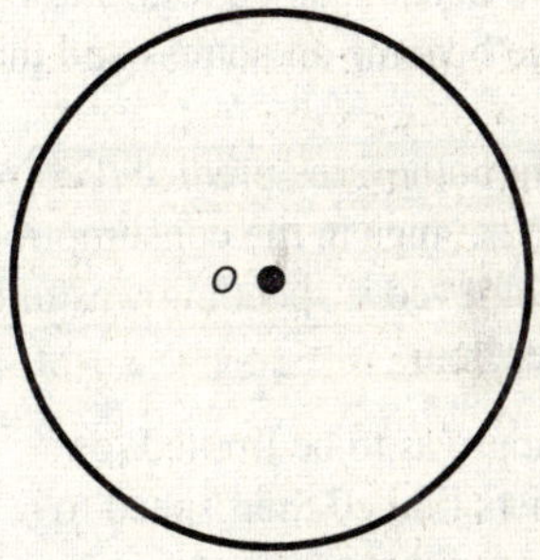

STOP

IF THERE IS STILL TIME REMAINING,
YOU MAY REVIEW THE QUESTIONS IN THIS SECTION ONLY.
YOU MAY NOT TURN TO ANY OTHER SECTION OF THE TEST.

4 4 4 4 4 4 4 4 4 4 4

Section 4

TIME: 25 minutes
21 Questions

Directions: This test consists of a number of sentences, in each of which some part or the whole is underlined. Each sentence is followed by five alternative versions of the underlined portion. Select the alternative you consider both most correct and most effective according to the requirements of standard written English. Answer A is the same as the original version; if you think the original version is best, select answer A.

In considering the answer choices, be attentive to matters of grammar, diction, and syntax, as well as clarity, precision, and fluency. Do not select an answer which alters the meaning of the original sentence.

1. In her candid autobiography, the author discusses her early years, her desire to become an actress and how she made her debut on the stage.

    (A) to become an actress, and how she made
    (B) that she become an actress, and how she made
    (C) to become an actress, and
    (D) that she become an actress, and
    (E) that she become an actress and that she make

2. Government authorities predicted correctly that tremendous savings in the consumption of gasoline would be achieved if speeding was to be limited to 55 miles per hour.

    (A) speeding was to be limited to
    (B) motorists limited their speed to
    (C) speeding did not exceed
    (D) a motorist was to limit his speed to
    (E) speeding by motorists was to be limited to

3. The word processor has revolutionized office procedures more than any machine of modern times.

    (A) any machine
    (B) has any machine
    (C) any other machine
    (D) has any other machine
    (E) any other machine has

4. The possibility of expropriation was believed to be unlikely in the near future due to the lack of mining technology and capital available in this small South American country.

    (A) due to the lack of mining technology and
    (B) because of the lack of mining technology and
    (C) because there was no mining technology and
    (D) because of the lack of mining technology and there was no
    (E) due to the lack of mining technology and there was no

5. The doctrine applies in Canada, where there is a federal law and a provincial law that are each valid and consistent.

    (A) is a federal law and a provincial law that are each valid and
    (B) are a federal law and a provincial law that are each valid and
    (C) are a federal law and a provincial law both of which are each valid and
    (D) is a federal law and a provincial law both of which are each valid and
    (E) are a federal law and a provincial law that are each valid or

GO ON TO THE NEXT PAGE ➤

4 4 4 4 4 4 4 4 4 4 4

6. Former Postal Service employees who believe they may be affected by this settlement should contact their last place of USPS employment, the department advised.

(A) may be affected
(B) may be effected
(C) will have been affected
(D) will be effected
(E) will have been effected

7. Blake is among the very few individuals who critics regard as genuinely significant in the history of both art and literature.

(A) who critics regard as genuinely significant in the history of both
(B) whom critics regard as genuinely significant in the history of both
(C) whom critics regard as genuinely significant both in the history of
(D) who critics regard as genuinely significant both in the history of
(E) who is regarded by critics as genuinely significant in the history of both

8. Many scientists are alarmed over the interest in such pseudo-scientific topics as ESP, flying saucers, and the occult, fearing that this interest may herald a new dark age of gullibility, ignorance, and thinking in superstitious ways.

(A) this interest may herald a new dark age of gullibility, ignorance, and thinking in superstitious ways
(B) it may herald a new dark age of gullibility, ignorance, and thinking in superstitious ways
(C) it may herald a new dark age of gullibility, ignorance, and superstition
(D) this interest may herald a new dark age of gullibility, ignorance, and superstition
(E) they may herald a new dark age of gullibility, ignorance, and superstition

9. Having broken with Freud, Jung's later writings nevertheless bore signs of the continued influence of Freudian doctrine and theories.

(A) Having broken with Freud, Jung's later writings nevertheless bore signs of the continued
(B) Since breaking with Freud, Jung's later writings nevertheless bore signs of the continued
(C) Although he had broken with Freud, in his later writings Jung nevertheless showed signs of the continued
(D) Having broken with Freud, Jung's later writings nevertheless bore signs of the continual
(E) Having broken with Freud, later writings by Jung nevertheless bore signs of the continued

10. That Giotto's paintings are significant in the history of the early Renaissance is undeniable, but Giotto cannot scarcely be considered the equal of such masters as Leonardo and Raphael.

(A) cannot scarcely be considered
(B) can scarcely be considered
(C) cannot hardly be considered
(D) cannot scarcely be considered to be
(E) isn't hardly to be considered

11. Although the theory of continental drift was not widely accepted until the mid-twentieth century, the basic concept had been described as early as 1620.

(A) was not widely accepted until the mid-twentieth century, the basic concept had been
(B) was not widely accepted until the mid-twentieth century, the basic concept was
(C) was not widely accepted until the mid-twentieth century, the basic concept has been
(D) had not been widely accepted until the mid-twentieth century, the basic concept has been
(E) had not been widely accepted until the mid-twentieth century, the basic concept was

GO ON TO THE NEXT PAGE ➤

4 4 4 4 4 4 4 4 4 4 4

12. The reason I am supporting Senator Blandings is because her extensive background in foreign affairs has made her uniquely qualified for a seat on this important subcommittee.

(A) because her extensive background in foreign affairs has made her uniquely qualified for
(B) that her extensive background in foreign affairs have made her uniquely qualified for
(C) that her extensive background in foreign affairs has made her uniquely qualified for
(D) that her extensive background in foreign affairs has made her uniquely qualified to
(E) because her extensive background in foreign affairs have made her uniquely qualified for

13. Fear of future nationalistic feelings and a conviction that natural resource endowments should be exploited for the welfare of the residents of the country, rather than for private profit, are shared by all managers of extractive industries there.

(A) rather than for private profit, are
(B) rather than for private profit, is
(C) irregardless of private profit, are
(D) as opposed to private profit, is
(E) and not necessarily for private profit, is

14. The lieutenant reminded his men that the only information to be given to the enemy if captured was each individual's name, rank, and serial number.

(A) the only information to be given to the enemy if captured was each individual's name, rank, and serial number
(B) the only information to be given to the enemy if they were captured was each individual's name, rank, and serial number
(C) the only information to be given to the enemy if captured were each individual's name, rank, and serial number
(D) , if captured, the only information to be given to the enemy was each individual's name, rank, and what his serial number was
(E) , if they were captured, the only information to be given to the enemy was each individual's name, rank, and serial number

15. Writing a beautiful sonnet is as much an achievement as to finish a 400-page novel.

(A) to finish
(B) it is to finish
(C) finishing
(D) if you finished
(E) to have finished

16. Anyone interested in computer programming can find a job in contemporary industry if you learn the basic programming languages, such as COBOL and FORTRAN.

(A) if you learn
(B) if you will learn
(C) if he would learn
(D) by the study of
(E) by studying

17. During the gasoline shortage of the 1970s caused by the actions of the OPEC nations, the number of accidents on our highways decreased markedly.

(A) the number of accidents on our highways decreased markedly
(B) the amount of accidents on our highways decreased markedly
(C) there were less accidents on our highways
(D) there were a fewer amount of accidents on our highways
(E) they found there were many fewer accidents on our highways

18. Being that only twenty-four states have ratified the proposed amendment, we can assume that it will not be adopted.

(A) Being that only twenty-four states
(B) Since twenty-four states only
(C) Being as only twenty-four states
(D) Seeing as how only twenty-four states
(E) Inasmuch as only twenty-four states

GO ON TO THE NEXT PAGE ➤

4 4 4 4 4 4 4 4 4 4 4

19. I have studied the works of George Bernard Shaw not only for their plots but also because they are very witty.

(A) also because they are very witty
(B) because they are also very witty
(C) for their wit also
(D) because they are very witty also
(E) also for their wit

20. The noise at the airport was deafening, which made conversation difficult if not impossible.

(A) The noise at the airport was deafening, which made conversation
(B) The noise at the airport was deafening, and it made conversation
(C) The deafening noise at the airport made conversation
(D) The airport noise was deafening, which made conversation
(E) The noise at the airport was deafening, conversation being

21. Inflation in the United States has not and, we hope, never will reach a rate of 20 percent a year.

(A) and, we hope, never will reach
(B) reached and, we hope, never will
(C) and hopefully never will reach
(D) reached and, we hope, never will reach
(E) reached and hopefully never will

STOP

IF THERE IS STILL TIME REMAINING, YOU MAY REVIEW THE QUESTIONS IN THIS SECTION ONLY. YOU MAY NOT TURN TO ANY OTHER SECTION OF THE TEST.

5 5 5 5 5 5 5 5 5 5 5

Section 5

TIME: 25 minutes
17 Questions

Directions: For each question, choose the best answer among the listed alternatives.

1. In almost all developing countries, the initial thrust of their respective trade policies was to foster domestic industries whose production would replace imports. This was a natural and logical strategy, given that import-substituting production could count on an existing known domestic demand, promised some mitigation of national economic dependence, and could be protected easily from external competition through high tariffs, quotas, or subsidies of various kinds.

   Which of the following, if true, would weaken the strategy above?

   (A) Domestic demand may be unknown.
   (B) Quotas are more regressive than tariffs.
   (C) Subsidies and import constraints keep domestic prices high and impose a burden on consumers.
   (D) Fast economic growth fosters inequality of income.
   (E) A protectionist policy may be beneficial to the developing country, but disliked by economically advanced countries.

2. The quantitative supply of labor (as well as its qualitative composition) depends on the following variables: the size of the population, its age-sex composition, marital structure, and participation rates in the labor force in accordance with these factors.

   Each of the following, if true, could affect the supply of labor except:

   (A) Birth and death rates.
   (B) Immigration and emigration.
   (C) Educational level of the population.
   (D) Number of employment agencies.
   (E) Marital status of females.

3. In order to discourage present surburban growth patterns, which because of their low densities are uneconomic to service and wasteful of land and resources, land use policy studies should include research into innovative forms of high density, low-rise housing.

   The above statement is a response to all of the following problems except:

   (A) The tendency to exclude light industry from residential areas means that people have to go outside their communities to seek work.
   (B) The traditional practice of using land as a commodity rather than a resource has meant that the location of new communities is often solely governed by a developer's economic convenience.
   (C) There is a lack of coordination between the planning and structure of communities and their relation to transportation networks.
   (D) Present patterns of urban growth have squandered agricultural and rural lands.
   (E) In houses designed for the standard family, there is a lack of inter and intra-unit privacy.

4. Over the last 20 years the rate of increase in total production in Workland has been second to none in the world. However, the growth is more modest when calculated per capita of total population. Over the last ten years progress has been much slower.

   If the information above is accurate, which of the following must be true?

   (A) Workland has a very large population.
   (B) Productivity per capita has not grown as fast during the past ten years.
   (C) Total production has increased faster than population growth.
   (D) The birth rate has declined.
   (E) The per capita production rate has not declined.

GO ON TO THE NEXT PAGE ➤

5 5 5 5 5 5 5 5 5 5 5

5. The earliest known proto-Eskimos are those of the Cape Denbigh Flint complex of northwestern Alaska, including adjacent Baffin Island. Denbigh people and their descendants were well equipped to survive in the Arctic. Their adaptive success is obvious in the speed with which they spread eastward across arctic Canada to northeast Greenland, which they reached by 2000 B.C.

   Which of the following, if true, would refute the above?

   (A) The Cape Denbigh Flint complex dates back to 3000 B.C.
   (B) The Vikings populated Greenland between 800 and 1100 A.D.
   (C) Denbigh artifacts of early settlements in northeast Greenland date back further than Denbigh artifacts found on Baffin Island.
   (D) Denbigh origin lies in the Paleolithic and the Mesolithic period—say about 4000 B.C. of Siberia.
   (E) The Denbigh people are known almost solely from their flint tools.

6. Harry Dyner was the Minister of Petroleum in a small oil-producing country. His country's oil exports were approximately 2 percent of total world oil sales. The Minister of Finance was anxious to maximize petroleum production and export to earn foreign exchange. Dyner, however, believed that increased sales would only drive down the world price of petroleum and lower his country's foreign exchange revenue.

   Which of the following would best exemplify an error in Dyner's reasoning?

   (A) Price of crude v. price of refined petroleum.
   (B) Production goals v. financial goals.
   (C) The supply produced by a single country v. aggregate supply on the market.
   (D) Seasonal v. long-term supply.
   (E) Long-term v. short-term demand.

7. There is no clear line between health and illness; it is easy to forget what it feels like to be really well and to get gradually used to often having a headache, feeling irritable, or tired. There is an unrecognized proportion of the population that has been tipped over the brink into ill health by ubiquitous contaminants.

   Which of the following statements best describes the purpose of the above?

   (A) The public must be encouraged to have regular medical examinations.
   (B) The public must be warned to be aware of various physical and chemical hazards.
   (C) The public must be warned to treat seriously such symptoms as headaches, irritability, and tiredness.
   (D) The medical professional is not always capable of diagnosing illness.
   (E) No one can really be sure if he is healthy or ill.

8. Administrators and executives are members of the most stable occupation.

   The stability mentioned in the above statement could be dependent on each of the following factors except

   (A) Training and skills.
   (B) Nature of the occupation.
   (C) Status.
   (D) Relatively high income.
   (E) Rate of turnover.

GO ON TO THE NEXT PAGE ➤

9. By far the chief export in the 15th century was textiles. Among these, woolens and worsteds predominated; linens were far less important and silks played an insignificant part. Outside this group, the only important item in the first half of the century was corn, though the exports of fish, lead, and tin were by no means negligible.

   Given the above information which of the following statements is correct?

   (A) Corn, though not as important an export as textiles, was still an important component of the export trade.
   (B) Corn was nearly as important an export as linen.
   (C) Silk was a valuable export in the 15th century.
   (D) Fishing was a bigger industry than wool production in the 15th century.
   (E) Nontextile items were one of the chief elements in the list of products exported in the 15th century.

10. Self-employment is found more often among men and women in the 25- to 44-year-old group than among their older or younger counterparts. Some 31 percent of the men and only 19 percent of the women who operate unincorporated businesses on a full-time basis completed four or more years of college. And while self-employed men are generally better educated than their wage-and-salary counterparts, the same cannot be said of self-employed women.

    If the information above is accurate, which of the following must be true?

    (A) Self-employed women are generally younger than self-employed men.
    (B) Self-employed men have more education than self-employed women.
    (C) Women wage earners have more education than men wage earners.
    (D) Salaried men are younger than self-employed men.
    (E) Self-employed men and women have more education than wage-earning men and women.

11. Between 1940 and 1945 gasoline consumption in the U.S. dropped about 35 percent because of wartime rationing. In the same period, lung cancer in U.S. white males declined by approximately the same percentage. Between 1914 and 1950 lung cancer mortality increased nineteenfold and the rate of gasoline consumption increased at the same rate.

    Which of the following facts, if true, would weaken the above argument?

    (A) For each of the years between 1939 and 1949, lung cancer among urban blacks in the United States remained at the same level.
    (B) The amount of lead in gasoline increased between 1916 and 1944.
    (C) After 1950 gasoline consumption jumped.
    (D) During World War II, people suffering from cancer were forbidden to drive.
    (E) Women first began driving in large numbers between 1941 and 1951.

12. From 1920 to 1950, the amount of food production per worker and per hour increased twofold. From 1950 to 1980, food production per worker and per hour increased 13 times.

    Each of the following, if true, could help to account for this trend except

    (A) The number of farm workers increased.
    (B) The use of mechanical technology in food production decreased.
    (C) The use of chemical fertilizers decreased.
    (D) The number of hours worked per unit of output decreased.
    (E) More workers were needed to produce the same unit of output.

GO ON TO THE NEXT PAGE ➤

13. "Some men are certainly tall, others are certainly not tall; but of intermediate men, we should say, 'tall'? Yes, I *think* so or no, I shouldn't be inclined to call him tall."

    Which of the following most accurately reflects the intention of the writer of the above?

    (A) Men intermediately tall, partake of "tallness" to a moderate degree.
    (B) To call men tall who are not strikingly so must be to use the concept with undue imprecision.
    (C) Every empirical concept has a degree of vagueness.
    (D) There is really no need to be as indecisive as the writer of the above.
    (E) Calling someone tall or short depends upon one's whim.

14. There are many reasons why individuals want to run their own businesses. Some foresee more personal satisfaction if they are successful in launching their own business, while others are interested mainly in the prospect of larger financial rewards. Since the late 1970s and early 1980s, tax regulations and other changes have encouraged increasing numbers of venture capitalists and entrepreneurs to start new enterprises. Since 1980, some one-half million new ventures have been started. Not all have succeeded, of course.

    The above statement makes which of the following assumptions?

    (A) Success in starting a new business depends in large part on sound financial planning.
    (B) Social incentives motivate investors just as much as financial rewards.
    (C) Financial incentives are associated with new business starts.
    (D) Most new business ventures succeed initially but fail later on.
    (E) Venture capitalists are motivated by nonmonetary gains.

15. A highly cohesive work group is a prerequisite for high team performance. Sociologists posit that the association between group cohesion and success is owing to the support individual team members give to one other and their acceptance of the group's goals and activities.

    Each of the following, if true, either provides support for or cannot weaken the sociologists' assumption about the relationship between cohesion and success except

    (A) A group of West German researchers found that successful work teams were headed by dominant leaders.
    (B) Industrial psychologists in England found that work groups who tended to participate in after hours social activities were more productive.
    (C) University researchers found that there was a significant correlation between team productivity and the extent to which team members understood and complied with the group's objectives.
    (D) American researchers found that successful team members tended to rate their fellow members more favorably.
    (E) The winning team in a computerized business game rated their peers generally low on "stick by the rules," "extrovert," "friendly," and "positive" and high on "egocentric," "individualistic," and "discord."

GO ON TO THE NEXT PAGE ➤

16. Before the middle of the 14th century, there were no universities north of Italy, outside France and England. By the end of the 15th century, there were 23 universities in this region, from Louvain and Mainz to Rostock, Cracow, and Bratislava and the number of universities in Europe as a whole had more than doubled.

    Given the above information, which of the following statements is correct?

    (A) Until the age of university expansion in the 15th century, there were perhaps 11 universities in the whole of Europe.
    (B) South of Italy there were 23 universities in the 14th century.
    (C) In the 13th century, France and England were the only countries in Europe with universities.
    (D) After the great age of university expansion in the 14th and 15th centuries, France and England were not the only northern European countries to have such centers of learning.
    (E) Italy was the cradle of university expansion.

17. Between 1979 and 1983, the number of unincorporated business self-employed women increased five times faster than the number of self-employed men and more than three times faster than women wage-and-salary workers. Part-time self-employment among women increased more than full-time self-employment.

    Each of the following, if true, could help to account for this trend except:

    (A) Owning a business affords flexibility to combine work and family responsibilities.
    (B) The proportion of women studying business administration courses has grown considerably.
    (C) There are more self-employed women than men.
    (D) Unincorporated service industries have grown by 300 percent over the period; the ratio of women to men in this industry is three to one.
    (E) The financial reward of having a second wage earner in the household has taken on increased significance.

STOP

IF THERE IS STILL TIME REMAINING,
YOU MAY REVIEW THE QUESTIONS IN THIS SECTION ONLY.
YOU MAY NOT TURN TO ANY OTHER SECTION OF THE TEST.

6 6 6 6 6 6 6 6 6 6 6

Section 6

TIME: 25 minutes
21 Questions

Directions: This test consists of a number of sentences, in each of which some part or the whole is underlined. Each sentence is followed by five alternative versions of the underlined portion. Select the alternative you consider both most correct and most effective according to the requirements of standard written English. Answer A is the same as the original version; if you think the original version is best, select answer A.

In considering the answer choices, be attentive to matters of grammar, diction, and syntax, as well as clarity, precision, and fluency. Do not select an answer which alters the meaning of the original sentence.

1. Since neither of the agencies had submitted the necessary documentation, each were required to reapply for the grant the following year.
   (A) each were required to reapply for the grant the following year
   (B) each were required, the following year, to reapply for the grant
   (C) each was required to reapply for the grant the following year
   (D) both were required to reapply, the following year, for the grant
   (E) it was required to reapply for the grant the following year

2. Stationary missile launching sites are frequently criticized by military experts on the ground that, in comparison to mobile units, they are the most vulnerable to preemptive attack.
   (A) they are the most
   (B) such sites are the most
   (C) they are rather
   (D) stationary sites are most
   (E) they are more

3. The qualities needed in a president are scarcely tested in today's political campaigns, which call instead for showmanship, good looks, and being able to seem eloquent while saying nothing.
   (A) being able to seem eloquent
   (B) the ability to seem eloquent
   (C) having eloquence
   (D) a certain eloquence
   (E) that he seem eloquent

4. Anyone who would speak with authority on the poets of the Renaissance must have a broad acquaintance with the writers of classical antiquity.
   (A) Anyone who would speak
   (B) If one would speak
   (C) He which would speak
   (D) Anyone desirous for speaking
   (E) Those who have a wish to speak

5. In its final report, the commission proposed, among other measures, that the legal drinking age be raised from eighteen to twenty-one.
   (A) that the legal drinking age be raised
   (B) a rise of the legal drinking age
   (C) that the legal drinking age should be raised
   (D) raising the age of drinking legally
   (E) to raise legally the drinking age

6. Since neither her nor the Dean were willing to veto the curriculum changes, they went into effect as of September 1.
   (A) her nor the Dean were willing
   (B) she nor the Dean was willing
   (C) her nor the Dean wished
   (D) she or the Dean was willing
   (E) she nor the Dean were willing

GO ON TO THE NEXT PAGE ➤

6 6 6 6 6 6 6 6 6 6 6

7. A broad range of opinions was represented between the various members of the steering committee.

   (A) A broad range of opinions was represented between
   (B) A broad range of opinions were represented between
   (C) A broad range of opinions had been held by
   (D) A broad range of opinions was represented among
   (E) Varying opinions were represented by

8. Undaunted by the political repercussions of his decision, the new gasoline rationing plan was announced by the Governor at the state office building last Friday.

   (A) the new gasoline rationing plan was announced by the Governor
   (B) the Governor's new gasoline rationing plan was announced
   (C) the Governor made the announcement concerning the new gasoline rationing plan
   (D) the new gasoline rationing plan of the Governor was announced
   (E) the Governor announced the new gasoline rationing plan

9. Mario had already swum five laps when I jumped into the pool.

   (A) had already swum five laps when I
   (B) already swam five laps when I
   (C) already swam five laps when I had
   (D) had already swum five laps when I had
   (E) had already swam five laps when I

10. Despite their avowed opposition to the strike, no one from among the dozens of nonunion workers were willing to cross the picket line.

   (A) from among the dozens of nonunion workers were willing
   (B) of the dozens of nonunion workers were willing
   (C) was willing from among the dozens of nonunion workers
   (D) from among the dozens of nonunion workers was willing
   (E) from the dozens of nonunion workers were willing

11. The poetry of George Herbert is regarded by many critics as equal in quality, though less influential, than the work of his more famous contemporary John Donne.

   (A) equal in quality, though less influential, than the work
   (B) equal in quality to, though less influential than, the work
   (C) qualitatively equal, though less influential than, that
   (D) equal in quality, though less influential, then the work
   (E) of equal quality, though of less influence, than that

12. If it is the present administration whom we should blame for the economic crisis, the first step toward a solution is to reject the incumbent at the polls this November.

   (A) whom we should blame
   (B) whom is to blame
   (C) who we should blame
   (D) who should be blamed
   (E) who one should blame

13. The assembly speaker has called for a shorter fall session of the legislature in hopes that less amendments of a purely symbolic nature will be proposed by the state's lawmakers.

   (A) in hopes that less amendments of a
   (B) hoping that fewer amendments that have a
   (C) in hopes that fewer amendments of a
   (D) in order that less amendments of a
   (E) in hope that fewer amendments of

14. Parker's testimony made it clear that he appointed Ryan before he had become aware of Ryan's alleged underworld connections.

   (A) he appointed Ryan before he had become aware
   (B) he appointed Ryan before his awareness
   (C) he had appointed Ryan prior to his having become aware
   (D) his appointment of Ryan preceded awareness
   (E) he had appointed Ryan before becoming aware

GO ON TO THE NEXT PAGE ➤

6 6 6 6 6 6 6 6 6 6 6

15. Despite its being smaller in size than are conventional automobile engines, the new Alcock Engine can still deliver the horsepower needed for most short-distance city driving.

(A) Despite its being smaller in size than are
(B) In spite of its being smaller than
(C) Although smaller than
(D) Despite its size relative to
(E) Though not comparable in size to

16. Seventy-four applications were received, of whom the better were selected for detailed review.

(A) of whom the better were selected
(B) from which were selected the better
(C) the best of which were selected
(D) from whom were selected the best
(E) from which they selected the best

17. If the British government had had no fear of the increasing hostility of the Indian populace, Gandhi's nonviolent tactics would have availed little.

(A) If the British government had had no fear of
(B) If the British government did not fear
(C) Had the British government no fear
(D) If the British government did not have fear of
(E) Would the British government not have feared

18. The official imposition of "Lysenkoism" on Soviet biologists, with its chilling effects on scientists in countless related fields, illustrate vividly the dangers of government interference with science.

(A) illustrate vividly the dangers of government interference with science
(B) illustrate the dangers of government interference with science vividly
(C) illustrates vividly the dangers of government interference with science
(D) vividly illustrate the dangers of government interference with science
(E) vividly illustrates how dangerous can be government interference with science

19. Health care costs have been forced upward less by increases in the salaries of nurses, technicians, and other personnel than by increases in the amounts spent on diagnostic machinery and electronic equipment.

(A) than by increases in the amounts
(B) than the amounts
(C) but by increases in the amounts
(D) and more by increases in the amounts
(E) than by funds

20. The press secretary announced that neither himself nor the President would be available for questions until they had had more time to examine the report.

(A) neither himself nor the President would be
(B) neither he or the President was
(C) neither he nor the President would be
(D) he and the President will not be
(E) he nor the President would be

21. In routine cases, the Civilian Review Board receives all complaints about police misconduct, weighs the evidence and the seriousness of the charges, and then it decides whether a formal inquiry is needed.

(A) then it decides whether a formal inquiry is needed
(B) then decides if a formal inquiry would be needed
(C) then it decides whether to hold a formal inquiry
(D) then decides whether a formal inquiry is needed
(E) decides at that point if a formal inquiry is needed or not

STOP

IF THERE IS STILL TIME REMAINING.
YOU MAY REVIEW THE QUESTIONS IN THIS SECTION ONLY.
YOU MAY NOT TURN TO ANY OTHER SECTION OF THE TEST.

7 7 7 7 7 7 7 7 7 7 7

Section 7

TIME: 25 minutes
17 Questions

Directions: Solve each of the following problems; then indicate the correct answer on your answer sheet.

A figure that appears with a problem is drawn as accurately as possible unless the words "figure not drawn to scale" appear next to the figure. Numbers in this test are real numbers.

1. Dictionaries weigh 6 pounds each and a set of encyclopedias weighs 75 pounds. 20 dictionaries are shipped in each box. 2 sets of encyclopedias are shipped in each box. A truck is loaded with 98 boxes of dictionaries and 50 boxes of encyclopedias. How much does the truck's load weigh?

   (A) 588 pounds
   (B) 7,500 pounds
   (C) 11,750 pounds
   (D) 19,260 pounds
   (E) 22,840 pounds

2. Mary is paid $600 a month on her regular job. During July in addition to her regular job, she makes $400 from a second job. Approximately what percentage of her annual income does Mary make in July? Assume Mary has no other income except the income mentioned above.

   (A) 8
   (B) $8\frac{1}{3}$
   (C) $12\frac{1}{2}$
   (D) 13
   (E) 14

3. A train travels at an average speed of 20 mph through urban areas, 50 mph through suburban areas, and 75 mph through rural areas. If a trip consists of traveling half an hour through urban areas, $3\frac{1}{2}$ hours through suburban areas, and 3 hours through rural areas, what is the train's average speed for the entire trip?

   (A) 50 mph
   (B) $53\frac{2}{7}$ mph
   (C) $54\frac{3}{7}$ mph
   (D) $58\frac{4}{7}$ mph
   (E) $59\frac{2}{7}$ mph

GO ON TO THE NEXT PAGE ➤

7 7 7 7 7 7 7 7 7 7 7

4. $(x - y)(y + 3)$ is equal to

 (A) $x^2 - 3y + 3$
 (B) $xy - 3y + y^2$
 (C) $xy - y^2 - 3y + 3x$
 (D) $xy - 3y + y^2 + 3x$
 (E) $y^2 - 3y + 3x - xy$

5. If $x < y$, $y < z$, and $z > w$, which of the following statements is always true?

 (A) $x > w$
 (B) $x < z$
 (C) $y = w$
 (D) $y > w$
 (E) $x < w$

6. What is the ratio of $\frac{2}{3}$ to $\frac{5}{4}$?

 (A) $\frac{1}{4}$
 (B) $\frac{10}{12}$
 (C) $\frac{8}{15}$
 (D) $\frac{20}{6}$
 (E) $\frac{2}{7}$

7. Of the numbers, 7, 9, 11, 13, 29, 33, how many are prime numbers?

 (A) none
 (B) 3
 (C) 4
 (D) 5
 (E) all

8. A worker's daily salary varies each day. In one week he worked five days. His daily salaries were $40.62, $41.35, $42.00, $42.50, and $39.53. What was his average daily salary for the week?

 (A) $40.04
 (B) $40.89
 (C) $41.04
 (D) $41.20
 (E) $206.00

9. One dozen eggs and ten pounds of apples are currently the same price. If the price of a dozen eggs rises by 10% and the price of apples goes up by 2%, how much more will it cost to buy a dozen eggs and ten pounds of apples?

 (A) 2%
 (B) 6%
 (C) 10%
 (D) 12%
 (E) 12.2%

GO ON TO THE NEXT PAGE ➤

10. How many two-digit prime numbers have a remainder of 2 when divided by 7?

    (A) none
    (B) one
    (C) two
    (D) three
    (E) more than three

11. A car gets 20 miles per gallon of gas when it travels at 50 miles per hour. The car gets 12% fewer miles to the gallon at 60 miles per hour. How far can the car travel at 60 miles per hour on 11 gallons of gas?

    (A) 193.6 miles
    (B) 195.1 miles
    (C) 200 miles
    (D) 204.3 miles
    (E) 220 miles

12. Feathers cost \$500 a ton for the first 12 tons and \$$(500 - x)$ a ton for any tons over 12. What is x, if it costs \$10,000 for 30 tons of feathers?

    (A) 270.00
    (B) 277.00
    (C) 277.70
    (D) 277.78
    (E) 280.00

13. The angles of a triangle are in the ratio 2 : 3 : 4. The largest angle in the triangle is

    (A) 30°
    (B) 40°
    (C) 70°
    (D) 75°
    (E) 80°

14. Find the area of the trapezoid $ABCD$. $AB = CD = 5$, $BC = 10$, $AD = 16$, and BE is an altitude of the trapezoid.

    (A) 50
    (B) 52
    (C) 64
    (D) 80
    (E) 160

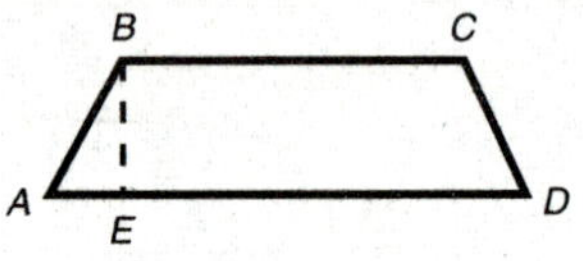

GO ON TO THE NEXT PAGE ➤

15. If x is less than 2, which of the following statements are always true?

    I. x is negative.
    II. x is positive.
    III. $2x$ is greater than or equal to x.
    IV. x^2 is greater than or equal to x.

    (A) III only
    (B) IV only
    (C) I and III only
    (D) I, III, and IV only
    (E) none of the statements

16. A worker is digging a ditch. He gets 2 assistants who work $\frac{2}{3}$ as fast as he does. If all 3 work on a ditch they should finish it in what fraction of the time that the worker takes working alone?

    (A) $\frac{3}{7}$
    (B) $\frac{1}{2}$
    (C) $\frac{3}{4}$
    (D) $\frac{4}{3}$
    (E) $\frac{7}{3}$

17. In a survey of political preferences, 78% of those asked were in favor of at least one of the proposals: I, II, and III. 50% of those asked favored proposal I, 30% favored proposal II, and 20% favored proposal III. If 5% of those asked favored all three of the proposals, what percentage of those asked favored more than one of the three proposals?

    (A) 5
    (B) 10
    (C) 12
    (D) 17
    (E) 22

STOP

IF THERE IS STILL TIME REMAINING,
YOU MAY REVIEW THE QUESTIONS IN THIS SECTION ONLY.
YOU MAY NOT TURN TO ANY OTHER SECTION OF THE TEST.

Answers
SAMPLE TEST 5

Section 1 [Problem Solving]

1 E	6 D	11 D	16 B	21
2 B	7 A	12 C	17 B	22
3 E	8 C	13 C	18	23
4 C	9 D	14 B	19	24
5 E	10 E	15 B	20	25

Section 2 [Reading Comprehension]

1 E	6 A	11 C	16 C	21 B
2 C	7 C	12 C	17 E	22 C
3 B	8 D	13 C	18 B	23 D
4 B	9 B	14 C	19 E	24 B
5 A	10 C	15 D	20 B	25 C

Section 3 [Data Sufficiency]

1 A	6 C	11 A	16 A	21 A
2 E	7 C	12 A	17 E	22
3 E	8 E	13 E	18 D	23
4 A	9 A	14 E	19 C	24
5 D	10 D	15 D	20 A	25

Section 4 [Sentence Correction]

1 C	6 A	11 A	16 E	21 D
2 B	7 B	12 C	17 A	22
3 C	8 D	13 A	18 E	23
4 B	9 C	14 E	19 E	24
5 B	10 B	15 C	20 C	25

Section 5 [Critical Reasoning]

1 C	6 C	11 A	16 D	21
2 D	7 B	12 D	17 C	22
3 E	8 E	13 C	18	23
4 B	9 A	14 C	19	24
5 C	10 B	15 E	20	25

Section 6 [Sentence Correction]

1 C	6 B	11 B	16 C	21 D
2 E	7 D	12 A	17 A	22
3 B	8 E	13 C	18 C	23
4 A	9 A	14 E	19 A	24
5 A	10 D	15 C	20 C	25

Section 7 [Problem Solving]

1 D	6 C	11 A	16 A	21
2 D	7 C	12 D	17 D	22
3 D	8 D	13 E	18	23
4 C	9 B	14 B	19	24
5 B	10 D	15 E	20	25

Self-Scoring Guide—Analytical Writing

Evaluate your writing tests (or have a friend or teacher evaluate them for you) on the following basis. Read each essay completely, paying special attention to its logical organization and use of examples and facts to buttress its claims or position. Assign a holistic score between 0 and 6, using the scale below. Your writing score will be the average of the scores of the two essays.

6	**Outstanding**	Cogent, well-articulated analysis of the issue or critique of the argument. Develops a position with insightful reasons and persuasive examples. Well organized. Superior command of language and variety of syntax. Only minor flaws in grammar, usage, and mechanics.
5	**Strong**	Well-developed analysis or critique. Develops a position with well-chosen examples or reasons. Generally well organized. Clear control of language and variety of syntax. Minor flaws in grammar, usage, and mechanics.
4	**Adequate**	Competent analysis or critique. Develops a position with relevant reasons or examples. Adequately organized. Adequate control of language, but may lack syntactic variety. May have some flaws in grammar, usage, and mechanics.
3	**Limited**	Competent but clearly flawed analysis or critique. Vague or limited in developing a position. Poorly organized. Weak in using relevant examples or reasons. Language used imprecisely or lacking in sentence variety. Contains major errors or frequent minor errors in grammar, usage, and mechanics.
2	**Seriously Flawed**	Serious weaknesses in analysis and organization. Unclear or seriously limited in presenting or developing a position. Disorganized. Few relevant examples or reasons. Frequent serious problems in language and sentence structure. Numerous errors in grammar, usage, or mechanics that interfere with meaning.
1	**Fundamentally Deficient**	Little evidence of ability to organize and develop a coherent response to issue or argument. Severe and persistent errors in language and sentence structure. Pervasive pattern of errors in grammar, usage, and mechanics that severely interfere with meaning.
0	**Unscorable**	Illegible or not written on the assigned topic.

Analysis

Section 1
Problem Solving

(Numbers in parentheses at the end of each explanation indicate the section in the Mathematics Review where material addressed in the question is discussed.)

1. An angle of x degrees has the property that its complement is equal to $\frac{1}{6}$ of its supplement where x is

(A) 30
(B) 45
(C) 60
(D) 63
(E) 72

(E) The complement of x is an angle of $90 - x$ degrees, and the supplement of x is an angle of $180 - x$ degrees. Thus, we have $90 - x = \frac{1}{6}(180 - x) = 30 - \frac{1}{6}x$, so $60 = \frac{5}{6}x$ or $x = 72$. (III-1, II-2)

2. If $y = \frac{3}{(x^2)} + x$ and $x = 3$, then y is

(A) $\frac{2}{3}$

(B) $\frac{10}{3}$

(C) $\frac{12}{3}$

(D) $\frac{18}{3}$

(E) $\frac{36}{6}$

(B) If $x = 3$, then $x^2 = 9$, and $\frac{3}{(x^2)} = \frac{3}{9} = \frac{1}{3}$. So $\frac{3}{(x^2)} + x = \frac{1}{3} + 3 = \frac{10}{3}$. (II-1)

3. Which of the following numbers is the least common multiple of the numbers 2, 3, 4 and 5?

(A) 12
(B) 24
(C) 30
(D) 40
(E) 60

(E) Since 4 is a multiple of 2, the least common multiple of 3, 4, and 5 will be the least common multiple of 2, 3, 4, and 5. Since 3, 4, and 5 have no common factors, the least common multiple is 3 • 4 • 5 = 60. (I-1)

4. In a certain town 40% of the people have brown hair, 25% have brown eyes, and 10% have both brown hair and brown eyes. What percentage of the people in the town have neither brown hair nor brown eyes?

(A) 35
(B) 40
(C) 45
(D) 50
(E) 55

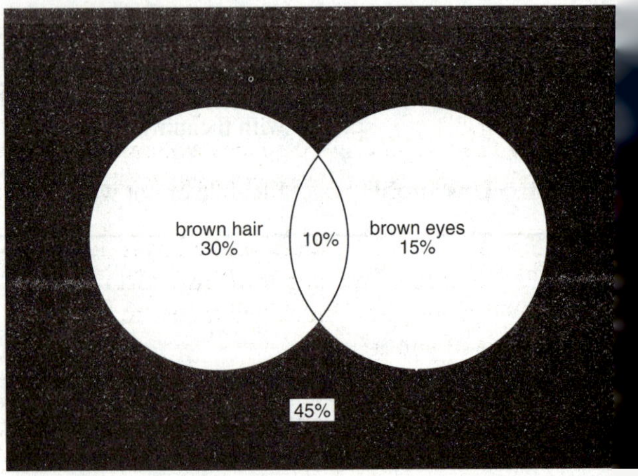

(C) Since 10% have both brown eyes and brown hair, and 25% have brown eyes, 15% of the people have brown eyes but do not have brown hair. Thus, 40% + 15% or 55% of the people have brown eyes or brown hair or both. Therefore, 100% – 55% or 45% of the people have neither brown eyes nor brown hair. (II-4)

5. If the altitude of a triangle increases by 5% and the base of the triangle increases by 7%, by what percent will the area of the triangle increase?

(A) 3.33%
(B) 5%
(C) 6%
(D) 12%
(E) 12.35%

(E) Area = $\frac{1}{2}$(altitude)(base). The increased altitude is (1.05) altitude and the increased base is (1.07) base. Therefore, the increased area is $\frac{1}{2}$ (1.05)(1.07)(altitude) (base). So the increased area is (1.1235) area. Thus, the area has increased by 12.35%. (III-7, I-4)

6. A shipping firm charges 2¢ a pound for the first 20 pounds of package weight and 1.5¢ for each pound or fraction of a pound over 20 pounds of package weight. How much will it charge to ship a package which weighs $23\frac{1}{2}$ pounds?

(A) 6¢
(B) 8¢
(C) 45¢
(D) 46¢
(E) 47¢

(D) The first 20 pounds cost 20 • 2¢ = 40¢. The package weighs $3\frac{1}{2}$ pounds more than 20 pounds, so there are 3 pounds and one fraction of a pound over 20 pounds. The weight over 20 pounds will cost 4 • (1.5)¢ = 6¢. Therefore, the total cost will be 46¢. (II-3)

7. If paper costs 1¢ a sheet, and a buyer gets a 2% discount on all the paper he buys after the first 1,000 sheets, how much will it cost to buy 5,000 sheets of paper?

(A) $49.20
(B) $50.00
(C) $3,920.00
(D) $4,920.00
(E) $5,000.00

(A) Since 5,000 – 1,000 = 4,000, there are 4,000 sheets which will be discounted. The 4,000 sheets cost 4,000¢ or $40.00 before the discount, so they will cost (.98)($40.00) or $39.20 after the 2% discount. The first 1,000 sheets cost 1¢ each so they cost 1,000¢ or $10.00. Therefore, the total cost of the 5,000 sheets will be $49.20. (I-4)

8. Tom's salary is 150% of John's salary. John's salary is 80% of Steve's salary. What is the ratio of Steve's salary to Tom's salary?

(A) 1 to 2
(B) 2 to 3
(C) 5 to 6
(D) 6 to 5
(E) 5 to 4

(C) Let T be Tom's salary, J be John's salary, and S be Steve's salary. Then the given information is $T = (1.5)J$ and $J = (.8)S$. Changing to fractions we get $T = \frac{3}{2}J$ and $J = \frac{4}{5}S$ so $S = \frac{5}{4}J$. Therefore, $\frac{S}{T} = \frac{\frac{5}{4}J}{\frac{3}{2}J} = \frac{\frac{5}{4}}{\frac{3}{2}}$ $= \frac{5}{4} \bullet \frac{2}{3} = \frac{5}{6}$. The ratio is 5 to 6. (II-3, II-5)

9. A charity solicited P persons over the phone who agreed to an average pledge of $\$R$ each. Q of these people who had pledged an average of $\$S$ each never sent in the pledged amount. Which of the following expressions represents the percentage of pledged money that the charity received?

(A) $100 \times \frac{PR}{QS}$

(B) $100 \times \frac{QS}{PR}$

(C) $100\,PR - 100\,QS$

(D) $100 - \frac{100\,QS}{PR}$

(E) $100\,PR - \frac{100\,QS}{PR}$

(D) The amount pledged is $P \times \$R$ and the amount that was not received is $Q \times \$S$. Therefore, the charity received $PR - QS$. So the percentage received is

$$\% = 100 \times \frac{(PR - QS)}{(PR)}$$

$$\% = 100 \times \left(1 - \frac{QS}{PR}\right)$$

$$\% = 100 - \frac{100QS}{PR} \qquad \text{(II-3)}$$

10. If it takes 50 workers 4 hours to dig a sewer, how long should it take 30 workers to dig the same sewer?

(A) 2 hrs., 24 min.
(B) 5 hrs., 12 min.
(C) 6 hrs., 12 min.
(D) 6 hrs., 20 min.
(E) 6 hrs., 40 min.

(E) 30 workers are $\frac{3}{5}$ of 50 workers, so it should take the 30 workers $\frac{5}{3}$ as long as the 50 workers. Therefore, the 30 workers should take $\frac{5}{3} \cdot 4 = \frac{20}{3} = 6\frac{2}{3}$ hours = 6 hours and 40 minutes. (II-3)

11. Three pounds of 05 grass seed contain 5 percent herbicide. A different type of grass seed, 20, which contains 20 percent herbicide, will be mixed with the three pounds of 05 grass seed. How much grass seed of type 20 should be added to the three pounds of 05 seed so that the resulting mixture contains 15 percent herbicide?

(A) 3 pounds
(B) 3.75 pounds
(C) 4.5 pounds
(D) 6 pounds
(E) 9 pounds

(D) Call x the amount of type 20 grass seed that will be added. Then the total amount of grass seed will be $3 + x$ pounds. Since the resulting mixture should contain 15 percent herbicide, the total amount of herbicide will be $.15(3 + x)$. However, the total amount of herbicide is also the herbicide from type 05 plus the herbicide from type 20. This is $.05 \times 3$ plus $.20 \times x$, which gives $.15 + .2x$. Therefore, we have the equation $.15(3 + x)$ or $.45 + .15x$, which $= .15 + .2x$. Solving for x gives $.3 = .05x$ or $x = 6$. So the correct answer is 6 pounds of type 20 must be added to the original 3 pounds. (II-3)

12. A car is traveling on a straight highway. At 10 o'clock, it passes a truck traveling in the same direction. The truck continues on the highway traveling at 50 mph while the car travels at 65 mph. How far apart are the car and the truck at 2 o'clock?

(A) 15 miles
(B) 30 miles
(C) 60 miles
(D) 200 miles
(E) 260 miles

(C) The car is traveling 15 mph faster than the truck. Since the car and truck were in the same place at 10 o'clock, 4 hours later at 2 o'clock the car will be 4 hours $\times$ 15 mph = 60 miles from the truck. (II-3)

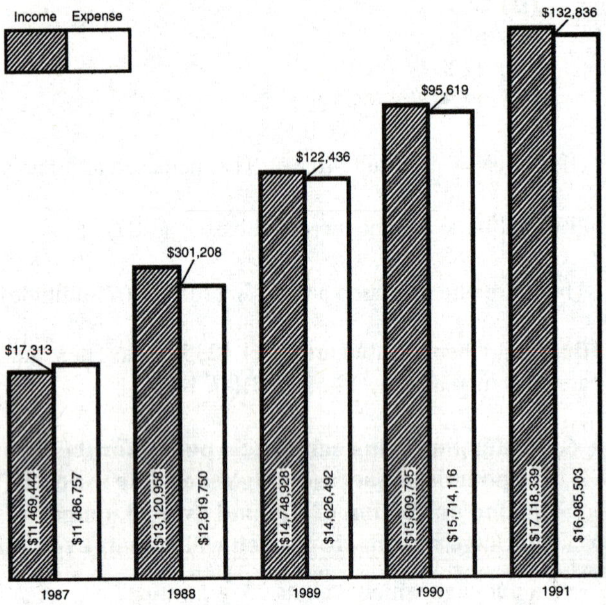

13. Which of the following statements can be inferred from the graph?

I. The company made a profit in all the years shown on the graph.
II. The company's profit increased in every year between 1989 and 1991.
III. The company's expenses increased in each year shown on the graph.

(A) I only
(B) II only
(C) III only
(D) I and III only
(E) I, II, and III

(C) Statement I is false since there was a loss in 1987. II is false since the profits decreased from 1989 to 1990. (IV-4)

14. Wheat costs $2.00 a bushel and corn costs $2.62 a bushel. If the price of wheat rises 10% a month and the price of corn is unchanged, how many months will it take before a bushel of corn costs less than a bushel of wheat?

(A) 2
(B) 3
(C) 4
(D) 5
(E) 6

(B) The price of wheat (in dollars) will be $2(1.1)^n$ after n months. This will be greater than 2.62 when $(1.1)^n$ is greater than $\frac{2.62}{2} = 1.31$. Since $1.1 \times 1.1 = 1.21$ and $1.1 \times 1.1 \times 1.1 = 1.331$, after three months the price of a bushel of corn will be less than the price of a bushel of wheat. (I-8)

15. If $\frac{1}{2} + \frac{1}{4} = \frac{x}{15}$, then x is

(A) 10
(B) 11.25
(C) 12
(D) 13.75
(E) 14

(B) If $\frac{1}{2} + \frac{1}{4} = \frac{x}{15}$, then since $\frac{1}{2} + \frac{1}{4} = \frac{3}{4}$, we have that $\frac{3}{4} = \frac{x}{15}$. So $x = \frac{45}{4} = 11\frac{1}{4} = 11.25$. (I-2)

16. If $x + y + z + w = 15$, then at least k of the numbers x, y, z, w must be positive where k is

(A) 0
(B) 1
(C) 2
(D) 3
(E) 4

(B) If three of the numbers were negative, then as long as the fourth is greater than the absolute value of the sum of the other three, the sum of all four will be positive. For example, $(-50) + (-35) + (-55) + 155 = 15$. (I-6)

17. Which of the following figures has the largest area?

I. A circle of radius $\sqrt{2}$.
II. An equilateral triangle whose sides each have length 4.
III. A triangle whose sides have lengths 3, 4, and 5.

(A) I
(B) II
(C) III
(D) I and II
(E) II and III

(B) The area of the circle is $\pi \times \sqrt{2} \times \sqrt{2} = 2\pi$. Since $3^2 + 4^2 = 5^2$, the triangle in III is a right triangle. So it has an altitude and base equal to 3 and 4. Therefore, its area is $\left(\frac{1}{2}\right) \times 3 \times 4 = 6$, which is less than 2π because π is greater than 3.

Let ABC be the equilateral triangle of II. Then if AD is an altitude of ABC, the right triangles ABD and ACD are congruent. So BD must equal CD, which means $BD = \frac{4}{2} = 2$. Now we can compute the length of the altitude AD by the Pythagorean relation. AD is the square root of AC squared minus CD squared. So AD is the square root of $(4^2 - 2^2 = 16 - 4 = 12)$. Hence, the area of ABC is $(\frac{1}{2}) \times 4 \times \sqrt{12} = 2 \times 2 \times \sqrt{3} = 4\sqrt{3}$. Thus II has the largest area since $4\sqrt{3}$ is larger than 2π. ($4\sqrt{3}$ is about 6.93 and 2π is only about 6.28.) (III-7)

Section 2
Reading Comprehension

The passage for questions 1–9 appears on page 502.

1. The attitude of the report, as described in the passage, may best be expressed as

(A) harshly condemnatory, because industry is not more responsive to the business climate
(B) optimistic that government will induce industry to make needed changes
(C) critical of labor unions
(D) pessimistic that anything can be done to reduce the trade gap
(E) objective in assessing the influence of free trade on employment

(E) The report (on which the passage is based) is certainly not optimistic (B), but rather pessimistic in its assessment, although not specifically about the trade gap (D). Nor can the report be characterized as harshly condemnatory (A) or critical of labor unions (C). After all, as pointed out in the passage, it is labor that will suffer. The answer is (E). This is specifically supported by the first and second paragraphs.

2. What is the meaning of *free trade* in line 13?

(A) unlimited sale of goods in Europe
(B) trade on a barter basis
(C) the elimination of tariffs
(D) sale of price-discounted goods to European countries
(E) trade with only the so-called "free countries," i.e., Western Europe

(C) Free trade is the reduction or elimination of tariffs and duties on exports. See lines 4–5 and 28–30.

3. It can be inferred that the term *adjustment assistance* in line 31 refers mainly to

(A) unemployment compensation
(B) some sort of financial assistance to manufacturers hurt by free trade
(C) help in relocating plants to Europe
(D) aid in reducing work stoppages
(E) subsidy payments to increase exports

(B) Manufacturers that cannot increase productivity in order to lower prices will not be able to compete with duty-free imports, and will not receive adjustment assistance, i.e., subsidies or some other financial payments to buttress them in the face of foreign competition.

4. The author's central recommendation seems to be that

(A) unemployment should be avoided at all costs
(B) redundant labor should be removed in all sectors
(C) government should control the service sector
(D) tariffs should not be lowered
(E) workers should be retrained

(B) The author's recommendation is that redundant labor should be removed. See lines 59–61.

5. Which of the following titles best describes the content of the passage?

(A) *The Prospects of Free Trade*
(B) *Government Intervention in World Trade*
(C) *Trade with the Common Market*
(D) *What Lies Ahead?*
(E) *Unemployment and Adjustment Assistance*

(A) Even though the subject of trade with the Common Market (C) is discussed, the major thrust of the passage is on the consequences of free trade—in this case, with the Common Market.

6. Which of the following will occur because of duty-free imports?

I. Twelve billion dollars of capital will be idled.
II. Thirty-five thousand workers will be unemployed.
III. Fifteen thousand firms will face bankruptcy.

(A) I only
(B) II only
(C) I and II only
(D) II and III only
(E) I, II, and III

(A) Only alternative I was mentioned in paragraph 1. II is incorrect because the workers will be *displaced,* not unemployed.

7. According to the passage, the government is responsible for

(A) increasing tariffs
(B) subsidizing exports
(C) not explaining its position
(D) adjustment assistance
(E) overmanned ships

(C) The author blames the government for not making its position clear with regard to trade policy. See line 26.

8. Tariffs will be reduced on

(A) all manufactured goods
(B) manufactured and agricultural goods
(C) all goods
(D) industrial goods
(E) industrial and consumer goods

(D) The passage specifically mentions industrial goods on line 29.

9. Which industries will be affected by tariff reductions?

I. Services
II. Manufacturing
III. Extracting

(A) I only
(B) II only
(C) I and II only
(D) II and III only
(E) I, II, and III

(B) The manufacturing sector only will be impacted. The indifferent attitude of the service sector (paragraphs 5 and 6) is owing to the fact that it will not be affected by tariff reductions.

The passage for questions 10–17 appears on page 504.

10. According to the passage, scientists are not interested in theological explanations because

(A) scientists tend to be atheists
(B) theology cannot explain change
(C) theological explanations are not empirical
(D) theology cannot explain social behavior
(E) scientists are concerned primarily with data gathering

(C) This is stated in paragraph 3 of the passage.

11. The major objective of the passage is to

(A) show that explanation is more important than discovery
(B) prove that sociology is a science
(C) explain the major objectives of sociology
(D) discuss scientific method
(E) describe social behavior

(C) The major objective is to explain the objectives of sociology, which are the same as those of science. See line 1.

12. Which of the following statements best agrees with the author's position?

(A) Science is the formulation of unverified hypotheses.
(B) Explanation is inferred from data.
(C) Causation is a basis for explanation.
(D) Generalization is a prerequisite for explanation.
(E) Empiricism is the science of discovery.

(C) A discussion of this point is given in paragraph 3. The other answers are either factually incorrect or incomplete.

13. Judging from the contents of the passage, the final step in a study of social behavior would be to

(A) discover the problem
(B) establish principles
(C) offer an explanation of the data by determining causation
(D) collect data
(E) establish generalizations

(C) The final step or objective of science—according to the passage—is explanation (line 3), best stated as a causal proposition. See lines 66–68.

14. According to the passage, which of the following activities contribute to the advance of science?

I. Finding data relationships
II. Expanding the limits of the empirical
III. Establishing ultimate causes of phenomena

(A) I only
(B) II only
(C) I and II only
(D) I and III only
(E) I, II, and III

(C) I and II are mentioned in the first and second paragraphs. III is mentioned in lines 54–57 as one of the activities in which the scientist is *not* interested.

15. The author's main point in the first paragraph may best be described by which of the following statements?

(A) Science and sociology are interdisciplinary.
(B) The first objective of sociology is discovery.
(C) Discovery without explanation is meaningless.
(D) Both discovery and explanation are fundamental to building a science.
(E) It takes a long time before relationships of data are discovered.

(D) Answers (B) and (E) are mentioned in the passage, but are secondary in importance to (D). Answer (C) is not correct, and answer (A) is not mentioned in the passage.

16. According to the author, which of the following explanations would a scientist accept?

I. Snow falls because angels are having a pillow fight.
II. Suicide is caused by weak character.
III. Babies weigh 20% more than the average weight of newborns if their mothers take a 2-hour nap every day during the last 3 months of pregnancy.

(A) I only
(B) II only
(C) III only
(D) II and III only
(E) I, II, and III

(C) The scientist would not accept I since angels are not considered empirical (see the last paragraph). He would not accept II; since the term *weak character* is not defined, it cannot be observed. The scientist would accept III since all the terms involved in the explanation are observable.

17. The major objective of the second paragraph is

(A) to show that electrons are empirical data
(B) to show that science changes as time passes
(C) to demonstrate the difference between chemistry and sociology
(D) to explain how science expands the frontiers of the observable world
(E) to explain what the term *empirical order* means

(E) All the other answers are mentioned in the paragraph but they are not the main topic.

The passage for questions 18–25 appears on page 506.

18. It can be inferred from the passage that polytheism means a belief in

(A) Greek gods
(B) more than one god
(C) a god-centered world
(D) powerful deities
(E) infinite numbers of gods

(B) This is mentioned in the first and the final paragraphs. In any case, the prefix *poly* means many and the suffix *theist* means one who believes in a god or gods.

19. The author's statement in lines 13–14 that "you could tell a good deal about a person's frame of mind by the gods he favored" means that

(A) those who believed in gods were superstitious
(B) worship was either anthropocentric or theocentric
(C) gods were chosen to represent a given way of life
(D) the way a person thinks depends on the power of deities
(E) in certain cultures, the gods served as representations of what people thought of themselves

(E) Answers (A), (B) and (D) cannot be inferred from the passage. Answer (C) is roughly consonant with what the author has to say, but (E) is a stronger example of the question statement.

20. It may be inferred from the passage that the author would most likely agree that ancient cultures

I. symbolized their deities only in human form
II. symbolized the gods in many forms
III. were mainly self-worshippers

(A) I only
(B) II only
(C) I and II only
(D) I and III only
(E) I, II, and III

(B) I is incorrect since they worshipped gods in both human and other forms. See lines 39ff.

21. The main point the author makes about anthropomorphism in lines 34 and 35 is that

(A) certain cultures are inclined to antropomorphism
(B) those who demean anthropomorphism may themselves practice it
(C) the disparagement of anthropomorphism is common to both ancient and modern cultures
(D) the Germans tend to be more theocentric than the English
(E) anthropomorphism is a practice common to all cultures

(B) Although the author states that certain cultures are more inclined to anthropocentric worship (A), he mentions it while making the point that there are those who attribute it to others, even though practicing it themselves.

22. It may be inferred from the last paragraph that polytheism entails

(A) a commonality of interests among the deities
(B) predictable consequences
(C) incoherence and conflict among the "powers"
(D) an orderly universe
(E) worshipping one god at a time

(C) The paragraph indicates that if the universe is partly controlled by the "wet-god" (it rains), then the "dry-god" lacks control. This is an example of incoherence. If you pray for rain, you must also pray to prevent the "dry-god" from exercising his powers, an example of potential conflict. Hence there is hardly a commonality of interests or order in a polytheistic system.

23. Which people worshipped animals?

(A) Romans
(B) Greeks
(C) Egyptians
(D) Celts
(E) Pagans

(D) See lines 42–44.

24. Anthropomorphism may be said to be symbolizing

(A) a deity in one's own image
(B) a human form
(C) any form
(D) both human and spiritual forms
(E) an abstract form

(B) See paragraph 2.

25. A polytheist

I. has favorite gods
II. simultaneously worships more than one god
III. lived in Greece

(A) I only
(B) II only
(C) I and II only
(D) II and III only
(E) I, II, and III

(C) Alternative I is found in line 1; alternative II, in lines 58–59. Alternative III is incorrect; the passage also mentions Romans.

Section 3
Data Sufficiency

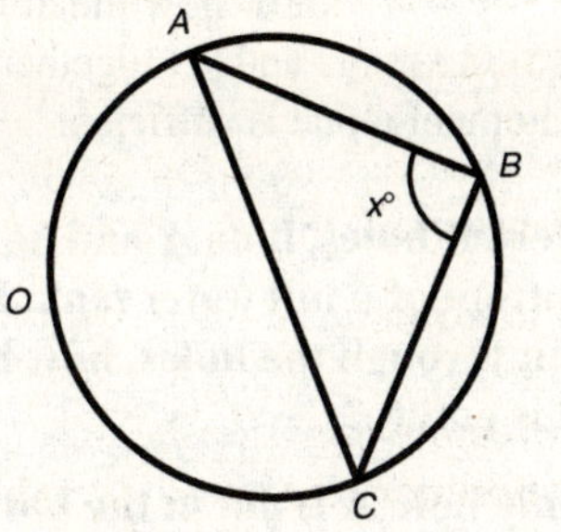

1. *ABC* is a triangle inscribed in circle *AOCB*. Is *AC* a diameter of the circle *AOCB*?

(1) Angle *ABC* is a right angle.
(2) The length of *AB* is $\frac{3}{4}$ the length of *BC*.

(A) STATEMENT (1) alone is sufficient. If angle *ABC* is a right angle, then *AOC* is a semicircle. Therefore, *AC* is a diameter.

STATEMENT (2) alone is insufficient. There are many (an infinite number) triangles we can inscribe in the circle such that $AB = \frac{3}{4}BC$. Not all of these will have *AC* as a diameter.

Therefore, STATEMENT (1) alone is sufficient, but STATEMENT (2) alone is not sufficient.

2. How many books are on the bookshelf?

(1) The average weight of each book is 1.2 pounds.
(2) The books and the bookshelf together weigh 34 pounds.

(E) STATEMENT (1) alone is not sufficient. We still need the total weight of the books; then we can divide by the average weight to obtain the number of books.

STATEMENT (2) tells us how much the books and the bookshelf together weigh, but we don't know how much the books weigh.

So STATEMENTS (1) and (2) together are not sufficient.

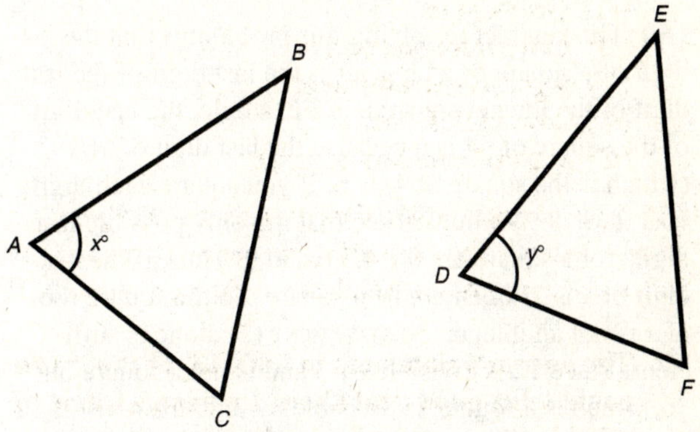

3. Is the triangle *ABC* congruent to the triangle *DEF*? *x* is equal to *y*.

(1) *AB* is equal to *DE*.
(2) *BC* is equal to *EF*.

(E) STATEMENT (1) alone is not sufficient, since many noncongruent triangles can have a side and an angle which are equal.

By the same reasoning, STATEMENT (2) alone is not sufficient.

STATEMENTS (1) and (2) together are not sufficient. For two triangles to be congruent, they must have two pairs of corresponding sides and the *included* angles equal. For example, the following two triangles satisfy STATEMENTS (1) and (2) and $x = y$ but they are not congruent.

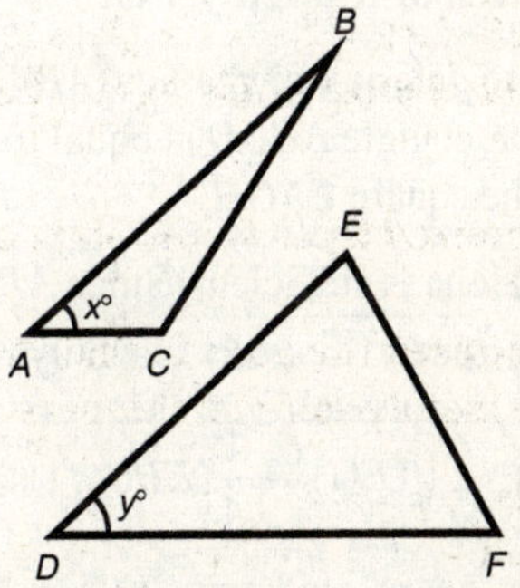

Therefore, STATEMENTS (1) and (2) together are not sufficient.

4. Decide whether the square root of the integer x is an integer.

(1) The last digit of x is 2.
(2) x is divisible by 3.

(A) The key fact to solving this problem is that the last digit of a square of an integer is the last digit of the last digit of the integer squared. For example, the last digit of the square of 94 is 6 because the last digit of 16 (which is the square of 4) is 6. If you square each digit {0,1,2, ... 8,9}, you will see that the only possible last digits for a square are 0,1,4,5,6 and 9. Thus, if the last digit of x is 2, x can *not* be a square. So the square root of x is not an integer. So STATEMENT (1) alone is sufficient. Since 12 is divisible by 3 and is not a square but 36, which is a square, is divisible by 3, STATEMENT (2) alone is not sufficient.

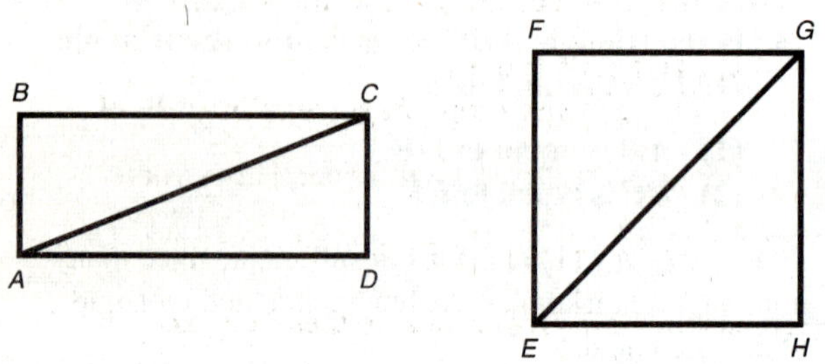

5. Do the rectangle *ABCD* and the square *EFGH* have the same area?

(1) $AC = EG, AB = \frac{1}{2}EH$

(2) The area of triangle *ABC* is not equal to the area of triangle *EFG*.

(D) We have to determine whether $(AB)(BC)$ which is the area of the rectangle *ABCD* is equal to $(EH)^2$ which is the area of the square *EFGH*.

STATEMENT (1) alone is sufficient. Since *ABC* is a right triangle, $BC = \sqrt{(AC)^2 - (AB)^2}$, and using STATEMENT (1) we have $BC = \sqrt{(EG)^2 - \frac{1}{4}(EH)^2}$. Using the fact that *EFGH* is a square, we know $(EG)^2 = 2(EH)^2$, so we can express BC in terms of EH. Using STATEMENT (1) we can express AB as $\frac{1}{2}EH$, so $(AB)(BC)$ can be expressed as a multiple of $(EH)^2$. Notice that to answer the question you don't have to actually set up the equation. If you work it out you will find that the area of *ABCD* is $\frac{\sqrt{7}}{4}(EH)^2$, so the areas are not equal.

Don't waste time carrying out the extra work on the test.

STATEMENT (2) alone is sufficient since the diagonal of a rectangle divides the rectangle into two congruent triangles. Therefore, the area of *ABCD* is equal to the area of *EFGH* if and only if the area of *ABC* is equal to the area of *EFG*.

6. How much does Susan weigh?

(1) Susan and Joan together weigh 250 pounds.
(2) Joan weighs twice as much as Susan.

(C) STATEMENT (2) says $J = 2S$, where J = Joan's weight and S = Susan's weight. But since we don't know Joan's weight, STATEMENT (2) alone is not sufficient.

STATEMENT (1) says $J + S = 250$; so if we use STATEMENT (2) we have $2S + S = 250$, which can be solved for S. Don't waste time actually solving the equation. But STATEMENT (1) alone is not sufficient. If we use only STATEMENT (1), we don't know how much Joan weighs. Therefore, STATEMENTS (1) and (2) together are sufficient, but neither statement alone is sufficient.

7. Two different holes, hole *A* and hole *B*, are put in the bottom of a full water tank. If the water drains out through the holes, how long before the tank is empty?

(1) If only hole *A* is put in the bottom, the tank will be empty in 24 minutes.
(2) If only hole *B* is put in the bottom, the tank will be empty in 42 minutes.

(C) In each minute, hole *A* drains $\frac{1}{24}$ of the tank according to STATEMENT (1). Since we have no information about *B*, STATEMENT (1) alone is not sufficient.

In each minute, hole *B* drains $\frac{1}{42}$ of the tank according to STATEMENT (2), but STATEMENT (2) gives no information about hole *A*. So STATEMENT (2) alone is not sufficient.

If we use STATEMENTS (1) and (2), then both holes together will drain $\frac{1}{24} + \frac{1}{42}$ or $\frac{7+4}{6 \times 28}$ or $\frac{11}{168}$ of the tank each minute. Therefore, it will take $\frac{168}{11}$ or $15\frac{3}{11}$ minutes for the tank to be empty. So STATEMENTS (1) and (2) together are sufficient, but neither statement alone is sufficient.

8. Find $x + y$

(1) $x - y = 6$
(2) $-2x + 2y = -12$

(E) STATEMENTS (1) and (2) are equivalent, since $x - y = 6$ if and only if $-2x + 2y = -2(x - y) = (-2)(6) = -12$. Each statement tells us only what $x - y$ is, and we have no other information. Therefore, each statement alone is insufficient. But since the two statements are the same, even together they are not sufficient.

9. *C* is a circle with center *D* and radius 2. *E* is a circle with center *F* and radius *R*. Are there any points which are on both *E* and *C*?

(1) The distance from *D* to *F* is $1 + R$.
(2) $R = 3$.

(A) STATEMENT (2) alone is not sufficient, since we must know how close the circles are and we know only the radius of each circle.

STATEMENT (1) alone is sufficient. The centers of the two circles are closer than the sum of the radii. (So we can form a triangle with *DF* as one side and the two other sides with length 2 and *R* respectively; but this means that the third vertex of the triangle will be on both circle *E* and circle *C*.)

So STATEMENT (1) alone is sufficient, but STATEMENT (2) alone is not sufficient.

10. Mr. Parker made $20,000 in 1967. What is Mr. Parker's average yearly income for the three years 1967 to 1969?

(1) He made 10% more in each year than he did in the previous year.
(2) His total combined income for 1968 and 1969 was $46,200.

(D) It is sufficient to be able to find his total income for the years 1967 through 1969 since we divide the total income by 3 to obtain the average income.

STATEMENT (1) alone is sufficient. Since we know his income for 1967, we can find his income in 1968 and 1969 by using STATEMENT (1). Therefore, we can find the total income. STATEMENT (2) alone is sufficient. Add the combined income from 1968 and 1969 to the income from 1967 (which is given), and we have the total income.

Therefore, STATEMENTS (1) and (2) are each sufficient.

11. Is the integer *n* divisible by 9? *n* is a two digit number.

(1) When *n* is divided by 3 the remainder is 2.
(2) When *n* is divided by 7 the remainder is 1.

(A) STATEMENT (1) alone is sufficient. If *n* is divisible by 9, it must be divisible by 3. Since (1) implies that *n* is not divisible by 3, (1) alone is sufficient.

STATEMENT (2) alone is not sufficient. Some numbers with a remainder of 1 when divided by 7 are: 1, 8, 15, 22, 29, and 36. Of these numbers, 36 is divisible by 9 and its remainder is 1 when divided by 7. However, 15 is not divisible by 9 and its remainder is 1 when divided by 7. So the correct choice is (A).

12. John and Paul are standing together on a sunny day. John's shadow is 10 feet long. Paul's shadow is 9 feet long. How tall is Paul?

(1) John is 6 feet tall.
(2) John is standing 2 feet away from Paul.

(A) STATEMENT (1) alone is sufficient. If P = Paul's height, then we can write a proportion $\frac{P}{6} = \frac{9}{10}$ since their shadows are proportional to their heights.

$$\left[\text{Thus, } P = \frac{54}{10} = 5.4 \text{ feet.}\right]$$

STATEMENT (2) alone is not sufficient. The distance they are apart does not give us any information about their heights.

Therefore, STATEMENT (1) alone is sufficient, but STATEMENT (2) alone is not sufficient.

13. A dozen eggs cost 90¢ in January 1980. Did a dozen eggs cost more than 90¢ in January 1981?

(1) In January 1980, the average worker had to work 5 minutes to pay for a dozen eggs.
(2) In January 1981, the average worker had to work 4 minutes to pay for a dozen eggs.

(E) STATEMENTS (1) and (2) together are insufficient. You need to know whether the wages of the average worker changed. 4 minutes of work in January 1981 could be worth more or less than 90¢.

14. At 7 o'clock how many people are on line to buy tickets at a theater box office?

(1) People are getting on the line at the rate of 2 people per minute at 7 o'clock.
(2) People are buying tickets and leaving the line at the rate of 4 people every 2 minutes at 7 o'clock.

(E) Both STATEMENTS (1) and (2) tell you how the line is changing at 7 o'clock. However, you need information about the length of the line at some time in order to use information about how it changes to get the length of the line. For example, if 100 people were on line (1) and (2) could be true, but both (1) and (2) could also be true if 50 people were on line. So, (1) and (2) together are not sufficient to answer the question.

15. What is the value of $\frac{x}{y}$? $x > 0$.

(1) $x = \frac{1}{4}y$

(2) y = 400% of x

(D) STATEMENT (1) alone is sufficient. Since $x > 0$, (1) implies $y > 0$. Hence, we can divide the equations $x = \frac{1}{4}y$ by y to get the value of $\frac{x}{y}$.

STATEMENT (2) alone is sufficient since $y = 4x$ is equivalent to STATEMENT (1). When STATEMENTS (1) and (2) are equivalent to each other, the only possible choices are (D) or (E). Therefore, you should guess (D) or (E), if you know the STATEMENTS are equivalent.

16. How many of the numbers x, y, and z are positive? x, y, and z are all less than 30.

(1) $x + y + z = 61$
(2) $x + y = 35$

(A) STATEMENT (1) alone is sufficient. Since all the numbers are less than 30, all three must be positive for their sum to be larger than 60.

STATEMENT (2) alone is insufficient. (2) implies that x and y are positive, but gives no information about z.

17. How far is it from town A to town B? Town C is 15 miles west of town A.

(1) It is 10 miles from town B to town C.
(2) There is a river between town A and town B.

(E) STATEMENTS (1) and (2) together are not sufficient. You need to know what direction it is from town B to town C, besides the distance between the towns.

18. Is $2 < x < 4$?

(1) $x^2 - 5x + 6 < 0$
(2) $5x^2 - 25x > 0$

(D) The key to this problem is to factor the expressions. You can factor STATEMENT (1) into $(x - 3)(x - 2)$. If the expression is negative that means $x - 3$ and $x - 2$ must have *opposite* signs. This can only happen if $2 < x < 3$. Thus, (1) alone is sufficient.

STATEMENT (2) alone is sufficient since the expression factors into $5x(x - 5)$. To be positive both $5x$ and $x - 5$ must have the same sign. This will happen if $x < 0$ or if $x > 5$. This means x does *not* satisfy $2 < x < 4$. So (2) alone is sufficient.

Remember answering the question does not only mean answering yes. Deciding that a statement can not be true also answers the question.

19. What percentage of families in the state have annual incomes over $25,000 and own a sailboat?

(1) 28% of all the families in the state have an annual income over $25,000
(2) 40% of the families in the state with an annual income over $25,000 own a sailboat.

(C) STATEMENTS (1) and (2) are sufficient. 40% of the 28% are families who both have income over $25,000 and own a sailboat. Note that STATEMENT (2) alone is not sufficient. The percentage of families who own a sailboat and have an income over $25,000 is a percentage of families in the state. In STATEMENT (2), the percentage given is a percentage of families with income over $25,000.

20. What is the two-digit number whose first digit is a and whose second digit is b? The number is greater than 9.

(1) The number is a multiple of 51.
(2) The sum of the digits a and b is 6.

(A) Two digit numbers are the integers from 0 to 99. Since you are told that the number is greater than 9, the only possible choices are integers 10, 11 . . . . . 99.

STATEMENT (1) alone is sufficient since there is only one multiple of 51 ($51 = 51 \times 1$) in the list of possibilities.

STATEMENT (2) alone is not sufficient since 15 and 51 both satisfy (2) and are two digit numbers greater than 9.

21. What is the radius of the circle with center O?

(1) The area of the circle is 25π.
(2) The area of the circle divided by the diameter of the circle is equal to π times $\frac{1}{2}$ of the radius of the circle.

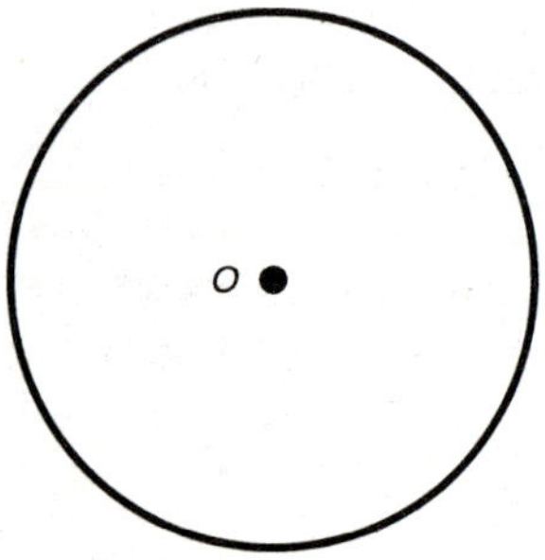

(A) Since the area of a circle is equal to πr^2 and the radius is positive, STATEMENT (1) alone is sufficient.

STATEMENT (2) is true for all circles, so it gives no information about the radius of this particular circle.

Section 4 Sentence Correction

1. **In her candid autobiography, the author discusses her early years, her desire to become an actress and how she made her debut on the stage.**

   (A) to become an actress, and how she made
   (B) that she become an actress, and how she made
   (C) to become an actress, and
   (D) that she become an actress, and
   (E) that she become an actress and that she make

(C) Choices (A), (B), and (E) lack parallel structure; parallel nouns should be used: *years, desire,* and *debut.* Choice (D) unnecessarily changes the infinitive to *become.*

2. **Government authorities predicted correctly that tremendous savings in the consumption of gasoline would be achieved if speeding was to be limited to 55 miles per hour.**

   (A) speeding was to be limited to
   (B) motorists limited their speed to
   (C) speeding did not exceed
   (D) a motorist was to limit his speed to
   (E) speeding by motorists was to be limited to

(B) Choices (A), (C), and (E) imply that driving a car at any speed is speeding. Choice (D) is wrong, because the subjunctive mood is required in the *if* clause.

3. **The word processor has revolutionized office procedures more than any machine of modern times.**

   (A) any machine
   (B) has any machine
   (C) any other machine
   (D) has any other machine
   (E) any other machine has

(C) Choices (A) and (B) contain a faulty comparison. The word processor *is* a modern machine, and so the word *other* must be included. In choices (D) and (E), the word *has* is unnecessary and awkward.

4. **The possibility of expropriation was believed to be unlikely in the near future due to the lack of mining technology and capital available in this small South American country.**

   (A) due to the lack of mining technology and
   (B) because of the lack of mining technology and
   (C) because there was no mining technology and
   (D) because of the lack of mining technology and there was no
   (E) due to the lack of mining technology and there was no

(B) *Due to* should not be used in place of the compound preposition *because of.* Choice (C) has an error in agreement between the singular verb (*was*) and the compound subject *(technology* and *capital).* Choice (D) is wordy and awkward.

5. **The doctrine applies in Canada, where there is a federal law and a provincial law that are each valid and consistent.**

   (A) is a federal law and a provincial law that are each valid and
   (B) are a federal law and a provincial law that are each valid and
   (C) are a federal law and a provincial law both of which are each valid and
   (D) is a federal law and a provincial law both of which are each valid and
   (E) are a federal law and a provincial law that are each valid or

(B) The compound subject requires a plural verb. Choice (C) uses incorrect language: *both of which are each,* and choice (E) changes the meaning by using *or* instead of *and.*

6. **Former Postal Service employees who believe they may be affected by this settlement should contact their last place of USPS employment, the department advised.**

   (A) may be affected
   (B) may be effected
   (C) will have been affected
   (D) will be effected
   (E) will have been effected

(A) *Affected* (*influenced by* or *acted upon*) is the correct word. Choice (C) uses the wrong tense.

7. Blake is among the very few individuals who critics regard as genuinely significant in the history of both art and literature.

(A) who critics regard as genuinely significant in the history of both
(B) whom critics regard as genuinely significant in the history of both
(C) whom critics regard as genuinely significant both in the history of
(D) who critics regard as genuinely significant both in the history of
(E) who is regarded by critics as genuinely significant in the history of both

(B) The pronoun *who* is the object of the verb *regard;* therefore, it should be in the objective case, *whom.* Choice (C) misplaces the modifier *both.*

8. Many scientists are alarmed over the interest in such pseudo-scientific topics as ESP, flying saucers, and the occult, fearing that this interest may herald a new dark age of gullibility, ignorance, and thinking in superstitious ways.

(A) this interest may herald a new dark age of gullibility, ignorance, and thinking in superstitious ways
(B) it may herald a new dark age of gullibility, ignorance, and thinking in superstitious ways
(C) it may herald a new dark age of gullibility, ignorance, and superstition
(D) this interest may herald a new dark age of gullibility, ignorance, and superstition
(E) they may herald a new dark age of gullibility, ignorance, and superstition

(D) To maintain parallel construction, the noun *superstition* should replace the gerund phrase *thinking in superstitious ways.* The reference of *it* or *they* in choices (B), (C), and (E) is not completely clear.

9. Having broken with Freud, Jung's later writings nevertheless bore signs of the continued influence of Freudian doctrine and theories.

(A) Having broken with Freud, Jung's later writings nevertheless bore signs of the continued
(B) Since breaking with Freud, Jung's later writings nevertheless bore signs of the continued
(C) Although he had broken with Freud, in his later writings Jung nevertheless showed signs of the continued
(D) Having broken with Freud, Jung's later writings nevertheless bore signs of the continual
(E) Having broken with Freud, later writings by Jung nevertheless bore signs of the continued

(C) All the choices but (C) include a dangling modifier, since Jung's *writings* had not broken with Freud.

10. That Giotto's paintings are significant in the history of the early Renaissance is undeniable, but Giotto cannot scarcely be considered the equal of such masters as Leonardo and Raphael.

(A) cannot scarcely be considered
(B) can scarcely be considered
(C) cannot hardly be considered
(D) cannot scarcely be considered to be
(E) isn't hardly to be considered

(B) *Cannot scarcely, cannot hardly,* and *isn't hardly* are considered double negatives.

11. Although the theory of continental drift was not widely accepted until the mid-twentieth century, the basic concept had been described as early as 1620.

(A) was not widely accepted until the mid-twentieth century, the basic concept had been
(B) was not widely accepted until the mid-twentieth century, the basic concept was
(C) was not widely accepted until the mid-twentieth century, the basic concept has been
(D) had not been widely accepted until the mid-twentieth century, the basic concept has been
(E) had not been widely accepted until the mid-twentieth century, the basic concept was

(A) The past perfect tense *had been described* is needed to make clear the order in which the events occurred.

12. The reason I am supporting Senator Blandings is because her extensive background in foreign affairs has made her uniquely qualified for a seat on this important subcommittee.

(A) because her extensive background in foreign affairs has made her uniquely qualified for
(B) that her extensive background in foreign affairs have made her uniquely qualified for
(C) that her extensive background in foreign affairs has made her uniquely qualified for
(D) that her extensive background in foreign affairs has made her uniquely qualified to
(E) because her extensive background in foreign affairs have made her uniquely qualified for

(C) The correct expression is *the reason is that.* Choice (B) has an error in agreement: *background . . . have.* The idiom is *qualified for,* not *qualified to* (D).

13. Fear of future nationalistic feelings and a conviction that natural resource endowments should be exploited for the welfare of the residents of the country, rather than for private profit, are shared by all managers of extractive industries there.

(A) rather than for private profit, are
(B) rather than for private profit, is
(C) irregardless of private profit, are
(D) as opposed to private profit, is
(E) and not necessarily for private profit, is

(A) With a compound subject *(feelings* and *conviction),* the plural verb *are* is called for. In choice (C), *irregardless* is nonstandard English.

14. The lieutenant reminded his men that the only information to be given to the enemy if captured was each individual's name, rank, and serial number.

(A) the only information to be given to the enemy if captured was each individual's name, rank, and serial number
(B) the only information to be given to the enemy if they were captured was each individual's name, rank, and serial number
(C) the only information to be given to the enemy if captured were each individual's name, rank, and serial number
(D) , if captured, the only information to be given to the enemy was each individual's name, rank, and what his serial number was
(E) , if they were captured, the only information to be given to the enemy was each individual's name, rank, and serial number

(E) Choices (D) and (E) correct the misplaced modifier, but choice (D) has an error in parallel structure. The noun clause *what his serial number was* is not parallel with *name* and *rank.*

15. Writing a beautiful sonnet is as much an achievement as to finish a 400-page novel.

(A) to finish
(B) it is to finish
(C) finishing
(D) if you finished
(E) to have finished

(C) *Finishing* is parallel to *writing.*

16. Anyone interested in computer programming can find a job in contemporary industry if you learn the basic programming languages, such as COBOL and FORTRAN.

(A) if you learn
(B) if you will learn
(C) if he would learn
(D) by the study of
(E) by studying

(E) Choices (A) and (B) suffer from the change of persons (from *anyone* to *you).* In choice (C) *would learn* is the wrong tense. Choice (D) is wordy.

17. During the gasoline shortage of the 1970s caused by the actions of the OPEC nations, the number of accidents on our highways decreased markedly.

(A) the number of accidents on our highways decreased markedly
(B) the amount of accidents on our highways decreased markedly
(C) there were less accidents on our highways
(D) there were a fewer amount of accidents on our highways
(E) they found there were many fewer accidents on our highways

(A) The word *number* is used when the quantity can be counted. Choices (C) and (D) incorrectly use *less* and *fewer; fewer accidents* and *lesser amount* would be correct. In choice (E) *they* has no reference.

18. Being that only twenty-four states have ratified the proposed amendment, we can assume that it will not be adopted.

(A) Being that only twenty-four states
(B) Since twenty-four states only
(C) Being as only twenty-four states
(D) Seeing as how only twenty-four states
(E) Inasmuch as only twenty-four states

(E) *Being that* in choices (A) and (C) is incorrect. The placement of *only* in choice (B) is wrong. Choice (D), *Seeing as how. . .* .is nonstandard.

19. I have studied the works of George Bernard Shaw not only for their plots but also because they are very witty.

(A) also because they are very witty
(B) because they are also very witty
(C) for their wit also
(D) because they are very witty also
(E) also for their wit

(E) Parallel structure is violated in choices (A), (B), and (D). The placement of *also* in choice (C) is poor, for it ends the sentence on an anticlimactic note.

20. The noise at the airport was deafening, which made conversation difficult if not impossible.

(A) The noise at the airport was deafening, which made conversation
(B) The noise at the airport was deafening, and it made conversation
(C) The deafening noise at the airport made conversation
(D) The airport noise was deafening, which made conversation
(E) The noise at the airport was deafening, conversation being

(C) In choices (A) and (D) *which* refers to the entire sentence rather than to a specific antecedent. (B) is not as strong a sentence as (C). Choice (E) has a dangling modifier.

21. Inflation in the United States has not and, we hope, never will reach a rate of 20 percent a year.

(A) and, we hope, never will reach
(B) reached and, we hope, never will
(C) and hopefully never will reach
(D) reached and, we hope, never will reach
(E) reached and hopefully never will

(D) Choices (A), (B), and (E) omit important parts of the verb. *Hopefully* in choices (C) and (E) is wrong; although many people use it this way, most grammarians do not accept it as a substitute for *we hope.* (Strictly speaking, *hopefully* should only be used to mean *in a hopeful way,* as in *The farmer searched the skies hopefully looking for signs of rain.*)

Section 5
Critical Reasoning

1. In almost all developing countries, the initial thrust of their respective trade policies was to foster domestic industries whose production would replace imports. This was a natural and logical strategy, given that import-substituting production could count on an existing known domestic demand, promised some mitigation of national economic dependence, and could be protected easily from external competition through high tariffs, quotas, or subsidies of various kinds.

Which of the following, if true, would weaken the strategy above?

(A) Domestic demand may be unknown.
(B) Quotas are more regressive than tariffs.
(C) Subsidies and import constraints keep domestic prices high and impose a burden on consumers.
(D) Fast economic growth fosters inequality of income.
(E) A protectionist policy may be beneficial to the developing country, but disliked by economically advanced countries.

(C) An import substitution policy is designed to develop local industry and is frequently promoted by a protectionist policy, i.e. tariffs, quotas, and other constraints that either prohibit imports or tax them highly. By restricting imports or increasing their cost, locally produced products may be priced more highly than if import competition were allowed. Therefore, consumers ultimately pay the cost of higher priced (and often inferior) locally produced goods. Alternative (E) is partially correct. A protectionist policy (limiting imports) may benefit developing countries by allowing local industry to develop and may be an anathema to trading partners, but this hardly weakens the argument for a policy of economic independence as given in the statement. If answer choice (A) were true, there would be nothing to protect because there could be no imports. Answer (B) is, in fact, true, but the quotas may be even more protective than tariffs. In any case, both quotas and tariffs are only the means to carry out the strategy. The inequality issue (D) cannot be deduced from the passage.

2. **The quantitative supply of labor (as well as its qualitative composition) depends on the following variables: the size of the population, its age-sex composition, marital structure, and participation rates in the labor force in accordance with these factors.**

   Each of the following, if true, could affect the supply of labor except:

   (A) Birth and death rates.
   (B) Immigration and emigration.
   (C) Educational level of the population.
   (D) Number of employment agencies.
   (E) Marital status of females.

(D) The birth and death rates and the immigration and emigration rates affect the size of the population, so choices (A) and (B) obviously affect the supply of labor. The educational level (C) affects the participation rate, in the labor force, and marital status (E) is said in the given paragraph to be a factor in the labor force. The only factor that could not, according to the passage, affect the supply of labor is the number of employment agencies (D). Employment agencies are involved in the distribution and direction of the labor supply, but they do not affect the quantitative supply of labor.

3. **In order to discourage present surburban growth patterns, which because of their low densities are uneconomic to service and wasteful of land and resources, land use policy studies should include research into innovative forms of high density, low-rise housing.**

   The above statement is a response to all of the following problems except:

   (A) The tendency to exclude light industry from residential areas means that people have to go outside their communities to seek work.
   (B) The traditional practice of using land as a commodity rather than a resource has meant that the location of new communities is often solely governed by a developer's economic convenience.
   (C) There is a lack of coordination between the planning and structure of communities and their relation to transportation networks.
   (D) Present patterns of urban growth have squandered agricultural and rural lands.
   (E) In houses designed for the standard family, there is a lack of inter and intra-unit privacy.

(E) Choices (A), (B), (C), and (D) all refer to the community and land use and are relevant to the given statement. Statement (E) relates to housing design, a topic not referred to in the given paragraph.

4. **Over the last 20 years the rate of increase in total production in Workland has been second to none in the world. However, the growth is more modest when calculated per capita of total population. Over the last ten years progress has been much slower.**

   If the information above is accurate, which of the following must be true?

   (A) Workland has a very large population.
   (B) Productivity per capita has not grown as fast during the past ten years.
   (C) Total production has increased faster than population growth.
   (D) The birth rate has declined.
   (E) The per capita production rate has not declined.

(B) Two factors are noted in the given passage. First, the per capita production rate has not been as high as the production increase, without regard to population size. Second, the rate of increase over the last ten years has been slower. Therefore (B) is correct. Productivity per capita has not grown as fast during the past ten years. There is no indication about the size of the Workland population given in the paragraph, and so we cannot know whether or not (A) is true. The paragraph says that growth in production is more modest when calculated per capita of total population; we can infer that population growth has increased faster than total production, so (C) is incorrect. We can also infer that the birth rate has not declined and that per capita production has declined, so (D) and (E) are also incorrect.

5. The earliest known proto-Eskimos are those of the Cape Denbigh Flint complex of northwestern Alaska, including adjacent Baffin Island. Denbigh people and their descendants were well equipped to survive in the Arctic. Their adaptive success is obvious in the speed with which they spread eastward across arctic Canada to northeast Greenland, which they reached by 2000 B.C.

Which of the following, if true, would refute the above?

(A) The Cape Denbigh Flint complex dates back to 3000 B.C.
(B) The Vikings populated Greenland between 800 and 1100 A.D.
(C) Denbigh artifacts of early settlements in northeast Greenland date back further than Denbigh artifacts found on Baffin Island.
(D) Denbigh origin lies in the Paleolithic and the Mesolithic period—say about 4000 B.C. of Siberia.
(E) The Denbigh people are known almost solely from their flint tools.

(C) Alternative (C) implies a westward migration—from Greenland to Baffin Island into Alaska proper—instead of an eastward migration as stated in the passage. Answer choice (A) supports the statement chronologically. Even if answer choice (B) is true, the Eskimos or their descendants inhabited Greenland before the Vikings. Answer (E) is not associated with the movement of Eskimos or their descendants.

6. Harry Dyner was the Minister of Petroleum in a small oil-producing country. His country's oil exports were approximately 2 percent of total world oil sales. The Minister of Finance was anxious to maximize petroleum production and export to earn foreign exchange. Dyner, however, believed that increased sales would only drive down the world price of petroleum and lower his country's foreign exchange revenue.

Which of the following would best exemplify an error in Dyner's reasoning?

(A) Price of crude v. price of refined petroleum.
(B) Production goals v. financial goals.
(C) The supply produced by a single country v. aggregate supply on the market.
(D) Seasonal v. long-term supply.
(E) Long-term v. short-term demand.

(C) Since Dyner's country produces only 2% of the world petroleum supply, its output can hardly affect world prices. If this is true, then answers (A), (D), and (E) cannot falsify his reasoning. Answer (B) has some connection to the argument—production goals (i.e., increased production) v. financial goals (i.e., foreign exchange savings)—but it does not signify an error in Dyner's reasoning.

7. There is no clear line between health and illness; it is easy to forget what it feels like to be really well and to get gradually used to often having a headache, feeling irritable, or tired. There is an unrecognized proportion of the population that has been tipped over the brink into ill health by ubiquitous contaminants.

Which of the following statements best describes the purpose of the above?

(A) The public must be encouraged to have regular medical examinations.
(B) The public must be warned to be aware of various physical and chemical hazards.
(C) The public must be warned to treat seriously such symptoms as headaches, irritability, and tiredness.
(D) The medical professional is not always capable of diagnosing illness.
(E) No one can really be sure if he is healthy or ill.

(B) Choice (B) is the best answer. The statement is an admonition for people to be aware of "contaminants," a reference to physical and chemical hazards. Alternatives (A) and (C) might be implied, but they are not such good choices as (B). Alternative (D) is not implied. Alternative (E) might be implied, but it is not the major message of the statement.

8. Administrators and executives are members of the most stable occupation.

The stability mentioned in the above statement could be dependent on each of the following factors except

(A) Training and skills.
(B) Nature of the occupation.
(C) Status.
(D) Relatively high income.
(E) Rate of turnover.

(E) The factors listed in (A), (B), (C), and (D) all affect occupational mobility. The rate of turnover (E) is another way of measuring mobility; it is not an explanatory variable, or, in other words, it is not a factor that affects stability or mobility.

9. By far the chief export in the 15th century was textiles. Among these, woolens and worsteds predominated; linens were far less important and silks played an insignificant part. Outside this group, the only important item in the first half of the century was corn, though the exports of fish, lead, and tin were by no means negligible.

Given the above information which of the following statements is correct?

(A) Corn, though not as important an export as textiles, was still an important component of the export trade.
(B) Corn was nearly as important an export as linen.
(C) Silk was a valuable export in the 15th century.
(D) Fishing was a bigger industry than wool production in the 15th century.
(E) Nontextile items were one of the chief elements in the list of products exported in the 15th century.

(A) Textiles are mentioned as the major export, and among textiles, woolens and worsteds as the most important. Apart from textiles, corn is mentioned as the only other significant export. Therefore, (A) is correct. Linen and silks were mentioned as insignificant exports, so choices (B) and (C) are not appropriate. Since textile export was the most important export, and woolens an important component of the textile export, it can be inferred that wool production was more important an industry than fishing, which produced only an insignificant export; therefore, choice (D) is incorrect. Choice (E) is clearly incorrect: the first sentence of the passage states that by far the chief export in the 15th century was textiles.

10. Self-employment is found more often among men and women in the 25- to 44-year-old group than among their older or younger counterparts. Some 31 percent of the men and only 19 percent of the women who operate unincorporated businesses on a full-time basis completed four or more years of college. And while self-employed men are generally better educated than their wage-and-salary counterparts, the same cannot be said of self-employed women.

If the information above is accurate, which of the following must be true?

(A) Self-employed women are generally younger than self-employed men.
(B) Self-employed men have more education than self-employed women.
(C) Women wage earners have more education than men wage earners.
(D) Salaried men are younger than self-employed men.
(E) Self-employed men and women have more education than wage-earning men and women.

(B) 31% of men who operate unincorporated businesses (self-employed), completed four or more years of college, against 19% of women in the same category. We can then conclude that self-employed men have more education than self-employed women. The passage states that self-employed people are often in the 25-to-44-year-old group; no distinction is made between the sexes, so we cannot know whether or not self-employed women are generally younger than self-employed men, so choice (A) is not appropriate. The passage compares the education of self-employed men and wage-earning men and the education of self-employed women and wage-earning women, but it does not compare wage-earning women with wage-earning men, so we cannot know if statement (C) is true. According to the passage, salaried men are often younger or older than self-employed counterparts, so (D) is not necessarily true. The last part of the passage states that self-employed women do not have more education than their wage-earning counterparts, so (E) cannot be true.

11. Between 1940 and 1945 gasoline consumption in the U.S. dropped about 35 percent because of wartime rationing. In the same period, lung cancer in U.S. white males declined by approximately the same percentage. Between 1914 and 1950 lung cancer mortality increased nineteenfold and the rate of gasoline consumption increased at the same rate.

Which of the following facts, if true, would weaken the above argument?

(A) For each of the years between 1939 and 1949, lung cancer among urban blacks in the United States remained at the same level.
(B) The amount of lead in gasoline increased between 1916 and 1944.
(C) After 1950 gasoline consumption jumped.
(D) During World War II, people suffering from cancer were forbidden to drive.
(E) Women first began driving in large numbers between 1941 and 1951.

(A) The statement implies a correlation between a decline in gasoline consumption (less pollution) and a decrease in the incidence of lung cancer among white males. If lung cancer among blacks did not decrease over the same time period, one could assume that another causal or intermediate variable—other than gasoline consumption—may explain the decrease in lung cancer among white males. Answer choice (C) does not explain associations in variables occurring between 1914 and 1950. Answer choices (D) and (E) do not explain the relationship between gasoline consumption and cancer. Choice (B) supports the argument.

12. From 1920 to 1950, the amount of food production per worker and per hour increased twofold. From 1950 to 1980, food production per worker and per hour increased 1.3 times.

Each of the following, if true, could help to account for this trend except

(A) The number of farm workers increased.
(B) The use of mechanical technology in food production decreased.
(C) The use of chemical fertilizers decreased.
(D) The number of hours worked per unit of output decreased.
(E) More workers were needed to produce the same unit of output.

(D) The statement is evidence of declining productivity. If fewer hours are needed to produce the same output, productivity should increase. In choice (A), an increase in the number of workers to achieve the same output indicates a decline in productivity. Using less technology (B) and fertilizers (C) will lower productivity. Using more workers to achieve the same output (E) is a decrease in productivity.

13. "Some men are certainly tall, others are certainly not tall; but of intermediate men, we should say, 'tall'? Yes, I *think* so or no, I shouldn't be inclined to call him tall."

Which of the following most accurately reflects the intention of the writer of the above?

(A) Men intermediately tall, partake of "tallness" to a moderate degree.
(B) To call men tall who are not strikingly so must be to use the concept with undue imprecision.
(C) Every empirical concept has a degree of vagueness.
(D) There is really no need to be as indecisive as the writer of the above.
(E) Calling someone tall or short depends upon one's whim.

(C) Choice (C) reflects the intention of the writer of the passage, which stresses the facts of usage. Choice (A) implies a metaphysical (platonic) theory about the use of the word tall. Choice (B) is an opinion opposed to that of the writer. Alternative (D) is a judgment on the behavior described in the abstract. Choice (E) is a judgment based on fantasy.

14. There are many reasons why individuals want to run their own businesses. Some foresee more personal satisfaction if they are successful in launching their own business, while others are interested mainly in the prospect of larger financial rewards. Since the late 1970s and early 1980s, tax regulations and other changes have encouraged increasing numbers of venture capitalists and entrepreneurs to start new enterprises. Since 1980, some one-half million new ventures have been started. Not all have succeeded, of course.

The above statement makes which of the following assumptions?

(A) Success in starting a new business depends in large part on sound financial planning.
(B) Social incentives motivate investors just as much as financial rewards.
(C) Financial incentives are associated with new business starts.
(D) Most new business ventures succeed initially but fail later on.
(E) Venture capitalists are motivated by nonmonetary gains.

(C) While personal satisfaction is a motivating factor, the statement shows that business starts increased—since 1980—along with a set of tax changes, promoting financial gains. (B) is the second best answer. However, it cannot be inferred that social motives are "just as" strong as the financial motive, given that the passage states that tax regulations motivated increasing numbers of entrepreneurs to invest. Answer choice (A) may be correct, but there is nothing in the passage to substantiate it. Choice (D) may be eliminated because of the word "most." There is no evidence in the passage to support answer choice (E).

15. A highly cohesive work group is a prerequisite for high team performance. Sociologists posit that the association between group cohesion and success is owing to the support individual team members give to one other and their acceptance of the group's goals and activities.

Each of the following, if true, either provides support for or cannot weaken the sociologists' assumption about the relationship between cohesion and success except

(A) A group of West German researchers found that successful work teams were headed by dominant leaders.
(B) Industrial psychologists in England found that work groups who tended to participate in after hours social activities were more productive.
(C) University researchers found that there was a significant correlation between team productivity and the extent to which team members understood and complied with the group's objectives.
(D) American researchers found that successful team members tended to rate their fellow members more favorably.
(E) The winning team in a computerized business game rated their peers generally low on "stick by the rules," "extrovert," "friendly," and "positive" and high on "egocentric," "individualistic," and "discord."

(E) Answer choice (E) weakens the argument. Team members rated their peers low on characteristics of cohesion and high on characteristics of group discord and lack of harmony. Answer choices (B), (C), and (D) support the statement's assumption. Choice (A) neither supports nor weakens it. A dominant leader may or may not contribute to cohesion, depending on whether or not he or she unites or divides the group.

16. Before the middle of the 14th century, there were no universities north of Italy, outside France and England. By the end of the 15th century, there were 23 universities in this region, from Louvain and Mainz to Rostock, Cracow, and Bratislava and the number of universities in Europe as a whole had more than doubled.

Given the above information, which of the following statements is correct?

(A) Until the age of university expansion in the 15th century, there were perhaps 11 universities in the whole of Europe.
(B) South of Italy there were 23 universities in the 14th century.
(C) In the 13th century, France and England were the only countries in Europe with universities.
(D) After the great age of university expansion in the 14th and 15th centuries, France and England were not the only northern European countries to have such centers of learning.
(E) Italy was the cradle of university expansion.

(D) The passage states that university expansion—north of Italy outside France and England—took place between the mid-14th century and the end of the 15th century. There is nothing in the passage about the number of universities in the whole of Europe, so we have no way of knowing if (A) is correct. Statement (B) is not substantiated by what is in the passage—namely, that "by the end of the 15th century, there were 23 universities" in a wide region. There is nothing in the passage that states that France and England were the only countries with universities in the 13th century, so (C) is not appropriate. Similarly, nothing in the passage states or implies that Italy was the cradle of university expansion (E).

17. Between 1979 and 1983, the number of unincorporated business self-employed women increased five times faster than the number of self-employed men and more than three times faster than women wage-and-salary workers. Part-time self-employment among women increased more than full-time self-employment.

Each of the following, if true, could help to account for this trend except:

(A) Owning a business affords flexibility to combine work and family responsibilities.
(B) The proportion of women studying business administration courses has grown considerably.
(C) There are more self-employed women than men.
(D) Unincorporated service industries have grown by 300 percent over the period; the ratio of women to men in this industry is three to one.
(E) The financial reward of having a second wage earner in the household has taken on increased significance.

(C) Even if it were true that there are more self-employed women than men it does not explain why this number increases five times faster than men. Answer choice (A) supports the argument by showing that it has become more convenient for women to be self-employed. Choice (B) gives a means to that end. Answer (D) provides evidence to support the claim, and (E) is an example of a motivating factor that induced more women to work.

Section 6
Sentence Correction

1. Since neither of the agencies had submitted the necessary documentation, each were required to reapply for the grant the following year.

(A) each were required to reapply for the grant the following year
(B) each were required, the following year, to reapply for the grant
(C) each was required to reapply for the grant the following year
(D) both were required to reapply, the following year, for the grant
(E) it was required to reapply for the grant the following year

(C) The pronoun *each* is singular, and requires the singular verb *was required.*

2. Stationary missile launching sites are frequently criticized by military experts on the ground that, in comparison to mobile units, they are the most vulnerable to preemptive attack.

(A) they are the most
(B) such sites are the most
(C) they are rather
(D) stationary sites are most
(E) they are more

(E) When only two things are being compared (in this case, stationary sites and mobile units), the word *more* rather than *most* should be used.

3. The qualities needed in a president are scarcely tested in today's political campaigns, which call instead for showmanship, good looks, and being able to seem eloquent while saying nothing.

(A) being able to seem eloquent
(B) the ability to seem eloquent
(C) having eloquence
(D) a certain eloquence
(E) that he seem eloquent

(B) To maintain parallel structure, a phrase beginning with a noun (*ability*) is needed.

4. Anyone who would speak with authority on the poets of the Renaissance must have a broad acquaintance with the writers of classical antiquity.

(A) Anyone who would speak
(B) If one would speak
(C) He which would speak
(D) Anyone desirous for speaking
(E) Those who have a wish to speak

(A) The original wording is the clearest and simplest.

5. In its final report, the commission proposed, among other measures, that the legal drinking age be raised from eighteen to twenty-one.

(A) that the legal drinking age be raised
(B) a rise of the legal drinking age
(C) that the legal drinking age should be raised
(D) raising the age of drinking legally
(E) to raise legally the drinking age

(A) No error.

6. Since neither her nor the Dean were willing to veto the curriculum changes, they went into effect as of September 1.

(A) her nor the Dean were willing
(B) she nor the Dean was willing
(C) her nor the Dean wished
(D) she or the Dean was willing
(E) she nor the Dean were willing

(B) The pronoun *she* is needed, since it is part of the compound subject of the verb *was willing*; the verb must be singular to agree with the nearest subject (*Dean*).

7. A broad range of opinions was represented between the various members of the steering committee.

(A) A broad range of opinions was represented between
(B) A broad range of opinions were represented between
(C) A broad range of opinions had been held by
(D) A broad range of opinions was represented among
(E) Varying opinions were represented by

(D) Use *among* when three or more people or things are involved.

8. Undaunted by the political repercussions of his decision, the new gasoline rationing plan was announced by the Governor at the state office building last Friday.

(A) the new gasoline rationing plan was announced by the Governor
(B) the Governor's new gasoline rationing plan was announced
(C) the Governor made the announcement concerning the new gasoline rationing plan
(D) the new gasoline rationing plan of the Governor was announced
(E) the Governor announced the new gasoline rationing plan

(E) The underlined phrase must begin with *the Governor*; otherwise, the phrase which precedes it has no clear reference. Choice (C) is verbose and rather vague.

9. Mario had already swum five laps when I jumped into the pool.

(A) had already swum five laps when I
(B) already swam five laps when I
(C) already swam five laps when I had
(D) had already swum five laps when I had
(E) had already swam five laps when I

(A) No error.

10. Despite their avowed opposition to the strike, no one from among the dozens of nonunion workers were willing to cross the picket line.

(A) from among the dozens of nonunion workers were willing
(B) of the dozens of nonunion workers were willing
(C) was willing from among the dozens of nonunion workers
(D) from among the dozens of nonunion workers was willing
(E) from the dozens of nonunion workers were willing

(D) The pronoun *no one* is singular, and requires the singular verb *was*. Choice (C) is awkward in comparison to choice (D).

11. The poetry of George Herbert is regarded by many critics as equal in quality, though less influential, than the work of his more famous contemporary John Donne.

(A) equal in quality, though less influential, than the work
(B) equal in quality to, though less influential than, the work
(C) qualitatively equal, though less influential than, that
(D) equal in quality, though less influential, then the work
(E) of equal quality, though of less influence, than that

(B) The comparative phrases *equal . . . to* and *less . . . than* must be complete in order for the sentence to make sense.

12. If it is the present administration whom we should blame for the economic crisis, the first step toward a solution is to reject the incumbent at the polls this November.

(A) whom we should blame
(B) whom is to blame
(C) who we should blame
(D) who should be blamed
(E) who one should blame

(A) Correct as originally written. The pronoun *whom* is correct, since it is the object of the verb *should blame*.

13. The assembly speaker has called for a shorter fall session of the legislature in hopes that less amendments of a purely symbolic nature will be proposed by the state's lawmakers.

(A) in hopes that less amendments of a
(B) hoping that fewer amendments that have a
(C) in hopes that fewer amendments of a
(D) in order that less amendments of a
(E) in hope that fewer amendments of

(C) Use *fewer* for countable items (such as amendments); use *less* for noncountable substances (for example, sand, water, or time).

14. Parker's testimony made it clear that he appointed Ryan before he had become aware of Ryan's alleged underworld connections.

(A) he appointed Ryan before he had become aware
(B) he appointed Ryan before his awareness
(C) he had appointed Ryan prior to his having become aware
(D) his appointment of Ryan preceded awareness
(E) he had appointed Ryan before becoming aware

(E) The past perfect tense *had appointed* is needed to clarify the order in which the events occurred.

15. Despite its being smaller in size than are conventional automobile engines, the new Alcock Engine can still deliver the horsepower needed for most short-distance city driving.

(A) Despite its being smaller in size than are
(B) In spite of its being smaller than
(C) Although smaller than
(D) Despite its size relative to
(E) Though not comparable in size to

(C) The other choices are verbose, vague, or both.

16. Seventy-four applications were received, of whom the better were selected for detailed review.

(A) of whom the better were selected
(B) from which were selected the better
(C) the best of which were selected
(D) from whom were selected the best
(E) from which they selected the best

(C) Use the pronoun *whom* only for people, never for things. Choice (E) introduces *they*, a pronoun without a reference. *Best* is needed here.

17. If the British government had had no fear of the increasing hostility of the Indian populace, Gandhi's nonviolent tactics would have availed little.

(A) If the British government had had no fear of
(B) If the British government did not fear
(C) Had the British government no fear
(D) If the British government did not have fear of
(E) Would the British government not have feared

(A) No error. In most *if* clauses, the past subjunctive form of the verb—with *had*—must be used.

18. The official imposition of "Lysenkoism" on Soviet biologists, with its chilling effects on scientists in countless related fields, illustrate vividly the dangers of government interference with science.

(A) illustrate vividly the dangers of government interference with science
(B) illustrate the dangers of government interference with science vividly
(C) illustrates vividly the dangers of government interference with science
(D) vividly illustrate the dangers of government interference with science
(E) vividly illustrates how dangerous can be government interference with science

(C) The singular verb *illustrates* is needed, since the subject is the singular *imposition*.

19. Health care costs have been forced upward less by increases in the salaries of nurses, technicians, and other personnel than by increases in the amounts spent on diagnostic machinery and electronic equipment.

(A) than by increases in the amounts
(B) than the amounts
(C) but by increases in the amounts
(D) and more by increases in the amounts
(E) than by funds

(A) Correct as originally written. Parallelism calls for repetition of the pronoun *by (less by . . . than by . . .)*.

20. The press secretary announced that neither himself nor the President would be available for questions until they had had more time to examine the report.

(A) neither himself nor the President would be
(B) neither he or the President was
(C) neither he nor the President would be
(D) he and the President will not be
(E) he nor the President would be

(C) The pronoun should be *he*, since it is part of the compound subject of the verb *would be*.

21. In routine cases, the Civilian Review Board receives all complaints about police misconduct, weighs the evidence and the seriousness of the charges, and then it decides whether a formal inquiry is needed.

(A) then it decides whether a formal inquiry is needed
(B) then decides if a formal inquiry would be needed
(C) then it decides whether to hold a formal inquiry
(D) then decides whether a formal inquiry is needed
(E) decides at that point if a formal inquiry is needed or not

(D) The pronoun *it* is unnecessary, since the subject of the verb—*the Civilian Review Board*—has already appeared.

Section 7 Problem Solving

(Numbers in parentheses at the end of each explanation indicate the section in the Mathematics Review where material addressed in the question is discussed.)

1. Dictionaries weigh 6 pounds each and a set of encyclopedias weighs 75 pounds. 20 dictionaries are shipped in each box. 2 sets of encyclopedias are shipped in each box. A truck is loaded with 98 boxes of dictionaries and 50 boxes of encyclopedias. How much does the truck's load weigh?

(A) 588 pounds
(B) 7,500 pounds
(C) 11,750 pounds
(D) 19,260 pounds
(E) 22,840 pounds

(D) Each box of dictionaries weighs $6 \times 20 = 120$ pounds. Each box of encyclopedias weighs $2 \times 75 = 150$ pounds. So the load weighs $98 \times 120 + 50 \times 150 = 19{,}260$ pounds. (II-3)

2. Mary is paid $600 a month on her regular job. During July in addition to her regular job, she makes $400 from a second job. Approximately what percentage of her annual income does Mary make in July? Assume Mary has no other income except the income mentioned above.

(A) 8
(B) $8\frac{1}{3}$
(C) $12\frac{1}{2}$
(D) 13
(E) 14

(D) Mary makes $600 a month on her regular job. Therefore, she receives $\$600 \bullet 12 = \$7{,}200$ a year from her regular job. Her only other income is $400. So her total yearly income is $7,600. She makes $\$600 + \$400 = \$1{,}000$ during July, so she makes $\frac{1{,}000}{7{,}600} = \frac{5}{38}$ which is about .13 of her annual income during July. Therefore, Mary makes about 13% of her annual income in July. (I-4)

3. A train travels at an average speed of 20 mph through urban areas, 50 mph through suburban areas, and 75 mph through rural areas. If a trip consists of traveling half an hour through urban areas, $3\frac{1}{2}$ hours through suburban areas, and 3 hours through rural areas, what is the train's average speed for the entire trip?

(A) 50 mph
(B) $53\frac{2}{7}$ mph
(C) $54\frac{3}{7}$ mph
(D) $58\frac{4}{7}$ mph
(E) $59\frac{2}{7}$ mph

(D) The train will average 50 mph for $3\frac{1}{2}$ hours, 75 mph for 3 hours and 20 mph for half an hour. So the distance of the trip is $\left(3\frac{1}{2}\right)(50) + (3)(75) + \left(\frac{1}{2}\right)(20) =$ $175 + 225 + 10 = 410$ miles. The trip takes 7 hours. Therefore, the average speed is $\frac{410}{7} = 58\frac{4}{7}$ mph. (I-7)

4. $(x - y)(y + 3)$ is equal to

(A) $x^2 - 3y + 3$
(B) $xy - 3y + y^2$
(C) $xy - y^2 - 3y + 3x$
(D) $xy - 3y + y^2 + 3x$
(E) $y^2 - 3y + 3x - xy$

(C) $(x - y)(y + 3) = x(y + 3) - y(y + 3)$
$= xy + 3x - y^2 - 3y$
$= xy - y^2 - 3y + 3x$

(II-1)

5. If $x < y$, $y < z$, and $z > w$, which of the following statements is always true?

(A) $x > w$
(B) $x < z$
(C) $y = w$
(D) $y > w$
(E) $x < w$

(B) If $x < y$ and $y < z$, then $x < z$. All the other statements may be true but are not always true. (II-7)

6. What is the ratio of $\frac{2}{3}$ to $\frac{5}{4}$?

(A) $\frac{1}{4}$
(B) $\frac{10}{12}$
(C) $\frac{8}{15}$
(D) $\frac{20}{6}$
(E) $\frac{2}{7}$

(C) The ratio is $\frac{\frac{2}{3}}{\frac{5}{4}}$ which is equal to $\frac{2}{3} \cdot \frac{4}{5} = \frac{8}{15}$.

(I-2, II-5)

7. Of the numbers, 7, 9, 11, 13, 29, 33, how many are prime numbers?

(A) none
(B) 3
(C) 4
(D) 5
(E) all

(C) 3 divides 9 evenly and 3 divides 33 evenly, so 9 and 33 are not primes. 7, 11, 13, and 29 have no divisors except 1 and themselves, so they are all primes. Thus, the set of numbers contains 4 prime numbers. (I-1)

8. A worker's daily salary varies each day. In one week he worked five days. His daily salaries were \$40.62, \$41.35, \$42.00, \$42.50, and \$39.53. What was his average daily salary for the week?

(A) \$40.04
(B) \$40.89
(C) \$41.04
(D) \$41.20
(E) \$206.00

(D) Add up all the daily wages for the week: \$40.62 + 41.35 + 42.00 + 42.50 + 39.53 = \$206.00. Divide \$206.00 by 5 to get the average daily wage, \$41.20. (I-7)

9. One dozen eggs and ten pounds of apples are currently the same price. If the price of a dozen eggs rises by 10% and the price of apples goes up by 2%, how much more will it cost to buy a dozen eggs and ten pounds of apples?

(A) 2%
(B) 6%
(C) 10%
(D) 12%
(E) 12.2%

(B) If the price of a pound of apples rises 2%, then the price of ten pounds of apples rises 2%. This is because the percentage change is the same for any amount sold. Since a dozen eggs and ten pounds of apples currently cost the same, each costs one half of the total price. Therefore, one half of the total is increased by 10% and the other half is increased by 2%, so the total price is increased by $\frac{1}{2}(10\%) + \frac{1}{2}(2\%) = 6\%$. (I-4)

10. How many two-digit prime numbers have a remainder of 2 when divided by 7?

(A) none
(B) one
(C) two
(D) three
(E) more than three

(D) The best way to do this problem is to look at all the two-digit numbers that have a remainder of 2 when divided by 7 and see how many are prime. It is easy to look at this list, since each successive entry is 7 more than the previous entry. The list is 16, 23, 30, 37, 44, 51, 58, 65, 72, 79, 86, 93. To check whether a number is prime you only have to see if it is divisible by primes that are less than or equal to the number's square root. Since these are all two-digit numbers, their square roots are all less than 10. The only primes less than 10 are 2, 3, 5 and 7. Now, since 16, 30, 44, 58, 72 and 86 are even, they are not prime. 51 and 93 are divisible by 3 and 65 is divisible by 5 so the only possible primes are 23, 37 and 79. Since none of these is divisible by 7, they are all prime. The correct choice is (D). (I-1)

11. A car gets 20 miles per gallon of gas when it travels at 50 miles per hour. The car gets 12% fewer miles to the gallon at 60 miles per hour. How far can the car travel at 60 miles per hour on 11 gallons of gas?

(A) 193.6 miles
(B) 195.1 miles
(C) 200 miles
(D) 204.3 miles
(E) 220 miles

(A) The car gets 100% – 12% or 88% of 20 miles to the gallon at 60 miles per hour. Thus, the car gets (.88)(20) or 17.6 miles to the gallon at 60 mph. Therefore, it can travel (11)(17.6) or 193.6 miles. (I-4, II-3)

12. Feathers cost \$500 a ton for the first 12 tons and \$(500 – x) a ton for any tons over 12. What is x, if it costs \$10,000 for 30 tons of feathers?

(A) 270.00
(B) 277.00
(C) 277.70
(D) 277.78
(E) 280.00

(D) The first 12 tons cost (12)(\$500) or \$6,000. When you purchase 30 tons, you are buying 18 tons in addition to the first 12 tons so the additional 18 tons will cost \$(500 – x)(18). Since \$10,000 – \$6,000 = \$4,000, we get \$9,000 – 18x = \$4,000, and 18x = \$5,000. So x = 277.78. (II-3)

13. The angles of a triangle are in the ratio 2 : 3 : 4. The largest angle in the triangle is

(A) 30°
(B) 40°
(C) 70°
(D) 75°
(E) 80°

(E) The sum of the angles of a triangle is 180°. Let x be the number of degrees in the largest angle; then the other angles are $\frac{1}{2}x$ and $\frac{3}{4}x$ degrees. Therefore, $\frac{1}{2}x + \frac{3}{4}x + x = \frac{9}{4}x = 180°$, so $x = 80°$. (II-5, III-4)

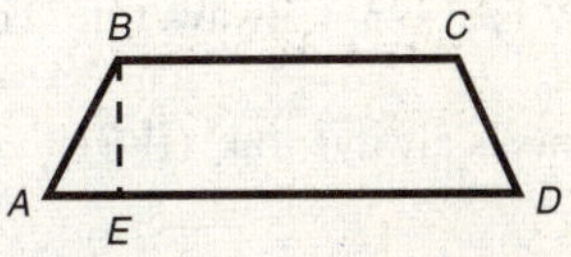

14. Find the area of the trapezoid $ABCD$. $AB = CD = 5$, $BC = 10$, $AD = 16$, and BE is an altitude of the trapezoid.

(A) 50
(B) 52
(C) 64
(D) 80
(E) 160

(B) If we draw $CF \perp AD$, then $\Delta ABE \cong \Delta DCF$ and $AE = FD = 3$. Then $BE = 4$. Thus the area of the trapezoid, which equals the product of the altitude and the average of the bases, equals $(4)\left(\frac{1}{2}\right)(10 + 16) = 52$. (III-7)

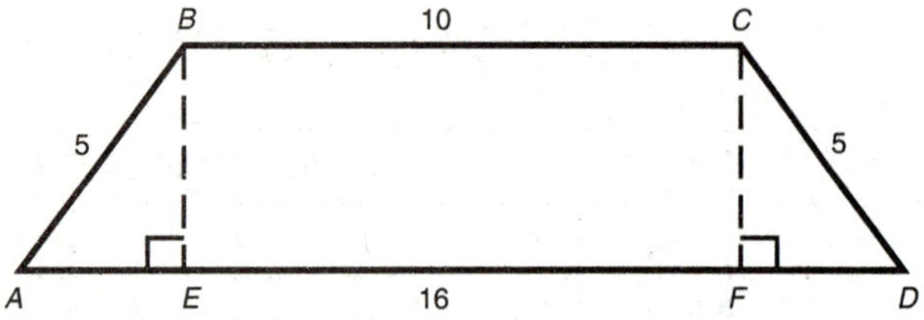

15. If x is less than 2, which of the following statements are always true?

I. x is negative.
II. x is positive.
III. $2x$ is greater than or equal to x.
IV. x^2 is greater than or equal to x.

(A) III only
(B) IV only
(C) I and III only
(D) I, III, and IV only
(E) none of the statements

(E) Since -1 (a negative number) is less than 2, and 1 (a positive number) is less than 2, neither I or II is always true.

Since -1 is less than 2 and $2 \times -1 = -2$, which is less than -1, III is not true.

Finally, since $\frac{1}{2}$ is less than 2 but $\frac{1}{2} \times \frac{1}{2} = \frac{1}{4}$, which is less than $\frac{1}{2}$, IV is also not always true. Therefore, none of the statements is always true. (II-7)

16. A worker is digging a ditch. He gets 2 assistants who work $\frac{2}{3}$ as fast as he does. If all 3 work on a ditch they should finish it in what fraction of the time that the worker takes working alone?

(A) $\frac{3}{7}$

(B) $\frac{1}{2}$

(C) $\frac{3}{4}$

(D) $\frac{4}{3}$

(E) $\frac{7}{3}$

(A) Since each assistant does $\frac{2}{3}$ as much as the worker, all 3 will accomplish $1 + 2\left(\frac{2}{3}\right)$ or $\frac{7}{3}$ as much as the worker by himself. So they will finish the job in $1 \div \frac{7}{3}$ or $\frac{3}{7}$ as much time as it would take the worker by himself. (II-3)

17. In a survey of political preferences, 78% of those asked were in favor of at least one of the proposals: I, II, and III. 50% of those asked favored proposal I, 30% favored proposal II, and 20% favored proposal III. If 5% of those asked favored all three of the proposals, what percentage of those asked favored more than one of the three proposals?

(A) 5
(B) 10
(C) 12
(D) 17
(E) 22

(D) The percent favoring at least one of the proposals is NOT the sum of 50, 30, and 20 because someone favoring 2 of the proposals will be counted twice and someone favoring all three will be counted 3 times. The correct relation is 78 = 50 + 30 + 20 – (percent favoring 2 of the proposals) – 2 (percent favoring all 3). Thus 78 = 100 – (percent favoring 2) – 2(5), which can be solved to give the percentage favoring 2 of the proposals or 100 – 10 – 78 = 12. Therefore the percentage favoring more than one proposal is 12 + 5 = 17. (II-4)

Evaluating Your Score

Tabulate your score for each section of Sample Test 5 according to the directions on pages 6–7 and record the results in the Self-Scoring Table below. Then find your rating for each score on the Self-Scoring Scale and record it in the appropriate blank.

Self-Scoring Table

SECTION	SCORE	RATING
1		
2		
3		
4		
5		
6		
7		

***Self-Scoring Scale*—RATING**

SECTION	POOR	FAIR	GOOD	EXCELLENT
1	0 – 8+	9 – 11	11+ – 14	14+ – 17
2	0 – 12+	13 – 17+	18 – 21+	22 – 25
3	0 – 9+	10 – 13+	14 – 17+	18 – 21
4	0 – 9+	10 – 13+	14 – 17+	18 – 21
5	0 – 8+	9 – 11	11+ – 14	14+ – 17
6	0 – 9+	10 – 13+	14 – 17+	18 – 21
7	0 – 8+	9 – 11+	11+ – 14	14+ – 17

Study again the Review sections covering material in Sample Test 5 for which you had a rating of FAIR or POOR.

To obtain an approximation of your actual GMAT score, see page 6.

APPENDIX
A List of Schools Requiring the GMAT

Listed below are graduate schools of business that *require* the GMAT as part of their admissions procedure.

United States

Alabama

Alabama Agricultural and Mechanical University
School of Business
Normal, AL 35762

Auburn University
Auburn School of Business
Graduate School
Auburn, AL 36830

Samford University
School of Business
Birmingham, AL 35229

Spring Hill College
MBA Program
Mobile, AL 36608

Troy State University
School of Business and Commerce
Troy, AL 36081

Troy State University at Dothan
Fort Rucker School of Business and Commerce
Dothan, AL 36301

Troy State University at Montgomery
MBA Program
Montgomery, AL 36082

University of Alabama/Birmingham
Graduate School of Management
Birmingham, AL 35294

University of Alabama/Huntsville
School of Administrative Science
Huntsville, AL 35899

University of Alabama/Tuscaloosa
Graduate School of Business
Tuscaloosa, AL 35487

University of North Alabama
School of Business
Florence, AL 35630

University of South Alabama Graduate School
College of Business and Management Studies
Mobile, AL 36688

Alaska

University of Alaska/Anchorage
School of Business and Public Affairs
Anchorage, AK 99508

University of Alaska/Fairbanks
School of Management
MBA Program
Fairbanks, AK 99701

University of Alaska/Juneau
Division of Business
Juneau, AK 99801

Arizona

American Graduate School of International Management
Graduate Business Program
Glendale, AZ 85306

Arizona State University
College of Business Administration
Tempe, AZ 85287

Grand Canyon University
College of Business
Phoenix, AZ 85017

Northern Arizona University
College of Business Administration
Flagstaff, AZ 86011

University of Arizona
College of Business and Public Administration
Graduate Programs
Tucson, AZ 85721

Arkansas

Arkansas State University
College of Business
Graduate Programs
State University, AR 72467

Harding University
Graduate School of Business
Searcy, AR 72143

University of Arkansas/Fayetteville
College of Business Administration
Fayetteville, AR 72701

University of Arkansas/Little Rock
The Graduate School
Little Rock, AR 72204

University of Central Arkansas
Graduate Business Programs
Conway, AR 72032

California

Azusa Pacific University
Division of Business Administration
Azusa, CA 91702

California Lutheran College
Graduate Program in Business Administration
Thousand Oaks, CA 91360

California Polytechnic State University//San Luis Obispo
School of Business
San Luis Obispo, CA 93407

California State Polytechnic University/Pomona
School of Business Administration
Graduate Programs
Pomona, CA 91768

California State University/Bakersfield
School of Business and Public Administration
Graduate Programs
Bakersfield, CA 93309

California State University/Chico
School of Business
MBA Program
Chico, CA 95929

California State University/Dominguez Hills
School of Management
Carson, CA 90747

California State University/Fresno
School of Business
Graduate Program
Fresno, CA 93740

California State University/Fullerton
School of Business Administration and Economics
Fullerton, CA 92634

California State University/Hayward
School of Business and Economics
Graduate Programs
Hayward, CA 94542

California State University/Long Beach
School of Business Administration
Graduate Programs
Long Beach, CA 90801

California State University/Los Angeles
School of Business and Economics
Graduate Programs
Los Angeles, CA 90032

California State University/Northridge
School of Business Administration and Economics
Northridge, CA 91330

California State University/Sacramento
School of Business and Public Administration
Sacramento, CA 95819

California State University/San Bernardino
School of Administration
Graduate Programs
San Bernardino, CA 92346

California State University/Stanislaus
Division of Business Administration
MBA Program
Turlock, CA 95380

Chapman College
School of Business and Management
MBA Programs
Orange, CA 92666

Claremont Graduate School
Business Administration Department
Claremont, CA 91711

College of Notre Dame
Graduate School
Belmont, CA 94002

Golden Gate University
Graduate College and School of Accounting
San Francisco, CA 94105

Holy Names College
The MBA in Weekend College
Oakland, CA 94619

Humboldt State University
College of Business and Economics/MBA Program
Arcata, CA 95521

La Sierra University
School of Business and Management
Riverside, CA 92515

Lincoln University
Department of Business Administration
San Francisco, CA 94118

Loyola Marymount University
College of Business Administration
MBA Program
Los Angeles, CA 90045

Monterey Institute of International Studies
Division of International Management
Graduate Programs
Monterey, CA 93940

Northrop University
College of Business and Management
Graduate Programs
Inglewood, CA 90306

Pacific Christian College
Graduate School of Business
San Diego, CA 92111

Pacific States University
College of Business Administration
Los Angeles, CA 90006

Pepperdine University
School of Business and Management
Graduate Programs
Los Angeles, CA 90044

Saint Mary's College of California
Graduate Business Programs
Moraga, CA 94575

San Diego State University
College of Business Administration
San Diego, CA 92182

San Francisco State University
School of Business
San Francisco, CA 94132

San Jose State University
School of Business
MBA Program
San Jose, CA 95192

Santa Clara University
Leavey School of Business and Administration
Santa Clara, CA 95053

Sonoma State University
School of Business and Economics
Rohnert Park, CA 94928

Stanford University
Graduate School of Business
Stanford, CA 94305

United States International University
School of Business and Management
Graduate Programs
San Diego, CA 92131

University of California/Berkeley
Graduate School of Business Administration
Berkeley, CA 94720

University of California/Davis
Graduate School of Administration
Davis, CA 95616

University of California/Irvine
Graduate School of Management
Irvine, CA 92717

University of California/Los Angeles
Graduate School of Management
Los Angeles, CA 90024

University of California/Riverside
Graduate School of Administration
Riverside, CA 92521

University of California/San Diego
Graduate School of Business Administration
San Diego, CA 92110

University of Judaism
Graduate School of Management
Public Management and Administration
Los Angeles, CA 90077

University of La Verne
School of Business and Economics
La Verne, CA 91750

University of San Diego
School of Business Administration
Alcala Park
San Diego, CA 92110

University of San Francisco
McLaren College of Business
MBA Program
San Francisco, CA 94117

University of Southern California
Graduate School of Business Administration
Los Angeles, CA 90007

University of the Pacific
School of Business and Public Administration
Stockton, CA 95211

Colorado

Colorado State University
College of Business
MBA Program
Fort Collins, CO 80523

Regis College/Colorado Springs Campus
Graduate Program
Colorado Springs, CO 80904

Regis College/Denver Campus
Special Programs
MBA Program
Denver, CO 80221

University of Colorado
Graduate School of Business Administration
Boulder, CO 80309

University of Colorado at Colorado Springs
Graduate School of Business Administration
Colorado Springs, CO 80933

University of Colorado at Denver
Graduate School of Business
Denver, CO 80202

University of Denver
Graduate School of Business and Public Management
Denver, CO 80208

University of Southern Colorado
Graduate School of Business
Pueblo, CO 81001

Connecticut

Central Connecticut State University
Organization and Management
New Britain, CT 06050

Fairfield University
School of Business
Graduate Program
Fairfield, CT 06430

Quinnipiac College
Graduate Studies
School of Business
Hamden, CT 06518

Sacred Heart University
Division of Graduate Studies
Bridgeport, CT 06606

Southern Connecticut State University
School of Business Economics
New Haven, CT 06515

University of Bridgeport
Graduate School of Management
Bridgeport, CT 06601

University of Connecticut
School of Business Administration
Storrs, CT 06269
(Note: The MBA program is offered at the Stamford and Hartford campuses.)

University of Hartford
Austin Dunham Barney School of Business and Public Administration
West Hartford, CT 06117

Western Connecticut State University
Ancell School of Business
Danbury, CT 06810

Yale University
School of Organization and Management
New Haven, CT 06520

Delaware

Delaware State College
Graduate School of Business
Dover, DE 19901

Goldey-Beacom College
Office of Graduate Studies
Wilmington, DE 19808

University of Delaware
College of Business and Economics
Newark, DE 19711

Wilmington College
MBA Program
New Castle, DE 19720

District of Columbia

American University
The Kogod College of Business Administration
Washington, DC 20016

George Washington University
School of Government and Business Administration
Washington, DC 20052

Georgetown University
School of Business Administration
Washington, DC 20057

Howard University
School of Business and Public Administration
Washington, DC 20001

Southeastern University
School of Business and Public Administration
Washington, DC 20024

Strayer College
Graduate School, Business Administration
Washington, DC 20005

University of the District of Columbia
College of Business and Public Management
Washington, DC 20004

Florida

Barry University
School of Business
Graduate Division
Miami Shores, FL 33161

Florida Agricultural and Mechanical University
Graduate Business Program
Tallahassee, FL 32307

Florida Atlantic University
College of Business and Public Administration
Boca Raton, FL 33431

Florida International University
Graduate Business Program
Miami, FL 33199

Florida State University
College of Business
Tallahassee, FL 32306

Jacksonville University
College of Business Administration
Jacksonville, FL 32211

Nova University
Center for the Study of Administration
Fort Lauderdale, FL 33314

Palm Beach Atlantic College
School of Graduate Studies
West Palm Beach, FL 33416

Rollins College
Roy E. Crummer Graduate School of Business
Winter Park, FL 32789

Saint Thomas University
Division of Human Resources
Program in Advanced Accounting
Miami, FL 33054

Stetson University
School of Business Administration
DeLand, FL 32720

University of Central Florida
College of Business Administration
Orlando, FL 32816

University of Florida
Graduate School of Business Administration
Gainesville, FL 32611

University of Miami
School of Business Administration
Graduate Studies
Coral Gables, FL 33124

University of North Florida
College of Business Administration
Jacksonville, FL 32216

University of South Florida
College of Business Administration
Tampa, FL 33620

Georgia

Albany State College
School of Business
Albany, GA 31705

Augusta College
School of Business Administration
Augusta, GA 30910

Berry College
Graduate Studies
Mount Berry, GA 30149

Clark Atlanta University
School of Business Administration
Atlanta, GA 30314

Columbus College
School of Business
Columbus, GA 31993

Emory University
Graduate School of Business Administration
Atlanta, GA 30322

Georgia College
School of Business
Milledgeville, GA 31061

Georgia Institute of Technology
College of Management
Atlanta, GA 30332

Georgia Southern College
Graduate School of Business
Statesboro, GA 30460

Georgia State University
Graduate Division
College of Business Administration
Atlanta, GA 30303

Kennesaw College
Graduate School of Business
Marietta, GA 30061

LaGrange College
MBA Program
LaGrange, GA 30240

Mercer University/Atlanta
Division of Business and Economics
MBA Program
Atlanta, GA 30341

Mercer University/Macon
School of Business and Economics
MBA Program
Macon, GA 31207

Savannah State College
School of Business
MBA Program
Savannah, GA 31404

Southern College of Technology
School of Management
Marietta, GA 30060

University of Georgia
Graduate School of Business Administration
Athens, GA 30602

Valdosta State College
School of Business Administration
Valdosta, GA 31698

West Georgia College
School of Business
Carrollton, GA 30118

Hawaii

Chaminade University of Honolulu
Business Administration Division
MBA Program
Honolulu, HI 96816

University of Hawaii at Hilo
Graduate School of Business
Hilo, HI 96720

University of Hawaii at Manoa
College of Business Administration
Honolulu, HI 96822

Idaho

Boise State University
College of Business
Graduate Programs
Boise, ID 83725

Idaho State University
College of Business
MBA Program
Pocatello, ID 83209

Illinois

Aurora University
Graduate Management Center
Aurora, IL 60506

Bradley University
College of Business Administration
MBA Program
Peoria, IL 61625

DePaul University
Graduate School of Business
Chicago, IL 60604

Eastern Illinois University
School of Business
Graduate Business Studies
Charleston, IL 61920

Governors State University
College of Business and Public Administration
Graduate Programs
Park Forest South, IL 60466

Illinois Benedictine College
MBA Program
Lisle, IL 60532

Illinois Institute of Technology
Stuart School of Management and Finance
Chicago, IL 60616

Illinois State University
College of Business
Graduate Programs
Normal, IL 61761

Lake Forest Graduate School of Management
Graduate Business Program
Lake Forest, IL 60045

Lewis University
College of Business
Romeoville, IL 60441

Loyola University of Chicago
Graduate School of Business
Chicago, IL 60611

North Central College
MBA Program
Naporville, IL 60566

Northeastern Illinois University
College of Business and Management
Chicago, IL 60625

Northern Illinois University
The Graduate School
College of Business
DeKalb, IL 60115

North Park College
MBA Programs
Chicago, IL 60625

Northwestern University
J. L. Kellogg Graduate School of Management
Evanston, IL 60201

Olivet Nazarene University
MBA Program
Kankakee, IL 60901

Quincy College
Graduate School of Business
Quincy, IL 62301

Roosevelt University
Walter E. Heller College of Business Administration
Graduate Programs
Chicago, IL 60605

Rosary College
Graduate Business Programs
River Forest, IL 60305

Saint Xavier College
Graham School of Management
Chicago, IL 60655

Sangamon State University
Graduate Programs
Springfield, IL 62708

Southern Illinois University/Carbondale
Graduate School and College of Business Administration
Carbondale, IL 62901

Southern Illinois University/Edwardsville
School of Business
Graduate Programs
Edwardsville, IL 62026

University of Chicago
Graduate School of Business
Chicago, IL 60637

University of Illinois at Chicago
Graduate School of Business
Chicago, IL 60680

University of Illinois at Urbana
Graduate School of Business
Urbana, IL 61801

Western Illinois University
College of Business
Graduate Programs
Macomb, IL 61455

Indiana

Anderson University
School of Business
Anderson, IN 46012

Ball State University
College of Business
Graduate Programs
Muncie, IN 47306

Butler University
College of Business Administration
Graduate Programs
Indianapolis, IN 46208

Indiana State University
School of Business
Graduate Programs
Terre Haute, IN 47809

Indiana University/Bloomington
Graduate School of Business
Bloomington, IN 47401

Indiana University/Gary
Division of Business and Economics
Gary, IN 46408

Indiana University/Purdue University
Division of Business and Economics
Graduate Program
Fort Wayne, IN 46805

Indiana University/Purdue University
School of Business
Indianapolis, IN 46202

Indiana University/South Bend
Division of Business and Economics
Graduate Program
South Bend, IN 46615

Indiana University Southeast
Division of Business and Economics
New Albany, IN 47150

Manchester College
Graduate Program
North Manchester, IN 46962

Purdue University
Graduate School
Department of Management
Hammond, IN 46323

Purdue University
Krannert Graduate School of Management
West Lafayette, IN 47907

Saint Francis College
Department of Business Administration
Fort Wayne, IN 46808

University of Evansville
Graduate School of Business Administration
Evansville, IN 47702

University of Indianapolis
Graduate Business Programs
Indianapolis, IN 46227

University of Notre Dame
College of Business Administration
Graduate Division
Notre Dame, IN 46556

University of Southern Indiana
Office of Graduate Studies/School of Business
Evansville, IN 47712

Iowa

Drake University
College of Business Administration
Graduate Programs
Des Moines, IA 50311

Iowa State University
College of Business Administration
Ames, IA 50011

Maharishi International University
Department of Business Administration
Fairfield, IA 52556

Saint Ambrose College
MBA Program
Davenport, IA 52803

University of Dubuque
MBA Program
Dubuque, IA 52001

University of Iowa
College of Business Graduate Programs
Iowa City, IA 52242

University of Northern Iowa
School of Business
Graduate Programs
Cedar Falls, IA 50614

Kansas

Emporia State University
Division of Business
Graduate Programs
Emporia, KS 66801

Fort Hays State University
School of Business
MBA Program
Hays, KS 67601

Friends University
College of Business Graduate Programs
Wichita, KS 67213

Kansas State University
College of Business Administration
Graduate Programs
Manhattan, KS 66506

Pittsburg State University
Kelce School of Business and Economics
MBA Program
Pittsburg, KS 66762

University of Kansas
School of Business
Graduate Programs
Lawrence, KS 66045

Washburn University
School of Business
MBA Program
Topeka, KS 66621

Wichita State University
College of Business Administration
Graduate Studies in Business
Wichita, KS 67208

Kentucky

Bellarmine College
Graduate Business Program
Louisville, KY 40205

Eastern Kentucky University
Graduate School
College of Business
Richmond, KY 40475

Morehead State University
School of Business and Economics
Morehead, KY 40351

Murray State University
College of Business and Public Affairs
Murray, KY 42071

Northern Kentucky University
Master of Business Administration
Highland Heights, KY 41076

University of Kentucky
College of Business and Economics
Lexington, KY 40506

University of Louisville
School of Business
Louisville, KY 40292

Western Kentucky University
Graduate College
Bowling Green, KY 42101

Louisiana

Centenary College of Louisiana
School of Business
MBA Program
Shreveport, LA 71104

Grambling State University
Graduate School of Business
Grambling, LA 71245

Louisiana State University/Baton Rouge
College of Business Administration
Graduate Division
Baton Rouge, LA 70803

Louisiana State University/Shreveport
College of Business Administration
MBA Program
Shreveport, LA 71115

Louisiana Tech University
College of Administration and Business
Graduate Programs
Ruston, LA 71272

Loyola University
College of Business Administration
Graduate Programs
New Orleans, LA 70118

McNeese State University
The Graduate School
MBA Program
Lake Charles, LA 70609

Nicholls State University
College of Business Administration
MBA Program
Thibodaux, LA 70310

Northeast Louisiana University
College of Business Administration
MBA Program
Monroe, LA 71209

Northwestern State University of Louisiana
Division of Business
Natchitoches, LA 71497

Southeastern Louisiana University
School of Graduate Studies
MBA Program
Hammond, LA 70402

Southern University
Graduate Accountancy Program
Baton Rouge, LA 70813

Tulane University
School of Business
MBA Program
New Orleans, LA 70118

University of New Orleans
College of Business Administration
Graduate Programs
New Orleans, LA 70122

University of Southwestern Louisiana
College of Business Administration
MBA Program
Lafayette, LA 70504

Maine

Husson College
Graduate Studies Division
Bangor, ME 04401

Thomas College
Graduate School of Management
Waterville, ME 04901

University of Maine
College of Business Administration
The Graduate School
Orono, ME 04469

University of Southern Maine
School of Business Economics and Management
Portland, ME 04103

Maryland

Loyola College
School of Business and Management
Baltimore, MD 21210

Morgan State University
School of Graduate Studies
Baltimore, MD 21239

Mount Saint Mary's College
Graduate School of Business
Emmitsburg, MD 21727

Salisbury State College
School of Business
Salisbury, MD 21801

University of Baltimore
School of Business
Baltimore, MD 21201

University of Maryland/College Park
College of Business and Management
College Park, MD 20742

Massachusetts

American International College
School of Business Administration
Graduate Program
Springfield, MA 01109

Anna Maria College for Men and Women
Graduate Division, Department of Business Administration
Paxton, MA 01612

Assumption College
Graduate School
MBA Program
Worcester, MA 01609

Babson College
Graduate School of Business
Wellesley, MA 02157

Bentley College
Graduate School
Waltham, MA 02254

Boston College
Graduate School of Management
Chestnut Hill, MA 02167

Boston University
School of Management
Graduate Programs
Boston, MA 02215

Boston University
MBA Program
Boston, MA 02215

Brandeis University
Heller School
Waltham, MA 02254

Clark University
Graduate School of Management
Worcester, MA 01610

Fitchburg State College
Program in Management
Fitchburg, MA 01420

Massachusetts Institute of Technology
Alfred P. Sloan School of Management
Cambridge, MA 02139

Nichols College
MBA Program
Dudley, MA 01570

Northeastern University
Graduate School of Business Administration
Boston, MA 02115

Salem State College
Program in Business Administration
Salem, MA 01970

Simmons College
Graduate School of Management
Boston, MA 02115

Suffolk University
Graduate School of Management
Boston, MA 02108

University of Massachusetts at Amherst
School of Business Administration
Graduate School
Amherst, MA 01003

University of Massachusetts at Boston
Graduate Business School
Boston, MA 0210X

University of Massachusetts at Dartmouth
MBA Program
North Dartmouth, MA 02747

University of Massachusetts at Lowell
College of Management
Lowell, MA 01854

University of Massachusetts/ Worcester Medical Center
Graduate School of Nursing
Worcester, MA 01605

Western New England College
School of Business
Springfield, MA 01119

Worcester Polytechnic Institute
Evening School
MBA and MSA Programs
Worcester, MA 01609

Michigan

Andrews University
School of Business
Berrien Springs, MI 49104

Aquinas College
Graduate Management Program
Grand Rapids, MI 49506

Central Michigan University
School of Business Administration
Graduate Programs
Mt. Pleasant, MI 48859

Eastern Michigan University
College of Business
Graduate Programs
Ypsilanti, MI 48197

GMI Engineering and Management Institute
Master of Science in Manufacturing Management Program
Flint, MI 48504

Grand Valley State Colleges
F.E. Seidman Graduate School of Business and Administration
Allendale, MI 49401

Lake Superior State College
Department of Business and Economics
MBA Program
Sault Ste. Marie, MI 49783

Madonna College
Graduate Studies Program
Livonia, MI 48150

Michigan State Unversity
Graduate School of Business Administration
East Lansing, MI 48824

Michigan Technological University
School of Business and Engineering Administration
Graduate Program
Houghton, MI 49931

Northern Michigan University
School of Business and Management
MBA Program
Marquette, MI 49855

Oakland University
School of Economics and Management
Rochester, MI 48063

Saginaw Valley State College
School of Business and Management
University Center, MI 48710

University of Detroit
College of Business and Administration
Graduate Programs
Detroit, MI 48207

University of Michigan/Ann Arbor
Graduate School of Business Administration
Ann Arbor, MI 48109

University of Michigan/Dearborn
School of Management
MBA Program
Dearborn, MI 48128

University of Michigan/Flint
School of Management
MBA Program
Flint, MI 48503

Wayne State University
School of Business Administration
MBA Program
Detroit, MI 48202

Western Michigan University
College of Business
Kalamazoo, MI 49008

Minnesota

Mankato State University
College of Business Administration
Graduate Programs
Mankato, MN 56001

Metropolitan State University
Program in Management and Administration
St. Paul, MN 55101

Moorhead State University
MBA Program
Moorhead, MN 56560

Saint Cloud State University
College of Business
Graduate Programs
St. Cloud, MN 56301

University of Minnesota/Duluth
School of Business and Economics
MBA Program
Duluth, MN 55812

University of Minnesota/ Minneapolis/St. Paul
Graduate School of Management
Minneapolis, MN 55455

University of St. Thomas
Graduate Programs in Management
St. Paul, MN 55105

Winona State University
Department of Business Administration and Economics
MBA Program
Winona, MN 55987

Mississippi

Delta State University
School of Business
Graduate School
Cleveland, MS 38732

Jackson State University
School of Business and Economics
The Graduate School
Jackson, MS 39217

Millsaps College
School of Management
Jackson, MS 39210

Mississippi College
School of Business and Public Administration
Clinton, MS 39058

Mississippi State University
College of Business and Industry
Division of Graduate Studies
Mississippi State, MS 39762

University of Mississippi
School of Business and Administration
University, MS 38677

University of Southern Mississippi/ Hattiesburg
College of Business Administration
Graduate Studies
Hattiesburg, MS 39401

University of Southern Mississippi/ Long Beach
Coordinator of Graduate Business Studies
Long Beach, MS 39560

William Carey College
Graduate Center for Management Development
Hattiesburg, MS 39401

Missouri

Avila College
Department of Business and Economics
MBA Program
Kansas City, MO 64145

Central Missouri State University
College of Business and Economics
Warrensburg, MO 64093

Drury College
Breech School of Business Administration
MBA Program
Springfield, MO 65802

Lincoln University
School of Graduate Studies
MBA Program
Jefferson City, MO 65101

Maryville College
Division of Management
St. Louis, MO 63141

Northeast Missouri State University
Division of Business
Graduate Programs
Kirksville, MO 63501

Northwest Missouri State University
School of Business Administration
Graduate Programs
Maryville, MO 64468

Rockhurst College
Graduate Business Program
Kansas City, MO 64110

Saint Louis College of Pharmacy
Director of Graduate Studies
St. Louis, MO 63110

Saint Louis University
MBA Program
St. Louis, MO 63108

Southwest Missouri State University
School of Business
Graduate Programs
Springfield, MO 65802

University of Missouri/Columbia
College of Business and Public Administration
Graduate Programs
Columbia, MO 65211

University of Missouri/Kansas City
School of Administration
Kansas City, MO 64110

University of Missouri/St. Louis
School of Business Administration
Graduate Programs
St. Louis, MO 63121

Washington University
Graduate School of Business Administration
St. Louis, MO 63130

Montana

University of Montana
School of Business Administration
Graduate Programs
Missoula, MT 59812

Nebraska

Bellevue College
Masters of Art in Management
Bellevue, NE 68005

Chadron State College
School of Graduate Studies
Chadron, NE 69337

Creighton University
College of Business Administration
Graduate Programs
Omaha, NE 68178

University of Nebraska/Lincoln
College of Business Administration
Lincoln, NE 68588

University of Nebraska/Lincoln at Offutt Air Force Base
MBA Program
Offutt Air Force Base, NE 68113

University of Nebraska/Omaha
College of Business Administration
Graduate Programs
Omaha, NE 68182

Wayne State College
Division of Business
Wayne, NE 68787

Nevada

University of Nevada/Las Vegas
College of Business and Economics
Las Vegas, NV 89154

University of Nevada/Reno
College of Business Administration
Reno, NV 89557

New Hampshire

Dartmouth College
Amos Tuck School of Business Administration
Hanover, NH 03755

Plymouth State College
Master of Business Administration Program
Plymouth, NH 03264

Rivier College
Graduate Department of Business Administration
Nashua, NH 03060

University of New Hampshire
Whittemore School of Business and Economics
Durham, NH 03824

New Jersey

Fairleigh Dickinson University
Samuel J. Silberman College of Business Administration
Madison, NJ 07940

Fairleigh Dickinson University
Graduate School of Business
Rutherford, NJ 07070

Fairleigh Dickinson University
Graduate School of Business
Teaneck, NJ 07666

Glassboro State College
Department of Business Administration
Graduate Studies
Glassboro, NJ 08028

Monmouth College
MBA Program
West Long Beach, NJ 07764

Montclair State College
School of Business Administration
MBA Program
Upper Montclair, NJ 07043

Rider College
Division of Graduate Studies School of Business
Lawrenceville, NJ 08648

Rowan College of New Jersey
Graduate Office
Glassboro, NJ 08028

Rutgers University/Camden
Master of Business Administration Program
Camden, NJ 08102

Rutgers University/Newark
Graduate School of Business Administration
Newark, NJ 07102

Seton Hall University
W. Paul Stillman School of Business
South Orange, NJ 07079

Stevens Institute of Technology
Department of Management Science
Hoboken, NJ 07030

William Paterson College of New Jersey
School of Management
MBA Program
Wayne, NJ 07470

New Mexico

College of Santa Fe
Graduate School of Business
Santa Fe, NM 87501

Eastern New Mexico University
College of Business
Graduate Programs
Portales, NM 88130

New Mexico Highlands University
Division of Business and Economics
MBA Program
Las Vegas, NM 87701

New Mexico State University
College of Business Administration and Economics
Graduate Programs
Las Cruces, NM 88003

University of New Mexico
Robert O. Anderson Graduate School of Management
Albuquerque, NM 87131

Western New Mexico University
Department of Business and Public Administration
Silver City, NM 88061

New York

Adelphi University
School of Business Administration
Garden City, NY 11530

Canisius College
School of Business Administration
Buffalo, NY 14214

City University of New York/ Baruch College
School of Business and Public Administration
Graduate Studies
New York, NY 10010

City University of New York/ Graduate School and University Center
Program in Business
New York, NY 10036

Clarkson University
School of Management
Potsdam, NY 13676

College of Insurance
Graduate Program
Business Division
New York, NY 10038

College of Saint Rose
Graduate School
Social Science Division
Albany, NY 12203

Columbia University
Graduate School of Business
New York, NY 10027

Cornell University
Graduate School of Management
Ithaca, NY 14853

Cornell University
Graduate School, Hotel Administration
Ithaca, NY 14853

Dowling College
Master of Business Administration Program
Oakdale, NY 11769

Fordham University
Martino Graduate School of Business Administration
New York, NY 10023

Hofstra University
School of Business
Hempstead, NY 11550

Iona College
Hagan Graduate School of Business
New Rochelle, NY 10801

Iona College at Orangeburg
MBA Program
Orangeburg, NY 10962

Long Island University/ Brooklyn Center
Graduate School of Business and Public
Administration
Brooklyn, NY 11201

Long Island University/ C.W. Post Center
Graduate Programs
Greenvale, NY 11548

Long Island University/Westchester
School of Business and Public Administration
Graduate Studies
Dobbs Ferry, NY 10522

Manhattan College
Graduate Division
School of Business
Riverdale, NY 10471

Marist College
Graduate Programs
Poughkeepsie, NY 12601

Mercy College
Master of Science Program in Human Resource Management
Dobbs Ferry, NY 10522

Mount Saint Mary College
MBA Program
Newburgh, NY 12550

New York Institute of Technology
Center for Business and Economics
Old Westbury, NY 11568

New York University
Leonard N. Stern School of Business
New York, NY 10006

Niagara University
College of Business Administration
MBA Program
Niagara University, NY 14109

Pace University
Lubin Graduate School of Business
New York, NY 10038

Pace University at White Plains
Graduate School of Business
White Plains, NY 10603

Polytechnic University
Division of Management
Brooklyn, NY 11201

Rensselaer Polytechnic Institute
School of Management
Troy, NY 12181

Rochester Institute of Technology
College of Business, Graduate Business Program
Rochester, NY 14623

Russell Sage College
MBA Program
Albany, NY 12208

Saint Bonaventure University
School of Business Administration
School of Graduate Studies
St. Bonaventure, NY 14778

Saint John Fisher College
Graduate School of Business
Rochester, NY 14618

Saint John's University
Graduate Division, College of Business Administration
Jamaica, NY 11439

Saint John's University
College of Business Administration
Staten Island, NY 10300

State University of New York at Albany
School of Business
Albany, NY 12222

State University of New York at Binghamton
School of Management
Binghamton, NY 13905

State University of New York at Buffalo
School of Management
Buffalo, NY 14214

State University of New York/ College at Oswego
Graduate Program in Business Administration/Management
Oswego, NY 13126

State University of New York/ Institute of Technology at Utica/ Rome
P.O. Box 3050
Utica, NY 13504

State University of New York, Maritime College
Office of Continuing Education
Throgs Neck, NY 10465

Syracuse University
School of Management
Syracuse, NY 13210

Syracuse University at Corning Center
College Center of Finger Lakes
Corning, NY 14830

Union College and University
Institute of Administration and Management
Schenectedy, NY 12308

University of Rochester
Graduate School of Management
Rochester, NY 14627

North Carolina

Appalachian State University
John A. Walker College of Business
Boone, NC 28608

Campbell University
Department of Business
Buies Creek, NC 27506

Duke University
Fuqua School of Business
Durham, NC 27706

East Carolina University
School of Business
Greenville, NC 27834

Elon College
Graduate Program in Business
Elon College, NC 27244

Fayetteville State University
Graduate School of Business
Fayetteville, NC 28301

High Point University
School of Business
High Point, NC 27262

Meredith College
Department of Business and Economics
Raleigh, NC 27607

North Carolina Central University
School of Business
Durham, NC 27707

Pfeiffer College
MBA Program
Charlotte, NC 28204

Queens College
The Graduate School
MBA Program
Charlotte, NC 28274

University of North Carolina/ Chapel Hill
Graduate School of Business Administration
Chapel Hill, NC 27514

University of North Carolina/ Charlotte
College of Business Administration
Charlotte, NC 28223

University of North Carolina/ Greensboro
School of Business and Economics
Greensboro, NC 27412

University of North Carolina/ Wilmington
MBA Program
Wilmington, NC 28406

Wake Forest University
Babcock Graduate School of Management
Winston-Salem, NC 27109

Western Carolina University
School of Business
Graduate School
Cullowhee, NC 28723

Wingate College
School of Business
Wingate, NC 28174

North Dakota

North Dakota State University
MBA Program
Fargo, ND 58105

University of North Dakota
Graduate Business Programs
Grand Forks, ND 58202

Ohio

Air Force Institute of Technology
Director of Admissions
Wright Patterson, OH 45433

Ashland College
MBA Program
Ashland, OH 44805

Baldwin-Wallace College
Master of Business
Administration Program
Berea, OH 44017

Bowling Green State University
College of Business Administration
Bowling Green, OH 43403

Case Western Reserve University
Weatherhead School of Management
Cleveland, OH 44106

Cleveland State University
James J. Nance College of Business
Administration
Cleveland, OH 44115

Franciscan University of Steubenville
MBA Program
Steubenville, OH 43952

John Carroll University
School of Business
Cleveland, OH 44118

Kent State University
Graduate School of Management
Kent, OH 44242

Miami University
School of Business Administration
Oxford, OH 45056

Ohio State University
College of Administrative Science
Columbus, OH 43210

Ohio University
College of Business Administration
Athens, OH 45701

Tiffin University
Division of Business
Tiffin, OH 44883

University of Akron
College of Business Administration
Akron, OH 44325

University of Cincinnati
College of Business Administration
Cincinnati, OH 45221

University of Dayton
MBA Program
School of Business Administration
Dayton, OH 45469

University of Toledo
College of Business Administration
Toledo, OH 43606

Walsh University
Graduate Program
North Canton, OH 44720

Wright State University
College of Business Administration
School of Graduate Studies
Dayton, OH 45435

Xavier University
Graduate Programs
Cincinnati, OH 45206

Youngstown State University
Graduate School of Business
Youngstown, OH 44555

Oklahoma

Northeastern State University
The Graduate College
Tahlequah, OK 74464

Oklahoma City University
School of Management and
Business Sciences
Graduate Programs
Oklahoma City, OK 73106

Oklahoma State University
College of Business Administration
Graduate Programs
Stillwater, OK 74078

Oral Roberts University
School of Business
Tulsa, OK 74171

Phillips University
Center of Business and Communication
MBA Program
Enid, OK 73702

Southern Nazarene University
Graduate Management Program
Bethany, OK 73008

University of Central Oklahoma
College of Business Administration
Edmond, OK 73034

University of Oklahoma
College of Business Administration
Graduate Programs
Norman, OK 73019

University of Tulsa
College of Business Administration
Graduate Programs
Tulsa, OK 74104

Oregon

Oregon State University
School of Business
Graduate Programs
Corvallis, OR 97331

Portland State University
School of Business Administration
Graduate Programs
Portland, OR 97207

Southern Oregon State College
School of Business
Graduate Programs
Ashland, OR 97520

University of Oregon
Graduate School of Management
Eugene, OR 97403

University of Portland
School of Business Administration
MBA Program
Portland, OR 97203

Willamette University
Geo. H. Atkinson Graduate School
of Management
Salem, OR 97301

Pennsylvania

Bloomsburg University of Pennsylvania
School of Graduate Studies
Bloomsburg, PA 17815

Bucknell University
Department of Management
Graduate Program
Lewisburg, PA 17837

California University of Pennsylvania
Department of Business and Economics
California, PA 15419

Carnegie-Mellon University
Graduate School of Industrial Administration
Pittsburgh, PA 15213

Clarion University of Pennsylvania
School of Business Administration
Graduate School
Clarion, PA 16214

Drexel University
College of Business and Administration
Philadelphia, PA 19104

Duquesne University
Graduate School of Business and Administration
Pittsburgh, PA 15282

Eastern College
Graduate Program in Business Administration
St. Davids, PA 19087

Gannon University
Master of Business Administration Program
Erie, PA 16541

Indiana University of Pennsylvania
School of Business
Graduate School
Indiana, PA 15705

Kings College
Graduate Office
Wilkes Barre, PA 18711

Kutztown University of Pennsylvania
College of Graduate Studies
Kutztown, PA 19530

La Roche College
Graduate Studies
Pittsburgh, PA 15237

La Salle University
School of Business Administration
Philadelphia, PA 19141

Lebanon Valley College
MBA Program
Annville, PA 17003

Lehigh University
College of Business and Economics
Bethlehem, PA 18015

Marywood College
Graduate Program in Business and Managerial Science
Scranton, PA 18509

Moravian College
MBA Program
Bethlehem, PA 18017

Pennsylvania State University at Erie, Behrend College
Graduate Admissions
Erie, PA 16563

Pennsylvania State University/ The Capitol Campus
Master of Administration Program
Middletown, PA 17057

Pennsylvania State University/ University Park
Graduate Studies
College of Business Administration
University Park, PA 16802

Philadelphia College of Textiles and Science
MBA Program
Philadelphia, PA 19144

Point Park College
MIBM Program
Pittsburgh, PA 15222

Robert Morris College
Graduate School
Coraoplis, PA 15108

Saint Joseph's University
MBA Program
Philadelphia, PA 19131

Temple University
School of Business Administration
Graduate School
Philadelphia, PA 19122

University of Pennsylvania
The Wharton School, Graduate Division
Philadelphia, PA 19104

University of Pittsburgh
Graduate School of Business
Pittsburgh, PA 15260

University of Scranton
School of Management, Graduate School
Pittsburgh, PA 18510

Villanova University
College of Commerce and Finance
MBA Program
Villanova, PA 19085

Waynesburg College
Graduate Program in Business
Waynesburg, PA 15370

West Chester University of Pennsylvania
School of Administration and Public Affairs
West Chester, PA 19380

Widener University
Graduate Program in Business Administration
Cheater, PA 19013

Wilkes University
MBA Program
Wilkes Barre, PA 18766

York College of Pennsylvania
Department of Business Administration
York, PA 17405

Rhode Island

Bryant College
Graduate School
Smithfield, RI 02917

Providence College
Graduate School
Department of Business Administration
Providence, RI 02918

University of Rhode Island
College of Business Administration
Kingston, RI 02881

South Carolina

Central Wesleyan College
Leadership Education for Adult Professionals
Central, SC 29630

Charleston Southern University
Director of Graduate Studies in Business
Charleston, SC 29423

Citadel, The
MBA Program
Department of Business Administration
Charleston, SC 29409

Clemson University
College of Industrial Management and Textile Science
Clemson, SC 29631

Clemson University-Furman University
MBA Program
Greenville, SC 29613

Francis Marion University
School of Business
Florence, SC 29501

University of South Carolina
College of Business Administration
Columbia, SC 29208

Winthrop College
School of Business Administration
Rock Hill, SC 29733

South Dakota

Huron University
Master of Business Administration
Huron, SD 57350

Northern State University
MBA Program
Aberdeen, SD 57401

University of South Dakota
School of Business
Graduate Programs
Vermillion, SD 57069

Tennessee

Belmont College
The Jack C. Massey Graduate School of Business
Nashville, TN 37212

Christian Brothers College
Graduate School of Business
Memphis, TN 38104

East Tennessee State University
College of Business
The School of Graduate Studies
Johnson City, TN 37601

Memphis State University
Fogelman College of Business and Economics
Graduate School
Memphis, TN 38152

Middle Tennessee State University
Graduate Studies
School of Business
Murfreesboro, TN 37132

Rhodes College
Department of Economics and Business Administration
Memphis, TN 38112

Tennessee State University
School of Business
Nashville, TN 37203

Tennessee Technological University
The Graduate School, Division of MBA Studies
Cookeville, TN 38501

Trevecca Nazarene College
Graduate Studies in Organizational Management
Nashville, TN 37210

University of Tennessee/Chattanooga
School of Business Administration
Chattanooga, TN 37402

University of Tennessee/Knoxville
College of Business Administration
Knoxville, TN 37916

University of Tennessee/Martin
School of Business Administration
Martin, TN 38238

Vanderbilt University
Owen Graduate School of Management
Nashville, TN 37203

Texas

Abilene Christian University
College of Business Administration
Abilene, TX 79699

Angelo State University
MBA Program
San Angelo, TX 76909

Baylor University
Hankamer School of Business
Graduate Programs
Waco, TX 76798

Corpus Christi State University
College of Business
Corpus Christi, TX 78412

East Texas State University/Commerce
College of Business and Technology
Commerce, TX 75428

East Texas State University/Texarkana
College of Business Administration
Master's Programs
Texarkana, TX 75501

Houston Baptist University
College of Business and Economics
Graduate Programs
Houston, TX 77074

Lamar University
College of Business
MBA Program
Beaumont, TX 77710

Prairie View A&M University
College of Business
Graduate Program
Prairie View, TX 77445

Rice University
Jesse H. Jones Graduate School of Administration
Houston, TX 77001

Saint Mary's University
School of Business and Administration
Graduate Programs
San Antonio, TX 78284

Sam Houston State University
College of Business Administration
Graduate Programs
Huntsville, TX 77341

Southern Methodist University
Edwin L. Cox School of Business
Graduate Programs
Dallas, TX 75275

Southwest Texas State University
School of Business, Graduate Division
San Marcos, TX 78666

Stephen F. Austin State University
Graduate School of Business
Nacogdoches, TX 75962

Sul Ross State University
Division of Business Administration
MBA Program
Alpine, TX 79830

Texas A&M University
College of Business Administration
Graduate Programs
College Station, TX 77843

Texas Christian University
M.J. Neeley School of Business
Fort Worth, TX 76129

Texas Southern University
School of Business
Graduate Programs
Houston, TX 77004

Texas Tech University
College of Business Administration
Graduate Programs
Lubbock, TX 79409

University of Dallas
Graduate School of Management
Irving, TX 75062

University of Houston/Clear Lake
School of Business and Public Administration
Graduate Programs
Houston, TX 77058

University of Houston/ University Park
College of Business Administration
Graduate Programs
Houston, TX 77004

University of Mary Hardin-Baylor
Graduate Program—Business
Belton, TX 76513

University of North Texas
College of Business Administration
Graduate Programs
Denton, TX 76203

University of St. Thomas
Cameron School of Business
MBA Program
Houston, TX 77006

University of Texas/Arlington
College of Business Administration
Graduate Programs
Arlington, TX 76019

University of Texas/Austin
Graduate School of Business
Austin, TX 78712

University of Texas/Brownsville
Graduate School
Brownsville, TX 78520

University of Texas/Dallas
School of Management and Administration
Graduate Programs
Richardson, TX 75080

University of Texas/Pan American
School of Business Administration
Edinburg, TX 78539

University of Texas/San Antonio
College of Business
Graduate Program
San Antonio, TX 78285

University of Texas/Tyler
School of Business Administration
MBA Program
Tyler, TX 75701

West Texas State University
School of Business
Graduate Programs
Canyon, TX 79016

Utah

Brigham Young University
Graduate School of Management
Provo, UT 84602

Southern Utah State College
Graduate School of Business
Cedar City, UT 84720

University of Utah
Graduate School of Business
Salt Lake City, UT 84112

Utah State University
College of Business
Graduate Programs
Logan, UT 84322

Weber State College
Graduate School of Business
Ogden, UT 84408

Vermont

University of Vermont
Division of Engineering
Mathematics and Business Administration
Burlington, VT 05405

Virginia

College of William and Mary in Virginia
School of Business Administration
Williamsburg, VA 23185

George Mason University
Graduate School
School of Business Administration
Fairfax, VA 22030

Hampton University
Graduate Studies in Business
Hampton, VA 23668

James Madison University
School of Business
Harrisonburg, VA 22807

Liberty University
School of Business and Government
MBA Program
Lynchburg, VA 24501

Lynchburg College
Department of Business Administration
Lynchburg, VA 24501

Mary Washington College
Graduate Business Programs
Fredericksburg, VA 22401

Marymount University
MBA Program
Arlington, VA 22207

Old Dominion University
School of Business Administration
Norfolk, VA 23508

Radford University
College of Business and Economics
Radford, VA 24142

Regent University
College of Administration and Management
Virginia Beach, VA 23464

Shenandoah College and Conservatory
MBA Program
Winchester, VA 22601

University of Richmond
Graduate Division
Richmond, VA 23173

University of Virginia
Colgate Darden Graduate School of Business
Charlottesville, VA 22906

Virginia Commonwealth University
School of Business
Richmond, VA 23284

Virginia Polytechnic Institute and State University
College of Business
Blacksburg, VA 24061

Washington

Eastern Washington University
MBA Program Office, School of Business
Cheney, WA 99004

Gonzaga University
School of Business Administration
Graduate Programs
Spokane, WA 99258

Pacific Lutheran University
School of Business Administration
MBA Program
Tacoma, WA 98447

Saint Martin's College
Graduate Studies in Management
Lacey, WA 98503

Seattle Pacific University
Master of Business Administration Program
Seattle, WA 98119

Seattle University
Albers School of Business
MBA Program
Seattle, WA 98122

University of Washington, Seattle
Graduate School of Business Administration
Seattle, WA 98195

Washington State University
College of Business and Economics
Graduate Programs
Pullman, WA 99163

Western Washington University
College of Business and Economics
Graduate Programs
Bellingham, WA 98225

West Virginia

Marshall University
Graduate School
College of Business
Huntington, WV 25701

University of Charleston
Graduate School of Business
Charleston, WV 25304

West Virginia University
College of Business and Economics
Morgantown, WV 26506

West Virginia Wesleyan College
MBA Program
Buckhannon, WV 26201

Wheeling Jesuit College
Graduate Business Program
Wheeling, WV 26003

Wisconsin

Marquette University
Robert A. Johnston College of Business Administration
Graduate Programs
Milwaukee, WI 53233

University of Wisconsin/Eau Claire
School of Business
MBA Program
Eau Claire, WI 54701

University of Wisconsin/La Crosse
College of Business Administration
MBA Program
La Crosse, WI 54601

University of Wisconsin/Madison
Graduate School of Business
Madison, WI 53706

University of Wisconsin/Milwaukee
Milwaukee School of Business Administration
Milwaukee, WI 53201

University of Wisconsin/Oshkosh
College of Business Administration
Oshkosh, WI 54901

University of Wisconsin/Parkside
Division of Business and Administrative Science
MBA Program
Kenosha, WI 53141

University of Wisconsin/Whitewater
College of Business and Economics
Whitewater, WI 53190

Wyoming

University of Wyoming
College of Commerce and Industry
Graduate Business Programs
Laramie, WY 82071

Guam

University of Guam
College of Business and Public Administration
Mangilao, GU 96913

Puerto Rico

Universidad del Turabo
Program in Accounting
Caguas, PR 00626

University of Puerto Rico, Mayaguez
College of Business Administration
Mayaguez, PR 00708

University of Puerto Rico/Rio Piedras
Graduate School of Business Administration
Rio Piedras, PR 00931

World University
Graduate School of Management and Accounting
Carolina, PR 00628

Virgin Islands

University of the Virgin Islands
Division of Business Administration
St. Thomas, VI 00801

Canada

Carleton University
Graduate School of Business
Ottawa, ON K1S5B

Concordia University
Faculty of Commerce and Administration
Montreal, PQ H3G1M

Dalhousie University
Faculty of Graduate Studies
International Business
Halifax, NS B3H31

Lakehead University
School of Business Administration
Thunder Bay, ON P7B5E

McGill University
Faculty of Management
Montreal, PQ H3A2T

McMaster University
Faculty of Business Program in Management Science
Hamilton, ON L8S4M

Memorial University of Newfoundland
Faculty of Business Administration
St. John's, NF A1B3X

Queen's University at Kingston
School of Business
Kingston, ON K7L3N

Saint Mary's University
Faculty of Commerce
Halifax, NS B3H3C

Simon Fraser University
Faculty of Business Administration/
Finance
Burnaby, BC V5A1S

University College of Cape Breton
Sydney, NS B1P 6L2

Université de Sherbrooke
School of Business
Sherbrooke, PQ J1K2R

University of Guelph
Office of Graduate Studies
Guelph, ON N1G 2WI

University of Alberta
Faculty of Business
Edmonton, AB T6G2R

University of British Columbia
Faculty of Commerce and
Business Administration
Vancouver, BC V6T1Z

University of Calgary
Faculty of Management
Calgary, AB T2N1N

Université du Québec à Montréal
Département des sciences
administratives
Montréal, PQ H3C 3P8

University of Manitoba
Faculty of Administrative Studies
Winnipeg, ON R3T2N

University of New Brunswick
Graduate School of Business
Fredericton, NB E3B5A

University of Ottawa
MBA Program
Ottawa, ON K1N 6N5

University of Saskatchewan
College of Commerce
Saskatoon, SK S7NOW

University of Toronto
School of Graduate Studies
Department of Management
Toronto, ON M5SMB

University of Victoria
School of Business
Victoria, BC V8W 3P2

Documentation

If you have purchased the version of this book that is packaged with computer disks, please read the following instructions for installation of the software into your computer.

This documentation applies to both the Windows and Macintosh versions of the computer program packaged with this book.

Hardware Requirements

The program will run on a Macintosh with
- minimum of 2MB of RAM
- System 6 or better
- hard disk with 2.5MB

The program on Windows requires
- minimum of 4MB of RAM
- 486 IBM or equivalent
- VGA monitor

Hard Drive Installation

The program must be installed on the hard drive of your computer before you can run it.

Macintosh Installation

To install the program on the hard disk, first boot the machine in the normal way.

1. Put the *Barron's GMAT for Macintosh Computers* disk into the floppy disk drive. Double-click on the disk icon to open it.
2. Double-click on the Barron's GMAT Installer icon.
3. After the opening screen, a "finder" dialog will open. If the settings are okay, click the Save button.
4. Follow the on-screen instructions and choose *Quit* when you get the message that installation was successful.
5. Eject the disk from your floppy disk drive and store in a safe place.
6. Open the Barron's GMAT folder on your hard drive and double-click on the Quest Study Guide icon to begin the program.

Windows Installation

To install the program on the hard disk, first boot the machine in the normal way.

1. Put the *Barron's GMAT for Windows* disk into the A drive.
2. From the Program Manager, choose *Run* from the File menu.
3. At the command line, type *A:\ install.exe,* then click *OK.*
4. Follow the on-screen instructions to complete installation.
5. To run the program, double-click on the GMAT icon and wait about ten seconds for the program to load.

Model Test and Practice Questions

The disk accompanying this GMAT book includes one Model Test and numerous Practice Questions. The test may be taken in Testing or in Learning Mode.

Testing Mode

Testing Mode most nearly replicates actual timed test conditions. The test is scored and a Score Analysis, based on the GMAT Skill Areas (see below), is provided. Then you are directed to Practice Questions within those Skill Areas, which will strengthen your weaknesses.

It is recommended that the user take a complete test at one sitting in this mode. However, if time constraints do not permit that, you can receive a score analysis for completion of either all of the verbal skill areas or all of the quantitative skill areas.

Scores and analyses are not saved when the computer is turned off, so it's a good idea to save a print copy.

Learning Mode

In Learning Mode, the user controls the pace and receives feedback for every answer choice—right or wrong—and is also given a second and third opportunity to arrive at the right answer.

Practice Questions

The Practice Questions are organized by Skill Area, and they provide the same kind of instruction as Learning Mode. Every answer is explained, and you have second and third chances to determine the correct answer.

Skill Areas

The Skill Areas have been identified as follows:

Verbal

1. Reading Comprehension
2. Sentence Correction
3. Critical Reasoning

Quantitative

4. Problem Solving
 a. Arithmetic
 b. Algebra
 c. Geometry
 d. Tables and Graphs
5. Data Sufficiency

SPECIAL OFFER TO PURCHASERS OF THE BOOK:

Order *Extra* Help for the GMAT—Then Put Your Personal Computer to Work for You

Here's extra help on the GMAT for both Macintosh and Windows users. Barron's software program gives you all this and more:

- A full-length practice test has been taken from this volume and programmed for your computer. Now you can take a practice test at your computer keyboard.
- Activate the practice test in the timed *Testing Mode* and you can take the test under the same conditions you'll encounter when you take the actual GMAT. When you've finished, an automatic scorer tells you how well you've done and categorizes your incorrect answers by topic. That way you'll know the areas where you need to do more studying.
- Activate the practice test in the *Learning Mode* and you discover right away whether you've answered each question correctly. If you've chosen an incorrect answer, your computer will tell you so and give you another chance. The reasons why your answers are correct or incorrect are explained to you.
- You also get hundreds of extra questions for drill and review, complete with answers and explanations.

Hardware Requirements: Windows requires 486 IBM or equivalent with 4 MB RAM, Windows 3.1, and VGA monitor. Macintosh requires 2 MB RAM, System 6 or better, and 2.5 MB free on hard disk.

BARRON'S

Barron's Educational Series, Inc.
250 Wireless Boulevard, Hauppauge, NY 11788
In Canada: Georgetown Book Warehouse
34 Armstrong Avenue, Georgetown, Ont. L7G 4R9

Please send me ________copy (copies) of Barron's **GMAT Computer Test Prep Disk at $20.00 each (Canada $25.95).** New York State residents, please add sales tax to total.

Please specify one:

☐ ISBN 0-8120-9578-2 for Windows (3½" disk) ☐ ISBN 0-8120-9201-5 for Macintosh (3½" disk)

I enclose a check or money order for $_______ which includes applicable sales tax plus 15% for postage and handling (minimum charge $4.95).

Credit card orders

Bill my: ☐ MasterCard ☐ Visa ☐ Amex ☐ Carte Blanche ☐ Diners Club

Account #________________________________

Signature____ Exp. Date_____/_____/_____

Name________________________________ Address________________________________

City________________________________ State________________ Zip____________

Price subject to change without notice.

(#5a) R 2/97

More selected BARRON'S titles:

Dictionary of Accounting Terms
(1918-0) $11.95, Canada $15.95
Dictionary of Banking Terms
(1530-4) $12.95, Canada $16.95
Dictionary of Business Terms
(1833-8) $11.95, Canada $15.95
Dictionary of Computer Terms
(9023-3) $9.95, Canada $12.95
Dictionary of Finance & Investment Terms
(9035-7) $11.95, Canada $15.95
Dictionary of Insurance Terms
(3379-5) $10.95, Canada $14.50
Dictionary of Marketing Terms
(1783-8) $11.95, Canada $15.95
Dictionary of Real Estate Terms
(1434-0) $11.95, Canada $15.95
Dictionary of Tax Terms
(1780-3) $9.95, Canada $12.95

BARRON'S FOREIGN LANGUAGE BUSINESS DICTIONARIES

Seven bilingual dictionaries translate about
3000 business terms not found in most foreign phrasebooks.

French for The Business Traveler
(1768-4) $9.95, Canada $12.95
German for The Business Traveler
(1769-2) $9.95, Canada $12.95
Italian for The Business Traveler
(1771-4) $9.95, Canada $12.95
Japanese for The Business Traveler
(1770-6) $11.95, Canada $15.95
Korean for The Business Traveler
(1772-2) $11.95, Canada $15.95
Russian for The Business Traveler
(1784-6) $11.95, Canada $15.95
Spanish for The Business Traveler
(1773-0) $10.95, Canada $14.50

All prices are in U.S. and Canadian dollars and subject to change without notice. At your bookseller, or order direct adding 15% postage (minimum charge $4.95)
N.Y. state residents add sales tax. All books are paperback editions. ISBN PREFIX 0-8120

BARRON'S

Barron's Educational Series, Inc.
250 Wireless Boulevard, Hauppauge, NY 11788
In Canada: Georgetown Book Warehouse
34 Armstrong Ave., Georgetown, Ontario L7G 4R

(#12) R 11/96

More selected BARRON'S titles:

BARRON'S ACCOUNTING HANDBOOK, 2nd EDITION,
Joel G. Siegel and Jae K. Shim
Provides accounting rules, guidelines, formulas and techniques etc. to help students and business professionals work out accounting problems.
Hardcover: $29.95, Canada $38.95/ISBN 0-8120-6449-6, 880 pages

REAL ESTATE HANDBOOK, 3rd EDITION,
Jack P. Friedman and Jack C. Harris
A dictionary/reference for everyone in real estate. Defines over 1500 legal, financial, and architectural terms.
Hardcover, $29.95, Canada $39.95/ ISBN 0-8120-6330-9, 810 pages

HOW TO PREPARE FOR THE REAL ESTATE LICENSING EXAMINATIONS SALESPERSON AND BROKER, 5th EDITION,
Bruce Lindeman and Jack P. Friedman
Reviews current exam topics and features updated model exams and supplemental exams, all with explained answers.
Paperback, $12.95, Canada $16.95/ISBN 0-8120-2994-1, 340 pages

BARRON'S FINANCE AND INVESTMENT HANDBOOK, 4th EDITION,
John Downes and Jordan Elliot Goodman
This hard-working handbook of essential information defines more than 3000 key terms, and explores 30 basic investment opportunities. The investment information is thoroughly up-to-date.
Hardcover $35.00, Canada $45.50/ISBN 0-8120-6465-8, approx. 1200 pages

FINANCIAL TABLES FOR MONEY MANAGEMENT
Stephen S. Solomon, Dr. Clifford Marshall, Martin Pepper, Jack P. Friedman and Jack C. Harris
Pocket-sized handbooks of interest and investment rate tables used easily by average investors and mortgage holders.
Each book: Paperback.
Real Estate Loans, 2nd Ed., $6.95, Canada $8.95/0-8120-1618-1, 336 pages
Mortgage Payments, 2nd Ed., $6.95, Canada $8.95/0-8120-1386-7, 304 pages
Bonds, 2nd Ed., $5.95, Canada $7.50/0-8120-4995-0, 256 pages
Canadian Mortgage Payments, 2nd Ed., Canada $8.95/0-8120-1617-3, 336 pages
Adjustable Rate Mortgages, 2nd Ed., $6.95, Canada $8.50/0-8120-1529-0, 288 pages

Books may be purchased at your bookstore or by mail from Barron's. Enclose check or money order for total amount plus sales tax where applicable and 15% for postage and handling (minimum charge $4.95). Prices subject to change without notice.

BARRON'S

Barron's Educational Series, Inc.
250 Wireless Blvd., Hauppauge, NY 11788
In Canada: Georgetown Book Warehouse
34 Armstrong Ave., Georgetown, Ontario L7G 4R9

(#11) R10/96